D1806337

MOTORING
IN
WESTERN EUROPE

Editorial:	Patricia Kelly
Compilation:	Publications Research Unit
Maps:	Cartographic Department
Advertising:	Peter Whitworth Tel Basingstoke 20123

YOUR PASSPORT TO TROUBLE-FREE TRAVEL

BARCLAYS TRAVELLERS CHEQUES

Take Barclays travellers cheques
wherever you go... whenever you go.
They're welcomed throughout the world.
Safer than cash.
A world-wide network of refund agents
helps you in case of loss or theft.
Choose US dollars or sterling.

Buy them at
Automobile Association Travel Agencies

BARCLAYS

Contents

Abbreviations & symbols

Hotels and garages listed by the AA are shown in the gazetteer for each country. The figures shown after the town and province names give the population. Hotel and garage names in italics indicate that particulars have not been confirmed by the management. Establishments are open all the year round unless otherwise stated.

★★★★★	Hotel classification	⮂	Logis de France (see page 152)
☆☆☆☆☆	(See page 8)	♨	Repair service available Sundays. Dates in parentheses indicate when service is available
⮂	Private baths		
🚿	Private showers		
P	Parking for cars	M/c	Motorcycle repairs undertaken
🏠	Garage and/or lock-up	(GB)	Some English spoken (garages only)
☽	Night porter	Beach	Hotel has private beach
⚲	Tennis court(s) (private)	Pool	Hotel has private pool
♌	Golf (private)	Sea/	Rooms overlook sea, mountain(s) or a lake
∩	Riding stables (private)	mountains/	
⮞⮜	Breakdown service* available 24hrs per day 7 days per week	lake	
⮜⮞	Breakdown service* available usually weekdays only during business hours	†	Town in France for which there is a town plan in the AA Road Book of France
		Plan	Number gives location of hotel on town plan
🛢	Petrol and oil, but not necessarily stores and mechanic available 24hrs per day 7 days per week		
🛢	Petrol and oil available weekdays	*Breakdown services have no connection with the AA Free Breakdown Service in this country. See the AA 5-Star Service, page 10).	
☎	Telephone number. Where there is a dialling code it is shown in parentheses against the town entry		
☎	Night telephone number (24hr breakdown service only)	▶ All charges are in local currency. Those shown are given by the hotels at the time of going to press, and they may be increased. You are advised to confirm prices at the time of booking.	
sB	Single room including breakfast per person per night		
sB⮂🚿	Single room with private bath/shower and breakfast per person per night	**Service Agencies** held by garages are indicated by the following abbreviations:	

sB⮂🚿	Single room with private bath/shower and breakfast per person per night		
dB	Double room (two persons) including breakfast	AM	Aston Martin	MB	Mercedes-Benz

dB	Double room (two persons) including breakfast	AM	Aston Martin	MB	Mercedes-Benz
dB⮂🚿	Double room (two persons) with private bath/shower and breakfast	AR	Alfa Romeo	Opl	Opel
		†Bed	Bedford	Peu	Peugeot
L	Lunch price	BL	Austin, MG, Morris,		
D	Dinner price		Vanden Plas,	Por	Porsche
alc	à la carte		Wolseley	Ren	Renault
DP	Demi-pension (see page 9)	BMW	BMW	Rov	Rover/Landrover
Pn	Pension (see page 9)	Chy	Commer, Hillman	RR	Rolls-Royce,
St%	Service and/or tax charge (service and tax is included unless otherwise stated)		Humber, Singer		Bentley
			Sunbeam	Sab	Saab
Map	Followed by the atlas page number and appropriate square reference (eg Map 5 C2) (See gaz. entry page 9)	Cit	Citroën	Sim	Simca
		Dat	Datsun	Ska	Skoda
		Fia	Fiat	Toy	Toyota
n rest	Hotel does not have own restaurant (ie hôtel garni or hôtel meuble)	Frd	Ford	Tri	Triumph
		Hon	Honda	†Vau	Vauxhall
ta	Telegraphic address	Jag	Jaguar, Daimler	VW	Volkswagen/
tx	Telex	Lnc	Lancia		Audi, NSU
rm	Number of bedrooms (including annexe)	Lot	Lotus	‡Vlo	Volvo, Daf
A	Annexe followed by number of rooms (see Rooms page 10)	Maz	Mazda		
(English breakfast)	English type breakfast available (see page 9)	†Where no Vau or Bed dealer is available owners could approach the nearest Opl agency listed. ‡All Daf dealers are now incorporated into the Volvo network.			

Produced by the Publications Division of the Automobile Association, Fanum House, Basingstoke, Hampshire RG21 2EA.

We acknowledge the kind help of all the tourist offices, boards and departments for the countries covered, who supplied photographs.

Filmset by Vantage Photosetting Co Ltd., Southampton and London

Printed in Great Britain by Fletcher and Sons Ltd., Norwich and bound by Richard Clay (The Chaucer Press) Ltd., Bungay, Suffolk
© The Automobile Association 1979

ISBN 0 901088 98 6

55770

Paul Hughes at large in Europe

'Once you get to a destination, you have to find somewhere else to travel to . . .'

Gadding about in Europe behind the wheel of a car is one of the nicest things I know.

Mind you, I am not one of those people who dash across Europe with white knuckles and staring eyes. I like to dawdle, to linger a while and get the feel of places I visit. As a matter of fact, I am an *aficionado* of *quincaillerie*. (If I knew what that meant I'd probably be better at it). But I do have a liking for Continental ironmongers shops. I can browse for hours in them, prodding and sniffing the baffling stock of weird implements, sacks of seeds, and the extraordinary gadgets that make French agricultural village life so complex and enchanting.

In Brittany, I nearly bought a straw *skep*. It is a thing for keeping bees in, shaped just like the cartoonists' idea of what a bee-hive should look like. Every home should have one.

Incidentally, does anyone need a wire face mask with a little gate in the cage at the mouth? I bought it somewhere in a Continental street market because I thought it was some sort of fencing mask. I made questioning gestures to the stall holder when I confirmed what it was and he nodded gleefully in agreement. Only when I got it home did I realise he thought I was imitating a threatening bee, and the gate was for the beekeeper to smoke to ward off the bees.

But the *fugheiria* I brought back from Portugal is more useful. It is a small cast-iron charcoal brazier which the local people use for grilling fresh sardines. We use it for our Continental picnics. It is handy to have the car, if you are inclined, like me, to buy heavy souvenirs. That's probably why we have so many of those large terracotta vases in our garden.

Of course, you *can* drive quickly about on wonderful motorways in Europe if you need to hurry. Try driving on the E6 Euroroute from Rome to the North Cape right up in Norway in the Arctic Circle for instance. That's a good run. I was at the North Cape last summer, and when I got there – the most northerly point of Europe – I must confess I was mildly surprised, even disappointed, that there was nowhere further to go.

I suppose that's the point of it all really. Once you get to your destination you have to find somewhere else to travel to. Now, I am a professional traveller and I spend a lot of my time on the road. Between you and me, I like it and the *Daily Mirror* even pays me to do it. What did that canny Scot Robert Louis Stevenson say?

'To travel hopefully is a better thing than to arrive, and the true success is to labour.'

I don't know about the last phrase. Swanning about among the country byways across the Channel is very pleasant work. I was a foreign correspondent based in Paris and I often had to rush off on important stories at a moment's notice, often working with the keen and dedicated European newshounds.
Those boys knew a lot about fast driving, and their cars were built to be driven hard. But the most urgent chase would be brought to a screeching halt if one of the hatchet-faced newshawks looked at his watch at about midday and said;

'Alors, c'est l'heure du repas. On me dit qu'on peut manger pas mal prés d'ici. Je crois qu'il y a un petit restaurant . . . '

That's how once when it was the hour of the repast, the missing diplomat we wanted to interview was forgotten and I came to be eating *lampreys** near Bordeaux. (Ugh, they're dreadful). A Frenchman feels he's lost face if he does not know the speciality of the region. So, as the stranger, I had to be the one to try it.

Well into the woods up in the Ardennes hills of Belgium once, famished, I tracked down a remote restaurant that specialised in back of hare, *rable de lievre.* The young chef was desolated, he said, for the hare was not fit to eat. Nonsense, we said, we like our hare a bit gamey in England. That was the trouble, he explained. The back of the hare had not been long enough in the marinade to do justice to such an animal. Solemnly we proceeded to the kitchen, stomachs caved in with hunger. A stern jury, we examined the evidence.

We held a colourful post mortem in the kitchen. We bared our arms, plunged our hands into a barrel of red wine, herbs and juniper berries and dragged out the blue carcass. After much prodding we persuaded the chef that in England, after all, we did *not* like our game too hairy. It was delicious.

In Italy I plunged right into the crowd scene when I took a side turning in Ventimiglia and found myself trapped in the biggest open-air market in that part of the country. The locals were voluble. A number of excited merchants waved their hands in expressive gestures and shouted. Now, I didn't understand a word. But I could imagine what a Cockney street trader in London's Petticoat Lane would have said if I had tried to drive through there on a crowded market day.

But , *'Me no provoke'* is the best adage for travellers abroad. So you wear them down with nods and smiles until eventually you all become quite good friends. They moved their vans and even some of their stalls, gave me a melon and a bunch of onions and advised on the best place to eat.

Talk about food to anyone in Europe and their faces will light up as though they have had a revelation that the English really did join the human race when they joined the Common Market.

And it's always worth trying to speak a few words of the local language.

A friend of mine, fevered with an extravagant desire to buy a gift both exciting and feminine in Paris, dragged me out of the car in a tricky parking area and into the many-storeyed emporium of *Galeries Lafayette.*

'Ask the lady for me,' he urged. 'Tell her what I want.'

'Er-excuse-moi, madame,' I hesitated, *'mais, où se trouve les frilly knickers?'*

The French saleswoman directed us without batting one cynical Parisien eyelid to where the frillies found themselves.

A stop for a drink and a stretch every couple of hours seems about right for my life style. I know people who hit the *autobahn* and drive flat out for hours on end, but that does not suit me. Mind you, don't make every stop an excuse for an alcoholic drink. The police in Europe are putting into effect now stiffer regulations to stop drinking and driving. Anyway, coffee abroad is usually so good that it makes a refreshing drink accompanied by a glass of water as a chaser.

You do need to keep your wits about you because, on the whole, I reckon the Continentals are better drivers than the British. They seem to drive with rather more flair. We possibly err on the side of prudence. But whatever your temperament, it

* eel like fish

pays to use your mirrors. I like to feel that I am driving in a sort of flexible plastic bubble like a large observation dome with all-round vision.

In slow traffic, it contracts fore and aft, but bulges out sideways to take in what people on either side are up to. For fast driving, the imaginary bubble extends well ahead so that I can anticipate what anything else within range might do. Sounds a bit fanciful, I suppose, but it works for me.

Headlamps on British cars dip to the left, our edge of the road, but, of course, abroad when you dip your lights that brings the beam right into the eyes of approaching drivers. So do take a few minutes to clip on plastic headlamp converters. Remember, too, that if you have a heavy load weighing down the rear of the car this will bring up your headlamps at the front end, so check that the beam is aligned correctly with a full holiday load aboard. Keep a spanner handy, too, for tightening up the roof rack if you have to use one. They usually loosen a little after a few hours of jigging up and down on the road.

Different countries have different styles of driving. Frankly, though, it is the British drivers that terrify me. They adopt a bulldog attitude and really come straight on and hit you if they think thay are in the right. Most Continentals dash up, then stop at the last moment.

Watch out for fork roads leading in from the right in Europe joining what appears to be the main road. The old *'priorité à droite'* rule, giving priority to vehicles coming from the right, is still firmly entrenched in many rustic minds in rural areas. So be prepared for them to swing out slap in front of you from some byway.

I'm a byways man myself, of course – I love exploring the meandering back lanes. And finding accommodation for the night is simple, too, if you stick to the villages and avoid the busy towns. What you eat is usually more memorable than where you sleep, so I prefer to ring ahead and book a table for dinner at some off-the-beaten-track place and ask them if they know of a family hotel nearby where I can take a room for the night. The odds are that the restaurateur or one of the family lets rooms in the village. Before you know where you are, you are in the middle of the village life chatting over a nightcap with your new friends.

That's how I discovered the 'trou Normande'. It is a tot of fiery Calvados apple spirit taken in the 'hole' between courses in Normandy. Normandy cooking is rich with cream sauces, so it is not a bad idea to drink a *'digestif'* with it. But after a long chat and a *trou* with the hotelier's wife who ran the cash desk another *trou* with the husband, the chef, and others with the daughter and sons I was glad I had a bed for the night there and did not have to drive.

Enjoying your car journey and your driving is only half the battle. As well as giving you extra challenges, the long distance you will cover, with the extra load, will put unaccustomed stresses on the engine too.

Remember the old nemonic 'POWER'. That stands for petrol, oil, water, electrics and rubber. (Rubber means tyres). The least you can do is to attend to those basics. Hire a box of spares from your garage or the AA (see page 28), already prepared for your model of car. You get your deposit back when you return the box after your holiday. Book your car in for a thorough service before you set off.

Driving on the different side of the road can have its problems. The main dangers are when you are overtaking and coming out of garages, hotel exits and approaching roundabouts.

A useful reminder is to tell yourself: *I am a visitor in their country. I am humble. I sit in the gutter.* Then you can be sure that you are driving your British right-hand drive car on the correct side of the road.

Distracted by trying to count your foreign currency as you leave the petrol service station, it is dangerously easy to swing the car the wrong way, directly into the on-coming traffic. Fortunately, at most roundabouts there are arrows pointing the way. But when in doubt, and when you feel the heavy hand of mental fatigue coming on, don't try to work it out. Follow the other traffic. And if you are really panicked, stop, no matter where you are, and have a think.

Planning ahead is fun, but do not be too ambitious. Take time to look at the view as you go along. I reckon the more stops we have the more pleasant the journey. But then, I know the trouble that writers of guide books go to, so I like to use maps and guide books to wander and explore where-ever I go.

General information

The 1979 edition of *Motoring in Western Europe* aims to provide practical reading. Essentially, two major information sections are provided, one of a general nature and one dealing with European motoring regulations. These two divisions are maintained throughout the country sections but are specific to the countries with which they deal. Thus, the tourist has a broad background picture to all countries and specific detail concerning the country in which he is travelling.

If you are travelling to Greece and Yugoslavia or countries in Scandinavia or Eastern Europe separate booklets are available to you. These are *Motoring in Scandinavia, Motoring in South-East Europe* and *Motoring in North-East Europe.* They may be obtained on application to any AA office.

AA agents

The Association does not maintain offices outside Britain but is represented by allied motoring clubs throughout Europe. Additionally it has appointed port agents at the more popular ports whose particular function is to assist and advise motorists embarking or disembarking. Recovery agents have also been appointed throughout Europe and their activities are restricted to vehicle recovery. European motoring clubs allied to the AA will extend a courtesy service to AA members but this will be commensurate with their facilities. Agents will operate within their limitations and none would be able to extend the wider range of AA services. An exception would be the AA Continental Emergency Centre in Boulogne (see page 149), which is equipped for wider operations.

Accommodation

Hotels and motels The lists of hotels and motels for each country have been compiled from information given by members, by the motoring organisations and tourist offices of the countries concerned, and from many other sources.

Your comments concerning the whole range of hotel information – whether included in this Guide or not, and whether in praise or in criticism – will always be most welcome; a special form will be found on page 394, and all information will be treated in the strictest confidence.

Gazetteer entry The gazetteer entry is complied from information supplied by the proprieter. The establishments shown in italics indicate that particulars have not been confirmed by management.

Complaints *You are advised to bring any criticism to the notice of the hotel management immediately. This will enable the matter to be dealt with promptly to the advantage of all concerned.* If a personal approach fails, members should inform the AA. You are asked to state whether or not your name may be disclosed in any enquiries we may make.

Classification Although the system of classification in Europe is similar to the AA system in this country, the variations in the traditions and customs of hotel-keeping abroad often made identical grading difficult.

Hotels and motels are classified by stars. The definitions are intended to indicate the type of hotel rather than the degree of merit. Meals, service, and hours of service should be in keeping with the classification, and all establishments with restaurants must serve meals to non-residents and are expected to give good value for money.

★ Hotels simply furnished but clean and well kept; all bedrooms with hot and cold running water; adequate bath and lavatory facilities.
★★ Hotels offering a higher standard of accommodation; adequate bath and lavatory facilities on all main floors and some private bathrooms and/or showers.
★★★ Well-appointed hotels; at least 40 per cent of bedrooms with private bathrooms and bidets.
★★★★ Exceptionally well-appointed hotels offering a very high standard of comfort and cuisine, room and night service; at least 80 per cent of bedrooms with private bathrooms; suites available on request.
★★★★★ Luxury hotels offering the highest standard of accommodation, service, and comfort.

Motels, etc Motels, motor hotels and some purpose-built hotels are indicated by white stars (eg ☆☆).
These establishments conform to the major requirements of their star classification but their facilities are designed to cater particularly for overnight stays. In some cases, porterage and

room service may be rather restricted for the classification but this is offset by studio-type bedrooms, a higher proportion of private bathrooms to bedrooms, extended meal hours, and more parking space.

A list of motels, published by the European Motel Federation, is obtainable by AA members from Hotel and Information Services, AA, Basingstoke, Hants RG21 2EA.

Charges The gazetteer normally quotes terms minimum and maximum for one and two persons with Continental breakfast price added to the room tariff to give inclusive terms for bed and breakfast with and without private facilities. If an English breakfast is also available, this will be indicated by (English breakfast) in the gazetteer entry.

However, in some cases, proprietors have indicated that English breakfast *only* is available; although this may mean that the price for Continental breakfast has already been included in the room tariff.

DP indicates *demi-pension* (half-board) terms only available which means that in addition to the charge for rooms, guests are expected to pay for one main meal whether it is taken or not.

Pn indicates *pension* (full board) terms only available. Both these terms are shown minimum and maximum with and without private facilities for one and two persons. See page 4 'Symbols and Abbreviations' for further information.

Example of a gazetteer entry

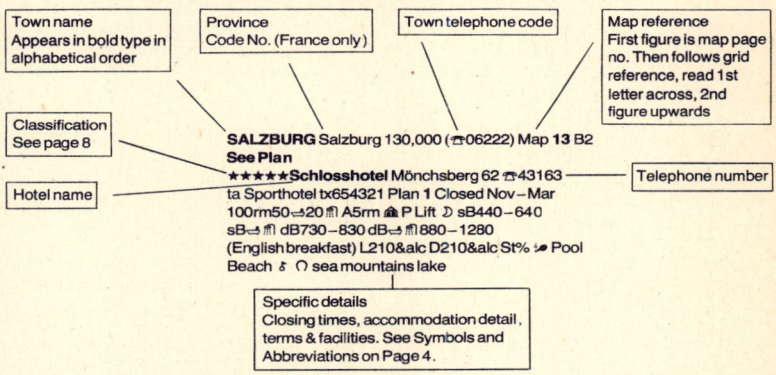

Hotels are not required by law to exchange travellers' cheques for guests, and many small hotels are unable to do so. You must expect to pay a higher rate of commission for this service at a hotel than you would at a bank.

Every effort is made to get up-to-the-minute prices, but tariffs may be increased due to changes in taxes or economic circumstances and during public holidays, festivals, etc. You are advised to confirm prices when making reservations.

Town plans Listed below are major towns and cities for which there are town plans, followed by page numbers. A list of hotels showing the plan no. can be found adjacent to the relevant plan. In addition, the appropriate plan number will appear following the telephone number in the hotel entry. These numbers correspond to the number on the plan thereby giving the location of the hotel.

Reservations The practice is the same in Europe as it is this country; rooms are booked subject to their still being available when confirmation is received. It is therefore most important that confirmation should be sent to the hotel as soon as possible after the rooms have been offered. Unfortunately, many hotels will not accept bookings for one or two nights only. Sometimes a deposit is required which can be arranged through your bank. Many hotels do not hold reservations after 19.00hrs, and you should advise hotels if you anticipate a late arrival or if you are unable to take up your booking for any reason. Unwanted rooms can then often be relet and you will be saved the expense of paying for them, as a confirmed booking represents a legal contract.

Hotel telephone numbers are given in the gazetteer.

The AA regrets that it cannot make reservations on your behalf, except in conjunction with one of the holiday schemes, details of which are available from any AA travel agency.

When writing direct, it is advisable to enclose an international reply coupon; these are available from any post office.

When reservations are made on the spot, it is the custom to inspect the rooms offered and to ask for the price before accepting them. No embarrassment is caused by this practice, and British visitors are urged to adopt it in their own interests.

Double rooms may not be reduced in price when let to one person; however, a double room is generally cheaper than two rooms. Accommodation in an annexe may be of a different standard from rooms in the main hotel building; it is advisable to check the exact nature of the accommodation at the time of reservation.

AA signs The AA issues signs on request to hotels listed in this Guide. You are advised, however, not to rely solely on the sign, but to check that the establishment still appears in this edition.

Villas and chalets Full details of this AA service can be obtained from any AA travel agency.

Camping and caravanning Information is given separately in the guide to *Camping and Caravanning in Europe*.

Annual events

The short list of events provided in the country sections gives only those which recur annually at about the same time. A complete list of notable events throughout the year is available from the appropriate national tourist office and is usually available during March.

Breakdown

If your car breaks down, endeavour to move it to the side of the road or to a position where it will obstruct the traffic flow as little as possible. Place a warning triangle at the appropriate distance on the road behind the obstruction. Bear in mind road conditions and if near or on a bend the triangle should be placed round the bend. If the car is fitted with hazard warning lights these may be switched on but they will only warn on the straight and will have no effect at bends or rises in the road. If the fault is electrical, the lights may not operate and it is for these reasons that they cannot take the place of a triangle. Having taken these first precautions, seek assistance if you cannot deal with the fault yourself. The local motoring club should be called for 'first aid' and in obtaining their assistance the local police may be helpful. If you use the service of a garage and are holding AA credit vouchers always ensure that the garage will accept these before you commit yourself to any expense. See the country sections and 5-Star information for more details.

In order to obtain free roadside assistance from the main European motoring clubs which are affiliated to the Alliance Internationale de Tourisme (AIT), it is necessary to be an AA member and to possess AA travel insurance – 5-Star Service.

The AA *5-Star Service* provides a wide range of service, insurance and credit facilities within certain specified limits and is divided into three parts:

1 *Vehicle Security* includes vehicle recovery, the location and delivery of spare parts, free roadside assistance from AIT patrols*, the use of the AA Continental Emergency Centre based at Boulogne, AIT credit vouchers*, legal assistance*, financial assistance toward the turnout of a breakdown vehicle and towage, comprehensive service booklet, emergency repatriation voucher, and chauffeur service following illness.

2 *Touring Security* includes cover for car hire, travel and accommodation expenses following the loss of the use of a vehicle due to breakdown, accident or theft.

3 *Personal Security* includes cover for luggage, medical expenses, loss of deposits, loss of money and personal accident.

Items starred are available to full AA members only.

If an AA member has not taken 5-Star Service and he requires the vehicle recovery and/or spare parts service, the AA will help but assistance cannot be provided until a deposit to cover service fees and all estimated costs has been made. In addition a charge is made for arranging emergency medical assistance.

British Consulates

Consulates overseas will help or advise British travellers only if they are in serious trouble or distress. They will not advance money or finance a traveller for any reason, nor will they do the work of travel agents, information bureaux, banks or police. The loss of valuables including passports, is a police matter and should be reported to them, not a consulate. In most countries there is usually more than one British Consulate with varying degrees of status. In the country sections the address of the most important will be given but the towns in which other consulates will be found are also given.

Currency

As all countries (including the United Kingdom) have regulations controlling the import and export of currency, you are advised to consult your bank for full information before making final arrangements.

Customs concessions

Visitors to the countries listed in this Guide may assume as a general rule that they may temporarily import personal articles duty free, providing the following conditions are met:

1. that the articles are for personal use and are not to be sold or otherwise disposed of;
2. that they may be considered as being in use and in keeping with the personal status of the importer;
3. that they are taken out when the importer leaves the country;
4. that the importer stays less than 6 months in any 12-month period.

Customs officers may withhold concessions at any time and may ask the traveller to deposit enough money to cover possible duty especially on portable items of apparent high value such as television sets, radios, cassette recorders, pocket calculators, musical instruments etc (which must be declared). Any deposit paid (for which a receipt must be obtained) is likely to be high but is recoverable, but only at the entry point at which it was paid, on leaving the country and exporting the item. Before making any deposit it is as well to enquire whether it is possible to take any Customs document to cover the temporary importation or whether an entry can be made on the importer's passport. If such a Customs document is taken or a passport entry made ensure that it is cancelled when the item is exported. Concessions may not apply if the traveller enters the country more than once a month, or if he is under 17 years of age (an alternative age may apply in some countries). Should you be taking a large number of personal effects with you, it would be a wise measure to prepare in advance, an inventory to present to the Customs authorities on entry. All dutiable articles must be declared when you enter a country, otherwise you will be liable to penalties. It is generally accepted that the following quantities can be taken into most European countries without payment of duty or purchase tax:

1. **Tobacco** 200 cigarettes or 250 grammes of other manufactured tobaccos;
2. **Wine** 1 litre of wine with the exception of Austria and Switzerland (2 litres);
3. **Spirits** 1 litre of spirits with the exception of Portugal (half a litre);
4. **Toilet water** 0.25 litre;
5. **Cameras** 1 camera, 1 cine-camera.

Customs concessions for the United Kingdom

If, when leaving Britain, you export any items of new appearance, such as watches, items of jewellery, cameras etc, particularly of foreign manufacture, which you bought in the UK, make sure you carry the retailer's receipt, otherwise you may experience difficulty when re-importing the items on your return.

Returning to the United Kingdom When returning to the United Kingdom you must declare everything (purchases or gifts) in excess of the duty-free allowances (set out below) which you have obtained abroad or on the journey, or free of duty or tax in this country. You must also declare any alterations or additions which have been made to your motor car while abroad.

Prohibitions and restrictions The importation of certain goods into the United Kingdom is prohibited or restricted. These include controlled drugs, counterfeit coins, firearms (including gas pistols), ammunition, explosives, gold coins, medals, medallions and similar gold pieces, horror comics, indecent and obscene books, magazines, films and other articles, live animals and birds, derivatives of rare species including certain fur skins, and garments thereof, and plumage, meat and poultry (not fully cooked), plants, potatoes, bulbs, trees and certain vegetables and fruit, radio transmitters (including walkie-talkies) radio microphones and microbugs.

Stop at Thomas Cook before you start to travel.

You'll be taking the car, naturally. So the way to avoid those extra tickets as you flit between travel agencies looking for the service you want, call in at the bank, have a word with your insurance brokers, check on the visa situation, is to call in at **Thomas Cook** Your one-stop travel shop. They can sort out all your problems.

Consider your car booked
Car ferries and motor-rail links are no problem. Once we've confirmed you're on, you're on.

We'll put the right money in your pocket
As a motorist abroad, you'll need currency as well as the usual Travellers Cheques.

You'll be hard put to find a better exchange rate than in your **Thomas Cook** travel shop. And you'd have to drive hard to find a country where **Thomas Cook** Travellers Cheques are not recognised.

Vis-a-Vis Passports
Red tape doesn't daunt us. Passport renewals, visas, international driving licences, even camping carnets – we can advise you on all aspects of official documentation.

And should you break down...
Not only do you have the facilities of local **Thomas Cook** and affiliate offices throughout Europe, but you can also get the potentially invaluable benefits of all the 24-hour emergency services of Europ Assistance – with their protection you need never be stranded by breakdown or accident.

And remember, when you make a car ferry booking with us, you also get our exclusive Holiday Bonus offer, which adds up to savings of up to £40 on all your holiday needs. As well as the greatest saving and borrowing plan ever: The **Thomas Cook** Budget Travel Plan.

So make sure you stop at **Thomas Cook** before you start to travel and let us sort out all your problems.

Thomas Cook
The trusted name in travel. Everywhere.

Duty and tax-free allowances   You are entitled to the allowances in either column 1 or column 2.
The countries of the EEC (Common Market) are Belgium, Denmark, France, West Germany, the Irish Republic, Italy, Luxembourg, the Netherlands and the United Kingdom (but not the Channel Islands).

	Goods obtained duty and tax-paid in the EEC.	Goods obtained outside the EEC, or duty or tax-free in the EEC.	
Tobacco goods			
Cigarettes	300	200	double if you live outside Europe
or			
Cigarillos	150	100	
or			
Cigars	75	50	
or			
Tobacco	400 grammes	250 grammes	
Alcoholic drinks			
Over 38.8° proof (22° Gay Lussac)	1½ litres	1 litre	
or			
not over 38.8° proof or fortified or sparkling wine	3 litres	2 litres	
plus			
still table wine	3 litres	2 litres	
Persons under 17 are not entitled to tobacco and drinks allowances.			
Perfume	75 grammes (3fl oz or 90cc)	50 grammes (2fl oz or 60cc)	
Toilet water	375cc (13fl oz)	250cc (9fl oz)	
Other goods	£50 worth	£10 worth	

Customs Notice No. 1 is available to all travellers at the point of entry or on the boat and contains useful information of which returning tourists should be aware.

Customs offices

Many Customs offices at the main frontier crossings are open 24 hours daily to deal with touring documents.

Those with restricted opening times are listed below. The hours shown are for the handling of tourist documents. At all frontier crossings, other transactions, such as the payment of duty, can be carried out during normal business hours only.

The table can be read in either direction; eg for France–Belgium read from left to right, for Belgium–France read from right to left.

Nearest town	Map ref	Road number	Frontier post	Opening times		Frontier post	Road number	Map ref	Nearest town
France						**Belgium/Luxembourg**			
Dunkirk	3 A1	N16A	Oest-Capel	06.20-22.00		Kapelhoek (Stavele)	N9	3 A1	**Ypres**
Lille	3 B1	D941	Baisieux	08.00-12.00 14.00-18.00 Mon-Fri		Hertain	N8	3 B1	**Tournai**
Valenciennes	3 B1	D169	Maulde	06.00-22.00		Bléharies	N71	3 B1	**Tournai**
Maubeuge	3 B1	D936	Cousolre	07.00-21.00		Leugnies	N36	3 B1	**Beaumont**
Avesnes	3 B1	D962	Hestrud	07.00-22.00		Grandrieu	N21	3 B1	**Beaumont**
Rocroi	10 C4	D949	Givet	08.00-21.00		Petit Doische	N46	10 C4	**Philippeville**
Rocroi	10 C4	D949	Givet	08.00-21.00		Dion	N46	10 C4	**Beauraing**
France						**Germany**			
Metz	11 A3	D954	Villing	06.00-22.00 (1 Oct-31 Mar)	04.00-23.00 (1 Apr-30 Sep)	Ittersdorf Villinger Strasse	269	11 A3	**Saarlouis**

Inside
it's unbeatable.
Outside
it's unbreakable.

These days St. Ivel Fivepints is better value than ever.

Altogether more delicious whether you use it for cooking or in drinks.

And of course, the lightweight, unbreakable bottle's tailormade for the outdoor life. It's even got a resealable lid that means your Fivepints stays fresh for weeks.

So make sure you stock up with plenty before you go on holiday.

The next best thing to fresh milk.

Nearest town	Map ref	Road number	Frontier post	Opening times	Frontier post	Road number	Map ref	Nearest town
France					**Italy**			
Bourge St-Maurice	28 C4	N90	Col du Petit St-Bernard	Always (when pass is open)	Col Du Petit St-Bernard	26	28 C4	**Aosta**
St Michel de-Maurienne	28 C3	N6	Grand-Croix	Always (when pass is open)	Molaretto	25	28 C3	**Susa**
France					**Spain**			
Bayonne	20 C3	D20	Ainhoa	1 May-30 Sep 07.00-24.00 / 1 Oct-30 Apr 07.00-22.00	Dancharinea	N121	20 C3	**Pamplona**
St-Jean-Pied-de-Port	20 C3	D933	Arnéguy	as above	Valcarlos	C135	20 C3	**Pamplona**
Oloron-Ste-Marie	20 C3	N134	Urdos	16 Jun-30 Sep Always / 1 Oct-15 Jun 08.00-21.00	Canfranc	N330	20 C3	**Jaca**
Pau	20 C3	N134 bis	Eaux-Chaudes	1 Jun-31 Oct 07.00-24.00 / 1 Nov-31 May 08.00-21.00	Sallent-de-Gallego	C136	20 C3	**Huesca**
Montrejeau	20 D3	D125	Bagnères de Luchon	08.00-22.00	Bosost-El Portillón	D27	20 D3	**Viella**
St-Béat	20 D3	N618C	Fos	As above	1 May-30 Sep Always / 31 Oct-30 Apr 08.00-24.00	Lés	N230	20 D3	**Viella**
Amélie-les-Bains	22 D4	D115	Prats-de-Mollo	1 Jun-30 Sep Always / 1 Oct-31 May 08.00-16.30	Camprodón	C151	22 D4	**Ripoll**
Belgium					**Netherlands**			
Maldegem	3 B2	68	Stroobrugge	Summer: 07.00-24.00 Winter: 07.00-21.00	Eede	N97	3 B2	**Breskens**
Gent	3 B2	56	Watervliet	07.00-19.00	Veldzigt	Unclass	3 B2	**Breskens**
Turnhout	4 C2	20	Weelde	07.00-24.00	Baarle-Nassau	Unclass	4 C2	**Breda**
Netherlands					**Germany**			
Emmen	4 D3	N92	Coevorden	06.00-24.00	Escherbrügge	403	4 D3	**Nordhorn**
Zutphen	4 D2	Unclass	's-Heeren-berg	06.00-24.00	Heerenber-gerbrücke	E36	4 D2	**Emmerich**
Venlo	4 D2	Unclass	Herungerweg	06.00-22.00	Niederdorf	60	4 D2	**Moers**
Italy					**Switzerland**			
Aosta	28 C4	27	Grand St Bernard Pass Tunnel	Always (when pass is open) / Always	Grand St Bernard Pass Tunnel	21	28 C4	**Martigny**
Domodóssola	28 D4	337	Ponte Ribellasca	05.00-24.00/01.00	Camedo	69	28 D4	**Locarno**
Luino	28 D4	394	Zenna	06.00-23.00 Hols 06.00-24.00	Dirinella	Unclass	28 D4	**Locarno**
Luino	28 D4	Unclass	Fornasette	Weekdays–06.00-23.00 Holidays–06.00-24.00	Fornasette	Unclass	28 D4	**Lugano**
Porlezza	28 A4	340	Valsolda	05.00-02.00 (Oct-Mar 05.30-01.00)	Gandria	Unclass	28 A4	**Lugano**
Chiavenna	12 C1	36	Montespluga	05.00-01.00 (when pass is open)	Splügen Pass	64	12 C1	**Thusis**
Tirano	29 A4	38	Piattamala	1 May-30 Sep 05.00-02.00 / 1 Oct-30 Apr 05.00-01.00	Campocologno	29 via Bernina Pass	29 A4	**Pontresina**
Bormio	12 D1	38	Giogo di Maria (Stelvio)	05.00-24.00 (when pass is open)	Umbrail Pass	28	12 D1	**Sta Maria**
Glorenza	12 D1	41	Tubre	04.00-24.00	Mustair	28	12 D1	**Sta Maria**
Switzerland					**Austria**			
Zernez	12 D1	27	Martina	04.00-24.00	Nauders (Zolhaus)	185	12 D1	**Nauders**
Italy					**Austria**			
Merano	12 D1	448	Passo del Rombo	07.00-20.00 (when pass is open)	Timmelsjoch	186	12 D1	**Sölden**
Tolmezzo	13 B1	52 bis	Timau (Monte Croce Carnico) Always	May-Sep; Oct 08.00-20.00; Nov-Apr 08.00-18.00 (when pass is open)	Mauthen via Plöcken Pass	110	13 B1	**Ober-Drauburg**

Nearest town	Map ref	Road number	Frontier post	Opening times		Frontier post	Road number	Map ref	Nearest town
Pontebba	13 B1	Unclass	Passo di Pramollo	Always (when pass is open)		Nassfeld	Unclass	13 B1	**Hermagor**

Portugal   ## Spain

Nearest town	Map ref	Road number	Frontier post	Opening times		Frontier post	Road number	Map ref	Nearest town
Oporto	17 A3	N13	Valenca do Minho	1 Jul-30 Sep 07.00-01.00 1 Oct-30 Jun 07.00-01.00	1 Apr-31 Oct 07.00-01.00 1 Nov-31 Mar 08.00-24.00	Tuy	550	17 A3	**Vigo**
Vila Real	17 B3	N103-5	Vila Verde da Raia	1 Jul-30 Sep 07.00-24.00 1 Oct-30 Jun 08.00-21.00	May-Oct 07.00-24.00 Nov-Apr 08.00-21.00	Feces de Abajo	N525	17 B3	**Orense**
Bragança	18 C2	N218-1	Quintanilha	1 Jul-30 Sep 07.00-23.00 1 Oct-30 Jun 07.00-20.00	Apr-Oct 07.00-24.00 Nov-Mar 08.00-21.00	San Martin del Pedroso/ Alcañices	N122	18 C2	**Zamora**
Guarda	17 B1	N16	Vila Formoso	1 Jul-30 Sep 07.00-24.00 1 Oct-30 Jun 07.00-23.00	Apr-Oct 07.00-01.00 Nov-Mar 08.00-24.00	Fuentes de Oñoro	N620	17 B1	**Salamanca**
Castelo Branco	23 B4	N355	Segura	1 Jul-30 Sep 08.00-24.00 1 Oct-30 Jun 08.00-24.00	1 May-1 Oct 07.00-24.00 2 Oct-30 Apr 09.00-21.00	Piedras Albas	C 523	23 B4	**Caceres**
Portalago	23 B4	N246-1	Galegos	1 Jul-30 Sep 07.00-20.00 1 Oct-30 Jun 07.00-20.00	1 Apr-31 Oct 07.00-24.00 1 Nov-31 Mar 08.00-21.00	Valencia de Alcantara	N521	23 B4	**Caceres**
Elvas	23 B3	N4	Caia	1 Jul-30 Sep 07.00-01.00 1 Oct-30 Jun 07.00-23.00	Apr-Oct 07.00-01.00 Nov-Mar 08.00-24.00	Caya	N5	23 B3	**Merida**
Maurão	23 B3	N256	Sâ Leonardo	1 Jul-30 Sep 07.00-24.00 1 Oct-30 Jun 07.00-20.0	1 Apr-31 Oct 07.00-24.00 1 Nov-31 Mar 08.30-21.00	Villanueva del Fresno	C436	23 B3	**Zafra**
Beja	23 B3	N260	Vila Verde de Ficalho	1 Jul-30 Sep 07.00-24.00 1 Oct-30 Jun 07.00-20.00	1 Apr-30 Sep 07.00-24.00 1 Oct-31 Mar 08.00-21.00	Resal de La Frontera	N433	23 B3	**Seville**
Faro	23 B3	N125	Vila Real de Santo Antonio	1 Jul-30 Sep 08.30-24.00 1 Oct-30 Jun 08.00-20.00	1 May-31 Oct 08.00-24.00 1 Nov-30 Apr 09.00-21.00	Ayamonte	N431	23 B2	**Huelva**

Denmark   ## Germany

Nearest town	Map ref	Road number	Frontier post	Opening times		Frontier post	Road number	Map ref	Nearest town
Abenrå	1 A1	A10 (E3)	Krusâ Padborg		Always 06.00-24.00	Kupfer-mühle Harrislee	76(E3)	1 A1	**Flensburg**

NB For crossings between Northern Ireland and the Republic, see page 257.

WARNING

Overseas visitors should not bring pets of any kind with them to Britain unless they are prepared for the animals to go into lengthy quarantine. Because of the continuing threat of rabies, penalties for ignoring the regulations are extremely severe.

Have the time of your life...

with an AA Members Holiday Loan.

Why put off that fabulous holiday of your dreams? Or reduce your savings, when an AA Members Holiday loan can spread the cost? Loans are arranged simply, quickly and confidentially. And interest rates are *specially reduced for AA members*.

Whether you're planning a motoring tour, a camping trip, a package holiday, a cruise, or a visit to loved ones far away, we can cover all your expenses...fares, accommodation, new clothes, equipment, and spending money. With our help you could have the time of your life and plenty of time to pay. Just fill in and post the coupon below for details. You don't even need to buy a stamp.

Documents required

As well as a current passport, a tourist temporarily importing a motor vehicle should carry either an International Driving Permit or a valid national driving licence, the registration document of the car or an International Certificate for Motor Vehicles, and evidence of insurance. The proper international distinguishing sign should be affixed to the rear of the vehicle. The appropriate papers must be carried at all times and secured against loss. The practice of spot checks on foreign cars is widespread and to avoid inconvenience or an on-the-spot fine ensure that your papers are in order and that the registration distinguishing sign is of approved standard design. The notes under the country headings will detail the requirements for individual countries where these depart from the following general information.

British Driving Licence Provided you are over 18 years of age you may drive in all the countries covered by this guide on a valid British driving licence (not a provisional) for a limited period and provided you are a *bona fide* tourist without any residential qualifications in the country you are visiting. Austria, Italy and Spain differ from this general statement.

International driving permit An internationally recognised document which enables the holder to drive a motor vehicle without local formality for a limited period in a country in which he is a visitor. Its full validity is one year from the date of its issue and it is not renewable. Its issue is necessary for some countries who do not accept the visitor's national driving licence.
The Permit, for which a charge is made, is issued by the AA to an applicant who holds a valid British (or Irish) driving licence and who is over 18 years old. It cannot be issued to the holder of a foreign licence who must make his application in the country where his driving licence was issued.

Registration document This must show that the vehicle is registered in the name of the importer. Clearly this would not be the case if the car is hired or borrowed when it is better to carry an International Certificate for Motor Vehicles, together with a letter signed by the registered owner authorising the importer to have the use of the vehicle.

International Certificate for Motor Vehicles A general licence which, when used in conjunction with recognised nationality plate, makes it unnecessary to register the vehicle in the country to be visited. It is valid for one year from the date of its issue and it is not renewable. The Certificate, for which a charge is made, is issued by the AA for some countries who do not accept foreign registration papers or to avoid complication if the vehicle is not registered in the importer's name.

Insurance Motor insurance is compulsory by law in all the countries covered in this Guide with the exception of Portugal (where it is likely to be during 1979). But you are strongly advised to ensure that you are adequately covered for all countries in which you will travel. It is best to seek the advice of your insurance company regarding the extent of cover and full terms of your existing policy. Not all insurers will be willing to offer cover in the countries that you intend to visit and it may be necessary to seek a new, special policy for the trip from another company. Should you have any difficulty, AA Insurance Services will be pleased to help you.

International Green Card of Insurance Is recognised in most countries as evidence that you are covered to the minimum extent demanded by law and the AA recommends its use. It will be issued by your own insurers but since its provisions are an extension to an existing policy, an additional premium will be charged. It will name all the countries for which it is valid and should be specially endorsed for a caravan or trailer if one is to be towed. The document will not be accepted until you have signed it.

If your cover is inadequate, temporary policies may be effected at all frontiers but this is a most expensive way of covering yourself. Austria is an exception.

Green Cards and the Common Market (EEC) In accordance with a Common Market Directive, the production and inspection of Green Cards at the frontiers of Common Market countries is no longer a legal requirement and the principle has been accepted by other European countries who are not members of the EEC. The Community countries concerned are Belgium, Denmark, France, West Germany, Republic of Ireland, Luxembourg, and the Netherlands. The non-EEC countries also subscribing to the Directive are Austria, Czechoslovakia, the German Democratic Republic, Finland, Hungary, Norway, Sweden and Switzerland. Italy, although a member of the EEC, prefers tourists to be able to produce a Green Card if required. You are advised to consult your insurer regarding the matter.

The fact that Green Cards will not be inspected does not remove the necessity of having insurance cover as required by law in the countries concerned. All private car policies issued by British Insurance companies should now provide cover for the minimum legal requirement in the countries mentioned. This does not mean that the full extent of your cover at home is automatically extended, however, and in some circumstances you may find yourself without adequate cover. You are therefore strongly advised to contact your insurers in good time prior to any trip abroad to ensure that the cover you have is satisfactory.

Although Green Cards are not legally required in EEC countries or those listed above, and that they may not be inspected at the frontiers of those countries, does not mean that they have been abolished altogether. They will still be required for other countries in Europe (eg Spain) and for such countries as Turkey, Israel, Morocco and Tunisia. In addition, they may prove more effectively than an Insurance Certificate that the minimum insurance requirements operative in the country visited have been met. They are internationally recognised by police and other authorities and may save a great deal of inconvenience in the case of an accident.

Spain – extra insurance is recommended in the form of a Bail Bond.

Nationality plate A nationality plate of the approved pattern, oval with black letters on a white background, and size (GB at least 6.9in by 4.5in), must be displayed on a vertical or near vertical surface at the rear of your vehicle (and caravan or trailer if you are towing one). On the Continent checks are made to ensure that a vehicle's nationality plate is in order. In some countries fines are imposed for failing to display a nationality plate, or for not displaying the correct nationality plate. A list of international distinguishing signs appears on pages 21 and 22.

Carnet de Passages en Douane This is a valuable document which enables a motorist to temporarily import certain vehicles into another country without having to deposit duty. The cost of this document, which can be issued by the AA, depends on the number of countries to be visited which require a *Carnet de Passages en Douane*. Generally the document is not required for motor vehicles temporarily imported into European countries for periods not exceeding six months by *bona fide* tourists. Any other category of person should refer to the AA to ascertain if a Carnet can be issued.

Belgium – a Carnet is required for towed pleasure craft over 18ft (5.5 metres) long, motor boats, and outboard motors without boats.

France – a Carnet is required for outboard engines exceeding 92cc (5cv as applied to marine engines) with or without boats.

Luxembourg – a Carnet is required for all towed pleasure craft.

If you are issued with a *Carnet de Passages en Douane,* you must ensure that it is properly discharged as you cross each frontier in order to avoid inconvenience and expense, possibly including payment of Customs charges, at a later date.

Electrical information

The public electricity supply in Europe is predominantly AC (alternating current) of 220 volts (50 cycles) but can be as low as 110 volts. In some isolated areas low voltage DC (direct current) is provided. European circular two-pin plugs and screw-type bulbs are usually the rule. However, before connecting any appliances, it is advisable to consult the hotel or campsite proprietor, or check the voltage stamp on a light bulb.
Useful electrical adaptors (not voltage transformers) which can be used in Continental shaver points and light bulb sockets are available in the United Kingdom, usually from the larger electrical appliance retailers.

Ferry crossing

From Britain the shortest sea crossing from a southern port would be obvious but it might not always be the best choice bearing in mind how it places you on landing for main roads to your destination. Your starting point is important because if you have a long journey to a southern port then a service from an eastern port might be more convenient. Perhaps a Motorail service to the south might save time and possibly an overnight stop? In some circumstances the south-western ports may offer a satisfactory service and before making bookings it may be worth seeking advice so that the journey can be as economic and as comfortable as possible. The AA provides a full information and booking service on all sea, motorail and hovercraft services and instant confirmation is available on many by ringing one of the numbers listed below (Monday to Friday, 09.00 – 17.00). Ask also if you want information and booking on Continental car-sleeper and ferry services.

The South-East	01-977 0177	The North	061-486 0777
The West & Wales	Bristol 24417	Scotland	041-812 2888
The Midlands	021-550 7648	Northern Ireland	Belfast 26242
		Republic of Ireland	Dublin 777004

Garages

The garages listed in the gazetteer for each country are those which are most likely to be of help to members on tour, because of their situation and the services they have stated they can provide. Although the AA cannot accept responsibility for difficulties over repairs to members' cars, any unsatisfactory cases will be noted for amendment in later editions of the guide to *Motoring in Western Europe*.

It cannot be emphasised too strongly that disputes with garages on the Continent must be settled on the spot. It has been the AA's experience that subsequent negotiations can seldom be brought to a satisfactory conclusion.

In selecting garages, preference has been given to those which provide a breakdown service (see below), good garaging space in major cities and in the Channel ports and those accepting AIT Credit Vouchers. The number of garages holding each agency reflects, as far as possible, the relative popularity of the various makes of cars. Although firms normally specialise in the makes for which they are accredited agents, they do not necessarily hold stocks of spare parts. Certain garages will repair only the make of car for which they are officially agents as indicated in the text.

A complete list of service agencies for your own make of car is generally available through your own dealer. It has been found on occasions that some garages in Europe make extremely high charges for repairing tourists' cars; always ask for an estimate before authorising a repair.

France All prices must be displayed on the premises so that they are clearly visible and legible. When you have had a repair carried out, you should receive an invoice stating the labour charge, *ie* the hourly rate (displayed) multiplied by the time spent or the time shown on the time schedule for each operation, and not just a lump sum. The price of supplies and spares, shown separately. Parts which have been replaced must be returned to you, unless it is a routine replacement or the repair is carried out free during the guarantee period.

Spain Garages are officially classified. Blue signs displayed outside garages indicate the classification I to III as well as the type of work that can be dealt with, by means of symbols. There must be set prices for common repair jobs and these must be available to customers so that they may authorise repairs. A complaints book must also be available and this is inspected during official visits by representatives of the local authority.

Breakdowns An explanation of the breakdown service symbols is given on page 4. *Breakdown services operated by European garages have no connection with the AA Continental Breakdown Service.*

Details of services operated by clubs affiliated to the AA are given under the Motoring Club section in the countries concerned.

Hours of opening In most European countries normal business hours are 08.00–18.00hrs; these times may be altered on Sundays and public holidays, when repairs, breakdown service, and petrol are often unobtainable. An indication of service outside normal business hours is given by abbreviations (see page 4).

In many countries, especially France, it may be difficult to get a car repaired during August because many garages close down for annual holidays.

International time

All Continental countries are ahead of GMT as follows:

Country	Hours ahead of GMT		Country	Hours ahead of GMT	
	Winter	Summer		Winter	Summer
United Kingdom	**0**	**1**	Luxembourg	1	2
Austria	1	1	Netherlands	1	2
Belgium	1	2	Portugal	0	1
France and Monaco	1	2	Spain and Andorra	1	2
Germany	1	1	Switzerland and		
Italy and San Marino	1	2	Liechtenstein	1	1

International distinguishing signs

(Established by international conventions and/or as notified to the United Nations) The standardisation of distinguishing signs to two letters is being considered at international level but it is likely to be several years before any decision is reached and implemented. The suggested new signs, which are given in parentheses, will be used on a national basis ie for aircraft, radio, and boats, etc.

A	(AT)	Austria*
ADN	(YD)	Democratic Yemen (formerly Aden)*
AFG	(AF)	Afghanistan[1]
AL		Albania
AND	(AD)	Andorra
AUS	(AU)	Australia*
B	(BE)	Belgium
BDS	(BB)	Barbados*
BG		Bulgaria
BH	(BZ)	Belize (formerly Honduras)
BR		Brazil
BRN	(BH)	Bahrain
BRU	(BN)	Brunei*
BS		Bahamas*
BUR	(BU)	Burma
C	(CU)	Cuba[1]
CDN	(CA)	Canada
CH		Switzerland
CI		Ivory Coast
CL	(LK)	Sri Lanka (formerly Ceylon)*
CO		Colombia[1]
CR		Costa Rica
CS		Czechoslovakia
CY		Cyprus*
D	(DE)	German Federal Republic[1]
DDR	(DD)	German Democratic Republic
DK		Denmark
DOM	(DO)	Dominican Republic
DY		Benin (formerly Dahomey)
DZ		Algeria
E	(ES)	Spain (including African localities and provinces)
EAK	(KE)	Kenya*
EAT	(TZ)	Tanzania (formerly Tanganyika)*
EAU	(UG)	Uganda*
EC		Ecuador
ET	(EG)	Arab Republic of Egypt
F	(FR)	France (including overseas departments and territories)
FJI	(FJ)	Fiji*
FL	(LI)	Liechtenstein[1]
GB		United Kingdom of Great Britain & Northern Ireland*
GBA		Alderney* ⎫ Channel
GBG		Guernsey* ⎬ Islands
GBJ		Jersey* ⎭
GBM		Isle of Man*[1]

GBZ	(GI)	Gibraltar
GCA	(GT)	Guatemala
GH		Ghana
GR		Greece
GUY	(GY)	Guyana* (formerly British Guiana)
H	(HU)	Hungary
HK		Hong Kong*
HKJ	(JO)	Jordan
I	(IT)	Italy
IL		Israel
IND	(IN)	India*
IR		Iran[1]
IRL	(IE)	Ireland*
IRQ	(IQ)	Iraq[1]
IS		Iceland
J	(JP)	Japan*
JA	(JM)	Jamaica*
K	(KH)	Khmer Republic (formerly Cambodia)
KWT	(KW)	Kuwait[1]
L	(LU)	Luxembourg
LAO	(LA)	Laos
LAR	(LY)	Libya[1]
LB	(LR)	Liberia[1]
LS		Lesotho (formerly Basutoland)*
M	(MT)	Malta*
MA		Morocco
MAL	(MY)	Malaysia*
MC		Monaco
MEX	(MX)	Mexico
MS	(MU)	Mauritius*
MW		Malawi*
N	(NO)	Norway
NA	(AN)	Netherlands Antilles
NIC	(NI)	Nicaragua
NL		Netherlands
NZ		New Zealand*
P	(PT)	Portugal
P	(AO)	Angola
P	(CV)	Cape Verde Islands
P	(MZ)	Mozambique*
P	(GN)	Guinea
P	(ST)	São Tomé and Principe
PA		Panama[1]
PAK	(PK)	Pakistan*
PE		Peru
PL		Poland
PY		Paraguay
R	(RO)	Romania
RA	(AR)	Argentina

RB	(BW)	Botswana (formerly Bechuanaland)*	SYR	(SY)	Syria	
RC	(TW)	Taiwan (Formosa)	T	(TH)	Thailand*	
RCA	(CF)	Central African Republic	TG		Togo	
RCB	(CG)	Congo	TN		Tunisia	
RCH	(CL)	Chile	TR		Turkey	
RH	(HT)	Haiti	TT		Trinidad and Tobago*	
RI	(ID)	Indonesia*				
RIM	(MR)	Mauritania[1]	U	(UY)	Uruguay	
RL	(LB)	Lebanon	USA	(US)	United States of America	
RM	(MG)	Malagasy Republic (formerly Madagascar)	V	(VA)	Holy See (Vatican City)	
RMM	(ML)	Mali	VN	(VD)	Republic of Vietnam	
ROK	(KP)	Korea (Republic of)				
RP	(PH)	Philippines	WAG	(GM)	Gambia	
RSM	(SM)	San Marino	WAL	(SL)	Sierra Leone	
RSR	(RH)	Rhodesia (formerly Southern Rhodesia)*	WAN	(NG)	Nigeria	
			WD	(DM)	Dominica*	Windward Islands
RU	(BI)	Burundi[1]	WG	(GD)	Granada*	
RWA	(RW)	Rwanda	WL	(LC)	St Lucia*	
			WS		Western Samoa*	
S	(SE)	Sweden	WV	(VC)	St Vincent (Windward Islands)*	
SD	(SZ)	Swaziland*				
SF	(FI)	Finland				
SGP	(SG)	Singapore*	YU		Yugoslavia	
SME	(SR)	Surinam (Dutch Guiana)*	YV	(VE)	Venezuela	
SN		Senegal	Z	(ZM)	Zambia*[1]	
SU		Union of Soviet Socialist Republics	ZA		South Africa*	
SY	(SC	Seychelles*	ZR		Zaire (formerly Congo Kinshasha)	

*In countries marked with an asterisk the rule of the road is drive on the left; otherwise drive on the right.

Notes
[1] Not included in the United Nations list of signs established according to the 1949 Convention on Road Traffic.

Medical treatment

Travellers who are in the habit of taking certain medicines should make sure that they have a sufficient supply to last for their trip since they may be very difficult to get abroad.

Those who suffer from certain diseases (diabetes or coronary artery diseases, for example) should get a letter from their doctor giving treatment details. Some Continental doctors will understand a letter written in English, but it is better to have it translated into the language of the country that it is intended to visit. The AA cannot make such a translation.

Travellers, who for legitimate health reasons carry drugs or appliances (hypodermic syringe etc) may have difficulty with Customs or other authorities. Others may have a diet problem which would be understood in hotels but for a language problem. The letter which such persons carry should therefore supply treatment details, a statement for Customs, and diet requirements.

The National Health Service is available in the United Kingdom only and medical expenses incurred overseas cannot be reimbursed by the United Kingdom Government. However, there are reciprocal health agreements with some of the countries covered by this Guide. The country sections will provide further details concerning local arrangements. You are strongly advised to take out comprehensive and adequate insurance cover before leaving the United Kingdom. The AA offers excellent cover under personal security and will be pleased to offer advice.

Reciprocal Health Agreements If you are visiting any of the European community countries, the EEC Social Security Regulations will probably entitle you to receive treatment on the same basis as insured people in that country. However, not everyone is covered. A form E111, Certificate of Entitlement, is usually required in order to benefit from these arrangements. Further details and the application form for Form E111 are contained in leaflet SA28. Leaflet SA30 lists all of the countries, in addition to the EEC countries, with which the UK has health agreements and states what documents must be carried in order to receive urgent medical treatment free or at a reduced cost. Leaflets SA28 and SA30 are available from local offices of the Department of Health and Social Security.

Further information about health care arrangements overseas is obtainable from the Department of Health and Social Security, Alexander Fleming House, Elephant and Castle, London SE1 6BY, tel/01-407 5522 ext 6641 (non-EEC countries), ext 6681 (EEC countries).

Stop the miseries of Travel Sickness

Travel Sickness: what makes it even more sickening is that if one member of your holiday party suffers from it, then everybody suffers!

Whether you go by car, coach, plane, boat or hovercraft – take SEA-LEGS.

Pleasant to take, virtually tasteless, and suitable for all the family, SEA-LEGS stays effective long enough for you to take it on the night before you set out!

As soon as you've seen your travel agent, see your chemist about SEA-LEGS.

If you can't take the ups and downs of travel, take

sea-legs

and settle down to a good journey.

DF Sea-Legs is a Trade Mark of Duncan, Flockhart & Co. Ltd. DF75 59 HN

Vaccination requirements Guidance about international vaccination requirements and other medical advice is given in the leaflet *Notice to Travellers* obtainable from the Department of Health and Social Security at the address on page 22 and telephone number ext 6749/6711.

Metric conversion tables

To convert miles to kilometres, read the appropriate number in the central column as the measurement in miles, and its equivalent in kilometres opposite in the left-hand column. To convert kilometres to miles, read the appropriate number in the central column as the measurement in kilometres, and its equivalent in miles opposite in the right-hand column. Use the tables in similar fashion for other conversions.

Kilometres		Miles	Metres		Feet	Kilograms		Pounds
1.609	1	0.621	0.305	1	3.281	0.454	1	2.205
3.219	2	1.243	0.610	2	6.562	0.907	2	4.409
4.828	3	1.864	0.914	3	9.843	1.361	3	6.614
6.437	4	2.486	1.219	4	13.123	1.814	4	8.818
8.047	5	3.107	1.524	5	16.404	2.268	5	11.023
9.656	6	3.738	1.829	6	19.685	2.722	6	13.228
11.265	7	4.350	2.134	7	22.966	3.175	7	15.432
12.875	8	4.971	2.438	8	26.247	3.629	8	17.637
14.484	9	5.592	2.743	9	29.528	4.082	9	19.842
16.093	10	6.214	3.048	10	32.808	4.536	10	22.046
32.187	20	12.427	6.096	20	65.617	9.072	20	44.092
48.280	30	18.641	9.144	30	98.425	13.608	30	66.139
64.374	40	24.855	12.192	40	131.233	18.144	40	88.185
80.467	50	31.069	15.240	50	164.042	22.680	50	110.231
96.561	60	37.282	18.288	60	196.850	27.216	60	132.277
112.654	70	43.496	21.336	70	229.658	31.751	70	154.324
128.748	80	49.710	24.384	80	262.467	36.287	80	176.370
144.841	90	55.923	27.432	90	295.275	40.823	90	198.416

Kilograms per sq cm		Pounds per sq in	Litres		Gallons	Litres		Pints
0.070	1	14.224	4.546	1	0.220	0.568	1	1.76
0.141	2	28.447	9.092	2	0.440	1.136	2	3.52
0.211	3	42.671	13.638	3	0.660	1.705	3	5.28
0.281	4	56.894	18.184	4	0.880	2.273	4	7.04
0.352	5	71.118	22.730	5	1.100	2.841	5	8.80
0.422	6	85.341	27.276	6	1.320	3.410	6	10.56
0.492	7	99.565	31.822	7	1.540	3.978	7	12.32
0.562	8	113.788	36.368	8	1.760	4.546	8	14.08
0.633	9	128.012	40.914	9	1.980			
0.703	10	142.235	45.460	10	2.200			

Motoring Clubs in Europe

Alliance Internationale de Tourism The AIT is the largest confederation of touring associations in the world and it is through this body that the AA is able to offer its members the widest possible touring information service. Its membership consists not of individuals, but of associations or groups of associations having an interest in touring. The Alliance was formed in 1919 – the AA was a founder member and is represented on its Administrative council and Management Committee. The General Secretariat of the AIT is in Geneva.

Tourists visiting a country where there is an AIT club may avail themselves of its touring advisory services upon furnishing proof of membership of their home AIT club. AA members making overseas trips should, whenever possible, seek the advice of the AA before setting out and should only approach the overseas AIT clubs when necessary.

Passports and Visas

Every person in the vehicle must hold an up-to-date passport valid for all countries through which it is intended to travel. There are various types of passport, including a limited British visitor's passport available from the main post office, depending upon the user's requirements. Further information can be obtained from any of the passport offices listed below. Applications in the United Kingdom should be made to your nearest passport office allowing four weeks for passport formalities to be completed and should be accompanied by two identical photographs.

Channel Islands
Guernsey   White Rock, St Peter Port
Jersey   Victoria Chambers, St Helier

England
Liverpool   Passport Office, 5th Floor, India Buildings, Water Street, L2 OQZ, *tel* 051-227 3461
London   Passport Office, Clive House, 70 Petty France, SW1H 9HD *tel* 01-222 8010
Peterborough   Passport Office, 55 Westfield Road, PE3 6TG *tel* 0733 263636

Isle of Man
Isle of Man   Government Office, Douglas

Northern Ireland
Belfast 1   F & C Office, Passport Agency, Marlborough House, 30 Victoria Street, BT1 3LY *tel* 32371 (Personal applications only)

Scotland
Glasgow   Passport Office, 1st floor, Empire House, 131 West Nile Street, G1 2RY *tel* 041-332 0271

Wales
Newport   Passport Office, Olympia House, Upper Dock Street, NPT 1XA, Gwent (Mon) *tel* 0633 52431

Irish Passport   Irish citizens resident in the Dublin Metropolitan Area or in Northern Ireland should apply to the Passport Office, 39 Dawson Street, Dublin 2. If resident elsewhere in Ireland, application should be made through the nearest Garda Station. Irish citizens resident in Britain should apply to the Irish Embassy, 17 Grosvenor Place, London SW1X 7HR.

Visas   Holders of a British passport bearing on the cover the name of a colony, protectorate, trust territory, or showing the national status as 'British Protected Person' should consult the embassy or consulate of the countries to be visited.

Petrol and oil

In Western Europe, and indeed throughout the world, grades of petrol compare favourably with those in UK. International brands are usually available on main tourist and international routes, but in the more remote districts named brands may not be so readily available. In Eastern Europe international brands are not always on sale but an equivalent standard will be found. The minimum amount of petrol which may be purchased is usually five litres (just over one gallon). It is advisable to keep the petrol tank topped up, particularly in remote areas or if wishing to make an early start when garages may be closed. Some garages may close between 12.00 and 15.00hrs for lunch.
Cars hired in countries where petrol coupons are available will not be entitled to coupons. You are strongly advised to secure your petrol with a locking filler cap.

Octane rating   The international method of denoting the grade of petrol is by an octane number. In Britain this rating is related to a star method, 2-Star – 90/93 octane; 3-Star – 94/96 octane; 4-Star – 97/99 octane and 5-Star – 100/101 octane. The range will vary with individual brands so that if 2-Star is used it will be not less than 90 and not higher than 93 octane.
In Britain the motorist uses a fuel recommended by the vehicle manufacturers and this is expressed by an octane number. Overseas he should use a grade in the recommended range. If a car requires a fuel in the high octane range (100 or higher) and he is visiting a country where he suspects that this may not be available then it is possible that engine adjustments may be made for a satisfactory performance on a lower grade. If such adjustments are contemplated then the advice of the vehicle manufacturer or his agent must be sought. If a lower grade petrol than that recommended by the manufacturer is used then the speed of the car must be restricted.

Petrol prices   A list of petrol prices is given on the chart on page 73. These are an average of the varying prices in the different districts of the country and are given in local currency per litre. Although there is a tendency for these prices to increase the rise is usually gradual but it would be misleading to quote them in sterling per gallon because the exchange rates fluctuate frequently and often violently. Thus it is more reliable to make a conversion when you have bought your currency and know what rate you were given. By multiplying the litre price by 4.55 you will have the price per gallon in the local currency. By applying the current rate of exchange you will have a reasonable guide to the current sterling price per gallon. Petrol prices at filling stations on motorways will be higher than elsewhere whilst at self-service pumps it will be slightly cheaper.

Remember that the fuel which is contained in the tank may be temporarily imported duty free, but that duty may have to be paid on any carried in cans. On sea and air ferries and European car-sleeper trains operators insist that spare cans must be empty.

Note: a roof rack laden with luggage increases petrol consumption, which should be taken into consideration when calculating mileage per gallon.

Liquified Petroleum Gas/LPG

The availability of this gas in Europe makes a carefully planned tour, with a converted vehicle, limited but feasible. The gas is retailed by several companies in Europe who will supply information as to where their product may be purchased. A motorist regularly purchasing the fuel in UK could possibly obtain lists of European addresses from his retailer but in cases of difficulty the AA may be able to help.

According to information available there are two such filling stations in Austria, both in Vienna, as many as 700 in the Benelux countries, few in France where the fuel was illegal until 1979, 16 in W Germany, about 24 in Italy (mainly in the north), 25 in Spain, and 1 in Switzerland, in Lausanne.

Engine oil

Brands and grades of engine oil familiar to the British motorist are usually available in Western Europe but may be difficult to find in remote country areas. When available they will be much more expensive than in the UK and generally packed in 2-litre cans (3½ pints). A motorist can usually assess the normal consumption of his car and should be strongly advised to carry with him what oil he is likely to require for his trip. Automatic transmission fluid is not always readily available and the tourist should carry an emergency supply with him.

Preparing your vehicle for a holiday abroad

We know as well as anyone how expensive mechanical repairs and replacement parts can be in Europe. A vast number of the breakdowns we have dealt with have occurred simply because people did not take the trouble to prepare their cars before setting off. Remember that a holiday abroad is not just another day trip, but often involves many miles of hard driving over roads completely new to you, perhaps without the facilities you have come to take for granted in this country. Many people think 'it can never happen to me', but it can and will if the car is not properly prepared or if it is overloaded.

We recommend that a major service be carried out shortly before your holiday or tour abroad. In addition it is advisable to give the car a general check to see that there are no visible or audible defects. It is impracticable for us to provide you with an itemised check list in view of the differences that exist between the various makes and types of car but using the manufacturer's handbook for your particular car, it should be possible to ensure that no obvious faults are missed. If AA members would like a thorough check of their car made by one of the AA's experienced engineers, any service centre can arrange this at a few days' notice. Our engineer will then submit a written report complete with a list of the repairs required. There is a fee for this service; for more detailed information please ask for our leaflet *Tech 8*.

The following tips should prove useful:

Tyres

Inspect your tyres carefully; if you think they are likely to be more than three-quarters worn before you get back, it is better to replace them before you start out. Expert advice should be sought if you notice uneven wear, scuffed treads or damaged walls, or whether the tyres are suitable for further use. In some European countries, drivers can be fined if tyres are badly worn.

When checking tyre pressures, remember that if the car is heavily loaded the recommended pressures may have to be raised a few pounds per square inch above normal. This should also be done for high-speed driving. Check the recommendations in your handbook. Don't check the pressure immediately after a run, as the tyres will still be hot and pressure will have increased quite a lot, even after a short trip. Don't forget about your spare. Many unfortunates know how embarrassing it is to have a blowout miles from anywhere, only to find that the spare, which they last pumped up a year ago, is flat!

Tubeless tyres

In some countries, tubeless tyres are not in general use. It is a good idea to take an inner tube of the correct size and type so that this can

LUCAS SERVICE.
YOU CAN GO A LONG WAY FOR IT.

Right to the toe of Italy if you have to.
Because Lucas have an agent there,
ready to help you with any electrical service you
may need.

So however far from home you are, you
can rely on Lucas' European network of 2,500
distributors and sub-distributors to keep you on the
right track.

Simply ring any main Lucas Service
distributor, and he'll direct you to the nearest sub-
distributor.

Send for your free copy of our booklet
which lists all Lucas European distributors.

And find out
just how far you can go
to get Lucas service.

Lucas Service

Miss M. King, Lucas Service Overseas Ltd.,
Windmill Rd, Haddenham, Aylesbury, Bucks. HP17 8JB.

be fitted if all else fails. When the tube is inserted it is advisable to put this wheel on the rear axle, in case a blowout should occur. Moderate speeds only should be used until the tyre has been properly repaired.

Warm-climate touring

In hot weather and at high altitudes, excessive heat in the engine compartment can cause carburation problems. It is advisable, if you are towing a caravan, to consult the manufacturers about the limitations of the cooling system, and the operating temperature of the gearbox fluid if automatic transmission is fitted.

Cold-weather touring

If you are planning a winter tour in Europe, make sure that you fit a high-temperature (winter) thermostat and make sure that the strength of your anti-freeze mixture is correct for the low temperatures likely to be encountered.

If you are likely to be passing through snow-bound regions, it is important to remember that for many resorts and passes the authorities insist on wheel chains, spiked or studded tyres, or snow tyres. In some countries, such as Austria and Germany, however, the use of spiked or studded tyres is banned. See Road conditions page 30.

Note: The above comments do not apply where severe winter conditions prevail. It is doubtful whether the cost of preparing a car, normally used in the UK, would be justified for a short period. However, the AA's Technical Services Department will be pleased to advise on specific enquiries.

Brakes

The brakes are one of the really vital parts of the car and yet they are very often neglected. Like other mechanical parts, brakes become worn with use and unless they are regularly checked and maintained, worn linings and pads, or hydraulic fluid leaking from faulty cylinders or perished hoses could prove lethal.

If you are about to start a long European trip and the brake linings of your vehicle are more than half worn, it is in your interests – and other people's – to change them before you leave. It is also advisable to have your brake fluid changed if it is more than two years old. Fluid that has absorbed moisture can lead to brake failure in arduous conditions, such as descending long mountain passes.

Engine and mechanical

Consult your vehicle handbook for servicing intervals. Unless the engine oil has been changed recently, drain and refill with fresh oil and fit a new filter. Deal with any significant leaks by tightening up loose nuts and bolts and renewing faulty joints or seals.

If you suspect that there is anything wrong with the engine, however insignificant it may seem, it should be dealt with straight away. Even if everything seems in order, don't neglect such commonsense precautions as checking valve clearances, sparking plugs, and contact breaker points, and make sure that the distributor cap is sound. The fan belt should be checked for fraying and slackness. If some of the items mentioned previously are showing signs of wear but are still serviceable, it is a good idea to replace them and take the displaced parts with you as spares.

Any obvious mechanical defects should be attended to at once. Look particularly for play in steering connections and wheel bearings and, where applicable, ensure that they are adequately greased. A car that has covered a high mileage will have absorbed a certain amount of dirt into the fuel system and as breakdowns are often caused by dirt, it is essential that all filters (petrol, oil and air) should be cleaned or renewed.

The cooling system should be checked for leaks and any perished hoses or suspect parts replaced.

Electrical

Don't begin a journey without first making a check of the electrics. This applies particularly if the car is not so new and perhaps a light or a switch is not working. Any malfunction can very easily go unnoticed until the battery is run flat or even a fire occurs, so it is very important to trace any small fault.

Check that all the connections are sound and that the wiring is in good condition. Should any problems arise with the charging system, it is essential to obtain the services of a qualified auto-electrician.

Lighting adjustments

Left dipping headlights are not permitted. However, there are several adaptors which can be used, but owing to the variety both of bulbs and headlamps, manufacturers should be consulted for the best method of adapting either of these for European use. In France, yellow headlights are used.

Remember to have the lamps set to compensate for the load being carried.

Spares

The problem of what spares to carry is a difficult one; it depends on how long you are likely to be away. It is possible to hire an AA Spares Kit; full information about this service is available from any AA service centre.

In addition to the items contained in the spares kit, the following would also prove useful:

A pair of windscreen wiper blades;   a torch;
a length of electrical cable;   a fire extinguisher;
an inner tube of the correct type;   a tow rope;
a roll of insulating or adhesive tape.

It is compulsory in some countries to carry a set of spare bulbs. Remember that when ordering spare parts for dispatch abroad you must be able to identify them as clearly as possible and by the manufacturer's part numbers if known. When ordering spares, always quote the engine and chassis numbers of your car.

General   Make sure that you have clear all-round vision. See that your seat belts are securely mounted and not damaged, and remember that in most European countries their use is compulsory.

If you are carrying skis, remember that their tips should point to the rear. You must be sure that your vehicle complies with the regulations concerning dimensions for all the countries you intend to pass through (see country sections). This is particularly necessary if you are towing a trailer of any sort. If you are planning to tow a caravan, you will find advice and information in the AA's guide to *Camping and Caravanning in Europe.*

Photography

Photography in European countries is generally allowed without restriction, with the exception of photographs taken within the vicinity of military or government establishments.
Signs are usually prominent where the use of cameras is prohibited. These are obvious – mostly a picture of a camera with a diagonal line across it is shown.

Public holidays

Public holidays, on which banks and shops are closed, vary from country to country, but generally fall into two categories; those which are fixed on the calendar by some national festival or religious date and those which are moveable. The latter, usually religious, are based on a moveable Easter Sunday, and the actual dates will be given in any current diary.

The following lists give the moveable and fixed holidays and also the dates of moveable ones for the next few years.

Fixed holidays

Epiphany	Jan 6
St Joseph	Mar 19
St Peter and St Paul	Jan 29
Assumption	Aug 15
All Saints	Nov 1
Christmas	Dec 25

Moveable holidays

	1979	1980	1981
Easter	Apr 13	Apr 4	Apr 17
Easter Day (Sun)	Apr 15	Apr 6	Apr 19
Ascension	May 24	May 15	May 28
Whit Sun	Jun 3	May 25	Jun 7
Trinity	Jun 10	Jun 1	Jun 18
Corpus Christi	Jun 14	Jun 5	Nov 29
Advent	Dec 2	Nov 30	

Religious services

Refer to your religious organisation in the British Isles. A directory of British Protestant churches in Europe, North Africa and the Middle East entitled *English Speaking Churches,* can be purchased from the Commonwealth and Continental Church Society, 175 Tower Bridge Road, London SE1 2AO *tel* 01-407 4588.

Report forms

We would appreciate your comments on accommodation, garages and roads to help us to prepare future publications. Please list your comments on the report forms provided at the back of the guide. The accommodation report form is for your comments on hotels and motels which you have visited, whether they are listed in the handbook or not.

Similarly, the garage report form can be used for your reports on garages which you have visited. The road report form can be used for particularly bad stretches and road works.

Road conditions

Main roads are usually in good condition but often not finished to our standards. The camber is often steeper than that usually found in the United Kingdom, and edges may be badly corrugated and surfaces allowed to wear beyond the customary limits before being repaired. In France such stretches are sometimes signposted *chaussée deformée*. However, there are extensive motorway systems in Germany and Italy, and many miles of such roads in other countries. When roads under repair are closed, you must follow diversion signs – often inadequate – such as *deviation* and *umleitung*. To avoid damage to windscreens or paintwork, drive slowly over loose grit and take care when overtaking. Further information on roads is also given under country sections.

The months of July and August are at the peak of the touring season particularly in Austria, Belgium, France and Germany when school holidays start, and during this period motorways and main roads are heavily congested. Throughout the summer there is a general exodus from the cities, particularly at weekends and tourists should be prepared for congested roads and consequent hold-ups.

Tolls are charged on most motorways in France, Italy, Spain and sections in Austria and you may feel they are expensive. Over long distances the toll charges could be quite considerable. For example, for a journey from Calais to Nice and return, the toll charges amount to about £40. Cars with caravans are charged about £60. A motorised caravan, due to its height, on which tolls are based, attracts even higher charges in France. No doubt you will weigh the cost against time and convenience, (eg overnight stops) particularly as the alternative all-purpose roads are often fast. In addition to the toll motorways, tolls are charged on some bridges, tunnels and mountain roads. The more important ones are given in the country sections. All toll charges should be used as a guide only as they are subject to change.

Route planning

The AA European Route Planning Service, available only to AA members, consists of a series of route planning maps and town plans for which a charge is made. In addition the popular route books have been up-dated and re-introduced for 1979. A charge is also made for these. The whole series is complementary (see map on page 31) and can be supplied as a complete pack or separately. They may be obtained by completing the application form on page 397 and sending it, with an appropriate remittance, to the address given.

Throughroute Maps: (scale approximately 33 miles to 1 inch)

A series of six maps each based on a different main European cross-Channel port: Boulogne, Calais, Cherbourg, Dieppe, Le Havre and Ostend/Zeebrugge. These maps are not ordinary road maps but are designed to give guidance on straightforward journeys by indicating the easiest and quickest AA-recommended route plus the mileage from each port to a large number of destinations, in Western Europe.

European Route   (scale approximately 33 miles to 1 inch)
Planning Map:

Suitable for general planning purposes, this map covers Western Europe excluding Scandinavia. It shows motorways, main roads, distances and road numbers and includes an index of placenames.

Country Maps: (scale approximately 16 miles to 1 inch)

A new series of motorists' maps covering France (No. 1), Spain and Portugal (No. 2), Benelux and Germany (No. 3) and Switzerland, Austria, and Italy (No. 4). They show classes of roads, road numbers, distances in kilometres, mountain pass information, toll roads, bridges and tunnels, ferries, airports, scenic roads etc.

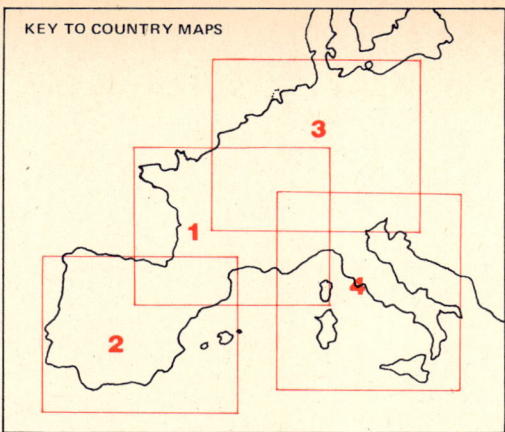

KEY TO COUNTRY MAPS

Two Scandinavian maps (No. 8, Southern, No. 9, Northern) are available, scale approximately 16 miles to 1 inch except Finland, Northern Norway and Northern Sweden. They are the same as those issued in 1978 and include town plans, internal ferry information, a mileage chart, touring advice and an index of placenames.

Any of these country maps can be especially marked on request, to indicate a suggested route.

Town Plans
A series of four books of town plans of the larger European towns. Book 1 covers France, 2 Spain and Portugal, 3 Belgium, Netherlands, Luxembourg and Germany, 4 Switzerland, Austria and Italy. A plan of Paris (city centre and environs) is also available.

Route Books
Each book describes all main routes and a large proportion of other routes, for the area covered. The itineraries include a description of the scenery, road conditions and gradients, road numbers and distances.

Passes and tunnels

Principal mountain passes

It is best not to attempt to cross mountain passes at night, and daily schedules should make allowance for the comparatively slow speeds inevitable in mountainous areas.

Gravel surfaces (such as grit and stone chips) vary considerably; they are dusty when dry, slippery when wet. Where known to exist, this type of surface has been noted. Road repairs can be carried out only during the summer, and may interrupt traffic. Precipitous sides are rarely, if ever, totally unguarded; on the older roads stone pillars are placed at close intervals. Gradient figures take the mean on hairpin bends, and may be steeper on the insides of the curves, particularly on older roads.

Before attempting late-evening or early-morning journeys across frontier passes, check the times of opening of the Customs offices. A number of offices close at night, eg the Timmelsjoch border crossing is closed between 20.00 and 07.00hrs.

Caravans
Passes suitable for caravans are shown. Those shown to be *negotiable* by caravans are best used only by experienced drivers driving cars with ample power. The remainder are probably best avoided. A correct power-to-load ratio is always essential.

Conditions in winter
Winter conditions are given in italics in the last column. *UO* means usually open, although a severe fall of snow may temporarily obstruct the road for 24–48 hours, and wheel chains are often necessary; *OC* means occasionally closed between the dates stated; *UC* usually closed between the dates stated. Dates for opening and closing the passes are approximate only. Warning notices are usually posted at the foot of a pass if it is closed, or if chains or snow tyres should or must be used. Wheel chains may be needed early and late in the season and between short spells (a few hours) of obstruction. At these times conditions are usually more difficult for caravans.

In fair weather, wheel chains or snow tyres are only necessary on the higher passes, but in severe weather you will probably need them (as a rough guide) at altitudes exceeding 2,000ft. (See also Winter conditions page 65).

Pass and height	From To	Distances from summit and max gradient		Min width of road	Conditions
*Albula 7,595ft Switzerland (Map 12 C1)	Tiefencastel (2,821ft) La Punt (5,546ft)	31km 9km	1 in 10 1 in 10	12ft	UC Nov–late May. An inferior alternative to the Julier; tar and gravel; fine scenery. Alternative rail tunnel (see page 56).
Allos 7,382ft France (Map 28 C2)	Barcelonnette (3,740ft) Colmars (4,085ft)	20km 24km	1 in 10 1 in 12	13ft	UC early Nov–late May. Very winding, narrow, partially unguarded but not difficult otherwise; passing bays on southern slope, good surface.
Aprica 3,875ft Italy (Map 29 A4)	Tresenda (1,220ft) Edolo (2,264ft)	14km 15km	1 in 11 1 in 16	13ft	UO. Fine scenery; good surface, well graded; suitable for caravans.
Aravis 4,915ft France (Map 28 C4)	La Clusaz (3,412ft) Flumet (3,008ft)	8km 12km	1 in 11 1 in 11	13ft	OC Dec–late Mar. Outstanding scenery, and a fairly easy road.
Arlberg 5,912ft Austria (Map 12 C1/2)	Bludenz (1,905ft) Landeck (2,677ft)	33km 35km	1 in 8 1 in 7½	20ft	OC Nov–Apr. Modern road; short, steep stretch from west, easing towards the summit; heavy traffic; negotiable by caravans; parallel new road tunnel opened Dec 1978.
Aubisque 5,610ft France (Map 20 C3)	Eaux Bonnes (2,461ft) Argelès-Gazost (1,519ft)	11km 32km	1 in 10 1 in 10	11ft	UC early Nov–Jun. A very winding road; continuous but easy ascent; the descent incorporates the Col de Soulor (4,757ft); 8km of very narrow, rough, unguarded road, with a steep drop.
Ballon d'Alsace 3,865ft France (Map 11 A2)	Giromagny (1,830ft) St-Maurice-sur-Moselle (1,800ft)	17km 9km	1 in 9 1 in 9	13ft	OC Dec–Mar. A fairly straightforward ascent and descent, but numerous bends; negotiable by caravans.
Bayard 4,094ft France (Map 28 C3)	Chauffayer (2,988ft) Gap (2,382ft)	18km 8km	1 in 12 1 in 7	20ft	UO. Part of the Route Napoléon. Fairly easy, steepest on the southern side; negotiable by caravans from north to south.
*Bernina 7,644ft Switzerland (Map 12 C1)	Pontresina (5,915ft) Poschiavo (3,317ft)	15.5km 17km	1 in 10 1 in 8	16ft	OC Nov–late Apr during the day, but closed at night. A good road on both sides; negotiable by caravans.
Bonaigua 6,797ft Spain (Map 22 C4)	Viella (3,150ft) Esterri del Aneu (3,185ft)	23km 16km	1 in 12 1 in 12	14ft	UC Nov–Apr. A sinuous and narrow road with many hairpin bends and some precipitous drops; the alternative route to Lérida through the Viella tunnel is open in winter.
Bracco 2,018ft Italy (Map 29 A2)	Riva Trigoso (141ft) Borghetto di Vara (318ft)	15km 18km	1 in 7 1 in 7	16ft	UO. A two-lane road with continuous bends; passing usually difficult; negotiable by caravans; alternative toll motorway available.
Brenner 4,495ft Austria-Italy (Map 13 A1)	Innsbruck (1,885ft) Vipiteno (3,115ft)	39km 14.5km	1 in 12 1 in 7	20ft	UO. Parallel toll motorway open; heavy traffic may delay at Customs; suitable for caravans; Resia Pass and Felbertauern Tunnel possible alternatives.
†Brünig 3,304ft Switzerland (Map 11 B1)	Brienzwiler Station (1,886ft) Giswil (1,601ft)	6km 13km	1 in 12 1 in 12	20ft	UO. An easy but winding road; heavy traffic at weekends; suitable for caravans.

*Permitted maximum width of vehicles 7ft 6in
†Permitted maximum width of vehicles 8ft 2½in

Spotlight on the Algarve

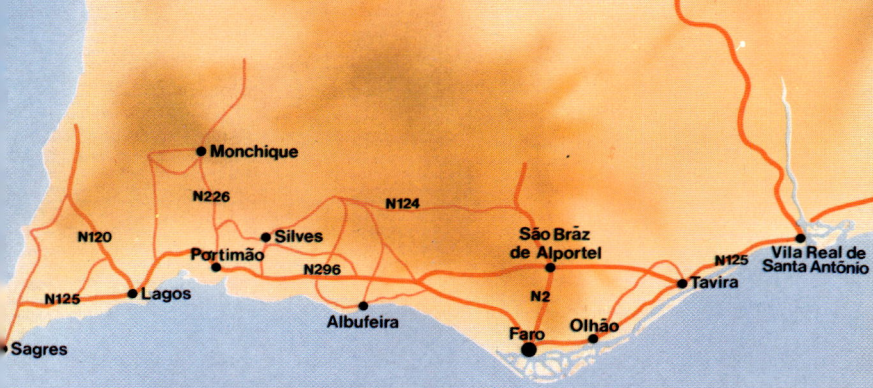

Monchique

N226

N120

Silves

Portimão

N296

N125 Lagos

Sagres

Albufeira

N124

São Brás
de Alportel

N2

Faro

Olhão

N125 Tavira

Vila Real de
Santa António

The Algarve is still relatively new to British tourists – and yet it is an ideal holiday destination for all seasons. The temperature is uniform all the year round, the winter is short and mild, spring arrives in January and the summer is warm and bright. The whole area is fortunate in facing south, and also in being protected from the north by the long range of Monchique hills which slope down gently to the sea to the east and by the River Guadiana which separates it from Spain. Because of this protection, the Algarve has remained very much a land apart from the rest of Portugal. Its name, taken from the Arabic *el gharb*, means 'the west' or 'the beyond'. The region bears the unmistakable marks left by 500 years of Moorish domination, not only in its placenames, like Alfambra, Faro or Bensafrim, but in its architecture and most importantly, in the characteristics of its people.

The personality of the Algarve people cannot help but impress itself on the visitor. A quality of spontaneous friendship is always present. Generally dressed in black, the older generation present a dramatic contrast to their surroundings, but many villagers embroider their dresses with flowers or wear one tucked in the brim of their hats to add a splash of colour.

Porto Cordo – photo by courtesy of the Portuguese National Tourist O

A hardworking race, hardened in the continuous struggle with the sea and by the rough work of the land, the Portuguese relax with music and dancing. In the Algarve these folk dances are as distinctive as the people, reflecting their mixed history. *Fado,* haunting songs rendered by black-clad *prima donnas* must be heard. There are many theories about Fado's origins, but the word itself means fate and *fadistas* take tragedy, unrequited love and the inevitability of it all as their themes. In direct contrast is the 'Corridino' music played on a type of accordian which has an extremely catchy rhythm. On feast days, when the villages have their fairs, everyone is expected to join in and the thought of a religious festival without dances, singing, fireworks and processions is incredible to them. (See Yearly Events).

The capital city of this Moorish empire was Chelb, known today as Silves. At the height of its power, it was a river port with direct access to the sea, and in its heyday, the city's population topped 30,000 but its value as a port diminished with the silting of the River Arade. When Silves fell, so fell the empire, although Faro and part of the coastline remained under domination for another 60 years.

Between the sombre greatness of noble Cape St Vincent and the frontier town of Vila Real de Sto Antonio – a distance of almost 150km – there are dozens of fishing villages and small inland towns whose public buildings, churches and domestic architecture reflect their

varied backgrounds. There are lovely drives to be taken through the countryside with views of seemingly endless beaches, broken by secluded coves. Among the sights one often sees are roadside stalls displaying masses of pottery. Some will have been hand-painted with simple designs but most merely have a dark brown glaze.

A hardworking race

The NEW
International Map Series
from Geographia

**Available from map retailers,
booksellers, newsagents etc. or
Geographia Ltd.**
63 FLEET STREET,
LONDON EC4Y 1PE

The early morning sardine catch

Most of the larger villages and towns have restaurants, nightclubs and discos and the main hotels pride themselves on their restaurants that usually offer international cuisine, but the tourist should not hesitate to explore and sample the excellent seafood specialities of the smaller bars in the towns. (A guide to the most usual Portuguese dishes can be found on page 47 under Glossary).

For the sporting enthusiast, the Algarve is a holiday haven. It is the nearest thing to a golfing paradise to be found in Europe, with six superb courses. There are ample opportunities to rent horses for trekking all along the coastline and all manner of water-sports including water-skiing, snorkling and scuba-diving. Deep-sea fishing for shark or swordfish is available and boats can be hired by the day, usually for four persons. And for the less energetic, those who prefer shopping trips, Portuguese street markets and the country fairs and carnivals provide great scope for browsing.

The Algarve has long been noted for the excellent value of its leather products and quality workmanship has been combined with good design in the manufacture of shoes, bags and belts. Local marble is available in goods ranging from vases, ashtrays to lamp bases. A wide range of embroidered work (some imported from Madeira) can be found in many shops. The finer work encompasses tablemats, cloths and dresses. In Portimão one may even purchase wool embroidery and tapestry work such as chair covers.

The manufacture of jewellery by hand is one of the ancient Portuguese art forms and lovely gold pieces make relatively inexpensive mementoes. Quite often these are modern interpretations of traditional styles, as the art is handed down the generations.

The intricate pattern of filigree, made with the finest wire, is a technique that takes many years to master. The Arabs brought this art from North Africa and today Portugal is one of the few places where it survives and flourishes. Pieces such as bracelet charms, galleons and brooches are particularly delightful.

FARO – VILA REAL DE SANTO ANTONIO

Since the middle of the 16th century, Faro has been the capital of the Algarve and it is to here that most visitors travel at some time during their stay. Liberated from Moorish domination in 1249, it has a bronze statue in the main square honouring King Alfonso III who led the conquering Christian forces.

The old quarter of the town is still surrounded by parts of the ancient defensive walls and is worth a visit, quite apart from the Cathedral there. Other notable sights include the Nuns' Chapel; the Town Hall; the Church of Our Lady of Carmo, the blue-and-white tiled Church of St Francis and the old town gate 'Arco de Repuso'.

Refreshments can be obtained at 'Alfaghar', located in the city centre, and one of Faro's oldest and most attractive houses, or at 'Kappra' – a family-run establishment with a friendly atmosphere.

Take the Lisbon road (N2) to S Bras de Alportel, stopping on the way at Estoi.
Here can be seen the Roman and early Christian remains of Milréu. Roman baths, some attractive mosaics and fragments of columns are worth noting and close by are the palace and formal park and fountains.

Continue to S Bras de Alportel, a typical country village, and then on to Tavira by the N296.

Tavira lies at the mouth of the Ribeira de Asseca, and is said to be the most picturesque town in the Algarve. Its harbour has been silted up and the town is cut off from the sea by a long spit of land. The town has two interesting churches: that of the Misericordia and the 18th-century church of Santa Maria do Castelo.
(At Santa Luzia, 1km to the S, and at Ilha de Tavira, there are excellent beaches).

Keep with the N296 for Vila Real de Santo Antonio.
Standing on the bank of the Guadiana River, Vila Real de Santo Antonio marks Portugal's frontier with Spain and car and pedestrian ferries run regularly across the river to Ayamonte on the Spanish side.
(By taking the road to the N, Castro Marim can be reached. Here one can see the remains of the old fortress belonging to the period of Alfonso II, which was restored in 1940 by the Portuguese Government).

Return by the coastal route to Monte Gordo, which has one of the most unusual and delightful beaches in the entire Province, and then along the N125 for Olhão.
This is very much like a North African town, with the houses and church built in the shape of white cubes, sometimes two or three storeys high. It is the result of modern trading links between its merchants and those of the North African coasts; similar buildings being found in Tunisia and Libya. The old part of the city is most attractive.

The village of Tavira – photo by courtesy of J Allan Cash Ltd

Local brown glazed pottery

FARO – ALBUFEIRA

Travel by the N125 to Vale do Lobo.
Situated some 10m W of Faro, this is a unique, complete village of
differently shaped houses around which villas are interspersed
between pine woods and one of Europe's finest golf courses. Mosaic
walkways give direct access to the sea.

Continue to Vilamoura.
The climate and natural beauty here are exceptional – long, sandy
beaches with surrounding hills covered in pine and almond trees. The
choice of holiday activities is wide and varied; two 18-hole golf courses,
a riding centre, tennis courts, a gambling casino and a Marina.
(A detour can be made to Loulé, a market town best known for its
craftsmen. Generally descendants of the Moslem community, it is
possible to view the coppersmiths at work beating the sheets of copper
in the narrow streets leading from Dom Alfonso III square, and in
particular the Rue 9 de Abril. The most distinctive of local industries,
however, is the decoration of harnesses – braided reins, ropes, saddles
and bridles).

Stay with the main road to Albufeira.
The largest resort on the coast. Though the main square is surrounded
by souvenir shops, the atmosphere is essentially Moorish. Situated
right on the seashore, its main beach is reached through a tunnel close
by the luxurious Sol e Mar hotel which dominates the beach.
Great character is provided by the fish market, around which there are
many small restaurants, the best of which include 'Alfredos', 'Antonio
Catunes', one of the most famous rustic eating places and the 'Ruina'.
The 'Cabraz de Praia' is sited on a cliff-side terrace and offers mouth-
watering desserts.

*The small, interesting village of Armacão de Pera lies a few kilometres to
the W.*
Lays claim to the largest beach in the whole of the Algarve. Set among
huge sandstone cliffs and rock formations, the village is close to the
ruins of an 18th-century fort whose chapel is worthy of attention. The
Praia Senhora da Rocha (the beach of Our Lady of the Rocks) takes its
name from the Romanesque chapel which is perched above.
Immediately west of this beach the sea has carved a series of caverns,
vaults and grottoes, in the area of Furnas.

Albufeira beach and town

PORTIMÃO – MONCHIQUE

Apart from being the busiest town along the coast, Portimão is also the largest. Set alongside the long bridge which spans the River Arade are the fish quays where dozens of boats unload their early morning catches. It is thought the town was built on the site of a Phoenician or Carthaginian trading post and is well known for the quality of its rush and furniture work.

Horse-drawn transport in Praia da Rocha

'A Lanterna' specialises in seafood and has been catering for years, 'A Feitoria' is a famous local landmark and 'Porta de Abrigo' is yet another establishment offering good fish dishes.
(Carvoeiro, which has become fashionable in recent years, is a delightful detour to make. Part of its attraction lies in its secluded beaches. Neat cottages are clustered around a harbour and during the holiday season fishermen grill and sell some of their catch from the beach.)

(A further detour can be made to Praia da Rocha. One of the most esteemed of resorts and a playground of the rich. Its beaches are divided by huge and weirdly-shaped rocks. A long promenade runs along the cliff top above the beach, and it is here that the villas, hotels and other establishments are to be found, giving the town its truly international flavour. Excellent views may be had from the old Fortress of St Catherine.)

Continue by the N226 and then the N124 to Silves.
Placed at the junction of the Odelouca and Arade rivers, some 20Km N of Portimão. Practically all of its former glory was destroyed in the earthquake of 1755 but fortunately the Cathedral of Santa Maria survived, though badly damaged. Built in the 13th century, it has the remnants of a Moorish mosque behind its altar and a fine doorway.

Head northwards to Monchique.
The hills are the setting for one of the most interesting excursions to be made. Here the countryside is rugged, with breathtaking views of rolling hills dotted with heather, arbutus, olives and oleanders. The Caldas de Monchique is a small thermal resort whose waters, tasting slightly warm, were used by the Romans for the treatment of rheumatic conditions and respiratory disorders. The cool breezes provide a welcome relief to the heat of the coast.

LAGOS – CAPE ST VINCENT

With its deep harbour and wide bay, Lagos is a fascinating and historic town. At the time of Moorish occupation, it was the centre for trade between Portugal and Africa. In the old part of the town visitors may still see sections of the early Roman walls and admire the ancient fortress which guards the harbour. Also to be seen is the site of the first slave market to be established in Europe, and close to it, the former palace of Dom Henrique, now a hospital. The Chapel of St Antonio, a fine example of Portuguese 18th-century Baroque, is also worth seeing. So ornate are its gilded wood carvings that it is known as the 'Golden Chapel'.

Praia da Luz and Praia dona Ana are two of several attractive beaches on the promontory lying to the S of the town. There are numerous outstanding bars that serve food, notably 'Os Arcos', which has an informal, welcoming atmosphere, 'Bar Barroca' and 'O Trovador'.

Continue along the N125 to Sagres.
As one travels westwards the landscape becomes noticeably harder. The Algarve came to real prominence in the 15th century when Prince Henry the Navigator established his School of Navigation here, which led to monumental voyages of discovery. In the course of a single century, Portugal discovered and explored nearly two thirds of the inhabited globe. Prince Henry was Grand Master of the Order of Christ

View of the harbour at Lagos

under whose flag the caravels sailed. Vasco da Gama and Christopher Columbus both learned their skills here.

The fortress of Sagres was built in the 17th century and visitors can see the old School of Seamanship within its walls. A giant compass (the famous 'Compass Rose') has been laid out in stones and it is said that Henry used this for his mathematical calculations. His house and the Graca chapel are also to be seen.
Don't miss the typical fisherman's bar 'A Tasca', which gives superb views of the Bay of Baleeira, and specialises in fish straight from the sea.

Carry on to Cape St Vincent.
Often referred to as *O Fim do Mundo* – the end of the world – this is unquestionably one of the grandest, wildest geographical features in Europe. Seas are always rough here and there is a constant flow of shipping rounding the Cape. A tour of the lighthouse is a must, its strong light throwing a beam some sixty miles out to sea.

GETTING TO THE ALGARVE

Since the opening of the international airport at Faro, travel to the Algarve has been made easy. There are frequent flights direct from London (Heathrow) by British Airways and TAP.

Outward flights:

Dep	Mon, Thu, Sat, Sun	arrive Faro
London	16.25	19.50
Also	Sun	
	11.30	14.05

Return flights:

Dep	Mon, Thu, Sat, Sun	arrive London
Faro	14.50	17.20
Also	Sun	
	12.50	15.25

Normal scheduled fare (economy single)	£101.50*
(economy return)	£203.00
Infant up to 2 not taking a seat	10% off adult fare
Child over 2 years of age	Half adult fare

Excursion fares (off peak *ie* Apr-Jun, Oct-Mar)	£72.00
(peak *ie* Jul-Sep)	£97.50

* Prices correct at time of going to press (Dec 1978).

All manner of water sports are available

GETTING ABOUT THE ALGARVE

Local bus services are very good and the regular service between Lisbon and the Algarve is fast and reliable. Below are some of the distances between the more important centres with stopping off and picking up points:

Lisbon – Lagos (Albergaria Beira-mar)	246Km
Lisbon – Sagres	279Km
Lisbon – Praia da Rocha (Hotel Jupiter)	283Km
Lisbon – Albufeira (Hotel Baltum)	318Km
Lisbon – Faro (Hotel Faro)	282Km

There is one main railway line in the Algarve which runs from Vila Real de Santo Antonio to Lagos with a junction at Tunes (near Albufeira) for the line to Lisbon. A ferry boat connects with the train at Barreiro Station to take passengers across the river to Lisbon (Terreiro do Paco) Station. The local railway is a very good way to see the Algarve and it also enables one to meet the local people.

But if you prefer to go it alone, why not take advantage of the several car hire firms in the area?

Albufeira: AUTO CERRO Tel 52425
AUTO JARDIM Duarte Pacheco, 23 and Rua 5 de Outubro, 65
  Tel 52415
AVIS Rua da Igreja Nova, 6 Tel 52678
CONTAUTO EUROPCAR Rua Diogo Leote Tel 52444

Faro: Airport Tel 24538 AVIS
CONTAUTO EUROPCAR RENT A CAR Rua Aboim

Ascensao 111-113
  Tel 23777/8
EVA RENT A CAR Tel 26195
Lagos: CONTAUTO EUROPCAR Tel 63173
Portimão: AVIS Tel 22029
CONTAUTO EUROPCAR Tel 24465
Praia da AVIS Tel 22029
Rocha: CONTAUTO EUROPCAR Tel 24465/24115

Procession of children in Lagos

GLOSSARY

Sardinha Assada	Fresh grilled sardines eaten straight from the charcoal grill with a salad and washed down with a strong red wine.
Caldo Verde	A simple potato soup with finely shredded green cabbage.
Cataplana	A mixture of clams, ham and Portuguese sausage, flavoured with onions, malaguetas and paprika.
Bolo Algarvio	(Algarve Cake) A rich cake with the principal ingredients being eggs, sugar and almonds.
Morgado de figos do Algarve	(Fig sweetmeat)

SHOPPING

Faro	**Madeira Superbia** 22 1 de Dezembro Madeira embroideries and tapestries.
Loulé	**Pinto Furniture** Located off the main street. One of the best stores in the Algarve, with furniture in every style and variety.
Albufeira	**Nau Sta Maria** Rua 5 de Outubro 27 High quality gold filigree. Select pieces of porcelain. **Topazio Shoe Shop** Located next to the 'Tribunal', Rua Igreja Nova. Ladies and mens handmade shoes. A good selection of handbags and other accessories.
Portimão	**Confortalis Furniture** Rua de Comercio. Items of hand-painted furniture. **Galeria Portimão** Rua Sta Isabel Fine selection of paintings, sculpture, tapestries and ceramics.

YEARLY EVENTS

January	Float display competition, Sta Barbara de Nexe—Bordeira. Amateur Golf Tournament—Vilamoura and Quinta do Lago.
February	Carnival celebrations—Loulé, Olhão, Moncarapacho and Vila Real de Sto António. Golf Tournaments.
March	Pro/Am Golf Tournament—Vilamoura. International Tennis Tournament—Vilamoura.
April	Easter Concert—Faro. Easter Week—all Algarve.
May	Photographic competition—Vilamoura. Table Tennis—Vilamoura. International Fishing Contest—Olhão.
June	Popular Festivals in various towns. Tourist Fair—Alte. Military Band Music—all Algarve.
July	Book Fair—Portimão. Popular Festivals—in various towns.
August	National Folklore Festival. Silves Castle Festival. Vila de Loulé Festival.
September	Music Festival—all Algarve. Popular Festivals—in various towns.
October	Golf Tournaments. Regional Cooking Week—all Algarve hotels. Popular Festivals—in various towns.
November	Standard Car Rally—around Algarve. Fishing Competition.
December	International Photographic Competition—Silves. Christmas Festivals Algarvia.

Special note: The Algarve Tourist Office publishes a monthly programme folder giving full details of all activities. These can be found at the local tourist office and hotels.

Almond blossom time in the Algarve

TOSSA DE MAR SPAIN

The most typical and beautiful holiday resort of the Costa Brava

Wide beaches and magnificent, natural landscapes. Mild climate
throughout the year. Blue, sunny skies, no mass tourism.
"Villa Vella" (the old village) — walled area dating from the
XII century, now a National Monument.
Hotels, pensions and accommodation of all categories.
Holiday apartments, bungalows, villas.
Camping and Caravanning Sites.
Many water sports. Horse-riding, tennis courts, boating.
Typical "fiestas". Regional, folklore shows.
Many social, cultural and touristic activities.
All roads leading to Tossa allow breathtaking, unique
views over sea and land.
Season mainly from April to October but also ideal for
restful winter holidays.
Information: Oficina Municipal de Turismo
Tossa de Mar (Costa Brava), Spain

Pass and height	From To	Distances from summit and max gradient		Min width of road	Conditions
Bussang 2,365ft France (Map 11 A2)	Thann (1,115ft) St-Maurice-sur-Moselle (1,800ft)	22km 8km	1 in 10 1 in 14	13ft	*UO*. A very easy road over the Vosges; beautiful scenery; *suitable for caravans.*
Campolongo 6,152ft Italy (Map 13 A1)	Corvara (5,145ft) Arabba (5,253ft)	6km 4km	1 in 8 1 in 8	16ft	*OC Jan–Mar.* A winding easy ascent; long level stretch on summit followed by easy descent; good surface; *suitable for caravans.*
Cayolle 7,631ft France (Map 28 C2)	Barcelonette (3,740ft) Guillaumes (2,687ft)	32km 33km	1 in 10 1 in 10	13ft	*UC early Nov–May.* Narrow and winding road with blind bends.
Costalunga (Karer) 5,752ft Italy (Map 13 A1)	Cardano (925ft) Pozza (4,232ft)	23km 10km	1 in 8 1 in 7	16ft	*UO*. A good, well-engineered road; *caravans prohibited.*
Croix-Haute 3,858ft France (Map 27 B3)	Monestier-de-Clermont (2,776ft) Aspres-sur-Buech (2,497ft)	36km 28km	1 in 14 1 in 14	18ft	*UO*. Well engineered; several hairpin bends on the north side; *suitable for caravans.*
Envalira 7,897ft Andorra (Map 22 C4)	Pas de la Casa (6,851ft) Andorra (3,375ft)	6km 30km	1 in 12 1 in 10	20ft	*OC Nov–Apr.* A good two-lane road with wide bends on ascent and descent; fine views; *negotiable by caravans.*
Falzarego 6,945ft Italy (Map 13 A1)	Cortina d'Ampezzo (3,958ft) Andraz (4,622ft)	17km 9km	1 in 12 1 in 12	16ft	*OC Jan–May.* Well-engineered; bitumen surface; many hairpin bends on both sides; *negotiable by caravans.*
Faucille 4,331ft France (Map 10 D1)	Gex (1,985ft) Morez (2,247ft)	11km 28km	1 in 10 1 in 12	13ft	*UO*. Fairly wide, winding road across the Jura mountains; *negotiable by caravans* but it is probably better to folow La Cure-St-Cergue-Nyon.
Fern 3,969ft Austria (Map 12 D2)	Nassereith (2,742ft) Lermoos (3,244ft)	9km 10km	1 in 10 1 in 10	20ft	*UO*. An easy pass but slippery when wet; *suitable for caravans.*
***Flüela** 7,818ft Switzerland (Map 12 C1)	Davos-Dorf (5,174ft) Susch (4,659ft)	13km 13km	1 in 10 1 in 8	16ft	*OC Nov–May.* Tolls levied in winter to pay for snow clearance (Nov 16-May 15); 5 Swiss francs per car. Easy ascent from Davos; some acute hairpin bends on the eastern side; bitumen surface; *negotiable by caravans.*
†Forclaz 5,010ft Switzerland France (Map 28 C4)	Martigny (1,562ft) Argentière (4,111ft)	13km 19km	1 in 12 1 in 12	16ft	*UO Forclaz; Montets OC Nov-early Apr.* A good road over the pass and to the frontier; in France narrow and rough over Col des Montets (4,793ft); *negotiable by caravans.*
Fugazze 3,802ft Italy (Map 29 B4)	Rovereto (660ft) Valli del Pasubio (1,148ft)	27km 12km	1 in 8 1 in 8	10ft	*UO*. Bitumen surface; several hairpin bends, narrow on northern side.
***Furka** 7,972ft Switzerland (Map 11 B1)	Gletsch (5,777ft) Realp (5,066ft)	10km 13km	1 in 10 1 in 10	13ft	*UC Oct-Jun.* A well-graded modern road, but with narrow sections and several sharp hairpin bends on both ascent and descent. Fine views of the Rhône Glacier.
Galibier 8,385ft France (Map 28 C3)	Lautaret Pass (6,751 ft) St-Michel-de-Maurienne (2,336ft)	7km 34km	1 in 14 1 in 8	10ft	*UC Oct-Jun.* Mainly wide, well surfaced but unguarded. Ten hairpin bends on descent then 5km narrow and rough. Rise over the Col du Télégraphe (5,249ft), then eleven more hairpin bends. (Tunnel under Galibier summit caved in; new, longer road over summit rises to 8,678ft).

* Permitted maximum width of vehicles 7ft 6in
† Permitted maximum width of vehicles 8ft 2½in

See page 31 for other abbreviations

Pass and height	From To	Distances from summit and max gradient		Min width of road	Conditions
Gardena (Grödner-Joch) 6,959ft Italy *(Map 13 A1)*	Val Gardena (6,109ft) Corvara (5,145ft)	68km 10km	1 in 8 1 in 8	16ft	*OC Nov–late May*. A well-engineered road, very winding on descent.
Gavia 8,604ft Italy *(Map 12 D1)*	Bormio (4,019ft) Ponte di Legno (4,140ft)	25km 16km	1 in 5½ 1 in 5½	10ft	*UC early Nov–late Jun*. Steep and narrow but with frequent passing bays; many hairpin bends and a gravel surface; not for the faint-hearted; extra care necessary.
Gerlos 5,341ft Austria *(Map 13 A2)*	Zell am Ziller (1,886ft) Wald (2,890ft)	29km 15km	1 in 12 1 in 11	14ft	*OU*. Hairpin ascent out of Zell to modern toll road; the old, steep, narrow, and winding route with passing bays and 1-in-7 gradient is not recommended, but is *negotiable with care*.
†**Grand St Bernard** 8,114ft Switzerland– Italy *(Map 28 C4)*	Martigny (1,562ft) Aosta (1,913ft)	44km 33km	1 in 9 1 in 9	13ft	*UC late Oct–early Jun*. Modern road to entrance of road tunnel (usually open) see page 55; then narrow but bitumen surface over summit to frontier; also good in Italy; *suitable for caravans,* using tunnel. Pass road closed for vehicles towing trailers.
*****Grimsel** 7,100ft Switzerland *(Map 11 B1)*	Innertkirchen (2,067 ft) Gletsch (5,777ft)	25km 6km	1 in 10 1 in 10	16ft	*UC late Oct–Jun*. A fairly easy, modern road, but heavy traffic at weekends. A long ascent, finally hairpin bends; then a terraced descent with six hairpins into the Rhône valley.
Grossglockner 8,212ft Austria *(Map 13 B2)*	Bruck an der Glocknerstrasse (2,480ft) Heiligenblut (4,268ft)	33km 15km	1 in 8 1 in 8	16ft	*UC late Oct–early May*. Numerous well-engineered hairpin bends; moderate but very long ascents; toll road; very fine scenery; heavy tourist traffic; *negotiable preferably from south to north,* by caravans.
Hochtannberg 5,510ft Austria *(Map 12 C2)*	Schröcken (4,163ft) Warth (near Lech) (4,921ft)	6km 4km	1 in 7 1 in 11	13ft	*OC Jan–Mar*. A reconstructed modern road.
Ibañeta (Roncesvalles) 3,468ft France–Spain *(Map 20 A/B2)*	St-Jean-Pied de-Port (584ft) Pamplona (1,380ft)	26km 53km	1 in 10 1 in 10	13ft	*UO*. A slow and winding, scenic route; *negotiable by caravans*.
Iseran 9,088ft France *(Map 28 C4)*	Bourg-St-Maurice (2,756ft) Lanslebourg (4,587ft)	49km 33km	1 in 12 1 in 9	13ft	*UC mid Oct–late Jun*. The second highest pass in the Alps. Well-graded with reasonable bends, average surface; several unlit tunnels on northern approach.
Izoard 7,743ft France *(Map 28 C3)*	Guillestre (3,248ft) Briançon (4,396ft)	32km 20km	1 in 8 1 in 10	16ft	*UC late Oct–mid Jun*. A fairly easy but winding road with many hairpin bends.
*****Jaun** 4,948ft Switzerland *(Map 11 B1)*	Broc (2,378ft) Reidenbach (2,759ft)	25km 8km	1 in 10 1 in 10	13ft	*UO*. A modernised but generally narrow road; some poor sections on ascent, and several hairpin bends on descent; *negotiable by caravans*.
†**Julier** 7,493ft Switzerland *(Map 12 C1)*	Tiefencastel (2,821ft) Silvaplana (5,958ft)	36km 7km	1 in 10 1 in 7½	13ft	*UO*. Well-engineered road approached from Chur by Lenzerheide Pass (5,098ft); *suitable for caravans*.
Katschberg 5,384ft Austria *(Map 13 B2)*	Spittal (1,818ft) St Michael (3,504ft)	35km 6km	1 in 5½ 1 in 6	20ft	*UO*. Steep though not particularly difficult; parallel toll motorway, including tunnel, now open; *negotiable by light caravans,* using tunnel.
*****Klausen** 6,404ft Switzerland *(Map 12 C1)*	Altdorf (1,512ft) Linthal (2,165ft)	25km 23km	1 in 11 1 in 11	16ft	*UC early Nov–late May*. Easy in spite of a number of sharp bends; *no through route for caravans as they are prohibited on part of*

*Permitted maximum width of vehicles 7ft 6in
†Permitted maximum width of vehicles 8ft 2½in

See page 31 for other abbreviations

Pass and height	From To	Distances from summit and max gradient		Min width of road	Conditions
					road in Canton of Glarus.
Larche (della Maddalena) 6,545ft France – Italy (Map 28 C3)	Condamine (4,291ft) Vinadio (2,986ft)	19km 32km	1 in 12 1 in 12	10ft	*OC Nov – Mar.* An easy, well-graded road; narrow and rough on ascent, wider with better surface on desccent; *suitable for caravans.*
Lautaret 6,752ft France (Map 28 C3)	Le Bourg-d'Oisans (2,359ft) Briançon (4,396ft)	38km 28km	1 in 8 1 in 10	14ft	*OC Dec – Apr* during the day, but closed between 19.00 – 07.00hrs Nov – Apr. Modern, evenly graded, but winding, and unguarded in places; very fine scenery;* *suitable for caravans.*
Loibl (Ljubelj) 3,500ft Austria – Yugoslavia (Map 14 C1)	Unterloibl (1,699ft) Kranj (1,263ft)	10km 29km	1 in 5½ 1 in 8	20ft	*UO.* Steep rise and fall over Little Loibl Pass to tunnel under summit; from south to north just *negotiable by experienced drivers with light caravans.* The old road over the summit is closed to through traffic.
*Lukmanier (Lucomagno) 6,289ft Switzerland (Map 12 C1)	Olivone (2,945ft) Disentis (3,772ft)	18km 22km	1 in 11 1 in 11	16ft	*UC early Nov – early Jun.* Rebuilt, modern road; *suitable for caravans.*
†Maloja 5,960ft Switzerland (Map 12 C1)	Silvaplana (5,958ft) Chiavenna (1,083ft)	11km 32km	level 1 in 11	13ft	*UO.* Escarpment facing south; fairly easy but many hairpin bends on descent; *negotiable by caravans, possibly difficult on ascent.*
Mauria 4,258ft Italy (Map 13 B1)	Lozzo Cadore (2,470ft) Ampezzo (1,837ft)	14km 31km	1 in 14 1 in 14	16ft	*UO.* A well-designed road with easy, winding ascent and descent; *suitable for caravans.*
Mendola 4,475ft Italy (Map 12 D1)	Appiano (1,365ft) Sarnonico (3,208ft)	15km 8km	1 in 8 1 in 10	16ft	*UO.* A fairly straightforward, but winding road; well guarded; *suitable for caravans.*
Mont Cenis 6,834ft France – Italy (Map 28 C3)	Lanslebourg (4,587ft) Susa (1,624ft)	11km 28km	1 in 10 1 in 8	16ft	*UC Nov – May.* Approach by industrial valley. An easy, broad highway but with poor surface in places; *suitable for caravans;* alternative rail tunnel (see page 56).
Monte Croce di Comélico (Kreuzberg) 5,368ft Italy (Map 13 A/B1)	San Candido (3,847ft) Santo Stefano di Cadore (2,978ft)	15km 22km	1 in 12 1 in 12	16ft	*UO.* A winding road with moderate gradients; beautiful scenery; *suitable for caravans.*
Montgenèvre 6,100ft France – Italy (Map 28 C3)	Briançon (4,396ft) Cesana Torinese (4,429ft)	11km 8km	1 in 14 1 in 11	16ft	*UO.* An easy, modern road; *suitable for caravans.*
Monte Giovo (Jaufen) 6,869ft Italy (Map 12 D1)	Merano (1,063ft) Vipiteno (3,115ft)	41km 19km	1 in 8 1 in 11	13ft	*UC Nov – early May.* Many well-engineered hairpin bends; *caravans prohibited.*
*Mosses 4,740ft Switzerland (Map 11 A1)	Aigle (1,378ft) Château-d'Oex (3,153ft)	18km 15km	1 in 12 1 in 12	13ft	*UO.* A modern road; *suitable for caravans.*
Nassfeld (Pramollo) 5,092ft Austria – Italy (Map 13 B1)	Tröpolach (1,972ft) Pontebba (1,841ft)	10km 12km	1 in 5 1 in 10	13ft	*UO.* An alternative to the Plöcken Pass, which is often closed for long periods during the winter. The Austrian section is mostly narrow and winding, with tight, blind bends; the winding descent in Italy has been improved.
Nufenen 8,130ft Switzerland (Map 11 B1)	Ulrichen (4,416ft) Airolo (3,745ft)	13km 24km	1 in 10 1 in 10	13ft	*UC mid Oct – mid Jun.* The approach roads are narrow, with tight bends, but the road over the pass is good; *negotiable by light caravans* (limited 1.5 tons).

*Permitted maximum width of vehicles 7ft 6in
†Permitted maximum width of vehicles 8ft 2½in

See page 31 for other abbreviations

Pass and height	From To	Distances from summit and max gradient		Min width of road	Conditions
*Oberalp 6,709ft Switzerland (Map 12 C1)	Andermatt (4,737ft) Disentis (3,772ft)	10km 22km	1 in 10 1 in 10	16ft	UC early Nov–mid May. A much improved and widened road with a modern surface; many hairpin bends but long level stretch on summit; negotiable by caravans.
*Ofen (Fuorn) 7,070ft Switzerland (Map 12 D1)	Zernez (4,836ft) Santa Maria im Münstertal (4,547ft)	22km 14km	1 in 10 1 in 8	12ft	UO. Good, fairly easy road through the Swiss National Park; suitable for caravans.
Petit St Bernard 7,178ft France–Italy (Map 28 C4)	Bourg-St-Maurice (2,756ft) Pré St-Didier (3,335ft)	31km 23km	1 in 20 1 in 12	16ft	UC late Oct–Jun. Outstanding scenery; a fairly easy approach but poor surface and unguarded broken edges near the summit; good on the descent in Italy; negotiable by light caravans.
Peyresourde 5,128ft France (Map 20 D3)	Arreau (2,310ft) Luchon (2,067ft)	18km 14km	1 in 10 1 in 10	13ft	UO. Somewhat narrow with several hairpin bends, though not difficult.
*Pillon 5,070ft Switzerland (Map 11 B1)	Le Sépey (3,212ft) Gsteig (2,911ft)	14km 7km	1 in 11 1 in 11	13ft	UO. A comparatively easy modern road; suitable for caravans.
Plöcken (Monte Croce-Carnico) 4,468ft Austria–Italy (Map 13 B1)	Kötschach (2,316ft) Paluzza (1,968ft)	14km 16km	1 in 7 1 in 14	16ft	OC Dec–Apr; Nassfeld Pass possible alternative. A modern road with long reconstructed sections; heavy traffic at summer weekends; delay likely at the frontier; negotiable by caravans; to avoid congestion caravans are prohibited at summer weekends.
Pordoi 7,346ft Italy (Map 13 A1)	Arabba (5,253ft) Canazei (4,806ft)	9km 12km	1 in 10 1 in 10	16ft	OC Nov–May. An excellent modern road with numerous hairpin bends; negotiable by caravans.
Port 4,098ft France (Map 22 C4)	Tarascon (1,555ft) Massat (2,133ft)	18km 13km	1 in 10 1 in 10	14ft	OC Nov–Apr. A fairly easy road but narrow on some bends; negotiable by caravans.
Portet-d'Aspet 3,507ft France (Map 20 D3)	Audressein (1,625ft) Fronsac (1,548ft)	19km 38km	1 in 7 1 in 7	11ft	UO. Approached from the west by the easy Col des Ares (2,611ft) and Col de Buret (1,975ft); well-engineered road, but calls for particular care on hairpin bends; rather narrow.
Pötschen 3,221ft Austria (Map 13 B2)	Bad Ischl (1,535ft) Bad Aussee (2,133ft)	17km 8km	1 in 11 1 in 11	23ft	UO. A modern road; suitable for caravans.
5,879ft France–Spain (Map 20 C3)	Eaux-Chaudes (2,152ft) Biescas (2,821ft)	23km 34km	1 in 10 1 in 10	11ft	UC late Oct–early Jun. A fairly easy, unguarded road, but narrow in places; poor but being rebuilt on Spanish side.
Puymorens 6,281ft France (Map 22 C4)	Ax-les-Thermes (2,362ft) Bourg-Madame (3,707ft)	29km 27km	1 in 10 1 in 10	18ft	OC Nov–Apr. A generally easy modern tarmac road, but narrow, winding, and with a poor surface in places; not suitable for night driving; suitable for caravans. Alternative rail service available between Ax-les-Thermes and La Tour-de-Carol.
Quillane 5,623ft France (Map 22 C4)	Quillan (955ft) Mont-Louis (5,135ft)	63km 5km	1 in 12 1 in 12	16ft	OC Nov–Mar. An easy, straightforward ascent and descent; suitable for caravans.
Radstädter-Tauern 5,702ft Austria (Map 13 B2)	Radstadt (2,808ft) St Michael (3,504ft)	21km 26km	1 in 6 1 in 7	16ft	UO. Northern ascent steep but not difficult otherwise; parallel toll motorway including tunnel now open; negotiable by light caravans, using tunnel.

*Permitted maximum width of vehicles 7ft 6in

See page 31 for other abbreviations

Pass and height	From To	Distances from summit and max gradient		Min width of road	Conditions
Resia (Reschen-Scheideck) 4,954ft Italy–Austria *(Map 12 D1)*	Spondigna (2,903ft) Prutz (2,841ft)	30km 35km	1 in 10 1 in 10	20ft	*UO.* A good straightforward alternative to the Brenner; *suitable for caravans.*
Restefond (La Bonette) 9,193ft France *(Map 28 C2/3)*	Jausiers (near Barcelonnette) (3,986ft) St-Etienne-de-Tinée (3,766ft)	23km 27km	1 in 9 1 in 9	10ft	*UC early Oct–early Jun.* The highest pass in the Alps, completed in 1962. Narrow, rough, unguarded ascent with many blind bends, and nine hairpins. Descent easier; winding with twelve hairpin bends.
Rolle 6,463ft Italy *(Map 13 A1)*	Predazzo (3,337ft) Mezzano (2,126ft)	21km 25km	1 in 11 1 in 14	16ft	*OC Nov–Mar.* Very beautiful scenery; bitumen surface; a well-engineered road; *negotiable by caravans.*
Rombo (see Timmelsjoch)					
Route des 4,210ft France *(Map 11 A/B2)*	St-Dié (1,125ft) Cernay (902ft)	— —	1 in 8 1 in 8	13ft	*UC Nov–Apr.* A renowned scenic route crossing seven ridges, with the highest point at Hôtel du Grand Ballon.
†St Gotthard 6,860ft Switzerland *(Map 11 B1)*	Göschenen (3,704ft) Airolo (3,745ft)	19km 15km	1 in 10 1 in 10	20ft	*UC mid Oct–early Jun.* Modern, fairly easy; a new road avoids top twenty-five hairpin bends of the famous terraced descent of thirty-seven bends. Heavy traffic; *negotiable by caravans* (max height vehicles 11ft 9in). Alternative rail tunnel (see page 56).
*San Bernardino 6,778ft Switzerland *(Map 12 C1)*	Mesocco (2,549ft) Hinterrhein (5,328ft)	22km 8km	1 in 10 1 in 10	13ft	*UC Nov–mid Jun.* Easy, modern roads on northern and southern approaches to tunnel (see page55); narrow and winding over summit; via tunnel *suitable for caravans.*
Seeberg (Jezersko) 3,990ft Austria–Yugoslavia *(Map 14 C1)*	Eisenkappel (1,821ft) Kranj (1,263ft)	14km 33km	1 in 8 1 in 10	16ft	*UO.* An alternative to the steeper Loibl and Wurzen passes; moderate climb with winding, hairpin ascent and descent.
Sella 7,264ft Italy *(Map 13 A1)*	Plan (5,269ft) Canazei (4,806ft)	9km 9km	1 in 9 1 in 9	16ft	*OC Nov-May.* A finely engineered, winding road; exceptional views of the Dolomites.
Semmering 3,215ft Austria *(Map 14 D2)*	Mürzzuschlag im Mürztal (2,205ft) Gloggnitz (1,427ft)	13km 16km	1 in 6 1 in 6	20ft	*UO.* A fine, well-engineered highway; *suitable for caravans.*
Sestriere 6,660ft Italy *(Map 28 C3)*	Casana Torinese (4,429ft) Pinerolo (1,234ft)	12km 55km	1 in 10 1 in 10	16ft	*UO.* Mostly bitumen surface; *negotiable by caravans.*
Silvretta (Bielerhöhe) 6,666ft Austria *(Map 12 C1)*	Partenen (3,451ft) Galtür (5,195ft)	15km 10km	1 in 9 1 in 9	16ft	*UC late Oct-early Jun.* For the most part reconstructed; thirty-two easy hairpin bends on western ascent; eastern side more straightforward. Toll road; *caravans prohibited.*
†Simplon 6,578ft Switzerland–Italy *(Map 28 D4)*	Brig (2,231ft) Domodóssola (919ft)	22km 41km	1 in 9 1 in 11	23ft	*OC Nov-Apr.* An easy, reconstructed modern road, but 13 miles long, continuous ascent to summit; *suitable for caravans.* Alternative rail tunnel (see page 56).
Somport 5,350ft France-Spain *(Map 20 C3)*	Bedous (1,365ft) Jaca (2,687ft)	31km 30km	1 in 10 1 in 10	12ft	*UO.* A favoured, old established route; generally easy, but in parts narrow and unguarded; fairly good-surfaced road; *suitable for caravans.*

*Permitted maximum width of vehicles 7ft 6in
†Permitted maximum width of vehicles 8ft 2½in

See page 31 for other abbreviations

Pass and height	From To	Distances from summit and max gradient		Min width of road	Conditions
*Splügen 6,930ft Switzerland–Italy (Map 12 C1)	Splügen (4,790ft) Chiavenna (1,083ft)	9km 30km	1 in 9 1 in 7½	10ft	*UC Oct.-early Jun*. Mostly narrow and winding, with many hairpin bends, and not well guarded; care also required at many tunnels and galleries.
††Stelvio 9,080ft Italy (Map 12 D1)	Bormio (4,019ft) Spondigna (2,903ft)	22km 28km	1 in 8 1 in 8	13ft	*UC Oct–Jun*. The third highest pass in the Alps; the number of acute hairpin bends, all well-engineered, is exceptional – from forty to fifty on either side; the surface is good, the traffic heavy. Hairpin bends are too acute for long vehicles.
†Susten 7,300ft Switzerland (Map 11 B1)	Innertkirchen (2,067ft) Wasser (3,018ft)	28km 19km	1 in 11 1 in 11	20ft	*UC Nov–Jun*. A very scenic route and a good example of modern road engineering; easy gradients and turns; heavy traffic at weekends; *negotiable by caravans*.
Tenda (Tende) 4,331ft Italy-France (Map 28 C2)	Borgo S Dalmazzo (2,103ft) La Giandola (1,059ft)	24km 29km	1 in 11 1 in 11	18ft	*UO*. Well guarded, modern road with several hairpin bends; road tunnel at summit; suitable for caravans; *but prohibited during the winter*.
Thurn 4,177ft Austria (Map 13 A/B2)	Kitzbühel (2,502ft) Mittersill (2,588ft)	19km 11km	1 in 12 1 in 16	16ft	*UO*. A good road with narrow stretches; northern approach rebuilt, *suitable for caravans*.
Timmelsjoch (Rombo) 8,232ft Austria-Italy (Map 12 D1)	Obergurgl (6,322ft) Moso (3,304ft)	14km 23km	1 in 7 1 in 8	12ft	*UC mid Oct-late Jun*. Roadworks on Italian side still in progress. The pass is open to private cars (without trailers) only as some tunnels on the Italian side are too narrow for larger vehicles; toll road.
Tonale 6,181ft Italy (Map 12 D1)	Edolo (2,264ft) Dimaro (2,513ft)	30km 27km	1 in 14 1 in 8	16ft	*OC Jan–Apr*. A relatively easy road *suitable for caravans*.
Tosas 5,905ft Spain (Map 22 C4)	Puigcerdá (3,708ft) Ribas de Freser (3,018ft)	25km 25km	1 in 10 1 in 10	16ft	*UO*. Now a fairly straightforward, but continuously winding two-lane road with many sharp bends; some unguarded edges; *negotiable by caravans*.
Tourmalet 6,936ft France (Map 20 D3)	Luz (2,333ft) Ste-Marie-de-Campan (2,811ft)	19km 16km	1 in 8 1 in 8	14ft	*UC Oct–late Jun*. The highest of the French Pyrenees routes; the approaches are good though winding and exacting over summit; sufficiently guarded.
Tre Croci 5,935ft Italy (Map 13 A1)	Cortina d'Am-pezzo (3,983ft) Pelos (2,427ft)	7km 48km	1 in 9 1 in 9	16ft	*UO*. An easy pass; very fine scenery; *suitable for caravans*.
Turracher Höhe 5,784ft Austria (Map 13 B1)	Predlitz (3,024ft) Reichenau (3,281ft)	20km 8km	1 in 5½ 1 in 4½	13ft	*UO*. Formerly one of the steepest mountain roads in Austria, now much improved; steep, fairly straightforward ascent, followed by a very steep descent; good surface and mainly two-lane width; fine scenery.
*Umbrail 8,205ft Switzerland–Italy (Map 12 D1)	Santa Maria im Münstertal (4,547ft) Bormio (4,019ft)	13km 19km	1 in 11 1 in 11	14ft	*UC early Nov–mid May*. Highest of the Swiss passes; narrow; mostly gravel surfaced with thirty-four hairpin bends but not too difficult.
Vars 6,919ft France (Map 28 C3)	St-Paul-sur-Ubaye (4,823ft) Guillestre (3,246ft)	8km 20km	1 in 10 1 in 10	16ft	*OC late Nov–late Apr*. Easy winding ascent with seven hairpin bends; gradual winding descent with another seven hairpin bends; good surface; *negotiable by caravans*.
Wurzen (Koren) 3,510ft Austria–Yugoslavia (Map 13 B1)	Riegersdorf (1,752ft) Kranjska Gora (2,657ft)	7km 6km	1 in 5½ 1 in 5½	13ft	*UO*. A steep two-lane road which otherwise is not particularly difficult; caravans prohibited.

Pass and height	From To	Distances from summit and max gradient		Min width of road	Conditions
Zirler Berg 3,310ft Austria *(Map 12 D2)*	Seefeld (3,870ft) Zirl (2,041ft)	7km 5km	1 in 7 1 in 6½	20ft	*UO.* An escarpment facing south, part of the route from Garmisch to Innsbruck; a good modern road but heavy tourist traffic and a long steep descent, with one hairpin bend, into the Inn Valley. Steepest section from the hairpin bend down to Zirl.

*Permitted maximum width of vehicles 7ft 6in
†Permitted maximum width of vehicles 8ft 2½in

††Maximum length of vehicle 30ft
See page 31 for other abbreviations

Major road tunnels

All charges listed below should be used as a guide only.

In addition to the nine road tunnels below, more are being planned. The Frejus road tunnel between France and Italy (12.7km long) and the St Gotthard road tunnel in Switzerland (16.3km long) may now not open until 1980.

Pyrenees
France–Spain
Map 21 B4

This new trans-Pyrenean tunnel is now open. The tunnel is 3km (2 miles) long, and runs nearly 6,000ft above sea level between Aragnouet and Bielsa. It is probable that there will be a toll.

Grand St Bernard
Switzerland–Italy
Map 28 C4

The tunnel is over 6,000ft above sea level; although there are covered approaches, wheel chains may be needed to reach it in winter. The Customs, passport control, and toll offices are at the entrance. The tunnel is 5.9km (3½ miles) long. The permitted maximum dimensions of vehicles are – *height* 4m (13ft 1in) *width* 2.5m (8ft 2in). The minimum speed is 40kph (24mph) and the maximum 80kph (49mph). Do not stop or overtake. There are breakdown bays with telephones on either side.

Charges
(in Swiss francs
or Italian lire)

The toll charges are calculated according to the wheelbase.

	Fr	L
motorcycles	4	1,400
Cars: wheelbase up to 6ft 10in	12	4,150
wheelbase from 6ft 10in to 10ft 6in	18	6,200
Wheelbase over 10ft 6in	27	9,350
with caravan	27	9,350
minibuses	27	9,350
coaches	54–90	18,700–31,800

Mont Blanc
Chamonix
(France)–
Courmayeur (Italy)
Map 28 C4

The tunnel is over 4,000ft above sea level. It is 11.6km (7 miles) long. Customs and pasport control are at the Italian end. The permitted maximum dimensions of vehicles are: *height* 4.15m (13ft 7in); *length* 18m (59ft); *width* 2.5m (8ft 2in). *Total weight* 35 metric tons (34 tons 9cwt); *axle weight* 13 metric tons (12 tons 16cwt). The minimum speed is 50kph (31 mph) and the maximum 80kph (50mph). Do not stop or overtake. Keep 100m (110 yd) between vehicles. Turn side and rear lights on, but not headlights. There are breakdown bays with telephones.

Charges

The tolls are calculated according to the wheelbase (in French francs).

		Fr
cars:	wheelbase up to 2.3m (7ft 6½in)	32
	wheelbase from 2.3m to 2.63m (7ft 6½in to 8ft 7½in)	49
	wheelbase from 2.64m to 3.3m (8ft 7½in to 10ft 10in) and cars with caravans	66
	wheelbase over 3.3m (10ft 10in)	150
vehicles:	with three axles	230
	with four, or more axles	300

San Bernardino
Switzerland
Map 12 C1

This tunnel is over 5,000ft above sea level. It is 6.6km (4 miles) long, 4.8m (15ft 9in) high, and the carriageway is 7m (23ft) wide. Do not stop or overtake in the tunnel. Keep 100m (110yd) between vehicles. Switch on side and rear lights, but not headlights.

There are breakdown bays with telephones.
No tolls are charged.

Arlberg
Austria
Map 12 C1

This new tunnel (opened December 1978) is 14km (8¾ miles) long, and runs at about 4,000ft above sea level, to the south of and parallel to the Arlberg pass. Toll charges are not available at the time of going to press.

Felbertauern
Austria
Map 13 B2

This tunnel is over 5,000ft above sea level; it runs between Mittersill and Matrei, to the west of and parallel to the Grossglockner Pass.

The tunnel is 5.2km (3¼ miles) long, 4.5m (15ft) high, and the two-lane carriageway is 7m (23ft) wide.

From November to April wheel chains are usually needed on the approach to the tunnel.

Charges
(in Austrian schillings)

	Single Sch	Return Sch
cars/caravans	190	330
motorcycles	50	
coaches	540–1080	920–1840

Return tickets are issued. Those for cars are interchangeable between the Grossglockner Hochalpenstrasse, Felbertauern Strasse, and Tauernautobahn.

Gleinalm
Austria
Map 14 C2

This new tunnel (opened August 1978) is 8.3km (5 miles) long and runs between St Michael and Friesach, near Graz. The tunnel forms part of the A9 Pyhrn Autobahn which will, in due course, run from Linz via Graz to Yugoslavia. Charges: The toll charges for cars are 90 Austrian Schillings for a single journey.

Katschberg
Austria
Map 13 B2

This tunnel is 3,642ft above sea level, and forms an important part of the Tauern autobahn between Salzburg and Carinthia. The tunnel is 5.4km (3½ miles) long, 4.50m (15ft) high, and the two-lane carriageway is 7.50m (25ft) wide. For charges see Tauern autobahn page 116.

Radstädter
Tauern
Austria
Map 13 B2

This tunnel is 4,396ft above sea level. It is 6.4km (4 miles) long, and runs to the east of and parallel to the Tauern railway tunnel. With the Katschberg Tunnel (see above) it forms an important part of the Tauern autobahn between Salzburg and Carinthia. For charges see Tauern autobahn page 116.

Rail tunnels

Vehicles are conveyed throughout the year through the St Gotthard Tunnel (Göschenen-Airolo), the Simplon Tunnel (Brig-Iselle) and the Lötschberg Tunnel (Kandersteg-Goppenstein-Brig). Services are frequent and no advance booking is necessary and although the actual transit time is 15/20 minutes, some time may be taken by the loading and unloading formalities.

The operating company issues a full timetable and tariff list which is available from the AA, the Swiss National Tourist Office or at most Swiss frontier crossings.

Albula Tunnel
Map 12 C1

Thusis (2,372ft)/Tiefencastel (2,821ft)-Samedan (5,650ft) 5.9km (3½ miles) long.

Motor vehicles can be conveyed through this tunnel, but you are recommended to give notice. Thusis *tel* (081) 811113, Tiefencastel (081) 711112, Samedan (082) 65404.

Services

Six daily in each direction.

Charges

These are given in Swiss francs and are likely to increase.

		Fr	
cars (up to eight passengers)		63 (including driver)	
motorcycles		14.00 per 100kg	
caravan		52	
	1st class	2nd class	
passengers	21	14	

France–Italy
The Mont Cenis
Tunnel
(Fréjus Tunnel)
Italy Map 28 C3

Modane (3,524ft) France–Bardonecchia (4,305ft) 13.6km (8½ miles) long.

The following information is liable to change without notice.

Booking Advance booking is unnecessary, but motorists should report at least 15 minutes before the train is due to start.

All Customs formalities are carried out at Modane, but there is passport control at both stations.

The driver must drive his vehicle on and off the wagon. Trailer caravans and baggage trailers are accepted only if accompanied by a towing vehicle.

Maximum dimensions The maximum overall length permitted is 10m (32ft 10in); the maximum permitted height decreases as the width increases, according to the dimensions, shown below;

Width	6ft 7in	6ft 11in	7ft 2in	7ft 6in	7ft 10in	8ft 2in
Height	9ft 1in	9ft 0in	8ft 11in	8ft 9in	8ft 8in	8ft 7in

Services There are trains from both stations all the year round hourly between 07.00 and 21.00hrs.

Charges The rates quoted are payable at Modane for journeys in either direction; they cannot be paid in advance in sterling.

(in French francs or Italian lire)

	Fr	L
cars		
up to 12ft (3.80m)	30	5,600
up to 14ft (4.42m)	36	6,700
over 14ft (4.42m)	42	7.800
caravan trailers*	30	5,600
luggage trailers*	20	3,700
motorcycles, solo and scooters	13	2,400
with sidecar	20	3,700

Passengers: fares are included in the freight rates up to a maximum of eight including the driver.
*Accepted only if accompanied by towing vehicle.

Austria Motor vehicles can be conveyed through the following tunnels:

Arlberg Tunnel Langen (3,990ft) – St Anton (4,222ft) Map 12 C1/2.
Tauern Tunnel Böckstein (3,711ft) (near Bad Gastein) – Mallnitz Map 13 B1/2.

Karawanken Tunnel Rosenbach-Jesenice (Yugoslavia) Map 34 A4.
Arlberg Tunnel 10.2km (6½ miles) long.

Booking Advance booking is unnecessary (except for request trains), but motorists must report at least 30 minutes before the train is due to start. The driver must drive his vehicle on and off the wagon.

Maximum dimensions
They are: Height 11ft
    width 10ft 4in

Services From November to March, when the Arlberg Pass is closed, trains operate in each direction every two hours between 08.00 and 21.00hrs. When the pass is open, there are three trains daily from Langen to St Anton, plus two trains operating on request only.

From St Anton to Langen there are three scheduled trains per day, operating on a request basis.

The minimum trainload acceptable is Sch 1,200 and any surcharge necessary to make up this sum is shared. It is very rare that these request services are used by a sufficient number of vehicles to make up the minimum surcharge of Sch 1,200.
Duration 15 minutes.

None of the rates given can be paid in advance in sterling.

Charges	single Sch	Return Sch
cars (including passengers)	160	240
motorcycles (with or without sidecar)	30	
*caravans	100	140
*boat trailers	100	140
per passenger	11	

*These are not accepted without a towing vehicle.

Tauern Tunnel 8.5km (5½ miles) long.
Booking As for the Arlberg Tunnel.
Maximum dimensions For caravans and trailers these are: height 8ft 10½in width 8ft 2½in

Services
In summer, trains run approximately every half-hour in both directions, 07.40–23.00 hrs; and every hour during the night providing there is sufficient traffic; additional trains are run during the day when necessary. In winter, there is a service approximately every hour 04.45–22.05hrs.
Duration 10 minutes.

Charges
As for the Arlberg Tunnel.

Karawanken Tunnel
8.5km (5½ miles) long.
Since the opening of the Loibl Tunnel, see page 51, assuring an all-year-round link between Klagenfurt and Ljubljana, the use of the Karawanken Tunnel by motorists is not an economic proposition.

Tourist Offices

National tourist offices are especially equipped to deal with enquiries relating to their countries. They are particularly useful for information on current events, tourist attractions, car hire, equipment hire and information on specific activities such as skin-diving, gliding, horse-riding etc.

The offices in London are most helpful but the local offices overseas reward a visit because they have information not available elsewhere and tourists are advised to visit the office when they arrive at their destination. Hotels etc will be able to supply the address.

TOURIST INFORMATION CENTRES

You never have to worry about where to go, what to do or where to stay as you travel around Britain — help and guidance are never far away.

To help you explore Britain, to see the major sights and the fascinating attractions off the beaten track, there is a countrywide service of Tourist Information Centres (TICs) ready and able to give advice and directions on how best to enjoy your holiday in Britain.

When you arrive at your holiday destination, look for this sign:

 Tourist information

All centres are located in key positions: in town centres; on major roads and well-known tourist routes; at ports and airports; at resorts and holiday attractions.

Motor accidents don't just happen ~ they are caused

Telephone – use abroad

It is really no more difficult to use the telephone abroad than at home but it may be confusing because you will not be familiar with the equipment or system. Further, you may not be able to read the instructions or speak to the operator. It is therefore a good idea to try to get a local person to help you.

Call boxes should normally only be used for local calls. For calls outside the district or international calls you should go to the local telegraph office or use a telephone at a garage or hotel. Hotels will charge for the use of their phones, sometimes quite heavily. Systems vary from country to country and it is not possible to give full details but the following chart may be helpful with elementary principles.

Country	Insert coin before or after lifting receiver	Dialling tone	Ringing tone	Engaged tone	Coins needed to operate a call box
Andorra	Before	Continuous tone	As UK engaged	Series of pips	5 peseta piece or *jeton* from point where call made
Austria	Instructions in English in all call boxes	Same as UK		Series of short tones	1 schilling piece
Belgium	After	Same as UK	Series of long tones	Series of short tones	5 franc piece
France	Before – grey coinbox After – yellow coinbox	Continuous tone	As UK engaged	Series of short tones	50 centimes or *jeton* from point where call made
Germany (W)	After	Short & long tones	Long tones	Series of short tones	2 × 10 pf pieces
Italy		Continuous tone	Series of long tones	Series of short tones	50 lire coin or *gettoni* from bars, tobacco shops or PO
Luxembourg	After	Same as UK	Series of long tones	Series of short tones	3 single francs
Netherlands	Instructions in English in all coin boxes				
Portugal	Automatic same as UK. Manual, turn handle to raise operator				80 centavos
Spain	After		Series of long tones	Series of short tones	peseta coins or if in a bar get *fichas* from barman
Switzerland	After	Continuous tone	Long single tone	Series of short tones	20 cents

Useful words and phrases

This is not meant to be a comprehensive vocabulary and has been compiled specifically for the non-linguist. The AA publication 'Car Components Guide' written in twelve languages, will also prove useful.

English	French	German	Italian	Spanish
Essential information				
Please where is the toilet?	S'il vous plaît, où sont les toilettes?	Bitte, wo ist die Toilette?	Per favore, dove sono i gabinetti?	¿Por favor, donde està el WC?
Male	Messieurs Hommes	Herren	Signori Uomini	Caballeros
Female	Dames Femmes	Damen	Signore Donne	Señoras
Route directions				
motorway	autoroute	Autobahn	autostrada	autopista
street; road	rue	Strasse	strada	calle
Main road				carretera
left	gauche	links	sinistra	izquierda
right	droite	rechts	destra	derecha
fork; branch; bear	talonnement	Abzweigung	forca di strada	bifurcación
turn	tourner	ein-, abbeigen	voltare	volver; girar; dar la vuelta
forward	tout droit	gerade aus	diretta	todo sequida
crossroads	croisement	Kreuzung	incrocio; croce	cruce; encrucijada
roundabout	sens giratoire	Rondell; Kreisverkehr	giro	giratoria
bridge	pont	Bruecke	ponte	puente
church	église	Kirche	chiesa	iglesia
public house	café; taverne	Gasthaus	osteria	fonda; café; hosteriá
level crossing	passage à niveau	Bahnuebergang	passaggio a livello	paso a nivel
Greetings				
Good morning (afternoon), Sir	Bonjour, monsieu	Guten Morgen, (Guten Tag) (Herr X)	Buon giorno, Signore	Buenos dias, señor
Good evening, Madam	Bonsoir, madame	Guten Abend, (Frau X)	Buona sera, Signora	Buenas noches, señora
Good-bye, Miss X	Au revoir, mademoiselle	Auf Wiedersehen, (Fräulein X)	Arrivederci, Signorina	Hasta la vista, Señorita
Excuse me	Excusez-moi	Entschuldigen Sie	Mi scusi	Dispénseme Vd
If you please	S'il vous plaît	Bitte	Per favore	Hágame Vd el favor
Thank you	Merci	Danke	Grazie	Gracias
Yes. No	Oui. Non	Ja. Nein	Si. No	Si. No
Speaking the language				
Do you speak…?	Parlez-vous…?	Sprechen Sie…?	Parla…?	¿Habla Vd…?
I speak…	Je parle…	Ich spreche…	Io parlo…	Yo hablo…
I do not speak…	Je ne parle pas…	Ich spreche nicht…	Io non parlo…	Yo no hablo…
French	français	französisch	francese	francés
English	anglais	englisch	inglese	inglés
Spanish	espagnol	spanisch	spagnolo	español
Portuguese	portugais	portugiesisch	portoghese	portugués
German	allemand	deutsch	tedesco	aleman
Italian	italien	italienisch	italiano	italiano
Dutch	hollandais	holländisch	olandese	holandés
Do you understand…?	Comprenez-vous…?	Verstehen Sie…?	Capisce…?	Comprende Vd…?
I do not understand…	Je ne comprends pas…	Ich verstehe nicht…	Non capisce…	No comprendo…
Speak slowly	Parlez lentement	Sprechen Sie langsam	Parli adagio	Hable Vd despacio
Could you repeat it?	Répétez	Wiederholen Sie	Ripeta	Repita

English	French	German	Italian	Spanish

At the shops

English	French	German	Italian	Spanish
How much?	Combien?	Wieviel?	Quanto?	¿Cuánto cuesta?
Cheaper	Meilleur marché	Biliger, preiswerter	A miglior prezzo	Lo ma barato
Too dear	Trop cher	Zu teur	Troppo caro	Demasiado caro

Telling the time

English	French	German	Italian	Spanish
Yesterday	Hier	Gestern	Ieri	Ayer
Yesterday evening	Hier soir	Gestern Abend	Ieri sera	Ayer tarde
Tonight	Cette nuit	Heute Nacht	Questa notte	Esta noche
This morning	Ce matin	Heute Morgen	Questa mattina	Esta mañana
Today	Aujourd'hui	Heute	Oggi	Hoy
This afternoon	Cet après-midi	Heute Nachmittag	Questo pomeriggio	Esta tarde
At noon	A midi	Mittags	A mezzogiorno	A mediodïa
At midnight	A minuit	Um Mitternacht	A mezzanotte	A medianoche
This evening	Ce soir	Heute Abend	Questa sera	Esta noche
Tomorrow	Demain	Morgen	Domani	Mañana
Tomorrow morning	Demain matin	Morgen früh	Domani mattina	Mañana por la mañana
Tomorrow evening	Demain soir	Morgen Abend	Domani sera	Mañana por la tarde
The day after tomorrow	Après-demain	Übermorgen	Dopo domani	Pasado mañana
Early. Late	Tôt. Tard	Früh. Spät	Presto. Tardi	Temprano. Tarde
At once	Toute de suite	Sofort	Subito	En seguida
Second (in time)	Seconde	Sekunde	Secondo	Segundo
Minute (in time)	Minute	Minute	Minuto	Minuto
Hour	Heure	Stunde	Ora	Hora
What time is it?	Quelle heure est-il?	Wieviel Uhr ist es?	Che ore sono?	¿Qué hora es?
Monday	Lundi	Montag	Lunedì	Lunes
Tuesday	Mardi	Dienstag	Martedì	Martes
Wednesday	Mercredi	Mittwoch	Mercoledì	Miércoles
Thursday	Jeudi	Donnerstag	Giovedì	Jueves
Friday	Vendredi	Freitag	Venerdì	Viernes
Saturday	Samedi	Samstag	Sabato	Sábado
Sunday	Dimanche	Sonntag	Domenica	Domingo

Using the telephone

English	French	German	Italian	Spanish
Can I use your phone please?	Puis je utiliser votre téléphone s'il vous plaît?	Kann ich Ihr Telefon benutzen bitte?	Prego, posso servirmi del Vestro telefono?	¿Puedo usar su telefono, por favor?
Have you any coins?	Avez-vous des pièces?	Haben sie Munzen?	Avete delle monete?	¿Tiene monedas?
Operator is there anything wrong with the line?	Operatrice y a-t-il quelque chose qui ne va pas dans cette ligne?	Ist etwas mit dieser heiting nicht in Ordnung?	C'e qualcosa che non bene con la linea?	¿Pasa algo raro en esta linea?

Dining out

English	French	German	Italian	Spanish
Please show me . . . a good restaurant	Indiquez-moi un bon restaurant	Wollen Sie mir . . . nennen (angeben) ein gutes Restaurant	Mi indichi un buon ristorante	Indíqueme un buen restaurant
What time is . . .	A quelle heure est . . .	Um wieviel Uhr servieren Sie (gibt es)?	A che ora é . . .?	¿A qué hora se sirve . . .?
breakfast	le petit déjeuner	das Frühstück	la prima colazione	el desayuno
lunch	le déjeuner	das Mittagessen	la colazione	el almuerzo
dinner	le dîner	das Abendessen	il pranzo	la comida
Can you serve me quickly	pouvez-vous me préparer rapidement à manager?	Können Sie mir schnell etwas zu essen zubereiten?	Può prepararmi presto da mangiare?	¿Puede servirme de prisa?

English	French	German	Italian	Spanish
How much is the meal?	Quel est le prix du repas?	Was kostet die Mahlzeit?	Qual è il prezzo del pasto?	¿Cuánto cuesta el cubierto?
Is the price of drink included?	Boisson comrise?	Ist das Getränk inbegriffen?	Bevanda compresa?	¿Está incluida la bebida?
Show me the menu	Montez-moi le menu?	Zeigen Sie mir das Menü	Mi faccia vedere la lista delle vivande	Muéstreme el menú
Give me the wine list	Donnez-moi la carte des vins	Geben Sie mir die Weinkarte	Mi dia la lista dei vini	Déme Vd la lista de vinos
What is the special dish of the region?	Quelle est la spécialité du pays?	Welches ist die hiesige Spezialität?	Qual'è la specialità del paese?	¿Cuál es el plato especial de la región?

Something to eat

English	French	German	Italian	Spanish
I should like . . .	Je voudrais . . .	Ich möchte . . .	Vorrei . . .	Yo quería . . .
some soup	de la soupe	Suppe	della zuppa, della minestra	Sopa
some clear soup	du bouillon	Freischbrühe	del brodo	caldo o consomé
some fish	du poisson	Fisch	del pescu	pescado
fried fish	une friture de poisson	Gebratenen Fisch	una frittura di pesce	pescado frito
a lobster	du homard	Hummer	dei gamberi	langosta
some meat	de la viande	Fleisch	della carne	carne
a chop or a cutlet	une côtelette	ein Kotelett	una cotoletta	una chuleta
some veal	du veau	Kalbfleisch	del vitello	ternera
some beef	du boeuf	Rindfleisch	del manzo	vaca
some lamb	du mouton	Hammelfleisch Schaffleisch	dell' agnello	cordero
some pork	du porc	Schweinefleisch	del maiale	cerdo
some ham	du jambon	Schinken	del prosciutto	jamón
some chicken	du poulet	Huhn	del pollo	pollo
some beefsteak	du beefsteak	beefsteak	una bistecca	bistek . . .
. . . underdone,	. . . saignant	. . . blutig (englisch)	. . . al sangue	. . . poco pasado
. . . well done	. . . cuit	. . . durch durchgebraten, gar	. . . ben cotta	. . . pasado
. . . medium done	. . . à point	. . . halbenglisch	. . . cotta a puntino	. . . a punto
some bread	du pain	Brot	del pane	pan
some butter	du beurre	Butter	del burro	mantequilla
an omelette	une omellette	eine Omelette	une frittata	una tortilla
a ham omelette	. . . au jambon	eine Schinken-omelette	. . . prosciutto	. . . con jamón
a mushroom omelette	. . . aux champignons	eine Omelette mit Champignons	. . . coi funghi	de setas
a savoury omelette	. . . aux fines herbes	eine Omelette mit	. . . con verdura	de finas hierbas
a salad	une salade	Salat	. . . una insalata	ensalada
some vegetables	des légumes	Gemüse	dei legumi	legumbres
tomatoes	des tomates	Tomaten	dei pomodori	tomates
some potatoes	des pommes de terre	Kartoffeln	delle patate	patatas
Cabbage	du chou	Kohl	cavolo	coles
Cauliflower	du chou-fleur	Blumenkohl	cavolfiori	coliflores
Green peas	des petits pois	Grüne Erbsen	dei pisellini	guisantes
Beans	des haricots	Bohnen	dei fagiuoli	habichuelas, judías
some salt and pepper	de sel et du poivre	Salz und Pfeffer	del sale e del pepe	sal y pimienta
some oil and vinegar	de l'huile et du vinaigre	Öl und Essig	dell'olio e dell'aceto	aceite y vinagre
some mustard	de la moutarde	Senf, Mostrich	della senape	mostaza
(with) no garlic please	(avec) sans ail, s'il vous plait	(mit) ohne Knoblauch bitte	per favore (con) senza aglio	por favor (con) sin ajo
Cheeses	Fromages	Käse	Formaggio	Queso
Fruits	Fruits	Früchte	Frutta	Frutas
Pastries	Pâtisseries	Feines Gebäck	Pasticceria	pastelería
Chocolate	Du chocolat	Schokolade	Della cioccolata	Chocolate
Ice creams	Glaces	Eis	Gelato	Helados

English	French	German	Italian	Spanish

Something to drink

English	French	German	Italian	Spanish
A bottle	Une bouteille	Eine Flasche	Una bottiglia	Una botella
Half a bottle	Une demi-bouteille	Eine Halbe Flasche	Una messa bittiglia	Media botella
Water	De l'eau	Wasser . . .	Dell'acqua	Aqua
Iced water	. . . glacée	geeistes Wasser	. . . ghiacciata	. . . helada
Hot water	. . . chaude	warmes Wasser	. . . calda	. . . caliente
White wine	Du vin blanc	Weisswein	Del vino bianco	Vino blanco
Red wine	Du vin rouge	Rotwein	Del vino rosso	Vino tinto
Cider	Du cidre	Obstwein, Most	Del sidro	Sidra
Orangeade	De l'orangeade	Orangeade	Una aranciata	Naranjada
Lemonade	De la citronnade	Zitronensaft	Una limonata	Limonada
Beer	De la bière	Bier	Della birra	Cerveza
Mineral water	De l'eau minérale	Mineralwasser	Dell'acqua minerale	Agua mineral
Liquers	Des liquers	Liköre	Dei liquori	Licores
Coffee	Du café	Kaffee	Del caffè	Café
Tea	Du thé	Tee	Del tè	Té
Milk	Du lait	Milch	Del latte	Leche
Sugar	Du sucre	Zucker	Dello zucchero	Azúcar
Jam	De la confiture	Konfitüre	Della marmaletta	Dulce
Cream	De la crème	Sahne	Della panna	Crema

The finale

English	French	German	Italian	Spanish
Waiter! the bill	Garçon! l'addition	Kellner! die Rechnung	Cameriere! Il conto	¿Camarero! la Cuenta
Are tips included?	Pourboire compris!	Ist das Trinkgeld inbegriffen?	Mancia compresa?	¿Está incluída la propina?

At the garage

English	French	German	Italian	Spanish
Fill up the tank, Please . . . with petrol with oil	Faites le plein s'il vous plaît . . . d'essence d'huile	Füllen Sie den Tank . . . mit Benzin mit Öl	Mi faccia il pieno . . . di benzina d'olio	Sírvase llenar el depósito . . . de gasolina de aceite
Give me five, ten, twenty, thirty litres of petrol	Mettez-moi cinq, dix, vingt, trente litres d'essence	Geben Sie mir fünf, zehn, zwanzig, dreissig Liter Benzin	Mi metta cinque, dieci, venti, trenta litri di benzina	Póngame cinco, diez, veinte, treinta litros de gasolina
Check the water	Vérifiez l'eau	Sehen Sie bitte das Wasser nach	Verifichi l'acqua	Compruebe el agua
Fill the radiator	Remplissez le radiateur	Füllen Sie den Kühler auf	Riempia il radiatore	Llene el radiador
Have you a can with some water?	Avez-vous un arrosoir avec de l'eau?	Haben Sie eine Kanne mit Wasser?	Avete un innaffiatoio con acqua?	¿Tiene usted una regadera con agua?
Check the tyre-pressure	Vérifiez le pneus	Sehen Sie die Reifen nach	Verifichi le gomme	Compruebe los neumáticos
I wish to garage my car here; what is the charge per night?	Je désire garer ma voiture ici; qule est le prix par nuit?	Ich möchte meinen Wagen hier einstellen; was kostet das pro Nacht?	Vorrei lasciare qui la mia automobile; quanto costa per notte?	Deseo dejar mi automóvil aquí; ¿cuánto me cobrará por una noche?
I have a puncture; please mend it	J'ai crevé un pneu; veuillez le réparer	Ein Pneu ist geplatz; bitte reparieren Sie ihn	Ho bucato una gomma; me la ripari	He reventado un neumático; sírvase repararlo
I want . . . a tyre an inner tube	Je désire . . . un pneu une chambre à air	Ich wünsche . . . einen Reifen einen Schlauch	Vorrei . . . una gomma una camera d'aria	Deseo . . . un neumático una cámara de aire

English	French	German	Italian	Spanish
a sparking plug	une bougie	eine Kerze	una candela	una bujía
Please check (rest) The battery	Veuillez vérifier la batterie	Wollen Sie bitte die Batterie nachsehen	Verifichi la batteria	Haga el favor de comprobar la batería
Will you please Adjust . . .	Veuillez régler . . .	Wollen Sie bitte . . . einstellen	Regoli . . .	Quiere Vd reglar . . .
The brakes	les freins	die Bremsen	i freni	los frenos
the ignition	l'allumage	die Zündung	l'accensione	el encendido
the steering	la direction	die Steuerung	lo sterzo	la dirección
Something is wrong with . . . my car	Quelque chose ne va pas . . . à ma voiture	Es funktioniert etwas nicht . . . an meinem Wagen	Qualche cosa non va . . . alla mia Automobile	Hay algo que no va bien . . . en mi coche,
my engine	dans mon moteur	an meinem Motor	nel motore	en mi motor
My car won't start	Ma voiture ne démarre pas	Mein Wagen Fährt nicht an	La mia automobile non si mette in moto	Mi coche no arranca
The starter motor is faulty	Le démarreur est détraqué	Der Anlasser funktioniert nicht	La messa in moto è guasta	El motor de arranque de mi automóvil está averiado
The radiator is leaking	Le radiateur a une fuite	Der Kühler hat ein Leck (ist undicht)	Il radatore perde	El radiador pierde
My engine knocks; will you please look at it?	Mon moteur cogne; veuillez l'examiner	Mein Motor klopft; würden Sie ihn nachsehen?	Il motore batte; lo guardi	Mi motor golpea; sírvase examinarlo
My engine has seized up; will you please repair it	Mon moteur est grippé; réparez- le, s'il vous plaît	Mein Motor sitzt fest; reparieren Sie ihn, bitte	Il mio motore è guasto; lo ripari, per favore	Mi motor está agarrotade; quierre Vd proceder a repararlo
The clutch does not work	L'embrayage ne foncitionne plus	Die Kupplung funktioniert nicht mehr	La frizione non funziona più	El embrague no funciona
The fuses are blown	Les fusibles ont sauté	Die Sicherungen sind durchgebrannt	Le valvole sono saltate	Los fusibles se han quemado
I want some new bulbs	Il me faut des ampoules neuves	Ich brauche neue Birnen	Mi occorrono delle nuove lampadine	Me hacen falta lámparas nuevas
How long will this repair take?	Combien de temps prendra cette réparation?	Wie lange wird diese Reparatur dauren?	Quanto tempo occorre per questa riparazione?	¿Quánto tiempo durará esta reparación?
How much will it cost?	Combien coûtera-t-elle?	Wieviel kostet sie?	Quanto costerà?	¿Cuánto costará?
I wish to hire a car	Je désire louer une automobile . . .	Ich möchte ein Auto . . . mieten	Vorrei noleggiare un'automobile	Deseo alquilar un automóvil

At the chemist's

Please make up this prescription	Veuillez préparer cette ordonnance	Wollen Sie bitte dieses Rezept zu-bereiten	Mi prepari, per favore, questa ricetta	Sirvase prepararme esta receta
How much?	Quel en est le prix?	Was kostet es?	Quanto costa?	¿Cuánto cuesta?
Have you a remedy for . . .	Avez-vous un médicament . . .	Haben Sie eine Arznei . . .	Ha una medicina . . .	Tiene Vd un medicamento . . .
a cough?	contre la toux?	gegen Husten	contro la tosse?	para la tos?
a toothache?	contre les maux de dents?	gegen Zahn-schmerzen	contro il mal di denti?	para el dolor de muelas?
a headache?	contre les maux de tête?	gegen Kopf-schmerzen	contro il mal di testa?	para el dolor de cabeza?
insomnia?	contre l'insomnie?	gegen Schlaflosig-keit	contro l'insonnia?	para el insomnio?
sea-sickness?	contre le mal de mer?	gegen Seekrank-heit	contro il mal de mare?	para el mareo?

English	French	German	Italian	Spanish
indigestion?	contre les troubles digestifs?	gegen Verdau-ungsstörungen,	contro i disturbi digestivi?	para el dolor de estómago?
diarrhoea?	contre les coliques?	gegen Kolik?	contro la colica?	para los cólicos?
I want . . .	J'aimerais . . .	Ich möchte . . .	Vorrei . . .	Desearía . . .
a laxative	un laxatif	ein Abführmittel	un lassativo,	un laxante
a packet of cotton wool	un paquet d'ouate	ein Paket Watte	un pacchetto di ovatta	un paquete de algodón
tampons	tampons	tampons	tamponi	tampones
toilet paper	du papier hygiénique	Toilettenpapier	della carta igiencia	papel higiénico
razor blades	des lames de rasoir	Rasierklingen	delle lamette da rasoio	hojos de afeitar
sun lotion	un produit anti-solaire	ein Sonnenschutz-mittel	un prodotto anti-solare	un producto antisolar

Valuables

Tourists should pay particular attention to the security of their money and items of value while touring. Whenever possible excess cash and travellers' cheques should be left with the hotel management **against a receipt**. In some areas, children and youths cause a diversion to attract tourists' attention while pickpockets operate in organised gangs. Unusual incidents, which are more likely to occur in crowded markets or shopping centres, should be avoided.

It cannot be stressed too strongly that all valuables should be removed from a parked car even if it is parked in a supervised car park or lock-up garage.

Visitors' registration

All visitors to a country must register with local police which is a formality usually satisfied by the completion of a card or certificate when booking into an hotel, camp site or place offering accommodation. If staying with friends or relations then it is usually the responsibility of the host to seek advice from the police within 24 hours of the arrival of his guests.

For short holiday visits the formalities are very simple but most countries place a time limit on the period that tourists may stay after which a firmer type of registration is imposed. Where necessary the country sections will give fuller information in this respect.

Winter conditions

Motoring in Europe during the winter months is restricted because of the vast mountain ranges – the Alps sweeping in an arc from the French Riviera, through Switzerland, northern Italy, and Austria to the borders of Yugoslavia, the Pyrenees which divide France and Spain – as well as extensive areas of Spain, France and Germany which are at an altitude of well over 1,000ft. However, matters have been eased with improved communications and modern snow-clearing apparatus.

Where comment is warranted, this will be given under the winter conditions section of each country. Details of road and rail tunnels which can be used to pass under the mountains are given on pages 55-58, and the periods when the most important mountain passes are usually closed are given on pages 31-32, 49-55. If you want a conventional seaside holiday between October and March, you will probably have to travel at least as far south as Lisbon, Valencia, or Naples to be reasonably certain of fine weather.

Weather information   Any AA service centre can give general information about winter weather conditions in Europe, but detailed information about conditions on mountain passes and main roads is available from the AA London Operational Centre, Stanmore, tel 01-954 7373. Information is received from the European Road Information Centre, which gets daily reports from all associated motoring clubs. You can also get information about current European conditions from the weather centres of the Meteorological Offices in:

London	01-836 4311
Manchester	061-832 6701
Newcastle upon Tyne	Newcastle upon Tyne 26453
Southampton	Southampton 28844
Glasgow	041-248 3451
Nottingham	Nottingham 384091

Climatological information is available from the World Climatology Branch of the Meteorological Office at Bracknell, Berkshire, tel 20242. For detailed information a charge is made, the amount depending on the work involved in answering the specific enquiry.

When you are abroad, you should contact the nearest office of the appropriate national motoring club. It is advisable to check on conditions ahead as you go along and hotels and garages are often helpful.

Winter-sports centres   You can usually reach these, as at least one main approach road is swept, but you may need wheel chains, spiked or studded tyres, or snow tyres.

Winter tyres   In fair weather, wheel chains, spiked or studded tyres, or snow tyres are only necessary on the higher passes, but in severe weather you will probably need them (as a rough guide) at altitudes exceeding 2,000ft.

If you think you will need any of these devices, it is better to take them with you from home. They may be purchased at motor accessory shops to whom an early approach should be made in case the size you require is not in stock.

Information on hiring wheel chains (where such a service exists) in the countries where they are most needed is given under the heading 'Tyres' in the country sections.

Wheel chains and spiked or studded tyres damage the road surface if it is free of snow or ice; there are definite periods when these may be used and in certain countries the use of spiked or studded tyres is illegal.

If wheel chains, spiked or studded tyres, or snow tyres are compulsory, this is usually signposted.

See also Cold-touring weather touring, page **28**.

Wheel chains   These are chains which fit over the tyres to enable the wheels to grip on snow or icy surfaces. Wheel chains are sometimes called snow chains or anti-skid chains. Full-length chains which fit right round a tyre are the most satisfactory, but they must be fitted correctly. Check that the chains do not foul your vehicle bodywork; if your vehicle has front-wheel-drive put the steering on full lock while checking. If your vehicle has radial tyres it is essential that you contact the manufacturers of your vehicle and tyres for their recommendations in order to avoid damage to your tyres. Chains should only be used when compulsory or necessary as prolonged use on hard surfaces will damage the tyres.

Spiked or studded tyres   These are tyres with rugged treads onto which spikes or studs have been fitted. For the best grip they should be fitted to all wheels. Spiked or studded tyres are sometimes called snow tyres.

Snow tyres   These are usually heavy-duty tyres with rugged treads. Snow tyres (preferably fitted to all wheels) are suitable for some level surfaces and some very gradual slopes. Of the devices mentioned above, they are the least effective.

Journey time   As there are several aspects of a journey to consider it will be difficult to reach a good conclusion on the time a journey will take. Customs clearance, traffic and weather conditions, the time of day, the negotiating of mountain passes and other factors will effect calculations. However, an approximate travelling time can be arrived at by considering the kilometre distance as minutes ie 60Km (37½ miles) takes about 60 minutes. Thus to travel 300Km will take about 300 minutes or 5 hours. Allowance will, of course, have to be made in the light of your experience when travelling along motorways (where an average speed of 55 mph is possible) and secondary roads. The table below is a guide to journey times at average speeds expressed in kilometres.

Always take a pride in your driving and remember that fatigue increases the risk of accidents. An alert driver is more likely to drive safely. He is able to concentrate fully, enabling him to react quickly. A tired driver loses concentration consequently his judgement becomes less reliable and his reactions slower. Fatigue is often aggravated at dusk or after dark, so try and plan journeys to avoid long hours of driving extending after daylight has begun to fade. Do not drive for long unbroken periods. Stop in a safe and convenient place at regular intervals and walk around to stretch your limbs.

REMEMBER DRIVING AND DRINKING JUST DO NOT MIX

Distance in kilometres	Average speed in mph									
	30		40		50		60		70	
	hrs	mins	hrs	mins	hrs	mins	hrs	mins	hrs	mins
20		25		19		15		13		11
30		37		28		22		19		16
40		50		37		30		25		21
50	1	2		47		37		31		27
60	1	15		56		45		38		32
70	1	25	1	5		52		43		36
80	1	39	1	15	1	0		50		42
90	1	52	1	24	1	7		56		48
100	2	4	1	33	1	15	1	2		53
150	3	6	2	20	1	52	1	33	1	20
200	4	8	3	6	2	30	2	4	1	46
250	5	10	3	53	3	7	2	35	2	13
300	6	12	4	40	3	44	3	6	2	40
350	7	14	5	27	4	21	3	37	3	7
400	8	16	6	12	5	0	4	8	3	32
450	9	18	6	59	5	37	4	39	3	59
500	10	20	7	46	6	14	5	10	4	26

Motoring regulations

Motoring laws in Europe are just as wide and as complicated as those in the UK but they should cause little difficulty to the average British motorist. He should however, take more care and extend greater courtesy than he would normally do at home, and bear in mind the essentials of good motoring – avoiding any behaviour likely to obstruct traffic, to endanger persons or cause damage to property. It is also important to remember that when travelling in a country the tourist is subject to the laws of that country.

Road signs are mainly international and should be familiar to the British motorist (see inside front cover and inside back cover) but in every country there are a few exceptions. He should particularly watch for signs indicating crossings and speed limits. Probably the most unusual aspect of motoring abroad to the British motorist is the universal and firm rule of giving priority to traffic coming from the right and unless this rule is varied by signs, it must be strictly observed.

The following information will be common to the countries covered in this Guide but any national variations will be indicated in the country sections.

Accidents

The country sections give individual country regulations and information on summoning the fire, police and ambulance services. The international regulations are similar to those in the UK; the following recommendations are usually advisable.

If you are involved in an accident you *must* stop. A warning triangle should be placed on the road at a suitable distance to warn following traffic of the obstruction. The use of hazard warning lights in no way affects the regulations governing the use of warning triangles. Medical assistance should be obtained for persons injured in the accident. If the accident necessitates calling the police, leave the vehicle in the position in which it comes to rest; should it seriously obstruct other traffic, mark the position of the vehicle on the road and get the details confirmed by independent witnesses before moving it.

The accident must be reported to the police if it is required by law (see country sections); if the accident has caused death or bodily injury; or if an unoccupied vehicle or property has been damaged and there is no one present to represent the interests of the party suffering damage. Notify your insurance company by letter if possible, within 24 hours of the accident; see the conditions of your policy. If a third party is injured, the insurance company or bureau, whose address is given on the back of your Green Card or frontier insurance certificate, should be notified; the company or bureau will, if necessary, pay compensation to the injured party.

Make sure that all essential particulars are noted, especially details concerning third parties and co-operate with police or other officials taking on-the-spot notes by supplying your name and address or other personal details as required. It is also a good idea to take photographs of the scene endeavouring to get good shots of other vehicles involved, their registration plates and any background which might help at later enquiries. This record may be useful when completing the insurance company's accident form.

If you are not involved in the accident but feel your assistance as a witness or in any other useful capacity would be helpful then stop and park your car carefully well away from the scene. If all the help necessary is at the scene then do not stop out of curiosity nor park your car at the site.

First aid Expert assistance should be summoned immediately. Unless you have a knowledge of first aid you should be extremely cautious about attending anyone injured in an accident. The following notes may be useful.

Bleeding and wounds To stop bleeding apply pressure to the sides of the wound. Cleanse around and away from the wound, taking care not to disturb any blood clot. Apply and maintain pressure to the bleeding part with dressing, cover with pad, and bandage firmly.

Broken bones Fractures should be moved as little as possible. Support the injured part at once.

Exhaled air resuscitation Lay patient on his back. Tilt the head and chin away from the chest to clear airway, making sure that it is not obstructed by the tongue or foreign matter. Open your mouth and take a deep breath. Pinch the casualty's nostrils together, then seal your lips around the mouth. Blow into his lungs until the chest rises, then remove your mouth and watch the chest deflate. Repeat giving the first four inflations as rapidly as possible. Lung inflation can also be carried out through the nose. The casualty's mouth should be sealed with the thumb holding the lower jaw.

Fainting Lay patient down and raise lower limbs, EXCEPT IN CASE OF FRACTURE. Loosen tight clothing about neck, waist, and chest, and ensure fresh air.

First-aid kit It is always advisable to carry a first-aid kit.

Shock Loosen any tight clothing, wrap the casualty in a blanket or coat and lay him down at absolute rest.

Alterations to vehicles

If a vehicle constructionally satisfies the law in its country of registration then it should be acceptable in any country into which it has been temporarily imported. Thus no changes should be necessary but there are regulations in some countries which, in the interests of courtesy or safety, should be observed. Where appropriate these will be mentioned in the country sections.

Caravan and luggage trailers

Carry a list of contents, as this may be required at a frontier. A towed vehicle should be readily identifiable by a plate in an accessible position showing the name of the maker of the vehicle and his production or serial number.

Common Law Claims

In Spain, particularly, and to a lesser extent, in some other countries common law ie claims to be made against other parties following, for example, a road accident – not to be confused with claims made under the benefits of 5-Star Service – are frequently not recoverable in full. Claims for vehicle hiring charges are invariably reduced, and, in certain cases, may not be admissible at all.

If an accident occurs in Spain and your vehicle is repaired in the United Kingdom you are generally only entitled to recover, subject to liability, an amount equal to the cost of repairing the vehicle in Spain which is usually considerably less than the UK cost. AA members may contact the Association's Legal Services, Head Office, for advice on such matters.

Compulsory equipment

All countries have differing regulations as to how vehicles circulating on their roads should be equipped but generally domestic laws are not enforced on visiting foreigners. However, where a country considers aspects of safety or other factors are involved they will impose some regulations on visitors and these will be mentioned in the country sections.

Crash helmets

All riders of motorcycles, irrespective of the capacity of their machine, should wear crash helmets.

Dimension and weight restrictions

For an ordinary private car a height limit of 4 metres and a height limit of 2.5 metres is generally imposed. Apart from a laden weight limit imposed on commercial vehicles every vehicle, private or commercial, has an individual weight limit and as this effects private cars see Overloading page 70. See also Road tunnels, page 55, as some dimensions are restricted by the shape of the tunnels.
If you have any doubts consult the AA.

Drinking and driving

There is only one safe rule – if you drink, don't drive. The laws are strict and penalties severe.

Hazard warning lights

Although four flashing indicators are allowed in the countries covered in this Guide, they in no way affect the regulations governing the use of warning triangles.

Level crossings

Practically all level crossings are indicated by international signs. Most guarded ones are the lifting barrier type, sometimes with bells or flashing lights to give warning of an approaching train.

Lights

For driving abroad, lights must be so adjusted that they do not dip to the left. The easiest way to achieve this is to use an adapter.

Dipped headlights should be used in conditions of fog, snowfall, heavy rain and when passing through a tunnel, irrespective of its length and its lighting. In some countries police will wait at the end of a tunnel, checking this requirement.

Headlight flashing is generally used as a warning of approach or a passing sign at night. In other circumstances it is accepted as a sign of annoyance or irritation and should be used with caution lest it be misunderstood.

Minibus

A minibus, equipped to carry more than eight passengers (in addition to the driver) is classed as a commercial passenger carrying vehicle, and, as such, attracts special regulations including the keeping of a special log recording the driver's hours and a minimum age for driving such vehicles. It is also a legal requirement that all such vehicles be fitted with a Tachograph. If you plan to tour in EEC countries with a vehicle in the category described you should contact the local Traffic Area Office of the Department of Transport, or, if in Northern Ireland, The Ministry of Development, Belfast, well in advance of your departure.

Mountain passes

Always engage a low gear before either ascending or descending steep gradients, keep well to the right side of the road and avoid cutting corners. Avoid excessive use of brakes. If the engine overheats, pull off the road, making sure you do not cause an obstruction, leave the engine idling, and put the heater controls, including the fan, into the maximum heat position. Under no circumstances remove the radiator cap until the engine has cooled down. Do not fill the coolant system of a hot engine with cold water.

Always engage a lower gear before taking a hairpin bend, give priority to vehicles ascending and remember that as your altitude increases so your engine power decreases. Priority must always be given to postal coaches travelling in either direction. Their route is usually signposted.

Overloading

This can create safety risks, and in most countries committing such an offence can involve on-the-spot fines. It would also be a great inconvenience if your car was stopped because of overloading – you would not be allowed to proceed until the load had been reduced. The maximum loaded weight, and its distribution between front and rear axles is decided by the vehicle manufacturer and if your owner's handbook does not give these facts you should seek the advice of the manufacturer direct. There is a public weighbridge in all districts and when the car is fully loaded (not forgetting the passengers, of course) use this to check that the vehicle is wihin the limits. When loading a vehicle, care should be taken that lights, reflectors, or number plates are not masked or that the driver's view is in no way impaired. All luggage loaded on a roof rack must be tightly secured and should not upset the stability of the vehicle. Any projections beyond the front, rear, or sides of a vehicle that might not be noticed by either driver must be clearly marked.

Overtaking

When overtaking on roads with two lanes or more in each direction, always signal your intention in good time, and after the manoeuvre, signal and return to the inside lane. Do not remain in any other lane.

Always overtake on the right and use horn as a warning to the driver of the vehicle being overtaken (except in areas where the use of the horn is prohibited). Do not overtake whilst being overtaken or when vehicle behind is preparing to overtake. Do not overtake at level crossings, at intersections, the crest of a hill or at pedestrian crossings. When being overtaken keep well to the right and reduce speed if necessary – never increase speed.

Parking

Parking is a problem everywhere in Europe and the police are extremely strict with offenders. Heavy fines are inflicted as well as the towing away of unaccompanied offending cars. This can cause inconvenience and heavy charges are imposed for the recovery of impounded vehicles. You should acquaint yourself with local parking regulations and endeavour to understand all relative signs. As a rule always park on the right-hand side of the road or at an authorised place. As far as possible park off the main carriageway but not on cycle tracks, pedestrian verges, railway lines or tram tracks.

Passengers

It is an offence in all countries to carry more passengers in a car than the vehicle is constructed to seat, but some have regulations as to how the passengers shall be seated. Where such regulations are applied to visiting foreigners it will be mentioned in the country sections.

For passenger carrying vehicles constructed and equipped to carry more than eight passengers in addition to the driver there are special regulations (see Minibus page 69).

Police fines

Often called on-the-spot fines, police fines can be imposed in one form or another in most countries in Europe by policemen, for minor traffic offences. They are sometimes paid in cash to the policeman and sometimes at a post office against a 'ticket' issued by the policeman. Once paid they cannot be recovered. Such fines are intended to keep minor motoring offences out of courts thus reducing administrative costs to the advantage of the motorist and the police. Nevertheless such fines are very high and punitive. If the motorist disputes the charge he can opt to go before a court but this, in the case of a tourist, can lead to delays, inconvenience and extra expense. Further, as a measure of guarantee or surety, particularly in more serious cases, the policeman is often authorised to demand a sum of money to cover anticipated fines and costs. If the depositing of cash is refused then the police officer is empowered to confiscate property or even the car to cover any deposits he considers necessary. In most cases it is more straightforward to accept the fine but a receipt should always be obtained for deposits on fines. Should AA members feel they require assistance in any matter involving local police they should appeal to the Legal Department of the AA at HO, Basingstoke.

Priority

The general rule is to give way to traffic entering a junction from the right which is sometimes varied at roundabouts. This is the one aspect of European driving which may cause the British driver the most confusion because his whole training and experience makes it unnatural. Road signs indicate priority or loss of priority and tourists are well advised to make sure that they understand such signs.

Great care should be taken at intersections and tourists should never rely on receiving the right of way, particularly in small towns and villages where local traffic, often slow moving, such as farm tractors etc. will assume right of way regardless of oncoming traffic.

Always give way to public services and military vehicles. Blind or disabled people, funerals and marching columns must always be allowed right of way.

Vehicles such as buses and coaches carrying large numbers of passengers will expect and should be allowed priority.

Road signs

Most road signs through Europe are internationally agreed and the majority would be familiar to the British motorist. Please refer to the inside front and inside back covers for signs relating to the countries covered by this guide. Watch also for road markings – do not cross a solid white or yellow line marked on the road centre.

Roundabouts

Priority at roundabouts is given to vehicles entering the roundabout unless signposted to the contrary. This is a complete reversal to the United Kingdom rule, and particular care should be exercised when manoeuvring while circulating in an anti-clockwise direction on a roundabout. It is advisable to keep to the outside lane on a roundabout if possible, to make your exit easier.

Rule of the road

In all European countries, drive on the right and overtake on the left.

Seat belts

All countries in this guide with the exception of Italy require visitors to wear seat belts. If your car is fitted with belts then in the interest of safety, wear them, otherwise you may run the risk of a police fine.

Signals

Signals of a driver's intentions must be given clearly, within a reasonable distance, and in good time. In built-up areas, the general rule is not to use horns unless safety demands it; in many large towns and resorts, as well as in areas indicated by the international sign, the use of the horn is totally prohibited.

Speed limits

It is important to observe speed limits at all times. Offenders may be fined and driving licences impounded on the spot, thus causing great inconvenience and possible expense. The chart (on page 73) gives limits for private cars which are standard legal limits. These may be varied by road signs and where such signs are displayed the lower limit should be accepted. At certain times limits may also be temporarily varied and information would be available at the frontier. It can be an offence, without good reason to travel at so slow a speed as to obstruct traffic flow.

Temporary importation

A motor vehicle, caravan, boat, or any other type of trailer is subject to strict control on entering a country and attracts Customs duty and a variety of taxes, but much depends upon the circumstances and the period of the import and also upon the status of the importer. A person entering a country in which he has no residence, with a private vehicle for holiday or recreational purposes and intending to export the vehicle within a short period enjoys special privileges and the normal formalities are reduced to an absolute minimum in the interests of tourism. Importers of any type of commercial vehicle or one to be used to support commercial enterprises do not have the same tolerance.

A person entering a country with a motor vehicle for a period of generally more than three months or to take up residence, employment, or with the intention of disposing of the vehicle should seek advice concerning his position well in advance of his departure. Any AA service centre will be pleased to help.

A temporarily imported vehicle should not:

a   be left in the country after the importer has left;
b   be put at the disposal of a resident of the country;
c   be retained in the country longer than the permitted period;
d   be lent, sold, hired, given away, exchanged or otherwise disposed of.

A *bona fide* tourist will generally be allowed to import anything considered in use or in keeping with his status, but such articles, where not consumable, must be exported when the importer leaves the country. In the case of some portable items of high value *ie* a portable television set, the Customs may make a note in the importer's passport and in his own interest he should ensure the entry is cancelled when exporting the item.

Traffic lights

In principle cities and towns operate in a way similar to those in the United Kingdom, although they are sometimes suspended overhead. The density of the light may be so poor that lights could be missed. There is usually only one set on the right-hand side of the road some distance before the road junction, and if you stop too close to the corner the lights will not be visible. Watch out for 'filter' lights which will enable you to turn right at a junction against the main lights. If you wish to go straight ahead do not enter a lane leading to 'filter' lights otherwise you may obstruct traffic wishing to turn right.

Trams

Trams take priority over other vehicles. Always give way to passengers boarding and alighting. Never position a vehicle so that it impedes the free passage of a tram. Trams must be overtaken on the right except in one-way streets.

Tyres

If the tyres on your car conform to British regulations then they would be acceptable abroad but if you are found with tyres not up to standard then you face a fine and the possibility of being held until the tyres are changed.

Amongst other things, the British regulations state that tyres must display a clearly visible tread and pattern with a tread of at least one millimetre throughout the entire breadth and around the whole circumference.

Warning triangles

In all the countries in this book the use of warning triangles is compulsory, except for two-wheeled vehicles. It should be placed on the road behind a stopped vehicle to warn traffic approaching from the rear of an obstruction ahead. Warning triangles should be used when a vehicle has stopped for any reason – not only breakdowns.

The triangle should be placed in such a position as to be clearly visible up to 100m (109yds) by day and by night, about 2ft from the edge of the road but not in such a position as to present a danger to on-coming traffic. It should be set about 30m (33yds) behind the obstruction but this distance should be increased up to 100m (109yds) on motorways.

Hazard warning lights should not be used in place of a triangle but may complement it in use. Triangles can be purchased from the AA.

SPEED LIMITS – In KM/H, MPH in brackets   PETROL

	In Built-up Areas	Outside Built-up Areas	On Motorways	With Trailer	Currency	Per Litre at Pump		Per Litre at Pump		Seat Belts	Warning Triangle
						Super	Octane	Regular	Octane		
Austria	50(31)	100(62)	130(80)	*100(62)	Schilling	7	96/99	6.60	87/92	X	X
Belgium	60(37)	90(56)	120(74)		Franc	16.97	98	16.56	92/94	X	X
France	60(37)	90(56)	130(80)		Franc	2.68	98	2.48	90	X	X
Germany	50(31)	100(62)	130(80)	80(49)	Mark	0.91/1.00	97/99	0.84/0.96	91/92	X	X
Ireland Rep	48(30)	97(60)	—	—	Pound	0.92	99	0.90	90	R	R
Italy	50(31)				Lire	†500	96/100	485	84/86	R	X
Up to 600cc		80(49)	90(56)								
601cc to 900cc		90(56)	110(68)								
901cc to 1300cc		100(62)	130(80)								
Over 1300cc		110(68)	140(87)								
Luxembourg	60(37)	90(56)	120(74)		Franc	13.26	97/99	12.88	90/92	X	X
Netherlands	50(31)	80(49)	100(62)	80(49)	Florin	1.13	98	1.09	96	X	X
Portugal	60(37)	90(56)	120(74)	70(43)	Escudos	31.00	98	28.00	85	X	X
Spain	60(37)	90(56)	100(62)	70(43)	Pesetas	37/40	96/98	31.00	90	X	R
Switzerland	60(37)	100(62)	130(80)	80(49)	Franc	0.99/1.05	98/99	95/101	90/92	R	X

X Compulsory
R Recommended

* See speed limit Austria country section.

† Subject to coupon reduction – see country section.

Limits may be varied by road signs in which case the lower limit must be observed.

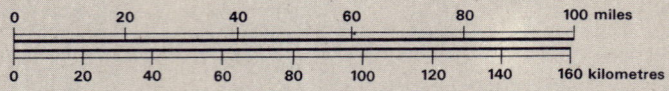

AA

Motoring in Western Europe

| 0 | 20 | 40 | 60 | 80 | 100 miles |

| 0 | 20 | 40 | 60 | 80 | 100 | 120 | 140 | 160 kilometres |

SCALE OF ATLAS: 33 MILES TO ONE INCH (APPROX)

Map Legend

Motorway and junction	
Toll motorway	
Motorway under construction	
Transit route (GDR)	
Single carriage motorway	
Principal route	
Main road	
Other road	
Mountain road tunnel	
Mountain pass	
Mountain railway tunnel connection	
Road snowbound during winter	
Road number	E4
Distance in kilometres	22
Frontier	
Place with AA hotels, sometimes garages	●
Place with AA listed garage only	◉
Town	○
Hovercraft ferry	Ⓗ
Vehicle ferry	- - - Ⓥ OSLO
River and lake	Drava
Canal	
Mountain/Volcano	▲
Overlaps and numbers of continuing pages	6

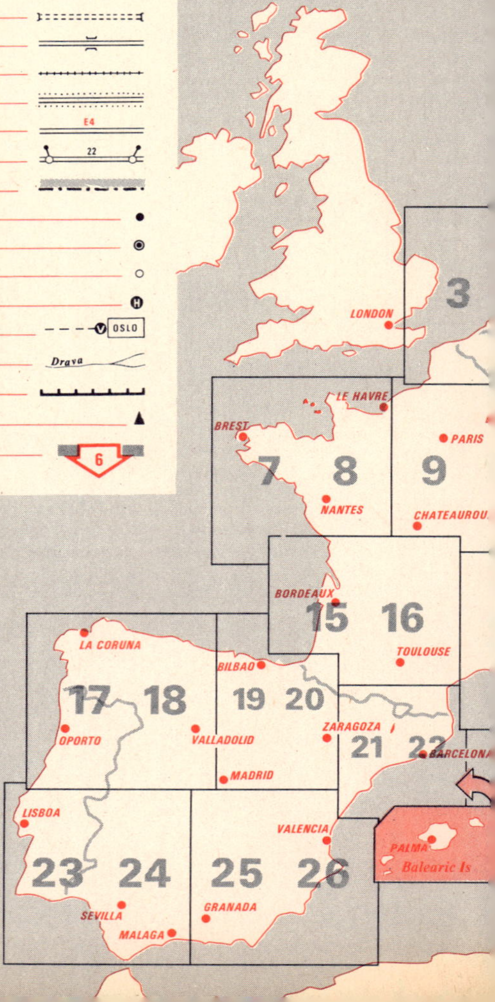

LONDON

LE HAVRE

BREST · · PARIS

7   8   9

NANTES   CHATEAUROU

BORDEAUX

15   16

LA CORUNA   TOULOUSE

BILBAO

17   18   19   20   ZARAGOZA

OPORTO   VALLADOLID   21   22   BARCELONA

MADRID

LISBOA

VALENCIA

PALMA

23   24   25   26   Balearic Is

SEVILLA   GRANADA

MALAGA

3

Key to atlas pages

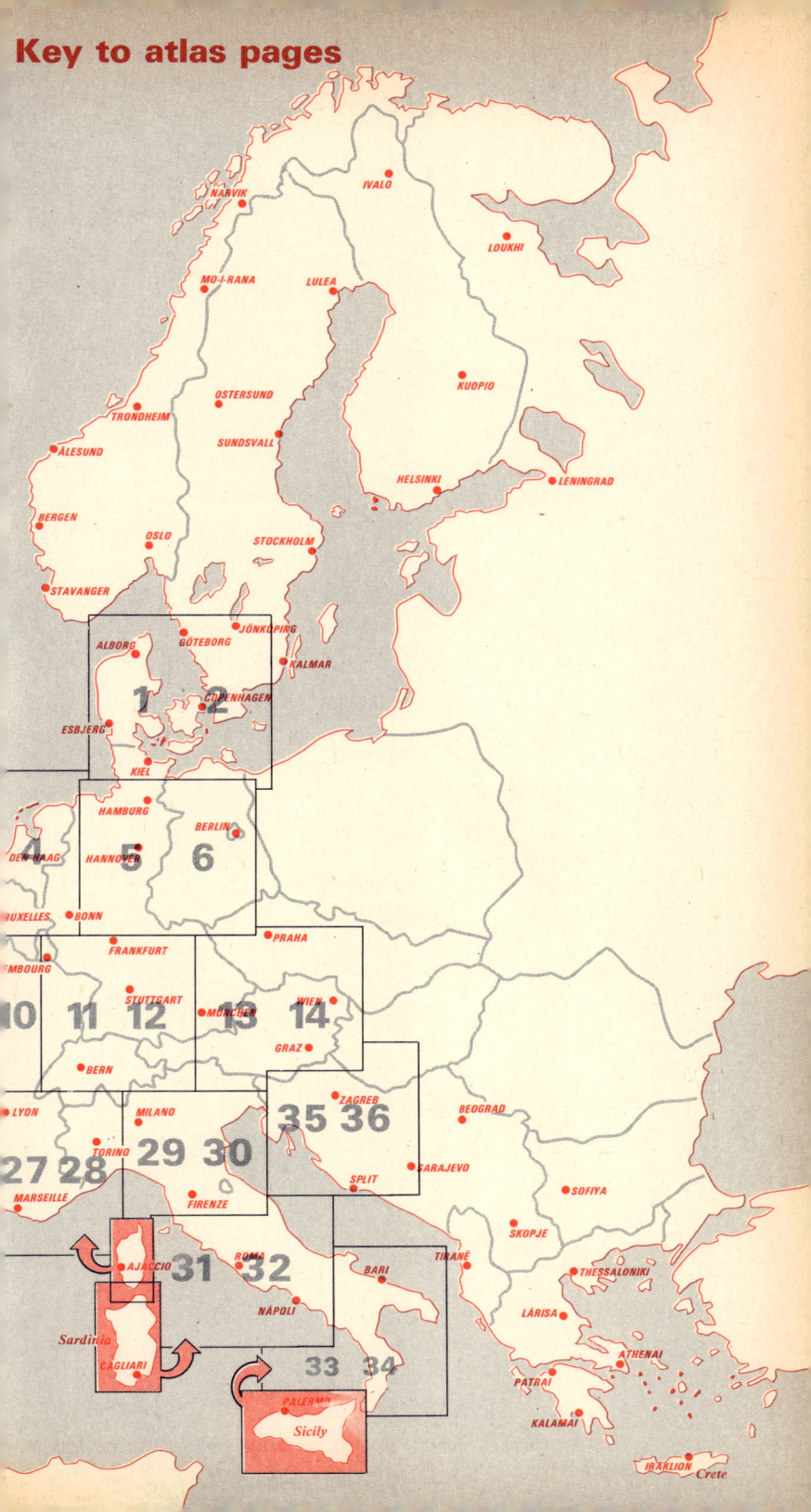

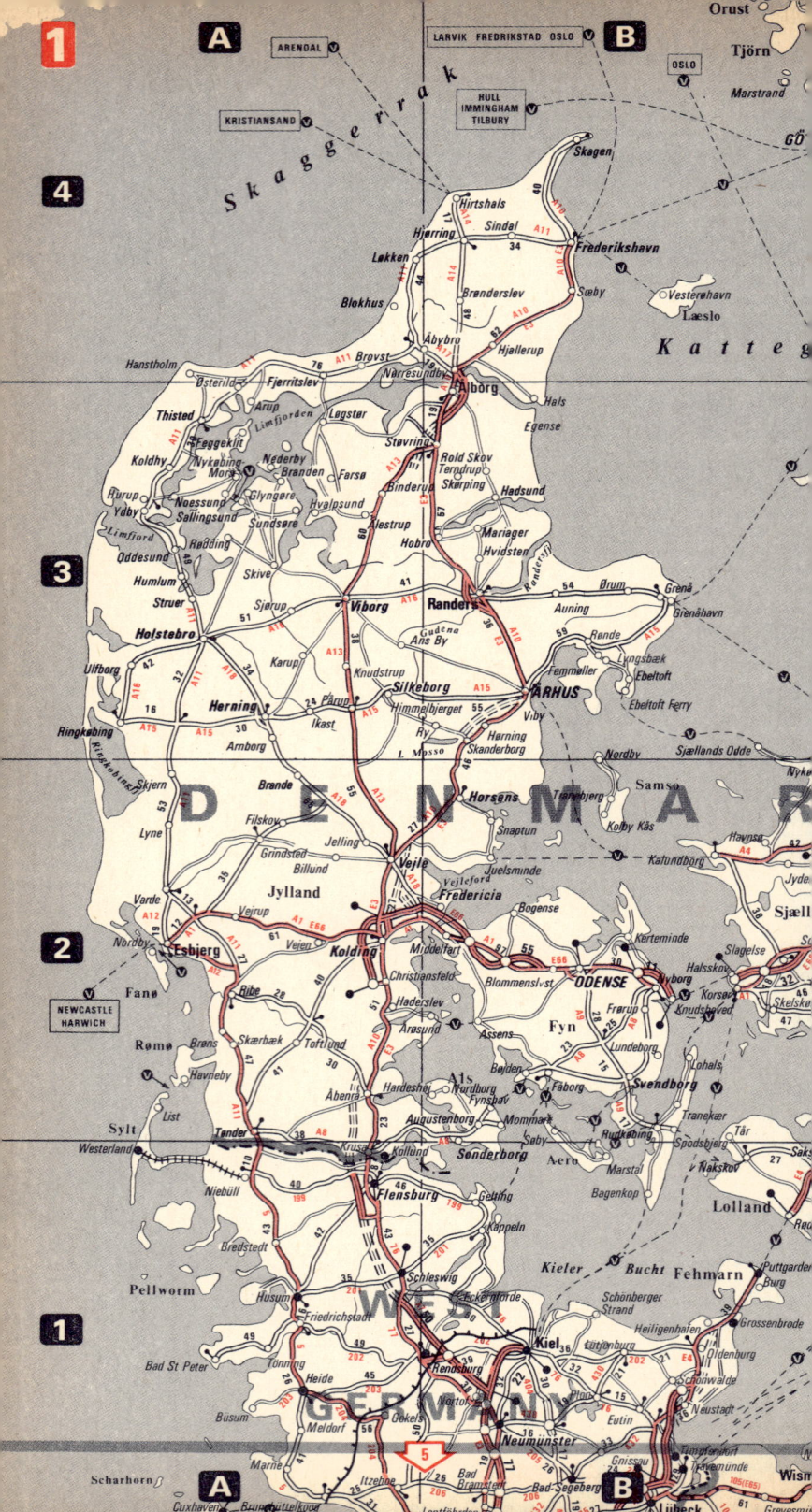

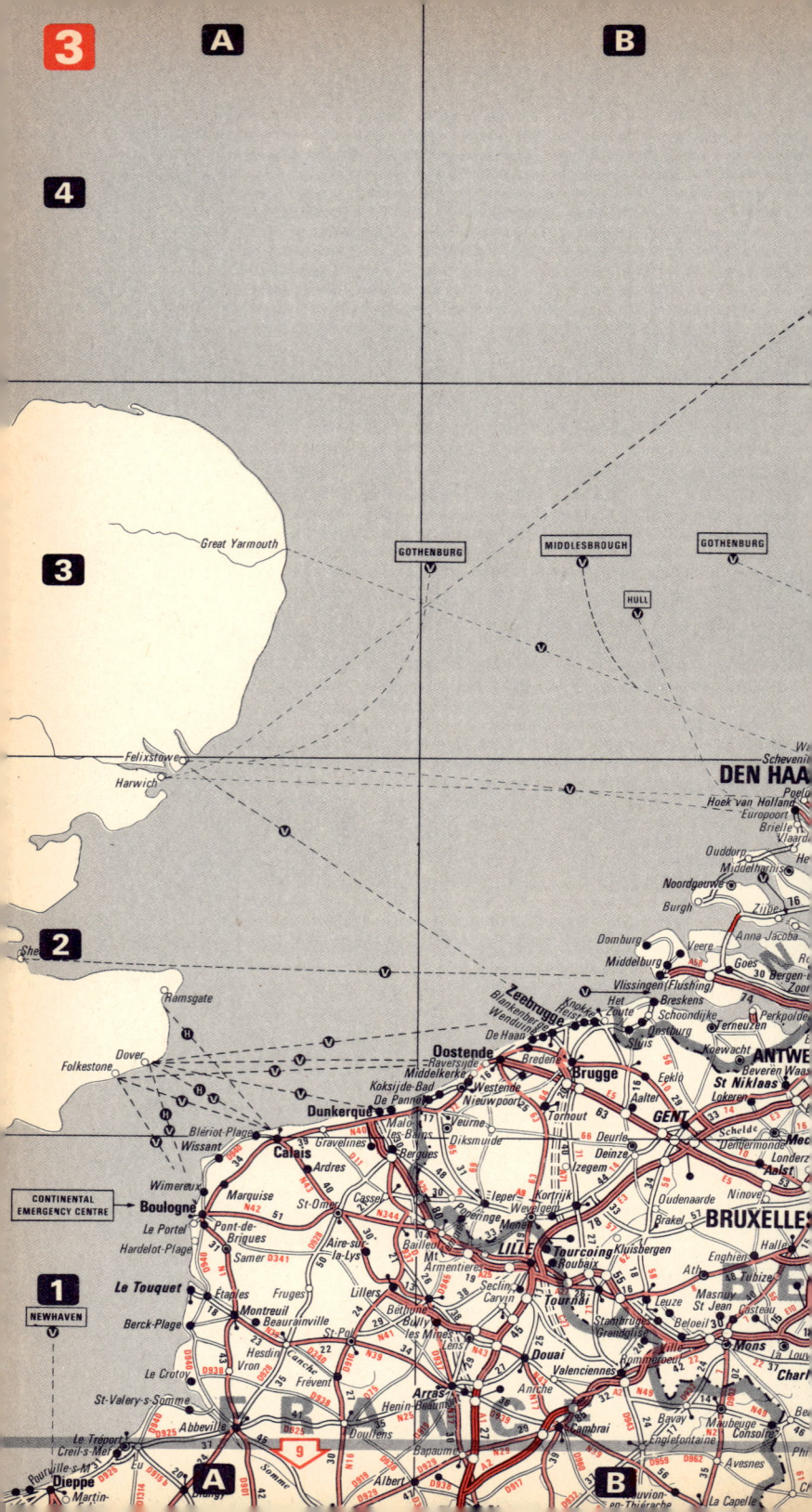

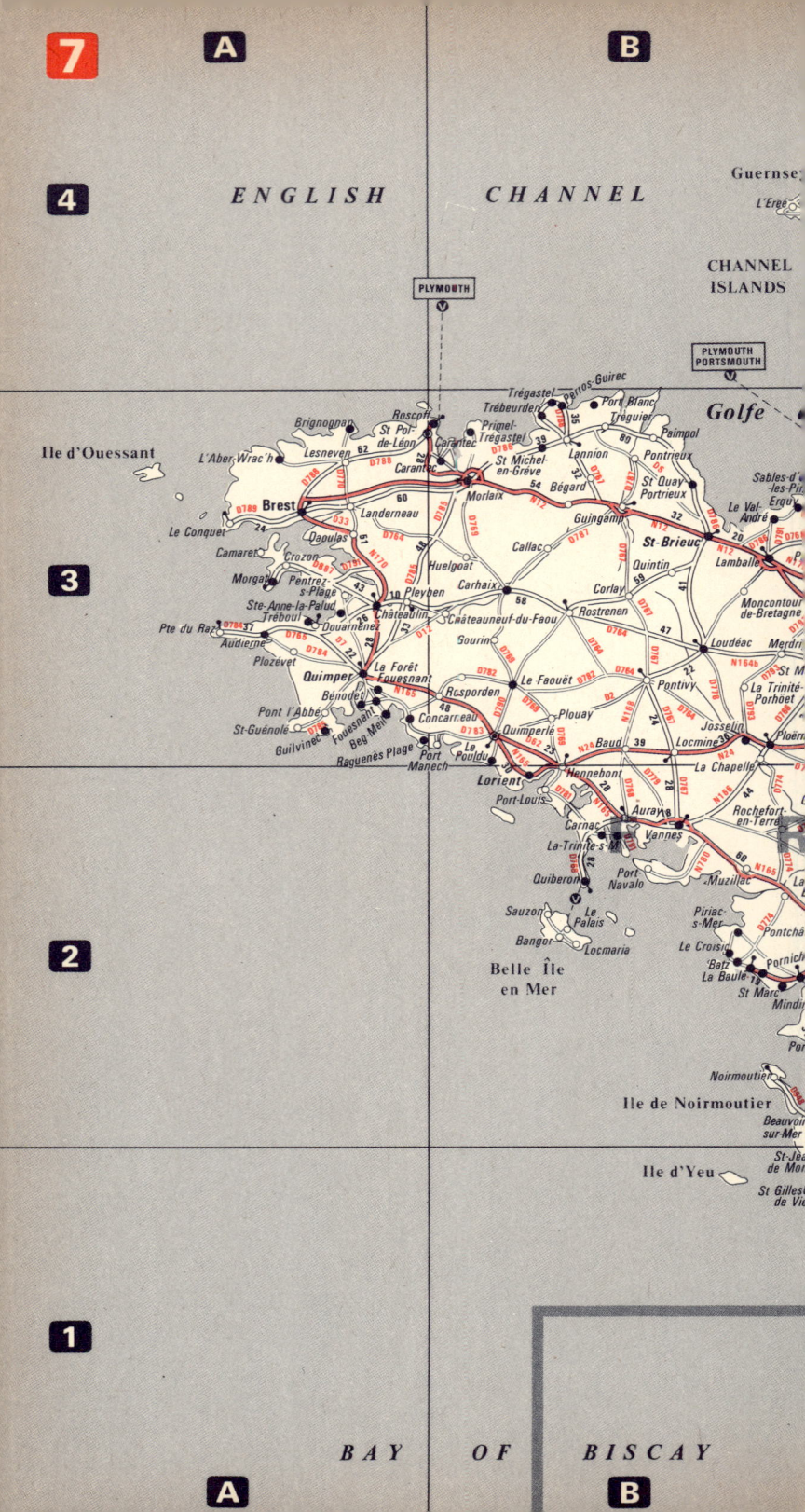

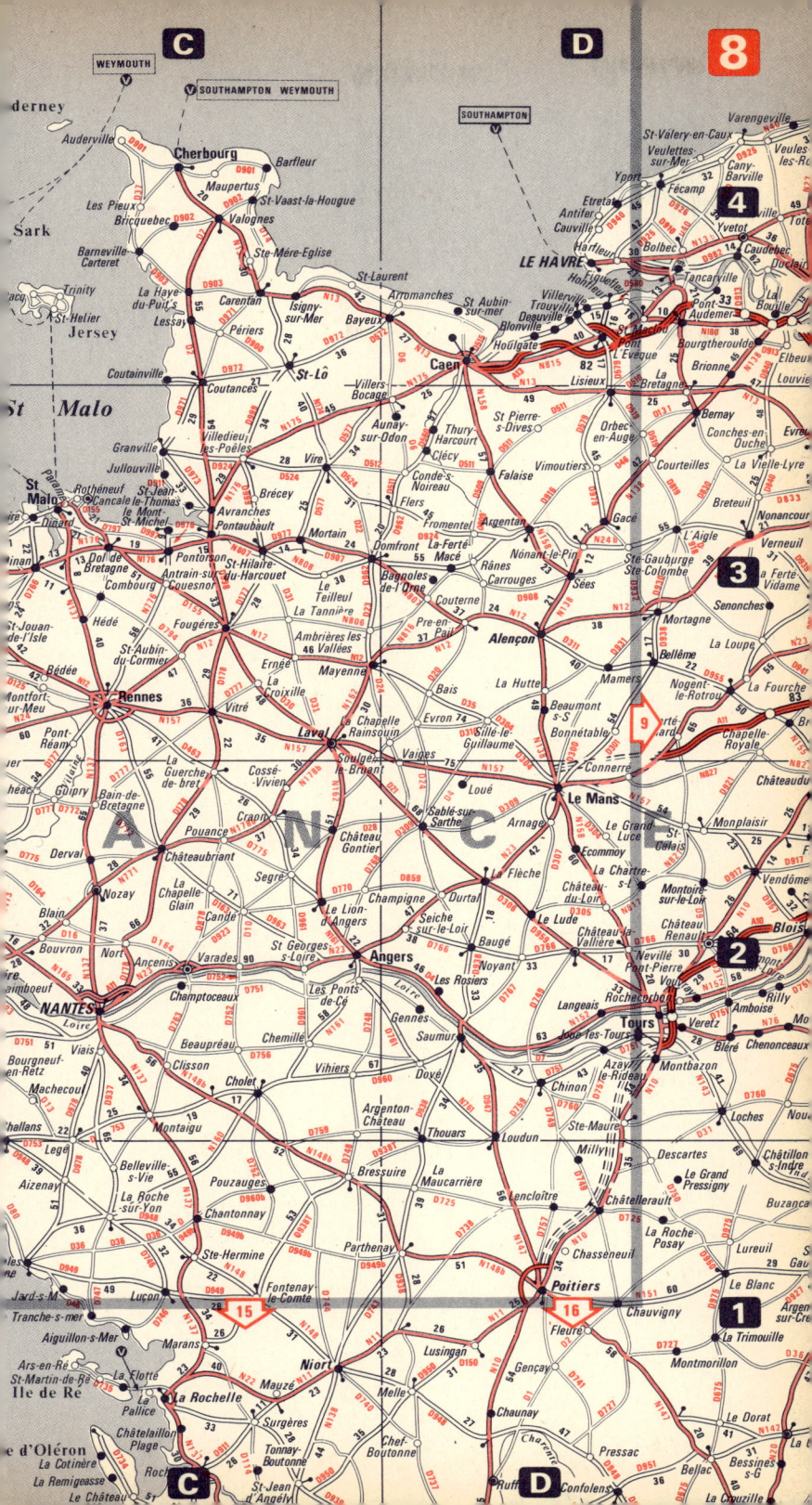

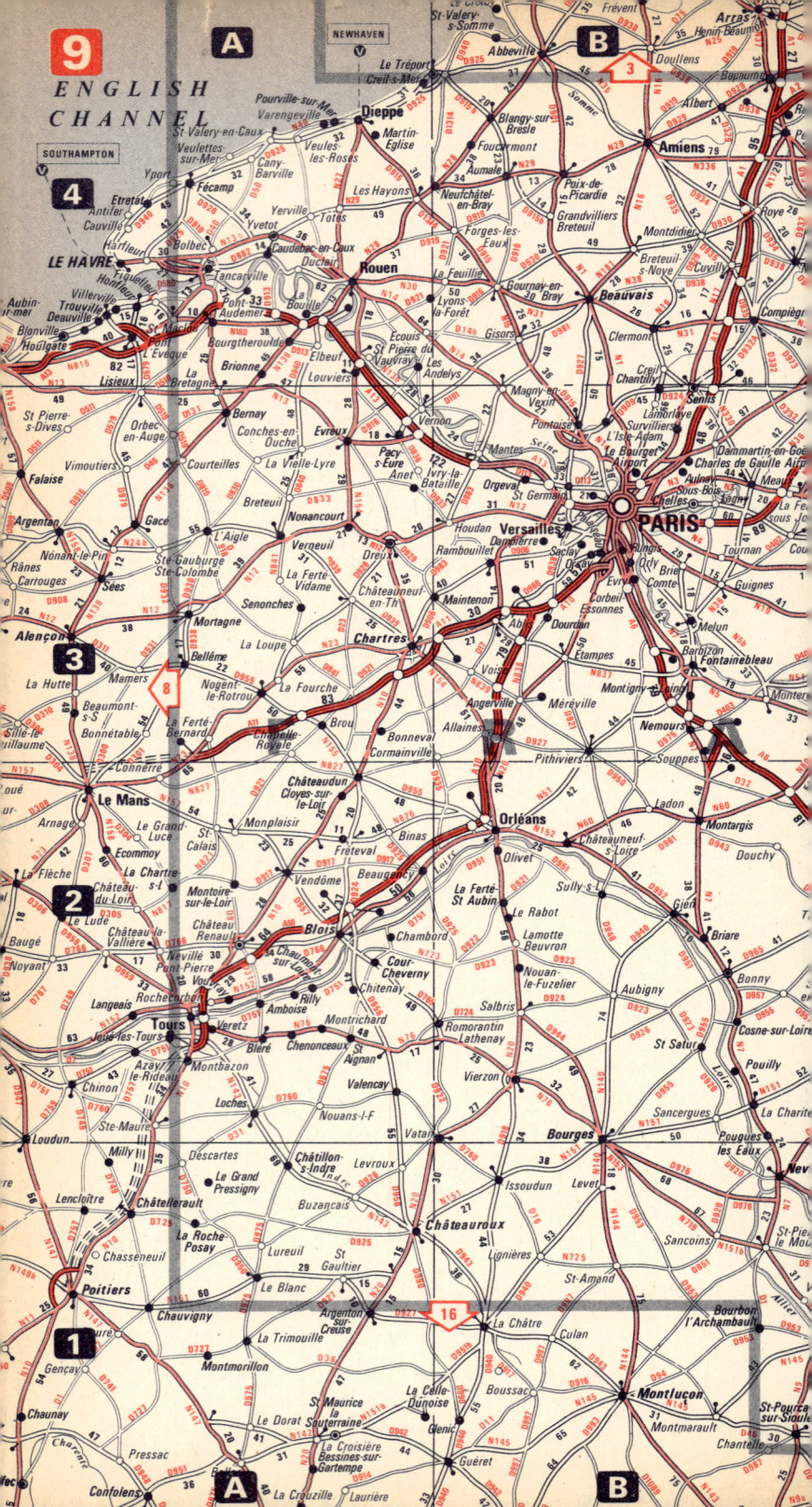

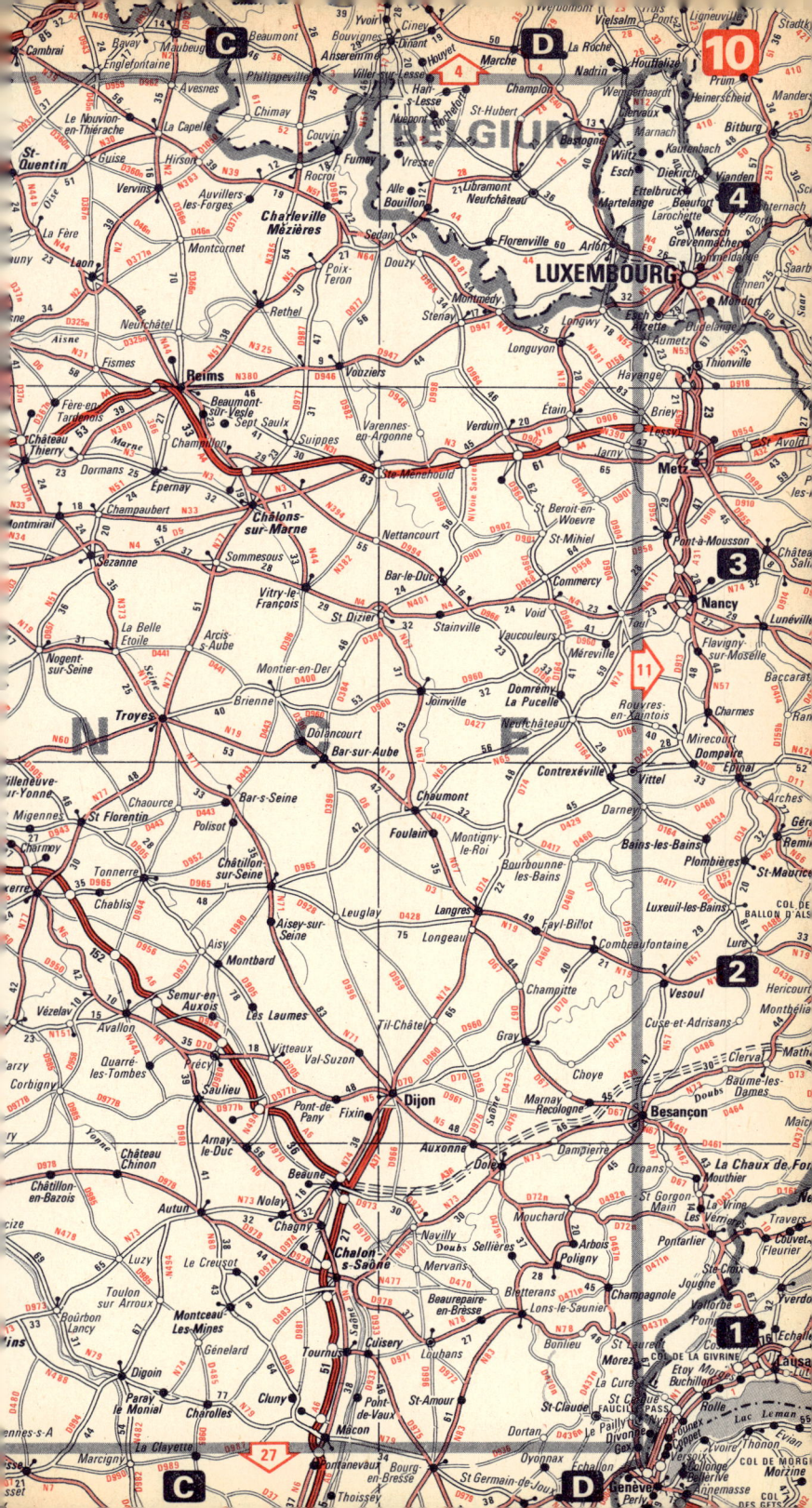

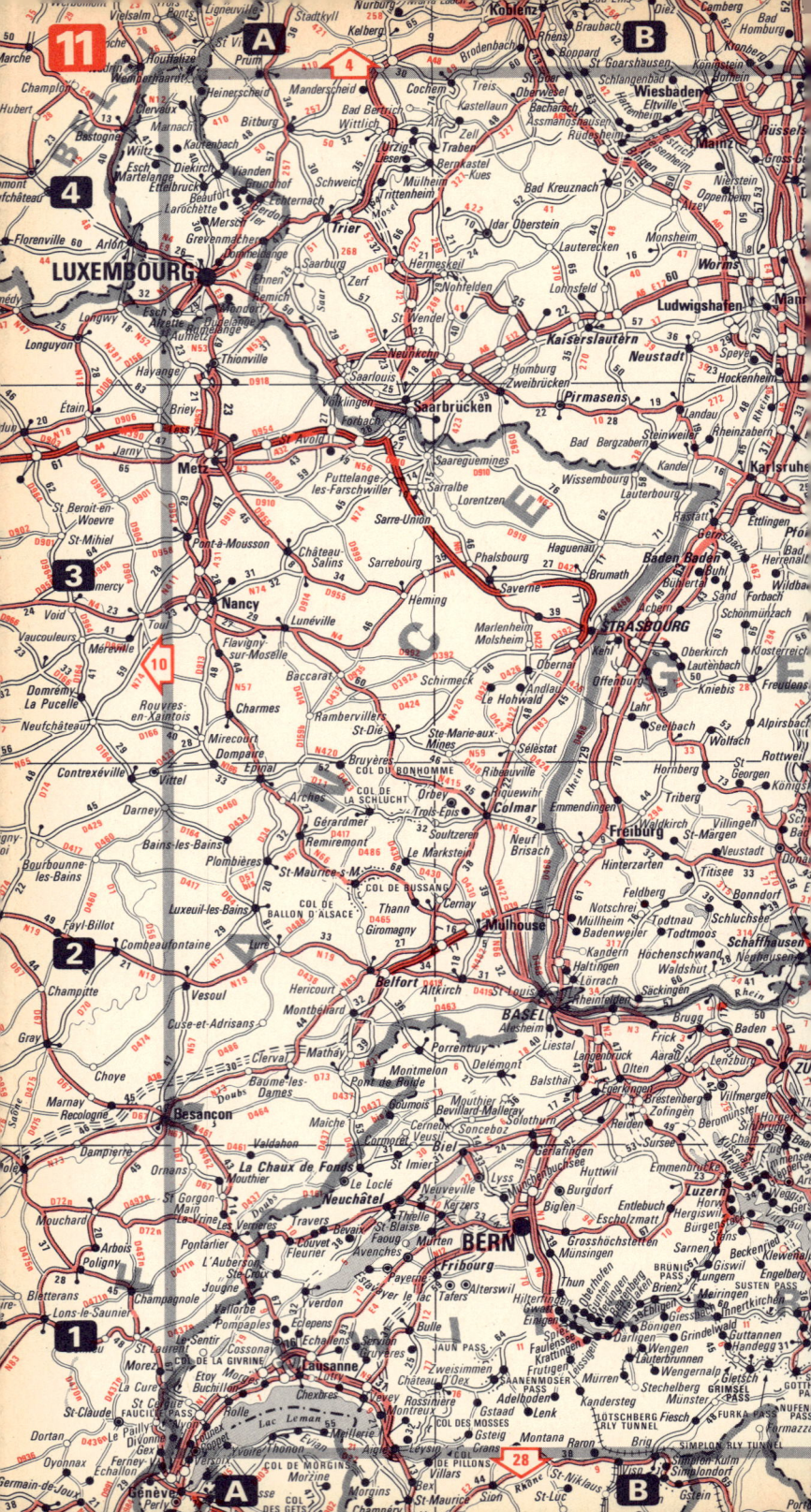

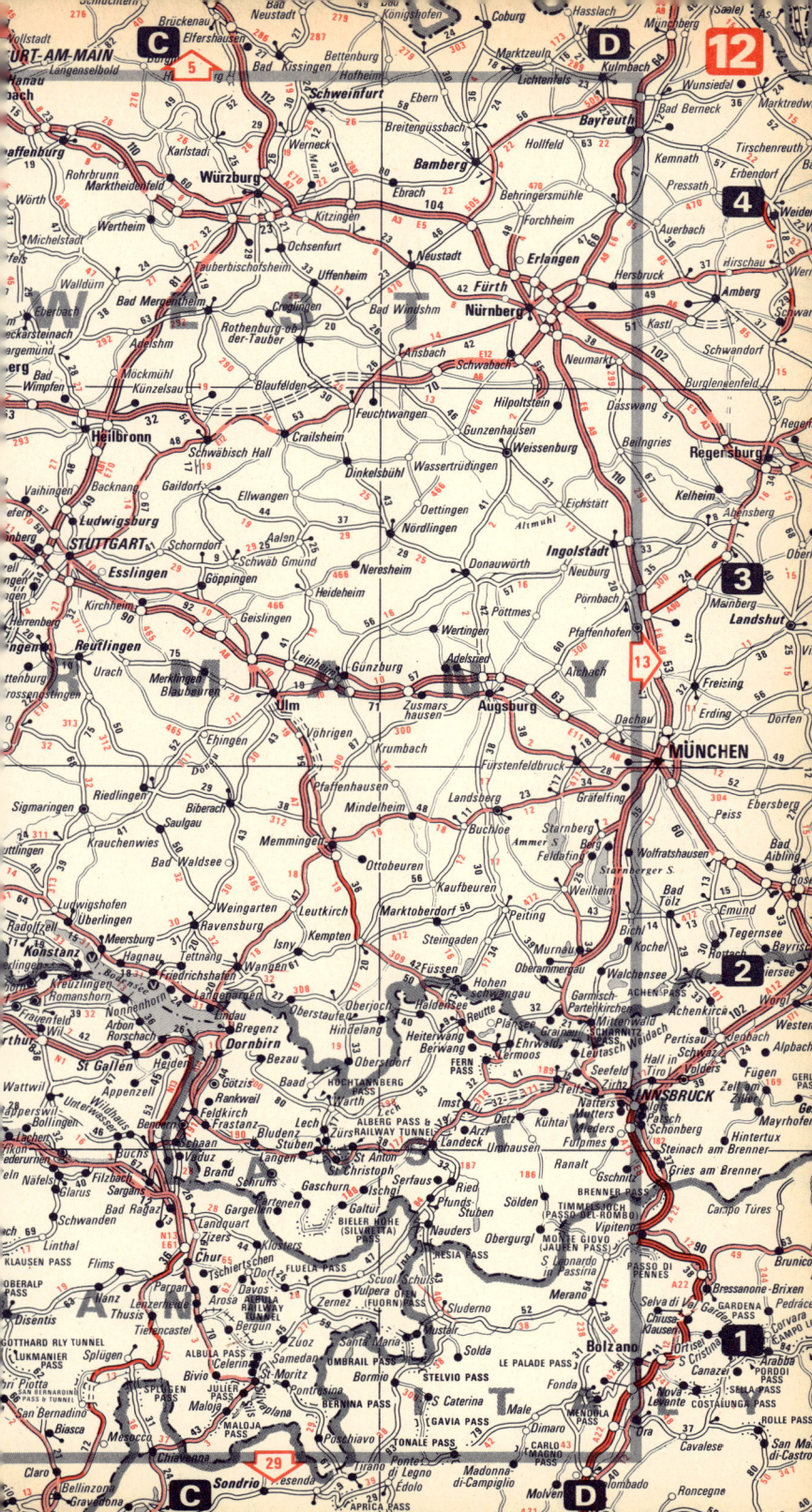

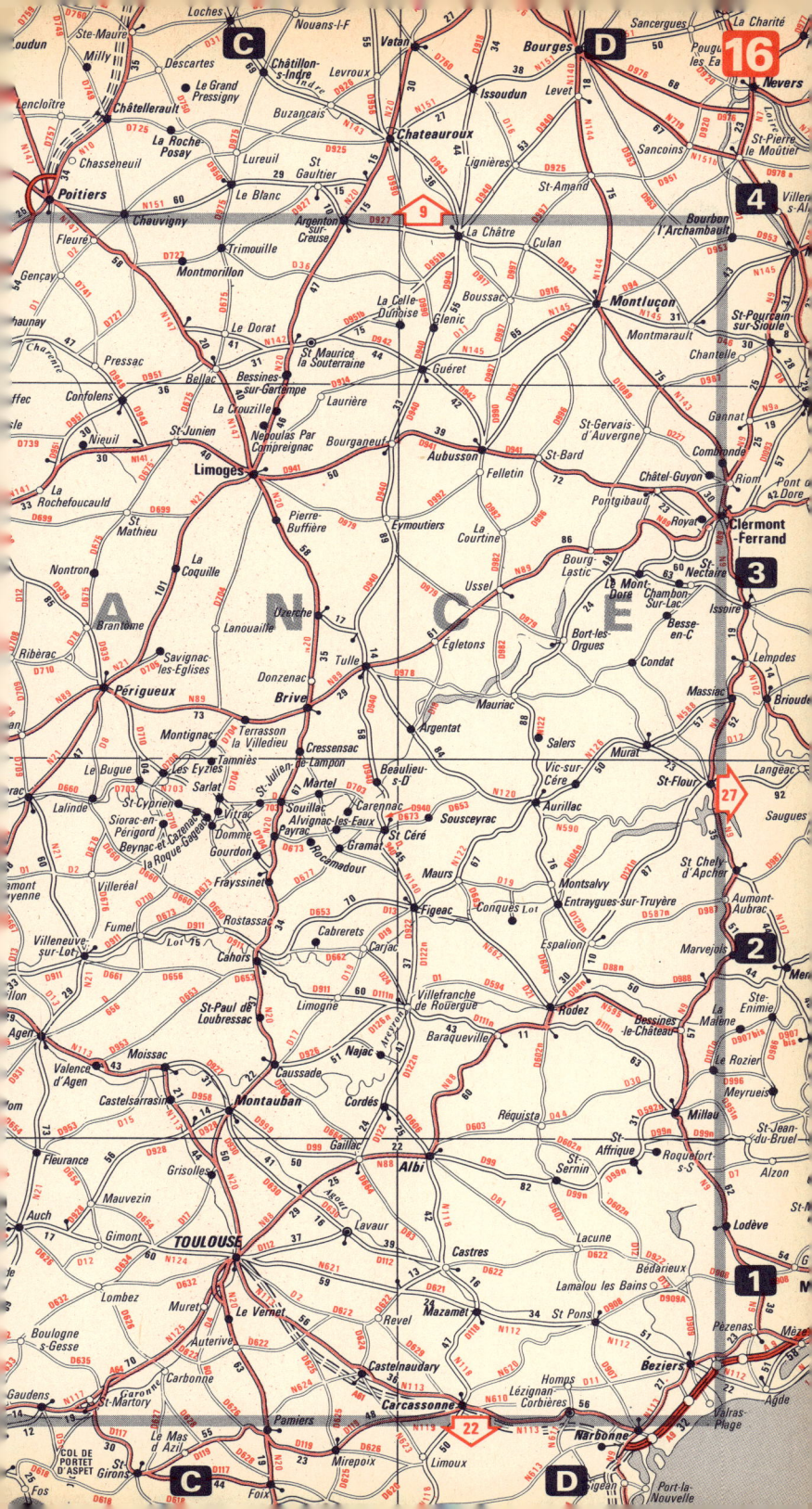

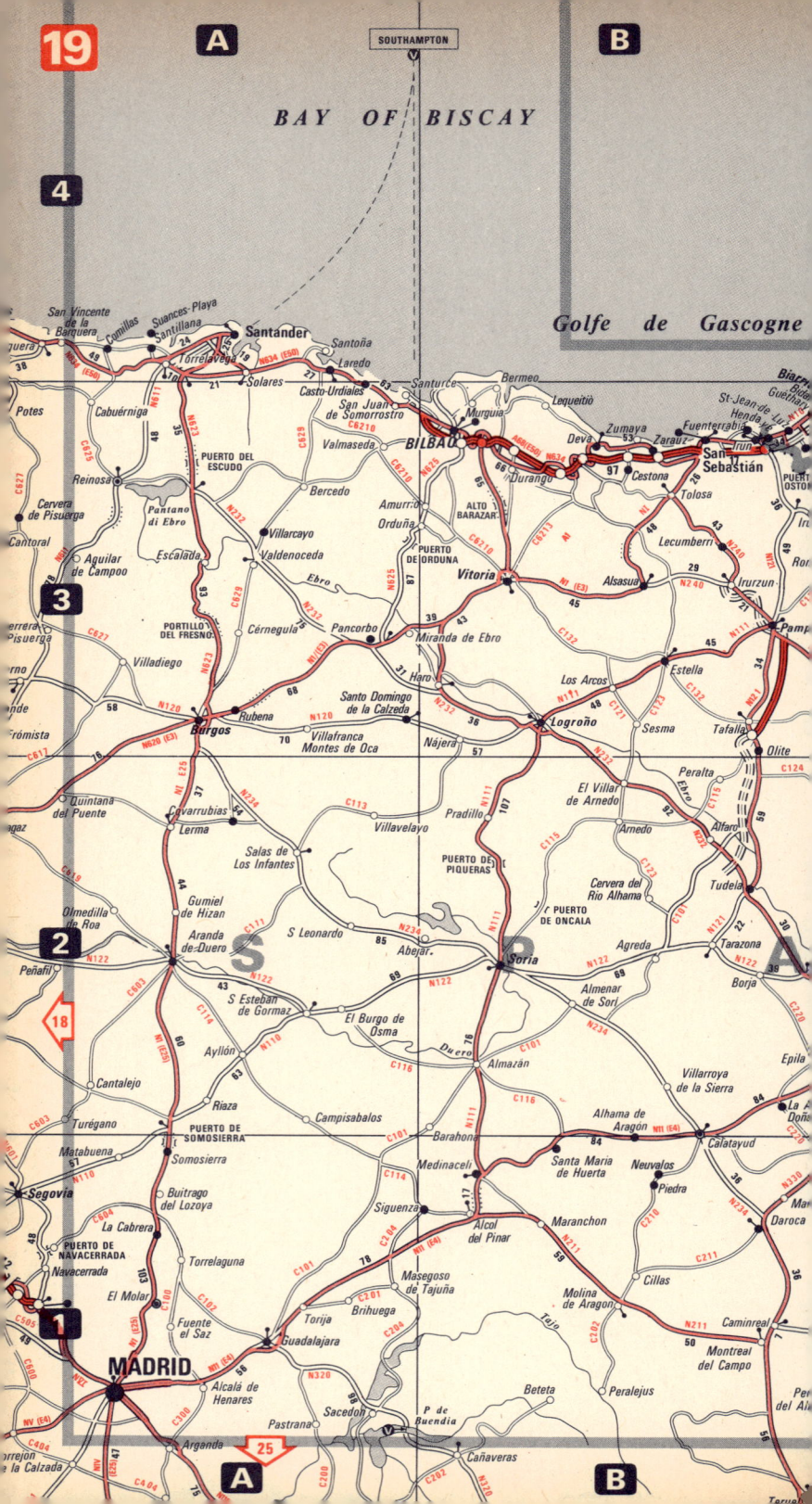

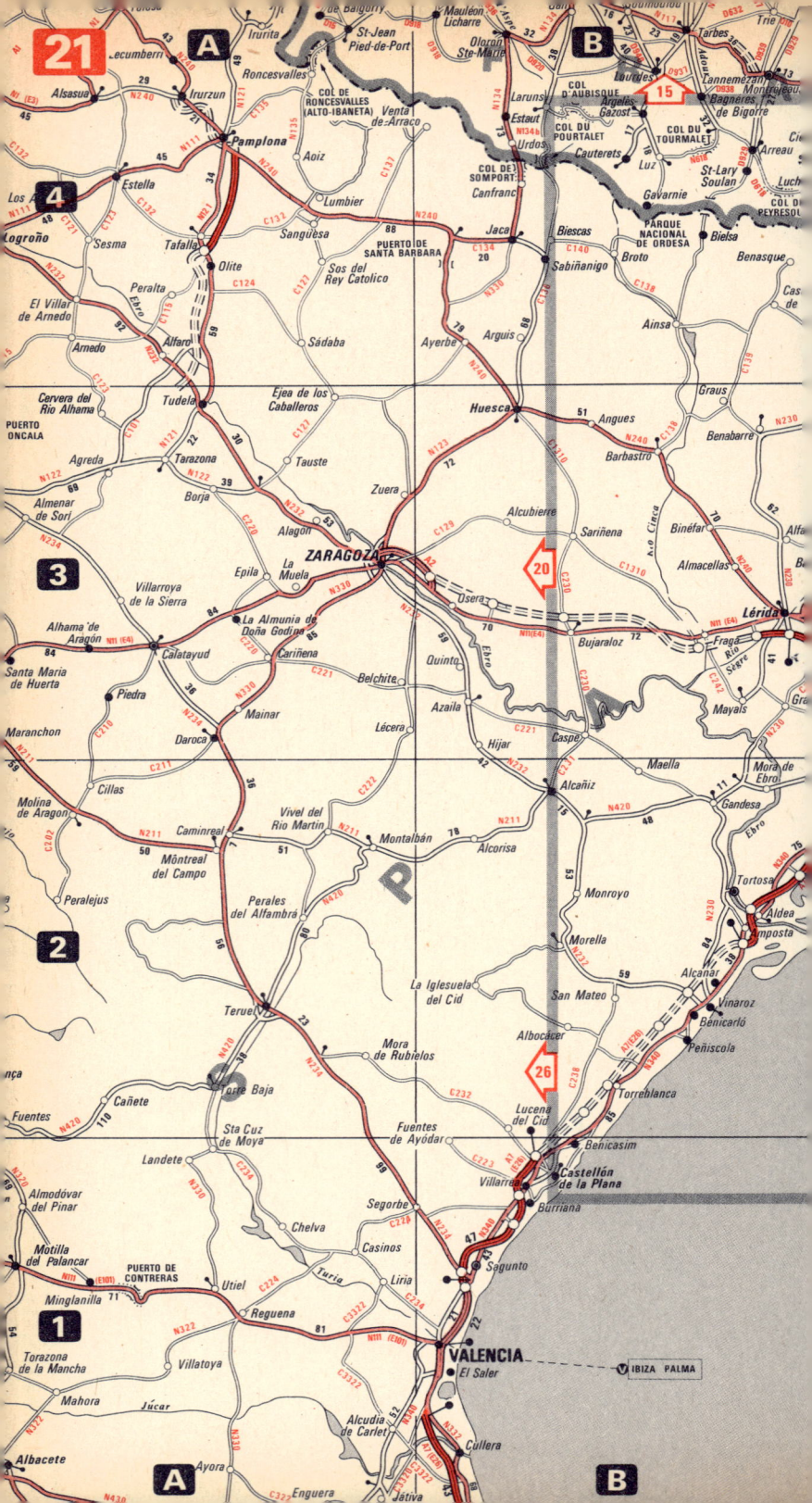

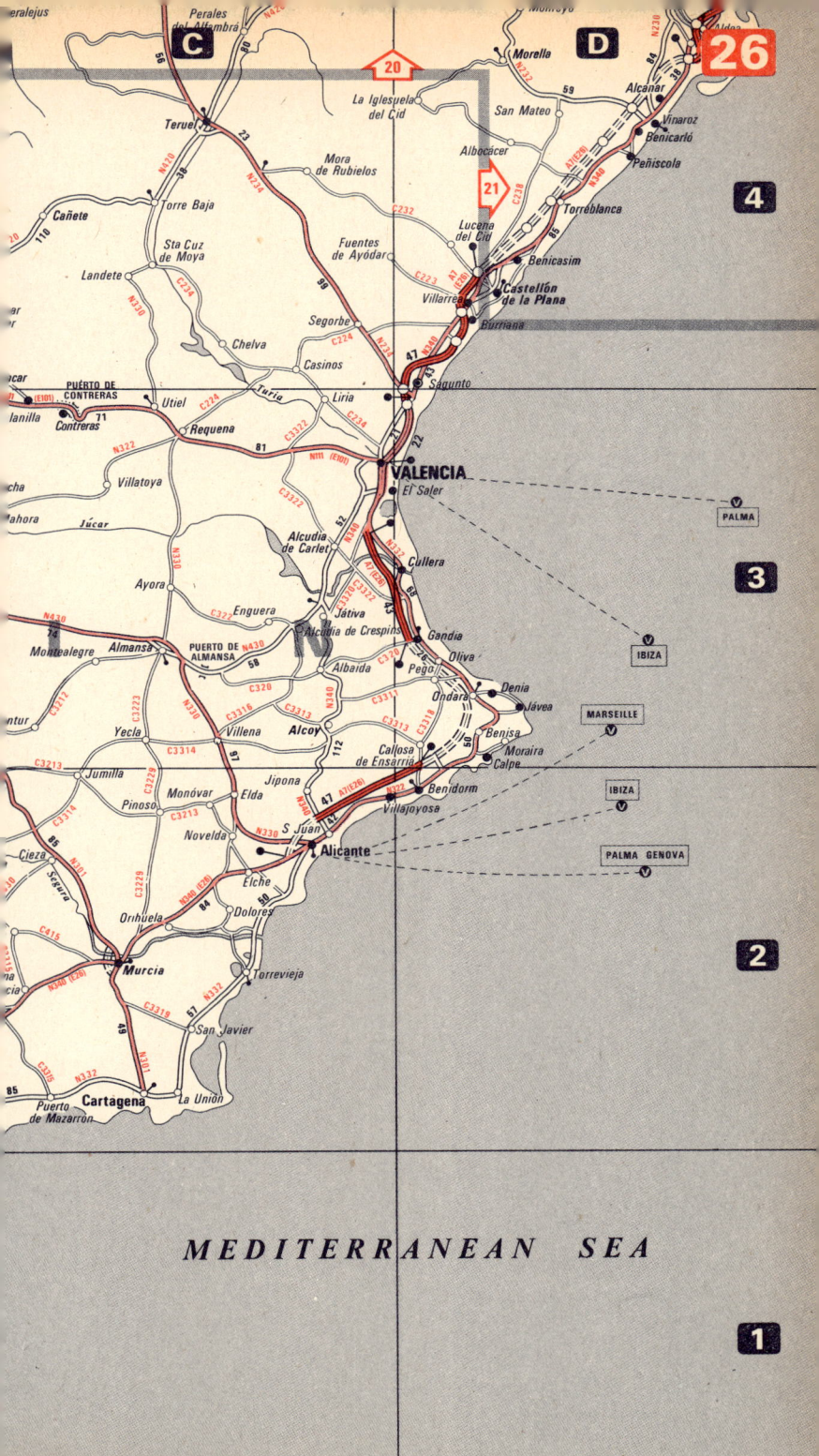

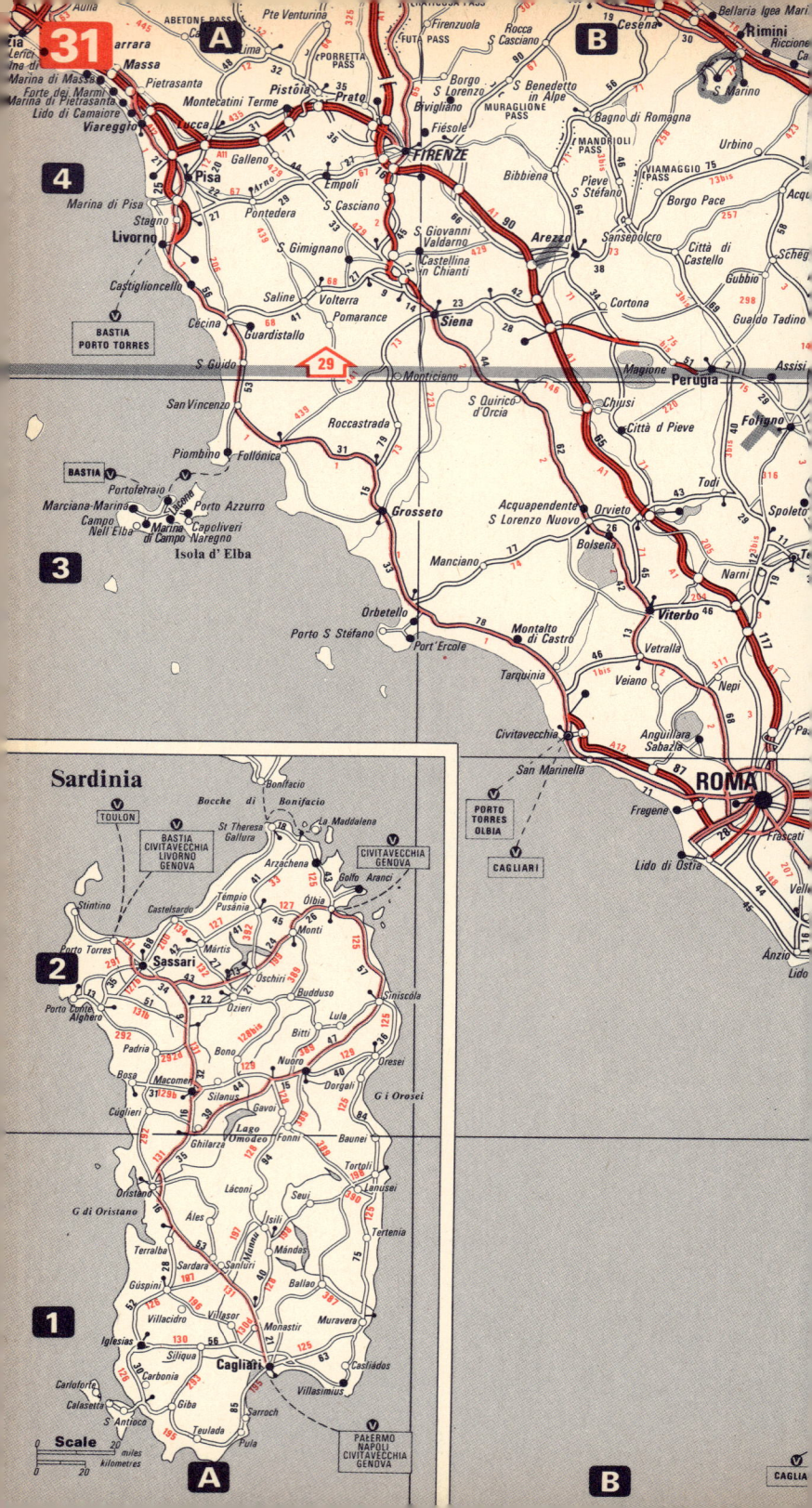

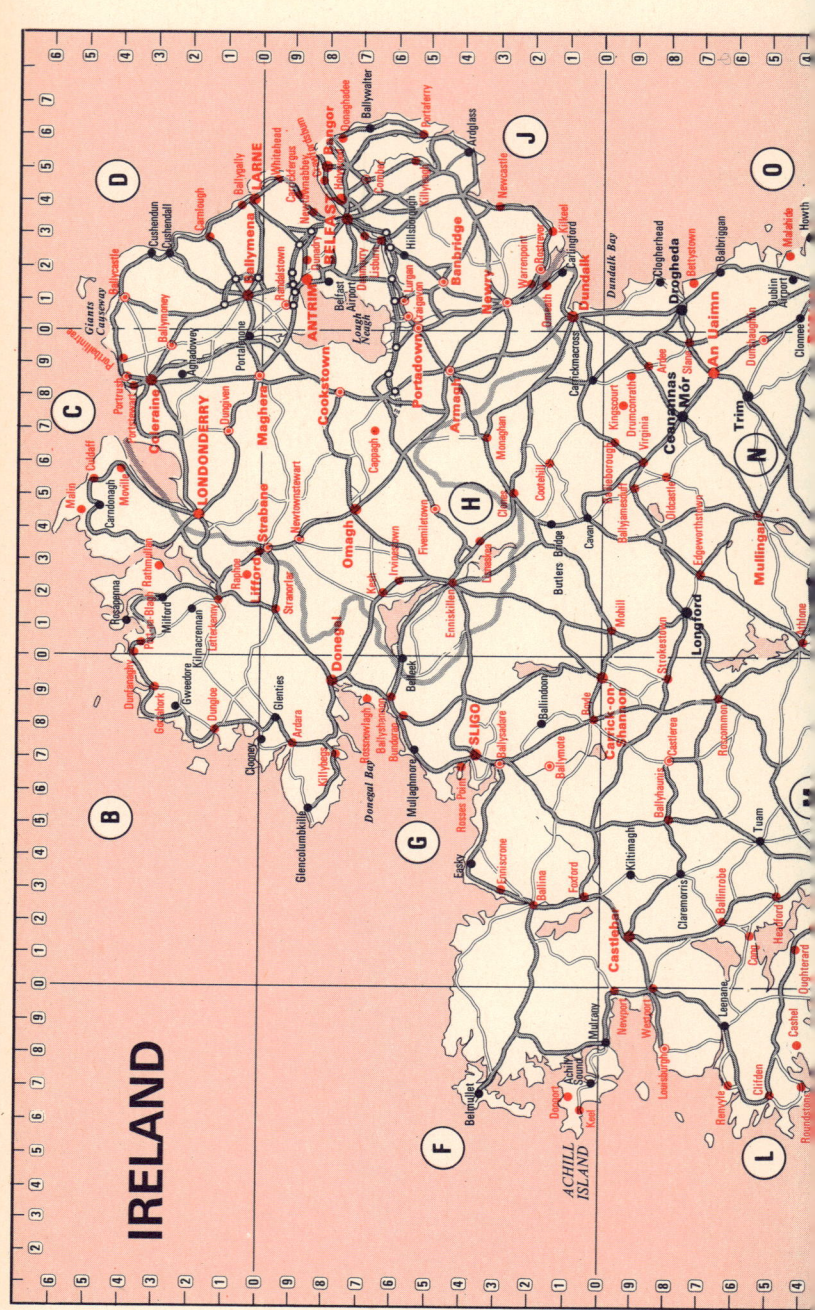

35

IRELAND

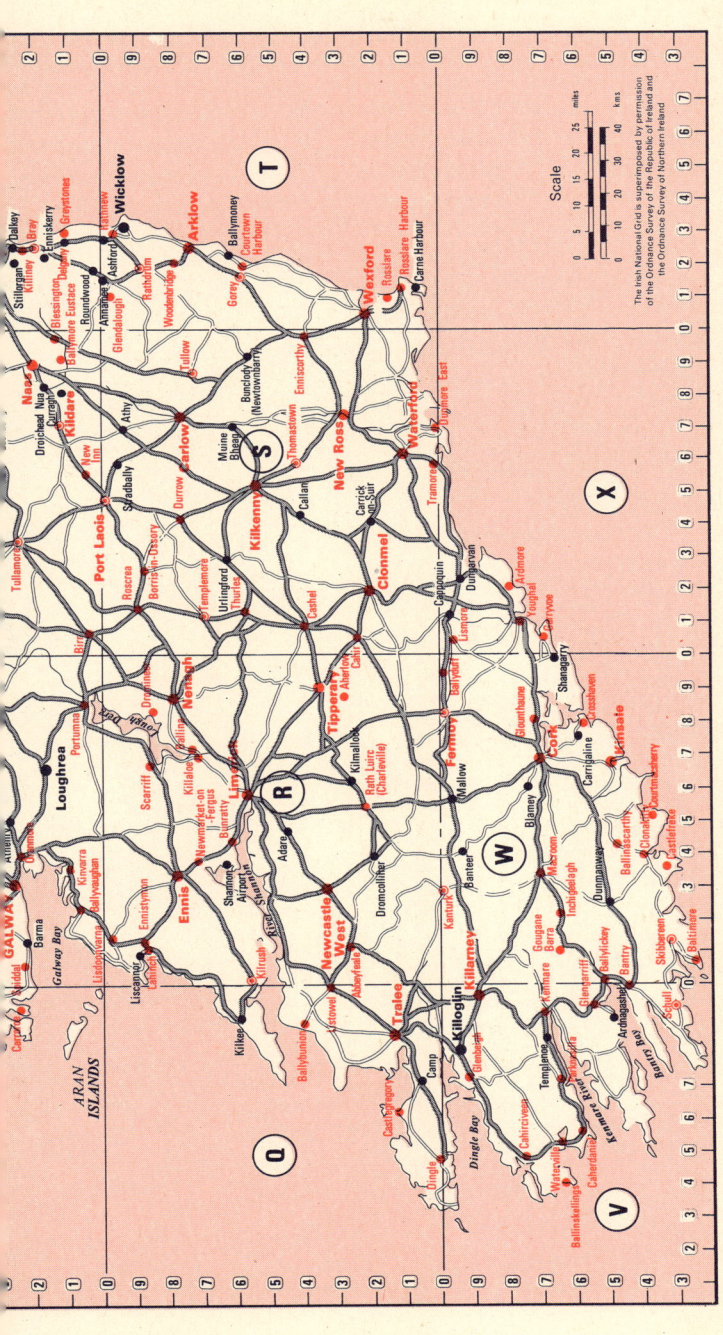

Scale

The Irish National Grid is superimposed by permission
of the Ordnance Survey of the Republic of Ireland and
the Ordnance Survey of Northern Ireland

● Hotel and / or Garage

◉ Garage only

AUSTRIA

Population 7,460,000 **Area** 32,376 sq miles **Maps** 12, 13 & 14

How to get there

The usual approach from Calais, Ostende, and Zeebrugge is via Belgium to Aachen to join the German *Autobahn* network, then onwards via Cologne to Frankfurt; here the routes branch southwards via Karlsruhe and Stuttgart for Innsbruck and the Tirol, or eastwards via Nürnberg and Munich to Salzburg for central Austria. The distance to Salzburg is about 700 miles and usually requires two night stops. Vienna, the capital, is a further 200 miles east. Travelling via Holland is a straightforward run joining the German *Autobahn* system near Arnhem. Alternatively, Austria can be reached via northern France to Strasbourg and Stuttgart, or via Basle and northern Switzerland. This is also the route if travelling from Dieppe, Le Havre, and Cherbourg.

General information

Information in this section is specific to Austria. A wider background is provided in the notes on page 8 with other information which you are advised to read.

Accommodation   The official hotel guide is available from the Tourist Office in London. Additional information on accommodation at small inns, in private homes, and at farmhouses may be obtained from local and regional tourist information offices. Hotels are officially classified from A1 (luxury) to D (simple hotels). Room, pension, service, and heating charges are exhibited in bedrooms.

Annual events		
	January	**Innsbruck** International Ski Jumping
		Salzburg Mozart Week
		Imst Tobogganing Competition
		Kitzbühel International Hahnenkamm Skiing Race
		Winter Sports (January/April)
	February	**Tirol** Processions of Tirolese bands in traditional costumes; Tirolean folklore evenings (all year)
	March	**Vienna** International Spring Fair
	April	**Salzburg** Easter Festival

These are not recommended routes:
the distances are given as a guide only.

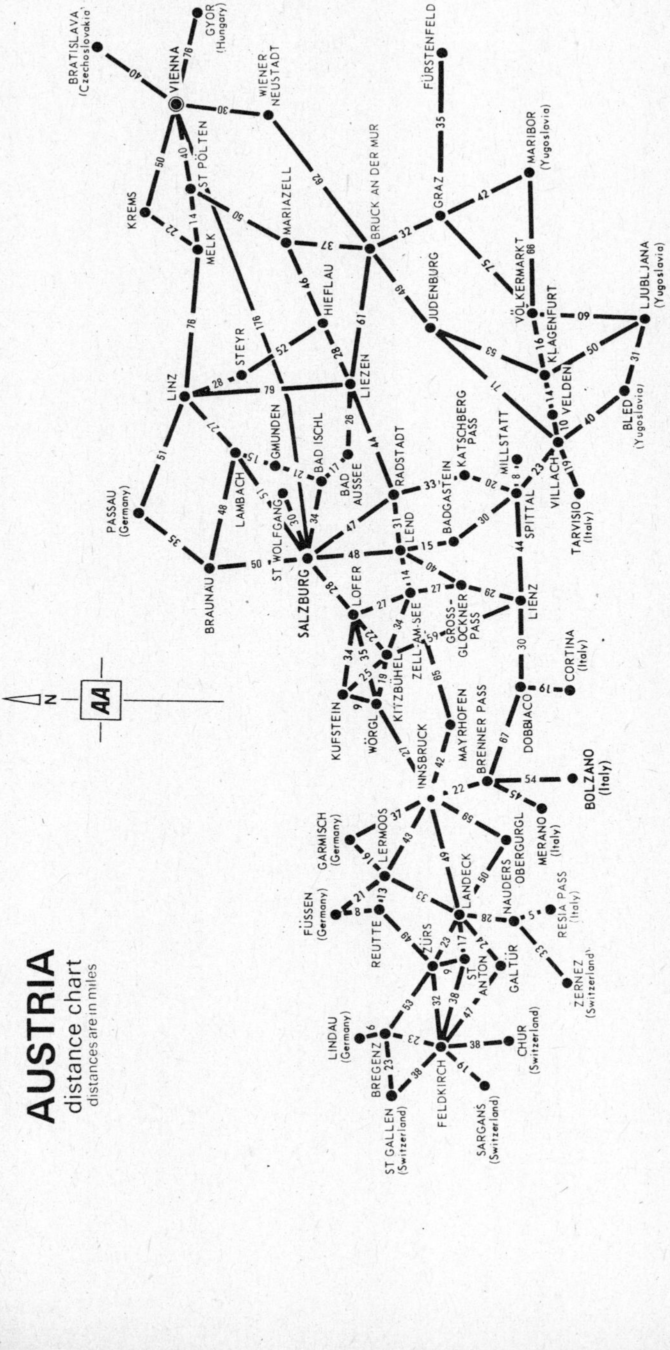

AUSTRIA
distance chart
distances are in miles

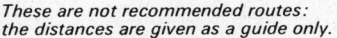

N

AA

BRATISLAVA (Czechoslovakia)
GYOR (Hungary)
VIENNA
WIENER NEUSTADT
FÜRSTENFELD
MARIBOR (Yugoslavia)
KREMS
ST PÖLTEN
MELK
MARIAZELL
BRUCK AN DER MUR
GRAZ
VÖLKERMARKT
KLAGENFURT
LJUBLJANA (Yugoslavia)
STEYR
HIEFLAU
JUDENBURG
VELDEN
BLED (Yugoslavia)
LINZ
LIEZEN
GMUNDEN
BAD ISCHL
BAD AUSSEE
RADSTADT
KATSCHBERG PASS
MILLSTATT
VILLACH
PASSAU (Germany)
LAMBACH
ST WOLFGANG
LEND
BADGASTEIN
SPITTAL
TARVISIO (Italy)
BRAUNAU
SALZBURG
LOFER
ZELL AM SEE
GROSS-GLOCKNER PASS
LIENZ
CORTINA (Italy)
KUFSTEIN
WÖRGL
KITZBÜHEL
MAYRHOFEN
BRENNER PASS
DOBBIACO
BOLZANO (Italy)
GARMISCH (Germany)
INNSBRUCK
FÜSSEN (Germany)
LERMOOS
MERANO (Italy)
OBERGURGL
REUTTE
LANDECK
NAUDERS
RESIA PASS (Italy)
LINDAU (Germany)
BREGENZ
FÜRS
ST ANTON
GALTÜR
ZERNEZ (Switzerland)
ST GALLEN (Switzerland)
FELDKIRCH
CHUR (Switzerland)
SARGANS (Switzerland)

113

Austria

May	**Vienna** Vienna Festival
	Salzburg Whitsun Concerts
June	**Forchtenstein** Castle plays
	Baden Operetta weeks
	Ossiach Carinthian Summer festival
July	**Bad Iscki** Operetta weeks
	Vienna Youth Festival
	Spittal Comedy plays
	Bregenz Bregenz Festival (plays on lake)
	Salzburg Salzburg Festival
	Marleisch Lake Festival
	Vienna Musical Summer
August	**Alpbach** European Forum
	Hollabrunn Folk Festival
	Klagenfurt Timber Fair
September	**Vienna** Autumn Fair
	Innsbruck Fair
	Graz Autumn Fair
October	**Graz** Styrian Autumn Festival

The national opera and theatre season lasts from September to June and the concert season from October to June.

Breakdowns (ÖAMTC) If your car breaks down, try to move it to the side of the road so that it obstructs the traffic flow as little as possible, and place a warning triangle on the road 50 metres from the rear of the vehicle. If you require assistance you should telephone the nearest centre of the ÖAMTC who will help you but they will charge for their services. Roadside service is available to AA members upon production of their *5-Star Service Booklet*. The ÖAMTC usually operate between 07.00 and 19.00hrs with the exception of Vienna which operates 24 hours and Graz, between 07.00 and 24.00hrs. The telephone number of the breakdown service in Vienna is 0222/9540.

Patrol service (Strassenwacht) This operates around Vienna and on the south and west motorways when the volume of traffic demands it. The patrols are in radio contact with the ÖAMTC offices.

Note: The ARBÖ, known also by other names eg Automobile Club of Vienna, is not recognised by AIT or FIA, and AA members using their assistance will almost certainly be charged and no reimbursement can be claimed under 5-Star Service.

British Consulates 1010 Vienna, Wallnerstrasse 8 ☎637502
There is also a consulate in Innsbruck.

Currency and banking The unit of currency is the Austrian schilling, divided into 100 groschen. There is no restriction on the amount of foreign or Austrian money that a *bona fide* tourist may import into the country. On export there is a limit of Sch 26,000 in foreign currency and Sch 15,000 in Austrian currency.

Banking hours Monday, Tuesday, Wednesday and Friday 08.00–12.30hrs, 13.30–15.00hrs; Thursday 08.00–12.30hrs, 13.30–17.30hrs. The bank counter at the ÖAMTC head office (Schubertring 3, Vienna 1) is open on Monday–Friday 08.00–17.00hrs, Saturdays 08.00–12.00hrs; exchange offices at some main railway stations are open on Saturdays, Sundays, and public holidays.

Shopping hours Generally these are 08.00–18.00hrs with a 2–4hr break around midday. Saturdays, 08.00–12.00hrs.

Documents
Driving licence Although a valid British licence is accepted in Austria it may present some language difficulty and to overcome this the ÖAMTC will provide a translation into German which is available from any of the Club's frontier or provincial offices. You are recommended to take advantage of this facility which is free. A licence issued in the Republic of Ireland is not accepted and an International Driving Permit is necessary.

Insurance **Frontier insurance** Short-term third-party insurance cover cannot be arranged at the frontier. A motorist who does not hold insurance cover will have to take out a Claim Settlement Insurance which costs Sch 200. Under this scheme a visiting motorist is not himself insured, but the arrangement authorises the Austrian Bureau of Insurance to deal with any claims resulting from an accident. Damages awarded following a court action are repayable to the Bureau.

Trailers must be covered by a separate policy, not the policy covering the towing vehicle.

Ferries
River Danube

The following particulars may change:

Cars are not carried on the pleasure boats passing down the Danube between Passau and Vienna. A car pilot service or transportation by low-loader is in operation between Passau and Linz or Passau and Vienna for the benefit of motorists who want to make the boat journey. The service is operated from Passau by Autovermietung Lermer, Neuburger Strasse 64, Passau 839 and Garage Josefine Graswald, Schmiedgasse 10. Enquiries in Vienna should be made at the Erste Donau-Dampfschiffahrts-Gesellschaft, Zollamts-strasse 1, Vienna 111.

Medical treatment

In-patient hospital treatment may be free if you produce your UK passport, although a small charge will be made for dependants. Other medical services must be paid for. There is an emergency medical service and if this is required an appeal must be made to the local police.

Motoring club

The Österreichischer Automobil-Motorrad-und-Touring-Club (ÖAMTC) which has its headquarters at 1/3 Schubertring, 1010 Vienna 1 has offices at the major frontier crossings and is represented in most towns either direct or through provincial motoring clubs. They will assist motoring tourists generally and supply information on touring matters, road and traffic conditions and offer breakdown and technical services. To assist British motorists the frontier offices supply a German translation of the British driving licence which is most useful and helps local police who might otherwise have difficulty if presented with a driving licence only in the English language.

The offices are usually open between 08.00 and 17.00hrs weekdays, 09.00 to 12.00hrs on Saturdays and are closed on Sundays and public holidays. However, a telephone service (0222/7299) for information is available, including weekends and public holidays, from the Head Office in Vienna between 06.00 and 20.00hrs. The Club's 24-hour breakdown service is available from the Vienna office on telephone number 0222/9540.

Post and telephone

		Sch
Rates for mail to the UK;		
Air mail	Postcards	4.00
	Letters up to 20gm	6.00
	20–50gm	10.00
	50–100gm	15.00
	100–250gm	30.00
	250–500gm	55.00

Hours Post offices are usually open from Monday to Friday 08.00–18.00hrs, with a break between 12.00–14.00hrs.

Telephone rates
A 3-minute call to the UK costs Sch45.00. Calls are 33% cheaper between 19.00 and 08.00hrs.

Public holidays

Holidays based on religious festivals are not always fixed on the calendar but any current diary will give actual dates. The Whit period (a religious holiday) should not be confused with the British Spring Holiday.

Fixed holidays

1 January	New Year's Day
6 January	Epiphany
1 May	Public holiday – Labour Day
15 August	Assumption Day
26 October	National Holiday
1 November	All Saints' Day
8 December	Immaculate Conception
24, 25, 26 December	Christmas

Moveable holidays

Good Friday
Easter Monday
Ascension Day (early May)
Whit Monday
Corpus Christi (early June, always a Thursday).

Roads

The motorist crossing into Austria from any frontier enters a network of well-engineered roads. A circular tour taking in the main places of interest can be made in one or two weeks. Old roads have been systematically improved and new ones built. The most famous is the Grossglockner highway (maximum gradient 12%) on which a toll is levied.

The main traffic artery runs from Bregenz, in the west, to Vienna, in the east, via the Arlberg Pass, Innsbruck, Salzburg, and Linz. Long stretches of this road have been duplicated by an

Austria

Autobahn (Motorways; see below). Most of the major Alpine roads are excellent, although some are being reconstructed, and a comprehensive tour can be made through the Tirol, Salzkammergut, and Carinthia without difficulty. Service stations are fairly frequent, even on mountain roads.

Holiday traffic   In July and August, several roads across the frontier become congested, particularly at weekends and on German public holidays (see Germany section); try to cross before 10.00hrs. The points are on the Lindau-Bregenz road; at the Brenner Pass (possible alternative – the Resia Pass); at Kufstein; on Munich-Salzburg *Autobahn* and on the Villach-Tarvisio road. For details of mountain passes, see page 31.

Motorways   About 518 miles of the planned 1,157 miles of the *Autobahnen* (motorways) have now been opened and more stretches are under construction. Tolls are levied on the Brenner and Tauern motorways and on the Gleinalm Tunnel of the Pyhrn autobahn.

To join a motorway, follow the signposts bearing the motorway symbol. The regulations are usually similar to those in Great Britain. Vehicles unable to travel at a minimum of 40kph (24mph) on the level, and motorcycles under 50cc are prohibited.

Motorway telephones   There are emergency telephone posts sited at 2km (1¼-mile) intervals. To use the telephone lift the speaking flap and you will be automatically connected to the motorway control. The location of the post is printed inside the speaking flap; read this into the telephone, standing from 6 to 8in away from the microphone. If you ask for help and then find you do not need it, you must tell the motorway control.

On the Brenner motorway emergency callposts of a different type have been installed. They are coloured red and orange and are furnished with a speaking tube and four levers bearing the symbols for police, Red Cross, repair service, and telephone connection. By pressing the appropriate lever, a motorist will be connected with the required emergency service. When one of the first three levers is used, sufficient indication of what type of help is needed is conveyed to the headquarters in Innsbruck; when the telephone connection lever is used a motorist can talk direct to headquarters, which will send help if required.

At the top of each telephone post there is an orange/yellow light which flashes if there is danger on that stretch of the motorway.

Toll roads   There are about 40 roads throughout Austria on which tolls are charged but these are mainly minor roads and often lead only to beauty spots or places of particular interest. However, the following are important roads on which tolls are charged. The charges, given in Austrian schillings, should be taken as a guide only since they are subject to change.

Return tickets for cars are interchangeable between the Grossglockner Hochalpenstrasse Felbertauern Tunnel.

Salzburg and Carinthia

Felbertauern Tunnel (see page 56)
Grossglockner-High Alpine road
(Grossglockner–Hochalpenstrasse)

	single
car with or without trailer/caravan	200
motorcycle	60
coach	600–1,200

Tauern Autobahn

	single
car with or without trailer/caravan	200
motorcycle	60
coach	400–800

Salzburg

New Gerlos road

	single
car	60
car and trailer	90
motorcycle	20
coach	300–600

Styria

Pyhrn Autobahn (Gleinalm Tunnel)

	single
car with or without trailer/caravan	90
motorcyle	50
coach	240

Tirol and Vorarlberg

Arlberg Tunnel (see page 56)
Silvretta-High Alpine road
(Hochalpenstrasse)

20 per person. If the return journey is made on the same day, the return fare is an extra 8 per person with original ticket.
Group of 26 people: 17 per person; extra 8 per person for the return journey with original ticket.

Tirol

Brenner Autobahn

	single
car with or without trailer/caravan	120
motorcycle	40
coach	300

Timmelsjoch road

	single
car	70
minibus per person 5	40 (minimum fare)
motorcycle per person	10

Only private cars without trailers or minibuses are allowed on the Italian part of the road. All other vehicles and trailers are prohibited.

Winter conditions   *Entry from southern Germany* The main approaches to Innsbruck and to Salzburg and Vienna are not affected.

Entry from Switzerland The approach to Vorarlberg and Tirol is available at all times, as the Arlberg Pass is swept and kept open as much as possible, and there is an alternative rail service.

From Austria into Italy The Resia and Brenner Passes are usually open throughout the year, but snow chains may be necessary in severe weather. The Plöcken Pass is occasionally closed in winter, but the Nassfeld Pass is likely to be kept open. Roads entering Italy at Dobbiaco and Tarvisio are usually clear, providing an unobstructed throughroute from Vienna to Venice.

From Austria into Yugoslavia It is best to travel via Tarvisio (Italy) and Jesenice, via Lavamünd and Dravograd, or via Graz and Maribor. Entry via the Wurzen and Seeberg Passes and the Loibl Pass road tunnel is possible but not advised. *Within Austria* In the provinces of Upper Austria and Lower Austria, and in Burgenland, motoring is unaffected by winter conditions; elsewhere, because of the altitude, it is restricted.

When the Grossglockner Pass is closed, Ost Tirol and Carinthia can be reached by either the Felbertauern road tunnels, the Tauern Autobahn, or the Tauern railway tunnel between Bockstein (near Bad Gastein) and Mallnitz (see page 57 and 55).

Winter-sports resorts The main approach roads are swept and are closed only in the most severe weather. Zürs and Lech can be reached via the Arlberg Pass only.

Wheel/snow chains   If you plan to motor in areas of high altitude during winter you may find wheel chains are compulsory in certain local conditions. It is probably better to consider purchasing these at home prior to departure, they are stocked by multiple car accessory retailers, and you will have the advantage of ensuring a proper fit and their availability when you want them. Further, they may be useful at home in certain winter conditions. Alternatively they may be hired from the ÖAMTC for a maximum period of 60 days on deposit of between £15 and £30. They are delivered in a packed condition and if they are returned unused then the deposit is returned, less a percentage reduction, according to the length of hire. If the seal is broken and the chains used then 65% of the deposit is retained.

The conditions of hire are fully described in a leaflet issued by the ÖAMTC from any of their offices.

Tourist information offices   The Austrian National Tourist organisation maintains two fully-equipped information offices in the UK – in London at 30 St George Street, W1R 9PP and Manchester at 19 Mosley Arcade, Piccadilly Plaza 1. Either of these will be pleased to assist you with any information regarding tourism, whilst in most towns in Austria there will be found a local or regional tourist office who will supply detailed local information.

Visitors' registration   A visitor staying at a hotel or supervised camp site must sign the guest book. They need not report to the police.

Motoring regulations

Information in this section is specific to Austria. A wider background is provided in the notes on page 67 with other regulations which you are advised to read.

Accidents   **Fire** ☎122 **police** ☎133 **ambulance** ☎144
A driver who is involved in an accident must stop and exchange particulars with the other party. If personal injury is sustained it is obligatory that you obtain medical assistance for the injured persons, and immediately report the incident to the police. All persons who arrive at the scene of an accident are obliged to render assistance, unless it is obvious that everything necessary has already been done.

Compulsory equipment
First-aid kit   In Austria all motorists are required to carry a first-aid kit by law and visitors are expected to comply. This item will not be checked at the frontier and foreigners will not be penalised if they are not carrying one. However, at the scene of an accident any motorist can be stopped and his first-aid kit demanded and if this is not forthcoming the police may take action.

Dimensions and weight restrictions   Vehicles must not exceed:
height 4 metres;
width 2.5 metres;
length vehicle/trailer combination 18 metres; weight trailers without brakes may weigh up to 750kg and may have a total weight up to 50% of the towing vehicle.

Drinking and driving   A driver convicted of driving while under the influence of alcohol is severely punished: a minimum fine of Sch5,000 may be imposed,

Austria

together with either the withdrawal of his licence or one week's imprisonment. Police are entitled to remove the ignition keys from motorists who are apparently under the influence of drink and also from drivers who are showing signs of exhaustion.

Hitch-hiking   In Austria, hitch-hiking is generally prohibited on motorways and highways. There are special provisions in Styria and Vorarlberg; in both Federal lands hitch-hiking is prohibited for boys under the age of 16 and for girls under the age of 18.

Lights

Although it is prohibited to drive with undipped headlights in built-up areas, motorists may give warning of approach by flashing their lights. It is prohibited to drive on illuminated urban motorways with sidelights only. In poor visibility motorists may use foglights in conjunction with both sidelights and dipped headlights. parking lights are not required if the vehicle can be seen from 50 metres (55yd). Lights on lampposts which are ringed with red do not stay on all night and parking lights will be required. Motor cyclists must keep their headlights on all day in all weather conditions.

Parking

Parking is forbidden on a main road or one carrying fast-moving traffic; on or near tram lines; within 15 metres (16yd) of bus and tram stops; opposite another stationary vehicle, and on the left-hand side of one-way streets with only two driving lanes. In addition, parking is prohibited wherever there is a sign reading *Beschränkung für Halten oder Parken* (restriction for stopping or parking).

On roads which have priority (as a rule Federal Roads), if there is fog or any other impediment to visibility, there is a total ban on stopping.

Motorists who park their car in front of a house or an entry to a property must remain near the vehicle. Cars must be parked facing in the direction of traffic flow.

In blue zones or restricted parking areas there are no signs other than those on entering the zone so tourists, unfamiliar with the area, should be alert to the fact that they will have no reminders.

Vienna   Parking on roads with tram lines is prohibited at all times from 15 December to 31 March; from 1 April to 14 December it is prohibited from 05.00 to 20.00hrs. There is no parking in the centre of the city as it is a pedestrian zone.

In some towns short-term parking is allowed in areas known as blue zones where parking is free, except in Vienna where a charge is made for parking tickets available from some banks, tobacco shops and the ÖAMTC. These tickets allow parking for periods of ½, 1, or 1½ hours. Outside Vienna parking for up to 1½ hours in blue zones is free. Parking tickets are not used but a parking disc is necessary which is available free of charge from tobacco shops.

In Vienna parked vehicles which obstruct traffic will be towed away and their drivers pay costs arising. A visitor's car will only be towed away if serious obstruction is caused.

Spending the night in a vehicle or trailer on the roadside is not prohibited, except on a priority road.

Passengers

No vehicle may carry more adult passengers than the number for which it was constructed, and passengers must allow the driver free movement. Children under 14 years of age are considered as half persons, and children under 6 years are not counted at all.
Note: Children under 12 years of age must not be transported in the front seats of a vehicle.

Police fines

The Austrian police are authorised to impose on-the-spot fines for infringement of minor traffic regulations and once such a fine is paid it is not refunded even if it is established that the fine was unjustified. The policeman is required to issue an official receipt when collecting the fine.

If you refuse to pay the fine then you will be charged to appear in a court which may lead to inconvenience and likely a higher fine. Unless you strongly dispute an on-the-spot fine your best course is to pay and dispose of the matter.

Priority

On mountain roads, vehicles travelling uphill have priority. Vehicles which continue straight ahead or make a right-hand turn at a crossroads or intersection have priority over oncoming vehicles turning left, provided that there are no signs to the contrary; in this case, even trams cede priority.

If you wish to turn across the flow of traffic at a junction controlled by a policeman, pass in front of him unless otherwise directed.

Buses must not be prevented from leaving a recognised stopping point.

Seat belts   If your car is fitted with seat belts it is compulsory to wear them. Although it is rare for penalties to be imposed for failing to do so there are laws relating to insurance claims and if it is established that at the time of any accident, front-seat passengers were not wearing seat belts then they are held to have contributed to any injuries sustained.

Speed   The beginning of a built-up area is indicated by the placename sign and the end by a sign bearing the inscription *Ortsende von* (end of area) followed by the name of the place. In these areas the maximum speed for all vehicles (except mopeds) is 50kph (31mph); mopeds 40kph (24mph). Outside built-up areas, private cars are subject to a speed limit of 100kph (62mph) which is increased to 130kph (80mph) on motorways unless lower speed limits are indicated. Private vehicles towing trailers with a total weight of less than 750kg (1,650lb) are restricted to 100kph (62mph) on all roads, including motorways, outside built-up areas. If the trailer is over 750kgs then the limit is 100kph on motorways and 80kph (49mph) on main roads outside built-up areas. At certain periods during the summer, lower speed restrictions are imposed.

Traffic lights   A flashing green light indicates that the green phase is about to end.

Tyres   Should show a continuous depth of tread of 1.6mm. It is an offence to use tyres not up to this standard and Austrian police may carry out a check taking drastic action against offenders which may include halting the vehicle until new tyres are fitted.

Warning triangles   These are compulsory for all vehicles outside built-up areas. A triangle must be placed on the road behind the vehicle or obstacle, and must be clearly visible from 200 metres (219yd).

Region of Pontauer

Austria/hotels and garages

Prices are in Austrian Schillings

Abbreviations:

pl	platz
str	strasse

ACHENKIRCH AM ACHENSEE Tirol 1,595
(☎05246) Map **13** A2

★★*Achenseehof* ☎209 Closed Oct–Nov & Apr–
14 May 40⇄ 🏠 ✒ Pool lake

★*Sporthotel Imhof* ☎309 Closed Nov 26rm6⇄20 ⋔
🏠 P Lift sB⇄218–278 dB⇄ ⋔416–536
(English breakfast) L50–80 D50–80 lake

ADMONT Steiermark 3,400 (☎03613) Map **14** C2

★★*Post* (DP) ☎2416 35rm4⇄11 ⋔ 🏠

ALPBACH Tirol 1,576 (☎05336) Map **13** A2

★★★★*Böglerhof* Dorfpl ☎5227 tx051160 Closed
Apr & Nov 64rm41⇄13 ⋔ 🏠 P Lift sB220–300
sB⇄280–350 dB210–260 dB⇄ ⋔270–370
(English breakfast) L100 D100 ✒ Pool mountains

★★*Alpbacher-Hof* ☎5237 Closed Apr–19 May &
Oct–14 Dec 34rm30⇄34 ⋔ 🏠 P sB⇄ ⋔270–300
dB⇄ ⋔500–600 L80–100 D110–130 Pool
mountains

★*Gasthof Jakober* ☎5223 Closed Oct–Nov
61rm22⇄1 ⋔ 🏠

ALTAUSSEE Steiermark 2,500 (☎06152)
Map **13** B2

★★★*Tyrol* ☎7636 24⇄ 🏠 P ♪ sB⇄250–350
dB⇄500–700 (English breakfast) L150 D150
mountains lake

★★*Kitzer* Haupstr 21 ☎7227 21rm4⇄5 ⋔ 🏠 P
sB150–170 sB⇄ ⋔170–200 dB300–340
dB⇄ ⋔340–400 (English breakfast) L70 D70–90 ✒
Pool mountains lake

◥◥ *E Plasonig* ☎7327 ☎2458 M/c P BL/Maz/Peu
(GB)

ALTMÜNSTER Oberösterreich 7,480 (☎07612)
Map **13** B2

★★*Alpen* ☎8377 46rm39 ⋔ Lift lake

★★*Reiberstorfer* Ebenzweier 27 ☎8105
41rm17⇄18 ⋔ 🏠 Lift lake

★*Seewies* ☎8137 30rm lake

AMSTETTEN Niederösterreich 21,850 (☎07472)
Map **14** C3

★★★*Hofmann* Bahnhofstr 2 ☎2516 tx19212
60rm12⇄23 ⋔ 🏠 P Lift sB160–180 sB⇄180–200
dB300–340 dB⇄ ⋔340–350 (English breakfast)
L50–75 D50–75

🛢 ◥◥ *P Bacher* Ardaggerstr 91 ☎2690 P
Chy/Sim/Ska

🛢 ◙◘ *K Laumer* Linzerstr 112 ☎2525 M/c Peu (GB)

ANIF Salzburg 2,930 (☎06246) Map **13** B2

★★*Friesacher* ☎2075 tx062943 48rm41⇄6 ⋔ P Lift
♪ sB⇄ ⋔fr355 dB⇄ ⋔fr490 (English breakfast)
L90–150 D90–150 ✒ mountains

★★*Schlosswirt* ☎2175 36rm23⇄3 ⋔ A17rm 🏠 P
Lift sB210–280 sB⇄ ⋔300–380 dB310–400
dB⇄ ⋔480–650 (English breakfast) L80–130
D80–130 mountains

ARZL IM PITZTAL Tirol, 1,910 (☎05412) Map **12** D2

★★*Post* ☎3111 Closed Oct–6 May 62rm27⇄12 ⋔
🏠 P Lift sB126–168 sB⇄ ⋔161–217 dB224–308
dB⇄ ⋔322–434 L40–100 D40–100 Pool mountains

AURACH Tirol 830 (☎05356) Map **13** A2

★★★*International* ☎4507 Closed Nov
20rm15⇄5 ⋔ Pool

★★*Gstrein* ☎2459 20⇄ 🏠 lake

AUSSEE (BAD) Steiermark 5,200 (☎06152)
Map **13** B2

★★*Erzherzog Johann & Kristina* Kurhausplatz 62
☎2017 38rm15⇄12 ⋔ 🏠 P ♪ sBfr195 sB⇄ ⋔fr255
dBfr400 dB⇄ ⋔fr510 (English breakfast) Lfr85 Dfr95
mountains

★*Stadt Wien* ☎2068 30rm8⇄5 ⋔ A10rm

🛢 ◙◘ *H Obermeyr* Wiedleithe 100–102 ☎2413 M/c P
Opl/Vau (GB)

Bad Each name preceded by Bad is listed under the
name that follows it.

BADEN BEI WIEN Niederösterreich 24,300
(☎02252) Map **14** D3

★★★*Herzoghof* Theresiengasse 5 ☎2117 tx14480
111rm107⇄4 ⋔ Lift Pool

★★★*Krainerhütte* Helenental ☎4511 tx14303
68rm55⇄13 ⋔ 🏠 P Lift ♪ sB⇄ ⋔fr410 dB⇄ ⋔fr360
✒ Pool mountains

★★*Sacher* Helenental ☎2100 Closed Oct–Apr
25rm10⇄ ✒

★★*Wald* Helenstr 92 ☎2916 30rm3⇄12 ⋔ 🏠 ✒

★*Cholerakapelle* Helenental 40 ☎2850 Closed Jan
& Feb 13rm6 ⋔ A2rm 🏠 P sB190–270 sB⇄ ⋔230–270
dB310–400 dB ⋔360–450 (English breakfast)
L80–100 D80–100

🛢 ◙◘ *A Gramsel* Hotzendorfpl 2 ☎2989 Aud/VW

BADGASTEIN Salzburg 5,800 (☎06434) Map **13** B2

★★★★*Elisabethpark* ☎676613 Closed Apr
& Oct–Nov 135⇄ ⋔ Lift Pool ♪

★★★*Parkhotel Bellevue* ☎2571 tx0676621 Closed
16 Oct–14 Dec 150rm110⇄ ⋔ P Lift ♪ sB270–450
sB⇄350–600 dB540–900 dB⇄700–1200
L100–120 D140–180 Pool ♪ ○ mountains

★★★*Savoy* (Pn) ☎2588 tx67688 Closed
21 Oct–14 Dec 63rm32⇄10 ⋔ 🏠 Lift Pool

★★★*Straubinger* ☎2012 tx67670 Closed
10 Oct–22 Dec & 1 Apr–10 May 72rm28⇄3 ⋔ P Lift
♪ sB220–320 sB⇄ ⋔350–500 dB400–600
dB⇄ ⋔580–880 (English breakfast) L50–100
D50–100 mountains

★★*Grüner Baum* ☎2516 tx6776611 Closed
4 Apr–14 May & 17 Oct–16 Dec 97rm61⇄2 ⋔ 🏠

★★*Kurhotel Eden* (Pn) ☎2076 36rm11⇄ Lift

★*Bristol* ☎2219 Closed Nov 30rm9⇄11 ⋔ 🏠 Lift

BERWANG Tirol 550 (☎05674) Map **12** D2

★★★*Singer* Haus am Sonnenhang ☎8181 Closed
11 Apr–19 May & 21 Sep–17 Dec 49rm32⇄2 ⋔ P Lift
sB200–250 sB⇄ ⋔290–390 dB380–480
dB⇄ ⋔480–680 L100–130 D110–150 mountains

BEZAU Vorarlberg 1,500 (☎05514) Map **12** C2

★★*Gams* ☎2220 tx59144 40rm16⇄12 ⋔ P Lift
sBfr200 sB⇄ ⋔fr295 dBfr180 dB⇄ ⋔260–320
(English breakfast) L70–150 D70–150 ✒ Pool
mountains

★★*Post* Hauptstr ☎2207 Closed Nov–22 Dec
41rm25⇄16 ⋔ 🏠 P Lift Pool mountains

BISCHOFSHOFEN Salzburg 8,900 (☎06462)
Map **13** B2

★*Tirolerwirt* Gasteinerstr 3 ☎2776 8rm1⇄ A2rm 🏠
P sB110–125 sB⇄135–150 dB220–250
dB⇄250–270 (English breakfast) mountains

BLUDENZ Vorarlberg 12,000 (☎05552) Map **12** C2

★★*Herzog Friedrich* Mutterstr 6 ☎2703 18rm2⇄ ⋔
🏠 P Lift sBfr135 dBfr390 dB⇄ ⋔fr410
(English breakfast) L40–150 D20–150 mountains

★★*Schlosshotel Dörflinger* ☎3016 30rm10⇄20 ⋔
🏠 P sBfr245 sB⇄ ⋔fr245 dB⇄ ⋔fr480
(English breakfast) L100–150 D100–150 ♪
mountains

★*Hoher Frassen* Obdorfweg 54 (n rest) ☎2264
16rm 🏠

◙◘ *H Zimmermann* Brunnenfeld ☎2554 BL/Chy/Sim
(GB)

BRAND Vorarlberg 550 (☎05559) Map **12** C1

★★★*Scesaplana* ☎221 tx5234121 Closed Etr–14
May & Oct–14 Dec 40rm34⇄ P Lift sB300–400
sB⇄420–550 dB300–400 dB⇄400–660 ✒ Pool
mountains

★★*Hammerle* ⇄213 Closed 23 Sep–27 May
55rm13⇄14 ⋔ A21rm

★*Valbona* ☎226 21rm2⇄6 ⋔ A11rm

★*Zimba* ☎219 Closed 21 Apr–24 May & Oct–14
Dec 20rm13⇄4 ⋔ 🏠 P sB⇄ ⋔190 dB260 dB⇄ ⋔320
(English breakfast) L 70–90 D70–90 mountains

BRAUNAU AM INN Oberösterreich (☎07722)
Map **13** B3

★★*Post* ☎3492 30rm9⇄9 ⋔ 🏠 P Lift sB120
sB⇄ ⋔ fr215 dB fr220 dB⇄ ⋔ fr315
(English breakfast) L fr85 D fr85

BREGENZ Vorarlberg 23,530 (☎05574) Map **12** C2
★★*Central* Kaiserstr 24 (n rest) ☎22947 tx57779
42rm 6㎖
★★**Weisses Kreuz** Römerstr 5 ☎22488 tx57741
40rm18⇔8㎖ P Lift ♪ sB215–265 sB⇔㎖255–375
dB390–450 dB⇔㎖450–600 (English breakfast)
L170–180 D90 ✍ mountains lake
★*Germania* ☎22766 15rm2⇔5㎖㎡
  🛏 ☈☈ **Central** (G Böhler) Weiherstr 13
☎22208☎22208 MB (GB)
BRUCK AN DER GLOCKNERSTRASSE Salzburg
3,300 (☎06545) Map **13** B2
★★*Lukashansl* (DP) ☎458 80rm40⇔ ㎡ Lift
★*Höllern* ☎1240 40rm12⇔14㎖ A3rm㎡
BRUCK AN DER MUR Steiermark 17,634
(☎03862) Map **14** C2
★★**Bauer zum Schwarzen Adler** Mittergasse 23
☎51331 60rm33⇔9㎖ ㎡ P ♪ sB140–165
sB⇔㎖240–315 dB250–300 dB⇔㎖415–490
L70–100 D70–100
★★**Bayer** ☎51218 tx36639 32rm10⇔4㎖ P
sB180–205 sB⇔㎖210–245 dB320–370
dB⇔㎖380–570 (English breakfast) L60–120
D60–120 mountains
★★*Schreiner* Bahnhofstr 16 ☎51220 60rm6⇔6㎖
㎡
  🛏 ☈☈**R Reichel** Grazerstr 17 ☎51633 M/c Frd/MB
(GB)
BURGAU AM ATTERSEE Salzburg 3,000 (☎07663)
Map **13** B2
★★*Seehotel Burgau* Salzkammergut ☎266 Closed
Nov–Mar 42rm8⇔ A2rm㎡ lake
DELLACH AM WÖRTHERSEE Kärnten 1,300
(☎04274) Map **13** B1
★★★*Gesundheits Centrum Golf Hotel* ☎2511
Closed Oct–Apr 70rm40⇔㎡ 🜂 ♪ lake
DELLACH MILLSTÄTTERSEE See **MILLSTATT**
DEUTSCHLANDSBERG Steiermark 5,230
(☎03462) Map **14** C1
★*Rainer* ☎2318 28rm6⇔3㎖ ㎡ ✍
DIENTEN AM HOCHKÖNIG Salzburg 820
(☎06416) Map **13** B2
★*Pesentheiner* ☎207 Closed Etr–May & Oct–14
Dec 25rm17㎖ ㎡ P sB160–190 sB㎖180–210
dB180–210 dB㎖200–230 L65–80 D45–60 Pool
mountains
DÖBRIACH Kärnten (☎04246) Map **13** B1
  🛏 ☈☈ **F Burgstaller** Millstätter See ☎7736 M/c Frd
(GB)
DÖLLACH-SAGRITZ Kärnten 1,405 (☎04824)
Map **13** B1
★★*Post* ☎0428 Closed 16 Oct–14 Dec 46rm5⇔3㎖
㎡ ✍
★★*Schlosswirt* (Pn) ☎211 Closed Apr, May & Nov
30rm13⇔4㎖ ㎡ ✍ Pool ○
DORNBIRN Vorarlberg 34,850 (☎05572) Map **12** C2
★★★*Park* Goethestr 6 ☎62691 tx59109
40rm15⇔10㎖ ㎡ P Lift ♪ sB310–350
sB⇔㎖410–465 dB fr520 dB⇔㎖620–730
(English breakfast) L140 D140 ✍ mountains
★★*Zum Hirschen* Marktpl 12 ☎62157 38rm4⇔8㎖
A15rm ♪ Sb fr140 sB⇔㎖ fr165 dB fr280
dB⇔㎖ fr330 (English breakfast) L50–90 D50–150
mountains
  🛏 ☈☈ **F Mäser** Lustenauerstr 97 ☎65601 P Fia (GB)
DÜRNSTEIN AN DER DONAU Niederösterreich
1,000 (☎02711) Map **14** C3
★★★*Schloss Dürnstein* ☎212 Closed 16 Nov–
14 Mar 34rm30⇔3㎖ P Lift ♪ sB330–440 sB⇔㎖440
dB460 dB⇔㎖570–850 (English breakfast) L130
D155 Pool
★★*Richard Löwenherz* ☎222 Closed mid Nov–Feb
40rm30⇔10㎖ P sB310–350 sB⇔㎖410–450
dB⇔㎖480–650 L120 D120 Pool
EHRWALD Tirol 2,000 (☎05673) Map **12** D2
★★*Halali* (Pn) ☎2101 Closed Dec 12rm2⇔10㎖ ㎡
★★*Schönrun* ☎2322 Closed Oct–19 Dec
46rm35⇔2㎖ A15rm ㎡ P sB fr175 sB⇔㎖ fr205
dB fr190 dB⇔㎖ fr130 (English breakfast) L fr80 D fr80
mountains

★★*Sonnenspitze* Kirchel 14 (Pn) ☎2208 Closed
Nov 33rm2⇔6㎖ ㎡
★★*Spielmann* Wettersteinstr 24 ☎2225 Closed Nov
40rm17⇔4㎖ A4rm ㎡ Pool
★★ *Tannenhof* (DP) ☎2288 Closed 21 Apr–May &
11 Oct–19 Dec 15⇔
EISENSTADT Burgenland 10,000 (☎02682)
Map **14** D2
★★*Schwechaterhof* F-Lisztgasse 1 ☎2879 tx1722
63rm2⇔10㎖ ㎡
★*Eisenstadt* Sylvesterstr 5 (n rest) ☎3350
14rm2⇔3㎖ ㎡ P sB125–170 sB⇔㎖210–250
dB250–300 dB⇔㎖350–450
ENGELHARTSZELL Oberösterreich (☎07717)
Map **13** B3
★★*Ronthalerhof* ☎8083 9rm5⇔4㎖ P
sB⇔㎖215–252 dB⇔㎖350–414
(English breakfast) L50–80 D50–80
ENNS Oberösterreich 9,000 (☎07223) Map **14** C3
★*Drei Mohren* Hauptpl 5 (n rest) ☎351 22rm ㎡
EUGENDORF Salzburg (☎06212) Map **13** B2
☆☆*Wallersee* ☎8282 12rm3⇔9㎖ ㎡ P sB fr180
sB⇔㎖180–295 dB⇔㎖310–490
(English breakfast) D30–100 mountains
  🛏 ☈☈ **Auto-Hilfe** (Wagner) Bundesstr 1 ☎79560
☎338914 P
FELD AM SEE Kärnten (☎04246) Map **13** B1
★★*Lindenhof* ☎2274 27rm5⇔14㎖ A10rm ㎡ P
sB140–170 aB⇔㎖190–240 dB240–300
sB⇔㎖340–440 (English breakfast) D60–70
mountains
FELDKIRCH Vorarlberg 22,000 (☎05522)
Map **12** C2
★★★*Central – Löwen* Neustadt 17 ☎22070 tx52311
59rm27⇔12㎖ ㎡ P Lift ♪ sB fr180 sB⇔㎖ fr250
dB fr340 dB⇔㎖ fr470 (English breakfast) L70–130
D70–130 mountains
★★*Alpenrose* Rosengasse 6 ☎22175 16rm8⇔ ㎡
★★*Hochhaus* Reichsstr 177 ☎22479 19rm4⇔4㎖
㎡ P Lift ♪ sB144 sB⇔㎖174 dB278 dB⇔㎖318
  🛏 ☈☈**P Fehr** Bundesstr 2 ☎23373 Frd (GB)
FELDKIRCHEN Kärnten 7,770 (☎04276)
Map **14** C1
★★*Dauke* ☎2413 20⇔ ㎡
FERLEITEN AN DER GLOCKNERSTRASSE
Salzburg 830 (☎06546) Map **13** B2
★★*Lukashansl* (DP) ☎220 Closed mid Oct – mid
May 32rm4⇔2㎖ A10rm
FERNPASS Tirol (☎05265) Map **12** D2
★★ *Fernpass* (DP) ☎5201 23rm12⇔2㎖ A9rm ㎡
FRASTANZ Vorarlberg 5,000 (☎05522) Map **12** C2
☆☆ *Galina* Bundesstr 1 ☎22781 Closed Nov 30⇔ ㎡
Lift
★★*Stern* ☎22717 17rm1⇔3㎖ A7rm ㎡ P
sB155–195 sB⇔㎖110–250 dB190–210
dB⇔㎖230–260 (English breakfast) L85–90
D85–90 mountains
FREISTADT Oberösterreich 6,000 (☎07942)
Map **14** C3
★*Goldenen Hirsch* (Gasthof Deim) ☎2258
25rm14⇔10㎖ A8rm P sB150–160 sB⇔㎖180–225
dB300–410 dB⇔㎖420–440 (English breakfast)
L70–90 D60–100
FÜGEN Tirol 2,300 (☎05288) Map **13** A2
★*Post* ☎2286 Closed Nov–14 Dec 60rm50⇔10㎖ P
Lift sB⇔㎖230–260 dB⇔㎖420–480 (English
breakfast) L65 D85 Pool mountains
FULPMES Tirol 2,500 (☎05225) Map **12** D2
★★*Holzmeister* ☎2260 Closed 16 Oct–Nov
32rm16⇔3㎖
FÜRSTENFELD Steiermark 6,300 (☎03382)
Map **14** D2
★*Hitzl* ☎2144 43rm5㎖ ㎡
★*Brauhaus* Grazerpl 2 ☎2429 20rm4⇔4㎖
☈☈ *M Koller* Fehringerstr 13 ☎2527 M/c P Frd/MB
☈☈*H Marth* Ledergasse 27 ☎3298 M/c P Cit
FUSCH AN DER GROSSGLOCKNERSTRASSE
Salzburg 790 (☎06546) Map **13**B2

Austria

★★**Post Hofer** ☎226 42rm5⇌20🛁 🏠 P sB110–130
dB200–240 dB⇌🛁260–300 (English breakfast)
L130 D60 ⊸ mountains
★**Lampenhäusl** ☎215 Closed Nov–8 Dec
32rm1⇌8🛁 A18rm 🏠 P sB110–130
sB⇌🛁130–150 dB180–220 dB⇌🛁210–230
(English breakfast) L60–90 D50–80 mountains

FUSCHL AM SEE Salzburg 700 (☎06226)
Map **13** B2
★★**Seehotel Schlick** ☎237 50rm20⇌ 🏠 P
sB150–170 sB⇌🛁180–200 dB190–200
dB⇌🛁210–230 (English breakfast) L70–80 D75–90
mountains lake

GAISBERG Salzburg (☎06222) Map **13** B2 **See
Salzburg plan**
★★★**Kobenzl** (DP) ☎21776 tx63833 Salzburg
plan **9** Closed Nov–14Mar 38rm33⇌ 🏠 Pool ◯
★★★**Zistelalm** ☎20104 Salzburg plan **12** Closed 16
Nov–14 Dec 24rm3⇌12🛁 🏠 P ♪ sB150–175
sB⇌🛁235–265 dB280–300 dB⇌🛁400–550
L50–100 D50–200 Pool mountains

GALTÜR Tirol 535 (☎05443) Map **12** C1
★★**Berghaus Franz Lorenz** ☎206 Closed Oct–
14 Dec 24⇌🛁 🏠 P Lift ♪ sB⇌🛁235–305
dB⇌🛁454–610 (English breakfast) L50–110
D50–110 mountains
★★**Fluchthorn** ☎202 Closed Oct–May
50rm23⇌27🛁 🏠 P Lift ♪ sB⇌🛁240–300
dB⇌🛁400–640 (English breakfast) L90 D120
mountains
★**Paznaunerhof** ☎234 Closed May 18rm 6🛁 🏠

GARGELLEN Vorarlberg 600 (☎05557) Map **12** C1
★★**Alpenrose** ☎314 Closed 21 Apr–May &
Oct–Nov 18rm4⇌7🛁 🏠
★★**Feriengut Gargellenhof** (DP) ☎274 tx52299
Closed May & Nov 34rm7⇌ 🏠
★★**Madrisa** Ortsmitte ☎6331 tx52269 Closed
21 Sep–22Jun 50rm22⇌1🛁 P sB220–250
dB190–290 dB⇌🛁290–420 (English breakfast)
L80–140 D80–140 Pool mountains

GARS AM KAMP Niederösterreich (☎02985)
Map **14** C3
O Moser J–Stausskasse 307 ☎2259 M/c P
Chy/Sim

GASCHURN Vorarlberg 1,180 (☎05558) Map **12** C1
★★★**Sporthotel Epple** (DP & Pn) ☎251 tx52389
Closed 24Apr–May & Oct–25Nov 81rm39⇌25🛁 🏠
P Lift ♪ sB380–550 sB⇌🛁470–820 dB760–1100
dB⇌🛁940–1640 L100–120 D100–120 ⊸ Pool
mountains

GERLOS Tirol 550 (☎05284) Map **13** A2
★★**Kroller** (DP) ☎202 40rm30⇌10🛁 🏠
★**Jägerhof** ☎203 38rm3⇌6🛁 P ♪ sB125–140
sB⇌🛁155–170 dB250–280 dB⇌🛁290–320
(English breakfast) L45–80 D40–65 ⊸ mountains

GMUNDEN Oberösterreich 12,700 (☎07612)
Map **13** B2
★★★**Post** Badgasse 8 ☎3651 20rm11⇌9🛁
★★**Seehotel Schwan** Rathauspl 8 ☎3391
45rm28⇌8🛁 🏠 P Lift ♪ sB190–220
sB⇌🛁250–300 dB380–420 dB⇌🛁550–650
mountains lake
⚙ J Beham Georgstr 5 ☎3838 ☎3838 Ren (GB)

GOLLING Salzburg 2,900 (☎06244) Map **13** B2
★**Goldener Stern** Hauptstr ☎220 Closed Nov
25rm5⇌10🛁 🏠 P sB110–130 sB⇌🛁135–155
dB100–120 dB⇌🛁130–155 mountains

GÖTZIS Vorarlberg (☎2202) Map **12** C2
🛢 ⚙ *Auto beck* Dr A-Heinzlestr 61 ☎2203 Peu Vau

GRAZ Steiermark 252,850 (☎0316) Map **14** C2
★★★**Daniel** Europl 1 ☎911080 tx31182
100rm53⇌19🛁 🏠 P Lift ♪ sB 245–310
sB⇌🛁395–475 dB490–520 dB⇌🛁580–710
L90–145 D90–145
★★★**Park** Leonhardstr 8 ☎33511 tx31498 63rm48⇌
🏠 P Lift ♪ sB240–280 sB⇌🛁420–470 dB420–450
dB⇌🛁580–660 Lalc Dalc

★★★**Steirerhof** Jakominipl 12 ☎76356 tx31282
98rm95⇌ Lift
★★★**Weitzer** Griesgasse 15 ☎913801 tx31284
178rm66⇌49🛁 A84rm P Lift ♪ sB245–310
sB⇌🛁395–475 dB490–520 dB⇌🛁580–710
(English breakfast) L90–145 D90–145
★★★**Wiesler** Grieski 4 ☎913241 tx31130
90rm50⇌6🛁 🏠 P Lift ♪ sB180–250
sB⇌🛁400–450 dB350–400 dB⇌🛁600–700
(English breakfast) L80 D80
★★**Mariahilf** Mairiahilferstr ☎913163 tx31087
44rm10⇌16🛁 🏠 P Lift ♪ sB180–190
sB⇌🛁350–400 dB340–360 dB⇌🛁500–600
(English breakfast) L80–100 D80–100
🛢 ⚙ **W Denzel** Wetzelsdorferstr 35 ☎53580 M/c
BMW/Vlo (GB)
⚙ **J Jacomini** Kärntnerstr 115 ☎22188 BL/Jag/Tri
(GB)
🛢 ⚙ **H Krajacic** Idlhofgasse 17 ☎912823 BL/Rov
(GB)
⚙⚙ **Dr K Repitsch** Harmsdorfgasse 44 ☎42111
☎492784 M/c Bed/Maz/Vau (GB)
🛢 ⚙ **Autozentrale** (G von Salis & M Braunstein)
Wienerstr 34 ☎911680 Bed/Opl (GB)

GRIES AM BRENNER Tirol 1,300 (☎05274)
Map **13** A1
★**Intertouring** ☎216 Closed 7 Oct–9 Dec 40rm
A20rm
★**Weisses Rössl** Hauptstr ☎214 Closed
15Oct–20Dec 30rm5🛁 P sB190–210 sB🛁220–240
dB330–360 dB🛁380–410 (English breakfast)
L80–120 D80–120 mountains

GRIESKIRCHEN Oberösterreich (☎07248)
Map **13** B3
At **Neumarkt im Hausruckkeis** (5.5km NW)
🛢 ⚙⚙ **H Edtstadler** Marktpl 22 ☎227 ☎227 M/c P
BMW/Vlo (GB)

GRÖBMING Steiermark 1,920 (☎03685) Map **13** B2
🛢 ⚙ **A Franz** Bundesstr 324 ☎2359 M/c P Fia/MB
(GB)

GROSSGLOCKNERSTRASSE Kärnten (☎04824)
Map **13** B2
★★**Kaiser-Franz-Josef-Haus** ☎2363 Closed
Nov–Apr 70rm15⇌13🛁

GRUNDLSEE Steiermark 1,400 (☎06152)
Map **13** B2
★**Backenstein** (n rest) ☎8545 15rm12⇌ 🏠 P
sB145–175 sB⇌225–295 dB235–370
dB⇌370–470 L100–120 D50–60 mountains lake

GSCHNITZ Tirol 300 (☎05272) Map **12** D1
★★**Gschnitzer Hof** ☎23113 Closed Oct–17 Dec &
11 Apr–May 32rm3⇌6🛁 🏠 Pool

GSTATTERBODEN Steiermark 700 (☎03613)
Map **14** C2
★★**Gesäuse** ☎245519 76rm12⇌

HAIBACH Oberösterreich (☎07713) Map **13** B3
★★**Donauhotel Faberhof** ☎8144 Closed Jan & Dec
21rm7⇌13🛁 🏠 P sB⇌🛁200–265 dB⇌🛁360–455
L60–80 D60–90

HALDENSEE Tirol (☎05675) Map **12** D2
★**Rot-Fluh** ☎465 tx05546 Closed Nov–14 Dec
73rm40⇌6🛁 🏠 P Lift sB175–240 sB⇌🛁350–460
dB310–440 dB⇌🛁530–720 (English breakfast)
L50–130 D50–130 ⊸ Pool mountains lake

HALL IN TIROL Tirol 11,940 (☎05223) Map **13** A2
★★★**Park** Kurpark ☎2566 45rm17⇌1🛁 🏠 Lift
★★**Maria Theresia** Reimmichlstr 25 ☎6313
25rm3⇌ Lift
★**Tyrol** ☎6621 tx54223 36rm14⇌22🛁 P Lift
sb⇌🛁235–270 dB280–360 dB⇌🛁410–480 Pool
mountains

HALLEIN Salzburg 14,000 (☎06245) Map **13** B2
★★**Kurhaus St-Josef** ☎2509 Closed 26 Nov–
28 Dec 90rm7⇌ 🏠 Lift Pool
★**Stern** (n rest) ☎2610 Closed Oct–Apr 35rm2⇌3🛁
🏠 P sB140–185 dB350–330 dB⇌🛁360–410
(English breakfast) mountains

HALLSTATT AM SEE Oberösterreich 1,340
(☎06134) Map **13** B2
★★**Grüner Baum** Marktpl 104 ☎263 Closed
Nov–Mar 42rm18⇆2🛏 🏠 lake

HEILIGENBLUT Kärnten 1,400 (☎04824)
Map **13** B1/2
See also **Grossglocknerstrasse**
★★**Glocknerhof** ☎2244 tx48154 Closed
21 Apr–19 May & 16 Oct–7 Dec 75rm45⇆15🛏
A20rm 🏠 P Lift sB200–280 sB⇆🛏300–490
dB400–560 dB⇆🛏600–980 (English breakfast)
L80–150 D120–150 Pool mountains
★★**Rupertihaus** ☎2247 tx4652 33rm11⇆11🛏 P
sB100–130 sB⇆🛏130–160 dB200–260
dB⇆🛏260–320 L70alc D80alc mountains
★**Post** ☎2245 Closed 11 Oct–May 35rm13⇆14🛏
🏠 P sB170–200 sB⇆🛏220–250 dB140–170
dB⇆🛏180–240 (English breakfast) L75–95
D85–100 ◯ mountains

HEITERWANG Tirol 380 (☎05674) Map **12** D2
★**Fischer am See** ☎29116 Closed Nov–Feb except
Xmas 13rm9⇆ 🏠 P sB175–205 sB⇆210–240
dB350–410 dB⇆420–480 mountains lake

HINTERSTODER Oberösterreich 1,000 (☎07564)
Map **13** B2
★**Dietlgut** (DP & Pn) ☎248 25rm12⇆13🛏 🏠 P
sB190–280 sB⇆🛏270–340 dB380–560
dB⇆🛏540–680 Pool mountains

HINTERTHAL AM HOCHKÖNIG Salzburg
(☎06584) Map **13** B2
★★★**Wachtelhof** ☎288 Closed May & Oct–Nov
27rm23⇆4🛏 A2rm 🏠 Pool

HINTERTUX Tirol 1,400 (☎05287) Map **13** A2
★★**Berghof** (DP) ☎304 26rm7⇆7🛏 🏠 P
sB210–220 sB⇆🛏230–250 dB190–200
dB⇆🛏210–230 mountains

HOF BEI SALZBURG Salzburg 1,240 (☎06229)
Map **13** B2
★★★★**Schloss Fuschl** ☎253 tx63454 Closed
Nov–mid Apr 69rm45⇆1🛏 🏠 Lift ✒ Pool ♨ ◯ lake
★★**Baderluck** ☎216 28rm9⇆

HOFGASTEIN (BAD) Salzburg 5,200 (☎06432)
Map **13** B2
★★★**Grand Park** Kurgartenstr 26 ☎356 tx67756
96rm90⇆ 🏠 P Lift 𝄞 sB385–500 sB⇆485–550
dB⇆870–1300 (English breakfast) L110–150
D120–150 Pool mountains
★★**Astoria** ☎277 Closed 16 Oct–21 Dec 55rm
10⇆15🛏 🏠 Pool
★★**Österreichischer Hof** Kurgartenstr 9 ☎216
Closed Apr & 4 Oct–19 Dec 59rm19⇆40🛏 🏠 P Lift
sB⇆315–405 dB560–760 L80 D80 Pool
🗃 ✂ **P Schober** Anger 104 ☎532 Fia/Lnc

HUNGERBURG See **Innsbruck**

IGLS Tirol 1,400 (☎05222) Map **13** A2
★★★**Aegidihof** Bilgeristr 1 ☎7108 Closed 21
Oct–14 Dec 30rm26⇆ 🏠 P Lift 𝄞 sB200–580
sB⇆280–580 dB200–500 dB⇆260–700
(English breakfast) L95 D105
★★★**Iglerhof** Patscherstr ☎7331 tx53480 Closed
16 Mar–14 May & Nov–14 Dec 93rm65⇆ 🏠 Lift
Pool ♨
★★★**Park** ☎7305 tx53576 Closed Nov 64rm54⇆ 🏠
P Lift 𝄞 sB395–445 sB⇆495–745 dB390–440
dB⇆490–690 Lfr130 Dfr150 ✒ Pool ♨ mountains
★★★**Sport** ☎7241 tx53314 Closed Nov–14 Dec.
90rm80⇆ 🏠 Lift ✒ Pool
★★**Alpenhof Kittler** ☎7491 Closed Nov
38rm34⇆2🛏 🏠 P Lift 𝄞 sB265–330
sB⇆🛏325–380 dB240–310 dB⇆🛏300–360
(English breakfast) L70–90 D70–90 ♨ mountains
★★**Batzenhäusl** ☎7104 Closed 16 Oct–14 Dec
24rm17⇆4🛏 🏠 P Lift sB180–240 sB⇆🛏230–340
dB200–260 dB⇆🛏260–360 (English breakfast)
L70–90 D70–100 mountains
★★**Tiroler Hof** ☎7194 Closed 16–19 May &
16Sep–19Dec 50rm8⇆2🛏 🏠

★★**Waldhotel** ☎7272 Closed Nov 20rm8⇆12🛏 P
Lift sB⇆🛏320–440 dB⇆🛏540–780 (English
breakfast) L78–110 D78–110 Pool mountains
★**Bon-Alpina** Hilberstr 8 ☎7219 closed 16 Oct–
14 Dec 52rm5⇆ A6rm
★**Gothensitz** (n rest) ☎7211 15rm4⇆3🛏 P
sB150–185 (room only) sB⇆🛏205–230 (room only)
dB250–320 (room only) dB⇆🛏380–420
(room only) mountains
★**Oswald** ☎7262 13rm3⇆
★**Romedihof** ☎7141 Closed Oct & Nov 22rm21⇆ P
sB⇆175–195 dB⇆180–210 L80 D70–80
mountains

IMST Tirol 5,920 (☎05412) Map**12** D2
★★**Linserhof** ☎2415 40rm30🛏 🏠 Pool
★★**Post** Postpl 3 ☎2554 Closed 16 Oct–14Dec
43rm20⇆2🛏 🏠 Lift Pool

INNSBRUCK Tirol 116,000 (☎05222)
Map **13** A2 **See Plan overleaf**
The Herzog–Friedrich Str area is now a pedestrian
precinct and only open to vehicular traffic at certain
times of the day.
★★★★**Tyrol** Südtirolerpl 1 ☎21781 tx53424 Plan**1**
Closed Nov–Apr 121rm101⇆20🛏 🏠 P Lift 𝄞
sB⇆🛏550–700 dB⇆🛏800–1200
(English breakfast) L140 D140 mountains
★★★**Europa** Südtirolerpl 2 ☎35571 tx53424 Plan **2**
133rm100⇆ 🏠 P Lift 𝄞 sB300–380 sB⇆550–700
dB490–580 dB⇆800–1200 (English breakfast)
L140 D140 mountains
★★★**Goldener Adler** Herzog–Friedrichstr 6
☎26334 tx54217 Plan **4** 37rm16⇆21🛏 P Lift 𝄞
sB⇆🛏400–500 dB⇆🛏600–800 L 100 D 130
mountains
★★**Binder** Dr. Glatzstr 20 ☎42236 Plan **5** 34rm9⇆
🏠 Lift sB170 sB⇆230 dB340 dB⇆420
(English breakfast) L70 D70 ✒ Pool
★★**Central** Erlerstr II ☎24866 Plan **6** 60rm12⇆35🛏
🏠 P Lift 𝄞 sB245–275 sB⇆🛏375–445
dB 360–440 dB⇆🛏520–700 L90 D70 mountains
★★**Goldene Rose** Herzog–Friedrichstr 39 ☎22041
Plan **7** 27rm7⇆ P Lift 𝄞 sB200–250 sB⇆330–380
dB340–380 dB⇆520–580 (English breakfast)
L90–220 D90–220
★★**Grauer Bär** Universitätsstr 5 ☎34531 tx53387
Plan **8** 159rm67⇆21🛏 🏠 P Lift 𝄞 sB355–385
sB⇆🛏445–505 dB550–610 dB⇆🛏730–810
(English breakfast) L80 D80 mountains
★★**Hufeisen** An-der-Lanstr 33 ☎51841 Plan **10**
28rm20⇆8🛏 🏠 Lift
★★**Maria Theresia** M-Theresienstr 31 ☎35615
tx53300 Plan **12** 77rm60⇆17🛏 🏠 Lift 𝄞
sB360–420 sB⇆🛏360–420 dB300–330
dB⇆🛏300–330 (English breakfast) L80 D80
Mountains
★★**Schwarzer Adler** Kaiserjägerstr 2 ☎27109
Plan **14** 22rm16⇆6🛏 P 𝄞 sB⇆🛏360 dB⇆🛏560
L90 D90 mountains
★**Goldener Stern** Innstr 37 ☎27167 Plan **15**
100rm10🛏 Lift
★**Greif** Leopoldstr 3 ☎27401 tx53111 Plan **16**
58rm14⇆29🛏 Lift
★**Putzker** Höttingerau 41 (n rest) ☎29163 Plan **17**
15rm
★**Touringhaus** Brunecker Str 12 (n rest) ☎21781
tx53424 Plan **18** Closed 7 Jan–Apr & 16 Oct–19 Dec
35rm1⇆ 🏠 Lift
🗃 ✂ **Linser-Auto** Hallerstr 119A ☎62421
Bed/Opl/Vau/(GB)
🗃 ✂**F Niederkofler** Grassmayrstr 23 ☎25759 P
Dat/Ska/(GB)
🗃 ✂**G Plörer** Griesauweg 33 ☎45451 M/c P
BMW/Vlo/(GB)
M Steger & Sohn Haymongasse 9A ☎27377
Electrical repairs (Lucas Agent) (GB)

At **Hungerburg** (4KmN) also funicular from
Innsbruck

Austria

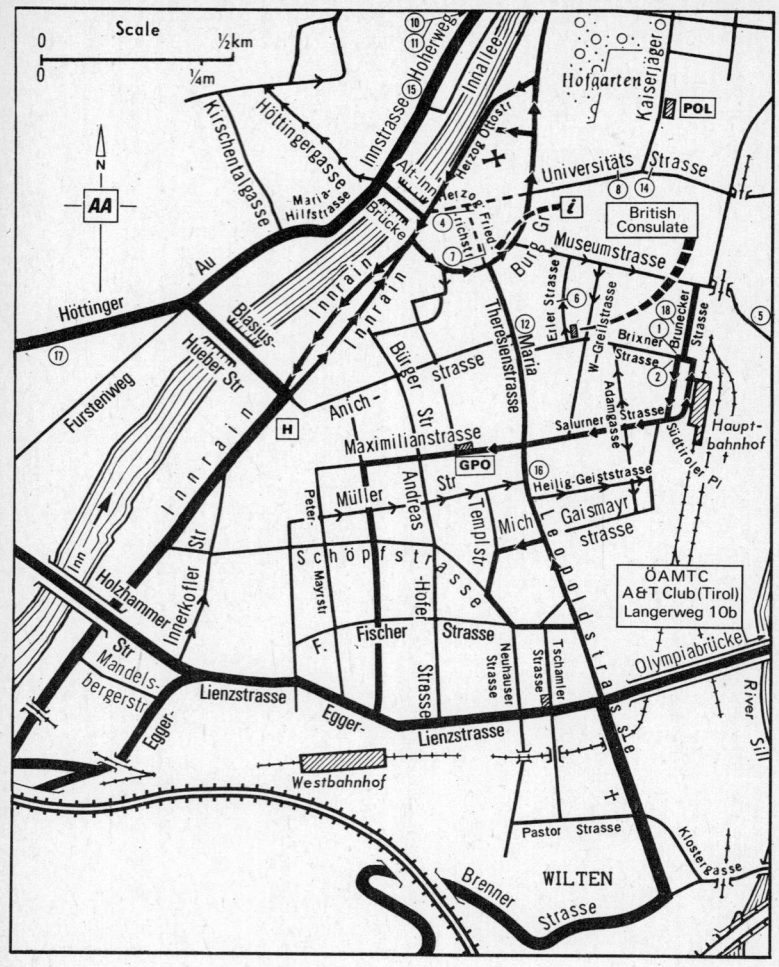

Innsbruck

1	★★★★ Tyrol
2	★★★ Europa
4	★★★ Goldener Adler
5	★★ Binder
6	★★ Central
7	★★ Goldene Rose
8	★★ Grauer Bär

10	★★ Hufeisen
11	★★ Mariabrunn
12	★★ Maria Theresia
14	★★ Schwarzer Adler
15	★ Goldener Stern
16	★ Greif
17	★ Putzker
18	★ Touringhaus

Austria

★★*Mariabrunn* ☎33161 tx53194 Plan **11**
Closed 16Oct – 14 Dec 32⇌ 🏨
At **Völs** (5Km 3 on No. 1A)
🛏 🏍 **Meisinger** Innsbruckerstr 57 ☎34516 ☎34516
P Jag/Peu/RR (GB)

ISCHGL Tirol 980 (☎05444) Map **12** C1
★*Post* Paznautal ☎233 Closed May – 9 Jun & 16
Sep – Nov 61rm35⇌6🏻 🏨 Lift Pool

ISCHL (BAD) Oberösterreich 14,000 (☎06132)
Map **13** B2
★★★*Golf* ☎3590 tx68124 48rm30⇌18🏻 🏨 P Lift ♪
sB⇌🏻475 – 525 dB⇌🏻830 – 1350 (English
breakfast) L100 – 120 D100 – 140 Pool ঌ mountains
★★**Freischütz** 96 Rettenbach ☎3354 Closed
Nov – Mar 25 rm8⇌ 🏨 P sB160 – 190 sB⇌270 – 300
dB320 – 380 dB⇌500 – 550 (English breakfast)
L90 – 100 D100 mountains
★★**Post** Kaiser F-Josefstr 3 – 5 ☎3441 Closed
21Oct – 19Dec 63rm32⇌3 P Lift ♪ sB180 – 220
sB⇌🏻280 – 310 dB320 – 440 dB⇌🏻460 – 600
L80 – 110 D70 – 100 mountains
★*Bayerischer Hof* Schröpperpl 1 ☎3360 Closed
11Dec – Feb 16rm 🏨
ITTER Tirol (☎05332) Map **13** A2
★★**Schloss Itter** ☎2561 tx5117124 Closed 16
Oct – 14 Dec 24rm11⇌ P Lift sB250 sB⇌320 dB420
dB⇌560 L100 D100 Pool mountains

JUDENBURG Steiermark 11,360 (☎03572)
Map **14** C2
🛏 🏍 **W Denzel** Weisenweg 4 ☎2477 M/c BMW/Vlo
(GB)
🏍 *A Gauper Gabelhof* Hetzendorferstr 53 ☎2430 P
Cit/Peu

KANZELHÖHE-ANNENHEIM Kärnten 300
(☎04249) Map **13** B1
★★★*Berghotel & Sonnenhotel* ☎2713 Closed 16
Apr – May & 16 Oct – 19 Dec 60rm40⇌2🏻 Lift Pool
lake
KIRCHBERG Tirol (☎05357) Map **13** A2
★★*Spertenhof* ☎411 11rm7🏻 🏨
KITZBÜHEL Tirol 7,750 (☎05356) Map **13** A2
★★★*Hirzingerhof* Schwarzseestr 12 ☎3211
tx17124 Closed Apr & Nov 26rm26⇌2🏻 A10rm 🏨 P
Lift ♪ sB⇌🏻410 – 550 dB⇌🏻700 – 1000 (English
breakfast) L95 D110 mountains
★★★★*Tennerhof* Griesenauweg 26 ☎3181
tx5118426 Closed 11 Oct – 19 Dec & 2 Apr – May
47rm41⇌2🏻 P ♪ sB⇌🏻350 – 600
dB⇌🏻560 – 1050 (English breakfast) L140 – 160
D150 – 185 mountains
★★★*Goldener Greif* ☎4311 tx5117118
Closed Apr – May & 16 Oct – 14 Dec 49rm40⇌ Lift
Pool
★★**Erika** J – Pirchlstr 21 (DP & Pn) ☎4885 Closed
May 74rm72⇌ 🏨 P sB⇌300 – 550 dB⇌600 – 1100
(English breakfast) Pool mountains
★★*Hummer* Hammerschmiedstr 7 ☎2813 41rm6⇌
★★**Klausner** Bahnhofstr ☎2136 tx5118418 Closed
Nov 52rm21⇌15🏻 🏨 P Lift ♪ sB255 – 265
sB⇌🏻325 – 345 dB300 – 310 dB⇌🏻340 – 360 L90
D110 mountains
★★**Schweizerhof** Hahnenkampstr 4 ☎2735 Closed
Nov 37rm16⇌15🏻 🏨 P ♪ sB200 – 280
sB⇌🏻240 – 380 dB⇌🏻400 – 750 (English
breakfast) L80 – 95 D95 – 120 mountains
★★**Sonnenhof** ☎2721 Closed Oct – 19 Dec & Apr
29rm20⇌2🏻 🏨
★★*Zum Jägerwirt* Jochbergstr 12 ☎4281
tx5117114 Closed Apr – Nov 60rm30⇌ Lift
🛏 🏍 *Herz* J – Pirchlstr 30 ☎4638 M/c P Frd (GB)
KLAGENFURT Kärnten 75,000 (☎04222)
Map **14** C1
★★★ **Sandwirt** Pernhartgasse 9 ☎82431 tx42329
55rm35⇌ 🏨 Lift ♪ sB280 sB⇌420 – 450 dB480
dB⇌670 – 750 (English breakfast) L110 D110
★★*Dermuth* Kohldorferster 52 ☎21247
51rm47⇌4🏻 🏨 Pool
★★**Kurhotel Carinthia** 8 Maistr 41 ☎70883 tx42399
23⇌ P Lift ♪ sB⇌370 – 470 dB⇌580 – 760

★★**Moser-Verdino** Domgasse 2 ☎83431 tx42467
100rm56⇌14🏻 P Lift ♪ sB220 – 260
sB⇌🏻350 – 400 dB390 – 460 dB⇌🏻630 – 680
(English breakfast) L170 D170 mountains
★*Janach* Bahnhofstr 5 ☎85114 30rm6⇌ P ♪
sB110 – 170 sB⇌240 dB260 – 340 dB⇌390 – 440
(English breakfast)
🛏 🏍 *A Krainer* Rosentalerstr 162 ☎21415 P Por
🏍 *K Kropiunig* Reinholdweg 7 ☎22796 P
BL/Rov/Toy
🛏 🏍 *A Luger* Völkermarkterstr 58 ☎31684
BL/Jag/Rov/Tri
Mandl St-Veiterstr 209 ☎43200 Chy/Sim (GB)
🛏 🏍 *J Sintschnig* Südbahngürtel 8 ☎32144 Frd
(GB)
🛏 🏍 *A Wiesner & Sohne* Rosenthalerstr 205
☎22206 BL/Rov/Tri
🔧 🏍 *R Wurm* St-Veiterring 27 ☎80991 P Peu/Ren
(GB)
KOFLACH Steiermark (☎03144) Map **14** C2
🛏 🏍 *J Suppanz* Dillacherstr 4 ☎293 M/c P Chy/Sim
KÖTSCHACH-MAUTHEN Kärnten 2,830 (☎04715)
Map **13** B1
★★**Post** ☎221 32rm8⇌10🏻 🏨 sB140 – 180
sB⇌🏻180 – 220 dB360 – 400 dB⇌🏻360 – 400
(English breakfast) L60 – 100 D60 – 100 St% ✆ Pool
ঌ mountains
KREMS AN DER DONAU Niederösterreich 22,950
(☎02732) Map **14** C3
★★★*Park* E-Hofbauerstr 19 ☎3266 tx71130
70rm50⇌ 🏨 P Lift ♪ sB180 – 230 sB⇌270 – 340
dB340 – 400 dB⇌440 – 500 (English breakfast) L85
D95
★★**Weisse Rose** Obere Landstr 19 ☎3457
31rm12⇌6🏻 🏨
🛏 *J Auer* Wienerstr 82 ☎3501 Bed/Opl
🏍 *H Starkl* Wienerstr 48 ☎3030 M/c Peu/Ren (GB)
KRIMML Salzburg 670 (☎06564) Map **13** A2
★★**Klockerhaus** ☎208 Closed Nov 40rm4⇌15🏻 P
sB180 – 200 dB200 – 240 dB⇌🏻260 – 280
mountains
KUFSTEIN Tirol 12,000 (☎05372) Map **13** A2
★★**Andreas Hofer** Pirmoserster 8 ☎3281
ta Sapplhotel 130rm8⇌8🏻 🏨 P ♪ sB193 sB⇌🏻273
dB366 dB⇌🏻546 (English breakfast) L90 D90
mountains
★★*Egger* ☎2535 52rm3⇌3🏻 Lift
★*Post* ☎2024 Closed Nov 30rm1🏻
🛏 🏍 *H Gaderbauer* Zellerstr 29 ☎4740 ☎30795 P
Aud/VW (GB)
🛏 🏍 *Krimbacher* K-Kraftstr2 ☎2236 P Frd/MB
🛏 🏍 *A Reibmayr* Fischergries 16 ☎2141 Opl
KÜHTAI Tirol 50 (☎05229) Map **12** D2
★★★*Astoria* (Pn) ☎215 Closed mid Apr – Nov
45rm32⇌5🏻 🏨 P Lift sB380 – 630 sB⇌🏻440 – 730
dB880 – 1380 dB⇌🏻880 – 1380 Pool mountains
LANDECK Tirol 6,600 (☎05442) Map **12** D2
★★*Post* Malserstr 19 ☎2383 79rm A21rm
At **Zams** (2km NE)
🏍 **Plaseller** Buntweg 8 ☎2304 Frd (GB)
LANGEN AM ARLBERG Vorarlberg 825 (☎05582)
Map **12** C1/2
★★*Arlbergerhof* ☎213 18rm2⇌2🏻 🏨
LECH AM ARLBERG Vorarlberg 10,920 (☎05583)
Map **12** C2
★★**Arlberg** ☎134 Closed May – mid Jun & Oct – mid
Nov 46rm40⇌4🏻 🏨 P Lift sB451 – 495
sB⇌🏻495 – 607 dB⇌🏻556 – 666
(English breakfast) L120 – 150 D140 – 150 ✆ Pool
mountains
★★**Schneider** ☎601 ta Almhof Closed May – Nov
70rm66⇌ 🏨 P Lift sB820 – 1050 sB⇌🏻1000 – 1180
dB⇌🏻1180 – 1500 (English breakfast) L fr160
D fr280 ✆ mountains
★★*Tannbergerhof* (DP) ☎202 tx5239117 Closed
18 Apr – 14 Jun & Oct – 26Nov 32rm26⇌6🏻 🏨 Lift
LEIBNITZ Steiermark (☎03452) Map **14** C1
☆☆*ATS* ☎2163 tx34430 55rm5⇌50🏻 Lift

Austria

LEOBEN Steiermark 37,800 (☎03842) Map **14** C2
★★**Baumann** F-Josefstr 10 ☎2565 tx33402
90rm19⇄26🕭 🏠 P Lift ♪ sB140–246
sB⇄🍴346–456 dB260–370 dB⇄🍴550–670 L fr70
D fr70
　🍴 🅿 **J Puntinger** Kerpelyster 14 ☎2206 M/c P Fia
　🍴 **J Wiedner** Kärntnerstr 130 ☎4896 M/c P Ren/Vlo

LEONDING See **LINZ AN DER DONAU**

LERMOOS Tirol (☎05673) Map **12** D2
★★★**Drei Mohren** (DP) ☎2362 tx5558 Closed 3
Nov–16 Dec 50rm36⇄5🍴 🏠 Lift
★★**Post** ☎2281 Closed Nov–19 Dec 60rm30⇄ 🏠 P
sB204–234 sB⇄254–284 dB194–224
dB⇄234–274 Pool mountains
★**Loisach** ☎2394 Closed Nov 47rm24⇄18🍴 🏠 P
Lift sB240–280 sB⇄🍴285–325 dB250–290
dB⇄🍴295–335 L50–100alc D50–100alc
mountains lake

LEUTASCH WEIDACH Tirol 1,500 (☎05214)
Map **12** D2
★**Waldheim** ☎288 14rm7⇄

LIENZ Tirol 12,500 (☎04852) Map **13** B1
★★★**Traube** Hauptpl 14 ☎2551 tx4618 Closed
Nov–14 Dec 55⇄🍴 🏠 P Lift ♪ sB⇄🍴370–420
dB⇄🍴770 (English breakfast) L120 D150 mountains
★★**Glocknerhof** Schillerstr 4 ☎2167 18rm3⇄7🍴
P ♪ sB140–157 dB280–314 dB⇄🍴340–374
(English breakfast) Pool mountains
★★**Post** Südtirolerpl 7 ☎2505 26rm2⇄7🍴 P ♪
sB205–245 sB⇄🍴255–305 dB350–430
dB⇄🍴450–550 L80–90 D80–90 mountains
★★**Sonne** ☎3311 tx4661 Closed 16 Oct–14 Dec
57rm41⇄9🍴 🏠 P Lift ♪ sB380–440
sB⇄🍴440–500 dB420–490 dB⇄🍴480–550
L95–110 D110–130 mountains
★★**Tyrol** ☎3482 35rm10⇄25🍴 A30rm 🏠 P
sB⇄🍴120–140 dB⇄🍴220–280 (English breakfast)
L50–70 D50–70 Pool mountains
　🍴 🅿 **E Plössnig** Stadion ☎3110 Ren
　🍴 🅿 **W Rogen** Kärntnerstr 36 ☎2335 Opl (GB)
　🅿 **J Thum** Industriestr ☎3935 ☎3335 M/c P
AR/Chy/Sim
　🅿 **G Troger** Dr-K-Rennerstr 12 ☎3411 ☎3057 &
2026 Frd (GB)

LIEZEN Steiermark 6,110 (☎03612) Map **14** C2
★★**Karow** Bahnhofstr 4 ☎2381 33rm9⇄1🍴 🏠 P
sB135–200 dB270–300 dB⇄🍴370–400
(English breakfast) L70–100 D50–100 mountains
　🍴 🅿 **A Böhm** Ausseerstr 29 ☎2330 M/c P AR/Ren
　🍴 🅿 **T Manner** Salzburgerstr 30 ☎2313 Fia/Lnc/MB

LINZ AN DER DONAU Oberösterreich 206,000
(☎07222) Map **14** C3
☆☆☆**EuroCrest** Wankmüllerhofstr 39 ☎42361
tx12/1795 105rm61⇄44🍴 🏠 Lift
★★**Oberdorfer** Schubertstr 1 (n rest) ☎27555
22rm3⇄
★★**Schwechaterhof** Landstr 18 ☎72255 36rm12⇄
P Lift ♪ sB190–205 sB⇄300–350 dB345–365
dB⇄435–530 L65 D65
★★**Wolfinger** Hauptpl 19 ☎23401 25rm9⇄ 🏠 Lift
　🍴 **M Eibl** Friedhofstr 30 ☎58300 P Maz
　🍴 🅿 **H Günther** Hamerlingstr 13 ☎55025 M/c Opl
　🍴 🅿 **A Jetzinger** Schiffbaustr 16 ☎78225 Closed
weekends Vau
　🍴 🅿 **H Mayer** Industriezelle 72 ☎79161 Aud/VW

At **Leonding** (5km SW)
　🍴 🅿 **G Schoeller** Kremstal Bundesstr ☎55586 P
Ren
　🍴 🅿 **Seidl-Weibold** Kremstal Bundesstr ☎55360
M/c BL/Jag/Tri

LOFER Salzburg 1,500 (☎06248) Map **13** B2
★★**Brau** ☎207 tx63745 Closed Nov–Apr 25rm6⇄
🏠 P sB150–160 dB260–330 dB⇄🍴380–440 (English
Breakfast) L65–80 D65–80 mountains
★★**Post** ☎303 tx63745 38rm14⇄9🍴 🏠 P
sB160–170 sB⇄🍴230–270 dB260–330
dB⇄🍴400–460 L65–80 D65–80 mountains

★★**St-Hubertus** 26rm4⇄ 🏠

MALLNITZ Kärnten 1,200 (☎04784) Map **13** B1
★★**Alpen** ☎262 Closed 1–24 May & Nov–19 Dec
60rm26⇄8🍴 A25rm 🏠 Lift

MARIA WÖRTH Kärnten 1,000 (☎04273)
Map **14** C1
★★★**Linde** ☎2278 50rm36⇄11🍴 🏠 Lift Pool lake
★★**Ebner** ☎2283 86rm21⇄12🍴 🏠 Pool

MAYRHOFEN Tirol 2,600 (☎05285) Map **13** A2
★**Strass** Hauptstr 198 ☎205 66rm12⇄3🍴 A24rm 🏠
Lift

MILLSTATT Kärnten 1,400 (☎04766) Map **13** B1
★★**Forelle** ☎2050 Closed 16 Oct–Apr 55rm32⇄5🍴
P Lift ♪ sB162–220 sB⇄🍴294–385 dB282–440
dB⇄🍴474–798 L70–130 D95–130 ⚓ Pool
mountains lake

At **Dellach/Millstätter See** (5km SE)
★★**Harring** (DP & Pn) ☎2507 30rm7⇄20🍴 A15rm P
sB⇄210–420 dB⇄🍴420–840 D70–90
mountains lake

MONDSEE Oberösterreich 2,100 (☎06224)
Map **13** B2
☆☆☆**Euromotel Mondsee** Innerschwand 150
☎(06232)2876 tx63357 46rm⇄ P Lift ♪ sB⇄fr285
dB⇄fr495 (English breakfast) Lfr75 Dfr75 mountains
lake
★**Leitnerbräu** Marketpl 9 ☎(06232)2219
17rm1⇄4🍴 A30rm P sBfr137 sB⇄fr187 dBfr166 dBfr274
dB⇄🍴fr332 L65–100 D50–100 mountains
　🅿 **W Berger** Poststr 2–4 ☎2303 Opl/Vau
　🍴 🅿 **M Widlroither** Südtirolerstr ☎(06232)2612 M/c
BL/Toy

MUTTERS Tirol 1,350 (☎05222) Map **12** D2
★★**Berktold** ☎25021 21rm9⇄ 🏠 P ♪ sBfr205
sB⇄fr245 dB370 dB⇄430 L90–110 D90–110 St%
mountains
★**Muttererhof** ☎27491 Closed May–15 Dec
24rm11⇄ 🏠 P sB160–180 dB320–360
dB⇄400–440 L160–200 D80–100 mountains

NATTERS Tirol 1,020 (☎05222) Map **12** D2
★**Eichhof** ☎266555 Closed Nov–Apr 20rm P
sB100–120 dB200–220 (English breakfast) L50–70
D50–70 mountains
★**Steffi** ☎29402 Closed 16 Sep–14 Jun 12rm1⇄6🍴
P sB130 sB⇄🍴145 dB240 dB⇄🍴270 mountains

NAUDERS Tirol 1,200 (☎05473) Map **12** D1
★**Sporthotel** ☎236 Closed Nov–14 Dec
70rm30⇄5🍴 🏠 Lift Pool
★**Hochland** ☎272 Closed 16 Apr–May & Oct–
14 Dec 20rm6⇄21🍴 A10rm P sB160–180
sB⇄200–220 dB280–320 dB⇄🍴370–400
(English breakfast) L65–90 D65–90 mountains
★**Post** ☎202 Closed 17 Apr–May & Oct–16 Dec
42rm4⇄11🍴 A34rm 🏠 P sB150–200
sB⇄🍴180–250 dB260–320 dB⇄🍴320–420
(English breakfast) L65–105 D65–105 mountains
★**Verzasca** (n rest) ☎237 Closed 23Apr–May &
Oct–14 Dec 20rm1⇄5🍴 🏠 P sB140–210
sB⇄🍴190–260 dB180–300 dB⇄🍴280–440
mountains

NEUMARKT Steiermark 1,871 (☎03584) Map **14** C2
★★**Gasthof Strimitzhof** ☎2106 18rm4⇄ 🏠

NEUMARKT AM WALLERSEE Salzburg 1,880
(☎06216) Map **13** B2
★**Lauterbacher** ☎456 Closed Jan & Feb
15rm8⇄7🍴 🏠 P sB130–150 dB⇄🍴220–250 lake
　🍴 🅿 **Poller** Haupestr 12 ☎207 M/c P Fia/Lnc

OBERGURGL Tirol 300 (☎05256) Map **12** D1
★★★**Edelweiss & Gurgl** ☎223 100rm45⇄15🍴 🏠
Lift

OBERTAUERN Salzburg 180 (☎06466) Map **13** B2
★★★**Schütz** ☎204 Closed 25 Apr–14 Dec
38rm4⇄34🍴 🏠 P ♪ sB⇄🍴291–435
dB⇄🍴582–870 (English breakfast) mountains
★★**Pohl** ☎209 Closed 23 Apr–14 Jun & 16 Sep–
24 Nov 18rm8🍴 P sB320–340 sB🍴340–370

dB460–560 dB 490–920 (English breakfast)
L70–90 D70–90 mountains

ÖETZ Tirol 1,549 (☎05252) Map **12** D2
★★**Alpen** ☎6232 Closed Nov 49rm25⇌7 P Lift
sB125–255 sB⇌ 265–295 dB240–270
dB⇌ 280–310 (English breakfast) L70–90
D70–90 mountains
★★**Drei Mohren** Hauptstr ☎6301 30rm10⇌12
P sB185–215 sB⇌ 215–285 dB370–430
dB⇌ 430–570 (English breakfast) L88–130
D88–150 ● mountains
PARTENEN Vorarlberg 610 (☎05558) Map **12** C1
★★★**Silvrettasee** ☎246 tx52245 Closed 26
Apr–May & 16 Oct–14 Dec 60rm11⇌20 P Lift
sBfr219 sB⇌ fr276 dBfr314 dB⇌ fr506
(English breakfast) L65–170 D100–170 mountains
PATSCH Tirol 670 (☎05474) Map **12** D1
★★*Grünwalderhof* ☎7304 Closed 16 Mar–14 May
& Oct–14 Dec 30rm16⇌ ● Pool
PERTISAU AM ACHENSEE Tirol 1,300 (☎05243)
Map **13** A2
★★**Kristall** (Pn) ☎5490 tx53440 37rm7⇌18 P
sB285–375 dB240–350 dB⇌ 300–420 mountains
★★**Pfandler** ☎5223 Closed 16 Oct–14 Dec
53rm40⇌14 P Lift mountains lake
PFUNDS-STUBEN Tirol 1,852 (☎05474) Map **12** D1
★★**Post** ☎202 tx58172 Closed Nov–15 Dec
111rm93⇌ P Lift ♪ sB190–240 sB⇌ 220–280
dB160–210 dB⇌ 190–240 Pool mountains
PICHL-AUHOF AM MONDSEE Oberösterreich 850
(☎06224) Map **13** B2
★★**Seehof am Mondsee** ☎2550 tx63670 Closed
Oct–Apr 23rm20⇌1 A6rm P sB240–280
sB⇌ 260–450 dB460–540 dB⇌ 480–1.200
(English breakfast) L60–100 D100–150 ●
mountains lake
PÖRTSCHACH AM WÖRTHERSEE Kärnten 2,700
(☎04272) Map **14** C1
★★★★*Park* ☎2621 tx42344 Closed 11 Oct–Apr
150⇌ Lift ● lake
★★★**Schloss Leonstein** ☎2816 tx442019 Closed
21 Oct–11 May 44rm29⇌6 P ♪ sB280–370
sB⇌ 300–495 dB250–325 dB⇌ 310–510
L100–130 D120–150 ● ○ mountains lake
★★★**Sonnengrund** Annastr 9 (Pn) ☎2343 Closed
11 Oct–19 Apr 45rm21⇌20 P Lift sB300–460
sB⇌ 300–580 dB600–920 dB⇌ 600–1160
L fr100 d fr100 Pool mountains lake
★★**Schloss Seefels** ☎2377 tx42153 Closed
Nov–22 Mar 75rm61⇌6 A39rm P ♪
sB350–560 sB⇌ 470–920 dB420–630
dB⇌ 480–4140 (English breakfast) L80–150 D150
● Pool mountains lake
★★**Werzer Astoria** Bundesstr 1 ☎2231 Closed
Oct–4 May 175rm59⇌17 A6rm P Lift ♪
sB175–275 sB⇌ 285–345 dB350–550
dB⇌ 535–655 L fr80 D fr95 Pool lake
RADENTHEIN Kärnten (☎04246) Map **13** B1
★★**Metzgerwirt** ☎2052 19 P sB 220–260
(room only) dB 370–400 (room only) Pool
mountains
 W Flath Millstatterstr 30 ☎351 ☎344 M/c P
Opl/Toy
 G Tusch Schattseite 101 ☎389 M/c Ren
RADSTADT Salzburg 3,500 (☎06465) Map **13** B2
 W Pfleger ☎312 Frd (GB)
RAMSAU AM DACHSTEIN Steiermark (☎03687)
Map **13** B2
 K Knaus Hauptstr 49 ☎2941 BMW/Opl/Vau/Vlo
RANKWEIL Vorarlberg 8,500 (☎05522) Map **12** C2
★*Rankweiler Hof* ☎44113 8rm
RAURIS Salzburg (☎06544) Map **13** B2
★★*Rauriserhof* (DP) ☎213 94rm23⇌33 A90rm
Lift Pool
REUTTE Tirol 4,500 (☎05672) Map **12** D2
★★**Hahnenkamm** ☎2595 25rm20⇌5 Pool
★★**Tirolerhof** Bahnhofstr 16 ☎2557 Closed 21
Jan–Mar 40rm3⇌9 P sB175–205

sB⇌ 205–255 dB370–420 dB⇌ 430–490
(English breakfast) L65–150 D65–150 mountains
 J Breschjak Innsbruckerstr 18–27 ☎2627
☎2472 M/c P BL/BMW/Cit/Fia/Sab/Ska/Vlo
 K-Hiebl Lindenstr 3 ☎2385 ☎2385 P MB (GB)
 Schlaffer Allgäuerstr 68 ☎2622 M/c P Cit/Frd
(GB)

RIED Tirol 700 (☎05472) Map **12** D1
★*Post* ☎274 Closed 16 Oct–14 May 14rm

SAALBACH Salzburg 1,800 (☎06586) Map **13** B2
★★★**Kendler** (DP) ☎225 Closed May & 19 Sep–
17 Dec 43rm15⇌12 Pool
★★**Berger's Sporthotel** (DP & Pn) ☎577 tx6668515
Closed Oct–Nov 55rm40⇌15 P Lift ♪
sB210–440 sB⇌ 240–660 dB420–880
dB⇌ 480–1320 (English breakfast) L70–110
D70–110 mountains
★★*Reiterhof* ☎257 Closed 11 Apr–19 Dec
26rm4⇌5
★★**Saalbacherhof** ☎7111 tx68513 Closed
Oct–Nov 100rm80⇌20 P Lift ♪
sB⇌ 445–665 dB⇌ 440–660 (English breakfast)
L100–140 D105–140 ● Pool mountains
SAALFELDEN Salzburg 10,450 (☎06582)
Map **13** B2
★★**Dick** Bahnhofstr 106 ☎2215 30rm14⇌8 P
sB190–240 sB⇌ 250–300 dB360–400
dB⇌ 460–540 (English breakfast) L70–110
D80–120 Pool mountains
★★*Oberbräu* ☎2442 20rm4⇌
 Rieger Bundesstr 64 ☎2031 M/c P Frd/Jag/MB
(GB)

ST ANTON AM ARLBERG Tirol 1,980
★★★**Mooserkreuz** ☎2230 Closed 16 Apr–May, Oct
& Nov 40rm25⇌15 P Lift sB⇌ 270–600
dB260–600 dB⇌ 200–500 L100–150 D100–150
Pool mountains
★★★**Post & Alte Post** ☎2214 tx17512 Closed Oct &
Nov 108rm68⇌ P Lift ♪ sB160–180
sB⇌ 260–280 dB320–360 dB⇌ 520–560
(English breakfast) L110–130 D110–130 mountains
★★*Alpenhof* ☎2495 Closed 11 Apr–May &
Oct–Nov 32rm15⇌2
★★*Arlberg* Hauptstr ☎2210 Closed 16 Sep–May
60rm45⇌ Lift ●
★★**Montjola** ☎2302 Closed 16 Apr–Nov
18rm9⇌2 A9rm P sB330 dB540 dB⇌ 660
(English breakfast) L100 D100
★ *Alpenheim* ☎2389 Closed Oct–Nov 28rm14
★*Bergheim* ☎2255 Closed May–19 Jun & 16
Sep–Nov 30rm16⇌1
 Tyrol (H Schulter) ☎2353 N P (GB)
ST CHRISTOPH AM ARLBERG Tirol (☎05446)
Map **12** C1/2
★★★**Hospiz** (DP & Pn) ☎2611 tx5817515 Closed
May & Oct 100rm80⇌ P Lift sB⇌ fr288 sB⇌ fr328
dB fr576 dB⇌ fr656 L fr78 D fr90 ● Pool mountains

ST GILGEN AM WOLFGANGSEE Salzburg 2,620
(☎06227) Map **13** B2
★★★**Parkhotel Billroth** ☎217 Closed 21 Sep–
14 May 47rm30⇌5 P Lift sB235–325
sB⇌ 235–385 dB470–650 dB⇌ 650–770
(English breakfast) L200–240 D100–120 St% ●
mountains lake
★★**Alpenland am See** (n rest) ☎330 Closed
11 Sep–Jun 17rm1⇌4 P ♪ sB110 sB⇌ 140
dB200–260 dB⇌ 280–340 (English breakfast)
mountains lake
★★**Hollweger** ☎226 Closed Nov–14
Dec29rm18⇌7 P sB203–228 sB⇌ 238–268
dB176–271 dB⇌ 231–316 L fr80 D fr80 mountains
lake
★★**Post** ☎239 Closed Oct 48rm9⇌2 P
sB144.50–169 sB⇌ 231–256 dB289–338
dB⇌ 461–512 Pool mountains
★★**Radetzky** Streicherpl 1 ☎232 Closed 16 Oct–14
Dec & 16 Jan–Apr 45rm25⇌ P sB176.50 dB340
dB⇌ 375–394 L80–90 D80–90 mountains lake

Austria

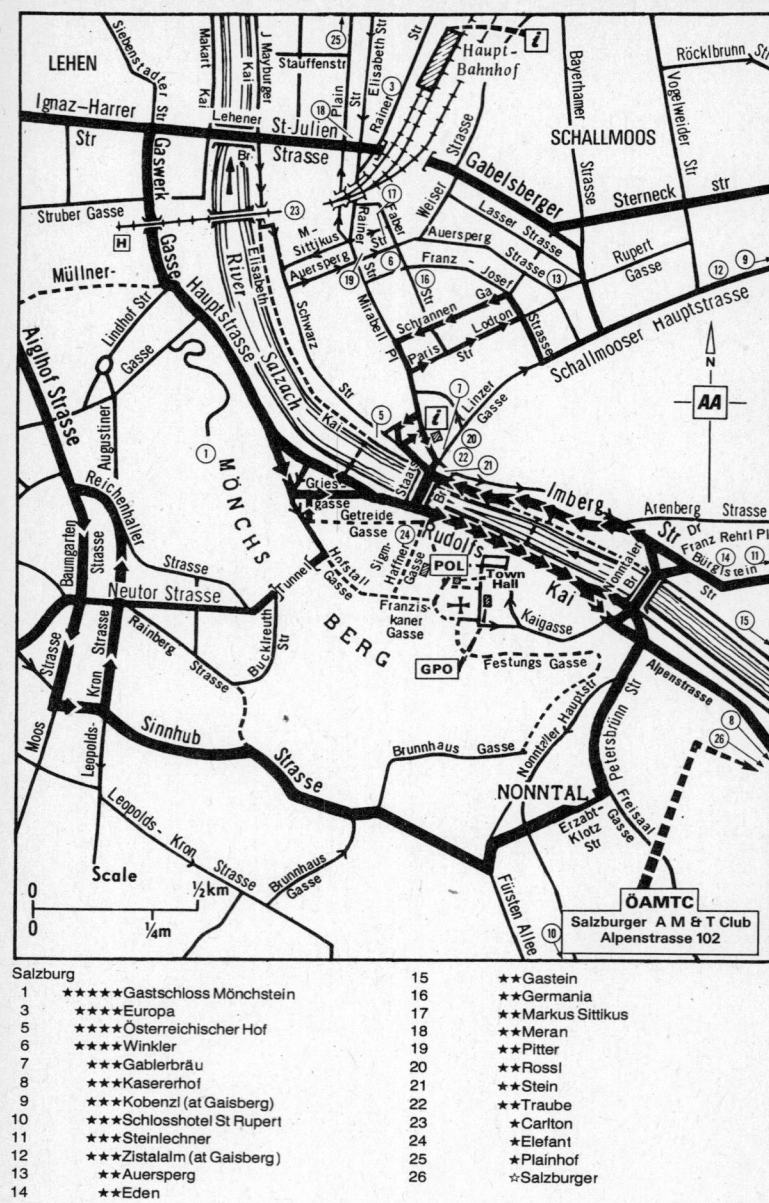

Salzburg

1	★★★★★Gastschloss Mönchstein	15	★★Gastein
3	★★★★Europa	16	★★Germania
5	★★★★Österreichischer Hof	17	★★Markus Sittikus
6	★★★★Winkler	18	★★Meran
7	★★★Gablerbräu	19	★★Pitter
8	★★★Kasererhof	20	★★Rossl
9	★★★Kobenzl (at Gaisberg)	21	★★Stein
10	★★★Schlosshotel St Rupert	22	★★Traube
11	★★★Steinlechner	23	★Carlton
12	★★★Zistalalm (at Gaisberg)	24	★Elefant
13	★★Auersperg	25	★Plainhof
14	★★Eden	26	☆Salzburger

★**Mozartblick** (n rest) ☎403 23rm4⇆16🏠 A10rm 🏠
P sB95–120 dB190–240 dB210–260 mountains
lake
ST JOHANN IM PONGAU Salzburg 6,670 (☎06412)
Map **13** B2
★**Prem** ☎207 52rm14⇆2🏠 🏠
ST JOHANN IN TIROL Tirol 5,300 (☎05352)
Map **13** A2
★★★**Sporthotel Austria** Speckbacherstr 57 (DP)
☎2507 Closed Apr–14 May & Oct–14 Dec
50rm40⇆ 🏠 Lift Pool
★★**Kaiserhof** ☎2545 Closed Oct–14 Dec 40rm15⇆
🏠 P Lift sB235–275 sB⇆275–315

dB430–510 dB⇆570–670 (English breakfast)
L70–100 D70–100 mountains
🍴 **E Foidl** Pass-Thurnstr 11 ☎2129 BL/Dat/Jag
Rov/Tri

ST OSWALD BEI FREISTADT Oberösterreich
(☎07945)Map **14** C3
🍴 **H Reindl** ☎225 P Bed/Vau

ST-POLTEN Niederösterreich 40,000 (☎02742)
Map **14** C3
★★**Pittner** Kremsergasse 18 ☎2006 77rm17⇆1🏠 P
Lift ♪ sB210–330 sB⇆🏠330–390 dB380–510
dB⇆🏠510–580 (English breakfast) L70 D25–100

Auto-Dinstl Stifterstr ☎2644 P Cit
⏢ ⬩⬩ **W Denzel** Linzerstr 52 ☎63281 M/c BMW/Vlo
⬩⬩*Huber* Mariazellerstr 85 ☎7566 Aud/VW
⏢ ⬩⬩*F Lutzenberger* Kremserlandstr 8 ☎2475 M/c P
Dat/Sab/Ska/Toy

ST WOLFGANG AM WOLFGANGSEE
Oberösterreich 2,200 (☎06138) Map **13** B2
★★★**Weisses Rössl** ☎358 tx68148 Closed
Dec–Feb 65rm32⇌8🏠 A15rm 🏠 P Lift 𝄞
sB170–360 sB⇌🏠310–480 dB320–560
dB⇌🏠480–860 (English breakfast) L190 D110 ⬩
Pool mountains lake
★★**Appesbach** ☎209 Closed Oct–Mar 15rm7⇌3🏠
P sB130–180 sB⇌🏠260–320 dB115–180
dB⇌🏠190–300 ⬩ mountains lake
★★**Post & Schloss Eibenstein** ☎346 Closed
Nov–mid Apr 155rm48⇌17🏠 P Lift sB170–210
sB⇌🏠195–235 dB300–380 dB⇌🏠370–450 L70
D50 Pool mountains lake

SALZBURG Salzburg 130,000 (☎06222) Map **13** B2
See Plan
★★★★★**Gastschloss Mönchstein** Mönchsberg 26
☎41363 Plan **1** Closed 16 Oct–14 Mar 11rm10⇌1🏠
A3rm 🏠 P Lift 𝄞 sB⇌🏠800–1500 ⬩
★★★**Europa** Rainerstr 31 ☎73391 tx63424 Plan **3**
104rm65⇌39🏠 P Lift 𝄞 sB⇌🏠455–565
dB⇌🏠840–1090 (English breakfast) L110 D110
★★★**Österreichischer Hof** Schwarzstr 5–7
☎72541 Plan **5** 130⇌ 🏠 P Lift sB⇌405–705
dB⇌640–1400 (English breakfast) L195 D195
★★★★**Winkler** F-Josefstr 7–9 (n rest) ☎73513
tx63961 Plan **6** 103⇌ sB⇌420–650 dB⇌670–1100
(English breakfast) St% ⬩ Pool ᐃ ᐯ mountains lake
★★★*Gablerbräu* Linzergasse 9 ☎73441 Plan **7**
62rm26⇌ Lift
★★★*Kasererhof* Alpenstr 6 ☎21265 tx63477 Plan **8**
54rm45⇌5🏠 🏠 P Lift 𝄞 sB450 sB⇌🏠700
dB⇌🏠1200 (English breakfast) L150 D150
mountains
★★★**Schlosshotel St Rupert** Morzgerstr 31
☎43231 Plan **10** Closed Nov–Mar 30rm24⇌1🏠 🏠
P 𝄞 sB560–660 sB⇌🏠660–760 dB680–800
dB⇌🏠960–1280 (English breakfast) L fr210
mountains
★★★**Steinlechner** Aignerstr 14 ☎20061 Plan **11**
31rm15⇌ P 𝄞 sB180–230 sB⇌230–250
dB360–460 dB⇌460–500 L70–80 D70–80
★★**Auersperg** Auerspergstr 61 ☎71757 tx63817
Plan **13** 65rm24⇌28🏠 🏠 P Lift 𝄞 sB310–350
sB⇌🏠330–435 dB600–620 dB⇌🏠680–790
L fr170 D fr85
★★*Eden* Gaisbergstr 38 ☎20118 Plan **14** 12⇌10🏠
A3rm 🏠
★★**Gastein** Ignaz-Rieder-Kai 25 (n rest) ☎22565
Plan **15** 13⇌ 🏠 P 𝄞 sB⇌300–600 dB⇌500–1200
mountains
★★**Germania** Faberstr 10 ☎71200 Plan **16** 35rm6⇌
Lift
★★**Markus Sittikus** M.-Sittikusstr 20 (n rest)
☎71121 Plan **17** 40rm11⇌18🏠 P Lift 𝄞 sB205–260
sB⇌🏠250–350 dB360–470 dB⇌🏠450–650
(English breakfast)
★★*Meran* Plainstr 14 ☎72214 Plan **18** 56rm7⇌ Lift
★★*Pitter* Rainerstr 6–8 ☎78571 tx63532 Plan **19**
210rm90⇌40🏠 P Lift 𝄞 sB280–350
sB⇌🏠340–500 dB540–640 dB⇌🏠600–960
(English breakfast) L110–120 D110–120 mountains
★★*Rössl* Priesterhausgasse 6 ☎74426 tx 74832
Plan **20** Closed Oct–Jun 55rm7⇌ Lift
★★**Stein** Staatsbrücke ☎74346 Plan **21** Closed
Nov–21 Dec 80rm41⇌ Lift 𝄞 sB250–290
sB⇌🏠300–390 dB440–520 dB⇌🏠540–660 L100
D100
★★**Traube** Linzergasse 4 ☎74063 Plan **22** Closed
Nov–Mar 50rm11⇌9🏠 P Lift 𝄞 sB200–250
sB⇌🏠250–300 dB390–440 dB⇌🏠450–580
★*Carlton* M-Sittikus Str 3 ☎74343 Plan **23** Closed 21
Dec–6Jan 47rm6⇌5🏠 🏠 Lift Pool

★*Elefant* S-Haffner Gasse 4 ☎43397 Plan **24**
39rm12⇌3🏠 Lift
★*Plainhof* Plainstr 55 (n rest) ☎72181 Plan **25**
32rm3⇌2🏠 🏠
☆*Salzburger* Alpenstr 48 & Friedensstr 6 (n rest)
☎20871 Plan **26** Closed 25 Dec–Jan 27rm13🏠 🏠 P
𝄞 sB150–160 dB260–280 dB🏠300–320
mountains
⏢ ⬩⬩**Eibl** Linzer Bundestr 39 ☎78435 BL (GB)
⏢ ⬩⬩**Intermotor Handelsgembh** Imbergstr 23
☎77151 Dat/Sab/Ska (GB)
⏢ ⬩⬩**Öfag** Innsbrucker Bundesstr 128 ☎44501
Bed/Opl/Vau (GB)
⏢ ⬩⬩**G Pappas** Siebenstädterstr 46 ☎31531 ⬩ MB
(GB)
⏢ ⬩⬩*Pletzer* Schallmooser Hauptstr 52 ☎795270 P
Fia/Ren
⏢ ⬩⬩**Porsche-Inter Auto** Alpenstr 175 ☎20911
☎72581 P Aud/Por/VW (GB)
⏢ ⬩⬩**Porsche-Inter Auto** Sterneckstr 17 ☎75230
☎72581 P Aud/Por/VW (GB)
⬩⬩**E Scheidinger** Schallmooser Hauptstr 24 ☎71176
P Frd (GB)
SCHLADMING Steiermark 3,300 (☎03687)
Map **13** B2
★★*Alte Post* ☎2571 45rm15⇌5🏠 🏠
SCHÖNBERG/STUBAI Tirol 590 (☎05225)
Map **13** A2
★★*Jägerhof* ☎2560 Closed 11 Oct–19 Dec
90rm30⇌30🏠 A71rm 🏠 Lift ⬩
SCHRUNS Vorarlberg 2,340 (☎05556) Map **12** C1
⬩⬩*R Lins* Silvrettastr ☎2540 MG
SCHUTTDORF See **ZELL AM SEE**
SEEBODEN Kärnten 3,324 (☎04762) Map **13** B1
★★★★**Royal Hotel Seehof** ☎81714 tx48122 Closed
11 Oct–Mar 95rm90⇌5🏠 🏠 P Lift 𝄞
sB⇌🏠400–610 dB⇌🏠600–920 L80–100
D80–100 ⬩ Pool mountains lake
★★*Seehotel Steiner* (DP) ☎81713 Closed 6
Oct–mid Apr 50rm 🏠 Pool lake
SEEFELD Tirol 2,050 (☎05212) Map **12** D2
★★★★**Astoria** ☎2272 tx385523 Closed early
Oct–16 Jun 60rm51⇌1🏠 P Lift 𝄞 sB⇌🏠360–365
sB⇌🏠490–590 dB fr295 dB⇌🏠425–570 L150
D160 Pool mountains
★★★★*Eden* Münchnerstr 136 ☎2258 tx53885511
Closed Apr & 21 Sep–Nov 51⇌ 🏠 Lift ⬩
★★★*Dreitorspitze* Speckbacherstr 182 ☎2951
tx5385525 Closed 26 Sep–14 Jun 53rm17⇌16🏠 🏠
Lift Pool
★★★**Gartenhotel Tümmlerhof** ☎2571 Closed Nov
74rm63⇌1🏠 🏠 P Lift 𝄞 sB280–360
sB⇌🏠400–580 dB560–640 dB⇌🏠700–1160
L120–150 D120–160 mountains
★★★**Karwendelhof** Bahnhofstr ☎2655 tx5385513
Closed Apr–19 Dec 53rm40⇌1🏠 mountains
★★★*Klosterbräu* (Pn) ☎2621 tx5385517 Closed
Apr–May & Oct–Nov 106rm50⇌18🏠 A53rm 🏠 Lift
Pool
★★★*Philipp* Münchnerstr 68 ☎2301 Closed Apr &
Oct & Nov 60rm15⇌45🏠 🏠 Lift
★★★*Schlosshotel* ☎2658 tx5385513 Closed
Apr–May & Oct 18 Dec 21rm17⇌ 🏠 Lift
★★*Kurhotel* ☎2671 Closed Oct–14 Dec 52rm35⇌
🏠 P Lift 𝄞 sB230–280 sB⇌310–380 dB310–380
dB⇌410–480 (English breakfast) L90–120
D90–120 Pool mountains
★★*Regina* Claudiastr 171 ☎2270 Closed
26 Sep–9 Jun 28rm6⇌2🏠 🏠 P (English breakfast)
L80–100 D80–100 mountains
SEMMERING Niederösterreich 1,400 (☎02664)
Map **14** D2
★★★*Silvana* ☎309 25⇌ Lift
★★*Südbahn* ☎455 114rm40⇌ 🏠 Lift ⬩ Pool
SERFAUS Tirol 800 (☎05476) Map **12** D1
★★*Maximilian* ☎255 Closed Oct–10 Jun 30⇌ 🏠
Lift
★*Furgler* ☎201 Closed 16 Oct–Nov &
29 Apr–14May 42rm40⇌2🏠 🏠 P Lift

sB⇌ ⋔300–530 dB⇌ ⋔300–530 (English breakfast) D100–120 mountains
SILLIAN Tirol 2,000 (☎04856) Map **13** A1
★***Post*** ☎273 60rm10⇌10⋔ ⌂
SÖLDEN Tirol 1,900 (☎05254) Map **12** D1
★★***Hochsölden*** (Pn) ☎2229 Closed May–Nov 90rm70⇌ ⌂ Lift
SPITTAL AN DER DRAU Kärnten 12,300 (☎04762) Map **13** B1
★★★**Salzburg** Tirolerstr 12 ☎3165 55rm16⇌11⋔ A26rm ⌂ P ☽ sB fr170 sB⇌ ⋔ fr280 dB fr300 dB⇌ ⋔ fr500 (English breakfast) L70 D alc mountains
∞**Auto Nowak** Villacherstr 72 ☎3447 M/c P BMW/Peu/Vlo (GB)
»**W Riebler** Koschatstr 13 ☎2561 ☎2561 P Frd (GB)
STAINACH Steiermark (☎03684) Map **13** B2
⊡ ∞**W Denzel** ☎2304 M/c P BMW/Vlo
STEINACH AM BRENNER Tirol 2,560 (☎05272) Map **13** A1/2
★★**Steinacherhof** ☎6241 Closed 16 Oct–17 Dec 64rm51⇌8⋔ ⌂ P Lift ☽ sB⇌ ⋔310–370 dB400–520 dB⇌ ⋔520–640 (English breakfast) L80–105 D80–105 ↗ Pool mountains
★★**Wilder Mann** ☎6210 tx53245 Closed 5 Oct–19 Dec 62rm32⇌4⋔ A8rm ⌂ P Lift sB fr180 sB⇌ ⋔fr220 dB fr340 dB⇌ ⋔fr400 (English breakfast) L fr75 D fr75 mountains
★**Weisses Rössl** ☎6206 Closed Nov–14 Dec 45rm15⇌17⋔ A29rm ⌂ P Lift sB160–170 sB⇌ ⋔210–220 dB280–290 dB⇌ ⋔380–390 (English breakfast) L70 D70 Pool mountains
STEYR Oberösterreich 41,200 (☎07252) Map **14** C3
★★***Minichmayr*** Haratzmüllerstr 1 ☎3419 tx28134 45rm15⇌5⋔
⊡ ∞**F Hilbert** Madlsederstr 1 ☎63460 M/c P Frd/Vau (GB)
STUBEN Vorarlberg 700 (☎05582) Map **12** C1/2
★★**Post** ☎84516 51rm21⇌14⋔ ⌂ P sB125–155 sB⇌ ⋔ 155–190 dB220–260 dB⇌ ⋔300–335 mountains
TELFS Tirol 5,800 (☎05262) Map **12** D2
★***Hohe Munde*** Untermarkstr 17 ☎2408 23rm5⇌8⋔ ⌂
⊡ » ***H Harting*** Bundesstr 1 ☎2854 P Aud/MB/VW
THIERSEE Tirol 1,800 (☎05376) Map **13** A2
★★**Haus Charlotte** ☎207 45rm12⇌11⋔ ⌂ P Lift sB200–250 sB⇌ ⋔300 dB370–410 dB⇌ ⋔480–520 L88–120 D88–120 Pool mountains lake
⊡ ∞***KFZ Service*** (S Mairhofer) ☎255 Ren
THUMERSBACH See **ZELL AM SEE**
TRAUNKIRCHEN AM TRAUNSEE Oberösterreich 1,600 (☎07617) Map **13** B2
★★***Post*** ☎307 65⇌ Lift lake
TURRACHER-HÖHE Kärnten (☎04275) Map **13** B1
★★**Hochschober** ☎8213 tx42152 Closed Nov & May 72rm ⌂ P sB fr270 dB fr648 (English breakfast) L160 D80 ↗ Pool lake
VELDEN AM WÖRTHERSEE Kärnten 3,200 (☎04274) Map **14** C1
★★★**Schloss Velden** am Corso 24 ☎2655 Closed 26 Sep–14 may 160rm100⇌ A60rm ⌂ P ☽ sB240–410 sB⇌340–640 dB400–680 dB⇌520–920 (English breakfast) L100 D100 ↗ Pool mountains lake
★★★**Seehotel Europa** Wrannpark 1 (DP) ☎2770 tx4294522 Closed Oct–9 May 70rm48⇌10⋔ A18rm P Lift ☽ sB280–400 sB⇌ ⋔350–530 dB500–740 dB⇌ ⋔700–1020 D100–130 ↗ mountains lake
★★★**Seehotel Veldnerhof–Mösslacher** am Corso 17 ☎2018 180rm35⇌33⋔ P Lift ☽ sB198–338 sB⇌ ⋔248–478 dB376–626 dB⇌ ⋔456–796 (English breakfast) L80–95 D80–95 ↗ lake
★★**Seehotel Hubertushof** ☎2676 Closed 16 Oct–14 Mar 55rm18⇌23⋔ A38rm P sB180–265 sB⇌ ⋔230–370 dB160–265 dB⇌ ⋔180–370 Pool lake
★★**Wrann** Europapl 4 (DP&Pn) ☎2021 tx4294522 Closed Oct–Apr 43rm5⇌15⋔ ⌂ P sB210–290 sB⇌ ⋔280–350 dB280–360 dB⇌ ⋔350–420 (English breakfast) L70–90 D70–90 ↗ Pool mountains
⊡ ∞**O Matschnig** am Corso 18 ☎2067 M/c P Ren (GB)
VIENNA See **WIEN**
VILLACH Kärnten 34,000 (☎04242) Map **13** B1
★★★***Park*** Moritschstr 2 ☎23300 tx45582 170rm133⇌ ⌂ Lift
★★**Mosser** Bahnhofstr 7 ☎24115 30rm5⇌5⋔ P ☽ sB177–210 sB⇌ ⋔387–310 dB334–360 dB⇌ ⋔454–510 (English breakfast) L70–90 D70–90
★★***Post*** Hauptpl 26 ☎26101 tx45723 80rm31⇌1⋔ ⌂ Lift
⊡ ∞**FA Bruder Brodnik** Klagenfurterstr 37 ☎24388 Chy/Sim/Ska (GB)
⊡ »**H Gram** Tirolerstr 51 ☎24092 ☎24092 P Jag/Peu
⊡ ∞***W Lackner*** Siedlerstr 25 ☎24825 M/c P BL/Jag/Rov Tri
⊡ ∞**S Papp** Steinwenderstr 15 ☎24826 Frd (GB)
At **WARMBAD** (5km S)
★★★**Josefinenhof** ☎25531 tx45563 61rm42⇌8⋔ ⌂ P Lift ☽ sB320–370 sB⇌ ⋔390–650 dB520–560 dB⇌ ⋔700–1020 (English breakfast) L90–100 D90–100 ↗ Pool mountains
★★★**Kurhotel Warmbaderhof** ☎25501 tx45583 129rm104⇌20⋔ ⌂ P Lift ☽ sB⇌310–540 sB⋔310–690 sB⋔500–880 dB⋔500–1200 (English breakfast) L fr120 D fr120 ↗ Pool
VOLDERS Tirol (☎05224) Map **13** A2
⊡ ∞**H Federer** Fiegerstr 2 ☎2398 P Aud/Peu/VW
WAIDHOFEN-AN-DER-YBBS Niederösterreich (☎07442) Map **14** C2
∞***K Plank*** Weyrerstr 51A ☎2442 M/c P Opl
WAIDRING Tirol (☎05353) Map **13** B2
★★**Tiroler Adler** ☎311 Closed 26 Oct–Nov 33⇌ ⋔ ⌂ P Lift sB⇌ ⋔240–275 dB⇌ ⋔420–470 (English breakfast) L alc D40–180
WARMBAD See **VILLACH**
WEISSKIRCHEN IN STEIERMARK Steiermark (☎03577) Map **14** C2
»***R Kocher*** Bahnhofstr 21 ☎2567 Closed weekends P Bed/Cit/Vau
WELS Oberösterreich 48,160 (☎07242) Map **13** B3
★★★***Greif*** Kaiser Josef pl 50 ☎5361 tx25566 125rm40⇌ ⌂ Lift
★★**Parzer** Kaiser Josef pl 52 (n.rest) ☎6472 55rm5⇌6⋔ ⌂ P sB 155–183 sB⇌ ⋔205–233 dB 245–276 dB⇌ ⋔345–416 (English breakfast)
» **K Huber** Hamerlingstr 9 ☎7650 ☎3423 P BL/Peu/(GB)
WESTENDORF Tirol 2,350 (☎05334) Map **13** A2
★***Jakobwirt*** (DP) ☎6245 Closed Apr–9 May & Oct–19 Dec 60rm44⇌ Lift
WIEN (VIENNA) 1,649,000 Map **14** D3 **See Plan**
Bold Roman numbers after hotel addresses are district (Bezirk) numbers. Garages are listed below under Bezirk headings.
★★★★★**Ambassador** Neuer Markt 5 **I** ☎527511 tx1906 Plan **1** 105⇌ ⋔ P Lift ☽ sB⇌ ⋔690–850 dB⇌ ⋔1250–1620
★★★★★**Bristol** Kärntner Ring 1 **I** ☎529552 tx12474 Plan **2** 130rm126⇌4⋔ Lift ☽ sB⇌ ⋔700–1000 dB⇌ ⋔1000–1800 (English breakfast) L235–275 D235–275
★★★★★**Imperial** Kärntner Ring 16 **I** ☎651765 tx12630 Plan **3** 160rm150⇌10⋔ ⌂ Lift ☽ sB⇌ ⋔650–1050 dB⇌ ⋔1000–1800 (English breakfast)
★★★★★**Intercontinental** Johannesgasse 28 **III** ☎563611 ta Inhotelcor tx11235 Plan **4** 500rm500⇌ ⌂ P Lift ☽ sB⇌870–1320 dB⇌1140–1640 (English breakfast) L 150–180 D150–180

★★★★★**Sacher** Philharmonikerstr 4 I ☎525575
tx12520 Plan **5** 119rm 113⇄3🛁 P Lift ♪ sB450
sB⇄🍴760–950 dB⇄🍴1400–1800
(English breakfast) Lalc Dalc

★★★★*Europa* Neuer Markt 3 I ☎521594 tx12292
Plan **6** 100⇄ Lift

★★★★**Parking** Parking 12 I ☎526524 tx
Terrassenhotel tx13420 Plan **7** 65rm63⇄ 🏛 P Lift ♪
sB⇄490–600 dB⇄780–960 (English breakfast)
L 135 D135

★★★★**Prinz Eugen** Wiedner Gürtel 14 IV ☎651741
tx12483 Plan **8**106rm65⇄41🍴 P Lift ♪
sB⇄🍴506–676 dB⇄🍴922–1076
(English breakfast) L 160 D160

★★★★**Royal** Singerstr 3 I ☎524631 tx12870 Plan **9**
66⇄ P Lift ♪

★★★★**Stephansplatz** Stephanspl 9 I ☎635605
tx74334 Plan **10** 68rm49⇄13🍴 P Lift ♪ sB345
sB⇄🍴590 dB⇄🍴795–860 L 120 D120

★★★*Astoria* Kärntnerstr 32 I ☎526585 tx12856
Plan **11** 115rm73⇄4🍴 Lift

★★★**Bellevue** Althanstr 5 IX (n rest) ☎345631
tx74906 Plan **12** 86rm33⇄17🍴 🏛 P Lift ♪
sB 280–320 sB⇄🍴430–490 dB 480–530
dB⇄🍴740

★★★**Erzherzog Rainer** Wiedner Hauptstr 27 IV
☎654646 tx132329 Plan **13** 85rm 70⇄15🍴 🏛 P Lift
♪ sB 440–510 sB⇄🍴580–630 dB 750–655
dB⇄🍴960–1000 (English breakfast) L 180–175
D180–175

★★★*Kahlenberg* Kahlenberg XIX ☎321251 Plan **14**
33rm14⇄15🍴 🏛 Lift

★★★*Kaiserhof* Frankenberggasse 10 IV ☎651701
tx76872 Plan **15** 74rm28⇄46🍴 Lift

★★★**Kärntnerhof** Grashofgasse 4 I (n rest)
☎521923 tx12535 Plan **16** 43rm32⇄ 🏛 P Lift ♪
sB 280 sB⇄🍴395 dB 470 dB⇄🍴590–680

★★★*Palais Schwarzenberg* Schwarzenbergpl 9 III
☎725125 tx76124 Plan **17** 35⇄ A10rm Lift ✍

★★★**Park Schönbrunn** Hietzinger Hauptstr 10 XIII
☎822676 tx12513 Plan **18**395rm325⇄ 🏛 P Lift ♪
sB⇄695–775 dB⇄990–1280 (English breakfast)
L 180 D180 Pool

★★★**Römischer Kaiser** Annagasse 16 I (n rest)
☎527751 tx13696 Plan **19** 26rm20⇄4🍴 Lift ♪
sB⇄🍴480–680 dB 580 dB⇄🍴680–980
(English breakfast)

★★★*Stefanie* Taborstr 12 II ☎242412 tx74589
Plan **20** 160rm100⇄ 🏛 Lift

★★★**Tyrol** Mariahilfer Str 15 VI (n rest) ☎572423
tx11885 Plan **21** 35rm20⇄15🍴 🏛 Lift sB 250–280
sB⇄🍴400–480 dB 450–500 dB⇄🍴680–750
(English breakfast)

★★★**Wandl** Peterspl 9 I (n rest) ☎636317 Plan **22**
137rm38⇄33🍴 Lift ♪ sB 222–257 sB🍴⇄ 327–412
dB 384–494 dB⇄🍴 574–664

★★★**Weisser Hahn** Josefstädter Str 22 VIII (n rest)
☎423648 tx75533 Plan **23** 68rm24⇄23🍴 Lift ♪
sB 290–330 sB⇄🍴450–475 dB 490–520
dB⇄🍴680–830 (English breakfast)

★★**Austria** Wolfengasse 3 I ☎527439 tx112848
Plan **24** 60rm24⇄4🍴 P Lift ♪ sB 310–340
sB⇄🍴495–530 dB 505–530 dB⇄🍴750–790

★★**Graben** Dorotheergasse 3 I ☎521531 Plan **25**
46rm22⇄ P Lift ♪

★★**Madeleine** Geblergasse 21 XVII (n rest)
☎434741 tx75121 Plan **26** 78rm42⇄20🍴 🏛 P Lift ♪
sB280–320 sB⇄🍴380–480 dB490–520
dB⇄🍴580–850

★★**Regina** Rooseveltpl 15 IX ☎427681 tx74700
Plan **27** 127rm79⇄19🍴 P Lift ♪

★★**Stieglbräu** Mariahilferstr 156 XV ☎833621
Plan **28** 61rm37⇄2🍴 Lift ♪ sB280 sB⇄🍴380
dB480 dB⇄🍴680

Bezirk II
🛏 ⚙ *E Glaser* Czerningasse 11 ☎243148 P Rov

Bezirk III
⚙ **F Eckl** Untere Viaduktgasse 3 ☎738105 Ren

🛏 ⚙ **H & E Lehmann** Steingasse 14 ☎733787 BL
(GB)

Bezirk VI
🛏 ⚙ **W Denzel** Gumpendorferstr 19 ☎571571
BMW/Vlo (GB)

🛏 ⚙*G Wittek* Liniengasse 28 ☎564283 Frd

Bezirk IX
🛏 **Votivpark** Universitätsstr ☎423518 (GB)

Bezirk X
🛏 *F M Tarbuk* Davidgasse 90 ☎641631
Chy/Sab/Sim

🛏 ⚙ *Teha* Gudrunstr 144 ☎6445080 M/c Closed
weekends AR/Chy/Sim

Bezirk XII
🛏 ⚙*Felber* Arndtstr 46–48 ☎838204 Opl/Vau

Bezirk XV
🛏 **W Denzel** Tautenhayngasse 22 ☎920306 Vlo

Bezirk XVIII
⚙*G Molnar* 1180 Thimigasse 50 ☎474128 P BL

Bezirk XX
🛏 **A Geiszler & Söhne** Sachsenpl 10 ☎333166
BL/BMW/Maz/Vlo (GB)

Bezirk XXII
🛏 *Auto-Martin* Hirschstettnerstr 92 ☎225147 P
BL

WEINER NEUSTADT Niederösterreich (☎02622)
Map **14** D2

🛏 ⚙**W Denzel** Neunkirchnerstr 129 ☎3766 M/c
BMW/Vlo (GB)

WÖRGL Tirol 7,650 (☎05332) Map **13** A2

★★**Central** Bahnhofstr 27 ☎2459 100rm14⇄3🍴 Lift

WOLFSBERG Kärnten (☎04352) Map **14** C1
🛏 ⚙**Grohs & Kainbacher** Ritzing ☎2316 M/c
Bed/Vau

YBBS AN DER DONAU Niederösterreich 6,000
(☎07412) Map **14** C3

★★**Royal Weisses Rössel** ☎2292 32rm P Lift
sB170–270 sB⇄220–270 dB290 dB⇄390
(English breakfast) L75–85 D75–85

★**Steiner** Burgpl 2 ☎2629 20rm2⇄14🍴 🏛 P
sB131–180 sB⇄🍴160–211 dB240–280
dB⇄🍴310–360 (English breakfast) L70 D70

ZAMS See **LANDECK**

ZELL AM SEE Salzburg 7,000 (☎06542) Map **13** B2

★★**Berner** N-Gassner-Prom 1 ☎2557 Closed Nov
18rm11⇄ 🏛 P sB120–160 sB⇄160–200
dB200–290 dB⇄280–370 (English breakfast)
L60–75 D60–75 lake

★★**Zauner** ☎2504 Closed Oct, Nov & Apr
30rm10⇄2🍴 🏛 P ♪ sB190–230 sB⇄🍴240–290
dB340–440 dB⇄🍴440–580 (English breakfast)
L75–150 D75–150 lake

★★*Zum Hirschen* ☎2447 Closed Nov 37rm12⇄ 🏛
Lift

★*Victoria* ☎2694 33rm1⇄14🍴 Lift

🛏 ⚙**G Altendorfer** Bruckner Bundesstr 108 ☎3283
M/c Opl (GB)

⚙*Glocknergarge* (F Gottwald) Flugplatzstr 3
☎2490 Ren

At Schuttdorf (2km S)

🛏 ⚙**Moser** Brucker Bundesstr 90 ☎2628 ☎2628 P
MB/Sim (GB)

At Thumersbach (2km E)

★★**Bellevue** ☎3104 Closed Oct–19 May
50rm13⇄10🍴 A18rm P sB80–140 sB⇄🍴150–180
dB150–260 dB⇄🍴320–400 L65–75 D65–75 Pool
lake

ZELL AM ZILLER Tirol 1,750 (☎05282) Map **13** A2

★*Bräu* Dorfpl 1 ☎2313 37rm5⇄ 🏛

ZIRL Tirol 4,050 (☎05228) Map **12** D2

★★★**Zirler Weinhof** ☎2444 Closed 16 Nov–14 Dec
20rm9⇄11🍴 A13rm 🏛 Lift

★★**Goldener Löwe** Hauptpl ☎2330 tx53350
18rm12⇄ 🏛 P sB150–170 sB⇄🍴220–260
dB300–340 dB⇄🍴440–520 (English breakfast) L80
D80

Austria

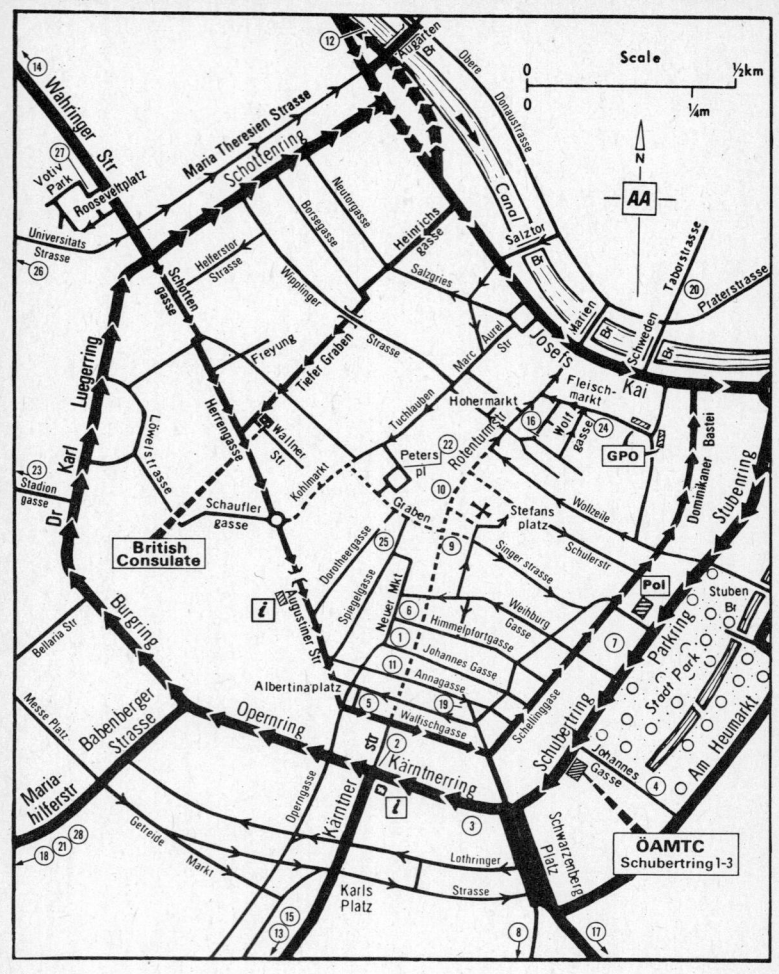

Wien (Vienna)

1	★★★★★Ambassador
2	★★★★★Bristol
3	★★★★★Imperial
4	★★★★★Intercontinental
5	★★★★★Sacher
6	★★★★Europa
7	★★★★Parking
8	★★★★Prinz Eugen
9	★★★★Royal
10	★★★Stephansplatz
11	★★★Astoria
12	★★★Bellevue
13	★★★Erzherzog Rainer
14	★★★Kahlenberg
15	★★★Kaiserhof
16	★★★Kärntnerhof
17	★★★Palais Schwarzenberg
18	★★★Park Schönbrunn
19	★★★Römischer Kaiser
20	★★★Stefanie
21	★★★Tyrol
22	★★★Wandl
23	★★★Weisser Hahn
24	★★Austria
25	★★Graben
26	★★Madeleine
27	★★Regina
28	★★Stieglbräu

★★Post Meilstr 2 ☎2207 15⇌27🛏 🏠 P Lift
sB125–200 sB⇌🛏185–220 dB200–260
dB⇌🛏280–340 (English breakfast) L50–90
D50–90 mountains

ZÜRS AM ARLBERG Vorarlberg 400 (☎05583)
Map 12 C2
★★★Zürserhof ☎513 Closed May–Nov
120rm60⇌5🛏 🏠 Lift

Oberau in the Tirol

BELGIUM

Population 9,651,000 **Area** 11,775 sq miles **Maps** 3, 4, 10 & 11

How to get there

Many cross-Channel ferries operate direct from Dover and Folkestone to Ostend or from Dover, Felixstowe and Hull to Zeebrugge. Alternatively, it is possible to use the shorter Channel crossings from Dover or Folkestone to France and drive along the coastal road to Belgium. Fast hovercraft services operate from Dover or Ramsgate to Calais and from Dover to Boulogne.

General information

Information in this section is specific to Belgium. A wider background is provided in the notes on page 8 with other information which you are advised to read.

AA Port agent B-8400 Ostende G E Huyghe & Son, ☎(059)702855

Accommodation There is no official classification, but hotels exhibiting the distinctive sign issued by the National Tourist Office, included in the official hotel guide, must satisfy regulations which lay down standards of comfort and amenities. Room prices are exhibited in hotel reception areas, and full details of all charges including service and taxes are shown in each room. There are few luxury hotels outside Brussels and the major resorts.

*These are not recommended routes:
the distances are given as a guide only.*

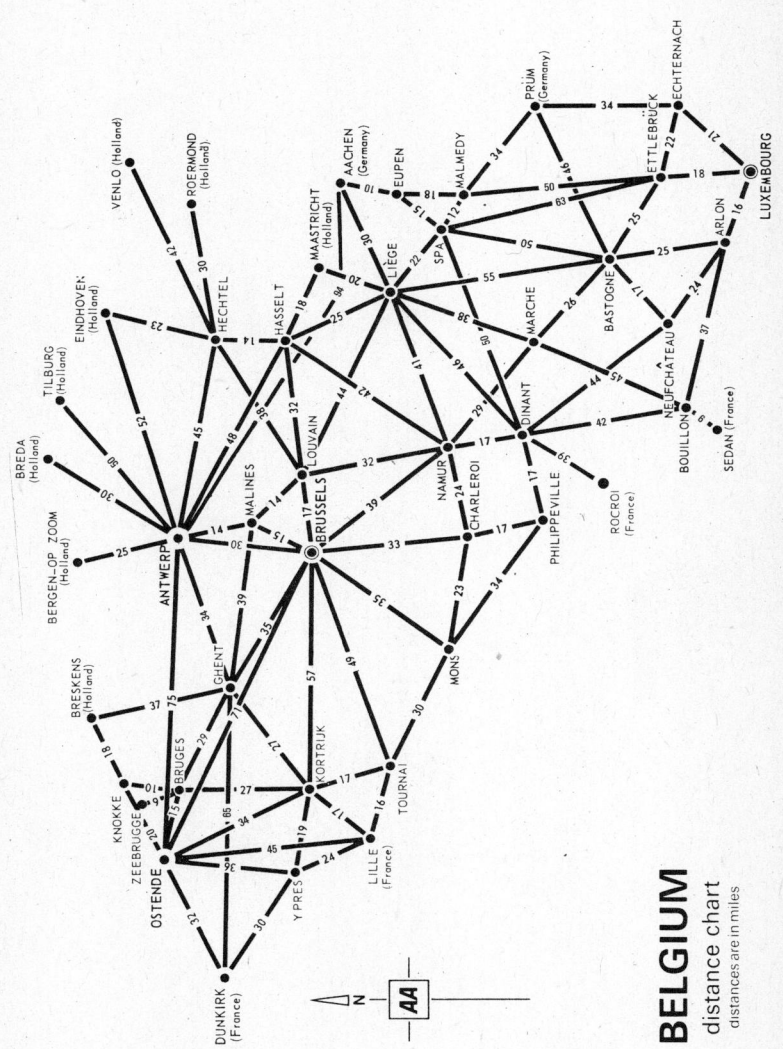

BELGIUM
distance chart
distances are in miles

Belgium

Annual events	April	**Antwerp, Kortrijk, Tongeren and St Truiden** Flanders Spring Festival (April/July)
	May	**Nationwide** May Day celebrations **Ieper** Grand Festival of Cats **Bruges** Procession of the Holy Blood **Antwerp** Fair (May/June)
	June	**Chimay** Music Festival at the castle (June/July)
	July	**Bruges** *Son et Lumière* (July/September) **Schoten** International Festival of Folk Dances **Visé** Summer Festival of the Guild of Crossbowmen
	August	**Bruges, Brussels, and Leuven** Flanders Summer Festival (August/September) **Bree** Touristic Month (many events) **Overijse** Grape and Wine Festival
	September	**Antwerp** Liberation festivities **Wieze** Beer Festival

A more comprehensive list of events is obtainable from the Belgian National Tourist Office (see page 138).

Breakdowns

The Belgian motoring club (TCB) maintains an efficient breakdown service known as Touring Secours/Touring Wegenhulp. Service is available to AA members on production of the *5-Star Service Booklet*.

Patrols

The Touring Secours/Touring Wegenhulp operates a breakdown service daily between 07.00 and 23.00hrs. If you need help, telephone the number relevant to the zone in which you have broken down (this is indicated on the map on this page) and the Touring Secours will send a patrol to assist you.

The Flemish Automobile Club (VAB-VTB operates only in the Antwerp area) and the Royal Automobile Club of Belgium (RACB) each have patrol cars displaying the signs 'Wacht op de Weg' or (RACB). However, neither is associated with the AA and motorists will have to pay for all services.

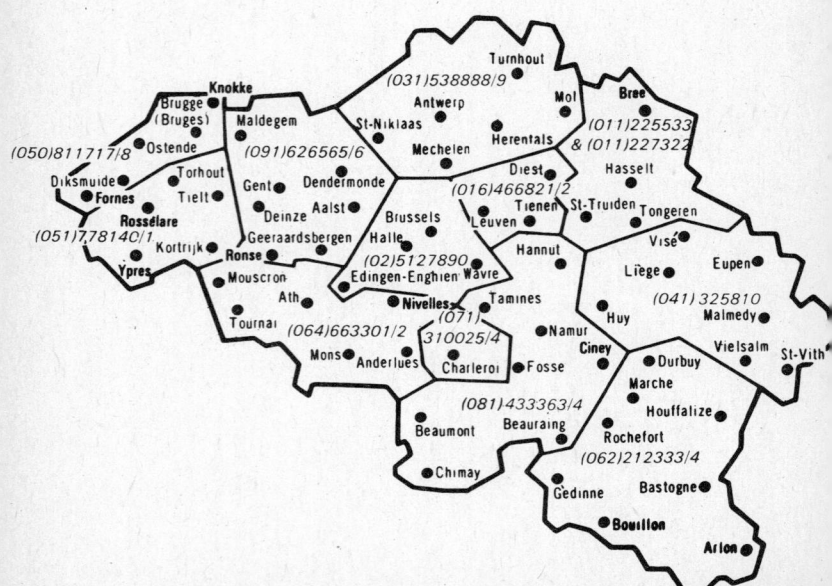

Belgium

British Consulates	1040 Bruxelles 4, rue Joseph II 28, Britannia House ☎(02)2191165. There are also British Consulates in Liege, Ghent, Antwerp and Ostend.

Currency and Banking

The unit of currency is the Belgian franc, divided into 100 centimes. There is no restriction on the amount of currency which may be taken into or out of Belgium, whether in the form of travellers' cheques or Belgian and foreign banknotes. As Belgian currency regulations are subject to change, intending visitors should familiarise themselves with the current exchange regulations before leaving Britain.

Banking hours

Banks are generally open 09.00–15.30hrs from Monday to Friday. Many close for lunch. They are closed on Saturdays. Outside banking hours currency can be changed in Brussels at special offices at the Gare du Nord, open 07.00–23.00hrs daily and the Gare du Midi, open 10.00–24.00hrs daily, and at Zaventem Airport, open 07.00–22.00hrs daily.

Shopping hours

Shops are usually open 09.00–18.00hrs from Monday to Saturday. Supermarkets are open 09.00–20.00hrs (21.00hrs on Friday).

Documents

Certain documents may be necessary for a vehicle temporarily imported by a person staying in Belgium for longer than 6 months. Pleasure craft (boats) more than 5.5 metres in length must be imported under cover of a Customs carnet except craft, with or without motor, of any length which enter and must leave by water, *ie* through a port.

Medical treatment

The provision of medical benefits in Belgium is administered by friendly societies (*Mutualités*) or by regional offices of the Auxiliary Fund for Sickness and Invalidity Insurance (*La Caisse Auxiliaire d'Assurance Maladie – Invalidité*) whose address is 10 boulevard Saint-Lazare, 1030 Brussels, ☎2182300. The address of the nearest local office of the friendly societies may be obtained by local enquiry or from the national federation of friendly societies. You go direct to any doctor or dentist and show him form E111. You will have to pay for treatment and will be given a receipt which will show the service provided (*Attestation de soins donnés*). You can take the doctor's prescription to any chemist, but again you should obtain a receipt for the charge the chemist makes and also make sure he stamps and returns your copy of the doctor's prescription. You will be able to obtain a refund of approximately 75% of the cost on presentation of form E111, together with the receipts from the doctor and chemist, at the nearest office of the insurance societies.

If you or your dependants need hospital treatment, then you should present form E111 to one of the local offices of the friendly societies which will authorise part payment of the cost and advise you where you can obtain the treatment. If you enter hospital urgently and thus are unable to contact the local office beforehand, you should present form E111 to the hospital authorities and ask them to obtain an undertaking to pay part of the cost from the appropriate insurance authority.

Motoring club

The Touring Club Royal de Belgique has its head office at 44 rue de la Loi, 1040 Bruxelles and branch offices in most towns.

Office hours

The Brussels head office is open weekly 09.00–18.00hrs; Saturday 09.00–12.00hrs. Regional offices are open weekdays 09.00–12.00hrs (Monday from 09.15hrs) and 14.00–18.00hrs; Saturday 09.00–12.00hrs. All offices are closed on Saturday afternoons and Sundays.

Post and telephone	**Surface mail**		BFr
		Postcards to France, Germany, Italy, Netherlands and Luxembourg	6.00
		other countries	10.00
		Letters 20g to those countries listed above	8.00
		other countries	14.00
		50g	25.00
		100g	33.00

Belgium

Air mail There is an extra charge if the country of destination is outside Europe.

Telephone rate A telephone call to the UK costs BFr22.50 for each minute. In Brussels the *poste restante* address is: Centre Monnaie, 1000 Brussels.

Public holidays

Holidays based on religious festivals are not always fixed on the calendar but any current diary will give the actual dates. The Whit holiday should not be confused with the British Spring Holiday.

Fixed holidays

1 January	New Year's Day
1 May	Labour Day
21 July	National holiday
15 August	Assumption of the Virgin Mary
1 November	All Saints' Day
11 November	Armistice Day
25 December	Christmas Day

Moveable holidays

Easter Monday
Ascension Day
Whit Monday

Roads

The main roads are generally good. The road numbers of the all-purpose main roads are prefixed 'N'. Motorways (Autoroute/Autosnelweg) are prefixed 'A', or 'E' if the section is part of the European road network. The road system in Brussels is first-class, incorporating underpasses and other modern features, and the signposting for through-traffic is now better. If travelling to Ostende from Louvain (Leuven) or Namur (Namen), you have to follow signs Gent-Gand, as Ostende appears at the exits of the city only.

Motorways

Approximately 734 miles of motorways (*autoroutes*) are open, and more stretches of the planned 1,488-mile network are under construction. Nearly all motorways are part of the European international network.

To join a motorway, follow signposts bearing the motorway symbol; no tolls are charged. Bicycles and motorcycles under 50cc are prohibited but, with certain exceptions, all other vehicles with pneumatic tyres, including those for invalids, are permitted.

Winter conditions

From 1 November to 31 March, motorists may telephone (02)5116667 any time of the day or night for a pre-recorded general report on road conditions, which is constantly brought up to date. They may obtain information concerning a specific section of road in Belgium or a main route abroad by telephoning (02)5127890 between 07.30 and 20.00hrs.

Road signs

Translations of some written signs to be seen on the road are given below:

Passage difficile *Moeilijke doorgang*	} Difficult passage
Disque obligatoire *Schijf verplicht*	} Disc obligatory
Excepte circulation locale *Uitgezonderd Plaatselijk* *Verkeer*	} No entry except for local traffic

Tourist information offices

The Belgian National Tourist Office is at 66 Haymarket, London SW1 4RB. Their telephone number is 01–930 9618 and they will be pleased to supply information on all aspects of tourism. In Belgium the National Tourist organisation is supplemented by the Provincial Tourist Federation, whilst in most towns there are local tourist offices. These organisations will help tourists with information and accommodation.

Visitors' registration

All visitors staying for more than three months must obtain a *Permis de séjour* before entering Belgium.

Motoring regulations

Information in this section is specific to Belgium. A wider background is provided in the notes on page 67 together with other regulations which you are advised to read.

Accidents

Fire and **ambulance** ☎900, **police** ☎901 and in large towns ☎906 Vehicles must be removed, after the drivers have exchanged particulars, where damage to

Belgium

vehicles only has occurred. The police must be called if an unoccupied stationary vehicle is damaged or if injuries are caused to persons; in the latter case the car must not be moved (see the recommendations on pages 67 and 68).

Dimensions Restrictions	Vehicles must not exceed:
	height 4 metres;
	width 2.5 metres;
	length vehicle/trailer combinations 15 metres.

Drinking and driving
A driver with 0.8gr of alcohol per litre of blood is punishable by a fine of between BFr4,000 and BFr40,000 and/or a prison sentence of between 15 days and three months; in addition the driver may be disqualified.

Lights
Between dusk and dawn and in all cases where visibility is restricted to 200m, dipped or full-beam headlights must be used. However, headlights must be dipped: where street lighting is continuous permitting clear vision for 100m; at the approach of oncoming traffic (including vehicles on rails); when following another vehicle and, where the road is adjacent to water, at the approach of oncoming craft if the pilot is likely to be dazzled.

Parking lights
Vehicles parked on the public highway must use position lights (parking lights) both day and night if vehicles are not visible from 100 metres.

In built-up areas the position lights may be replaced by a single parking light displayed on the side nearest to the centre of the road providing the vehicle is not more than 6 metres long and 2 metres wide, has no trailer attached to it, its maximum carrying capacity is not more than eight persons excluding the driver.

Parking
Regulations differentiate between *waiting* (long enough to load or unload goods or for passengers to get in or out) and *parking*.
Vehicles must be left on the right-hand side of the road, except in one-way streets when they can be left on either side. Where possible the vehicle must be left on the level shoulder inside built-up areas and on the shoulder, level or otherwise, outside these areas. If the shoulder is used by pedestrians then at least 1 metre must be left for them on the side farthest away from the traffic.

It is illegal to wait or park on: cycle tracks and cycle crossings; level crossings, pedestrian crossings and 5 metres each side of these crossings; a hill, a bend, in tunnels and underpasses; less than 5 metres from an intersection; less than 20 metres on either side of traffic lights and road signals in general except where the vehicle is less than 1.65 metres high and the lower edge of the sign or signal is 2 metres above ground.

Parking is prohibited: at less than 1 metre in front of or behind another stationary vehicle, or in a position where the vehicle causes an obstruction to other vehicles which would prevent their movement; less than 15 metres either side of a bus or tram stop; in front of an entrance to a private or public building; at any place where pedestrians must use the carriageway to avoid an obstacle; if the vehicle would hinder the passage of a vehicle on rails; on roads where there is fast-moving traffic; on a carriageway marked in traffic lanes or where broken yellow lines are painted; opposite another stationary vehicle and on the central reservation of dual carriageways.

In many towns and cities there are short-term parking areas known as blue zones where parking discs must be displayed. Outside these areas a parking disc must be used where the parking sign has an additional panel showing a parking disc. In some disc areas parking meters may also be found in which case the parking disc is not valid in the meter bay.

Parking meters
Where these are used the instructions for use will be on the meter.

Passengers
Children under the age of 12 years are not permitted to travel in the front seat of a vehicle.

Police fines
The police are authorised to impose fines, which must be paid within 48 hours with special stamps which are on sale at post offices.

Priority
In built-up areas, a driver must give way – by slowing down or, if need be, by stopping – to bus drivers who have used their direction indicators to show they intend driving away from a bus stop.

Cyclists taking part in an authorised race, should be given priority – motorists should stop and allow the cyclists free passage.

Belgium

Speed In all towns and built-up areas at the beginning of which a sign with the name of the town (white sign with black letters) is placed, there is an overall maximum speed limit of 60kph (37mph). Both inside and outside built-up areas, and on motorways, vehicles using makeshift or secondary ropes for towing after breakdowns or accidents are limited to 25kph (15½mph). Outside built-up areas, there is a maximum limit of 90kph (56mph) for private vehicles except on motorways and four-lane roads where the speed limit is 120kph (74mph). Mopeds are limited to 40kph (24mph) everywhere. There is a minimum limit of 70kph (43mph) on straight, level stretches of motorway.

Traffic lights The three-colour traffic light system operates in Belgium. However, the lights may be replaced by arrows of the individual colours and these have the same meaning as the lights, but only in the direction in which the arrow points.

Tyres **Spiked tyres** These are permitted during the winter months. You should enquire the dates when their use is authorised before using these tyres.

They must be fitted to all four wheels and also to a trailer over 500kg and vehicles under 3.5 tonnes. They may not be used on motorways and speed on other roads may not exceed 60kph (37mph). See also winter conditions page 65.

Warning triangles These are compulsory for all vehicles except two-wheeled vehicles. They must be placed, at least 30m on ordinary roads and 100m on motorways, behind the vehicle to warn following traffic, and they must be visible at a distance of 50m.

Panorama of Bouillon

Prices are in Belgian francs

St% Service and tax charge
Supplementary local taxes are payable in addition to the charges shown. These vary from town to town.

Abbreviations:
av	Avenue	r	rue
bd	boulevard	rte	route
pl	place, plein	str	straat

AALST (ALOST) Oost-Vlaanderen 45,250 (☎053) Map **3** B1
★ *Bourse van Amsterdam* Grote Markt 26 ☎211581 6rm1⇆

AALTER Oost-Vlaanderen 10,250 (☎091) Map **3** B2
★*Memling* Markt II (n rest) ☎741013 10rm3⇆7⋔ sB⇆⋔550–600 dB⇆⋔900–1000 (English breakfast)

AARLEN See **ARLON**

AARTSELAAR See **ANTWERPEN (Anvers)**

ALBERT PLAGE See **KNOKKE-HEIST**

ALLE Namur 850 (☎061) Map **10** D4
★*Charmille* r Liboichant 12 ☎500363 Closed 15 Jan–15 Feb 11rm5⇆

ALOST See **AALST**

ANSEREMME Namur (☎082) Map **4** C1
★*Lesse* r des Forges 4 (DP) ☎222078 Closed Nov–Mar 32rm2⇆ ⌂

ANTWERPEN (Anvers) Antwerpen 662,350 (☎031) Map **4** C2
☆☆☆**EuroCrest** G-Legrellelaan 10 ☎372900 tx33843 314⇆ P Lift ♪ sB⇆1525 dB⇆1985 (English breakfast) L fr 195 D fr195
☆☆☆**Eurotel Antwerpen** Copernicuslaan 2 ☎316780 ta Oteleur tx33965 350rm200⇆150⋔ ⌂ P Lift ♪ sB⇆⋔1370–1510 dB fr1780 dB⇆⋔2180 (English breakfast) L250–450 D250–450 Pool
☆☆☆**Novotel Antwerpen** Luithagen 6 ☎420320 tx32488 119⇆ P Lift sB⇆fr1076 dB⇆fr1565 English breakfast only ✍ Pool
★★★*Plaza* Charlotta-Lei 43 (n rest) ☎395970 tx31531 80rm75⇆5⋔ ⌂ Lift
★★★**Waldorf** Belgielei 36 ☎309950 tx32948 100⇆ ⌂ P Lift ♪ sB⇆1150–1900 dB⇆1600–2000
★*Métropole* Handschoenmarkt 5–7 ☎329248 Closed 21 Dec–5 Jan 20rm6⇆1⋔ ♪ sB535–645 sB⇆⋔645–700 dB680–950 dB⇆⋔845–950 (English breakfast) L fr215 D fr320
▮ ᵴᵅ*Autostrade Motors* Boomesesteenweg 441 ☎277910 Frd
▯ ᵴᵅ*Centrauto* St-Josefstr 48 ☎301815 BMW/Jag (GB)
▯ ᵴᵅ*Leyland Motors* Haringrodestr 104 ☎393980 BL/Jag/Rov/Tri
▮ ᵴᵅJ **Lins** Grote Tunnelpl 3 ☎339928 Bed/BL (GB)
▯ ᵴᵅ*Servais & Collin* Haringrodestr 54 ☎395990 M/c AR (GB)
At **Aartselaar** (8km S)
☆☆☆☆*Sofitel* Boomsesteenweg 15 ☎876850 tx33619 125⇆ ⌂ Lift Pool
At **Berchem** (1km S)
▯ ᵴᵅ*Acker* Uitbreidingstr 92 ☎309999 M/c Fia/Vau (GB)
At **Deurne** (4km NE)
★★*Rivierenhof* Turnhoutsebaan 244 ☎242564 15rm5⇆ ⌂ P Lift ♪ sB430 sB⇆635–860 dB⇆1013 (English breakfast) L300 D300 ✍ lake

ARLON (Aarlen) Luxembourg 13,850 (☎063) Map **10** D4
★★★*Arly* av Luxembourg 81 ☎215381 Closed 1–14 Jan 27⇆ ⌂ Lift ✍ Pool
★★*Ecu de Bourgogne* pl Leopold 9 (n rest) ☎211167 Closed 18 Dec–16 Jan 22rm10⇆2⋔ Lift
★★*Nord* r Faubourgs 2 ☎212293 Closed 18 Dec–4 Jan 25rm7⇆2⋔ P sB476 sB⇆⋔678–690 dB660–690 dB⇆⋔996–1100

▯ ᵴᵅ **Beau Site** av de Longwy 167 ☎212916 Frd (GB)

ATH Hainaut 11,262 (☎068) Map **3** B1
▯ ᵴᵅ **Center** chaussée de Bruxelles 45 ☎224283 P BL (GB)

BASTOGNE Luxembourg 6,950 (☎062) Map **10** D4
★★*Lebrun* r de Marche 8 ☎211193 Closed Jan & Feb 27rm8⇆8⋔ ⌂ P sB460–540 sB⇆⋔1040–1090 dB840–875 dB⇆⋔1235–1370 L350–680 D350–680
★*Luxembourg* pl Mac-Auliffe 25 ☎211226 Closed 16 Nov–14 Mar 13rm
➻F *Luc-Nadin* chemin des Scieries 16 ☎211806 P BL (GB)

BELOEIL Hainaut (☎069) Map **3** B1
★★*Couronne* r Durieu 8 ☎679567 Closed 16 Sep–8 Oct 10rm5⇆

BERCHEM See **ANTWERPEN (Anvers)**

BEVEREN-WAAS Oost-Vlaanderen 16,850 (☎031) Map **3** B2
☆☆*Beveren* Grote Baan 280 ☎758623 19⇆

BLANKENBERGE West-Vlaanderen 14,325 (☎050) Map **3** B2
★★*Idéal* Zeedijk 244 ☎411691 Closed 21 Sep–mid Apr 50⇆ ⌂ Lift sB⇆790–870 dB⇆1378–1540 L340 D310 Pool sea
★★*Petite Rouge* Zeedijk 127 ☎411032 60rm20⇆4⋔ ⌂ P Lift ♪ sB525–685 sB⇆⋔895–1020 dB1050–1350 dB⇆⋔1590–1820 L450–560 D400 sea
★*Pacific* J-de Troozlaan 48 ☎411542 Closed Xmas 24rm12⋔
★*Park & Cygne* de Smet de Nayerlaan 133 ☎411811 Closed 21 Oct–19 Mar 29rm
★*Suisse* J-de Troozlaan 33 ☎41747 Closed Oct–mid Apr 30rm ⌂

BOOM Antwerpen 16,780 (☎03) Map **4** C2
▯ ᵴᵅ*E Roofthooft* Antwerpsestr 12 ☎880891 Closed weekends Frd

BOUILLON Luxembourg 2,900 (☎061) Map **10** D4
★★*Tyrol* r Haut de la Ville ☎466293 Closed Jan–14 Feb 10⇆ P sB⇆830 dB⇆1110 L400 D400
★*Semois* r Collège 46 (DP) ☎466027 45rm12⇆2⋔ Lift

BOUSSU See **MONS (Bergen)**

BOUVIGNES See **DINANT**

BRASSCHAAT-POLYGOON Antwerpen 27,720 (☎031) Map **4** C2
☆☆*Dennenhof* Bredebaan 940 ☎630509 25rm20⋔

BREDENE West-Vlaanderen 7,292 (☎059) (3km NE of **Ostende**) Map **3** B2
★*Zomerlust* P-Benoitlaan 26 ☎320340 20rm sB341 dB517–567 D fr230

BRUGGE (Bruges) West-Vlaanderen 119,750 (☎050) Map **4** B2
★★★*Portinari* Garenmarkt 15 ☎331612 50⇆ P Lift ♪ sB⇆700–945 dB⇆1115–1450 D360
★★*Duc de Bourgogne* Huidenvettverspl 12 ☎332038 Closed Jan & 1–14 Jul 10⇆ sB⇆1025 dB⇆1650–1800 L1350&alc D1350&alc
★★*Europ* Augustijnenrei 18 (n rest) ☎337975 Closed Dec–Feb 28rm6⇆17⋔ P Lift sB575 sB⇆⋔745–945 dB910 dB⇆⋔1100–1360
★★*Sablon* Noordzandstr 21 ☎333902 48rm18⇆ Lift ♪ sB595 sB⇆700 dB1040 dB⇆1190
★*Févéry* Collaert Mansionstr 3 (n rest) ☎331269 14rm7⋔ Lift ♪ sB470 sB⋔610 dB675 dB⋔815
★*Jacobs* Baliestr 1 (n rest) ☎339831 Closed Oct–14 Mar 34rm17⇆ Lift

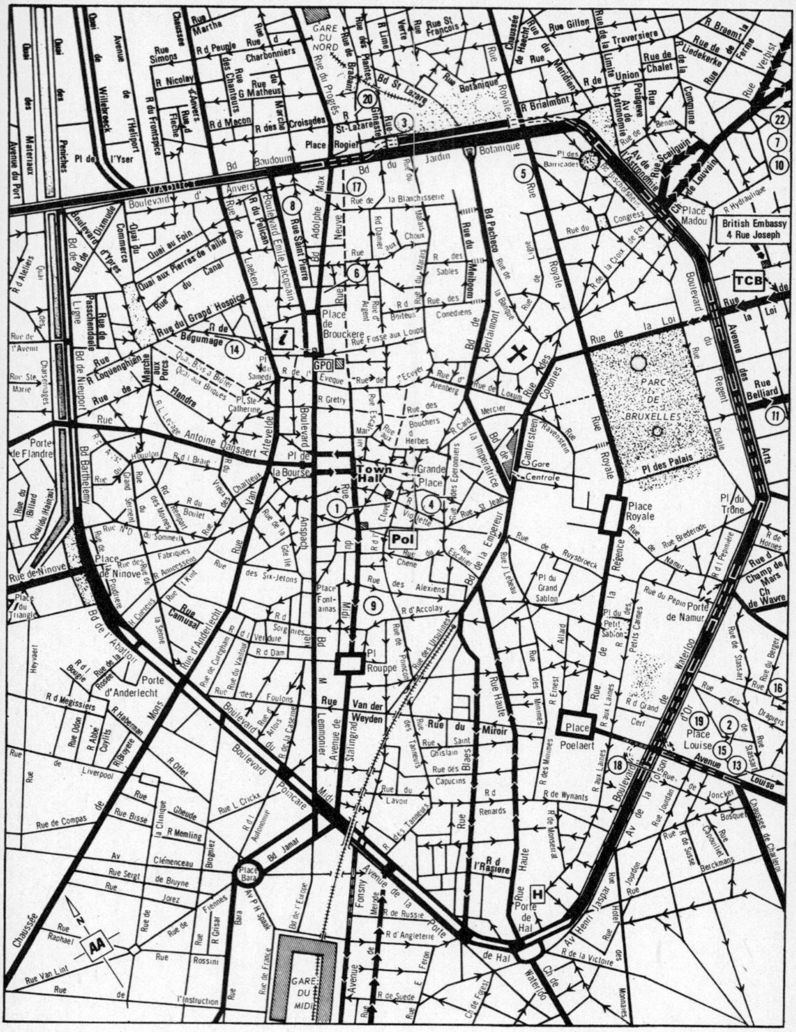

Brussel (Bruxelles)

1	★★★★★Amigo
2	★★★★★MacDonald
3	★★★★★Palace
4	★★★★★Royal Windsor
5	★★★★Astoria
6	★★★★Atlanta
7	☆☆☆☆Sofitel see Bruxelles Airport (at Diagem 8km NE)
8	★★★Bedford
9	★★★Brand Whitlock's
10	☆☆☆Novotel see Bruxelles Airport (at Diagem 8km NE)
11	★★★Queen Anne
13	★★Concorde-Louise
14	★★Noga
15	★★Résidence du Bois
16	★★Richmond House
17	★★Scheers
18	★Albergo
19	★Astor
20	★Monico-Nord
22	★Vignette (at Tervuren 13km E)

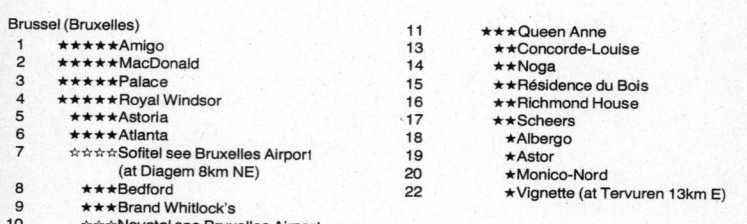

★**Londres** 't Zand 11 (off Zuidzandstr) ☎333074 25rm1⇨2 ⩋ sB450 dB850–925 dB⇨ ⩋925–1050 L315 D315 ∩

★**Lybeer** Korte Vuldersstr 31 (nr Cathedrne) (n rest) ☎334355 Closed 6 Nov–Feb 30rm sB425 dB750

★**Pauw** St-Gilliskerhof 8 (n rest) ☎337118

8rm1⇄2🛏 ♪ sB460 dB700 dB⇄ 🛏850

🅟 ⋈ **Canada** (L Huy) St-Pickerskaai 36 ☎317370 Frd (G.B.)

🅟 ⋈**Vandeplas** Komvest 16 ☎332506 P BL (G.B.)

At **OOSTKAMP** (8KM S)

★★★**Château des Brides** Breidels 1 (n rest) ☎822001 Closed Oct☞14 Apr 10rm5⇄ P Lift sB600 sB⇄1200 dB900 dB⇄1300–1600

BRUSSEL-BRUXELLES Brabant 1,050,800 (☎02) Map **4** C1 **See Plan**

★★★★★**Amigo** r de l'Amigo 1 (by town hall) ☎51155910 tx21618 Plan **1** 183rm172⇄11🛏 🏛 Lift

★★★★**Mac Donald** av Louise 321 ☎6498030 tx23322 Plan **2** 76⇄ 🏛 Lift

★★★★★**Palace** pl Rogier 22 ☎2176200 tx21248 Plan **3** 356⇄ Lift

★★★★★**Royal Windsor** r Duquesony ☎5114215 tx62905 Plan **4** 300⇄ 🏛 Lift

★★★★**Astoria** r Royale 103 ☎2176290 tx25040 Plan **5** 110⇄ Lift sB⇄1800 sB2350 (English breakfast) L760 D760

★★★★**Atlanta** bd A-Max 7 ☎2170120 tx21475 Plan **6** 244rm225⇄ 🏛 P Lift sB⇄1800–2000 dB⇄1975–2570 L315–500 D315–500

★★★**Bedford** r du Midi 135 ☎5127840 tx24059 Plan **8** 220rm200⇄20🛏 🏛 P Lift ♪ sB1040 sB⇄🛏1460 dB1460 dB⇄🛏1850 (English breakfast) L430 D430

★★★**Brand Whitlock** bd Brand Whitlock 156 (n rest) ☎7332966 Plan **19** 15rm12🛏 🏛

★★★**Queen Anne** bd E-Jaćqmain 110 (off pl Brouchěre) ☎2171600 Plan **11** 57rm53⇄ Lift sB665 sB⇄765 dB⇄1150 (English breakfast)

★★**Concorde-Louise** r de la Concorde 59 (n rest) ☎5128610 Plan **13** 27rm9⇄5🛏 Lift sB660 sB⇄🛏715–835 dB895 dB⇄🛏965–1085

★★**Noga** r du Béguinage 38 ☎2185032 Plan **14** 19rm9⇄8🛏 Lift sB505–805 sB⇄🛏655–805 dB⇄🛏930–1080

★★**Résidence du Bois** av L-Georges 12 (off S end of av Louise) ☎470162 Plan **15** 15rm4⇄6🛏 Lift

★★**Richmond House** r de la Concorde 21 (n rest) (off av Louise) ☎5124824 ta Britburo Plan **16** 27rm15⇄2🛏 Lift sB450–550 sB⇄🛏650–750 dB700–800 dB⇄🛏975–1000

★★**Scheers** bd A-Max 132 ☎217761 tx21675 Plan **17** 62rm44⇄ Lift

★**Albergo** av de la Toison d'Or 57 ☎5382960 Plan **18** 70rm60⇄4🛏 Lift

★**Astor** r Capt Crespel 9 (n rest) ☎5116086 Plan **19** 13rm6⇄

★ **Monico Nord** r de Brabant 2 ☎173293 Plan **20** 26rm10⇄10🛏

Berg Chaussée de Waterloo 532–538 ☎3441546 Ren

🅟⋈**J Decat** chaussée de louvain 677 ☎7339890 Maz

🅟 ⋈**D'Leteren Centre** chaussée de Mons 95 ☎5222000 Aud/VW (G.B.)

🅟 ⋈**Leyland Motors** r de Hennin 18–22 ☎6492020 BL/Rov/Tri

🅟**P Plasman** Chaussée de Waterloo 567 ☎3451950 M/c Frd (G.B.)

🅟⋈**C F Wismeyer** r Vanderkindere 467 ☎3435050 Bed/Vau

At **Tervuren** (13km E)

★**Vignette** Chaussée de Louvain 12 ☎573056 Plan **22** closed Jan 18rm6⇄1🛏 🏛

BRUSSEL-BRUXELLES AIRPORT

At **Diegem** (8km NE)

☆☆☆☆**Sofitel** Bessenveldstr 15 ☎7206050 tx26595 Plan **7** 125⇄🛏 P sB⇄🛏 1535–2060 dB⇄🛏2070–2630 (English breakfast) L235–850 D138–1000 Pool

☆☆☆☆**Novotel Brussel Airport** ☎7205830 tx26751 162⇄ P Lift sB⇄🛏 fr1220 dB⇄🛏 fr1543 English breakfast only Pool

CASTEAU Hainaut 2,750 (☎065) Map **3** B1

☆☆**Casteau Euro Crest** Chaussée de Bruxelles 38 ☎728741 tx57164 71rm35⇄36🛏 P ♪ sB⇄🛏885–1015 dB⇄🛏1255–1725 (English breakfast) L fr295 D Fr295

CHAMPLON Luxembourg 800 (☎084) Map **4** C1

★★**Hostellerie de la Barrière** Barrière 1 ☎455155 21rm12⇄2🛏 🏛 P sB⇄🛏 780–900 dB875–915 dB⇄🛏915–1275 L alc D alc

CHARLEROI Hainaut 268,650 (☎071) Map **4** C1

See also **Gosselies**

★★★**Siebertz** quai de Brabant 6 (n rest) ☎314487 tx51200 33rm15⇄9🛏 Lift

🅟 ⋈**Leteren** r de Montigny 145 ☎322232 P Aud/VW

CHAUDFONTAINE Liège 2,800 (☎041) Map **4** C1

★★★**Bains** av Thermes 7 ☎653895 35rm11⇄ P Lift ♪ sB445–560 sB⇄560–635 dB655 dB⇄870–1420 L fr535 D fr535 Pool

CINEY Namur 7,600 (☎083) Map **4** C1

★★**Château du Domaine St-Roch** r Sainfoin 8 ☎21055 12rm5🛏 🏛

COQ-SUR-MER (LE) See **HAAN (DE)**

COURTRAI See **KORTRIJK**

COXYDE-SUR-MER See **KOKSIJDE**

DEURLE Oost-Vlaanderen 2,100 (☎091) Map **3** B1

★★**Auberge de Pêcheur** Pontstr 42 ☎824444 Closed Oct 15rm11⇄

DEURNE See **ANTWERPEN (Anvers)**

DIEGEM See **BRUSSEL-BRUXELLES AIRPORT**

DIEST Brabant 10,650 (☎013) Map **4** C1

★**Modern** Chaussée de Louvain 4 ☎331066 13rm5⇄8🛏 P sB⇄🛏525–675 dB⇄🛏750–1100 D260–800

🅟 ⋈**Meelberghs** av E-Robeyslaan 10 ☎333388 Frd

DINANT Namur 9,850 (☎082) Map **4** C1

★★**Couronne** r A-Sax 1 ☎222441 25rm4⇄2🛏 P Lift sB410–450 sB⇄🛏600 dB720–780 dB⇄🛏895–1100 L260–500 & alc D260–500 & alc

★★**Gare** r de la Station 39–41 ☎222056 Closed 16 Nov– Mar 22rm6⇄ 🏛 P Lift sB302 sB⇄480 dB420–460 dB⇄620–640 L230–550 D280–550 St%

★★**Thermidor** r de la Station 3 ☎223135 6rm2⇄

★**Banque** pl Gare 49 ☎22020 12rm2⇄ 🏛

★**Belle Vue** r de Philippeville 3 ☎222924 7rm5⇄1🛏 P dB670 dB⇄🛏820 (English breakfast) L200–500 D200–500

★**Collégiale** r A-Sax 2 ☎22372 18rm

★**Commerce** pl St-Nicolas 12 ☎222744 Closed Nov–14 Mar 24rm Lift

🅟 ⋈ **Dinant Motors** rte de Bouvignes 53 ☎223026 P Opl

🅟 ⋈**S A Etamenco** r A-Caussin 95 ☎222254 Lnc Fia

🅟⋈**M Jaumotte** quai JB-Culot 18 ☎223007 Hon (GB)

At **Bouvignes** (2km NW)

★★**Auberge de Bouvignes** r Fétis 2 (DP) ☎611600 Closed Dec 5rm3⇄

At **Payenne-Coustinne** (12km SE)

★**Host Grisons** Gd Route (DP) ☎666355 Closed Feb 14rm8⇄

DOLEMBREAUX See **LIÈGE**

DOORNIK See **TOURNAI**

EEKLO Oost-Vlaanderen 19,400 (☎091) Map **3** B2

★**Rembrandt** Koningin Astridplein 2 ☎772570 7rm2🛏

🅟 ⋈**Baets** Markt 85 ☎771285 Aud/VW (G.B.)

🅟 ⋈**Wolf** Leopoldlaan 4 ☎771440 M/c P Frd

ENGHIEN Hainaut 4,000 (☎02) Map **3** B1

★★**Vieux Cèdre** av Elisabeth 1 ☎3952061 Closed 16 Aug–6 Sep 6rm3⇄6🛏 A4rm P sB610–850 sB⇄🛏960–1250 dB920–1150 dB⇄🛏1070–1500 (English breakfast) L350–800 D350–800

🅟 ⋈**Chapelle** r d'Hoves 132 ☎3951509 Cit (GB)

EUPEN Liège 15,000 (☎087) Map **4** D1

★★**Bosten** Verwierstr 2–4 ☎552209 14rm6⇄ 🏛 P sB430–450 sB⇄490–525 dB860–900 dB⇄880–1050 L250–625 D250–625

Belgium

FLORENVILLE Luxembourg 2,650 (☎061)
Map **10** D4
★★**France** r Généraux Cuvelier 28 ☎311032 Closed
Jan – 15 Feb 38rm8⇄ ⋒ P Lift sB475 – 480
sB⇄575 – 610 dB700 – 750 dB⇄800 – 850
L350 – 500 D350 – 500 St%
  🛏 **Mauxhin & Fils** r de la Station 32C ☎311055 P
Cit

GEEL Antwerpen 30,000 (☎014) Map **4** C2
  🛏 ⏳**Dierckx Puba** Passtr 170 ☎588020 P BL (GB)

GENT (Gand) Oost-Vlaanderen 218,550 (☎091)
Map **3** B2
☆☆☆**Holiday Inn** Ottgemsesteenweg 600
☎225885 tx11756 120⇄ P Lift sB⇄fr1350
dB⇄fr1750 Pool
★★★**Europa** Gordunakaai 59 ☎226071 tx11547
40⇄ ⋒ P Lift sB⇄1020 dB⇄1275 – 1380 L fr370
D fr370
★★★**Park** Wilsonplein 1 ☎251781 39rm44⇄18 ⋒ Lift
★★**St Jorishof** Botermarkt 1 (off St-Baafsplein)
☎236791 72rm44⇄3 ⋒ ⋒ P Lift sB575 – 675
sB⇄ ⋒875 dB950 dB⇄ ⋒1150 (English breakfast)
L alc D alc
★★**Terminus** Koningin M-Hendrikaplaal 6 ☎225545
tx11339 Closed Sat 23rm5⇄6 ⋒ P Lift
sB460 – sB⇄ ⋒fr665 dB fr880 dB⇄ ⋒fr935 L alc D alc
St%
  🛏 ⏳**Center & Docks Motors** Vliegtuiglaan 18
☎510033 P Bed/Vau (GB)
  🛏 ⏳**W Roelens** Doornzelestr 21 ☎232476 M/c Toy
  🛏 ⏳**A Vandersmissen** Fievestr 26 ☎257637 Frd
  🛏 ⏳**Leyland Vernaeve** Doornzelestr 31 ☎230384
BL (GB)

GEMBLOUX Namur 11,500 (☎081) Map **4** C1
  🛏 ⏳**Croisée** (A Denis) Chaussée de Namur 18
☎611626 P Frd (GB)

GOSSELIES Hainaut 10,700 (☎071) Map **4** C1
★**John's** pl Station 4 ☎350838 Closed Jul
18rm10⇄10 ⋒ P lift ⫯ sB fr415 sB⇄ ⋒540 – 1015
dB830 – 1330 dB⇄ ⋒805 – 1330 (English breakfast)
L alc D alc St%

HAAN (DE) (Coq-sur-Mer) West-Vlaanderen 3099
(☎059) Map **3** B2 (12.5km NE of **Ostende**)
★★**Belle Vue** Koningspl 5 ☎233439 Closed
Oct – mid Apr 51rm17⇄5 ⋒ P Lift sB530 ⫯685
sB⇄ ⋒680 – 885 dB860 – 1070 dB⇄ ⋒960 – 1170
(English breakfast) L300 – 350 D300 – 350

HALLE (HAL) Brabant 20,400 (☎02) Map **3** B1
★**Eleveurs** Basiliekstr 136 ☎3565309 Closed Jul
14rm8⇄3 ⋒ P sB500 sB⇄ ⋒600 – 950 dB750
dB⇄ ⋒800 – 1300 (English breakfast) L500 D500

HAN-SUR-LESSE Namur 800 (☎084) Map **10** D4
★★**Voyageurs** rte de Rochefort 1 ☎377237 tx42079
45rm20⇄10 ⋒ P Lift sB545 – 650 sB⇄ ⋒645 – 775
dB790 – 1000 dB⇄ ⋒990 – 1200 (English breakfast)
L300 – 800 D300 – 800

HASSELT Limburg 40,175 (☎011) Map **4** C2
★**Century** Leopoldpl 1 ☎224799 Closed
23 Dec – Jan 10rm1⇄ ⋒ P sB495 – 550 dB820 – 1000
L225 – 600 D225 – 600
  🛏 ⏳**Hoffer** Demerstr 66 ☎224911 Ren (GB)
  🛏 ⏳**The Jerrycan** (A Slegers) Luikersteenweg
316 – 320 ☎278699

HERBESTHAL Liège (☎087) Map **4** C1
★**Herren** r Mitoyenne 82 ☎80101 14rm1⇄

HERENTALS Antwerpen 18,350 (☎014) Map **4** C2
  🛏 ⏳**Tuerlinx** St Janstr 116 ☎212312 ☎272312
Bed/Opl (GB)

HERSTAL See **LIÈGE**

HOEI See **HUY**

HOUFFALIZE Luxembourg 1,325 (☎062) Map **4** C1
★**Clé des Champs** rte de Libramont 22 ☎288044
9rm4 ⋒ P sB530 sB ⋒640 dB725 dB ⋒840 L255
D255
  🛏 ⏳**Lambin** pl du roi Albert 23 ☎288035 P BL (GB)

HOUYET Namur 1,000 (☎082) Map **4** C1

★**Lesse** r de la Gare 12 (DP) ☎666402 10rm

HUY (HOEI) Liège 12,750 (☎085) Map **4** C1
★★★**Aigle Noir** quai Dautrebande 8 ☎211064
Closed 16 – 31 Aug 13rm6⇄3 ⋒ Lift sB585
sB⇄ ⋒760 – 860 dB870 – 1120 dB⇄ ⋒1180 – 1320
(English breakfast) L600 D400 St%
★**Wagram** chaussée de Napoléon 2 ☎212679 8rm
  🛏 ⏳**Vandevliedt** r de la Motte 21 ☎213134
Bed/Opl/Vau (GB)

IEPER (Ypres) West-Vlaanderen 21,350 (☎057)
Map **3** B1
★**St Nicolas** G-de Stuerstr 6 ☎200622 Closed Sun
Eve & Mon & 15 Jul – 8 Aug 6rm4⇄ sB550 sB⇄550
dB800 dB⇄800 L alc D alc St%
★**Sultan** Grote Markt 33 ☎200193 20rm9⇄ ⋒
  🛏 ⏳**Devos & Dewanckel** Menesteenweg 30
☎201335 M/c P Frd (GB)

KASTERLEE Antwerpen 6,275 (☎014) Map **4** C2
★**Dennen** Lichtaartsebaan 89 ☎556107 10rm5⇄ ⋒

KNOKKE-HEIST West-Vlaanderen 28,700 (☎050)
Map **3** B2
At Albert Plage
★★★**Lido** Zwaluwenlaan 16 ☎601925 Closed
6 Jan – 1 Feb 37rm14⇄4 ⋒ ⋒ P Lift ⫯ sB460 – 670
sB⇄ ⋒510 – 720 dB1020 – 1140 dB⇄ ⋒1120 – 1240
(English breakfast) L350 – 400 D400 – 450 sea
★★★**Sofitel la Reserve** Elizabethlaan 132 ☎600606
tx81657 Closed Feb 120rm115⇄ ⋒ P Lift ⫯
sB1435 – 1840 dB⇄ ⋒2170 – 2850 L650 D650 ⇸
Pool lake
At Heist
★★**Royal** Zeedijk 228 ☎51050 Closed 7 Sep – Whit
49rm9⇄4 ⋒ Lift sea
At Knokke
★★**Cecil** Elizabethlaan 20 ☎601033 Closed
Oct – mid Apr 45rm10⇄ Lift sea
At Zoute (Le)
★★★**Majestic** Zeedijk 688 ☎611144 Closed Oct – Etr
60rm52⇄ ⋒ P Lift ⫯ sB745 – 820 sB⇄ ⋒795 – 870
dB1390 – 1540 dB⇄ ⋒1490 – 1840 L fr75 D fr475 sea
★★**Nouvel** van Bunnenpl 1 ☎601861 tx81272
Closed Oct – Etr 50rm2⇄22 ⋒ P Lift sB725 – 775
sB⇄ ⋒875 – 975 dB1150 – 1250 dB⇄ ⋒1450 – 1550
(English breakfast) L350 D350 sea
★**Florida** A-Bréartstr 9 ☎611124 20rm5⇄1 ⋒ Lift
sB525 – 625 sB⇄ ⋒825 dB950 – 1050
dB⇄ ⋒1050 – 1150 (English breakfast) L240 D280
St% sea

KOKSIJDE (Coxyde-sur-Mer) West-Vlaanderen
7,900 (☎058) Map **3** B2
★★**Royal** Zeedijk 65 ☎511300 Closed Oct – mid Apr
30rm7⇄ Lift sea

KORTRIJK (COURTRAI) West-Vlaanderen 43,400
(☎056) Map **3** B1
★★★**Damier** Grote Markt 41 ☎221547 40rm19⇄ Lift
⫯ sB430 – 600 sB⇄700 – 950 dB1000 – 1180
dB⇄1600 – 2000 L400 – 550 D400 – 500 St%

La Each name preceded by La is listed under the
name that follows it

Le Each name preceded by Le is listed under the
name that follows it

LEOPOLDSBURG Limburg (☎011) Map **4** C2
  🛏 ⏳**W Heeren** Diestersteenweg 144 ☎341295
☎341295 P Bed/Vau (GB)

LEUVEN (LOUVAIN) Brabant 29,800 (☎016)
Map **4** C1
★**Industrie** Martelarenpl 7 ☎221349 18rm4 ⋒
  🛏 **Hergon** Diestsestr 133 ☎223506 Frd

LEUZE Hainaut 7,250 (☎069) Map **3** B1
★**Couronne** pl de la Gare ☎16691 Closed Aug 10rm

LIBRAMONT Luxembourg (☎061) Map **10** D4
  🛏 ⏳**Etienne** av de Bouillon 6 ☎222060 P BL (GB)

LIÈGE (LUIK) Liège 432,600 (☎041) Map **4** C1
☆☆☆**Ramada Inn** bd de la Sauvenière 100
☎325919 tx41896 rm105⇄ P Lift sB⇄1600 – 1700
dB⇄2000 – 2200 (English breakfast)

★★**Angleterre** r des Dominicans 2 (nr pl de la République Français) ☎234303 40rm15⇆ Lift sB550 sB⇆865 dB800 dB⇆1160

★**Cygne d'Argent** r Beeckman 49 ☎237001 19rm10⇆9 ▥ Lift sB⇆ ▥697–812 dB902 dB⇆ ▥1164–1248 L300 D300

🛏 ➾**Britannique** pl St-Paul 7 ☎322050 Rov (GB)

🛏 ➛**Brondeel** quai de Coronmeuse 28 ☎271820 Chy/Ska

🛏 **S A Sodia** r L-Boumal 24 ☎526862 BL (GB) At **Herstal** (8km on E5)

★★★**Post House** ☎646400 tx41103 93⇆ ▥ Lift ♪ sB⇆1325 dB⇆1750 (English breakfast) L310 D310–600 St% Pool

☆☆**Euromotel** r de l'Abbaye 99 ☎644590 tx41459 58rm48⇆10 ▥ P sB⇆ ▥1050 dB⇆ ▥1350 (English breakfast) L350 D350

LIER Antwerpen 27,850 (☎031) Map **4** C2

🛏 ➾**G Guwy** F-van Cauwenbergstr 19 ☎800139 Frd

LIGNEUVILLE Liège 1,110 (☎080) Map **4** D1

★★**Moulin** ☎570081 Closed Dec–14 Jan 20rm7⇆ ▥ P sB500 sB⇆ ▥675 dB875 dB⇆ ▥1150 Lalc D700⇆

LOKEREN Oost-Vlaanderen 27,150 (☎091) Map **3** B2

★★**Park** Antwerpsesteenweg 1 (DP) ☎482046 Closed Mon & 5–27 Jul 10rm5⇆5 ▥ ▥

🛏 ➾**Mees** Gentsesteenweg 263 ☎555759 P Fia

🛏 ➾**Moderne** Weverslaan 14 ☎481400 BMW (GB)

LORCE Liège 300 (☎080) Map **4** C1

★**Vallée** ☎85826 Closed Jan–Feb 6rm

LOUVAIN See **LEUVEN**

LOUVIÈRE (LA) Hainaut 22,850 (☎064)

🛏 ➾**J Dupire et Fils** r L-Dupuis 10 ☎224031 ☎228653 BL/Jag/Rov (GB)

MALINES See **MECHELEN**

MALMÉDY Liège 6,400 (☎080) Map **4** D1

★★**Bristol** pl Albert-1er 47 ☎777476 9rm2⇆9 ▥ sB450–550 dB⇆ ▥795–975 L350–525 D350–525

MARCHE-EN-FAMENNE Luxembourg 4,950 (☎084) Map **4** C1

★★**Cloche** r Luxembourg 2 ☎311579 10⇆ ▥ lake

🛏 ➾**Leunen & Cie Sprl** rte de Bastogne 51A ☎311582 Fia/Lnc (GB)

🛏 ➾**Verhulst A & Fils** rte de Liege 50 ☎311673 M/c P BL (GB)

MARIAKERKE See **OOSTENDE (Ostende)**

MASNUY-ST-JEAN Hainaut (☎065) Map **3** B1

★★★**Amigo** chaussée Brunehault 4 ☎728721 tx57313 52⇆ Lift Pool

MECHELEN (MALINES) Antwerpen 64,650 (☎015) Map **3** B2

★**Memling** Onder de Toren 12 ☎211218 10rm1⇆1 ▥ A1rm

🛃 ➾**Festraets NV** M Sabbestr 123 Ver koop Administration en Service ☎202752 Bed/Vau (GB)

MENEN (Menin) West-Vlaanderen 21,800 (☎056) Map **3** B1

🛏 ➾**Descamps** Brugsestr 349 ☎513053 ☎513053 P Dat

🛏 ➾**Vanhoo** Kortrijkstr 269 ☎513535 ✿ Ren

MONS (BERGEN) Hainaut 61,750 (☎065) Map **3** B1

🛏 ➾**Automons** (G Vienne) r du chemin de Fer 163 ☎311126 P Fia (GB)

🛏 ➾**A Wattier** au du Grand Jour 3 ☎335173 Frd (GB) At **Boussu** (12km W on N22)

🛏 ➾**Amand** rte de Mons 20–30 ☎773831 P BL/Tri (GB)

MONT KEMMEL West-Vlaanderen 1,410 (☎057) Map **3** B1

★★★**Hostellerie Mont Kemmel** Bergstr 339C ☎44145 Closed Feb–14 mar 22rm17⇆ ▥ ▥

NADRIN Luxembourg 500 (☎084) Map **4** C1

★★**Ondes** ☎444111 15rm7⇆1 ▥ ▥

NAMUR (NAMEN) Namur 31,350 (☎081) Map **4** C1

🛏 ➾**L Labenne & M Franceschini** av F-Golenvaux 23–29 ☎223000 P Bed/Hon/Opl/Vau

NEUFCHÂTEAU Luxembourg 2,750 (☎061) Map **10** D4

🛏 ➾**L Guillaume** av de la Victoire 46 ☎27211 M/c P

NEU-MORESNET (KELMIS) Liège (☎087) Map **4** C/D1

★★**Sélect** r de Liege 75 ☎59005 Closed Oct–15 Dec 7rm1⇆ ▥

NEUPONT Luxembourg 358 (☎084) Map **10** D4

★★**Baligan** Neupont par Wellin ☎388166 Closed Feb–mid Apr 11rm ▥

★**Ry des Glands** rte de Libin 93 ☎388133 Closed Jan–Feb 12rm ▥ P sB590 dB1180 L450–600 D450–600 lake

NIL-ST-VINCENT Brabant 1,150 (☎010) Map **4** C1

★**Manoir** chaussée de Namur 18 ☎655325 Closed Sep 6rm1⇆ P sB450–700 sB⇆900 dB600–900 dB⇆1200 (English breakfast) L575–795 D575–900

NIVELLES (Nijvel) Brabant 18,100 (☎067) Map **4** C1

🛏 ➾**F Havaux** pl E-de-Lalieux 25 ☎222208 P BL/Jag/Rov/Tri

OOSTENDE (Ostende) West-Vlaanderen 71,750 (☎059) Map **3** B2 **See Plan**

★★★**Impérial** Van Iseghemlaan 76–78 ☎705481 tx81167 Plan **1** 61rm50⇆7 ▥ ▥ P Lift sB⇆ ▥790–850 dB1070 dB⇆ ▥1230–1450 (English breakfast) L420 D420 sea

★★★**Ambassadeur** Wapenplein 8A ☎700941 Plan **2** 21⇆ ▥ P Lift ♪ sB⇆1150–1450 dB⇆1600–1800 (English breakfast) L435–535 D400–500

★★★**Bellevue-Britannia** prom Albert 1er 55–56 ☎706373 Plan **3** 58rm49⇆ Lift ♪ sBfr800 sB⇆900–1050 dBfr1600 dB⇆1800–2100 L440–535 D535 sea

★★★**Prado** Léopold II Laan 22 ☎705306 tx18193 Plan **4** 28⇆ Lift ♪ sB⇆910 dB⇆1310 (English breakfast)

★★★**Riff** Léopold II Laan 20 ☎707663 Plan **5** 48rm47⇆1 ▥ Lift sB⇆810 dB⇆ ▥1290

★★★**Ter Streep** Léopold II Laan 14 (n rest) ☎700911 Plan **6** 38rm30⇆8 ▥ Lift Pool

★★★**Westminster** Van Iseghemlaan 22 ☎702411 Plan **7** 60⇆ Lift dB

★★**Derby** Van Iseghemlaan ☎72030 Plan **8** 20rm3⇆ Lift

★★**Ensor** Kapucijnenstr 27 ☎802857 Plan **9** Closed 16 Nov–14 Feb 24rm23⇆1 ▥ ▥ P Lift ♪ sB⇆ ▥700–850 dB⇆ ▥900–1100 (English breakfast) sea

★★**Europe** Kapucijnenstr 52 ☎701012 Plan **10** Closed 4 Nov–Feb 65rm25⇆25 ▥ ▥ P Lift ♪ sB425–450 sB⇆ ▥650 dB750–800 dB⇆ ▥850–900 L200–245 D200–245

★★**Motor Inn** Vlisserskaai 7 ☎706362 Plan **11** Closed 19 Dec–4 Jan 23rm7 ▥ ▥ Lift sea

★★**Parc** M.-Josépl 3 ☎701680 Plan **12** 53rm7⇆5 ▥ Lift sB640–750 sB⇆ ▥835–975 dB970–1135 dB⇆ ▥1145–1305

★**Glenmore** Hofstr 25 ☎702022 Plan **14** Closed Oct–Etr 50rm16⇆3 ▥ Lift ♪ sB405–485 sB⇆ ▥525–605 dB680–840 dB⇆ ▥920–1080 (English breakfast) L250 D250 sea

★**Niewe Sportsman** de Smet de Nayerlaan 9 ☎702384 Plan **15** 10rm1⇆ sB300 dB600

★**Pacific** Hofstr 11 ☎701507 Plan **16** Closed Nov–Feb 51rm35 ▥ ▥ Lift ♪ sB475 sB⇆ ▥525 dB850 dB⇆ ▥950

★**Regent** prom Albert-1er 3 ☎703457 Plan **18** Closed 16 Nov–14 Dec 40rm2⇆ Lift sea

★**Strand** Vlisserskaai 1 ☎703383 tx81357 Plan **19** ▥ Lift sB550 sB⇆ ▥925–1000 dB1100 dB⇆ ▥1325 L325–695 D325–695

🛏 ➾**Casino Kursaal** Van Iseghemlaan 83 ☎703240 P Peu

🛃 ➾**Ocean** Koningster 27 ☎702820 P

🛏 ➾**Oostende-Motors** (m de Four) Torhoutsteenweg 473–475 ☎704840 P BL (GB)

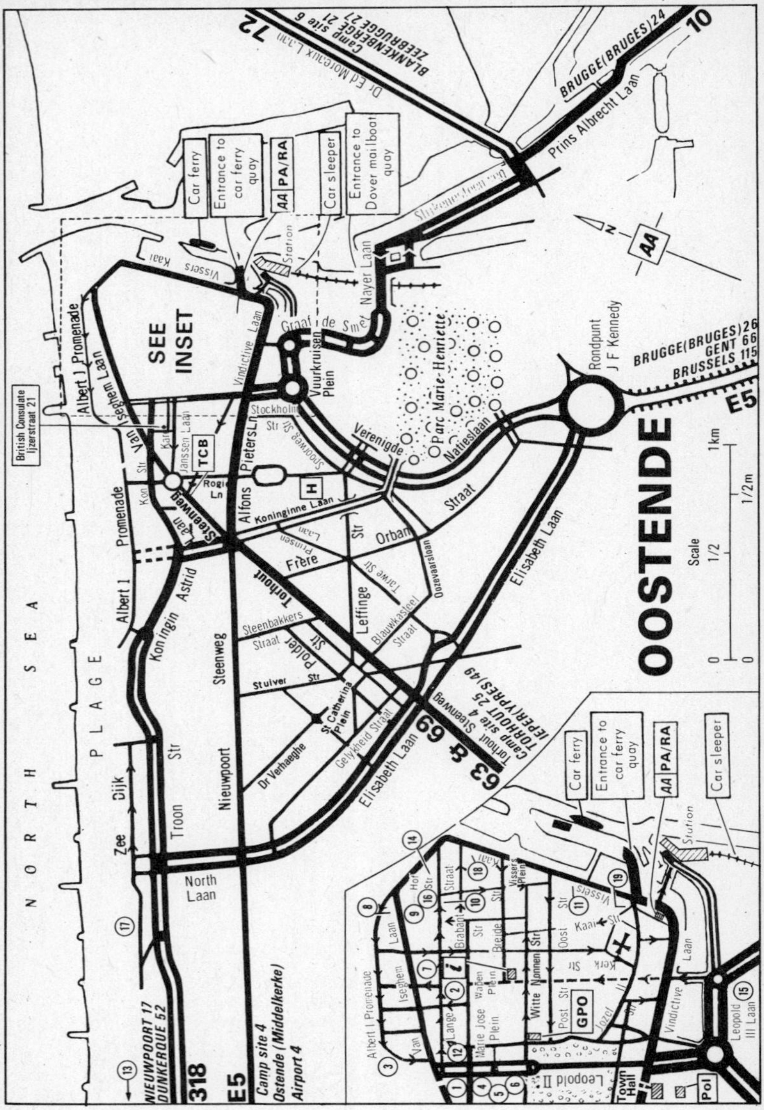

Belgium

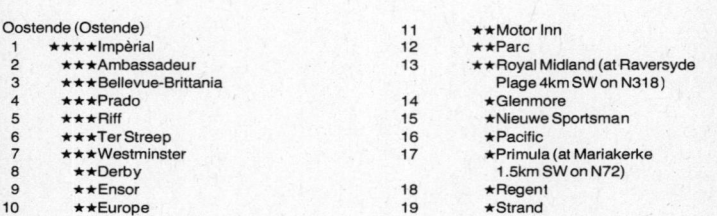

Oostende (Ostende)

1	★★★★Impèrial	11	★★Motor Inn
2	★★★Ambassadeur	12	★★Parc
3	★★★Bellevue-Brittania	13	★★Royal Midland (at Raversyde Plage 4km SW on N318)
4	★★★Prado	14	★Glenmore
5	★★★Riff	15	★Nieuwe Sportsman
6	★★★Ter Streep	16	★Pacific
7	★★★Westminster	17	★Primula (at Mariakerke 1.5km SW on N72)
8	★★Derby	18	★Regent
9	★★Ensor	19	★Strand
10	★★Europe		

i ๖๏Phare/Verhaeghe r Longue 91 ☎701364
☎701364 P (GB)

🛏 ๖๏Royal Auto NV Koninginnelaan 52 ☎707635
Chy/Sim (GB)

🛏 ๖๏F Stoops chaussée de Torhoutsteenweg 54
☎702472 AR/Sab/Toy (GB)

At **Mariakerke** (1.5km SW on N72)

★**Primula** Raversijdestr 48 ☎705191 Plan **17** Closed
Oct – 14 Mar 15rm2⇌9🍴 sB375 – 400
dB⇌🍴750 – 800 L150 D150

At **Raversyde Plage** (4km SW on N318)

★★**Royal Midland** Digue de Mer 354 ☎702138
Plan **13** Closed 16 Oct – Mar 34rm8⇌ sB450 – 600
sB⇌🍴550 – 650 dB900 dB⇌🍴975
(English breakfast) L250 D250 sea

OOSTKAMP See **BRUGGE (Bruges)**

PANNE (DE) (La Panne) West-Vlaanderen 7,100
(☎058) Map **3** B2

★★★**Parc** A-Dumontlaan 30 ☎41407 Closed
Oct – Feb 48rm22⇌ P Lift 𝄞 sB710 – 810
sB⇌🍴1010 – 1060 dB1070 dB⇌🍴1220 – 1420
(English breakfast) L560 D560

★★**Royal** Zeelaan 178 ☎411116 Closed
16 Nov – 14 Feb 35rm29⇌ P Lift sB655 – 685
sB⇌🍴735 – 765 dB1050 – 1140 dB⇌🍴1160 – 1230
(English breakfast) L410 D390 sea

★**Mon Bijou** Zeelaan 94 ☎41105 35rm3🍴 🐕 Lift 𝄞

★**Regina Maris** av Bortier 11 ☎411222 Closed
6 Jan – 4 Feb 71rm25⇌25🍴 Lift Pool

PAYENNE-COUSTINE See **DINANT**

PHILIPPEVILLE Namur 2,400 (☎071) Map **4** C1

★★**Croisée** r de France 45 ☎666231 Closed
13 Dec – Jan 11rm5⇌ 🐕 P sB510 – 775
sB⇌590 – 775 dB710 – 1100 dB⇌805 – 1100
L550alc D550alc St% Pool

★**Princes de Liège** rte de Giver 1 ☎666104 9⇌ 🐕 P
𝄞 sB⇌600 – 700 dB⇌1300 (English breakfast)
L575 – 875 D575 – 875

🛏 ๖๏Michaux Quatre Bras ☎666567 🛠 Ren

PROFONDEVILLE Namur 2,350 (☎081) Map **4** C1

★**Auberge d'Alsace** av Gl-Gracia Boreuville 42
☎412228 6⇌ 🐕 P sB⇌550 dB⇌950 L500 D500
mountains lake

RAVERSYDE PLAGE See **OOSTENDE**

ROCHE-EN-ARDENNE (LA) Luxembourg 1,800
(☎084) Map **4** C1

★★★**Air Pur** rte de Houffalize 11 ☎411223 Closed
Jan – Etr 14rm9⇌ P sB810 sB⇌1660 dB970 – 1240
dB⇌1820 – 2220 L alc D alc St%

★★★**Ardennes** r de Beausaint 2 (DP) ☎411112
Closed Jan – mid Apr & 16 Nov – Xmas 12⇌ 🐕

★★**Belle-Vue** av du Hadja 10 ☎411187 25rm6⇌

★**Merlettes** r Val du Pierreux (DP Pn) ☎411159
Closed 11 Sep – Mar 13rm 🐕 L Pool

🛏 ๖๏C Bechet pl Chanteraine 8 ☎411119 P Frd/Toy

ROCHEFORT Namur 4,550 (☎084) Map **10** D4

★★★**Central** pl Albert1-er 30 ☎211044 Closed Oct
7rm2⇌ P sB590 – 790 sB⇌790 – 890 dB980 – 1580
dB⇌1180 – 1780 L220 – 570 D220 – 570

★**Bristol** pl Albert-1er 27 (DP) ☎211170 7rm

★**Fayette** r Jacquet 87 ☎211024 Closed 16 Sep – 6
Oct 22rm5⇌7🍴 A15rm P sB450 – 550
sB⇌550 – 650 dB620 – 880 dB⇌🍴780 – 1040
(English breakfast) L280 – 680 D280 – 680

SINT NIKLAAS (St-Nicolas) Oost-Vlaanderen
48,850 (☎031) Map **3** B2

★★★**Serwir** Koningin Astridlaan 49 ☎765311
tx32422 28rm9⇌19🍴 P Lift sB⇌🍴770 – 975
dB⇌🍴1490

★★**Arend** O-L-Vroupl 8 ☎760126 10rm2⇌1🍴 P
sB380 sB⇌🍴530 dB660 dB⇌🍴760 L200 D200

🛏 ๖๏Sint Christoffel (J H Streat) Wegvoeringstr 88
☎761338 BL/Rov/Tri (GB)

SINT TRUIDEN (St-Trond) Limburg 22,300 (☎011)
Map **4** C1

🛏 ๖๏Celis Bevingenstweg 1C ☎677951 BL/Rov/Tri

🛏 ๖๏P Burghardt & Nicolai Hasseltsesteenweg 21G

☎673387 P AR/Toy (GB)

SPA Liège (☎087) Map **4** C1

★★★**Château Sous-Bois** chemin de la Platte 22
☎72300 Closed Nov – mid Nov 20⇌ Lift

★★★**Vieille France** rte du Lac 5 ☎771731 Closed
Sep – Dec 6rm4⇌ 🐕 🏊 Pool lake

★★**Grand Cerf** rte Sauvenière 111 (DP) ☎772565
Closed 14 Nov – 14 Dec 7⇌

At **Lac de Warfaz** (2.5km NE)

★★**Lac** ☎771074 12rm5⇌ 🐕 P dB666 – 697
dB⇌819 – 890 L560alc D560alc lake

At **Tiège-lez-Spa** (5km NE)

★★★**Charmille** r de Tiège 38 ☎474313 Closed Jan &
Feb 40rm25⇌ 🐕 Lift 🏊

SPONTIN Namur 600 (☎083) Map **4** C1

★**Cheval Blanc** chaussée de Dinant 26 ☎699471
12rm

STAMBRUGES-GRANDGLISE Hainaut 2,450
(☎069) Map **3** B1

★**Château Vert Gazon** rte de Mons 1 ☎575984
Closed 1 – 15 Jan & 15 Jun – 1 Jul 7rm6⇌1🍴 🐕 P
sB⇌🍴660 dB⇌🍴1010 – 1340 L940alc D940alc

STROMBEEK See **BRUSSELS – BRUXELLES**

TERVUREN See **BRUSSEL-BRUXELLES**

THOUROUT See **TORHOUT**

TIÈGE-LEZ-SPA See **SPA**

TIENEN (Tirlemont) Brabant 23,950 (☎016)
Map **4** C1

🛏 ๖๏Delaisse Leuvensestr 115 – 117 ☎811077
☎811652 M/c P Toy (GB)

TONGEREN Limburg 20,700 (☎012) Map **4** C1

★**Lido** Grote Markt 19 ☎231948 9rm2⇌1🍴

🛏 ๖๏Alberto Henisstr 121 ☎231291 P

TORHOUT (Thourout) West-Vlaanderen 15,750
(☎050) Map **3** B2

🛏 ๖๏Deketclaere Vredelaan 91 ☎212623 ☎212623
(night phone) P Bed/Vau (GB)

At **WYNENDAELE** (3km)

★**'t Gravenhof** Oostendestr 335 ☎212314
11rm5⇌3🍴 🐕

TOURNAI (Doornik) Hainaut 33,200 (☎069)
Map **3** B1

🛏 ๖๏American av Van Cutsem 23 ☎221921 Frd
(GB)

🛏 ๖๏R Blancquart chaussée de lille 18B ☎222162 P
Toy

TURNHOUT Antwerpen 38,200 (☎014) Map **4** C2

★**Terminus** Grote Markt 72 ☎42078 13rm 4⇌2🍴
Lift

🛏 ๖๏Perfect Nieuwekaai 9 – 11 ☎413588 Ren (GB)

VERVIERS Liège 31,450 (☎087) Map **4** C1

★★★**Amigo** r Herla 1 ☎221121 tx49128
59rm50⇌9🍴 🐕 Lift 🏊

★★**Grand** r du Palaise 145 ☎223177 28rm8⇌4🍴
A16rm P Lift 𝄞 sB540 sB⇌🍴690 dB755
dB⇌🍴1330

🛏 ๖๏F Spirlet Fils r S–Lobet 62 – 66 ☎223111 Frd

🛏 ๖๏Stevens r de Liège 18 – 19 ☎221069 P Lot/Vau
(GB)

VEURNE (Furnes) West-Vlaanderan 9.500 (☎058)
Map **3** B2

🛏 ๖๏R Sierens D de Haenelaan 2 ☎311205 Aud/VW
(GB)

VILLE-POMMEROEUL Hainaut 2,460 (☎065)
Map **3** B1

★★**Relais** rte de Mons 10 ☎620561 Closed
16 Aug – 4 Sep 6⇌ 🐕 P sB⇌975 – 1075
dB⇌1950 – 2150

VILLERS-SUR-LESSE Namur 500 (☎084)
Map **4** C1

★**Beau Séjour** r Village 15 (DP) ☎377115 Closed
16 Jan – Feb 23rm9⇌10🍴 A5rm 🐕

VRESSE Namur 500 (☎061) Map **10** D4

★★★**Eau Vive** r de Petit Fays 52 ☎500471 Closed
Jan & Feb 33rm31⇌ A6rm P Lift sB795 sB⇌865
dB1350 dB⇌1450 – 1550 L575 – 700 D575 – 700

WENDUINE West-Vlaanderen 2,200 (☎050)
Map **3** B2

★★*Mouettes* Zeedijk 7 ☎411514 Closed Oct–Mar 28rm8⇌16🛏 Lift sea

WEPION Namur 4,800 (☎081) Map **4** C1

☆☆☆☆**Sofitel** chaussée de Dinant 195 ☎715811 tx59031 120⇌ P sB⇌1200–1680 dB⇌1710–2150 L275 D275 Pool

★*Frisia* chaussée de Dinant 311 ☎411106 9rm2⇌ 🏨

WESTENDE West-Vlaanderen 5,100 (☎059) Map **3** B2

★★*Rotonde* Zeedijk 400 ☎300495 closed 16 Sep–mid Apr 16rm9⇌ Beach sea

WEVELGEM West-Vlaanderen 14,500 (☎056) Map **3** B1

★★★*Park Cortina* Lauwestr 55 ☎4125222 tx85203 Closed 1–15 Aug 36rm15⇌5🛏 A6rm 🏨 Lift

WYNENDAELE See **TORHOUT (THOUROUT)**

XHOFFRAIX Liège (☎080) Map **4** D1

★★**Trôs Marets** Point de Vue Albert -1er ☎777917 Closed 16 Nov–22 Dec 7⇌ P sB⇌1345–2545 dB⇌2690–5090 L900–1350 D900–1350

YPRES See **LEPER**

YVOIR Namur 2,650 (☎082) Map **4** C1

★★**Vachter** chaussée de Manur 140 ☎611314 Closed Jan & Feb 10rm9⇌ 🏨 P sB⇌895 dB⇌1185 L998 D998

ZEEBRUGGE West-Vlaaderen (☎050) Map **3** B2

★*Victoire* P-Trooslaan 5 ☎544025 22rm3⇌ sea

ZOLDER Limburg 12,000 (☎011) Map **4** C2

★*Pits* Omloop Terlaemen ☎225520 12rm11⇌1🛏 Pool

ZOUTE (LE) See **KNOKKE HEIST**

View of a Spa

FRANCE & MONACO

Population 52,346,000 **Area** 210,038 sq miles **Maps** 3, 7, 8, 9, 10, 11, 15 & 16

How to get there

Motorists can cross the Channel by ship or hovercraft services. Short sea crossings operate from Dover and Folkestone to Boulogne and Calais (1½–1¾hrs). Longer Channel crossings operate from Dover to Dunkirk (2½hrs). Newhaven to Dieppe (3¾hrs). Portsmouth to Le Havre (5½hrs), Cherbourg (4–6½hrs), or St Malo (8–10hrs). Southampton to Le Havre (6½–8½hrs) or Cherbourg (5hrs), Plymouth to Roscoff (7–8hrs) and St Malo (7–9hrs), and Weymouth to Cherbourg (4hrs). Fast hovercraft services operate between Dover and Boulogne or Calais (30–35mins) and between Ramsgate and Calais (40mins).

General information

Information in this section is specific to France. A wider background is provided in the notes on page 8 with other information which you are advised to read.

AA Port agents
33076 Bordeaux Cedex Mory SA, Zone Portuaire d'Entrepots de Bordeaux-Nord 1 rue Surcouf ☎508400. (56)

62201 Boulogne-sur-Mer G A Gregson & Sons. The Automobile Association, Gare Maritime BP No.21 ☎(21)302222.

62100 Calais G A Gregson & Sons, The Automobile Association, Gare de Transit ☎(21)964720; ta Gregson-Calais.

50100 Cherbourg Agence Maritime Tellier, Gare Maritime 50100 ☎532427; Port office (when ferries operating), car ferry terminal ☎532038.

76200 Dieppe G A Gregson & Sons, The Automobile Association, car ferry terminal, Esplanade ☎841941.

76600 Le Havre G A Gregson & Sons, The Automobile Association, 47 boulevard John Kennedy ☎(35)420566.

13002 Marseille Watson Brown SA, 10 Place de la Joliette ☎(91)903860; ta Energy-Marseille.

AA Continental Emergency Centre
Control of AA operations in Europe is centred at the AA office operated by G A Gregson & Sons, Gare Maritime, Boulogne-sur-Mer 62201 ☎(21)302222. 24-hour service is available daily (including Sundays) from 1 July to 30 September. During other months, service is available daily (including Sundays but excluding Christmas) from 09.00-18.00hrs and also for scheduled boat sailings.

France

*These are not recommended routes:
the distances are given as a guide only.*

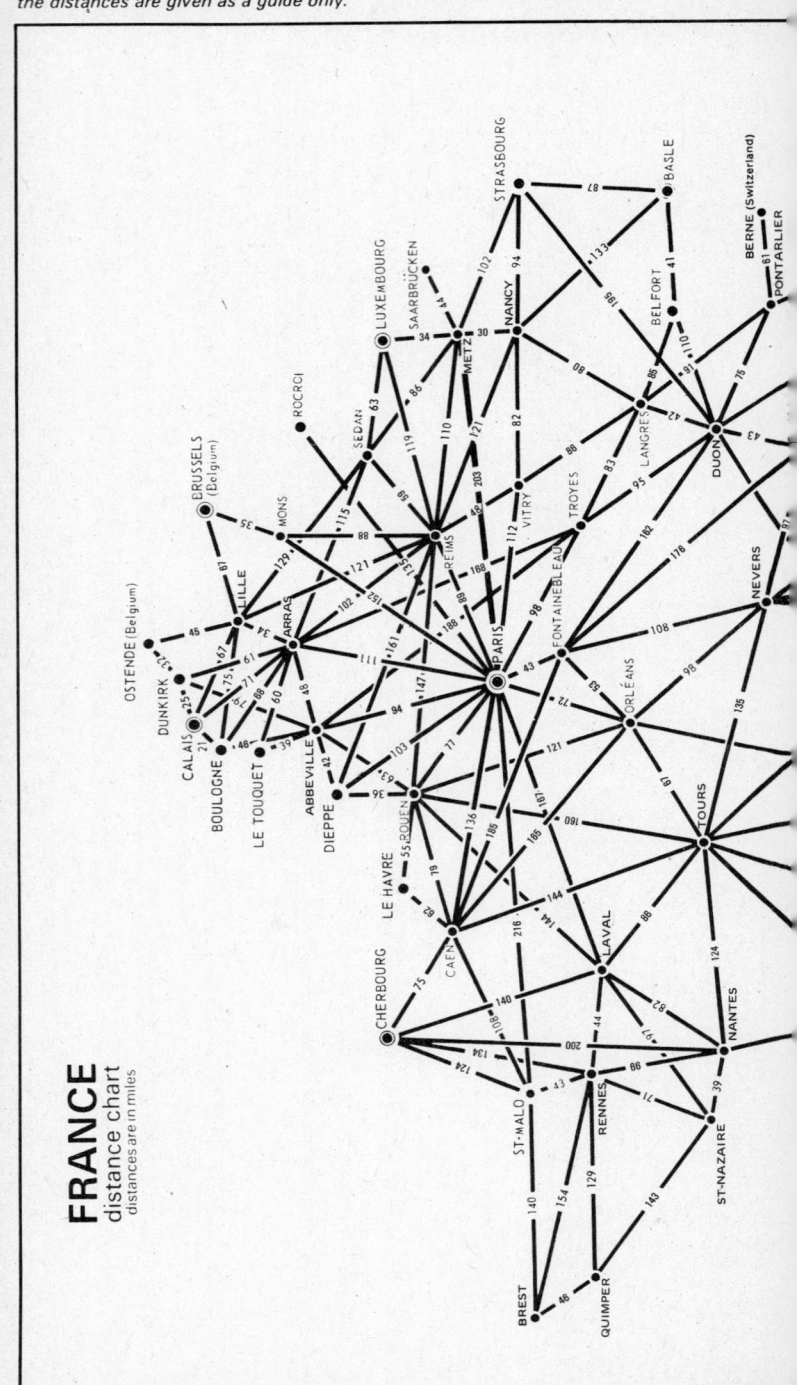

FRANCE
distance chart
distances are in miles

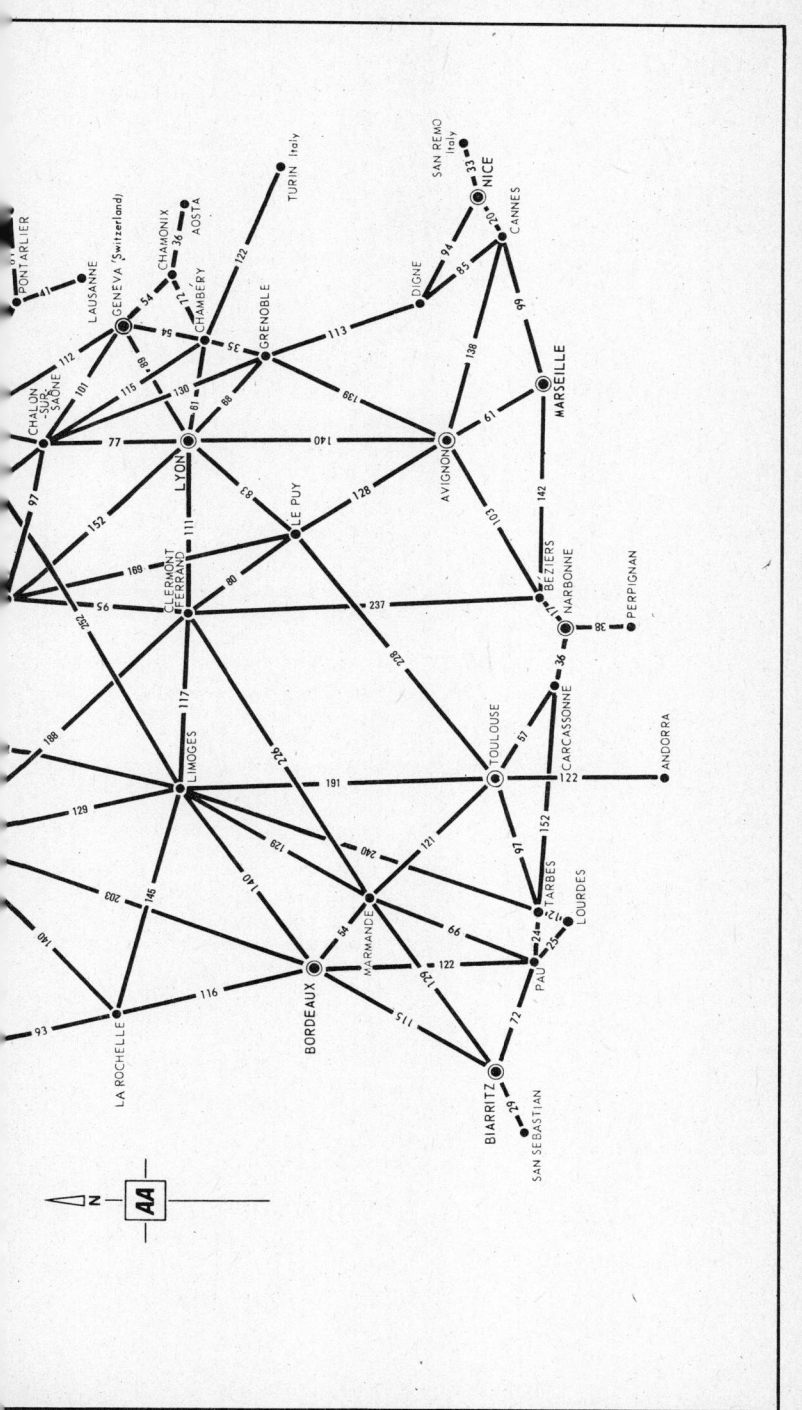

France

Accommodation   There is a large selection of hotels of all categories. The Commissariat de Tourisme classifies hotels in five categories; one-star to *de luxe*. Local tourist information offices (see page 159) can provide details of hotels and restaurants in the area.

Rates for rooms are usually officially controlled and must be displayed in each room, but the cost of meals is not controlled. Many hotels, particularly along the French Riviera, offer full board terms only, as indicated in the gazetteer DP.

Logis de France These are Government-sponsored tourist inns equivalent to the one-star or two-star categories. They are generally located off the beaten track and offer a high standard for their type and good value for money. There are nearly 4,000 Logis, some of which are listed in the gazetteer, and they are marked by the symbol **L**.
The *Logis de France Guide* is published annually, and can be purchased through bookshops.

Relais Routier These are restaurants situated on main roads offering simple accommodation and providing a good meal at a reasonable price. The *Relais Routier Guide* issued each year, can be purchased through bookshops.

Gites de France This is furnished accommodation in rural France, often at farms, for those who prefer to cater for themselves. There are some 23,000 Gites in 4,000 villages, created with the financial support of the French Government and governed by a charter laid down by the Fédération National de Gites de France.

Personal callers at the office at 178 Piccadilly, London can book a holiday Gite by joining the British section of the Federation, membership costs £3.50, in addition to the booking service, includes a free copy of the *French Farm and Village Guide*. This Guide can also be purchased through bookshops.

Annual events

January	**Nationwide** Ski-ing events
February	**Nice** Carnival with dancing, fireworks, and processions (February/March) **Amelie les Bains** Carnival with flower-decked vehicles and the burning of King Carnival
March	**Vichy** Carnival
April	**Ajaccio, Bastia, Bonifacio, Sartene** (Corsica) Good Friday processions **Biarritz** Folklore Festival
May	**Reims** and **Orleans** Festival of Joan of Arc **Saintes-Maries-de-la-Mer** Festival of the Gypsies **Saint-Tropez** 'La Bravade' celebration of 17th-century naval victory **Cannes** Film Festival
June	**Le Mans** 24-hour Race **Rouen** Joan of Arc Festival **Brie-Comte-Robert** Festival of Roses **Toulouse** Traditional Fair **Lyon** International Music Festival
July	**Nationwide** Tour de France world-famous cycling race **Aix-en-Provence** Music Festival **Nationwide** Bastille Day
August	**Aix-les-Bains** Flower Fair **Biarritz** Sea Fair **Confolens** International Folklore Festival
September	**Dijon** International Folk Festival **Anduze** Assembly of the Desert, Protestant meeting **Lourdes** Festival of the Virgin
November	**Beaune** etc Burgundy Wine Festival

Further information can be obtained from the French Government Tourist Office (see page 159).

Breakdowns   If your car breaks down, try to move it to the verge of the road so that it obstructs the traffic flow as little as possible. Place a warning triangle to the rear of the vehicle to warn following traffic.

On most of the major routes, at intervals of 2–3 miles, signs that say *'Touring Club de France, Secours Automobile, poste d'appel en cas d'urgence'*, outside shops, cafés, garages etc, indicate that a telephone call may be made from there to the nearest garage providing breakdown service. The police will also help by calling assistance.

Touring Secours   This is a radio-controlled breakdown service operated by the Touring Club de France. It is available for 24 hours daily in Paris and from 07.00 to 23.00hrs through a network of regional offices. AA members calling upon the service should produce their *5-Star Service Booklet*, otherwise a charge will be made. In any case towage, spare parts and fuel will be charged for.

British Consulates   75008 Paris, 105/109 rue du Faubourg St-Honore ☎2669142. There are also British Consulates in Epernay, Le Havre, Cherbourg, Nantes, Bordeaux, Biarritz, Lille, Calais, Boulogne, Dunkirk, Lyons, Metz, Marseilles, Strasbourg, Perpignan, Ajaccio (Corsica).

Currency and banking   The unit of currency is the French franc, which is divided into 100 centimes. There is no restriction on the amount of foreign currency which may be taken into France. Travellers are, however, restricted to taking Fr5,000 with them when leaving the country, unless, of course, they imported more currency on entry and completed the appropriate form at the time.

Banking hours   In most large towns banks are open from Monday to Friday 09.00–16.00hrs; they close on Saturdays and Sundays. Banks close at midday on the day prior to a national holiday and all day on Monday if the holidays falls on a Tuesday.

The *Credit Lyonnais* has offices at the Invalides air terminal in Paris open daily from 07.30hrs until midnight for cashing travellers' cheques. The *Société Générale* has two offices at Orly airport which are open between 07.00 and 23.00hrs. At the Charles de Gaule airport exchange facilities are available between 07.15 and 19.00hrs.

Shopping hours   Department stores are usually open from Monday to Saturday, 09.00–18.30hrs. Some foodshops open 07.00 and 20.00hrs and are open Sunday morning. Most shops are closed on Monday morning and all shops usually close for two or three hours at lunchtime.

Documents   A Carnet is necessary for outboard engines exceeding 92cc (5cv, French rating, as applied to marine engines) imported without boats.

Medical treatment   The provision of medical benefits in France is administered by local Social Security offices (*Le Caisse Primaire de Securité Sociale*). The address of the local office may be obtained from the Social Service Department of the Town Hall (Hotel de Ville). You may consult any doctor or dentist who will issue a sickness document (*feuille de maladie*) on which he will enter his fee after you have paid him. It should then be taken to the chemist together with the doctor's prescription. After you have paid him, the chemist will enter the cost of the medicines supplied and return the document and prescription to you.

You will be able to obtain a refund or part of the costs of treatment and medicines from the nearest local Social Security Office on presentation of form E111, the receipted sickness document and prescription. On entering hospital, produce form E111 and advise the hospital authorities that you are an insured person. They will carry out the necessary formalities (*prise en charge*) with the Social Security office. A percentage of the cost will be met direct by the local Social Security.

Motoring clubs   Although there are many motoring clubs and organisations in France, the most active as regards to general services to foreign visitors is the TCF (Touring Club de France) whose head office is at 65 avenue de la Grande-Armée, 75782 Paris Cedex 16. They also maintain branch offices in main towns throughout France. They have a wide range of services available to their members but will extend a courtesy service to foreign tourists. When requesting service AA members should produce their *5-Star Service Booklet*.

Automobile Club du Nord de la France   The Automobile Club du Nord de la France will assist AA members whenever possible. Produce your *5-Star Service Booklet*. 59 Roubaix (head office) 40–42 rue de Maréchal-Foch ☎Lille (20)530000. Office hours: 24-hour emergency service.

Automobile Club de l'Ouest   The Automobile Club de l'Ouest will also assist AA members whenever possible. Produce your *5-Star Service Booklet*. 72 Le Mans (head office) Les Raineries ☎840130. Office hours: weekdays 09.00–12.00hrs, and 14.00–18.00hrs; Saturdays 09.00–12.00hrs.

France

Post and telephone	Rates for foreign postage are:		Fr
	postcards		1.00
	letters up to	20gm	1.50
		20–50gm	3.00
		50–100gm	4.00
		100–250gm	7.50

Telephone rates   The charge for a 3-minute call to the UK is about Fr7.80 with a surcharge if the call is made from a hotel. There are very few public telephone boxes. Local calls can be made from a café or restaurant, but for toll or trunk calls you will need to go to a post office. Some public telephones are operated by coins, others by discs called *jetons*. You can buy a *jeton* from the place where you make the call – a café, restaurant, underground or railway station, etc, or from the post office.

To make a call, insert the coins or *jeton* before lifting the receiver, then lift and dial in the normal way; if there is no reply, the coins or *jeton* are returned when you replace the receiver.

Local calls cost 60 centimes from post office call boxes and are untimed. Other calls are based upon time and distance and the time of day that the call is made. If you are not familiar with the system and wish to make a long distance call it is better to do this from a hotel or café where there may be someone on hand to help you.

The address of the Paris post office, which is open 24 hours a day, is 52, rue du Louvre, Paris.

Public holidays   Holidays based on religious festivals are not always fixed on the calendar and any current diary will give actual dates. The Whit period should not be confused with the British Spring Holiday.

Fixed holidays	1 January	New Year's Day
	1 May	Labour Day
	14 July	Bastille Day
	15 August	Assumption
	1 November	All Saints' Day
	25 December	Christmas

Moveable holidays	Good Friday
	Easter Monday
	Ascension Day
	Whit Monday

Roads   France has a very comprehensive network of roads. They are classified into four main grades – the *autoroutes* (motorways), prefixed A; the *routes nationales* (national roads), prefixed N; *routes departémentales* (departmental roads), prefixed D; *chemins vicinaux* (local roads), prefixed V. *Routes nationales* allow high average speeds on long journeys, although a few (*eg* N1, N6, and parts of N7) carry heavy traffic. Their subsidiary branches are indicated by various references, for example N5bis, N6a, and No 10 ter. Road surfaces are normally good; exceptions are often signposted *chaussée deformée*. The cobble (*pavé*) stretches in the north are gradually being replaced by tarmac. The camber is often severe and the edges rough. It is a widespread practice to surface roads by spreading loose chippings on sprayed tar; too high a speed or careless overtaking can lead to a broken windscreen. The gradients of mountain passes are usually moderate; in some places at high altitudes road edges are not well protected.

Road number changes As part of a decentralisation scheme, many national highways have been transferred to the departments. Some road numbers were simply changed by replacing the prefix N with D, but in some cases the figure 9 has been used to precede the last two figures of the old number, eg N315 is now D915, N77 is now D977 and N1 is now D901.

It now appears that many of the local authorities have adopted the recommendation of the Ministry of the Interior to use the figure 9 as the first digit of the new D numbers, but regrettably there are many exceptions where any number between 3 and 9 has been used.

Holiday traffic   *Itinéraires bis (Emeraude)* and *Itinéraires de delestage*. Special green and yellow signs (arrows) are used to indicate alternative routes to avoid heavy traffic routes and/or traffic hold-ups in towns. The signs on these roads are continuous and when they appear it is usually advantageous to follow them, although you cannot be absolutely sure of gaining time.

Traffic lanes (Paris)   There are special lanes for buses and taxis only in some streets; they are marked by a continuous yellow line painted one vehicle-width from the kerb. Usually, buses and taxis in the special lane travel in the opposite direction to other traffic.

Motorways   There are about 3,001 miles of motorway (*autoroute*) open, and 318 miles under construction and due to open 1979. A total of 3,728 miles of motorways are expected to be in use by the end of 1980. To join a motorway, follow signs with the words *par autoroute* added. Motorcycles of 50cc or less are prohibited; commercial vehicles weighing more than 3 tons are prohibited at weekends. Tolls are charged

on most motorways according to the distance travelled. Most cars (including Minis) pay the tolls quoted below if the entire motorway is used. Where only one toll charge is quoted, the same toll applies to all cars with or without caravans.
NB Motorised caravans are charged at a more expensive rate.

Toll payment (Péage)   On the majority of the toll motorways a travel ticket is issued on entry, and toll is paid on leaving the motorway. The travel ticket gives all relevant information about the toll charges, including the toll category of the vehicle. At the exit point, the ticket is handed in. On some motorways the toll collection is automatic; have the correct amount ready to throw into collecting basket.

If change is required use marked, separate lane.

The main toll motorways are:

Autoroute du Nord
A1   *Paris (Porte de la Chapelle)–Roissy-en-France* **(no toll)**
Roissy–Roye–Fresnes (nr Arras)
(toll: car Fr22.50; with caravan Fr33.50)
Fresnes–Lille **(no toll)**
A1/A2   *Roissy-en-France–Cambrai*
(toll: car Fr23.00; with caravan Fr34.50)

Autoroute de l'Est
A4   *Paris–Lagny* **(no toll)**
Lagny–Reims **(toll:** car Fr25.00; with caravan Fr37.50)
Reims–Metz **(toll:** car Fr36.00; with caravan Fr54.00)

Autoroute du Sud (Soleil)
A6   *Paris–Fleury (near Fontainebleau)* **(no toll)**
Fleury (near Fontainebleau)–Lyon **(toll:** car Fr53.00; with caravan Fr80.00)
A7   *Lyon–Vienne* **(no toll)**
Vienne–Orange **(toll:** car Fr28.00; with caravan Fr43.00)
Vienne–Marseille **(toll:** car Fr41.00; with caravan Fr64.00)
A7/A8   *Vienne–Aix-en-Provence*
(toll: car Fr41.00; with caravan Fr64.00)

Autoroute Esterel–Côte d'Azur (La Provencale)
A8   *Aix-en-Provence–Puget-sur-Argens (Fréjus)*
(toll: Car Fr22.50; with caravan Fr34.00)
Aix-en-Provence–Nice
(toll: car Fr34.50; with caravan Fr52.00)
Nice-La Turbue **(toll:** Fr7.00; with caravan Fr10.00)
Roquebrune (nr Menton)–Italian frontier **(toll:** car Fr2.50; with caravan Fr4.00)

Autoroute Orange–Narbonne (La Languedocienne)
A9   *Orange–Montpellier* **(toll:** car Fr15.00; with caravan Fr23.00)
Montpellier–Narbonne **(toll:** car Fr15; with caravan Fr23)

Autoroute La Catalane
B9   *Narbonne–Le Perthus* **(toll:** car Fr17.00; with caravan Fr26.00)

Autoroute Paris–Orléans–Tours (L'Aquitaine)
A10/A11   *Paris (Palaiseau)–La Folie Bessin* **(no toll)**
A10   *La Folie Bessin–Orléans Ouest* **(toll:** car Fr17.00; with caravan Fr25.00)
Orléans–Tours **(toll:** car Fr20.00; with caravan Fr30.00)
Tours–Poitiers **(toll:** car Fr20.00; with caravan Fr30.00)

Autoroute Paris–Chartres (L'Océane)
A10/A11   *Paris (Palaiseau)–La Folie Bessin* **(no toll)**
A11   *La Folie Bessin–Chartres* **(toll:** car Fr10.50; with caravan Fr16.00)
Paris–Le Mans **(toll:** car Fr33.00; with caravan Fr50.00)

Autoroute de L'Ouest and Normandie
A13   *Paris–Mantes* **(no toll)**
Mantes–Les Essarts (nr Rouen) **(toll:** Fr10)
Mantes–Bourneville (nr Pont Audemer) **(toll:** Fr14.50)
Mantes–Caen **(toll:** Fr26.50)

Autoroute Calais–Arras
A26   *Lillers–Arras* **(toll:** car Fr8.00; with caravan Fr12.00)

Autoroute Metz–Saarbrücken
A32   *Metz–Freyming* **(toll:** Fr6.00)
Freyming–Saarbrücken **(no toll)**

Autoroute Freyming–Strasbourg
A34   *Freyming–Strasbourg* **(toll:** car Fr17; with caravan Fr25.50)

France

Autoroute Beaune–Mulhouse
A36 *Besançon–Montbéliard* (**toll:** Fr17.50/26.00)
Montbéliard–Belfort (**no toll**)
Belfort–Mulhouse (**toll:** car Fr5; with caravan Fr7.50)

Autoroute Dijon–Beaune
A37 *Dijon–Beaune* (**toll:** car Fr5.50; with caravan Fr9)

Autoroute Grenoble–Annecy
A41 *Annecy–Chambéry* (**toll:** car Fr12.00; with caravan Fr18.00)
Grenoble–Pontcharra (**toll:** car Fr8.00; with caravan Fr12.00)

Autoroute Blanche
B41 *Geneva–Le Fayet* (**toll:** car Fr12.00; with caravan Fr18.00)

Autoroute Lyon–Chambéry
A43 *Lyon–Chambéry* (**toll:** car Fr26.00; with caravan Fr39.00)

Autoroute Lyon–Grenoble
A48 *Lyon–Grenoble* (**toll:** car Fr20.00; with caravan Fr30.00)

Autoroute Marseille–Aubagne–Toulon
A/B52 *Marseille–Aubagne* (**no toll**)
Aubagne–Toulon (**toll:** car Fr9; with caravan Fr14)
Aix-en-Provence–Toulon (**toll:** car 16.00; with caravan Fr25.00)

Autoroute des deux Mers
A61 *Bordeaux–La Prade* (**no toll**)
La Prade–Langon (**toll:** car Fr10.00; with caravan Fr14.50)

Autoroute de la Côte Basque
A63 *Bayonne–Spanish frontier* (**toll:** car Fr10; with caravan Fr14.50)
A64 *Orthez bypass* (**toll:** car Fr2.00; with caravan Fr3.00)
B71 *Thiers bypass* (**toll:** car Fr3.00; with caravan Fr4.50)

Toll bridges

Tancarville toll bridge *Map 9 A 4*
29km (18 miles) from Le Havre
Charges

Vehicles		
	cars up to 4cv	Fr4
	4–9cv	Fr6.50
	over 9cv	Fr9
	motorcycles and scooters with or without sidecars	Fr1
	coaches up to 29 seats	Fr16
	coaches over 29 seats	Fr22
	lorries	Fr6.50–23
	caravan	Fr2.50
Vehicle passengers		free

Ile d'Oleron toll bridge *Map 15 B3*
Charges (including return)

Vehicles		
	cars	Fr19
	motorcycles	Fr4
	coaches (including passengers)	Fr50
	car/caravan combination	Fr38

Ile de Noirmoutier toll bridge *Map 7 B2*
Charges

Vehicles		
	cars under 1500kg	Fr8
	caravans and cars over 1500kg	Fr10
	motorcycles	Fr1

Seudre toll bridge *Map 15 B3*
5km (3 miles) from Marennes
Charges

Vehicles		
	car	Fr7
	caravan	Fr7
	motorcycle	Fr1

St Nazaire toll bridge *Map 7 B2*
Charges

Vehicles		
	car	Fr28
	car and caravan	Fr31
	motorcycle	Fr5
	moped	Fr1

Motorway telephones

For assistance on a motorway use one of the telephone boxes sited at 2.4km (1½-mile) intervals; they are connected to police stations.

Ferries (internal)	All particulars are subject to alteration.
Rhine ferries	*See Germany, page 229*
Seine ferries	**Port Jérôme-Quillebeuf** *Map 9 A4*
(between Le Havre	40.5km (25 miles) from Le Havre ☎Tancarville (Seine Maritime)
and Rouen)	397711
	The service is liable to interruption at certain tides.

Service Departures from Port Jérôme at 05.40 and 06.10hrs; hourly on the half-hour between 06.30 and 22.30hrs. Additional services at 10 and 50mins past the hour during morning, midday and evening peaks.

Departures from Quillebeuf at 05.30hrs; hourly on the hour between 06.00 and 22.00hrs and at 22.20hrs. Additional services at 20 and 40mins past the hour during morning, midday and evening peaks.

The following ferries also operate a half-hourly service during the winter months from 06.00 to 21.00hrs, and during the summer, 22.00hrs.

1	**Le Trail–La Maillerave** *Map 9 A4*
2	**Yainville–Heurteauville** *Map 9 A4*
3	**Jumieges–Port Jumieges** *Map 9 A4*
4	**Mesnil–sous–Jumieges** *Map 9 A4*
5	**Duclar–Berville-sur-Seine** *Map 9 A4*
6	**Sahurs–La Bouille** *Map 9 A4*
7	**Le Val-de-la-Have–Grand Couronne** *Map 9 A4*
8	**Dieppedale–Le Grand Quevilly** *Map 9 A4*

North and West	St-Malo–Dinard *Map 8 C3*
Coast ferries	☎Dinard 461592

Service It is now usual to cross by the dam of the Rance hydro-electric generating station. There is no toll and the distance is 10km (6 miles).

Quiberon–Le Palais (Belle-Ile-en-Mer) *Map 7 B2* ☎Quiberon (97) 526013: Le Palais (97) 528001.

Service

From October to March 2–3 daily
From March to May 3–6 daily
June 4–6 daily
From July to August 10 daily

September 3–6 daily
Duration 1 hour
Car space must be booked in advance

France

La Pallice (La Rochelle 5km)–Sablanceaux
(Ile de Re) *Map 8 C1* ☎La Rochelle 356148

Service From 05.45–00.40hrs approximately every 15 or 20 mins.
Winter departures 06.20–00.30hrs operating every 30 mins.
Duration 15 minutes

Royan–Pointe de Grave (across the Gironde) *Map 15 B3*
☎ Royan 052903; Le Verdon (56) 596084 and 596049
This service may be suspended during adverse weather conditions.

Service From June to September hourly or every 40mins between 08.00–22.20hrs (approx),
from Royan; hourly or every 40mins between 07.00–21.20hrs (approx), from Pointe de Grave.
Out of season 8 crossings daily between 08.00–21.00hrs (approx), from Royan; 8 crossings
daily between 07.00–22.00hrs (approx) from Pointe de Grave.
Duration 30 minutes

Blaye–Lamarque (across the Gironde) *Map 15 B3* ☎(56) 420449

Service From morning to evening; from July to end of August, 7 sailings daily; from September
to June 4–6 sailings daily.
Duration 30 minutes

South Coast ferries	To **Ile de Port-Cros** and **Ile du Levant** *Map 28 C1*
Passengers only	**Service** Frequent daily services during the summer (limited in winter) from Le Lavandou.

Duration 30–45 minutes
Four sailings daily during the season (limited in winter) from Port d'Hyères.
Duration 1hr to Port Cros; 1hr 15mins to Levant
To **Ile de Porquerolles** *Map 28 C1*
Service Frequent daily services during the summer (limited in winter) from La Tour-Fondue and
from Port d'Hyères.
Duration 20 mins from La Tour-Fondue; 30mins from Port d'Hyères
To **Iles de Lerins** *Map 28 C1*
Service 9 daily services from Cannes during summer months; 5 daily services from Cannes
during winter months. Additional services operate on Sundays and public holidays.
Full details are available from Compagnie Esterel – Chanteclair, Gare Maritime des Iles, 06400
Port de Cannes ☎(93) 391182.

Winter conditions Although there are five mountain regions – the Vosges, Jura,
Central Plateau, Alps and Pyrenees – motoring in winter is not
severely restricted. The main channels for south-bound traffic wanting to avoid the Alps and
Central Plateau are the N7 (A7) route along the Rhône Valley, the N20 from Limoges to
Toulouse, and the highways farther west. Roads into Belgium, Luxembourg and Germany are
generally unaffected.
All-the-year-round approaches to Strasbourg and Basle avoiding the Vosges and Jura are
routes N4 and N19 respectively. The approach to Switzerland via Pontarlier is very seldom
obstructed, and during very severe weather is a better route to Geneva than over the Faucille
Pass; alternatively the road via Bourg to Geneva is always open. Italy can be entered via the
Mont Blanc tunnel, the Fréjus railway tunnel (avoiding the Mont Cenis Pass), or along the French
Riviera via Menton. The main routes to Spain via Biarritz and Perpignan avoid the Pyrenees.

Whenever possible, roads are swept and kept clear.

In certain circumstances of thaw, some barred roads may be used by certain classes of traffic at
the driver's risk; passenger vehicles without trailers being used privately may proceed provided
they do not exceed 80kph (49mph).

Road signs Signposting is most efficient, but in open country there are not
always advance warning signs. Signs tend to point across the roads
they indicate, which is confusing at first. Loopways for heavy vehicles (*poids lourds*) are often
useful for avoiding town centres.

Allumez vos lanternes	Use headlights
Arbres inclinés	Overhanging trees
Arrêt d'autocar présentant un danger particulier	Bus stop causing a particular danger
Barriere de dégel	Thaw barrier
Carriere exploitée a la mine	Mining works
Cassis	150 metres (164yd) from the sign – road deterioration
Chaussée deformée	Bad road surface
Couloir d'avalanches	Avalanche region
Cylindrage	Road roller in use

French	English
Fin d'interdiction de stationner	End of no-parking area
Fin ou traversée de piste cyclable	End of crossing of cycle path
Gravillons	Loose chippings
Halte gendarmerie	Halt police
Hauteur limitée a 4m50	Vehicles under 4.5 metres in height only
Interdit au piétons	Pedestrians prohibited
Passage de hauteur limitée	Restricted passage to vehicles of certain height
Passage protégé	Crossroads protected by stop signs on side roads (proceed with caution)
Priorité a droite	Yield to traffic from the right
Poids lourds	Loopway for heavy vehicles
Poste suivant a 50km	Next callbox 50km away
Route barrée a 300m	Road closed after 300 metres
Route déviée	Diversion
Sens unique	One-way street
Serrez a droite	Keep right
Sortie d'usine	Factory exit
Suppression point noir	Black-spots notorious for accidents
Verglas	Glazed frost
Zone a stationnement réglementé	Regulated parking zone
Zone bleue	Blue-zone parking
Zone du chute de pierres	Danger from falling rocks

Tourist information offices

The French National Tourist Office maintains a full information service in London at 178 Piccadilly, London W1V 0AL and will be pleased to answer any enquiries on touring in France.

Once in France you should contact the local tourist office, *Syndicat d'Initiative* which will be found in all larger towns and resorts. They all have English-speaking staff and are pleased to give advice on local events, amenities and excursions. They can also answer specific local queries such as bus timetables and local religious services (all denominations) not available in the UK.

A further source of information within the country, is the *Accueil de France* (welcome office) who will also book hotel reservations within their area for the same night, or 24 hours in advance for personal callers only. There are not so many of these offices and mainly they are located at important stations and airports.

The hours of opening vary considerably depending upon the district and the time of year. Generally the offices are open between 09.00–12.00hrs and 14.00–18.00hrs from Monday to Saturday but in popular resort areas *Syndicats d'Initiative* are sometimes open later and on Sunday mornings.

Visitors' registration

A visitors' registration form will be completed by hotel or camp site management. If staying with friends at a private address, the host should notify the authorities.

Motoring regulations

Information in this section is specific to France. A wider background is provided in the notes on page 67 with other regulations which you are advised to read.

Accidents

Fire, police, ambulance Contact the police (*brigade de gendarmerie*), particularly in cases of injury. Police station telephone numbers are written in each telephone box. In Paris the number is 17. Emergency telephone boxes are stationed every 20km on some roadways and are connected direct to the local police station. In the larger towns emergency help can be obtained from the *police secours* (emergency assistance department).

Motorists involved in an accident must immediately obtain a written report (*constat*) from a bailiff (*huissier*), a number of whom are usually to be found in towns of any importance. The *constat* should be obtained, if possible, before the vehicle is moved. These reports for the most part constitute *prime facie* evidence in a court of law, or otherwise are valuable in establishing the facts of responsibility in support of claims for damages. The authorised charge for establishing a *constat* is Fr300–400 depending upon the length, and the circumstances of the accident. An official receipt should always be obtained. Motorists are urged to obtain these reports whenever

France

appropriate, especially if they do not consider themselves responsible for the accident. At the discretion of the authorities a sum of money may have to be deposited after the accident to cover court costs or fines. Otherwise the recommendations on page 67 are advisable.

Caravans and trailers Only one trailer may be towed. Due to their size, cars towing trailers may neither circulate nor park in the blue zone between 14.00 and 23.30hrs, excluding Sundays and public holidays. If you wish to cross Paris between these hours when towing a trailer you are recommended to use the boulevard Périphérique. Vehicles or vehicle-trailer combinations which are longer than 7 metres (23ft), or weigh more than 3,500kg (3tons 8cwt 100lb), must stay at least 50 metres (55yd) behind the vehicle in front when driving outside built-up areas. They must also keep to the two right-hand lanes on roads with three lanes or more in each direction.

Crash helmets It is obligatory for drivers and passengers of all motorised bicycles over 50cc or motorcycles to wear crash helmets.

Dimensions Private cars and trailers are restricted to the following dimensions:
Vehicles height – no restrictions; width – 2.50 metres;
Vehicle trailer combinations total length – 18 metres.

Drinking and driving A driver having 0.08% or more alcohol in his blood is considered to be under the influence of alcohol and is therefore automatically subject to a penalty.

Lights Headlights should be adapted so that they do not dip to the left. Motorists are also advised to comply with the French law which requires all vehicles to be equipped with headlights which emit a yellow beam. This may be accomplished by using amber lens converters.

Alternatively, the outer surface of the headlamp glass can be coated with yellow plastic paint which is removable with a solvent.

Unless street lighting is adequate, cars must have two headlights alight at night whether dipped or otherwise; dipping to one light is not permitted, even for visitor's cars.

In fog, mist, or poor visibility during the day or night, either two foglights or two dipped headlights must be switched on *in addition to* two sidelights. Failure to comply with this regulation will lead to a fine of Fr160–600.

Parking lights must be used in badly lit areas and when visibility is poor.

Parking As a general rule all prohibitions are indicated by road signs or by red markings on the kerb. It is prohibited to leave a vehicle parked in the same place for more than 24 consecutive hours in Paris and surrounding departments. It is prohibited to park a vehicle on a road with a continuous centre line if the width of the road between the line and a parked vehicle would not allow unimpeded movement of a line of traffic. Parking is forbidden in places where it would obstruct traffic or view.
On some roads in built-up areas, parking is allowed from the 1st to the 15th day of each month on the side of the road where the numbers of the buildings are odd, and from the 16th to the last day of the month on the side of the road with even numbers. This is called alternate unilateral parking.

There are short-term parking areas known as blue zones in most principal towns; in these areas discs must be used (placed against the windscreen) every day, except Sundays and public holidays, between 09.00 and 12.30hrs and 14.30 and 19.00hrs. They permit parking up to one hour. Discs are sold at police stations, but at tourist offices and some clubs and commercial firms they are available free of charge. Due to their size, cars towing trailers may neither circulate nor park in the blue zones between 14.00 and 20.30hrs, except on Sundays and public holidays. There are grey zones where parking meters are in use; in these zones a fee must be paid between 09.00 and 19.00hrs. Motorists using a ticket issued by automatic machines must display the ticket behind the windscreen or nearside front window of their car.

Paris In some parts of the blue zone parking is completely forbidden. It is prohibited to park caravans even for a limited period, not only in the blue zone but in almost all areas of Paris.

Violation of parking regulations Vehicles which are parked contrary to regulations are liable to be removed by the police at the owner's risk and the driver will be liable for any costs incurred.

Passengers Children under ten years of age are not allowed to travel in the front seats of a vehicle unless the vehicle does not have rear seats, or if it is impossible to accommodate the children in the rear.

Police fines The police usually exercise their extensive powers of levying summary fines on motorists. The officer collecting the fine should issue an official receipt. The police officers may give the offender a card and instruct him to affix stamps to the value of the fine. The stamps are sold by licensed tobacconists.

A driver may refuse to pay a fine and prefer to go for trial. Unless a motorist strongly disputes the alleged infringement, his best course is to pay the fine, thereby avoiding inconvenience and extra cost. A motorist fined for a serious offence must deposit the money with the police pending proceedings; if he is unable or unwilling to make the deposit, his car may be impounded.

Priority Motorists should be extra careful when driving in France. New regulations and signs for priority are being enforced. If there are no priority signs (a blue arrow on a yellow triangle), give way to traffic from the right, but you have priority on roads bearing the sign *Passage Protégé*. Secondary roads are marked with a stop sign or a yellow triangle with a red border. International priority signs will still be in use. On steep gradients, vehicles travelling downhill must give way to vehicles travelling uphill. Give way to street-cleaning vehicles. See also page 70.

Speed The beginning of a built-up area is indicated by a sign bearing the placename, and the end of the placename sign with a thin red line diagonally across it; the limit in these areas, unless otherwise signposted, is 60kph (37mph) for all vehicles except mopeds (vehicles not over 50cc), which are restricted to 45kph (28mph).

On the approach to a built-up area, the limit is often decreased by stages. In open country, mopeds are limited to 45kph (28mph).

Outside built-up areas speed limits are:
on normal roads 90kph (56mph)
on dual carriageways and toll-free motorways 110kph (68mph)
on toll motorways 130kph (80mph)

There are no special limits for a private car towing a caravan. All lower speed limits must be adhered to. Different maximum speed limits can be fixed on a permanent or temporary basis. Special speed limits are enforced where there are road works; these limits are indicated by signs. Both French residents and visitors to France, who have held a driving licence for less than one year, must not exceed 90kph (56mph) – or any lower limit which is signposted; a plastic disc bearing the figure 90 is displayed at the rear of vehicles driven by the relevant French residents.

Traffic lights The three-colour system, as in the United Kingdom, is in operation, with the addition of miniatures set at eye-level and with the posts placed in irregular positions, sometimes overhead and possibly without a set on the opposite side of the junction. It must be stressed that the lights themselves are extremely dim, and easily missed.

A flashing amber light is a warning that the intersection or junction is particularly dangerous. A flashing red light indicates no entry, or may be used to mark obstacles.

Tyres **Spiked or studded tyres** These may be used from 15 November to 15 March provided that a speed of 90kph (56mph) is not exceeded. Vehicles must display at the rear a speed limitation disc bearing the figure 90. The disc can be obtained at road frontier posts.

Wheel chains These can be purchased from vehicle accessory shops in large towns. In other places wheel chains can be purchased, and in some cases hired, from some garages. Establishments have only small supplies. In Paris wheel chains can be hired from: Paris 4, Etablissements Dethy, 20 place des Vosges; Paris 13, Etablissements Vertadier, 1–3 Rue Paul Bourget. Deposits are about Fr100–150, and charges are about Fr35–96.

Warning triangles It is compulsory to use a warning triangle or the vehicle's flashing hazard warning lights. The triangle must be placed on the road 30 metres (33yd) behind the vehicle or obstacle and must be visible to following traffic from 100 metres (109yd). In certain circumstances, such as electrical failure or accident damage, it may not be possible to use hazard warning lights and a warning triangle is, therefore, recommended at such times.

Monaco

Map 28 C2
The Principality of Monaco has a population of 24,000 and an area of 8 sq miles. The official Monaco Information Centre in the UK is at 34 Sackville Street, London W1X 1DB ☎ 01 – 437 3660. Although a sovereign state, it is very much under the influence of France and its laws are similar to those of the major country. Monaco is one large city/state but Monaco Town and Monte Carlo are the two towns of the State.

Motoring regulations are the same as in France but it should be stated that whilst caravans are permitted to pass through the Principality they are not allowed to stop or park.

Auron (Alpes-Maritimes)

France/hotels and garages

Prices are in French Francs
For additional information on French hotels, see page 152.
The number following the town name is the department number; the department name is in brackets. Towns for which there is a town plan in the *AA Road Book of France* are marked †.

Abbreviations:
av	Avenue
bd	boulevard
espl	esplanade
fbg	faubourg
Gl	Général
Ml	Marshal, Maréchal
r	rue
rte	route
sq	square

ABBEVILLE† 80 (Somme) 26,600 (☎22) Map **3** A1
★★*Relais Vauban* 2 bd Vauban ☎240285 22⇄
★*Chalet* 2 av de la Gare ☎242157 Closed 16 Dec – 14 Jan 12rm 4🏠 🏛 P sB39 sB🏠47 dB63 dB🏠65 – 77 L24 – 42 D24 – 42
★*Conde* 14 pl de la Libération ☎240633 8rm sB fr36 dB44 – 50 L 28 – 48 D28 – 48
★*Gare* 20 av de la Gare ☎240409 27rm9⇄ 🏛

ABER-WRAC'H (L') 29 (Finistère) (☎98) Map **7** A3
★★*Baie des Anges* ☎049004 Closed Oct 17rm⇄2🏠 A10rm P sB62 – 104 sB⇄🏠 62 – 104 dB⇄🏠104 – 118 L 38 – 120 D38 – 120 sea

ABRETS (LES) 38 (Isère) 2,450 (☎76) Map **27** B4
★*Belle-Étoile* 🆑 pl de la République ☎320497 15rm3⇄2🏠 🏛 P sB34 – 66 sB⇄🏠58 – 66 dB58 – 111 dB⇄🏠89 – 111 L 25 – 48 D25 – 48 ⏴
★*Hostellerie Abrésienne* 🆑 r Gambetta (DP) ☎320428 22rm1⇄ 🏛

AGAY 83 (Var) (☎94) Map **28** C2
★★★*Baumette* ☎440015 Closed 6 Oct – Feb 80rm60⇄6🏠🏛 P Lift ♪ sB73 – 113 sB⇄🏠113 – 163 dB 126 – 176 dB⇄🏠146 – 256 L60 D70 ⏴ Pool Beach sea
★*Santa Monica* ☎440141 Closed Oct-May 17rm 5⇄12🏠 sea
At **Camp Long** (1km SW on N98)
★*Beau Site* (n rest) ☎440045 Closed Oct – Mar 24rm4⇄10🏠 P sB35 – 50sB⇄🏠 54 – 73 dB 58 dB⇄🏠64 – 76 sea
At **Dramont** (2km SW)
★★★*Sol et Mar* ☎952560 Closed mid Oct – mid Mar 47⇄ P Lift ♪ sB⇄🏠163 – 173 dB⇄🏠176 – 193 L 50 – 80 D50 – 80 Pool Beach sea

AGDE 34 (Herault) 11,800 (☎67) Map **27** A2
★★*Tamarissiere* ☎942087 closed 16 Dec – 14 Mar 24rm17⇄7🏠 sea
At **Cap d'Agde** (7km SE)
☆☆*Ibis* r du Tambour (n rest) ☎94766 tx490034 30⇄ P Lift sB⇄fr102 dB⇄fr122

AGEN† 47 (Lot et Garonne) 35,850 Map **16** C2
★★*Perigord* pl XIV Juillet (n rest) ☎661004 Closed 21 Dec – Jan 22rm3⇄19🏠 🏛 P Lift ♪ sB🏠55 – 85 dB83 – 106 dB⇄🏠93 – 109
★★*Residence Jacobins* 1pl Jacobins (n rest) ☎470331 18rm16⇄2🏠 🏛 P ♪ sB⇄🏠78 – 90 dB⇄🏠96 – 130 (English breakfast)
🛢 🗤 *France Auto* 33 cours de Belgique ☎473207 Frd
🛢 🗤*R Lange* 14 bd de la Liberté ☎472084 Chy
🛢 🗤*Palissy* 1 r Palissy ☎470239 Opl
🛢 🗤*F Tastets* 182 bd de la Liberté ☎471063 BL/Jag/Tri/(GB)

AIGLE (L') 61 (Orne) 10,250 (☎34) Map **9** A3
★★★*Dauphin* pl de la Halle (DP) ☎241244 30rm21⇄1🏠 🏛

AIGUEBELLE 83 (Var) 1,170 (☎94) Map **98** C1
★★★★*Roches Fleuries* (4km on N559 to Le Lavandou) ☎71057 Closed 26 Sep – 14May 50⇄ 🏛 P ♪ sB⇄132 – 144 dB⇄256 – 313 L 60 – 68 D60 – 68 Pool Beach sea

★★★*Bains* (14km NE of Le Lavandou on N559) ☎728149 Closed Oct – May 35rm12⇄18🏠 Beach sea
★★*Plage* (n rest) ☎058074 Closed Oct – May 52rm21⇄27🏠 A31rm sB 58 – 64 sBe⇄🏠81 – 121 dB⇄🏠178 – 258

AIGUILLON-SUR-MER 85 (Vendée) 2150 (☎51) Map **15** B4
★★*Port* 2 r Belle Vue ☎564008 Closed Oct – 14 Mar 33rm12⇄11🏠 P SB44 – 48 sB⇄🏠80 – 92 dB56 – 66 dB⇄🏠100 – 106 (English breakfast) L 23 – 50 D23 – 50 Pool sea

AINHOA 64 (Pyrénées Atlantiques) 550 (☎59) Map **20** C3
★★★*Argi – Eder* ☎299104 Closed 16 Jan – 15 Mar 38rm36⇄2🏠 A4rm P sB111 – 131 dB122 – 144 dB⇄🏠122 – 144 L 50 – 90 D50 – 90 ⏴ Pool mountains
★★*Ithurria* ☎299211 Closed 12 Nov – 24 Dec 30rm20⇄9🏠 🏛

AIRE-SUR-L'ADOUR 40 (Landes) 6,950 (☎57) Map **15** C1
At **Segos** Gers (32) (8km SW on N134)
★★*Domaine du Bassibé* ☎(62)094671 Closed 16 Nov – Dec 10rm7 ⇄3🏠 🏛 P ♪ sB130 – 160 (English breakfast) L 70 D70 St% Pool mountains

AIRE-SUR-LA-LYS 62 (Pas-de-Calais) 9,700 (☎21) Map **3** A1
★*Europ* 14 Grand pl (n rest) ☎390432 16rm6🏠 🏛 P sB30 – 33 dB44 – 47 dB🏠56 – 69
🙌H *Delgery* 5 pl J – d'Aire ☎390298 ☎390298 P Ren (GB)

AISEY-SUR-SEINE 21 (Côte-d'Or) 160 (☎80) Map **10** C2
★*Roy* 🆑 ☎932163 Closed 16 Nov – 14 Dec 10rm1⇄5🏠 P sB 44 – 60 sB⇄🏠45 – 60 dB52 – 60 dB⇄🏠69 – 80 L 25 – 50 D25 – 50

AIX-EN-PROVENCE† 13 (Bouches-du-Rhône) 114,050 (☎91) Map **27** B2
★★★★*Roy René* 14 bd du R – René ☎260301 tx41888 66rm47⇄12🏠 🏛 Lift
★★★*Manoir* 8 r Entrecasteaux (n.rest) ☎262720 43rm21⇄22🏠 Lift
☆☆☆*Novotel Beaumanoir* Rèsidence Beaumanoir (A8) ☎(42)274750 tx400244 97⇄ P Lift sB⇄fr136 dB⇄fr172 English breakfast only Pool
☆☆☆*Novotel Sud* Arc de Meyran ☎(42)279049 tx420517 80⇄ P Lift sB⇄fr136 dB⇄fr172 English breakfast only Pool
★★★*Paul Cézanne* 40 av V-Hugo (n rest) ☎263473 44rm26⇄18🏠 🏛 Lift sB⇄🏠 123 – 154 dB⇄🏠154 – 251
★★★*PLM le Pigonnet* av Pigonnet (off rd N8 towards Marseille) ☎(42)590290 tx410629 50rm38⇄12🏠 A14rm 🏛 P Lift ♪ sB⇄🏠146 – 170 dB⇄🏠206 – 253 (English breakfast) L 80 D 80 Pool
★★*Nègre-Coste* 33 cours Mirabeau (n rest) ☎(42)277422 36rm25⇄11🏠 🏛 Lift
★★*Renaissance* 4 bd de la République (n rest) ☎(42)260422 Closed Jan 32rm12⇄ ♪ sB53 sB⇄76 dB74 dB⇄101 (English breakfast)
★★*Rotonde* 15 av de Belges (n rest) ☎262988 42rm14⇄28🏠 🏛 P Lift ♪ sB65 – 87 sB⇄🏠105 – 114 dB102 – 113 dB⇄🏠113 – 132
🛢 *Azur-Pneu* 7 cours Gambetta ☎262387
🛢 *Clinique Auto* 16 r F-Dol ☎262118 P Ren
🛢 🗤*Côte d'Azur* 2 cours Gambetta ☎261960 Frd
🛢 🗤*Sextius Electric Auto* (Maurin & Polbni) 50 av P-Brossolette ☎276238 Ren
At **Celony** (3km SW on N7)

France

☆☆*Relais du Soleil* r d'Avingnon (N7) ☎233309
25⇌ 🏠 ⌂

At **Eguilles** (11km NW)

★★*Belvedere* ☎(42)246292 20rm8⇌12🛏 A14rm P
sB⇌🛏109 – 162 dB119 – 185 dB⇌🛏119 – 185 L35
D35 Pool

AIX-LES-BAINS† 73 (Savoie) 22,300 (☎79)
Map **27** B4

★★★★*Albion* av d'Albion ☎610244 Closed Oct – 4
May 110rm95⇌ 🏠 P Lift sB83 – 98 sB⇌143 – 163
dB⇌201 – 326 L60 D60 St% Pool mountains lake

★★★*Iles Britanniques* pl de l'Establishment
Thermal ☎350002 Closed Oct – 1 May
88rm43⇌20🛏 A8rm 🏠 Lift lake

★★★*International Hotel Rivollier* 18 av C-de-
Gaulle ☎352100 tx320410 62rm53⇌ P Lift ♪
sB51 – 71 sB⇌91 – 111 dB⇌122 – 162
(English breakfast) L fr40 D fr40 mountains

★★*Parc* 28 r de Chambéry ☎612911 Closed 16
Oct – 14 Apr 50rm12⇌ 🏠 P Lift ♪ sB43 – 89
sB⇌79 – 99 dB98 – 118 dB⇌118 – 130
(English breakfast) L fr32 D fr32 Pool ↄ ⌂

★★*Pavillon* pl Gare ☎351904 Closed Oct – Mar
40rm19⇌8🛏 🏠 P Lift ♪ sB44 – 59 sB⇌84 – 89
dB72 – 94 dB⇌🛏103 (English breakfast) L32 D32
mountains lake

★*Beaulieu* 29 av C-de-Gaulle (Pn) ☎350102 Closed
Oct – Mar 31rm15⇌ Lift

🅂 ៛◎*Seigle* 41 av Marlioz ☎610955 Frd (GB)

AJACCIO See **CORSE (CORSICA)**

ALBERT 80 (Somme) 11,159 (☎22) Map **9** B4

★*Basilique*🅻 3 – 5 r Gambetta ☎750471 10rm6⇌
sB39 – 54 sB⇌54 dB57 – 61 dB⇌75 – 79
(English breakfast) L25 – 57 D25 – 57&alc

★*Paix* 43 r V-Hugo ☎750164 14rm2⇌2🛏 P
sB40 – 46 sB⇌🛏59 dB49 – 55 dB⇌🛏68
(English breakfast) L26 – 70 D11 – 70

ALBERTVILLE 73 (Savoie) 17,550 (☎79)
Map **28** C4

★★*Million* ☎322515 30rm26⇌ 🏠 Lift sBfr69
sB⇌99 – 104 dB⇌128 – 148 (English breakfast)
L50&alc D50&alc

At **Venthon** (2km NE on N525)

★*Chez Teddy* (n rest) ☎322383 12rm P dB40 – 46
(English breakfast) mountains

ALBI† 81 (Tarn) 49,500 (☎63) Map **16** D1

★★★*Grand St-Antoine* 17 r St-Antoine ☎540404
tx520850 56rm35⇌21🛏 🏠 P Lift ♪ sB⇌🛏97 – 137
dB⇌🛏119 – 184 L35 – 50 D35 – 50

★★*Chiffre* 50 r Séré de Rivières ☎540460
40rm12⇌16🛏 P Lift ♪ sB50 – 65 sB⇌🛏75 – 110
dB65 – 80 dB⇌🛏95 – 140 (English breakfast) L29 – 90
D29 – 90

★*Orléans* pl Stalingrad ☎541656 Closed 20
Dec – 14 Jan 68rm56🛏 Lift

🅂 ៛◎*Brison* rte de Castres ☎544910 P BL

🅂 ៛◎*E Puech* 179 – 185 av Gambetta ☎541400 P
Ren

At **Fonvialane** (3km N on N606)

★★★*Réserve* ☎607979 tx520850 Closed Dec & Jan
20rm10⇌10🛏 P ♪ sB⇌🛏115 – 155
dB⇌🛏155 – 210 (English breakfast) L35 – 50
D35 – 50 ⚓ Pool lake

ALENÇON† 61 (Orne) 34,700 (☎33) Map **8** D3

★★★*Grand Cerf* 21 r St Blaise ☎260051 Closed 16
Dec – 14 Jan 33rm12⇌9🛏 🏠 P Lift ♪ dB⇌🛏
dB⇌🛏76 – 101 (English breakfast) L25 – 60alc
D25 – 60alc

★★*France* 3 r St-Blaise (n rest) ☎262636
31rm7⇌7🛏 P ♪ sBfr38 sB⇌🛏fr69 dBfr62
dB⇌🛏fr82

★*Gare*🅻 50 av Wilson ☎290393 tx61000 Closed
24 Dec – 2 Jan 22rm5⇌8🛏 🏠 P ♪ sB52 – 64
sB⇌🛏74 – 86 dB⇌🛏82 – 106 L fr28 D fr28

★*Paris* 26 r D-Papin, Face de la Gare (n rest)
☎290164 Closed Aug 18rm4🛏 P sB37 – 41
sB🛏45 – 50 dB40 – 49 dB🛏48 – 57

🅂 ៛◎*Guerin* 13 – 15 r Demees ☎261328 P Frd

🅂 ៛◎*B Koselleck* 45 – 49 r de Paris ☎264067 Fia/Lnc
(GB)

🅂 ៛◎*Paris* 132 av de Quakenbruck ☎260582
Chy/Sim

🅂 ៛◎*Sodiac* (on N12 3km E of town) ☎260322 P Ren
(GB)

ALÈS† 30 (Gard) 45,800 (☎66) Map **27** A2

★★★*Christel* r E-Quinet ☎522707 75⇌ 🏠 Lift

★★*Grand* 1 pl G-Péri ☎861901 45rm10⇌16🛏 🏠
Lift

★★*Orly* 10 r Avejan (n rest) ☎864327 44rm32⇌9🛏
A8rm 🏠 Lift

🅂 ៛◎*Auto Service* 914 rte d'Uzés ☎522569 BL/Hon
(GB)

At **St-Hilaire-de-Brethmas** (2.5km SE)

🅂 ◎◎*Sud-Auto* rte de Nimes ☎864964 M/c Ren

ALPE-D'HUEZ (L') 38 (Isère) 330 (☎76) Map **28** C3

★★★*Chamois d'Or* ☎803132 Closed 25 Apr – 16
Dec 40rm21⇌4🛏 P Lift sB81 – 96 sB⇌🛏101 – 156
dB177 – 192 dB⇌🛏197 – 207 (English breakfast)
L50 – 70 D50 – 70 mountains

ALTKIRCH 68 (Haut-Rhin) 6,300 (☎89) Map **11** B2

★*Sundgovienne* (3.5km W on N19) ☎409718
Closed Jan 31rm 🏠 Lift

★*Terrasse* 🅻 ☎409802 20rm10⇌10🛏 🏠 P ♪
sB39 – 78 sB⇌🛏57 – 78 dB44 – 91 dB⇌🛏63 – 91
(English breakfast) L18 – 43 D18 – 45

ALVIGNAC-LES-EAUX 46 (Lot) 550 (☎60)
Map **16** C2

★★*Palladium* av de Padirac ☎386023 Closed
Oct – 14 May 27rm14⇌4🛏 P ♪ sB61 dB106
dB⇌🛏106 – 133 L33 – 58 D33 – 58 ⚓ Pool

AMBERT 63 (Puy-de-Dôme) 8,100 (☎73)
Map **27** A4

★★*Livradois* pl du Livradois ☎821001 Closed Oct
14rm4⇌3🛏 🏠 P sB51 sB⇌🛏93 – 99 dB63 – 73
dB⇌🛏108 – 138 L45 – 65 D45 – 65 mountains

★*Terminus* pl de la Gare ☎820803 tx39794 Closed
Jan 12rm2⇌6🛏

🅂 ◎◎*Mavel* 22 av ML-Foch ☎820050 P Chy/Sim

AMBOISE 37 (Indre-et-Loire) 11,150 (☎47)
Map **9** A2

★★★★*Choiseul* 36 quai Violettes ☎572383 17⇌ 🏠
sB⇌🛏139 – 245 dB⇌🛏222 – 299 L55 – 85

★★*Bellevue* quai C-Guinot ☎570226 Closed
Jan – 14 Mar 25rm10⇌5🛏

★★*Château de Pray* (2km NE on N751) (DP)
☎572367 Closed Jan – 4 Feb 16rm11⇌4🛏 🏠 sea

★★*Lion d'Or* 17 quai C-Guinot ☎570023 Closed
Dec – Feb 23rm13⇌2🛏 🏠 sB49 – 106
sB⇌🛏76 – 106 dB66 – 115 dB⇌🛏85 – 115
(English breakfast) L40 – 120&alc D40 – 120&alc river

★*Brèche* 26 r J-Fery ☎570079 Closed Jan & Feb
15rm4⇌1🛏 🏠 sB37 – 39 sB⇌🛏67 – 74 dB47 – 60
dB⇌🛏59 – 93 (English breakfast) L24 – 28 D24 – 28

★*France & Cheval Blanc* 6 – 7 quai C-de-Gaulle
☎570244 Closed Dec – Feb 22rm9⇌ 🏠 sB35
sB⇌52 dB42 – 50 dB⇌79 – 98 L24 – 35 D24 – 35

★*Parc* 8 r L-de-Vinci (DP) ☎570693 Closed
Jan – Feb 15rm8⇌5🛏 A1rm

🅂 ◎◎*Moderne Sport* (J Lamond) 12 r de Blois
☎571132 Dat/Opl/Vlo

AMÉLIE-LES-BAINS 66 (Pyrénées-Orientales)
4,050 (☎69) Map **22** D4

★★★*Thermes* r des Thermes ☎300100
83rm28⇌14🛏 🏠 Lift

AMIENS† 80 (Somme) 136,800 (☎22) Map **9** B4

★★★*Grand Hotel de L'Univers* 2 r Noyon (n rest)
☎915251 41rm24⇌17🛏 Lift ♪ sB75 – 98
sB⇌🛏98 – 125 dB88 – 112 dB⇌🛏112 – 148

★★*Calton-Belfort* 42 r de Noyon ☎922644
tx140754 41rm20⇌8🛏 P Lift ♪ sB85 – 111
sB⇌🛏110 – 120 dB110 – 120 dB⇌🛏146 – 158
(English breakfast) L50 – 80 D50 – 80

★★*Francitel* 8 pl A-Fiquet ☎913632 tx81962 20rm
10🛏 P sB52 sB🛏78 dB60 dB🛏86
(English breakfast) L fr40 Dfr40

★★**Nord-Sud** 11 r Gresset ☎915903 26rm20⇌ P sB62–97 sB⇌107 dB109 dB⇌159

★★**Normandie** 1 bis r Lamartine ☎917499 23rm2⇌8 ⋔ 🏠 P sBfr42 sB⇌ ⋔fr80 dBfr53 dB⇌ ⋔fr98 (English breakfast)

★**Paix** 8 r de la République (n rest) ☎913921 Closed 16 Dec–4 Jan 26rm12⇌12 ⋔ P sB50–74 sB⇌74 dB65–83 dB⇌ ⋔83

☖ ⪢**Leroux** 48–92 r G-de-Rumilly ☎953720 Frd (GB)

At **Boves** (7km SE on D934)

☆☆☆**Novotel Amiens Est** ☎462222 tx140731 92⇌ P Lift sB⇌fr147 dB⇌fr177 English breakfast only Pool

At **Dury** (5km S on N16)

☖ ⪢**Renel** (N16) ☎954242 Bed/Lnc/Opl/Vau (GB)

ANCENIS 44 (Loire-Atlantique) 7,300 (☎40) Map **8** C2

☖ ⪢**Moderne** 339 av F-Robert ☎830275 Cit

ANDELYS (LES) 27 (Eure) 8,300 (☎32) Map **9** A4

★**Chaine d'Or** pl St Sauveur ☎540031 Closed Mon, Tue & Jan 6⇌1 ⋔ 🏠 P dBfr49 dB⇌ ⋔72–95 (English breakfast) L 36–75 alc D36–75 alc river

ANDLAU 67 (Bas-Rhin) 1,900 (☎88) Map **11** B3

★★**Kastelberg** ⌷ r du Gl-Koenig (n rest) ☎089783 31rm30⇌ A10rm P sB57–61 dB⇌97–117

ANDREZIEUX-BOUTHÉON See **ST-ETIENNE**

ANGERS† 49 (Maine-et-Loire) 143,000 (☎41) Map **8** C2

★★★**Anjou** 1bd Ml-Foch ☎882482 tx720521 50rm34⇌16 ⋔ 🏠 Lift ♪ sB 95–120 sB⇌120 dB⇌ ⋔139 (English breakfast) L 40–61 D40–61

★★**Boule d'Or** 27 bd Carnot ☎437656 tx72930 28rm16⇌6 ⋔ 🏠 P sB42–83 sB⇌ ⋔61–83 dB50–91 dB⇌ ⋔69–91 L 30–73 D30–73

★★**Croix de Guerre** 23 r Château-Gontier ☎886659 tx720930 28rm8⇌6 ⋔ 🏠 P sB49–61 sB⇌ ⋔fr87 dBfr57 dB⇌ ⋔fr95 L 36–52

★★**France** 8 pl de la Gare ☎884942 tx720895 61rm28⇌14 ⋔ Lift ♪ sB⇌ ⋔108–114 dB65–72 dB⇌ ⋔117–139 L 42 alc D42 alc

★★**Progrès** (n rest) ☎881014 tx720982 42rm27⇌15 ⋔ Lift ♪ sB⇌ ⋔70–95 (room only) dB⇌ ⋔78–95 (room only)

★★**Univers** 16 r de la Gare (n rest) ☎884358 tx720930 45rm8⇌16 ⋔ P Lift ♪ sB38–42 dB56–68 dB⇌ ⋔70–109

☖ ⪢**GAMA** 17 quai F-Faure ☎436456 BMW/Chy/Lnc/Sim (GB)

☖ ➤➤**Grand Angers** 49 rte de Paris St Sylvan d'Anjou ☎802066 ☎802066 P Opl/Vau (GB)

☖ ➤➤**Rallye Service** 5 r St-Maurille ☎880339 BL

ANGLET 64 (Pyrénées-Atlantiques) 26,500 (☎59)

★★**Biarritz Golf** av Guynemer à la Chambre d'Amour ☎038302 Closed Oct–mid Apr 25rm8⇌4 ⋔ P sB fr42 sB⇌ ⋔fr67 dB fr59 dB⇌ ⋔fr74 L fr30 Dfr30 sea

★**Fauvettes** 69 r Moulin Barbot, à la Chambre d'Amour ☎037558 Closed Oct–Mar 10rm3 ⋔ 🏠 sB⇌40 dB 44 dB⇌ ⋔57 (English breakfast) L 25 D25 sea

☖ ⪢**Aylies** 54 av d'Espagne ☎039813 Ren

ANGOULÊME† 16 (Charente) 50,525 (☎45) Map **15** B3

★★★**Grand France** 1 pl des Halles ☎954795 tx791020 60rm33⇌14 ⋔ P Lift ♪ sB 59 sB⇌ ⋔104 dB81 dB⇌ ⋔141 (English breakfast) L 50 D50

★★**Epi d'Or** 66 bd R-Chabasse (n rest) ☎956764 30⇌

★★**Palais** 4 pl F-Louvel ☎954145 53rm15⇌12 ⋔ 🏠 Lift

★★**Terminus** av de L-de-Tassigny (n rest) ☎923900 38rm Lift

★**Flore** 414 rte de Bordeaux ☎928055 Closed 24 Dec–9 Jan 57rm6⇌7 ⋔ A16rm 🏠 P sB35–37 sB⇌ ⋔49–55 dB49 dB⇌ ⋔63–83

(English breakfast) L24–60 & alc D24–60 & alc

➤➤**H Boutin** 74 r de Paris ☎950493 P

☖ ⪢**Richeboeuf** 3 zone Industrielle, La Madeleine ☎923788 Frd

⪢**Sport** 157 r St-Roch ☎928966 BL (GB)

At **Champniers** (7km NE)

☆☆**Novotel Angoulême Nord** (N10) ☎920040 tx790153 100⇌ P Lift sB⇌fr142 dB⇌fr162 English breakfast only Pool

☆☆**PM16**⌷ rte de Poitiers (n rest) ☎957377 30⇌ P ♪ sB⇌89–94 dB⇌119–124 (English breakfast)

☖ ⪢**Angoulême Nord Auto** (N10) ☎958139 Bed/Opl/Vau (GB)

ANNECY† 74 (Haute Savoie) 55,000 (☎50) Map **28** C4

See also: **Menthon-St-Bernard**
            Talloires
            Veyrier-du-Lac

★★★★**Albigny Sofitel** av d'Albigny ☎452010 70rm62⇌8 ⋔ 🏠 Lift

☆☆☆**Mercure** Le Champ Fleuri, Seynod ☎510347 tx385303 69⇌ P Lift sB⇌fr134 dB⇌fr168 English breakfast only Pool

★★★**Splendid** 4 quai E-Chappuis ☎452000 tx385233 50rm25⇌25 ⋔ Lift sB 89 sB⇌ ⋔109–119 dB⇌ ⋔146

★★**Faisan Doré** ⌷ 34 av d'Albigny ☎230246 tx74000 42rm13⇌13 ⋔ 🏠 P Lift ♪ sB60–62 sB⇌ ⋔110–130 dB72–75 dB⇌ ⋔150–160 L fr45 Dfr45 lake

★★**Jeanne d'Arc** 26 r Vaugelas (n rest) ☎455337 42rm14⇌7 ⋔ Lift sB33 (room only) sB⇌ ⋔58–72 (room only) dB40 (room only) dB⇌ ⋔58–72 (room only)

★★**Robinson** ☎510943 Closed Oct–Apr 32rm24⇌ 🏠 Lift ⚓ Pool lake

☖ ⪢**Ducros** 21 r de l'Isernon ☎454265 BL/Jag/Rov/Tri

☖ ⪢**Parmelan** av du Petit Port ☎231285 P Opl

At **Puya (La)**

★★★**Trésoms & Forêt** 3 bd Corniche ☎514384 tx385201 Closed 16 Dec–Jan 48rm34⇌1 ⋔ P Lift ♪ sB 101–171 sB⇌ ⋔101–171 dB112–182 L 68–98 D68–98 lake

ANNEMASSE 74 (Haute-Savoie) 23,700 (☎50) Map **28** C4

★★**National** pl J-Deffaught ☎386022 tx385417 45rm26⇌16 ⋔ 🏠 P Lift sBfr66 sB⇌ ⋔79–89 dBfr87 dB⇌ ⋔104–116 (English breakfast) L 30–50 D30–50 mountains

★★**Parc** 19 r de Genève (n rest) ☎384460 30rm6⇌24 ⋔ 🏠 P Lift ♪ sB⇌ ⋔86–107 dB⇌ ⋔98–127 mountains

☖ ⪢**SADAL** rte de Taninges Vétraz ☎374245 Cit (GB)

ANTHÉOR 83 (Var) 200 (☎94) Map **28** C2

★★**Réserve d'Anthéor** ☎448005 Closed 11 Oct–Jan 12rm9⇌3 ⋔ P sB66–81 sB⇌ ⋔81 L25–45 D25–45 Beach sea

ANTIBES† 06 (Alpes Maritimes) 56,350 (☎93) Map **28** C2

☆☆**Côte d'Azur** (3km E on N7) ☎342479 Closed 4 Nov–14 Dec 51rm45⇌ Pool

★★**Josse** bd J-Willye ☎614724 Closed Nov–14 Dec 30rm28⇌2 ⋔ A12rm P ♪ sB⇌ ⋔140 dB⇌ ⋔150 (English breakfast) L45 D45 sea

★★**Laverne** av Chênes Antibes (n rest) ☎615423 16rm9⇌1 ⋔ sea

☆☆**Mercator** quartier de la Brague (4km N via N7) ☎335075 18⇌ A2rm P ♪ sB⇌122–137 dB⇌132–147 (English breakfast) ⚓

At **Cap d'Antibes**

★★★**Gardiole** chemin de la Garoupe (n rest) ☎613503 Closed Nov–Feb 20rm5⇌18 ⋔ A4rm sB39–40 (room only) sB⇌ ⋔53–66 (room only) dB⇌ ⋔90–149 (room only)

★★★**Résidence du Cap** 161 bd J F-Kennedy

France

🏨610944 tx470892 Closed Nov–Mar 44⇌ A6rm P Lift dB⇌200–400 L80–100 D80–100 🏊 Pool
★★**Beau Site** bd du Cap 🏨615343 Closed Nov–mid Apr 29rm8⇌16 🏠 A9rm P sB48–72 sB⇌ 🏠48–72 dB⇌ 🏠97–120 L fr35 D fr35 sea

APT 84 (Vaucluse) 11,600 (🏨90) Map **27** B2
★★**Ventoux** 67 av V-Hugo 🏨740758 Closed 16 Jan–14 Feb 15rm3⇌12 🏠 P Lift sB⇌ 🏠80 dB61–87 dB⇌ 🏠87 (English breakfast) L fr26 D fr26
🛢 **Germain** 56 av V-Hugo 🏨741017 Frd

ARBOIS 39 (Jura) 4,250 (🏨82) Map **10** D1
★★**Messageries** 🏨 2 r Courcelles 🏨661545 26rm8⇌4 🏠 🏩
★ **Paris** 🅻 r de l'Hotel de Ville 🏨660567 Closed mid Nov–mid Mar 20rm11⇌7 🏠 A7rm P dB76–126 dB⇌ 🏠76–126 L45–130 D45–130

ARCACHON 33 (Gironde) 14,350 (🏨56) Map **15** B2
See also **Pyla-Sur-Mer & Pilat-Plage**
★★★**Arc** 89 bd Plage (n rest) 🏨830685 tx570503 30⇌ P Lift 🌙 sB⇌ 🏠100–211 dB⇌110–224 Pool sea
★★**Maris-Stella** 8 av Ste-Marie (n rest) 🏨830331 Closed Nov–Feb 14rm7⇌4 🏠 🏩 sea
🛢 👀**F Dagut** 19 bd Ml-Leclerc 🏨830601 🏨834686 Cit (GB)
🛢 👀**Dupin** 61 bd Mestrezat 🏨831328 🏪 (Jul & Aug) P MB/VW
👀**Integral Station** (M G Maurel) 59 cours Lamarque 🏨834096 Frd

ARDRES 62 (Pas-de-Calais) 3,200 (🏨21) Map **3** A1
★★**Clément** pl du Gl-Leclerc 🏨354066 Closed 16 Jan–14 Feb 19rm9⇌4 🏠 P Lift sB50–62 sB⇌ 🏠95–110 dB70–80 dB⇌ 🏠105–120 (English breakfast) L60–150 D60–150
★★**Relais** 🅻 bd C-Senlecy 🏨354200 Closed 7–31 Jan 11rm3⇌7 🏠 sBfr44 sB⇌ 🏠83 dB⇌ 🏠77–105 (English breakfast) L30–51 D30–51
★**Chaumière** (n rest) 🏨354124 12rm4⇌4 🏠 P sB49–59 sB⇌ 🏠69–88 dB58–68 dB⇌ 🏠78–123

ARGELÈS-GAZOST 65 (Hautes Pyrénées) 3,700 (🏨62) Map **21** B4
★**Bernède** 51 r Foch 🏨970664 tx53535 35rm3⇌6 🏠 A5rm
★**Marie-Bernadette** 🅻 39 r de l'Arieulat (n rest) 🏨970793 Closed Oct–May 18rm
★**Mon Cottage** 3 r Yser 🏨970792 21rm10⇌ A5rm 🏩 P Lift sB43 sB⇌53 dB53 dB⇌64 (English breakfast) L24 D24

ARGELÈS-SUR-MER 66 (Pyrénées-Orientales) 5,115 (🏨68) Map **22** D4
★★**Plage des Pins** a la Plage 🏨360022 tx500911 Closed Oct–May 37⇌ 🏩 P Lift 🌙 sB⇌121–128 dB⇌130–137 L35–50 D35–50 sea
★**Commerce** 22 la rte de Libramont (DP) 🏨351017 Closed 1–19 Jan 46rm6⇌14 🏠 🏩 Lift

ARGENTAN 61 (Orne) 17,450 (🏨34) Map **8** D3
★★**Renaissance** 🅻 av de la 2E D-B 🏨671611 Closed Sun evening & Mon 15rm2⇌4 🏠 P sB59–77 sB⇌ 🏠58–77 dB59–87 dB⇌78–87 (English breakfast) L25–35 D25–35
★**Gilbert** 🅻 av J-Vachal (DP) 🏨280162 Closed Oct 30rm11⇌6 🏠 🏩 Lift

ARGENTEUIL See **PARIS**

ARGENTIÈRE 74 (Haute-Savoie) 102 (🏨50) Map **28** C4
★★**Couronne** 🏨2 Closed 27 Sep–14 Dec 35rm13⇌7 🏠

ARGENTON-SUR-CREUSE 36 (Indre) 6,800 (🏨54) Map **16** C4
★★**Manoir de Boisvillers** 11 r Moulin de Bord (n rest) 🏨041388 20rm6⇌6 🏠 🏩 P 🌙 sB58–63 sB⇌ 🏠78–86 dB66–76 dB⇌ 🏠86–96 river
★**France** 🅻 8 r J-J-Rousseau 🏨040331 26rm4⇌5 🏠 A10rm 🏩 P sB33–36 sB⇌ 🏠55–63 dB48–57 dB⇌75–85 L20–35 D20–35
At Vivier (2.5km SE on D48)
★★**Moulin du Vivier** 🏨040323 Closed Jan–20 Feb 15rm3⇌3 🏠 🏩

ARLES†13 Bouches-du-Rhône 50,350 (🏨90) Map **27** B2
★★★★**Jules César** bd des Lices 🏨964976 tx400239 Closed 21 Nov–19 Dec 60rm30⇌30 🏠 🏩 🌙 sB⇌ 🏠145–195 dB⇌ 🏠200–330 (English breakfast) L80–120 D80–120
☆☆☆**Cantarelles** Ville Vielle 🏨964410 tx401582 35⇌ P 🌙 sB⇌88–122 dB⇌115–160 (English breakfast) L45 D45 Pool
★★★**Europa** Pont de Crau (n rest) 🏨961754 tx440096 32rm27⇌5 🏠 A5rm P dB⇌ 🏠99–108 (English breakfast) L28 D28 Pool
★★★**Forum** 10 pl Forum (n rest) 🏨960024 Closed 21 Dec–Jan 45rm36⇌ Lift sB⇌94–140 dB⇌125–165 Pool
★★**Arlatan** 26 r Sauvage (n rest) 🏨963675 tx440096 49rm32⇌13 🏠 A8rm 🏩 🌙 sBfr71 sB⇌ 🏠fr126 dB⇌ 🏠137–158
★★**Cloitre** 10 r du Cloitre 🏨962950 35rm9⇌18 🏠 A10rm P sB38 sB⇌ 🏠45–49 dB61 dB⇌ 🏠81–90 D25
★★**Mireille** 2 pl St Pierre 🏨964161 Closed Jan 34rm26⇌5 🏠 A3rm 🏩 P 🌙 sB51–105 sB⇌ 🏠100–130 dBfr74 dB⇌ 🏠110–152 (English breakfast) L fr35 D fr35 Pool
★★**Regence** 5 r M-Jouveau (n rest) 🏨963985 18rm6⇌2 🏠
★**Lamartine** 1 r M-Jouveau 🏨1383 32rm7 🏠
🛢 👀**Comercial Auto** rte de Tarascon 🏨963220 🏨960815 P Cit

ARMENTIÈRES 59 (Nord) 28,500 (🏨20) Map **3** B1
🛢 👀**Delabie** 37 r J-Ferry 🏨770957 Aud/VW
👀**Duretz** 1 r J-Ferry 🏨770952 P BMW/Dat/Opl (GB)

ARNAY-LE-DUC 21 (Côte-d'Or) 2,500 (🏨80) Map **10** C1/2
★**Terminus** 🅻 r Arquebuse 🏨900033 12rm5 🏠 🏩 P sB32 sB⇌ 🏠37 dB45 dB⇌ 🏠50 L27–58 D27–68

ARRAS†62 (Pas-de-Calais) 50,400 (🏨21) Map **3** B1
★★★**Univers** 3 pl Croix Rouge 🏨213401 38rm16⇌9 🏠 A1rm 🏩 P 🌙 sB63–65 sB⇌ 🏠012–107 dB 74–80 dB⇌ 🏠116–120 (English breakfast) L37–65 D37–65
★★**Grandes Arcades** 8 Grand pl 🏨233089 22rm8⇌ sB36–43 sB⇌61 dB69–85 (English breakfast) L34–62 D34–62
★**Astoria-Carnot** pl de la Gare (DP) 🏨210814 32rm6⇌8 🏠
★**Chanzy** 🅻 8 r Chanzy 🏨210202 20rm6⇌4 🏠 A8rm 🏩 P sB fr46 sB⇌ 🏠53–69 dBfr61 dB 🏠72–109 L36–83 D36–83
👀**Central** 163 av Kennedy 🏨230824 Opl (GB)
🛢 👀**Grands Garages de l'Arton's** 40 voie N-Dame de Lorrette 🏨230256 Ren (GB)
🛢 👀**Houviez** 17 r de Lens 🏨215441 AR/Hon
🛢 👀**Leclercq** 38 bd de Strasbourg 🏨216233 BL
At Fresnes-les-Montauban (13km N)
☆☆☆**Grill** (N 50) 🏨216549 tx120945 40⇌
At Tilloy-les-Nofflaines (3.5km)
🛢 👀**Nord Service** (Le Frere) 7r de Cambrai 🏨212474 P Ren

ARREAU 65 (Hautes-Pyrénées) 950 (🏨62) Map **21** B4
At Cadéac (2km S)
★★**Val d'Aure** 🏨63 28rm4⇌8 🏠 A9rm P sB65 dB73 dB⇌ 🏠100 (English breakfast) L26–75 D26–75 mountains

ARSY See **COMPIÈGNE**

ARTEMARE 01 (Ain) 850 (🏨79) Map **27** B4
★**Berrard** 🅻 🏨873010 32rm A16rm 🏩 P 🌙 sB33–42 dB44–52 (English breakfast) L18–75 D18–75

ARVERT 17 (Charente-Maritime) 2,400 (🏨46) Map **15** B3
★★**Villa Fantaisie** 🅻 (DP) 🏨364009 23rm7⇌2 🏠

ASCAIN 64 (Pyrénées-Atlantiques) 1,900 (🏨59) Map **19** B3

★★*Etchola* ☎540008 Closed Oct–May
28rm7⇄16🛏 A7rm 🏚
★★*Rhûne* pl d'Ascain ☎540004 Closed 16 Oct–Mar
33rm23⇄2🛏 🏚
★*Pyrenees Atlantique* (2km E on N618) ☎540222
37rm23⇄12🛏 P dB⇄🛏65–88 L fr35 Dfr30
mountains

ASSEVILLERS See PERONNE

AUBENAS 07 (Ardèche) 13,750 (☎75) Map **27** A3
🛏 &O*R Nave* bd St-Didier ☎352676 P AR/BL/MB

AUBIERE See CLERMONT-FERRAND

AUBUSSON 23 (Creuse) 6,850(☎55) Map **16** D3
★★*France* ᄂ 6 r Déportés-Politiques (DP) ☎661022
30rm9⇄8🛏 A4rm 🏚
★*Lion d'Or* ᄂ 11 pl d'Espagne ☎661388 Closed Jan
14rm4⇄2🛏 P sB35–40 sB⇄🛏48 dB47
dB⇄🛏59–69 (English breakfast) Lfr30 Dfr30

AUCH†32 (Gers) 25,100 (☎62) Map **16** C1
★★★*France* pl de la Libération ☎050044 tx520474
Closed Jan 32rm20⇄10🛏 🏚
★★*Poste* 5 r C-Desmoulins (n rest winter) ☎050236
32rm10⇄15🛏 🏚 sB⇄🛏69–94 dB⇄🛏98–128
L fr30 Dfr30

AUDIERNE 29 (Finistère) 3,700 (☎98) Map **7** A3
★★*Cornouaille* ᄂ Face au Port (n rest) ☎700913
Closed 26 Sep–24 Jun 20rm13⇄5🛏 A10rm 🏚
dB 63–85 dB⇄🛏92–119 sea

AULNAY-SOUS-BOIS 93 (Seine) 78,210 Map **10** B3
☆☆☆*Novotel* rte de Gonesse (N370) ☎9292297
tx691568 140⇄ P Lift sB⇄fr163 dB⇄fr178
English breakfast only Pool

AUMALE 76 (Seine-Maritime) 3,160 (☎35)
Map **9** B4
★*Dauphin* r St Lazare ☎934192 Closed 25 Jul–10
Aug & 20 Dec–10 Jan 11rm2⇄4🛏 P sB fr41
dBfr70 dB⇄🛏fr59 (English breakfast) L 28–53
D28–53

AUNAY-SUR-ODON 14 (Calvados) 2,950 (☎31)
Map **8** D3
★*St Michel* 6–8 r Caen ☎776316 tx14260 7rm P
sB fr36 dB fr43

AURILLAC†15 (Cantal) 33,400 (☎71) Map **16** D2
★★*Grand Bordeaux* ᄂ 2 av de la République
☎480184 tx990316 50rm13⇄15🛏 A13rm P Lift
sB61 sB⇄🛏90 dB 80 dB⇄🛏114 (English breakfast)

AURON 06 (Alpes-Maritimes) 1,610 (☎93)
Map **28** C2
★★★*Pilon* ☎022015 tx470300 Closed 21 Apr–Jun
& Sep–14 Dec 36rm23⇄10🛏 P Lift 🅳
sB190–240 sB⇄🛏190–240 dB240–280
dB⇄🛏240–280 (English breakfast) L 80 D80 Pool
mountains

AUTUN†71 (Saône-et-Loire) 22,950 (☎85)
Map **10** C1
★★*Tête Noire* ᄂ 1–3 r de l'Arquebuse (DP)
☎522539 (DP) 20rm4⇄9🛏 🏚
★*Vieux Moulin* ᄂ Porte d'Arroux ☎521090
11rm3⇄3🛏 🏚

AUVILLERS-LES-FORGES 08 (Ardennes) 800
(☎24) Map **10** C4
★★*Hostellerie Lenoir* ᄂ ☎363011 Closed 2
Jan–14 Feb 24rm12⇄12🛏 🏚 Lift sB94 sB⇄🛏149
dB 162 dB⇄🛏162 (English breakfast) L 125 D125

AUXERRE†89 (Yonne) 40,000 (☎86) Map **10** C2
★★★*Maxime* 2 quai de la Marine ☎521419
25rm23⇄2🛏 🏚 P Lift 🅳 sB 101–130
dB⇄🛏142–154 L80&alc
★★*Cygne* 14 r 24 Août (n rest) ☎522651
24rm10⇄14🛏 🏚 P 🅳 sB⇄🛏73–90 dB⇄🛏91–134
★★*Fontaine* 12 pl C-Lepère (off r de Paris) ☎524080
Closed 16 Dec–14 Jan 33rm23⇄1🛏 🏚 Lift
★★*Normandie* 41 bd Vauban (n rest) ☎525780
46rm14⇄18🛏 🏚 P 🅳 sB62 sB⇄🛏83–88 dB70
dB⇄🛏95–101 (English breakfast)

&O*Bourgogne Grizeau* 38–40 av de la Tournelle
☎523716 Ren
🛏 *St Amatre* (G Lelouche) 46 r du 24 Août ☎520836
BL (GB)

AUXONNE 21 (Côte-d'Or) 6,950 (☎80) Map **10** D1/2
★*Corbeau* ᄂ 1 r de Berbis ☎363210 Closed Jan
10⇄ P dB⇄🛏63–85 L26–75 D26–75 St%
🛏 &O*Ste Cone* ☎363220

At **Villiers les Po s** (5km NW)
★★*Auberge du Cheval Rouge* ᄂ ☎363411
10rm6⇄4🛏 P sB44–68 sB⇄🛏56–68 dB88–136
dB⇄🛏112–136 L19–38 D19–38

AVALLON 89 (Yonne) 9,300 (☎86) Map **10** C2
★★★★*Poste* 13 pl Vauban ☎340612 Closed Dec &
Jan 25rm22⇄2🛏 🏚 P 🅳 dB175–225
sB⇄🛏205–275 dB230–300 dB⇄🛏250–400 L alc
D alc St%
★★*Chapeau Rouge* 11 r de Lyon ☎341434
40rm30⇄ 🏚
★★*Relais Fleuri* ᄂ (3.5km E on N6) ☎340285 30⇄
P sB⇄100–105 dB⇄120–130 L fr43 D fr43
🛏 &O*M Gueneau* 26 r de Paris ☎341927 M/c P Ren
🛏 &O*Porte du Mowan* 2 rte de Paris ☎341303 P Toy
At **Cousin Valley** (3km W on D427)
★★*Moulin des Ruats* ☎340714 Closed Nov–10 Mar
21rm13⇄ P dB fr60 dB⇄fr135 L alc D alc

AVIGNON†84 (Vaucluse) 93,050 (☎90) Map **27** B2
See also Villeneuve-les-Avignon
★★★★*Europe* 12 pl Crillon (n rest Jan) ☎826692
ta Horope tx431965 65rm46⇄8🛏 🏚 Lift 🅳 sB104
sB⇄🛏149–169 dB138 dB⇄🛏183–278
(English breakfast) L55 D55
☆☆☆☆*Holiday Inn* rte Marseille ☎829910 tx431994
104⇄ P Lift sB⇄132–158 dB⇄162–196 L alc D alc
Pool
☆☆☆*Novotel Avignon-Sud* rte de Marseille (N7)
☎826009 tx432278 79⇄ P Lift sB⇄fr131 dB⇄fr166
(English breakfast only) Pool
★★*Angleterre* 29 bd de Raspail 1 (n rest) ☎863431
32rm6⇄13🛏 🅳 sB32–62 sB⇄🛏56–62 dB54–69
dB⇄🛏64–82
★★*France* 28 pl Clemenceau (off pl de l'Horloge)
☎825886 Closed 9–24 Jan & 9–24 Jun
21rm11⇄7🛏
★★*Midi* 53 r de la République (n rest) ☎810876
tx431074 Closed 16 Dec–14 Jan 60rm20⇄20🛏 Lift
★★*Regina* 6 r de la République (n rest) ☎864945
41rm14⇄15🛏 Lift sBfr57 sB⇄🛏fr94 dB66–71
dB⇄🛏fr103
★*Jaquemart* 3 r F-David (n rest) ☎863471
20rm3⇄5🛏 sB34–38 sB⇄🛏60–70 dB55
dB⇄🛏fr78
★*Mistral* bd du Metz (n rest) ☎822995 tx42033
15rm1⇄8🛏
Parking 77A av P-Sémard ☎822196 P BMW
🛏 &O*SARVIA* 124 av P-Sémard ☎820180 Opl
At **Avignon Nord Autoroute Junction (A7)** (8km E
by D942)
☆☆☆☆*Sofitel* ☎311643 tx432869 100⇄ 🏚 Lift ✈
Pool

AVRANCHES 50 (Manche) 11,350 (☎33) Map **8** C3
★★*Croix d'Or* 83 r de la Constitution ☎580488
26rm12⇄5🛏 A6rm 🏚 P sBfr40 sB⇄🛏fr40 dBfr130
dB⇄🛏fr130 L35–120 D35–120
★★*St Michel* 5 pl GI-Patton ☎580191 Closed
Nov–Mar 26rm11⇄4🛏 P sBfr45 sB⇄🛏fr45
dBfr110 dB⇄🛏fr110 L35–110 D35–110
🛏 &O*Poulain* pl Patton ☎580900 P Ren (GB)
At **Val St Père (Le)** (4km SW)
🛏 &O*Mazet Avranches* bd du Luxembourg ☎582315
P Cit

AX-LES-THERMES 09 (Ariège) 1,600 (☎61)
Map **22** C4
★★*Moderne* ᄂ 20 av du Dr-Gomma ☎642024
Closed Nov–Mar 22rm10⇄6🛏 🏚 P Lift sB35–53
sB⇄🛏53 dB53–73 dB⇄🛏73 L19–31 D19–31
mountains

France

★★*Paix* 2 av A-Authie ☎642261 Closed Nov–21 Mar 47rm15⇌6🍴 🏠

★★*Roy René* L☆ ☎642228 Closed 16 Oct–3 Feb 28rm6⇌20🍴 P Lift sB60–86 sB⇌🍴73–86 dB68–94 dB⇌🍴81–94 (English breakfast) L24–55 D24–55 mountains

★*Lauzerale* L☆ ☎642070 Closed Nov–Mar 24rm2⇌5🍴 P sB36–42 sB⇌🍴58–72 dB49–54 dB⇌🍴65–97 L22–48 D22–48 mountains

AZAY-LE-RIDEAU 37 (Indre-et-Loire) 2,755 (☎47) Map **8** D2

★★★*Grand Monarque* L☆ ☎433008 Closed Dec–Feb 30rm9⇌7🍴 🏠 P sB50–58 sB⇌🍴105–110 dB68–78 dB⇌🍴115–140 (English breakfast) L38–100 D38–100

BAGNÈRES-DE-BIGORRE 65 (Hautes-Pyrénées) 10,600 (☎62) Map **21** B4

★★★★*Résidence* ☎950397 Closed 11 Oct–mid Apr 45rm11⇌15🍴 A10rm P sB64–74 sB⇌🍴94–109 dB72–83 dB⇌🍴102–118 (English breakfast) L32–38 D32–38 Pool mountains

★★*Vignaux* 16 r de la République (n rest) ☎950341 Closed Nov–Feb 18rm2⇌ sB38–41 sB⇌🍴62–64 dB46–49 dB⇌70–72

BAGNOLES-DE-L'ORNE 61 (Orne) 700 (☎34) Map **8** D3

★★★★*Thermes* ☎371500 Closed 21 Sep–4 May 69rm51⇌ P Lift ♪ sB84–114 sB⇌🍴134–109 dB123–188 dB⇌🍴168–278 (English breakfast) L65 D65

★★★*Lutetia-Reine Astrid* bd P-Chalvet ☎370311 Closed Oct–14 Apr 28rm14⇌ A8rm 🏠

★★*Bois Joli* av P-du-Rozier ☎370933 Closed Oct–mid Apr 20rm13⇌2🍴

★★*Ermitage* 23 bd A-Christphle (n rest) ☎371813 Closed Oct–27 Apr 38rm12⇌8🍴 🏠 P dB56–77 dB⇌🍴71–88 (English breakfast)

BAGNOLES-EN-FORÊT 83 (Var) 560 Map **28** C2

★★*Auberge Bagnolaise* rte Fayence ☎406024 12rm2⇌ P sB⇌frc57 dBfr90 dB⇌frc104 L25–40 D30alc mountains

★*Miresterel* r de l'Ancienne Mairie ☎406049 Closed 16 Oct–Jan 7rm2⇌1🍴 dB42 dB⇌🍴67 L23–40 D23–40 mountains

BAGNOLET See **PARIS**

BAGNOLS-SUR-CÈZE 30 (Gard) 17,800 (☎66) Map **27** B2

★★*Château de Coulorgues* rte Avignon ☎895278 Closed Oct–19 Mar 25⇌ 🌳 Pool

🏠*Stolard* rte de Tresques ☎895636 Ren

BAINS-LES-BAINS 88 (Vosges) 1,800 (☎29) Map **11** A2

★★*Beau Site* 2 pl de la 2E D-B ☎363174 Closed Oct–Apr 45rm18⇌ P sB45–52 sB⇌55–61 dB73 dB⇌73 (English breakfast) L27 D25

BAIX 07 (Ardèche) 550 (☎75) Map **27** B3

★★★*Cardinale* quai du Rhône ☎628588 Closed 16 Oct–Mar 15⇌ A10rm P sB⇌190–290 dB⇌230–330 (English breakfåst) L100–120 D100–120 Pool mountains

BANDOL 83 (Var) 6,250 (☎94) Map **27** B1

★★★★*PLM Ile Rousse* bd L-Lumiere ☎294686 tx400372 55⇌ 🏠 P Lift ♪ sB⇌185–285 dB⇌225–340 (English breakfast) L85 D85 Pool Beach sea

★★*Baie* 62 r Marçon (n rest) ☎294082 14⇌ sB⇌140 dB⇌150

★★*Golf* Plage de Renecros ☎294583 Closed Nov–Mar 23rm9⇌21🍴 P sB63–85 sB⇌🍴fr85 dB71–143 dB⇌🍴106–143 (English breakfast) L29–35 Dfr38 Beach sea

★★*Provencal* r Raimu ☎295211 tx400308 22rm11⇌11🍴 sB⇌🍴67 dB⇌🍴120–130 (English breakfast) L36 D36

★★*Reserve* rte de Sanary ☎294271 16rm12⇌1🍴 P dB68–134 dB⇌🍴fr87 L55 D55 sea

BANYULS-SUR-MER 66 (Pyrénées-Orientales)

4,300 (☎68) Map **22** D4

★★★*Catalan* ☎383244 Closed 16 Oct–Apr 36⇌ 🏠 P Lift ♪ sB⇌140–170 dB⇌160–190 (English breakfast) L50 D50 🏊 Pool ∩ sea

BAPAUME 62 (Pas-de-Calais) 4,250 (☎21) Map **9** B4

★*Paix* av A-Guidet ☎071103 Closed 21 Dec–3 Jan & 1–14 Aug 15rm9⇌ 🏠 P sB36–67 sB⇌73 dB80 dB⇌80 L25–55 D25–55

🏠M Lectez 38 r de Péronne ☎071413 P Peu

BARBEREY See **TROYES AIRPORT**

BARBEZIEUX 16 (Charente) 5,500 (☎45) Map **15** B3

★★*Boule d'Or* 11 bd Gambetta ☎780011 28rm10⇌4🍴 🏠 dB64–68 (English breakfast) L28–90 D28–90

🏠*Gaboriaud* 13 bd Gambetta ☎781213 ☎781213 Opl

BARBIZON 77 (Seine-et-Marne) 1,200 (☎1) Map **9** B3

★★★★*Bas-Breau* Grande r ☎0664005 tx690953 Closed 19 Nov–28 Dec 19⇌ 🏠 P ♪ sB326–376 dB652–752 L190–230 D190–230 St%

★★★*Pléiades* Grande r ☎4374025 Closed Feb–14 Mar 18⇌ 🏠

★★*Charmettes* Grande r ☎0664021 39rm31⇌8🍴 🏠 P sB⇌🍴78–103 dB⇌🍴87–189 (English breakfast) L alc D alc

BARBOTAN-LES-THERMES 32 (Gers) 450 (☎62) Map **15** B2

★★*Château de Bégué* (2km SW on N656) ☎095008 Closed Nov–mid Apr 35rm18⇌ 🏠 P sB58–106 sB⇌106 dB67–125 dB⇌125 L alc D alc ∩ lake

BARCELONNETTE 04 (Alpes de Hautes-Provence) 2,350 (☎92) Map **28** C3

★★*Grand* 6 pl Manuel ☎810314 30rm21⇌2🍴 🏠

BARFLEUR 50 (Manche) 750 (☎33) Map **8** C4

★*Moderne* pl de Gl-de-Gaulle ☎540016 20rm2⇌ A12rm

★*Phare* L☆ r St-Thomas ☎540207 Closed Dec–Feb 19rm5⇌4🍴 A5rm

BAR-LE-DUC 55 (Meuse) 20,550 (☎28) Map **10** D3

🏠*Billet* 83 r Bradfer ☎790130 Peu

BARNEVILLE-CARTERET 50 (Manche) 2,000 (☎33) Map **8** C4

At **Barneville Plage**

★★*Isles* L☆ bd Maritime ☎549076 Closed 16 Sep–19 Mar 36rm14⇌14🍴 🏠 P Lift sB47.50–52.50 sB⇌🍴87.50–92.50 dB100 dB⇌🍴100 (English breakfast) L fr38 D fr38 🏖 Beach sea

At **Carteret**

★★*Angleterre* L☆ 4 r de Paris ☎548604 tx17593 Closed Nov–Feb 46rm19⇌4🍴 sea

★★*Marine* L☆ 2 r de Paris ☎548131 Closed Oct–19 Jun 29rm16⇌7🍴 sea

★★*Plage et du Cap* L☆ le Cap ☎548696 15rm11⇌ A4rm dB39–60 (room only) dB⇌60–73 (room only) L25–50 D25–50 sea

BAR-SUR-AUBE 10 (Aube) 7,450 (☎25) Map **10** C3

★*Commerce* L☆ 38 r Nationale ☎270876 Closed mid Jan–mid Feb 16rm 🏠 P sB43–90 dB47–120

BAR-SUR-SEINE 10 (Aube) 3,450 (☎25) Map **10** C2

★★*Barséquanais* 7 av Gl-Leclerc ☎388275 Closed 21 Dec–19 Jan 24rm4⇌10🍴 A14rm P sB36–43 sB⇌🍴45–53 dB47–53 dB⇌🍴64–79 (English breakfast) L25–45 D25–45

BASTIA See **CORSE (CORSICA)**

BASTIDE (LA) 48 (Lozère) 200 (☎66) Map **27** A3

★★*Pins* ☎334007 Closed Nov–14 Mar 27rm6⇌4🍴 🏠 🏠*Naud Jean-Mar* ☎334018 ☎334018 🚗 Ren (GB)

BATZ-SUR-MER 44 (Loire-Atlantique) 2,250 (☎40) Map **7** B2

★*Calme Logis* pl du Murier ☎239016 Closed Nov–mid Apr 22rm10⇌ 🏠

BAUGÉ 49 (Maine-et-Loire) 4,500 (☎41) Map **8** D2

★*Boule d'Or* r Cygne ☎891202 Closed 16 Feb–14
Mar 14rm1⇔3🍴 🏠

BAULE (LA)† 44 (Loire-Atlantique) 15,200 (☎40)
Map **7 B2**

★★★*Pléiades* 28 bd d'Armor (DP) ☎602024 Closed
16 Sep–May 40rm27⇔3🍴 🏠 Lift
★★★*Royal* espl Casino ☎603306 Closed Nov–mid
Apr 120rm60⇔25🍴 🏠 Lift sea
★★*Bellevue-Plage* 27 bd Océan ☎602855 Closed
16 Oct–14 Feb 34⇔🍴 P Lift ♪ sB⇔🍴107–152
dB⇔144–174 L fr60 D fr60 ⌐ Pool sea
★★*Welcome* 7 av des Impairs (off allée IX Monettes)
☎603025 Closed Oct–Apr 18rm7⇔11🍴
dB⇔🍴87–99 L38 D38 sea
★*Ar Vro & Terrasse* 49 av Gl-de-Gaulle ☎602144
Closed 21 Sep–May 44rm8⇔8🍴
★*Concorde* 1 av de la Concorde ☎602309 Closed
Oct–mid Apr 44rm22⇔22🍴 sb⇔🍴74–81
dB⇔🍴104–110 L46 D40 sea
🛢 🗪*Minot* 237 av du MI-du Lattre de Tassigny
☎602071 M/c Cit (GB)

At Baule-les-Pins (La)

★*Villa d'Azur* Ⅼ 28 av de la Mer ☎601258 Closed
Dec–Feb 10rm6🍴

BAUX-DE-PROVENCE (LES) 13 (Bouches-du-
Rhône) 400 (☎90) Map **27 B2**

★★★*Baumanière* ☎973307 tx42203 25rm19⇔6🍴
Lift ⇒ Pool ⌐

BAYEUX 14 (Calvados) 14,550 (☎31) Map **8 D4**

★★★*Lion d'Or* 71 r St-Jean ☎920690 Closed 21
Dec–19 Jan 30rm13⇔12🍴 🏠 P ♪ sB70–75
sB⇔🍴100–115 dB80–90 dB⇔🍴130–146
(English breakfast) L40–100 D40–100
🛢 🗪*St-Patrice* 54 r St-Patrice ☎920681 Cit

BAYONNE† 64 (Pyrénées-Atlantiques) 44,750
(☎59) Map **20 C3**

★★*Capagorry* 14 r Thiers (n rest) ☎254822
tx540376 48rm24⇔21🍴 Lift ♪ sB⇔🍴86–116
dB⇔🍴114–152
★*Basses-Pyrénées* 12 r Tour de Sault ☎250029
46rm11⇔13🍴 A10rm 🏠 Lift ♪ dB52 dB⇔🍴90
L fr21.50 D fr21.50 St% mountains
🛢 🗪*Centre Auto* 19 r D-Etcheverry ☎551334
Bed/Opl (GB)

BEAUCAIRE 30 (Gard) 13,000 (☎66) Map **27 B2**

★★*Vignes Blanches* rte de Nîmes (DP) ☎591312
tx480690 Closed 16 Oct–Mar 55rm45⇔5🍴 Lift Pool

BEAUGENCY 45 (Loiret) 6,850 (☎38) Map **9 A2**

★★*Ecu de Bretagne* Ⅼ pl du Martroi ☎446760
Closed 16 Jan–14 Feb 26rm8⇔8🍴 A11rm P
sB43–78 sB⇔🍴68–78 dB85 dB⇔🍴85–106
L35–100 D35–100

BEAULIEU-SUR-DORDOGNE 19 (Corrèze) 1,715
(☎55) Map **16 C2**

★★*Central* ☎910134 Closed Dec 34rm9⇔6🍴 P Lift
sB32–37 dBfr56 dB⇔🍴73–89 L23–48 D23–48
★*Turenne* pl Marbot ☎911016 Closed Oct–Mar
21rm5⇔18🍴 🏠

BEAULIEU-SUR-MER 06 (Alpes Maritimes) 4,300
(☎93) Map **28 C2**

★★★★★*Réserve de Beaulieu* 5 bd Gl-Leclerc
☎010001 tx470301 Closed Dec–9 Jan 50⇔ 🏠 P Lift
♪ sB⇔202–444 dB⇔314–594 (English breakfast)
L alc D alc St% Pool sea
★★★★*Métropole* bd Gl-Leclerc (DP) ☎010008
tx470304 Closed 21 Oct–19 Dec 50rm40⇔10🍴 P
Lift ♪ sB⇔🍴345–465 dB⇔🍴370–480 Pool Beach
sea
★★★*Résidence* 9 bis av Albert 1er (n rest) ☎010602
21⇔ Lift sea
★★★*Victoria* 47 bd Marinoni (DP) ☎010220
tx470303 Closed Oct–17 Dec 80rm48⇔17🍴 Lift ♪
sB72–80 sB⇔🍴80–102 L28 D28 sea

BEAUMONT-SUR-SARTHE 72 (Sarthe) 2,250
(☎43) Map **8 D3**

★*Barque* ☎970016 26rm6⇔10🍴 🏠 sB39 sB⇔🍴62
dB43 dB⇔🍴71 L25 D25

★*Chemin de Fer* ⅬⅬ à la Gare ☎970005 16rm2⇔4🍴
🏠 sBfr37 dB50–75 L24–60 D24–60

BEAUMONT-SUR-VESLE 51 (Marne) 500 (☎26)
Map **10 C3**

★*Maison du Champagne* ☎616245 10rm6⇔1🍴 P
sB36–53 sB⇔🍴fr53 dB51–80 dB⇔🍴fr80
(English breakfast) L25–46 D25–46

BEAUNE† 21 (Côte-d'Or) 20,000 (☎80) Map **10 C1**

★★★*Poste* 3 bd Clémenceau ☎220811 Closed 19
Nov–19 Mar 27rm17⇔2🍴 🏠 Lift
★★★*Cep* 27 r Maufoux ☎223548 tx350690 Closed
Nov & Dec 21rm17⇔3🍴 ♪ sB⇔🍴77–152
dB⇔🍴124–189 D alc
☆☆*PLM* A6 ☎221612 tx350627 120⇔ P sB⇔130
dB⇔151 L fr45&alc D fr45&alc
☆☆*Samotel* rte de Chalon-sur-Saône ☎223555
66⇔ P sB⇔104–120 dB⇔124–140 Pool
★*Central* ⅬⅬ 2 r V-Millot ☎222423 22rm
11⇔11🍴
🛢 *Bolatre* 41 fbg Bretonnière ☎222803 Fia
🛢 🗪*Monnot* 146 rte de Dijon ☎221102 Frd (GB)

At Ladoix-Serrigny (5km NE)

★★*Paulands* ☎214105 20rm15⇔ P sB85–90
sB⇔90 dB95–100 dB⇔115–140 D alc

BEAURAINVILLE 62 (Pas-de-Calais) 1,950 (☎21)
Map **3 A1**

★*Val de Canche* ⅬⅬ ☎903222 10rm1⇔ 🏠 P
sB34–61 sB⇔61 dB46–69 dB⇔69
(English breakfast) L24–40 D24–40

BEAUREPAIRE 38 (Isère) 3750 (☎74) Map **27 B3**

★*Fiard* 25 de la République ☎846202 Closed Oct
21rm7⇔10🍴 sB65–95 sB⇔🍴90–95 dB80
dB⇔🍴100–120 (English breakfast) L35–85
D35–85

BEAUREPAIRE-EN-BRESSE 71 (Saone-et-Loire)
550 (☎85) Map **10 D1**

★★*Croix Blanche* (N78) ☎741322 15⇔ 🏠 P
sB⇔74 dB⇔87 L fr25 D fr25

BEAUVAIS† 60 (Oise) 56,750 (☎4) Map **9 B4**

☆☆☆*Mercure* ZAC du quartier St-Lazare, av
Montaigne ☎4020336 tx150210 60⇔ P Lift
sB⇔fr139 dBfr172 English breakfast only Pool
★*Palais* 9 r St-Nicolas (n rest) ☎4451258
14rm3⇔11🍴 P sB60–71 sB⇔🍴82–99 dB79–107
dB⇔🍴90–112 (English breakfast)
🚙 🗪*Beauvais Dépannage* 14 r de Buzenval
☎4450413 ☎4450413 Sab/Ska/Vlo (GB)
🛢 🗪*Porte de Paris* 12 bd A-Briand ☎4452326
BL/Tri

BEAUVALLON 83 (Var) Map **28 C2**

★*Marie Louise* ☎960605 Closed Nov–Feb
14rm12🍴 A5rm sea

BEAUVEZER 04 (Alpes-de-Hautes-Provence) 250
(☎94) Map **28 C2**

★★*Alp* (DP) ☎1 tx04440 Closed Sep–May
65rm20⇔ A14rm 🏠 ⇒

BEDARRIDES 84 Vaucluse 2,030 Map **27 B2**

☆☆*Motel 7* ☎843892 tx42033 20rm5⇔2🍴 Pool

BEG-MEIL 29 (Finistère) 3,850 (☎98) Map **7 A3**

★★*Bretagne* ☎949804 Closed 21 Sep–mid Apr
45rm6⇔14🍴 A19rm P dB54–57 dB⇔🍴117–124
L30–60
★★*Duchesse Anne* ☎949107 Closed Oct–mid Apr
30rm9⇔14🍴 🏠
★★*Thalamot* ⅬⅬ Le Chemin Creux Fouesnant
☎949738 Closed Oct–mid Apr 33rm18🍴 A4rm
sB48–65 sB⇔🍴70 dB79–86 dB⇔🍴91–100 L32–65
D32–65
★*Au-Bon-Accueil* (DP) ☎949814 Closed
21 Sep–mid Apr 14rm
★*Plage* ☎949806 Closed Oct–mid May 45rm3⇔4🍴

BELFORT† 90 (Territoire-de-Belfort) 57,350 (☎84)
Map **11 A2**

★★★*Lion* r G-Clemenceau ☎211700 tx360914
82rm44⇔38🍴 P Lift sB⇔🍴97–136 dB⇔🍴132–146
(English breakfast) L alc D alc mountains
★★*Europe* (n rest) ☎216389 50rm20⇔6🍴 Lift

France

🛇 ⋈*Centre* 21 av Wilson ☎214233 Opl
At **Danjoutin** (3km S)
☆☆☆*Mercure* r Dr-Jacquot ☎215501 tx360801 59⇌
P Lift sB⇌fr138 dB⇌fr150 English breakfast only
Pool

BELIN 33 Gironde 2,250 (☎56) Map **15** B2
★*Aliénor d'Aquitaine* ☎880123 12rm3⇌9 ⋔ 🏛 P
sB⇌ ⋔68 – 93 dB⇌ ⋔75 – 100 D28 alc ○
★*Hostellerie de Pins* 7 Gimenez ☎23 Closed
Jan – 2 Feb 12rm 🏛
🛇 ⋈*Auto* (A Dubourg) ☎84 P Ren
BELLÊME 61 (Orne) 1,850 (☎34) Map **9** A3
★*Relais St-Louis*1bd Bansart-des Bois ☎331221
Closed 23 Dec – Jan 9rm5⇌2 ⋔ ⋔ P sB36 – 59
sB⇌ ⋔36 – 59 dB43 – 66 dB⇌ ⋔66
(English breakfast) L 26 – 54 D26 – 54 ○
BELLEY 01 Ain 8,250 (☎79) Map **27** B4
★★*Pernollet* 9 pl de la Victoire ☎243 Closed 16
Nov – 14 Dec 26rm17⇌ 🏛
BELLEVUE See **HOUCHES (LES)**
BÉNODET 29 (Finistère) 2,100 (☎98) Map **7** A3
★★★*Gwell-Kaer* av de la Plage (DP) ☎910438
24rm14⇌10 ⋔ 🏛 Lift sea
★★*Ancre de Marine*⅃ 6 av l'Odet ☎910529 Closed
Nov – Feb 25rm14⇌ a15rm sB62 – 115 sB⇌95 – 115
dB79 – 94 dB⇌99 – 139 (English breakfast) L 42 – 72
Dfr42 sea
★★*Grand* 4 av l'Odet ☎910002 Closed 16 Sep – May
54rm17⇌ Lift sB52 – 54 sB⇌72 dB 73 – 90
dB⇌114 – 126
★★*Ker Moor* av Plage ☎910448 Closed 21
Sep – May 70rm30⇌10 ⋔ 🏛 ➹ Pool sea
★*Bellevue* 14 av playe (n rest) ☎910423 Closed
Nov – mid Apr 40rm5⇌ A10rm 🏛 sea
BERCK-PLAGE 62 (Pas-de-Calais) 16,500 (☎21)
Map **3** A1
★★*Comme Chez Soi* 44 – 48 pl de l'Entonnair
☎090465 Closed 21 Dec – 19 Jan 19rm10⇌6 ⋔
sB58 sB⇌ ⋔81 – 89 dB66 – 81 dB⇌ ⋔92 – 103
L37 – 55 D37 – 55 sea
BERGERAC 24 (Dordogne) 28,650 (☎53)
Map **16** C2
★★*Bordeaux*⅃ 38 pl Gambetta ☎571283 Closed
Jan 42rm12⇌14 ⋔ 🏛 P ◗ sB⇌fr55 sB⇌ ⋔84 dBfr72
dB⇌ ⋔102 L 32 – 65 D32 – 65
🛇 ⋈*Bergerac Auto* 109 r Neuve ☎574211
BERGUES 59 (Nord) 4,850 (☎20) Map **3** A1
☆☆☆*Novotel Dunkerque* (5km NW off D916 on
D252B) ☎659733 tx820916 64⇌ P Lift sB⇌fr132
dB⇌fr153 English breakfast only Pool
★*Tonnelier* 4 r de Mont-de Piété ☎687005 10rm P
sB37 – 43 dB57 – 80 (English breakfast) L 27 – 38
D27 – 38
BERNAY 27 (Eure) 11,300 (☎32) Map **9** A3
★*Angleterre & Cheval Blanc*⅃ 10 r Gl-de-Gaulle
☎431259 Closed Feb 23rm1⇌2 ⋔ 🏛 P sB50 – 80
sB⇌ ⋔75 – 80 dB65 – 85 dB⇌ ⋔85 – 95
(English breakfast) L 42 – 45 D42 – 45
★*Lion d'Or*⅃ 48 r Thiers ☎431206 29rm5⇌9 ⋔ P
sB36 – 70 sB⇌ ⋔42 – 70 dB56 – 96 dB⇌ ⋔62 – 96
(English breakfast) L 34 – 70 D34 – 70
🛇 ⋈*J. Robillard* rte de Broglie, zone Industrielle
☎430999 P BL/Opl (GB)
BESANÇON† 25 (Doubs) 126,200 (☎81) Map **11** A2
★★★*Frantel* av E-Droz ☎801444 tx360268
96rm67⇌29 ⋔ 🏛 Lift sB⇌ ⋔167 – 192
dB⇌ ⋔219 – 254 L62 – 120 D62 – 120
☆☆*Novotel* r de Trey ☎501466 tx360009 107⇌ P
Lift sB⇌fr144 dB⇌fr177 English breakfast only Pool
★*Gambetta* 13 r Gambetta (n rest) ☎820233
26rm12⇌5 ⋔ ◗ D sB51 sB⇌ ⋔61 – 93 dB5 – 9
dB⇌ ⋔69 – 111
🛇 ⋈*Bever* 4 r Pergaud ☎812801 BMW
🛇 ⋈*Fournier* 81 r de Dôle ☎820522 BL (GB)
At **Château – Farine** (6km SW)
☆☆☆*Mercure* chemin des Essarts – l'Amour
☎880400 tx360167 59⇌ P Lift sB⇌fr141 dB⇌fr156
English breakfast only Pool

BESSE-EN-CHANDESSE 63 (Puy-de-Dome) 1,950
(☎73) Map **16** D3
★★*Beffroy*⅃ ☎795008 17rm8⇌5 ⋔ 🏛 P sB fr48
dB⇌ ⋔111 L 36 – 80 D36 – 80 mountains
BESSINES-SUR-GARTEMPE 87 (Haute-Vienne)
3,000 (☎55) Map **16** C3/4
★★*Manoir Henri IV* ☎760056 Closed Oct 6rm4⇌ 🏛
P dB 64 dB⇌81 – 91 L28 – 45 D28 – 45 mountains
☆☆*Toit de Chaume* (5km S on Limoges rd)
☎760102 tx580915 Closed 16 Nov – 14 Mar 20⇌
Pool
★★*Vallée* (N20) ☎760166 Closed 10 – 27 Feb 8
7 – 23 Oct 20rm8⇌ 🏛 P sB37 – 40 sB⇌55 – 62
dB43 – 46 dB⇌61 – 68 L22 – 110 D22 – 110
BÉTHUNE† 62 Pas-de-Calais 28,300 (☎21)
Map **3** B1
★★*Vieux Beffroi* 48 Grand pl ☎251500
63rm22⇌21 ⋔ P Lift D sB48 – 57 sB⇌ ⋔57 – 74
dB⇌ ⋔78 – 101 (English breakfast) L 31 – 100
D31 – 100
★★*Bernard & Gare*⅃ 3 pl de la Gare ☎252002 34rm
sB34 – 68 dB51 – 85 L 28 – 60
🛇 ⋈*Automobiles Bethunoise* 255 bd Thiers
☎252430 Ren
🛇 ⋈*Mizon* av Kennedy ☎251205 Peu
BEYNAC-ET-CAZENAC 24 (Dordogne) 410 (☎53)
Map **16** C2
★★*Bonnet*⅃ ☎295001 Closed 16 Oct – Mar 21rm 🏛
P sB56 sB⇌ ⋔56 dB⇌ ⋔95 – 125 L 50 – 105
D50 – 105 river
BÉZIERS† 34 (Herault) 85,700 (☎67) Map **16** D1
★★★*Compagnie du Midi* 20 bis bd de Verdun
☎287859 taMapotel tx51837 35rm18⇌11 ⋔ Lift
★★★*Imperator* 28 allées P-Riquet (n rest) ☎285485
tx490608 45rm12⇌25 ⋔ 🏛 Lift
🛇 ⋈*Chapat* 1 av du Prés-Wilson ☎765534 P Frd (GB)
🛇 ⋈*Foch* 117 – 119 av Ml-Foch ☎287318 BL/Tri
BIARD See **POITIERS**
BIARRITZ† 64 (Pyrénées-Atlantiques) 27,700 (☎59)
Map **20** C3
★★★★*Miramar* 13 r des Vagues ☎240440 ta
Miramartel Closed Nov – mid Apr 200⇌ Lift sea
★★★★*Palais* av de l'Impératrice ☎2409040
tx570000 Closed Nov – Apr 150rm130⇌6 ⋔ P Lift D
sB⇌240 – 320 dB⇌ ⋔360 – 470
(English breakfast) L alc D alc Pool sea
★★★*Plaza* av Edouard VI ☎247400 tx570048 60⇌
P Lift D sB⇌fr147 dB⇌ ⋔204 L alc D alc sea
★★★*Regina & Golf* 52 av de l'Impératrice ☎240960
Closed Nov – mid Apr 54⇌ P Lift D sB⇌115 – 175
dB⇌150 – 230 (English breakfast) L60alc D60alc sea
mountains
★★★*Windsor* Grande Plage (DP) ☎240852 Closed
Dec – 14 Mar 37rm27⇌10 ⋔ Lift sea
★★*Beaulieu* pl du Port-Vieux ☎242359 Closed
Nov – mid Apr 28rm dB60 – 95 L30alc D30alc sea
★*Marbella* 11 r Port-Vieux ☎240604 Closed
Oct – Mar 40rm21⇌ Lift
★★*St-Julien* 20 av Carnot (DP) ☎242039 Closed 16
Dec – 16 Jan 21rm7⇌2 ⋔
★*Palacito* 1 r Gambetta (n rest) ☎240489
26rm9⇌9 ⋔ P sB60 – 87 sB⇌ ⋔74 – 81 dB73 – 108
dB⇌ ⋔89 – 102 (English breakfast)
★*Washington* 34 r Mazagrau (off pl G-Clemenceau)
☎241080 Closed Oct – Mar 20rm4⇌5 ⋔ sB42 – 64
sB⇌ ⋔66 – 89 dB56 – 67 dB⇌ ⋔81 – 96
(English breakfast)
🛇 ⋈*Eskualduna Fourneau* 33 av Prés-J F-Kennedy
☎231082 Maz/Ska (GB)
🛇 *Franco-Américain* av Prés-J F-Kennedy
☎231542 M/c Fia (GB)
🛇 ⋈*Paris Biarritz Automobiles* 48 av du Ml-Foch
☎241945 Aud/VW
🛇 ⋈*Régina* 50 av de l'Impératrice ☎242020 P MB
BIDART 64 (Pyrénées Atlantiques) 3,000 (☎59)
Map **20** C3
★★★*Bidartea* (N10) ☎549468 30rm26⇌4 ⋔ P Lift

sB⇌ 🍽70–80 dB⇌ 🍽106–126 (English breakfast)
L fr30 D fr40 Pool Beach sea mountains
BITSCHWILLER See **THANN**
BLANC (LE) 36 (Indre) 8,450 (☎54) Map **9** A1
★*Promenade* 36 r St-Lazare ☎371007 Closed 26
Sep–4 Oct & 24 Dec–13 Jan 20rm1⇌ 🏠
BLANGY-SUR-BRESLE 76 (Seine-Maritime) 3,450
(☎35) Map **9** B4
★*Poste* 44 Grand r ☎935020 Closed 21 Dec–19 Jan
14rm P sB36–41 dB45–58 L29–38 D29–38
★*Ville* 2 r N-Dame ☎935157 Closed 6–27 Aug 6rm
sB49–55 dB62–89 (English breakfast) L24–60
D24–60 St%
BLAYE 33 (Gironde) 4,300 (☎56) Map **15** B3
🛢 ⚙*Ferandier* rte de Cars ☎420341 P Peu (GB)
BLÉRÉ 37 (Indre-et-Loire) 4,150 Map **9** A2
★*Cher* 9 r Pont ☎297515 Closed Jan & Feb
21rm1⇌18🍽 A8rm sB⇌ 🍽50–63 dB⇌ 🍽57–70
L35–50 D35–50
BLÉRIOT-PLAGE 62 (Pas-de-Calais) 74,905 (☎21)
Map **3** A1
★*Dunes* ☎345430 13rm4⇌ A4rm 🏠 P sB48–70
sB⇌63–85 dB66–80 dB⇌81–110
(English breakfast) L25–100 D25–100
BLOIS†41 (Loir-et-Cher) 51,977 (☎39) Map **9** A2
★*Bellay* 12 r Minimes (n rest) ☎782362 12rm5⇌1🍽
sB32 dB45 dB⇌ 🍽59
★*Cheverny* 🅻 ☎780670 Closed Oct 10rm P
sB27–37 dB44–54 L22–28 D22–28
★*Gerbe d'Or* 1 r Bourg-Neuf ☎780088 22rm4⇌8🍽
🏠
★*St Jacques* 🅻 pl Gare ☎780415 tx75935 Closed
4–26 Nov & 23–30 Dec 28rm1⇌1🍽 🌙 sB39–52
sB⇌ 🍽59 dB51–65 dB⇌ 🍽67 L26–45 D26–45
★*Viennois* 🅻 5 quai Amédée-Contant ☎741280
26rm8⇌2🍽 A15rm sBfr41 sB⇌ 🍽fr56 dBfr48
dB⇌ 🍽fr69 L25–51 D25–51
🛢 ⚙*SERVA* 148 av Maunoury ☎784285 Ren
BLONVILLE-SUR-MER 14 (Calvados) 800 (☎31)
Map **8** D4
★*Mer* 🅻 93 av de la République (n rest) ☎879323
Closed 18 Sep–24 Mar 20rm13⇌ P sB45–50
(room only) dB50–60 (room only) dB⇌90–105 (room
only) sea
BOLLÈNE 84 (Vaucluse) 11,550 (☎90) Map **27** B2
★★*Relais Belle Ecluse* r Suze ☎341514 Closed 16
Oct–Mar 16rm8⇌5🍽 P sB79–116 sB⇌ 🍽116
dB127 dB⇌ 🍽127 L alc D alc
⚙*Marignan* av M-Coulon ☎301151 P
🛢 ⚙*Portes de Provence* (R Ladame) sortie de
l'Autoroute ☎301046 M/c P Peu
BONNEVAL 28 (Eure-et-Loir) 4,900 (☎37) Map **9** A3
★★*Bois Guibert* (N10) ☎982233 Closed 21
Dec–Jan 14rm6⇌2🍽 P dB62 dB⇌ 🍽77–93 L38–50
D38–50
BONNY-SUR-LOIRE 45 (Loiret) 1,700 (☎38)
Map **9** B2
🛢 ⚙*Route Bleue* (Parot) ☎316332 Ren
BORDEAUX†33 (Gironde) 226,300 Map **15** B2
AA agents; see page 149
★★★★*Aquitania PLM* Parc des Expositions
☎508380 tx570557 210⇌ Lift Pool lake
★★★*Frantel* 5 r R-Lateaulade ☎909237 tx540565
196⇌ Lift sB⇌203 dB⇌246–266 L70–140
D70–140
★★★*Normandie* 7 cours 30-Juillet (n rest) ☎521680
tx540320 100rm50⇌50🍽 P Lift 🌙 sB⇌ 🍽78–92
dB⇌ 🍽110–142
☆☆*Novotel Bordeaux-le-Lac* quartier du lac
☎509970 tx570274 173⇌ P Lift sB⇌fr143
dB⇌fr156 English breakfast only Pool
☆☆☆*Sofitel* quartier du Lac ☎509014 tx540097
100⇌ P Lift sB⇌ 🍽153–197 dB⇌ 🍽212–234
(English breakfast) L45–90 D45–90 Pool lake
★★*Bayonne* 15 cours de l'Intendance (n rest)
☎480088 37rm11⇌12🍽 Lift 🌙 sB43–91
sB⇌ 🍽64–91 dB71–98 dB⇌ 🍽71–98
(English breakfast)

★★*Français* 12 r Temple (off cours de l'Intendance)
(n rest) ☎481035 36rm8⇌23🍽 Lift
☆☆*Ibis* quartier du Lac ☎509650 tx550346 122⇌ P
Lift sB⇌88 dB⇌108 L35 D35 lake
★*Seze* 23 allées Tourny (n rest) ☎526555
25rm12⇌8🍽 Lift 🌙 sB66–69 sB⇌ 🍽106–119 dB77
dB⇌ 🍽127 (English breakfast)
★*Etche-Ona* 11 r Mautrec (n rest) ☎443649 Closed
21 Dec–3 Jan 30rm10⇌15🍽
🛢 ⚙*A Baillac* 31 r Tastet (off cours d'Albert)
☎960010 BL/Chy/Dat Sim/Tri (GB)
🛢 ⚙*A Pigeon* 469 rte du Médoc ☎288428
Bed/Opl/Vau (GB)
🛢 ⚙*Stewart & Arden* 126 cours de l'Argonne
☎913104 BL/Jag/Rov/Tri
At **Bruges** (5km NW)
🛢 ⚙*J Palau* 419 rte du Médoc ☎288466
At **Gradignan** (8km SW on N10)
☆☆*Bordeaux Vielmur* 1 r Prof-Villemin
☎891011 tx550922 147⇌ P Lift sB⇌fr155
dB⇌fr185 L fr35 Dfr55 Pool
At **Merignac** (4km W on D106E)
☆☆*Novotel Bordeaux Aéroport* av Kennedy
☎474040 tx540320 100⇌ P Lift sB⇌fr145
dB⇌fr159 English breakfast only Pool
BORMES-LES-MIMOSAS 83 (Var) 3,100 (☎94)
Map **28** C1
★★*Grand* Closed Nov–Feb 38rm11⇌4🍽 🏠 ⚓ sea
★★*Safari* rte Stade (n rest) ☎710983 Closed
Nov–Jan 32rm15⇌17🍽 P dB⇌ 🍽174–244 Pool
sea
★*Belle Vue* pl Gambetta ☎711515 15rm2⇌10🍽
sB33–38 dB45 dB⇌ 🍽63–80 L fr38 Dfr38 sea
BOSSONS (LES) See **CHAMONIX-MONT-BLANC**
BOUILLE (LA) 76 (Seine Maritime) 700 (☎35)
Map **9** A4
★★*Bellevue* quai H-Malot ☎796057 Closed Jan
20rm2⇌ 🍽
BOULOGNE-SUR-MER†62 (Pas-de-Calais) 49,300
(☎21) Map **3** A1 **See Plan**
AA Continental Emergency Centre; see page
149
★★*Alexandra* 93 r Thiers (n rest) ☎313208 Plan**1**
20rm4⇌6🍽 P 🌙 dBfr48 dB59–72 dB⇌ 🍽72–92
★★*Faidherbe* 12 r Faidherbe (n rest) ☎316094
Plan **2** 35rm10⇌10🍽 dB⇌
☆☆*Ibis Boulogne* quai L-Danrémont ☎301240
tx160485 Plan **3** 80⇌ 🏠 P Lift sB⇌fr94 dB⇌fr114
L30–45 alc D30–45 alc
★★*Lorraine* 7 pl de Lorraine (n rest) ☎313478
Plan **4** 21rm5⇌7🍽 P sB44–49 sB⇌ 🍽59–79
dB55–60 dB⇌ 🍽65–85 (English breakfast)
★★*Marmin* 10 r Monsigny ☎316115 Plan **5**
24rm12⇌8🍽 Lift
★★*Métropole* 51 r Thiers (n rest) ☎315430 Plan **6**
30rm2⇌15🍽 Lift
★*Hamiot* 🅻 1 r Faidherbe ☎314420 Plan **7** 24rm Lift
★*Londres* 22 pl de France (n rest) ☎313563 Plan **8**
20rm4⇌4🍽 P Lift sBfr50 sB⇌ 🍽fr65 dBfr60
dB⇌ 🍽fr70
★*Menestrel* 21 r de Brequerecque (DP) ☎316016
Plan **9** 15rm 🏠 Lift
⚙*Gare* 1 bd Beaucerf ☎317189 Chy/Sim
🛢 ⚙*Paris* 33 av J-Kennedy ☎300522 Frd (GB)
🛢 ⚙*St Christophe* bd de la Liane ☎300911
AR/Bed/Opl/Vau (GB)
At **Portel (Le)** (1km SW)
★*Beau Rivage & Armada* bd Pasteur ☎315982 Not
on plan 11rm5⇌5🍽 P sB32 dB38–46
dB⇌ 🍽59–69 L22–55 D22–55
BOULOU (LE) 66 (Pyrénées-Orientales) 3,750
(☎68) Map **22** D4
★*Richelieu* r Arago (n rest) ☎374223 Closed
Nov–Feb 20rm4⇌9🍽
⚙*Carrosserie Nouvelle* av du Gl-de-Gaulle (N4)
☎374169 P
BOURBON-L'ARCHAMBAULT 03 (Allier) 2,600
(☎70) Map **16** D4

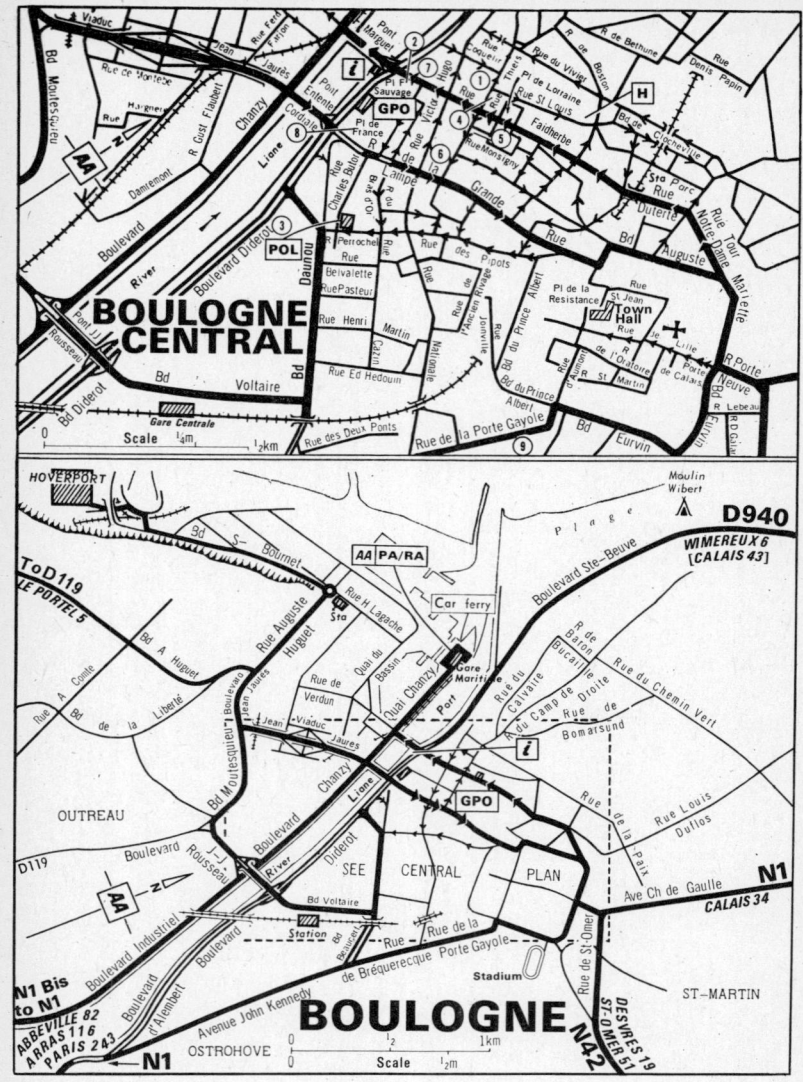

Boulogne			
1	★★Alexandra	5	★★Marmin
2	★★Faidherbe	6	★★Métropole
3	☆☆Ibis Boulogne	7	★Hamiot
4	★★Lorraine	8	★Londres
		9	★Menestrel

★★**Parc** r du Parc ☎14 Closed 11 Oct–24 Apr
65rm15⇄3🍴 🏠 Lift
BOURG-EN-BRESSE† **01** (Ain) 45,000 (☎74)
Map **27** B4
★★★**Logis de Brou** 132 bd Brou (n rest) ☎221155
30rm18⇄12🍴 🏠 P Lift sB⇄🍴72–122
dB⇄ 🍴104–144
🛢 ♨**ARNO** bd E-Herriot, zone Industrielle Nord
☎212297 Ren
♨**Bugey** (F Jullien) 28 av de Pont d'Ain ☎215512 P
Frd
BOURGES† **18** (Cher) 80,500 (☎36) Map **9** B1/2
★★★**Angleterre** 1 pl 4 Pillers ☎246851
33rm12⇄9🍴 P Lift ♪ sB 45–58 sB⇄🍴67–98
dB fr67 dB⇄🍴76–107 L30–49 D30–49
★★**D'Artagnan** 19 pl Séraucourt ☎246751 33⇄ 🏠
Lift
★★**Berry** 3 pl du Gl-Leclerc ☎244358 21rm10⇄4🍴
🏠 P Lift ♪ sB fr58 sB⇄🍴fr62 dB fr70 dB⇄🍴fr124
(English breakfast) L33 & alc D33&alc
★★**Boule d'Or** 13 pl Gordaine ☎705587 Closed 21
Dec & 19 Jan 48rm6⇄5🍴 🏠
★★**Christina** 5 r Halle ☎705650 (n rest)
76rm41⇄30🍴 🏠 P Lift ♪ sB44–88 sB⇄🍴50–68
dB56 dB⇄🍴87–95 (English breakfast)
★★**Poste** 22 r Moyenne (n rest) ☎700806
34rm4⇄9🍴 A6rm 🏠 P Lift ♪ sB42–119 sB🍴⇄fr63
dB fr58 dB⇄🍴fr70
BOURGET AIRPORT (LE) See **PARIS**
BOURGOIN-JALLIEU 38 (Isère) 22,350 (☎74)
Map **27** B4
★**Negociants** 📍 22 av des Alpes (DP) ☎930204
17rm4🍴
🛢 ♨**Parenton** 15 r Pontcottier ☎933410 Frd
BOURG-ST-MAURICE 73 (Savoie) 5,730 (☎79)
Map **28** C4
★★**Petit St-Bernard** av Stade ☎070432 Closed
May, Oct & Nov 24rm8⇄4🍴 🏠

BOURGTHEROULDE 27 (Eure) 1,350 (☎35)
Map **9** A4
★**Corne d'Abondance** pl de la Mairie ☎776008
Closed Feb & Aug 12rm1⇄ 🏠 P sB38–44 sB⇄73
dB51–60 dB⇄ L24–33 D24–33
BOVES See **AMIENS**
BREST† **29** (Finistére) 172,200 (☎98) Map **7** A3
☆☆**Novotel** (N 788) ☎023283 tx940470 85⇄ P Lift
sB⇄fr145 dB⇄fr175 English breakfast only Pool sea
★★★**Voyageurs** 15 av G-Clemenceau ☎802573
40rm14⇄22🍴 Lift sB fr53 sB⇄🍴fr110 dB75
dB⇄🍴139 L35–80 D35–80
At **Plougastel-Daoulas** (9.5km SE)
☆**Ibis Brest** rte de Quimper, quartier de Ty-Menez
☎405028 tx940731 46⇄ P Lift sB⇄🍴fr94 dB
dB⇄🍴fr114 L30–45 alc D30–45 & alc
BREVIANDES See **TROYES**
BRIANCON† **05** (Hautes-Alpes) 11,500 (☎92)
Map **28** C3
At **Ste-Ca herine**
★★★**Mont Brison** 1 av Gl-de-Gaulle (n rest)
☎211455 32rm10⇄22🍴 🏠 P Lift sB50 sB⇄🍴88
dB71 dB⇄🍴99 mountains
★★★**Vauban** av Gl-de-Gaulle ☎211211 Closed 16
Nov–14 Dec 45rm24⇄14🍴 🏠 P Lift sB82–122
sB⇄🍴92–122 dB104 dB⇄🍴124–144 L48–70
D48–70 mountains lake
★★**Moderne** 3 r Alphand ☎555 60rm20⇄20🍴 🏠 Lift
BRIARE 45 (Loiret) 5,700 (☎38) Map **9** B2
★**Cerf** 22 bd Buyser ☎012038 Closed 6 Jan–4 Feb
20rm4⇄4🍴 🏠
BRICQUEBEC 50 (Manche) 3,200 (☎33) Map **8** C4
★**Taverne Oudinet** 📍 9 pl Ste-Anne ☎522315 7rm
sB36–39 dB42–54 L22–38 D22–38

France

★**Vieux Château** L̲ 4 cour du Château ☎522449 20rm12⇌12 🕭 🏠 P sB42–44 sB⇌ 🕭67–76 dB51–59 dB⇌ 🕭74–83 (English breakfast) L28–52 D28–52 ⚇

BRIGNOGAN-PLAGES 29 (Finistère), 1,050 (☎98) Map **7** A3
★★**Chalet** 44 av Gl-de-Gaulle ☎830624 tx74884 Closed 16 Sep–May 40rm10⇌7 🕭 🏠

BRIGNOLES 83 (Var) 10,500 (☎94) Map **28** C2
★**Univers** L̲ pl Caramy ☎691108 Closed 1–14 Oct 10rm2⇌8 🕭 🏠
🚗**J Brun** 13 chemin de la Burlière ☎690627 Peu (GB)

BRIONNE 27 (Eure), 4,900 (☎32) Map **9** A4
Logis de Brionne L̲ 1 pl St-Denis ☎448173 15rm4 🕭 🏠
★**Vieux Donjon** 19 r de la Soie ☎448062 9rm1⇌1 🕭 🏠 P sB40–63 sB⇌ 🕭61–73 dB47–80 dB⇌ 🕭68–80 L fr30 D fr30

BRIOUDE 43 (Haute-Loire), 8,450 (☎71) Map **27** A3
★★**Brivas** rte Puy ☎501049 Closed 21 Nov–19 Dec 30rm8⇌10 🕭 P sB50–73 sB⇌ 🕭65–73 dB62–80 dB⇌ 🕭70–92 (English breakfast) L27–51&alc D27–51&alc mountains
★**Moderne** L̲ 12 av V-Hugo ☎500730 tx39794 21rm4⇌11 🕭 🏠

BRIVE-LA-GAILLARDE† 19 (Corrèze), 54,800 (☎55) Map **16** C3
★★**Chapon Fin** 1 pl Ml-de-Lattre-de-Tassigny ☎742340 30rm15⇌15 🕭 🏠
★★**Crémaillère** L̲ 53 av Ml-Staline ☎743247 11⇌ sB⇌46–54 dB⇌53–61 L25–90 D25–90
★★**Quercy** 8 bis quai Tourny (n rest) ☎740926 80rm42⇌38 🕭 Lift
★★**Truffe Noir** 22 bd A-France ☎743532 31rm28⇌3 🕭 Lift
★**Montauban** L̲ 6 av E-Herriot ☎240038 Closed Jan 21rm2⇌8 🕭 🏠 P sB40–48 sB⇌ 🕭66 dBfr55 dB⇌ 🕭73 L23–52 D23–52
🛏 🚗**G Cremoux** 20 av Ml-Bugeaud ☎240913 P BL (GB)
🚗**International** 23 av des Toulouse ☎742542 P BMW
🛏 🚗**Lavigne** 13 av L-Blum ☎240475 P
At **Varetz** (14km NW)
★★★Château de Castel Novel ☎850001 tx580709 Closed 4 Nov–Apr 28⇌ P Lift sB⇌ 🕭 dB⇌185–280 L55–110&alc D55–110&alc ⚇ Pool

BRON See **LYON**

BROU 28 (Eure-et-Loir) 3,650 (☎37) Map **9** A3
★**Plat d'Etain** L̲ pl des Halles ☎980398 18rm6⇌6 🕭 A8rm 🏠 P L25–55 D25–55 mountains lake

BRUGES See **BORDEAUX**

BRUYÈRES 88 (Vosges), 4,050 (☎29) Map **11** A3
★**Renaissance** L̲ pl Collège ☎575014 18rm3⇌3 🕭 🏠

BUGUE (LE) 24 (Dordogne), 2,800 (☎53) Map **16** C2
★★★**Mapotel Royal Vezere** pl H-de-Ville ☎062001 tx540710 Closed Oct–Apr 52rm41⇌11 🕭 Lift sB⇌ 🕭110–160 dB⇌ 🕭125–175 (English breakfast) L41–81 D41–61 Pool river

BULLY-LES-MINES 62 (Pas-de-Calais) 12,300 (☎21) Map **3** B1
★**Moderne** 144 r de la Gare ☎291422 38rm4⇌8 🕭 🏠 P sB37 sB⇌ 🕭62 dB64 dB⇌ 🕭69 (English breakfast) L25–80 D25–80

CABRERETS 46 (Lot) 250 (☎65) Map **16** C2
★**Grottes** L̲ ☎312702 Closed Nov–Mar 17rm3⇌3 🕭 A5rm Pool

CADÉAC See **ARREAU**

CAEN† 14 (Calvados), 122,800 (☎31) Map **8** D4
★★★★**Relais des Gourmets** 15 r Geole ☎860601 tx170353 26rm16⇌10 🕭 P Lift ⚇ sB⇌ 🕭82–122 dB⇌ 🕭104–144 (English breakfast) L60–100 D60–100 St%

★★★**Malherbe** pl Ml-Foch (n rest) ☎844006 tx170555 45rm38⇌ Lift
★★★**Moderne** 116 bd Gl-Leclerc ☎860423 tx170353 60rm15⇌33 🕭 🏠 Lift
☆☆**Novotel** av de la Côte de Nacre ☎930588 tx170563 86⇌ P Lift sB⇌fr148 dB⇌fr171 English breakfast only Pool
★★**Bristol** 31 r du Xl-Novembre (off pl Ml-Foch) ☎845976 Closed 21 Dec–14 Jan 24rm4⇌8 🕭 P Lift dB61–63 dB⇌ 🕭80–100
★★**Metropole** 16 pl de la Gare (n rest) ☎822676 Closed 21 Dec–5 Jan 38rm11⇌6 🕭 Lift
★★**Place Royale** 1-3 pl de la République (n rest) ☎818533 40rm9⇌8 🕭 🏠 Lift ⚇ sBfr54 sB⇌ 🕭109 dB⇌ 🕭118
★**Bernières** 50 r de Bernières (n rest) ☎760126 Closed 23 Dec–4 Jan 16rm1⇌7 🕭 sBfr45 sB⇌ 🕭66–73 dB52 dB⇌ 🕭73–80
★**St-Jean** 20 r des Martyrs (off r St-Jean) ☎816873 15rm6⇌ P sB36–53 sB⇌53 dB43–60 dB⇌60
🛏 🚗**Chubilleau et Cie** 43 quai de Juillet ☎845738 (GB)
🛏 🚗**Eden** 24 r du Xl-Novembre ☎844032 BL/Tri
🚗**G Viard** 1 av de Paris ☎820998 Frd (GB)
At **Herouville St Clair**
☆☆**Ibis Caen** av du Grand Parc ☎935446 tx170735 95⇌ P Lift sB⇌fr102 dB⇌fr122 L30–45alc D30–45alc

CAGNES-SUR-MER 06 (Alpes-Maritimes), 29,550 (☎93) Map **28** C2
★★★★**Tierce** angle bd de la Plage et Kennedy (n rest) ☎200209 Closed 21 Oct–19 Nov 23⇌ 🏠 P Lift ⚇ sB⇌ 🕭113–147 dB⇌152–170 Beach sea mountains
★★**Cagnard** ☎207321 18⇌ 🏠 Lift
★★**Savournin** 15 av Renoir ☎206058 tx46041 Closed 16 Sep–14 Nov 32rm7⇌11 🕭
🚗**J Estre** 48 bis av de Verdun ☎206155 P Ren
At **Cros-de-Cagnes** (2km SE)
☆☆**Horizon** 111 bd de la Plage ☎310995 tx460938 Closed 16 Nov–14 Dec 43rm22⇌18 🕭 P Lift sB 85 sB⇌ 🕭140 dB 110 dB⇌ 🕭185 sea
At **Villeneuve-Loubet** (3km SW)
☆☆**Mediterranée** (N 559) ☎200007 (n rest) 16⇌ P dB⇌ 🕭56–89 (room only) sea

CAHORS† 46 (Lot) 21,950 (☎65) Map **16** C2
★★**France** L̲ 252 av J-Jaures (n rest) ☎351676 tx520394 78rm36⇌42 🕭 🏠 P Lift sB⇌ 🕭78–135 dB⇌ 🕭87–144 sea
★**Terminus** L̲ 5 av C-de Freycinet ☎352450 31rm7⇌19 🕭 P Lift ⚇ sB 75–82 sB⇌ 🕭100–106 dB91–104 dB⇌ 🕭115–126 (English breakfast) mountains
🛏 🚗**Quercy** (R Marcel) Pech d'Angély ☎353118 P Opl/VW
🚗**Recuper Auto** ☎351516 ☎353503 M/c P BL/Dat/Frd/Tri
At **Laroque-des-Arcs** (5km N)
★**Beau Rivage** ☎353058 15rm1⇌14 🕭 P dB fr39 dB⇌ 🕭fr39 (English breakfast) L 36.60 alc D36.60 alc river
At **Mercués** (8km NW by N20 & N111)
★★★**Château de Mercués** ☎360001 tx520602 Closed Nov–Mar 23⇌ P Lift ⚇ sB⇌320–370 dB⇌390–540 L alc D alc ⚇ Pool mountains
CALAIS† 62 (Pas-de-Calais) 79,400 Map **3** A1 **See Plan**
AA agents; see page 149
★★★**Meurice** 5 r E-Roche (n rest) ☎345703 Plan **1** 45rm35⇌15 🕭 🏠 P Lift ⚇ sB 80 sB⇌ 🕭100 dB⇌ 🕭109–124
★★**Bellevue** 25 pl d'Armes (n rest) ☎345375 Plan **2** 40rm11⇌7 🕭 🏠 P Lift sB38–54 sB⇌ 🕭59–78 dB54–62 dB⇌ 🕭67–86
★★**George-V** 36 r Royale (n rest) ☎344029 Plan **3** Closed Dec–14 Mar 50rm10⇌8 🕭 P sB fr 42 sB⇌ 🕭84–91 dB fr58.50 dB⇌ 🕭 92.50–100
★★**Sauvage** 46 r Royale ☎340606 Plan **4** 40rm15⇌ P dBfr77 dB 🕭fr116 Lfr31 Dfr31

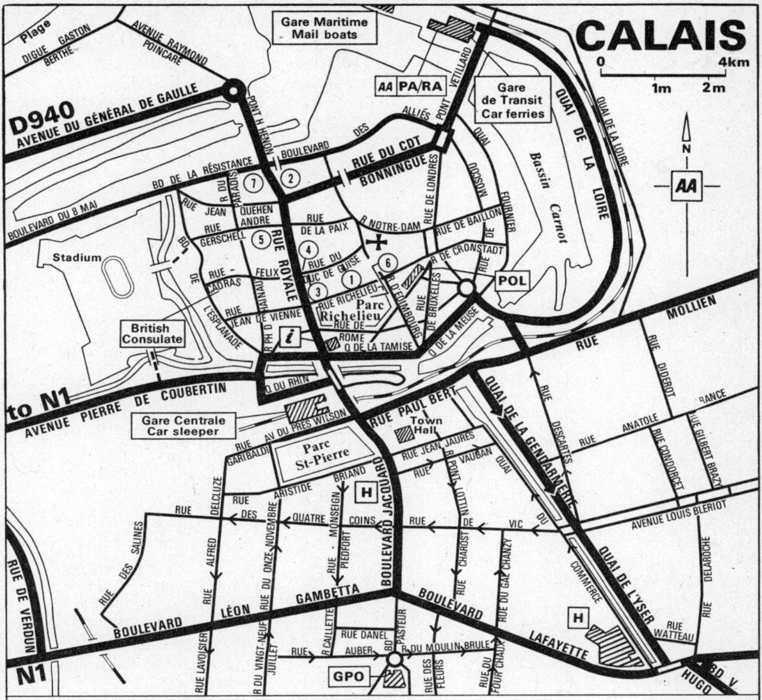

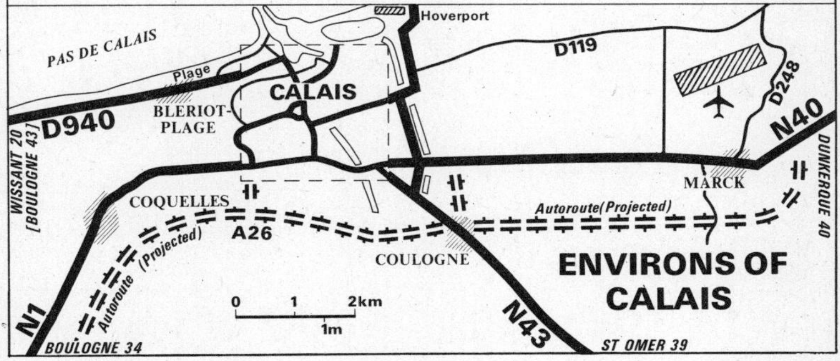

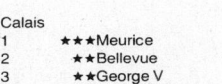

Calais

1	★★★Meurice	5	★Beffroi
2	★★Bellevue	6	★Richelieu
3	★★George V	7	★Sole Meunière
4	★★Sauvage		

France

★**Beffroi** 10 r A-Gerschel (n rest) ☎344751 Plan **5**
20rm4⇄6🛏 P sB39–46 dB44–65 dB⇄🛏80–94
★**Richelieu** 17 r Richelieu (DP & Pn) ☎346160
Plan **6** 15rm2⇄3🛏 A8rm P sB47 sB⇄🛏60 dB61
dB⇄🛏74 (English breakfast)
★**Sole Meurière** 53 r de la Mer ☎343608 Plan **7**
14rm7⇄7🛏 P sB74–100 sB⇄🛏94–105
dB92–119 dB⇄🛏112–119 (English breakfast)
L30–70 D30–70
🖪 ⴥ**Calaisienne d'Automobiles** 361 av de St
Exupery ☎347242 Peu (GB)
Commerce 79 quai du Commerce ☎347323 Fia
🖪 ⴥ**Minne** 229 bd V-Hugo ☎344408 P Aud/VW
ⴥ**Pierre** 4 r Dolain ☎345894 Dat

CALIGNAC 47 (Lot-et-Garonne) (☎58) Map **15** B2
★**Palmiers**🖳 ☎651102 14rm4⇄10🛏 P dB54–60
dB⇄🛏65–84 L22–48 D22–48 ◠ lake

CALVI See **CORSE (CORSICA)**

CAMBO-LES-BAINS 64 (Pyrénées-Atlantiques)
5,5150 (☎59) Map **20** C3
★**Bellevue**†† r des Terrasses ☎257322 24rm4⇄10🛏
🏠

CAMBRAI† 59 (Nord) 41,150 (☎20) Map **3** B1
★★★**Beatus** 38 rte de Paris (n rest) ☎814570
tx820211 26rm24⇄2🛏 🏠 P Ɒ sB⇄🛏95–118
dB⇄🛏105–130 (English breakfast)
★★**Motte Fenelon** sq du Château ☎836138
tx120285 60rm54⇄ A30rm Lift 🖢 Pool
★★**Mouton Blanc** 33 r Alsace-Lorraine ☎813016
tx820211 Closed Aug 36rm P Lift Ɒ sB45–58
dB72–121 L38–126 D38–126
★**Poste** 58–60 av de la Victoire (n rest) ☎813469
32rm11⇄18🛏 🏠 P Lift sB56 sB⇄🛏66–88
dB⇄🛏84–119 (English breakfast)
★**France** 37 r Lille (n rest) ☎813880 Closed Aug
24rm2⇄5🛏 sB44 dB56 dB⇄🛏63
(English breakfast)
🖪 ⴥ**Beffroi** 8 r XI Novembre ☎812176 P BL/Tri (GB)
ⴥ**Vente** 132 bd Faidherbe ☎815705 Opl

CAMP LONG See **AGAY**

CANCALE 35 (Ille-et-Vilaine) 4,900 (☎99) Map **8** C3
★★**Continental**🖳 au Port ☎896016 Closed 16
Nov–Feb 18rm4⇄4🛏 P sB44–103 sB⇄🛏97–103
dB52–111 dB⇄🛏105–111 L28–65 D28–65 sea
★**Mar-i-Cel** pl Centrale ☎803216 60⇄ P Lift Ɒ
sB73–88 dB⇄🛏101–136 sea

CANNES† 06 (Alpes-Maritimes) 71,000 (☎93)
Map **28** C2
★★★★★**Carlton** 60 bd Croisette ☎689168 tx470720
328⇄ 🏠 P Lift Ɒ sB⇄🛏180–380 dB⇄🛏290–500
(English breakfast) L alc D95 & alc St% Beach sea
★★★★★**Majestic** 163 bd Croisette ☎ 🏠 Lift Ɒ
sB⇄🛏280–420 dB⇄🛏320–480
(English breakfast) L alc D alc St% Beach sea
★★★★**Martinez-Concorde** 73 bd Croisette
☎689191 tx470708 Closed Oct–Dec 400⇄🛏 P Lift
Ɒ Beach
★★★★**Grand** 45 bd Croisette ☎381545 tx470727
77⇄ P Lift Ɒ sB⇄🛏226–346 dB⇄🛏307–417
Beach sea
★★★★**Méditerranée** 1 bd J-Hibert ☎992275
tx470723 150⇄ 🏠 Lift Ɒ sB⇄🛏160–210
dB⇄🛏180–310 (English breakfast) L60–65
D60–65 Pool sea
★★★★**Reserve Miramar** 64 bd Croisette ☎382470
tx47767 63rm59⇄4🛏 A6rm Lift
★★★**Embassy** 8 r de Bone ☎387902 tx47081 50⇄
🏠 Lift
★★★**Savoy** r F-Einesy (off bd Croisette) ☎381774
Closed Nov–14 Dec 55rm35⇄13🛏 Lift
sB⇄🛏125–170 dB⇄🛏240 L fr60 Dfr60
★★★**Suisse** r B-Lépine ☎385367 Closed 21 Oct–14
Jan 73rm58⇄ A7rm Lift

★★**France** 85 r d'Antibes (n rest) ☎392334
34rm⇄8🛏 🏠 Lift Ɒ sB⇄🛏80–100
dB⇄🛏100–125 (English breakfast)
★★★**Iles Britanniques** 9 bd d'Alsace (n rest)
☎390585 40rm15⇄5🛏 Lift
★★**Roches Fleuries** 92 r G-Clemenceau (n rest)
☎392878 Closed 16 Nov–14 Dec 24rm8⇄ 🏠 P Lift
sB39–80 sB⇄🛏72–80 dB58–88 dB⇄🛏81–88
mountains
ⴥ**Croisette** 30 bd d'Alsace ☎393071 Opl
ⴥ**MA Gras** 96-98 r G-Clemenceau ☎393861 Por
(GB)
🖪 ⴥ**Romeo** 1 bd J-Hibert ☎475541 Frd (GB)

CANNET (LE) 06 (Alpes-Maritimes) (☎93)
Map **28** C2
ⴥ**Europa** Bretelle de l'Autoroute ☎451700 AR/RR
(GB)

CAPBRETON 40 (Landes) 4,600 (☎58) Map **20** C4
★★**Océan** av de la plage ☎721022 Closed 16
Oct–14 Mar 47rm34⇄13🛏 A20rm Lift sea

CAP BRUN See **TOULON**

CAP D'AIL 06 (Alpes-Maritimes) 4,300 (☎93)
Map **28** C2
★★**Cigogne**🖳 r de la Gare ☎068257 Closed
Dec–Feb 15rm8⇄7🛏 P sB⇄🛏122–142
dB⇄🛏154–174 (English breakfast) L50&alc
D50&alc sea mountains
★**Miramar** av du 3-Septembre (n rest) ☎068023
Closed 16 Nov–Jan 27rm20🛏 dB53–88 dB🛏53–88
sea

CAP D'ANTIBES See **ANTIBES**
CAP-FERRAT See **ST-JEAN-CAP-FERRAT**
CAP-MARTIN See **ROQUEBRUNE-CAP MARTIN**
CAP SARDINAUX See **STE-MAXIME-SUR-MER**

CARANTEC 29 (Finistère), (☎98) Map **7** B3
★**Falaise** ☎670053 Closed 17 Sep–Apr 27rm6⇄ 🏠
P sB32 dB47–53 dB⇄🛏62–79 L27–37 D27–37
Beach sea
★**Pors-Pol**🖳 ☎670052 Closed Oct–mid Apr 40rm
3⇄18🛏 dB42–53 dB⇄🛏59–79 L25–45 D25–45
sea

CARCASSONNE† 11 (Aude) 44,650 (☎68)
Map **16** D1
★★★**Cité** pl St-Nazaire (n rest) ☎250334 Closed 16
Oct–14 Apr 64rm36⇄14🛏 🏠 Lift
★★★**Donjon** 2 r Comte Roger (n rest) ☎251113
16rm4⇄12🛏 🏠 P sB⇄🛏81–105 dB⇄🛏94–122
★★★**Terminus** 2 av Ml-Joffre ☎252500 tx535135
110rm70⇄30🛏 🏠 Lift
★☆**Croque Sel** rte Narbonne ☎251415 Closed Jan
11⇄ P sB⇄🛏85 dB⇄🛏92 L24–40 D24–40 mountains
★**Logis de Trencavel**🖳 286 av du Gl-Leclerc
☎251953 Closed 21 Jan–Feb 12rm3⇄6🛏 🏠 P
dB99–134 L65 D65
★★**Montsegur** 1 av Bunau-Varilla (n rest) ☎253141
Closed 16 Dec–14 Jan 21rm6⇄15🛏 P Lift Ɒ
sB⇄🛏61–94 dB⇄🛏86–122 (English breakfast)
★**Residence & Auter** 26r A-Marty ☎250896
tx51857 27rm13⇄2🛏 Lift
★★**Royal** 22 bd J-Jaurés (n rest) ☎251912
27rm3⇄10🛏 🏠 P Ɒ sB39–44 sB⇄🛏57–65
dB49–57 dB⇄🛏67–73
i ⴥ**Alaux et Gestin** rte Narbonne ☎257712 Ren
🖪 ⴥ**Audoise Auto** rte de Montréal ☎478200
Chy/Sim

CARENNAC 46 (Lot) 400 (☎65) Map **16** C2
★**Fenelon**🖳 ☎384716 Closed Feb 24rm6⇄5🛏 P
sB37–42 sB🛏52–62 dB50–55 dB🛏70–76
L19–60 D19–60 river

CARENTAN 50 (Manche) 6,600 (☎33) Map **8** C4
★**Auberge Normande**🖳 bd Verdun ☎420299
12rm6⇄4🛏 A1rm P sB36–65 sB🛏52–72 dB72
dB⇄🛏72

CARHAIX 29 (Finistère) 8,950 (☎98) Map **7** B3
★★**France**🖳 14 r des Martyrs ☎930015 Closed 21
Dec–19 Jan 20rm5⇄5🛏 P sB39–52 sB⇄🛏68–77
dB60–63 dB⇄🛏76–91 L32–57 D32–57
🖪 ⴥ**Saux** av V-Hugo ☎930466 P Sim

176

CARNAC 56 (Morbihan) 3,750 (☎97) Map **7** B2
At Carnac-Plage
★★*Armoric* 53 av de la Poste (DP) ☎521347 Closed
Oct–mid Apr 25rm6⇌9⋔ ✎
★*Celtique* 17 av Kemario ☎521149 Closed 16
Sep–mid Apr 35rm6⇌17⋔ P sBfr53 db67–101
dB⇌⋔fr106 (English breakfast) L fr36 D fr36
★*Genêts* 45 av Kermario ☎521101 Closed Oct–May
31rm14⇌6⋔ P sBfr69 sB⇌⋔93 dB77–89
dB⇌⋔101–125 L42–45 D42–45

CARQUEFOU See NANTES

CARQUEIRANNE 83 (Var) 5,250 (☎94) Map **27** B1
★★*Plein Sud* rte des Salettes (n rest) ☎665286
Closed 6–31 Nov 17rm6⇌11⋔ P sB⇌⋔78–90
dB⇌⋔86–98

CARTERET See BARNEVILLE-CARTERET

CASSIS 13 (Bouches-du-Rhône) 5,850 (☎91)
Map **27** B1
★★★*Plage* pl Bestouan ☎010570 Closed 16 Oct–14
Mar 29rm13⇌16⋔ P Lift ⅅ sB70 sB⇌⋔70
dB⇌⋔108–179 sea
★★*Liautaud* av V-Hugo (DP) ☎017537 Closed
Nov–19 Dec 32rm14⇌15⋔ ⋔ Lift sea

CASTELJALOUX 47 (Lot-et-Garonne) 5,450 (☎58)
Map **15** B2
★*Grand Cadets de Gascogne* pl Gambetta
☎930059 Closed 2–19 Nov 14rm8⇌2⋔ ⋒ P
sB42–46 sB⇌⋔73–88 dB54–56 dB⇌⋔86–104
(English breakfast) L35–100 D35–100 ◯
🛢 ✎*A Gloriant* (N133) ☎930596 P Ren

CASTELLANE 04 (Alpes-de-Hautes-Provence)
1,300 (☎92) Map **28** C2
★*Ma Petite Auberge* pl M-Sauvaire ☎836206
Closed 16 Oct–14 Mar 18rm4⇌9⋔ sB43–65
sB⇌⋔58–70 dB51–75 dB⇌⋔66–80 L30–50
D30–50 mountains
🛢 ✎*J Trinquard* (N85) ☎142 Ren

CASTELNAUDARY 11 (Aude) 10,850 (☎68)
Map **16** C1
★★*France & Notre Dame* 2 av F-Mistral ☎231018
32rm10⇌7⋔ ⋒
★★*Palmes & Industrie* ㏇ 10 r Ml-Foch ☎230310
tx49935 Closed Jan 20rm12⇌4⋔ ⋒ Lift
★*Fourcade* 14 r des Carmes ☎230208 Closed 16
May–14 Jun 19rm13⇌2⋔ A5rm ⋒ P sB33
sB⇌⋔50–107 dB57–114 dB⇌⋔57–114
(English breakfast) L30–70 D30–70

CASTELSARRASIN 82 (Tarn-et-Garonne) 12,250
(☎63) Map **16** C2
★*Moderne* 54 r de L'Egalité (n rest) ☎043010
ta Marceillac 12rm2⇌⋔ ⋒ P ⅅ sBfr23 dBfr28 dB⋔fr36
(English breakfast)

CASTRES† 81 (Tarn) 47,550 (☎63) Map **16** D1
★★*Grand* 11 r de la Libération ☎590030 tx530905
Closed 16 Dec–14 Jan 36rm20⇌10⋔ ⋒ Lift ⅅ
sB49–69 sB⇌⋔69–79 dB⇌⋔108–128
(English breakfast) L28–48 D28–48

CAUDEBEC-EN-CAUX 76 (Seine-Maritime) 2,750
(☎35) Map **9** A4
★★*Marine* 18 quai Guilbaud ☎962011 tx770404
34rm16⇌13⋔ P Lift sB61–67 dB92–97
dB⇌⋔142–167 (English breakfast) L42–64
D42–64 ✎ river
★★*Normandie* quai Guilbaud ☎962511
11rm2⇌3⋔ P sB45–72 sB⇌⋔66–72 dB56–80
dB⇌⋔74–80 (English breakfast) L25–60 D25–60
river

CAUSSADE 82 (Tarn-et-Garonne) 5,900 (☎63)
Map **16** C3
★★*Dupont* 12 r Recollets ☎021202 34rm8⇌2⋔ :
A8rm ⋒ P sB47 sB⇌⋔74 dB54 dB⇌⋔81
(English breakfast) L23–77 D23–77&alc
★★*Larroque* av de la Gare ☎021014 30rm15⇌10⋔
⋒ P sB43–53 sB⇌⋔60–78 dB64–80
dB⇌⋔79–90 (English breakfast) L26–48 D26–48
🛢 ✎*Mousquetaires-Auto* (M A Roumignuie) 25 bd
L-Grand ☎021026 Ren

CAUTERETS 65 (Hautes-Pyrénées) 1,100 (☎62)
Map **21** B4
★★*Belfort* ㏇ r Belfort (n rest) ☎975018 Closed 2
Oct–14 May 20rm ⋒ P Lift sB⇌⋔58–63
dB⇌⋔81–86 (English breakfast) mountains
★★*Mouré* 19 r de Belfort ☎975109 tx530337 Closed
Oct–14 Dec 40rm17⇌10⋔ Lift
At Pont d'Espagne (8km SE by N21C)
★*Pont d'Espagne* ☎300 Closed Nov–Mar 18rm

CAVAILLON 84 (Vaucluse) 21,550 (☎90)
Map **27** B2
★★★*Christel* Boscodomini ☎710779 tx431547
Closed Jan 109⇌7⋔ P Lift sB⇌⋔103–118 dB⇌⋔122–134
(English breakfast) L35–50 D35–50 Pool river
mountains

CAVALAIRE-SUR-MER 83 (Var) 2,750 (☎94)
Map **28** C1
★★*Bonne Auberge* 400 av des Allies ☎720296
Closed Oct–mid Apr 35rm3⇌20⋔ P sB70 dB68–77
dB⇌⋔86–107

CAVALIÈRE 83 (Var) 850 (☎94) Map **28** C1
★★★*Surplage* ☎728419 Closed 21 Oct–21 Mar
96rm75⇌9⋔ Lift Pool Beach sea
★*Cap Negre* (DP) ☎728046 Closed Oct–mid Apr
30⇌ Lift sea

CELLE-DUNOISE (LA) 23 (Creuse) 750 (☎55)
Map **16** C/D4
★*Pascaul* ㏇ ☎891066 Closed Oct 13rm4⋔ ⋒
sB30 dB42–44 dB⋔50–52 (English breakfast)
L20–60 D20–60

CELONY See AIX-EN-PROVENCE

CERGY See PONTOISE

CHABLIS 89 (Yonne) 2,450 (☎86) Map **10** C2
★*Étoile* 4 r Moulins ☎531050 Closed 16 Dec–14 Feb
16rm3⇌6⋔ ⋒
🛢 ✎*Route Service* ☎531046 ☎531046 ⚙ M/c P Cit
(GB)

CHAGNY 71 (Saône-et-Loire) 5,950 (☎85)
Map **10** C1
★★*Lameloise* 36 pl d'Armes ☎490210
35rm15⇌12⋔ ⋒
★*Capucines* ㏇ rte Chalon ☎870817 Closed Dec
12rm8⇌2 P sB70–100 sB⇌⋔75–102 dB85–112
dB⇌⋔85–112 (English breakfast) L fr60 D fr60
★*Paris* 6 r de Beaune ☎870838 Closed Jan
13rm1⇌4⋔ A5rm P sBfr30 dBfr47 dB⇌⋔fr54
L22–29

CHALLANS 85 (Vendée) 12,250 (☎51) Map **8** C1/2
★*Marais* 16 pl Gl-de-Gaulle (DP) ☎681513
17rm4⇌13⋔

CHALLES-LES-EAUX 73 (Savoie) 2,600 (☎79)
Map **27** B4
★★★*Château de Challes* r du Château ☎251145
Closed 25 Sep–14 May 70rm36⇌3⋔ A50rm P ⅅ
sB47–53 sB⇌⋔99–104 dB72–78 dB⇌⋔118–134
(English breakfast) L31–55 D31–55 ✎ Pool
mountains

CHÂLONS-SUR-MARNE† 51 (Marne) 55,750 (☎26)
Map **10** C3
★★*Angleterre* 19 pl Mgr-Tissier ☎682151 Closed 16
Feb–14 Mar 18rm9⇌4⋔ P ⅅ sB57–77
sB⇌⋔96–134 dB74–87 dB⇌⋔106–155 L32–81
D32–81
★★*Bristol* 77 av P-Semard (n rest) ☎682463
24rm11⇌13⋔ ⋒ P sB⇌⋔fr50 dB⇌⋔67–85
★*Mon des Loges* ☎694117 23rm1⇌2⋔
★★*Pasteur* 46 r Pasteur (n rest) ☎681000
26rm8⇌8⋔ P dB47–86
★★*Pot d'Etain* 18 pl République (n rest) ☎680909
Closed 21 Dec–19 Jan 24rm3⇌5⋔ P ⅅ sBfr39
sB⇌⋔fr78 dBfr59 dB⇌⋔fr94 (English breakfast)
🛢 ✎*Centre* (Halloz) 21–23 r Thiers ☎644937 P Frd
🛢 ✎*G Poiret* 16 Ter r des Martyrs de la Résistance
☎680845 BL (GB)
✎*Raige* 17 r Clovis Jacquiert ☎681431 ☎681431 ⚙
P
🛢 ✎*Rennesson Garage de l'Avenue* 133 av de
Paris ☎681163 P Opl

France

At **Epine (L')** (8.5km E on N3)

★★Armes de Champagne ☎681043 Closed 16 Jan–14 Feb 40rm9⇌19🛁 A12rm⇌ P ⅅ sB67 sB⇌🛁68–119 dB83 dB⇌🛁84–135 L32–82&alc D32–82&alc

CHALON-SUR-SAÔNE 71 (Saone-et-Loire) 60,500 (☎85) Map **10** C1

☆☆☆**Mercure** av de l'Europe ☎465189 tx800132 88⇌ P Lift ⅅ sB⇌fr119 dB⇌fr156 English breakfast only Pool

★★★Royal 8 r du Port Villiers ☎481586 tx601610 52rm34⇌14🛁 🏠 P Lift ⅅ sB⇌🛁120–160 (room only) dB⇌🛁130–230 (room only)

★★★St-Regis 22 bd de la République ☎480728 tx801624 40rm20⇌10🛁 🏠 Lift ⅅ sBfr71 sB⇌🛁fr106 dB⇌🛁162 L42 D42

★★Europe 11–13 r du Port-Villiers ☎480386 21rm5⇌3🛁 🏠 P sB50–103 sB⇌🛁78 dB66 dB⇌🛁86–111 L fr32 D fr32

★★St-Rémy pl Pont-Paron (n rest) ☎483804 40rm20⇌20🛁 P sB73 sB⇌🛁79 dB81 dB⇌🛁87–110

★Laurentides 30 quai St-Cosme ☎482985 33rm14⇌12🛁 Lift sBfr50 sB⇌🛁fr58 dB⇌🛁75–120 L25–40&alc D25–40&alc

🗓 **B Picard** 26 rte d'Oslon, St-Marcel ☎488523 P Aud/VW (GB)

🗓 **Rocade Automobile** 91 av de Paris ☎483476 Chy

CHAMBÉRY† 73 (Savoie) 58,800 (☎79) Map **27** B4

★★★ ♦Grand 6 pl de la Gare ☎695454 tx320910 60rm50⇌10🛁 🏠 P Lift ⅅ sB⇌🛁134–194 dB⇌🛁178–288 (English breakfast) L60–120 D60–120 mountains

★★★France 22 fbg Reclus (n rest) ☎335118 tx320937 48rm42⇌6🛁 🏠 P Lift sB⇌🛁92–112 dB⇌🛁139–172

★★★Touring 12 r Sommeiller ☎623726 43rm8⇌24🛁 🏠 P Lift ⅅ sB61–106 sB⇌🛁76–106 dB88–141 dB⇌🛁141 L fr30 D fr30 mountains

🗓 **♦Actual Autos** 381 av du Covet ☎340500 ➌ BL (GB)

🗓 **R Blumet** 1 av de Lyon ☎694473 P Lnc/Toy

🗓 **Gare** 29 av de la Boisse ☎344161 Fia (GB)

🗓 **Gauthier et Coudurier** 15 quai de la Rize ☎332809 P Peu

At **Chamnord**

☆☆**Ibis Chambéry** ☎692836 tx320457 91⇌ P Lift sB⇌fr88 dB⇌fr112 L30–45 alc D30–45 alc

CHAMBON (LAC) 63 (Puy-de-Dôme) 566 (☎73) Map **16**D3

★★Bellevue 🅻🅴 (DP) ☎886106 Closed Oct–Apr 25rm5⇌7🛁 A8rm P sB62–75 sB⇌🛁79–95 dB124–150 dB⇌🛁158–190 L32–65 D32–65 lake

★★Grillon 🅻🅴 ☎886066 18rm7🛁 🛁 lake

CHAMBORD 41 (Loir-et-Cher)250 (F39) Map **9** A2

★★St-Michel 🅻🅴 ☎463131 Closed 16 Nov–14 Dec 40rm18⇌4🛁 🏠 P

CHAMNORD See **CHAMBÉRY**

CHAMONIX-MONT-BLANC† 74 (Haute-Savoie) 9,050 (☎50) Map **28** C4 See also **Argentière**

★★★★Croix Blanche 7 r Vallot (n rest) ☎530011 tx385614 Closed 30 May–Jun 36rm25⇌11🛁 A18rm P Lift ⅅ sB⇌🛁70–95 dB⇌🛁100–140 (English breakfast) 🛁 mountains

★★★Mont-Blanc pl d'Eglise ☎530564 tx385614 Closed Nov–15Dec 60rm53⇌2🛁 🏠 P Lift ⅅ sBfr152 sB⇌🛁fr152 dB fr234 dB⇌🛁fr234 L fr55 Dfr55 🛁 Pool mountains

★★★Richemond r Dr-Paccard ☎530885 Closed 18 Apr–14 Jun & 18 Sep–19 Dec 54rm36⇌ P Lift ⅅ sB47–59 sB⇌🛁69–83 dB84–96 dB⇌🛁113–136 (English breakfast) L40 D40 mountains

★★Sapinière-Montana 85 r Mummery ☎530763 tx385410 Closed 16 Oct–14 Dec 30rm23⇌1🛁 A9rm 🏠 P Lift ⅅ sB80–100 sB⇌🛁100–130 dB100–115 dB⇌🛁120–170 L45–50 D45–50 mountains

🗓 **♦Bouchet** pl du Mont-Blanc ☎530175 P Ren (GB)

At **Bossons (Les)** (3.5km S)

★★Aiguille du Midi 🅻🅴 ☎530065 Closed 26 Sep–Xmas & mid Apr–14 May 45rm22⇌5🛁 🏠 Lift 🛁

CHAMPAGNOLE 39 (Jura) 10,750 (☎82) Map **10** D1

★★★Ripotot 54 r MI-Foch ☎521545 Closed 16 Sep–Apr 65rm35⇌ 🏠 P Lift ⅅ sB45–55 sB⇌ 79–99 dB63–78 dB⇌ 108–138 (English breakfast) L60 D60 mountains

CHAMPILLON See **EPERNAY**

CHAMPNIERS See **ANGOULÊME**

CHAMPTOCEAUX 49 (Maine-et-Loire) 1,300 (☎40) Map **8** C2

★★Côte 🅻🅴 ☎835039 tx700610 29rm12⇌6🛁 🏠 P sBfr45 sB⇌🛁84 dBfr56 dB⇌🛁101 (English breakfast) L26–46 D25–46

CHANTEMERLE 05 Hautes-Alpes 1,500 (☎92) Map **28** C3

★★Clos 🅻🅴 ☎240013 Closed 21 Apr–14 June & 21 Sep–19 Dec 35rm19⇌1🛁

CHANTILLY 60 (Oise) 10,700 (☎4) Map **9** B3/4

★Angleterre 9 pl Omer Vallan ☎4570059 Closed 6 Jan–14 Feb 20rm4⇌4🛁 A4rm 🏠 P sB43–48 sB⇌🛁63–73 dB50–60 dB⇌🛁80–85 (English breakfast) L35–40 D30–40

At **Lys Chantilly** (7km S)

★★★Lys Rond-Point de la Reine ☎4215019 tx150298 35rm25⇌10🛁 A21rm P sB⇌🛁125–150 dB⇌🛁135–160 (English breakfast) L fr52 Dfr52

CHANTONNAY 85 (Vendee) 7,450 (☎30) Map **8** C1

★Chêne Vert 2 av Mgr-J-Batiot ☎388013 Closed Feb 20rm2⇌2🛁

★Mouton 31 r Nationale ☎943022 Closed Oct 12rm2⇌5🛁 P sB40–65 sB⇌🛁72 L25–43 D25–43

🗓 **Chauveau-Puaud** 20 av G-Clemenceau ☎313255 P Cit

CHAPELLE-EN-VERCORS (LA) 26 (Drôme) 850 (☎75) Map **27** B3

★Bellier ☎482003 Closed 26 Sep–9 Jun 13rm7⇌1🛁

CHARAVINES 38 (Isère) 1,200 (☎76) Map **27** B4

★★Hostellerie Lac Bleu 🅻🅴 (1.5km N on D50) ☎066048 Closed Nov–Feb 15rm2⇌8🛁 P sBfr43 dBfr58 dB⇌🛁74–92 L34–65 D34–65 mountains lake

CHARBONNIERES-LES-BAINS See **LYON**

CHARLEVILLE-MÉZIÈRES† 08 (Ardennes) 63,350 (☎24) Map **10** C4

🗓 **♦C Cailloux** 50 chaussée de Sedan ☎570101 Frd

🗓 **♦Central** 20 av J-Jaurès ☎332211 Closed Sat Sim (GB)

At **Villers-Semeuse** (5km E)

☆☆☆**Mercure** r L-Michel ☎570529 tx840076 67⇌ P Lift sB⇌fr136 dB⇌fr170 English breakfast only Pool

CHARMES 88 (Vosges) 6,000 (☎29) Map **11** A3

★Central 🅻🅴 10 r des Capucins ☎380240 Closed Jan 12rm9🛁 🏠 dB50–52 dB⇌🛁59–65 L25–70 D25–70

CHARMOY 89 (Yonne) Map **10** C2

★Relais de Charmoy ☎732319 Closed Jan 10rm2⇌4🛁 P dB46 dB⇌🛁51–65 L25–49 D25–49

CHAROLLES71 (Saone-et-Loire) 4,350 (☎85) Map **10** C1

★Moderne 🅻🅴 10 av de la Gare ☎240702 Closed 24 Dec–Jan 19rm12⇌4🛁 A7rm P dB60–65 dB⇌🛁90–120 L35–85 D35–85 Pool

CHARTRES† 28 (Eure-et-Loir) 41,300 (☎37) Map **9** A3

★★★Grand Monarque 22 pl des Epars ☎210072 43rm22⇌8🛁 🏠 Lift

☆☆☆**Novotel** av M-Proust, la Madeleine ☎218030 tx781298 78⇌ P Lift sB⇌🛁137–147 dB⇌🛁161–171 L fr45 Dfr45 Pool

★Jehan-de-Beauce 19 av J-de-Beauce ☎21041 46rm29⇌ Lift

★★Paris 🅻🅴 6 pl de la Gare ☎211013 Closed 1–15 Feb & 19 Aug–2 Sep 12rm5🛁 P sB36–41 sB🛁fr60

178

dB56−62 dB🍴67−77 L30−54 D30−54

★**Ouest** 3 pl Semard (n rest) 🕿214327 26rm15🛏
P Lift ♪ sB42−67 sB🛏🍴67−83 dB49−65
dB🛏90−115 L33−45 D33−45

🅿 🛵**Bellenger** 8 av J-de-Beauce 🕿213383 Sim

🅿 🛵**Paris-Brest** 80 r F-Lepine 🕿211388 Frd

🅿 🛵**Ruelle Guy 'Beaulieu'** 104 r fbg la Grappe
🕿215119 Ren

At **Lucé** (SW on N27)

🅿 🛵**Chartres Auto Sport** rte d'Illiers 🕿212479
Closed Mon BL

CHARTRE-SUR-LE-LOIR (LA) 72 (Sarthe), 1,950
(🕿43) Map 8 D2

★★**France** 🇱 20 pl de la République 🕿444016
Closed Feb 32rm11🛏14🍴 🏠 P sB42−47
sB🛏🍴53−77 dB🛏75−88 L26−65 D26−65

CHASSENEUIL See **POITIERS**

CHÂTEAU-ARNOUX 04 (Alpes-de-Hautes-
Provence) 6,250 (🕿92) Map 27 B2

★★★**Bonne Étape** (N85) 🕿640009 tx430605
Closed 4 Jan−14 Feb 20rm17🛏3🍴 🏠 P
dB🛏🍴116−256 L62−160 D62−160 Pool mountains
lake

At **St-Auban** (4km SE on N96)

🅿 🛵**Guillaume** (N96) 🕿641710 P Ren

CHÂTEAUBRIANT 44 (Loire-Atlantique) 13,850
(🕿40) Map 8 C2

★★★**Hostellerie de la Ferrière** rte de Nantes
🕿811012 15rm11🛏3🍴 A4rm P sB52−130
dB🛏🍴110−130 dB61−139 dB🛏🍴119−139
L fr25&alc D fr25&alc lake

★**Armor** 19 pl Motte (n rest) 🕿811119 20rm6🛏7🍴
Lift sB40 sB🛏🍴47−74 dB🛏🍴74

CHÂTEAU CHINON 58 (Nièvre) 2,950 (🕿86)
Map 10 C1

★★**Vieux Morvan** pl Ancienne Mairie (n rest)
🕿850501 Closed 16 Nov−9 Jan 23rm11🍴 sB41−74
sB🍴58−74 dB52−57 dB🍴66−84 L26−42 D26−42
mountains

CHÂTEAUDUN 28 (Eure-et-Loir) 16,150 (🕿37)
Map 9 A2

★★**Beauce** 50 r de Jallans 🕿451475 Closed 19
Dec−8 Jan 22rm8🛏8🍴 🏠 sBfr47 sB🛏🍴60−82
dB54−71 dB🛏🍴82−92 (English breakfast) L34−75
D34−75

★**Trois Pastoureaux** 31 r A-Gillet 🕿450162 Closed
Mon & Feb 10rm2🛏 A7rm 🏠 P sB36 sB🛏68 dB43
dB🛏75 L29.50

🅿 🛵**Touchard** bd du 8 Mai 🕿450332 P Aud/VW

CHÂTEAUFARINE See **BESANÇON**

CHÂTEAU-GONTIER 53 (Mayenne), 8,650 (🕿43)
Map 8 C2

★★**Mirwault** (1.5km N by r Basse-du-Rocher)
🕿071012 Closed 25 Dec−Jan 10rm3🍴 P Lift
sB49−69 dB57−77 L32−70 D32−70 river

★**Anglais** 🇱 10 pl Gare 🕿071034 16rm1🛏1🍴 🏠 P
sB35−38 sB🛏🍴45−48 dB46−51 dB🛏🍴58−59
L22−24 D22−24

CHÂTEAULIN 29 (Finistère) 5,700 (🕿98) Map 7 A3

At **Port-Launay** (2.5km NE)

★★**Bon Accueil** 🇱 rte de Brest 🕿861577 tx94501
59rm17🛏25🍴 🏠 P Lift sB50−57 sB🛏🍴90−107
dB60−69 dB🛏🍴100−119 (English breakfast)
L30−100 D30−100 lake

CHÂTEAUNEUF-SUR-LOIRE 45 (Loiret) 5,700
(🕿38) Map 9 B2

★**Nouvel du Loiret** 4 pl A-Briande (DP) 🕿894228
Closed 19 Dec−2 Jan 21rm4🛏5🍴 🏠

CHÂTEAU RENAULT 37 (Indre-et-Loire) 6,000
(🕿47) Map 9 A2

🅿 🛵**Traveau Gilles** 24 r de la République 🕿565105
🕿565105 🛵 M/c P Cit (GB)

CHÂTEAUROUX† 36 (Indre) 55,650 (🕿54)
Map 9 A/B1

★★**France** 16 r V-Hugo 🕿340080 44rm20🛏20🍴 🏠
P Lift ♪ sBfr61 sB🛏111−153 dB🛏🍴121−165
(English breakfast) L alc

★**Central** 19 av de la Gare (n rest) 🕿340100 6rm

🅿 🛵**Caberry** 124 rte de Blois 🕿342362 Aud/VW

🛵🛵**Pabariel** 54 av de la Gare 🕿340796 Closed Mon
Frd (GB)

🅿 🛵**J Sarraf** 34 rte d'Argenton 🕿222222 P Ren

CHÂTEAU-SALINS 57 (Moselle) 2,570 (🕿87)
Map 11 A3

★**Vallet** 50 av Napoleon 1er 🕿051048 Closed Oct
16🛏 🏠

CHÂTEAU-THIERRY 02 (Aisne) 13,900 (🕿23)
Map 10 C3

★★**Ile de France** (3km N on N37) 🕿831012
31rm6🛏16🍴 P Lift sBfr47 sB🛏🍴fr76 dBfr60
dB🛏🍴fr96 Lfr24

☆**Girafe** pl A-Briand (n rest) 🕿830206 29rm3🛏9🍴
🏠 P sB43−44 sB🛏🍴73−74 dB61−63 dB🛏🍴91−93
(English breakfast) river

🅿 🛵**Bachelet** av Gl-de-Gaulle à Essômes 🕿832178
M/c P Bed/Lnc/Opl

🅿 **Tourisport** Nogentel 🕿831128 P BL

CHÂTELAILLON-PLAGE 17 (Charente-Maritine)
5,400 (🕿46) Map 15 B4

★★**Grand** 13 av Gl-Leclerc 🕿351239 Closed 16
Sep−May 27rm9🛏9🍴

★★**Hostellerie Select** 1 r G-Musset 🕿351059
23rm6🛏5🍴 🏠

★**Majestic** 🇱 pl de St-Marsault 🕿351014 Closed 21
Dec−4 Jan 30rm9🛏12🍴 🏠 P sB39−54 dB65
dB🛏🍴77−94 L25−60 D25−60

🅿 🛵**M Aguillon** av d'Angoulins 🕿351449 Toy

CHÂTEL GUYON 63 (Puy-de-Dôme) 3,700 (🕿73)
Map 16 D3

★★★**Hermitage** 18 r Brocqueville 🕿860034 Closed
Oct−May 70rm35🛏 Lift

★★★**International** r A-Punnet 🕿860672 Closed
Oct−Apr 70rm50🛏7🍴 Lift ♪ sB54−84
sB🛏100−110 dB94 dB🛏🍴110−130
(English breakfast) L35−58 D35−58

CHÂTELLERAULT† 86 (Vienne) 38,300 (🕿49)
Map 8 D1

★★★**Moderne** 74 bd Blossac 🕿213011 tx791061
38rm9🛏19🍴 🏠 Lift

★★**Croissant** av J-F-Kennedy 🕿210177 20rm8🛏
Lift

★★**Escale** 17 av d'Argenson (n rest) 🕿211350
32rm9🛏 P Lift sB47−58 sB🛏🍴54−58 dB54−80
dB🍴61−80 (English breakfast)

☆**Ibis Chatellerault** quartier de la Forêt 🕿217577
tx791488 72🛏 P Lift sB🛏fr94 dB🛏fr114 L35−45alc
D35−45alc

★★**Univers** 4 av G-Clemenceau 🕿212353 Closed 2
wks Dec 30rm4🛏13🍴 A5rm 🏠 P Lift ♪ sB34−37
dBfr72 dB🛏🍴fr100 L25−80 D25−80

🅿 🛵**Tardy** 32−42 bd d'Estrées 🕿214844 Frd

CHÂTILLON-EN-BAZOIS 58 (Nièvre) 1,120 (🕿83)
Map 10 C1

★**Poste** Grande r 🕿23 14rm 🏠 Lift

CHÂTILLON-SUR-INDRE 36 (Indre) 3,700 (🕿54)
Map 9 A1

★**Auberge de la Tour** 🇱 🕿387217 Closed 16
Dec−Jan 10rm2🍴 🏠 P sB42−44 sB🍴61 dB49−54
dB🍴68 L26−48 D26−48

★**Promenade** 88 r Grande 🕿387195 Closed Feb
12rm1🛏 🏠

🅿 🛵**J-Goullier** 5 rte du Blanc 🕿387109 P Ren

CHÂTILLON-SUR-SEINE 21 (Côte-d'Or) 7.950
(🕿80) Map 10 C2

★★**Côte d'Or** r C-Ronot 🕿911329 Closed 7 Jan−24
Feb 12rm7🛏2🍴 🏠 P sB75−84 sB🛏🍴124−129
dB146−166 (English breakfast) L52−95 D52−95

★★**Sylvia** 9 av de la Gare (n rest) 🕿910244
20rm8🛏5🍴 A8rm 🏠 P sB45−54 sB🛏🍴59−83
dB53−63 dB🍴67−92

★**Jura** 19 r Dr-Robert (n rest) 🕿911402 Closed
Oct−mid Apr 12rm1🛏4🍴

★*Montagne* pl Joffre Closed 9−31 Dec 16rm 🏠

🛪 ⏚ *Centre* 3 r Marmont ☎910144 P Frd

🛪 ⏚ *Châtillonnais* (Ferrier) 20 av de la Gare
☎911113 P Fia

CHÂTRE (LA) 36 (Indre) 5,250 (☎54) Map **16** D4

★*St-Germain* 86 r Nationale ☎15 26rm1⇌1 🛁 🏠

CHAUMONT 52 (Haute-Marne) 29,350 (☎25)
Map **10** D2

★★★*Terminus Reine* pl de la Gare ☎036666
tx840920 67rm21⇌27 🛁 🏠 P Lift ♪ sB46−92
sB⇌🛁62−92 dB58−110 dB⇌🛁81−110 L55 D55

★★*Grand Val* rte de Langres (N19) ☎031590
64rm6⇌26 🛁 🏠 P Lift sB46−53 sB⇌🛁78−83 dB62
dB⇌🛁89−94 L30−50 D30−50

★*France* 25 r Toupot de Béveaux ☎030111 40rm6⇌
A5rm 🛁

🛪 ⏚ *Boni* 11 r P-Burello ☎030455 Frd (GB)

🚗 ⏚ *François* 11 av de la République ☎030888
☎030888 P Chy (GB)

CHAUMONT-SUR-LOIRE† 41 (Loir-et-Cher) 800
(☎39) Map **9** A2

★★★*Château*💶 (DP) ☎469804 Closed 16 Nov−14
Mar 20⇌ 🏠

★*Moutier St-Martin* ☎469813 7rm4⇌3🛁 P Lift
dB⇌🛁58−65 L30−60 D30−60

CHAUNAY 86 (Vienne) 1,300 (☎49)
Map **15/16** B4/C4

★★*Central* ☎492504 Closed Feb 12⇌ 🏠

CHAUVIGNY 86 (Vienne) 6,850 (☎49) Map **16** C4

★*Lion d'Or*💶 8 r Marche ☎463028 Closed 16
Dec−14 Jan 12rm 🏠 P sBfr39 dBfr56 L25−42&alc
D25−42&alc

CHELLES 77 (Seine-et-Marne) 36,500 (☎1)
Map **1** B3

🛪 ⏚ *Chelles* av de Sylvie, zone Industrielle
☎9575302 P Bed/BL/Opl (GB)

🛪 ⏚ *Dubos* 92 av du Ml-Foch ☎9573558 Frd

CHENEHUTTE-LES-TUFFEAUX See **SAUMUR**

CHENONCEAUX 37 (Indre-et-Loire) 350 (☎47)
Map **9** A2

★★★*Ottoni* (N76) ☎299009 Closed 16 Oct − mid Apr
35rm17⇌ A16rm 🏠 P sB62−82 sB⇌🛁92−107
dB79−89 dB⇌🛁114−139 (English breakfast) L47alc
D47alc

★★*Bon Laboureur et Château* (N76) ☎299002
Closed 6 Nov−19 Mar 26rm16⇌3🛁 🏠 P sB52−102
sB⇌🛁102 dB80−146 dB⇌🛁132−146 L40−75
D40−75

★*Roy* r Dr-Bretonneau ☎299017 Closed Dec & Jan
26rm4⇌5🛁 A5rm P sB31−38 dB48−51 dB⇌🛁67
L20−41 D20−41

CHERBOURG† 50 (Manche) 34,650 (☎33)
Map **8** C4 **See Plan**

AA̲ | **agents; see page 149**

★★★*Sofitel* Gare Maritime ☎533011 tx170613
Plan **1** 62⇌ 🏠 Lift sea

★★*Caligny* 41 r Ml-Foch (n rest) ☎531024 Plan **2**
Closed 16 Dec−9 Jan 46rm6⇌10🛁 🏠 P sBfr42
dB⇌🛁fr73

★★*Louvre* 28 r de la Paix (n rest) ☎530228 Plan **3**
42rm9⇌14🛁 🏠 Lift ♪ sB46−50 sB⇌🛁71−86
dB53−61 dB⇌🛁79−117

★★*Torgistorps* 14 pl de la République (n rest)
☎433232 Plan **4** 14rm8⇌4🛁 P sB51−90 sB⇌🛁90
dB82−97 dB⇌🛁97 (English breakfast) sea

★*Renaissance* 4 r de l'Eglise (n rest) ☎532306
Plan **5** 14rm10🛁 P sB42 sB🛁70 dB52 dB🛁80 sea

🛪 ⏚ *Ganche* 47 r du Val-de-Saire ☎532868
☎537105 Ren

🛪 ⏚ *Manche* 5 av Carnot ☎531870 Peu (GB)

🛪 ⏚ *Poste* (Leprévost) 46 bis r Ancien-Quai
☎530334 Chy/Sim

🛪 ⏚ *Vikings* 12 av de Paris ☎532219 Aud/VW

At **Tourlaville** (4km E)

🚗 ⏚ *Moderne* 13 r P-Desprès ☎533310 M/c P

CHINON 37 (Indre-et-Loire) 8,350 (☎47) Map **8** D2

★*Boule d'Or* 66 quai J-d'Arc (DP) ☎930313 Closed
16 Dec & Jan 20rm2⇌7🛁 🏠

★*Gargantua* 73 r Voltaire ☎930471 Closed 6
Nov−Feb 16rm12⇌ A4rm P sB fr54 dB65−127
dB⇌🛁89−127 L60 D60

★*Lion d'Or* 10 pl J-d'Arc ☎930741 Closed Jan
15rm2⇌3🛁 A5rm P Lift sB36−69 sB⇌🛁fr53
dB43−96 dB⇌🛁60−96 L23−40 D23−40

At **Marcay** (7km S on D116)

★★★*Château de Marcay* ☎930347 tx750806
Closed Jan & Feb 26rm16⇌10🛁 A11rm P ♪
sB⇌🛁136−176 dB⇌🛁227−307
(English breakfast) L alc D alc 🏊 Pool

CHITENAY 41 (Loir-et-Cher) 700 (☎39) Map **9** A2

★*Clé des Champs*💶 rte de Fougères ☎792203
Closed 16 Jan−14 Feb 10rm1⇌2🛁 P sB40
sB⇌🛁65 dB47 dB🛁72 L55 D55

CHOLET 49 (Maine-et-Loire) 54,050 (☎41)
Map **8** C2

★★★*Chotel* av Sables d'Olonne (2km S) ☎624545
Closed 1−14 Aug & 25−31 Dec 42⇌ 🏠 P Lift ♪
sB⇌🛁86−128

★★*Poste* 20 bd Gl-Richard ☎620720 Closed 2−23
Aug 65rm13⇌20🛁 🏠 Lift

★*Boule d'Or* 49 r Commerce ☎620178 17rm3⇌6🛁
🏠 P sB35−52 sB⇌🛁52 dB51−72 dB⇌🛁72 L30−90
D30−90

CHONAS L'AMBALLAM See **VIENNE**

CIBOURE See **ST-JEAN-DE-LUZ**

CIOTAT (LA) 13 (Bouches-du-Rhône) 32,750 (☎91)
Map **27** B1

★★★*Rose Thé* 4 bd Beau Rivage (n rest) ☎830923
41rm9⇌15🛁 A6rm P ♪ sB49−90 sB⇌🛁84−100
dB78−110 dB⇌🛁98−128 (English breakfast) Beach
sea

🛪 ⏚ *Electric* rte de Marseille ☎084867 Frd (GB)

CIVRIEUX-D'AZERGUES 69 (Rhône) 800 (☎78)
Map **27** B4

★★*Roseraie* ☎430178 Closed 1−14 Sep
12rm2⇌6🛁 🏠 sB48 sB⇌🛁61 dB55−83
dB⇌🛁68−73 L23−70 D23−70

CLAIX See **GRENOBLE**

CLAYETTE (LA) 71 (Saone-et-Loire) 3,000 (☎85)
Map **27** A4

★*Gare* 14rm3🛁 🏠

CLÉCY 14 (Calvados) 1,200 (☎31) Map **8** D3

★★*Site Normand* 💶 ☎697105 10rm5⇌7🛁
dB76−145 dB⇌🛁76−145 L30−70 D30−70

CLELLES 38 (Isère) 300 (☎76) Map **27** B3

★★*Ferrat* (N75) ☎344270 17rm6⇌1🛁 🏠 P sBfr54
dBfr63 dB⇌🛁108 L fr45 D fr35 mountains

CLERMONT 60 (Oise) 8,700 (☎4) Map **9** B4

★*France* ☎4500056 16rm 🏠

CLERMONT-FERRAND† 63 (Puy-de-Dôme)
161,250 (☎73) Map **27** A4

★★★*PLM Arverne* 16 pl Delille ☎919206 tx390741
57rm55⇌5🛁 P Lift sB⇌🛁91−131 dB⇌🛁157
(English breakfast) L40alc D40alc mountains

★★★*Frantel* 82 bd Gergovia ☎930575 tx390656
124⇌ 🏠 Lift ♪ sB⇌🛁167−192 dB⇌🛁219−237
L62−100&alc D62−100&alc

★★★*Gallieni* 51 r Bonnabaud ☎935969 tx390990
80rm56⇌24🛁 P Lift ♪ sB⇌🛁70−140
dB⇌🛁120−165 (English breakfast) L alc D alc

★★*Minimes* 10 r des Minimes (n rest) ☎933149
28rm13⇌13🛁 P ♪ sB48 sB⇌🛁66 dB73 dB⇌🛁80
mountains

★*Foch* 22 r Ml-Foch (n rest) ☎934840 15rm3🛁
sB39−47 sB🛁fr47 dBfr45 dB🛁fr53

★*Ravel* 8 r de Maringues ☎915133 tx390794
20rm10🛁 sB47−59 sB🛁59−64 dB56−68
dB🛁68−78 (English breakfast) L fr35 D fr35

🛪 ⏚ *Auvergne* 17 r Bonnabaud ☎931818 P Fia (GB)

🛪 ⏚ *Dugat* 20 rte de Lyon ☎924724 Frd

🛪 ⏚ *R Portier* rte de Issoire (N9) ☎924523 MB (GB)

CLICHY See **PARIS**

CLOYES-SUR-LE-LOIR 28 (Eure-et-Loir) 2,600
(☎37) Map **9** A2

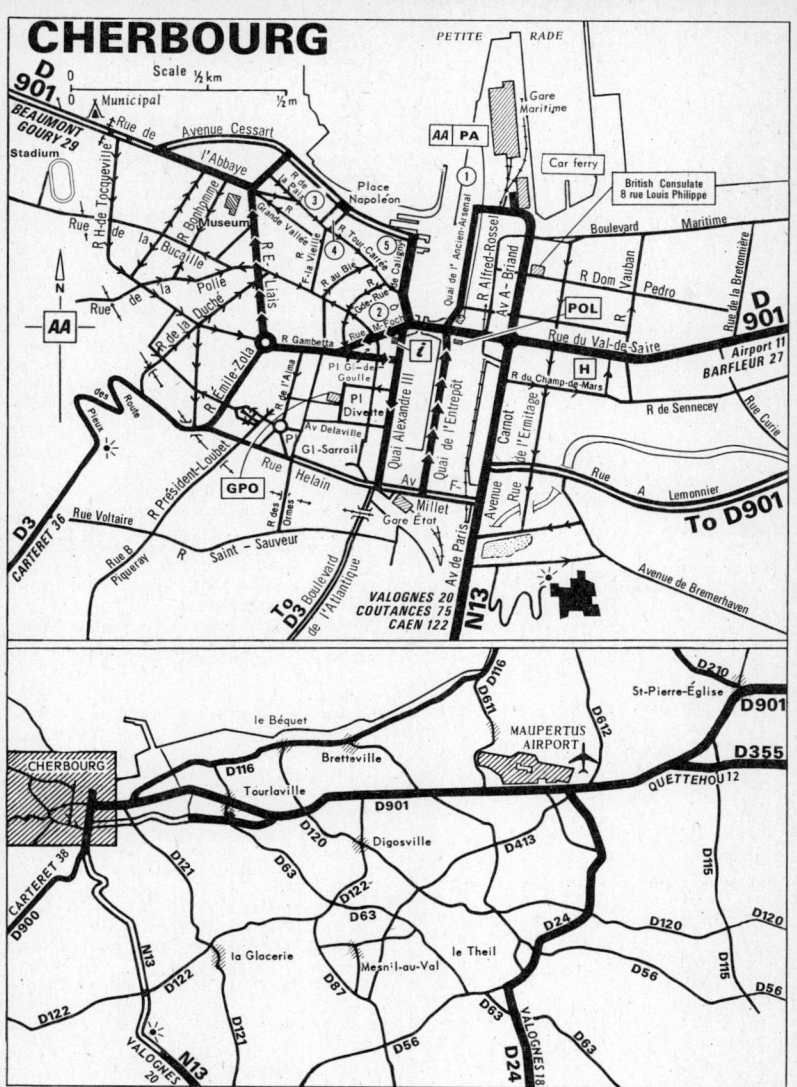

CHERBOURG

Scale ½ km

Cherbourg
1 ★★★Sofitel
2 ★★Caligny
3 ★★Louvre
4 ★★Torgistorps
5 ★Renaissance

France

★★*St-Jacques* 35 r Nationale ☎985008 Closed 21
Dec–14 Jan 21rm7⇌6🍴 ✒ lake

CLUNY 71 (Saone-et-Loire) 4,700 (☎85) Map **10** C1

★★**Bourgogne 🅛** pl de l'Abbaye ☎590058 Closed
16 Nov–9 Feb 17rm8⇌5🍴 🏛 P sB62
sB⇌🍴111–116 dB122–127 dB⇌🍴122–127
L58–95 D58–95

★★**Moderne** Pont d l'Etang (1km S) ☎590565
Closed 11 Oct–9 Dec 15rm8⇌ 🏛 P sB45–79
sB⇌79–99 dBB63–90 dB⇌90–108 L30–60
D30–60

★**Abbaye 🅛** av de la Gare ☎591114 Closed 15
Dec–5 Feb 20rm4⇌4🍴 A6rm 🏛 P sB34–73
sB⇌🍴73 dB50–64 dB⇌🍴80 L26–45 D26–45

CLUSAZ (LA) 74 (Haute-Savoie) 1,700 (☎50)
Map **28** C4

★★★★*Beauregard* ☎024017 tx30132 Closed 16
Sep–14 Dec & 16 Apr–14 Jun 43⇌ Lift Pool

COARAZE 06 (Alpes-Maritimes) 350 (☎93)
Map **28** C2

★★**Petite Auberge** ☎913091 7⇌ P Lift sB⇌63
dB96–101 dB⇌96–101 (English breakfast) L45–55
D40–45 mountains

COGNAC† 16 (Charente) 22,600 (☎45) Map **15** B3

★★**Auberge** 13 r Plumejeau ☎820659 27rm9⇌12🍴
sB40–62 sB⇌🍴55–62 dB47–105 dB⇌🍴62–105
L fr25 D fr25

★★**Moderne 🅛** 24 r E-Mousnier (n rest) ☎821953
Closed 25–31 Dec 26⇌ 🏛 P Lift sB⇌63–72
dB⇌74–83

At **St-Laurent-de-Cognac** (6km W)

★★**Logis de Beaulieu 🅛** ☎823050 21rm15⇌6🍴 🏛
P 𝄞 sB⇌🍴fr39 (English breakfast) L32–66 D32–66

COL DE CUREBOURSE See **VIC-SUR-CERE**

COLLIOURE 66 (Pyrénées-Orientales) 2,700 (☎68)
Map **22** D4

★★**Frégate** bd C-Pelletan 30rm8⇌2🍴

★★**Madeloc** r R-Rolland (n rest) ☎820756 Closed
Oct–Apr 22rm9⇌13🍴 P sB⇌🍴49–59
dB⇌🍴103–133 mountains

★★**Méditerranée** av A-Maillol (n rest) Closed
Nov–mid Apr 23rm3⇌15🍴 🏛

★★**Terrasses** rte Port-Vendres ☎820652
20rm2⇌14🍴 P dB55–67 dB⇌🍴81 sea mountains

COLMAR† 68 (Haut Rhin) 67,450 (☎89) Map **11** B2

★★★**Champs de Mars** 2 av de la Marne ☎415454
tx880928 75⇌ P Lift sB⇌120 dB⇌144 Lalc D alc

☆☆**Novotel Colmar** 49 rte de Strasbourg
☎414914 tx880915 60⇌ P Lift sB⇌fr132 dB⇌fr152
English breakfast only Pool

★★★**Terminus Bristol** 7 pl de la Gare ☎412038
tx87998 95rm47⇌17🍴 Lift

★★**Majestic** 1 r de la Gare ☎414519 Closed Dec
34rm12⇌3🍴 Lift sB61–63 sB⇌🍴63 dBfr68
dB⇌🍴79–87 L fr30 D fr20

🛏 🕭*Bolchert* 77 r Morat ☎413125 (closed wknds)
Frd

COMBEAUFONTAINE 70 (Haute-Saone) 400
(☎84) Map **10** D2

★**Balcon 🅛** rte de Paris ☎786234 Closed 15–23
Sep & 26 Dec–15 Jan 17rm2⇌3🍴 🏛 P sB30
sB⇌🍴44 dB42 dB⇌🍴51 L27–60 D27–60

COMBOURG 35 (Ille-et-Vilaine) 4,750 (☎99)
Map **8** C3

★**Château & Voyageurs 🅛** 1 pl Châteaubriand
☎730038 24rm15⇌4🍴 A9rm 🏛 P sB47–118
sB⇌🍴75–118 dBfr55 dB⇌🍴83–126 L30–65
D30–65 lake

COMBRONDE 63 (Puy-de-Dôme) Map **16** D3

★*Family* ☎971001 Closed 16 Dec–14 Jan 17rm4🍴

COMMERCY 55 (Meuse) Map **10** D3

🛏 🕭*Billet* 112 r du 155E ☎910154 Peu

COMPIÈGNE† 60 (Oise) 40,750 (☎44) Map **9** B4

★★**Harlay** 3 r Harlay (n rest) ☎4230150
18rm14⇌4🍴 P Lift sB⇌🍴fr103 dB⇌🍴111–143
(English breakfast)

★★*Résidence de la Forêt* 112 r St-Lazare (Dp)
☎4202286 Closed 16 Dec–14 Jan 20rm9⇌7🍴 🏛

🛏🕭*SOVA* 9 r de Soissons ☎4403307 P BL/Toy/Vlo
At **Margy** (2km W on D935)

🛏🕭*Ile de France* 36 av O-Butin ☎4404694 Frd

CONCARNEAU 29 (Finistère) 19,050 (☎98)
Map **7** A/B3

★★**Grand** 1 av P-Guéguen ☎970028 Closed
Nov–Apr 33rm9⇌12🍴 P 𝄞 sBfr50 dB58–73
dB⇌🍴77–102 L40 D40 sea

★*Sables Blancs* 🅛 Plages des Sables ☎970139
Closed 16 Oct–22 Mar 48rm8⇌34🍴 sea

🛏 🕭*Odet* rte Quimper, Penanguer ☎971075 Ren

CONDAT 15 (Cantal) 1,730 (☎71) Map **16** D3

★*Voyageurs* rte de Clermont ☎785115 Closed 16
Oct–12 Nov 24rm 🏛

CONDRIEU 69 (Rhône) 3,200 (☎74) Map **27** B4

★★★**Beau Rivage** quai St-Abdon ☎595224 Closed
6 Jan–19 Feb 25⇌ 🏛 P sB⇌112–147 dB⇌163
(English breakfast) L100–140 D100–140 mountains
lake

CONFOLENS 16 (Charente) 3,200 (☎45)
Map **16** C3

★*Auberge Belle Étoile* 🅛 151 bis rte Angoulême
☎840235 Closed 1–15 Oct 14rm5⇌1🍴 🏛

CONQUES 12 (Aveyron) 450 (☎65) Map **16** D2

★*Ste-Foy* ☎698403 Closed 4 Nov–14 Mar
20rm16⇌4🍴 🏛

CONTREXÉVILLE 88 (Vosges) 4,600 (☎29)
Map **10** D2

★★★**Souveraine** ☎080959 tx961254 Closed 16
Sep–19 May 31rm13⇌12🍴 P 🏛 sB55–57
sB⇌🍴101 dB83–75 dB⇌🍴121–134
(English breakfast) ✒

COQUILLE (LA) 24 (Dordogne) 1,700 (☎53)
Map **16** C3

★*Voyageurs* 🅛 r de la République (N21) ☎558013
Closed Nov–Mar 10rm7⇌ 🏛 P sB45 sB⇌64–75
dB68 dB⇌73–95 (English breakfast) L33–83
D33–83

CORDÉS 81 (Tarn) 1,100 (☎63) Map **16** C2

★★*Grand Ecuyer* ☎560103 17rm16⇌ 🏛 ✒ Pool

★★*Vieux Cordés* 🅛 ☎12 20rm8⇌1🍴 🍴 🏛

CORPS 38 (Isère) 550 (☎76) Map **27** B3

★★**Poste 🅛** pl de la Mairie ☎300003 40rm8⇌2🍴
A25rm 🏛 P sB31 sB⇌🍴59 dB⇌🍴74 L28 D28
mountains lake

★*Roseraie* rte du Sautet ☎949111 Closed 16
Oct–31 Dec 22rm12⇌5🍴 🏛 ✒

CORSE (CORSICA) 20 293,300 (☎95) Map **28** Inset

Ajaccio Corse du Sud 51,800

★★★★*Dolce Vita* rte des Sanguinaires ☎213520
34⇌ Pool Beach sea

★★★★*Sofitel Porticcio* (DP) ☎250034 tx460708
Closed 16 Oct–Mar 100⇌ P Lift 𝄞 sB⇌380–465
dB⇌560–670 L70 D70 ✒ Pool Beach sea

★★★*Continental* 22 cours Grandval ☎214116
tx460085 Closed Nov 80rm45⇌14🍴 A27rm 🏛 Lift
Pool sea

★★*Etrangers* 2 r Rossi ☎210126 47rm21⇌5🍴 🏛
Lift sea

☆☆*Stella di Mare* 🅛 rte des Sanguinaires (7km S on
N193) ☎213608 60⇌ Pool Beach sea

Bastia Haute Corse 52,023

★★★*Ile de Beauté* 9 r G-Péri (n rest) ☎311556
Closed Nov–Feb 55⇌ Lift

Calvi Haute Corse 3,700

★★★★*Grand* bd Wilson (n rest) ☎650974 tx460718
Closed Oct–Mar 60rm48⇌12🍴 Lift 𝄞
sB⇌🍴178–278 dB⇌🍴216–336
(English breakfast) mountains

Ile-Rousse (L') Haute Corse 2,700

🛏 🕪*Cyrnos* av P-Doumer ☎600942 ☎601195 M/c
P Cit

Porto Corse du Sud

★*Kalliste* 🅛 la Marine ☎261031 Closed 16 Oct–Mar
40rm21⇌19🍴 🏛 sea

182

Porto-Vecchio Corse du Sud 7,850
★★★*Ziglione* (5km on N198) (DP) ☎469 Closed 16 Oct–14 Mar 32⇄ Beach sea
Propriano Corse du Sud 2,950
★★★*Arena Bianca* rte du Rizzanese ☎20110 Closed Nov–Mar 104rm40⇄65🍽 Lift Beach sea
★★★*Marinca* (5km N on N196) (DP) ☎Marinca11 Closed Oct–Mar 58⇄ A10rm Beach sea
St-Florent Haute Corse 1,400
★★★*Lauriers Roses* ☎370014 Closed Nov–mid Apr 18rm5⇄9🍽

COSNE-SUR-LOIRE 58 (Nièvre) 12,350 (☎86)
Map 9 B2
★★*Grand Cerf* 43 r St-Jacques ☎280446 Closed 13 Dec–9 Jan 21rm3⇄8🍽 🏠 sBfr47 sB⇄🍽fr57 dBfr59 dB⇄🍽fr79 L22–50 D22–50
★*Vieux Relais* ☜ 11 r St-Agnan ☎282021 Closed 16 Dec–Jan 11rm4🍽6⇄ P sB50 sB⇄🍽70–90 dB64 dB⇄🍽114 (English breakfast) L29–115 D29–115

CONTINIÈRE (LA) See OLÉRON (ILE D')

COUR-CHEVERNY 41 (Loir-et-Cher) 1,900 (☎39)
Map 9 A2
★★*St-Hubert* ☜ (DP) ☎799660 Closed 6 Dec–14 Jan 21rm11⇄10🍽 Lift
★★*Trois Marchands* ☜ 3 pl Eglise ☎799644 Closed 7 Jan–Feb 45rm15⇄9🍽 A12rm

COURTABEUF See ORSAY

COUSIN VALLEY See AVALLON

COUSOLRE 59 (Nord) Map 3 B1
★★*Viennois* rte National ☎642173 Closed Tue 11⇄ 🏠

COUTAINVILLE 50 (Manche) (☎33) Map 8 C4
★*Hardy* ☜ 28 pl-Juillet ☎470411 27rm8⇄1🍽 A15rm 🏠

COUTANCES 50 (Manche) 11,950 (☎33) Map 8 C4
★*Moderne* bd A-Lorraine ☎451377 Closed Feb 17rm1⇄ 🏠 P sB34–36 dB45–49 dB⇄68 L22–48 D22–48
★*Parvis* (DP) ☎451355 12⇄
🛏 &*Bernard* rte de Lessay ☎451633 BL/Tri
🛏 &*SODIAM* rte de St-Lô ☎450255 P Ren

CRÈCHES-SUR-SAÔNE See MÂCON

CRESSENSAC 46 (Lot) 650 (☎65) Map 16 C3
★*Chez Gilles* ☜ (N20) ☎377006 Closed Feb 19rm2⇄4🍽 🏠 sB45 sB⇄🍽64 dB52–72 dB⇄🍽71–76 L25–70 D25–70

CRÉTIL See PARIS

CREUSOT (LE) 71 (Saône-et-Loire) 33,500 (☎85)
Map 10 C1
At Monchanin (8km E off D28)
☆☆☆*Novotel Montchanin-Creusot-Montceau* 30 r du Pont J-Rose ☎557211 tx800588 87⇄ P Lift sB⇄fr125 dB⇄fr164 English breakfast only Pool

CRIEL-SUR-MER 76 (Seine-Maritime) (☎35)
Map 9 A4
★★*Hostellerie de la Vieille Ferme* ☎867218 Closed 16 Jan–6 Feb 36rm30⇄ P sB37–45 dB⇄99–128 L43–75 D43–75 🍽

CROISIC (LE) 44 (Loire-Atlantique) 4,350 (☎40)
Map 7 B2
★★*Océan* Port Lin (1km S) ☎230003 Closed Nov–Jan 24rm14⇄

CROISIÈRE (LA) See ST MAURICE LA SOUTERRAINE

CROIX DE LA MALEYRIE (LA) See DONZENAC

CROIX-VALMER 83 (Var) 1,900 (☎94) Map 28 C1
★★★*Mer* (2.5km SE on N559) ☎796061 Closed Oct–mid Apr 31rm15⇄12🍽 P dBfr69 dB⇄🍽125–140 L42–100 D42–100 Pool Beach

CROS-DE-CAGNES See CAGNES-SUR-MER

CROTOY (LE) 80 (Somme) 2,450 Map 3 A1
★*Baie* quai Léonard ☎278122 16rm8⇄2🍽 sea
★*Paris* 1 pl J-d'Arc ☎278046 14rm5⇄3🍽 sB39–70 sB⇄68–86 dB48–80 dB⇄🍽76–96 L35–60 D35–60 sea

CROUZILLE (LA) 87 (Haute-Vienne) (☎55)
Map 16 C3
★*Lac* Closed Oct–Mar 11rm2⇄ lake

At **Nantiat**
☆☆*Relais St-Europe* ☎399121 19⇄ P sB⇄100 dB⇄110 L alc D alc mountains

CUISERY 71 (Saône-et-Loire) 1,600 (☎85)
Map 10 C1
★*Voyageurs* r de la Gendarmerie (n rest) ☎401461 Closed 16 Sep–14 Jun 9rm 🏠

DAMPIERRE 78 (Yvelines) 750 (☎1) Map 9 B3
★★*Château* ☎0525289 Closed Thu, 6–19 Jan & Sep 15rm8⇄1🍽 🏠

DANJOUTIN See BELFORT

DAX†40 (Landes) 20,300 (☎58) Map 15A/B1
★★★*Parc* ☜ 1 pl Thiers (n rest) ☎741617 tx540481 44rm32⇄10🍽 🏠 Lift

At **St-Paul-lès-Dax** (2km W)
🛏 &*Duprat-Desclaux* rte de Bayonne (N124) ☎743804 Bed/BL/Opl/Vau (GB)
🛏 &*Thermal* av Foch ☎742334 Frd

DEAUVILLE† 14 (Calvados) 5,750 (☎31) Map 8 D4
★★★★★*Normandy* r J-Mermoz ☎880921 tx170617 380rm317⇄ Lift 🍽 Pool
★★★★*Royal* ☎881641 tx170549 Closed mid Sep–mid Apr 360⇄ P Lift ♪ sB⇄190–290 dB⇄215–390 L80 D80 St% 🍽 Pool sea
★★★*PLM* bd E-Cornuché, Port de Deauville (n rest) ☎886262 tx170364 64⇄ P Lift sB⇄89–167 dB⇄131–220 sea

DEVILLE-LES-ROUEN See ROUEN

DIEPPE† 76 (Seine-Maritime) 26,150 (☎35)
Map 9 A4 **See Plan overleaf**
　AA agents; see page 149
★★★*Aguado* 30 bd de Verdun (n rest) ☎842700 Plan 1 53rm24⇄22🍽 P Lift sB60–109 sB⇄🍽87–144 dB92–142 dB⇄🍽126–172 (English breakfast) sea
★★★*Présidence* bd de Verdun ☎843131 tx180865 Plan 2 89rm76⇄4🍽 🏠 Lift sBfr84 sB⇄🍽fr154 dBfr118 dB⇄🍽188–218 (English breakfast) L60 D60 sea
☆☆*Ibis Dieppe* le Val Druel ☎846530 Not on plan 42⇄ P Lift sB⇄fr94 dB⇄fr114 L30–45alc D30–45alc
★★*Rhin & Newhaven* 11–12 bd de Verdun ☎841018 tx770741 Plan 3 Closed 2 Jan–6 Feb 31rm9⇄4🍽 P Lift ♪ sB39–52 sB⇄🍽64–85 dB54–63 dB⇄🍽71–109 (English breakfast) L36–54 D36–54 sea
★★*Univers* 10 bd de Verdun (DP) ☎841255 Plan 5 Closed 16 Dec–19 Jan 28rm22⇄3🍽 Lift sea
★★*Windsor* ☜ 18 bd de Verdun ☎841523 Plan 6 46rm40⇄ P Lift ♪ sB60–72 sB⇄95–106 dB70–82 dB⇄105–116 L39–46 D39–46 sea
🛏 &*Casino* (Thiroux) 28 r Sygogne ☎842214 P AR/BL (GB)
🛏 &*Grands de Normandie* 33 r Thiers ☎842340 ☎842462 P Ren
🛏 &*Prince* 21 Voie Pénétraute ☎841677 ☎841677 P Cit
🛏 &*Plage* 4 r Bouzard ☎841036 Frd (GB)

DIGNE 04 (Alpes-de-Hautes-Provence) 16,600 (☎92) Map 28 C2
★★★*Ermitage Napoleon* bd Gambetta 60rm36⇄8🍽 🏠 Lift
★★*Aiglon* ☜ 1 r de Provence ☎310270 tx430605 Closed Dec & Jan 33rm3⇄9🍽 A9rm 🏠 P sB50–55 sB⇄🍽64–75 dB67–74 dB⇄🍽95–107 (English breakfast) L25–63 D25–63 mountains
★★*Grand Paris* 2 bd Thiers ☎311115 Closed 3 Jan–14 Feb 35rm28⇄2🍽 🏠 P Lift ♪ sB⇄102–122 dB⇄🍽144–164 L41–75 D41–75
★★*Mistre* 65 bd Gasserdi ☎310016 Closed 10 Nov–10 Dec 37rm15⇄10🍽 🏠 P ♪ sB48–88

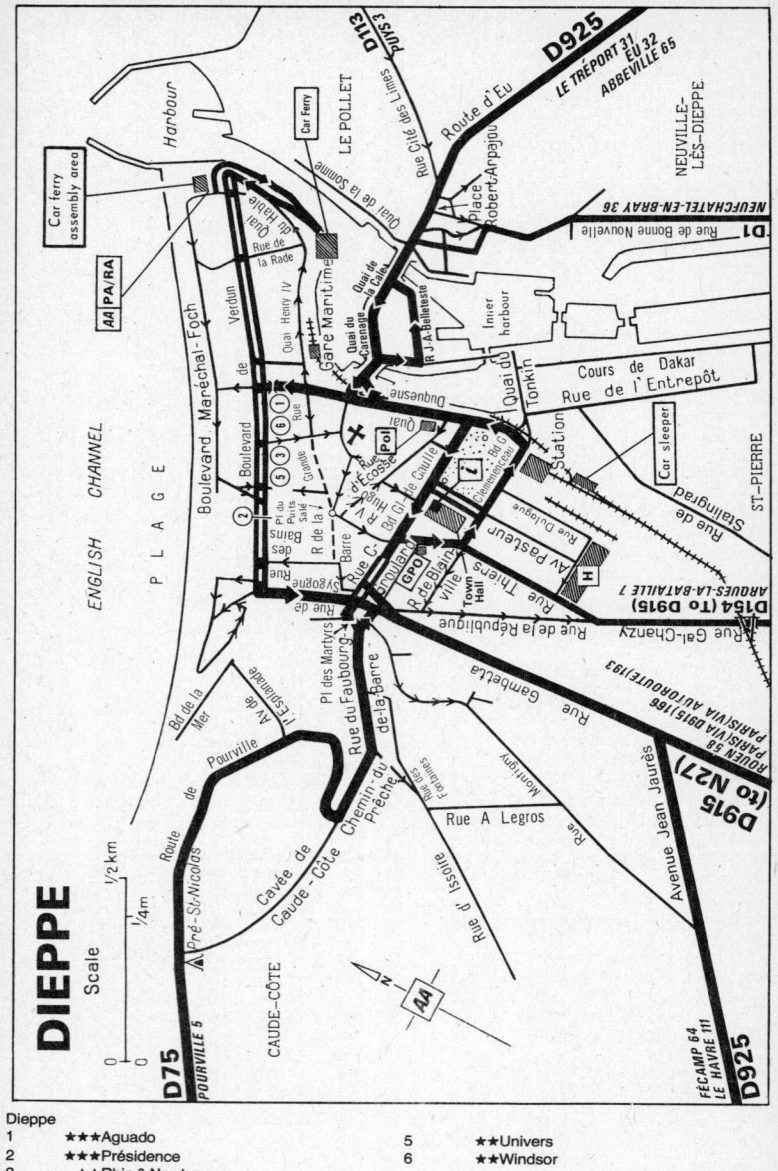

DIEPPE

Scale

ENGLISH CHANNEL

Dieppe
1	★★★Aguado	5	★★Univers
2	★★★Présidence	6	★★Windsor
3	★★Rhin & Newhaven		

sB⇨🍴78–108 dB66–136 dB⇨🍴116–156
(English breakfast) L50–95 D50–95 mountains
🛏 🅿️ **Auto B Hory** quartier de la Tour, rte de Marseille
☎313124 P Cit

DIGOIN 71 (Saone-et-Loire) 11,450 (☎85)
Map **10** C1
★**Gare** 79 av Gl-de-Gaulle ☎530304 Closed Dec
12rm8⇨7🍴 A4rm P sBfr55 sB⇨🍴55–90
dB95–120 dB⇨🍴95–120 L80alc D80alc
★**Moderne** r de la Fayencerie (n rest) ☎530580
Closed 25 Dec–25 Jan 12rm1⇨1🍴

DIJON† 21 (Côte d'Or) 156,800 (☎80) Map **10** D2
★★★**Central** 10 r Château ☎304400 tx350606
90rm35⇨35🍴 Lift sB64 sB⇨🍴121 dB74 dB⇨🍴141
L60 D60
★★★**Chapeau Rouge** 5 r Michelet ☎302810
tx350535 33rm28⇨5🍴 P Lift 🄳 sB⇨🍴111–148
dB⇨🍴141–216 (English breakfast) L70–120&alc
D70–120&alc
★★**Ducs** 5 r Lamonnoye (continuation of r Chabot-
Charny) ☎326946 56rm14⇨8🍴 🅿 Lift
★★**Jura** 14 av Ml-Foch (n rest) ☎416112 tx350912
75rm58⇨ A10rm Lift
★**Nord** 2 r Liberté ☎305520 24rm14⇨ Lift sB51–137
sB⇨🍴86–137 dB60–146 dB⇨🍴95–161
(English breakfast) L34–72 D34–72
🛏 🅿️ **Montchapet** 12 r Gagnereaux ☎323284 P Frd
(GB)

At **Hauteville-les-Dijon** (7km NE on D107)
★**Clos** ☎711120 13rm5⇨4🍴 🅿
(English breakfast) L fr24 D fr24

At **Marsanny** (8km SW)
☆☆**Novotel Dijon-Sud** rte de Beaune (N74)
☎412578 tx350728 122⇨ P Lift sB⇨fr154
dB⇨fr167 English breakfast only Pool

At **Talant** (4km NW)
🛏 🅿️ **Vernier** 58 bis bd de Troyes ☎415761 Peu

DINAN† 22 (Côtes-du-Nord) 16,400 (☎96) Map **8** C3
★★**Avaugour** 1 pl Champs-Clos ☎390749 tx951415
27⇨ P Lift sB⇨fr142 dB⇨fr174 L fr50 D fr50 St%
🛏 🅿️ **Meyer** 21 r des Pivents ☎391272 Opl/Vau

DINARD 35 (Ille-et-Vilaine) 9,600 (☎99) Map **8** C3
★★★★**Grand** 46 av George-V ☎461028 Closed
Oct–Mar 113rm95⇨ Lift sea
★★**Bains** 38 av George-V ☎461371 40rm11⇨10🍴
P Lift sB48–52 sB⇨🍴78–98 dB70–80
dB⇨🍴96–121 (English breakfast) L35 D35 sea
★★**Dinard** 5 r Levavasseur ☎461310 Closed
16 Oct–19 Mar 18⇨ sea
★★**Dunes** 5 r G-Clemenceau (continuation of r Prés-
Wilson) (DP) ☎461272 32rm16⇨1🍴
★★**Emeraude Plage** 1 av George-V ☎461579
Closed 21 Sep–mid Apr 50rm30⇨6🍴 A5rm 🅰 sea
★★**Printania** 5 av George-V ☎461307 tx74884
Closed Oct–mid Apr 100rm25⇨
★★**Roche Corneille** 4 r G-Clemenceau ☎461447
22rm18⇨4🍴
★**Hostellerie de la Marjolaine** 9 r Levavasseur (Pn)
☎461185 22rm2⇨3🍴 sB80–90 sB⇨🍴90
dB160–180 dB⇨🍴180
🛏 🅿️ **Parc** 10 r Yves Verney ☎461338 BL

DIVONNE-LES-BAINS 01 (Ain) 4,250 (☎50)
Map **11** A1
★★★**Château de Divonne** ☎500032 Closed
Oct–May 40rm30⇨ lake
★**Truite** 25 Grande r (n rest) ☎500441 22rm8⇨4🍴

DOLANCOURT 10 (Aube) 146 (☎25) Map **10** C3
★★**Moulin du Landion** 🛗 ☎261217 16⇨ P sB⇨83
dB⇨100–105 (English breakfast) L28–58&alc
D28–58&alc river

DOL DE BRETAGNE 35 (Ille-et-Vilaine) 5,050 (☎99)
Map **8** C3
★★**Bretagne** 🛗 17 pl Châteaubriand ☎480203
Closed Xmas & New Year 30rm1⇨8🍴 🅰 sB33–40
dB42–49 dB⇨🍴59–68 L20–38&alc D20–38&alc
★**Bresche Arthur** 🛗 bd Dominiac ☎480144
25rm3⇨9🍴 🅿 Lift 🄳 sB51–78 sB⇨🍴58–78
dB58–108 dB⇨🍴66–108 L fr32 D fr32

DOLE† 39 (Jura) 30,500 (☎82) Map **10** D1
★★★**Chandioux** pl Grévy ☎721757 tx360498
40rm4🍴 🅰 P 🄳 sB70–87 sB⇨🍴100–137 dB91–109
dB🍴145–179 L fr48 D fr48
🛏 🅿️ **Morilhat** 8 bd Wilson ☎722085 P Ren

DOMFRONT 61 (Orne) 4,550 (☎34) Map **8** C/D3
★★**Poste** 🛗 15 r Ml-Foch ☎385100 tx74884 Closed
8 Jan–24 Feb 24rm5⇨3🍴 🅰
★★**France** 🛗 r Mont St-Michel ☎385144 22rm3⇨4🍴
P sB fr33 sB⇨🍴39–47 dB47–55 dB⇨🍴57–78
(English breakfast) L25–43 D25–43 🌶

DOMME 24 (Dordogne) 900 (☎53) Map **16** C2
★**Nouvel** pl Halle ☎148 15rm1⇨ Lift

DOMPAIRE 88 (Vosges) 950 (☎29) Map **11** A3
★★**Commerce** 🛗 pl Ml-Leclerc ☎365028 tx960573
11rm4⇨1🍴 🅰 P sB55–60 sB⇨🍴74–83 dB63–68
dB⇨🍴82–91 L31–60 D31–60

DOMRÉMY-LA-PUCELLE 88 (Vosges) 300 (☎29)
Map **10** D3
★**Basilique** le Bois-Chenu (S 1.5km by D53)
☎940781 28rm7⇨ 🅰 P sB39–62 sB⇨fr62 dBfr66
dB⇨🍴69 L36–63 D36–63
★**Pucelle** ☎940460 Closed Nov & Dec 12rm6🍴
A7rm 🅰 P sB29–39 sB🍴39 dB45 dB🍴45 L18–35
D18–35

DONZÈRE 26 (Drôme) 3,400 (☎75) Map **27** B3
★**Roustan** Centre Ville ☎986127 Closed
13 Nov–Dec 10rm5⇨ 🅰 P sB⇨fr89 dB98–118 L65
D65

DOUAI† 59 (Nord) 47,600 (☎20) Map **3** B1
★★**Grand Cerf** 46 r St-Jacques ☎887960 36rm8⇨6🍴
P 🄳 sB47–91 sB⇨🍴62–91 L fr27 Dfr27

DOURDAN 91 (Essonne) 7,500 (☎1) Map **9** B3
★★★**Blanche de Castille** pl des Halles ☎4927548
tx69902 40⇨ Lift

DRAGUIGNAN 83 (Var) 22,450 (☎94) Map **28** C2
★★**Col de l'Ange** (rest evening only) ☎682301
tx970423 30⇨ P 🄳 sB⇨🍴101–111 dB⇨🍴131–151
D42 mountains
★★**Parc** 21 bd Liberté ☎685384 Closed 16 Dec–14
Jan 20rm5⇨15🍴 P sB⇨🍴79–84 dB⇨🍴89–94
(English breakfast) L33–65 D33–65
🅿️ **Azur** 748 rte de Lorgues ☎681871 M/c Frd

DRAMONT See AGAY

DREUX† 28 (Eure-et-Loir) 34,050 (☎37) Map **9** A3
🛏 🅿️ **Ouest** 51 av des Fenots ☎461145 BL (GB)

At **Montreuil** (8km NE)
★★**Auberge Gué des Grues** ☎385025 5rm3⇨2🍴
🅰 Lift

DUNKERQUE (DUNKIRK)† 59 (Nord) 83,800 (☎20)
Map **3** A2 See also **Bergues** and **Malo les Bains**
★★★**Europ** 13 r de Leughenaer ☎662907 tx120084
100⇨ P Lift sB⇨🍴70–105 dB⇨🍴109–134
(English breakfast)
★★★**Frantel Dunkerque** r J-Jaurès ☎659722
tx110587 126⇨ Lift sB⇨🍴157–174 dB⇨🍴177–193
(English breakfast) L62–100 D62–100 sea
★★**Arcades** pl J-Bart (n rest) ☎665015 tx820093
32rm25⇨ Lift sB89–106 sB⇨🍴111–138 dB123–146
dB⇨🍴154–180 (English breakfast)
★★**Borel** 6 r l'Hermitte ☎665180 tx820050 30⇨ Lift
★★**Moderne** r Gambetta ☎668024 Closed
16 Aug–7 Sep 20rm2⇨ P sB43 dB fr76 L33–55
D33–50
🛏 🅿️ **Flandres** 4 quai des Quatre-Écluses ☎666432
Frd (GB)
🛏 🅿️ **Gare Auto Sport** 9 r Belle Vue ☎667105
BL/Rov/Tri
🛏 🅿️ **Patfoort** 9 r du Leighenaer ☎665112 Fia (GB)

DURY See AMIENS

ECHELLES (LES) 73 Savoie) 1,200 (☎79)
Map **27** B4
★**Commanderie** r de Chambéry (DP) ☎366046
Closed 7–15 Oct 5rm 🅰

ECOMMOY 72 (Sarthe) 4,100 (☎43) Map **8** D2
★**Commerce** ⓛ 19 pl République ☎271034 Closed
16 Dec–14 Jan 13rm6🛏 🅿 P sBfr44 sB⇄🍴fr62
dB50–68 dB⇄🍴fr80 L25–35 D25–35

EGUILLES See **AIX-EN-PROVENCE**

ELNE 66 (Pyrénées-Orientales) 6,050 (☎69)
Map **22** D4
🚫**Subiros** rte de Pergignan, chemin de las Trilles
☎372132 ☎372132 🕭 P Cit (GB)

ENTRAYGUES-SUR-TRUYÈRE 12 (Aveyron) 1,600
(☎65) Map **16** D2
★**Truyère** ☎445110 tx53366 Closed Dec–Feb
21rm17⇄3🍴 🅿 P Lift sB44 sB⇄🍴67–89 dB63
dB⇄🍴80–132 L26 D26 mountains

EPERNAY† 51 (Marne) 31,150 (☎26) Map **10** C3
★★★**Berceaux** 13 r Berceaux ☎512884
24rm12⇄12🍴 Lift sB⇄🍴82–100 dB⇄🍴92–110
L60–90 D60–90 St%
★**Europe** 18 r Porte-Lucas ☎518028 31rm2⇄15🍴
🅿 P sB45–52 sB⇄🍴56–59 dB64 L48–72 D48–72
🛢 🚗**Citroën** rte de Reims, Dizy ☎512762 Cit
🚗**Eur' Autos** 4 Passage Fourché ☎513256
AR/BL/Tri

At **Champillon** (6km N on N51)
★★★**Royal Champagne** ☎512506 14⇄ P ♪
dB⇄156–186 L alc D alc

At **Vinay** (6km S on N51)
★★★**Briqueterie** rte de Sezanne ☎514712
42rm32⇄10🍴 🅿 P Lift ♪ sB76–105
sB⇄🍴82–105 dB106–144 dB⇄🍴112–144
(English breakfast) L45–75 &alc D45–75 &alc

EPINAL† 88 (Vosges) 42,850 (☎29) Map **11** A2
★**Point Central** 6 quai des Bons Enfants ☎822050
12rm5⇄3🍴
★★**Résidence** 39 av des Templiers (n rest)
☎824564 18rm10⇄8🍴
★★**Vosges & Terminus** pl de la Gare (n rest)
☎823578 48rm6⇄2🍴 🅿 P Lift sB30–33 dB52
dB⇄🍴69
★**Azur** 54 quai des Bons Enfants (n rest)
20rm2⇄2🍴 sB32–38 dB48–54 dB⇄🍴67
🛢 🚗**Epinal** 89 r d'Alsace ☎820594 Peu
🛢 🚗**Spinaliens** 17 r Ml-Lyautey ☎824747 Frd (GB)

EPINE (L) See **CHÂLONS-SUR-MARNE**

ERQUY-PLAGE 22 (Côtes-du-Nord) 3,300 (☎96)
Map **7** B3
★**Beauregard** ⓛ bd plage ☎323003 17rm A8rm sea

ETAPLES 62 (Pas-de-Calais) 10,600 (☎21)
Map **3** A1
★**Bellevue** 19 r Herambault ☎096932 Closed
16 Dec–14 Jan 7rm
★**Voyageurs** 11 pl Gare ☎946933 Closed Jan
23rm6⇄2🍴 🅿

ETRETAT 76 (Seine-Maritme) 1,550 (☎35)
Map **8** D4
★★★**Dormy House** rte Havre ☎270788 Closed
15 Nov–9 Mar 40rm26⇄ 🅿 ♪ 🕭 sea
★★**Windsor** 9 av George-V ☎270727 Closed
Nov–mid Apr 15rm4⇄3🍴

ETSAUT 64 (Pyrénées-Atlantiques) (☎59)
Map **20** C3
★**Pyrénées** ☎397862 20rm7⇄1🍴 A7rm 🅿 P
sB37–41 sB⇄🍴57 dB48 (English breakfast)
L25–50 D25–50 mountains

EVIAN-LES-BAINS 74 (Haute-Savoie) 6,200 (☎50)
Map **11** A1
★★★★**Royal** ☎751400 ta Casiroy tx385759
Closed Nov–14 Apr 200rm150⇄7🍴 🅿 P Lift ♪
sB⇄🍴170–400 dB⇄🍴240–590 L75alc D85alc 🏊
Pool 🕭 mountains lake
★★★**Splendide** ☎750485 tx34989 Closed
11 Sep–May 100rm80⇄ Lift
★★**Mateirons** ☎750416 Closed Oct–Feb 23rm16⇄
A3rm P dB64–68 dB⇄🍴101–111 L30 D30 lake

At **Maxilly-Petite-Rive** (2km E on N5)
★★★**Lumina** ☎752867 tx385661 Closed Oct–Apr

62⇄ 🍴 P Lift ♪ sB⇄100–180 dB⇄140–200 L50
D50 Pool Beach mountains lake

At **Verniaz (La)** (3km S)
★★★★★**Verniaz & ses Chalets** ☎750490 tx34069
Closed Jan 50⇄ 🅿 Lift 🏊 Pool lake

EVREUX† 27 (Eure) 50,400 (☎32) Map **9** A3
★★★**Grand Cerf** ⓛ 11 r de la Harpe ☎331401
tx770581 Closed Feb 26rm12⇄14🍴 🅿 P Lift ♪
sB72–182 sB⇄🍴137–157 dB94–154
dB⇄🍴134–224 L50&alc D50&alc
★★**Grenoble** 17 r St-Pierre (n rest) ☎330731
16rm3⇄2🍴 🅿
★★**Normandy** 37 pl Dupont de l'Eure ☎331440
25rm7⇄12🍴 🅿 P sB61–67 sB⇄🍴105–105
dB102–134 (English breakfast) L35–65 D35–65
★★**Orme** ⓛ 13 r Lombards (n rest) ☎393412
20rm4⇄6🍴 sB56–57 sB⇄🍴71–88 dB64–65
dB⇄🍴79–96
★**Beffroi** 2 r de l'Horloge (n rest) ☎390849 16rm 🆒
🛢 🚗**Stade** 35 rte de Conches ☎334450 BMW/Dat
(GB)
🚗**Vendôme Automobile** 180 rte d'Orléans
☎393810 P Chy/Sim (GB)
🛢 🚗**Victor-Hugo** 8 bis r V-Hugo ☎392721 Fia (GB)

EVRY 91 (Essonne) 15,600 (☎71) Map **9** B3
☆☆☆**Novotel paris-Evry** (A6) ☎0778270 tx600685
180⇄ P Lift sB⇄fr158 dB⇄fr170 English breakfast
only Pool

EYZIES-DE-TAYAC (LES) 24 (Dordogne) 900
(☎53) Map **16** C2
★★★**Cro-Magnon** ☎069706 Closed 9 Oct–7 Apr
28rm22⇄5🍴 A12rm P sB91–111 sB⇄🍴121–131
dB122–142 L45–110 D45–110 Pool
★★**Centenaire** ⓛ ☎069718 Closed 20 Mar–2 Nov
30⇄ A8rm 🅿 P sB⇄96 dB⇄132–172
(English breakfast) L70 D70
★★**Glycines** ☎069707 Closed 16 Oct–mid Apr
27rm22⇄3🍴 🅿 P sB65–110 sB⇄🍴70–110
dB84–139 dB⇄🍴89–139 (English breakfast)
L35–80&alc D35–80&alc
★**France** ⓛ ☎069723 Closed Mar–Oct 16rm4⇄8🍴
P sB42–53 sB⇄🍴61–86 dB60–66 dB⇄🍴68–93
L24–64 D24–64 mountains

EZE-BORD-DE-MER 06 (Alpes-Maritimes) 1,440
(☎93) Map **28** C2
★★★★**Cap Estel** (DP & Pn) ☎015044 tx470305
Closed Nov–Jan 47⇄ A6rm P Lift ♪ sB⇄290–550
dB⇄580–1100 (English breakfast) L90–110
D90–115 Pool Beach sea mountains
★★**Bananaraie** (n rest) ☎015139 tx470305 Closed
11 Sept–Apr 32rm15⇄7🍴 A10rm P sB35–38
sB⇄🍴64–72 dB56–59 dB⇄🍴99–105
★★**Cap Roux** ☎015123 Closed Oct–Feb
36rm16⇄20🍴 P Lift sB⇄🍴58–88 dB⇄🍴101–120
sea

FALAISE 14 (Calvados) 8,650 (☎31) Map **8** D3
★★**Normandie** 4 r Al-Courbet ☎901826 30rm5⇄9🍴
🆒 sBfr37 dBfr61 dB⇄🍴72–85 L19–27 D19–27
★★**Poste** 38 r G-Clemenceau ☎901314 22rm2⇄🍴
P sBfr37 sB⇄fr52 dBfr43 dB⇄fr58 L22–40 D22–40
★**Belle Épée** 1 r Gambetta ☎900529 Closed
16 Aug–9 Sep 12rm P sBfr32 dB32–39
(English breakfast) L18–29 D18–29
🛢 🚗**Poste** (Chesnes) 36 r G-Clemenceau ☎900100

FAOUËT (LE) 56 (Morbihan) 3,220 Map **7** B3
★**Croix d'Or** 9 pl Bellanger ☎230733 16rm 🆒 P
sBfr29 dBfr38 L20–70 D20–70

FAVERGES Haute-Savoie 5,400 Map **28** C4
At **Doussard** (7km NW)
★★**Marceau** Marceau-Dessus ☎443011 Closed
Dec & Jan 28rm10⇄ A8rm P sB56–71 dB74–92
dB⇄🍴132–142 L55–60 D55–60 🚤 mountains lake

FAYL-BILLOT 52 (Haute Marne) 1,850 (☎27)
Map **10** D2
★**Rose des Vents** ☎846301 11rm1⇄6🍴

FÉCAMP 76 (Seine-Maritime) 22,250 (☎35)
Map **9** A4

★*Plage* 87 r de la Plage Closed 16 Dec–14 Jan 17rm
🏠 sea
🗎 &⊃**Rouen** pl Bigot ☎281424 Cit (GB)
FÈRE-EN-TARDENOIS 02 (Aisne) 2,800 (☎23)
Map **10** C3
★★★**Château** ☎822113 Closed Jan & Feb 19⊃ P
sB175–215 sB⊃175–215 dB⊃250–310
(English breakfast) L fr135 D fr135 ✍
FERNAY-VOLTAIRE See **GENEVA AIRPORT**
(Switzerland)
FERTÉ-MACÉ (LA) 61 (Orne) 7,715 (☎34)
Map **8** D3
★★*Grand Turc* 12 r St-Denis ☎370044 Closed Oct
23rm2⊃4 🏠
FERTÉ-ST-AUBIN (LA) 45 (Loiret) 4,300 (☎38)
Map **9** B2
★★**Perron** 9 r du Gl-Leclerc ☎915336 33rm5⊃9🍴
A12rm P sB41–93 sB⊃🍴83–93 dB51–63
dB⊃🍴91–93 (English breakfast) L27–80 D27–80
🗎 &⊃**Gidoin** (N20) ☎915117 P Fia
🗎 &⊃**Relais de Sologne** 159 r du Gl-Leclerc
☎915711 P Ren
FIGEAC 46 (Lot) 10,900 (☎65) Map **16** D2
★★**Carmes** ⚿ 18 pl XII Mai ☎342078 tx520794
Closed 16 Dec–7 Jan 34rm26⊃8🍴 🏠 P Lift
sB71–106 sB⊃🍴71–106 dB97–137 dB⊃🍴97–137
L30–80 D30–80 Pool
FIRMINY 42 (Loire) 25,450 (☎77) Map **27** A4
★★*Firm* 37 r J-Jaurès ☎560899 20rm6⊃14🍴 🏠
FIXIN 21 (Côte d'-Or) 850 (☎80) Map **10** C2
★★**Chez Jeanette** ⚿ ☎343108 ta janethotel Closed
7–13 Jan 11rm9🍴 P sB 39 sB🍴50 dB46–57
dB57–64 (English breakfast) L36–52 D36–52
(English breakfast) (☎50) Map **28** C4
FLAINE 74 (Haute-Savoie) (☎50) Map **28** C4
★★★★**Sofitel Flaine** ☎908030 tx385965 Closed 16
Apr–14 Dec 60⊃ 🏠 P Lift ♪ sB⊃134–174
dB⊃208–278 L60 D60
FLÈCHE (LA) 72 (Sarthe) 16,400 (☎43) Map **8** D2
🗎 &⊃**Gambetta** 51 bd Gambetta ☎940620 BL
🗎 &⊃**Welcome** (R Bouttier) 14 av de Verdun
☎940408 Frd (GB)
FLEURANCE 32 (Gers) 5,800 (☎62) Map **16** C1
★★*Fleurance* rte d'Agen ☎061485 tx530416
25rm15⊃2🍴
FLORAC 48 (Lozère) 2,100 (☎66) Map **27** A3
★*Gorges du Tarn* ☎450063 Closed Oct–mid Apr
31rm13⊃4🍴 A12rm 🏠 sB fr39 sB⊃🍴64 dB fr46
dB⊃🍴71 L25–40 D25–40 mountains
★*Parc* ☎450305 Closed Dec–14 Mar
50rm12⊃25🍴 A26rm 🏠 sB41–43 dB⊃🍴86–101
L26–55 &alc D26–55 &alc mountains
FLORENSAC 34 (Herault) 3,050 (☎67) Map **27** A2
★★**Leonce** ⚿ 2 pl de la République ☎770305 Closed
16 Sep–9 Oct 30rm5⊃9🍴 A10rm 🏠 Lift sB fr44
dB78–80 dB⊃🍴78–99 L22–55 D22–55
FLOTTE (LA) See **RÉ (ILE DE)**
FOIX 09 (Ariège) 10,250 (☎61) Map **22** C4
★★★**Barbacane** av de Lerida (DP) ☎650044 Closed
16 Oct–Mar 22rm19⊃ 🏠
★★★**Tourisme** ☎650205 tx530972 30⊃
sB⊃55–118 dB⊃104–127 L fr27 D fr27 mountains
FONTAINE See **GRENOBLE**
FONTAINEBLEAU†77 (Seine-et-Marne) 19,600
(☎1) Map **9** B3
★★★**Aigle Noir** 27 pl N-Bonparte ☎4223265
tx600080 30⊃ 🏠 Lift ♪ sB⊃202–242
dB⊃244–312 (English breakfast) L fr80 &alc Dfr80
&alc
★★**Londres** 1 pl du Gl-de-Gaulle ☎4222021 Closed
Feb 22rm3⊃4🍴 P ♪ sB⊃🍴110–120
dB60–70 dB⊃🍴120–130 L45–100 D45–100 &alc
St%
★*Forêt* av Prés-Roosevelt (n rest) ☎4223926
30rm5⊃10🍴 🏠 P ♪ sB40 (room only)
sB⊃🍴51–63 (room only) dB40–60 (room only)
dB⊃🍴63–72 (room only)
★*Neuville* 196 r Grande ☎4222339 Closed Jan
20rm4⊃4🍴 A4rm 🏠

🗎 &⊃**François**-1er (P Laine) 9 r Chancellerie
☎4222034 Frd (GB)
🗎 &⊃**St Antoine** 11 r de France ☎42223188 BL
At **Ury** (6km SW on N51)
☆☆☆**Novotel Fontainebleau Ury** (N51) ☎4224825
tx600153 127⊃ P Lift 🏠⊃fr159 dB⊃fr173 English
breakfast only Pool
FONT ROMEU 66 (Pyrénées-Orientales) 3,050
(☎68) Map **22** C4
★★★**Bellevue** ☎300016 65rm30⊃ P Lift sB43–88
sB⊃88 dB56–116 dB⊃116 (English breakfast) L32
D32 mountains
★★*Carlit* ⚿ ☎300745 37rm4⊃19🍴
★*Pyrénées* (n rest) ☎300149 Closed May &
Oct–Dec 42rm10⊃12🍴 Lift sB⊃🍴53–76 (room
only) dB⊃🍴84–101 (room only) mountains
FONVIALANE See **ALBI**
FORÊT-FOUESNANT (LA) 29 (Finistère) 2,100
(☎98) Map **7** A3
★**Beauséjour** 47 r de la Baie ☎560208 Closed
Oct–Mar 30rm10🍴 P sB48–53 sB🍴58–64
dB55–65 dB🍴70–75 (English breakfast) L30–50
D25–50 sea
★**Espérance** ⚿ ☎560135 Closed 26 Sep–14 Mar
30rm7⊃10🍴 A18rm P sB43–53 dB58–64
dB⊃🍴76–88 L25–45 D25–45 sea
FOS-SUR-MER 13 (Bouches-du-Rhône) 6,750
(☎91) Map **27** B2
★★★**Frantel** ☎050057 146⊃ P sB⊃167–192
dB⊃219–254 L62–90 D62–90 alc Pool lake
FOUESNANT 29 (Finistère) 4,900 (☎98) Map **7** A3
★★**Pointe Mousterlin** ⚿ (at Pointe de Mousterlin-
6km SW by D145 & D134) ☎560412 Closed
21 Sep–24 May 50rm23⊃10🍴 🏠 P sB46 dB66–72
dB⊃🍴75–135 L25–40 D40 sea
★**Amorique** ⚿ ☎560019 Closed Oct–Mar 25rm8
⊃4🍴 A12rm P dB51–58 dB⊃🍴96–106
(English breakfast) L30–60 D30–60
🗎 **MJ Bourhis** rte de Quimper ☎560265 ✍ P Ren
FOUGÈRES 35 (Ile-et-Vilaine) 27,700 (☎99)
Map **8** C3
★★**Voyageurs** 10 pl Gambetta ☎990820 Closed
6 Dec–31 Dec 38rm8⊃9🍴 P sB38–53
sB⊃🍴62–69 dB fr60 dB⊃🍴69–87
★**Moderne** ⚿ 15 r Tribunal ☎990024 26rm1⊃10🍴
🏠 P sB40 sB⊃🍴53 dB60 dB⊃🍴79
(English breakfast) L28 D28
🗎 &⊃**Centre** 12 r J-Ferry ☎990207
FOULAIN 52 (Haute-Marne) 810 (☎27) Map **10** D2
★**Chalet** ☎021111 Closed Mon 12rm1⊃3🍴
🗎 **Maitre Et Fils** ☎021016 BL
FRAYSSINET 46 (Lot) 500 (☎65) Map **16** C2
★**Bonne Auberge** ⚿ ☎310002 Closed 12 Nov–Jan
10rm10🍴 A2rm 🏠 P sB🍴51–76 dB🍴60–85
(English breakfast) L25–60 D25–60 mountains
☆*Escale* ☎310001 10🍴 P ♪ dB🍴135 L fr30 Dfr30
St% mountains
FRÉJUS†83 (Var) 30,650 (☎94) Map **28** C2
🗎 &⊃**Moderne Chiotti** av de Verdun ☎954076 Cit
At **Colombier** (3km W)
★★★**Residences du Colombier** rte de Bagnols
☎954592 tx470328 Closed Oct–14 Apr
60rm40⊃20🍴 P sB fr170 sB⊃🍴fr160 dB⊃🍴fr230
L fr70 Dfr70 ✍ Pool
FRESNES-LES-MONTAUBAN See **ARRAS**
FRÉTEVAL 41 (Loir-et-Cher) 900 (☎39) Map **9** A2
★**Chalet du Loir** ☎926499 Closed Oct 9rm3⊃
sB42–61 sB⊃fr74 dB fr62 dB🍴fr102
FRÉVENT 62 (Pas-de-Calais) 4,450 (☎21) Map **3** A1
★**Amiens** ⚿ 7 r Doullens ☎042543 10rm1⊃3🍴 🏠
FUMAY 08 (Ardennes) 6,150 (☎24) Map **10** C4
★★**Roches** 28 av J-Jaurès ☎369012 Closed Feb
36rm8⊃8🍴 🏠 P sB fr44 sB⊃🍴fr71 dB52–67
dB⊃🍴78–93 L35–100 D35–70
GACÉ 61 (Orne) 2,700 (☎34) Map **8** D3
★★★**Champs** ⚿ rte d'Alençon ☎355145 Closed Tue
& 16 Jan–14 Feb 24rm16⊃2🍴

France

A9rm P sB58–69 sB⇄ 🍴71–120 dB68–81
dB⇄ 🍴81–132 L37–58 &alc D37–58 &alc Pool ◯
★Étoile d'Or 60 Grande r ☎355003 12rm 🏠 P
sB fr31 dB45–54 (English breakfast) L26–35
D26–35
🛏 ⁑**Moderne** (C Ducheone) 16 r de Rouen
☎356084 Ren

GAN 64 (Pyrénées-Atlantiques) (☎59) Map **15** B1
★Hostide l'Horizon ☎687272 17rm3⇄1 🍴 A6rm P
sB41–63 sB⇄ 🍴fr63 dB48–58 dB⇄ 🍴70–87 L fr27
Dfr27 mountains

GAP† 05 (Hautes-Alpes) 29,750 (☎92) Map **28** C3
★★Fons-Régina (2km S on N85) ☎510253 Closed
Oct21rm4⇄10 🍴 sB43 sB⇄ 🍴55–64 dB55
dB⇄ 🍴80–90 L fr34 Dfr34 mountains
★★Grille 2 pl F-Euzière ☎511484 30rm12⇄18 🍴 Lift
sB⇄ 🍴64–79 dB⇄ 🍴88–118 (English breakfast)
L25–80 D25–80
★Poyo pl F-Euzière ☎510413 7⇄10 🍴 P Lift
sB⇄ 🍴58–74 dB⇄ 🍴82 (English breakfast) L24–35
D24–35 mountains
🛏 ⁑**S Aurouze** pl de Verdun ☎512618 BL Rov Tri

GARDE-ST-CAST-(LA) See ST-CAST

GAVARNIE 65 (Haute-Pyrénées) 200 (☎62)
Map **21** B4
★Voyageurs ☎974801 Closed Nov–Mar 30rm4⇄
🏠

GÉMENOS 13 (Bouches-du-Rhône) 3,050 (☎91)
Map **27** B2
★★★Relais Magdeleine ☎822005 Closed 11
Jan–14 Mar 17rm14⇄3 🍴 🏠 Pool

GENNES 49 (Maine-et-Loire) 1,700 (☎41) Map **8** D2
★★Loire ☎518103 Closed 4 Jan–9 Feb
11rm4⇄2 🍴 🏠 P Lift sB40–70 sB⇄ 🍴70–86
dB60–78 dB⇄ 🍴78–94 L24–48 &alc D24–48 &alc
★★Naulets d'Anjou ☎518188 Closed Nov–Feb
15⇄7 P sB⇄56–92 dB⇄87–100 (English breakfast)
L fr50 Dfr50 ✇

GÉRARDMER 88 (Vosges) 10,000 (☎29)
Map **11** A2
★★★Beau Rivage esp du Lac ☎630028 Closed
21 Sep–9 May 56rm39⇄9 🍴 🏠 Lift
★Parc 🖂 av de la Ville-de-Vichy (n rest) ☎630243
Closed 16 Oct–mid Apr (except Xmas & New Year)
38rm2⇄10 🍴 A14rm 🏠 P sB38–55 sB⇄ 🍴60–82
dB46–63 dB⇄ 🍴68–90 L25–28 D28–75 lake
★Echo de Ramberchamp (n rest) ☎630227 Closed
11 Nov–19 Dec 17rm11⇄2 🍴 P sB43–48 sB⇄58–61
dB50–55 dB⇄65–70 mountains lake
★Lac Bout du Lac ☎630421 Closed Oct–23 Mar
17rm
🛏 ⁑**Choux Automobiles** 52 rte de Colmar
☎630088 ☎630088 Chy

At **Saut des Cuves** (3km NE on N417)
★★★Saut des Cuves ☎631024 Closed
6 Nov–Jan 27rm10⇄10 🍴 🏠 P Lift 🌙 sB fr80
sB⇄ 🍴131 dB fr101 dB⇄ 🍴101–144
(English breakfast) L fr44 Dfr44 mountains

GEX 01 (Ain) 4,400 (☎50) Map **10** D1
★★★Mainaz col de la Faucille (Pn) ☎417717 Closed
21–30 Jun & 4 Nov–14 Dec 25rm23⇄2 🍴 🏠
sB⇄ 🍴120–140 dB⇄ 🍴240–280 L37–80 D37–80
mountains lake
★Bellevue av de la Gare ☎415540 Closed Nov&
Dec 22rm12⇄4 🍴 🏠 P sB37–44 sB⇄ 🍴53–57
dB52–54 dB⇄ 🍴61–76 (English breakfast) L24–35
D24–38 mountains lake
🛏 ⁑**Modernes** les Vertes Campagnes ☎415424
Ren
🛏 ⁑**Prodon** 9 r des Terreaux ☎415517 Cit

GIEN 45 (Loiret) 15,350 (☎38) Map **9** B2
★★Rivage 🖂 1 quai Nice (DP) ☎672053
28rm15⇄2 🍴 🏠

GIVORS 69 (Rhone) 22,000 (☎78) Map **27** B4
At **Grigny** (3km N on D15)
★★Manoir ☎730543 Closed 16 Nov–Feb
11rm7⇄4 🍴

GLÉNIC 23 (Creuse) (☎55) Map **16** D4

★★Moulin Noyé (N140) ☎520911 32rm7⇄6 🍴

GLUGES See MARTEL

GOLFE-JUAN 06 (Alpes-Maritimes) 3,236 (☎93)
Map **28** C2
★★Stellamare 7 rte Cannes (N7) ☎637105 Closed
Nov–Jan 21rm6⇄12 🍴 sea

GORDES 84 (Vaucluse) 1,600 (☎90) Map **27** B2
★★Mayanelle r Combe ☎720028 Closed 6 Jan–4
Feb 10rm6⇄4 🍴

GOUMOIS 25 (Doubs) 150 (☎81) Map **11** A2
★★Taillard 🖂 (DP) ☎442075 Closed 11 Jan–9 Feb
& Nov–9 Dec 18rm8⇄7 🍴 A1rm 🏠

GRADIGNAN See BORDEAUX

GRAMAT 46 (Lot) 3,550 (☎65) Map **16** C2
★★Château de Roumégouse (4km NW on N681)
☎386381 Closed 16 Oct–Mar 12⇄9 sB92–130
dB⇄123–178 L45–60 &alc D45–60 &alc
★Lion d'Or 🖂 pl République ☎387318 Closed
16 Nov–14 Jan 18rm6⇄3 🍴 sB53–64
sB⇄ 🍴53–93 dB61–101 L35–90 D35–90
🛏 ⁑**Elias** ☎387106 P Ren

GRANDE-MOTTE (LA) 34 (Herault) ☎67)
Map **27** A2
★★★Frantel r du Pont ☎569081 tx480241
135rm135⇄10 🍴 🏠 P Lift sB⇄ 🍴183–250
dB⇄236–305 (English breakfast) L70–80
D70–75 ✇ Pool sea

GRAND-PRESSIGNY (LE) 37 (Indre-et-Loire) 1,300
(☎47) Map **9** A1
★Espérance (DP & Pn) ☎949012 10rm 🏠 P Lift
sB50–75 dB100–150 (English breakfast) L fr25
Dfr25 St% ✇

GRANVILLE 50 (Manche) 15,200 (☎33) Map **8** C3
★Gourments 1 r G-Clemenceau ☎501987 20rm6⇄
sBfr38 sB⇄fr63 dBfr47 dB⇄fr69 L fr38 D fr38
🛏 ⁑**A Haral** 5 r C-Desmaisons ☎500104 P Sim

GRASSE† 06 (Alpes-Maritime) 35,350 (☎93)
Map **28** C2
★★Beau Soleil 12 bd Crouët ☎360170 tx47844
50rm40⇄ Lift Pool
🛏 ⁑**Imperial** bd du Gl-Leclerc ☎365320 Ren

GRAY 70 (Haute-Saône) 9,650 (☎84) Map **10** D2
★Château de Rigny ☎652501 25rm20⇄ 🏠 P
sB⇄71–161 dB⇄172–222 L55–90&alc
D55–90&alc ✇
🛏 ⁑**Gray Automobiles** (Larue) av de Gl-de-Gaulle
☎652523 P Peu

GRENOBLE† 38 (Isère) 169,750 (☎76) Map **27** B3
★★★★Sofitel 1 av d'Innsbruck ☎095427 tx980470
100⇄ 🏠 P Lift 🌙 sB⇄196 dB⇄248
(English breakfast) L alc D alc ✇ Pool
★★★Angleterre 5 pl V-Hugo ☎873721
70rm30⇄40 🍴 P Lift 🌙 sB⇄105–140
dB⇄128–151 (English breakfast) mountains
★★★Louvre 3 r Clot-Bey (off bd E-Rey) (n rest)
☎442864 55rm30⇄10 🍴 Lift
★★Savole 52 av Alsace-Lorraine ☎440020
tx320635 84rm26⇄31 🍴 Lift sB65–82
sB⇄91–116 dB106 dB⇄138–156
(English breakfast) L32–60 D32–60
★★★Terminus 10 pl Gare (n rest) ☎872433 Closed
1–21 Aug 52rm12⇄25 🍴 Lift sB60–68
sB⇄78–130 dB68–140 dB⇄90–140
mountains
★★Alpazur 59 av Alsace-Lorraine (n rest) ☎444280
30rm6⇄11 🍴 sB45–68 sB⇄69–76 dB60–89
dB⇄79–89
★★Gallia 7 bd Ml-Joffré (n rest) ☎873921 tx980882
36rm16⇄12 🍴 Lift 🌙 sB62 sB⇄75–90 dB75
dB⇄88–118
★★Paris-Nice 61 bd J-Vallier (n rest) ☎463618
29rm6⇄13 🍴 🏠 P sB54 sB⇄65–76 dB69–90
dB⇄80–90 (English breakfast) mountains
🛏 ⁑**Albertiny** 146 av L-Blum ☎090087 BL (GB)

At **Claix** (2.5km W on N75 & D269)
★★★Oiseaux ☎980774 tx980718 Closed Dec–14
Jan 20rm5⇄10 🍴 🏠 P sB78 sB⇄ 🍴102–132 dB90
dB⇄ 🍴114–144 L35–65 D35–65 Pool mountains

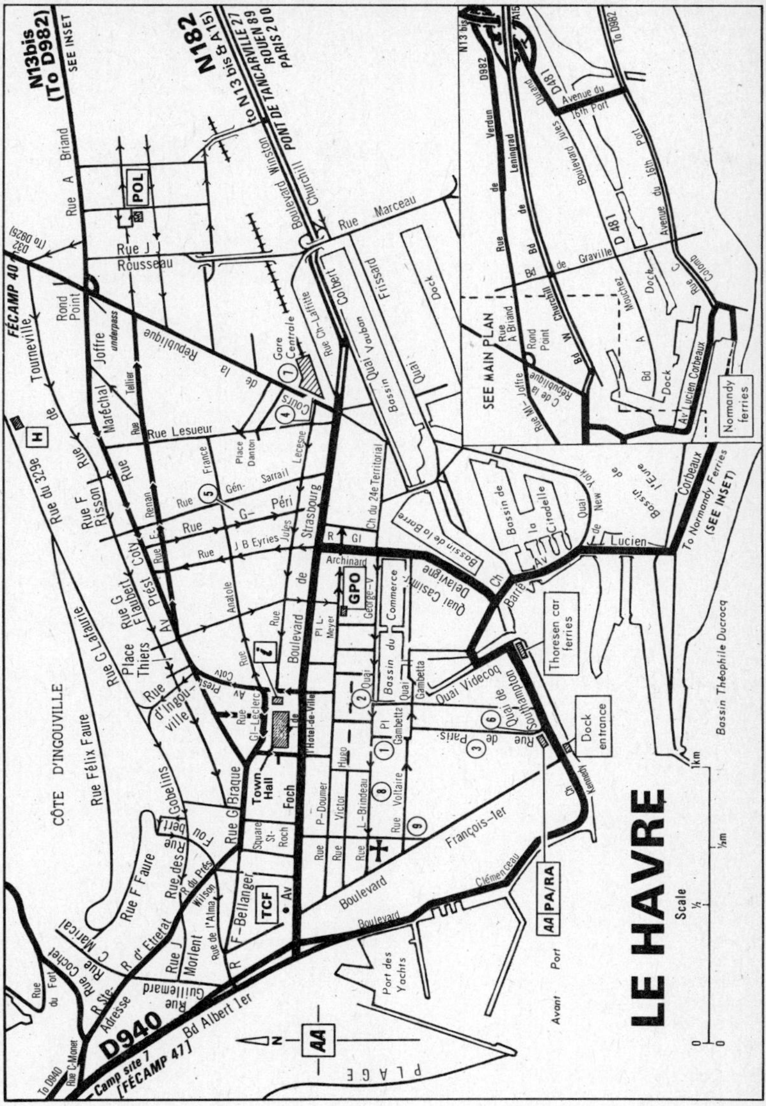

LE HAVRE

Havre (Le)

1	★★★Bordeaux	6	★★Monaco
2	★★★Normandie	7	Grand Hotel Terminus
3	★★★Marly	8	★Petit Vatel
4	★★France & Bourgogne	9	★Voltaire
5	★★Ile de france		

France

At **Pont-de-Claix** (8km S)
★**Globe** 1 cours St-André ☎980929 Closed Jan
12rm9🏠 🏛

At **St Martin d'Hères** (4km SE)
🍴 🐾**Majestic** 109 av G-Péri ☎423818 Opl

At **Voreppe** (12km NW by A48)
☆☆☆**Novotel Grenoble-Voreppe** Autoroute de Lyon
☎210327 tx3202731 14⇄ P Lift sB⇄fr132
dB⇄fr167 English breakfast only Pool

GRIGNY See GIVORS

GRIMAUD 83 (Var) 2,450 (☎94) Map 28 C2
★★★★**Kilal** ☎432002 tx470230 Closed Oct–Mar
50rm45⇄5🏠 🏛 P Lift ♪ sB⇄🏠160–265
dB⇄🏠220–430 (English breakfast) L80 D80
mountains

At **Port Grenoble** (5.5km E)
★★★**Giraglia** ☎563133 tx470494 Closed Nov 48⇄
🏛 P Lift ♪ sB⇄180 dB⇄194–306 Pool Beach sea

GRISOLLES 82 (Tarn-et-Garonne) 2,400 (☎63)
Map 16 C1
★★**Relais des Garrigues** ☎303159 Closed 11–24
Jan & 2–14 Dec 27rm20🏠 🏛 P ♪ sBfr56 sB🏠fr86
dBfr63 🏠93–98 (English breakfast) L25–40
D25–40

GUÉRET 23 (Creuse) 16,150 (☎55) Map 16 D4
★★**St-François** 31 pl Bonnyaud ☎524976
30rm9⇄7🏠 P Lift sB51 sB⇄🏠84 dB⇄🏠92
(English breakfast) L22–46 D22–46
★**Auclair** ⇚ 19 av Senatorerie ☎520126
33rm6⇄15🏠 A5rm 🏛 P sB46 sB⇄🏠86 dB52
dB⇄🏠92 L22–69 D22–69

GUÉTHARY 64 (Pyrénées-Atlantiques) 1,000 (☎59)
Map 20 C3
★★**Gurutzia** ☎265030 Closed Nov–14 Dec
27rm18⇄2🏠 🏛 sea
★★**Juzan** ☎265009 Closed Oct–May 28rm12⇄7🏠
P Lift sB39–42 dB49 dB⇄🏠81–87 L25–38 D25–38
sea
★★**Mariénia** (n rest) ☎265104 Closed Oct–May
14rm4⇄1🏠 P sB30 dB39–50 dB⇄🏠60–69 sea

GUILVINEC 29 (Finistére) 4,650 (☎98) Map 7 A3
At **Lechiagat** (1km E)
★★**Port** ☎911010 38rm10⇄28🏠 sea

HALLES (LES) 69 (Rhône) 250 (☎74) Map 27 A4
★**Charreton** rte de Bordeaux ☎3 Closed Jan & Feb
11rm 🏛

HAM 80 (Somme) 6,275 (☎22) Map 9 B4
★**France** 5 pl Hôtel de Ville (DP) ☎810022 Closed
Aug 16rm5⇄5🏠

HAUCONCOURT See METZ

HAUTEVILLE-LES-DIJON See DIJON

HAVRE (LE) 76 (Seine-Maritime) 219,600 (☎35)
Map 8 D4 **See Plan**
⊡ **AA** ⊡ agents; see page 189
★★★**Bordeaux** pl Gambetta (n rest) ☎226944
ta Borotel tx190428 Plan **1** 31rm20⇄11🏠 P Lift ♪
sB⇄🏠114–185 dB⇄🏠150–196 (English breakfast)
sea
★★★**Marly** 121 r de Paris (n rest) ☎428369
tx190369 Plan **3** 34rm14⇄16🏠 Lift ♪ sB58–79
sB⇄🏠90–132 dB68–89 dB⇄🏠121–149
★★★**Normandie** quai George-V (n rest) ☎424961
tx19354 Plan **2** 65rm40⇄15🏠 Lift
★★**France & Bourgogne** 21 cours de la République
☎212929 Plan **4** 33rm20⇄ Lift
★★**Ile de France** 104 r A-France (n rest) ☎424929
Plan **5** 17rm6⇄7🏠 sB34–59 sB⇄🏠44–59
dB50–62 dB⇄🏠50–65
★★**Monaco** 16 r de Paris ☎422101 Plan **6**
Closed Feb 11rm3⇄1🏠 P sB52–73 dB⇄🏠77–81
L45–100 D45–100 sea
★**Grand Hotel Terminus** 23 cours de la République
(n rest) ☎424275 Plan **7** 44rm17⇄4🏠 Lift sB48
sB⇄🏠79 dB⇄🏠86
★**Petit Vatel** 86 r L-Brindeau (n rest) ☎428510
Plan **8** 28rm9🏠 sB43–53 sB🏠53 dB50 dB🏠60

★**Voltaire** 14 r Voltaire (n rest) ☎429521 Plan **9**
24rm15🏠 Lift
🍴 🏠**Etablissements le Troadec** 93 r Lesueur
☎213303 Aud/VW (GB)
🍴 **Foch** 30–32 av Foch ☎428874 P
🍴 🐾**Ste Normande des Autos** 200 bd de Graville
☎252535 Chy/Sim (GB)
🍴 **J Tanguy** 19 r G-Braque ☎423380 P Vlo

HAYE-DU-PUITS (LA) 50 (Manche) 1,800 (☎33)
Map 8 C4
★**Gare** ⇚ ☎460422 Closed 10 Jan–8 Feb
11rm2⇄2🏠 A1rm 🏛 P sB39–55 sB⇄🏠47–55
dB54–64 dB⇄🏠62–64 (English breakfast) L25–50
D25–50

HAYONS (LES) See NEUFCHATEL-EN-BRAY

HÉDÉ 35 (Ille-et-Vilaine) 1,500 (☎99) Map 8 C3
★★**Hostellerie du Vieux Moulin** ⇚ (N137) ☎000414
15rm13⇄ P sB⇄🏠73 dB⇄🏠81
(English breakfast) L35–60 D35–60

HENDAYE-PLAGE 64 (Pyrénées-Atlantiques)
10,150 (☎59) Map 19 B3
★★**Paris** Rond-Point ☎267561 Closed 2 Oct–mid
Apr 39rm9⇄24🏠 Lift

HENIN BEAUMONT 62 (Pas-de-Calais) 26,500
(☎21) Map 3 B1
At **Noyelles Godault** (3km NE)
☆☆☆**Novotel Henin-Douai** (A1) ☎201601 tx110352
80⇄ P Lift sB⇄fr119 dB⇄fr148 English breakfast
only Pool

HEROUVILLE ST CLAIRE See CAEN

HESDIN 62 (Pas-de-Calais) 3,330 (☎21) Map 3 A1
At **Marconne** (1km E on N39)
🍴 🐾**J Hibon** 5 av d'Arras ☎069644 P Ren (GB)

HOHWALD (LE) 67 (Bas-Rhin) 500 (☎88)
Map 11 B3
★★★**Grand** ☎083103 Closed 16 Nov–19 Dec & 7
Jan–14 feb 74rm28⇄27🏠 🏛 Lift ✍
★**Idoux** ☎083120 Closed 16 Nov–14 dec 20rm 🏛

HONFLEUR 14 (Calvados) 9,200 (☎31) Map 8 D4
★★★**Ferme St-Siméon** ☎892361 Closed
3 Jan–14 Mar 8⇄ P dB⇄252–332 L alc D alc sea

HOSSEGOR 40 (Landes) 950 (☎58) Map 15 A1
★★**Beauséjour** av Tour-du-Lac ☎720107 Closed 19
Sep–May 46rm40⇄ 🏛 P Lift ♪ Pool
★★**Ermitage** ⇚ allées des Pins Tranquilles (DP)
☎720222 Closed 16 Sep–May 12rm2⇄10🏠 P
dB⇄🏠96–109 (English breakfast) D33 ✍

HOUCHES (LES) 74 (Haute-Savoie) 1,500 (☎50)
Map 28 C4
☆☆**Delta** (N506) ☎544503 30⇄ 🏛
★★**Piste Bleue** ⇚ rte les Chavants ☎544066 Closed
mid Apr–14 Jun & 21 Sep–14 Dec 25rm16⇄ P sB49
dB87–91 dB⇄95–98 L39 D39 mountains
At **Bellevue**
★**Hutte** ✍ St-Gervaise 549 Closed mid Apr–Jun &
Sep–24 Dec 25rm

HOUDEMENT See NANCY

HOULGATE 14 (Calvados) (☎31) Map 8 D4
★★**Centre** 31 r des Bains ☎911815 Closed Oct–mid
Apr 24rm4⇄7🏠 dB56–64 dB⇄🏠101

HYÈRES† 83 (Var) 39,600 (☎94) Map 28 C1
★**Central** 17 av J-Clotis ☎650345 15rm2⇄6🏠
🍴 🐾**Sapor** 17 av des Iles d'Or ☎651071 Opl

ILE-ROUSSE (L') See CORSE (CORSICA)

ILLKIRCH See STRASBOURG

INOR 55 (Meuse) (☎28) Map 10 D4
★**Faison Doré** (DP) ☎803545 15rm3🏠

ISIGNY-SUR-MER 14 (Calvados) 3,350 (☎31)
Map 8 C4
★★**France** ⇚ 17 r Demagny ☎220033 Closed
2 Dec–Jan 20rm12⇄ P sB51 sB⇄🏠89 dB59 dB⇄97
L28–40 D28–40

ISLE-D'ADAM (L') 95 (Val d'Oise) 10,050 (☎1)
Map 9 B3
★★**Cabouillet** ⇚ 5 quai de l'Oise (DP) ☎4690090
9rm6⇄ Lift ✍ Pool ᵬ

ISSOIRE 63 (Puy-de-Dome) 15,700 (☎73) Map **27** A4
★★**Pariou** ℒ 18 bd Kennedy ☎892211 Closed Sat 29rm8⇄15⋒ P sBfr47 sB⇄⋒56 dBfr60 dB⇄⋒80 L23–40 D alc
★***Paris*** r Espagne ☎892297 15rm3⇄4⋒ ⌂

ISSOUDUN 36 (Indre) 16,550 (☎54) Map **9** B1
★★**France & Commerce** 3 r P-Brossolette ☎210065 tx751422 Closed Jan 28rm20⇄8⋒ ⌂ P ☽ sB⇄⋒72–133 dB⇄⋒120–151 (English breakfast) L32–60 D32–60

ITXASSOU 64 (Pyrénées-Atlantiques) 1,250 (☎59) Map **20** C3
★***Arza Mendi*** pl Fronton (DP) ☎257529 Closed Nov–mid Apr 13rm1⇄4⋒

IVRY-LA-BATAILLE 27 (Eure) 2,350 (☎32) Map **9** A3
★★**Grand St-Martin** ℒ 9 r Ezy ☎364139 Closed Jan 10rm4⇄4⋒ sB⇄⋒68–88 dB⇄⋒98–145 L50–98 D50–98
★★***Moulin*** 10 r Henri-IV ☎364051 Closed Feb 14⇄

JARD-SUR-MER 85 (Vendée) 1,450 (☎30) Map **8** C1
★★***Coquille*** Le Port (DP) ☎334236 Closed 21 Sep–19 Mar 10rm2⇄7⋒ sea

JOIGNY 89 (Yonne) 11,950 (☎86) Map **10** C2
★★**Moderne** ℒ av R-Petit ☎621628 tx801693 22rm9⇄11⋒ ⌂ P dB124–156 dB⇄⋒142–186 (English breakfast) L80–110 D80–110 Pool
★★**St-Jacques** ℒ 14 fbg Paris (DP) ☎620970 Closed Jan 17rm sBfr140 dBfr180 L170&alc D170&alc
⚲⚒**Blondeau** 6 fbg de Paris ☎620502 P Opl/Vau

JOINVILLE 52 (Haute-Marne) 5,150 (☎27) Map **10** D3
★★**Grand Pont** ℒ r A-Briand ☎960986 27rm3⇄14⋒ A16rm ⌂ sB41–48 sB⇄⋒69–80 dB57–70 dB⇄⋒72–100 (English breakfast) L23–60 D23–60
★**Poste** ℒ pl Grève ☎961263 Closed 16 Jan–14 Feb 12rm2⇄2⋒ ⌂ P sB40–53 sB⇄⋒43–73 dB51–66 dB⇄⋒68–86 (English breakfast) Lfr25 Dfr25
★**Soleil d'Or** 9 r des Capucins ☎961566 121rm1⇄3⋒ ⌂ P sB35–50 sB⇄⋒50 dB42–67 dB⇄⋒57–67
⚲⚒**Duthoit** av de la Marne ☎961040 M/c Ren

JOSSELIN 56 (Morbihan) 3,000 (☎97) Map **7** B3
★★***Château*** ℒ r Gl-de-Gaulle ☎222011 tx74884 Closed Feb 41rm10⇄14⋒ ⌂

JOUÉ-LES-TOURS 37 (Indre-et-Loire) 6,448 Map **8** D2
★★***Cèdres*** Savonière (n rest) ☎430028 35rm9⇄26⋒ ⌂ Lift
★★**Château de Beaulieu** ☎285219 17rm9⇄7⋒ A8rm P sB63 sB⇄⋒98–163 dB111–176 dB⇄⋒111–176 L48–140 D48–140 ⚭ Pool

JOUGNE 25 (Doubs) 900 (☎81) Map **11** A1
★**Deux Saisons** ℒ ☎891386 Closed 26 Apr–14 Jun & 21 Sep–14 Dec 21rm4⇄9⋒ ⌂ Lift sB41 sB⇄⋒45 dB63 dB⇄⋒72–78 (English breakfast) L25–40 D25–40 mountains

JUAN-LES-PINS 06 (Alpes-Maritimes) 27,400 (☎93) Map **28** C2
★★★★★***Provençal*** bd Littoral ☎611980 tx470756 Closed Nov–Mar 220⇄ ⌂ Lift ⚭ Beach sea
★★★★**Belles Rives** bd Littoral ☎610279 tx470984 Closed Oct–mid Apr 46rm43⇄3⋒ A2rm Lift ☽ sB⇄⋒180–320 dB⇄⋒250–510 (English breakfast) L alc D alc St% Beach sea
★★★***Astoria*** av Ml-Joffre ☎612365 tx470800 60rm30⇄20⋒ ⌂ Lift sea
★★★***Helios*** 3 av Daucheville (DP) ☎615525 Closed Nov–Feb 70rm67⇄3⋒ ⌂ Lift
★★★***Juana*** la Pinède ☎610870 tx47778 Closed 21 Oct–19 Mar 50rm45⇄ ⌂ Lift Beach sea
★★**Alexandra** r Pauline (DP & Pn) ☎610136 Closed Oct–14 Mar 20rm8⇄8⋒ sB82–99 sB⇄⋒109–119 dB164–198 dB⇄⋒218–238 L34 D34 Beach
★★**Cyrano** av L-Gallet (n rest) ☎610483 Closed Nov–Feb 40rm12⇄16⋒ Lift ☽ sB72–76 sB⇄⋒116–120 dB72–76 dB⇄⋒126–130 Beach sea
★★**Emeraude** av Saramartel ☎610967 Closed Nov–mid Apr 20rm15⋒ sB42 dBfr65 dB⇄⋒92–150 mountains
★★**Noailles** av G-Gallice ☎611170 Closed Oct–May 22rm4⇄3⋒ P sBfr48 dBfr61 dB⇄⋒fr128 (English breakfast) Lfr28 Dfr28 sea
★★***Régence*** 2 av Al-Courbet ☎610939 Closed Oct–21 Mar 20rm10⇄10⋒
★**Midi** 93 bd Poincaré ☎613516 Closed Nov & Dec 18rm3⇄6⋒ A2rm ⌂ P sB48–58 dB66–71 dB⇄⋒81 (English breakfast) L25–45 D25–45 sea
⚲⚒**St Charles** 6 r St-Charles ☎610816 P Cit (GB)
⚲⚒**Wilson** 122 bd Wilson ☎612515 P Opl (GB)

JULLOUVILLE 50 (Manche) 4,000 (☎33) Map **8** C3
★★***Casino*** ℒ (DP) ☎618282 Closed 26 Sep–6 Apr 58rm17⇄17⋒

LA Each name preceded by La is listed under the name that follows it.

LABOUHEYRE 40 (Landes) 2,650 (☎58) Map **15** B2
⚲ **Lafargue** pl du Foirail ☎789111 M/c Aud/MB/VW

LADOIX-SERRIGNY See **BEAUNE**

LAFFREY 38 (Isère) 200 (☎76) Map **27** B3
★★**Grand Lac** ℒ ☎681290 A20⇄⋒ P sB⇄⋒49 dB⇄⋒68–75 L28 D28 mountains

LALINDE 24 (Dordogne) 3,100 (☎53) Map **16** C2
★★***Château*** ℒ r Verdun ☎610182 Closed Oct 10rm1⇄1⋒
★★**Résidence** 3 r Prof-Testut (n rest) ☎610181 Closed Nov–mid Apr 11rm2⇄9⋒ sB43–53 sB⇄⋒43–53 dB⇄⋒61–88

LAMASTRE 07 (Ardèche) 3,100 (☎75) Map **27** B3
★★★**Midi** pl Siegnobos ☎064150 Closed 16 Dec–Feb 22rm12⇄3⋒ sB54–64 sB⇄⋒fr79 dB108–118 L60–125 mountains
★★**Commerce** ℒ pl Rampon ☎064153 23rm5⇄10⋒ ⌂ P sB48–53 dB⇄⋒71–96 L30–90 D30–90

LAMBALLE 22 (Côtes-du-Nord) 10,200 (☎96) Map **7** B3
★★**Angleterre** ℒ 29 bd Jobert ☎310621 tx390794 35rm13⇄10⋒ A13rm ⌂ P Lift ☽ sB45–80 sB⇄⋒90–105 dB65–95 dB⇄⋒110–120 (English breakfast) L32–80 D32–80
★**Tour d'Argent** ℒ 2 r du Dr-Lavergue ☎310137 15rm1⇄5⋒ P sBfr41 sB⇄⋒fr49 dBfr48 dB⇄⋒56–79 (English breakfast) L25–40 D25–40

LANESTER See **LORIENT**

LANGEAIS 37 (Indre-et-Loire) 3,950 (☎47) Map **8** D2
★★***Family & Duchess-Anne*** ℒ 9 r Tours ☎558203 Closed Feb 22rm4⇄4⋒ ⌂
★★**Hosten** 2 r Gambetta ☎558212 tx7502189 Closed Jan 14rm12⇄2⋒ ⌂ P sBfr81 dB⇄⋒162 L115&alc D115&alc

LANGOGNE 48 (Lozère) 4,350 (☎66) Map **27** A3
★★***Poste*** 13 av Foch 40rm8⇄8⋒ ⌂ ⚭

LANGON 33 (Gironde) 6,150 (☎56) Map **15** B2
⚲⚒**Doux et Trouillot** 45 cours Sadi-Carnot ☎630047 M/c P Peu (GB)

LANGRES 52 (Haute-Marne) 12,500 (☎25) Map **10** D2
★★**Europe** 23 r Diderot ☎851088 Closed Oct 28rm8⇄8⋒ A9rm ⌂ P sB43–48 sB⇄⋒68–78 dB54–61 dB⇄⋒81–91 L22–55&alc D22–55&alc
★★**Lion d'Or** rte de Vesoul ☎850330 Closed Feb 17rm4⇄6⋒ ⌂ P sB58 sB⇄⋒70 dB78 dB⇄⋒81 L25 D25 Pool lake
★★***Amorial*** 16 r Gambetta (n rest) ☎850101 Closed Feb 12rm4⇄1⋒ ⌂
★**Cheval Blanc** ☎850700 Closed Jan & Feb 20rm6⇄7⋒ A7rm ⌂ P dBfr43 dB⇄⋒93 L22–50 D22–50

France

⬛ &⬩*Europe* rte Chaumont ☎850378 M/c P
Aud/BMW/VW
LANGUEUX See **ST-BRIEUC**
LANNEMEZAN 65 (Hautes-Pyrénées) 8,500 (☎62)
Map **15** B1
⬛ &⬩*Pyrénées* (J Barbet) 13 ter rte de Tarbes
☎989111 Bed/Opl
LANSLEBOURG 73 (Savoie) 550 (☎79) Map **28** C3
★*Belais des Deux Cols* 73 Val Cenis ☎052341
Closed Spring & Autumn 20rm10➾ A10rm sBfr37
sB➾fr45 dB60–94 dB➾fr74 L25–40 D25–40 Pool
mountains
LANSLEVILLARD 73 (Savoie) 350 (☎79) Map 28C3
☆☆*Étoile des Neiges* ☎050041 Closed 16 Sep–14
Dec & 16 Apr–14 Jun 20rm12➾4㎖ bsB59 sB➾㎖69
dB78 dB➾㎖93 (English breakfast) L45 D45
mountains
LAON†02 (Aisne) 30,200 (☎23) Map **10** C4
★★*Angleterre* 10 bd Lyon ☎230462 30rm16➾4㎖
🏠 P Lift ⅅ sB60 sB➾㎖97 dB89 dB➾㎖120
(English breakfast) L32 D32
★*Bannière de France* 11 r de F-Roosevelt ☎232144
Closed 21 Dec–9 Jan 18rm5➾7㎖ 🏠 sB38–53
sB➾㎖68–83 dB61–81 dB➾㎖76–111 L30–75
D30–75
★*Commerce* 18 pl de la Gare ☎230038 21rm4➾4㎖
🏠 P ⅅ sB44–84 dB51–91
&⬩*St-Marcel* (M G Leleu) 45 bd Gras-Brancourt
☎234172 AR/BL/Lnc (GB)
⬛ &⬩*SICB* 121 av de Belgique ☎232067 P Frd (GB)
LAPALISSE 03 (Allier) 3,800 (☎70) Map **27** A4
★*Galland* 20 pl de la République ☎990721
12rm2➾1㎖ 🏠 P sB34 dB51 dB➾㎖82 L fr30 D fr30
LARAGNE 05 (Hautes-Alpes) 3,900 (☎92)
Map 27 B2/3
★*Terrasses* av Provence ☎650854 Closed
Nov–Apr 17rm3➾4㎖ 🏠 P sB fr38 dB45–50
dB➾fr60 L24–38 D fr24 mountains
LARCENAC-ST-VINCENT 43 (Haute-Loire) (☎71)
Map 27 A3
★*Relais* ℒ ☎085109 10rm6㎖ 🏠 P ⅅ sB32–33
sB➾㎖45–46 dB43–44 dB➾㎖56–57
(English breakfast) L25–50 D35–50 mountains
LAROQUE-DES-ARCS See **CAHORS**
LAUMES (LES) 21 (Côte-d'Or) 2,906 (☎80)
Map **10** C2
★★*Gare* ℒ ☎960046 26rm3➾2㎖ 🏠 P ⅅ sB30–39
dB47–57 dB➾㎖67–70 (English breakfast) L25–65
D25–65
LAVAL†53 (Mayenne) 54,550 (☎43) Map **8** C3
⬛ &⬩*Boureau* 9 r Echelle Marteau ☎531314 &
533232 Frd
⬛ &⬩*Ouest* 95 quai P-Boudet ☎530969 AR/BL/Jag
Tri
⬛ ⬩*SEGL* 101 r V-Boissel ☎534481 ☎533232
Aud/VW (GB)
LAVANDOU (LE) 83 (Var), 3,826 (☎94) Map **28** C1
★★★*Calanque* 62 av Gl-de-Gaulle ☎710463
41rm26➾15㎖ P Lift 🏠 sB84–129 sB➾㎖84–129
dB102–156 L42–120 D42–120 sea
★★★*California* ☎710263 Closed 21 Sep–19 May
27rm15➾12㎖ P dB➾㎖73–120 L24–40 D24–40
★★★*Résidence-Beach* bd Front-de-Mer ☎710066
Closed 26 Sep–24 May 55rm48➾5㎖ P Lift
dB➾㎖177–252 L fr40 D fr50 ⚓ Beach sea
★★*Neptune* 26 av Gl-de-Gaulle ☎710101
33rm4➾18㎖ ⚓ Pool δ ◌
★★*Provençale* 11 r Parton Ravello ☎710044
Closed Oct–Mar 13rm3➾4㎖
★*Petite Bohème* av F-Roosevelt ☎711030 Closed
Oct–Whit 16rm10➾3㎖ P sB46 dB56–64
dB➾㎖89–103 L34 D34 sea
&⬩*Vieille* (M Costa) chemin du Repos ☎710804 Frd
(GB)
LAVAUR 81 (Tarn) 8,500 (☎63) Map **16** C1
At **St-Lieux-les-Lavour** (11km NE on D81 & D631)
★★*Château* ☎577619 17➾ A5rm
LAXOU See **NANCY**

LE Each name preceded by Le is listed under the
name that follows.
LECHIAGAT See **GUILVINEC**
LECQUES (LES) 83 (Var) (☎94) Map **27** B1
★*Terrasses* av des Lecques ☎262423 Closed Feb
13rm9➾4㎖ P dB➾㎖93–122 L32alc D32alc sea
LENS†62 (Pas-de-Calais) 40,300 (☎21) Map **3** B1
⬛ &⬩*Thirion* 60–68 av A-Maès ☎282008 P Bed/Opl
LES Each name preceded by Les is listed under the
name that follows it.
LESCAR See **PAU**
LESSAY 50 (Manche) 1,350 (☎33) Map **8** C4
★*Hostellerie de l'Abbaye* pl St-Cloud ☎464388
12rm7➾ P sB32–55 sB➾㎖55 dB➾㎖61–70
(English breakfast) L34–50 D34–50
LÉZIGNAN-CORBIÈRES 11 (Aude) 7,450 (☎68)
Map **16** D1
&⬩*Lézignan-Auto* (Sarraset) 63 av G-Clemenceau
☎270293 P Ren
LIBOURNE†33 (Gironde) 23,000 (☎56) Map **15** C2
★★★*Loubat* 32 r Chanzy ☎511758 52rm19➾8㎖ 🏠
⬛ &⬩*D Agulio* 25 r du Près-Wilson ☎511460 Ren
LILLE†59 (Nord) 177,300 (☎20) Map **3** B1
★★★*Bellevue* 5 r J-Roisin ☎574586 tx820790
66➾㎖ P Lift ⅅ sB➾㎖104–112 dB➾㎖134–157
St%
★★★*Carlton* 3 r de Paris ☎552411 tx110400
80rm70➾3㎖ Lift
★★★*Royal Concorde* 2 bd Carnot (n rest) ☎510511
tx820575 111rm65➾22㎖ P Lift sB64–76
sB➾㎖100–147 dB92–103 dB➾㎖138–188
(English breakfast)
⬛ ⬩*Delannoy* 208 fbg d'Arras ☎961513 BL/Tri (GB)
⬛ ⬩*Lilloise Autos* 58 r des Stations ☎938065 Sim
At **Englos** (7.5km W on D63)
☆☆*Motellerie* ☎923015 tx820302 95rm52➾43㎖
P sB98–104 sB➾㎖118–124 dB➾㎖152–164
L fr55 D fr55 ◌ Pool
☆☆*Novotel Lille-Lomme* (A25) ☎504700
tx120120 117➾ P Lift sB➾fr132 dB➾fr164 English
breakfast only Pool
At **Madeleine**
&⬩*Baillet* 201 r du Gl-de-Gaulle ☎515556 BL (GB)
At **Marcq en Baroeul** (4.5km N on N350)
☆☆☆*Holiday Inn* ☎721730 tx120785 125➾ Lift
Pool
LILLE AIRPORT
At **Lesquin** (8km SE)
☆☆☆*Novotel Lille Aéroport* (A1) ☎979225
tx820519 92➾ P Lift sB➾fr132 dB➾㎖165 English
breakfast only Pool
LILLERS 62 (Pas-de-Calais) 9,560 Map **3** A1
★*Commerce* 50 pl de la Gare ☎022077 Closed Aug
10rm 🏠 P sB28–30 dB37–45 (English breakfast)
L32–38 D22–30
LIMOGES†87 (Haute-Vienne) 147,450 (☎55)
Map **16** C3
★★★*Frantel* 1 pl République ☎321796 tx580771
75➾ Lift sB➾㎖167–192 dB➾㎖219–254 L40–100
D40–100
★★★*Luk* 29 pl Jourdan (DP) ☎334400 55➾ Lift
★★*Jourdan* 2 av du Gl-de-Gaulle ☎774962
45rm30➾10㎖ Lift
★*Relais Lamartine* ℒ 10 r des Coopérateurs (n rest)
☎775339 20rm2➾3㎖ 🏠
&⬩*Colin* 5 cours Gay-Lussac ☎772302 BL
&⬩*Sud Auto* rte de Toulouse ☎304830 P
BL/Jag/Opl/Rov/Tri/Vau
LINGOLSHEIM See **STRASBOURG**
LION-D'ANGERS (LE) 49 (Maine-et-Loire) 2,350
(f41) Map **8** C2
★*Voyageurs* quai Oudon ☎913008 Closed 16
Nov–7 Feb 13rm4➾2㎖ 🏠
LISIEUX†14 (Calvados) 26,700 (☎31) Map **8** D4
★★★*Grand Normandie* ℒ 11 bis r au Char ☎621605
tx170269 Closed 16 Oct–Apr 85rm20➾14㎖ 🏠 P Lift
sB63 sB➾㎖110 dB72 dB➾㎖119 L28–75 D28–75

France

★★**Lourdes** 4 r au Char (DP) ☎311948 39rm8⇌2🍴
🏚 Lift
★★**Regina** 14 r de la Gare (DP) ☎311533 tx170169
40⇌ 🏚 Lift
★**Coupe d'or** L 49 r Pont-Mortain ☎311684
tx170169 16rm2⇌5🍴 🏚
⚙️**Jonguard** 81 r H-Cheron ☎310942 Aud/VW (GB)
LOCHES† 37 (Indre-et-Loire)6,850 (☎47) Map **9** A2
★**France** 6 r Picois ☎590032 Closed 1 wk May & 16
Nov–14 Dec 23rm4⇌6🍴 🏚 P sB37–63
sB⇌🍴47–63 dB44–70 dB⇌🍴54–70 L 23–40
D23–40
At **Bridoré** (14km S on N143)
★★**Barbe Bleue** ☎947269 Closed Feb
12rm1⇌10🍴 P sB36–41 dB⇌🍴66–83
(English breakfast) L 30–56 D30–56
LODÈVE 34 (Herault) 8,200 (☎67) Map **27** A2
★★**Croix Blanche** ☎441087 Closed Dec–Mar
32rm12⇌3🍴 A13rm P sB35–44 dB51–62
dB⇌🍴66–70 (English breakfast) L 21–41 D21–41
mountains
★**Nord** 18 bd de la Liberté ☎441008 Closed Dec &
Jan 21rm2⇌3🍴 🏚 P sB33–36 sB⇌🍴42–51
dB42–58 dB⇌🍴83 L 19–70 D19–70 mountains
LONGUYON 54 (Meurthe-et-Moselle) 7,500 (☎28)
Map **10** D4
🛢️ ⚙️**M R Piquerez** 6 r Mazelle ☎445066 P Ren
LONS-LE-SAUNIER† 39 (Jura) 23,300 (☎82)
Map **10** D1
★★**Genève** pl XI-Novembre ☎241911 42rm26⇌6🍴
🏚 P Lift sBfr71 sB⇌🍴132 dBfr102 dB⇌🍴174
L35–48 D35–48
⚙️**Sports** 70 r des Salines ☎471970 Opl
🛢️ ⚙️**Thevenod** rte de Champagnole ☎244158
Aud/MB/VW
LORIENT 56 (Morbihan) 71,950 (☎97) Map **7** B2/3
★★★**Bretagne** 6 pl de la Libération ☎643465
34rm29⇌ 🏚 Lift
★★★**Richelieu** pl J-Ferry ☎213573 tx950810 58⇌ P
Lift sB⇌🍴136 dB 176 (English breakfast) L 60 & alc
D60alc
At **Lanester**
☆☆**Novotel Lorient** ☎760216 tx950026 60⇌ P Lift
sB⇌fr134 dB⇌fr169 English breakfast only Pool
LOUDEAC 22 (Côtes-du-Nord) 10,150 (☎96)
Map **7** B3
★**Voyageurs** L 10 r Cadélac ☎280047 Closed 21
Dec–19 Jan 32rm3⇌15🍴 🏚 Lift
LOUDUN 86 (Vienne) 8,470 (☎49) Map **8** D2
★**Roue d'Or** rte Saumur ☎220123 14rm4⇌1🍴 🏚 P
sBfr61 sB⇌🍴78 dB87 dB⇌🍴102
(English breakfast) L fr29 Dfr29
LOUÉ 72 (Sarthe) 1,900 (☎43) Map **8** D2
★★★**Ricordeau** 11r Libération ☎274003 Closed
3 Jan–9 Feb 21rm11⇌8🍴 A8rm 🏚 P sB67–135
sB⇌🍴fr103 dB 169–258 (English breakfast)
L75–90 D75–90
LOUHANS 71 (Saône-et-Loire) 11,050 (☎85)
Map **10** D1
🛢️ ➦**Chevrier** 11 r11 du Novembre P
LOURDES† 65 (Hautes-Pyrénées) 18,100 (☎62)
Map **15** B1
★★★**Grotte** 66 r de la Grotte ☎945887 tx531937
Closed 21 Oct–9 Apr 90⇌ 🏚 P Lift ⤴ sB⇌🍴114–144
dB⇌🍴158–218 (English breakfast) L 56 D56
mountains
★★★**Moderne** av B-Soubirous ☎941232
105rm42⇌15🍴
★★**Provençale** 4 r Baron-Duprat ☎943134 tx48518
60rm28 ⇌12🍴 Lift
★★**St-Roch** 4 pl J-d'Arc (DP) ☎940214 Closed 16
Oct–mid Apr 43rm3⇌1🍴 A10rm lift
🛢️ ➦**Boutes** rte de Tarbes ☎940168 ☎942193
Chy/Sim (GB)
🛢️ ⚙️**P Chartier** 14 av A-Marqui ☎942308 Opl
🛢️ ⚙️**Felices** 14 av du Gl-Leclerc ☎943149 BL/Tri
LOUVIERS 27 (Eure) 8,900 (☎32) Map **9** A4
At **St-Pierre de Vauvray**

★★★**Hostellerie de St-Pierre** ☎500329 Closed
Dec–Feb 17rm12⇌ P Lift sB80–202
sB⇌🍴132–202 dB 92–214 dB⇌🍴144–214
(English breakfast) L 80 D80
At **Vironvay** (4km SE on N182A)
★★**Salsons** ☎400256 Closed 10 Jan–10 Feb
12rm11⇌1🍴 🏚 P sB⇌🍴109–134 dB⇌🍴138–278
(English breakfast) L 80 D80
LUC (LE) 83 (Var) 5,650 (☎94) Map **28** C2
★**Hostellerie du Parc** 1 r J-Jaures ☎735001
10rm2⇌4🍴 🏚 P sB54–99 sB⇌🍴64–99 dB68–118
dB⇌🍴98–118 (English breakfast) L50–100
D50–100
LUCÉ See **CHARTRES**
LUCHON 31 (Haute-Garonne) 3,650 (☎61)
Map **21** B4
★★★**Poste & Golf** 29 allées d'Etigny ☎790040
tx520018 Closed 21 Oct–19 Dec 60rm55⇌2🍴 Lift ⤴
Pool
★★**Bains** 75 allées d'Etigny ☎790058 Closed
21 Oct–19 Dec 52rm 15⇌24🍴 P Lift sB59
dB⇌🍴108–118 L40 D40 mountains
LUCON 85 (Vendée) 9,600 (☎30) Map **8** C1
★**Croissant** 1 pl du Acacias ☎561115 Closed Oct
40rm15⇌15🍴 🏚 P sB35–42 sB⇌🍴50–65
dB48–58 dB⇌🍴57–75 (English breakfast) L22–38
D22–38
LUDE (LE) 72 (Sarthe) 4,150 (☎43) Map **8** D2
★**Maine** L 24 rte Saumur ☎946054 Closed 11 Jan–
9 Feb & Aug–7 Sep 19rm2⇌6🍴 🏚
LUNEL 34 (Herault) 13,600 (☎67) Map **27** A2
★**Palais** 12 av de Latte-de-Tassigny ☎711139
Closed 21 Dec–19 Jan 24rm2⇌4🍴 🏚
LUNÉVILLE† 54 (Meurthe-et-Mosel) 24,727 (☎28)
Map **11** A3
★★**Europe** 56 r Alsace (n rest) ☎731617
30rm8⇌10🍴
🛢️ ⚙️ **SAMIA** 111 bis r d'Alsace ☎731078 Peu
🛢️ ⚙️**R Turck** 95 fbg de Ménil ☎731501 P Ren
LUS-LA-CROIX HAUTE 26 (Drôme) 500 (☎75)
Map **27** B3
★**Touring** L (off N75) ☎585001 Closed Oct–Mar
17rm1⇌ 🏚 P sB31–38 dB42–56 L25–35 D25–30
mountains
LUXEUIL-LES-BAINS 70 (Haute-Saône) 11,00
(☎84) Map **11** A2
★★**Beau Site** L 18 r Thermes ☎401467
44rm25⇌11🍴 A14rm 🏚 P Lift sB53–72
sB⇌🍴73–108 dB76–96 dB⇌🍴96–156
(English breakfast) L fr30 D fr30
LYON† 69 (Rhône) 462,850 (☎78) Map **27** B4
★★★★**Grand** 11 r Grolée ☎425621 tx330244
143rm90⇌41🍴 🏚 P Lift ⤴ sB95 sB⇌🍴135–215
dB110 dB⇌🍴175–230 (English breakfast) L50 D50
★★★★**PLM Terminus** 12 cours de Verdun ☎375811
tx330500 140rm80⇌44🍴 🏚 P Lift sB76
sB⇌🍴116–186 dB112 dB⇌🍴142–197
(English breakfast) L43–55 D43–55 ⤴ Pool 🚸 ◯
★★★★**Royal Sogetel** 20 pl Bellecour ☎375731
tx310785 94rm65⇌24🍴 🏚 P Lift ⤴ sB85
sB⇌🍴118–273 dB⇌🍴130–285
(English breakfast) L40–90 D40–90
★★★★**Sofitel** 20 quai Gailleton ☎427250 tx33225
200⇌ 🏚 P Lift ⤴ sB⇌🍴255–280 dB⇌🍴370–405
(English breakfast) L85 D fr85 river
★★★**Beaux-Arts** 75 r Prés-Herriot (n rest) ☎380950
tx330440 80rm50⇌30🍴 Lift
★★★**Carlton Sogetel** pl de la République (n rest)
☎425651 tx310787 96rm52⇌22🍴 🏚 P Lift ⤴ sB80
sB⇌🍴110–195 dB⇌🍴119–204
(English breakfast)
★★**Globe et Cecil** 21 r Gaspanin ☎425895 tx310917
65rm22⇌11🍴 Lift sB44–55 sB⇌🍴92–99
dB65–70 dB⇌🍴102–109 (English breakfast)
🛢️ ⚙️**Générale** 32 quai Perrache ☎420705 Ren
🛢️ ➦**Denuzière** 5 r Denuzière ☎376843 P
🛢️ ⚙️**Ste Dumond Frères** 7 r Duhamel ☎375565 P
Peu (GB)
⚙️**Kennings** 70–76 r de Marseille ☎581653 BL

France

At **Bron** (10 km SE)
☆☆☆**Novotel Lyon Aéroport** 260 av St-Exupery
☎269748 tx340781 196⇄ P Lift sB⇄fr148 sB⇄fr173
English breakfast only Pool
★★**Hostel Lyon** 36 av du Doyen ☎543134 tx380694
140⇄ P Lift sB⇄ fr94 dB⇄fr108 L33−55&alc
D33−55&alc

At **Charbonnières-les-Bains** (8km NW on N7)
★★★**Christel** 78 bis rte de Paris ☎344140 tx380768
60⇄ Pool

At **Dardilly** (10 km on N6)
☆☆☆**Holiday Inn** Porte de Lyon ☎357020
tx900006 204⇄ 🛏 P Lift sB⇄ 🍴127 dB⇄ 🍴161
(English breakfast) L40 D40 Pool
☆☆☆**International** Porte de Lyon ☎352805 tx33045
200⇄ Lift
☆☆☆**Novotel Lyon Nord** Porte de Lyon ☎351341
tx330962 107⇄ 🛏 P Lift sB⇄fr148 dB⇄fr174 English
breakfast only Pool

At **St-Priest** (11km SE by D518)
🚗**Kennings** 190 rte de Grenoble ☎908200 BL
(GB)

LYONS-LA-FORÊT 27 (Eure) 900 (☎32)
Map **9** A/B4
★★**Licorne** 🛏 pl Benserade ☎496202 24rm15⇄2🍴
P Lift sB66−71 sB⇄ 🍴131−152 dB92−112
dB⇄🍴152−212 L60−110 D60−110

MÂCON† 71 (Saône-et-Loire) 40,500 (☎85)
Map **10** C1
★★★**Frantel Mâcon** 26 r de Coubertin ☎382806
tx800830 63rm48⇄15🍴 P Lift sB⇄ 🍴167−192
dB⇄ 🍴219−254 L62−120 D62−120 river
☆☆☆**Novotel Mâcon Nord** (A6) ☎370080 tx800869
60⇄ P Lift sB⇄fr124 dB⇄fr167 English breakfast
only Pool
★★**Bellevue** 36 quai Lamartine (DP) ☎380507
tx800837 41rm⇄14🍴14 🛏 Lift
★★**Champs-Elysées** 6 r V-Hugo, 2 pl de la Barrre
☎383657 51rm16⇄2🍴 🛏 P Lift 🐶 sB51−56
sB⇄🍴79 dB70−78 dB⇄ 🍴93−108 L33−70
D36−70
★★**Genève** 🛏 1 r Bigonnet ☎381810 tx800762
61rm32⇄ 🛏 Lift sB46−57 sB⇄77 dB65−70
dB⇄97−114 L32−63 D32−63
★★**Terminus** 91 r V-Hugo ☎380102 tx800831
34rm20⇄10🍴 🛏 P Lift 🐶 sB72−97 sB⇄ 🍴91−97
dB80−105 dB⇄ 🍴99−105 (English breakfast)
L42−63 D42−63
★**Charollais** 71 r. Rambuteau ☎383623 12rm1 🍴
P sB fr38 dB fr46 dB⇄fr68 L25−55 D25−55
🚗 ⊕**Bois** 39 r Lacretelle ☎386431 ☎386431 P BL
🚗 ⊕**Chauvot** r J−Mermoz, zone industrielle des
Bruyères ☎382859 P Maz/Vlo
🚗 ⊕**Ferret** 89 r de Lyon ☎388355 M/c Cit (GB)
🚗 **Renault** Carrefour de l'Europe, av E-Herriot
☎382550 Ren

At **Crèches-sur-Saône** (0.5km NW on D89)
★★**Château de la Barge** ☎371204 24rm18⇄4🍴 P
dB⇄ 🍴105−130 L40−63 D40−63

At **St-Albain** (10km N)
☆☆☆**Sofitel** (A6) ☎381617 tx800881 100⇄ 🛏 P Lift
🐶 dB175 dB 🍴249 (English breakfast) D52 Pool

At **St-Jean-le-Priche** (7km N on N6)
★★★**Château St-Jean** ☎370135 Closed Nov−Feb
24rm11⇄

At **Sancé-lès-Mâcon** (4km N on N6)
☆☆☆**Vieile Ferme** (N6) ☎384693 32⇄ P
dB⇄134−164 L38−85 D38−85 Pool

MADELEINE See LILLE

MAGESCQ 40 (Landes) 1,150 (☎58) Map **15** A1/2
★★**Relais Poste** 🛏 ☎577025 Closed mid Oct−mid
Nov 16⇄🍴 🛏 P sB⇄🍴162−112 dB⇄ 🍴74−124
L50−100 D50−100 🏊 Pool

MAINTENON 28 (Eure-et-Loir) 3,350 (☎37)
Map **9** A/B3
★**Aqueduc** 🛏 pl Gare ☎230005 tx720895 Closed 16
Jan−14 Feb 17rm2⇄6🍴 🛏

MALÈNE (LA) 48 (Lozère) 250 (☎66) Map **27** A3
★★★**Château Mâlène** ☎475112 Closed Oct−Apr
12rm5⇄7🍴 P dB⇄🍴105−155 L32&alc mountains
river
★**Grand** Closed Oct−Apr 31rm11⇄3🍴 🛏

MALO-LES-BAINS 59 (Nord) 15,220 (☎20)
Map **3** A2
★**Digue** 29 Digue de Mer ☎665828 21rm1⇄1🍴 sea

MAMERS 72 (Sarthe) 6,800 (☎43) Map **8** D3
★★**Croix Blanche** 🛏 2 r Dallier/7 r P-Bert ☎976263
7rm3⇄ P dB45−55 dB⇄67−84 L20−34 D20−34

MANDELIEU 06 (Alpes-Maritimes) 9,700 (☎93)
Map **28** C2
☆**Esterel** ☎389220 Closed Nov 31rm22🍴 P
sB⇄100−120 dB 🍴130−160 (English breakfast) D38
mountains
★**Pavillion des Sports** ☎479086 Closed Nov−
19 Dec 11rm6🍴 A4rm P dBfr66 dB 🍴101
(English breakfast) L25−60 D25−60

MANS (LE) 72 (Sarthe) 155,250 (☎43) Map **8** D2
★★★★**Concorde** 16 av Gl-Leclerc ☎847170
tx720487 64rm32⇄23🍴 P Lift 🐶 sB⇄ 🍴130
dB155−157 dB⇄ 🍴160
★★★**Moderne** 14 r Bourg Belé ☎843640
33rm17⇄11🍴 🛏
★★**Central** 5 bd R-Levasseur (off pl de la
République) (n rest) ☎240893 50rm10⇄30🍴 🛏 Lift
🐶 dB57 dB⇄ 🍴65
★**Rennes** 43 bd de Gare (n rest) ☎850070
23rm4⇄9🍴
Albion Auto 108 av F-Geneslay ☎843274 BL
🚗 ⊕**Charpentier** 132 av Bollée ☎844174 Toy
🚗⊕**Goutard** 20 bis r Barbier ☎243418 Vlo
🚗 **Leseul** bd P-Lefaucheux, Zone industrielle Sud
☎846170

MARCAY See CHINON

MARCONNE See HESDIN

MARGNY See COMPIÈGNE

MARGUERITTES See NÎMES

MARKSTEIN (LE) 68 (Haut-Rhin) (☎89) Map **11** A2
★**Belle Vue** 🛏 ☎826182 tx68610 16rm6🍴 P
sB37−44 sB🍴fr44 dBfr55 dB 🍴fr70 L35−50&alc
D35−50&alc mountains lake

MARLENHEIM 67 (Bas-Rhin) 1,850 (☎88)
Map **11** B3
★**Cerf** 🛏 179 r Gl-de-Gaulle ☎875006 Closed Feb
& 29 Jun−11 Jul 20rm6⇄4🍴 🛏
★★**Hostellerie Reeb** 🛏 (N4) (DP) ☎875270 Closed
16−31 Jan 26rm15⇄6🍴 🛏

MARMANDE 47 (Lot-et-Garonne) 17,750 (☎58)
Map **15** B2
★**France** pl Couronne (n rest) ☎642274 13rm
🚗 ⊕**Auto-Aquitaine** 95 rte de Bordeaux ☎640491
Frd

MARQUISE 62 (Pas-de-Calais) 5,050 (☎21)
Map **3** A1
★**Bon Sejour** 80 av Ferber (DP) ☎321107 Closed
16−30 Sep 8rm
★**Grand Cerf** 20 av Ferber ☎321039 Closed 16
Dec−14 Jan 10rm3⇄1🍴 🛏

MARSANNY See DIJON

MARSEILLE† 13 (Bouches-du-Rhône) 914,400
(☎91) Map **27** B2
| AA | agents; see page 149
★★★**Grand & Noailles** 66 Canebière ☎549148
tx430609 70⇄ P Lift sB⇄fr134 dB⇄262
(English breakfast) L60 D60
★★★**Splendide** 31 bd d'Athenes ☎397500 tx41939
138rm90⇄33🍴 🛏 Lift
★★★**Castellane** 31 r du Rouet ☎792754
47rm20⇄20🍴 🛏 P Lift sB61 sB⇄ 🍴85 dB78
dB⇄ 🍴105 (English breakfast) L29&alc D29&alc
★★★**Royal St George** 10 r du Capitaine Dessemond
(n rest) ☎525692 28⇄🍴 Lift sB⇄ 🍴78−94
dB⇄ 🍴107−128 (English breakfast)
★**Eden Corniche** 156 prom de la Corniche (n rest)
☎520189 18rm1⇄3🍴 🛏 🐶 sea

⌁ F Bertrand & ses Fils 243 bd National ☎625473 P
⌁ ⅏**Capucines** 59 allée L-Gambetta ☎640057 P
Ren (GB)
⌁ ⅏*Garcin* 72 r Monte Cristo ☎340766 P Sim
⌁ ⅏*Kennings* 69 bd N-Dame (Angle r Dragon)
☎376505 BL (GB)
At **Penne-St-Menet (La)** (10km E of A52)
☆☆☆*Novotel Marseille Est* (A52) ☎439060
tx400667 131⇌ P Lift sB⇌fr136 dB⇌fr172 English
breakfast only Pool
MARSEILLE AIRPORT
At **Marignane** (8km NW)
★★★**Sofitel** ☎899102 tx401980 180⇌ P Lift ♪
sB⇌184–205 dB⇌232–252 (English breakfast)
L fr50 D fr50 ✍ Pool
At **Vitrolles** (8km N)
☆☆☆ *Novotel Marseille Aéroport* (A7) ☎899044
tx420670 166⇌ P Lift sB⇌fr136 dB⇌fr172 English
breakfast only Pool
MARTEL 46 (Lot) 1,600 (☎65) Map **16** C2
At **Gluges** (5km SE on N681)
★★**Falaises** Ⅼ ☎373359 Closed 16 Dec–Jan
17rm4⇌ P sB36–57 dB48–54 dB⇌64–69 L25–75
D25–75
MARVEJOLS 48 (Lozère) 5,950 (☎66) Map **16** D2
★**Paix** Ⅼ 2 av de Brazza ☎321017 27rm5⇌11 ⋔
P sB55–69 sB⇌69–82 dB56–68 dB⇌67–84
(English breakfast) L18–36 D18–36 mountains
⌁ ⅏*Mairie* 16 av de Brazza ☎320086 Opl
MASSAT 09 (Ariège) 750 (☎61) Map **22** C4
★★**Trois Seigneurs** Ⅼ av de St-Girons ☎669589
Closed Nov–Feb 25rm20⇌ A10rm P ♪ sB47
sB⇌⋔52 dB59 dB⇌⋔88 (English breakfast)
L30–74 D30–74 mountains lake
MASSIAC 15 (Cantal) 2,100 (☎71) Map **16** D3
★★**Poste** av de Clermont Ferrand (N9) ☎230201
tx390794 Closed 11 Nov–14 Mar 37rm14⇌13 ⋔ P
Lift sB fr48 dB fr66
MAUBEUGE 59 (Nord) 35,500 (☎20) Map **3** B1
⌁ ⅏*Pont Rouge Willot* 2 av de Pont Rouge
☎647308 P Bed/Opl
MAULÉON-LICHARRE 64 (Pyrénées-Atlantiques)
4,500 (☎59) Map **20** C3
★★**Bidegain** 13 r de la Navarre ☎281605 Closed 16
Dec–14 Jan 30rm11⇌3 ⋔ P sB38–53
sB⇌⋔68–78 dB76–86 dB⇌⋔76–86 L32–55
D32–55 mountains
MAXILLY-PETITE-RIVE See **EVIAN-LES-BAINS**
MAYENNE 53 (Mayenne) 13,500 (☎43) Map **8** C3
★★**Grand** Ⅼ 2 r Ambroise de Loré ☎043735
29rm7⇌14 ⋔ P ♪ dB70–85 dB⇌⋔101–138
(English breakfast) L40 D40 river
★**Croix Couverte** rte de Paris ☎043248 11rm5⇌6 ⋔
A10rm ⋒ P dB103–118 dB⇌⋔103–118 L fr30
D fr30 ○
⌁ ⅏*Bassaler* 26 r P-Lintier ☎041584 P BMW (GB)
⌁ ⅏ F Blouin 17 bd Gl-Leclerc ☎041657 P
★★**Grand Balcon** sq G-Tournier ☎610114
tx520287 Closed 16 Dec–14 Jan 25rm8⇌14 ⋔ Lift
★**Fabre** 10 r Verdun ☎ 610269 18rm5⇌5 ⋔
MEAUX†77 (Seine-et-Marne) 43,150 (☎1)
Map **9** B3
★★**Sirène** 34 r Gl-Leclerc ☎4340780 16rm14⇌ P
Lift ♪ sB46–89 sB⇌69–89 dB121–133
dB⇌121–133
⌁ ⅏*Brie et Picardie* 44 r de la Crèche ☎4340651
Frd
⌁ ⅏*Vance* 37 av F-Roosevelt ☎4332976 Ren (GB)
MÉGÈVE 74 (Haute-Savoie) 5,300 (☎50) Map **28** C4
★★★*Edelweiss* ☎212526 Closed Apr–19 Dec
36rm24⇌2 ⋔ Lift ♪ sB⇌⋔140–170
dB⇌⋔160–200 (English breakfast) L50 mountains
★★★**Parc** (n rest in summer) ☎210574 Closed
Sep–Jun except Xmas & Etr 48⇌ P Lift ♪
sB⇌127–147 dB⇌164–194 L43–48 D43–48 St♧
mountains
★★★*Beauregard* rte d'Arbois ☎210556 Closed mid
Apr–Jun & Sep–14 Dec 28rm15⇌

MEILLERIE 74 (Haute-Savoie) 280 (☎50)
Map **11** A1
★*Terrasses* ☎760406 Closed Oct 16rm ⋒
MELUN†77 (Seine-et-Marne) 39,000 (☎1) Map **9** B3
☆☆**Ibis Melun** av de Meaux ☎0684245 40⇌ P Lift
sB⇌fr94 dB⇌fr114 L30–45alc D30–45alc
⌁ ⅏*Rolland* 44 av Thiers ☎4393640 Frd
MENDE 48 (Lozère) 12,000 (☎66) Map **27** A3
★★**France** Ⅼ 9 bd L-Arnault ☎650004 28rm21⇌2 ⋔
⋒ P sB38–48 sB⇌⋔63–73 dB82 dB⇌⋔82
L25–50 D25–50 mountains
★★**Lion d'Or** 12 bd Britexte ☎650646 tx480302
42rm22⇌20 ⋔ P Lift ♪ sB70–106 sB⇌⋔90–106
dB120–162 dB⇌⋔120–162 L35–75 D35–75 Pool
mountains lake
★★**Paris** 2 bd du Soubeyran ☎650003 Closed
Dec–Feb 50rm5⇌11 ⋔ ⋒ Lift
⌁ ⅏*Sevene* 19 av Ml-Foch ☎651737 ☎651620 P
Frd
MENTHON-ST-BERNARD 74 (Haute-Savoie) 850
(☎50) Map **28** C4
★★*Beau Sejour* ☎448204 Closed Oct–mid Apr
20rm3⇌15 ⋔ ⋒
MENTON†06 (Alpes-Maritimes) 25,300 (☎93)
Map **28** C2
★★★**Napoléon** 29 Porte de France ☎358950
tx470312 40⇌ P Lift ♪ sB⇌⋔124–169
dB⇌⋔158–228 L55 D55 Pool sea mountains
★★★**Princess & Richmond** 32 av Gl-de-Gaulle
(n rest) ☎358020 Closed 4 Nov–19 Dec
45rm39⇌6 ⋔ ⋒ P Lift ♪ sB⇌⋔85–105
dB⇌⋔110–130 sea
★★★**Viking** 2 av Gl-de-Gaulle (n rest) ☎358044
Closed 16 Oct–19 Dec 34⇌ ⋒ P Lift ♪
sB⇌⋔110–130 dB⇌⋔130–160
(English breakfast) Pool sea mountains
★★**Aiglon** 7 av de la Madone (n rest) ☎357523
Closed 21 Oct–19 Dec 30rm24⇌ P Lift ♪ sB60–70
sB⇌80–90 dB90–100 dB⇌115–140 Pool sea
mountains
★★**Floréal** cours du Centenaire (DP) ☎357581
62rm48⇌ P Lift sB53 sB⇌68 dB93 dB⇌105
mountains
★★**Londres** ☎357462 Closed 16 Oct–Dec
26rm5⇌15 ⋔ P Lift sB38 sB⇌⋔65 dB55 dB⇌⋔83
(English breakfast) L30 D30
★★**Parc** 11 av Verdun ☎357174 Closed 11 Oct–19
Dec 75rm60⇌8 ⋔ P Lift ♪ sB70–90
sB⇌⋔120–130 dB⇌⋔170–180
(English breakfast) L55–65 D55–65 mountains
★★**Prince de Galles** 4 av Gl-de-Gaulle (DP & Pn)
☎357101 Closed Nov 58rm28⇌3 ⋔ P Lift sB78–107
sB⇌⋔96–127 dB156–214 dB⇌⋔192–254
L40–45 D40–45 sea mountains
★★**Rives d'Azur** prom Ml-Joffre ☎357209
36rm15⇌3 ⋔ Lift ♪ sB fr48 sB⇌⋔98–109 dB75
dB⇌⋔125–137 L30–40 D30–40 Beach sea
mountains
★*Céline-Rose* 57 av Sospel (DP) ☎357469 36rm3⇌
⋒ Lift
⌁ ⅏*Ideal* 1 av Riviera ☎357920 Frd (GB)
MERCUES See **CAHORS**
MÉRÉVILLE 54 (Meurthe-et-Moselle) 1,908
Map **9** B3
★★**Maison Carrée** Ⅼ ☎470923 23rm13⇌9 ⋔ ⋒ P
sB65–90 sB⇌⋔65–90 dB84–99 dB⇌⋔84–99
(English breakfast) L20–81 D20–81
MERIGNAC See **BORDEAUX**
METZ†57 (Moselle) 117,200 (☎87) Map **11** A3
★★★★**Royal** 23 av Foch ☎683277 tx860425
76rm40⇌25 ⋔ Lift ♪ sB130 sB⇌⋔130 dB⇌⋔180
(English breakfast) L58 D58
★★★★*Sofitel* pl des Paraiges ☎745727 tx930328
115⇌ ⋒ P Lift sB⇌171–193 dB⇌222–252
(English breakfast) L35–70 D70 Pool
★★**Central** 3 bis r Vauban (n rest) ☎755343
tx930281 54rm36⇌18 ⋔ ⋒ Lift sB⇌⋔76–95
dB⇌⋔92–105 (English breakfast)

France

★★**Pergola**L̲ 103 rte Plappeville ☎302682
33rm7⇄11 📶 A8rm
🛢 🕬**A Kron** 4 r de l'Amphithéatre ☎742514 Maz
(GB)
🕬**Metz Automobiles** 11 r des Alliés ☎300244 P
BMW
At **Hauconcourt** (9.5km N on A31)
☆☆**Novotel** (A31) ☎305568 tx860191 128⇄ P Lift
sB⇄fr155 dB⇄fr167 English breakfast only Pool
At **Metz-Borny** (2km E)
🛢 🕬**Europe Automobiles** (N3) ☎741010 P Opl
MEYRUEIS 48 (Lozère) 1,100 (☎66) Map **27** A2
★★**Château d'Ayres** ☎456010 Closed Oct – 24 Mar
20rm8⇄6 📶
★★**Renaissance** (DP) ☎456019 30rm24⇄ A20rm
MIGENNES 89 (Yonne) 8,350 (☎86) Map **10** C2
★★**Paris**L̲ 57 av J-Jourès ☎802322 10rm4⇄ 📶 P
sB41 – 75 sB⇄73 dB55 – 91 dB⇄91 – 96
L25 – 60&alc D25 – 60&alc
MILLAU† 12 (Aveyron) 22,600 (☎65) Map **16** D2
★★★**International** 1 pl Tine ☎602066 100rm 📶 P
Lift 🌙 sB fr71 dB⇄ 📶 L121 L35 – 75
★★**Moderne** 11 av J-Jaurès ☎600123 Closed
Oct – 14 Mar 45rm 📶 P Lift 🌙 sB fr55 dB⇄ 📶92
L35 – 75
★**Causses** L̲ 26 av J-Jaurès ☎600319 24rm2⇄5 📶
📶 P sB fr34 dB fr43 dB⇄ 📶 fr58 L19 – 40 D19 – 40
mountains
MILLY 37 (Indre-et-Loire) (☎47) Map **8** D1
★**Château de Milly** ☎581456 Closed Jan 12rm8⇄
MIMIZAN 40 (Landes) (☎58) Map **15** A2
At **Mimizan Plage** (6km on D626)
★★**Côte d'Argent** av M-Martin ☎090708 Closed
Nov – mid Apr 73rm40⇄2 📶 A33rm P Lift 🌙 dB70
dB⇄ 📶131 D43 sea
MIRAIL (LE) See **TOULOUSE**
MIRAMAR 06 (Alpes-Maritimes) (☎93) Map **28** C2
★★★★**St-Christophe** (Pn) ☎903136 tx470878
40rm22⇄18 📶 📶 Lift Pool Beach sea
★★★**Tour de l'Esquillon** Rond-Point de l'Esquillon
☎903181 25⇄ 📶 Beach sea
MIRAMBEAU 17 (Charente-Maritime) 1,409 (☎46)
Map **15** B3
★**Union** ☎496164 14rm1 📶 A2rm 📶 P sB37 – 42
dB49 – 54 dB 📶64 – 69 L23 – 38 D23 – 38
MIREPOIX 09 (Ariège) 3,900 (☎61) Map **22** C4
★**Commerce** cours du Dr-Chabaud ☎681029
32rm7⇄9 📶 A7rm 📶 P sB42 – 69 sB⇄ 📶59 – 69
dB47 – 93 dB⇄ 📶65 – 93 L22 – 70 D22 – 70
MODANE 73 (Savoie) 5,150 (☎79) Map **28** C3
★**Europe** 33 r J-Ferry (DP) ☎050867 17rm 📶
MOISSAC 82 (Tarn-et-Garonne) 12,150 (☎63)
Map **16** C2
★★★**Moulin** 1 pl du Moulin ☎040355 Closed
16 Dec – Jan 37rm45⇄12 📶 P Lift sB⇄ 📶58 – 168
dB⇄ 📶116 – 181 (English breakfast) L40 – 70
D40 – 70 lake
★★**Chapon Fin** pl Recollets ☎040422 Closed Mar
33rm10⇄19 📶 📶
★**Pont Napoléon** ☎040155 Closed Nov – 14 Dec
20rm2⇄2 📶 📶 P dB43 – 47 dB⇄ 📶52 – 58
L24 – 60&alc D24 – 60&alc lake
MONESTIER-DE-CLERMONT 38 (Isère) 850 (☎76)
Map **27** B3
★**Major** (DP) ☎349111 Closed 21 Oct – 14 Nov 17rm
A11rm 📶
MONTARGIS 45 (Loiret) 19,900 (☎38) Map **9** B2
★★★**Poste** L̲ 2 pl V-Hugo (DP) ☎852277 tx780994
35rm9⇄12 📶 A4rm 📶
★**Tour d'Auvergne** 20 r J-Jaurès ☎850116 Closed
Feb 14rm8⇄4 📶 📶 P sB⇄ 📶63 – 78 dB45 – 55
dB⇄ 📶75 – 105 L25 – 70 D25 – 70
🛢 🕬**St-Christophe** 46 av d'Antibes Amilly ☎852284
Aud/VW
MONTAUBAN† 82 (Tarn-et-Garonne) 50,450 (☎63)
Map **16** C2
★★★**Ingres** 10 av Mayenne ☎633601 tx520319
36rm29⇄7 📶 📶 Lift

★★**Midi** 12 r N-Dame ☎631723 tx51630
62rm30⇄25 📶 A10rm 📶 P Lift 🌙 sB46 – 58
sB⇄ 📶60 – 120 dB56 – 72 dB⇄ 📶71 – 140
(English breakfast) L28 – 65 D28 – 65
★★**Trois Pigeons** 6 av du 11-Régt-d'Infantrie
(n rest Sat eve & 5 – 26 Aug) ☎034530
47rm10⇄24 📶 📶 Lift dB49 – 73 dB⇄ 📶55 – 80
L22 – 60 D22 – 60
★**Languedoc** 98 fbg Toulousain (n rest) ☎633215
14rm4 📶 A6rm 📶 P sB37 dB47 dB 📶55
★**Orsay** Face Gare ☎630057 Closed 1 – 19 Jun
30rm2⇄18 📶 📶 P sB37 – 63 sB⇄ 📶57 – 63 dB57 – 80
dB⇄ 📶64 – 82 L22alc D22alc
🕬**Delpoux** rte de Toulouse, zone Industrielle
☎630886 Aud/VW (GB)
🕬**J R Gardette** 111 quai Poult ☎633497 (GB)
🛢 🕬**SETAM** (P Gardette) 1724 av Toulouse
☎630483 P Frd
Sport 646 av J-Moulin ☎032750 P Closed Mon BL
(GB)
At **Montbeton** (3km W)
★★★**Hostellerie des Coulandrières** rte
Castlesarrasin ☎031809 22rm21⇄1 📶 P
sB⇄ 📶90 – 131 dB⇄ 📶97 – 164 (English breakfast)
L35 – 75 &alc D35 – 75 &alc lake
MONTBARD 21 (Côte-d'Or) 7,750 (☎80) Map **10** C2
★★**Gare** pl de la Gare ☎920212 16rm11 📶 📶
★★**Ecu** L̲ 7 r Auguste – Carré (DP & Pn) ☎921166
15rm9⇄4 📶 📶 P sB fr70 sB⇄ 📶70 dB fr140
dB⇄ 📶fr140 L35 – 100 D35 – 100
🛢 🕬**Montbard Automobile** 39 r d'Arbrantes
☎920623 ☎920623 Ren
MONTBAZON 37 (Indre-et-Loire) 2,450 (☎47)
Map **9** A2
★★★★**Château d'Artigny** ☎262424 tx750900
Closed 26 Nov – 9 Jan 58⇄ 📶 P Lift 🌙 sB⇄158 – 368
dB⇄186 – 396 (English breakfast) L72 – 160
D72 – 160 St% 🌙 Pool
★★★★**Tortinière** (1.5km N) ☎260019 tx750806
Closed Dec – 9 Mar 20⇄ sB⇄ 📶195 – 215 (room
only) dB⇄ 📶195 – 260 (room only) Pool
MONTBÉLIARD 25 (Doubs) 32,000 (☎81)
Map **11** A2
★★**Joffre** 35 av Joffre ☎912349 30rm11⇄9 📶 Lift
MONTCEAU-LES-MINES 71 (Saône-et-Loire)
28,250 (☎85) Map **10** C1
★★**Commerce** L̲ 16 quai J-Chagot ☎093418
33rm10⇄18 📶 📶 Lift
MONTCHANIN See **CREUSOT (LE)**
MONT-DE-MARSAN† 40 (Landes) 30,200 (☎58)
Map **15** B2
★★★**Richelieu** L̲ 3 r Château-Vieux ☎750016
75rm30⇄20 📶 📶 P Lift 🌙 sB41 – 48 sB⇄ 📶69 – 80
dB60 – 70 dB⇄ 📶96 – 105 (English breakfast)
L30 – 36 D30 – 36
☆☆**Motel le Bois Fleuri** rte de St-Sever (n rest)
☎752468 Pool
🛢 🕬**Continental** (G Fraresso) 839 av du MI-Foch
☎750677 BL
MONT-DORE (LE) 63 (Puy-de-Dôme) 2,350 (☎73)
Map **16** D3
★**Castelet** av M-Bertrand ☎210529 Closed Apr &
Nov 33rm11⇄
★**Mon Clocher** L̲ r M-Sauvagnat ☎210541 tx39794
Closed mid Apr – mid May & Oct – mid Dec 32rm4 📶
At **Pied du Sancy** (4km S on N683)
★★**Puy Ferrand** L̲ ☎210258 Closed Oct – 14 Dec
43rm23⇄12 📶 📶 P Lift sB35 – 95 sB⇄ 📶80 – 95
dB69 – 114 dB⇄ 📶94 – 114 L40 – 45 D40 – 45
mountains
MONTÉLIMAR† 26 (Drôme) 29,150 (☎75)
Map **27** B3
★★★**Relais de l'Empereur** pl M-Dormoy ☎012900
tx345537 Closed 10 N0v – 20 Dec 40rm30⇄5 📶
A1rm 📶 P 🌙 sB61 – 64 sB⇄ 📶165 – 117
dB⇄ 📶128 – 228 (English breakfast) L alc D alc
☆☆**Euromotel** rte de Marseille ☎011588 tx345126
Closed Nov – 14 Mar 51rm18⇄33 📶 Pool

★★**Sphinx** 19 bd Desmarais ☎018664 Closed
25–31 Dec 20rm13⇆7🛏 🏠 P sBfr68 sB⇆🛏78
dBfr76 dB⇆🛏86–145 (English breakfast)
🅿 &o*R Gros* 71 av du Teil ☎010807 Bed/Opl
🅿 &o*MR Magne* 7 fbg St-James ☎012055 Cit
🅿 &o*Peyrouse* pl d'Aygu ☎010231 M/c Frd (GB)
MONTIGNAC 24 (Dordogne) 3,250 (☎53)
Map **16** C3

★**Avenue** av J-Jaurès ☎518281 Closed Feb
16rm2⇆6🛏 P sB58–68 sB⇆68–74 dB48
dB⇆🛏81 L fr30 Dfr 30

★**Soleil d'Or**L2 16 r IV Septembre ☎518022 Closed
26 Nov–26 Dec 24rm7⇆4🛏A10rm 🏠 P sB33–42
sB⇆🛏52–60 dB48–54 dB⇆🛏63–84 L22–72
D22–72

★*Vanne Rouge* r Abbevoire ☎4248210 12rm9⇆
MONTLUCON† 03 (Allier) 58,850 (☎70) Map **16** D4
★★★**Terminus** 47 av M-Dormoy ☎052893
45rm8⇆25🛏 🏠 Lift
★★**Château St-Jean** parc St-Jean (1km S on rte de
Clemont-Ferrand) ☎050465 7rm5⇆1🛏 P
sB58–227 sB⇆🛏145–227 dB91–237
dB⇆🛏155–237 L43–85 D43–85 ○
★★**Univers** 38 av M-Dormoy (n rest) ☎053347
60rm24⇆24🛏 🏠 Lift
🅿 &o**Univers** 2 r de Valmy ☎051000 ❂ P BL
MONTMIRAIL 51 (Marne) 3,450 (☎26) Map **10** C3
★**Vert Galant** 2 pl Vert-Galant ☎422017 Closed Feb
14rm3🛏 🏠 P sB31–38 dB44–53 dB⇆🛏60–68
(English breakfast) L26–48 D26–48
🅿 &o**J Boussin** 4 pl R-Petit ☎422309 Cit
MONTMORILLON 86 (Vienne) 7,450 (☎49)
Map **16** C4
★★*France Mercier* 2 bd de Strasbourg (DP)
☎910051 Closed Jan–14 Feb 25rm7⇆4🛏 🏠
MONTOIRE-SUR-LE-LOIR 41 (Loir-et-Cher) 4,200
(☎39) Map **9** A2
★★**Cheval Rouge**L2 pl Ml-Foch ☎870705 Closed
Tue evening, Wed & Feb 17rm9⇆1🛏 🏠 P sB48–63
sB⇆🛏69–85 dB59–80 dB⇆🛏80–110 L37–88
D37–88 St%
MONTPELLIER 34 (Hérault) 195,650 (☎67)
Map **27** A2
★★★**Eden** av de la Pompignane ☎586024 tx48656
122⇆ Lift Pool
★★★**Frantel** 218 r du Bastian le Polygone ☎639063
tx480362 116⇆ 🏠 P Lift sB⇆🛏167–178
dB⇆184–212 (English breakfast) L62–120 &alc
D62–120 &alc
★★★**Grand Hotel & Midi** 22 bd V-Hugo (n rest)
☎926961 48rm34⇆8🛏
☆☆**Ibis** rte de Palavas ☎588230 tx480578 102⇆ P
Lift sB⇆fr102 dB⇆fr112 L30–45alc D30–45alc
🅿 &o**Auto Méditerranée** 49 av G-Clémenceau
☎921468 BMW (GB)
🅿 &o**Midi Automobile** r Mortels l'Eglise, zone
Industrialle ☎921986 P BL (GB)
At **Perols** (8km S adj to Montpellier Airport)
☆☆⇆**Euromotel** rte de Carnon ☎730304 tx480652
77⇆ Pool
At **St-Jean-de-Vedas** (5km W on N113)
&o**Imbert** rte de Sète ☎424622 P Frd (GB)
MONTREUIL (EURE-ET-LOIRE) See **DREUX**
MONTREUIL 62 (Pas-de-Calais) 3,200 (☎21)
Map **3** A1
★★★**Château de Montreuil** Chaussée des
Capucins ☎060011 14rm12⇆2🛏 A3rm 🏠 P ♪
sB⇆🛏100–140 dB⇆🛏120–160 L alc D alc ❂ Pool
★**Chez Edouard** 7–9 r de Change ☎061033 Closed
Oct 10rm2⇆1🛏 🏠 sB35–48 sB⇆🛏62–65
dB56–71 dB⇆🛏93–100 L25–40 D25–40
🅿 &o*Damour* av Gl-Leclerc ☎060691 Peu
MONTRICHARD 41 (Loir-et-Cher) 3,900 (☎39)
Map **9** A2
★★**Bellevue**L2 quai du Cher ☎320617 Closed 16
Nov–14 Dec 30rm27⇆3🛏 Lift sB⇆🛏77–134

dB⇆🛏121–143 (English breakfast) L fr55 D fr55 sea
river
★★*Croix Blanche* (N64) (DP) ☎320034
19rm3⇆3🛏 🏠
★★**Tête-Noir**L2 rte de Tours ☎320555 Closed Jan
42rm19⇆7🛏 A9rm P sB51–68 sB⇆🛏68 dBfr59
dB⇆🛏95 L49–63 D49–63
🅿 &o*Renault* 38 rte de Tours ☎320484 P Ren
MONT-ST-MICHEL (LE) 50 (Manche) 105 (☎33)
Map **8** C3
★★**Mère Poulard** ☎601401 Closed Oct–mid Apr
28rm16⇆6🛏 A14rm sB42–55 sB⇆🛏118–128
dBfr64 dB⇆🛏127–168 L75–155&alc
D75–155&alc
★★**Digue**L2 ☎601402 Closed Nov–mid Apr
35rm22⇆3🛏 P sB⇆🛏93–100 dB61–70
dB⇆🛏106–130 L30–50 D30–50
★★**Guesalin** L2 (DP) ☎601410 Closed Nov–Feb
13rm5⇆4🛏 sea
☆☆**K**L2 (2km on D976) ☎601418 tx170537 Closed
Nov–Feb 60⇆ sB⇆103 dB⇆136
MOREZ 39 (Jura) 7,200 (☎82) Map **10** D 1
★★**Central Modern** 106 r de la République
☎330307 52rm12⇆1🛏 A24rm 🏠 P sB41–43
sB⇆🛏64–74 dB53–63 dB⇆🛏87–102
(English breakfast) L31–65 D31–65 mountains
🅿 &o*Morez Autos* (Rathier & Cie) 74 r République
☎331470 P
MORGAT 29 (Finistère) 7,030 (☎98) Map **7** A3
★★**Ste-Marine** (DP) ☎810801 Closed 26 Sep–
24 Mar 36rm16⇆20🛏 Lift sea
★*Julia* ☎810589 Closed 21 Sep–May 30rm10⇆
MORLAIX† 29 (Finistère) 20,550 (☎98) Map **7** B3
★★★**Grand Hotel d'Europe** 1 r d'Aiguillon ☎882258
60rm38⇆5🛏 Lift
MORTAGNE-AU-PERCHE 61 (Orne) 5,150 (☎34)
Map **9** A3
★*Tribunal* pl Palais ☎250477 Closed Jan
14rm6⇆1🛏 A8rm P sBfr35 dBfr46 dB⇆🛏64–91
L27–44 D27–44
MORTAIN 50 (Manche) 3,150 (☎33) Map **8** C3
★*Cascades*L2 16 r du Bassin ☎590003 Closed Oct
14rm3⇆1🛏 🏠 sBfr35 dBfr49 dB⇆🛏fr79
(English breakfast) L25–75 D25–75
MORZINE 74 (Haute-Savoie) 2,657 (☎50)
Map **28** C4
★★**Dahu** ☎791112 tx385620 Closed 16 Apr–Jun
& Sep–17 Dec 26rm18⇆4🛏 P sB58–77
sB⇆🛏78–93 dB113–130 dB⇆🛏123–180
(English breakfast) L48–58 D46–56 mountains
MOUGINS 06 (Alpes-Maritimes) 8,500 (☎93)
Map **28** C2
★★★*Clos des Boyères* ☎900158 20rm15⇆ ❂ Pool
MOULINS† 03 (Allier) 26,950 (☎70) Map **9** B1
★★★**Paris** 21 r de Paris ☎440058 tx990512 Closed
1–21 Feb 29rm22⇆7🛏 🏠 P Lift ♪ sB92–182
sB⇆🛏107–182 dB104–194 dB⇆🛏119–194
(English breakfast) L fr80 D fr80
★★**Moderne** 5 pl J-Moulin ☎440506 44rm4⇆19🛏
🏠 Lift sBfr64 dB73–88 dB⇆🛏113 L35–55 D35–55
★**Parc**L2 24 pl République ☎441225 25rm3⇆21🛏
🏠 P ♪ sBfr69 sB⇆🛏fr69 dB fr78 dB⇆🛏fr78
L32–70 D32–70
MOUTHIER 25 (Doubs) 350 (☎81) Map **11** A1
★★**Manoir** 21 Grand r ☎870637 Closed Oct–Mar
17rm(5⇆🛏
★*Cascade*L2 ☎621900 16rm3⇆6🛏 🏠 P dB56–58
dB⇆🛏66–93 L30–65 D30–65 mountains
MOUTIERS 73 (Savoie) (☎79) Map **28** C4
☆☆**Ibis** Colline de Champoulet ☎242711 tx980611
64⇆ P Lift sB⇆fr88 dB⇆fr112 L30–45alc
D30–45alc mountains
MULHOUSE† 68 (Haut-Rhin) 119,350 (☎89)
Map **11** B2
★★★**Frantel** 4 pl Gl-de-Gaulle ☎460123 tx881807
96⇆ 🏠 Lift sB⇆167–192 dB⇆219–254 L62alc
D62alc

France

★★ *Bourse* 14 r de la Bourse (off av Ml-Foch) (n rest)
☎456685 50rm13⇌37 🖩 Lift

At **Rixheim** (5km E on N66)

Ott & Wetzel r de Mulhouse ☎440137 BL/Jag/Rov
Tri

At **Sausheim** (6km NE on D422)

☆☆☆***Mercure*** ☎445440 tx881757 99⇌ P Lift
sB⇌fr137 dB⇌fr147 Pool

☆☆☆***Novotel*** r de l'Ile Napoléon ☎444444 tx881673
77⇌ P Lift sB⇌fr137 dB⇌fr163 English breakfast
only Pool

MURAT 15 (Cantal) 3,050 (☎71) Map **16** D3
★★ *Grand Hotel & Messageries* ☎200404 Closed
Jan 30rm11⇌4 🖩 🏠

MUSE (LA) See **ROZIER (LE)**

NAJAC 12 (Aveyron) 950 (☎65) Map **16** C2
★★ *Miquel* ☎457080 Closed 16–28 Feb & 1–15 Nov
31rm12🖩 A7rm ☎ P sBfr30 sB🖩fr44 dBfr40
dB🖩fr55 L19–36 D19–36 mountains
★ *Belle Rive* (2km on D39) ☎457420 Closed
Nov–14 Mar 34rm6⇌16 🖩 A4rm ☎ P dBfr46
dB⇌🖩59–72 (English breakfast) L20–35 D20–35
mountains

NANCY† 54 (Meurthe-et-Mosel) 111,500 (☎28)
Map **11** A3
★★★ *Frantel Nancy* 11 r R-Poincare ☎356101
tx960034 192⇌ 🏠 Lift ♪ sB⇌185 dB⇌204–215
(English breakfast) L62–90 D62–90
★★★ *Grand Concorde* 2 pl Stanisles ☎350301
tx960367 60rm34⇌19 🖩 Lift ♪ sB74
sB⇌🖩130–150 dB fr118 dB⇌🖩180–198
(English breakfast) L fr50 D fr50
★★★ *Palais* 48 r St-Jean ☎354732 tx960525
70rm38⇌ Lift sB49–54 sB⇌75–93 dB70–76
dB⇌95–120
★★ *Americain* 61 r P-Sémard (n rest) ☎362853
tx961052 51rm26⇌25 🖩 Lift ♪ sB⇌🖩60–126
dB⇌🖩77–147 (English breakfast) L21–25 D21–25
★★ *Poincaré* 81 r R-Poincaré (n rest) ☎402599
25rm7 🖩 sB fr39 sB 🖩fr59 dB fr54 dB 🖩fr70
🛅 🕭*H Gras* 11 r A-Lebrun ☎365175 Frd (GB)
SOVAN av de Strasbourg ☎528801 P (Closed
wknds) MB/Opl

At **Houdemont** (6km S)

☆☆☆***Novotel Nancy-Sud*** rte d'Espinal (N57)
☎551198 tx961124 86⇌ P Lift sB⇌fr135 dB⇌fr177
English breakfast only Pool

At **Laxou** (3km SW)

☆☆☆***Mercure Nancy Ouest*** 10 r de Saone ☎963710
tx850014 100⇌ P Lift sB⇌fr138 dB⇌fr150 English
breakfast only Pool 🕭
☆☆☆***Novotel Nancy Ouest*** (N4) ☎966746
tx850988 119⇌ P Lift sB⇌fr137 dB⇌fr166 English
breakfast only Pool
☆☆☆***Sofitel*** r de la Saone ☎964221 tx850036 100⇌
P Lift sB⇌177–203 dB⇌224–244
(English breakfast) L alc D alc Pool

NANS-LE-PINS 83 (Var) 1,000 (☎94) Map **27** B2
★★★ *Châteauneuf* (3.5km N) ☎789006 Closed
Dec–Mar 30rm19⇌9 🖩 P sB57–62 sB⇌🖩86
dB⇌🖩134–194 L55 D55 ⨂ Pool

NANTES 44 (Loire-Atlantique) 263,700 (☎40)
Map **8** C2
★★★★ *Sofitel* r A-Millerand, Ile Beaulieu ☎476103
tx710990 100⇌ 🏠 P Lift sB⇌164–231
dB⇌212–277 (English breakfast) L fr26 D fr35 St%
Pool
★★★ *Central* 4 r Couedic ☎717105 tx700666
143rm90⇌43 🖩 Lift
★★★ *Frantel* 3 r du Dr Zamenhof, Ile Beaulieu
☎471058 tx711440 150⇌ 🏠 P Lift sB⇌167–192
dB⇌219–254 dB⇌219–254 L62alc D62alc
★★ *Bourgogne* 9 allée du Commandant Charcot
(n rest) ☎740334 tx700610 42rm20⇌22 🖩 P Lift ♪

sB⇌🖩64–95 dB⇌🖩81–123 (English breakfast)
★★ *Graslin* 1 r Piron (off pl Graslin) (n rest) ☎713561
46rm8⇌16 🖩 Lift
★ *Astoria* 11 r Richebourg (n rest) ☎743990
45rm12⇌32 🖩 P Lift ♪ sB64–85 sB⇌🖩94–110
dB⇌🖩103–124
🛅 🕭*Grimaud* 64 bd J-Verne ☎495141 Hon/Toy
🛅 🕭*Auto Selection* 42 bis r des Hautes-Pavés
☎733314 P Maz/Vlo

At **Carquefou** (4km E on D337, off N23)

☆☆☆***Mercure*** ☎492924 tx710962 78⇌ P lift
sB⇌fr147 Db⇌fr160 English breakfast only Pool
☆☆☆***Novotel Nantes Carquefou*** allée des Sapins
☎493284 tx711175 99⇌ P Lift sB⇌fr145 dB⇌fr157
English breakfast only Pool

NANTIAT See **CROUZILLE (LA)**

NANTUA 01 (Ain) 3,650 (☎74) Map **27** B4
★★★ *France* 44 r Dr-Mercier ☎765055 Closed 31
Oct–19 Dec 19⇌ 🏠 P sB⇌90–110 dB⇌120–170
L65–100alc D65–100alc St% mountains
★★ *Lac* 15 av de la Gare ☎765012 Closed Nov–14
Dec 18rm14⇌2 🖩 P sB53–86 sB⇌🖩58–86
dB61–98 dB⇌🖩90–111 (English breakfast)
L40–120 D40–120 mountains
★★ *Lyon* 19 r Dr-Mercier ☎765043 Closed Oct
18rm4⇌5 🖩 P dB60 dB⇌🖩74–105 L27–61
D27–61 mountains

NAPOULE-PLAGE (LA) 06 (Alpes-Maritimes) 3,000
(☎93) Map **28** C2
★★★★ *Ermitage du Riou* bd de Mer ☎389556
tx470072 40rm35⇌5 🖩 P Lift ♪ sB⇌🖩90–320
dB⇌🖩110–355 (English breakfast) L alc D alc Pool
sea mountains
★★★ *Beau Rivage* rte Cannes ☎389191 tx46878
Closed Nov–19 Dec 40rm38⇌8 🖩
★★ *Beele Auberge* bd H-Clews ☎389508 Closed 16
Nov–14 Dec 11rm1⇌9 🖩 Beach 🕊 ☌ sea
★★ *Rocomare* ☎389536 Closed 16 Oct–14 Mar
12rm 6 🖩 sea

NARBONNE† 11 (Aude) 40,550 (☎68) Map **22** D4
☆☆☆***Novotel Narbonne Sud*** zone Industrielle, rte
de Perpignon ☎325481 tx500480 96⇌ P Lift
sB⇌fr139 dB⇌fr161 English breakfast only Pool
★★ *Dorade* 44 r J-Jaures (n rest) ☎326595 tx500428
44rm6⇌8 🖩 P Lift ♪ sB34–38 (room only)
sB⇌🖩37–62 (room only) dB34–49 (room only)
dB⇌🖩62–81 (room only)
★★ *Languedoc* 22 bd Gambetta ☎322888 tx290987
45rm18⇌13 🖩 Lift
★★ *Residence* 6 r Premier Mai (n rest) ☎321941
tx500428 26rm14⇌12 🖩 🏠 ♪ sB⇌🖩78–93
dB⇌🖩100–135 (English breakfast)
★★ *Terminus* 2 av P-Sémard (n rest) ☎320275
33rm2⇌2 🖩
★ *Lion d'Or* 39 av P-Semard ☎320692 Closed Feb
25rm7⇌8 🖩 🏠 P dB50–54 dB⇌🖩59–74 L25–60
D25–60
🕭*Fralsse* 36 bd F-Mistral ☎320631 BL
🛅 🕭*J Gabriel* 4 bd M-Sembat ☎320246 Frd (GB)
🛅 🕭*Languedoclenne Distribution Autos* 84 av
Carnot ☎322720 P Ren

At **Narbonne Plage** (15km E on D68 & D168)

★★ *Caravelle* bd du Front de Mer (DP) ☎338038
Closed Nov–Mar 24 🖩 sea

NEMOURS 77 (Seine-et-Marne) 11,250 (☎1)
Map **9** B3
☆☆☆***Euromotel*** (A6) (n rest) ☎4281032 tx690243
102⇌ P sB⇌116 dB⇌152
★★ *Ecu de France* 3 r de Paris ☎4281154 28rm 🏠 P
♪ sBfr45 sB⇌🖩75–85 dBfr53 dB⇌🖩83–93
L32–110 & alc D32–110 & alc St%
★ *Roches* av d'Oremsson (at St Pierre) ☎4280143
Closed Oct 17rm7⇌6 🖩 A6rm 🏠 P sB40
sB⇌🖩65–87 dB74–96 dB⇌🖩96–119
(English breakfast) L29–70 D29–70
★ *St Pierre* 10 av Carnot (n rest) ☎4280157 Closed
16 Jan–14 Feb 25rm2⇌10 🖩 🏠 P sB46–49
sB⇌🖩72–80 dB54–57 dB⇌🖩80–89
🛅 🕭*Gambetta* 70 av Gambetta ☎4280546

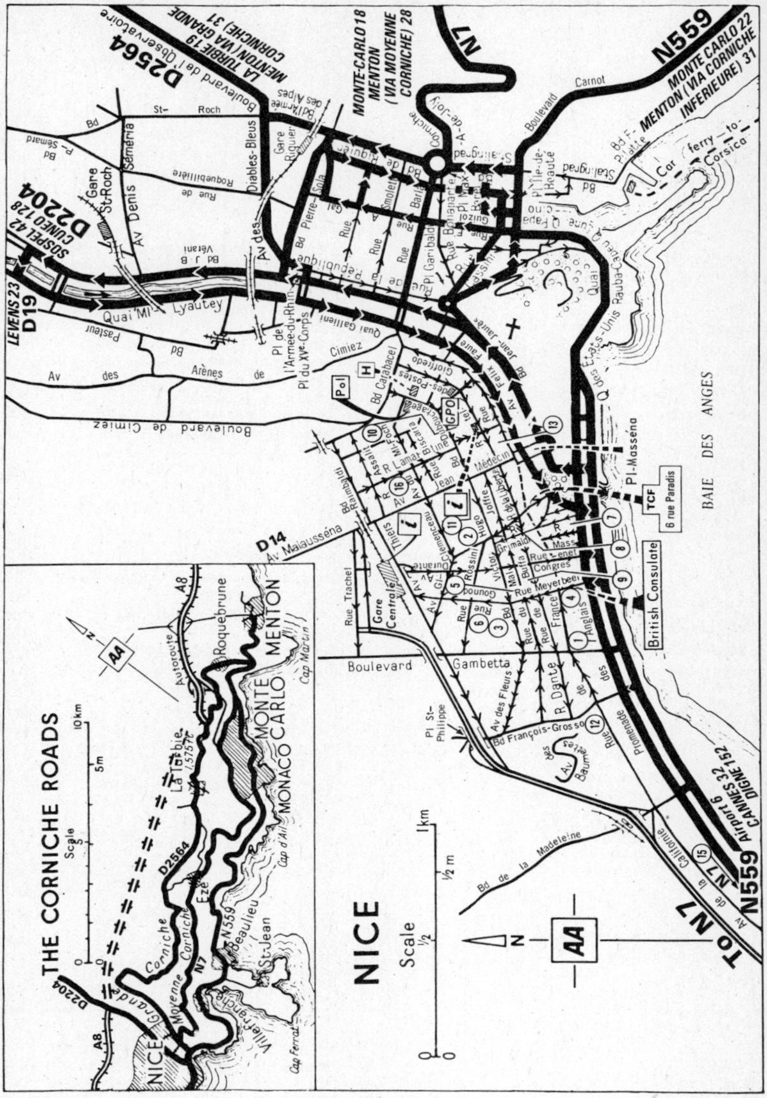

THE CORNICHE ROADS

NICE

Scale

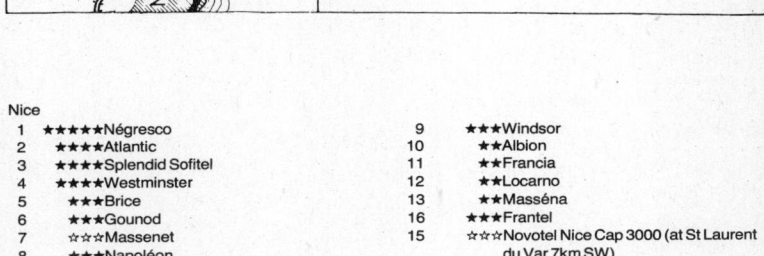

Nice
1 ★★★★★Négresco
2 ★★★★Atlantic
3 ★★★★Splendid Sofitel
4 ★★★★Westminster
5 ★★★Brice
6 ★★★Gounod
7 ☆☆☆Massenet
8 ★★★Napoléon

9 ★★★Windsor
10 ★★Albion
11 ★★Francia
12 ★★Locarno
13 ★★Masséna
16 ★★★Frantel
15 ☆☆☆Novotel Nice Cap 3000 (at St Laurent du Var 7km SW)

France

NEPOULAS PAR CAMPREIGNAC 87 (Haute-Vienne) Map **16** C3
☆☆*Motel Relais St-Eutrope* (N20) ☎399121 Closed 9 Jan – 7 Feb 20⇄

NEUF-BRISACH 68 (Haut-Rhin) 2,600 (☎89)
Map **11** B2
At **Volgelgrun** (5km E on N415)
☆☆*Motel l'Européen* (DP) ☎725157 22rm13⇄9🗄
Pool

NEUFCHÂTEL-EN-BRAY 76 (Seine-Maritime)
6,150 (☎35) Map **9** B4
★★*Grand Cerf* 9 Grand r (DP) ☎930002 Closed Dec
14rm1⇄4🗄 ▥
★*Mouton d'Or* 21 pl N-Dame ☎931460 Closed 16
Dec – 14 Jan 15rm
🛉 ●*Lechopler* 31 r St-Pierre ☎930082 ☎930476
Ren
At **Hayons (Les)** (7km W on N28)
★*Escale* Closed 16 Dec – 14 Jan 16rm7🗄 ▥

NEUVILLE-EN-FERRAIN See **TOURCOING**

NEVERS†58 (Nièvre) 47,750 (☎86) Map **9** B1
★★★*Magdalena* rte de Paris (n rest) ☎572141
40rm30⇄10🗄 ▥ P Lift 🌙 sB⇄🗄99 – 119
dB⇄🗄128 – 158 (English breakfast)
★★★*St-Louis* 🏷 2 pl Mosse ☎572710 Closed 7
Jan – 27 Feb 12⇄
★★*Molière* r Molière (n rest) ☎572996 18rm3⇄15🗄
★*Ste-Marie* 25 r Petit-Mouesse ☎611002 Closed 16
Jan – Feb 17rm5⇄3🗄 A9rm P sB44 – 73
sB⇄🗄58 – 73 dB66 – 81 dB⇄🗄87 – 102 L23 – 31
D23 – 31
🛉 ●*Nandrot & Verma* 4 av Colbert ☎610332 P
Bed/BMW/Opl (GB)
●*Tenailles* 18 r Pasteur ☎610674 BL

NICE†06 (Alpes-Maritimes) 346,650 (☎93)
Map **28** C2 **See Plan page 199**
★★★★★*Négresco* 37 prom des Anglais ☎883951
tx46040 Plan **1** 188⇄ Lift
★★★★*Atlantic* 12 bd V-Hugo ☎884015 tx460840
Plan **2** 120⇄ P Lift 🌙 sB⇄110 – 150 dB⇄160 – 220
(English breakfast) L fr45 D fr45
★★★★*Splendid Sofitel* 50 bd V-Hugo ☎886954
tx460938 Plan **3** 130⇄ ▥ Lift 🌙 sB⇄210 – 230
dB⇄240 – 260 (English breakfast) L fr50 D fr50 Pool
★★★★*Westminster* 27 prom des Anglais ☎882944
tx460872 Plan **4** Closed 6 Nov – 15 Dec
110rm103⇄7🗄 Lift 🌙 sB⇄🗄132 – 172
dB⇄🗄224 – 244 English breakfast only L55 D55 sea
★★★*Brice* 44 r MI-Joffre ☎881444 tx470658 Plan **5**
Lift 🌙 sB⇄🗄85 – 97 dB⇄🗄120 – 140
(English breakfast) L fr38 D fr38
★★★*Frantel* 28 av Notre-Dame ☎803024 tx470662
Plan **16** 201⇄ Lift ▥ sB⇄🗄203 – 266
dB⇄246 – 316 L62alc D62alc Pool
★★★*Gounod* 3 r Gounod (n rest) ☎882620
tx460938 Plan **6** 45rm35⇄10🗄 ▥ P Lift 🌙
sB⇄🗄110 – 120 dB⇄🗄130 – 150
(English breakfast)
☆☆*Massenet* 11 r Massenet ☎871131 Plan **7** 46⇄
▥ P Lift sB⇄🗄130 – 151 dB⇄155 – 206
(English breakfast)
★★★*Napoléon* 6 r Grimaldi ☎877007 tx460949
Plan **8** 80⇄ Lift 🌙 sB⇄109 – 129 dB⇄153 – 173
(English breakfast)
★★★*Windsor* 11 r Dalpozzo ☎885935 tx970072
Plan **9** 60rm33⇄22🗄 ▥ Lift 🌙 sB⇄🗄110 – 130
dB⇄🗄125 – 140 ●
★★*Albion* 25 bd Dubouchage (DP) ☎805733
tx46878 Plan **10** 87rm18⇄11🗄 ▥ Lift
★★*Francia* 4 bd V-Hugo ☎878945 tx46840 Plan **11**
42rm25⇄5🗄 Lift
★★*Locarno* 4 av des Baumettes (n rest) ☎885494
tx460979 Plan **12** 50rm25⇄25🗄 ▥ Lift
sB⇄🗄75 – 85 dB⇄🗄102 – 108 (English breakfast)
★★*Masséna* 5 r Gioffredo (n rest) ☎854925
tx470192 Plan **13** 115rm105⇄10🗄 Lift 🌙
sB⇄🗄110 – 155 dB⇄🗄155 – 210
(English breakfast)

🛉 ●*Albert 1er* 7 r Halévy ☎879948 Toy
●*Azur-Autos* (M R Heyberger) r G-Garaud, quartier
de Riquier ☎893629 P Closed Sat BMW (GB)
🛉 ●*Europ Motors* 5 r Maccarani (off r de France)
☎871181 Vlo (GB)
●*Michigan Motors* 3 bd de l'Armée des Alpes
☎890077 Closed Sat Opl (GB)
🛉 ●*PCA* 6 bis r Massingy ☎800447 Frd (GB)
At **St-Laurent du Var** (7km SW off N7)
☆☆☆*Novotel Nice Cap 3000* av de Verdun
☎316115 tx470643 103⇄ P Lift sB⇄fr143
dB⇄fr170 English breakfast only Pool

NIEUIL 16 (Vharente) 950 (☎45) Map **16** C3
★★★*Château de Nieuil* (E on N739) ☎713401
Closed 16 Nov – 14 Dec 12rm10⇄2🗄 ▥

NÎMES†30 (Gard) 134,000 (☎66) Map **27** A2
★★★★*Imperator* pl A-Briand ☎219030 tx490635
Closed Feb 64rm35⇄29🗄 A4rm ▥ Lift
★★★*Sofitel* chemin de l'Hostellerie, bd
Périphérique Sud ☎844044 tx490644 100⇄🗄 P Lift
sB⇄🗄161 – 192 dB⇄🗄203 – 235 L fr60 D fr60
★★★*Cheval Blanc et des Arènes* pl des Arènes
☎673205 48rm26⇄22🗄 Lift 🌙 sB⇄🗄95 – 125
dB⇄🗄119 – 134 L fr42 D fr42
☆☆*Novotel Nîmes Ouest* bd Peripherique
☎846020 tx480675 96⇄ P Lift sB⇄fr138 dB⇄fr172
English breakfast only Pool
★★*Carrière* 6 r Grizot ☎672489 tx49926
55rm15⇄35🗄 ▥ Lift
Automatic Station 11 bis bd Talabot ☎676048 Dat
(GB)
●*Mediterranée Autos* 64 r de la République
☎840801 (Closed wknds) Frd
🛉 ●*Renault* (RNUR) 1412 rte Montpellier ☎846000
Ren
At **Marguerittes** (7km on N86)
☆☆*Marguerittes* ☎844071 48🗄 A12rm P sB🗄66
dB🗄77

NIORT†79 (Deux-Sèvres) 64,000 (☎48) Map **15** B4
★★★*Brèche* 8 av Bujault ☎244178 tx790624 Closed
23 Dec – Mar 50rm19⇄26🗄 P Lift 🌙 sB55 – 69
sB⇄🗄91 – 109 dB⇄🗄122 – 133
★★*Grand* 32 av Paris (n rest) ☎242221 tx790624
40rm10⇄ ▥ P Lift 🌙 sB fr63 sB⇄fr86 dB⇄116
(English breakfast)
★*Terminus* 80 r de la Gare ☎240038
45rm20⇄15🗄 ▥ Lift
🛉 ●*Aumonier* 40 rte de Niort, Aiffres ☎244796 P BL
Hurtaud rte de la Rochelle ☎244469
MB/Opl (GB)

NOGENT-LE-ROTROU 28 (Eure-et-Loir) 13,600
(☎37) Map **9** A3
★★*Dauphin* 39 r Villette-Gate ☎521730 Closed 26
Jan – Feb 26rm5⇄6🗄 ▥ P 🌙 sB55 – 105
sB⇄🗄95 – 110 dB75 – 100 dB⇄🗄110 – 130 L38 – 60
D38 – 60

NOIRÉTABLE 42 (Loire) 2,000 (☎77) Map **27** A4
★★*Chaumière* r de la République ☎247300 Closed
Feb 28rm9⇄6🗄 A8rm
🛉 ●*Reparations* (C Dejob) ☎247031 🚗 P Ren

NOLAY 21 (Côte-d'Or) (☎80) 1,700 Map **10** C1
★*Ste-Marie* 36 r de la République ☎217319 Closed 3
Jan – 1 Feb 13rm4🗄 P sB36 – 52 sB🗄fr52 dB43 – 59
dB🗄59 – 72 (English breakfast) L22 – 50
D22 – 50

NONANCOURT 27 (Eure) 1,900 (☎32) Map **9** A3
★*Grand Cerf* 17 Grand r (DP) ☎581527 9rm5🗄 ▥

NONTRON 24 (Dordogne) 4,100 (☎53) Map **16** C3
★*Grand* 🏷 3 pl Agard ☎560001 Closed 16 – 31 Jan
26rm10⇄6🗄 ▥ P Lift 🌙 sB33 – 48 sB⇄🗄43 – 61
dB50 – 53 dB⇄🗄55 – 95 (English breakfast) L30 – 70
D20 – 70

NOUAN-LE-FUZELIER 41 (Loir-et-Cher) 2,300
(☎39) Map **9** B2
★*Moulin de Villiers* rte Chaon (3km NE by D44)
☎087227 Closed 6 Jan – 14 Mar & 1 – 14 Sep
20rm8⇄5🗄

NOUVION-EN-THIÉRACHE (LE) 02 (Aisne) 3,300
(☎23) Map **10** C4
★**Paix** 37 r V-Vicary ☎970455 Closed 14 Dec – 16
Jan 26rm6⇄6🛏 A2rm 🏠

NOVES 13 (Bouches-du-Rhône) 3,600 (☎90)
Map **27** B2
★★★**Auberge de Noves** ☎941921 tx431312 Closed
Feb 22⇄🛏 A5rm 🏠 P dB⇄🛏201 – 356 L90 – 132
D132 St% Pool

NOYELLES-GODAULT See **HENIN-BEAUMONT**
NOYON 60 (Oise) 14,050 (☎4) Map **9** B4
★★**Grillon** 37 – 39 r St-Éloi ☎4440087 Closed 6
Jun – 24 Jul & 24 – 29 Dec 38rm11⇄22🛏 A4rm 🏠
★**St-Eloi** 81 bd Carnot ☎4440149 25rm5⇄ A12rm P
sB29 – 87 sB⇄44 – 87 dB41 – 94 dB⇄51 – 94
L25 – 60&alc D25 – 60&alc

NOZAY 44 (Loire-Atlantique) 3,250 (☎40) Map **8** C2
🛢 🛱**Renault** 1 rte de Nantes ☎794802 Ren

NYONS 26 (Drôme) 5,950 (☎75) Map **27** B3
★★**Colombet** ℒℰ pl de la Libération ☎260366 Closed
26 Oct – 9 Dec 32rm9⇄9🛏 🏠 Lift ⅅ sB44 – 49
sB⇄🛏89 – 99 dB63 – 68 dB⇄🛏108 – 148 L35 – 70
D35 – 70 mountains

OBERNAI 67 (Bas-Rhin) 8,411 (☎88) Map **11** B3
★★**Duc d'Alsace** ℒℰ 6 pl de la Gare ☎955534 Closed
15 Jan – 15 Mar 16rm⇄🛏 P sB⇄fr128 dB⇄fr136
(English breakfast) L21 – 90 D21 – 90 St%

OLÉRON (ILE D') 17 (Charente-Maritime) (☎46)
Map **15** B3/4

Cotinière (la)
☆☆☆**Motel Ile de Lumière** (n rest) ☎471080 Closed
Nov – Mar 46rm20⇄26🛏 Pool Beach sea

Remigeasse (La)
★★★**Grand Large** ☎470818 Closed Dec – Feb 12rm
S4rm sB128 – 218 🏊 Pool sea

St-Trojan-les-Bains
☆☆☆**Novotel Oléron St Trojan** ☎760246 tx790910
80⇄ P Lift Pool sea

OLIVET 45 (Loiret) 12,400 (☎38) Map **9** B2
★★★**Beauvoir** r Beauvoir ☎635757 25rm9⇄6🛏 🏊
★★**Rivage & Reine Blanche** ℒℰ r Reine Blanche
☎660293 taOrleans tx760926 90rm80⇄4🛏 P Lift ⅅ
sB⇄🛏108 – 134 dB⇄🛏138 – 155
(English breakfast) L fr51 D fr51 St%

OLLIÈRES-SUR-EYRIEUX 07 (Ardèche) 800 (☎75)
Map **27** B3
★**Vallée** ℒℰ ☎652032 11rm

OLORON-STE-MARIE 64 (Pyrénées Atlantiques)
13,150 (☎59) Map **20** C3
★**Béarn Lardonnere** 4 pl de Mairie ☎390099
Closed Feb 27rm10⇄ A6rm 🏠

ORANGE† 84 (Vaucluse) 26,500 (☎90) Map **27** B2
☆☆☆☆**Euromotel Orange** rte de Caderousse
☎342410 98⇄ P sB⇄117 dB⇄149
(English breakfast) L fr40 D fr40 Pool mountains
★★**Louvre & Terminus** 89 av F-Mistral (n rest)
☎341008 Closed 16 Dec – 14 Jan 40rm23⇄17🛏 🏠
Lift
★★**Princes** 7 av de l'Arc de Triomphe ☎343016
47rm11⇄5🛏 Lift
🛢 ♦**G Ameller Station Bon Soleil** rte de Avignon
☎341234 Opl/Vau (GB)
🛢 ♦♦**Chaix** 20 av Gl-Leclerc ☎345101 P Toy (GB)
🛢 ♦**Princes** 2 – 10 av de l'Arc ☎340747 BL/Dat

ORLÉANS† 45 (Loiret) 110,000 (☎38) Map **9** B2
★★★★**Sofitel** 44 – 46 quai Barentin ☎621739
tx780073 110⇄ 🏠 P ⅅ sB⇄187 – 242
dB⇄244 – 309 (English breakfast) L fr55 D fr55 Pool
★★★**Arcades** 14 quai Cypierre (n rest) ☎627410
29rm14⇄6🛏 Lift

★★★**Cedres** 17 r du Ml-Foch (n rest) ☎622292
tx760912 32rm22⇄4🛏 Lift ⅅ sB63 sB⇄🛏81 – 99
dB72 dB⇄🛏90 – 119
★★**Grand** 21 r Bannier ☎871979 32rm8🛏 Lift
★★**Terminus** 40 r de la République ☎872464
55rm38⇄6🛏 P Lift ⅅ sB fr73 sB⇄🛏fr93 dB fr86
dB⇄🛏fr106 L fr30 D fr30
🛢 🛱**Gare** 38 r A-Dessaux, Fleury-les-Aubrais
☎872354 Frd
🛢 **Lion Fort** 44 bd J-Jaurès ☎625829 BL/Tri
At **St Jean-de-Braye** (3km E on N152)
🛢 🛱**Auto Sport** rte de Gien, St-Jean-de-Braye
☎891547 AR
At **Saran** (2km NW adj to A10 autoroute)
☆☆**Ibis** La Chiperie ☎883993 tx760902 108⇄ Lift
At **Source (La)** (10km S of N20)
☆☆☆**Novotel Orléans-Sud** r H-de Balzac ☎630428
tx760619 118⇄ P Lift sB⇄fr153 dB⇄fr163 English
breakfast only Pool

ORSAY 91 (Essonne) 19,500 (☎1) Map **9** B3
At **Courtaboeuf** (3km S on D35)
☆☆☆**Mercure** ☎9076386 tx691247 114⇄ P Lift
sB⇄fr159 dB⇄fr172 English breakfast only Pool

OUTREAU See **BOULOGNE-SUR-MER**
OYONNAX 01 (Ain) 23,350 (☎74) Map **27** B4
★**Nouvel** 31 r R-Nicod (n rest) ☎772811 37rm6⇄8🛏
🏠 Lift

PACY-SUR-EURE 27 (Eure) 3,600 (☎32) Map **9** A3
★★**Etape** r Isambard ☎361277 10rm6⇄ P sB46 – 58
sB⇄161 – 161 dB85 dB⇄127 – 192
(English breakfast) L50 – 120 D50 – 120 river

PALAISEAU 91 (Essonne) 23,431 (☎1) Map **9** B3
☆☆☆**Novotel Massy Palaiseau** 18 – 20 r Emile
Baudot, zone d'Activite ☎9208491 tx691595 151⇄ P
Lift sB⇄fr145 dB⇄fr157 English breakfast only Pool

PAMIERS 09 (Ariège) 15,200 (☎61) Map **22** C4
★★**Parc** ℒℰ (DP) ☎670258 12rm6⇄3🛏 🏠
🛢 🛱**Generale Automobile Appameenne** (N20)
☎671208 Bed/Opl (GB)

PARAMÉ See **ST MALO**
PARAY-LE-MONIAL 71 (Saône-et-Loire) 12,150
(☎85) Map **10** C1
★★**Vendanges de Bourgogne** ℒℰ 5 r D-Papin
☎811343 Closed Sun eve – Mon midday & Feb
15rm2⇄8🛏 🏠 P sB57 dB66 – 72 dB⇄🛏102
(English breakfast) L34 – 105 D34 – 105
★**Trois Pigeons** 2 r d'Argaud (DP) ☎810377 Closed
Jan 33rm6⇄14🛏 A15rm 🏠
🛢 🛱P **Henry** Les Carres (N79) ☎811365 P MB/Peu

PARIS† 75 2,350,000 (☎1) Map **9** B3 **See Plan**
pages 202 – 203 See also **Aulnay-sous-Bois, Evry,
Orgeval, Orsay, Palaiseau, Pontoise,
Rambouillet, St Germain-en-Laye & Surviilliers**
1st Arrondissement Opéra, Palais Royal, Halles,
Bourse
★★★★★**Meurice** 228 r de Rivoli ☎2603860
tx230673 Plan **45** 212⇄ Lift ⅅ sB⇄345 – 385
dB⇄460 – 490 Lalc D2alc St%
★★★★★**Ritz** 15 pl Vendôme ☎2603830 tx220262
Plan **54** 209⇄ Lift
★★★**Lotti** 7 r Castiglione ☎2603734 tx240066
Plan **40** 130rm122⇄ Lift ⅅ sB⇄🛏220 – 280
dB⇄🛏330 – 410 L fr70&alc D fr70&alc St%
★★★**Cambon** 3 r Cambon (n rest) ☎2603809
tx240814 Plan **16** 44rm21⇄21🛏 Lift
★★★**Castille** 37 r Cambon ☎2615520 Plan **18**
56rm48⇄5🛏 Lift ⅅ sB58 sB⇄🛏137 – 187
dB⇄🛏168 – 247 (English breakfast) L24 – 32
D24 – 32
★★★★**Louvre-Concorde** pl Théatre-Français
☎2615601 tx220412 Plan **41** 226rm120⇄86🛏 🏠 P
Lift ⅅ sB⇄🛏220 – 250 dB⇄🛏260 – 300
(English breakfast) Lalc D alc
★★**Duminy** 3 r Mont-Thabor (n rest) ☎2603280
Plan **21** 62rm33⇄ Lift sB45 – 50 (room only)
sB⇄90 – 125 (room only) dB80 (room only) dB⇄135
(room only)
★★**Family** 35 r Cambon (n rest) ☎2615484 Plan **24**
24rm16⇄4🛏 Lift

France

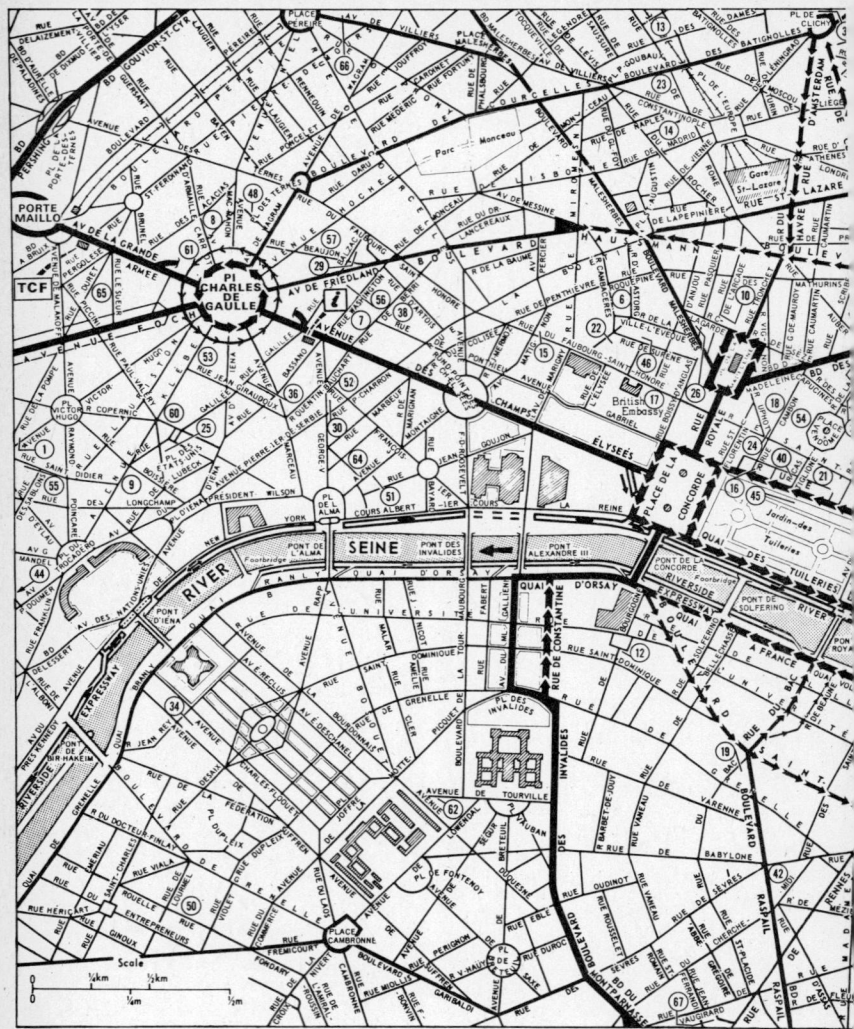

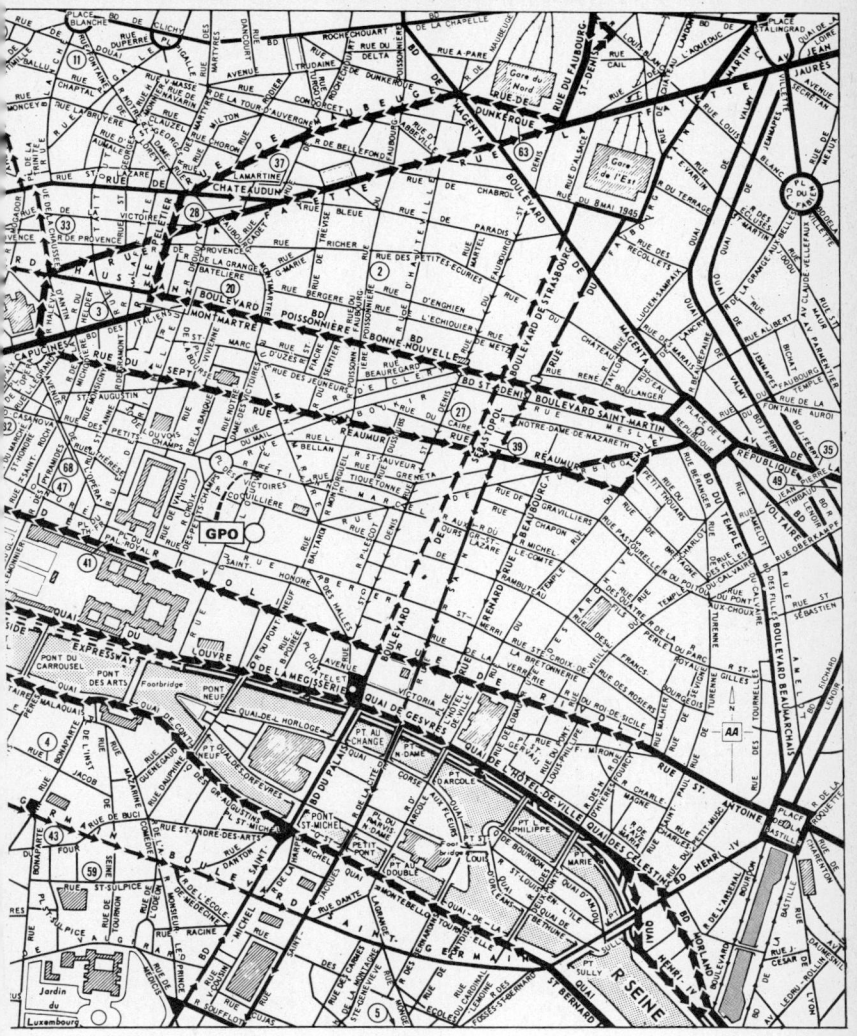

France

★★**Montana-Tuileries** 12 r St-Roch (n rest)
☎2604510 tx210311 Plan **47** 25rm22⇆1 🍽 Lift ♪
sB81 sB⇆ 🍽149 dB⇆ 🍽193 (English breakfast)

2nd Arrondissement Opéra, Palais-Royal, Halles, Bourse

★★★★**Westminster** 13 r de la Paix ☎2615746
tx680035 Plan **68** 102rm97⇆5 🍽 P Lift ♪
sB⇆ 🍽300-380 dB⇆ 🍽350-380
(English breakfast) L alc D alc

★★**France** 4 r du Caire (n rest) ☎2333098 Plan **27**
55rm12⇆3 🍽 Lift

3rd Arrondissement Bastille, République, Hôtel de Ville

★★*Little Palace* 4 r Salomon-de-Caus (n rest)
☎2720815 Plan **39** 60rm20⇆10 🍽 Lift

5th Arrondissement Quartier Latin, Luxembourg, Jarden des Plantes

⊗*Latin* 196 r St-Jacques ☎3261655 BL/Tri

6th Arrondissement Quartier Latin, Luxembourg, Jarden des Plantes

★★★★**Lutetia Concorde** 45 bd Raspail ☎5443810
tx270424 Plan **42** 300rm246⇆60 🍽 Lift ♪
sB⇆ 🍽235-265 dB⇆ 🍽290-330
(English breakfast)

★★★**Madison** 143 bd St-Germain (n rest)
☎3297250 Plan **43** 56⇆ Lift ♪ sB⇆98-157
dB⇆114-168

★★★*Senat* 22 r St-Sulpice (n rest) ☎3265348
Plan **59** 32rm23⇆9 🍽 🏠

★★★**Victoria Palace** 6 r Blaise-Desgoffe ☎5443816
tx270557 Plan **67** 113⇆ 🏠 P Lift ♪ sB⇆195
(room only) dB⇆225-240 (room only)
(English breakfast) L alc D alc

★★**Angleterre** 44 r Jacob (n rest) ☎2603472 Plan **4**
31rm26⇆ Lift sB75 sB⇆135 dB⇆155

7th Arrondissement Faubourg-St-Germain, Invalides, École Militaire

★★★**Bourgogne & Montana** 3 r de Bourgogne
☎5512022 tx270854 Plan **12** 35rm28⇆6 🍽 Lift ♪
sB⇆ 🍽143-210 dB⇆ 🍽161-220 L48-80 D48-80

★★★**Cayre** 4 bd Raspail (n rest) ☎5443888
tx270577 Plan **19** 131rm116⇆15 🍽 Lift ♪
sB⇆ 🍽195 dB⇆ 🍽233 (English breakfast)

★★*Splendid* 29 av de Tourville (n rest) ☎5512477
Plan **62** 45rm10⇆8 🍽 🏠 Lift

8th Arrondissement Champs-Élysées, St Lazare, Madeleine

★★★★★**Bristol** 112 fbg St-Honoré ☎2669145
tx280961 Plan **15** 220⇆ 🍽 P Lift ♪ sB⇆ 🍽360-600
dB⇆ 🍽535-900 L145alc D145alc

★★★★★*George-V* 31 av George V ☎7235400
tx650082 Plan **30** 359⇆ Lift

★★★★★**Plaza-Athénée** 25 av Montaigne
☎3598523 tx650092 Plan **51** 213⇆ Lift
sB⇆456-536 dB⇆fr642 L alc D alc St%

★★★★★**Prince de Galles** 33 av George-V
☎7235511 tx280627 Plan **52** 203⇆ Lift ♪
sB⇆345-385 dB⇆460-490 (English breakfast)
L fr90 D fr90 St%

★★★★★**Royal Monceau** 35 av Hoche ☎2277800
tx650361 Plan **57** 200⇆ Lift ♪ sB⇆296-351
dB⇆392-482 L alc D alc

★★★★**Bedford** 17 r de l'Arcade ☎2662232
tx290506 Plan **10** 144⇆ 🍽 Lift ♪ sB⇆ 🍽159
dB⇆ 🍽198-208 (English breakfast) L fr50 D fr50

★★★★*Castiglione* 40 r du fbg St-Honoré ☎2650750
tx210500 Plan **17** 110⇆ Lift

★★★★**Frantel Windsor** 14 r Beaujon ☎2277300
tx650902 Plan **29** 135rm133⇆2 🍽 Lift ♪
sB⇆ 🍽352-517 dB⇆ 🍽439-594
(English breakfast)

★★★**Lancaster** 7 r de Berri ☎3599043 tx640991
Plan **38** 57⇆ Lift

★★★★*Trémoille* 14 r Trémoille (n rest) ☎2256495
Plan **64** 106rm91⇆15 🍽

★★★**Astor** 11 r d'Astory ☎2665656 Plan **6**
141rm94⇆30 🍽 Lift

★★★**Atala** 10 r Châteaubriand ☎2250162 tx640576
Plan **7** 50rm35⇆15 🍽 Lift ♪

sB⇆ 🍽145-190 dB⇆ 🍽156-235 L55 D55

★★★**Royal** 33 av de Friedland ☎3590814 tx280965
Plan **56** 57rm46⇆9 🍽 Lift ♪ sB⇆ 🍽156-179
dB⇆ 🍽205-233 (English breakfast)
L alc D alc

★★**Elysée** 12 r Saussaies (n rest) ☎2652925
Plan **22** 31rm8⇆8 🍽 Lift ♪ sB48-57 sB⇆ 🍽105
dB57-66 dB⇆ 🍽114-121

★★**Europe** 15 r de Constantinople (n rest)
☎5228080 Plan **23** Closed Aug 49rm16⇆7 🍽 Lift
sB45-61 sB⇆ 🍽85-90 dB70 dB⇆ 🍽94-99

★★*Florida* 12 bd Malesherbes ☎2657206 Plan **26**
47rm27⇆6 🍽 Lift

★★**Ministère** 31 r Surène (n rest) ☎2662143 Plan **46**
34rm21⇆4 🍽 Lift ♪ sB fr66 sB⇆ 🍽94-144 dB fr75
dB⇆ 🍽103-155

★**Brescia** 16 r d'Edimbourg (n rest) ☎5221431
Plan **14** 34rm9⇆7 🍽 Lift sB53 sB⇆ 🍽67-92
dB61-73 dB⇆ 🍽99-119

9th Arrondissement Opéra Gare du Nord Gare de l'Est Grands Boulevards

★★★★**Ambassador** 16 bd Haussmann ☎2469263
tx650912 Plan **3** 300⇆ Lift sB⇆260 dB⇆335
(English breakfast) L fr75 Dfr75

★★★★*Commodore* 12 bd Haussmann ☎7709300
tx28601 Plan **20** 180⇆ Lift

★★★★*Grand* 2 r Scribe ☎2603350 tx220875
Plan **32** 600⇆ Lift ♪ sB⇆260-300 dB⇆350-390
(English breakfast) L 70 D70

★★★**Blanche Fontaine** 34 r Fontaine (n rest)
☎5267232 tx260717 Plan **11** 50rm47⇆3 🍽 Lift
sB⇆ 🍽137-142 dB⇆ 🍽158-163
(English breakfast)

★★★**Franklin & du Bresil** 19 r Buffault ☎2802727
tx640988 Plan **28** 65rm32⇆3 🍽 Lift
sB⇆ 🍽130-170 dB⇆ 🍽175-189 L fr50 Dfr50

★★★**Hélios** 75 r de la Victoire (n rest) ☎8742864
tx210500 Plan **33** 51rm24⇆22 🍽 Lift ♪ sB⇆ 🍽111
dB⇆ 🍽141

★**Laffon** 25 r Buffault (n rest) ☎8784991 Plan **37**
47rm13⇆14 🍽 Lift ♪ sB57-67 sB⇆ 🍽73-112
dB86-93 dB⇆ 🍽93-135

🏍**Ardennes** 3-5 r des Ardennes ☎2033075
☎2033075 BL/Vlo (GB)

10th Arrondissement Opéra, Gare du Nord, Gare de l'Est, Granders Boulevards

★★★**Terminus Nord** 12 bd Denain (n rest)
☎2802000 tx660615 Plan **63** 230rm74⇆113 🍽 Lift
sB⇆ 🍽150-210 dB⇆ 🍽170-240
(English breakfast)

★★*Altona* 166 r du fbg Poissonière (n rest)
☎8786824 Plan **2** 57rm27⇆ Lift

11th Arrondissement Bastille, République, Hôtel de Ville

⊗**Como Automobile** 82-84 bd Voltaire
☎3553917 BL/MB (GB)

Rochebrune 58-60av Parmentier ☎8052902 Frd

12th Arrondissement Bastille, Gare de Lyon, Place d'Italie, Bois de Vincennes

⊗*Porte Dorée* 268 av Daumesnill ☎6281033 P Ren

13th Arrondissement Bastille, Gare de Lyon, Gare d'Italie, Bois de Vincennes

★**Arts** 8 r Coypel (n rest) ☎3312230 Plan **5**
42rm1⇆15 🍽 Lift sB40-45 sB⇆ 🍽98 dB53-61
dB⇆ 🍽106

15th Arrondissement Vaugirard, Gare Montparnasse, Grenelle, Denfert-Rocherau

★★★★**Hilton** 18 av Suffren ☎2739200 tx200955
Plan **34** 489⇆ P Lift ♪ sB⇆295-355 dB⇆365-425

★★★**Sofitel Paris** 8-12 r L-Armand ☎5549500
tx200432 Not on plan 635⇆ 🏠 P Lift sB⇆ 🍽330-370
dB⇆410-450 (English breakfast) L alc Dalc Pool

★★**Pacific** 11 r Fondary (n rest) ☎5752049 Plan **50**
66rm37⇆2 🍽 Lift sB fr62 (room only) sB⇆ 🍽fr82
(room only) dB fr72 (room only) dB⇆ 🍽fr120 (room only)

⊗**Fremicourt** 146 bd de Grenelle ☎7576280
Chy/Sim (GB)

16th Arrondissement Passy, Auteuil, Bois de
Boulogne, Chaillot, Porte Maillot
★★★★★*Raphaël* 17 av Kléber ☎5530770 tx610356
Plan 53 90⇌ Lift
★★★*Alexander* 102 av V-Hugo (n rest) ☎5536465
tx610373 Plan 1 62rm49⇌13♒ Lift ♪
sB⇌♒180–200 dB⇌♒240
★★★*Baltimore* 88 av Kléber ☎5538333 tx611591
Plan 9 119⇌ P Lift sB⇌195–245 dB⇌260–295
★★★*Massenet* 5 r Massenet ☎5244303 tx620682
Plan 44 41rm34⇌2♒ P Lift ♪ sB⇌♒160 dB⇌♒180
(English breakfast)
★★*Farnese* 32 r Hamelin (n rest) ☎7205666
tx611732 Plan 25 37rm32⇌5♒ Lift ♪ sB⇌♒143
dB⇌♒180 (English breakfast)
★★*Keppler* 12 r Keppler (n rest) ☎7206505
tx260717 Plan 36 50rm21⇌15♒ Lift ♪ sBfr60
sB⇌♒fr103 dBfr112 dB⇌♒fr118
(English breakfast)
★★*Rond-Point de Longchamp* 86 r de Longchamp
(n rest) ☎7279627 tx620635 Plan 55 33rm10⇌13♒
Lift ♪ sB75 sB⇌♒160 dB107
dB⇌♒158–171 (English breakfast)
★★*Sevigné* 6 r de Belloy (n rest) ☎7208890
tx610219 Plan 60 30rm13⇌17♒ P Lift
sB⇌♒156–209 dB⇌♒186–220
(English breakfast)
★★*Vermont* 11 r Bois de Boulogne (n rest)
☎5000497 Plan 65 29rm23⇌5♒ Lift ♪ sB68
sB⇌♒149–156 dB⇌♒164–171
(English breakfast)

17th Arrondissement Clichy, Ternes, Wagram
★★★*Balmoral* 6 r du Gl-Lanrezac (n rest)
☎3803050 Plan 8 60rm27⇌18♒ Lift
★★★*Splendid* 1 bis av Carnot ☎3801456 tx280773
Plan 61 60rm44⇌16♒ Lift
★★*Neva* 14 r Brey (n rest) ☎380286 Plan 48
33rm24⇌ Lift ♪ sBfr73 sB⇌♒fr114 dB81 dB⇌127
Boursault 15 r Boursault (n rest) ☎5224219
Plan 13 13rm5⇌2♒
Verniquet 3 r Verniquet (n rest) ☎3802630 Plan 66
25rm5⇌15♒ Lift
&O*Boursault* 11-13 r Boursault ☎2936565 BL (GB)

18th Arrondissement Montmartre, La Villette,
Belleville
& &O*Chapelle* 20bd de la Chapelle ☎2061940 P Frd
& &O*Grand Pajol* 43 r Pajol ☎6071359 P Dat
*The distances shown after Argenteuil, Bagnolet,
Clicky, Créteil, Meudon-la-Forêt, Montrouge &
Vincennes, is that from the Place de la Concorde in
Paris*
At **Argenteuil** (14km NW)
& &O*Fontaines* 69 r A-Labrierre ☎9824003 Frd
At **Bagnolet** (7km E adj to Boulevard
Périphérique)
☆☆*Novotel Paris Bagnolet* 1 av de la République
☎8589010 tx670216 Plan 49 607⇌ P Lift sB⇌fr161
dB⇌fr173 English breakfast only Pool
☆☆*Ibis* r J-Jaurès ☎8589026 tx240830 Plan 35
414⇌ Lift
At **Clichy** (4km NW)
★*Girbal* 14 r Dagobert (n rest) ☎7375424 Plan 31
30rm24⇌6♒ Lift
& &O*GPM* 8 r de Belfort ☎7399940 P
At **Créteil** (12km SE off N5)
☆☆*Novotel Créteil-le-Lac* rte de Choissy (N186)
☎2079102 tx670396 Not on plan 110⇌ P Lift
sB⇌fr160 dB⇌fr175 English breakfast only Pool
At **Meudon-la-Forêt** (10km SW)
★★*Royal Chantecler* 29 av de Gl-de-Gaulle
☎6317628 Not on plan 15⇌
At **Montrouge** (6km S adj to *Boulevard Périphérique*)
☆☆*Ibis Paris Porte d'Orléans* 33 r Barbès
☎6565255 tx202527 Not on plan 407⇌ ♒ Lift
sB⇌fr120 dB⇌fr146 L35–50alc D35–50alc
At **St Denis** (4km N)
& *Neubauer* 227 bd A-France ☎2430243 Peu (GB)
At **Vincennes** (11km E off N34)

&O*L Deshayes et Fils* 232 r Fontenay ☎3749740 Frd
(GB)
& &O*Pacaud* 47 r de Strasbourg ☎3287056
PARIS AIRPORTS
BOURGET AIRPORT (LE) Map 9 B3
☆☆*Novotel Paris Nord Aéroport* r de Pont Yblon
(N2) ☎9314888 tx691527 140⇌ P Lift sB⇌fr162
dB⇌fr176 English breakfast only
CHARLES-DE-GAULLE AIRPORT Map 9 B3
At **Roissy** (2km E)
☆☆☆*Sofitel* ☎8622323 352⇌ P Lift ♪
sB⇌177–217 dB⇌204–264 L fr40 D fr40 St% *≈*
Pool
ORLY AIRPORT Map 9 B3
★★★★*Air* ☎7260310 56rm40⇌16♒ 🏛 Lift
★★★★*Hilton* ☎6873388 tx250621 388⇌ Lift ♪
sB⇌201–298 dB⇌255–352 L fr65 D fr65 Pool
PAU† 64 (Pyrénées-Atlantiques) 85,900 (☎59)
Map 15 B1
★★★*Continental* 2 r ML-Foch ☎276931 tx57906
110rm70⇌20♒ 🏛 Lift
★★★*Roncevaux* 25 r L-Barthou (n rest) ☎270844
tx570929 44rm20⇌18♒ 🏛 P Lift ♪ sB43–49
sB⇌♒69–110 dB58 dB⇌♒90–133
(English breakfast)
★*Central* 15 r L-Daran (n rest) ☎277275
27rm5⇌11♒ ♪ sB37–76 sB⇌♒63–76 dB66–96
dB⇌♒83–96
& *J Broqué* rte de Tarbes ☎027971 Ren
& &O*Forsans* 52 bd Champetier de Ribes ☎324669
BL/Vlo (GB)
& &O*Lavillauroy* 82 r d'Etigny ☎320312 Frd
At **Lescar** (7.5km NW on D945)
☆☆☆*Novotel Pau Lescar* (N117) ☎321732
tx570939 61⇌ P Lift sB⇌fr137 dB⇌fr149 English
breakfast only Pool
PASSENANS See **SELLIÈRES**
PAYRAC 46 (Lot) 512 (☎60) Map 16 C2
★★*Hostellerie de la Paix*L ☎376515 Closed Jan &
Feb 26rm9⇌ 🏛 P Lift sB48–61 sB⇌61–70
dB58–67 dB⇌68–77 L27–62 D27–62 mountains
PEN-GUEN See **ST-CAST**
PENNE-ST-MENET (LA) See **MARSEILLE**
PÉRIGUEUX† 24 (Dordogne) 37,700 (☎53)
Map 16 C3
★★*Boule d'Or* 8 pl Francheville ☎080251
42rm8⇌12♒ 🏛
☆☆*Ibis* bd Saumande ☎536458 tx550159 89⇌ P Lift
sB⇌fr88 dB⇌fr112 L35–45alc D35–45alc
& *Brout* 18 cours St-Georges ☎082855 ☎082611
≈ P Chy/Sim (GB)
&O*Cecasmo* 147 rte de Lyon ☎531773 AR
& *G Lacoste* rte de Bergerac ☎533901 Sim/Vlo
PEROLS See **MONTPELLIER**
PÉRONNE 80 (Somme) 9,450 (☎22) Map 9 B4
★★*St-Claude*L 42 pl L-Daudré ☎840002 Closed
Feb 30rm5⇌10♒ sB50–54 sB⇌♒80–92 dB57–61
dB⇌♒87–99 L34alc D34alc
★*Remparts*L 23 r Beaubois ☎840122 Closed 8–27
Aug 16rm5⇌7♒ 🏛 P sB48–83 sB⇌♒68–93
dB76–101 dB⇌♒76–101 (English breakfast)
L25–65 D25–65
At **Asservillers** (adj to Autoroute A1)
☆☆☆*Sofitel* ☎841276 tx140943 100⇌ P Lift ♪
sB⇌164–191 dB⇌215–247 D fr52 Pool
PÉROUGES 01 (Ain) 550 (☎74) Map 27 B4
★★★*Vieux Pérouges* ☎610088 22rm18⇌ 🏛
PERPIGNAN† 66 (Pyrenees-Orientales) 108,000
(☎68) Map 22 D4
★★★*Grand* quai Sadi-Carnot ☎340994 tx50969
62rm25⇌26♒ Lift
★★★*Windsor* 8 bd Wilson (n rest) ☎511865
tx500024 58rm27⇌31♒ P Lift ♪ sB⇌♒79–127
dB⇌♒106–147 (English breakfast)
★★*Baléares* 20 av GL-Guillot ☎850493
48rm7⇌20♒ P Lift dBfr59 dB⇌♒fr78 L26 D26
★★*Christina* 50 cours de Lassus (n rest) ☎614264
35rm25⇌5♒ 🏛 P Lift dB62–71 dB⇌♒82–94

★★**France** 16 quai Sadi-Carnot ☎349281 tx50950 40rm14⇌15 🏠 Lift

🛏 ⊶**FA** 4 bd St-Assiscle ☎347050 P Frd

🛏 ⊶**Monopole** rte de Narbonne, km 4 ☎612293 MB

At **Rivesaltes** (5km NW by N9)

☆☆☆**Novotel Perpignan** (N9) ☎640222 tx500851 85⇌ P Lift sB⇌fr120 dB⇌fr157 English breakfast only Pool

PERROS-GUIREC 22 (Côtes-du-Nord) 7,800 (☎96)
Map **7** B3

★★★**Printania** r des Bons-Enfants (n rest) ☎352100 Closed 16 Sep – 14 Apr 65rm38⇌10 🏠 Lift ⇌ sea

★★★**Trestraou** bd J-le-Bihan, Trestraou ☎352405 73rm46⇌12 🏠 A5rm Lift Pool sea

★★**Morgane** ⪩ 46 av Casino ☎352280 Closed Oct – May 28rm24⇌4 🏠 P Lift sB fr65 sB⇌🍴fr79 dB fr114 dB⇌🍴144 – 154 L43 – 100 D43 – 80 Pool sea

★**Riva-Bella** bd Clemenceau, Plage de Trestignel ☎352275 Closed 21 Sep – mid Apr 28rm10⇌ sea

🛏 ⊶**Côte** 39 r Ml-Joffre ☎352207 ⊕ P Bed/Opl/Vau (GB)

At **Ploumanach** (6km W on D788)

★**Roc'h-Hir** r St-Guirec (DP) ☎352324 Closed Oct – 14 Mar 24rm5 🏠

PEYREHORADE 40 (Landes) 3,100 (☎57)
Map **20** C4

★★**Central** pl A-Briand ☎730322 10rm3⇌4 🏠

PIERRE-BUFFIÈRE 87 (Haute-Vienne) 1,250 (☎55)
Map **16** C3

★**Providence** (N20) ☎006016 tx580091 12rm6⇌2 🏠 sB47 – 81 sB⇌🍴71 – 81 dB64 – 112 dB⇌🍴92 – 112 L34 – 100 D34 – 100

🛏 ⊶**Gauthier et Fils** ☎006024 Cit (GB)

PIERRELATTE 26 (Drôme) 10,050 (☎75)
Map **27** B3

★★**Hostellerie Tom** ⪩ 5 av Gl-de-Gaulle (N7) ☎040035 Closed Nov 12rm10⇌ 🏠 dB fr57 dB⇌🍴77 – 94 (English breakfast) L alc D alc

PILAT-PLAGE 33 (Gironde) 540 (☎56) Map **15** A2

See also **Arcachon & Pyla-sur-Mer**

★★**Brisants** 192 bd de l'Océan (n rest) ☎227335 Closed Oct – mid Apr 18rm8⇌4 🏠 Beach sea

PIRIAC-SUR-MER 44 (Loire-Atlantique) 1,150 (☎40) Map **7** B2

★**Plage & Port** ⪩ quai de Verdun ☎235009 24rm6⇌5 🏠 A14rm sB31 dB43 dB⇌🍴81 L28 – 75 D28 – 75 sea

PITHIVIERS 45 (Loiret) 10,450 (☎38) Map **9** B3

★**Poste** 10 Mail Ouest ☎020014 20rm6⇌ 🏠

PLOËRMEL 56 (Morbihan) 7,050 (☎97) Map **7** B3

★**Commerce** 70 r de la Gare ☎740532 20rm1⇌4 🏠 🏠

PLOMBIÈRES-LES-BAINS 88 (Vosges) 3,400 (☎29) Map **11** A2

★**Abbesses** pl Eglise ☎660040 tx88370 Closed Oct – Apr 45rm12⇌2 🏠 Lift sB⇌🍴86 – 91 dB94 – 99 dB⇌🍴94 – 99 L31 D31 mountains

PLOUMANACH See **PERROS-GUIREC**

POITIERS† 86 (Vienne) 85,500 (☎94) Map **8** D1

★★★**France** 28 r Carnot ☎413201 tx790526 86rm40⇌36 🏠 P Lift 🌙 sB60 – 85 sB⇌🍴120 – 160 dB95 dB⇌🍴100 – 190 L40 – 50 D40 – 50

★★★**Royal Poitou** rte de Paris ☎417286 32rm30⇌2 🏠 P 🌙 sB⇌🍴96 – 123 dB⇌🍴133 (English breakfast) L31 – 55 D31 – 55

★★**Europe** 39 r Carnot (n rest) ☎410088 44rm7⇌8 🏠 🏠

🛏 ⊶**Poitou-Auto** 99 av de Bordeaux ☎421792 Frd

At **Biard** (2km W)

🛏 ⊶**J P Barrault** Zone Industrielle, av de Nantes ☎880294 ☎416302 P Vlo (GB)

At **Chasseneuil** (8km N by N21)

☆☆☆**Relais Poitiers** ☎414141 tx790502 100rm42⇌32 🏠 A74rm P Lift 🌙 sB69 – 78 sB⇌🍴90 – 123 dB84 – 92 dB⇌🍴105 – 142 (English breakfast) L25 – 50 D25 – 50 ⊶ Pool

POIX-DE-PICARDIE 80 (Somme) 2,200 (☎22)
Map **9** B4

★**Cardinal** pl de la République ☎900823 Closed 2 wks Feb 23rm 🏠 P sB38 – 47 dB56 – 64 (English breakfast) L25 – 70 D32 – 42

★**Poste** pl de la République ☎900033 Closed 2 wks Jan 19rm1⇌2 🏠 P sB47 sB⇌🍴59 dB55 dB⇌🍴65 L23 – 60 D23 – 60

🛏 ⊶**Gressier** r C-Mehaye ☎900044 P Peu

POLIGNY 39 (Jura) 4,900 (☎84) Map **10** D1

★**Hostellerie Monts de Vaux** (DP) ☎371250 Closed Nov – 26 Dec 10rm9⇌ 🏠 P sB fr130 sB⇌🍴fr200 dB fr260 dB⇌🍴fr400

★★**Paris** ⪩ 7 r Travot ☎371387 27rm8⇌12 🏠 🏠 sB⇌🍴52 – 66 dB88 dB⇌🍴85 – 100 L23 – 65 D23 – 65 Pool mountains

★★**Vallée Heureuse** ⪩ ☎371213 9rm3⇌2 🏠 A1rm P sB48 – 54 sB⇌🍴58 – 69 dB61 – 68 dB⇌🍴76 – 93 L20 – 60 D20 – 60 mountains

POLISOT 10 (Aube) 300 (☎25) Map **10** C2

★**Hostellerie Seine** ☎385441 Closed Jan 21rm2⇌7 🏠 P sB48 – 88 sB⇌🍴78 – 88 dB66 – 106 dB⇌🍴96 – 106 river

PONS 17 (Charente-Maritime) 5,450 (☎46)
Map **15** B3

★★**Auberge Pontoise** r Gambetta ☎940099 Closed 21 Dec – 19 Jan 17rm5⇌7 🏠 P sB fr59 sB⇌🍴fr89 dB fr77 dB⇌🍴fr102 L fr37 D fr37

PONT-A-MOUSSON 54 (Meurthe-et-Mosel) 15,100 (☎28) Map **11** A3

★**Européen** 158 av Metz ☎810757 28rm6⇌2 🏠 A6rm 🏠 P sB fr50 sB⇌🍴81 – 94 dB59 dB⇌🍴90 – 103 D2fr26

★**Poste** 42 bis r V-Hugo ☎810116 24rm2⇌8 🏠 A8rm 🏠 P sB37 – 43 sB⇌🍴55 – 95 dB63 – 79 dB⇌🍴104 L35 – 100&alc D35 – 100&alc

PONTANEVAUX 71 (Saône-et-Loire) Map **27** B4

★★★**Campagnons de Jéhu** ☎372282 Closed Dec – Feb 25rm11⇌

PONTARLIER† 25 (Doubs) 18,850 (☎81)
Map **11** A1

★★**Bon Gite** ⪩ 12 r Salins ☎390872 Closed Mar 22rm2 🏠 P sB44 sB🍴46 dB57 dB🍴60 (English breakfast) L23 – 45 D23 – 45

★★**Poste** 55 r de la République ☎391812 Closed 16 Oct – 14 Dec 55rm15⇌5 🏠 🌙 sB35 – 58 sB⇌🍴74 dB57 – 77 dB⇌🍴77 – 115 (English breakfast) L28 – 75 D28 – 75

★★**Terrasse** 1 r de la République ☎390515 Closed May 32rm7⇌6 🏠 P sB48 – 53 sB⇌🍴fr68 dB59 – 66 dB⇌🍴78 L34 – 38 D34 – 38

🛏 ⊶**Belle Rive** 80 r de Besançon ☎391442 Chy/Sim

PONTAUBAULT 50 (Manche) 500 (☎33) Map **8** C3

★**13 Assiettes** ⪩ (N176) ☎581403 tx170537 Closed Dec – Feb 36rm2⇌25 🏠 P sB38 – 73 sB⇌🍴45 – 73 dB45 – 80 dB⇌🍴52 – 80 L19 – 70 D19 – 70

PONT-AUDEMER 27 (Eure) 10,050 (☎32) Map **9** A4

★★**Auberge Vieux Puits** 6 r N-Dame du Pré ☎410148 Closed 16 Dec – 14 Jan 8rm5 🏠 sB36 – 54 dB41 – 78 dB🍴66 – 84 L alc D alc

★**Palais** 8 r S-Dela Quaize (DP) ☎410947 14rm2⇌

★**Risle** 16 quai R-Leblanc ☎411457 18rm Lift sB37 – 45 dB55 – 60 L28 D28

PONT-D'AIN 01 (Ain) 2,300 (☎74) Map **27** B4

★★**Alliés** ⪩ ☎390009 18rm6⇌6 🏠 P sB54 sB⇌🍴68 – 81 dB62 – 72 dB⇌🍴76 – 101 L38 – 70 D38 – 70

★★**Paris-Nice** rte de Lyon ☎390380 Closed Thu 20rm5⇌2 🏠 sB38 sB⇌🍴57 dB52 dB⇌🍴68 D34

PONT-DE-BRIQUES 62 (Pas-de-Calais) 3,475
Map **3** A1

★**Cascade** 3 r P-Doumer (n rest) ☎322125 9rm 🏠

PONT-DE-CLAIX (LE) See **GRENOBLE**

PONT-DE-L'ISERE 26 (Drôme) 1,350 (☎75)
Map **27** B3

☆**Portes du Midi** (N7) ☎586026 Closed Nov 18rm5 🏠

PONT-DE-PANY 21 (Côte-d'Or) 190 (☎80)
Map **10** C2
★**Pont-de-Pany** L̶ ☎236059 Closed 20 Nov – 19
Dec 8rm3⇌ A8rm ⋒ P Lift sB43 sB⇌61 dB51
dB⇌69 (English breakfast) L26 D26 mountains
PONT D'ESPAGNA See **CAUTERETS**
PONT-DE-VAUX 01 (Ain) 2,150 (☎85) Map **10** C1
★**Reconnaissance** L̶ 9 pl Jaubert ☎373055
12rm3⇌5 ⋒ ⋒ P sB⇌fr44 dB fr63 dB⇌ ⋒73 – 93
L25 – 70 D25 – 70
PONT-DU-GARD 30 (Gard) (☎66) Map **27** A/B2
★★**Pont du Gard** ☎870110 Closed 21 Dec – Feb
11rm5⇌6 ⋒
★★**Vieux Moulin** (DP) ☎870135 Closed Oct – Feb
14rm8⇌4 ⋒ ⋒
PONTET D'EYRANS (LE) 33 (Gironde) (☎56)
Map **15** B3
⌂ ✷**Ferandier** ☎427107 ☎427107 P Peu (GB)
PONT-EVÊQUE See **VIENNE**
PONT-L'EVÊQUE 14 (Calvados) 3,800 (☎31)
Map **8** D4
★**Lion d'Or** L̶ pl Calvaire ☎640038 16rm10⇌ P
sB54 – 108 sB⇌76 – 108 dB62 – 117 dB⇌84 – 117
(English breakfast) L25 – 80 D25 – 80
PONTOISE 95 (Val d'Oise) (☎1) Map **9** B3
At **Clergy** (4km SW)
☆☆☆**Novotel** Ville Nouvelle ☎0303947 tx697264
196⇌ P Lift sB⇌fr139 dB⇌fr171 English breakfast
only Pool
PONTORSON 50 (Manche) 5,550 (☎33) Map **8** C3
★★**Poste & Croix d'Or** L̶ 92 r Couesnon ☎600045
Closed Jan 32rm6⇌12 ⋒ ⋒
★**Bretagne** L̶ 59 r Couesnon ☎601055 Closed Feb
29⇌ ⋒
⌂ ✷**Doré Rent** 43 r de la Libération ☎601110 Sim
PONT-ST-ESPRIT 30 (Gard) 6,850 (☎66)
Map **27** B2
★**Europe & Poste** 10 bd Gambetta ☎827124
23rm2⇌3 ⋒ ⋒
PONT-STE-MARIE See **TROYES**
PORNIC 44 (Loire-Atlantique) 8,200 (☎40) Map **7** B2
★**Family** r de l'Océan ☎820132 Closed Nov 18 ⋒
sea
PORNICHET 44 (Loire-Atlantique) 5,000 (☎40)
Map **7** B2
★★**Fleur de Thé** av Sellier ☎610496 Closed
17 Sep – 14 May 35rm14⇌ ⋒
★**Sud-Bretagne** 42 bd de la République ☎610268
Closed 16 Oct – 14 Mar 35rm20⇌2 ⋒ P sB59 – 108
sB⇌ ⋒fr108 dB70 – 119 dB⇌ ⋒fr119
(English breakfast) L37 – 75 D37 – 75
PORT-BLANC 22 (Côtes-du-Nord) 2,430 (☎96)
Map **7** B3
★**Grand** ☎203702 Closed Sep – 14 Jun
30rm12⇌4 ⋒ P sB⇌ ⋒54 dB⇌ ⋒77 L26 D26 ✷ sea
PORT-CROS (ILE DE) 83 (Var) (☎94) Map **28** C1
★★**Manoir** (DP) ☎719052 Closed Oct – Apr
29rm8⇌8 ⋒ A1rm
PORTEL (LE) See **BOULOGNE-SUR-MER**
PORT GRIMAUD See **GRIMAUD**
PORT-LAUNAY See **CHÂTEAULIN**
PORTO See **CORSE (CORSICA)**
PORT-VENDRES 66 (Pyrénées-Orientales) 5,860
(☎69) Map **22** D4
★★★**Compagnie du Midi** quai de la Douane
☎380033 60rm30⇌30 ⋒ ⋒ Lift sea
★★**Résidence** rte de Banyuls (Pn Jul & Aug only)
☎380068 Closed Nov – Jan 21rm12⇌4 ⋒ A4rm P Lift
sB48 – 88 sB⇌ ⋒82 dB55 – 222 dB⇌ ⋒72 – 222
L30 – 62 & alc D30 – 62 &alc Pool sea mountains
POUILLY-SUR-LOIRE 58 (Nièvre) 1,850 (☎86)
Map **9** B2
★**Neuf** 44 r W-Rousseau (n rest) 10rm3⇌1 ⋒ ⋒
★**Relais Fleuri** L̶ (0.5km SE on N7) ☎391299
Closed 16 Jan – 14 Feb 10rm8⇌2 ⋒ P
sB⇌ ⋒64 – 101 dB⇌ ⋒99 – 109 (English breakfast)
L26 – 94 D26 – 94 river

POULDU (LE) 29 (Finistère) 600 (☎98) Map **7** B3
★★**Castel Treaz** ☎969111 Closed 13 Sep – May
28rm11⇌11 ⋒ P Lift sB54 sB⇌ ⋒93 – 121 dB62
dB⇌ ⋒101 – 129 L40 – 60 D40 – 60 sae
✷**Quatres Chemins** L̶ ☎969044 35rm14⇌10 ⋒ P
sB47 sB⇌ ⋒59 dB60 dB⇌ ⋒69 – 108 L26 – 55
D26 – 55
POURVILLE-SUR-MER 76 (Seine-Maritime) 800
(☎35) Map **9** A4
★**Normandy** ☎841805 Closed 16 Nov – Jan
16rm1⇌2 ⋒ sea
POUZAUGES 85 (Vendée) 5,600 (☎51) Map **8** C1
★★**Bruyère** L̶ r Dr-Barhanneau ☎571346
30rm13⇌13 ⋒ P Lift sB fr55 sB⇌ ⋒67 – 77 dB fr77
dB⇌ ⋒88 – 113 (English breakfast) L26alc
D26alc
PRECY-SOUS-THILL 21 (Côte-d'Or) 583 Map **10** C2
A Durey (N70) P
PRÉMERY 58 (Nièvre) 2,800 (☎86) Map **9** B2
★**Poste** 4 Grand r ☎681230 Closed Feb 16rm1⇌1 ⋒
⋒
PRIMEL-TRÉGASTEL 29 (Finistère) 1,521
Map **7** B3
★**Grand** ☎673501 Closed Sep – Jun 36rm sea
PRIVAS 07 (Ardèche) 11,250 (☎75) Map **27** B3
★★**Croix d'Or** 3 cours de l'Esplanade 14rm3⇌2 ⋒ ⋒
PROPRIANO See **CORSE (CORSICA)**
PROVINS 77 (Seine-et-Marne) 13,118 (☎1)
Map **10** C3
★★**Croix d'Or** 1 r des Capucins ☎4000196 7rm4⇌
⋒
⌂ ✷**Griffon** 21 r E-Nocard ☎4000123 Frd (GB)
PUY (LE)† **43** (Haute-Loire) 29,050 (☎71)
Map **27** A3
★★★**Cris'tel** 15 bd A-Clair ☎094121 tx39679 30⇌
⋒ Lift
★★**Bristol** av Ml-Foch ☎091338 Closed
16 Nov – 14 Jan 35rm15⇌10 ⋒ A20rm ⋒ Lift ♪
sB40 – 76 sB⇌ ⋒71 – 76 dB79 – 84 dB⇌ ⋒79 – 90
L22 – 55 D22 – 55
★★**Lafayette** 17 bd St-Louis ☎093285 Closed
16 Nov – Feb 24rm5⇌1 ⋒ ⋒ Lift
★**Vervelne** L̶ 6 pl Cadelade ☎093539 28rm3⇌20 ⋒
dB⇌ ⋒64 (English breakfast) L25 D25
PUYA (LA) See **ANNECY**
PUY GUILLAUME 63 (Puy-de-Dôme) 2,320
Map **27** A4
★**Larivaut** 1 r E-Vaillant ☎2 13rm3⇌3 ⋒ ⋒
PYLA-SUR-MER 33 (Gironde) (☎56) Map **15** A2
See also **Arcachon & Pilat-Plage**
★★★**Guitoune** bd de l'Océan ☎227010 Closed
16 Nov – 14 Jan 21rm15⇌6 ⋒ ⋒ sea
★★**Beau Rivage** 10 bd de l'Océan ☎225241 Closed
16 Sep – May 16rm5⇌12 ⋒ A4rm sB48
sB⇌ ⋒68 – 94 dB63 dB⇌ ⋒81 – 111 L40 – 50
D40 – 50
QUARRÉ-LES-TOMBES 89 (Yonne) 900 (☎86)
Map **10** C2
★**Nord & Poste** L̶ (DP) ☎7 35rm4⇌6 ⋒ A24rm
QUIBERON 56 (Morbihan) 4,750 (☎97) Map **7** B2
★★★**Sofitel Thalassa** Pointe de Goulvas ☎502000
tx730712 Closed Jan 113⇌ P Lift ♪ sB⇌213 – 312
dB⇌281 – 410 (English breakfast) L70 D70 Pool sea
★★**Beau Rivage** 11 r de Port Maria ☎500839 Closed
Oct – Mar 48rm36⇌ Lift sB73 – 74 sB⇌92 – 96
dB81 – 82 dB⇌100 – 109 sea
★**Ty Breiz** bd Chanard ☎500990 Closed Oct – mid
Apr 32rm5⇌20 ⋒ sea
At **St-Pierre-Quiberon** (4.5km N on D786)
★★**Plage** ☎509210 Closed Nov – mid Apr
41rm23⇌18 ⋒ A4rm ⋒ Lift sB⇌88 – 109
dB⇌ ⋒96 – 127 (English breakfast) L31 – 49 D31 – 49
sea
QUILLAN 11 (Aude) 5,150 (☎68) Map **22** D4
★★**Chaumière** L̶ bd Ch-de-Gaulle ☎200679
40rm30⇌6 ⋒ ⋒

France

★**Cartier** 31 bd Ch-de-Gaulle ☎200514
30rm10⇄9 🏠 sB fr42 sB⇄ 🍴 sB85 dB fr49 dB⇄ 🍴104
(English breakfast) L22 – 60 D22 – 60
🚗**Escur** ☎200666 ☎200176 Ren (GB)

QUIMPER† **29** (Finistère) 60,500 (☎98) Map **7** A3
★★**Celtic** 13 r de Douarnenez ☎940297 33rm4⇄4 🍴
P sB29 – 73 sB⇄ 🍴70 dB50 – 55 dB⇄ 🍴80 L25 – 55
D25 – 55
★★**Gradlon** 30 r Brest (n rest) ☎950439 Closed 17
Dec – 15 Jan 25rm10⇄8 🍴 sB48 sB⇄ 🍴72 – 89
dB80 – 97 dB⇄ 🍴97 – 103 (English breakfast)
★★**Tour d'Auvergne** 11 r des Réguaires
☎950870 45rm22⇄11 🍴 A2rm 🏠 P Lift sB48 – 95
dB67 – 103 dB⇄ 🍴185 – 109 L30 – 75 D30 ✿75
🚗**Bozec** (ZAC de Kernevez) K3 rte de Douarnenez
☎959040 P BL (GB)
🅱 🚗**Bretagne Auto** rte de Concarneau, Ty-Bos
☎903200 Frd (GB)
🚗**Vigouroux** rte de Bénodet ☎901344 BMW/Toy
(GB)

QUIMPERLÉ 29 (Finistère) 11,750 (☎98) Map **7** B3
🅱 **Quimperlois** 22 rte de Lorient ☎960456 Aud/VW
RABOT (LE) 41 (Loir-et-Cher) (☎39) Map **9** B2
☆**Bruyeres** (N20) ☎080570 38rm24⇄14 🍴 P
sB⇄ 🍴56 – 94 dB⇄ 🍴63 – 101 L29 – 50 D29 – 50 Pool
RAGUENÈS PLAGE 29 (Finistère) (☎98) Map **7** A3
★**Chez Pierre** ☎978106 Closed Oct – Feb
20rm4 🍴 🏠 sea
RAMBOUILLET 78 (Yvelines) (☎1) Map **9** B3
★**St Charles** 1 r Groussay (n rest) ☎4830634 Closed
1st 2 wks Jul 14rm6⇄6 🍴 A2rm P sB41 – 79
sB⇄ 🍴63 – 79 dB49 – 109 dB⇄ 🍴71 – 109
RANCOURT 80 (Somme) (☎22) Map **9** B4
★★**Prieuré** (N37) ☎841023 23⇄ 🍴 🏠 P
dB⇄ 🍴84 – 91 (English breakfast) L fr30 D fr30
RAYOL (LE) 83 (Var) 850 (☎94) Map **28** C1
★★★**Baïlli de Suffren** ☎056038 tx420535 Closed
Oct – Apr rm50⇄ P Lift sB⇄320 – 410 dB⇄320 – 410
(English breakfast) L70 – 100 D70 – 100 sea
RÉ (ILE DE) 17 (Charente-Maritime) (☎46)
Map **15** B4
FLOTTE (LA) (1,750)
★★**Richelieu** av Plage ☎096070 Closed 3 – 31 Jan
30⇄ sB133 – 200 sB⇄ 🍴133 – 200 dB⇄ 🍴186 – 290
L80 – 150 D80 – 150 ✿ Pool sea
★**Ilot** 10 cours F-Faure ☎090602 27rm9⇄5 🍴 sea
RECOLOGNE 25 (Doubs) 260 Map **10** D2
★**Escale** ☎863213 Closed Nov – mid Apr
15rm4⇄7 🍴 A4rm sB28 – 45 sB⇄ 🍴45 – 52 dB51 – 61
dB⇄ 🍴51 – 61 (English breakfast) L18 – 28 D18 – 28
REIMS† **51** (Marne) 183,650 (☎26) Map **10** C3/4
★★★**Frantel** 31 bd P-Doumer ☎885354 tx830629
125⇄ 🏠 P Lift 🌙 sB⇄ 🍴149 – 189 dB⇄ 🍴188 – 228
L fr70 D fr70
☆☆☆**Mercure Reims Est** rte de Chalons ☎404787
tx830782 98⇄ P Lift sB⇄fr138 dB⇄fr150 English
breakfast only Pool
★★★**Paix** 25 – 27 pl Drouet d'Erlon ☎400408
tx830974 100⇄ 🏠 Lift sB⇄ 🍴116 – 150 dB⇄ 🍴116 – 170
L fr41 D fr41
★★**Crystal** 86 pl Drouet-d'Erlon (n rest) ☎475988
28rm3⇄8 🍴 Lift
★★**Europa** 8 bd Joffre (n rest) ☎473329 Closed
24 Dec – 5 Jan 32rm5⇄6 🍴 sB25 – 50 sB⇄ 🍴74 – 80
dB58 dB⇄ 🍴83 – 88
★★**Grand du Nord** 75 pl Drouet-d'Erlon (n rest)
☎473903 50rm22⇄28 🍴 Lift sB⇄ 🍴66 – 87
dB⇄ 🍴74 – 99
★★**Univers** 41 bd Foch (n rest) ☎475271
44rm18⇄3 🍴 Lift 🌙 sB50 – 90 sB⇄ 🍴90 dB98
dB⇄ 🍴82 – 98
★**Foch** 37 bd Foch ☎474822 Closed 16 Jan – 14 Feb
15rm7⇄
★**Welcome** 29 r Buirette (n rest) ☎474114 tx830600
Closed 21 Dec – 14 Jan 70rm8⇄32 🍴 A20rm Lift
🅱 🚗**SODIVA** 45 bis N44 à La Neuvilette ☎478863
(Closed wknds) MB/Por

🅱 🚗**Depann' Autos** (MJ Prott) 40 av d'Epernay
☎080108 ☎080108
At **Tinqueux** (4km W off N31)
☆☆☆**Novotel** rte de Soisson (N31) ☎081161
tx830034 125⇄ P Lift sB⇄fr137 dB⇄fr158 English
breakfast only Pool
🅱 🚗**Reims Automobiles** 2 av R Salengro ☎082108
Dat/Opl
REMIGEASSE (LA) See **OLÉRON (ILE D')**
REMIREMONT 88 (Vosges) 11,500 (☎29)
map **11** A2
At **St-Nabord** (5km N on N57)
★★★**Claire Fontaine** ☎622396 Closed Nov – 14 Mar
15 rm13⇄2 🍴 Lift
★★★**Montlroche** (N57) (n rest) ☎620659 Closed
Nov – Feb 14rm13⇄ 🍴 P Lift sB⇄ 🍴fr85 dB 100 – 115
dB⇄ 🍴100 – 115 mountains
RENAISON 42 (Loire) 2,050 (☎77) map **27** A4
★**Jacques Coeur** rte vichy ☎044005 10rm6 🍴 sB 46
dB44 dB⇄ 🍴62 – 70 (English breakfast) L 45 – 130
D45 – 130 mountains
RENNES† **35** (Ille-et-Vilaine) 205,750 (☎99)
Map **8** C3
★★★**Central** 6 r Lanjuinais (off quai Lamennais)
(n rest) ☎302359 tx74728 Closed 4 – 25 Aug
43rm19⇄9 🍴 Lift
★★★**Frantel** pl du Colombier ☎795454 tx730905
140⇄ P Lift sB⇄ 🍴167 – 192 dB⇄ 🍴219 – 254 L 62 alc
D62 alc
★★★**Guesclin** 5pl de la Gare ☎302801 75rm60⇄ 🍴
Lift
☆☆☆**Novotel Rennes Alma** av du Canada
☎506132 tx740144 99⇄ P Lift sB⇄fr139 dB⇄fr161
English breakfast only Pool
★★★**Président** 27 av Janvier (n rest) ☎309950
tx73004 34rm26⇄8 🍴 🏠 Lift
★★**Angelina** 1 quai Lemennais (n rest) ☎307139
25rm6⇄4 🍴 Lift
★**Angleterre** 19 r MI-Joffre (n rest) ☎307766
28rm3⇄9 🍴 sB41 sB⇄ 🍴50 – 54 dB 48
dB⇄ 🍴57 – 69
🅱 🚗**Mail** 30 av du Mail ☎591224 BL
🅱 🚗**Ouest** 5 r Gutemberg ☎362964 Ren
🅱 🚗**Ste Rennaise Auto** 137 rte Lorient ☎591014
Chy
RETHEL 08 (Ardennes) 9,200 (☎24) Map **10** C4
★★**Moderne** pl Gare ☎390454 25rm8⇄5 🍴 🏠
sB60 – 95 sB⇄ 🍴70 – 90 dB 75 – 85 dB⇄ 🍴85 – 105
(English breakfast) L &alc D &alc
RIGNAC See **GRAMAT**
RILLY-SUR-LOIRE 41 (Loire-et-Cher) 400 (☎39)
Map **9** A2
★**Château de la Haute-Borde** ☎469809 Closed
16 Nov – Feb 16rm5⇄2 🍴 🏠
RIQUEWIHR 68 (Haut-Rhin) 1,200 (☎89) Map **11** B2
★★**Jules Schmidt** ☎479218 Closed Jan & Feb
10rm6 🍴
Rive De Gler **42** (Loire) (☎77) Map **27** B4
★★**Hostellerie de la Renaissance** 43 r Marrel
☎750431 Closed Aug 10rm7⇄1 🍴 🏠 P sB fr49
dB⇄ 🍴92 – 115 (English breakfast) L 58 – 180
D58 – 180
RIVESALTES See **PERPIGNAN**
RIXHEIM See **MULHOUSE**
ROANNE† **42** (Loire) 56,500 (☎77) Map **27** A4
★★**France** 19 r A-Roche (n rest) ☎712117 Closed
1 – 15 Aug 44rm10⇄15 🍴 🏠
★★**Troisgros** 22 cours de la République ☎716697
Closed Jan 19rm18⇄1 🍴 🏠 🍸
■ 🚗**Gobelet** 54 av Gambetta ☎723022 P Vlo
🅱 🚗**Lafay** 13 pl Diderot ☎710408 Ren
ROCAMADOUR 46 (Lot) 750 (☎65) Map **16** C2
★★**Beau Site & Notre Dame** r R-le-Preux
☎386308 tx520421 Closed Nov – Mar 61rm27⇄25 🍴
A10rm 🏠 P Lift sB56 sB⇄ 🍴61 – 71 dB77
dB⇄ 🍴99 – 152 (English breakfast) L 31 – 95 D40 – 95
mountains

★★**Ste Marie** ⌐ 386307 Closed Nov – Mar
22⇌A5rm 🏛 P sB64 – 74 dB71 – 99 L28 – 70
D28 – 70 mountains
☆**Motel Château** rte de Château ⌐386222 Closed
6 Nov – 19 Mar 50rm18⇌14 🏛 A18rm
★**Lion d'Or** ⌐ porte Figuier ⌐386204 taDuclos
Closed 16 Oct – mid Apr 21rm6⇌8 🏛 A7rm sB38 – 88
dB45 – 95 L35 – 50 D40
ROCHE-CHALAIS (LA) 24 (Dordogne) 3,100 (⌐53)
Map **15** B3
★**Soleil d'Or** ⌐904237 Closed Oct – Feb
17rm4⇌3 🏛 🏛
ROCHEFORT 17 (Charente-Maritime) 32,900 (⌐46)
Map **15** B3/4
ⓑ **Central** 31 r Lafayette ⌐990065 BL (GB)
ⓑ ⑊**G Zanker** 76 r Gambetta ⌐993733 Frd (GB)
ROCHELLE (LA)† 17 (Charente-Maritime) 77,500
(⌐46) Map **15** B4
★★★**Brises** Chemin Digue Richelieu (n rest)
⌐348937 46rm38⇌8 🏛 P Lift ♪ sB90 – 185
sB⇌ 🏛 fr185 dB 150 – 190 dB⇌ 🏛182 – 190 sea
★★★**France & Angleterre** 22 r Gargouleau
⌐285624 tx79717 79rm37⇌26 🏛 🏛 Lift
★★★**Yachtman** 23 quai Valin ⌐412068 tx790762
36rm35⇌1 🏛 🏛 P Lift ♪ sB⇌ 🏛196 dB⇌ 🏛232 Pool
★**Trianon et Plage** 6 r de la Monnaie ⌐412135
Closed Feb 18rm5⇌8 🏛 🏛 P ♪ sB55 – 58 dB64 – 67
dB⇌ 🏛90 – 103 (English breakfast) L33 – 48 D33 – 48
ⓑ **A Chagneau & Fils** 124 bd A Sautel ⌐344225 Frd
ROCHE-POSAY (LA) 86 (Vienne) 1,450 (⌐49)
Map **9** A1
★**Parc** av Fontaines ⌐862002 Closed 26 Sep – 4
May 80rm25⇌13 🏛 🏛 Lift
RODEZ† 12 (Aveyron) 28,200 (⌐65) Map **16** D2
★★★**Tour Maje** bd Gally (n rest) ⌐683468
46rm23⇌19 🏛 Lift
★★**Grand Broussey** 1 av V-Hugo ⌐681871
taMapotel 78rm48⇌8 🏛 P Lift ♪ sB46 – 54
sB⇌ 🏛69 – 94 dB63 – 73 dB⇌ 🏛83 – 118
(English breakfast) L40 – 55 D40 – 55 mountains
★★**Moderne** ⌐ 9 r Abbé-Bessou ⌐680310
30rm4⇌13 🏛 Lift sea
★**Poste** ⌐ 2 r Béteille ⌐680147 25rm6⇌7 🏛 P Lift
sB48 sB⇌ 🏛71 dB55 dB⇌ 🏛78 L22 – 45 D22 – 45
ROISSY See **PARIS**
ROMANS-SUR-ISÈRE 26 (Drôme) 34,250 (⌐75)
Map **27** B3
★★**Terminus** 48 av P-Sémard (n rest) ⌐024688
Closed 7 – 23 Aug & 25 Dec – 7 Jan 32rm10⇌8 🏛 Lift
sB42 sB⇌ 🏛108 dB60 dB⇌ 🏛117
(English breakfast)
ROMORANTIN-LANTHENAY 41 (Loir-et-Cher)
17,050 (⌐39) Map **9** A/B2
★★**Lion d'Or** ⌐ 69 r G-Clemenceau ⌐760028
Closed 11 Jan – 14 Feb 18rm3⇌8 🏛 P sB78
dB⇌ 🏛156 L fr150 D fr150 St%
★**Orleans** pl du Gl-de-Gaulle ⌐760165 10rm5⇌1 🏛
sB51 sB⇌ 🏛63 dB89 dB⇌ 🏛109 (English breakfast)
L fr30 D fr30
ROQUEBRUNE-CAP-MARTIN 06 (Alpes-
Maritimes) 11,250 (⌐93) Map **28** C2
★★★**Victoria** 7 prom du Cap Martin (n rest)
⌐356590 Closed Oct – Jan 32⇌ 🏛 Lift sea
★★★**Vistaëro** Grande Corniche ⌐350150 27⇌ P
Lift ♪ sB⇌273 dB⇌376 – 546 L fr130 D fr130 St%
Pool sea
★★**Princessias** 15 av G-Drin ⌐350342 Closed
Nov – Jan 14⇌ P sB⇌100 – 120 dB⇌110 – 130 L58
D58 sea
★**Westminster** 14 av L-Laurens ⌐350068 Closed
Oct – Jan 30rm13⇌15 🏛 A4rm 🏛 P sB⇌ 🏛43 – 53
dB56 dB⇌ 🏛76 – 96 L35 – 40 D35 – 40 sea
ⓑ ⑊**Quatre Chemins** 57 av J-Jaurès ⌐350040 P
(GB)
ROQUEFORT-SUR-SOULZON 12 (Aveyron) 950
(⌐65) Map **16** A1
★★★**Grand** av de Lauras ⌐609020 Closed Oct – mid
Apr 20rm8⇌4 🏛

ROQUE-GAGEAC (LA) 24 (Dordogne) 400 (⌐53)
Map **16** C2
★★**Gardette** ⌐295158 Closed 12 Nov – mid Apr
16rm10⇌6 🏛 A4rm P sB45 – 59 sB⇌ 🏛99
dB⇌ 🏛62 – 107 (English breakfast) L28 – 90 D28 – 90
★**Belle Étoile** ⌐295144 Closed 16 Oct – 14 Mar
15rm3⇌10 🏛 🏛 P Lift dB54 – 64 dB⇌ 🏛54 – 64
L20 – 39 D20 – 39
ROSCOFF 29 (Finistère) 3,750 (⌐98) Map **7** B3
★★★**Gulf-Stream** r Marquix de Kergariou ⌐697319
Closed 11 Oct – 24 Mar 32⇌ 🏛 P Lift dB⇌ 🏛109 – 120
D47 – 130 sea
★**Bains** 25 pl Lacaze Duthiers ⌐697012 Closed
Nov – mid Apr 60rm1⇌10 🏛 A30rm Lift sB43
dB55 – 84 dB⇌ 🏛89 – 113 L25 – 50 D25 – 50 sea
ROSIERS (LES) 49 (Maine-et-Loire) 1,850 (⌐41)
Map **8** D2
★★**Jeanne de Laval** pl Eglise ⌐518017 Closed
11 Nov – 24 Dec 15rm13⇌ 🏛 🏛 P sB fr61 sB⇌ 🏛92
dB⇌ 🏛107 – 174 L70 – 120 D70 – 120 ⤴
ROUBAIX 59 (Nord) 109,800 (⌐20) Map **3** B1
★★★**PLM Grand** 22 av J-Lebas (n rest) ⌐701590
tx120301 95⇌ Lift sB⇌ 🏛115 – 125 dB⇌ 🏛145 – 158
(English breakfast)
ⓑ ⑊**Colisée** 6 r Molière ⌐751341 Opl
⑊**Pouthieux** av R-Salengro ⌐752992 M/c Hon
ROUEN† 76 (Seine-Maritime) 118,350 (⌐35)
Map **9** A4
★★★**Dieppe** pl B-Tissot ⌐719600 tx180413 44⇌ P
Lift ♪ sB⇌ 🏛120 – 140 dB⇌ 🏛140 – 175 L60 D60
★★★**Frantel** r de la Croix de 1er ⌐980698 tx180949
125⇌ 🏛 Lift ♪ sB⇌ 🏛172 – 200 dB⇌ 🏛240 – 267
(English breakfast) L65 D65
★★★**Poste** 72 r J-d'Arc (DP) ⌐882088 tx180674
85rm55⇌8 🏛 Lift
★★**Astrid** 121 r J-D'Arc (n rest) ⌐717588
40rm10⇌4 🏛 Lift
★★**Cardinal** 1 pl Cathédral (n rest) ⌐702442 Closed
Feb 20rm4⇌11 🏛 Lift sB49 – 81 sB⇌ 🏛56 – 81
dB56 – 88 dB⇌ 🏛63 – 81 (English breakfast)
★★**Cathédrale** 12 r St-Romain (n rest) ⌐715795
25rm23⇌ Lift
★★**Europe** 87 r aux Ours (n rest) ⌐708330
27rm6⇌4 🏛 Lift
★★**Nord** 91 r Gros-Horloge (n rest) ⌐704141
60rm19⇌28 🏛 Lift sB fr41 sB⇌ 🏛62 – 65 dB58 – 80
dB⇌ 🏛83 – 94
★★**Paris** 12 – 14 r de la Champmeslé (off quai de la
Bourse) (n rest) ⌐700926 22rm9⇌9 🏛 🏛 P Lift
sB fr51 sB⇌ 🏛60 – 82 dB fr62 dB⇌ 🏛84 – 89
★★**Viking** 21 quai du Havre (n rest) ⌐708498
37rm16⇌11 🏛 P Lift dB57 – 62 dB⇌ 🏛70 – 89 river
★**Arcades** 52r des Carmes (n rest) ⌐701030
16rm4 🏛
★**Normandie** 19 r du Bec (off r aux Juifs) (n rest)
⌐715577 23rm7⇌14 🏛 Lift sB⇌ 🏛61 – 84
dB⇌ 🏛78 – 107
★**Quebec** 18 – 24 r Quebec (off r de la République)
(n rest) ⌐700938 Closed 25 Dec – 9 Jan 38rm12⇌ 🏛
Lift
★**Vielle Tour** 42 pl Haute Vieille Tour (n rest)
⌐700327 23rm2⇌6 🏛 Lift ♪ sB44 – 51
sB⇌ 🏛56 – 71 dB51 – 55 dB⇌ 🏛64 – 83
ⓑ **Guez** 135 r Lafayette ⌐727684 Frd (GB)
At **Déville les Rouen** (3km NW off N13 bis)
ⓑ ⑊**Anova** 16 av Carnot ⌐741565 Toy (GB)
At **St Etienne du Rouvray** (2km S off N138)
☆☆☆**Novotel Rouen Sud** Le Madrillet ⌐665850
tx180215 135⇌ P Lift sB⇌ fr141 dB⇌ fr170 English
breakfast only Pool
ROUFFILLAC See **ST-JULIEN-DE-LAMPON**
ROUSSILLON 84 (Vaucluse) 1,100 (⌐90)
Map **27** B2
★★**Rose d'Or** ⌐756021 Closed 6 Nov – 14 Dec
10rm7⇌2 🏛
ROYAN† 17 (Charente-Maritime) 18,700 (⌐46)
Map **15** B3

France

★★★**Embruns** 18 bis bd Garnier (n rest) ☎050217
Closed 16 Nov–Feb 27rm1 🏛 A12rm P Lift 🌙 sB66
sB⇄🍴102–110 dB111–140 sea

★★**Grand de Pontaillac** 195 av de Pontaillac (n rest)
☎380044 Closed 16 Sep–May 55rm25⇄25🍴
A10rm 🏛 Lift 🌙 sB52–109 dB⇄🍴117–152 sea

★★**Océanie** bd F-Garnier ☎051495 40rm18⇄18🍴
🏛 Lift sea

🛏 **Barlbeaud** 50 bis av de la Grand Conche
☎050462 AR

▌ 🕸**E Marché** 75 av de Pontaillac ☎051153 Frd
(GB)

🛏 🕸**Thomas** rte de Saintes ☎050549 P MB (GB)

ROYAT 63 (Puy-de-Dôme) 4,500 (☎73) Map **16** D3

★★★**Métropole** 4 bd Vaquez ☎358018 Closed
Oct–Apr 80rm50⇄10🍴 Lift

ROZIER (LE) 48 (Lozère) 150 (☎65) Map **16** D2
At **Muse (La)** (on D107n)

★★★**Rozler & Muse** La Muse ☎606001 Closed
16 Oct–Mar 40rm25⇄3🍴 🏛 P Lift dB⇄🍴135–200
Beach

RUFFEC 16 (Charente) 4,700 (☎45) Map **15** B/C4

🛏 🕸**Lavaud** av A-Blanc ☎310145 P Fia

RUNGIS 94 (Val-de-Marne) 2,686 (☎1) Map **9** B3

★★★**Frantel** 20 av C-Lindberg ☎6873636
tx260738 206⇄ 🏛 P Lift sB⇄223 dB⇄281
(English breakfast) L68alc D68alc

SABLES-D'OLONNE (LES)† 85 (Vendée) 18,250
(☎30) Map **8** C1

★★**Beau Rivage** 40 prom de la Plage ☎320301
Closed 16 Dec–14 Feb 35rm13⇄4🍴 sea

★★**Charmettes** 22 prom de la Plage ☎320042
Closed Oct–14 May 8⇄ Lift Beach sea

★★**Résidence** 36 prom Clémenceau (n rest)
☎320666 35rm17⇄7🍴 🏛 sB46–56 (room only)
sB⇄🍴90–124 (room only) dB46–90 (room only)
dB⇄🍴100–163 (room only) sea

SABLES-D'OR-LES-PINS 22 (Côtes-du-Nord)
1,550 (☎96) Map **7** B3

★★★**Bon Accueil** 🅛 allée des Acacias ☎414219
Closed Oct–Whit except Etr 46rm25⇄5🍴 P
sB44–55 sB⇄🍴49–65 dB60–88 dB⇄🍴78–118
(English breakfast) L30–48 D30–48 sea

★★★**Diane** 🅛 av Brouard ☎414207 Closed
Oct–Whit except Etr 45rm22⇄6🍴 P sB44–55
sB⇄🍴49–65 dB60–80 dB⇄🍴78–118
(English breakfast) L30–48 D30–48 sea lake

★★**Ajoncs d'Or** ☎414212 Closed 26 Sep–14 May
(except Etr) 75rm25⇄15🍴 A45rm 🏛 P Lift sB44–59
sB⇄🍴59–84 dB62–77 dB⇄🍴77–92
(English breakfast) L40–52 D40–52 🍴 sea

★★**Dunes d'Armor** ☎414206 Closed Oct–May
65rm40🍴 A18rm P sB44–54 sB🍴fr67 dB63–76
dB⇄🍴93–112 (English breakfast) L27–55 D27–65
sea mountains

★★**Voile d'Or** r des Acacias ☎414249 Closed
16 Nov–Feb 16rm5⇄5🍴 P dB62–90 dB⇄🍴90
L26–57 D26–57&alc sea

SABLÉ-SUR-SARTHE 72 (Sarthe) 11,800 (☎43)
Map **8** D2

★**St Martin** 3 r Haute St-Martin ☎950003 Closed Mar
10rm1⇄4🍴 sB40–53 sB⇄🍴fr53 dB⇄🍴60–65
L25–45 D25–45

SACLAY 91 (Essonne) (☎1) Map **9** B4

☆☆☆**Novotel** Christ-de Saclay ☎9418140 tx691856
36⇄ P Lift sB⇄fr160 dB⇄fr172 English breakfast
only 🏊 Pool

ST-AFFRIQUE 12 (Aveyron) 9,250 (☎65)
Map **16** D1

★★**Moderne** av A-Pezet ☎990131 37rm9⇄16🍴
A11rm 🏛 P sB43–63 sB⇄🍴70 dB50–70 dB⇄🍴78
L21–60&alc D21–60&alc mountains

ST-AGRÈVE 07 (Ardèche) (☎75) 2,750 Map **27** A3

🛏 🕸**M Courtial** 26 av des Cévennes ☎301334 P Peu

ST-AIGNAN 41 (Loir-et-Cher) 3,700 (☎39) Map **9** A2

★★**St-Aignan** 🅛 7–9 quai J-J-Delorme ☎751804
Closed mid Dec–Jan 23rm2⇄12🍴 sB41–57

sB⇄🍴97–114 dB55–66 dB⇄🍴106–123
L28–70&alc D28–70&alc

ST-ALBAIN See **MÂCON**

ST-AMOUR 39 (Jura) 2,900 (☎82) Map **10** D1

★**Alliance** ☎251003 Closed 10 Oct–Mar
16rm8⇄5🍴 🏛 P sB60–90 sB⇄🍴70–90 dB70–100
dB⇄🍴80–110 L32–65 D32–65

★**Commerce** pl Chevalerie ☎251206 22rm4⇄3🍴
🏛 sB34–48 sB⇄🍴43–48 dB43–47
dB⇄🍴56–62 (English breakfast) L26–65 D26–65
mountains

ST-AUBAN See **CHÂTEAUX-ARNOUX**

ST-AUBIN-SUR-MER 14 (Calvados) 1,200 (☎31)
Map **8** D4

★**St Aubin** 🅛 r Verdun ☎973039 Closed Oct–21
Mar 26rm12⇄ sea

ST AVOLD 57 (Moselle) 18,950 (☎87) Map **11** A3

☆☆☆**Novotel St-Avold** (N3A) ☎922593 tx860966
60⇄ P Lift sB⇄fr131 dB⇄fr143 English breakfast
only Pool 🌙 lake

ST-BRIEUC† 22 (Côtes-du-Nord) 56,300 (☎96)
Map **7** B3

★★★**Alexandre 1er** 19 pl du Guesclin (n rest)
☎337945 43⇄ 🏛 P Lift sB⇄91–103 dB⇄114–140

★★★**Griffon** r de Guernsey ☎334003
44rm32⇄12🍴 🏛 P Lift 🌙 sB79 dB⇄🍴109–152
(English breakfast)

🛏 🕸**Moderne** 44 r du Dr-Rahuel ☎334015 (Closed
Sat) Frd

🛏 🕸**Royal Auto** 121 r J-Ferry ☎611091 (closed
weekends)

ST-CAST 22 (Côtes-du-Nord) 3,250 (☎96) Map **8** C3

★★★**Royal Bellevue** bd de la Mer ☎410004 Closed
Jul & Aug 107rm49⇄8🍴 Lift

★**Angleterre & Panorama** ☎410044 Closed
8 Sep–5 Jun 40rm 🏛 sea

At **Garde-St-Cast (La)** (2km SE)

★★★**Ar Vro** 🅛 ☎410001 Closed Oct–May
47rm30⇄12🍴 🏛 P Lift sB⇄🍴92 dB⇄🍴174–204
L65–110 D65–110 sea

At **Pen-Guen** (2.5km S)

★★**Pins** ☎410781 Closed Sep–24 Jun 38rm7⇄5🍴
sea

ST-CÉRÉ 46 (Lot) 4,400 (☎60) Map **16** C2

★★**Paris et Coq Arlequin** 🅛 bd du Dr-Roux
☎380213 Closed 4 Jan–Feb 32rm14⇄18🍴 🏛 P
sB⇄🍴82–115 dB⇄🍴92–165 L35–85 D35–85

★★**Touring** 7 pl de la République ☎380108 tx51626
Closed 16 Oct–May 31rm6⇄1🍴 🏛

ST-CHÉLY-D'APCHER 48 (Lozère) 5,350 (☎66)
Map **27** A3

★**Lion d'Or** 132 r T-Roussel ☎310014 Closed Jan
30rm5⇄5🍴 🏛 sB35 sB⇄🍴46 dB47 dB⇄🍴55
(English breakfast) L18–33 D18–33

🛏 🕸**Moderne** (Chauvet) 42 av de la République
☎310612 ☎310327 P Ren

ST-CLAUDE 39 (Jura) 14,100 (☎82) Map **10** D1

🛏 🕸**Grenard** 23 r Carnot ☎450648 P Frd (GB)

ST-CYPRIEN 24 (Dordogne) 1,800 (☎53)
Map **16** C2

★★**Abbaye** ☎292048 Closed Jan 18rm7⇄10🍴

ST DENIS See **PARIS**

ST-DIÉ† 88 (Vosges) 26,540 (☎29) Map **11** A3

★**Nouvel** 10 r Gambetta ☎562221 32rm5⇄1🍴 P
sB43–48 sB⇄🍴48–66 dB⇄🍴85 L30–45 D30–45

★**Vosges** 57 r Thiers ☎561621 17rm10🍴 🏛

🛏 🕸**Thouzet** rte de Raon ☎562330 Frd

ST-DIZIER† 52 (Haute-Marne) 39,850 (☎25)
Map **10** C/D3

★★★**Gambetta** ☎052210 33rm30⇄ 🏛 P Lift 🌙
sBfr56 sB⇄🍴109–120 dB⇄🍴127–145
(English breakfast) L fr34 Dfr36

★**Auberge la Babotte** (3m W on N4) ☎052075 10🍴
🏛 P Lift sB⇄🍴58–68 dB⇄🍴66–96 (English breakfast)
L28–60 &alc D28–60 &alc

★**Soleil d'Or** rte de Bar-le-Duc ☎050310 tx840946
🏛 Lift Pool

🛏 🕸**Clabaut** rte de Bar le Duc ☎051512 Peu

210

France

&ọ *Sport Auto* av Gl-Sarrail ☎051050 BL/Tri
Ⓑ &ọ *Triangle Motors* rte de Bar-le-duc (N401)
☎052398 Frd
ST-EMILION 33 (Gironde) 3,400 (☎56) Map **15** B2
★★**Hostellerie de la Plaisance** pl Clocher ☎517232
Closed 16 Jan–14 Feb 12↩

ST-ÉTIENNE 42 (Loire) 221,800 (☎77) Map **27** A4
★★★**Christel** r Bergson (n rest) ☎740221 tx300086
107↩ sB↩fr117 (English breakfast)
★★★**Frantel** r de Wuppertal ☎252275 tx300050
120↩ 🏤 P Lift sB↩151–180 dB↩165–194 L fr62
Dfr62
★★★**Grand** 10 av Libération (n rest) ☎329977
tx330811 86rm55↩31 🏠 Lift 🄓 sB75–136
sB↩🏠130–136 dB90–187 dB↩🏠175–187
(English breakfast)
★★★**Terminus du Forez** 31 av Denfert-Rochereau
☎324847 Closed 14–27 Aug 66rm25↩37 🏠 A1rm
🄓 sB↩🏠100 dB↩🏠115 L fr33 Dfr33
&ọ **St Etienne Automobile** 50 r Desire-Claude
☎325025 Opl (GB)

ST ETIENNE AIRPORT 52 (Haute-Marne)
Map **27** A4
☆☆☆**Novotel St-Etienne Aéroport** Centre de Vie,
(W of airport off N82) ☎551074 tx900722 98↩ P Lift
sB↩fr134 dB↩fr166 English breakfast only Pool

ST-ÉTIENNE-DE-BAIGORRY 64 (Pyrénées-
Atlantiques), 1,800 (☎59) Map **20** C3
★★**Arcé** (formerly, Trinquet) ☎374014 Closed
12 Nov–Feb 28rm14↩10 🏠 🏤 P sB70–90
dB80–100 L38–50 D38–50 mountains

ST-FLORENT See **CORSE (CORSICA)**

ST-FLORENTIN 89 (Yonne) 7,250 (☎86) Map **10** C2
★**Est** 7 r fbg St-Martin ☎351035 Closed Dec & Jan
29rm A6rm 🏤 P sB fr40 dB47–57 L 20–55

ST-FLOUR 15 (Cantal) 8,800 (☎71) Map **16** D2
★★★**Europe** 12–13 cours Spy-des-Ternes ☎600364
Closed 16 Jan–9 Feb 48rm18↩5 🏠 Lift
★★**Nouvel Bonne Table** 16 av République (DP)
☎600586 tx990218 48rm40↩ A30rm 🏠 Lift
★★**St Jacques** 6 pl Liberté ☎600920 30rm4↩15 🏠
🏤
★★**Voyageurs** 25 r Collège ☎601551 Closed
Oct–Apr 40rm16↩1 🏠 🏠 Lift sB53–58
sB↩🏠71–88 dB66–76 dB↩🏠76–106
(English breakfast) L25–60 D25–60 mountains
★**Parc & Terminus** av de la République (DP)
☎600829 Closed 11 Oct–Nov 48rm5↩5 🏠 🏠 Lift
Ⓑ **Nègre et Fils** av du Lioran ↩600243 ☎600643
🏤 P Peu (GB)

ST-GALMIER 42 (Loire) 3,250 (☎77) Map **27** A4
★★★**Charpinière** (formerly Christel) ☎541020
Closed Jan 35↩ P 🄓 sB↩94–138 dB↩117–167
(English breakfast) L48 &alc D45 &alc Pool

ST-GAUDENS 31 (Haute-Garonne) 12,950 (☎61)
Map **16** C1
★★**Ferrière & France** 1 r Gl-Leclerc ☎891457
18rm12↩ P 🄓 sB38 dB↩56–76 (English breakfast)
D22 mountains
At **Villeneuve de Rivière** (6km W on N117)
★★**Cedres** ☎891204 20↩ P Lift sB↩90–100 (room
only) dB↩125–140 room only)

ST-GEORGE d'AURAC 43 (Haute-Loire) Map **27** A3
Ⓑ **L Giraud** rte du puy (N102) ☎779111 P Cit

ST-GEORGES-DE-DIDONNE 17 (Charente-
Maritime), 4,000 (☎46) Map **15** B3
★**Bellevue** ☎050742 Closed Oct–Feb 19rm6↩
A5rm sB44 dB60 dB↩75 L27–40 D27–40 sea

ST-GERMAIN-DE-JOUX 01 (Ain) 550 (☎50)
Map **27** B4
★**Reygrobellet** Ⓛ (N84) (DP) ☎598113 Closed 26
Sep–14 Nov 20rm13↩4 🏠 🏠

ST-GERMAIN-EN-LAYE 78 (Yvelines) 42,000 (☎1)
Map **9** B3
Ⓑ &ọ **GUYNEMER Auto** 1 pl Guynemer ☎9631340
Fia/Lnc (GB)

ST-GERVAIS-LES-BAINS 74 (Haute-Savoie) 4,800
(☎50) Map **28** C4

★★★**Alpenrose** ☎782955 tx34414 Closed 16
Oct–14 Dec 47rm28↩19 🏠 Lift Pool
★★★**Splendid** ☎782133 Closed 16 Apr–Jun & 11
Sep–19 Dec 20rm12↩4 🏠 Lift sB79
sB↩🏠101–121 dB fr90 dB↩🏠132–142 mountains

ST-GILLES 30 (Gard) 9,800 (☎66) Map **27** A2
At **Saliers** (4km E on N572)
★★★**Cabanettes en Camargue** ☎873153 tx480451
29↩ 🏠 P dB↩164–189 L fr55 Dfr55 Pool

ST-GILLES-CROIX-DE-VIE 85 (Vendée) 6,900
(☎30) Map **7** B1
★★**Embruns** 16 bd de la Mer ☎551140 23rm9↩6 🏠
sB53–73 sB↩73 dB51–84 (English breakfast)
L fr31 Dfr31 sea

ST-GIRONS 09 (Ariège) 8,800 (☎61) Map **22** C4
★★★**Eychenne** 8 av P-Laffant ☎662055 Closed
1–26 Dec 50rm30↩10 🏠 🏠 🄓 sB66–131
sB↩🏠111–131 dB42–162 dB↩🏠147–162
(English breakfast) L37 D37 mountains
★★★**Truite Dorée** Ⓛ rte d'Aulus (1km S) ☎661689
Closed Oct–Apr 12rm6↩6 🏠 P sB99–119
sB↩🏠104–124 dB198–238 dB↩🏠203–243
(English breakfast) L35–70 D35–70 mountains lake

ST-HILAIRE-DE-BRETHMAS See **ALÈS**

ST-HILAIRE-LE-CHATEL See **MORTAGNE-AU-
PERCHE**

ST-HILAIRE-DU-HARCOUET 50 (Manche) 5,750
(☎33) Map **8** C3
★**Lion d'Or** Ⓛ 120 r Avranches ☎491082
20rm6↩11 🏠 sB43 sB↩🏠60–79 dB51
dB↩🏠68–87 L29–40 D29–40
★**Relais de la Poste** 11 r de Mortain (DP) ☎491031
12rm ↩🏠

ST-JEAN-CAP-FERRAT 06 (Alpes-Maritimes)
2,400 (☎93) Map **28** C2
★★★★**Grand Cap Ferrat** bd Gl-de-Gaulle ☎010454
tx47184 Closed Oct–Feb 80rm52↩12 🏠 🏠 Lift 🏊
Pool sea
★★★**Della Robbia** bd Gl-de-Gaulle (DP & Pn)
☎013307 Closed Oct–19 Dec 12rm9↩3 🏠 P
dB↩🏠250–337 L45 D45 sea
Ⓑ &ọ **Toso** Le Pont St-Jean ☎010589 P Ren (GB)

ST-JEAN-DE-BRAY See **ORLEÁNS**

ST-JEAN-DE-LUZ 64 (Pyrénées-Atlantiques)
121,000 (☎59) Map **19** B3
★★★**Chantaco** rte d'Ascain ☎261476
Closed Nov–Mar 24↩ 🏠 P 🄓 sB↩129–156
dB↩198–272 (English breakfast) L70–80 D70–80
🏊 ⓢ mountains lake
★★★★**Miramar** rte Ste-Barbe ☎260994
Closed 16 Nov–14 Dec 25↩ 🏠 sea
★★★★**Moderne** 43 bd Thiers ☎261461
Closed Sep–Jun 82rm77↩ Lift sea
☆☆☆**Motel Basques** Rond-Point Ste-Barbe
☎260424 Closed 23 Sep–21 Mar 55rm21↩15 🏠
★★★**Poste** 83 r Gambetta ☎260453
Closed Nov–Feb 34rm18↩9 🏠 🄓 sB59–65
dB97–105 dB↩🏠107–115
★★**Paris** 1 bd Passicot (n rest) ☎260062
Closed 16 Dec–Feb 23rm19↩9 🏠 sB45–52
sB↩🏠63–68 dB60–66 dB↩🏠76–84 mountains
lake
★★**Plage** 33 r Garat ☎260646 Closed mid Oct–mid
Apr 24rm17↩4 🏠 🏠 sB56 sB↩🏠77
dB↩🏠103–125 L32 D32 sea
★**Continental** 15 av Verdun ☎260123 24rm5↩15 🏠
sB69 sB↩🏠69 dB fr67 dB↩🏠95 D28–35
mountains
Ⓑ &ọ **Lamerain** 4–6 bd V-Hugo ☎260402 Ren (GB)
At **Ciboure** (1 km SW off N10)
★**Hostellerie de Ciboure** rte d'Espagne ☎260057
22rm 8↩7 🏠 P sB fr38 sB↩🏠68 dB fr57 dB↩🏠88
(English breakfast) L30 D30 Pool

ST-JEAN-DE-MAURIENNE 73 (Savoie) 10,450
(☎79) Map **28** C3
★★**St-Georges** 344 r République (n rest) ☎640105
24rm16↩5 🏠 P sB fr36 sB↩🏠 fr51 dB fr50
dB↩🏠67–82 mountains

France

⬛ ➤➤*Duverney* av du Mont-Cenis ☎641233 P Ren

ST-JEAN-DE-MONTS 85 (Vendée) 5,550 (☎30)
Map **7** B1

★★*Plage* espl de la Mer (DP) ☎580035 closed 16
Sep–14 May 56rm22⇌15🏠 Lift

🛏 ➤➤**M G Vrignaud** ☎586144 ⊜(Jun–15Sep) P Ren

ST-JEAN-DE-PRICHE See **MÂCON**

ST-JEAN-DE-VEDAS See **MONTPELLIER**

ST-JEAN-LE-THOMAS 50 (Manche) (☎33)
Map **8** C3

★★*Bains*L̃ (opp Post Office) ☎488420 Closed
16 Oct–14 Mar 30rm12⇌5🏠 A8rm P dB41
dB⇌🏠70 L21–55 D21–55 Pool ♡ sea

ST-JEAN-PIED-DE-PORT 64 (Pyrénées-
Atlantiques) 1,900 (☎59) Map **20** C3

★★★*Continental* 3 av Renaud (n rest) ☎370025
Closed 6 Nov–Mar 19⇌ Lift

★★*Central* 1 pl C-de-Gaulle ☎370022 14rm7⇌6🏠
Lift

★★*Pyrénées* pl Marché ☎370101 Closed
21 Nov–19 Dec 29rm20⇌3🏠

ST-JULIEN-DE-LAMPON 24 (Dordogne) 500 (☎53)
Map **16** C2

At **Rouffillac** (N of R Dordogne)

★*Cayre* ☎297024 14rm4⇌10🏠 A5rm P
dB⇌🏠70–85 L24–70 D24–70 ♣ Pool mountains

ST-JULIEN-EN-BEAUCHÈNE 05 (Hautes-Alpes)
150 (☎92) Map **27** B3

★★*St-Bermond-Gauthier* (N75) ☎580352
21rm4⇌21🏠 🏠 P sB⇌🏠30–55 dB⇌🏠43–69
(English breakfast) L23–55 D23–55 mountains

ST-JULIEN-EN-GENEVOIS 74 (Haute-Savoie)
6,400 (☎50) Map **28** C4

★*Savoyarde* rte de Lyon ☎492579 10rm1⇌ P sB36
sB⇌60 dB48 dB⇌67 L26 D26

ST-JULIEN-LES-VILLAS See **TROYES**

ST-LARY-SOULAN 65 (Hautes-Pyrénées) 750
(☎62) Map **21** B4

★★*Sporting* tx51617 Closed 16 Apr, Jun,
& Sep–14 Dec 72rm13⇌59🏠 Lift ♣ Pool

ST-LAURENT-DE-COGNAC See **COGNAC**

ST-LAURENT-DU-VAR See **NICE**

ST-LÔ 50 (Manche) 25,050 (☎33) Map **8** C4

★★*Terminus*L̃ 3 av Briovère ☎571471 15rm3⇌8🏠
🏠 P sB48–50 sB⇌🏠68–73 dB57 dB⇌🏠75–83
(English breakfast) L35 D35

★★*Univers*L̃ 1 av Briovère ☎571153
25rm12⇌10🏠 P sB42–53 sB⇌🏠53 dB⇌🏠84–86
(English breakfast) L31–60 D31–60

★*Armoric* 15 r de la Marne (n rest) ☎571747 Closed
27 Dec–4 Jan 21rm2⇌4🏠 P Lift sB fr36 sB⇌🏠55
dB⇌🏠42–61

★*Cremaillère* pl de la Préfecture ☎571468 Closed
Jan 12rm2⇌1🏠 P sB fr36 sB⇌🏠68–81 dB47–52
dB⇌🏠 fr84 (English breakfast)

★*Gare* pl de la Gare ☎571515 Closed 1–14 Feb
18rm2⇌2🏠 🏠 P sB34–57 sB⇌🏠57 dB49–63
dB⇌🏠63 (English breakfast) L27–70 D27–70

🛏 ➤➤**Elizabeth** rte de Coutances ☎571258 P
Bed/Opl

ST-LOUIS 68 (Haut-Rhin) 18,150 (☎89) Map **11** B2

★★*Pfiffer* 77 r Mülhouse ☎677444 Closed 6–20
Aug & 24 Dec–5 Jan 36rm 14⇌7🏠 🏠 P Lift sB fr63
sB⇌🏠105–120 dB fr73 dB⇌🏠130 L45–65 D alc

🛏 ➤➤**Bader** 81 av Gl-de-Gaulle ☎670015 Ren (GB)

ST-MALO†35 (Ille-et-Vilaine) 46,300 (☎99)
Map **8** C3

★★★*Central* 6 Grand r ☎408770 47rm 21⇌16🏠 🏠
Lift

★★*Grotte aux Fees* 36 chaussée du Sillon ☎348312
Closed Oct–Apr (except Xmas) 42rm6⇌ sea

★★*Louvre* 2–4 r de Marins ☎408662 Closed
Oct–Mar 45rm2⇌16🏠 Lift

★*Celtic* 25 chaussée du Sillon (n rest) ☎560948
Closed 16 Sep–14 May 15rm6⇌ sB45–60
dB80–100 dB⇌🏠140–150 sea

★*Noguette* 9 r de la Fosse ☎408357 13rm 4⇌5🏠 P
Lift sB51–88 sB⇌🏠168–88 dB59–116
dB⇌🏠76–136 L20–42 D20–42

🛏 ➤➤**Corsaires** 2 av L-Martin ☎561866 Frd (GB)
At **Paramé** (1km E)

★★*Rochebonne* 15 bd Châteaubriand ☎560172
39rm7⇌32🏠 Lift dB⇌🏠95–113 L36 D36 sea

ST-MARC 44 (Loire-Atlantique) (☎40) Map **7** B2

★★*Plage* ☎709282 Closed Oct & Nov 40rm9⇌15🏠

ST-MARTIN-DE-BELLEVILLE 74 (Haute-Savoie)
(☎50) Map **28** C4

☆☆☆**Novotel Val-Thorens** ☎000139 tx980230
104⇌ P Lift Pool

ST-MARTIN D'HÈRES See **GRENOBLE**

ST-MAURICE LA SOUTERRAINE 23 (Creuse)
(☎55) Map **16** C4

⬛ ➤➤**Larraud** carrefour (5km W at N20 & N142) La
Croisière ☎631503 M/c P

ST-MAURICE-SUR-MOSELLE 88 (Vosges) 1,900
(☎29) Map **11** A2

★★*Relais des Ballons*L̃ 22 r de la Gare ☎615109
Closed 13 Dec–14 Mar 19rm19⇌1🏠 🏠 P ♪
sB⇌🏠85–100 dB⇌🏠106–140 (English breakfast)
L60–150 D60–150 St% mountains

★*Bonséjour* ☎615233 18rm4⇌2🏠 🏠 P sB40–57
dB71–82 dB⇌🏠71–100 (English breakfast)
L30–40 D28–40 mountains

ST-MAXIMIN-LA-STE BAUME 83 (Var) 4,050 (☎94)
Map **27** B2

★*Chez Nous* 3 bd J-Jaurès ☎780257 tx83470
Closed 4 Dec–14 Jan 7rm1⇌2🏠 🏠 P sB fr30 dB fr47
dB⇌🏠 fr66 (English breakfast)

🛏 ➤➤**Centrauto** (N7) ☎780104 Ren

ST-MICHEL-DE-MAURIENNE 73 (Savoie) 3,900
(☎79) Map **28** C3

★★*Savoy*L̃ 25 r Gl-Ferrié ☎71 Closed 19 Jun–10
Jul 24rm12⇌4🏠 🏠 P sB51–55 sB⇌🏠65–77
dB59–67 dB⇌🏠73–114 (English breakfast)
L34–65 D34–65

🛏 ➤➤**Baudin** 18 r du Temple ☎15 Sim

ST-MICHEL-EN-GRÈVE 22 (Côtes-du-Nord) 400
(☎96) Map **7** B3

★★*Plage*L̃ ☎357443 Closed Jan–7 Feb 45rm5⇌
sea

ST-NABORD See **REMIREMONT**

ST-NAZAIRE 44 (Loire-Atlantique) 69,800 (☎40)
Map **7** B2

★★*Dauphin* 33 r J-Jaurès (n rest) ☎225685
22rm4⇌12🏠 🏠 ♪ sB fr49 sB⇌🏠62–82 dB75–94
dB⇌🏠75–94 (English breakfast)

🛏 ➤➤**Carnot** (Pauloin) 10 bd R-Coty ☎225425 Frd

ST-PALAIS-SUR-MER 17 (Charente-Maritime)
2,250 (☎46) Map **15** B3

★★★*Courdouan* av Pontaillac ☎026051
36rm16⇌18🏠 P ♪ dB⇌🏠131–151 L53 D53 sea

ST-PAUL-DE-LOUBRESSAC 46 (Lot) Map **16** C2

★*Relais de la Madeleine*L̃ ☎319808 Closed
11 Dec–9 Jan 20rm1⇌6🏠 sB33–44 sB⇌🏠44
dB49–61 dB⇌🏠61 (English breakfast) L22alc
D22alc

ST-PAUL-LÈS-DAX See **DAX**

ST-PIERRE-D'ALBIGNY 73 (Savoie) 2,550 (☎79)
Map **28** C4

★*Vieux Moulin* ☎22 11rm1🏠

ST-PIERRE-DE-CHARTREUSE 38 (Isère) 600
(☎76) Map **27** B3

★★*Beau Site*L̃ ☎086134 34rm16⇌8🏠 P Lift
sB49–54 dB⇌🏠108–123 L fr35 D fr35 Pool
mountains

ST-PIERRE-QUIBERON See **QUIBERON**

ST-POL-DE-LÉON 29 (Finistère) 8,775 (☎98)
Map **7** A/B3

🛏 ➤➤**M J Charetteur** pl du Créisker ☎690208
☎690208 Ren

ST-POL-SUR-TERNOISE 62 (Pas-de-Calais) 6,550
(☎21) Map **3** A1

★**Lion d'Or** 74 r Hesdin ☎031044 16rm8⇄5🅿 A5rm P sB47 sB⇄🅿68–78 dB54 dB⇄🅿75–85 (English breakfast) L24–44 D24–44 St%

🍴 ⋈**Bailleul** (MH Ets) 35 r Bethune ☎030655 ☎030655 P Ren

ST-PONS 34 (Hérault) 3,450 (☎67) Map **16** D1

★★*Château de Ponderach* (1.2km S) ☎970257 Closed 3 Nov–mid Apr 12rm 9⇄ 🏠 ✎ Pool

🅿 ⋈**J M Prax** rte de Castres ☎970142 Ren

ST-POURÇAIN-SUR-SIOULE 03 (Allier) 5,600 (☎70) Map **9** B1

★**Chêne Vert** 35 bd Ledru-Rollin ☎454065 tx390794 Closed 3 Jan–9 Feb 35rm16⇄11🅿 A15rm 🏠 P sB32–75 sB⇄🅿50–75 dB41–48 dB⇄🅿58–93 L30–120 D30–120

★**Deux Ponts** Îlot de Tivoli ☎454114 Closed Dec 27rm6⇄10🅿 🏠 P sB42–48 sB⇄🅿74–90 dB55–67 dB⇄🅿82–99 L35–70 D35–70 lake

ST-PRIEST See **LYON**

ST-QUAY-PORTRIEUX 22 (Côtes-du-Nord) 3,600 (☎96) Map **7** B3

★★**Bretagne** 36 quai de la République (n rest) ☎704091 15rm6🅿 sB49–59 sB🅿59 dB🅿67–72 (English breakfast) sea

★**Gerbot d'Avoine** 2 bd Littoral ☎704009 Closed 3 wks Oct 26rm2⇄8🅿 sB41–52 dB64–69 dB⇄🅿84–109 L28–90 D28–90 sea

★**Plage** ☎704004 Closed Oct–mid Apr 25rm9⇄1🅿 dB47–56 dB⇄🅿64–69 L23–45 D23–45 sea

ST-QUENTIN†02 (Aisne) 69,200 (☎23) Map **10** C4

★★**Grand** 6 r Dachery ☎626977 tx140225 40rm33⇄7🅿 P sB⇄🅿70 dB⇄🅿81–120

★★**Paix & Albert-1er** pl de Huit Octobre ☎627762 tx140225 64rm23⇄13🅿 🏠 P Lift sB fr49 sB⇄🅿74–96 dB fr56 dB⇄🅿103–110

🅿 ⋈*Danton* 48–50 r Danton ☎624119 P

🅿 ⋈*Gueudet* (Centre Technique) rte d'Amiens ☎627079

🍴 ⋈**Rassinoux** 267 rte de Paris ☎623227 ☎623227 🚲 P Ren

ST-RAPHAËL 83 (Var) 21,400 (☎94) Map **28** C2

★★★*Continental* 25 bd de la Libération (n rest) ☎950014 50rm23⇄10🅿 Lift sea

★★**Beau Séjour** prom Prés-Coty ☎950375 Closed 16 Nov–Jan 52rm16⇄5🅿 A8rm Lift dB⇄🅿fr101 L fr46 D fr46 sea

★★**Plage & Méditerranée** 39 bd de la Libération (n rest) ☎950160 Closed Nov–Mar 50rm27⇄12🅿 Lift sea

★**Genève** 92 bd F-Martin (Pn) ☎952335 30rm

★**Vieux Port** 108 av Colt-Guildbaud ☎952312 15rm4⇄ sea

🅿 ⋈**Bains** r J-Barbier ☎951672 P Cit (GB)

🅿 ⋈**Valescure** (M E Vagneur) 142 av de Valescure ☎954939 Frd/Ren (GB)

ST-RÉMY-DE-PROVENCE 13 (Bouches-du-Rhône) 8,000 (☎90) Map **27** B2

★★★*Antiques* av Pasteur (DP) ☎920302 27rm18⇄9🅿 Pool ◯

★★*Castelet des Alpilles* pl Mireille (DP) ☎920721 Closed 15 Jan–20 Feb 19rm13⇄4🅿

ST-SATUR 18 (Cher) 1,760 (☎36) Map **9** B2

★★**Laurier** r du Commerce ☎541720 Closed Feb 10rm5🅿 P sB38 dB65–77 dB🅿65–77 L27–60 D27–60

ST-SERNIN-SUR-RANCE 12 (Aveyron) 700 (☎65) Map **16** D1

★★**France** pl du Fort ☎996026 25rm5⇄10🅿 🏠 P sB38 sB⇄🅿52 dB45–76 dB⇄🅿59–76 (English breakfast) L35–59 D21–59 mountains

ST-TROPEZ 83 (Var) 5,450 (☎94) Map **28** C1/2

★★★★*Byblos* av P-Signac ☎970004 tx470235 Closed Nov–14 Dec 59⇄🅿 P Lift ♪ sB⇄220–410 dB⇄250–560 (English breakfast) St% Pool sea

★★★*Coste* Port du Pilon (n rest) ☎970064 30rm20⇄4🅿 P ♪ sB59–74 sB⇄🅿89–99 dB77–89 dB⇄🅿102–114 (English breakfast) sea

★★★**Ermitage** av P-Signac (n rest) ☎970152 Closed Oct–Mar 29rm5⇄24🅿 P sB109–133 sB⇄🅿133 dB118–142 dB⇄🅿142–165 sea

ST-VAAST-LA-HOUGUE 50 (Manche) 2,400 (☎33) Map **8** C4

★*France & Fuchsias* 18 r Ml-Foch (DP) ☎544226 16rm3⇄7🅿 ◯

ST-VALERY-SUR-SOMME 80 (Somme) 3,150 (☎22) Map **3** A1

★★*Relais Guillaume de Normandy* quai Romerel ☎275236 Closed Nov 15rm7⇄ sea

🅿 ⋈**J-Lefèvre** 7 quai du Romeral ☎275017 Cit (GB)

ST-VALLIER-SUR-RHÔNE 26 (Drôme) 5,450 (☎75) Map **27** B3

At **Sarras** (2km W on N86)

★★**Vivarais** av de Vivarais ☎230188 Closed Feb 10rm9⇄1🅿 P sB37–53 (room only) sB⇄🅿53 (room only) dB⇄🅿53 (room only)

STE-ANNE-LA-PALUD 29 (Finistère) (☎98) Map **7** B3

★★★**Plage** ☎925012 Closed Oct–21 Mar 35rm30⇄ 🏠 sea

STE-CATHERINE See **BRIANÇON**

STE-ENIMIE 48 (Lozère) 650 (☎66) Map **27** A3

★*Paris* ☎475002 Closed Oct–Apr 20rm6⇄3🅿

STE-MARIE See **VARS (COL DE)**

STE-MAXIME-SUR-MER 83 (Var) 6,650 (☎94) Map **28** C2

★★★*Beau Site* 10 bd des Cystes (DP) ☎961963 tx970080 Closed Oct–Mar 38rm20⇄16🅿 A26rm 🏠 Lift ✎ Pool sea

★★★*Belle Aurore* 3 la Croisette ☎960245 Closed Nov–Jan 18rm11⇄7🅿 A4rm P ♪ sB⇄🅿110–170 (room only) dB⇄🅿110–170 (room only) St% Beach sea

★★★*Chardon Bleu* 2 allée du Chardon-Bleu ☎960208 Closed Nov–Mar 15rm7🅿 sea

★★*Palmiers* pl 15 Août (n rest) ☎960041 35rm10⇄8🅿 sea

☆☆**Royal Bon Repos** r J-Alcard (n rest) ☎960874 Closed 16 Oct–14 Mar 25🅿 🏠 P dB🅿106–154 sea

SAINTES†17 (Charente-Maritime) 28,450 (☎46) Map **15** D3

★★★**Commerce Mancini** r des Messageries ☎930661 tx791012 Closed 15 Dec–15 Jan 44rm32⇄12🅿 🏠 P ♪ sB62–115 sB⇄🅿65 dB83–168 dB⇄🅿129–168 L38–85 D38–85

★★**Nouvel** 1 r Pasteur (off cours National) (n rest) ☎930172 29rm6⇄3🅿 🏠

★★**Terminus** espl de la Gare (n rest) ☎930162 37rm12⇄ 🏠 P ♪ sB43–46 sB⇄🅿65–67 dB51–61 dB⇄🅿75–86

★**Messageries** r des Messageries (n rest) ☎936499 37rm6⇄13🅿 P sB51–59 sB⇄🅿79–94 dB63–70 dB⇄🅿93–108

🅿 ⋈**Savia** rte de Bordeaux ☎934344 Frd

SAINTES-MARIES-DE-LA-MER (LES) 13 (Bouches-du-Rhône) 2,245 (☎90) Map **27** A2

★**Mirage** r C-Pelletan ☎978043 Closed Nov–Feb 27rm6⇄21🅿 dB⇄🅿97–117

SALERS 15 (Cantal) 550 (☎71) Map **16** D3

★**Beffroi** (n rest) ☎407011 Closed Nov–mid Apr 10⇄🅿 P sB56–58 dB⇄🅿76–85

SALLANCHES 74 (Haute-Savoie) 8,450 (☎50) Map **28** C4

☆☆*Ibis* av de Genève ☎581442 tx380271 60⇄🅿 Lift

SALON-DE-PROVENCE 13 (Bouches-du-Rhône) 35,000 (☎90) Map **27** B2

★*Grand Poste* 1 r Prés-Kennedy ☎560194 Closed Nov–Jan 29rm2⇄11🅿

At **Barben (La)** (8km SE)

★*Touloubre* ☎551685 tx430156 14rm6⇄1🅿 sB51–86 sB⇄🅿68–86 dB59–94 dB⇄🅿76–94

At **Lançon de Provence** (9km SE on A7)

☆☆☆*Sofitel* ☎539070 tx440183 100⇄🅿 P Lift ♪ sB⇄🅿170–207 dB⇄🅿213–251 D50 ✎ Pool

213

France

SALSES 66 (Pyrénées-Orientales) 2,100 (☎69)
Map **22 D4**
☆☆☆**Euromotel Roussillon** (N9) ☎386067
tx500092 Closed winter 56⇔
SAMER 62 (Pas-de-Calais) 2,035 Map **3 A1**
⚬ **⇆Roussel** 21 av C-de Gaulle ☎335144 P
SANARY-SUR-MER 83 (Var) 10,450 (☎94)
Map **27 B1**
★★**Tour** quai Gl-de-Gaulle ☎741010 Closed 16
Nov–14 Jan 25rm10⇔9🍴 sB47 sB⇔🍴83 dB56
dB⇔🍴97 L34 D34 sea
SANCÉ-LES-MÂCON See **MÂCON**
SARAN See **ORLÉANS**
SARLAT 24 (Dordogne) 10,900 (☎53) Map **16 C2**
★★★**Hostellerie de Meysset** ☎590829 Closed 16
Oct–7 Apr 30rm26⇔4🍴 P sB⇔🍴148–153
dB⇔🍴176–206 (English breakfast) L60 D60
★★★**Madeleine** 1 pl de la Petite Rigaudie ☎591041
Closed Jan 22rm18⇔4🍴 sB⇔🍴100–120
dB⇔🍴130–160 (English breakfast) L35–66
D35–66
★★**St-Albert** 🗺 10 pl Pasteur ☎590109
55rm22⇔18🍴 A24rm
★**Lion d'Or** 48 av Gambetta (n rest) ☎590083
Closed Nov–mid Apr 26rm4⇔4🍴 sB44 sB⇔🍴68
dB52 dB⇔🍴94 (English breakfast)
⚬ **⇆Fournet** rte de Vitrac ☎590523 M/c P Frd/Hon
SARRAS See **ST-VALLIER-SUR-RHÔNE**
SAULIEU 21 (Côte-d'Or) 3,200 (☎80) Map **10 C2**
★★★**Poste** 🗺 2 r Grillot (n rest) ☎640567 tx350540
48rm42⇔🏛 P 🌓 sB⇔🍴75–101 sB⇔🍴101–114 dB64
dB⇔🍴110–143 (English breakfast)
★★**Côte d'Or** 🗺 2 r Argentine ☎640766 Closed
3 Nov–1 Dec 22rm16⇔5🍴 A4rm 🏛
★**Quatre Vents** 47 r J-Ferry (X-rds Nevers–Autun)
(DP) ☎640079 Closed Jan 11rm 🏛
⚬ **⇆Fontaine** av de la Gare ☎640087 ☎640087 P
Peu (GB)
SAUMUR†49 (Maine-et-Loire) 34,200 (☎41)
Map **8 D2**
★★★**Budan** 3 quai Carnot ☎512876 80rm45⇔30🍴
🏛 Lift sea
★★**Roi René** 94 av Gl-de-Gaulle ☎504530 Closed
16 Nov–Feb 40rm9⇔12🍴 P Lift sB47–95
sB⇔🍴75–95 dB83–103 L33–57 D33–57 river
★**Bretagne** 🗺 55 r St-Nicolas ☎512638 9rm 🏛
sB34–36 dB41–58
★**Croix-Verte** 49 r de Rouen ☎503931 Closed Jan
18rm3⇔1🍴 P sB46–59 sB⇔🍴59–64 dB58–63
dB⇔🍴71–78 (English breakfast) L25–50 D25–50⚬
⚬ **M M Charbonneau** 103 r du Pont Fouchard
☎501133 P Peu (GB)
At **Chenehutte-les-Tuffeaux** (8km NW)
★★★**Prieuré** ☎501531 tx720183 Closed Feb
36rm31⇔4🍴 A15rm P Lift 🌓 sB94–174
sB⇔🍴94–174 dB118–243 dB⇔🍴118–243
(English breakfast) L65–135 D65–135 St% Pool
river
SAUSHEIM See **MULHOUSE**
SAUT-DES-CUVES See **GÉRARDMER**
SAVERNE 67 (Bas-Rhin) 10,450 (☎88) Map **11 B3**
★★**Geiswiller** 🗺 17 r Côte ☎911851 Closed 16–31
Jan 18rm2⇔7🍴
★**Boeuf Noir** 🗺 22 Grand r ☎911053 20rm5⇔8🍴 🏛
P sB48–70 (English breakfast) L27–70 D27–70
mountains
★**Chez Jean** 🗺 3 r de la Gare ☎911019
22rm15⇔3🍴 Lift dB55–75 dB⇔🍴75–93 L24–80
D24–80
⇆Wallior 21 r St-Nicolas ☎911752 ☎911752 Cit
(GB)
At **Stambach** (4.5km SW)
★★**Fameuse Truite** rte de Lutzelbourg ☎911861
32rm6⇔🏛
SAVIGNAC-LES-EGLISES 24 (Dordogne) 750
(☎53) Map **16 C3**
★**Parc** 🗺 ☎050012 Closed Jan & Feb
14rm10⇔4🍴 A11rm P sB⇔🍴134–214
dB⇔🍴148–228 L60–130 D60–130 ⚬

SÉES 61 (Orne) 5,250 (☎34) Map **8 D3**
★**Cheval Blanc** 🗺 1 pl St-Pierre ☎278048 9rm2🍴
sB fr37 sB🍴37–45 dB43–53 L20–36&alc
D20–36&alc
★**Dauphin** 31 pl Halls (DP) ☎278007 13rm1⇔2🍴
A6rm
SEGOS See **AIRE-SUR-L'ADOUR**
SELLIÈRES 39 (Jura) 930 Map **10 D1**
See also **Poligny**
At **Passenans** (6km SE)
★★**Domaine Touristique du Revermont** 🗺
☎852066 Closed 1–15 Feb & 1–15 Nov 28rm24⇔🍴
🏛 Lift Pool
SEMUR-EN-AUXOIS 21 (Côte-d'Or) 5,400 (☎80)
Map **10 C2**
★★**Lac** 🗺 (3km S on D103B at Lac de Pont)
☎971111 Closed 16 Dec–Jan 22rm9⇔2🍴 🏛 lake
★★**Côte d'Or** 3 pl G-Gaveau ☎970313 Closed Feb &
11–31 Dec 15rm2⇔5🍴 🏛 P sB31 sB⇔🍴56–61
dB44–47 dB⇔🍴63–68 (English breakfast) L26–54
D26–54
★**Gourmets** 4 r Varenne ☎970941 Closed 26
Oct–24 Nov 15rm3🍴 🏛 Lift sB fr34 dB47–56
dB🍴57 L31–55 D31–55
⚬ **M J Girard** 21 r du Cours ☎970510 P Ren
SÉNAS 13 (Bouches-du-Rhône) 3,300 (☎90)
Map **27 B2**
★**Luberon** (N7) ☎572010 Closed 16 Oct–Nov
7rm1⇔3🍴 P dB41–45 dB⇔🍴59–68 L25–65
D25–65
SENLIS 60 (Oise) 14,400 (☎4) Map **9 B3/4**
★★**Nord** 66 r République ☎4530116 Closed
24 Dec–19 Jan 16rm3⇔5🍴 🏛
⚬ **⇆P Delacharlery** rte de Crépy ☎4530818
☎4530818 P Ren (GB)
SENONCHES 28 (Eure-et-Loir) 3,500 (☎37)
Map **9 A3**
★**Forêt** 🗺 pl Champ-de-Foire ☎377850 Closed
Nov–3 Mar 14rm3⇔3🍴 P sB28–36
sB⇔🍴51–61 dB42–47 dB⇔🍴57–84
(English breakfast) L26–35 D26–35
SENS†89 (Yonne) 27,950 (☎86) Map **10 C3**
★★★**Paris & Poste** 97 r de la République ☎651743
Closed 16 Nov–14 Dec 38rm23⇔6🍴 A3rm 🏛 P 🌓
sB fr80 sB⇔🍴100–160 dB100–170
dB⇔🍴110–170 (English breakfast) L fr75&alc
D fr75&alc
★★**Croix Blanche** 9 r V-Guichard ☎651533
25rm2⇔6🍴 🏛
⚬ **⇆Senonaise d'Auto** Carr Ste-Colombe (N5 à St
Denis-sur-Sens) ☎651833 P Ren
SEPT-SAULX 51 (Marne) 350 (☎26) Map **10 C3**
★★**Cheval Blanc** ☎616027 Closed 16 Jan–14 Feb
25rm23⇔1🍴 A2rm 🏛 P Lift sB52–91 sB⇔🍴68–97
dB80–83 dB⇔🍴83–118 (English breakfast) L fr85
&alc Dfr85 &alc St% ⚬ Pool
SERRES 05 (Hautes-Alpes) 1,400 (☎92) Map **27 B3**
★**Alpes** av Grenoble ☎670018 18rm2⇔4🍴 🏛 P
sB35–44 sB⇔🍴63–64 dB51–52 dB⇔🍴71–77
L27–50 D27–50 mountains
⚬ **M P Reynaud** av de la Gare ☎670011 ☎670011
⚙ M/c P Ren
SERRIÈRES 07 (Ardèche) 1,450 (☎75) Map **27 B3**
★**Schaeffer** quai J-Roche ☎340007 Closed
Dec–Feb 13rm7🍴 L25–60 D25–60 St% river
SÈTE†34 (Hérault) 40,200 (☎67) Map **27 A2**
★★★**Grand** quai Ml-Lattre-de-Tassigny ☎742164
tx480225 51rm24⇔19🍴 Lift 🌓 dB60–73
dB⇔🍴96–125 (English breakfast) L26–35 D26–35
sea
⚬ **⇆Cano & Milano** 40 quai du Gl-Durand ☎742944
Ren
SEVRIER 74 (Haute-Savoie) 2,200 (☎50)
Map **28 C4**
At **Machevaz** (2km S by N512)
★★**Châtalgniers** ☎686329 tx385417 Closed
Oct–Apr 61rm23⇔11🍴 A35rm P sB fr37 dB fr67

France

dB⇄ 🍴fr78 (English breakfast) L29−80 D29−80 ⚓
Pool mountains

SEZANNE 51 (Marne) 6,550 (☎26) Map **10** C3

★★**Croix d'Or** 53 r N-Dame ☎420127 Closed 2 wks
Jan 13rm7⇄2🍴 ⌂ P sB40−44 sB⇄ 🍴40−44
dB⇄🍴52−60 L28−45 D28−45

★★**France** 25 r L-Jolly ☎420025 Closed 16 Jan−14
Feb 25rm7⇄10🍴 ⌂

SIORAC-EN-PÉRIGORD 24 (Dordogne) 800 (☎53)
Map **16** C2

★**Scholly** 🔙 r de la Poste ☎296002 Closed 16
Nov−14 Mar 30rm14⇄13🍴 A5rm P sB66−127
sB⇄ 🍴116−127 dB127−138 dB⇄🍴127−138
L42−100 D42−100

SISTERON 04 (Alpes-de-Hautes-Provence) 7,450
(☎92) Map **27** B2

★★★**Grand du Cours** av de la Libération (n rest)
☎610451 Closed 16 Nov−Feb 50rm20⇄30🍴 ⌂ P
Lift ♪ sB⇄🍴78−104 dB⇄🍴103−134
(English breakfast) mountains lake

★★**Select** pl de la République (n rest) ☎250 Closed
Nov−mid Apr 14rm3⇄2🍴

★★**Touring** 85 av de la Libération ☎6 Closed Nov &
Dec 30rm2⇄3🍴 ⌂

★**Arcades** pl de la République ☎209 10rm

🚗 **Alpes Automobiles** (Decaroli) av de la
Libération ☎610164 P AR/Ren

SOISSONS† 02 (Aisne) 32,150 (☎23) Map **10** C4

★★**Picardie** 6 r Neuve St-Martin (n rest) ☎532193
33rm6⇄27🍴 P Lift ♪ sB⇄🍴83−94
dB⇄🍴108−120

★**Rallye** 10 bd de Strasbourg (n rest) ☎530047
12rm1⇄4🍴 ⌂ dB64−111 dB⇄🍴86−111

🚗 **Jeanne d'Arc** 96 bd J-d'Arc ☎530414 ☎530414
Peu

🚗 **Lach** 7 r de la Bannière ☎533003 M/c
BMW/Hon/Peu (GB)

SOUFFELWEYERSHEIM See **STRASBOURG**

SOUILLAC 46 (Lot) 4,400 (☎65) Map **16** C2

★★**Ambassadeurs** 🔙 12 av du Gl-de-Gaulle
☎377836 Closed Oct 24rm10⇄9🍴 sB38−69
sB⇄🍴62−69 dB60−95 dB⇄🍴71−95 L28−90
D28−90

★★**Grand** pl allée Verninac ☎377830 Closed
Oct−14 May 17rm10⇄ ⌂ sB45−58 sB⇄🍴75−79
dB62−71 dB⇄🍴82−106 L25−80 &alc D25−80 &alc

★★**Granges Vieilles** rte de Sarlat (1.5km W on
N703) (n rest) ☎378092 Closed Oct−Mar 10⇄

★★**Périgord** 🔙 av de Paris ☎377828 tx390794
Closed Nov−Apr 50rm15🍴15🍴 A20rm ⌂ P
sB48−108 sB⇄🍴58−118 dB65−125
dB⇄🍴65−125 L28−75 D28−75 St%

★★**Renaissance** 🔙 av J-Jaurès ☎377804 tx390794
24rm12⇄12🍴 P Lift sB⇄🍴68−108
dB⇄🍴81−121 L28−75 D28−75

★★**Trufflère** ☎378895 Closed 11 Jan−9 Mar
20rm14⇄6🍴 ⌂

★**Nouvel** 🔙 21 av du Gl-de-Gaulle ☎377958
30rm11⇄11🍴 ⌂

SOUPPES SUR-LOING 77 (Seine-et-Marne) 4,460
Map **9** B3

★**Mouton** 72 av Gl-Leclerc ☎4297008 12rm ⌂ P
sB37−42 dB50−54 L26−60 &alc D26−60 &alc

SOURCE (LA) See **ORLÉANS**

SOUSCEYRAC 46 (Lot) 1,050 (☎65) Map **16** D2

★**Déjeuner de Sousceyrac** 🔙 ☎380256 Closed
Dec−mid Apr 15rm3⇄4🍴 A4rm sB fr31 dB42−45
dB⇄🍴55−66 (English breakfast) L22−25 D22−25

SOUSTONS 40 (Landes) 5,150 (☎57) Map **15** A1

★★**Bergerie** av du Lac ☎480143 Closed Oct−Apr
27⇄ A15rm P sB⇄🍴96 dB⇄🍴106 (English breakfast)
L38 D38

🚗 **Dufour** ☎480022 P Ren (GB)

STAINVILLE 55 (Meuse) 400 (☎28) Map **10** D3

★★★**Grange** 🔙 ☎786015 9rm8⇄3🍴 ⌂ P Lift sB56
sB⇄🍴66 dB74 dB⇄🍴74 (English breakfast)
L32−53alc D32−53alc

STAMBACH See **SAVERNE**

STRASBOURG† 67 (Bas-Rhin) 257,350 (☎88)
Map **11** B3

★★★★**Sofitel Strasbourg** pl St-Pierre-le-Jeune (off r
Nuée Bleue) ☎329930 tx870894 180rm160⇄20🍴
⌂ Lift sB fr143 sB⇄🍴190−305 dB⇄🍴240−390
(English breakfast) L fr65 Dalc

★★★★**Terminus-Gruber** 10 pl de la Gare ☎328700
tx87998 85rm46⇄21🍴 Lift

★★★**France** 20 r Jeu des Enfants (n rest) ☎323712
tx890084 70rm11⇄59🍴 ⌂ Lift sB⇄🍴120−160
dB⇄🍴130−170

★★★**Grand** 12 pl de la Gare (n rest) ☎324690
tx870011 100⇄ P Lift sB⇄🍴138−163 dB⇄🍴166−196
(English breakfast)

★★★**Monopole-Métropole** 🔙 14 r Kuhn ☎321194
tx89366 100⇄ Lift

☆☆☆**PLM-Pont de l'Europe** Parc du Rhin ☎610323
tx870833 93⇄ P ♪ sB⇄🍴115 dB⇄🍴141 L fr26

★★★**Union** 8 quai Kellermann (corner of r Nuée
Bleue) (n rest) ☎327041 58rm25⇄14🍴 Lift

★★**Couronne** 26 r du fbg de Saverne (off bd Prés-
Wilson) (n rest) ☎323545 43rm5⇄13🍴 ⌂

☆☆**Ibis Strasbourg** av Sebastopol ☎221499
tx880399 97⇄ P Lift sB⇄fr113 dB⇄fr141
L30−50alc D30−50alc

★★**Rhin** 7 pl de la Gare (n rest) ☎323500 Closed 24
Dec−1 Jan 63rm10⇄9🍴 Lift

★★**Vendôme** 9 pl de la Gare (n rest) ☎324523
39rm14⇄21🍴 Lift sB48−83 sB⇄🍴70−92
dB82−100 dB⇄🍴82−100

🚗 **Grand Dierstein** 164A rte de Schirmeck ☎300272
BI/Rov/Tri

🚗 **Société Nouvelle Strasbourgeoise des Autos**
270 rte de Colmar ☎399905 Chy/Sim (GB)

At **Cronenbourg** (4km NW on D41)

🚗 **Goetzmann Motors** 60−64 r du Marché-Gare
☎292000 Opl

At **Illkirch-Graffenstaden** (10km SW on A35 near
Colmer Interchange)

☆☆☆**Mercure Strasbourg Sud** r de 23 Novembre
☎660300 tx890277 97⇄ P Lift sB⇄fr142 dB⇄fr158
English breakfast only Pool

☆☆☆**Novotel Strasbourg-Sud** rte de Colmar (N83)
☎662156 tx890142 76⇄ P Lift sB⇄fr148 dB⇄fr164
English breakfast only Pool

At **Souffelweyersheim**

🚗 **Hess** 46 rte de Brumath ☎209090 Lnc/Por

SULLY-SUR-LOIRE 45 (Loiret) 5,050 (☎38)
Map **9** B2

★★**Poste** 11 r fbg St-Germain ☎352622 Closed Feb
30rm5⇄6🍴 A10rm ⌂ P Lift sB38−58 sB⇄🍴63−88
dB76−96 dB⇄🍴96−116 (English breakfast)
L35−80 D35−80

SURVILLIERS 95 (Val-d'Oise) 2,750 (☎1) Map **9** B3

☆☆☆**Mercure St-Witz** chemin de Montmelian
☎4719203 tx695917 118⇄ P Lift sB⇄fr159
dB⇄fr172 English breakfast only Pool

☆☆☆**Novotel Paris Survilliers** (A1/D16) ☎4710652
tx695910 79⇄ P Lift sB⇄fr160 dB⇄fr173
English breakfast only Pool

TALANT See **DIJON**

TALLOIRES 74 (Haute-Savoie) 850 (☎50)
Map **28** C4

★★★★**Abbaye** rte Port Talloires ☎447081 tx385201
Closed 16 Oct−Apr 37rm29⇄2🍴 ⌂ P ♪
sB110−130 sB⇄🍴210−250 dB⇄🍴280−360
(English breakfast) L80−95 D80−95 mountains lake

★★★**Cottage** rte G-Bise ☎447110 Closed 16
Oct−14 Mar 40rm28⇄4🍴 A10rm ⌂ P Lift ♪
sB85−265 dB⇄🍴230−330 L70 D70 ⚓ mountains
lake

★★**Beau Site** ☎447104 Closed Oct−14 May
38rm22⇄5🍴 A27rm ⌂ ⚓ lake

★★**Vivier** ☎447054 Closed 16 Oct−Mar
34rm24⇄10🍴 ⌂ P sB⇄🍴69−82 dB76−89
dB⇄🍴65−76 L23−43 D23−43 mountains lake

TAMNIES 24 (Dordogne) 300 (☎53) Map **16** C2

★**Laborderie** 🔙 ☎296859 Closed Dec−Jan

17rm9⇄6🛏 dB⇄🛁 🛁64–84 L25–60 & alc
D25–60 & alc 🍴 ♎

TANCARVILLE 76 (Seine-Maritime) (☎35)
Map 9 A4

★**Marine** ☎948915 Closed 16 Jan–14 Feb
16rm4⇄2🛁 🏠

TARARE 69 (Rhône) 12,200 (☎74) Map 27 B4

★**Mère Paul** (2km W on N7) ☎631457 Closed 21
Sep–14 Oct 14rm7⇄1🛁 A4rm 🏠

TARASCON-SUR-ARIÈGE 09 (Ariège) 4,300 (☎61)
Map 22 C4

★★**Poste** 🇱 16 av V-Pilhes ☎646041 Closed
Nov–mid Apr 30rm14⇄4🛁 P sB40–83 sB⇄🛁83
sB55–91 dB⇄🛁91 (English breakfast) L alc D alc
mountains

TARASCON-SUR-RHÔNE 13 (Bouches-du-Rhône)
10,700 (☎90) Map 27 B2

★★**Terminus** ☎911895 Closed 16 Nov–14 Feb
27rm4⇄8🛁 sB36 dB50 dB⇄🛁75–95 L32–50
D32–50

★**Provençal** 12 cours A-Briand ☎911141
22rm6⇄6🛁 🏠 P sB fr25 sB⇄🛁 fr55 dB fr54
dB⇄🛁78–85 L22–48 D22–48

TARBES† 65 (Hautes-Pyrénées) 57,800 (☎62)
Map 15 B1

★★★**Mapotel President** 1 r G-Faure ☎939840
tx530522 57⇄ 🏠 P Lift sB⇄🛁 fr120 dB⇄🛁 fr190
L40–65 D40–65 Pool

★★**Croix Blanche** pl Verdun r Verdun ☎930854
30rm5⇄7🛁

★**Royal Henri-IV** 7 bd B-Barrère (n rest) ☎340168
22rm10⇄10🛁 🏠

🚩 ⋈**Laffole** 1 av B-Barrere ☎340059 P Fia (GB)

TERRASSON-LA-VILLEDIEU 24 (Dordogne) 6,250
(☎53) Map 16 C3

★★★★**Rush** av V-Hugo ☎500374 tx57575 Closed
Jan & Feb 48⇄ 🏠 Lift

THANN 68 (Haut-Rhin) 8,550 (☎89) Map 11 A2

★**Parc** 🇱 23 r Kléber ☎371098 Closed Nov
21rm19⇄4🛁 🏠 P sB fr36 sB⇄🛁 fr50 dB fr48
dB⇄🛁 fr68 L20–65 D20–65 mountains

At **Bitschwiller** (2km N on N66)

🚩 ⋈**L Klein** r du Rhin ☎370134 P Ren (GB)

THÉOULE 06 (Alpes Maritimes) 800 (☎93)
Map 28 C2

★★**Guerguy la Galère** ☎389671 Closed Nov–Jan
rm14⇄ 🏠 P dB⇄🛁240–280 sea

★**Hermitage Jules César** Théoule Plage (n rest)
☎389612 Closed Oct–Jan 18rm 12🛁 sea

THIERS 63 (Puy-de-Dôme) 17,850 (☎73) Map 27 A4

★**Centre** 10 r Traversiès ☎801912 12rm1⇄ sB fr35
dB45–48 dB fr71 (English breakfast)

★**Nouvel & Grand** pl Belfort ☎800061 22rm1⇄5🛁
🏠

THIONVILLE 57 (Moselle) 44,200 (☎87) Map 11 A4

🚩 ⋈**Central Auto** 17 Impasse du Viaduct ☎880809
Frd

THOISSEY 01 (Ain) 1,500 (☎74) Map 27 B4

★★**Chapon Fin** ☎040474 Closed 6 Jan–19 Feb
29rm16⇄8🛁 🏠 P Lift sB fr71 sB⇄🛁96–156
dB92–122 dB⇄🛁122–232 L70–150&alc
D70–150&alc

★**Beau-Rivage** av Port ☎040166 Closed Nov–Feb
10🛁 P sB fr46 sB🛁 fr54 dB fr70 dB🛁 fr77 L32–60
D32–60 mountains

THONON-LES-BAINS 74 (Haute-Savoie) 27,150
(☎50) Map 11 A1

★★**Clos Savoyard** 50 av Genève ☎710391 Closed
Oct 19rm8⇄8🛁

THOUARS 79 (Deux-Sevres) 12,650 (☎48)
Map 8 D2

★**Cheval Blanc** 53 r Tremoile ☎660021 38rm6⇄2🛁
🏠 P sB36–48 sB⇄🛁59–73 dB66–81
dB⇄🛁66–81 L22–50 D22–50

🚩 ⋈**Chauvin & Fouchereau** 41 r P-Curie ☎662178
Ren

THURY-HARCOURT 14 (Calvados) 1,450 (☎31)
Map 8 D3

★**Poste** rte Caen ☎797212 Closed 16 Jan–24 Feb
11rm5⇄6🛁 🏠

TILLOY-LES-NOFFLAINES See **ARRAS**

TILQUES See **ST-OMER**

TINQUEUX See **REIMS**

TONNAY-BOUTONNE 17 (Charente-Maritime)
1,100 (☎46) Map 15 B4

★**Beau Rivage** r du Passage ☎332001 7rm 🏠 P
dB40–54 (English breakfast) L25–60 D25–60

🚩 ⋈**M A Seureau** Grand r ☎332065 P Ren (GB)

TONNERRE 89 (Yonne) 6,550 (☎86) Map 10 C2

★★**Abbaye St-Michel** 🇱 r St-Michel (DP) ☎550599
Closed 21 Dec–Jan 12rm8⇄1🛁 ♎

TOULON† 83 (Var) 185,075 (☎94) Map 27 B1

★★★**Frantel Tour Blanche** bd Admiral Vence
☎244157 tx400347 100rm77⇄100🛁 P Lift ⅅ
sB⇄🛁167–192 dB⇄🛁219–284
(English breakfast) L fr62alc D fr62alc Pool sea

⋈**Carrefour-Auto** 49 av du Gl-Pruneau ☎415986
BL/Jag/Tri

At **Cap Brun** (4km SE on D42)

★★**Résidence du Cap Brun** chemin P-Guegrand
☎412946 Closed Nov 23rm11⇄6🛁 sea

At **Valetta (La)** (4km NE)

🚩 ⋈**Azur** av de l'Universite ☎233648 Frd (GB)

TOULOUSE† 31 (Haute-Garonne) 382,200 (☎61)
Map 16 C1

★★★**Caravelle** 62 r Raymond-IV (n rest) ☎627065
tx530438 30rm18⇄12🛁 🏠 P Lift ⅅ sB117–134
sB⇄🛁117–134 dB⇄🛁146–174
(English breakfast)

★★★**Compagnie du Midi** Matabiau ☎628493
tx530171 65rm33⇄13🛁 P Lift sB84 sB⇄🛁129
dB107 dB⇄🛁158 (English breakfast) L31alc D31alc

★★★**Concorde** 16 bd Bon Repos (n rest Aug)
☎624860 tx531686 97rm70⇄27🛁 🏠 P Lift ⅅ
sB⇄🛁110–155 dB⇄🛁140–210 L fr40 D fr40

☆☆**Ibis** quartier du Mirail ☎408686 tx520805 89⇄ P
Lift sB⇄fr94 dB⇄fr114 L30–45alc D30–45alc

TOULOUSE AIRPORT

★★★**Frantel Wilson** 7 r de Labeda (n rest) ☎212175
tx530550 95rm53⇄42🛁 Lift ⅅ sB⇄🛁173–193
dB⇄🛁246–306

☆☆☆**Novotel Toulouse Purpan** 23 chemin de
Maubec ☎493410 tx520640 123⇄ P Lift sB⇄fr142
dB⇄fr173 English breakfast only ♎ Pool

TOUQUET-PARIS-PLAGE(LE) 62 (Pas-de-Calais)
5,600 (☎21) Map 3 A1

★★★★**Mer** 2 r St-Louis (off bd de la Mer) Closed
Oct–mid May (except Etr) 80⇄ Lift sea

★★★**Bristol** 17 Grande r Closed Nov–Feb
60rm35⇄32🛁 Lift

★★★**Côte d'Opale** bd de la Mer ☎050811 Closed 16
Nov–14 Mar 28rm22⇄ ⅅ sB76 sB⇄136 dB87
dB⇄147 (English breakfast) L65 D70 sea

★★★**Westminster** av Verger (n rest) ☎051966
Closed Nov–Feb 145⇄ P Lift ⅅ sB⇄160–215
dB⇄🛁180–235 St%

★★**Forêt** 73 r de Moscou (n rest) ☎050988 10⇄
sB⇄86–95 dB⇄94–103 (English breakfast) sea

★★**Plage** 13 bd de la Mer (n rest) ☎050322 Closed 4
Nov–Feb 25rm9⇄3🛁 sea

★**St Christophe** 45 r Bruxelles (off bd de la Mer)
☎052376 Closed 16 Sep–May (except Etr) 20rm8⇄
dB73–76 dB⇄84–98 L37–42 D37

★★**Universal** 10 r Bruxelles (off bd de la Paix) (n rest)
☎051199 Closed Oct–mid Apr 19rm7⇄7🛁

★**Windsor** 7 r St-Georges (off r de la Paix)
☎050544 28rm8⇄4🛁 Lift dB58–97 dB⇄🛁fr97
L fr41 D fr41 sea

★**Chalet** 15 r de la Paix ☎051299 Closed Oct–Feb
15rm5⇄1🛁 sB41 (English breakfast) L fr35 D fr35
sea

★**Robert's** 66 r de Londres ☎051198 Closed
Oct–Mar 14rm3⇄ sB37–44 sB⇄🛁57 dB51–66
dB⇄🛁66 L27–35 D27–35

★**Touquet** 17 r de Paris ☎052254 16rm2⇄5🛁
sB42–47 sB⇄🛁72–77 dB59–64 dB⇄🛁84–94
At the **Golf Links** (3km S)

★★★**Manoir** av du Golf ☎052022 Closed Nov–Feb 47rm45⇌A10rm P Lift ♪ sB82 sB⇌96 dB⇌144–158 L55 D55 Pool ♿

TOURCOING† 59 (Nord) 102,550 (☎20) Map **3** B1

☆☆☆**Novotel Neuville-en-Ferrain** Autoroute Lille-Gand (N near Halluin Interchange) ☎940770 tx110656 118⇌ P Lift sB⇌fr137 dB⇌fr181 English breakfast only Pool

☆☆**Ibis** ctr Gl-de-Gaulle ☎768458 tx120694 104⇌ P Lift sB⇌96 dB⇌116 L35alc D35alc

🅱 🏍**Ponthieux** 75 r Roubaix ☎266705 M/c Frd (GB)

TOURNUS 71 (Saône-et-Loire) 7,850 (☎85)

Map **10** C1

★★★**Sauvage** pl Champ-de-Mars (DP) ☎511445 tx800726 Closed 11 Nov–14 dec 30rm25⇌ 🏛 Lift

★★**Gare** 4 av Gambetta ☎511056 15rm3⇌6🏵 🏛 P sB48–72 sB⇌56–72 dB56–84 dB⇌64–84 (English breakfast) L30–70 D30–70

★**Terrasses** 🅻 18 av du 23-Janvier ☎510174 12rm2⇌1🏵 P sB34–56 sB⇌56–62 dB52–54 dB⇌🏵63–74 L24–50 D244–50

TOURS† 37 (Indre-et-Loire) 145,450 (☎47)

Map **9** A2 We have been informed that during the currency of this publication Tours telephone numbers are liable to change.

★★★**Armor** 🅻 26 bis bd Heurteloup (n rest) ☎052437 50rm16⇌17🏵 🏛 P Lift sB67–84 sB⇌🏵93–151 dB78–95 dB⇌🏵104–162 (English breakfast)

★★★**Bordeaux** 🅻 3 pl du Ml-Leclerc ☎054032 tx750008 54rm19⇌26🏵 P Lift ♪ sB fr80 sB⇌🏵110–120 dBfr105 dB⇌🏵150–155 L29–42&alc D29–42&alc St%

★★★**Central** 21 r Berthelot (n rest) ☎054644 42rm21⇌11🏵 🏛 P Lift ♪ sB86–90 sB⇌🏵130–150 dB156–160 dB⇌🏵105–132

★★★**Châteaux de la Loire** 12 r Gambetta (n rest) ☎051005 32rm10⇌6🏵 Lift

★★★**Métropole** 14 pl J-Jaurès ☎054051 tx75508 80rm40⇌16🏵 🏛 Lift

★★★**Royal** 65 av Grammont (n rest) ☎647178 32⇌ 🏛 P Lift ♪ sB⇌131–141 dB⇌152

★★★**Univers** 5 bd Heurteloup ☎053712 tx750806 76rm60⇌16🏵 🏛 Lift ♪ sB⇌🏵113–125 dB⇌🏵131–155 L43 D43

★★**Cygne** 6 r du Cygne (off r Colbert) ☎666641/(052325) tx750008 20rm9⇌2🏵 A1rm 🏛 sBfr55 sB⇌🏵fr70 dBfr69 dB⇌🏵94–144

★**Cholseuil** (n rest) ☎208576 16rm8⇌1🏵 sB45–47 sB⇌🏵68 dB⇌🏵66–80

★**Colbert** 78 r Colbert (n rest) ☎052763 15rm6⇌6🏵 🏛

★**Foch** 20 r Ml-Foch (off r National) (n rest) ☎057059 tx750004 15rm2⇌6🏵 sBfr58 sB⇌🏵74–92 dBfr81 dB⇌🏵85–105

🅱 🏍**Gaillard** 7 r G-Sand ☎206980 P

🅱 🏍**Gauron** 33 r Febvotte ☎284345 BL/Jag/Rov/Tri

🅱 🏍**Pont** 32 r James, Menneton ☎202533 Frd

🅱 🏍**St-Simon** 215–217 av de Grammont ☎054865 P BMW (GB)

🅱 🏍**Tourangelle Auto** 20–28 r d'Entraigues ☎203057 P Chy/Sim (GB)

TRANCHE (LA) 85 (Vendée) 2,150 (☎30)

Map **15** A/B4

★**Ker Paulette** av Plage Closed 26 Sep–May (except Etr) 29rm1⇌6🏵 🏛

TRÉBEURDEN 22 (Côtes-du-Nord) 2,909 (☎96)

Map **7** B3

★★**Family** 🅻 22 r des Plages ☎355031 27rm15⇌15🏵 🏛 dB80–93 dB⇌🏵90–100 (English breakfast) D35–50 sea

TRÉBOUL 29 (Finistère) 6,020 (☎98) Map **7** A3

★★**Bains** (DP) ☎920221 Closed 21 Sep–May 30rm2🏵 A4rm 🏛 sea

TRÉGASTEL-PLAGE 22 (Côtes-du-Nord) 2,050 (☎96) Map **7** B3

★**Beau Séjour** 🅻 ☎388802 Closed 16 Oct–14 Mar 23rm10⇌7🏵 P sB52–58 sB⇌🏵80–100 dB69–87 dB⇌🏵129–144 L32–70 D32–70 sea

★**Belle Vue** 🅻 ☎238818 Closed Oct–mid Apr 33rm11⇌21🏵 A5rm P Lift sB⇌🏵71–101 dB⇌🏵102–162 L37–68 D37–68 sea

★**Mer & Plage** (DP) ☎388803 Closed Oct–Mar 40rm20⇌4🏵 sea

TRELISSAC See **PÉRIGEUX**

TRÉPORT (LE) 76 (Seine-Maritime) 6,900 (☎35)

Map **3** A1

🅱 🏍**Moderne** (G Renault) 8–9 quai Sadi-Carnot ☎861390 ☎861390 P Ren

TRIMOUILLE (LA) 86 (Vienne) 1,300 (☎49)

Map **16** C4

★**Paix** pl Eglise et de la Mairie ☎916050 Closed 26 Jan–19 Feb 20rm4⇌4🏵 🏛 P sB54–56 sB⇌🏵75–77 dB62–80 dB⇌🏵83–107 (English breakfast) L28–73 D28–73

TRINITÉ-SUR-MER (LA) 56 (Morbihan) 1,450 (☎97)

Map **7** B2

★★**Rouzic** 17 cours de Quais ☎527206 Closed 16 Nov–14 Dec 28rm13⇌14🏵 Lift sea

★**Ostrea** ☎527323 12rm sea

TROIS-ÉPIS (LES) 68 (Haut-Rhin) (☎89) Map **11** B2

★★★★**Grand** ☎498065 tx880229 48rm44⇌4🏵 P Lift ♪ sB⇌🏵145–295 dB⇌🏵170–330 (English breakfast) L alc D alc Pool mountains

★★★**Marchal** 🅻 ☎498161 Closed 16 Dec–14 Jan 45rm31⇌5🏵 🏛 lift

TROUVILLE 14 (Calvados) 6,700 (☎31) Map **8** D4

★★★★**Bellevue** pl du Casino ☎881485 tx170187 Closed 6 Nov–14 Mar 100rm90⇌3🏵 🏛 P Lift ♪ sB89–94 sB⇌🏵174–194 dB108–118 dB⇌🏵218–278 (English breakfast) L alc St% sea

★★★**Flaubert** r G-Flaubert (DP) ☎883723 Closed 16 Nov–14 Feb 34rm17⇌8🏵 P Lift ♪ sB127–202 sB⇌🏵202 dB195–278 dB⇌🏵270–278 L39–56 D39–56 sea

★★★**Résidence** r de la Plage (n rest) ☎880466 Closed Oct–14 Mar 30rm 🏛 Lift ♪ sB84–89 sB⇌🏵124–144 dB103–108 dB⇌🏵138–178 (English breakfast) St% sea

★**Dunes** 3 r de la Plage ☎881649 23rm16⇌3🏵

🏍**Chantecler** 113 av du Gl-de-Gaulle ☎880040 P BL (GB)

TROYES† 10 (Aube) 75,550 (☎25) Map **10** C3

★★★**Grand** av Ml-Joffre (opp station) ☎439284 taGrantel tx840582 102rm55⇌25🏵 P Lift sB67 sB⇌🏵124 dB78 dB⇌🏵135 L35 D35

★★★**Royal** 22 bd Carnot ☎436801 41rm22⇌12🏵 🏛 P Lift sB70–80 sB⇌🏵85–100 dB85–95 dB⇌🏵105–125 (English breakfast) L30–45 D30–45

★★**France** 18 quai Dampierre ☎433830 61rm26⇌18🏵 Lift

★★**Paris** 56 r Salengro (n rest) ☎433713 tx840809 Closed Nov–9 Jan 30rm1⇌9🏵 🏛 P sB43–53 sB⇌🏵63–82 dB58–73 dB⇌🏵71–102 (English breakfast)

🅸 🏍**Contant Automobiles** 15bd Danton ☎434819 ☎434819 Ren (GB)

🅱 🏍**M Roy** 6 r P-Gillon ☎438293 P Lnc/Por

At **Brevlandes** (4km)

★★**Grand Fermière** ☎824565 15rm14🏵 P sB61–67 dB🏵83–92 (English breakfast) L22–42 St%

At **Pont-Ste-Marie** (3km E)

🅸 🏍**14 Juillet** r R-Salengro ☎811245 Frd

At **St-Jullen-les-Villas** (2km SE)

🏍**Selection-Auto** 43 bd de Dijon ☎435684 P

TROYES AIRPORT

At **Barberey** (6km NW on N19)

☆☆☆**Novotel Troyes Aéroport** rte de Paris (N19) ☎721214 tx840759 60⇌ P Lift sB⇌143 dB⇌155 English breakfast only Pool

TULLE† 19 (Correze) 21,650 (☎55) Map **16** C3

★★**Toque Blanche** 29 r J-Jaurès et pl Brigouleix ☎267541 11⇌ sB53–60 sB⇌🏵53–63 dB74–78 dB⇌🏵74–78

France

URIAGE-LES-BAINS 38 (Isère) (☎76) Map **27** B3
★★**Alpes** Grand allée ☎891028 Closed Oct–Apr
42rm10⇆ 🏠 P sB43–58 sB⇆99–107 dB66–77
dB⇆116 (English breakfast) L fr34 D fr34 mountains
★★**Manoir ᴸ** ☎891088 19rm2⇆4🏠 P sB45–54
dB62 dB⇆94 L32–50 D32–50 St% mountains
URY See **FONTAINEBLEAU**

UZERCHE 19 (Corrèze) 3,250 (☎55) Map **16** C3
★★**Amboise** av de Paris ☎731008 20rm5⇆15🏠 🏠
P sB fr40 sB⇆🏠 fr53 dB47–61 dB⇆🏠 fr60
(English breakfast) L18–58 D18–58
★★**Teyssier** r Pont-Turgot ☎731005 Closed 11
Jan–Feb 25rm10⇆ A8rm 🏠 P sB40–47
sB⇆🏠58–68 dB48–55 dB⇆🏠66–91 L35–77
D35–77

UZÈS 30 (Gard) 7,400 (☎66) Map **27** A2
★**Hostellerie Provençale** 3 r Grande Bourgade
☎221106 Closed Nov & Dec 10rm1⇆3🏠 P

VAISON-LA-ROMAINE 84 (Vaucluse) 5,250 (☎90)
Map **27** B2
★★★**Beffroi** r de l'Eveche ☎360471 Closed 11
Jan–9 Feb & 1–16 Dec 20rm4⇆10🏠 A10rm P
sB fr44 sB⇆🏠69–94 dB fr67 dB⇆🏠77–103
L35–65

VAL-ANDRÉ (LE) 22 (Côtes-du-Nord) (☎96)
Map **7** B3
★★**Grand du Val André** 80 r Al-Charner (DP)
☎722056 Closed Oct–Mar 45rm6⇆11🏠 🏠 Beach
sea
★**Bains** pl Gl-de-Gaulle ☎722011 Closed 21
Sep–19 Mar 26rm3⇆4🏠 P sB35–38 sB⇆🏠44–53
dB50–55 dB⇆🏠61–81 (English breakfast) L29–40
D29–40 sea

VALDAHON 25 (Doubs) 3,600 (☎81) Map **11** A1
★★**Franche Centre ᴸ** ☎592318 Closed 21 Dec–9
Jan 20⇆ 🏠 P sB⇆fr73 dB⇆fr102 L25–87 D25–87
mountains

VAL-D'ISÈRE 73 (Savoie) 1,350 (☎79) Map **28** C4
★★★★**Sofitel le Val d'Isère** (DP) ☎060830
tx980558 Closed 3 May–Nov 52⇆ 🏠 P Lift ♪
sB⇆220–290 dB⇆400–500 L fr80 D fr80 Pool
★★★**Aiglon** ☎060405 Closed 11 May–Jun &
Sep–24 Nov 27rm14⇆4🏠 🏠
★★★**Bellier** ☎060377 Closed 6 Dec–4 May
20rm14⇆4🏠
★★★**Christiania** (DP) ☎060825 tx32077 Closed
May–Nov 44rm38⇆4🏠 Lift
★★★**Savoie** ☎060371 tx32077 Closed May–Nov
35rm19⇆12🏠 Lift Pool
★**Vieux Village** ☎060379 Closed Jun, Oct & Nov
23⇆ sB⇆101–111 dB⇆119–131
(English breakfast) D45 mountains

VALENÇAY 36 (Indre) 3,200 (☎54) Map **9** A2
★★★**Espagne** 8 r du Château ☎000002 Closed
Dec–Feb 18⇆ P sB⇆102–216 dB⇆144–268
(English breakfast) L2 fr100 D fr100
★★**Lion d'Or ᴸ** pl Marché ☎000087 Closed 6 Jan–4
Feb 15rm6⇆2🏠 🏠 P sB47–52 sB⇆🏠56–65
dB61–75 dB⇆🏠76–100 L28–75 D28–75

VALENCE-D'AGEN 82 (Tarn et Garonne) 4,450
(☎63) Map **12** C2
☆☆**Ibis** 355 av Provence ☎444254 tx345384 78⇆ P
Lift sB⇆fr94 dB⇆fr106 L35–45alc D35–45alc
★★**Tout-Va-Bien** 35–39 r de la République
☎395483 27rm20⇆7🏠 🏠

VALENCE-SUR-RHÔNE† 26 (Drôme) 70,350 (☎75)
Map **27** B3
☆☆☆**Novotel Valence Sud** av de Provence (N7)
☎422015 tx345823 107⇆ P Lift sB⇆fr143
dB⇆fr154 English breakfast only Pool
★★**Pic** 285 av V-Hugo ☎431532 Closed Wed & Aug
10⇆ 🏠
★**Lyon** 23 av P-Sémard ☎440063 47rm6⇆5🏠 🏠
🛏 ♨**Mollère** 164 av V-Hugo ☎441137 M/c
BL/Jag/Por/Rov/Tri
VALENCIENNES† 59 (Nord) 43,250 (☎20)
Map **3** B1

☆☆☆**Motellerie** ☎461626 tx11864 67rm30⇆37🏠
Pool
☆☆☆**Novotel Valenciennes-Ouest** ☎442080
tx120970 76⇆ P Lift sB⇆fr121 dB⇆fr151 English
breakfast only Pool
🛏 ♨**Marceau** 27 pl de l'Esplanade ☎466072 Frd

VALETTA (LA) See **TOULON**

VALLOIRE 73 (Savoie) 950 (☎79) Map **28** C3
★★**Grand Valloire & Galibier** ☎001 Closed 16
Sep–14 Jun 43rm26⇆10🏠 🏠 Lift

VALOGNES 50 (Manche) 6,100 (☎33) Map **8** C4
★**Louvre** 28 r des Religieuses ☎400007 Closed Dec
20rm4⇆2🏠 P sB37–57 sB⇆🏠54–62 dB44–69
dB⇆🏠61–84 (English breakfast) L19–30 D19–30

VAL-ST-PÈRE See **AVRANCHES**

VAL-SUZON 21 (Côte-d'Or) 150 (☎80) Map **10** C2
★★★**Val-Suzon** ☎316015 Closed 11 Jan–9 Feb
18rm5⇆13🏠 A10rm P sB⇆🏠41–51
dB⇆🏠101–111 L100–150 D100–150

VANNES† 56 (Morbihan) 43,550 (☎97) Map **7** B3
★★★**Marebandière** 4 r A-Briand ☎663429
40rm17⇆23🏠 P Lift ♪ sB93–98 sB⇆🏠93–98
dB⇆🏠101–124 L28–100 D28–100
★★**Richemont** 28 av Fravel & Lincy ☎661295
45rm17⇆ 🏠
★**Image Ste-Anne** 8 pl de la Libération ☎632736
Closed 16 Oct–31 Oct 31rm14⇆18🏠 🏠 P sB fr55
sB⇆🏠70–100 dB fr69 dB⇆🏠89–120 L30–100
D30–100
★**Marée Bleue** 8 pl B-R-Hakeim ☎662429 16rm4🏠
P sB38–55 sB⇆🏠55 dB46–63 dB⇆🏠63 L28 D28
★**Relais Nantals** 38 r A-Briand (n rest) ☎661585
14rm1⇆1🏠 P sB36–37 sB⇆🏠48–77 dB fr42
🛏 ♨**Autorep** 41 r du Vincin ☎631035 Frd (GB)
🛏 ♨**Lambert & Dupré** 95 av E-Herriot ☎542070 Ren
♨♨**Y Maheo** 48 av V-Hugo ☎661156 ☎632345 Opl

VARCES 38 (Isère) (☎76) Map **27** B3
★**Escale** ☎978019 Closed Mon & Jan 7⇆ 🏠 P
dB⇆160–220 L135–225 D135–225 mountains

VARENGEVILLE-SUR-MER 76 (Seine-Maritime)
1,000 (☎35) Map **9** A4
★★**Terrasse ᴸ** ☎851254 Closed Oct–14 Mar
28rm8⇆ 🏠 ✔ sea

VARETZ See **BRIVE-LA-GAILLARD**

VARS (COL DE) 05 (Hautes-Alpes) 800 (☎92)
Map **28** C3
At **Ste-Marie** (8km N on N202)
★★★**Ste-Marie** ☎455002 Closed 16 Apr–14 Jul &
16 Sep–14 Dec 18⇆🏠

VATAN 36 (Indré) 2,300 (☎54) Map **9** B2
★★**France** 16 pl de la République ☎497411 Closed
Feb 12rm2⇆2🏠 🏠

VENCE 06 (Alpes-Maritimes) 11,700 (☎93)
Map **28** C2
★★★★**Domaine St Martin** rte de Coursegoules
☎580202 tx470282 Closed Dec–Jan 28⇆ 🏠 P ♪
dB⇆428–568 (English breakfast) St% ✔ Pool sea
★★**Diana** av Poilus (n rest) ☎582856 25⇆ P Lift
♪ sB⇆🏠95–115 dB⇆🏠105–125 mountains
★★**Régina** av Alliés ☎580334 Closed 16 Oct–9 Dec
25rm6⇆7🏠
★★**Seigneurs** pl Frêne ☎580424 Closed 16 Oct–14
Nov 10🏠
★**Fleurs** 8 rte de Grasse (DP & Pn) ☎580307
7rm3⇆3🏠

VENDÔME† 41 (Loir-et-Cher) 18,550 (☎39)
Map **9** A2
★★**Grand St-Georges** 14 r Poterie ☎772542
35rm30⇆ Lift
★**Vendôme ᴸ** 15 fbg Chartrain ☎770288
20rm8⇆8🏠 🏠 P Lift sB fr54 sB⇆🏠44–111
dB72–82 dB⇆🏠98–139 L37–80&alc D37–80&alc
🛏 ♨**R Garcia** 68 fbg Chartrain ☎770938 Frd (GB)
🛏 ♨♨**Motoculture** 45 rte de Paris, St Ouen ☎770943
☎770853 P MB/ Opl (GB)

VENTHON See **ALBERTVILLE**

VENTAVON SUR SAÔNE 05 (Hautes-Alpes) (☎92)
Map **27** B3
★★★**Domaine de Faye** rte de Col de Faye ☎539111
Closed 16 Nov – 19 Apr 12rm12⇄1 🍴 A6rm P
sB⇄🍴95 dB⇄🍴180 – 210 (English breakfast)
L80alc D80alc

VERDUN† 55 (Meuse) 26,950 (☎28) Map **10** D3
★★★**Bellevue** Rond-Pont-de-Lattre-de-Tassigny
☎860424 tx86464 Closed Feb 82rm60⇄ 🏤 Lift
★★**Bourguignonne** rte Ciel ☎495145 Closed Jan
16rm10⇄1 🍴 A6rm

VERETZ 37 (Indre-et-Loire) 1,350 (☎47) Map **9** A2
★**St Hororé** ☎503006 Closed Dec – Feb 10rm3⇄1 🍴
sB44 – 81 sB⇄🍴63 – 81 dB51 – 54 dB⇄🍴70 – 88
L30 – 58 river

VERNET (LE) 31 (Haute-Garonne) 1,300 (☎61)
Map **16** C1
★**Platanes** (N 20) ☎080513 23rm4⇄4🍴 P 🄳 sB47
sB⇄🍴78 dB86 L28alc D28alc

VERNET-LES-BAINS 66 (Pyrénées-Orientales)
1,350 (☎68) Map **22** D4
★★**Alexandra** 35rm23⇄ 🏤

VERNEUIL-SUR-AVRE 27 (Eure) 6,900 (☎32)
Map **9** A3
★★**Clos** 4 r Ferté-Vidame ☎322181 Closed 16
Dec – 14 Jan 10rm4⇄8🍴

VERNIAZ (LA) See **EVIAN-LES-BAINS**

VERSAILLES† 78 (Yvelines) 97,150 (☎1) Map **9** B3
★★★★**Trianon Palace** 1 bd de la Reine ☎9503412
tx698863 130rm100⇄30🍴 Lift
★★**Clagny** 6 Impasse Clagny ☎9501809 Closed
Aug 19rm1⇄17🍴 dB⇄🍴76 – 118
★★**St Louis** 28 r St-Louis ☎9502355 8⇄8🍴 sB68
sB⇄🍴82 – 87 dB fr82 dB⇄🍴95 – 103
★**Cheval Rouge** 18 r A-Chernier (off r de la Paroise)
☎9500303 Closed 21 Dec – 9 Jan 41rm11⇄11🍴 P
sB50 – 76 dB86 dB⇄🍴110 – 120 L49 D45
🄶 M P Augereau 67 av St-Cloud ☎9501120 AR/BL
🄶 🛒**Deschamps** 5 r St-Simon ☎9500397MB/Toy
🄶 🛒**Soverdlin** 18 r de Vergennes ☎9502254
Chy/Sim (GB)

VERVINS 02 (Aisne) 3,300 (☎23) Map **10** C4
★★**Tour du Roy** ☎980011 Closed 16 Jan – 14 Feb
15rm12⇄3🍴 P sB60 sB⇄🍴95 dB105 – 220
dB⇄🍴105 – 220 (English breakfast) L50 D50

VESOUL 70 (Haute-Saône) 20,100 (☎84)
Map **11** A2
★★**Nord** 7 r Aigle Noir ☎750256 35rm27⇄7🍴 🏤 P
Lift 🄳 sB70 – 120 sB⇄🍴95 – 120 dB120 – 150
dB⇄🍴120 – 150 (English breakfast) L35 D35
★**Relais N19** rte de Paris ☎753656 Closed 23
Dec – 19 Jan 26rm13⇄7🍴 🏤 P sB74 – 115
sB⇄🍴109 – 135 dB83 – 130 dB⇄🍴138 – 170
(English breakfast) L30 – 75 D30 – 75 lake
🄶 🛒**Central** (Mazeau) 1 – 3 r L-Jobard ☎751229
Closed wknds Frd
🄶 🛒**Delamotte** 12 r Fleurier ☎756123 P Fia
🄶 🛒**Euro-Garage-Paillotet** 69 av A-Briand
☎752133 ☎755507 P BL

VEYRIER-DU-LAC 74 (Haute-Savoie) 1,720 (☎50)
Map **28** C4
★★**Acacias** ☎458160 Closed Nov – Feb 23rm 7⇄
★★**Chaumière** ☎448006 35rm15⇄2🍴 🏤
★**Col-Vert**L• ☎448023 Closed 16 Nov – mid Apr
12⇄ P Lift dB⇄🍴124 – 148 (English breakfast)
L50 – 65 D50 – 65 mountains lake

VICHY† 03 (Allier) 32,300 (☎70) Map **27** A4
★★★**Pavillon Sévigné** 10 pl Sévigné (off av A-
Briand) ☎321622 tx990256 Closed Oct – Apr
55rm35⇄9🍴 P Lift 🄳 sB⇄🍴112 – 191
dB⇄🍴141 – 256 L65 D65 🄴 Pool 🄳
★★★**Albert-Ier** av P-Doumer ☎987293 tx390064
35rm26⇄ P Lift 🄳 sB75 – 149 sB⇄🍴104 – 149
dB⇄🍴127 – 177 (English breakfast)
★★★**Ambassadeurs** 1 r du Parc ☎982526 tx990246
Closed Oct – Apr 94rm70⇄ P Lift 🄳 sB95 – 105
sB⇄🍴115 – 225 dB140 – 155 dB⇄🍴150 – 330
(English breakfast) L70 D70

★★★**Russie & Mediterranée** 12 av A-Briand
☎987685 Closed Oct – 14 May 80rm20⇄13🍴 🏤 Lift
★★**Amirauté** 20 r Prés-Wilson ☎986422 Closed
Oct – 1 May 82rm28⇄5🍴 Lift
🄶 🛒**Excelsior** 12 av Victoria ☎985556 ☎988109 P
Chy
🄶 🛒**Nimes** (Cottin) 102 av Poincaré ☎983432 Ren
🄶 🛒**Perfect** rte de l'Aéroport à Charmeil ☎983243
Lnc/MB (GB)
🄶 🛒**St-Blaise** 2 – 6 r de Lisbonne ☎986371 BL (GB)

VIC-SUR-AISNE 02 (Aisne) 1,600 (☎23) Map **9** B4
★**Lion d'Or** pl Gl-de-Gaulle (DP) ☎555020 Closed
Aug 17rm6🍴

VIC-SUR-CÈRE 15 (Cantal), 2,050 (☎71) Map **16** D2
At **Col de Curebourse** (6km SE on D54)
★**Auberge des Monts** (DP) ☎475171 Closed
Oct – mid Apr 27rm 20⇄ A4rm

VIENNE† 38 (Isère) 28,800 (☎74) Map **27** B4
★★**Nord** 9 pl Miremont ☎850196 Closed 16 Sep – 16
Jan 43rm10⇄14🍴 🏤 Lift
At **Chonas l'Amballon** (9km S on N7)
☆☆**Km 500** ☎588144 tx380343 44rm30⇄14🍴 P
dB⇄🍴107 – 141 L31 – 65 D31 – 65 Pool
At **Pont-Evêque** (3km E on N502)
★**Midi** pl Église ☎859011 30rm9⇄10🍴

VIERZON† 18 (Cher) 36,550 (☎36) Map **9** B2
★★**Boulevard** 3 r Dr P-Roux ☎753982 Closed Feb
23rm1⇄9🍴 🏤
★★**Continental** 104 av E-Vaillant (n rest) ☎753522
36rm15⇄18🍴 Lift
🄶 🛒**Perchaud** 58 av J-Jaurès ☎753757 Frd

VILLEFRANCHE-SUR-MER 06 (Alpes-Maritimes)
7,300 (☎93) Map **28** C2
★★★★**Versailles** r Ml-Foch ☎808956 tx970433
Closed 21 Oct – 19 Dec 50rm44⇄6🍴 P Lift 🄳 sB138
dB176 dB⇄🍴196 L60 D60 sea
★★★**Provençal** r Ml-Joffre (DP & Pn) ☎807142
tx970433 45rm30⇄13🍴 Lift 🄳 sB66 – 80
sB⇄🍴81 – 115 dB132 – 160 dB⇄🍴162 – 230 L30
D30
★★★**Welcome** quai Courbet (DP) ☎808881 Closed
Nov – 19 Dec 35rm30⇄1🍴 🏤 Lift sea
★**Coq-Hard** L• bd Corne d'Or ☎807106 Closed Nov
11rm6⇄ P sB37 sB⇄🍴58 dB56 dB⇄🍴85 L30 D30 sea

VILLEFRANCHE-SUR-SAÔNE† 69 (Rhône) 30,700
(☎74) Map **27** B4
★★★**Plaisance** 96 av Libération ☎653352 Closed
Xmas 60rm30⇄33🍴 🏤 P Lift sB⇄🍴78 – 95
dB⇄🍴97 – 114
☆☆**Ibis Villefranche-sur-Saone** le Péage
Commune de Limas ☎682223 tx370777 118⇄ P Lift
sB⇄fr98 dB⇄fr106 L30 – 45alc D30 – 45alc
★**Ecu de France** 35 r d'Anse ☎683448 28rm5⇄7🍴
🏤 P 🄳 sB39 – 75 sB⇄🍴56 – 75 dB47 – 83
dB⇄🍴77 – 83 (English breakfast)
🛒**Europe** 1000 r Ampère, Impasse Edison ☎655059
Aud/VW
🄶 🛒**Gambetta** 28 bd Gambetta ☎650406 P Frd (GB)
🛒**Sport** (G Benoit) 996 r Ampère ☎650469 BMW

VILLENEUVE-DE-MARSAN 40 (Landes) 2,150
(☎57) Map **15** B2
★**Europe** pl Foirail ☎582008 26rm10⇄10🍴 P
sB58 – 88 sB⇄🍴58 – 88 dB65 – 95 dB⇄🍴90 – 95
L38 – 75 D38 – 75 Pool

VILLENEUVE DE RIVIÈRE See **ST-GAUDENS**
VILLENEUVE-LÈS-AVIGNON 30 (Gard) 9,000
(☎90) Map **27** B2
★★★**Prieuré** pl Chapitre ☎251820 tx431042 Closed
Nov – Feb 30⇄ A17rm P Lift 🄳 sB⇄🍴177 – 277
dB⇄🍴229 – 364 L alc D alc 🄴 Pool
★★**Magnanerale** L• 37 r Camp de Bataille ☎251111
Closed 16 Jan – Feb 21rm16⇄5🍴 🏤 P 🄳
sB⇄🍴67 – 171 dB⇄🍴78 – 182 L38 – 80 D38 – 80
Pool

VILLENEUVE-LOUBET See **CAGNES-SUR-MER**
VILLENEUVE-SUR-LOT 47 (Lot-et-Garonne)
23,050 (☎58) Map **16** C2

France and Monaco

★★★**Parc** ⚏ 13 bd de la Marine ☎700168
46rm19⇌27🅵 🏠 P Lift ⅅ sB⇌🅵fr77 dB⇌🅵fr101
(English breakfast) L23–45 D23–45
★★**Prune d'Or** ⚏ pl de la Gare ☎700095 Closed Feb
18rm2⇌4🅵 🏠
▮ ⋈**Lompech** 29–31 bd Voltaire ☎702461
☎702461 P BMW/Opl (GB)

VILLENEUVE-SUR-YONNE 89 (Yonne) 4,850
(☎86) Map **10** C2
★**Boursine** ☎871426 Closed Oct 8rm sB fr37 dB fr44
(English breakfast) L30–45 D30–45
★**Dauphin** 14 r Carnot ☎871855 9rm6⇌ 🏠 P sB33
dB43–51 dB⇌73 L30–44 D30–44

VILLERS-LES-POTS See **AUXONNE**

VILLERS-SEMEUSE See **CHARLEVILLE-MÉZIÈRES**

VILLERVILLE 14 (Calvados) 750 (☎31) Map **8** D4
★**Bellevue** ⚏ r Clemenceau & rte Honfleur ☎872022
20rm9⇌3🅵 🏠

VINCENNES See **PARIS**

VIRE 14 (Calvados) 14,400 (☎31) Map **8** C3
★★**Cheval Blanc** ⚏ 2 pl du 6-Juin-1944 ☎680021
tx170428 Closed Jan 22rm11⇌2🅵 ⅅ S B fr59
sB⇌fr89 dB68–113 dB⇌🅵fr98
(English breakfast) L30–130 D30–130

VIRONVAY See **LOUVIERS**

VITRAC 24 (Dordogne) 650 (☎53) Map **16** C2
★**Plaisance** ⚏ au Port ☎293304 Closed Dec–Jan
20rm1⇌4🅵 🏠

VITRÉ 35 (Ille-et-Vilaine) 12,900 (☎99) Map **8** C3
★**Chêne Vert** 2 pl de la Gare ☎750058 Closed Sun &
23 Sep–29 Oct 22rm4⇌6🅵 P sB35–38 dB49–79
dB⇌🅵68–97 L22–45 D22–45

VITROLLES 13 (Bouches-du-Rhône) (☎42)
Map **27** B2
See also **Marseille Airport**
⑧ ◊**Kennings** 15 4ème av ☎890699 P BL (GB)

VITRY-LE-FRANÇOIS 51 (Marne) 20,100 (☎26)
Map **10** C3
★★**Poste** pl R-Collard ☎740265 30rm12⇌16🅵 Lift
★**Bon Séjour** rte de St Dizier ☎740236 28rm1⇌
A19rm 🏠 P Lift aB fr55 sB⇌🅵fr70 dB fr110
(English breakfast) L23 D23
★**Cloche** 34 r A-Briand ☎740384 24rm6⇌4🅵
A10rm 🏠

★**Étoile** 4 fbg Châlons ☎741256 22rm4⇌5🅵 A3rm
P sB fr35 sB⇌🅵fr56 dB fr42 dB⇌🅵63–67 L19–48
D19–48
⑧ ⋈**François 1er** 3 r du Vieux Port ☎740438
☎741794
⑧ ◊**Perthois** 22 r Domine de Verzet ☎741851 Ren

VIZILLE 38 (Isère) 7,300 (☎76) Map **27** B3
★**Parc** ⚏ 5 av A-Briand ☎680301 25rm7⇌10🅵
sB fr38 sB⇌🅵63–82 dB71–90 dB⇌🅵71–90
L25–70 D25–70 mountains

VOGELGRUN See **NEUF-BRISACH**

VOREPPE See **GRENOBLE**

VOUVRAY 37 (Indre-et-Loire) 2,750 (☎47) Map **9** A2
★**Grand Vatel** av Brûlé ☎561032 Closed 6–19 Jan &
16–30 Nov 12rm2⇌ A4rm

VOUZIERS 08 (Ardennes) 5,500 (☎24) Map **10** C4
★★**Rennes** 12 r Chanzy ☎308403 23rm6⇌3🅵 🏠 P
sB47–49 sB⇌🅵57 dB61 dB⇌🅵103 L20–65
D20–65

VRINE (LA) 25 (Doubs) (☎81) Map **11** A1
★**Hostellerie de la Vrine** ⚏ ☎382004
50rm40⇌10🅵 🏠 P sB43–58 sB⇌🅵48–68
dB⇌🅵66–86 (English breakfast) L30 D30 St% Ⓞ
mountains

WIMEREUX 62 (Pas-de-Calais) 6,750 (☎21)
Map **3** A2
★★**Atlantic** Digue de Mer ☎324101 10rm6⇌4🅵 🏠
P Lift sB⇌🅵fr100 dB⇌🅵120–140 L alc D alc sea
★**Centre** 78 r Carnot ☎324108 Closed 21 Dec–19
Jan 18rm1⇌ 🏠 sB fr36 sB⇌🅵fr60 dB fr46
dB⇌🅵fr83 (English breakfast) L25alc D25alc

WISSANT 62 (Pas-de-Calais) 5,241 Map **3** A2
★**Normandy** (DP & Pn) ☎359011 Closed Nov–Feb
33rm4⇌8🅵 🏠 P sB fr51 sB⇌🅵fr66 dB fr102
dB⇌🅵fr132 L fr25 D fr28 Pool sea

YENNE 73 (Savoie) 2,200 Map **27** B4
★**Logis Savoyard** pl C-Dullin ☎367038 13rm A4rm
P dB37–40 L22–40 D22–40 mountains

YVETOT 76 (Seine-Maritime) 10,750 (☎35)
Map **9** A4
⑧ ◊**Roussel Auto** rte de Havre (N13 bis) ☎950088
Ren

YVOIRE 74 (Haute-Savoie) 350 (☎50) Map **11** A1
★**Flots Bleus** ⚏ r du Port ☎8 Closed 16 Sep–14
May 20rm

Monaco/hotels and garages

Prices are in French francs.
MONTE-CARLO 24,650 (☎93) Map **28** C2
★★★★**Hermitage** sq Beaumarchais ☎506731
tx479432 210rm193⇌17🅵 P Lift ⅅ sB⇌🅵158–278
dB⇌🅵246–406 (English breakfast) L75 D75 St% ◗
Pool Beach 🜂 sea mountains
★★★★**Métropole** av Grand Bretagne ☎505741
tx469936 150rm130⇌ 🏠 P Lift ⅅ sB103–117
sB⇌🅵129–223 dB160–171 dB⇌🅵235–399
(English breakfast) L86&alc D86&alc St% Pool sea
★★★★**Paris** pl Casino ☎508080 tx469925 260⇌🅵
P Lift ⅅ sB⇌🅵fr100 D fr105 St% ◗ Pool Beach
🜂 sea
★★★**Alexandra** 35 bd Princesse Charlotte (n rest)
☎506313 55rm37⇌9🅵 Lift ⅅ sB67 sB⇌🅵97–122
dB100 dB⇌🅵125–169

★★**Europe** 6 av Citronniers ☎308365 tx47668
50rm20⇌20🅵 sea
★★**Reserve & Suisse** 7 av Princesse Grace
☎308244 40rm9⇌23🅵 Lift sea
⑧ ◊**British Motors** 4 Impasse des Carrières
☎302485 BL/RR
◊**Frontière** 1 bd Charles III ☎304905 MB
◊**Monaco Motors** 11 r Princesse-Florestine
☎302722 Hon/Opl/Rov (GB)
▮ ◊**Riviera** 6 r Genets ☎306326 P
◊**Vulca-Pneus Itiberti** 9–11 bd Charles III
☎304312 M/c

At Monte-Carlo Beach

★★★★**Old Beach** ☎350471 tx479432 Closed
Oct–Apr 46⇌ P Lift ⅅ sB⇌🅵209–250
dB⇌🅵288–348 (English breakfast) L alc D alc St%
◗ Pool Beach 🜂 sea

GERMANY

Population 62,101,400 *Area (Federal Republic)* 95,980 sq miles *Maps* 4, 5, 11, 12 & 13

How to get there

If you use one of the short-crossing Channel ferries and travel via Belgium, West Germany is just within a day's drive. The distance from Calais to Cologne is just under 260 miles.

By driving through northern France and entering Germany near Strasbourg, the journey usually takes two days. This entry point is also used if travelling by the longer Channel crossings: Cherbourg, Dieppe, or Le Havre to southern Germany. The distance from Le Havre to Strasbourg is just over 400 miles, a journey which will take at least one or two days. The longer-crossing car ferries operating across the North Sea to Holland can be an advantage if visiting northern Germany. Alternatively, it is possible to use the ferries operating between Harwich and Bremerhaven or Hamburg.

General information

Information in this section is specific to Germany. A wider background is provided in the notes on page 8 with other information which you are advised to read.

AA agents   **2800 Bremen 1** (PA) Multiport GmbH, Am Wall 102, POB 10.55.09
Port agent (PA)   ☎310011

                         2850 Bremerhaven (PA) Multiport GmbH, Bremerhaven
(Gatehouse 1), ☎0471–46954.

2000 Hamburg 11 (PA) Multiport GmbH, Katharinenfleet 5 ☎362721.

These are not recommended routes:
the distances are given as a guide only.

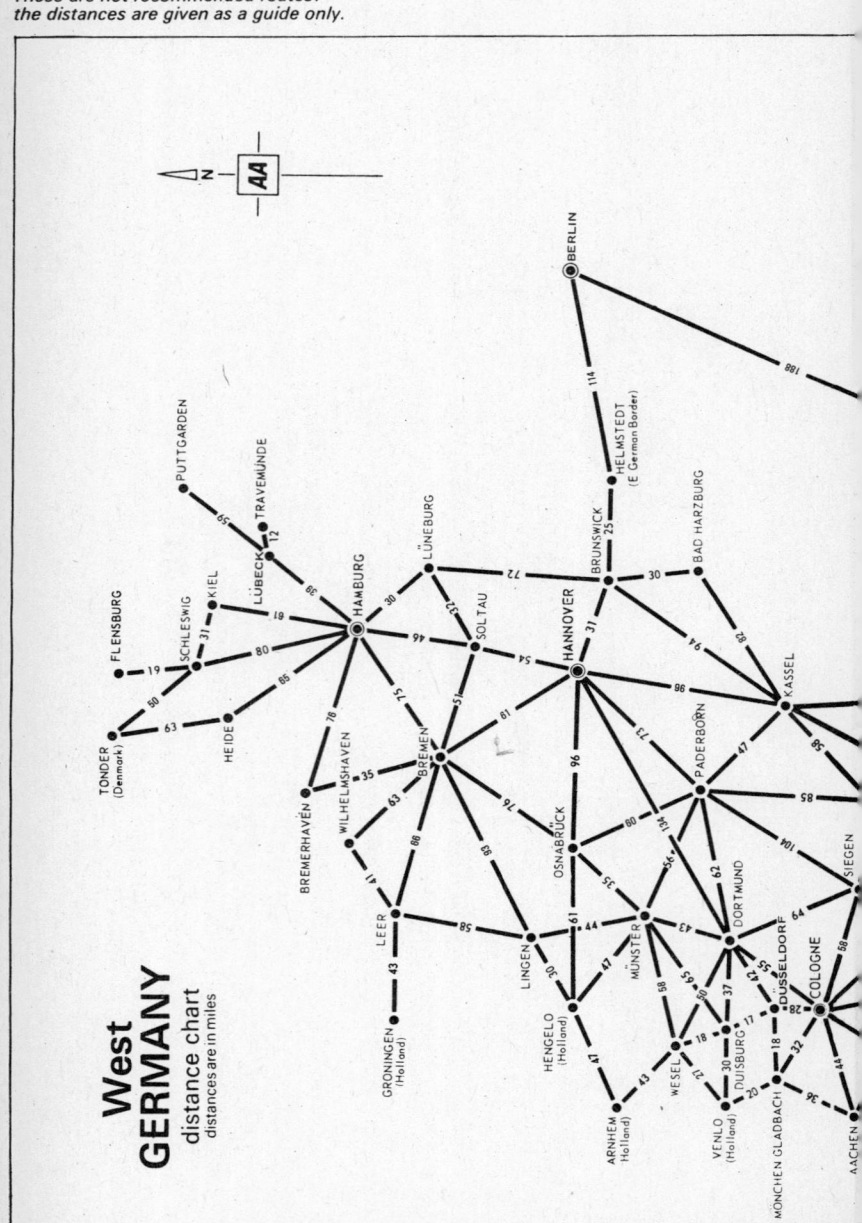

West
GERMANY
distance chart
distances are in miles

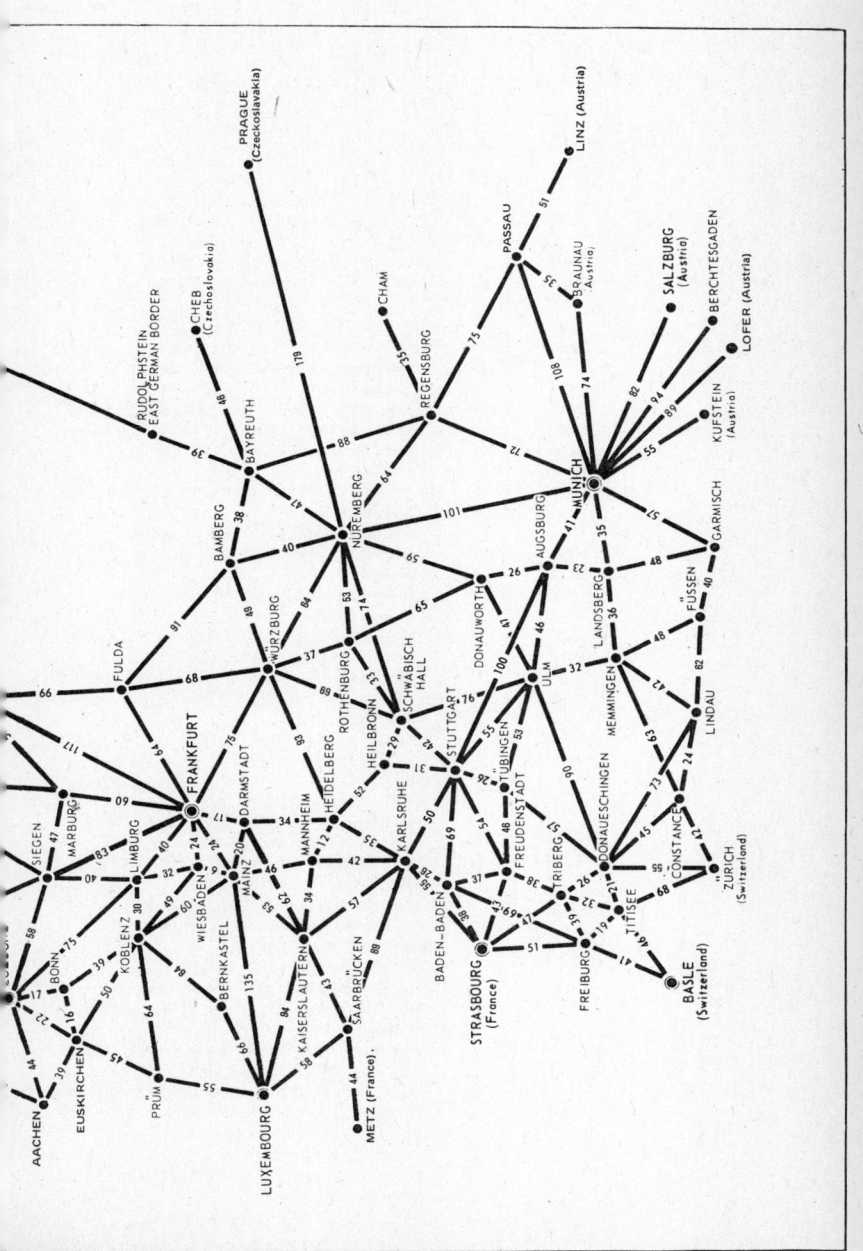

Germany

Accommodation   There is a good selection of hotels, most of which are listed in the Hotel Guide. This is distributed free by the Tourist Office in London, which can also provide details of accommodation in castles and stately homes. Regional and local tourist organisations also have details of inns and boarding houses.

For a nominal charge, tourist information offices will usually assist in finding hotel accommodation (see page 230). Enquiries by post should be accompanied by an international reply coupon (obtainable from the post office).

There is also a reservations service operated by the ADZ (Allgemeine Deutsche Zimmerreservierung). This organisation will make instantly confirmed bookings at hotels throughout the country. Full information about this service, including details of the hotels concerned, may be obtained from ADZ, Beethovenstrasse 61, Frankfurt/Main 1 ☎(0611) 1740767; tx 04–16666. Prices indicated normally include a service charge (10–15%) and VAT (11%). Reduced prices apply to children under ten years of age sharing a room with their parents.

Reservations are not normally held after 18.00hrs.

BAOR   Service personnel posted to Germany should consult their Standing Orders or Commanding Officer before taking a car to Germany or using it there. Although enjoying some privilege they will be regarded to some extent as residents in the country and tourist regulations (as outlined in this section) may not apply. For example, a tourist can use a warning triangle not strictly to the German regulations, but a service man will break local regulations unless his conforms.

Annual events		
	January	**Berlin** Agricultural Show
		Garmisch-Partenkirchen International winter sports
	February	**Frankfurt am Main** International Spring Fair
	March	**Wiesbaden** International Sports Goods Fair
	April	**Harz Mountains** Walpurgis Night celebrations
		Marburg May Market with singing in the market place
		Saarbrücken International Saar Fair
	May	**Dülmen** Round-up of wild horses in Merfelder Bruch
		Friedrichshafen International lake Constance Fair
		Weingarten Ancient equestrian procession of the Holy Blood
		Wiesbaden International May Festival
	June	**Berlin** International Film Festival
		Hamburg German Derby
		Hamelin Pied Piper plays (June/September)
		Heidelberg Castle Illumination and gala firework display
		Kiel Regatta Week
		Koblenz Operetta on the Rhine (June/September)
		Recklinghausen Ruhr Festival
		Würzburg Mozart festival
	July	**Bayreuth** Richard Wagner festival
		Hamburg Show Jumping Derby Week
		Munich Opera festival
		Ravensburg Birch Festival
	August	**Baden-Baden** Horseracing (week)
		Nürburgring German Grand Prix
		Mosel District Wine festivals
	September	**Berlin** Festival weeks: opera, ballet, theatre (September/October)
		Frankfurt am Main International Motor Show
		Munich Oktoberfest Beer festival (September/October)
		Southern & Western Germany Wine harvest festivities (September/October)
	October	**Mannheim** International Film Week

A more comprehensive list of events can be obtained from the German National Tourist Office (see page 230).

Breakdowns   If your car breaks down, try to move it to the verge of the road so that it does not obstruct traffic flow. A warning triangle must be placed to the rear of the vehicle and hazard warning lights, if fitted to the vehicle, must be used.

The ADAC operates a breakdown service, similar to that run by the AA, called the *Strassenwacht*. By courtesy of the ADAC, patrols will assist AA members upon production of their *5-Star Service Booklet*. Patrol cars operate on motorways, on the more important roads and in urban areas. On motorways, patrols are notified by the Motorway Authorities whom you can contact by using the emergency telephones. The direction of the nearest telephone is indicated by the point of the black triangle on posts alongside the motorways. If you break down on a road not equipped with emergency telephones or not covered by the *Strassenwacht* or if you need breakdown assistance in big cities, please call the nearest ADAC office, the telephone number of which is given on the cover of the official telephone directory. If there is nobody at the office, the automatic answering service will advise you of the nearest assistance point. Operating times on the main tourist routes are at least from 08.00 to 19.00hrs in summer and from 08.00 to 18.00hrs in winter, whereas in certain densely-populated urban areas there is a 24-hr service.

The following ADAC area centres can be called day and night:

Berlin	(030) 868686	Hannover	(0511) 8500222
Bremen	(0421) 446262	München	(089) 767676
Dortmund	(0231) 523052	Nürnberg	(0911) 551414
Düsseldorf	(0211) 434341	Saarbrücken	(0681) 63333
Frankfurt	(0611) 772222	Stuttgart	(0711) 233333
Hamburg	(040) 28999		

In addition, the Deutscher Touring Automobile Club (DTC), with which the AA is allied, has recently introduced a patrol service which provides a free daytime 30-minute repair service. The Automobile Club of Germany (AvD) and the Auto Club Europa (ACE) also operate a patrol service. The AA is not associated with these clubs and details are not available.

British Consulates   4 Dusseldorf, Nordsternhaus, 14 Georg-Glockstrasse ☎434281/5. There are also British Consulates in Berlin, Frankfurt/Main, Hamburg, Bremerhaven, Hannover, Munich, Stuttgart.

Currency and banking   The unit of currency is the Deutschmark, which is divided into 100 pfennigs.

Sterling travellers' cheques can be exchanged at all banks, savings banks, exchange offices at frontiers, main railway stations, and airports. There is no limit to the sum of money which may be imported or exported, either in German or in foreign currency.

Banking hours   Most banks are open from Monday to Wednesday and Friday 08.30–12.30hrs and 13.45–15.45hrs, and Thursday 08.30–12.30hrs and 13.45–17.30hrs; closed on Saturdays. Exchange offices of the Deutsche-Verkehrs-Kredit-Bank are located at most railway stations, and road and rail frontier crossing points. Generally they are open from early morning until late at night.

Shopping hours   Generally these are: *foodshops* from Monday to Friday 08.30–18.30hrs, Saturdays 07.30–13.00hrs; *department stores* from Monday to Friday 09.00–18.30hrs, Saturdays 09.00–14.00hrs (first Saturday each month 09.00–18.00hrs). Some shops close for lunch between 13.00 and 15.00hrs.

Medical treatment   The provision of medical benefits in Germany is administered by local sickness insurance offices *(Allgemeine Orskrankenkassen –* known as AOK), normally open Monday to Friday mornings only. Their address can be obtained by local enquiry, at the town hall, post offices etc.

You should first present form E111 to the local sickness insurance office, which will provide you with a sickness document *(Krankenschein)* and a list of names of doctors or dentists who operate within the sickness insurance scheme. The document should then be taken to the doctor or dentist you choose, who will treat you without charge. Any medicine prescribed by the doctor will be supplied by the chemist, but you will normally have to pay a small fixed charge for each item. This charge is not recoverable. If you or your dependants need hospital treatment, you should first obtain a certificate to this effect from a doctor, which you should then present with form E111 to the local sickness insurance office. A further certificate *(Kostenübernahmeschein)* entitling you to free hospital treatment (third class) will then be issued to you to take to the hospital authorities.

If you enter hospital urgently, and are thus unable to contact the local sickness insurance office beforehand, you should present form E111 to the hospital authorities, and ask them to obtain from the local sickness insurance office the further certificate *(Kostenübernahmeschein)*.

Germany

Motoring clubs

The principal German motoring clubs are the ADAC **(Allgemeiner Deutscher Automobil Club)** and the DTC **(Deutscher Touring Automobil Club)** who have offices at all major frontier crossings and larger towns. They will assist all foreign motorists in difficulties but may charge for their major services. AA members should produce their *5-Star Service Booklet* when requesting service.

All telephone directories in Germany contain information on how to call the ADAC road patrols and assistance. The ADAC also maintains a 24-hour emergency service at Munich on telephone number (089) 22 22 22.

Post and telephone

Rates for post to the United Kingdom are:

Air mail and surface mail		DM
Postcards		0.50
Letters up to	20gm	0.70
	20–50gm	1.20
	50–100gm	1.50

Telephone charges

The German telephone system is efficient and provides a dialling system to most European countries including the UK (for which the code is 0044). Charges are based on units of time which vary according to the distance and the time of day. Many hotels and garages provide, as a service, direct line telephones but charges are likely to be up to double the public rate. The cost per unit for a local call from post offices etc is DM0.23.

Public holidays

Holidays based on religious festivals are not always fixed on the calendar but any current diary will give actual dates. The Whit period (a religious holiday) should not be confused with the British Spring Holiday.

Fixed holidays

1 January	New Year's Day
6 January	Epiphany*
1 May	Labour Day
17 June	National Day
15 August	Assumption***
1 November	All Saints' Day** (not Hesse)
25/26 December	Christmas

Moveable holidays
Good Friday
Easter Monday
Ascension Day
Whit Monday
Corpus Christi**
Day of Prayer
(usually mid November)

The holidays marked with asterisks are holidays of the Roman Catholic faith and are only observed in the Catholic areas as follows:
*   Baden-Württemberg and Bavaria
**   Baden-Württemberg, Saarland, North Rhine-Westphalia, Rhineland, Palatinate Hesse and Bavaria
***   Saarland and Catholic areas of Bavaria.

Roads

The road system is dominated by a comprehensive network of motorways *(Autobahnen)*, which carry most of the long-distance traffic. The *Bundesstrassen* or state roads vary in quality. In the north and in the touring grounds of the Rhine Valley, Black Forest, and Bavaria, the roads are good and well graded.

Holiday traffic

Traffic at weekends increases considerably during the school holidays which are from July to mid September. In order to ease congestion, heavy lorries are prohibited on all roads at summer weekends, and on all Sundays and public holidays.

Motorways

Motorways *(Autobahnen)* and highways (indicated by a blue sign with white car) may be used only by those vehicles which are capable of exceeding 60kph (37mph) on the level. On motorways there is a recommended speed limit of 130kph (80mph).

There are about 14,395 miles of toll-free motorways *(Autobahnen)* open and more are under construction, or in preparation. The excellent system stretches in an unbroken line from the Belgian frontier to Berlin; from the Dutch frontier to Munich via Cologne, Frankfurt, Stuttgart, or Nürnberg; from the Danish frontier to Basle via Hamburg and Hannover. Nearly all motorways are part of the European international network. In general, motorways are two-lane dual carriageways, but in hilly areas there is an extra lane for lorries; these are sometimes signposted *Kriechspuren* (crawling lanes).

On certain hilly sections with only two lanes, lorries, coaches, and cars towing caravans are forbidden to overtake.

To join a motorway, follow the blue and white signposts; exits are indicated by an arrow-shaped sign bearing the word *Ausfahrt* in white letters on a blue background. The regulations are usually similar to those in Great Britain.

A well-planned chain of petrol stations and roadhouses is available in addition to many well-situated parking places. The usual distance between petrol stations is between 12 and 15 miles, but it is sometimes much farther; signposts give adequate warning of the distance to the next petrol station. Signs used are R for *Rasthaus* (roadhouse), T for *Tanken* (petrol station), and P for parking. Most motorways carry heavy traffic in the summer, particularly at weekends. delays are likely on the Cologne–Frankfurt–Karlsruhe, and Frankfurt–Nürnberg–Munich sections, and at the Salzburg and Kufstein frontiers leading into Austria.

Motorway telephone	Emergency telephone posts are placed at intervals of 2km (1¼ miles) along motorways. Black arrows on white safety posts show the

direction to the nearest post. When you lift the flap covering the voice tube, you are automatically connected with the motorway police. After you give details of the service required, the police will inform the ADAC patrol service. You should ask for *ADAC Strassenwachthilfe* (road patrol assistance). There is no charge for calls.

Pilot service	In Munich there is a pilot service *(Lotsendienst)*; pilots may be hired to guide motorists either to a place in the city or through to an exit

road. These pilots are licensed drivers covered by adequate insurance, and will drive the vehicle if requested.

Charges for this service are:

per hour	pilot	DM18
	pilot-driver	DM20
per 90min	guide	DM35

Rates are considerably reduced if the hire extends over several hours. Pilot stations are open daily from 08.00–20.00hrs in summer, and 08.30–19.00hrs in winter. They are located on the following main radial roads leading into Munich:

autobahn from Stuttgart–Obermenzing Station ☎8112412
autobahn from Nürnberg–Freimann Station ☎325417
autobahn from Salzburg–Ramersdorf Station ☎672755
autobahn from Garmisch–Unterdill Station ☎756330
federal road B13 from Holzkirchen–Harlaching Station ☎6909666

Pilot service stations will also supply tourist information and, for a fee, will make arrangements for accommodation.

Berlin	**Documents required for travel through the German Democratic Republic to West Berlin.**

Be sure you have a valid, standard passport (children over 16 years of age must have a separate passport), transit visa, national driving licence and registration book. The Green Card is now accepted, but make sure that it covers you for the GDR before you depart from the United Kingdom. Third party insurance can be arranged at the border crossings. Visas for journeys to West Berlin can be obtained at the frontier crossings at a cost of DM10.

Note Application for visas can be made to the Consular Section of the Embassy of the German Democratic Republic, 34 Belgrave Square, London SW1X 8QB ☎01–235 4465. Tourists travelling directly between West Germany and West Berlin are exempt from paying road tax, but must pay a visa charge.

Customs crossings	The main frontier Customs houses officially open for transit to West Berlin are listed below. The names printed in italics are within the

GDR, the others outside it.

Frankfurt	*Wartha*; Herleshausen
Hamburg	*Horst*; Lauenburg
Hannover	*Marienborn*; Helmstedt
Munich	*Hirschberg* Saalebrücke; Rudolphstein

Hours Crossings are open day and night.

West Berlin Entry is possible at Drewitz/Dreilinden on the routes from Frankfurt, Hannover and Munich, and at Staaken on the route from Hamburg.

East Berlin Entry for day visits from West Berlin is at Checkpoint Charlie on Friedrichstrasse/Zimmerstrasse. There are no restrictions for tourists of non-German nationality who wish to make a day trip from West to East Berlin, but make sure this is mentioned on the insurance policy.

Road signs	A blue rectangular sign with, for example '70/110km' in white – recommended speed range.

A blue rectangular sign with a white arrow pointing upwards and 'U' and a figure in white – diversion for motorway traffic.

Germany

A yellow circular sign with a green border and the letter 'H' in green – bus or tram stop.

Translations of some written signs are given below:

Anfang	Beginning
Ausfahrt	Exit
Baustofflagerung	Road works material
Durchfahrt verboten	No through traffic
Einbahnstrasse	One-way street
Einfahrt freihalten	Leave entrance free
Ende	End
Fahrbahnwechsel	Change traffic lane
Fahrt frei	Cancellation of previous restrictions
Freie Fahrt	No speed limit
Frostschäden	Frost damage
Gegenverkehr	Oncoming traffic
Glatteisgefahr	Ice on road
Haltestelle	Public transport stopping place
Landschafts-Schutzgebiet	Nature reserve
Langsam fahren	Drive slowly
Radweg kreuzt	Cycle-track crossing
Rollspit	Loose grit
Sackgasse } *Sackstrasse*	Cul-de-sac
Schlechte Wegstrecke	Bad surface
Seitenstreifen nicht befahrbar	Use of verge not advised
Starkes Gefälle	Steep down gradient
Strassenschäden	Road damaged
Taxenstand	Taxi rank
Umleitung	Diversion
Vorsicht beim Uberholen	Overtake with caution

Ferries (internal)
River Elbe

Cuxhaven–Brunsbüttelkoog *Map 5 A4/B4*
☎Cuxhaven (04721) 36026: Brunsbüttel (04852) 1270
Service Departures from either port at 08.00, 10.00, 12.00, 14.00, 16.00 and 18.00hrs with additional services at 06.00 and 20.00hrs in July and August.
Duration 75 minutes depending on tide
Charges

Vehicles	cars	DM11.50–18.50
	caravans	DM4.50 per metre
	motorcycles	DM5.50
	motorcycles with sidecar	DM9.50
Passengers		DM7.00

Glückstadt–Wischhafen *Map 5 B4*
☎Glückstadt (04124) 2430
Service Departures from Glückstadt summer weekdays 05.00, 05.40, 06.20, then every 20mins until 19.40 then 20.20, 21.00, 22.20 and 23.40. Sundays and holidays 05.00, 06.20, 07.00 then every 20mins until 21.40 then 22.20 and 23.40. Departures from Wischhafen summer weekdays 04.15, 05.00, 05.40, 06.20, then every 20mins until 19.40 then 20.20, 21.40 and 23.00. Sundays and holidays 04.15, 05.40, 06.20, 07.00, then every 20mins until 21.40 then 23.00. In winter service intervals are 20mins.
Duration 30 minutes
Charges

Vehicles	cars	DM5–8
	motorcycles	DM1.50
	motorcycles with sidecar	DM3.00
Passengers		DM1.20

River Weser

Bremerhaven–Nordenham/Blexen *Map 5 A4*
☎(0471) 21693
Service Departures from Bremerhaven daily throughout year 04.30, 05.30, *06.00, 06.30, *07.00, 07.30, *08.00, 08.30, then every 30mins until 19.30 then hourly until 23.30. Sundays and holidays 05.30, 06.30, 07.30, 08.30, then every 30mins until 19.30 then hourly until 23.30. Nordenham/Blexen 05.00, 06.00, *06.30, 07.00, *07.30, 08.00, *08.30, then every 30mins until 20.00 then hourly until 24.00. Sundays and holidays 06.00, 07.00, 08.00,

09.00, then every 30mins until 20.00 and hourly until 24.00.
*Not Saturdays.
Duration 10 minutes
Charges

Vehicles	cars	DM2–6
	motorcycles	DM0.60
	motorcycles with sidecar	DM1–2
Passengers		DM1.10

Reductions are available for return journeys.

Rhine

Cars are not carried on boats passing through the Rhine Gorge between Bonn and Mainz. One suggested method for incorporating a river trip is to take a day-return excursion on the Middle-Rhine between Mainz and Cologne and on the River Mosel. There are landing stages at nearly all towns and villages. For further information apply in the UK to G A Clubb Rhine Cruise Agency Ltd, 35 Dover Street, London W1K 3RA or when in Germany to KD Köln-Dusseldorfer Deutsche Rheinschiffahrt AG, Frankenwerft 15, 5000 Köln 7.

Cross-river services Unless otherwise stated, departures are at frequent intervals between the times given below:

1   Bad Godesberg – Nieder Dollendorf *Map 4 D1*
Service All year round 05.45–22.00hrs, except Sunday and public holidays: 07.45–22.00hrs.
Charges

Vehicles	cars	DM1.50–2.50
	motorcycles	DM1.50
Passengers		DM0.60

2   Königswinter – Mehlem *Map 4 D1*
Service All year round 05.45–22.50hrs, except Sunday and public holidays: 07.45–22.50hrs.
Charges as for No. 1

3   Bad Honnef – Rolandseck *Map 4 D1*
Service March to November: 06.30–22.00hrs; December to February: 06.30–21.00hrs.
Charges as for No. 1

4   Linz – Bad Kripp *Map 4 D1*
Service 06.00–24.00hrs all year round
Charges as for No. 1

5   Boppard – Filsen *Map 5 A1*
Service on demand

Jan–Mar	07.00–20.00hrs	Sun 08.00–20.00hrs
Apr–May	06.30–21.00hrs	Sun 08.00–21.00hrs
Jun–Aug	06.30–22.00hrs	Sun 07.30–22.00hrs
Sep	06.30–21.00hrs	Sun 08.00–21.00hrs
Oct–Dec	07.00–20.00hrs	Sun 08.00–20.00hrs

Charges as for No. 8

6   St Goar – St Goarshausen *Map 11 B4*
Service

Jan–Feb	06.00–20.00hrs
Mar–Apr	06.00–21.00hrs
May–Sep	06.00–22.00hrs
Oct–Nov	06.00–21.00hrs
Dec	06.00–20.00hrs

On Sundays services commence 1 hour later.
Charges as for No. 8

7   Lorch – Nieder Heimbach *Map 11 B4*
Service on demand

Apr–Sep	05.15–20.00hrs	Sun 07.00–20.00hrs
Oct–Mar	05.15–18.00hrs	Sun 07.30–18.00hrs

Charges as for No. 8

8   Rüdesheim – Bingen *Map 11 B4*
Service

Apr–Sep	05.45–22.15hrs
Oct–Mar	05.50–21.45hrs

Charges

Vehicles	cars	DM2–3
	motorcycles	DM1.50
	motorcycles with sidecar	DM2
Passengers	adults	DM0.80
	children (up to ten years)	DM0.30

Germany

9   Greffern–Drusenheim (France) *Map 11 B3*
See No. 11
10   Kappel-Rhinau (France) *Map 23 B3*
See No. 11
11   Plittersdorf–Seltz (France) *Map 11 B3*
Services 9–11
Mar–Oct   Mon to Fri   06.30–20.00hrs
            Sat, Sun and public holidays 06.30–22.00hrs
Nov–Feb   Mon to Fri   06.30–19.00hrs
            Sat, Sun and public holidays 07.00–19.00hrs
Charges Free
12   Weil–Huningue (France) *Map 11 B2*
Service departures from Weil every 15mins during greater part of
day 05.45–20.00hrs; half-hourly service early morning, midday and
evening. On Saturdays, Sundays and public holidays additional
services are provided at 20.30hrs, with a further service at 21.30hrs
during the summer months.
Departures from Huningue every 15mins during greater part of
day 05.55–20.10hrs; half-hourly service early morning, midday and
evening; on public holidays there are additional services at 20.35
and 21.35hrs.
Charges Free

**Bodensee
(Lake Constance)**

Konstanz–Meersburg *Map 12 C2*
Service 24-hour service every 15mins from early morning to late
evening; hourly at night.
Duration 20 minutes
Charges

Vehicles	cars	DM4–8.50
	motorcycles	DM1.60
	motorcycles with sidecar	DM2
Passengers adults		DM1.20

Friedrichshafen–Romanshorn (Switzerland) *Map 12 C2*
Service departures from Friedrichshafen every 2hrs between
07.00–19.00hrs;
departures from Romanshorn every 2hrs between 10.00–20.00hrs.
Duration 50 minutes
Charges

Vehicles	cars	DM12.00–15.20 (according to length, up to 4.10 metres and over)
	motorcycles	DM8.80
	motorcycles with sidecar	DM9.20
	caravans	DM12.00
Passengers		DM3.60

The vehicle charges above are 'high season rates' applicable from
July to September. At other times the charges are reduced by
DM1.60 for a motorcycle, DM2.40 for a large car.

Island of Sylt

Niebüll–Westerland *Map 1 A1*

No road exists between the mainland and the Island of Sylt, but
there is a railway over the Hindenburg Dam to Westerland. Cars are
loaded by ramp onto the trains. Vehicles must be alongside 20mins
before each departure.
Service There are 8–13 trains daily in each direction.
06.02–19.45   from Niebüll
06.10–22.35   from Westerland
Duration approx half-hourly
Charges

Vehicles	cars up to 1,100kg (1ton 1cwt 73lb)	DM37.00
	cars over 1,100kg	DM42.00
	motorcycles (solo)	DM3.60–7.50 according to weight
	moped	DM3.20
Passengers accompanying cars		free

**Tourist information
offices**

The UK office of the German National Tourist Board is in London at
61 Conduit Street, W1R 0EN. Their telephone number is 01–734
2600. In the Federal Republic there are regional tourist
associations–(DFV) whilst in most towns there are local tourist offices, usually situated near the
railway station or town hall. Any of these organisations will be pleased to help tourists with
information and hotel and other accommodation. The offices are usually open from 08.30 to
18.00hrs but in larger towns until 20.00hrs.

Visitors' registration A visitor staying overnight should report to the police, but this is usually done by the hotel or camp site management who complete the registration form. If staying with friends at a private address, the host should notify the authorities within seven days.

Motoring regulations

Information in this section is specific to the Federal Republic of Germany. A wider background is provided in the notes on page 67 with other regulations which you are advised to read.

Accidents In large towns dial 110 for **fire, police** and **ambulance**. For other areas, see the telephone directory.

You are generally required to call the police when individuals have been injured or considerable damage has been caused. Not to give aid to anyone injured will render you liable to a fine. Expert opinion should be sought to ascertain liability, when damage exceeds £150. This advice, however, will have to be paid for.

Crash helmets It is obligatory for all drivers and passengers of motorcycles which can exceed 40km (25mph) to wear crash helmets.

Dimensions Private cars and trailers are restricted to the following dimensions:
Cars   height   4 metres;
                width   2.5 metres;
Car/trailer combination 18 metres.

Drinking and driving If there is a definite suspicion that a driver is under the influence of alcohol, the police can compel him to undergo a blood test.
However, no one can be made to undergo a breath test (breathalyser). A driver is considered incapable of driving with an alcohol content in the blood of 0.8% but even a lower alcohol content can be considered to make a driver relatively incapable. A convicted driver is always punished by imprisonment, fine or suspension of driving licence if the blood-alcohol level is 1.3% or more.

A visiting motorist who is convicted will not be allowed to drive in Germany, and this will be noted on his driving licence.

Lights Driving on sidelights only is prohibited.
When fog, falling snow, or rain substantially affect driving conditions, dipped headlights or foglamps should be used even during daylight. The use of two foglamps together with dipped headlamps in such conditions is required by law. Motorcycles without sidecars may use foglights.

Rear foglights may only be used if, because of fog, the visibility is less than 50 metres.

Parking Parking is forbidden in the following places: on a main road or one carrying fast-moving traffic; on or near tram lines; within 15 metres (49ft) of a bus or tram stop; 5 metres (16ft) before or after an intersection, road junction or pedestrian crossing; within 10 metres (32ft) of traffic lights and 'give way' signs if the lights or the signs would be obscured by the parked vehicle; at taxi ranks; above manhole covers; on the left-hand side of the road (unless the road is one-way). A vehicle is considered to be parked if the driver has left it so that it cannot be immediately removed, if required. When stopping is prohibited under all circumstances, this is indicated by an international sign. Parking meters and special areas where parking discs are used, are indicated by signs which also show the permitted duration of parking. Disabled drivers may be granted special parking concessions; application should be made to the local traffic authority. Spending the night on the roadside in a vehicle or trailer is permitted for one night, provided that the vehicle is lit and parked in a lay-by. The sign showing an eagle in a green triangle prohibits both stopping and parking.

Passengers Children under twelve years old are not allowed to travel on the front seats of cars.

Police fines The police are empowered to impose and collect fines on the spot in cases of violation of traffic regulations. If a road user considers he is innocent of the alleged offence he can refuse to pay the fine and request his case be tried in court. If such a request is made then the police officer will demand a cash deposit against possible fines and costs. The case may be heard in the offender's absence. If the offence is considered serious then apart from the payment of the surety the accused must nominate an agent, resident in Germany, authorised to accept legal documents on his behalf. Any tourist who finds himself in such a position should seek help from the legal department of the nearest office of the ADAC.

Priority On pedestrian crossings (zebra crossings) pedestrians have the right of way over all vehicles except trams. Buses have priority when leaving public bus stops and other vehicles must give way to a bus driver who has signalled his intention to leave the kerb.

Germany

Speed   The speed limit in built-up areas is 50kph (31mph) unless otherwise indicated by signs. Outside built-up areas the limit for private cars is 100kph (62mph) unless signposted 120kph (75mph). Motorways *(Autobahnen)*, dual carriageways and roads with at least two marked lanes in each direction, which are not specifically signposted 130kph (81mph) have a recommended speed limit of 130kph. Vehicles towing a caravan or trailer are limited to 80kph (49mph) even on the *Autobahnen*. All lower limits must be adhered to. Anyone driving so slowly that a line of vehicles has formed behind him must permit the following vehicles to pass. If necessary he must stop at a suitable place to allow this.

Distance   Outside built-up areas, motor vehicles to which a special speed limit applies, as well as vehicles with trailers with a combined length of more than 7 metres (23ft), must keep sufficient distance from the preceding vehicle so that an overtaking vehicle may pull in.

Traffic lights   At some intersections with several lanes going in different directions, there are lights for each lane; watch the light for your lane.

Tyres   The legal requirement for tyres in Germany is a minimum tread depth of 1mm over the whole surface or whole width of the tyre.

Wheel chains   These must not be used on some free roads. In winter months the ADAC hires out chains, either special or the Kantenspur type, for cars and caravans. The construction of some vehicles allows only the use of the special chains. Chains can only be returned to ADAC offices and only during the hours of opening. On production of a valid AA membership card, chains may be hired at the following reduced charges.

Deposit	members (DM)	non-members (DM)
special	60	90
Kantenspur	120	180

Hire charge per day (days of collection and return are both counted as whole days)

	members (DM)	non-members (DM)
special (used)	1.50	3.00
Kantenspur (used)	3.00	4.50
special (unused)	0.75	1.50
Kantenspur (unused)	1.50	2.25

In addition, there is a basic fee of DM7.50 to members, DM15 to non-members.

If chain(s) are lost or damaged, or their wear exceeds the normal, the following amounts will be charged:

Special chains badly worn or damaged	up to DM15
Kantenspur chains badly worn or damaged	up to DM30
Packaging, badly soiled or torn	DM2
Fitting clamp missing	DM2
Fitting stretcher missing	DM2

Chains are sold in pairs and if one chain is lost, half the selling price will be charged; for loss of two chains, full selling price is charged.

If the deposit receipt is lost, the chains can be returned only to the station from which they were hired.

Chains are considered to have been used if the seal on the packaging has been removed in which case the hire charge is calculated on the basis of the fees for used chains for the whole period of hire, irrespective of the actual number of days in use. The maximum period for hire is 40 days. Reservations are not possible and the ADAC does not dispatch the chains by post.

Chains are available in several sizes, but, as foreign-made tyres may be different, it is not guaranteed that the appropriate size will be available; in this case alternative arrangements must be made. Further details may be obtained from the ADAC Head Office, department 'Strassendienste Schneeckettenverleih', 8 München 70, Baumgartnerstr 53 ☎(089) 76761. (No wheel chains are actually hired out from head office).

Warning triangles   Triangles are compulsory for all vehicles. They must be placed about 100 metres (109yd) behind a vehicle (or fallen object or load) on an ordinary road, and 200 metres (219yd) behind a vehicle on a motorway. Vehicles over 2,500kg (2tons 9cwt 24lb) must also carry a yellow flashing light.

Although the warning triangle sold by the AA does not correspond exactly to the type prescribed for Germany, it is legally acceptable for use by *bona fide* tourists.

Prices are in deutschmarks

A tax of 11% is payable on all accounts. This is usually added as a separate item on garage accounts but is included in the hotel charges quoted in this gazetteer, however certain spa (health) resorts eg Baden-Baden, have a special tax (kurtaxe) not included in hotel charges.

Abbreviations:
pl   Platz
str   Strasse

AACHEN Nordrhein-Westfalen 242,010 (☎0241)
Map **4** D1
★★★★**Parkhotel Quellenhof** Monheimsallee 52
☎48161 tx832864 150rm110➪10🛏 ♠ P Lift ♪
sB67–87 sB➪🛏98–127 dB➪🛏138–202
(English breakfast) L23–30 D23–30 ✎
★★**Benelux** Franzstr 21–23 ☎22343 40➪ ♠ P Lift
♪ sB➪fr59 dB➪fr84
★★**Brabant** Stolbergerstr 42 ☎500025 24rm3➪8🛏
♠ P Lift ♪ sB38–43 sB➪🛏43–53 dB61–75
dB➪🛏85 L8–18alc D8–18alc
★★**Buschhausen** Adenauerallee 215 ☎63071 75➪
A15rm ♠ Lift Pool
★**Braun** Lütticherstr 517 ☎74535 13rm5🛏 ♠ P
sB31–37 sB🛏35–42 dB51–56 dB🛏59–64
(English breakfast) L13–17 D7–13
★**Drei Türme** Ludwigsallee 25 ☎34219 10rm ♠
★**Hindenburg** Jülicherstr 141 ☎16093 Closed 21
Dec–14 Jan 40rm3➪10🛏 P Lift ♪ sB fr33
sB➪🛏fr43 dB fr63 dB➪🛏fr77 (English breakfast)
D11–25
★**Lousberg** Saarstr 108 (n rest) ☎20332 26rm8🛏 ♠
P Lift sB28–35 sB🛏40 dB55 dB🛏64–68
🛢 ►►**Cockerill** Herzogstr 13 ☎503870 M/c P Toy
🛢 ►►**Kuckarts** Viktoriastr 74 ☎503083 M/c P Ren
(GB)
🛢 ►►**Scharenberg & Jessen** Roermonderstr 62
☎31142 Frd

ACHERN Baden-Württemberg 20,610 (☎07841)
Map **11** B3
★★★**Seehotel** ☎3011 tx0742240 44rm24➪18🛏 P
Lift ♪ sB48–53 sB➪🛏63–68 dB➪🛏98–106
(English breakfast) L20–28 D13–28 Pool mountains
lake
★**Götz Sonne Eintracht** Haupstr 112 ☎5055
56rm32➪20🛏 ♠ P Lift sB31 sB➪🛏43–55
dB➪🛏70–120 L15–28 Pool

ADELSRIED Bayern 1,510 (☎08294) Map **12** D3
★**Schmid** Augsburgerstr 28 ☎891 100rm10➪40🛏
A35rm ♠ Lift Pool

ADENAU Rheinland-Pfalz 3,210 (☎02691)
Map **4** D1
★**Wilden Schwein** Hauptstr 117 ☎2055 7rm2🛏 ♠ P
sB26–28 sB➪🛏36–40 dB50–55 dB➪🛏65–75
(English breakfast) L9–28 D7–30

AHLHORN Niedersachsen 3,600 (☎04435)
Map **5** A3
☆**Nadermann** (B213) ☎302 10rm2➪2🛏
🛢 ►►**Auto Riemann** Wildeshauser Str ☎882 P
Aud/VW

AHRWEILER Rheinland-Pfalz 10,000 (☎02641)
Map **4** D1
★**Stern** Markpl 9 ☎34738 Closed 16 Dec–14 Jan
15rm3🛏 ♠ P sB23–27 dB42–48 dB🛏65–68
(English breakfast) L10–19 D10–22

AIBLING (BAD) Bayern 9,310 (☎08061) Map **13** A2
★★**Schuhbräu** Rosenheimerstr 6 ☎5831 Closed 26
Nov–25 Dec 45rm12➪8🛏 A9rm ♠ Lift
★**Lindner** Marienpl 5 ☎5295 Closed 24 Dec–4 Jan
47rm22➪11🛏 A14rm ♠ P sB35 sB➪🛏45 dB70
dB➪🛏90 (English breakfast) L10–25 D10–25

ALPIRSBACH Baden-Württemberg 7,050 (☎07444)
Map **11** B3
🛢 ►►**K Jautz** Hauptstr 29 ☎2345 ☎2345 Frd (GB)
At Ehlenbogen (4km N)
★★**Adler** Hauptstr 1 ☎2215 Closed 1–19 Dec & 16
Jan–14 Feb 22rm7🛏 ♠ 🛢

ALSFELD Hessen 17,815 (☎06631) Map **5** B1
☆☆**Rasthof-Pfefferhöhe** ☎759 tx49415
66rm18➪21🛏 ♠ P Lift ♪ sB25–26 sB➪🛏32–33
dB49–51 dB➪🛏58–60
★**Schwalbennest** Pfarrwiesenweg 14 ☎2964 16🛏
♠ P sB🛏26–28 dB🛏48–50 L6–8 D6–8
🛙 ►►**E Hartmann** Herfelderstr 81 ☎831☎831 M/c
Opl (GB)
🛙 ►►**W. Klöss** Grünbergerstr 72 ☎707☎708 M/c P
Frd (GB)

ALTENA Nordrhein-Westfalen 28,015 (☎02352)
Map **5** A2
K Lienkaemper Rahmedestr 141 ☎50430 M/c P
AR/BL

ALTENAHR Rheinland-Pfalz 2,210 (☎02643)
Map **4** D1
★**Lochmuhle** (near Mayschloss) ☎1345
65rm45➪35🛏 A15rm ♠ P Lift ♪ sB fr46 dB fr 50
dB➪🛏fr75 L13–16 D18–28 Pool mountains
★★**Post** Brückenstr 2 ☎2098 45rm15➪15🛏 ♠ P Lift
♪ sB27–33 sB➪🛏33–47 dB 52–58 dB➪🛏62–92
Pool mountains

AMBERG Bayern 50,000 (☎09621) Map **13** A4
★**Goldenes Lamm** Rathausstr 6 ☎12153 24rm5🛏
♠ P sB fr20 sB🛏 fr25 dB🛏 fr45 L6–16

ANDERNACH Rheinland-Pfalz 29,015 (☎02632)
Map **4** D1
★★**Rhein** Rhein prom, K-Adenauer Allee 20 ☎42240
Closed Nov–14 Mar 25rm10➪9🛏 ♠ P Lift sB fr25
sB➪🛏fr29 dB fr45 dB➪🛏fr60 L9–18 D9–18 river
★**Anker** K-Adenauer Allee 21 ☎42907 32rm4➪9🛏
♠ P sB29–34 sB➪🛏34 dB➪🛏69–71
(English breakfast) L8alc D8alc mountains river
🛙 ►►**E Kirsch** Fullscheuerveg 36 ☎42424 P Ren

ARNSBERG Nordrhein-Westfalen 82,010 (☎02931)
Map **5** A2
★★**Goldener Stern** Alter Markt 6 ☎3662 25rm 4🛏 ♠

AROLSEN Hessen (☎05691) Map **5** B2
★★★**Dorint Schlosshotel Arolsen** Grosse Allee 1
☎3091 tx994521 55➪ P Lift ♪ sB➪🛏64–78
dB➪🛏94–116 (English breakfast) L17–19 D17–19
Pool

ASCHAFFENBURG Bayern 55,550 (☎06021)
Map **12** C4
★★★**Aschaffenburger Hof** Frohsinnstr 11 ☎21441
tx4188736 59rm19➪40🛏 ♠ P Lift ♪ sB44 sB➪🛏58
dB77 dB➪🛏111 (English breakfast) L13 D13
★★★**Romantik-Hotel-Post** Goldbacherstr 19
☎21333 tx4188736 75rm54➪21🛏 ♠ P Lift ♪
sB➪🛏44–78 dB➪🛏80–120 (English breakfast)
L15–40 D15–40 Pool
🛙 ►►**Amberg** Würzburgerstr 67 ☎21418 P
AR/BL/Fia/Lnc (GB)
🛙 ►►**Auto-Haus** Pappelweg 8, Nilkheim ☎8588 P
Ren

ASSMANNSHAUSEN Hessen 3,015 (☎06722)
Map **11** B4
★★**Anker** Rheinstr 5 ☎2912 Closed Nov–Mar
48rm3➪2🛏 A18rm
★★**Krone** Rheinstr 10 ☎2236 Closed 11 Nov–14
Mar 84➪ ♠ P Lift ♪ sB38–48 sB➪🛏68–78 dB71–86
dB➪🛏96–156 (English breakfast) L fr4 D fr4 Pool
mountains lake

ATTENDORN Nordrhein-Westfalen 23,159
(☎02722) Map **5** A2
★★**Burghotel Schnellenberg** (3·5km W) ☎4081
Closed 6 Jan–14 Feb 42rm26➪16🛏 ♠ P
sB➪🛏45–60 dB➪🛏90–130 L13–35 D13–35 ✎
mountains

Germany

AUGSBURG Bayern 260,025 (☎0821) Map **12** D3
☆☆☆☆**Holiday Inn-Turmhotel** Wittelsbacher Park
☎577087 tx533225 185⇄🛏 P Lift ⓢ Bfr82
sB⇄🛏 fr82 dB⇄🛏 fr115 (English breakfast) L16−25
D16−50 Pool
★★★**Drei Mohren** Maximilianstr 40 ☎510031
tx53710 109rm85⇄16🛏 🏠 P Lift sB48
sB⇄🛏 68−85 dB⇄🛏 120−140
★★**Ost** Fuggerstr 4−6 ☎33088 tx533576 Closed 24
Dec−7 Jan 66rm12⇄22🛏 P Lift ⓢ sB30
sB⇄🛏 35−46 dB55−56 dB⇄🛏 59−76
★★**Parkhotel Weisses Lamm** Ludwigstr 36
☎35021 66rm17⇄17🛏 Lift ⓢ
★★**Post** Fuggerstr 7 ☎36044 50rm12⇄13🛏 🏠 P ⓢ
sBfr35 sB⇄🛏 fr41 dBfr60 dB⇄🛏 fr85
(English breakfast) Lfr12 Dfr12
🍴 ⓈⓄ**Listle** Kriegshaberstr 58 ☎403055 Ren (GB)

AURICH (OSTFRIESLAND) Niedersachsen 34,020
(☎04941) Map **5** A4
★**Piqueurhof** Bahnhofstr 1 ☎4118 48rm5⇄25🛏 🏠
P Lift ⓢ sB40−43 sB⇄🛏 56−58 dB68−74
dB⇄🛏 82−100 L10−25 D10−25

BRACHARACH Rheinland-Pfalz 2,941 (☎06743)
Map **11** B4
★★**Altkölnischer Hof** Blücherstr 2 ☎1339 Closed
Nov−Mar 20rm2⇄9🛏 🏠 P Lift sB28−34
sB⇄🛏 41−55 dB56−67 dB⇄🛏 70−84 L10−17
D12−19
★★**Engelsburg** (3km N) ☎(06744)243 Closed
Nov−Apr 14rm5⇄1🛏 🏠 P sBfr25 sB⇄🛏 fr30
dB45−55 dB⇄🛏 50−65 (English breakfast) D9−18
mountains lake

BAD each place preceded by Bad is listed under the
name that follows it.

BADEN-BADEN Baden-Wirttemberg 48,015
(☎07221) Map **11** B3
★★★★**Bellevue** Lichtentaler Allee ☎23721
tx781256 Closed 8 Jan−14 Mar 95rm68⇄18🛏 P Lift
ⓢ B50−70 sB⇄🛏 84−110 dB95−130
dB⇄🛏 105−200 (English breakfast) L26−30
D26−30 Pool mountains
★★★★**Selighof** Fremersbergstr 125 ☎23385
Closed Nov−mid Apr 58rm51⇄ 🏠 P Lift ⓢ sB50−66
sB⇄🛏 69−94 dB⇄🛏 102−158 (English breakfast)
L18−27 D20−29 Pool
★★★★**Steigenberger Bad Hotel Badischer Hof**
Langestr 47 ☎22827 tx781121 90rm70⇄ P Lift ⓢ
sB47−53 sB⇄🛏 75−101 dB⇄🛏 100−142 L22−28
D23−28
★★★**Europäischer Hof** Kaiserallee 2 ☎23561
tx784388 150rm132⇄ 🏠 Lift
★★★**Waldhotel Fischkultur** Gaisbach 91 ☎71025
taForellenhof 29rm 19⇄4🛏 A14rm 🏠 Lift
★★★**Golf** Fremersbergstr 113 (2km SW) ☎23691
tx781174 Closed Nov−Feb 85rm74⇄16🛏 🏠 P Lift
ⓢ B60−90 dB⇄🛏 90−115 (English breakfast)
L19−25 D19−25 ⚓ Pool mountains
★★★**Hirsch** Hirschstr 1 ☎23896 tx781193
101rm63⇄21🛏 🏠 P Lift ⓢ sB41−47 sB⇄🛏 71−87
dB⇄🛏 132−148 L25−35 D25−35 mountains
★★**Allee-Hotel-Bären** Hauptstr 36 ☎71046
80rm50⇄10🛏 🏠 Lift
★★**Müller** Langestr 34 ☎23211 32rm14⇄ P Lift ⓢ
sBfr35 sB⇄🛏 fr55 dBfr65 dB⇄🛏 fr90
★**Bischoff** Römerpl 2 ☎22378 Closed 16 Nov−Jan
21rm 🏠 P sB22−26 dB45
★**Römerhof** Sofienstr 25 ☎23415 Closed 16
Dec−Jan 27rm16🛏 🏠 P Lift sB22−30 sB🛏 40
dB50−60 dB🛏 68−70
🍴 ⓈⓄ**P Nagel** Langestr 104 ☎22672 BL/Jag
Rov/Tri
🍴 **Nippon** Aumattstr 8 ☎63527 P Dat/Hon/Maz

BADENWEILER Baden Wurttemberg 4,016
(☎07632) Map **11** B2
★★★★**Römerbad** Schlosspl 1 ☎701 tx772933
Closed 7 Jan−Feb 114rm100⇄ 🏠 P Lift ⓢ sB60−80
sB⇄🛏 95−120 dB130−150 dB⇄🛏 170−190
(English breakfast) Lfr30 Dfr35 ⚓ Pool mountains

★★★**Park** E-Eisenlohrstr 15 ☎5091 Closed mid
Nov−Feb 87rm78⇄6🛏 🏠 P Lift ⓢ sB40−49
sB⇄🛏 80−86 dB80−90 dB⇄🛏 140−160
(English breakfast) L12−20 D18−30 Pool mountains
BAMBERG Bayern 74,019 (☎0951) Map **12** D4
★★★**Bamberger Hof-Bellevue** Schönleinspl 4
☎22216 tx662867 42rm19⇄13🛏 🏠 P Lift ⓢ
sB35−45 sB⇄🛏 56−67 dB60−72 dB⇄🛏 78−98
(English breakfast)
★★**Straub** Ludwigstr 31 ☎25838 37rm5⇄2🛏 🏠 P
ⓢ B28−30 sB⇄🛏 38−42 dB52−56 dB⇄🛏 68−72
(English breakfast) L8−25 D8−25
🍴 ⓈⓄ**Schüberth** Siechenstr 87 ☎62253 M/c Ren
BAYREUTH Bayern 67,019 (☎0921) Map **12** D4
★★★**Bayerischer Hof** Bahnhofstr 14 ☎23061
tx642737 64rm37⇄12🛏 🏠 P Lift ⓢ sB28−32
sB⇄🛏 36−58 dB45−52 dB⇄🛏 52−95
(English breakfast) L12−18 D12−18 Pool
★★**Goldener Hirsh** Bahnhofstr 13 ☎23046
45rm15⇄3🛏 🏠 Lift
★★**Post** Bahnhofstr 21 (n rest) ☎5010 52rm12⇄6🛏
🏠 Lift
🍴 ⓈⓄ**R Keil** Markgrafenallee 28 ☎22622 BL/Fia/Vlo
BAYRISCHZELL Bayern 1,715 (☎08023)
Map **13** A2
★★**Alpenrose** Schlierseestr 100 ☎620
35rm5⇄25🛏 🏠 Pool
★★**Maria-Theresia** Tannermühlweg 358 ☎424
Closed 16 Oct−14 Dec 18rm8⇄2🛏
BERCHTESGADEN Bayern 24,450 (☎08652) Map
13 B2
★★★**Geiger** Stanggass ☎5055 55rm 43⇄55🛏 🏠 P
Lift sB53−68 sB⇄🛏 68−88 dB86−96
dB⇄🛏 96−166 (English breakfast) L18−30 D20−30
Pool mountains
🍴 ⓈⓄ**Buckwinkler** Bahnhofstr 21 ☎4087 Aud/Por/VW
(GB)
🚗 **G Köppl** Hindenburg Allee 1 ☎2615 ⚙ P Aud/VW
(GB)
At **Königssee**
★★**Königssee** ☎2343 tx56213 115rm35⇄ 🏠 Pool
★★**Schiffmeister** ☎3022 Closed 11 Oct−19 Dec
44rm12⇄ 🏠 Lift ⚓ Pool lake
BERG Bayern 6,311 (☎Starnberg 08151) Map **12** D2
★★**Strand Schloss Berg** Seestr 17 ☎5621
25rm8⇄1🛏 ⚓ Pool lake
BERGEN Niedersachsen 13,110 (☎05051)
Map **5** B3
★**Kohlmann** Lubenstr 6 ☎2012 15rm8🛏 A7rm 🏠 P
sB28 sB🛏 36 dB51 dB🛏 66 (English breakfast)
L6−25 D8−28
BERGZABERN (BAD) Rheinland-Pfalz 6,015
(☎06343) Map **11** B3
★★★**Park** Kurtalstr 83 ☎2415 Closed 7 Jan−14 Feb
40rm15⇄11🛏 A6rm 🏠 P Lift sB41−43
sB⇄🛏 52−72 dB82−86 dB⇄🛏 104−144 L11−32
D12−36 Pool mountains
BERLIN 2,050,010 (☎030) Map **6** D3
★★★★**Berlin Hilton** Budapesterstr 2 ☎261081
tx184380 343rm301⇄18🛏 Lift
★★★★**Bristol-Kempinski** Kurfürstendamm 27
☎881091 tx183553 335rm325⇄10🛏 P Lift ⓢ
sB⇄🛏 109−149 dB⇄🛏 138−188
(English breakfast) Lfr20 Dfr22 Pool
★★★★**Ambassador** Bayreutherstr 42−43 ☎240101
119rm110⇄8🛏 P Lift ⓢ sB111−119 sB⇄🛏 104
dB167−177 (English breakfast) L12−14 Dfr24 Pool
★★★**Berlin** Kurfürstenstr 62 ☎269291 tx184332
255rm185⇄70🛏 P Lift ⓢ sB⇄🛏 72−84
dB⇄🛏 110−120 (English breakfast) L16−23
D16−23
★★★★**Europäsccher Hof** Messedamm 10
☎302011 tx182882 179rm110⇄69🛏 Lift
★★★**Franke** A-Achillesstr57 ☎8921097 tx184857
69rm55⇄4🛏 P Lift ⓢ sB⇄🛏 50−69
dB⇄🛏 89−95 (English breakfast) L15−18 D15 Pool
★★★★**Parkhotel Zellermayer** Meinekestr 15
☎882051 tx184200 140⇄ 🏠 Lift

★★★★**Plaza** Knesebeckstr 63 ☎882081 tx184181 135rm121⇄11 🏠 🏦 Lift

★★★★*Savoy* Fasanenstr 9–10, Charlottenburg ☎310654 tx184292 115rm85⇄30 🏠 Lift

★★★★*Schweizerhof* Budapesterstr 21–31 ☎26691 tx185501 400rm316⇄84 🏠 🏦P Lift ♪ sB⇄ 🏠92–102 dB⇄🏠 144–154 (English breakfast) Pool

★★★*Kurfürstendamm* Eisenzahnstr 1 ☎8854025 tx183522 112rm45⇄67 🏠 🏦 Lift

★★★*Lichtburg* Paderbornerstr 10 ☎8919041 tx184208 65rm62⇄3 🏠 🏦 P Lift ♪ sB⇄🏠55–69 dB⇄🏠95 (English breakfast) L10–20 D8–18 Pool

★★★*Zoo* Kurfürstendamm 25 ☎883091 tx182835 144rm103⇄1 🏠 🏦 Lift

★★*Astrid* Bleibtreustr 20, Charlottenburg (n rest) ☎8815959 11rm 2 🏠 Lift

★★*Sachsenhof* Motzstr 7 ☎2162074 61rm13⇄1 🏠 Lift ♪ sB fr28 sB⇄🏠 fr33 dB fr56 dB⇄🏠 fr62 L fr9 D fr9

★★*Stephanie* Bleibtreustr 38, Charlottenburg (n rest) ☎8818073 14rm4⇄5 🏠 P Lift ♪ sB42–45 sB⇄🏠50–70 dB66–68 dB⇄🏠70–90

★*Charlottenburger Hof* Struttgarter pl 14 (n rest) ☎3244819 34rm P ♪ sB29 dB57

🛍 **Austin-Service** (W Hinz) Naumannstr 79 ☎7843051 BL (GB)

H Butenuth Forckenbeckstr 94 ☎82051 Frd (GB)

🚗 🛍*H Richtzenhain* Kantstr 126 ☎3124391 P BL/Rov/Tri

🛍 🛍*Sturm* Grünhofer Weg 30 ☎3311075 P Opl (GB)

🛍 *F Wacha* Stettiner Str 10 ☎4938967 P BL/Chy/Jag Rov/Tri

BERNKASTEL-KUES Rheinland-Pfalz 7,814 (☎06531) Map **11** A/B4

★★*Burg-Landshut* Gestade 11 ☎3019 Closed 16 Nov–Mar 35rm4⇄9 🏠 P ♪ sB34–46 sB⇄🏠36–46 dB62–72 dB⇄🏠77–92 L8–25 D8–25 river

★★*Drei Könige* Bahnhofstr 1 (n rest) ☎2327 Closed 16 Nov–14 Mar 40rm9⇄14 🏠 P Lift sB fr29 sB⇄🏠 fr 38 dB fr52 dB⇄🏠🏠 fr73river

★★*Post* Gestade 17 ☎300 Closed Jan 17rm4⇄1 🏠 A7rm 🏦

BIBERACH AN DER RISS Baden-Württemberg 28,920 (☎07351) Map **12** C2

★★★*Reith* Ulmerstr (n rest) ☎7828 43rm12⇄16 🏠 🏦 P Lift sB24–29 sB⇄🏠34–42 dB45–48 dB⇄🏠49–63

Schwaben Steigmühlstr 46 ☎7878 M/c P Frd

BIELEFELD Nordrhein-Westfalen 322,023 (☎0521) Map **5** A2

★★*Brand's Busch* Furtwengler Str 52 ☎22236 41rm5⇄31 🏠 A4rm 🏦 Lift

★★*Kaiserhof* Düppelstr 20 ☎65066 tx932656 145rm40⇄20 🏠 🏦 Lift

BIERSDORF See **BITBURG**

BINGEN Rheinland-Pfalz 26,940 (☎06721) Map **11** B4

★★★*Starkenburger Hof* Rheinkai 1 ☎14341 26rm13⇄ 🏠 P ♪ sB31 sB⇄🏠37–50 dB62 dB⇄🏠74–95 (English breakfast) Dfr8 river

🛍 🛍*L Honrath* Mainzer Str 71 ☎13131 Aud/Por/VW

🛍 🛍*Pieroth* Mainzerstr 439 ☎17355 Frd

BITBURG Rheinland-Pfalz 12,019 (☎06561) Map **11** A4

★*Mosella* Karenweg 11 ☎3147 16rm3⇄3 🏠 🏦

🛍 🛍*Auto-Jegen* Saarstr ☎3860 P Maz/Ren (GB)

🛍 🛍*C Metzger* Mötschertstr 49 ☎3462 AR/BL (GB)

At **Biersdorf** (12km NW)

★★★*Dorint Sporthotel Südeifel* am Stausee (☎06569) 841 tx4729607 240 🏠 Lift

BLANKENHEIM Nordrhein-Westfalen 8,110 (☎02449) Map **4** D1

★★*Schlossblick* Nonnenbacher Weg 2 ☎238 29rm1⇄12 🏠 🏦 P Lift sB21–23sB⇄🏠29–31 dB42–46 dB⇄🏠57–61 L11–22 D4–15 Pool mountains lake

BOCHOLT Nordrhein-Westfalen 49,900 (☎02871) Map **4** D2

🛍 🛍**Auto-Schreiber** Munsterstr 11 ☎8348 P BL (GB)

BOCHUM Nordrhein-Westfalen 433,623 (☎0234) Map **4** D2

🛍 **Reuter** Harpener Hellweg 7-11 ☎59881 Frd (GB)

BONN Nordrhein-Westfalen 287,015 (☎02221) Map **4** D1

★★★★**Königshof** Adenauerallee 9-11 ☎631831 taRoyal Hotel tx886535 83rm63⇄20 🏠 🏦 P Lift sB⇄🏠70–85 dB⇄🏠100–130 (English breakfast) L alc Dalc

★★★**Stern** Markt 8 ☎654455 tx886508 65rm33⇄24 🏠 P Lift sB43 sB⇄🏠59–75 dB64 dB⇄🏠85–114 L9–18 D9–18

★★**Beethoven** Rheingasse 26 ☎631411 tx886467 60rm9⇄38 🏠 P Lift sB33–43 sB⇄🏠53–73 dB63 dB⇄🏠73–93 (English breakfast) L12–20 D12–20

★★**Bergischer Hof** Münsterpl 23 ☎633441 28rm5⇄6 🏠 Lift

★*Eden* Hofgarten 6 ☎638071 33rm

★★**Savoy** Berliner Freiheit 17 (n rest) ☎651356 25rm8⇄2 🏠 P Lift sB30–35 sB⇄🏠 fr45 dB52–58 dB⇄🏠 fr70

🛍*J Bachem* Adenauer Allee 4-6 & Vorgbirgstr 100 ☎631151 (Closed wkends) Bed/Opl/Vau

🛍 🛍*Hessel* Putzchen chausse 43–51 ☎462088 M/c AR/Cit/Hon/Peu (GB)

🛍 🛍*J Knüfker* Lievelingsweg 2-4 ☎670444 P Chy/Sim

🛍 🛍*Mahlberg* K-Froweinstr 2 ☎636656 P BL

At **Röttgen**

☆☆☆*Bonn* Reichsstr 1 ☎251021 Closed 24 Dec–31 Dec34⇄ P ♪ sB⇄🏠52 dB⇄🏠84 L8–19 D8–19

BONNDORF Baden-Württemberg 5,213 (☎07703) Map **11** B2

★★★*Schwarzwald* Rothausstr 7 ☎421 67rm31⇄7 🏠 A27rm 🏦 P Lift sB24–26 sB⇄🏠30–36 dB46–52 dB⇄🏠60–72 Pool mountains

★*Germania* Martinstr 66 ☎281 8rm1⇄3 🏠

BOPPARD Rheinland-Pfalz 9,613 (☎06742) Map **5** A1

★★★*Bellevue* Rheinallee 41–42 ☎2081 tx426310 A84rm40⇄44 🏠 🏦 Lift Pool

☆☆*Ebertor* Heerstr (B 9) ☎2085 tx426310 Closed Dec–mid Apr 48rm48 🏠 A32rm 🏦

★★*Günther* Rheinallee 40 (n rest) ☎2335 Closed Dec–14 Jan 20rm4⇄13 🏠 P Lift sB⇄🏠23–31 dB⇄🏠45–62 river

★★*Rheinlust* Rheinallee 29 ☎3001 tx426319 Closed Nov–Apr 82rm9⇄30 🏠 A40rm 🏦 Lift

★★*Spiegel* Rheinallee 34 ☎2971 32rm14⇄9 🏠 P Lift sB fr30 sB⇄🏠34–46 dB60–64 dB⇄🏠72–87 (English breakfast) L9–20 D10–22 lake

★*Hünsrückerhof* Steinstr 26 ☎2433 26rm P sB24–28 dB27–31 (English breakfast) L7–17 D4–17

BRAUBACH Rheinland-Pfalz 4,210 (☎02627) Map **5** A1

★*Hammer* Untermarktstr 15 ☎336 12rm1⇄4 🏠 🏦

BRAUNLAGE Niedersachsen 8,020 (☎05520) Map **5** B2

★★★★**Maritim Congress und Sport** am Pfaffensteig ☎3051 tx96261 288⇄ 🏦 P Lift ♪ sB⇄🏠76–124 dB⇄🏠118–206 ⚓ Pool mountains

★★★**Weidmannsheil** Obere Bergstr 8 ☎3081 91rm30⇄16 🏠 P Lift ♪ sB39–64 sB⇄🏠58–73 dB 88–134 dB⇄🏠121–146 Pool mountains

BRAUNSCHWEIG (BRUNSWICK) Niedersachsen 270,005 (☎0531) Map **5** B3

★★★★**Atrium** Berliner Pl 3 ☎73001 tx0952576 130rm100⇄30 🏠 P Lift ♪ sB⇄🏠80–120 dB⇄🏠130–210 (English breakfast) L15 D15

★★★*Forsthaus* Hamburger Str 72 ☎32801 49rm4⇄24 🏠 Lift

★★*Frühlings* Bankpl 7 ☎49317 65rm18⇄31 🏠 🏦 P Lift sB36–46 sB⇄🏠54–67 dB fr73 dB⇄🏠78–97 (English breakfast) L9–16 D9–16

M Gottschling Ackerstr 34 ☎74546 BL/Jag/Rov/Tri

🛍 🛍*Könnecke* Gifhorner str 150 ☎311124 P Cit/Peu/Ren

ᵈ 🌢**Opel-Dürkop** Helmstedtstr 60 ☎703269 P
Bed/Opl (GB)

ᵈ 🌢*Sitte* Kurzestr 7 ☎76102 P

BRAUNSFELD See **KÖLN (COLOGNE)**

BREISIG (BAD) Rheinland-Pfalz 6,315 (☎02633)
Map **4** D1

★**Rheineck** Brunnenstr 10 ☎9180 31rm2⇌2📶 🏠 P
sB29–38 dB57–83 dB⇌ 📶77–91
(English breakfast) L8–28 D8–28) river

★**Vater und Sohn** Zehnerstr 78 ☎9148 8rm1⇌2📶 P
sB27–31 sB⇌📶33–37 dB54–62 dB⇌📶66–74
(English breakfast) L8–19 D8–19

BREMEN Bremen 572,050 (☎0421) Map **5** A3

⟦AA⟧ **agents; see page 221**

★★★★*Park* Bürgerpark ☎340031 tx244343 150⇌📶
🏠 P Lift ♪ sB⇌📶83–102 dB⇌📶155–160 lake

★★★**Columbus** Bahnhofspl 5 ☎314161 tx244688
136rm93⇌28 📶 Lift

☆☆☆**EuroCrest** A-Bebel Allee 4 ☎230041 tx244560
150rm60⇌90 📶 P Lift ♪ sB⇌📶83–86 dB⇌📶115
(English breakfast) D fr17 ♪

★★*Schaper-Siedenburg* Bahnhofstr 8 ☎310106
80rm7⇌18 📶 Lift

ᵈ 🌢*Harms* Hastedter Heerstr 303–305 ☎492074
Chy

Heins A-Noblestr 18 ☎490016 BL/Jag Rov/Tri (GB)

ᵈ 🌢**Motordienst** (R Lohrig) In der Vahr 66A
☎468033 AR/Hon/Peu (GB)

ᵈ 🌢**C Pollmann** Stresmannstr 9 ☎444131 P Frd
(GB)

At **Brinkum** (4km S)

☆*Atlas* G-Daimler Str 3 ☎874037 Closed 21 Dec–
9 Jan 30⇌ 🏠

BREMERHAVEN Bremen 150,020 (☎0471)
Map **5** A4

⟦AA⟧ **agents; see page 221**

★★★*Nordsee-Naber* T-Hensspl ☎47001 tx238881
125rm55⇌55 📶 🏠 Lift

★★★**Haverkamp-Seiffert** Schleswigerstr 27 ☎45031
tx238679.100rm30⇌40 📶 🏠 P Lift ♪ sB34–38
sB⇌📶47–70 dB59–65 dB⇌📶80–110
(English breakfast) L11–18 D13–20 Pool

🛢 🌢**Brem** Schonianstr 4 ☎22679 ☎22679 P AR
(GB)

BRINKUM See **BREMEN**

BRODENBACH Rheinland-Pfalz 610 (☎02605)
Map **4** D1

★*Post* Dorfstr 35 ☎ 348 Closed Nov–Mar 30rm
4⇌6📶 A12rm 🏠 P sB18–23 sB⇌📶26–30
dB36–46 dB⇌📶46–60 (English breakfast) L alc
D alc river

BRUCHSAL Baden Württemburg 40,025 (☎07251)
Map **11** B3

★★**Friedrichshof** Bahnhofspl 7 ☎2692 40rm9⇌8📶
🏠 P Lift sB fr22 sB⇌📶32–35 dB42–48
dB⇌📶54–60 L9–20 D9–20

ᵈ 🌢**Hetzel** Murgstr 12 ☎2283 🥄 M/c P BL/Maz (GB)

BRUNSWICK See **BRAUNSCHWEIG**

BÜDELSDORF See **RENDSBURG**

BÜHLERTAL Baden-Wüttemberg 8,215 (☎07223)
Map **11** B3

★**Rebstock** Hauptstr 110 ☎73118 Closed 16
Nov–14 Dec 32rm3⇌25 📶 🏠 P sB35–38
sB⇌📶36–39 dB65–73 dB⇌📶68–77
(English breakfast) L14–21 D12–26 mountains

CELLE Niedersachsen 80,021 (☎05141) Map **5** B3

★★**Celler Hof** Stechbahn 11 ☎28061 tx925117
52rm17⇌25 📶 🏠 P ♪ sB34–39 sB⇌📶62–68
dB68 dB⇌📶89–98 L10–19 D15–48

★★**Hannover** Wittingerstr 56 ☎34870 20rm4⇌16📶
🏠 P ♪ sB⇌📶40–60 dB⇌📶77–96 D5–12 🚾 river
🌢**Von Maltzan & Trebeljahr** Hohe Wende 3 ☎3921
Frd (GB)

CHAM Bayern 12,515 (☎09971) Map **13** A/B4

★★**Randsberger Hof** Randsberger-Hof-Str 15
☎1916 65rm12⇌37📶 🏠 P Lift ♪ sB27–28

sB⇌📶32–36 dB54–56 dB⇌📶64–72 L7–15
D7–15

COBLENCE See **KOBLENZ**

COBURG Bayern 46,713 (☎09561) Map **6** C1

★★**Der Festungshof** Festungsstr 1 ☎7781
19rm3⇌6📶 🏠 P Lift sB33–36 sB⇌📶46–61
dB66–70 dB⇌📶78 🛢 92 (English breakfast) L12–18
D12–25

COCHEM Rheinland-Pfalz 8,213 (☎02671)
Map **11** B4

★★**Alte Thorschenke** Brückenstr 3 ☎7059 Closed 6
Jan–9 Mar 55rm30⇌5📶 🏠 P Lift ♪ sB33–51
sB⇌📶50–70 dB69–93 dB⇌📶92–120
(English breakfast) L13–59 D13–59 mountains river

★★**Am Hafen** Uferstr ☎490 16rm1⇌ 🏠 P sB33–39
sB⇌📶38–44 dB32–41 dB⇌📶34–46
(English breakfast) L6–20 D5–15 river

★★**Germania** Moselprom 1 ☎261 tx869422 Closed
Jan–Mar 31rm13⇌4📶 P Lift sB fr42 sB⇌📶48–52
dB fr79 dB⇌📶90–99 L9–25 D12–25 river

ᵈ 🌢**Autohof Cochem** Sehler Anlagen 53 ☎626 P
Bed/Opl/Vau (GB)

ᵈ 🌢**M J Schneider** Moselprom 54 ☎7487 M/c P

CÖLBE See **MARBURG AN DER LAHN**

COLOGNE See **KÖLN**

CONSTANCE See **KONSTANZ**

CRAILSHEIM Baden Württemberg 25,024
(☎07951) Map **12** C3

★★*Post-Faber* Languestr 2–4 ☎8038
60rm20⇌14 📶 🏠 Lift

CREFELD See **KREFELD**

CREGLINGEN Baden-Württemberg 5,915
(☎07933) Map **12** C4

★★**Krone** Hauptstr 12 ☎558 Closed 21 Dec–Jan
25rm1⇌4📶 A8rm 🏠 P sB19–26 sB⇌📶26 dB fr38
dB⇌📶52–58 L6–14 D6–14

★★**Lamm** Hauptstr 31 ☎501 18rm 🏠

CUXHAVEN Niedersachsen 63,010 (☎04721)
Map **5** A4

★★★**Donners** Seedeich 2 ☎37014 85rm24⇌61📶
🏠 P Lift ♪ sB47–49 sB⇌📶53–85 dB85–92
dB⇌📶94–146 (English breakfast) L12–34 D6–30
Pool sea

DARMSTADT Hessen 138,024 (☎06151)
Map **11** B4

★★**Weinmichel** Schleiermacherstr 12 ☎26822
tx419275 Closed 24 & 25 Dec 75rm24⇌41📶 P Lift ♪
sB36 sB⇌📶54–60 dB⇌📶78–98 L12–22 D12–22

ᵈ 🌢*M J Wiest* Riedstr 5 ☎8641 Aud/Por/VW

DAUN Rheinland-Pfalz 7,021 (☎06592) Map **4** D1

★★**Hommes** Wirichstr 9 ☎538 Closed 21 Nov–19
Dec 41rm12⇌39📶 🏠 P Lift ♪ sB⇌📶52–56
dB⇌📶94–102 (English breakfast) L13–29 L13–29
Pool mountains

ᵈ 🌢*M Gessner* Abt-Richardstr 3 (B257) ☎2405
☎3293 Aud/VW

DECHSENDORF See **ERLANGEN**

DELMENORST Niedersachsen 70,015 (☎04221)
Map **5** A3

☆☆**Annenriede** Annenheider Damm 129 ☎6871
50rm2⇌48 📶 🏠 P ♪ sB⇌📶30–40 dB⇌📶50–70
L8–15 D5–15

★★**Central** Bahnhofstr 16 ☎19010 34rm8⇌6📶 🏠 P
♪ sB25–32 sB⇌📶37–42 dB43–47 dB⇌📶63–75
L8–18 D8–18

Sagehorn Bremerstr 41–43 ☎2001 Opl (GB)

DETMOLD Nordhein-Westfalen 65,013 (☎05231)
Map **5** A2

★★**Detmolder' Hof** Langestr 19 ☎28244
30rm2⇌8📶 🏠

★**Friedrichshöhe** Paderbornestr 6 (4km SE)
☎47053 14rm10 📶 🏠 P sB30 sB⇌📶33 dB57–59
dB⇌📶63–65 (English breakfast) L7–25 D5–25
mountains

ᵈ 🌢**Bergmann** Lageschestr 19–21 ☎25396 Frd
(GB)

🌢**H Budde** Marienstr 18 ☎22227 P BL/Rov/Tri (GB)

ᵈ 🌢*S Wagner* Grünstr 34 ☎27252 P Ren

DIEZ/LAHN Rheinland Pfalz 11,050 (☎06432)
Map **5** A1
★*Imperial* Rosenstr 42 ☎2131 17rm7🍴 🏠
At **Schaumberg** (4.5km SW)
★*Waldecker Hof* ☎2076 34rm 🏠 lake

DINKELSBÜHL Bayern 10,510 (☎09851)
Map **12** C3
★★*Deutches Haus* Weinmarkt 3 ☎2346 Closed
Dec–Feb 11rm3⇌5🍴 🏠
★★*Goldene Kanne* Segringerstr 8 ☎2363 Closed
16 Nov–14 Dec 24rm5⇌6🍴 🏠
★★*Goldene Rose* Marktpl 4 ☎2276 Closed 11
Nov–9 Mar 18rm5⇌6🍴 🏠 P sB28–30
sB⇌🍴40–45 dB49–54 dB⇌🍴64–79 L10 D10
🛢 ⇔*A Selferlein* Augsburgerstr 1 ☎2243 ☎2243
Opl (GB)

DOBEL See **HERRENALB (BAD)**

DONAUESCHINGEN Baden-Wurtleburg 18,215
(☎0771) Map **11** B2
🛢 ⇔*A Zimmermann* F-Ebertstr 76 ☎2246 P
Chy/Sim (GB)

DONAUWÖRTH Bayern 17,020 (☎0906) Map **12** D3
★★*Zur Traube* Kapellstr 14 ☎3142 33rm2⇌10🍴
A21rm 🏠 P Lift sB25–28 sB⇌🍴36–42 dB48–60
dB⇌🍴72–88 (English breakfast) L7–13 D7–12
★*Schwarzer Adler* Hindenburgstr 29 ☎825 15rm 🏠
★★*Vossen am Karlplatz* Bilkerstr 2 ☎325010
54rm11⇌14🍴 P Lift 🌙 sB51–57 dB85–90
dB⇌🍴95–114 (English breakfast) L8 D8
🛢 *H Dülpers* Volmerswerthstr 27 ☎391201 P Ren

DORTMUND Nordrhein-Westfalen 640,050 (☎0231)
Map **5** A2
★★★★*Romischer Kaiser* Olpestr 2 ☎528331
tx822441 Closed Sun 130rm90⇌20🍴 🏠 P Lift 🌙
sB⇌🍴91–96 dB⇌🍴136–141 L18–24 D18–25
★★*Westfalenhalle* Rheinlanddamm 200 ☎125063
tx822321 109rm6⇌46🍴 Lift ⚓
★★*Witteskindshef* Westfalendamm 270 ☎594049
tx822414 24rm3⇌8🍴 🏠
D Peters Arminiusstr 51–53 ☎17845 Frd

DUISBERG Nordrhein-Westfalen 602,040 (☎0203)
Map **4** D2
★★★*Duisburger Hof* Neckarstr 2 ☎331021
tx855750 128rm80⇌30🍴 🏠 P Lift 🌙 sB49–55
sB⇌🍴69–110 dB⇌🍴110–150 L alc D alc
P W Schwenke Buschstr 102 ☎50371 P BL/Rov
(GB)

DÜREN Nordrhein-Westfalen 88,915 (☎02421)
Map **4** D1
★★★*Germania* J-Schregal Str 20 ☎15005
58rm8⇌32🍴 🏠 lift
★*Nachtwächter* Kölner Landstr 12 ☎74031 Closed
19 Dec–9 Jan 40rm31🍴 A20rm P sB28–35
sB⇌🍴35 dB55 dB⇌🍴59–66 L15 D15

DURLACH See **KARLSRUHE**

DÜRRHEIM (BAD) Baden-Wurtlemberg 10,511
(☎07726) Map **11** B2
★★*Kreuz* Friedrichstr 2 ☎8044 tx7921312
59rm26⇌11🍴 A9rm 🏠 Lift Pool

DÜSSELDORF Nordrhein-Westfalen 680,009
(☎0211) Map **4** D2
★★★★★*Park* Cronelisupl 1 ☎8651 tx8582331 160⇌
P Lift 🌙 sB⇌99–131 dB⇌130–166
(English breakfast) 🏠
★★★*Börsen* Kreuzstr 19a (n rest) ☎363071
tx8587323 76rm19⇌55🍴 P Lift 🌙 sB⇌🍴84–105
dB⇌🍴110–140
★★★*Savoy* Breite str 2–6 ☎320541 tx8587324
90rm69⇌21🍴 P Lift sB⇌🍴89–110
dB⇌🍴135–160

EBERBACH AM NECKAR Baden-Wurtleberg
15,715 (☎06271) Map **12** C4
★★*Krone-Post* Hauptstr 1 ☎2310 50rm25⇌3🍴 P
Lift sB25–30 sB⇌🍴35–40 dB50–55 dB⇌🍴60–75
(English breakfast) L12–20 D14–22

★*Ochseb* Bahnhofstr 27 ☎2283 Closed 21 Dec–Jan
20rm10🍴 🏠 Lift

EBERNBURG See **KREWZNACH (BAD)**

EBRACH Bayern 2,410 (☎09553) Map **12** D4
★*Klosterbräu* Markt pl 4 ☎212 23rm15🍴 A6rm 🏠 P
sB23–26 sB🍴29–32 dB43–52 dB🍴52–58 L8–13
D12–15

ECHTERDINGEN See **STUTTGART**

EHLENBOGEN See **ALPIRSBACH**

ELFERSHAUSEN Bayern 2,210 (☎09704)
Map **17** B1
★★★*Gastehaus Ullrich* ☎281 tx672807
35rm22⇌14🍴 A5rm 🏠 P Lift sB29–32
sB⇌🍴46–51 dB54–56 dB⇌🍴72–76 Pool

ELTEN Nordrhein-Westfalen 3,600 (☎02828)
Map **4** D2
★★*Kur* Lindenallee 10 ☎2091 Closed Nov
24rm8⇌10🍴 P 🌙 sB43–52 sB⇌🍴45–55
dB85–104 dB⇌🍴89–110 (English breakfast) Pool
🛢 mountains

ELTVILLE AM RHEIN Hessen 15,050 (☎06123)
Map **11** B4
★*Rosenhof* Am Marktpl ☎3360 6rm2⇌2🍴
sB25–29 sB⇌🍴39–45 dB44 dB⇌🍴49–59
At **Erbach im Rheingau** (2km SW)
★★★★*Schloss Rheinhartshausen* Hauptstr 35
☎4081 Closed 16 Nov–14 Mar 42rm26⇌6🍴 Lift

EMDEN Niedersachsen 53,920 (☎04921) Map **4** D4
★*Deutsches Haus* Neuer Markt 7 ☎22048
27rm4⇌5🍴 🏠
★*Goldener Adler* Neutorstr 5 ☎24055 22rm 5⇌
10🍴 🏠
🛢 ⇔*Westermann* Auricherstr 227 ☎42051 P
Frd

EMMENDINGEN Baden-Württemberg 24,914
(☎07641) Map **11** B2
★*Park* Markrafenstr 9 (n rest) ☎8639 35rm2⇌5🍴
🏠 P sB26–31 sB⇌🍴31–38 dB50–62
dB⇌🍴59–72 (English breakfast) L6–8 D8–11 St%

EMMERICH Nordrhein-Westfalen 29,011 (☎02822)
Map **4** D2
★★*Zimmermann* Bahnhofstr 30 ☎70617
24rm3⇌12🍴 🏠

EMS (BAD) Rheinland-Pfalz 18,009 (☎02603)
Map **5** A1
★★★*Balzer* Villenprom 1 ☎2915 Closed Nov–Apr
110rm55⇌10🍴 🏠 P Lift sB30–40 sB⇌🍴35–40
dB60–70 dB⇌🍴70–80 L10–14 D11–15 Pool
mountains
★★★*Staatliches Kurhaus* Römerstr 3 ☎731
110rm45🍴 Lift
★★*Russischer Hof* Römerstr 23 ☎4462 25rm12☎
P Lift sB33 sB⇌🍴39–51 dB66 dB⇌🍴74–80 L9–15
D9–25 mountains

ENNEPETAL Nordrhein-Westfalen 38,104
(☎02333) Map **4** D2
★★*Burgmann* ☎71517 Closed 16 Dec–14 Jan
12rm8🍴 🏠 P sB31–37 sB🍴34–37 dB62–68
dB🍴68 English breakfast only L12–26 D11–15
mountains lake

ERBACH IM RHEINGAU See **ELTVILLE**

ERLANGEN Bayern 100,020 (☎09131) Map **12** D4
★★★★*Transmar Kongress* Beethoven Str 3 (DP)
☎87091 tx629750 138⇌ 🏠 Lift Pool
★★★*Grille* Bunsenstr 35 ☎6136 tx629839
65rm25⇌40🍴 🏠 P Lift 🌙 sBFr42 sB🍴52–83
dB Fr62 dB⇌🍴103–112
★*Luise* Pfälzerstr 15 ☎32835 Closed 29 Dec–10
Jan 69rm43⇌19🍴 🏠 P Lift sB37–44 sB⇌🍴67–70
dB72 dB⇌🍴83–100 English breakfast only Pool
🛢 ⇔*Lehner* G-Scharowsky Str 11–15 ☎33058
N☎65206 M/c P BL/Jag/Rov iTri
At **Dechsendorf** (5km NW)
★*Rasthaus am Heusteg* Heusteg 13 ☎41225
18rm3🍴 🏠 P Lift sB21 sB⇌🍴25 dB38 dB⇌🍴44
L8–25 D8–25

Germany

ESCHWEILER Nordrhein-Westfalen 50,000
(☎02403) Map **4** D1
★**Park** Parkstr 16 ☎6188 17rm4⇌7🍴 P sB Fr36
sB⇌🍴38 – 51 dB Fr60 dB⇌🍴Fr71 English breakfast
only L10 – 20 D8 – 20

ESSEN Nordrhein-Westfalen 685,024 (☎0201)
Map **4** D2
★★**Essen Touring** Frankenstr 379 (n rest) ☎42984
(Pn) 53rm24⇌ A26rm 🏛 P Lift ♪ sB36 sB⇌🍴48 – 51
dB62 dB⇌🍴87

📖 *Fischer* Altenessener Str 289 ☎352041 Frd
At **Essen-Rüttenscheid**
★★★**Arosa** Rüttenscheider Str 149 ☎795451
tx857354 68rm31⇌35🍴 P Lift ♪ sB52
sB⇌🍴79 – 93 dB⇌🍴116 – 175 L15 – 50

ETTLINGEN Baden-Wurtemberg 36,015 (☎07243)
Map **11** B3
★★★**Erbprinz** Rheinstr 1 ☎12071 tx782848
48rm44⇌4🍴 🏛 P Lift ♪ sB⇌🍴75 – 90
dB⇌🍴100 – 200 (English breakfast) Lalc Dalc
★**Rebstock** Leopoldstr 13 ☎12281 11rm P sB24 – 27
dB44 – 48 L7 – 15 D7 – 15

📖 ◗ *Walz & Zimmermann* Schleinkofer Str 2
☎16708 P BL/Jag/Rov Tri

FALLINGBOSTEL Niedersachsen 11,019
(☎05162) Map **5** B3
★★ *Berlin* Düeshorner Str 7 ☎532 Closed 16 – 24
Dec 10⇌ 🏛

📖 ◗ *F Kallbach* Michelsenstr 9 ☎578 P Chy/Cit/Vau
(GB)

FELDAFING Bayern 4,110 (☎08157) Map **12** D2
★★★**Kaiserin Elisabeth** Tutzinger Str 2 ☎1013
tx526408 70rm35⇌10🍴 A25rm 🏛 P Lift ♪ sB34 – 58
sB⇌🍴53 – 78 dB67 – 105 dB⇌🍴93 – 145 (English
breakfast) L16 – 20 D20 – 24 ◗ mountains lake

FELDBERG IM SCHWARZWALD Baden-
Württemberg 1,814 (☎07655) Map **11** B2
★★★**Dorint Hotel Feldberger Hof** Seebuck 12
☎311 tx77211224 80⇌ 🏛 P Lift ♪ sB⇌🍴55 – 75
dB⇌🍴76 – 120 L17 – 19 D17 – 19 Pool mountains
★★ *Albquelle* ☎213 17rm

FLENSBURG Schleswig-Holstein 93,110 (☎0461)
Map **1** A1
★★★**Europa** Rathausstr 1 – 5 ☎17522 70rm13⇌5🍴
🏛 P ♪ sB26 – 29 sB⇌🍴42 dB50 – 53 dB⇌🍴68
(English breakfast) L11 – 18 D18
★★★**Flensburger Hof** Süderhofenden 38 ☎17320
28rm23🍴 🏛 Lift

📖 ◗*H & M Patersen* Gutenbrstr 11 ☎17851 P BL
Cit Jag Peu Rov Tri
At **Kupfermühle** (9km N)
★★ *An der Grenze* (E3) ☎4098 45⇌ 🏛 Lift ◗ Pool
lake

FORBACH Baden-Württemberg 3,610 (☎07228)
Map **11** B3
★★ *Friedrichshof* Landstr 1 ☎2333 Closed Oct &
Nov 24rm1⇌7🍴 🏛

FRANKFURT AM MAIN Hessen 642,819 (☎0611)
Map **5** A1
★★★★★**Intercontinental** W-Leuschnerstr 43
☎230561 tx413639 814⇌ P Lift ♪ sB⇌101 – 196
dB⇌142 – 237 (English breakfast) L22 D25 Pool
★★★★**Frankfurter Hof** Kaiserpl (off Bethmannstr)
☎20251 tx411806 400⇌ P Lift ♪ sB⇌91 – 137
dB⇌138 – 178 (English breakfast) L alc D alc
★★★★**Hessischer Hof** F Ebert-Anlage 40 ☎740251
tx411776 107rm93⇌14🍴 A28rm 🏛 P Lift ♪
sB⇌🍴85 – 137 dB⇌🍴150 – 190 (English breakfast)
L alc D alc
★★★**Park** Wiesenhütten Pl 28 – 38 ☎230571
tx412808 270rm254⇌16🍴 🏛 P Lift ♪
sB⇌🍴93 – 133 dB⇌🍴151 – 191 (English breakfast)
L21 D21
★★★★**Savigny** Savignystr 14 ☎740481 tx4112061
90rm43⇌43🍴 P Lift ♪ sB Fr40 sB⇌🍴60 – 90
dB⇌🍴105 – 130 L7 – 16 D16
☆☆**EuroCrest** Isenburger Schneise 40 ☎678051
tx416717 300rm168⇌126🍴 P Lift ♪ sB⇌🍴92 – 95

---

dB⇌ 🍴115 – 125 (English breakfast) L Fr17 D Fr17
mountains
★★★**Monopol Metropole** Mannheimerstr 11
☎230191 tx411854 93rm63⇌3🍴 P Lift ♪ sB39 – 43
sB⇌🍴53 – 69 dB75 dB⇌🍴89 – 99 (English
breakfast) L13 D13
★★★**National** Baselerstr 50 ☎234841 tx412570
95rm60⇌20🍴 P Lift ♪ sB48 – 50 sB⇌🍴72 – 85
dB78 – 82 dB⇌🍴95 – 130 (English breakfast)
L20 – 25

B *Knelpel* Praunheimer Landstr 21 ☎785079
BL/Dat/(GB)
◗ *G Von Opel* Mainzer Landstr 330 ☎75031
Bed/Opl/Vau
📖 ◗*K H Steiger* Fritzlarer Str 18 ☎703041 Chy/Sim

FREIBURG IM BREISGAU Baden-Wurttemberg
180,005 (☎0761) Map **11** B2
★★★ *Colombi* Rotteckring 16 ☎31415 tx772750
84rm58⇌15🍴 🏛 Lift
★★★**Rappen** Munsterpl 13 ☎31353 Closed Feb
17rm6⇌7🍴 P Lift ♪ sB35 sB⇌🍴46 – 51 dB50
dB⇌🍴75 – 85 L14 – 26 D14 – 26
★★★**Victoria** Eisenbahnstr 54 ☎33211
52rm14⇌14🍴 🏛 P Lift ♪ sB46 – 54 sB⇌🍴75 – 78
dB58 – 80 dB⇌🍴95 – 120 L15 – 25
★★**Falken** Rathausgasse 32 ☎36984 Closed Aug
15rm8⇌ 🏛 sB36 – 40 sB⇌🍴49 – 54 dB54 – 68
dB⇌🍴72 – 96 L13 – 32 D13 – 32
★★ *Park Post* Eisenbahn Str 35 (n rest) ☎36077
Closed 16 Dec – 14 Jan 60rm8🍴 🏛 Lift
★★**Schlossbergblick** Ludwigstr 36 (n rest) ☎36927
42rm27⇌10🍴 P Lift sB43 – 47 sB⇌🍴53 – 57
dB76 – 83 dB⇌🍴83 – 113 mountains
★★ *Schotzky* Wendering 8 (n rest) ☎33171 Closed
21 Dec – 9 Jan 45rm6⇌2🍴
★★**Zum Roten Bären** Oberlinden 12
am Schwabentor ☎36969 24rm3⇌9🍴 🏛 P ♪
sB25 – 31 sB⇌🍴37 – 43 dB50 – 54 dB⇌🍴68 – 74
L12 – 23

📖 ◗*F Speck* Habsburgerstr 99 ☎31131 P BL (GB)

FREISING Bayern 32,000 (☎08161) Map **13** A3
★★**Bayerischer Hof** Untere Hauptstr 3 ☎3125
70rm19⇌18🍴 🏛 P Lift sB26 – 27 sB⇌🍴32 – 34
dB44 – 50 dB⇌🍴56 – 60 (English breakfast) L8 – 15
D8 – 15

FREUDENSTADT Baden-Württemburg 19,515
(☎07441) Map **11** B3
★★★**Rappen** Strassburgerstr 16 ☎3503
96rm52⇌1🍴 A35rm 🏛 Lift
★★★**Waldeck** Strassburgerstr 60 ☎2441
68rm33⇌15🍴 🏛 P Lift ♪ sB35 – 41 sB⇌🍴47 – 62
dB61 – 69 dB⇌🍴91 – 111 L12 – 21 D14 – 21
mountains
★★★**Waldlust** Lauterbadstr 92 ☎2051 tx764268
95rm86⇌27🍴 🏛 P Lift ♪ sB44 – 51 sB⇌🍴56 – 71
dB⇌🍴102 – 137 (English breakfast)
L18 D24
★★**Dreikönig** M-Luther str 3 ☎3333 19rm4⇌1🍴 P
sB23 sB⇌🍴26 dB43 dB⇌🍴51 L6 – 20 D3 – 20
★★**Krone** Markpl 29 ☎2007 25rm5🍴 🏛 P sB27
sB🍴27 dB54 dB⇌🍴54 L8 – 13 D8 – 13
★★ *Post* Stuttgarterstr 5 ☎2421 55rm25⇌15🍴 🏛
Lift
★★ *Waldhotel Stokinger* ☎2187 Closed Nov – 14
Dec 45rm9⇌9🍴 A35rm 🏛 Pool
★★**Württemberger Hof** Lauterbadstr 10 ☎2075
tx764388 Closed Nov 22rm2⇌11🍴 🏛 P Lift ♪
sB38 – 42 sB⇌🍴52 – 56 dB68 – 72 dB⇌🍴88 – 100
(English breakfast) L9 – 14 D9 – 14 Pool ◗
★ *Park* Lauterbadstr 103 ☎2318 26rm5🍴 🏛 ◗
★ *Zum See* Forststr 17 ☎2688 10rm A4rm 🏛 P
sB25 – 28 dB50 – 56 (English breakfast) L8 – 20
D12 – 20

📖 ◗**Hornberger & Schilling** Jetzt Deutzstr 2 ☎2429
P Opl (GB)

📖 ◗ *Oberndorfer & Knauf* Murgtalstr 35 ☎2278 Frd

FRIEDBERG Hessen 24,924 (☎06031) Map **5** A1

🏠 &◊ *G Von Opel* Frankfurter Str 9 ☎5548 Opl

FRIEDRICHSHAFEN Baden-Württemberg 53,011 (☎07541) Map **12** C2

★★**Buchhorner Hof** Friedrichstr 33 ☎21011 Closed 21 Dec – 9 Jan 56rm17⇆4🍴 🏛 P ♪ sB30–37 sB⇆🍴45–49 dB56–63 dB⇆🍴80–89 Lalc Dalc lake

🏠 **Frank** Meistershofenerstr 9 ☎21617 P Frd

FULDA Hessen 60,019 (☎0661) Map **5** B1

★★★**Lenz** Leipzigerstr 122 ☎77067 tx49733 60rm7⇆42🍴 A22rm P ♪ sB22–26 sB⇆🍴28–32 dB46–52 dB⇆🍴56–89 L8–26 D10–28

🏠 *W Fahr* Langebrückenstr-Andreasberg 4 ☎79078 Opl

FÜRSTENFELDBRÜCK Bayern 26,811 (☎08141) Map **12** D3

★**Post** Hauptstr 7 ☎2474 Closed 25–31 Dec 45rm8⇆13🍴 🏛 P Lift sB25–30 sB⇆🍴32–35 dB46–50 dB⇆🍴52–60 L7–18 D7–18

FÜSSEN Bayern 11,505 (☎08362) Map **12** D2

🏠 &◊ *G Gerhager* Oberleitnerstr 14 ☎7562

GARMISCH-PARTENKIRCHEN Bayern 27,525 (☎08821) Map **12** D2

★★★**Wittelsbach** Von Brugstr 24 ☎53096 tx59668 Closed 16 Oct – 19 Dec 60rm45⇆13🍴 🏛 P Lift ♪ sB49 sB⇆🍴53–65 dB82 dB⇆🍴94–114 English breakfast only L16–21 D21 Pool mountains

★★**Drei Mohren** Mohrenpl 7 ☎58088 Closed 31 Oct – 17 Dec 60rm16⇆5🍴 🏛 P ♪ sB30–39 sB⇆🍴46–51 dB66–75 dB⇆🍴82–94 (English breakfast) L10–20 D10–20 mountains

★★**Flora** Hauptstr 85 ☎4393 Closed Nov – 19 Dec 40rm15⇆10🍴 🏛 Lift

★★**Garmischer Hof** Bahnhofstr 51 (n rest) ☎51901 40rm9⇆7🍴 P Lift ♪ sB27–45 sB⇆🍴32–45 dB52–60 dB⇆🍴72–82 mountains

★★**Partenkirchner-Hof** Bahnhofstr 15 ☎58025 Closed 16 Nov – 14 Dec 75⇆ A21rm 🏛 P Lift ♪ sB⇆47–77 dB⇆83–113 (English breakfast) L17 D19–20 Pool mountains

Maier Unterfeldstr 3 ☎3776 Fia/Lnc/Peu (GB)

M Paulus Zugspitz Str 30 ☎54041 (GB)

Simson Haupstr 18 ☎53977 Ren

GELSENKIRCHEN Nordrhein-Westfalen 328,014 (☎0209) Map **4** D2

★★★★**Maritim** am Stadtgarlen 1 ☎15951 tx824636 250⇆ 🏛 P Lift ♪ sB⇆76–115 dB⇆112–157 Lalc D alc Pool

★★**Post** Bahnhofsvorpl 1–2 ☎21645 60rm12⇆18🍴 Lift

🏠 &◊ *E Hellmann* T-Otto Str 150 Hauptstr 50 Buer ☎54066 P Opl

GERNSBACH Baden-Württemberg 14,808 (☎07224) Map **11** B3

★**Ratsstuben** Hauptstr 34 ☎2141 Closed 16 Oct – 14 Nov 12rm2🍴 P sB fr (room only) sB🍴 fr22 (room only) dB fr40 (room only) dB⇆🍴 fr44 (room only)

GIESSEN Hessen 78,607 (☎0641) Map **5** A1

★★**Kuebel** Bahnhofstr 47 ☎77070 50rm30⇆17🍴 P ♪ sB40 sB⇆🍴45–60 dB60 dB⇆🍴70–86 L13–18&alc D alc Pool

☆**Ander Lahn** Lahnstr 21 ☎73516 20rm4🍴 🏛 P sB26–27 (room only) sB🍴32–38 (room only) dB🍴55–60 (room only)

🏠 ◗ *Mohr* Grunberger Str 85–87 ☎35051 P AR/Peu

GODESBERG (BAD) Nordrhein-Westfalen 72,000 (☎02229) Map **4** D1

★★★**Dreesen** Rheinstr 45–48 ☎364001 tx885417 85rm46⇆21🍴 🏛 P Lift ♪ sB31–43 (room only) sB⇆🍴65–83 (room only) dB60–80 (room only) dB⇆🍴106–116 (room only) L & alc D & alc

★★★**Godesberg** ☎363008 tx885503 14rm1⇆13🍴 P ♪ sB⇆🍴75–86 dB⇆🍴85–101 (English breakfast) L15–30 D15–30

★★★**Insel** Theaterpl 5 ☎364082 tx885592 69rm20⇆36🍴 P Lift ♪ sB40–42 (room only) sB⇆🍴52–68 (room only) dB70–75 (room only) dB⇆🍴90–100 (room only) L9–19 D9–19

★★★**Park** am Kurpark 1 (n rest) ☎363081 tx885463 58rm24⇆11🍴 P Lift ♪ sB45–50 (room only) dB⇆🍴58–70 (room only) dB fr75 (room only) dB⇆🍴95–150 (room only)

★★*Eden* Kaiserstr 5A ☎356034 tx885440 38rm28⇆ Lift

★★**Rheinland** Rheinallee 17 ☎366071 27rm7⇆10🍴 A12rm P ♪ sB36–57 sB⇆🍴fr63 dB66–76 dB⇆🍴fr98 L12–18 D12–18

★**Sonnenhang** Mainzerstr 275 ☎346820 11rm1⇆4🍴 🏛 P ♪ sB24 sB⇆🍴fr30 dB fr48 dB⇆🍴fr57 (English breakfast) L4–11 D4–11 mountains

GÖPPINGEN Baden-Württemberg 55,004 (☎07161) Map **12** C3

★★**Hohenstaufen** Obere Freihofstr 64 ☎73484 Closed Staff Hols 53rm6⇆17🍴 A12rm 🏛 P sB20–29 sB⇆🍴32–54 dB42–54 dB⇆🍴70–82 (English breakfast)

★**Apostel** Marktstr 7 (n rest) ☎73462 Closed 24 Dec – 6 Jan 28rm3⇆10🍴 P ♪ sB25–36 (room only) sB⇆🍴29–31 (room only) dB44–48 (room only) dB⇆🍴56–60 (room only)

GOSLAR Niedersachsen 52,014 (☎05321) Map **5** B2

★★★**Achtermann** Rosentorstr 20–21 ☎21001 tx953847 92rm34⇆58🍴 🏛 Lift

★★**Haus Riechenberg** am Grauhof ☎84001 tx53855 30rm22🍴 A10rm 🏛 P Lift sB34–38 sB⇆🍴50–56 dB61–71 dB⇆🍴87–97 (English breakfast)

GÖTTINGEN Niedersachsen 122,511 (☎0551) Map **5** B2

★★★**Gebhards** Goeth Alle 22-23 ☎56133 61rm15⇆24🍴 Lift Pool

★★**Kronprinz** Groner Torstr 3 (n rest) ☎44028 56rm4⇆4🍴 🏛

★★**Sonne** Paulinerstr 10–12 ☎56738 tx96787 Closed 21 Dec – 4 Jan 74rm30⇆20🍴 🏛 P Lift ♪ sB30–35 sB⇆🍴39–44 dB55–60 dB⇆🍴65–80 (English breakfast) L10–25 D10–25

&◊ *G Müller* Burgstr 6 ☎57587 M/c

◗◗ *W Richster* Benzstr 4 ☎73037 ☎77777 P Cit/Peu/Ren (GB)

🏠 ◗ *Rothe* am Lutteranger 8 ☎34304 P BL/Rov/Tri

GRÄFELFING Bayern 13,520 (☎089) Map **12** D2 At **Lochham** (1km NE)

★★**Würmtaler** Rottenbucherstr 55 ☎851281 60rm10⇆20🍴 A4rm 🏛 P Lift sB32–42 sB⇆🍴42–57 dB fr45 dB⇆🍴78 (English breakfast) L fr10 D fr15

GRAFENAU Bayern 5,011 (☎08552) Map **13** B3 At **Schlag** (1km S)

★★**Sonnenberg** am Schlag ☎203337 tx57413 196⇆🍴 🏛 P Lift ♪ sB⇆🍴39–77 (room only)

dB⇌ ⚿76–124 (room only) L14–16 ➶ Pool mountains

GRAINAU Bayern 3,209 (☎08821) Map **12** D2

★★★***Badersee*** ☎8686 Closed Nov 41rm20⇌6⚿ ⌂ Lift lake

★★**Post** Postgasse 10 ☎8853 Closed 26 Oct–19 Dec 35rm10⇌10⚿ ⌂ P sB34–37 sB⇌ ⚿46–49 dB62–66 dB⇌ ⚿88–98 (English breakfast) L fr14 D fr14 mountains

GRIMLINGHAUSEN
See **NEUSS-GRIMLINGHAUSEN**

GROSSENBRODE Schleswig-Holstein 2,000 (☎04367) Map **1** B1

★★***Baltic*** (E4) ☎371 80rm8⇌65⚿ ⌂ Lift Pool Beach sea

GROSS-GERAU Hessen 13,000 (☎06152) Map **11** B4

★**Adler** Frankenfurter Str 11 ☎2286 60rm5⇌43⚿ A7rm ⌂ P Lift sB25–30 sB⇌ ⚿34–43 dB50–60 dB⇌ ⚿68–80 (English breakfast) L5–30 D5–30

★★***Hirsch*** Marktpl 18 ☎5610 21rm1⇌12⚿ A10rm ⌂

GÜNZBURG Bayern 13,511 (☎08221) Map **12** C3

★★***Hirsch*** Marktpl 18 ☎5610 21rm1⇌12⚿ A10rm ⌂

HAGEN Nordrhein-Westfalen 243,324 (☎02331) Map **5** A2

★★***Deutsches Haus*** Bahnhofstr 35 ☎21051 tx823640 41rm4⇌31⚿ ⌂ Lift

HAGNAU Baden-Württemberg 1,321 (☎07532) Map **12** C2

★**Messmer** Meersburgerstr 12 (n rest) ☎6227 14rm4⇌4⚿ P sB28–31 sB⇌ ⚿38–45 dB56–70 dB⇌ ⚿70–80 lake

HALTINGEN Baden-Württemberg 5,300 (☎07621) Map **11** B2

★**Rebstock** Grosse Grasse 30 ☎62257 taBiechele 14rm6⚿ A4rm ⌂ P sB28–40 sB⇌ ⚿32–48 dB56–74 dB⇌ ⚿62–94 (English breakfast) L8–25

HAMBURG Hamburg 1,800,007 (☎040) Map **4** B4

[AA] **agents; see page 221**

★★★★★**Vier Jahreszeiten** Neuer Jungfernsteig 9–14 ☎34941 tx211629 200⇌6⚿ ⌂ P Lift ☽ sB⇌ ⚿146–109 dB⇌ ⚿197–302 (English breakfast) L alc D alc sea

★★★★**Atlantic** an der Alster 72 ☎248001 tx2163297 300⇌ ⌂ P Lift ☽ sB⇌131–171 dB⇌182–232 (English breakfast) Pool lake

★★★**Berlin** Borgfelderstr 1–9 ☎257211 tx213939 96rm53⇌27⚿ ⌂ P Lift ☽ sB54–64 sB⇌ ⚿94–113 dB⇌ ⚿127–147 (English breakfast) L fr20 D fr20

★★★**Central-Smolka** Isestr 98 ☎475057 tx215275 40rm20⇌18⚿ ⌂ P Lift ☽ sB fr50 sB⇌ ⚿66–108 dB fr90 dB⇌ ⚿115–140 (English breakfast) L alc D alc

☆☆☆**EuroCrest** Mexikoring 1 ☎6305051 tx217455 185rm127⇌58⚿ P Lift ☽ sB⇌ ⚿107 dB⇌ ⚿148 (English breakfast) L fr17 D fr17

★★★***Europäischer-Hof*** Kirchenallee 45 ☎248171 tx2162493 300rm120⇌180⚿ ⌂ ➶

★★★***Parkhochhaus*** Drehbahn 15 ☎341656 tx212475 107rm50⇌57⚿ ⌂ Lift

★★★**Reichshof** Kirchenallee 34 (off Steindamm) ☎248191 tx2163396 350rm150⇌200⚿ ⌂ P Lift ☽ sB⇌ ⚿89–100 dB⇌ ⚿120–150 (English breakfast) L fr19 D fr19

★★**Schümann** Langenhorner chausee 157 ☎5208025 22⇌ ⚿ ⌂ P sB⇌ ⚿52–57 dB⇌ ⚿85–90 (English breakfast)

☆**Hamburg** Hoheluftchaussee 119 (n rest) ☎473067 tx211645 37rm20⚿ ⌂ P ☽ sB fr48 sB⚿ fr68 dB fr75 dB⚿90–94

★**Pacific** Neuer Pferdemarkt 30 ☎4395094 60rm15⇌5⚿ ⌂ P Lift ☽ sB fr40 sB⇌ ⚿ fr50 dB fr61 dB⇌ ⚿ fr71

A Dannmeyer Grosslohering 66 ☎6724569 P BL

Hertzel Eppendorfer Landstr 51–53 ☎4603061 Peu (GB)

International Stresemannallee 54 ☎463579

Motor-Company Ruhrstr 63 ☎855011 Frd

L Nemeth Koppel 65 ☎244840 BL/Peu/RR (GB)

P Nitzschke Steinbeker Haupstr 84 ☎7128459 P BL/Rov/Tri

Touren & Sportwagen Goldbekpl 3–5 ☎271121 AR/BL/Jag/Rov/Tri

Vidal & Sohn Angerstr 20–22 ☎257901 ☎5402011 P Jag/MB/Ren Rov (GB)

HAMELN Niedersachsen 106,704 (☎05151) Map **5** B3

★★★**Dorint Hotel Weserbergland** Dingelstedtstr 3 ☎21044 tx924716 103⇌ ⌂ P Lift ☽ sB⇌54–75 dB⇌110 L17–19 D17–19 Pool

K Reissdorf Wallbaumstr 6/Berlinerpl ☎3764 M/c P Chy/Vlo

Hermann Struck Hastenbeckerweg 62 ☎12012 Frd (GB)

HANAU AM MAIN Hessen 90,022 (☎06181) Map **12** C4

Schäfer E-Kaiserstr 5 ☎24621 P Opl

HANNOVER Niedersachsen 575,030 (☎0511) Map **5** B3

☆☆☆**EuroCrest** Tiergarbier Str 17 ☎523092 tx922748 110rm78⇌32⚿ ⌂ P Lift ☽ sB⇌ ⚿92 dB⇌ ⚿115 (English breakfast) L fr17 D fr17

★★★***Europäischer Hof*** Luisenstr 4 ☎17644 taRummelshotel 56rm17⇌8⚿ Lift

★★★**Kastens Luisen Hof** Luisenstr 1–3 ☎16151 tx922325 210rm140⇌30⚿ ⌂ P Lift ☽ sB66–86 sB⇌ ⚿106–126 dB⇌ ⚿182–202 (English breakfast) L20–30 D20–30

☆☆☆**Park Kronsberg** Messeschnellweg ☎861086 tx923448 105rm31⇌68⚿ ⌂ P Lift ☽ sB43–50 (room only) sB⇌ ⚿60–80 (room only) dB fr70 (room only) dB⇌ ⚿82–110 (room only) (English breakfast) L12–22 D14–25

★★**Central Kaiserhof** Ernst-August-Pl 4 ☎327811 tx922810 86rm40⇌46⚿ P Lift ☽ sB⇌ ⚿63–74 dB⇌ ⚿106–138 (English breakfast) L14–22 D16–32

☆☆***Treffpunkt*** Hannoverschestr 109 ☎61721 56rm4⇌8⚿ ⌂

Deisterstrasse Deisterstr 33–37 ☎444016 Frd

E Gross Davenstedterstr 101 ☎451071 BL/Jag/Rov/Tri

Heidorn Viktoriastr 8–9 ☎441167 P BL (GB)

Jaguar-Automobile (G Koch) am Listholz 70 ☎691150 (GB)

W Rudhart am Klagesmarkt 3 ☎16531 P Bed/Opl/Vau (GB)

HANNOVER AIRPORT

☆☆☆☆**Holiday Inn** am Flughagen ☎730171 tx924030 150 ⇌ ⚿ P Lift ⚿ sB⇌ ⚿ fr90 dB⇌ ⚿ fr125 (English breakfast) L25alc D30alc Pool

HARZBURG (BAD) Niedersachsen 27,010 (☎05322) Map **5** B2

★★★**Bodes** Stadtpark 48 ☎2041 90rm40⇌30⚿ A40rm ⌂ P Lift ☽ sB37–47 sB⇌ ⚿53–67 dB78–88 dB⇌ ⚿100–124 (English breakfast) L12–25 D12–25 mountains

★★**Braunschweiger Hof** H-Willhelm Str 54 ☎7035 40rm3⇌28⚿ ⌂ P Lift sB28–32 sB⇌ ⚿42–45 dB49–52 dB⇌ ⚿72–78 L13–35 D13–35

★***Goldener Schlüssel*** ☎81313 7⚿ ⌂

HATTENHEIM Hessen 1,950 (☎06723) Map **11** B4

★★***Ress*** Hauptstr 25 (DP) ☎3013 taWeinress Closed 16 Dec–14 Feb 26rm4⇌2⚿ ⌂

HEIDE Schleswig-Holstein 23,500 (☎0481) Map **1** A1

W Leinweber Hamburgerstr 115 ☎3022 P Opl

HEIDELBERG Baden-Wurtlemberg 130,025 (☎06221) Map **11** B4

★★★★★**Europäischer Hof** F-Ebert Anlage 1A ☎27101 tx461840 127rm109⇌5⚿ P Lift ☽ sB59–79 sB⇌ ⚿79–119 dB100–120 dB⇌ ⚿144–176 English breakfast only L25–32 D25–32

★★★**Alt Heidelberg** Rohrbacher Str 29 ☎25575
tx461897 60rm19➪11 🏠 🛗 P Lift ♪ sB➪ 🏠55–59
dB➪ 🏠88–96 (English breakfast)
★★★**Bayrischer Hof** Bismarckpl ☎24646 Closed 23
Dec–9 Jan 46rm11➪9🏠 Lift
☆☆**EuroCrest** Pleikartsförster Str ☎71021
tx461650 70rm43➪27🏠 🏠 P Lift ♪ sB➪ 🏠91
dB➪ 🏠128 (English breakfast) L fr17 D fr18
★★**Neckar** Bismarckstr 19 (n rest) ☎23260
35rm9➪14🏠 P Lift ♪ sB36–42 sB➪ 🏠45–49
dB54–64 dB➪ 🏠75–88 (English breakfast)
★★**Schwarzes Schiff** Neuenheimer Landstr 5
☎46071 44rm27➪5🏠 P Lift ♪ sB fr35 sB➪ 🏠fr50
dB fr50 dB➪ 🏠 fr70 (English breakfast) L fr15 D fr15
★★**Stiftsmühle** in der Neckarhalle 129 ☎80555
35rm16➪ A5rm P Lift ♪ sB41 sB➪61 dB72–76
dB➪ 🏠87–126 mountains
★**Kohler** Goethestr 2 (n rest) ☎24360 Closed 16
Dec–8 Jan 43rm4➪26🏠 Lift ♪ sB26–34
sB➪ 🏠38–46 dB42–52 dB➪ 🏠60–72
(English breakfast)
★**Vier Jahreszeiten** Haspelgasse 2 ☎24164 Closed
16 Dec–14 Jan 25rm5➪6🏠 A3rm P ♪ sB30–35
(room only) sB➪ 🏠45–48 (room only) dB55–60
(room only) dB➪ 🏠75–85 (room only)
🛢 &▷**Auto-Center** Lanzstr 6 ☎28686 P Hon (GB)
Bosch-Dienst (L Fath-Trippmacher) Karl Benz Str 2
☎22171 (GB)
🛢 **Leyland** am Taubenfeld 39 ☎81091 P
BL/Jag/Rov/Tri
⊷&▷**J Pfotzer** Speyerer Str 11 ☎27191 Opl
🛢 ⊷**Raichle & Baur** Hebelstr 12 ☎24954 ☎71155
BL/Jag/Rov/Tri

HEILBRONN Baden-Wurtlemberg 117,015
(☎07131) Map **12** C3
★★★**Insel** F-Ebert Brücke ☎88931 tx728777
120rm100➪20🏠 P Lift ♪ sB➪ 🏠42–78
dB➪ 🏠68–118 (English breakfast) L fr16 D fr16 river
★★**Kronprinz** Bahnhofstr 29 (DP) ☎83941 tx728561
35rm4➪12🏠 🏠 Lift
🛢 ⊷**Autohaus Fend** Karlstr 49–51 ☎81081 P
BL/Jag/Rov/Tri

HELLERN See **OSNABRÜCK**

HELMSTEDT Niedersachsen 29,017 (☎05351)
Map **6** C3
★★**Petzold** Schöninger Str 1 ☎6001 28rm4➪7🏠 🏠
P sB31–35 sB➪ 🏠38–44 dB60–62 dB➪ 🏠72–82
(English breakfast) L10–18 D8–22
🛢 ⊷**Wagner** Grosser Stern 3 ☎3607 P Aud/VW

HEPPENHEIM AN DER BERGSTRASSE Hessen
24,041 (☎06252) Map **11** B4
★**Goldenen Engel** Gr Markt 2 ☎2563 24rm4➪12🏠
A12rm 🏠 P sB25–27 sB➪ 🏠30–37 dB47
dB➪ 🏠52–70 mountains

HERFORD Nordrheim-Westfalen 70,011 (☎05221)
Map **5** A3
★**Twachmann** Bügelstr 4 ☎56283 45rm 🏠 Lift

HERRENALB (BAD) Baden-Württemberg 4,720
(☎07083) Map **11** B3
★★★★**Mönchs Post** Doblerstr ☎2002 tx7245123
50rm30➪15🏠 🏠 Lift Pool 💲
At **Dobel** (6km E)
★★★**Mönchs Waldhotel** Neuenburgerstr 49 ☎8888
Closed 16 Nov–20 Dec 40rm8➪28🏠 🏠 P sB29–32
sB➪ 🏠42–47 dB37–40 dB➪ 🏠43–50
(English breakfast) L13–22 D13–22 mountains
★★**Funk** Hauptstr ☎2077 Closed 3 Nov–19 Dec
30rm3➪5🏠 A7rm 🏠 P sB32–37 sB➪ 🏠42–50
dB63–80 dB➪ 🏠93–100 L13–22 D14–25
mountains

HERRENBERG Baden-Wurttemberg 24,010
(☎07032) Map **12** C3
★**Neue Post** Wilhelmstr 48 ☎5156 Closed 24 Dec–9
Jan 7rm2➪🏠 P sB25–30 sB➪ 🏠fr30 dB fr50 dB➪ 🏠fr58
(English breakfast) L12–28 D6–14

HERSBRUCK Bayern 9,014 (☎09151) Map **12** D4

★**Schwarzer Adler** M-Lutherstr 26 ☎2231 Closed 21
Jun–9 Jul 10rm 🏠

HERSFELD (BAD) Hessen 30,025 (☎06621)
Map **5** B1
★★**Parkhotel Rose** am Kurpark 9 ☎4454 Closed 21
Dec–19 Jan 25rm12➪11🏠 🏠 P Lift sB30–45
(room only) sB➪ 🏠40–75 (room only) dB➪ 🏠60–95
(room only)
🛢 &▷**Auto Friedrich** Max-Beckerstr 3 ☎72001 P
Aud/VW (GB)

HILCHENBACH Nordrhein-Westfalen 16,029
(☎02733) Map **5** A1
★★**Deutscher Hof** Dammstr 10 ☎4339 25rm5➪5🏠
🏠

HILDESHEIM Niedersachsen 107,405 (☎05121)
Map **5** B3
★★★★**Rose** Markt 7 ☎1955 tx927126 50rm40➪5🏠
🏠 P Lift ♪ sB46–67 sB➪ 🏠46–67 dB59–99
dB➪ 🏠59–99 (English breakfast) L14–30alc
D14–30alc
🛢 &▷**Schwalenberg** Senkingstr 11 ☎53434/52163 P
🛢 **Touren & Sportwagen** (Erdmann & Felske)
Hildebrandstr 27 ☎56148 P BL (GB)

HILPOLTSTEIN Bayern 9,515 (☎09174) Map **12** D3
★**Post** Markstr 8 ☎207 16🏠 🏠 P sB➪21 dB🏠42
(English breakfast) L6–10 D6–12
🛢 ⊷**Auto-Sebesic** Heidecker Str 40 ☎500 P
Aud/VW

HINDELANG Bayern 5,056 (☎08324) Map **12** C/D2
★★**Luitpoldbad** A-Gross Weg ☎325 Closed 4
Nov–16 Dec 110rm70➪30🏠 🏠 P Lift ♪ sB27–30
sB➪ 🏠33–65 dB54–65 dB➪ 🏠90–110 L14–23
D14–23 ⊷ Pool mountains

HINTERZARTEN Baden-Württemberg 2,220
(☎07652) Map **11** B2
★★★★**Adler** ☎711 tx72692 90rm79➪74🏠 🏠 P Lift
♪ sB63–85 sB➪ 🏠85–110 dB129–144
dB➪ 🏠159–249 (English breakfast) L fr22 D fr28 ⊷
Pool ○ mountains
★★**Weisses Rössle** Freiburger Str 38 ☎1411
72rm33➪9🏠 A28rm 🏠 Lift ⊷ Pool
★**Linde** Rathausstr 2 ☎315 Closed 11 Nov–19 Dec
22rm4➪4🏠 🏠

HOCKENHEIM Baden-Württemberg 17,017
(☎06205) Map **11** B4
★★**Luxhof** an der Speyerer Brucke ☎32333
48rm12➪12🏠 A28rm 🏠 P sB30 sB➪ 🏠32–55
dB fr60 dB➪ 🏠75–90 (English breakfast) L10–18
D10–18 Pool

HÖCHENSCHWAND Baden-Württemberg 2,014
(☎St Blasien07672) Map **11** B2
★★★**Kurhaus** (DP) ☎354 tx7721212 54rm22➪22🏠
🏠 Lift ⊷ Pool
HOF Bayern 56,029 (☎09281) Map **6** C1
★★**Strauss** Bismarckstr 31 ☎2066 63rm6➪5🏠 🏠
Lift
🛢 ⊷**Autoverl** (Weissberg) C-Benzstr 4 ☎9067
☎9067 Frd (GB)

HOHELEYE See **LANGEWIESE**
HOHENSCHWANGAU Bayern 2,900 (☎08362)
Map **12** D2
★★**Müller** Alpseestr 14 ☎9256 30rm10➪1🏠 🏠
★★**Lisl und Jägerhaus** Neuschwansteinstr 1
☎9106 Closed Nov–14 Dec 44rm23➪5🏠 A16rm 🏠
HOLZMINDEN Niedersachsen 24,008 (☎05531)
Map **5** B3
🛢 **Kujath** Allersheimerstr 34 ☎2030 P Bed/Opl/Vau

HONNEF AM RHEIN (BAD) Nordrhein-Westfalen
23,500 (☎02224) Map **4** D1
At **Windhagen** (8km SE)
★★★**Sporthotel Waldbrunnen** Brunnenstr
☎(02645)3111 tx8579443 16➪ 🏠 P ♪ sB➪59–74
dB➪118–134 (English breakfast) L fr10 ⊷ Pool ○
mountains
HORNBERG Baden-Württemberg 5,021 (☎07833)
Map **11** B2
★★★**Bären** Hauptstr 85 ☎504 45rm21➪9🏠 🏠 Lift

HORSTMAR Nordrhein-Westfalen 6,411 (☎02558)
Map **4** D2
★**Crins** ☎7370 10rm A6rm ⌂ P sB24 dB48
(English breakfast) L5 – 19 D5 – 13

HUSUM Schleswig-Holstein 25,021 (☎04841)
Map **1** A1
★★★*Park Thordsen* Erichsenweg 23 ☎61061
tx28526 66rm30⇄30▥ ⌂ Lift ✒

IDAR-OBERSTEIN Rheinland-Pfalz 40,032
(☎06781) Map **11** B4
➋**Barth & Frey** Tiefensteinerstr 154 ☎31015 Opl
(GB)
H P Steuer Nahbollenbacherstr 90 ☎(06784) 565
M/c P AR/Hon (GB)

INGOLSTADT Bayern 90,005 (☎0841) Map **12** D3
★★**Rappensberger** Harderstr 3 ☎2307 93rm60⇄ ▥
P Lift ♪ sB32 – 37 sB⇄ ▥45 – 55 dB63 – 67
dB⇄ ▥75 – 98 L10 – 15 D10 – 15
★**Adler** Theresienstr 22 ☎2707 Closed 25 Dec – 14
Jan 50rm3⇄12 ▥ ⌂ P ♪ sB fr23 (room only)
sB⇄ ▥28 – 33 (room only) dB fr45 (room only)
dB⇄ ▥54 – 56 (room only) L alc D alc
★**Auwaldsee** ☎68484 Closed 31 Oct – 14 Mar
12rm2⇄ ▥ P sB24 sB⇄29 dB48 dB⇄58
(English breakfast) L fr9 D fr9 ✒ lake
🍴 ᴔ*Bacher* Goethestr 56 ☎56061 P Closed wkends
Frd
🍴 ➋*E Willner* Goethestr 61 ☎56005 Opl
At **Galmersheim** (☎08458) (on B13 7km W)
★★**Heidehof** Ingolstaedter Str 121 ☎711
18rm2⇄16▥ ⌂ P Lift sB▥56 – 58 dB⇄ ▥97 – 103
English breakfast only L9 20 D7 – 20 Pool

ISERLOHN Nordrhein-Westfalen 100,050 (☎02371)
Map **5** A2
★★**Deutsches Haus** Bahnhofstr 2 ☎23722
31rm6⇄21▥
★★**Korth** In der Calle 6 ☎40410 24rm4⇄10▥ ⌂ P
sB fr28 (room only) sB⇄▥fr52 (room only) dB fr52
(room only) dB⇄▥fr84 (room only) Pool
🛢 ᴔ**Spartcar Centre** (H Burschik) Baarstr 119
☎408078 P AR/BL/ (GB)

ISNY Baden-Württemberg 12,541 (☎07562)
Map **12** C2
★★**Hirsch** Bergtorstr 2 ☎543 Closed Nov
16rm1⇄1 ▥ A9rm ⌂
★★**Hohe Linde** Lindauerstr 75 ☎2401 Closed
Oct – 14 Nov 30rm5⇄13▥ ⌂ P sB30 – 35
sB⇄▥35 – 43 dB56 – 68 dB⇄ ▥68 – 80 L10 – 20
D8 – 16 Pool
Gruber Maierhofer Str 6 ☎2357 Frd

JÜLICH Nordrhein-Westfalen 32,290 (☎02461)
Map **4** D1
★★**Kratz** Kölnstr 5 ☎2408 24rm5⇄4▥ ⌂ P
sB32 – 38 sB⇄ ▥41 – 44 dB60 – 72 dB⇄ ▥80 – 85
(English breakfast) L12 – 20 D12 – 20
🍴 ᴔ*Schüsseler* Römerstr 9 ☎2539 P BL/Jag
Rov/Tri

KAISERSLAUTERN Rheinland-Pfalz 103,015
(☎0631) Map **11** B4
ᴔ**Schicht** Kaiserstr 74 ☎58233 P BL/BMW (GB)

KARLSRUHE Baden-Württemburg 285,021
(☎0721) Map **11** B3
★★★**Berliner Hof** Douglasstr 7 (n rest) ☎22242
41rm2⇄28▥ ⌂ P Lift ♪ sB38 – 44 sB⇄ ▥46 – 49
dB70 – 72 dB⇄ ▥78 – 84 English breakfast only
★★★*Kaiserhof* Marktpl ☎26615 40rm14⇄21▥ Lift
★★★**Parkhotel** Ettlingerstr 23 ☎60461 tx7825443
130rm⇄ P Lift ♪ sB⇄▥78 – 88 dB⇄115 – 130
English breakfast only L fr9 D fr9
★★★*Schloss* Bahnhofpl 2 ☎31805 tx7826746
100rm30⇄10▥ Lift
★★**Markt** Kaiserstr 76 (n rest) ☎27777 31rm4⇄6▥
P Lift ♪ sB38 – 43 sB⇄▥48 – 59 dB66 – 68
dB⇄▥83 – 86
🍴**Eden** Bahnhofstr 19 ☎28718 58rm14⇄23▥
A3rm ⌂ P Lift ♪ sB44 – 46 sB⇄ ▥61 – 71 dB81 – 86
dB⇄ ▥96 – 141 (English breakfast) L10 – 25 D10 – 25

★★**Hasen** Gerwigstr 47 ☎695079 37▥ ⌂ P Lift ♪
sB ▥48 – 56 dB ▥83 – 90 (English breakfast) D8 – 19
★**Kübler** Bismarckstr 39 – 43 (n rest) ☎26849 76rm
3⇄36▥ ⌂ P Lift sB32 – 37 sB⇄ ▥44 – 48 dB57 – 64
dB⇄▥74 – 78
➋ **Auto Böhler** Ottostr 6 ☎404051 ☎404051 ⌘ P
Vlo (GB)
Olm Rüpperrerstr 28 – 32 ☎661001 P BL/Jag
Rov/Tri
🍴 *F Opel* H-Billing Str 8 – 12 ☎27931 Opl
🍴 **Zentral** (K Vetter) Blumenstr 4 ☎27141 Sim (GB)
At **Durlach** (6km E)
★★★**Maison Suisse** Hildebrandstr 24 ☎406049
Closed 24 Dec – 14 Jan 15rm5⇄6▥ sB33 – 40
sB⇄ ▥50 – 54 dB⇄ ▥75 – 80 (English breakfast)
L16 – 25 D16 – 25

KASSEL Hessen 206,009 (☎0561) Map **5** B2
★★★★*Schloss Wilhelmshöhe* Schlosspark 2
☎30061 tx992261 149rm40⇄50▥ ⌂ Lift
★★★**Park-Hotel-Hessenland** Obere Königsstr 2
☎14974 tx99773 149rm40⇄50▥ ⌂ Lift
★★★**Reiss** W-Hilpert Str 24 ☎16203 tx99740
100rm43⇄34▥ ⌂ P Lift ♪ sB35 – 38 sB⇄ ▥60 – 65
dB⇄ ▥95 L13 – 18 D13 – 18
F Richter Schillerstr 46 – 48 ☎16464 Frd (GB)

KEHL Baden-Württemberg 30,011 (☎07851)
Map **11** B3
ᴔ**R Geiger** Strassburgerstr 11 ☎5046 Aud/Por/VW
(GB)

KELHEIM Bayern 12,617 (☎09441) Map **13** A3
★★**Ehrnthaller** Donaustr 22 ☎3333 71rm39⇄4▥ ⌂
P Lift ♪ sB23 – 27 sB⇄ ▥33 – 41 dB44 – 48
dB⇄ ▥60 – 70 L10 – 20 D8 – 15

KETTWIG Nordrhein-Westfalen 18,000 (☎02144)
Map **4** D2
★★★★*Hugenpoet* A-Thyssen Str 51 ☎6054
23rm18⇄1 ▥ ⌂ Lift ✒

KIEL Schleswig-Holstein 265,033 (☎0431)
Map **1** B1
★★★**Conti-Hansa** Schlossgarten 7 ☎40901
tx292813 59rm49⇄10▥ ⌂ Lift ✒
★★**Flensburger Hof** Grosser Kuhberg 9 – 13
☎91114 75rm15⇄20▥ ⌂ P Lift ♪ sB29 – 36
sB⇄ ▥50 – 55 dB⇄ ▥80 – 90 (English breakfast)
L fr14 D fr15
🍴 ᴔ**Herold** Zum Brook 1 ☎74066 Cit/Fia/Lnc

KIRCHHEIM Hessen 4,5015 (☎06625) Map **5** B1
☆☆☆**Center Kirchheim** ☎631 taMoki tx493337
140rm108⇄32▥ ⌂ P ♪ sB⇄ ▥50 – 66
dB⇄ ▥80 – 90 (English breakfast) L6 – 20 D10 – 25
Pool mountains

KIRCHHEIM UNTER TECK Baden-Württemberg
32,540 (☎07021) Map **12** C3
★★**Park Henzler** Eichendorffstr 99 ☎54900
72rm10⇄25▥ P Lift sB fr44 (room only)
sB⇄ ▥33 – 49 (room only) dB fr45 (room only)
dB⇄▥48 – 80 (room only)

KISSINGEN (BAD) Bayern 22,528 (☎0971)
Map **5** B1
★★★**Bristol** Bismarckstr 8 – 10 ☎4031 Closed
Dec – Feb 90rm35⇄35▥ ⌂ P Lift ♪ sB44 – 49
sB⇄ ▥66 – 76 dB82 – 110 dB⇄ ▥122 – 132
(English breakfast) L14 – 18 D14 – 18 Pool
★★**Fuerst Bismark** Bismarkstr 90 ☎3119 Closed 21
Dec – 19 Jan 40rm3⇄29▥ ⌂ P Lift sB34 – 40
sB⇄ ▥43 – 50 dB70 – 80 dB⇄ ▥85 – 102
(English breakfast) L10 – 17 D9 – 15 Pool
ᴔ**K H Fürsch** Kappellenstr 35 ☎61413 Toy (GB)

KLEVE Nordrhein-Westfalen 45,719 (☎02821)
Map **4** D2
★**König von Preussen** Bahnhofstr 1 (n rest)
☎24449 18rm
🍴 ➋ **W Könen** Kalkarerstr 92 ☎22081 P Opl

KLOSTERREICHENBACH Baden-Württemberg
(☎07442) Map **11** B3
★★**Sonne-Post** ☎2277 Closed 2 – 23 Dec
30rm12⇄7▥ ⌂ P sB38 – 44 sB⇄ ▥43 – 51 dB75 – 87
dB⇄ ▥85 – 101 (English breakfast) L12 – 30 D12 – 30
mountains

Germany

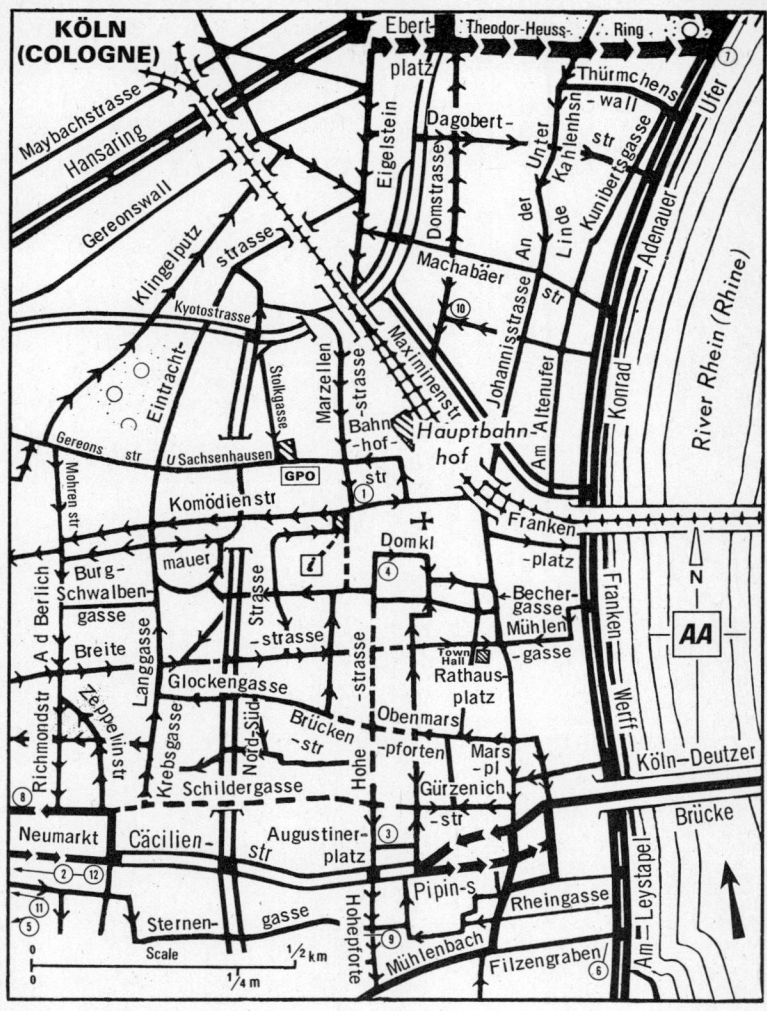

Köln (Cologne)

1	★★★★★ Excelsior-Ernst		7	★★★ Kaiser (Köln-Mülheim)
2	★★★★ Regent (Köln-Braunsfeld)		8	★★★ Rheingold
3	★★★ Augustinerplatz		9	★★ Ariane
4	★★★ Dom		10	★★ Berlin
5	☆☆☆ EuroCrest (Köln-Lindenthal)		11	★★ Bremer (Köln-Lindenthal)
6	★★★ Haus Lyskircher		12	★★ Conti

KNIEBIS Baden-Württemberg (☎07442) Map **11** B3
★★★**Lamm** ☎2077 72rm27⇌ 8🛁 A42 rm 🏠 P Lift
sB24−34 sB⇌🛁43−51 dB46−64 dB⇌🛁78−112
(English breakfast) L17−25 D17−25 Pool mountains

KOBLENZ (COBLENCE) Rheinland-Pfalz 119,023
(☎0261) Map **5** A1
★★★**Diehl's Rheinterrasse** Ehrenbreitstein
☎72010 63rm25⇌20🛁 🏠 Lift
★★★**Kleiner Riesen** Rheinanlagen 18 ☎32077
Closed 16 Dec−14 Jan 22rm10⇌ 🏠 P ⅅ sB30−35
sB⇌🛁50−55 dB64−74 dB⇌🛁83−93
(English breakfast) L18−20 D18−20 river

★★**Hohenstaufen** E-Schüllerstr 41 ☎35051
68rm6⇌7🛁 🏠 Lift
★**Scholz** Moselweisserstr 121 ☎42488 Closed 16
Dec−14 Jan 28rm10🛁 P sB26−30 (room only)
sB🛁32−34 (room only) dB43−47 (room only)
dB🛁53 (room only) L8−20 D10−20
G Schilling Andernacherstr 232 ☎85003 Ren (GB)
🛢 **P Wirtz** Bahnhofstr 32 ☎83028 P Bed/Opl (GB)
At **Stolzenfels** (8km S)
★**Cron** Rhenser Str 3 ☎37736 Closed 11 Oct−Mar
34rm2⇌ 🏠
KOCHEL AM SEE Bayern 3,515 (☎08851)
Map **12** D2

Germany

★★★**Schmied von Kochel** Schlehdorferstr 6 ☎216
45➡ 🍴 P Lift sB40-65 (room only) dB➡ 🍴90-130
(room only) mountains lake

KÖLN (COLOGNE) Nordrhein-Westfalen 985,050
(☎0221) Map 4 D1 **See Plan 243**

★★★★★*Excelsior-Ernst* Dompl ☎2701 tx8882645
Plan 1 146 ➡ 🏛 Lift

★★★**Augustinerplatz** Hohestr 30 (n rest) ☎236717
tx8882923 Plan 3 76rm90➡32🍴 P Lift 𝄞 sB38-55
sB➡ 🍴54-89 dB70-90 dB➡ 🍴100-200 L fr30
D fr15

★★★**Dom** Domkloster 2a ☎233751 tx8882919
Plan 4 🏛 P Lift 𝄞 sBfr86 sB➡🍴111-134
dB➡ 🍴164-212 (English breakfast) L25-37
D25-37

★★★**Lyskirchen** am Filzengraben 28-32 ☎234242
Plan 6 Closed 23 Dec-3 Jan 61rm13➡43🍴 🏛 P Lift
𝄞 sB53-58 sB➡🍴56-81 dB104-114
dB➡ 🍴127-142 Pool

★★★*Rheingold* Engelbertstr 33 (n rest) ☎248031
tx8882923 Plan 8 60rm10➡40🍴 🏛

★★**Ariane** Hohe Pforte 19-21 (n rest) ☎236033
Plan 9 44rm24🍴 🏛 P Lift 𝄞 sB32-41 sB🍴40-65
dB55-78 dB🍴70-98 (English breakfast)

★★**Berlin** Domstr 10-14 ☎123051 tx8885123
Plan 10 Closed 16 Dec-2 Jan 90rm4➡44🍴 🏛 P Lift
𝄞 sB33-39 sB➡🍴38-47 dB64-71 dB➡🍴78-83
(English breakfast) L10 D12

★★*Conti* Brüsseler Str 40 ☎212926 tx8881644
Plan 12 Closed 21 Dec-4 Jan 45rm25➡ 🏛 Lift
Kirschbaum Aachener Str 90 ☎514342 P

At Köln-Braunsfeld

★★★★**Regent** Melatengürtel 15 (n rest) ☎54991
tx8881824 Plan 2 181rm37➡121🍴 🏛 P Lift 𝄞
sB42-46 sB➡ 🍴59-85 dB85 dB➡ 🍴99-140
(English breakfast) L alc D alc

At Köln-Lindenthal

☆☆☆**EuroCrest** Dürenerstr 287 ☎435966
tx8882516 Plan 5 156rm75➡80🍴 🏛 P Lift
𝄞 sB➡🍴87-100 dB➡🍴110-130
(English breakfast) L fr17 D fr17 lake

★★**Bremer** Dürenerstr 225 ☎405013 tx8882063
Plan 11 100rm10➡85🍴 🏛 P Lift 𝄞 sB65-70
sB➡🍴65-70 dB➡🍴79-88 L18-28 D28-30 Pool
🛢 *Kierforl* Universitatsstr 91 ☎402061 Frd (GB)

At Köln-Mülheim

★★★**Kaiser** Genovevastr 10-14 (n rest) ☎623057
tx8873546 Plan 7 80rm 🏛 P Lift 𝄞 sB40-65 (room
only) sB➡ 🍴60-85 (room only) dB➡ 🍴85-150
(room only)

KÖNIGSSEE See **BERCHTESGADEN**

KÖNIGSFELD IM SCHWARZWALD Baden-
Wurttemberg 5,721 (☎07725) Map 11 B2

★★★**Schwarzwald** Volandstr 10 ☎7091
56rm16➡31🍴 🏛 P Lift 𝄞 sB44-47 sB➡🍴56-67
dB➡ 🍴104-130 (English breakfast) L18-25&alc
D19-27&alc Pool

KÖNIGSTEIN IM TAUNUS Hessen 16,211
(☎06174) Map 5 A1

★★★*Sonnenhof* Falkensteinerstr 7 ☎5033 tx41036
47rm34➡5🍴 🏛 Pool

★★**Parkhotel Bender** Frankfurterstr 1 ☎7105
40rm10➡10🍴 🏛 P sB32-47 sB➡🍴47-57
dB48-73 dB🍴73-98 L8-25 D8-25

KÖNIGSWINTER Nordrhein-Westfalen 36,434
(☎02223) Map 4 D1

★★★**Düsseldorfer-Hof** Rheinallee 14-15
☎22011 48rm11➡11🍴 A21rm 🏛 P Lift 𝄞 sB40-75
(room only) sB➡ 🍴45-50 (room only) dB80-90
(room only) dB➡ 🍴90-100 (room only)

★**Siebengebirge** Hauptstr 342 ☎21359 Closed 16
Dec-Jan 8rm2🍴 A2rm 🏛 P sB28-30 sB🍴30-32
dB56-58 dB🍴60-64 L9-17 D9-17

KONSTANZ (CONSTANCE) Baden-Wurttemberg
71,050 (☎07534) Map 12 C2

★★★**Steigenberger Insel** auf der Insel 1 ☎25011
tx733276 103➡ P Lift 𝄞 sB➡🍴69-99 (room only)
dB➡ 🍴88-138 (room only) lake

★★**Deutsches Haus** Marktstätte 15 (n rest) ☎27065
42rm6➡21🍴 🏛 Lift 𝄞 sB28-34 sB➡🍴40-48 dB52
dB🍴78-85

★★*Krone* Marktstätte 6 ☎23093 46rm10➡2🍴 🏛 Lift
🛢L *Vendrame* Radolfzellerstr 65 ☎79098 P
BL/Jag/Rov/Tri (GB)

KREFELD Nordrhein-Westfalen 23,270 (☎02151)
Map 4 D2

★★★**Park Krefelder Hof** Uerdinger Str 245 ☎59291
tx863748 157rm87➡70🍴 A67rm 🏛 P Lift 𝄞
sB➡🍴85-95 dB➡🍴150-180 (English breakfast)
L alc D alc Pool ♿

🛢 **Preckel** Virchowstr 139-145 ☎36033 Ren (GB)

KREUZNACH (BAD) Rheinland-Pfalz 44,010
(☎0671) Map 11 B4

🛢 ⋙**Auto-Holzhäuser** Mannheimerstr 183-185
☎30031 P Frd (GB)

At Ebernburg (6km S)

★★*Schoss & Reichsgräfin Von Sickingen* ☎2207
10rm2➡ 🏛

KREUZWERTHEIM See **WERTHEIM**

KRONBERG/TAUNUS Hessen 17,513 (☎06173)
Map 5 A1

★★★★**Schloss** Hainstr 25 ☎7011 tx415424
53rm51➡ P Lift 𝄞 sB➡🍴110-125 dB➡🍴185-200
(English breakfast) L alc D alc

KULMBACH Bayern 26,050 (☎09221) Map 6 C1

★★★**Hansa Hönsch** Weltrichstr 2 (n rest) ☎7995
29rm14➡11🍴 🏛 P Lift sBr30 (room only)
sB➡🍴32-42 (room only) dB fr64 (room only)
dB➡🍴fr74 (room only)

🛢 ⋙*A Dippold* Kronacher Str 2 ☎2017 P
Aud/Por/VW

KUPFERMÜHLE See **FLENSBURG**

LAASPHE Nordrhein-Westfalen 6,100 (☎02752)
Map 5 A1

★★★**Fasanerie** Lahnstr 55 ☎333 33rm6🍴 🏛 ♨

LAHNSTEIN Rheinland-Pfalz 22,014 (☎02621)
Map 5 A1

★★★*Dorint Rhein-Lahn* Im Kurzentrum ☎151
tx869827 210➡ 🏛 Lift ♨ Pool

⋙**Autoellehandel** Frankenstr 1, am Hafen ☎3630
M/c P (GB)

LAHR Baden-Wurttemberg 40,008 (☎07821)
Map 11 B3

★**Schulz** Alte-Bahnhofstr 6 ☎22674 22rm1➡15🍴 🏛
P sB20-36 (room only) sB🍴27-36 (room only)
dB44-50 (room only) dB➡🍴50-75 (room only)
L12-35 D12-35

⋙**Link** Lotzbecker 33 ☎24021 P Aud/Por/VW

LANDAU IN DER PFALZ Rheinland-Pfalz 39,516
(☎06341) Map 11 B3

★★**Körber** Reiterstr 11 ☎4050 Closed 13Dec-14
Jan 40rm10➡10🍴 🏛 P 𝄞 sB30 sB➡🍴35-45
dB50-55 dB➡🍴65-75 L15-20 D10-15

🛢 ⋙**R Kruppenbacher** A-Croissantstr 1-3 ☎5054
☎5053 ♿ Frd (GB)

LANDSBERG AM LECH Bayern 16,010 (☎08191)
Map 12 D2

🛢 ⋙**A Popp** Münchnerstr 34-36 ☎2288 ☎2288 P
Bed/Opl (GB)

Strobl Schongaver Str 15 ☎2433

LANDSHUT Bayern 56,021 (☎0871) Map 13 A3

🛢 **K Meusel** Ottostr 15 ☎72048 Frd

LANGENARGEN Baden-Württemberg 5,815
(☎07543) Map 12 C2

★★**Schiff** Markpl 1 ☎2407 Closed Nov-Feb
42rm7➡25🍴 P Lift sB35-40 sB➡🍴41-50
dB44-45 dB➡🍴46-58 L12-14 D12-14 lake

LANGENISARHOFEN Bayern (☎09938) Map 13 B3

★**Buhmann** ☎277 Closed 24 Dec-14 Jan 25rm1➡
🏛 P sB fr24 dB fr46 dB➡🍴fr49 English
breakfast only L6-13 D3-7

LAUTENBACH Baden-Württemberg 1,922
(☎07802) Map 11 B3

★**Sternen** Hauptstr 47 ☎3538 Closed Nov
40rm14➡15🍴 🏛 P Lift sB30-38 sB➡🍴38-40
dB36-44 dB➡🍴44-50 L8-15 D8-15

LENGFELD See **WÜRZBURG**

LEONBERG Baden-Württemberg 35,910 (☎07152)
Map **12** C3
★★★**Eiss** (Near the Autobahn) ☎43021 tx724141
75rm30⇌23🍴 A10rm 🏠 P Lift 🍴 sB43–52
sB⇌🍴64–69 dB70–75 dB⇌🍴95–100
(English breakfast) L fr7 d fr7
★★**Sonne** Stuttgarterstr 1 ☎27626 45rm15⇌10🍴
🏠 P 🌙 sB30–35 sB⇌🍴40–60 dB fr50
dB⇌🍴55–88 L10–20&alc D10–20&alc

LICHTENFELS Bayern 14,023 (☎09571) Map **6** C1
🛢 🏍**Auto Szymansky** Bambergerstr 43 ☎3654
☎3654 M/c P BL/Cit (GB)

LIEBENZELL (BAD) Baden-Württemberg 6,210
(☎07052) Map **11** B3
★★★**Krone** Badweg 7 ☎2081 42rm24⇌18🍴 Lift
★★**Kurhotel Helenbad** (n rest) ☎2091 Closed
Nov–Mar 39rm1⇌2🍴 🏠

LIESER Rheinland-Pfalz 1,419 (☎06531) Map **11** A4
★★**Mehn** Moselstr 2 ☎3011 Closed 16 Dec–14 Jan
25rm2⇌18🍴 🏠 P Lift sB27–29 sB⇌🍴31–35 dB54
dB⇌🍴68–72 L7–20 D8–15

LIMBURG AN DER LAHN Hessen 29,026 (☎06431)
Map **5** A1
★★**Dom** Grabenstr 57 ☎6249 57rm14⇌28🍴 🏠 P
Lift 🌙 sB37–40 sB⇌🍴55–63 dB68–80
dB⇌🍴93–120 L8–24 D8–24
★★**Zimmermann** Blumenröderstr 1 ☎42030
26rm5⇌12🍴 🏠 P sB29–32 sB⇌🍴45–52 dB54–60
dB⇌🍴70–90 D6–13
★**Huss** Bahnhofspl 3 ☎6638 38rm5⇌11🍴 🏠 P Lift
🌙 sB24–30 sB⇌🍴40–44 dB50–56 dB⇌🍴72–76

LINDAU IM BODENSEE Bayern 25,542 (☎08382)
Map **12** C2
★★★**Bayrischer Hof** Seepromenade ☎5055
tx54340 Closed Nov–Etr 87rm69⇌3🍴 🏠 P Lift 🌙
sB39–59 sB⇌🍴68–99 dB⇌🍴110–194
(English breakfast) L22–28 D22–28 Pool mountains
lake
Reutemann Seepromenade ☎5055 tx54340
40rm27⇌4🍴 🏠 P lift 🌙 sB36–48 sB⇌🍴47–73
dB70–80 dB⇌🍴97–145 (English breakfast)
L21–26 D21–26 Pool mountains lake
★★**Kellner** Alwindstr 7 (n rest) ☎5686 Closed
Oct–mid Apr 12rm3⇌3🍴 🏠 P sB25 (room only)
sB⇌🍴32 (room only) dB22–27 (room only)
dB⇌🍴32–34 (room only) mountains lake
★★**Seegarten** Seepromenade ☎5055 tx54340
Closed Dec–Feb 33rm4⇌20🍴 🏠 P Lift 🌙 sB34–45
sB⇌🍴48–60 dB⇌🍴84–106 (English breakfast)
L fr18 D fr18 Pool mountains lake
★**Lindauer Hof** Seehafen (harbour) ☎4064 35⇌ Lift
lake

LINDENFELS Hessen 4,609 (☎06255) Map **12** C4
★★**Hessisches Hous** Kurgarten ☎2405 Closed
Nov–Feb 24rm1⇌14🍴 A6rm 🏠 P Lift sB26–28
sB⇌🍴32–34 dB44–48 dB⇌🍴60–68 L8–15
D8–16 Pool

LINDENTHAL See **KÖLN (COLOGNE)**

LINGEN Niedersachsen 46,307 (☎0591) Map **4** D3
★**Nave** Marienstr 29 ☎4188 28rm4⇌4🍴 🏠

LIPPSTADT Nordrhein-Westfalen 67,050 (☎02941)
Map **5** A2
★★★**Koppelmann** Langestr 30 ☎3045
38rm10⇌6🍴 🏠 Lift
🛢 🏍**H Jathe** Erwitterstr 119 ☎12485 M/c P BL/Sab

LOCHHAM See **GRÄFELFING**

LÖRRACH Braden-Württemberg 45,020 (☎07621)
Map **11** B2
★★★**Binoth am Markt** Baslerstr 169 ☎2673
26rm5⇌10🍴 🏠 P Lift 🌙 sB23–30 (room only)
sB⇌🍴35–45 (room only) dB45 (room only)
dB⇌🍴55–70 (room only)
🛢 🏍**Büche & Tröndle** Tumringerstr 290 ☎8502
Aud/Por/VW (GB)

LÜBECK Schleswig-Holstein 234,033 (☎0451)
Map **5** B4

★★★**Lysia** auf der Wallhalbinsel ☎71077 tx26707
130rm17⇌113🍴 A59rm 🏠 P Lift 🌙 sB⇌🍴65–85
dB⇌🍴89–122
★★**Mühlenteich** Mühlenbrücke 6 (n rest) ☎77171
11rm5🍴 Lift lake
★**Kaiserhof** Kronsforder Alle 13 ☎791011
45rm11⇌28🍴 A12rm P Lift 🌙 sB37–45
sB⇌🍴48–75 dB68 dB⇌🍴85–105 D7–14
★**Lindenhof** Lindenstr 1a ☎84015 40rm5⇌2🍴 🏠 P
🌙 sB30–33 sB⇌🍴38–42 dB59–63 sB⇌🍴72–80
(English breakfast) L8–25 D8–25
🛢 🏍**Jäckel** Travemünder Allee 15–17 ☎33088 P
Cit/Ren (GB)
At **Ratekau** (10km N) (☎04504)
☆**Waldklause** (on E4) ☎1603 18rm 11🍴 A1rm 🏠

LUDWIGSBURG Baden-Württemberg 80,022
(☎07141) Map **12** C3
At **Monrepos (Schloss)** (5km NW)
★★★★**Monrepos** ☎30101 tx7264720
83rm40⇌43🍴 🏠 Lift

MAINZ Rheinland-Pfalz 190,009 (☎06131)
Map **11** B4
★★★**Central** Bahnhofsplatz 8 ☎674001 tx4187794
95rm33⇌18🍴 P Lift 🌙 sB40–48 sB⇌🍴50–67
dB71 dB⇌🍴85–125 (English breakfast) L19 D19
★★★**Europa** Kaiserstr 7 ☎63095 tx4187702
100rm48⇌32🍴 🏠 P Lift 🌙 sB⇌🍴74–77
dB⇌🍴105–115 L alc D alc
★★★**Mainzer Hof** Kaiserstr 98 ☎28471 tx4187787
72rm40⇌29🍴 P Lift 🌙 sB55 sB⇌🍴78 dB105
dB⇌🍴115 (English breakfast) L alc D alc
🛢 **Heinz** am Bismarckpl ☎676011 Frd

MALLERSDORF Bayern 5,031 (☎08772)
Map **13** A3
★**Ohne Sorge** Hofmark 5 (n rest) ☎272 8rm1⇌ P
sB18–20 (room only) sB⇌🍴20 (room only) dB36
(room only) dB⇌🍴45 (room only)

MANDERSCHEID Rhineland-Pfalz 1,310 (☎06572)
Map **11** A4
★★**Zens** Kurfurstenstr 35 ☎769 Closed 6 Nov–19
Dec 46rm11⇌13🍴 🏠 P Lift sB31–39 sB⇌🍴48
dB61–78 dB⇌🍴78–96 L15–22 D15–22 Pool
mountains

MANNHEIM Baden-Württemberg 320,048 (☎0621)
Map **11** B4
★★★★**Mannheimer Hof** A-Anlage 4 ☎45021
tx462245 200rm144⇌3🍴 🏠 P Lift
★★★**Augusta** Augusta Anlage 45 ☎408001
tx462394 100rm34⇌54🍴 🏠 P Lift 🌙 sB50
sB⇌🍴67–86 dB70–72 dB⇌🍴88–135
(English breakfast) L fr14 D fr15
★★★**Park** Friedrichspl 2 (n rest) ☎23841
56rm20⇌36🍴 Lift
★★**Bundesbahn** Hauptbahnhof ☎22926
45rm6⇌35🍴 Lift
★★**Mack** Mozartstr 14 (n rest) ☎23888 tx462116
Closed 16 Dec–9 Jan 75rm16⇌18🍴 A6rm 🏠 P Lift
🌙 sB35–51 sB⇌🍴47–51 dB64–68 dB⇌🍴68–80
(English breakfast)
🛢 **K R Bayer** Neckarauerstr 99 ☎852297
☎409602 P Ska/Vau
🏍**Kannenberg** Fahrlachstr 90–94 ☎408021 P
Bed/Opl/Vau
🛢 **H Kohlhoff** Obere Riedstr 117–119 ☎735083 Frd
(GB)
🏍**H Sebastuan** Sekenheim Autobahn-Tankstelle
☎475122 ☎475122 🏍 M/c P
At **Sandhofen** (10km N)
☆**Weber** ☎782021 51⇌🍴 🏠 P Lift sB⇌🍴45–70
dB⇌🍴70–120 L10–20 D10–30

MARBURG AN DER LAHN Hessen 70,040
(☎06421) Map **5** A1
★★★**Ortenberg** G-Voigtstr 21 ☎61049 44rm9⇌
A10rm 🏠 P 🌙 sB35–45 sB⇌🍴41–48 dB61–73
dB⇌🍴73–101 (English breakfast) L12–18&alc
D12–18&alc
★★**Europäscher Hof** Elisabethstr 12 (n rest)
☎64044 69rm14⇌58🍴 A20rm 🏠 P Lift 🌙 sB31–35
sB⇌🍴38–55 dB55–59 dB⇌🍴75–99
(English breakfast)

Germany

At **Cölbe** (7km N)
★★**Orthwein** Kasselerstr 48 an der B3 ☎82594
24rm🏠 🏨 P sB🚿19−21 dB🚿38−42 L6−15
D6−15 Beach mountains lake
MARIA LAACH Rheinland-Pfalz (☎02652)
Map **4** D1
★★**See** ☎251 77rm8🚿16🏠 🏨 P Lift ♪ sB21−36
(room only) sB🚿49−50 (room only) dB47−75
(room only) dB🚿🏠67−85 (room only) Pool lake
MARIENBERG (BAD) Rheinland-Pfalz 5,313
(☎02661) Map **5** A1
★★★**Kneipp-Kurhotel Wildpark** ☎269 Closed 16
Nov−19 Dec 40rm20🚿20🏠 P Lift🚿47−55
dB🚿🏠88−100 L12−18 D14−25 Pool mountains
MARKTHEIDENFELD Bayern 9,111 (☎09391)
Map **12** C4
★**Anker** Obertorstr 6−8 ☎3420 30rm10🚿8🏠 A14rm
🏨 P Lift sB fr24 sB🚿🏠36−40 dB fr45 dB🚿🏠60−69
(English breakfast) L fr9 D fr9
★**Schöne Aussicht** Brückenstr 8 ☎3455
45rm1🚿18🏠 🏨 P Lift sB fr28 sB🚿🏠36−44 dB fr52
dB🚿🏠68−78 L7−18 D5−18
MARKTOBERDORF Bayern 14,330 (☎08342)
Map **12** D2
★**Sepp** Bahnhofstr 13 ☎2414 (fr Oct 2048)
55rm50🚿50🏠 A30rm 🏨 P ♪ sB22−35
sB🚿🏠30−35 dB40−60 dB🚿🏠55−60 L8−17
D8−17 mountains
🛢 ➡**P Schmid** Hauptstr 33 ☎2837 ☎2837 P BL
MEERSBURG Baden-Württemberg 5,013 (☎07532)
Map **12** C2
★★★**Terrassen Weisshaar** S-Lochnerstr 24 ☎9006
Closed Nov 22rm18🚿4🏠 🏨 lake
★★**Brandners 3 Stuben** Winzergasse 1 ☎6019
14rm2🚿12🏠 🏨 P sB🚿46−51 dB🚿🏠80−90
(English breakfast) L12−20 D12−20 St%
★★**Weinstube-Löwen** Marktplatz 2 ☎6013 Closed
16 Dec−Jan 17rm2🚿17🏠 🏨 P sB🚿28−30
(room only) dB🚿🏠25−34 (room only) L13−25
D13−25
★**Zum Bären** Marktplatz 11 ☎6044 Closed 16
Nov−Feb 15rm7🏠 🏨 P sB23 sB🚿🏠32 dB42−46
dB🚿🏠54−62 L12−20 D12−20
MEMMINGEN Bayern 36,014 (☎08331) Map **12** C2
★★★**Adler** Maximilianstr 3 ☎87015 45rm13🚿13🏠
🏨 P Lift ♪ sB37−38 sB🚿🏠53−54 dB72−74
dB🚿🏠90−92 (English breakfast) L10−20 D9−18
🛢 **Draxler** Birkenweg 1 ☎4717 P BL/Jag/Rov Tri
🛢 **C Schenk** Donaustr 29 ☎86048 Opl
MERGENTHEIM (BAD) Baden-Württemberg 20,220
(☎07931) Map **12** C4
★★★★**Victoria** Poststr 2 ☎7036 tx74224
100rm75🚿7🏠 🏨 Lift Pool
MERKLINGEN Baden-Württemberg 1,402
(☎07931) Map **12** C3
★**Ochsen** Hauptstr 12 (07337)483 Closed Nov
13rm12🏠 🏨 P sB36 sB🚿🏠41 dB🚿🏠68
(English breakfast) L8−35 D8−35
MESCHEDE Nordrhein-Westfalen 33,030 (☎0291)
Map **5** A2
★★★**Hennesee** ☎7102 50🚿 🏨
MINDELHEIM Bayern 11,243 (☎08261) Map **12** D2
★★**Post** Maximilianstr 39 ☎203 Closed 21 Dec−9
Jan 60rm6🚿10🏠 🏨 Lift
🛢 ➡**E Schragl** Landsbergerstr 20 ☎1468 P Aud/VW
(GB)
MINDEN Nordrhein-Westfalen 84,011 (☎0571)
Map **5** A3
★★**Silke** Fischerglacis 21 (n rest) ☎23736
26rm10🚿12🏠 🏨 P Lift sB36 sB🚿🏠59 dB60
dB🚿🏠82 English breakfast only Pool
MITTENWALD Bayern 8,323 (☎08823) Map **12** D2
★★★**Post** Obermarkt 9 ☎1094 95rm45🚿22🏠 🏨 P Lift
♪ sB30−51 sB🚿🏠36−61 dB55−87 dB🚿🏠73−111
(English breakfast) L12−25 D12−25 🏊 Pool
mountains
★**Jagdhaus Drachenburg** Elmauerweg 20 ☎1249
Closed 21 Oct −19Dec 14rm8🚿2🏠 P sB31−34
sB🚿🏠35−40 dB54−57 dB🚿🏠70−84
(English breakfast) L13 D8

★**Zerhoch** H-Barth Weg 7 (n rest) ☎1508 Closed 4
Nov−14 Dec 19rm13🚿3🏠 🏨 P sB24−26
sB🚿🏠28−38 dB44−50 dB🚿🏠56−70 mountains
🛢 ➡**K Schober** Partenkirchnerstr 60 ☎8442 ☎8442
P Opl (GB)
MOGENDORF Rheinland-Pfalz 1,111 (☎02623)
Map **5** A1
★**Elser** Haupstr 11 ☎2410 10🚿 🏨
MÖHRINGEN See **STUTTGART**
MÖNCHENGLADBACH Nordrhein-Westfalen
265,050 (☎02161) Map **4** D2
★★★★**Dorint Park** Hohenzollernstr 5 ☎23054
tx852656 102rm69🚿33🏠 Lift 🏊 Pool
☆☆☆**Holiday Inn** am Geropl ☎31131 128🚿 Lift 🏊
Pool
★★**Coenen** Giesenkirchener Str 41−45
(02166)40171 Closed 2 wks Jul 22rm7🚿15🏠 🏨 P
Lift ♪ sB🚿🏠55−69 (room only) dB🚿🏠80−100
(room only) L12−19 D12−19
🛢 ➡**Issels** Rheydterstr 225 ☎13045 Fia/Ren (GB)
🛢 ➡**E Menke** Erkelenzer Str 8 ☎8991 P Fia/Vau
H Orth Erzbergerstr 173−177 ☎44141 Frd
MONREPOS (SCHLOSS) See **LUDWIGSBURG**
MONSCHAU Nordrhein-Westfalen 11,813
(☎02472) Map **4** D1
★★**Horchem** Kurstr 14 ☎490 Closed Jan−Feb
14rm4🚿3🏠 🏨 P sB28−35 sB🚿🏠36 dB34
dB🚿🏠41 (English breakfast) L12−22 D12−24
★**Alte Herrlichkeit** Haagweg 3a ☎3190 7rm6🏠 🏨 P
♪ sB🚿🏠26 dB48 dB🚿🏠52 D6−20 mountains
MONTABAUR Rheinland-Pfalz 11,010 (☎02602)
Map **5** A1
★★★**Montabaur** Autobahnausfahrt ☎5005 38rm
13🚿19🏠 A6rm P ♪ sB🚿35 sB🚿🏠57−102 dB fr69
dB🚿🏠80−159 L15−27 D15−27
☆☆**Heiligenroth** Heiligenroth (4·5km NE on
Autobahn) ☎5045 28🏠 P Lift ♪ sB🚿45−55
dB🚿🏠66−72
★**Post** Bahnhofstr 30 ☎3361 Closed 21 Dec−9 Jan
34rm2🚿9🏠 🏨 P Lift sB22−24 sB🚿🏠28−34
dB45−50 dB🚿🏠54−56 (English breakfast) L6−15
D6−15
★**Schlemmer** Kirchstr 18 ☎5022 Closed 21 Dec−9
Jan 25rm2🚿7🏠 🏨 P Lift sB29−33 sB🚿🏠38−41
dB55 dB🚿🏠65−70 (English breakfast) L8−20
D8−20 mountains
🛢 **Autozentrale** (K Arnst) Bohnhofstr 29 ☎3030 P
Opl (GB)
MÜLHEIM AN DER MOSEL Rheinland-Pfalz 1,002
(☎06534) Map **11** A4
★★**Moselhaus Selzer** Moselstr 7 ☎707 Closed 16
Nov−14 Mar 15rm2🚿6🏠 🏨 P sB25−33 sB🚿🏠33
dB🚿🏠54−80 L10−15 D7−15 mountains
MÜLHEIM AN DER RUHR Nordrhein-Westfalen
189,010 (☎02133) Map **4** D2
★★★**Noy** Schlossstr 28−30 ☎44671 50rm10🚿26🏠
P Lift sB48 (room only) sB🚿🏠75−88 (room only)
dB🚿🏠110−160 (room only)
MÜLLHEIM Baden-Württemberg 12,515 (☎07631)
Map **11** B2
☆☆☆**Euro** Bundesstr 3, Autobahnzufahrt ☎5522
tx772916 57rm6🚿45🏠 🏨
MÜNCHEN (MUNICH) Bayern 1,300,055 (☎089)
Map **13** A3 **See plan**
★★★★**Bayerischer Hof** Promenadepl 6 ☎228871
tx523409 Plan **1** 393rm393🚿70🏠 🏨 P Lift ♪
sB🚿🏠87−122 dB🚿🏠159−234 (English breakfast)
L25−27 D25−27 Pool
★★★★**Continental** M-Joseph Str 5 ☎557971
tx522603 Plan **2** 161rm120🚿6🏠 🏨 Lift ♪ sB74−94
dB🚿🏠99−149 dB138 dB🚿🏠163−223
English breakfast only L25 D25
★★★★**Excelsior** Schützenstr 11 ☎557906
tx522419 Plan **3** 105rm100🚿5🏠 P Lift ♪
sB🚿🏠70−90 dB🚿🏠120−145 L alc D alc
★★★★**Königshof** Karlspl 26 ☎558412 tx523616
Plan **4** 120🚿 🏨 Lift
★★★★**Vier Jahreszeiten** Maximilianstr 17
☎228821 tx523859 Plan **5** 365🚿 🏨 Lift

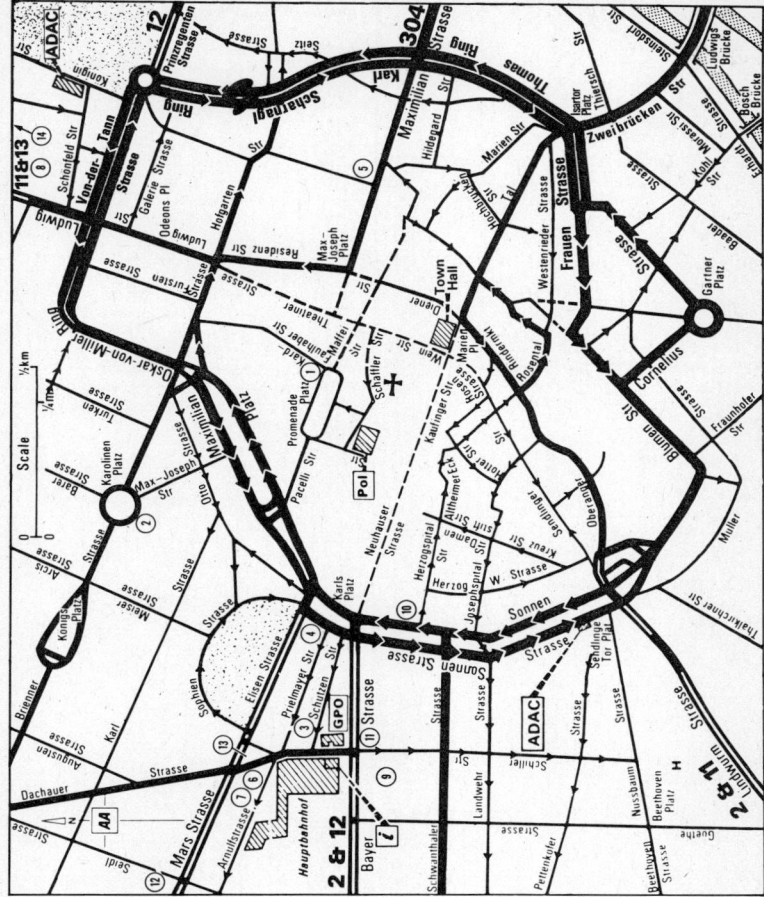

München (Munich)

1	★★★★Bayerischer Hof
2	★★★★Continental
3	★★★★Excelsior
4	★★★★Königshof
5	★★★★Vier Jahreszeiten
6	★★★Deutscher Kaiser
7	★★★Eden-Wolff
8	☆☆☆EuroCrest
9	★★★Mark
10	★★Daniel
11	★★Drei Löwen
12	★★Edelweiss
13	★★Feldhütter
14	★Leopold

★★★**Deutscher Kaiser** Arnulfstr 2 ☎558321
tx522650 Plan **6** 180rm90⇌20⋔ P Lift ♪ sB46
sB⇌⋔68 dB90 dB⇌⋔110 (English breakfast)
L22–25 D25

★★★**Eden-Wolff** Arnulfstr 4 ☎558281 tx523564
Plan **7** ⛾ P Lift ♪ sB50–55 sB⇌⋔86–98
dB⇌⋔110–160 L14–20 D16–20 mountains

☆☆☆**EuroCrest** Effnerstr 99 ☎982541 tx524757
Plan **8** 155rm66⇌89⋔ ⛾ P Lift ♪ sB⇌⋔94
dB⇌⋔128 (English breakfast) L fr17 D fr17
mountains

★★★**Mark** Senefelderstr 12 (off Vaverstr) ☎592801
tx522721 Plan **9** 74⇌44⋔ P Lift ♪ sB33–36
sB⇌⋔40–56 dB⇌⋔69–82 (English breakfast) L14
D14 St%

★★**Daniel** Sonnenstr 5 (n rest) ☎554945 tx523863
Plan **10** 81rm35⇌37⋔ P Lift ♪ sB34–38
sB⇌⋔45–48 dB51–58 dB⇌⋔66–79
(English breakfast)

★★**Drei Löwen** Schillerstr 8 ☎595521 tx523867
Plan **11** 160rm110⇌ ⛾ P Lift ♪ sB44–47
sB⇌⋔73–78 dB⇌⋔98–128 (English breakfast)
L16–18 D18–22

★★**Edelweiss** Menzingerstr 103 (n rest) ☎8111001
Plan **12** 28rm8⇌12⋔ ⛾ P ♪ sB45–49
sB⇌⋔55–62 dB65–74 dB⇌⋔83–92

★★**Feldhütter** Elisenstr 5 (off Luisenstr) ☎594126
tx523113 Plan **13** 58rm8⇌4⋔ Lift

★**Leopold** Leopoldstr 119 ☎367061 tx5215160
Plan **14** 83rm23⇌33⋔ ⛾ P Lift ♪ sB42
sB⇌⋔55–65 dB64–70 dB⇌⋔90 L15

🛢 &♢**P Behnke** Brennerstr 44–54 ☎521729 Lot/Peu
(GB)

🛢 &♢**Corso** Zielstattstr 63 ☎786087
Lot/Peu (GB)

🛢 **H Hanauer** Hilblestr 20 ☎183051 P Ren (GB)

🛢 &♢**Helbig** Friedenstr 30 ☎400277 BMW/Toy

&♢**Lotus** A Rosshaupterstr 104 ☎3592574

⌂ ⇝**Wilhelm** Freisinger Landstr 11 ☎328086 P BL/Jag/Rov (GB)

MÜNSTER/WESTFALEN Nordrhein-Westfalen 260,050 (☎0251) Map **5** A2

★★★**Kaiserhof** Bahnhofstr 14–16 (n rest) ☎40059 tx892141 100rm25⇋65🍴 P Lift ♪ sB39 (room only) sB⇋🍴60 (room only) dB68 (room only) dB⇋🍴98 (room only)

★★★★**Schloss Wilkinghege** Steinfurterstr 374 (4km NW) ☎213045 38rm18⇋20🍴 A17rm 🏛 P ♪ sB⇋🍴59–83 dB⇋🍴85–145 L17–27 D19–27 ⇗ ♨

★★**Mauritzhof** Eisenbahnstr 17 ☎42366 30🍴 P ♪ sB36–44 sB🍴38–44 dB66 dB🍴76–81 L fr10 D fr10

★**Conti** Berlinerpl 2A (n rest) ☎40444 tx892113 61rm6⇋36🍴 P Lift ♪ sB32–44 sB⇋🍴45–60 dB66–80 dB⇋🍴75–105 (English breakfast)

⌂ *Ing W Brandes* Altenbergerstr 32 ☎(02533)521 P BL/Rov/Tri

MURNAU Bayern 8,040 (☎08841) Map **12** D2

★★★*Alpenhof* Ramsachstr 8 ☎1045 52🍴 🏛 Lift Pool

NAGOLD Baden-Württemberg 19,231 (☎07452) Map **11** B3

★★**Post** Bahnhofstr 2 ☎4048 tx765948 42rm18⇋4🍴 A16rm 🏛 P Lift ♪ sB30–33 sB⇋🍴41–52 dB54–57 dB⇋🍴78–90 (English breakfast) L12–25 D12–25

NAUHEIM (BAD) Hessen 25,049 (☎06032) Map **5** A1

★★★**Hilbert's Park** Kurstr 2–4 ☎31945 ta Pahotel tx415514 112rm60⇋🍴 P Lift ♪ sB43–57 sB⇋67–85 dB79–94 dB⇋104–129 English breakfast only L18 D18

NECKARGEMÜND Baden-Württemberg 13,015 (☎06223) Map **12** C4 .

★★**Zum Ritter** Neckarstr 40 ☎7035 tx461837 60rm2⇋56🍴 P ♪ sB41–46 sB⇋🍴53–65 dB⇋🍴67–93 (English breakfast) L20–40 D10–20

NECKARSTEINACH Hessen 4,212 (☎06229) Map **12** C4

★★**Schiff** Neckargemünderstr 2 ☎324 Closed 16 Dec–14 Jan 22rm4⇋17🍴 P Lift sB⇋🍴30 (room only) dB⇋🍴60(room only) L13–30 D4–30

NERESHEIM Baden-Württemberg 6,707 (☎07326) Map **12** C3

★*Klosterhospiz* ☎6282 45rm13🍴 Lift

NEUBEUERN Bayern 2,511 (☎08035) Map **13** A2

★★**Burg** Marktpl 23 ☎2456 Closed 16 Jan–Feb 17rm1⇋10🍴 🏛 P Lift sB fr30 sB⇋🍴40–45 dB45–50 dB⇋🍴60–70 (English breakfast) L10–20 D10–20 mountains

NEUENAHR (BAD) Rheinland-Pfalz 28,034 (☎02641) Map **4** D1

★★★★**Kur** Kurgartenstr 1 ☎2291 tx861812 240rm160⇋🍴 P Lift ♪ sB49–55 sB⇋73–93 dB⇋106–140 (English breakfast) L fr19 D fr26 ⇗ Pool

★★★**Dorint** am Dahliengarten ☎2325 tx861805 118⇋🍴 P Lift ♪ sB⇋🍴74–78 dB⇋🍴104–112 (English breakfast) L19 D19 Pool

★★**Goldener Anker** Mittelstr 18 ☎2386 70rm60⇋5🍴 P Lift ♪ sB35–40 sB⇋🍴50–60 dB64–74 dB⇋🍴84–99 (English breakfast) L fr35 D fr15

★★*Hamburger Hof* Jesuitenstr 11 (n rest) ☎26017 33rm10⇋13🍴 🏛

⇝**J Waldecker** Heerstr 2 ☎2366 P Frd (GB)

NEUMÜNSTER Schleswig-Holstein 91,510 (☎04321) Map **1** B1

★★**Wappenklause** Gasstr 12 ☎45071 22rm16⇋1🍴 P sB22–31 sB⇋🍴35–44 dB62 dB⇋🍴67–72 L9–26alc D9–26alc

⌂ ⇝*H Fröhling* Kielerstr 239–245 ☎32031 P Frd

⌂ ⇝*E Landschoof* Rungestr 5 ☎31921 P BL (GB)

NEUSS Nordrhein-Westfalen 118,027 (☎02101) Map **4** D2

At **Neuss-Erfttal**

☆☆☆**Novotel Düsseldorf-Neuss** am Derikurner Hof ☎17081 tx8517634 115⇋🍴 P Lift sB⇋fr141 English breakfast only Pool

At **Neuss-Grimlinghausen** (4.5km SW on B5)

★**Kaisersaal** ☎37756 12🍴 P L7–17 D7–25

NEUSTADT AN DER AISCH Bayern 10,506 (☎09161) Map **12** D4

★★**Römerhof** R-Wagnerstr 1 ☎2498 38rm1⇋9🍴 🏛 P sB25–33 sB⇋🍴35–43 dB48–59 dB⇋🍴60–75 (English breakfast) L12–20 D8–15

NEUSTADT AN DER WEINSTRASSE Rheinland-Pfalz 52,543 (☎06321) Map **11** B2

⌂ ⇝**Naumer & Sohne** A-Kolpingstr 71 ☎13038 M/c P Frd

At **Schöntal** (3km W)

★**Königsmühle** Schöntalstr 10, ☎2487 25rm12⇋2🍴 A13rm P Lift sB23–26 sB⇋🍴28–40 dB44–50 dB⇋🍴62–70 L10–20 D5–20 mountains

NEUSTADT IM SCHWARZWALD Baden-Württemberg 11,500 (☎07651) Map **11** B4

★★★★**Adler-Post** Hauptstr 16 ☎5066 37rm25⇋🍴 P sB37–42 sB⇋🍴52–67 dB64–84 dB⇋🍴94–104 (English breakfast) L18–40 D18–40 Pool

NEUWIED Rheinland-Pfalz 63,013 (☎02631) Map **5** A1

P Wirtz Allensteinerstr 15 ☎5195 P Opl

NIEFERN Baden-Württemberg 9,710 (☎07233) Map **12** C3

★★**Decker** Pforzheimerstr ☎875 39rm5⇋23🍴 🏛 P ♪ sB32 sB⇋🍴46–54 dB45 dB⇋🍴85–97 L15–25 D15–25

NIERSTEIN Rheinland-Pfalz 6,613 (☎06133) Map **11** B4

★**Rhein** Mainzerstr 16 ☎5161 Closed 16 Dec–9 Jan 15rm4⇋11🍴 🏛 P sB⇋🍴40–62 dB⇋🍴63–99 (English breakfast) L9–50 D7–20 river

NONNENHORN Bayern 1,605 (☎08382) Map **12** C2

★★★**Strand** Wasserburgerstr ☎8223 Closed Nov–Mar 28rm20⇋5🍴 🏛 P sB40–54 sB⇋🍴53–70 dB⇋🍴93–125 L14–18 D15–20 Pool mountains lake

NORDEN Niedersachsen 24,208 (☎04931) Map **4** D4

★**Deutches Haus** Neuer Weg 26 ☎4271 Closed 1–14 Jan 45rm8⇋21🍴 🏛 P Lift sB fr29 sB⇋🍴fr38 dB fr54 dB⇋🍴fr74 L11–24 D11–24

NORDHORN Niedersachsen 50,051 (☎05921) Map **4** D3

★**Euregio** Dortmunderstr 20 ☎5077 26rm24🍴 🏛 P sB34 sB⇋🍴40–45 dB55 dB🍴64–71

NÖRDLINGEN Bayern 17,511 (☎08931) Map **12** D3

★★**Sonne** Markpl ☎5067 tx51749 40rm20⇋12🍴 🏛 P sB fr26 sB⇋🍴fr38 dB fr48 dB⇋🍴fr58

NORTHEIM Niedersachsen 34,025 (☎05551) Map **5** B2

★★*Sonne* Breitestr 59 ☎4071 34rm6⇋6🍴 🏛

NOTSCHREI Baden-Württemberg (☎07602) Map **11** B2

★★**Wald** ☎219 35rm16⇋14🍴 🏛 P Lift sB28–32 sB⇋🍴38 dB56–60 dB⇋🍴72–90 L10–20 D10–20 Pool mountains

NÜRBURG Rheinland-Pfalz 324 (☎02691) Map **4** D1

At **Nürburgring** (1km SW)

★★**Sport Tribune** ☎2035 tx863919 48rm4⇋23🍴 A20rm 🏛 P ♪ sB19–28 sB⇋🍴32–37 dB37–47 dB⇋🍴68–73 (English breakfast) L10–18 D11–22

NÜRNBERG (NUREMBERG) Bayern 515,047 (☎0911) Map **12** D4

★★★★**Grand** Bahnhofstr 1 ☎203621 tx622010 167rm121⇋22🍴 🏛 P Lift ♪ sB fr58 sB⇋🍴fr76 dB fr100 dB⇋🍴fr130

★★★★**Carlton** Eilgutstr 13 ☎203535 tx622329 117rm90⇋22🍴 P Lift ♪ sB⇋🍴fr68 dB⇋🍴fr110

☆☆☆**EuroCrest** Münchnerstr 283 ☎49441 tx622930 94rm70⇋24🍴 A45rm P Lift ♪

sB⇄ 🍴85–95 dB⇄ 🍴100–115 (English breakfast)
L fr17 D fr17

★★★Sterntor Tafelhofstr 8 ☎203101 tx622632
120rm60⇄ 🏛 Lift

★★★Victoria Königstr 80 ☎203801 63rm24⇄5🍴
Lift

★★Drei Linden Aussere Sulzbacherstr 1 ☎533620
30rm2⇄21🍴 🏛 P 🕩 sB36–39 sB⇄ 🍴44–66
dB⇄ 🍴72–100 L10–20 D12–25

★Kaiserhof Königstr 39 ☎203686 ta Kaiho
tx626012 66rm16⇄5🍴 🏛 P Lift 🕩 sB25–28
sB⇄ 🍴46–50 dB45–55 dB⇄ 🍴75–95

🍴 🗺**Motus** Sandreath Str 26 ☎42001 M/c P
Jag/Rov/Tri

OBERAMMERGAU Bayern 4,910 (☎08822)

Map 12 D2

★★Alte Post Dorfstr 19 ☎517 60rm16⇄8🍴 🏛

★★Bold König Ludwigstr 10 ☎520 49rm27⇄5🍴 🏛

★★Friedenshöhe König-Ludwigstr 31 ☎598 Closed
Nov–24 Dec 11rm4⇄7🍴 P sB⇄ 🍴40–43
dB⇄ 🍴70–76 English breakfast only L10–16
D10–16 mountains

★★Schilcherhof Bahnhofstr 17 ☎4740 Closed 16
Nov–24 Dec 25rm3⇄5🍴 A8rm 🏛 P sB26–28
sB⇄ 🍴32–34 dB46–50 dB⇄ 🍴54–62 D13

OBERHAUSEN Nordrhein-Westfalen 248,052
(☎02132) Map 4 D2

★★★Ruhrland Berlinerpl 2 ☎805031 tx856900
60rm25⇄25🍴 🏛 P Lift 🕩 sB42–47 sB⇄ 🍴57–72
dB84–99 dB⇄ 🍴104–124 (English breakfast)
L15–25 D15–25

🍴 🗺**Kupka** Duisbergerstr 188 ☎21824 P Opl

OBERKIRCH Baden-Württemberg 17,023
(☎07802) Map 11 B3

★★Obere Linde Hauptstr 25–27 ☎3038
34rm6⇄14🍴 A6rm 🏛 P sB fr25 sB⇄ 🍴fr33 dB fr45
dB⇄ 🍴fr58 L12–39 D12–45 🗺 mountains

🍴 🗺**L Müller** Appenweiererstr 11 ☎3356 Opl

At **Ödsbach** (3km S)

★★Grüner Baum Almstr 33 ☎2801 tx752627
Closed Feb 50rm20⇄25🍴 🏛 P sB30–33
sB⇄ 🍴39–42 dB56–62 dB⇄ 🍴76–82 L13–20
D13–20 🗺 Pool mountains

OBERSTAUFEN Bayern 6,410 (☎08386)

Map 12 C2

★★Kurhotel Hirsch Kalzhöferstr 4 (n rest) ☎2032
21rm8⇄10🍴 🏛 P sB37 sB⇄ 🍴40 dB⇄ 🍴53–54

OBERSTDORF Bayern 11,746 (☎08322)

Map 12 C2

★★★Wittelsbacher Hof Prinzenstr 24 ☎1018
Closed 16 Apr–12 May & 16 Oct–14 Dec
88rm50⇄32🍴 🏛 P Lift 🕩 sB28–38 sB⇄ 🍴50–66
dB⇄ 🍴72–112 (English breakfast) L20–24 D20–24
Pool mountains

🍴 🗺**Nebelhorn** Nebelhornstr 59 ☎4669 P Fia

OBERWESEL Rheinland-Pfalz 5,050 (☎06744)

Map 11 B4

★★Auf Schönburg ☎8198 Closed Dec–Feb
10rm5⇄3🍴 P dB55–110 dB⇄ 🍴88–110

★Goldner Pfropfenzieher ☎207 30rm7⇄1🍴 🏛 P
sB22–23 sB⇄ 🍴fr26 dB44–46 dB⇄ 🍴54–58
L10–20 D8–20 river

OCHSENFURT Bayern 11,400 (☎09331)

Map 12 C4

★Bären Hauptstr 74 ☎2282 Closed 26 Jul–24 Aug
29rm1⇄14🍴 🏛 P sB24–32 sB⇄ 🍴35–40 dB45–52
dB⇄ 🍴58–65 L10–24 D10–20

ÖDSBACH See **OBERKIRCH**

OESTRICH Hessen 9,210 (☎06723) Map 11 B4

★★★Schwan Rheinallee 5–7 ☎3001 tx42146
Closed 16 Dec–14 Feb 60rm28⇄26🍴 A17rm 🏛 P
Lift 🕩 sB52–54 sB⇄ 🍴57–79 dB104–108
dB⇄ 🍴104–158 (English breakfast) L15alc D15alc
river

OEYNHAUSEN (BAD) Nordrhein-Westfalen 45,045
(☎5731) Map 5 A3

★★Hahnenkamp Alte Reichsstr 4 (2.5km NE)
☎5041 tx9724836 25rm7⇄13🍴 🏛 P sB fr26
sB⇄ 🍴fr39 dB⇄ 🍴fr72 L10–30 D10–30 Pool

OFFENBACH Hessen 121,017 (☎0611) Map 11 B4

★★Graf Schlosstr 19 ☎811702 28rm4⇄11🍴 P
sB fr32 sB⇄ 🍴fr42 dB fr56 dB⇄ 🍴fr68
(English breakfast) L8–18 D8–18

OFFENBURG Baden-Württemberg 55,052 (☎0781)
Map 11 B3

★★★Palmengarten Okenstr 13 ☎25031 tx752849
Closed 24 Dec–3 Jan 66rm26⇄16🍴 🏛 P Lift 🕩
sB27–36 (room only) sB⇄ 🍴44–50 (room only)
dB54–68 (room only) dB⇄ 🍴80–90 (room only)
L16–20 D16–20

★★Park Waldhorn F-Volkstr 11 (n rest) ☎24517
35rm6⇄15🍴 P 🕩 sB26–29 (room only)
sB⇄ 🍴35–40 (room only) dB42–52 (room only)
dB⇄ 🍴55–70 (room only)

★Sonne Hauptstr 94 ☎71039 40rm6⇄11🍴 A15rm
🏛 P sB fr28 sB⇄ 🍴fr34 dB fr48 dB⇄ 🍴fr62 L7–19
D7–19

A Fandrich C-Benz Str 6 ☎25200 BL (GB)

🍴 🗺**A Linck** Freiburger Str 26 ☎25005 Opl (GB)

At **Ortenberg** (4km SE)

★Glattfelder ☎31219 Closed 1st two wks Nov
16rm6🍴 🏛 P sB20–25 (room only) sB🍴25
(room only) dB35–38 (room only) dB🍴45 (room only)

OLPE Nordrhein-Westfalen 23,032 (☎02761)

Map 5 A1

★★Tillmann Kölnerstr 15 ☎5252 20rm2⇄6🍴 🏛 P
sB31–32 sB⇄ 🍴34–47 dB55–62 dB⇄ 🍴62–94
(English breakfast) L9–18 D14–25

OPPENHEIM Rheinland-Pfalz 6,025 (☎06133)

Map 11 B4

★★Kurpfalz Wormserstr 2 ☎2291 Closed 16 Dec–9
Jan 20rm11⇄9🍴 🏛 P sB⇄ 🍴34–46 dB⇄ 🍴62–92
(English breakfast) L8–20 D7–20

ORTENBERG See **OFFENBURG**

OSNABRÜCK Niedersachsen 159,513 (☎0541)

Map 5 A3

★★★Hohenzollern H-Heinestr 17 (nr main rly sta)
☎27292 tx94776 100rm28⇄17🍴 P Lift 🕩 sB40–65
sB⇄ 🍴80–105 dB94 dB⇄ 🍴104–149
(English breakfast) L17–30 D11–30 Pool

🍴**H van Beers** Bahlweg 16 ☎73596 M/c AR/BL
(GB)

🍴 🗺**G Clupka** Pferdstr 2 ☎572629 BL (GB)

At **Hellern** (4km SW)

🍴 🗺**W Düling** Lengericher Landstr 2 ☎42381 🕩 M/c
P AR/Maz (GB)

OTTOBEUREN Bayern 7,015 (☎08332)

Map 12 C/D2

★★Hirsch Marktpl 12 ☎552 tx54504 67rm19⇄10🍴
🏛 Lift Pool

PADERBORN Nordrhein-Westfalen 104,047
(☎05251) Map 5 A2

🍴 **F-Kleine Automobile** Bahnhofstr 36 ☎24444 Frd
(GB)

🍴 🗺**R Sprenger** Detmolderstr 44 ☎56119 ☎56119
AR/BL/Fia (GB)

PASSAU Bayern 50,024 (☎0851) Map 13 B3

★★★Schloss Ort am Dreiflusseck ☎4072 Closed
21 Dec–14 Jan 34rm8⇄10🍴 🏛 Lift

★★Weisser Hase Ludwigstr 23 ☎34066
94rm14⇄10🍴 🏛 P Lift 🕩 sB29 sB⇄ 🍴42–45
dB46–49 dB⇄ 🍴55–85 L9–20 D5–20

🍴 🗺**O Hausmann** Theresienstr 27 & Neuburgerstr
99 ☎2998 BL/Peu

🍴 🗺**F Hofbauer** Neuburgerstr 141 ☎6017 Opl

PFAFFENHOFEN Bayern (☎08441) Map 12 D3

🍴 🗺**F X Stiglmayr** Scheyererstr 70 ☎894 P
BMW/Sim

PFORZHEIM Baden-Württemberg 110,033
(☎07231) Map 11 B3

★★★Ruf Bahnhofspl 5 (DP) ☎16011 tx783843
41rm25⇄3🍴 Lift

★★**Schwarzwald** am Schossgatter 7 ☎32818 26rm5⇌7🛁 P Lift sB26–36 sB⇌🛁48 dB53–58 dB⇌🛁75 (English breakfast) L12–18 D10–18
🛢 ✇***Brenk & Linkenheil*** Karlsruherstr 22 ☎17033 M/c Frd

PRIEN AM CHIEMSEE Bayern 7,213 (☎08051) Map **13** A2
★★**Bayerischer Hof** Bernauerstr 3 ☎1095 90rm33⇌4🛁 🏠 P Lift sB33–40 sB⇌🛁38–47 dB56–70 dB⇌🛁70–87 L9–17 D9–17 mountains

PRÜM Rheinland-Pfalz 5,621 (☎06551) Map **4** D1
★**Gebauer** Hahnpl 6 ☎2346 Closed 25 Sep–15 Oct 8rm P sB fr25 dB fr50 L6–20 D6–20

PUTTGARDEN Schleswig-Holstein 510 (☎04371) Map **1** B1
★***Dänia*** am Fährbahnhof ☎3016 tx29814 Closed Nov–Feb 66🛁 Lift sea

QUICKBORN Schleswig-Holstein 11,014 (☎04106) Map **5** B4
★***Jagdhaus Waldfrieden*** Bundesstr ☎3771 11rm1⇌10🛁

RASTATT Baden-Württemberg 41,031 (☎07222) Map **11** B3
★★**Blume** Kaiserstr 38 ☎32222 34rm5⇌9🛁 🏠 P sB29–31 sB⇌🛁35–44 dB55–65 dB⇌🛁69–87 (English breakfast) L9–20 D9–20
★★**Schwert** Herrenstr 3A ☎35984 22rm4⇌11🛁 🏠 P sB28–29 sB⇌🛁35–42 dB51 dB⇌🛁57–72 (English breakfast) L11–20 D12–21
★***Katzenberger's Adler*** Josefstr 7 ☎32103 Closed Oct 7rm1🛁 🏠

RATEKAU See **LÜBECK**

RATINGEN Nordrhein-Westfalen 87,000 (☎02102) Map **4** D2
☆☆☆**EuroCrest** Broichhofstr 3 ☎46046 tx8585235 200⇌ P ☽ sB⇌115–135 dB⇌160–195 (English breakfast) L fr17 D fr17 Pool
★★★***Krummenweg*** ☎17619 Closed 13 Dec–9 Jan 20rm15⇌ 🏠 Pool

RAVENSBURG Baden-Württemberg 43,018 (☎0751) Map **12** C2
★★**Waldhorn** Marienpl 15 ☎23017 24rm8⇌12🛁 🏠 P sB27 sB⇌🛁47 dB⇌🛁65–75 L15–60 D15–60

REGENSBURG Bayern 133,542 (☎0941) Map **13** A3
★★★**Avia** Frankenstr 1–3 ☎42093 tx65703 94rm15⇌68🛁 🏠 P Lift ☽ sB30 sB⇌🛁38–66 dB45 dB⇌45🛁50–87 (English breakfast) L fr13 D fr13
★★**Karmeliten** Dachaupl 1 ☎54308 tx65170 Closed 21 Dec–9 Jan 79rm 14⇌28🛁 P Lift ☽ sB38–42 sB⇌🛁55–57 dB66–70 dB⇌🛁90–94
★★***Straubinger Hof*** A-Schmetzer Str 33 ☎54462 68rm2⇌35🛁 🏠 Lift
🛢 ✇**Kellnberger** Kirchmeierstr 24 ☎26666 P Ren (GB)
O Seitz Alte Straubingerstr 19 ☎52872 BL

REICHENHALL (BAD) Bayern 14,516 (☎08651) Map **13** B2
★★★**Axelmannstein** Salzburgerstr 4 ☎4001 tx56112 156rm133⇌ A30rm 🏠 P Lift ☽ sB44–58 sB⇌74–100 dB94 dB⇌108–160 (English breakfast) L22 D23 St% 🎾 Pool mountains
★★★**Kurhotel Luisenbad** Ludwigstr 33 ☎5081 tx56131 Closed 31 Oct–19 Dec 86rm38⇌28🛁 🏠 P Lift ☽ sB39–55 sB⇌🛁67–92 dB78–86 dB⇌🛁146–186 (English breakfast) L22–26 D22–28 Pool mountains lake
🛢 ✇**Prechter** Innsbruckerstr Angerl 6 ☎2078 Frd

REIT IM WINKL Bayern 2,618 (☎08640) Map **13** A2
★★★***Unterwirt*** Kirchpl 2 ☎8811 65rm29⇌ 🏠 Lift Pool

REMAGEN Rheinland-Pfalz 14,516 (☎02642) Map **4** D1
★★**Fürstenberg** Rhein Prom ☎23066 14rm12⇌ P sB31–41 sB⇌41 dB62 dB⇌82 (English breakfast) L12–25 D12–25 Pool river
★**Fassbender** Marktstr 78 ☎23472 17rm 🏠 P sB20–22 dB40–44 L8–15 D8–15
★**Pinger** ☎22582 62rm40⇌8🛁 A15rm 🏠 P Lift sB22–30 sB⇌🛁25–35 dB22–50 dB⇌🛁50–60 L9–18 D10–20

RENDSBURG Schleswig-Holstein 34,511 (☎04331) Map **1** B1
★***Germania*** Parade pl 3 ☎22997 16rm 🏠
At **Büdelsdorf**
🛢 **J Suhr** Hollerstr 9 ☎3406 Frd

RENGSDORF BEI NEUWIED Rheinland-Pfalz 2,505 (☎02634) Map **5** A1
★★***Stern*** Hauptstr 56 ☎204 Closed 16 Oct–Mar 50rm7⇌3🛁 🏠

REUTLINGEN Baden-Württemberg 96,038 (☎07121) Map **12** C3
★★**Ernst** Leonhardspl ☎44081 tx729898 78rm18⇌54🛁 🏠 P Lift ☽ sB37–41 sB⇌🛁46–64 dB72–86 dB⇌🛁80–108 (English breakfast) L8–18 D8–18 Pool
★★***Reutlinger Hof*** Kaiserstr 33 (n rest) ☎17075 45rm3⇌18🛁 A12rm 🏠 Lift Pool
Auto-Specht Bühlweg 2, Ohmenhausen ☎54775 BL/Cit

RHEINZABERN Rheinland-Pfatz 3,400 (☎06344) Map **11** B3
★***Goldenes Lamm*** Hauptstr 53 ☎2377 Closed 21 Dec–9 Jan 20rm4🛁 A4rm

RHEYDT Nordrhein-Westfalen (☎02166) Map **4** D2
★★★**Besch Parkhotel** H-Junkersstr 2 ☎44011 33rm6⇌27🛁 🏠 P Lift ☽ sB⇌🛁56 dB⇌🛁82 (English breakfast) L15–56 D15–56

RIEDLINGEN Baden-Württemberg 8,814 (☎07371) Map **12** C2
★★***Brücke*** Hindenburg Str 4 ☎2449 Closed Nov 17⇌ 🏠

ROSENHEIM Bayern 38,527 (☎08031) Map **13** A2
★★★**Goldener Hirsch** Münchnerstr 40 ☎12029 43rm 12⇌6🛁 🏠 P Lift ☽ sB31–33 sB⇌🛁40–43 dB57–64 dB⇌🛁74–84 (English breakfast) L9–19 D9–19
🛢 ✇***Fink*** ☎37439 BL/Jag/ Rov/Tri
G Rupp Innstr 34 ☎13970 M/c BL

ROTENBURG (WÜMME) Niedersachsen 19,532 (☎04261) Map **5** B3
★**Deutsches Haus** Grossestr 51 ☎3300 A10rm P sB25 (room only) dB50 (room only) L8–20 D8–20
🛢 **Auto-Höhns** Waldweg 2–4 ☎2084 Frd (GB)
🛢 ✇***K-Lengen*** Harburgerstr 67 ☎809 P

ROTHENBURG OB DER TAUBER Bayern 12,550 (☎09861) Map **12** C4
★★★★**Eisenhut** Herrngasse 3 ☎2041 tx61367 Closed 11 Jan–Feb 85rm77⇌ 🏠 P Lift ☽ sB49–54 (room only) sB⇌🛁82–92 (room only) dB80–93 (room only) dB⇌🛁109–162 (room only)
★★★★**Goldener Hirsch** Untere Schmiedgasse 16 ☎2051 tx61372 Closed mid Dec– mid Jan 80rm50⇌16🛁 A20rm 🏠 P Lift ☽ sB35–46 sB⇌🛁49–80 dB60–90 dB⇌🛁80–150 (English breakfast) L15–30 D15–30
★★★**Burg** Klostergasse 1 (n rest) ☎2252 Closed Jan & Feb 20rm15⇌ 🏠 P sB27–33 sB⇌🛁46–48 dB55–59 dB⇌75–85
★★***Markusturm*** Rödergasse 1 ☎2370 30rm11⇌16🛁 🏠
★★**Reichs-Küchenmeister** Kirchpl 8 ☎3406 35rm10⇌9🛁 🏠 P Lift ☽ sB22–25 sB⇌🛁35–38 dB40–45 dB⇌🛁58–70 (English breakfast) L10–25 D10–25
★★**Tilman Riemenschneider** Georgengasse 11–13 ☎4606 ta Lowenhotel tx61384 50rm27⇌9🛁 🏠 P Lift ☽ sB29–32 sB⇌🛁39–49 dB56–62 dB⇌🛁72–94 (English breakfast) L8–22 D8–22
★★**Glocke** Plönlein 1 ☎3025 35rm12⇌13🛁 🏠 P Lift sB23–26 sB⇌🛁35–42 dB46–50 dB⇌🛁60–85 L10–22 D10–28
🛢 ✇**Central** (H Korn) Schützenstr 11 ☎3088 P Jag/MB (GB)

ⓑ ➽H **Döhler** Ansbacherst 35–40 ☎2084 ☎2084 P
GM/Opl (GB)
ROTTACH-EGERN Bayern 6,333 (☎08022)
Map **13** A2
★★★★ *Bachmair* Seestr 47 ☎6444 220➾ 🏦 Lift
Pool lake
ROTTENBURG Baden-Württemberg 30,053
(☎07472) Map **12** C3
★★*Martinshof* E-Bolzpl 5 ☎8081 30rm4➾14🍴 🏦
Lift
RÖTTGEN See **BONN**
ROTTWEIL Baden-Württemberg 24,015 (☎0741)
Map **11** B2/3
★*Johanniterbad* Johannsergasse 12 ☎6083 28rm
8➾10🍴 Lift
★**Lamm** Hauptstr 45 ☎45015 18rm2➾16🍴 🏦 P
sB28–35 sB➾🍴32–35 dB42–58 dB➾🍴45–60
L10–20 D6–20
ⓑ **F Bader** Tuttlingerstr 82 ☎8085 Frd (GB)
RÜDESHEIM Hessen 7,007 (☎06722) Map **11** B4
★★★ **Deutscher Hof** Rheinstr 21 ☎3016 tx42122
95rm35➾25🍴 🏦 Lift
★★★**Waldhotel Jagdschloss Niederwald**
(6·5km W) ☎1004 Closed 16 Dec–Jan
56rm34➾11🍴 🏦 P Ɗ sB31–35 sB➾🍴52–68 dB68
dB➾🍴85–98 (English breakfast) mountains
★★*Darmstädter Hof* Rheinstr 29 ☎2485 Closed
Dec–Mar 50rm10➾ 🏦 P Ɗ sB36–46 sB➾46
dB60–72 dB➾87–102 L8–19 D7–21 river
ⓑ *Corvers* Landstr 2 ☎2345 P Ren
ⓑ *Rüdesheim* Geisenheimerstr 18 ☎2542 P Opl
SAARBRÜCKEN Saarland 230,051 (☎0681)
Map **11** A3
★★★★**Berlin** Faktoreistr ☎33030 tx4421409
65rm35➾15🍴 🏦 P Lift Ɗ sB63–90 dB72–114
English breakfast only
☆☆☆**Novotel** Zinzingarstr ☎51071 tx4428836 100➾
P Lift sB➾🍴 fr79 dB➾🍴 fr104 English breakfast only
Pool
★★**Christine** Gersweilerstr 39 ☎55081 tx4428736
65rm65➾7🍴 🏦 P Lift Ɗ sB41–46 sB➾🍴54–79
dB60–80 dB➾🍴82–117 L8–25 D fr15 Pool
★★**Wien** Gutenbergstr 29 ☎55088 27rm20🍴 🏦 P
Lift Ɗ sB25–31 sB🍴39–41 dB35–38 dB🍴56 L alc
D alc
ⓑ ➽*Auto-Industrie* H-Böckingstr 16 ☎64011 P Frd
(GB)
ⓑ *Auto-Ritz* Sulzbachstr 33–35 ☎36529 P BL
ⓑ *Saar-Auto* Sulzbachstr ☎33001 Sim
SÄCKINGEN Baden-Württemberg 14,822 (☎07761)
Map **11** B2
★*Kater Hiddigeigel* Tanzenpl 1 ☎2818 21rm5➾2🍴
A5rm 🏦 P sB24–26 sB➾🍴26–36 dB45–52
dB➾🍴58–67 (English breakfast) L6–15 D8–18
ST GEORGEN Baden-Württemberg 15,012
(☎07724) Map **11** B2
★**Hirsch** Bahnhofstr 70 (n rest 3 wksJul) ☎7125
22rm8➾14🍴 🏦 P sB➾🍴34–38 dB➾🍴68–70 L alc
D alc
ST GOAR Rheinland-Pfalz 3,530 (☎06741)
Map **11** B4
★★**Goldenen Löwen** Heerstr 1 ☎274 Closed
Dec–14 Feb 11rm3➾4🍴 P sB28–30 sB➾🍴35–45
dB48 dB➾🍴65–80 L10–18 d8–28 river
★★**Hauser** Heerstr 160 ☎333 Closed 16 Dec–Jan
15rm2➾5🍴 🏦 P sB25 SB➾🍴32 dB46–50
dB➾🍴52–58 L9–18 D8–22 mountains river

★**Schneider am Markt** Herrstr 158 ☎289 Closed
Feb–14 Mar 17rm 7🍴 P sB29–36 sB🍴34–39
dB57–67 dB🍴67–87 L9–20 D8–22 mountains river
ST GOARSHAUSEN Rheinland-Pfalz 2,512
(☎06771) Map **11** B4
★★*Erholung* Nastätterstr 161 ☎684
95rm16➾14🍴 🏦
ST MÄRGEN Baden-Württemberg 1,613 (☎07669)
Map **11** B2
★★**Hirschen** Feldbergstr 9 ☎201 Closed 16 Nov–19
Dec 40rm26➾12🍴 A19rm 🏦 P sB27–38
sB➾ 🍴33–45 dB fr52 dB➾ 🍴55–76 L8–22 D9–22
mountains
SAND Baden-Württemberg 900 (☎07226)
Map **11** B3
★★**Plättig** ☎227 66rm30➾20🍴 🏦 P Lift
sB22–30sB➾🍴45–50 dB56 dB➾🍴66–94
(English breakfast) L18–25 D18–25 Pool mountains
SANDHOFEN See **MANNHEIM**
SAULGAU Baden-Württemberg 15,614 (☎07581)
Map **12** C2
★★**Kleber-Post** Hauptstr 100 ☎3051 49rm8➾19🍴
🏦 P sB38–40 sB➾🍴48–49 dB66–68
dB➾🍴80–85 (English breakfast) L11–19 D11–28
SCHACKENDORF See **SEGEBERG (BAD)**
SCHAUMBERG See **DIEZ/LAHN**
SCHLAG See **GRAFENAU**
SCHLANGENBAD Hessen 5,218 (☎06129)
Map **11** B4
★★**Stattliches Kurhaus** Rheingauerstr 47 ☎411
100rm48➾46🍴 🏦 P Lift Ɗ sB53–80 sB➾ 🍴77–98
dB fr113 dB➾ 🍴120–146 (English breakfast)
L18–25 D18–25
SCHLESWIG Schleswig-Holstein 32,532 (☎04621)
Map **1** A1
★★*Stadt Hamburg* Lollfuss 108 ☎7058
50rm8➾3🍴
★★*Strandhalle* am Jachthafen ☎22021
28rm18➾6🍴 🏦 lake
★**Weissen Schwan** Gottortstr 1 ☎32712 19rm4🍴
A4rm 🏦 P sB fr26 sB🍴fr30 dB fr52 dB🍴fr60
(English breakfast) L11–18 D fr10 sea
ⓑ **J Lorenzen** Flensburger Str 43 ☎23085 P Opl
ⓑ➽*A Wriedt* Flensburger Str 88 ☎23387 P Ren
SCHLUCHSEE Baden-Württemberg 2,109
(☎07656) Map **11** B2
★**Schiff** ☎252 Closed Nov–14 Dec 34rm5➾9🍴 🏦 P
Lift sB25–29 sB➾🍴30–38 dB47–54 dB➾🍴57–77
L7–12 D8–18 ⚓ Pool lake
SCHMIDEN See **STUTTGART**
SCHÖNBERG See **SEELBACH**
SCHÖNMÜNZACH Baden-Württemberg 950
(☎07447) Map **11** B3
★★**Post** Murgtalstr 635 ☎313 Closed 11 Nov–9 Dec
60rm26➾10🍴 Lift
SCHÖNTAL See **NEUSTADT AN DER
WEINSTRASSE**
SCHRIESHEIM Baden-Württemberg 11,840
(☎06203) Map **11** B4
★★**Luisenhöhe** Eichenweg ☎65617 28rm3➾17🍴
🏦 P sB27–29 sB➾🍴27–29 dB57–72
dB➾🍴62–75 (English breakfast) L9–14 D7–15
mountains
SCHWABACH Bayern 33,630 (☎09122) Map **12** D4
ⓑ ➽*Feser* Limbacherstr 26 ☎85035 P Aud/VW
SCHWÄBISCH HALL Baden-Württemberg 31,333
(☎0791) Map **12** C3

★★*Goldener Adler* am Markt 11 ☎6364 Closed
23 Dec – 14 Jan 18rm4⇌ 🏠
SCHWALENBERG Nordrhein-Westfalen 1,700
(☎05284) Map **5** B2
★★*Schloss Burg Schwalenberg* ☎167 9rm7🍴 🏠
SCHWARZENFELD Bayern 6,213 (☎09435)
Map **13** A4
★*Brauerel-Bauer* Hauptstr 30 ☎205 25rm 6🍴 🏠
SCHWEINFURT Bayern 57,038 (☎09721)
Map **12** C4
★★*Central* Zehntstr 20 (n rest) ☎1325 36rm20⇌9🍴
🏠 P Lift sB26 sB⇌🍴34 – 39 dB45 dB⇌🍴57 – 65
SCHWELM Nordrhein-Westfalen 34,523 (☎02125)
Map **4** D2
★★*Prinz von Preussen* Altmarkt 8 ☎13444
17rm14🍴 P sB24 – 28 sB🍴32 – 39 dB46 – 50
dB🍴60 – 71 L8 – 25 D8 – 25
SEELBACH Baden-Württemberg 4,410 (☎07823)
Map **11** B3
At **Schönberg** (6km NE)
★★*Geroldseck* ☎2044 25rm1⇌15🍴 🏠 P sB33 – 44
sB⇌🍴44 – 49 dB62 – 85 dB⇌🍴85 – 95 L10 – 20
D9 – 20 Pool mountains
SEESEN Niedersachsen 25,030 (☎05381)
Map **5** B2
★★*Goldener Löwe* Jacobsonstr 20 ☎1202
tx957316 25rm4⇌9🍴 A3rm 🏠 P sB25 – 40
sB⇌🍴50 – 55 dB50 – 55 dB⇌🍴65 – 75
(English breakfast) L9 – 24 D9 – 24
Auto-Hoffmann Autobahnizubringestr ☎1215 P Frd
(GB)
SEGEBERG (BAD) Schleswig-Holstein 14,013
(☎04551) Map **5** B4
At **Schackendorf** (5km NW on B404)
★★*Stefanie & Motel B404* ☎3600 36rm10⇌14🍴
A18rm 🏠 P sB20 – 30 sB⇌🍴30 dB38 – 51 dB⇌🍴51
(English breakfast) L30 – 38 D9 – 23
SIEGBURG Nordrhein-Westfalen 37,240 (☎02241)
Map **4** D1
★★*Stern* Marktpl 14 ☎60021 Closed 16 Dec – 14 Jan
50rm18⇌18🍴 🏠 P Lift ♪ sB26 – 30 (room only)
sB⇌🍴34 – 45 (rooms only) dB56 – 62 (room only)
dB⇌🍴63 – 79 (room only)
★★*Kaiserhof* Kaiserstr 80
☎50071 48rm2⇌ 🏠 Lift
🏠 *M Bässgen* Frankfurterstr 1 ☎66001 Opl
SIEGEN Nordrhein-Westfalen 121,550 (☎0271)
Map **5** A1
★★*Johanneshöhe* Wallhausenstr 1 ☎331088
26rm4⇌21🍴 🏠 P ♪ sBfr31 sB⇌🍴50 – 60
dB🍴74 – 100 (English breakfast) L15 – 30 D15 – 30
mountains
SIGMARINGEN Baden-Württemberg 15,425
(☎07571) Map **12** C2
🏠 🖘*J-Zimmermann* In den Burgwiesen 18 ☎1696
Opl
SINDELFINGEN Baden-Württemberg 56,048
(☎07031) Map **12** C3
☆☆☆*Stuttgart EuroCrest* W-Haspelstr 101 ☎81088
tx7265778 145rm56⇌89🍴 P Lift ♪ sB⇌🍴92 – 98
dB⇌🍴115 – 130 (English breakfast) Lfr17 Dfr17
mountains
SOEST Nordrhein-Westfalen 43,019 (☎02921)
Map **5** A2
★★*Andernach zur Börse* Thomästr 31 ☎3227
Closed Jul – 18 Aug & 23 Dec – 5 Jan 20rm1⇌12🍴
A4rm 🏠 P sB32 – 38 sB⇌🍴38 – 47 dB62 – 70
dB⇌🍴68 – 87 L12 – 25 D10 – 25
🏠 *H Siedler* Riga-Ring 15 ☎73051 Frd
SPEYER Rheinland-Pfalz 45,024 (☎06232)
Map **11** B4
★*Goldener Engel* Mühlturmstr ☎76732 Closed
24 Dec – 9 Jan 40rm11⇌18🍴 P Lift sB30 – 35 (room
only) sB⇌🍴34 – 44 (room only) dB53 – 58 (room
only) dB⇌🍴66 – 74 (room only)
Galant Tullastr 1 ☎33235 BL/Rov/Tri
STEINWEILER Rheinland-Pfalz (☎06349)
Map **11** B3

★*Zum Schwanen* ☎8369 10rm1⇌1🍴 🏠
STOLZENFELS See **KOBLENZ**

STRAUBING Bayern 44,520 (☎09421) Map **13** A3
★★*Seethaler* Theresienpl 25 ☎12022 25rm20⇌5🍴
🏠 P sB37 – 40 sB⇌🍴45 dB⇌🍴70 L alc D alc
★★*Wittelsbach* Stadtgraben 25 ☎1517
42rm4⇌10🍴 🏠 P Lift ♪ sB22 – 23 sB⇌🍴27 – 28
dB42 dB⇌🍴49 – 53 L8 – 12 D9 – 13
STUTTGART Baden-Württemberg 600,055
(☎0711) Map **12** C3
★★★★*Schlossgarten* Schillerstr 23 ☎299911
tx722936 125rm82⇌35🍴 🏠 P Lift ♪ sB70 – 75
sB⇌🍴85 – 115 dB⇌🍴125 – 150 (English breakfast)
L20 – 60 D20 – 60
★★★★*Steigenberger Graf Zeppelin* Arnulf-Klett-Pl
7 ☎299881 tx722418 280rm260⇌10🍴 P Lift ♪
sB60 – 70 sB⇌🍴95 – 130 dB🍴140 – 170
(English breakfast) L fr20 D fr20 Pool
★★★*Park* Villastr 21 ☎723405
81rm40⇌28🍴 P Lift ♪ sB40 – 46 sB⇌🍴62 – 95
dB⇌🍴100 – 130 (English breakfast) L19 – 25
D19 – 25
★★★*Reichsbahn* Bahnhofpl 2 ☎299801 tx723543
108rm45⇌34🍴 Lift
★★★*Rieker* Friedrichstr 3 (n rest) ☎221311 63⇌ 🏠
Lift
★★*Ketterer* Marienstr 3 ☎294151 tx722340
75rm20⇌28🍴 P Lift ♪ sB42 – 45 sB⇌🍴59 – 72
dB62 – 68 dB⇌🍴77 – 102 (English breakfast) L9 – 21
D9 – 21
🏠 *AVG Verkaufs* Chemnitzerstr 7 ☎722094 P
BL/Jag/Peu/Rov/Tri
W & M Krauss Hauptstätterstr 112 ☎602769
Jag/Peu/Ren Sim (GB)
Paullnen Stotzstr 8 ☎854551 BL/Jag/Rov/Sim/Tri
At **Echterdingen** (11km S)
★★★*Flughafen* ☎790211 tx7245677 128⇌ 🏠 Lift
★★*Graf Zeppelin* Stuttgarterstr 51 (n rest) ☎793433
Closed 21 Dec – 14 Jan 39⇌ 🏠 Pool
At **Möhringen** (7km S on rd 27)
🏠 🖘*Schwaben* Vaihingerstr 131 ☎713005 Frd
At **Schmiden** (9km NE)
🖘*Ceslik* Kanaistr 14 ☎511560 P Jag/Rov/Tri
TEGERNSEE Bayern 4,515 (☎08022) Map **13** A2
★★★*Eybhof* Schwaighofstr 53 ☎3141 Closed
Nov – 15 Dec 25rm14⇌1🍴 🏠 lake
TETTNANG Baden-Württemberg 14,042 (☎07542)
Map **12** C2
★★*Rad* Lindauerstr 2 ☎6001 45rm10⇌6🍴 🏠
TIMMENDORFER STRAND Schleswig-Holstein
10,520 (☎04503) Map **5** B1
★★*Villa Frieda* Höppnerweg 1 (n rest) ☎2304
Closed Oct – Mar 15rm7⇌ Pool
TITISEE Baden-Württemberg 12,008 (☎07651)
Map **11** B2
★★★*Brugger* ☎8239 tx7722332 55rm28⇌7🍴 🏠 P
Lift sB50 – 70 sB⇌🍴45 – 110 dB100 – 140
dB⇌🍴90 – 220 🍜 Pool lake view
★★★*Schwarzwald* Seestr 12 ☎8111 tx7722341
Closed Nov – 19 Dec 94rm82⇌ 🏠 P Lift sB46 – 56
sB⇌🍴56 – 86 dB72 – 92 dB⇌🍴92 – 172
(English breakfast) L21 – 26 🍜 Pool mountains lake
★★*Seehof* (n rest) ☎8314 Closed Nov – 19 Dec
22rm11⇌5🍴 🏠 P Lift sB27 – 30 (room only)
sB⇌🍴38 – 40 (room only) dB54 – 60 (room only)
dB⇌🍴68 – 80 (room only) mountains lake
★★*Waldlust* Neustädterstr 41 ☎8256 Closed Nov &
Dec 42rm23⇌4🍴 A22rm 🏠
☆*Rauchfang* Bärenhofweg 2 ☎8255 15rm6⇌9🍴 🏠
P sB27 – 30 (room only) sB⇌🍴30 – 35 (room only)
dB58 – 72 (room only) dB⇌🍴68 – 80 (room only)
(English breakfast) Pool mountains
★*Seerose* Seestr 21 (n rest) ☎8274 Closed
16 Oct – 19 Dec 20rm2⇌ A9rm
TODTMOOS Baden-Württemberg 2,220 (☎07674)
Map **11** B2
★★*Löwen* Hauptstr 505 Closed 16 Nov –

19 Dec 35rm3⇌14🛏 🏠 P Lift sB22 sB⇌ 🛏26–33
dB42 dB⇌ 🛏50–65 L6–18 D5–18 Pool mountains
TÖLZ (BAD) Bayern 13,019 (☎08041) Map **13** A2
★★★*Jodquellenhof* Ludwigstr 13 ☎891
70rm40⇌4🛏 🏠 Lift Pool
★*Gaissacher Haus* An der Umgehungstr ☎9583
Closed Nov 29rm10⇌13🛏 A10rm 🏠 P sB23–25
sB⇌🛏30–35 dB44–49 dB⇌🛏53–65 L8–17
D8–17 mountains
★*Kolberbräu* Marktstr 29 ☎9158 39rm20⇌ A20rm
🏠 Lift
🍴 *O Fussel* Ludwigstr 31 ☎3351 P
TRABEN-TRARBACH Rheinland-Pfalz 7,012
(☎06541) Map **11** A/B4
★★*Clauss Feist* Moselufer ☎6431 Closed Nov–Feb
24rm9⇌2🛏 A3rm 🏠 P sB28–30 sB⇌🛏33–38
dB46–56 dB⇌🛏60–76 (English breakfast) L12–26
D alc mountains
🍴 ⇖*H-Zündorf* Rissbacherstr ☎9266 Aud/VW (GB)
TRAUNSTEIN Bayern 14,118 (☎0861) Map **13** B2
★★*Parkhotel Traunsteiner Hof* Bahnhofstr 11
☎3623 65rm9⇌30🛏 🏠 P Lift ♪ sB32–37
sB⇌🛏42–46 dB56–73 dB⇌🛏76–83
(English breakfast) L9–18 D8–12
🍴 ⇖*K Schaffler* Wasserburgerstr 64–66 ☎3552
TRAVEMÜNDE Schleswig-Holstein 12,490
(☎04502) Map **5** B4
★★★*Golf* Helldahl 12–13 ☎4041 tx261434 60rm⇌
P Lift ♪ sB⇌55–95 dB⇌90–140 English breakfast
only D alc Pool sea
TREMSBÜTTEL Schleswig-Holstein 1,210
(☎04532) Map **5** B4
★★★*Schloss* ☎6544 19rm12⇌2🛏 🏠 P ♪
sB42–52 sB⇌🛏67–117 dB84–99 dB⇌🛏104–174
(English breakfast) L19–25 D19–24 ⇖
TRENDELBURG Hessen 6,021 (☎05675) Map **5** B2
★★*Burg* ☎1021 tx994812 Closed 11 Nov–24 Dec
21rm7⇌14🛏 P sB⇌🛏46–60 dB⇌🛏82–100 L9 D9
Pool
TRIBERG Baden-Württemberg 7,007 (☎07722)
Map **11** B2
★★★*Parkhotel Wehrle* ☎4081 60rm48⇌8🛏 A24rm
🏠 P ♪ sB34–43 sB⇌🛏50–77 dB65–77
dB⇌🛏97–117 (English breakfast) L20–32 D20–43
St% Pool mountains
TRIER Rheinland-Pfalz 101,043 (☎0651) Map **11** A4
★★★*Dorint Porta Nigra* Porta Nigra pl ☎78161
tx72895 67⇌ 🏠 Lift
★★*Dom* Hauptmarkt 18 (n rest) ☎74710 22rm5🛏 P
sB28–30 sB 🛏35 dB50–55 dB 🛏68
★★*Park Bürgerverein* Viehmarktpl 14 ☎43043
80rm22🛏 🏠 Lift
🍴 ⇖*J Arweiler* am Verteilerring ☎74577 ☎87070
Bed/Opl
C Metzger Im Siebenborn ☎87063 Closed Wknds
AR/BL/Jag/Rov/Sab/Tri
TRITTENHEIM Rheinland-Pfalz 1,504 (☎06507)
Map **11** A4
★*Moselperle* Moselweinstr 67 ☎2221 Closed 16
Dec–9 Jan 13rm6🛏 🏠 P sB20–25 sB⇌🛏25–27
dB35–37 dB⇌🛏44–48 (English breakfast) L8–15
D6–15 Pool mountains
TÜBINGEN Baden-Württemberg 73,633 (☎07122)
Map **12** C3
☆*Stadt Tübingen* Stuttgarterstr 97 ☎31071
39rm5⇌22🛏 🏠 P ♪ sB30–38 sB⇌🛏41–44
dB44–54 dB⇌🛏69–72 L alc D alc
TUTTLINGEN Baden-Württemberg 33,035
(☎07461) Map **12** C2
★*Ritter* Königstr 12 ☎8855 18rm 6🛏 🏠 P sB20
sB⇌🛏25–28 dB40 dB⇌🛏50–56 L11–25 D10–18
ÜBERLINGEN Baden-Württemberg 17,515
(☎07551) Map **12** C2
★★*Bad* Christophstr 2 ☎61055 tx733909
60rm20⇌20🛏 P Lift ♪ sB30–40 sB⇌🛏50–75
dB60–80 dB⇌🛏90–130 (English breakfast)
L12–20 D12–20 Pool mountains lake

★★*St Leonhard* St-Leonhardstr 83 ☎61041
43rm8⇌20🛏 🏠 Lift ⇖ Pool lake
★★*Seegarten* Seepromenade 7 ☎63498 Closed
Dec–Jan 28rm23⇌ 🏠 P Lift sB35–37 sB⇌53–58
dB73–81 dB⇌🛏105–135 (English breakfast)
L12–19 D12–24 mountains lake
UFFENHEIM Bayern 5,116 (☎09842) Map **12** C4
★*Traube* Am Markptl 3 ☎8288 Closed Nov–Dec
17rm 🛏 sB17–18 dB32–34 L8–11 D5–6
ULM Baden-Württemberg 98,314 (☎0731)
Map **12** C3
★★*Bundesbahn* Bahnhofspl ☎65151 tx712871
118rm72⇌16🛏 🏠 P Lift ♪ sB32–41 sB⇌🛏56–69
dB59–71 dB⇌🛏89–122 (English breakfast) L fr12
D fr12
★★*Goldenes Rad* Neuerstr 65 (n rest) ☎62421
22rm3⇌10🛏 P Lift sB30–37 (room only)
sB⇌🛏48–52 (room only) dB48–55 (room only)
dB⇌🛏75–89 (room only)
★*Neutor-Hospiz* Neuer Graben 23 (DP) ☎61191
tx712401 93rm27⇌49🛏 🏠 Lift
★*Münster* Münsterpl 14 (n rest) ☎64162
30rm5⇌10🛏
★*Roter Löwen* ☎64355 Ulmer Gasse 8
30rm5⇌15🛏 🏠 P Lift ♪ sB32–41 dB69
dB⇌🛏76–81 (English breakfast) L14–20 D14–20
★*Schlossbräustüble* Hintere Rebengasse 2
☎63839 Closed Jan–May 20rm
🍴 ⇖*Schwabengarage* Marchtalerstr 23 ☎61121
☎65549 M/c Frd (GB)
ÜRZIG/MOSEL Rheinland-Pfalz 1,400 (☎06532)
Map **11** A4
★*Moselschild* Haupstr 12–14 ☎3001 tx4721542
Closed 11–31 Jan 17rm3⇌13🛏 🏠 P sB39–41
sB⇌🛏46–51 dB61–67 dB⇌🛏83–91 L12–22
D12–22
★*Rotschwänzchen* ☎2183 10rm7🛏 P sB29–33
sB🛏31–43 dB52–57 dB⇌🛏62–70 L10–20 D6–20
mountains
VAIHINGEN See **STUTTGART**
VAIHINGEN AN DER ENZ Baden-Württemberg
22,027 (☎07042) Map **12** C3
★*Post* Franckstr 23 ☎4071 Closed 21 Dec–9 Jan
29rm2⇌9🛏 🏠 P Lift sB22–30 (room only)
sB⇌🛏35–38 (room only) dB45 (room only)
dB⇌🛏52–56 (room only)
VILLINGEN Baden-Württemberg 83,046 (☎07721)
Map **11** B2
★*Ketterer* Brigachstr 1 ☎22095 tx792554
35rm7⇌22🛏 🏠 P Lift ♪ sB37 sB⇌🛏45–51
dB⇌🛏84–96 (English breakfast) L31–51 D13–19
WAHLSCHEID Nordrhein-Westfalen 5,200
(☎02206) Map **4** D1
★★★*Schloss Auel* (1.5km NE) ☎2041 tx887510
23rm4⇌17🛏 P sB49–53 sB⇌🛏44–88 dB78–85
dB⇌🛏86–175 L18–38 D18–38 ⇖ Pool
WALCHENSEE Bayern 650 (☎08858) Map **12** D2
★★*Post* Seestr 52 ☎238 68rm5⇌5🛏 🏠 ⇖ lake
WALLDORF Baden-Württemberg 13,526 (☎06227)
Map **11** B4
☆☆☆*Holiday Inn* Roterstr (1.5km SW near
autobahn exit) ☎62051 tx466009 127⇌ P Lift ♪
sB⇌88 dB⇌118 (English breakfast) L15 D15 ⇖ Pool
★*Vorfelder* Bahnhofstr ☎2085 tx466246
40rm30⇌4🛏 🏠 Lift
WANGEN IM ALLGÄU Baden-Württemberg 23,333
(☎07522) Map **12** C2
★★*Alte Post* Postpl 2 (DP) ☎21019 42rm12⇌4🛏 🏠
★*Taube* Bindstr 47 ☎21338 14rm5🛏 🏠
🍴 ⇖*Dreher* Leutkircherstr 5–9 ☎3019 Opl
WASSERBURG AM INN Bayern 7,014 (☎08071)
Map **13** A2
★★*Fletzinger* Fletzingergasse 1 ☎3876 Closed 16
Dec–5 Jan 31rm14⇌1🛏 🏠 P sB23–26
sB⇌🛏30–35 dB42–51 dB⇌🛏58–68 L6–18
D6–18
WEIDEN IN DER OBERPFALZ Bayern 42,844
(☎0961) Map **13** A4

★★**Schmid** Obere Bachgasse 8 ☎42231 Closed Jun 18rm4⇆5🛏 ♨ P sB24–29 sB⇆ 🍴28–34 dB48–54 dB⇆ 🍴52–60 (English breakfast) D6–12

🛏 ↦**Auto Friedrich** Bahnhofstr 17 ☎44843 ☎44843 & 44806 P BL/Peu

🛏 ♨**Stegmann** Ohmstr 1 ☎43055 Aud/VW (GB)

WEINHEIM AN DER BERGSTRASSE Baden-Württemberg 42,015 (☎06201) Map **11** B4

★★**Fuchs' Sche Mühle** Birkenauer Talstr 10 (2km NE) ☎61031 28rm17⇆5🛏 ♨ P Lift sB35–37 sB⇆ 🍴39–55 dB54–60 dB⇆ 🍴74–80 (English breakfast) L10–24 D10–24

♨**Kellner** Augsburgerstr 48 ☎2638 P BL/Cit

WEISSENBURG IN BAYERN Bayern 16,520 (☎09141) Map **12** D3

WERTHEIM Baden-Württemberg 21,526 (☎09342) Map **12** C4

★★**Schwan** Mainpl 3 ☎1278 Closed 24 Dec–Jan 30rm3⇆17🛏 A25rm ♨ P sB31–37 sB⇆ 🍴41–47 dB58–65 dB⇆ 🍴69–81 (English breakfast) L10–25 D8–25

★**Badischer Hof** by the Tauberbrücke ☎1288 17rm1⇆3🛏 ♨

At Kreuwertheim

★**Herrnwlesen** Herrnwiesen 4 ☎7725 17rm2⇆13🍴 ♨ P sB⇆ 🍴30 dB38 dB⇆ 🍴48–51 mountains

WERTINGEN Bayern 4,218 (☎08272) Map **12** D3

★**Hirsch** Schulstr 7 ☎2083 28rm17🍴 A11rm ♨ P sB18 sB⇆ 🍴24 dB34 dB⇆ 🍴42 L10–14 D4–7

WESEL Nordrhein-Westfalen 60,040 (☎0281) Map **4** D2

★★★**Kaiserhof** F-Etzel pl 1 ☎21972 37rm5⇆16🍴 ♨ Lift

↦**Herzog** Schermbecker Landstr 18–20 ☎5405 ☎(02858) 529 P Frd

WESTERLAND AUF SYLT Schleswig-Holstein 11,111 (☎04651) Map **1** A1

★★★**Stadt Hamburg** Strandstr 2 ☎7058 80rm25⇆39🍴 Lift

WETZLAR Hessen 35,046 (☎06441) Map **5** A1

★★**Eulerhaus** Buderuspl 1 (n rest) ☎43549 31rm12⇆7🍴 P Lift sB28–31 sB⇆ 🍴41 dB53–55 dB⇆ 🍴66–71 (English breakfast)

WIEDENBRÜCK Nordrhein-Westfalen 16,100 (☎05242) Map **5** A2

☆**Wiedenbrück** Gütersloherstr 143 ☎8782 52rm3⇆21🍴 A21rm ♨

WIESBADEN Hessen 253,456 (☎06121) Map **11** B4

★★★★★**Nassauer Hof** Kaiser Friedrichpl 3 ☎39681 tx4186847 160⇆ ♨ P lift ♪ sB⇆95–155 (room only) dB⇆135–195 (room only) (English breakfast) L alc D alc mountains

★★★★★**Schwarzer Bock** Krauzpl 12 ☎3821 tx4186640 170rm114⇆37🍴 ♨ P Lift ♪ sB78–133 sB⇆ 🍴78–133 dB⇆ 🍴127–256 (English breakfast) L25 D30 Pool

★★★**Blum** Wilhelmstr 44 ☎39611 tx4186692 90rm58⇆13🍴 Lift

★★**Central** Bahnhofstr 65 ☎372001 tx4186604 70rm27⇆5🍴 P Lift ♪

★**Oranlen/VCH** Platterstr 2 ☎301058 tx4186217 90rm31⇆54🍴 ♨ P Lift ♪ sB⇆57–61 dB⇆ 🍴92–96 (English breakfast) D14

🛏 **Heine** Mainzerstr 141 ☎79780 AR/Peu (GB)

🛏 **W Rauch** Waldstr 134 ☎86594 Ren

🛏 ♨**Wiesbaden** Stresemannring (nr main rly station) ☎39401 Opl (GB)

At Wiesbaden-Dotzheim

Hell Stegerwaldstr 35 ☎420222 BL (GB)

At Wiesbaden-Sonnenberg

★**Köhler** König Adolfstr 6 ☎540804 12rm P sB fr24 dB fr42 L6–12 D5–13

WILDBAD IM SCHWARZWALD Baden-Württemberg 12,227 (☎07081) Map **11** B3

★★★★**Sommerberg** Heermannsweg 5 (2·5km SW) ☎644 tx724015 100⇆ ♨ Lift ✦ Pool

WILDUNGEN (BAD) Hessen 16,723 (☎05621) Map **5** B2

★★★**Staatliches Badehotel** Dr-Marcstr ☎4061 tx994612 59rm6⇆35🍴 ♨ Lift Pool ₺

WILHELMSHAVEN Niedersachsen 107,051 (☎04421) Map **5** A4

★★**Loheyde** Ebertstr 104 (n rest) ☎43048 80rm11⇆11🍴 ♨ P ♪ sB27–32 sB⇆ 🍴41–55 dB57–59 dB⇆ 🍴70–92

A Hillmann Rheinstr 202, Banter Weg 5–7 ☎26474 M/c P (GB)

↦**R Reuter** Bismarckstr 231 ☎26171 ☎26171 M/c P BL/Hon

WIMPFEN (BAD) Baden-Württemberg 6,009 (☎07063) Map **12** C3

★★**Weinmann** Marktpl 3 ☎8582 Closed Dec–1 Mar 20rm4⇆6🍴 ♨

WINTERBERG Nordrhein-Westfalen (☎02981) Map **5** A2

At Winterberg-Hoheleye (10km SW)

★**Hochsauerland** ☎313 tx875629 90rm60⇆30🍴 ♨ P Lift sB⇆ 🍴49–69 dB⇆ 🍴76–109 (English breakfast) L8–26 D8–26 Pool mountains

WOLFACH Baden-Württemberg 6,511 (☎07834) Map **11** B3

★★**Krone** Marktpl 33 ☎350 23rm5⇆9🍴 A9rm ♨ P Lift sB33–35 sB⇆ 🍴37–41 dB61–65 dB⇆ 🍴71–85 (English breakfast) L15–20 D15–30 mountains

★**Hecht** Hauptstr 51 ☎538 20rm4⇆ A10rm ♨ P sB25–28 sB⇆ 🍴30–32 dB55–57 dB⇆ 🍴60–64 (English breakfast) L10–12 D12–18 mountains

WOLFENBÜTTEL Niedersachsen 54,034 (☎05331) Map **5** B3

★**Stadtschenke** Grosse Kirchstr 9 ☎2359 26rm3⇆3🍴 P sB25–31 sB⇆ 🍴29–37 dB50–57 dB⇆ 🍴58–62 (English breakfast) L7–15 D7–15 St%

🛏 ♨**M Horter** Adersheimerstr 62–64 ☎43046 P Frd

WOLFRATSHAUSEN Bayern 11,022 (☎08171) Map **12** A2

★★**Haderbräu** Untermarkt 17 ☎1315 28rm2⇆1🍴 ♨

WORMS Rheinland-Pfalz 77,044 (☎06241) Map **11** B4

★**Dom** Obermarkt 10 ☎6277 tx467846 56rm17⇆36🍴 P Lift ♪ sB⇆ 🍴42–59 dB75 dB⇆ 🍴88–101 (English breakfast) L7–30 D7–30

★**Central** Kämmererstr 5 (n rest) ☎4718 25rm3⇆6🍴 ♨ Lift

🛏 ♨**Auto-Betriebe Berkenkamp** Speyererstr 88 ☎6343 P Frd (GB)

🛏 ♨**E K WIll** Karolingerstr 1–3 ☎23332 P BL/BMW (GB)

WUPPERTAL-BARMEN Nordrhein-Westfalen (☎0202) Map **4** D2

🛏 ♨**H Wilke** Stennert 8 ☎666517 P BL/Rov/Tri

WUPPERTAL-ELBERFELD Nordrhein-Westfalen (☎0202) Map **4** D2

★★★★**Kaiserhof** (n rest) Doppersberg 50 ☎450516 tx8591405 84⇆ Lift

★★**Post** Poststr 4 ☎450131 Closed 25 Dec–1 Jan 52rm3⇆39🍴 P Lift ♪ sB37–39 sB⇆ 🍴47–49 dB58 dB⇆ 🍴75 (English breakfast)

★★**Rathaus** Wilhelmstr 7 ☎450148 30rm6⇆24🍴 ♨ Lift

WUPPERTAL-LANGERFELD Nordrhein-Westfalen (☎0202) Map **4** D2

★**Neuenhof** Schwelmerstr 246 ☎602536 18rm7⇆2🍴 ♨

WÜRZBURG Bayern 112,454 (☎0931) Map **12** C4

★★★**Excelsior** Haugerring 2–3 ☎50484 54rm37⇆ ♨ P Lift ♪ sB31–41 sB⇆51–56 dB62–72 dB⇆86–96 (English breakfast) L alc D alc

★★★**Rebstock** Neubaustr 7 ☎50075 tx68684 81rm30⇆50🍴 P Lift ♪ sB⇆ 🍴53–82 dB⇆ 🍴96–125 (English breakfast) L16alc D alc

★★**Central** Koellikerstr 1 (n rest) ☎56952 21rm9🍴 ♨ Lift ♪ sB33 sB🍴40 dB62 dB🍴70–80

★★**Franziskaner** Franziskanerpl 2 ☎50360

47rm4⇌19🛏 P Lift ♪ sB30 sB⇌🛏 42–45dB48
dB⇌🛏60–75 L4–19
★★**Walfisch** am Pleidenturm 5 ☎50055
44rm11⇌22🛏 P Lift ♪ sB30–34 (room only)
sB⇌🛏40–46 (room only) dB55–60 (room only)
dB⇌🛏65–85 (room only) L10–19 alc D10–19 alc
🛢 **W Heinsen** Mainaustr 45, Mergentheimerstr 31
☎42046 Frd
🛢 **Auto-Körber** Sanderstr 31 ☎54646 Aud/VW (GB)
At **Lengfeld**
🛢 ♨**Stoy** Industrierstr ☎27646 P Chy/Sim (GB)
ZELL AN DER MOSEL Rheinland-Pfalz 5,515
(☎06542) Map **11** B4
★★**Schloss** ☎4084 Closed 16 Dec–14 Jan
11rm2⇌7🛏 P sB47–77 sB⇌🛏57–82 dB94–104
dB⇌🛏94–164 L50–70 D25–35
★**Marienburg** ☎2382 Closed 16 Nov–Feb
11rm1⇌5🛏 P sB fr30 sB⇌🛏 fr33 dB fr54

dB⇌🛏 fr64 L9–17 D9–17 mountains lake
ZUSMARSHAUSEN Bayern 2,213 (☎08291)
Map **12** D3
★★**Post** Augsbergerstr ☎302 Closed 29–31 Oct
30rm6⇌7🛏 🏠 P sB fr25 sB⇌🛏35 dB48–56
dB⇌🛏61–70 (English breakfast) L6–18 D6–18
Pool
ZWEIBRÜCKEN Rheinland-Pfalz 38,439 (☎06332)
Map **11** B3
★★**Rosen** Von Rosenstr 2 ☎2837 42rm7⇌17🛏 🏠 P
Lift ♪ sB22–29 (room only) sB⇌🛏31–39 (room
only) dB48 (room only) dB⇌🛏58–60 (room only)
🛢 ♨**Carbon** Zweibrückerstr 4 ☎3570 P Frd (GB)
ZWISCHENAHN (BAD) Niedersachsen 21,829
(☎04403) Map **5** A4
☆**Ferien** am Schlart (on B75 2km E) ☎2005
tx254713 31rm27⇌ P sB fr27 sB⇌42–47
dB⇌73–81 L fr15 D fr12

The historic town hall at Aachen.

IRELAND

Population *Northern 1,536,065; Republic 3,086,000*
Area *Northern 5,452 sq miles; Republic 27,136*
Maps *35 & 36*

General information

Politically, Ireland is divided into two, the Republic which is a sovereign independent state and Northern Ireland which forms part of the United Kingdom. Motoring conditions and regulations in the North are almost the same as in Great Britain and therefore these notes will apply only to the Republic. However some notes concerning the North are included where these are considered necessary.

How to get there

Car-carrying services operate from Britain to both the Republic and the Northern Counties. The services to the Republic are Fishguard to Rosslare; Fishguard to Dun Laoghaire; Holyhead to Dun Laoghaire; Liverpool to Dublin; Pembroke Dock to Rosslare; Pembroke Dock to Cork until May 1979 and thence Swansea to Cork. To the north the services are from Cairnryan to Larne; Stranraer to Larne; Liverpool to Belfast. There are also services to and from France: Le Havre and Cherbourg to Rosslare and Roscoff to Cork.

Accommodation   There is excellent accommodation of all types available from first-class luxury hotels to modest but comfortable inns. Boarding house and self-catering accommodation is widely available and fuller information can be obtained from the AA or from the Irish Tourist Board. In the gazetteer for Ireland, hotels are denoted by star classification (as in Great Britain) in either black, white or red. The AA's full-time, highly qualified team of inspectors regularly visit all listed establishments in Ireland.

Annual events   During the summer there are many open-air carnivals and festivals but one of Ireland's justifiable claims to world-wide fame is its horse breeding which leads to magnificent racing events. The track at Curragh in County Kildare is the scene of classic events between May and September. During the winter there is a busy steeplechasing and hurdling calendar with meetings at Leopardstown, Naas, Limerick, Mallow etc. The Dublin Horse Show, held during the first week in August, is the principal event of international interest. During early May, also in Dublin, is the Royal Dublin Society's Spring Show, whilst in July the Irish Open Tennis Championships is another Dublin attraction. In September the Irish Open Amateur Golf Championships are held in County Sligo.

The Irish Tourist Board will be pleased to supply a full list of events with details of dates and venues.

Breakdowns   The AA's Breakdown Service is available to members on terms similar to those in Britain. Patrols operate throughout the country and their services are complemented by garages. The service can be obtained from the following centres:

Location	Hours of Service	Telephone number
Belfast	08.00 – 01.00	Belfast 44538
*Coleraine, Co Londonderry	09.00 – 17.30	Coleraine 2596
Cork, Co Cork	08.00 – mdnt Mon – Sat 09.00 – mdnt Sun and Bank Holidays	(021) 55155
*Craigavon, Co Armagh	09.00 – 17.30	(0762) 41576
Dublin	08.00 – 01.00 Mon – Sat 09.00 – 01.00 Sun and Bank Holidays	(01) 779481
**Dundalk, Co Louth	09.00 – 17.30	(042) 32955
Galway, Co Galway	09.00 – 17.30	(091) 64438
Limerick, Co Limerick	09.00 – 17.30	(061) 48241
*Londonderry, Co Londonderry	09.00 – 17.30	Londonderry 43467
**Port Laoise, Co Leix	09.00 – 17.30	(0502) 21692
**Sligo, Co Sligo	09.00 – 17.30	(071) 5065
Waterford, Co Waterford	09.00 – 17.30	(051) 3765

*If no reply, ring Belfast 44538
**If no reply, ring Dublin 779481

Cats and Dogs   The importation of cats and dogs from Great Britain is not subject to any quarantine restrictions but the carrying of a certificate of good health is recommended. However, should any notifiable animal disease reach epidemic proportions these regulations may be temporarily changed.

Currency and banking   At the time of going to press some doubt exists concerning the position of the Republic and the UK in respect of entry to the proposed European Monetary System. You should approach your bank for current information.

Banking hours   In the Republic, banks open between 10.00 – 12.30hrs and 13.30 – 15.00hrs Monday to Friday. In Dublin late opening is on Thursday until 17.00hrs. Banks in other parts of the country have one evening during the week late opening until 17.00hrs but this varies from town to town.

Customs   The Republic is a separate Customs territory and the visitor will encounter a Customs barrier upon entry and when crossing the Northern Ireland land frontier only at approved crossings. It is prohibited to import tins or otherwise, any meat or poultry, meat or poultry products or milk or milk products. Any such commodities found will be confiscated and the owner may become liable to penalties.

Documents   Residents of the Republic of Ireland, Northern Ireland and Great Britain using private cars or motor cycles may cross the borders with the minimum of formality. There is inter-availability of driving licences for motorists on a

Ireland

temporary stay, but visitors to the Republic of Ireland should have full licences, not provisionals. Under EEC regulations, private motor insurers will provide the minimum legal cover required in all EEC countries, however, insurers may require prior notification of travel. It is necessary to carry the vehicle registration book, a full driving licence and insurance certificate. GB-registered vehicles should be fitted with a nationality plate. If your vehicle has more than nine seats (including the driver) then certain conditions apply as to the driver's age, qualifications and controlled driving hours. Full information is available from Traffic Area Offices of the Department of the Environment.

Ferries
Ferries in Northern Ireland and the Republic of Ireland are listed below. The information given is correct at the time of going to press; however, more details are available from the operating companies. At Christmas and Bank Holidays, services may be altered. Space cannot be reserved in advance and journeys are undertaken at vehicle owner's risk. Charges shown are for single journeys and are liable to increase without notice.

Killimer–Tarbert
Shannon Car Ferry Ltd
Kilrush, Co Clare
☎Kilrush 60

Services from Killimer every hour on the half hour: weekdays 08.30 – 21.30hrs; Sundays 09.30 – 21.30hrs.
Services from Tarbert every hour on the hour: weekdays 09.00 – 22.00hrs; Sundays 10.00 – 22.00hrs.
Car spaces 30
Charges (including passengers)

	Single	Return
Car	£2.50	£3.50
Caravan	£2.00	£3.00
Passenger on foot	50p	75p

Strangford/Portaferry
Ferry Superintendent
Strangford, Co Down
☎Strangford 637

Service Frequent service (every 30mins or less): weekdays 07.30 – 22.30hrs; Saturdays 08.00 – 23.30hrs; Sundays 09.30 – 22.30hrs.
Car spaces 23
Charges

Car	35p
3-wheeler	20p
Motorcycle	20p
Motor caravan	75p
2-wheel trailer	20p
4-wheel trailer	50p
Passenger	5p

Garages
Only those garages shown with the appropriate breakdown symbol have agreed to provide free breakdown service to members. The AA does not undertake to reimburse in full the charges made by other garages. The following symbols apply particularly to garages in Ireland:

◗◗	Free Breakdown Service available 7 days a week until 23.00hrs.
◗	Free Breakdown Service available Monday – Friday during normal working hours (08.00 – 18.00hrs) or until time shown.
R	Repair and servicing facilities during normal working hours or until time shown.

Medical treatment
Under EEC regulations, residents of Great Britain travelling in the Republic may claim free medical treatment although a charge may be made for dental services. Leaflet SA28, available from any office of the Department of Health and Social Security, provides fuller information. The National Health Service operates in Northern Ireland.

Offices of the AA
The AA Regional Headquarters for the Republic is at 23 Suffolk Street, Dublin with a branch office at 9 Bridge Street, Cork. In Northern Ireland there is an AA office at Fanum House, 108/110 Great Victoria Street, Belfast.

Public holidays
On the following holidays in the Republic, banks, offices and principal shops are closed for the whole day:

Fixed	1st January	New Year's Day
	17th March	St Patrick's Day
	First Monday in June	
	First Monday in August	
	Last Monday in October	
	25th December	Christmas
	26th December	Christmas
Moveable	Good Friday	
	Easter Monday	

May Day will also be a public holiday but a regular date has not yet been proclaimed. It will likely be during the first week in May.

Roads   The road numbering system in the Republic of Ireland has recently been changed and a new type of direction sign is gradually being brought into use. Roads are divided into four main categories. These are National Primary, National Secondary, Regional and County. The National Primary roads have the prefix N and a number between 1 and 25. Nearly all of these were in the former T (trunk) category. National Secondary roads also have a prefix N but a number above 50. Most of these were in the former L (link) category. Arrangements for Regional (prefix R) and County roads (prefix C) have yet to be finalised.

Tourist information   The Irish Tourist Authority maintains offices in Britain at 150 New Bond Street, London W1Y 0AQ, 19 Dixon Street, St Enoch Square, Glasgow G1 4AJ and 28 Cross Street, Manchester M2 3NH. They offer full information on tourist matters and visitors intending to visit the Republic are advised to contact them.

Motoring regulations

The main differences in motoring regulations between Great Britain and the Republic relate to speed limits and the use of warning triangles. In built-up areas private cars are subject to a limit of 30mph (48kph): outside built-up areas the limit is 60mph (96kph) on all roads not subject to a lower limit which will be indicated by road signs. Vehicles towing a trailer/caravan are limited to 35mph (56kph).

Private cars are not required to use a warning triangle but commercial vehicles exceeding 1½ tons (1,524kg) unladen weight must carry a red reflectorised triangle at all times and use it to give advance warning to other traffic when the vehicle is stopped due to breakdown or parked without lights.

Fermanagh viewed from Knockninney.

For ease of reference bed and breakfast (B & B) prices are shown by a system of price-banding, details of which follow.

The price-banding system indicates the range within each hotel's lowest charge for bed and breakfast (per single room, including VAT and service charge where applicable) is likely to fall. Note that where a hotel's prices are already close to the top of a band, the next higher band has also been given. If in doubt, always check with the hotel concerned before making your booking.

Price-band	Charges	Price-band	Charges
a	up to £5	d	£10 to £15
b	£5 to £7	e	£15 to £20
c	£7 to £10	f	over £20

We would point out that in this section the Red Star and Country house classifications differ from others used in the book:

Country house ♨ Hotels which display the characteristics of a traditional Country house, set in rural surroundings.

Red Star (Red) Hotels that are of outstanding merit within the normal star rating.

RS Restricted Service available on either accommodation or meals or both.

ABBEYFEALE Co Limmerick 1,337 Map 36 R12
★**Leen's** ☎(068)31121 Closed 25–31 Dec 15rm2⇆ 🏧 B&B(b)
ABBEYLEIX Co Laois 1,033 Map 36 S48 (19m W of Carlow)
⁑*Abbeyleix Motor Works* ☎(0502)31226
ACHILL ISLAND Co Mayo Map 35 F70
★**Achill Head** Keel ☎Keel 31 Closed Sep–May 24rm4⇆ 🏧 ♪ 100P ⚓ B&B(b)
★**McDowell's** Dugort ☎Dugort5 Closed 16 Sep–Apr 10rm2♨ B&B(b)
AHERLOW Co Tipperary Map 36 R83
★★★**Aherlow House** ☎Tipperary56153 Closed 24–25 Dec 9⇆ 🏧 A2rm 300P
ANTRIM Co Antrim 7,320 Map 35 J18
⁑*Hugh Tipping Mtrs* Ronaldstown Rd ☎2225 R
AN UAIMH Co Meath see NAVAN
ARDARA Co Donegal 683 Map 35 G79
★**Nesbitt Arms** ☎3 Closed Xmas 30rm B&B(b)
ARDEE Co Louth 3,096 Map 35 N99
★**Brophy's** ☎53331 Closed Xmas 10rm 2P ♨2 B&B(b)
ARDMORE Co Waterford 233 Map 36 X17
★★**Cliff House** ☎(024)41106 Closed Oct–23 Mar 21rm 30P B&B(c)(d)
ARKLOW Co Wicklow 6,984 Map 36 T27
★★**Arklow Bay** ☎2289 30rm 19⇆ 🏧 ♪ 60P B&B(c)
ARMAGH Co Armagh 12,297 Map 35 H84
⁑*Joshua White Ltd* College St ☎522467 R BL
ATHLONE Co Westmeath 11,611 Map 35 N04
★★**Royal** ☎2924 47rm19⇆ 🏧 Lift ♪ B&B(c)
⁑20.00 hrs *Bigley's* Cornafulla ☎(0902)37103 ⛽
AUGHNACLOY Co Tyrone 732 Map 35 H65 (18m NW of Armagh)
Watson & Hadden 138/144 Moore St ☎281 ☎220 R19.00 Toy
BAILIEBOROUGH Co Cavan 1,293 Map 35 N69
★★**Bailie** ☎34 Closed Xmas Day 20rm4⇆ 🏧 10P B&B(b)
BALLINA Co Mayo 6,369 Map 35 G21
★★★**Downhill** ☎21033 Closed 20–27 Dec 50rm25⇆ 🏧 ♪ 200P Pool B&B(c)
⁑24hrs *McAndrew Motors* ☎(096)21444 ⛽ Aud/Maz/VW
BALLINASCARTY Co Cork Map 36 44
★★★**Ardnavaha House** ☎(023) 49135 Closed Nov–Mar 24⇆ 🏧 24P ⚓ Pool
BALLINASLOE Co Galway 5,969 Map 35 M83
★★★**Hayden's** Dunloe St ☎(0905)2347 Closed 3 days Xmas 56rm 30⇆ 🏧 Lift ♪ 150P B&B(b)(c)
BALLINROBE Co Mayo 1,272 Map 35 M16
★**Lakelands** ☎20 18rm5⇆ 🏧
BALLINSKELLIGS Co Kerry Map 36 V46
★**Sigerson Arms** ☎4 RS 0ct–Apr 10rm ♪ 40P B&B(b)
BALLINSPITTAL Co Cork Map 36 W54 (7m SW of Kinsale)

⁑⁑**O'Regan's** ☎(021)73120 ⛽
BALLYBRITTAS Co Laois Map 36 N50 (8m NE of Port Laoise)
⁑22.00hrs *O'Reilly's* ☎(0502)26138 ☎(0502)26103 ⛽
BALLYBUNION Co Kerry 1,287 Map 36 Q84
★★**Marine** ☎(068)27139 Closed Oct–Apr RS May–Whit 21rm ♪ 50P 12♨ B&B(d)
BALLYCASTLE Co Antrim 2,895 Map 35 D14
⁑*JW McCaughan & Sons Ltd* Market St ☎62517 R BL
Starrs Colraine Rd ☎62460
BALLYCOTTON Co Cork 389 Map 36 W96 (20m SW of Youghal)
★★**Bay View** ☎(021)62746 20rm5⇆ 🏧 20P 4♨ B&B(a)(b)
BALLYDUFF Co Waterford Map 36 W99
★★**Blackwater Lodge** ☎35 Closed 2 Oct–29 Jan 10rm9⇆ 🏧 50P ♨1 B&B(c)
BALLYGALLY Co Antrim 487 Map 35 D30
★★★**Ballygally Castle** 274 Coast Rd ☎212 30⇆ 🏧 200P ⚓
★★**Coastway** Antrim Coast Rd ☎265 13rm4⇆ 🏧
BALLYGAR Co Galway 359 Map 35 M75 (10M SW of Roscommon)
⁑19.00hrs *Flynn Bros* ☎(0903)4583
BALLYGAWLEY Co Tyrone 572 Map 35 H65 (18m NW of Armagh)
J Loughran & Sons Ltd Main St ☎225 R VW
BALLYHAUNIS Co Mayo 1,093 Map 35 M47
★**Central** ☎30 16rm20P B&B(b)
⁑18.30hrs *BT Lynch* Main St ☎15 ⛽
BALLYJAMESDUFF Co Cavan 673 Map 35 N59
★**Percy French Arms** ☎24 Closed 22–31 Dec 12rm3⇆ 🏧 B&B(b)
BALLYLICKEY Co Cork Map 36 W05
★★★(Red) ♨ **Ballylickey House** ☎Bantry71 Closed Dec & Jan RS Oct–Nov & Feb–Mar 25⇆ 🏧 30P Pool B&B(d)
★★(Red) ♨**Sea View** ☎Bantry73 Closed 15 Oct–Mar 11rm4⇆ 🏧 A5rm 20P B&B(b)
BALLYMENA Co Antrim 16,487 Map 35 D10
★★★**Adair Arms** Ballymoney Rd ☎3674 28rm20⇆ 🏧 160P B&B(d)
⁑*General Mtr Wks Ltd* 197 Ballymoney Rd ☎2171 Rov/Tri/Vau
⁑⁑*R McMillan* 56 Balee West ☎3747 R24 ⛽
⁑*JJ Smith* Waveney Av ☎3557 R BL
BALLYMONEY Co Antrim 3,757 Map 35 C92
R Kennedy & Son 23 Ballymena Rd ☎3388 ☎3377 R Frd
JB McAteer & Son Queen St ☎2221 R
John McElderry (Motor Tractors) Victoria St ☎63324 R BL
Jack McLauglin Cafe Lane ☎3182 R
BALLYMORE EUSTACE Co Wicklow 433 Map 36 N91

★★**Ardenode** ☎(045)64198 Closed Sep–May 10rm4⇌ 🍴 120P B&B(**b**)(**c**)

BALLYMOTE Co Sligo 952 Map **35** G61
🏍19.00hrs *Alex Gilmore* ☎Ballymote 3343 🎔

BALLYNAHINCH Co Down 3,485 Map **35** J35 (10m S of Belfast)
🏍 *JF Walsh* 12 Downpatrick Rd ☎2958 **R**18.00hrs

BALLYSADARE Co Sligo Map **35** G62
🏍 *Park's* ☎(071)71291 🎔 Aud/Maz/VW

BALLYSHANNON Co Donegal 2,325 Map **35** G86
★**Dorrian's Imperial** ☎(072)65147 17rm12⇌ 🍴 10P B&B(**a**)
🏍 *Flood Mtrs* ☎(072)65131 Frd

BALLYVAUGHAN Co Clare Map **36** M20
★★(Red) **Gregan's Castle** ☎5 15rm10⇌ 🍴 50P B&B(**d**)
★★**Hyland's** ☎37 Closed Dec–Etr 12rm8⇌ 🍴 50P B&B(**c**)🌥

BALTIMORE Co Cork 200 Map **36** W02
★★**Baltimore House** ☎27 Closed mid Oct–Etr 15rm2⇌ 🍴26P B&B(**b**)

BANBRIDGE Co Down 6,864 Map **35** J14
JJ Henderson Scarva Rd ☎22655 ☎23307 Chy
🏍 *Wright & Co Ltd* 27 Dromore St ☎23641 ☎22377/2367 **R** Frd

BANDON Co Cork Map **36** W45 (20m SW of Cork)
🏍 *Star* ☎(023) 41514 🎔 Fia/Lnc

BANGOR Co Down 35,178 Map **35** J48
★★★**Royal** ☎3866 Closed Xmas Day 32⇌🍴 ♪ B&B(**d**)
★★**Winston** 19–23 Queens Pde ☎4575 30rm13 🍴 🍴 6P B&B(**d**)
Ballyrobert S/sta 402 Belfast Rd ☎Helensbay 2262 **R** Vau
🏍 *Charles Hurst (Mtrs) Ltd* 71/79 Newtownards Rd ☎4312 ☎Groomsport 288 BL/Rov/Tri
🏍 *Gael Mtrs Ltd* 62 Groomsport Rd ☎4211 **R** Frd
🏍 *PW Gethin & Sons* 118 Main St ☎65235 ☎63773 **R** 🎔 Dat
🏍 *JR Pringle* 33A Central Av ☎65623 **R**
🏍 *SC Taylor Ltd* 2 Ballyholme Rd ☎5307 **R**

BANGOR-ERRIS Co Mayo 165 Map **35** F82 (27m W of Ballina)
🏍 *Erris Motors* ☎3 🎔 Frd

BANTRY Co Cork 2,579 Map **36** V94
★★★**Westlodge** ☎360 60⇌🍴 ♪ 400P 🏠 Pool 🌥 B&b(**d**)
🏍 *Hurley Bros* ☎92 🎔 Ren
🏍 *O'Leary's* ☎127 Opl/Toy

BELFAST 358,991 Map **35** J367

Fanum House 108–110 Great Victoria St Belfast BT2 7AT ☎26242

☆☆☆☆**Belfast Europa** Great Victoria St ☎45161 tx74491 200⇌🍴 Lift ♪ 60P B&B(**e**)
★★**Bishopscourt** 149 Upper Newtownards Rd ☎658579 15rm3⇌🍴 ♪ 30P B&B(**c**)
🏍 *WH Alexander Ltd* 62–64 Great Victoria St ☎28424 ☎669491 🎔 BL
🏍 *AS Baird Ltd* Ormeau Rd ☎642972 **R** Chy
🏍 *Connsbrook F/sta* 125 Connsbrook Av ☎65300 **R**23.00hrs 🎔
🏍 *Dalys* 249–255 Falls Rd ☎26037 **R** Dat
🏍 *Dick & Co Ltd* 112 Donegal St ☎28551 **R** Fia Gowan 133 Lisburn Rd ☎661911 **R** Peu
Hills Engineering Wks Holywood Rd ☎656241 **R** Maz
🏍 *Charles Hurst Ltd* 10 Adelaide St ☎305566 **R** BL/Jag/Rov/Tri
🏍 *McLean & Bryce Ltd* Prince Regent Rd ☎51111 ☎Comber872670 🎔 BL
Loughside S/sta 809 Shore Rd ☎76951 **R**
🏍 *Maguires* 534 Falls Rd ☎613141 **R** 🎔 BL
🏍 *Orchard S/sta* 214 Holywood Rd ☎655149 ☎644683 **R** Chy
WJ McCrum Ltd 38–44 Clifton St ☎23065 **R** Rel
X Stanley Mtr Wks 27 Pakenham St ☎29399 **R** Dat/Vlo

BERAGH Co Tyrone 362 Map **35** H57 (21m SW of Cookstown)
🏍 *JJ Keenan* 51 Cooley Rd ☎317 **R**18.00hrs Chy

BETTYSTOWN Co Meath 1,882 Map **35** O17
★★**Village** ☎(041)127136 10rm4⇌ 🍴 100P B&B(**b**)

BIRR Co Offaly 3,881 Map **35** N00
★★**County Arms** ☎193 24rm2⇌ 🍴 ♪ 300P B&B(**c**)(**d**)
🏍 *A Bridge Ltd* Railway Rd ☎10 Frd
🏍18.30hrs *PL Doalan* ☎6 🎔

BLANCHARDSTOWN Co Dublin Map **35** O03
🏍21.00hrs *Ryan's* ☎(01)383446 🎔

BLESSINGTON Co Wicklow Map **36** N91
★★★**Downshire House** ☎(045)65199 Closed mid Dec–mid Jan 32rm25⇌ 🍴 ♪ 30P 🌥 B&b(**d**)
🏍 *Hughe's* ☎(045)65156

BOARDMILLS Co Down Map **35** J36 (6m E of Lisburn)
Temple S/sta 82 Carryduff ☎Bailliesmill 228 **R**18.00hrs

BORRIS-IN-OSSORY 276 Co Laois Map **36** S28
★**Leix County** ☎26 31⇌🍴 120P B&b(**b**)(**c**)

BORRISOKANE Co Tipperary 769 Map **36** R99 (10m N of Nenagh)
🏍 *Henderson & Bailey* ☎(067)27111

BOYLE Co Roscommon 1,339 Map **35** G80
★*Royal* Bridge St ☎16 23rm2⇌ 🍴 ♪ P
🏍18.15hrs *W Roe & Sons* ☎22 Frd

BRAY Co Wicklow 15,841 Map **36** O21
🏍 *Bray Mtr Eng* Vevay Rd ☎(01)867100 🎔 Peu

BUNDORAN Co Donegal 1,337 Map **35** G85
★*Maghery House* ☎(072)41234 31rm6⇌🍴25P
🏍 *TP O'Connell (Mtrs)* East End ☎(072)41300 🎔 Aud/Maz/MB/VW

BUNRATTY Co Clare Map **36** R46
★★★**Fitzpatrick's Shannon Shamrock Inn** ☎Shannon61177 tx6214 82⇌🍴 ♪ 200P Pool B&B(**e**)

CAHERDANIEL Co Kerry Map **36** V55
★★★**Derrynane** ☎36 Closed 4 Oct–21 Mar 62⇌🍴 ♪ 100P Pool B&B(**d**)

CAHIR Co Tipperary 1,747 Map **36** S02
★★★**Kilcoran Lodge** ☎261 23rm10⇌ 🍴 ♪ 60P 🛇 B&B(**c**)(**d**)
🏍 *Barry's* ☎270 BL

CAHIRCIVEEN Co Kerry 1,547 Map **36** V47
★★**Evan's** O'Connel St ☎10 Closed 10 Oct–Etr 16rm2⇌ 🍴 8🏠 B&B(**b**)

CAMLOUGH Co Down Map **35** J02 (6m W of Newry)
🏍22.30hrs *Charles Doyle Auto Engineers* ☎Bessbrock257 **R**18.00hrs

CAPPAGH Co Tyrone Map **35** H66
★★**Altmore House** ☎Pomeroy636 6rm2⇌ 🍴A1rm 60P B&B(**b**)

CARLOW Co Carlow 10,399 Map **36** S77
★★**Royal** Dublin St ☎(0503)41621 Closed Xmas Day RS 26 & 27 Dec 39rm10⇌ 🍴 ♪ 35P 13🏠 B&B(**c**)
🏍20.00hrs *RF Shirley & Co* ☎(0503) 41683

CARNLOUGH Co Antrim 1,385 Map **35** D21
★★**Londonderry Arms** ☎85255 10rm2⇌🍴 16P B&B(**b**)

CARRAROE Co Galway Map **36** L92
★★**Ostan Cheathru Rua** ☎(091)72105 Closed Xmas 24rm17⇌🍴 ♪ 150P 🔘 B&B(**c**)

CARRICKFERGUS Co Antrim 15,162 Map **35** J48
★★**Coast Road** ☎61021 20rm15⇌🍴 ♪ B&B(**d**)

CARRICKMORE Co Tyronne 398 Map **35** H67 (11m E of Omagh)
🏍 *J McElduff* ☎224 **R**18.00hrs
🏍 *Rockview S/sta* ☎244 **R**18.30hrs 🎔

CARRICK-ON-SHANNON Co Leitrim 1,854 Map **35** M90
★★**Bush** ☎14 tx4394 RS 20–30 Dec 28rm14⇌🍴 ♪ 25P B&B(**b**)(**c**)
★★**County** ☎42 Closed Xmas 20rm4⇌🍴 B&B(**b**)(**c**)
🏍24hrs *Wm Cox & Sons* Main St ☎217 ☎63 🎔

CARRYDUFF Co Down 2,279 Map **35** J36 (6m SE of Belfast)
ꝏ***Jamison of Carryduff Ltd*** 636 Saintfield Rd ☎812204 ☎813314 **R** Frd/Maz
CASHEL Co Galway Map **35** L84
★★★(Red) **Cashel House** ☎9 tx8812 Closed Nov–Feb;23rm20⇌ ⋒ 40PB&B(**c**)(**d**)
★★★**Zetland** ☎8 Closed Nov–Feb 18rm12⇌ ⋒ 20P 6🏠 B&B(**d**)(**e**)
CASHEL Co Tipperary 2,692 Map **36** S04
☆☆**Cashel Kings** ☎(062)61477 40⇌ ⋒ ☽ 300P B&B(**d**)
CASTLEBAR Co Mayo 5,979 Map **35** M19
★★★(Red)**Breaffy House** ☎(094)22033 Closed 20–27 Dec 43⇌ ⋒ ☽ 150P B&B(**d**)
★**Traveller's Friend** ☎(094)21919 Closed Xmas Day 21rm1⇌ ⋒ ☽ 300P B&B(**c**)
★***Welcome Inn*** ☎(094)22054 24rm7⇌ ⋒ 80P
ꝏ***Cathal Duffy*** ☎(094)21541/21905 Aud/Maz/MB/VW
CASTLECAULFIELD Co Tyrone 678 Map **35** H76 (16m NW of Armagh)
ꝏ***Fred Martin*** Ballygawley Rd ☎Donaghmore219 **R** ⚙
CASTLEDAWSON Co Londonderry 1,161 Map **35** H99 (13m NE of Cookstown)
Boyle Bros Magherafelt Rd ☎237 **R** Frd
CASTLEDERG Co Tyrone 1,684 Map **35** H28 (8m W of Newtownstewart)
ꝏ***Sharkeys*** Main St ☎278 **R** Frd
CASTLEDERMOT Co Kildare 583 Map **35** S78 (7m NE of Carlow)
ꝏ***M Hennessy & Sons*** ☎(0503)44114 BL/Daf/Peu
CASTLEFREKE Co Cork Map **36** W33
☆☆***Castlefreke*** ☎(023)48106 Closed Oct–Mar 15⇌ ⋒ 40P ⇝ Pool ∩
CASTLEGREGORY Co Kerry 216 Map **36** Q61
★★**Tralee Bay** ☎(066)39138 Closed Nov RS Dec–Etr 13rm6⇌ ⋒ P B&B(**c**)
CASTLEPOLLARD Co Westmeath 693 Map **35** N47 (13m N of Mullingar)
ꝏ***Doran's*** ☎(044)61145
CASTLEREA Co Roscommon 1,752 Map **35** M68
➡***Lavin's*** ☎96 ⚙
CHARLESTOWN Co Mayo 677 Map **35** G40 (16m N of Ballyhaunis)
ꝏ24hrs **Walsh's Auto Service** ☎16⚙
CLAUDY Co Londonderry 513 Map **35** C50 (10m SE of of Londonderry)
ꝏ***Browne & Day*** Hill Top Gar ☎234 **R**18.00hrs Frd
CLIFDEN Co Galway 790 Map **35** L65
★★★**Alcock & Brown** ☎134 Closed Nov–Etr 20⇌ ⋒ ☽ P ♿ B&B(**c**)
★★**Abbeyglen** ☎33 Closed 13 Oct–Etr 18rm16⇌ ⋒ 30P ⇝ Pool B&B(**c**)
★★***Celtic*** Main St ☎115 Closed Xmas 20⇌ ⋒
CLOGHER Co Tyrone 429 Map **35** H55 (16m S of Omagh)
ꝏ***Armstrong Bros*** Augher Bros ☎661 **R**
ꝏ21.00hrs ***McKenna Bros*** Main St ☎613 ⚙ Frd
CLONAKILTY Co Cork 2,430 Map **35** W34
★**Emmet** ☎(023)43394 11rm5⇌ ⋒ 6P B&B(**b**)(**c**)
ꝏ21.00hrs ***Western*** Western Rd ☎(023)43327 ⚙ BL
CLONES Co Monaghan 2,164 Map **35** H52
★★**Creighton** ☎55 Closed 25 Dec 19⇌ ⋒ 10P B&B(**b**)(**c**)
CLONMEL Co Tipperary 12,291 Map **36** S22
★★★**Clonmel Arms** ☎(052)21233 41rm20⇌ ⋒ Lift ☽ 10P B&B(**c**)
★★★**Minella** ☎(052)22388 40⇌ ⋒ ☽ P ∩ B&B(**d**)
★★***Hearns*** ☎(052)21611 Closed 23–31 Dec 28rm15⇌ ⋒ ☽ 40P
CLOUGHEY Co Down Map **35** J65
★★**Roadhouse** 204–208 Main Rd ☎Portavogie500 10rm4⇌ ⋒ 300P B&B(**c**)
COLERAINE Co Londonderry 14,871 Map **35** C83
☆☆☆**Bohill Auto Inn** Bushmills Rd ☎4406 30rm24⇌ ⋒ 50P B&B(**d**)
★★★**Lodge** Lodge Rd ☎4848 15⇌ ⋒ ☽ 150P B&B(**d**)
ꝏ ***George McAlister*** Glenlearey ☎4704 **R**24hrs ⚙
ꝏ***J W McCaughan & Sons Ltd*** Queen St ☎3449 **R**
ꝏ***T D McFarlane Ltd*** Church St ☎2361 **R** Frd
ꝏ***MacFarlane Mtrs Ltd*** Kingsgate St ☎2718 **R** BL
ꝏ***Strand S/sta*** 5–13 Strand Rd ☎3561/3753 ☎3578 **R**18.00hrs ⚙
COMBER Co Down 5,193 Map **35** J47
ꝏ***Kane of Comber Ltd*** The Square ☎872302 **R** BL/Rov/Tri
ꝏ***Lisbane Services Ltd*** 175 Killinchy Rd ☎396 **R**
CONG Co Mayo 233 Map **35** M15
★***Ryans*** ☎4 17rm 40P
CONVOY Co Donegal 654 Map **35** C20 (14m SE of Letterkenny)
➡***McGlinchey*** ☎36
COOKSTOWN Co Tyrone 6,673 Map **35** H87
ꝏ***Bradford Bros*** Northern Gar, Lissan Rd ☎3667 **R**18.00hrs Vau
ꝏ***T J Hamilton & Co*** 50 Union St ☎62488 **R** Peu/Toy
ꝏ***R A Patrick*** Orritor St ☎63601 **R**
COOTEHILL Co Cavan 1,542 Map **35** H51
★★**White Horse** ☎24 33rm3⇌ ⋒ 50P 8🏠 B&B(**c**)
CORK Co Cork 128,645 Map **36** W67
AA 9 Bridge St ☎(021)55155
★★★**Arbutus Lodge** Montenotte ☎(021)51237 Closed 24–29 Dec 20⇌ ⋒ ☽ 35P B&B(**d**)
★★★ **Jury's** Muskerry Island, Lancaster Quay, Western Rd ☎(021)26651 tx6073 100⇌ ⋒ ☽ 100P B&B(**e**)
★★★**Metropole** McCurtain St ☎(021)51301 Closed Xmas 120rm80⇌ ⋒ ☽ 50🏠 B&B(**d**)
★★★**Silver Springs** Lower Glenmire Rd, Tivoli ☎(021)51231 tx6111 Closed Xmas Day 72⇌ ⋒ Lift ☽ P B&B(**e**)
★★**Glengarriffe** Orchard Rd, Victoria Cross ☎(021)41608 Closed 21 Dec–20 Jan 12rm2⇌ ⋒ ⇝ Pool B&B(**d**)
★★**Moore's** Morrison's Island ☎(021)227361 38rm16⇌ ⋒ ☽ B&B(**c**)(**d**)
ꝏ***W M Canty & Son*** Anglesea St ☎(021)21285
ꝏ***Dennehy's*** Dennehy's Cross ☎(021)42846 ⚙ Frd
ꝏ***Johnson & Perrott*** Emmet Pl ☎(021)23295 ⚙ Peu/Toy/Vau
ꝏ***P J O'Hea & Co*** St Patrick's Quay ☎(021)26657 BL
ꝏ***Pope Bros*** Victoria Cross ☎(021)41851 BL
COSTELLO Co Galway Map **36** L92 (16m SW of Oughterard)
ꝏ19.00hrs ***Walsh's*** ☎(091)72169 Frd
COURTMACSHERRY Co Cork 210 Map **36** W54
★★(Red)**Courtmacsherry** ☎(023)46198 Closed mid Oct–mid Mar 16rm5⇌ ⋒ 50P ∩ B&B(**c**)
COURTOWN HARBOUR Co Wexford 291 Map **36** T15
★★**Bay View** ☎(055)25307 Closed Oct–Mar 20rm3⇌ ⋒ 20P B&B(**b**)(**c**)
★★**Courtown** ☎(055)25108 Closed Nov–Etr 28rm13⇌ ⋒ 30P Pool B&B(**c**)
➡***Doyle's*** Askigarron ☎Ballygarrett23 (Closed Mon) ⚙
CRAIGAVON Co Armagh 55,500 (with Lurgan & Portadown) Map **35** J05
➡***Irish Road Mtrs Ltd*** Highfield Rd ☎42424 ☎33751 ⚙ Frd
CRAWFORDSBURN Co Down 487 Map **35** J49
★★★**Old Inn** ☎Helen's Bay3255 Closed 2nd fortnight Jul 17rm14⇌ ⋒ ☽ 40P B&B(**c**)
CREESLOUGH Co Donegal 269 Map **35** C03 (16m NW of Letterkenny)
ꝏ***Friel Bros*** ☎7 ⚙ Frd
CROSSHAVEN Co Cork 1,222 Map **36** W36
★**Helm** ☎(021)831400 Closed 4 Sep–2 Jun 19rm1⇌ ⋒ ☽ 80P B&B(**b**)
CROSSMAGLEN Co Armagh 1,145 Map **35** H92 (10m NW of Dundalk)
ꝏ22.00hrs ***Donaghy Bros*** Newry St ☎228 **R**18.00hrs ⚙ Frd

CROSSMOLINA Co Mayo 1,077 Map **35** G11 (8m W of Ballina)
⚙️24hrs *Judge's Mtr Works* ☎16 ⬧ BL/Chy/Frd MB/Ren/Vau

DERRYGONNELLY Co Fermanagh 383 Map **35** H15 (10M NW of Enniskillen)
🚗 *Derrygonnelly Autos* Main St ☎217 ⬧ Lad

DERVOCK Co Antrim 600 Map **35** C93 (5m NE of Ballymoney)
⚙️23.00hrs *A Chestnut & Son* Ballymoney Rd ☎387 ☎314 **R**18.00hrs ⬧

DINGLE Co Kerry 1,401 Map **36** Q40
★★★**Sceilig** ☎104 tx6900 Closed Nov–14 Mar 79⇌🍴 150P 𝒟 ⚓ Pool B&B(d)
⚙️*O'Connor's* ☎38 ⬧

DOAGH Co Antrim 611 Map **35** J29 (4m NE of Dunadry)
⚙️*Fortfield Mtrs* Belfast Rd ☎310 ☎215 **R** Toy

DONAGHADEE Co Down 3,687 Map **35** J58
★★**Imperial** The Parade ☎882661 21rm 150P 𝒟 B&B(c)
⚙️*Hightrees* 28 New Rd ☎883363 **R**

DONEGAL Co Donegal 1,725 Map **35** G97
★★★**Central** The Diamond ☎4404 Closed 24–26 Dec 56⇌🍴 Lift 𝒟 B&B(c)(d)
★★**Abbey** ☎14 19rm5⇌🍴 P 𝒟 B&B(c)
⚙️*R E Johnston* ☎39/299 BL

DONEMANA Co Tyrone 610 Map **35** C40 (8m NE of Strabane)
⚙️23.00hrs *J L Cochrane & Son* ☎252 **R** ⬧ Opl

DOUGLAS Co Cork Map **36** W76 (2m SE of Cork)
⚙️*O'Mahony Bros* ☎(021)31861 Ren

DOWNPATRICK Co Down 7,403 Map **35** J44 (17m S of Belfast)
⚙️*Stewarts Mtr Wks Ltd* 23 St Patricks Av ☎2215 **R** BL/Rov/Tri

DROMINEER Co Tipperary Map **36** R88
★★**Sail Inn** ☎Puckane 3 6⇌🍴 60P B&B(c)

DROMORE Co Down 2,303 Map **35** J25 (7m N of Banbridge)
⚙️20.30hrs (17.30hrs Sat) *Dominic McClure* Hillsborough Rd ☎692325 **R**

DROMORE Co Tyrone 703 Map **35** H36 (9m SW of Omagh)
🚗*McGlones* Omagh Rd ☎228 **R**19.00hrs ⬧ Dat

DRUMCONRATH Co Meath Map **35** N89
★★ 🏵️ **Aclare House** ☎(041)54101 Closed 15 Dec–2 Jan RS 15 Oct–14 Dec & 3 Jan–15 Mar 16rm5⇌🍴 100P 11🏠 B&B(b)(c)

DUBLIN Co Dublin 679,748 Map **35** O13
| **AA** 23 Suffolk St, Dublin 2 ☎(01)779481 |
★★★☆(Red)**Shelbourne** St Stephen's Green ☎(01)766471 tx5184 172⇌🍴 60🏠 Lift 𝒟 B&B(f)
★★★★**Burlington** Leeson St ☎(01)785711 tx5517 420rm⇌🍴 P Lift 𝒟 Pool B&B(e)(f)
☆☆☆☆**International Airport** Cloghran ☎(01)379211 Closed Xmas 150⇌🍴 200P 𝒟 B&B(e) ⚓
★★★★**Jury's** Ballsbridge ☎(01)767511 tx5304 320⇌🍴 200P Lift 𝒟 B&B(f)
★★★**Royal Hibernian** Dawson St ☎(01)772991 tx5220 110rm96⇌🍴 Lift 𝒟 B&B(f)
★★★**Ashling** Parkgate St ☎(01)772324 tx5891 Closed 24–26 Dec 43⇌🍴 12🏠 45P 𝒟 B&B(d)
★★★**Green Isle** Crondalkin ☎(01)593406 tx5517 65⇌🍴 250P 𝒟 B&B(d)
★★★**Marine** Sutton ☎(01)322613 tx4858 Closed Xmas 22⇌🍴 Pool 100P B&B(d)
★★★**Montrose** Stillorgan Rd ☎(01)693311 tx5517 179⇌🍴 200P Lift 𝒟 B&B(d)
★★★**Royal Dublin** O'Connell St ☎749351 100⇌🍴 🏠60 Lift 𝒟 B&B(f)
★★★**Skylon** Drumcondra Rd ☎379121 88⇌🍴 20🏠 200P Lift 𝒟 B&B(d)
★★★**Tara Tower** Merrion Rd ☎(01)694666 tx5517 84⇌🍴 100P Lift 𝒟 B&B(d)

★★**Buswell's** 25 Molesworth St ☎(01)764013 tx4858 60⇌🍴 Lift 𝒟 B&B(d)
⚙️*Annamoe* Old Cabra Rd ☎(01)303293 ⬧
⚙️*R W Archer & Co* Sandwith St ☎(01)764131 Frd
⚙️*Autocars Ireland Ltd* Milltown Rd ☎(01)971098 ⬧ Fia
⚙️*Donore* Cork St ☎(01)751768
⚙️*Gorman Bros* 16 Maxwell Rd ☎(01)973338 Peu
⚙️*McCairns Mtrs* Swords Rd, Santry ☎(01)379933 Vau
⚙️*Walden Mtr Co* 173–174 Parnell St ☎(01)747831 Frd

DUNADRY Co Antrim Map **35** J28
★★★★**Dunadry Inn** ☎Templepatrick32474 58⇌🍴 200P 𝒟 B&B(e)

DUNDALK Co Louth 23,816 Map **35** J00
★★★**Ballymascanlon House** ☎(042)71124 Closed Xmas 44rm24⇌🍴 400P 𝒟 ⚓ ⌒ B&B(d)
★★**Fairways** Dublin Rd ☎(042)35425 47rm27⇌🍴 300P 𝒟 B&B(c)
★★★**Imperial** ☎(042)32241 tx4858 50⇌🍴 5🏠 100P Lift 𝒟 B&B(c)
⚙️*Byrne & Maguire* Dublin St ☎(042)34655 Frd
⚙️*Meehan's* Dublin Rd ☎(041)34256 Chy
⚙️*Smith's* ☎(042)34603 ⬧ Ren

DUNDONALD Co Down 7,978 Map **35** J47 (6m E of Belfast)
⚙️*T G Tinsley* 763 Up Newtownwards Rd ☎☎2651 **R** BL

DUNDRUM Co Down 807 Map **35** J44 (4m N of Newcastle)
⚙️20.00hrs *William Graham & Sons* Main St ☎250 **R**20.00hrs ⬧

DUNDRUM Co Tipperary Map **36** R95 (8mNE of Tipperary)
⚙️*Kennedy's* ☎(062)71126

DUNFANAGHY Co Donegal 303 Map **35** C03
★★**Arnold's** ☎7 Closed Jan–22 Mar & 2 Oct–Dec 37rm14⇌🍴 4🏠 55P ⚓ ⌒ B&B(b)
⚙️*Carrig Rua* ☎14 Closed Oct–Etr 9rm 12P

DUNGIVEN Co Londonderry 1,479 Map **35** C61 (19m E of Londonderry)
⚙️*Dunglven Mtrs* Railway Pl ☎245 **R**

DUNGLOE Co Donegal 940 Map **35** B71
★★**Ostan Na Rosann** 𝒟91 48⇌🍴 𝒟 200P Pool B&B(c)(d)
⚙️*24 Greene's* ☎14 ⬧

DUN LAOGHAIRE Co Dublin 98,379 Map **36** 022
★★★**Royal Marine** ☎(01)801911 115rm 100⇌🍴 10🏠 200P Lift 𝒟 ⚓ B&B(d)
★★**Victor** Rochestown Av ☎(01)853555 41⇌🍴 300P Lift 𝒟 ⚓ B&B(c)(d)
★**Abbey** ☎(01)805156 11rm B&B(b)

DUNMORE EAST Co Waterford 656 Map **36** S60
★★**Haven** ☎(051)83150 Closed Nov–Etr 17rm8⇌🍴 40P 𝒟 B&B(c)

DUNMURRY Co Antrim 6,078 Map **35** J26
★★★★**Conway** ☎Belfast612101 tx74281 77⇌🍴 250P Lift 𝒟 Pool B&B(e)

DUNSHAUGHLIN Co Meath 283 Map **35** N95
🚗 *Madden's Garage* ☎(01)259198 ⬧

DURROW Co Laois 596 Map **36** S47
★★**Castle Arms** ☎(0502)36117 14⇌🍴 40P

EDERNY Co Fermanagh Map **35** H26 (3m E of Kesh)
🚗 *John James McElhill* Market St ☎294 ☎Kesh348 **R**18 Lad

EDGEWORTHSTOWN Co Longford 546 Map **35** N27
★**Edgeworth** ☎18 16rm4⇌🍴 6🏠 50P B&B(b)
🚗24hrs *Kane's* ☎Edgeworthstown32 Opl/Sab

ELPHIN Co Roscommon 489 Map **35** M88 (9m SE of Boyle)
⚙️22.00hrs *McNally's* ⬧

ENNIS Co Clare 10,840 Map **36** R37
★★★(Red) **Old Ground** ☎(065)21127 tx8103 63rm61⇌🍴 100P 𝒟 B&B(e)
★★★**Auburn Lodge** ☎(065)21127 tx8103 63rm61⇌🍴 100P 𝒟 B&B(c)
★★★**West Country Inn** ☎(065)21421 50⇌🍴 350P 𝒟

Ireland

🕿22.00hrs *T Shiels & Co Ltd* ☎(065)21323 🔧 Frd
ENNISCORTHY Co Wexford 5,704 Map **36** S94
★**Murphy-Flood's** Town Centre ☎2413 Closed
Xmas Day & Good Fri 22rm5⇌ 🏛 3P B&B(**b**)
ENNISCRONE Co Sligo 582 Map **35** G22
★*Killala Bay* ☎(096)36269 19rm8⇌ 🏛 20P ⅅ
ENNISKILLEN Co Fermanagh 6,553 Map **35** H24
★★★**Kyllyhevlin** ☎(0861)3481 Closed Xmas Day
25rm15⇌ 🏛 30P ⅅ B&B(**c**)
★**Railway** ☎22084 17rm13⇌ 🏛 A6rm B&B(**b**)
🕿23.00hrs *T P Topping & Co Ltd* Dublin Rd ☎3475
☎3311 **R**18.00hrs BL
ENNISTYMON Co Clare 1,013 Map **36** R18
★★**Falls** ☎4 38rm16⇌ 🏛 P ⅋ B&B(**b**)(**c**)
FERMOY Co Cork 4,033 Map **36** W89
🕿 *Patrick O'Connor* MacCurtain St ☎(025)31700
Toy
🕿*O'Sullivan's* MacCurtain St ☎(025)31797
Aud/Maz/VW
FINAGHY Co Antrim 4,919 Map **35** J37 (4m S of
Belfast)
🕿23.00hrs *Finaghy* 87–89 Upper Lisburn Rd
☎Belfast611016/610196 **R**
FINTONA Co Tyrone 1,216 Map **35** H46 (8m S of
Omagh)
🕿23.00hrs *Coulters, Auto Engineers* 12–14 King
St ☎208 **R**18.00hrs
FIVEMILETOWN Co Tyrone 936 Map **35** H44 (17m S
of Omagh)
🚚 *R M Smith & Sons* Clugher Rd ☎238 **R**18.00hrs
🕿 *Wesley Irvine* ☎206/278 **R**18 Chy
FOXFORD Co Mayo 868 Map **35** G20
★★★**Pontoon Bridge** ☎20 Closed 15 Oct–14 Apr
24rm10⇌ 🏛 40P ⅅ B&B(**c**)
🕿22.00hrs *Reape's Auto Service* ☎19 🔧
GALWAY Co Galway 29,375 Map **36** M22
★★★★**Great Southern** Eyre Sq ☎(091)6404 tx8364
125⇌ 🏛 Lift Pool B&B(**e**)
★★★**Ardilaun House** Taylor's Hill ☎(091)65452
Closed Xmas 59rm42⇌ 🏛 100P ⅅ B&B(**e**)
★★★**Corrib Great Southern** ☎(091)65281
117rm115⇌ 🏛 Lift ⅅ B&B(**e**)
☆☆☆**Flannery's** Oranmore Rd ☎(091)6511 tx4404
72⇌ 🏛 200P Lift ⅅ B&B(**d**)
★★★**Odeon** Eyre Sq ☎(091)62041 60rm30⇌ 🏛 30P
Lift ⅅ B&B(**d**)
★★★**Warwick** Salthill ☎(091)64325 50rm30⇌ 🏛
40P ⅅ B&B(**d**)
★★**Anno Santo** Threadneedle Rd, Salthill
☎(091)62879 18rm16⇌ 🏛 9P Lift B&B(**c**)
★★**Galway Ryan** Oranmore Rd ☎(091)63181
tx8349 96⇌ 🏛 90P Lift ⅅ
★★**Skeffington Arms** Eyre Sq ☎(091)63173 Closed
Xmas 22rm13⇌ 🏛 50P ⅅ B&B(**c**)
★**Atlanta** Dominick Sq ☎(091)62241 20rm B&B(**b**)
★**Rockbarton Park** Salthill ☎(091)61717
11rm9⇌ 🏛 20P ⅅ B&B(**c**)
GARRISON Co Fermanagh 119 Map **35** G96 (9m SE
of Ballyshanon)
🚚 *Melvin* (A & S Rasdale) ☎Belleek246 **R**19.00hrs
GARRYVOE Co Cork Map **36** X06
★★**Garryvoe** ☎Cork62718 RS Xmas Day
20rm10⇌ 🏛 100P B&B(**a**)(**b**)
GLENBEIGH Co Kerry 266 Map **36** V69
★★**Falcon Inn** ☎56 17rm 40P ◯ B&B(**b**)
★★**Glenbeigh** ☎4 Closed mid Sep–mid Jun
22rm7⇌ 🏛 40P ⅅ ⅋ ◯
★**Towers** ☎12 Closed mid Oct–mid Nov
21rm4⇌ 🏛 50P ⅅ ◯ B&B(**a**)
🕿21.00hrs *John O'Sullivan* ☎7 Frd
GLENDALOUGH Co Wicklow Map **36** T19
★★**Royal** ☎(0404)5335 Closed mid Oct–mid Mar
34rm10⇌ 🏛 4 20P Lift B&B(**b**)
GLENGARRIFF Co Cork 244 Map **36** V95
★★**Casey's** ☎10 Closed 17 Oct–21 Mar 20rm5⇌ 🏛
20P ⅅ
🚚 *Arbutus* ☎22 🔧

GLOUNTHAUNE Co Cork 432 Map **36** W77
★★**Ashbourne House** ☎(021)821230 Closed Xmas
wk 24⇌ 🏛 A2rm P ⅅ Pool B&B(**d**)
GOREY Co Wexford 3,024 Map **36** T15
🕿*R H Nixon* ☎(055)21285
GORTAHORK Co Donegal Map **35** B93
★★**McFadden's** ☎Falcarragh 17 Closed Oct–15
Mar (except Xmas) 35rm7⇌ 🏛 20P B&B(**b**)
GORTEEN Co Sligo 165 Map **35** G60 (9m W of
Boyle)
🕿24hrs *Sherlock's* ☎25 ☎500
GORTIN Co Tyrone 261 Map **35** H48 (6m E of
Newtonstewart)
🕿21.00hrs *G G Pentland & Sons* Main St ☎201
R18.00hrs
GOUGANE BARRA Co Cork Map **36** W06
★★**Gougane Barra** ☎Ballingeary31 Closed 15
Oct–Mar 21rm13⇌ 🏛 A13rm3⇌ 🏛 35P B&B(**b**)(**c**)
GREYSTONES Co Wicklow 3,292 Map **36** O21
★★★**La Touche** ☎(01)874401 41rm15⇌ 🏛
A12rm4⇌ 🏛 100P ⅅ ⅋ B&B(**c**)(**d**)
HEADFORD Co Galway 673 Map **35** M24
★**Angler's Rest** ☎(093)21528 14rm3⇌ 🏛 50P
HELEN'S BAY Co Down 799 Map **35** J48 (8m NE of
Belfast)
🕿18.30hrs (Sat 13.00hrs) *Marshall Pritchard*
Helen's Bay Gar, Bridge Rd ☎3634 **R**18.30hrs
HILLTOWN Co Down 597 Map **35** J22 (8m E of
Newry)
🚚 *Mathews Mtrs* ☎Rathfriland326 **R**22.00hrs
HOLYWOOD Co Down 7,980 Map **35** J37
★★★★**Culloden** ☎5223 32rm31⇌ 🏛 300P Lift ⅅ ⅋
B&B(**e**)
🚚 *R Henderson* Redburn Sq ☎3795 **R**18.30hrs
🕿 *Leslie Innes* 131 High St ☎3044 **R**21.00hrs
(Sat&Sun 18.00hrs)
🕿*J E Meenely & Son* 69–75 High St ☎3132/5096
R18.00hrs BL
INCHIGEELA Co Cork Map **36** W26
★**Creedon's** ☎12 Closed 25–30 Dec 20rm5⇌ 🏛
20P ⅅ ◯ B&B(**a**)(**b**)
★**Lake** ☎10 10rm2⇌ 🏛 🏛2 10P B&B(**a**)
INNISHANNON Co Cork 190 Map **36** W55 (13m S of
Cork)
★★**Innishannon** ☎(021)75121 RS 1 Nov–6 Apr
10rm8⇌ 🏛 50P B&B(**c**)
IRVINESTOWN Co Fermanagh 1,286 Map **35** H25
★★**Mahons** ☎656 20rm7⇌ 🏛 🏛32 ⅅ B&B(**b**)(**c**)
KANTURK Co Cork 2,063 Map **36** R20 (13m W of
Mallow)
🚚 *Kanturk Mtr Wks* O'Brien St ☎12 🔧 Aud/Maz
MB/VW
KEEL Co Mayo See **ACHILL ISLAND**
KENMARE Co Kerry 903 Map **36** V97
★★★**Kenmare Bay** ☎(064)41300 tx5471 Closed
Jan–14 Mar 50⇌ 🏛 300P B&B(**d**)
★★★**Riversdale** ☎(064)41299 40⇌ 🏛 100P
🕿22.00hrs *Randles Bros* Shelbourne St
☎(064)42355 ☎(064)41230/41330 🔧 BL
KERRYKEEL Co Donegal Map **35** 23 (16m N of
Letterkenny)
🕿*John Ward* ☎3 Dat/Sab
KESH Co Fermanagh 311 Map **35** H16
★★**Lough Erne** Main St ☎275 Closed Xmas Day
11rm 100P B&B(**a**)(**b**)
KILCOCK Co Kildare 827 Map **35** N83 (19m W of
Dublin)
🚚 *Dermot Kelly* ☎(01)287311 ☎(01)287438
KILDARE Co Kildare 3,137 Map **36** N71
🕿19.00hrs *Robert Chapman & Son* ☎(045)21203
BL/BMW/Jag Rov/Vol
KILGARVAN Co Kerry 228 Map **36** W06 (7m E of
Kenmare)
🕿*John Mitchell Car Sales* ☎20
KILKEEL Co Down 2,884 Map **35** J31
★★**Kilmorey Arms** ☎62220 16rm1⇌ 🏛 🏛12 P ⅅ
🕿*D McAtee & Sons* 17–19 Greencastle St ☎62217 **R**

KILKENNY Co Kilkenny 13,306 Map **36** S55
★★★**Newpark** ☎(056)22122 46rm34⇄🖪 200P 🌙
🛏 B&B(**c**)
★★**Rose Hill House** ☎(056)21927 Closed Xmas
12rm 80P B&B(**b**)(**c**)
🏍 **Connolly's** Upr John St ☎(056)21140 Vau
🏍 **Statham (1974)** ☎(056)21016 Frd
KILLALOE Co Clare Map **36** R77
★★**Lakeside** ☎(061)76122 28rm 150P 🌙 Pool
B&B(**c**)
KILLARNEY Co Kerry 7,541 Map **36** V99
★★★★**Dunloe Castle** ☎(064)32118 tx8233 Closed
16 Oct–Apr 140⇄🖪 350P Lift 🌙 🛏 Pool ∩ B&B(**f**)
★★★★**Europe** ☎(064)31900 tx8213 Closed 16
Jan–Feb 175⇄🖪 350P Lift 🌙 Pool ∩ B&B(**f**)
★★★★**Great Southern** ☎(064)31262 tx6998
180⇄🖪 Lift 🌙 🛏 Pool B&B(**e**)
★★★**Aghadoe Heights** ☎(064)31766 tx 6942
Closed 21 Dec–13 Jan 46⇄🖪 300P 🌙 🛏 B&B(**d**)
★★★**Castlerosse** ☎(064)3114 tx4404 Closed Xmas
40⇄🖪 30🏠 50P 🌙 🛏 Pool B&B(**d**)(**e**)
★★★**Torc Great Southern** ☎(064)31611 94⇄🖪
140P 🌙 🛏 Pool B&B(**d**)
★★★**Lake** Mickross Rd ☎(064)31035 Closed Xmas
79rm44⇄🖪 200P 🌙 🛏 B&B(**c**)
★★**Arbutus** ☎(064)31037 Closed Xmas wk
35rm21⇄🖪 P 🌙 B&B(**b**)
★★**Glen Eagle** ☎(064)31870 53rm39⇄🖪 500P 🌙
🛏 B&B(**c**)
★★**Grand** ☎(064)31159 30rm3⇄🖪 🌙 P B&B(**a**)(**b**)
★★**Killarney Ryan** ☎(064)31555 tx6950 Closed 23
Oct–13 Mar 160⇄🖪 150P Lift 🌙
★★**Scotts** College St ☎(064)31060 Closed Dec &
Jan 27rm5⇄🖪 50P B&B(**b**)
🏍22.00hrs **Randles Bros** Muckross Rd
☎(064)31237 ☎(064)31977 BL
KILLINEY Co Dublin Map **36** 022
★★★★**Fitzpatrick's Castle** ☎(01)851535 48⇄🖪
2🏠 400P 🌙 🛏 Pool
★★★**Killiney Court** Station Rd ☎(01)851622 10⇄🖪
300P 🌙 B&B(**d**)
KILLYBEGS 1,094 Co Donegal Map **35** G77
★★★**Killybegs** ☎120 Closed Sep–10 Jun
31rm21⇄🖪 100P 🌙 🛏 B&B(**c**)(**d**)
🏍 **Bay View** ☎78 Closed 23–26 Dec 19rm b&b(**b**)(**c**)
KILLYLEAGH Co Down 2348 Map **35** J55
★**Dunmore** ☎258 RS Feb 10rm1⇄🖪 50P 🌙 B&B(**b**)
🏍 **T M Martin & Son** Dufferin Gar ☎203 R
KILMEADEN Co Waterford Map **36** S50 (8m W of
Waterford)
🏍 **Hennesey's** ☎(051)84129 ☎(051)84167
KILREA Co Londonderry 1,034 Map **35** C91 (15m S
of Coleraine)
🏍 **J T Proctor & Sons** 36-40 Bridge St ☎455/456
R18.00hrs Frd
KILRUSH Co Clare 2,671 Map **36** R05
🏍20.00hrs **Kilrush Mtr Co** ☎48 ⚙
KINAWLEY Co Fermanagh 531 Map **35** H23 (11m S
of Enniskillen)
🏍 **V G Brennan** Rockview Mtrs ☎ Derrylin603
☎ Derrylin314 R19.30hrs
KINGSCOURT Co Cavan 1,016 Map **35** N70
★**Mackin's** ☎18 Closed Xmas 14rm2⇄🖪 B&B(**b**)
KINSALE Co Cork 1,989 Map **36** W65
★★★**Acton's** ☎(021)72135 59rm42⇄🖪 90P Lift 🌙
Pool B&B(**d**)
★★★**Monastery** ☎(021)72624 10⇄🖪 12P B&B(**e**)
KINVARRA Co Galway 293 Map **36** M30
★**Winkles** ☎4 8rm 2🏠 25P
🏍22.00hrs **Patrick O'Loughlin** ☎20 ⚙
KIRCUBBIN Co Down 1,084 Map **35** J66 (8m N of
Portaferry)
🏍 **James Boyd** The Garage, 4 Main St ☎223 R
LAHINCH Co Clare 455 Map **36** R18
★★★**Aberdeen Arms** ☎20 tx6872 Closed 9 Oct–11
Apr 56rm41⇄🖪 50P 🌙 B&B(**c**)
LARNE Co Antrim 22,817 Map **35** D30
★★★**King's Arms** Broadway ☎3322 48rm33⇄🖪
500P Lift 🌙 B&B(**b**)(**c**)

🏍 **Cael Mtrs Ltd** Glynn Rd ☎5411 **R** Frd
🏍 **Harbour Eng Co** 104–106 Curran Rd ☎2071 **R**
BL
LETTERKENNY Co Donegal 5,207 Map **35** C11
★★★**Ballyraine** ☎411 tx33406 56⇄🖪 200P 🌙
B&B(**d**)
★★**Gallagher's** ☎8 20rm4⇄🖪 30P B&B(**a**)
★★**McCarry's** ☎61 16rm 3🏠 14P 🌙 B&B(**b**)
🏍 **Hegarty's Auto Service** ☎256 ⚙ Frd
LIFFORD Co Donegal 1,121 Map **35** H39
★★**Intercounty** ☎153 36rm⇄🖪 300P 🌙 B&B(**c**)
LIMAVADY Co Londonderry 5,555 Map **35** C62
(14m SW of Coleraine)
🏍 **Roe Mtrs Ltd** Catherine St ☎2322
LIMERICK Co Limerick 63,002 Map **36** R55
★★★**Jury's** Ennis Rd ☎(061)47266 tx8266 96⇄🖪
🌙 B&B(**e**)
★★**Hanratty's** Glentworth St ☎(061)43466
43rm29⇄🖪 🌙
★**Limerick Ryan** Ennis Rd ☎(061)45922 tx6920
180⇄🖪 100P Lift 🌙
☆☆**Parkway** Dublin Rd ☎(061)47599 tx6850 Closed
Xmas Day 103⇄🖪 1000P Lift 🌙 B&B(**d**)
★★**Royal George** O'Connell St ☎(061)44566
50⇄🖪 Lift 🌙 ⑂ B&B(**c**)
☆☆**Two Mile Motor Inn** Ennis Rd ☎(061)53122
47⇄🖪 500P 🌙 B&B(**c**)
🏍 **Bedford Mtr Co** Henry St ☎(061)45577 Vau/Vol
🏍 **Gleeson Bros** Ellen St ☎(061)45567 Chy
🏍 **F McNamara Mtrs** St Joseph's St ☎(061)49520
☎(061)53891
🏍 **A White & Co** 4 Shannon St ☎(061)44256
LISBURN Co Antrim 27,405 Map **25** J26
★★★**Woodlands** 3 Belfast Rd ☎2741 29rm18⇄🖪
500P 🌙
🏭 **Marsden Tailored Panels** 17A Chapel Hill ☎6943
☎70368 R (Body repairs only)
🏍 **John McLean & Son Ltd** Hillsboro Rd &
Longstone St ☎3201/4571 **R** BL
🏍 **Stevenson Bros Ltd** Seymour St ☎2214 **R** BL
LISDOONVARNA Co Clare 459 Map **36** R19
★★**Lynch's** ☎10 Closed 7 Oct–8 Jun 23rm 3🏠 10P
🌙 B&B(**b**)
★**Keane's** ☎11 Closed Oct–Mar 12rm5⇄🖪 5P
B&B(**b**)
★**Spa View** ☎26 Closed Oct–Mar RS Apr–Jun
19rm1⇄🖪 🏠2 40P B&B(**b**) 🛏
LISMORE Co Waterford 1,041 Map **36** X09
★★ 🛏 **Ballyrafter House** ☎(058)54002 Closed
Oct–Etr 14rm4⇄🖪 2🏠 20P ∩ B&B(**b**)(**c**)
LISKNASKEA Co Fermanagh 1,443 Map **35** H33
★★**Ortine** Main St ☎206 25rm17⇄🖪 2🏠 150P 🌙
B&B(**b**)(**c**)
LISTOWEL Co Kerry 3,021 Map **36** Q93
★★**Listowel Arms** ☎14 34rm22⇄🖪 Lift B&B(**b**)(**c**)
★**Stack's** Market St ☎(068)53 16rm3⇄🖪 A4rm 30P
🌙 B&B(**b**)
🏍 **Moloney's** Market St ☎(068)21033 Frd
LIXNAW Co Kerry 219 Map **36** Q92 (13m N of Tralee)
🏍20.00hrs **O'Keeffe** ☎(066)32157 ⚙
LONDONDERRY Co Londonderry 51,850
Map **35** C41
★★★★**Everglades** Prehan Rd ☎46722 tx747645
38⇄🖪 150P 🌙 Pool B&B(**d**)(**e**)
🏍 **Desmond Mtrs Ltd** 173 Strand Rd ☎67613
R18.00hrs Frd
🏍 **Chas Hurst Mtrs Ltd** 78 Strand Rd ☎64181/4 **R**
BL/MG/Rov/Tri
🏍 **G Nixon & Sons Ltd** Spencer Rd ☎42732/44760
R
🏍21.00hrs **Stewart & Irwin** 31C Abercorn Rd
☎61956 **R**18.00hrs
LOUGHBRICKLAND Co Down 349 Map **35** J14
(11m SW of Portadown)
🏭 **Frank McGrath** Main St ☎Banbridge2396
R22.00hrs ⚙23.00hrs
LOUISBURGH Co Mayo 310 Map **35** L87 (14m W of
Westport)
🏭24hrs **Harney's Garage** Chapel St ☎5

Ireland

LURGAN Co Armagh 24,055 Map **35** J05
&O*H Wilson & Sons* Portadown Rd ☎2278 ☎2874 **R** Chy

MACROOM Co Cork 2,256 Map **36** W37
★★*Castle* ☎74 20rm3⇌🍽 A11rm2⇌🍽 7🏠
★*Victoria* Main St ☎82 22rm4⇌🍽 10P B&B(**b**)
&O *Kelleher's* Main St ☎29 🍴 Frd

MAGHERA Co Londonderry 2,108 Map **35** C80
&O22.00hrs *Danny Otterson* Fair Hill ☎42651 **R**18.00hrs

MALAHIDE Co Dublin Map **35** 024
★★*Grand* ☎(01)450633 52rm20⇌🍽 🏠8 250P Lift ☽ ∩ B&B(**c**)

MANORHAMILTON Co Leitrim 858 Map **35** G83 (16m E of Sligo)
➥*Thompsons Service Gar* ☎26

MARKETHILL Co Armagh 954 Map **35** H93 (11m NW of Newry)
&O *R S Farson & Sons* Mtr Engineers ☎232 **R**18.00hrs

MILLTOWN Co Kerry 260 Map **36** V89 (4m N of Killorglin)
&O22.00hrs *Riordan's Garage* ☎33 🍴

MILTOWN MALBAY Co Clare 677 Map **36** R07 (7m S of Lahinch)
&O19.00hrs *McCarthy's* ☎29 🍴 BL

MOHILL Co Leitrim 868 Map **35** N09
★*Sportsmans* ☎12 11rm7⇌🍽 8🏠 300P ☽ B&B(**a**)(**b**)

MOIRA Co Down 754 Map **35** J16 (5m NE of Lurgan)
➥*Fernfield S/sta* (Brown Bros) Tummery ☎611266 ☎611389 **R** 🍴
Moira Auto Point Main St ☎611621 **R**

MONAGHAN Co Monaghan 5,256 Map **36** H63
★★★*Hillgrove* ☎(047)81288 30rm21⇌🍽 P ☽ 🍴 B&B(**c**)
&O *D & S Mtrs* North Rd ☎(047)81044 Aud/Maz/MB/VW
&O *Monaghan Mtr Works* Old Cross Square ☎(047)82011 BL

MONASTEREVIN Co Kildare 1619 Map **36** N61 (7m W of Kildare)
&O *Michael A Finlay & Sons* ☎(045)25331 🍴 Fia

MONEYMORE Co Londonderry 1,177 Map **35** H88 (5m N of Cookstown)
&O19.00hrs *Thomas John Boyce* 43 Lawford St ☎257 **R**19.00hrs (Sat18.00hrs)

MOUNTRATH Co Laois 1,098 Map **36** S39 (9m W of Port Laoise)
➥24hrs *Dooley Mtrs* Dublin Rd ☎(0502)32221

MOVILLE Co Donegal 1,089 Map **35** C53
★*Foyle* ☎25 20rm 🏠

MOY Co Tyrone 926 Map **35** H85 (6m SE of Dungannon)
➥*McMullan Bros* 15 – 19 Dungannon St ☎252 **R**19.30hrs

MULLINGAR Co Westmeath 9,245 Map **35** N45 (13m S of Castlepollard)
&O *Castle Mtrs* ☎(044)8263 Frd

NAAS Co Kildare 5,078 Map **36** N81 (12m NE of Kildare)
&O *Smiths* ☎(045)976675 🍴 Ren

NAVAN (An Uaimh) Co Meath 6,665 Map **35** N86
★★★*Ardboyne House* ☎(046)23119 26⇌🍽 200P ☽ B&B(**d**)
&O18.00hrs *Navan Engineering Works Ltd* ☎(046)21129 Frd

NEWCASTLE Co Down 4,621 Map **35** J33
★★ ♨*Enniskeen* ☎(03967)22392 Closed 5 Nov – 28 Feb 13rm7⇌🍽 4🏠 50P ☽ B&B(**b**)

NEWCASTLE WEST Co Limerick 2,680 Map **36** R23
☆☆*River Room Motel* ☎193 15⇌🍽 200P B&B(**c**)
&O *Nash's* ☎3 Frd

NEW INN Co Laois Map **36** N50
★★*Motel Montague* ☎(0502)26154 Closed Xmas 20⇌🍽 250P ☽ B&B(**c**)(**d**)

NEWMARKET-ON-FERGUS Co Clare 1,054 Map **36** R36
★★★★(Red) *Dromoland Castle* ☎(061)71144 Closed Nov – Mar 67⇌🍽 100P ☽ 🍴 & B&B(**f**)

NEWPORT Co Mayo 420 Map **35** L99
★★★ ♨*Newport House* ☎12 Closed Oct – Mar 13⇌🍽 A11rm 40P ☽ B&B(**d**)
➥*Kelly's* ☎3 🍴 BL

NEW ROSS Co Wexford 5,153 Map **36** S72
★★★*Five Counties* ☎(051)21703 36rm29⇌🍽 75P ☽ B&B(**b**)(**c**)
➥*Central* South St ☎(051)21205 BL
➥*O'Connor's* Marsh St ☎(051)21324 ☎(051)21353

NEWRY Co Down 11,393 Map **35** J02
➥*Cars Ltd* 19 Merchants Quay ☎3151 **R** Frd
&O*Hollywood Bros Ltd* Monaghan St ☎2208 **R** Vau/VW
&O21.00hrs *S H McCullogh & Sons* Downshire Rd ☎2144 **R**21.00hrs
&O*McGraths S/sta* Patrick St ☎2857 **R**19.00hrs
➥*Rowland & Harris Ltd* Railway Av ☎2201/2202 **R** BL

NEWTOWN ABBEY Co Antrim 57,936 Map **35** J38
☆☆*Chimney Corner Motel* 630 Antrim Rd ☎44925 48rm47⇌🍽 370P Lift B&B(**d**)
★★ ♨*Abbeylands* Whiteabbey ➥Whiteabbey64552 Cosed Xmas Day 12rm2⇌🍽 A4rm 60P B&B(**b**)(**c**)
★★*Glenavna House* ☎Whiteabbey64461 Closed Xmas RS 11 – 13 Jul 17rm7⇌🍽 60P ☽ B&B(**d**)
&O23.00hrs *Dick & Co Ltd* Glengormley ☎41515 **R** Fia
➥*Twinburn S/sta* 124 Monkstown Rd ☎Whiteabbey63656 ☎Whiteabbey65969 **R**18.00hrs
&O *William James Walker* Glenville Trucks, 151 Glenville Rd ☎Whiteabbey64897 ☎Whiteabbey65950 **R**

NEWTOWNARDS Co Down 15,387 Map **35** J47 (6m S of Bangor)
&O23.00hrs *David R Jeffers* Brae S/sta, Church St ☎3541 ☎3416 **R**18.00hrs

NEWTOWNHAMILTON Co Armagh Map **35** H92 (12m W of Newry)
&O*A Boyle & Co* 28 – 30 Newry St ☎207 **R**18.00hrs Toy

NEWTOWNSTEWART Co Tyrone 1,458 Map **35** H38 (10m N of Omagh)
➥*Wilson & Son* ☎239/489 **R**

OLDCASTLE Co Meath 759 Map **35** N58
★*Naper Arms* ☎124.10rm1⇌🍽 🏠6

OMAGH Co Tyrone 11,953 Map **35** H47
★★★*Knock-Na-Moe Castle* ☎3131 26rm11⇌🍽 100P ☽ B&B(**c**)
★★*Royal Arms* 51 High St ☎3262 28rm4⇌🍽 10🏠 200P ☽ B&B(**b**)
➥*Sean Duncan* 52 Brookmount Rd ☎44161 **R**
➥*Johnston King Mtrs Ltd* Derry Rd ☎2788 ☎2147 **R**18.00hrs VW

OMEATH Co Louth 331 Map **35** J11
★*Park* ☎(042)75115 17rm 200P B&B(**b**)

OUGHTERARD Co Galway 628 Map **35** M14
☆☆*Connemara Gateway Motel* ☎(091)82328 txDublin5818 Closed 20 Oct – 3 Apr 48⇌🍽 75P ☽ Pool B&B(**c**)(**d**)
★★*Egan's Lake* ☎82205 24rm17⇌🍽 20P ☽
★★*Oughterard House* ☎82207 33rm20⇌🍽 🏠4 35P Lift

PARKNASILLA Co Kerry Map **36** V76
★★★★(Red) *Great Southern* ☎Sneem3 60⇌🍽70P 8🏠 Pool & ☽ ∩ B&B(**e**)

PORTADOWN Co Armagh 21,906 Map **35** J05
&O*R Hewitt (Mtrs) Ltd* Church St ☎33286**R** BL/Rov/Tri
&O*Edwin May Ltd* Bridge St ☎32238/9 **R** Vau

PORTAFERRY Co Down 1,592 Map **35** J55
★★*Portaferry* Shore Rd ☎231 11rm

PORTBALLINTRAE Co Antrim 496 Map **35** C94 (5m E of Portrush)

★★**Bay View** ☎Bushmills31453 25rm3⇌ ᵐ 20P
16🏛 B&B**(c)**

★★**Beach** Bushmills ☎Bushmills31214 RS Jan – Etr
28rm14⇌ ᵐA15rm ♪ 100P B&B**(c)**

PORTLAOISE Co Laois 6,740 Map **36** S49

⏍*Cecil Lewis Mtrs* Mountrath Rd ☎(0502)21797
Frd

⏍22.00hrs *Portlaoise S/sta* Dublin Rd
☎(0502)21941 🚗

PORT-NA-BLAGH Co Donegal Map **35** C03

★★★**Port-Na-Blagh** ☎Dunfanaghy11 Closed
Oct – Etr 59rm30⇌ ᵐ Lift ♪ 80P ➤ B&B**(c)**

★★★**Shandon** ☎Dunfanaghy15 Closed mid
Sep – Etr & May 63rm36⇌ ᵐ Lift ♪ 150P ➤ B&B**(c)**

PORTRUSH Co Antrim 4,749 Map **35** C83

★★**Skerryban** Lansdowne Cres ☎822328 Closed
May – Sep RS Oct – Dec & Mar – 8 Apr 39rm10⇌ ᵐ
Lift ♪ P B&B**(b)(c)**

⏍*Glenvale Garages (B Boyd)* Coleraine Rd ☎3702
☎2460 **R** BL

⏍*JS Mtrs* 119 Eglinton St ☎2760 **R**18.00hrs

PORTSTEWART Co Londondery Map **35** C83

★★**Carrig** ☎2016 35rm10⇌ ᵐ S B&B**(c)(d)**

★**Windsor** 8 The Promenade ☎2523 Closed Jan &
Feb 26rm5⇌ ᵐ 9🏛 B&B**(b)(c)**

PORTUMNA Co Galway Map **36** M80

★★★**Westpark** ☎112 30⇌ ᵐ ♪ 200P ➤ B&B**(c)**
⏍*GA Claffev* ☎9 Frd

POYNTZPASS Co Armagh Map **35** J03 (9m N of
Newry)

⏍19.00hrs *Trainor Bros* Automobile Electrical
Engineers ☎219 **R**19.00hrs

RANDALSTOWN Co Antrim 2,462 Map **35** J09 (6m
NW of Armagh)

⏍*Robert Moore & Son* Main St ☎72286 ☎72287 **R**
BL/Rov/Tri

RAPHOE Co Donegal Map **35** C20

★**Central** ☎8 Closed 24 – 30 Dec 10rm 4P 2🏛
B&B**(a)(b)**

RATH LUIRC Co Cork 2,2323 Map **36** R52 (18m N of
Mallow)

⏍*Park Garage* ☎(063)367

⏍21.00hrs *Denis Duffy* ☎62 🚗

RATHCABBAN Co Offaly Map **36** M90 (7m W of Birr)

RATHDRUM Co Wicklow 1,141 Map **36** T18

⏍*Avonmore Service* ☎(0404)6130 Opl

RATHFRILAND Co Down 2,076 Map **35** J13 (10m
NW of Newry)

⏍*T Lylerea & Sons Ltd* Downpatrick St ☎223
R19.00hrs Frd

RATHMULLAN Co Donegal 486 Map **35** C22

★★★(Red)🏨**Rathmullan House** ☎4 Closed
Oct – Etr 21rm9⇌ ᵐ ♪ 80P ➤ B&B**(c)**

★★(Red)🏨**Fort Royal** ☎11 Closed Oct – Etr (except
4 days Xmas) 18rm7⇌ A11rm 50P ➤ ◯ B&B**(c)(d)**

★*Pier* ☎3 Closed Oct – Etr 16rm 50P

RATHNEW Co Wicklow 954 Map **36** T29

★★**Hunter's** ☎(0404)4106 17rm5⇌ ᵐ 40P 8🏛 ➤
B&B**(c)**

RENVYLE Co Galway Map **35** L66

★★★**Renvyle House** ☎3 tx8338 Closed Nov – Etr
74⇌ ᵐ ♪ 150P ♪ 🎿 ➤

RICHILL Co Armagh 658 Map **35** H94 (5m NE of
Armagh)

⏍*JH Hutchison* Ballyleaney Gar ☎871633
☎Portadown 34864 **R**18.00hrs

ROSCOMMON Co Roscommon 2,821 Map **35** M86

★★**Abbey** ☎(0903)6505 10rm2⇌ ᵐ 30P

ROSCREA Co Tipperary 3,855 Map **36** S18

★★**Pathe** ☎241 Closed Xmas Day 23rm8⇌ ᵐ 8P
B&B**(c)**

⏍*New Road Service Gar* ☎70

ROSSCAHILL Co Galway Map **35** M13

★★🏨**Ross Lake** ☎(091)80109 Closed Oct – Apr
13rm3⇌ ᵐ300P ➤ B&B**(c)**

ROSSES POINT Co Sligo 464 Map **35** G64

★★*Yeats Country Ryan* ☎(071)3251 tx6403 Closed

23 Oct – 10 Apr 80⇌ ᵐ ♪ 80P ➤

ROSSLARE Co Wexford 588 Map **36** T01

★★★(Red)**Strand** ☎(053)32114 Closed 16 Dec – 7
Feb 97rm87⇌ ᵐ Lift ♪ 200P Pool ➤ B&B**(c)(d)**

★★**Golf** ☎(063)32179 25rm13⇌ ᵐ 40P ➤ B&B**(c)**

ROSSLARE HARBOUR Co Wexford Map **36** T11

★★★**Great Southern** ☎(053)33233 tx8788 Closed 4
Jan – 9 Mar 100⇌ ᵐ ♪ 200P Pool ➤ B&B**(d)(e)**

ROSSNOWLAGH Co Donegal Map **35** G86

★★★(Red)**Sand House** ☎(072)65343 txDublin4858
Closed 2 Oct – Etr 40rm25⇌ ᵐ 60P ◯ B&B**(c)(d)**

ROSTREVOR Co Down 2,064 Map **35** J11

⏍*JC Campbell (NI) Ltd* 68 Shore Rd ☎391 **R**
BL/Rov/Tri

ROUNDSTONE Co Galway 204 Map **35** L74

★*Seal's Rock* ☎15 Closed Oct – Mar 40rm 40P 4🏛

SALTHILL Co Galway see Galway

SCARIFF Co Clare 619 Map **36** R68

★★**Clare Lakelands** ☎18 Closed Xmas wk 24⇌ ᵐ
♪ 100P ➤ B&B**(c)**

SCHULL Co Cork 457 Map **36** V93 (14m SW of
Bantry)

⏍18.30hrs *Schull Mtr Wks* 🚗

SHILLELAGH Co Wicklow 246 Map **36** S96 (16m
NW of Gorey)

⏍*Shillelagh Mtrs* ☎5 🚗 Fia

SKIBBEREEN Co Cork 2,104 Map **36** W13

⏍*Hurley Bros* ☎103/319 🚗 Fia

⏍24hrs Mon – Sat inc *Southern* ☎22 🚗 Ren

SLANE Co Meath 483 Map **35** N97

★*Conyngham Arms* ☎(041)24155 Closed Xmas
Day 14rm12⇌ ᵐ12P 12🏛 B&B**(c)**

SLIGO Co Sligo 14,456 Map **35** G63

★★★**Sligo Park** ☎(071)3291 tx4397 60⇌ ᵐ ♪ 200P
B&B**(d)**

★★**Silver Swan** Hyde Bridge ☎(071)3231 Closed
Xmas Day 24rm12⇌ ᵐ Lift ♪ 80P B&B**(c)**

⏍*Henderson's Mtrs* Wine St ☎(071)5286 Frd

SNEEM Co Kerry 285 Map **36** V66 (2m N of
Parknasilla)

⏍21.00hrs *Sneem Mtr Wrks* ☎26 🚗 Frd/VW

SPIDDAL Co Galway Map **36** M12

★★**Bridge House** ☎(091)83118 RS Oct – Apr
14rm8⇌ ᵐ20P 2🏛 B&B**(b)**

STEWARTSTOWN Co Tyrone 720 Map **35** H87 (6m
SE of Cookstown)

⏍*Megaw & McKeown* ☎224/217 **R**18.00hrs BL

STRABANE Co Tyrone 9,325 Map **35** H39

⏍*Autoservices* Lower Main St ☎882650

⏍Sionmills331 **R**18.00hrs

STRANORLAR Co 848 Map **35** H19

★★**Kee's** ☎Ballybofey18 24rm4⇌ ᵐ4P 10🏛

STROKESTOWN Co Roscommon 563 Map **35** M98

★★**Percy French** ☎46 22rm11⇌ ᵐ100P

SWINFORD Co Mayo 1,105 Map **35** M39 (9m E of
Foxford)

⏍19.00hrs *St Patrick's S/sta* ☎111 🚗 Fia

TEMPLEMORE Co Tipperary 2,174 Map **36** S17

⏍*Hassetts Mtr Works* ☎(0504)3105 BL

THOMASTOWN Co Kilkenny 1,270 Map **36** S54

⏍*Thomastown* ☎(056)24176 Toy

THURLES Co Tipperary 7,087 Map **36** S15

★★**Anner** ☎(0504)21799 15rm3⇌ ᵐ ♪ 300P
B&B**(b)**

★★**Hayes** ☎(0504)22122 38rm16⇌ ᵐ ♪ 20P 24🏛
B&B**(b)(c)**

⏍*Thurles Mtrs* The Mall ☎(0504)21355

TIMOLIN Co Kildare Map **36** S79 (13m N of Carlow)

⏍*Timolin Mtr Co* ☎(0507)24104 ☎(0507)24182

TIPPERARY Co Tipperary 4,717 Map **36** R83

★*Royal* Bridge St ☎(062)51204 20rm2⇌ ᵐ 10🏛
10P ♪

⏍*Hughe's* ☎(062)51371

TOBERMORE Co Londerry 570 Map **35** H89 (3m S
of Maghera)

⏍*Stockman & Sons* Maghera Rd ☎42320
R18.00hrs BL

Ireland

TOOMEBRIDGE Co Antrim 386 Map **35** H99 (7m E of Randalstown)
🛪 *Robert Murray & Sons* The Garage ☎240/317 **R** Aud/VW

TRALEE Co Kerry 13,263 Map **36** Q81
★★★ ⚐ **Ballyseede Castle** ☎(066)21585 13rm10⇄ 🏠 20P B&B(**d**)
★★★**Earl of Desmond** ☎(066)21299 52⇄ 🏠 350P 𝅘 ✎ B&B(**d**)(**e**)
★★★**Mount Brandon** ☎(066)21311 tx8211 62⇄ 🏠 500P Lift 𝅘 B&B(**d**)
★**Meadowlands** Listowel Rd ☎(066)21128 24rm2⇄ 🏠 50P
🛪 *Duggan's* Ashe St ☎(066)21124
🛪 *Kelliher's* ☎(066)21688 Peu Toy
🛪 *Rice's* 100 Rock St ☎(066)21877 ✿ BL
🛪 *Slattery's S/sta* Oak Park ☎(066)23133 ☎(066)22697 ✿

TRAMORE Co Waterford 3,792 Map **36** S50
★★★**Grand** ☎(051)81414 50⇄ 🏠 6P Lift 𝅘 B&B(**c**)

TRILLICK Co Tyrone 260 Map **35** H35 (15m S of Omagh)
🛪 *W Bell (Tractors) Ltd* The Garage, Kilskeery ☎218/434 **R**18.00hrs
🛪 *G J Tunney* The Garage, Main St ☎249 **R**18.00hrs Col/Frd/Hon Ren/Toy

TULAMORE Co Offaly 7,474 Map **36** N32
🛪 *Offaly Mtrs* Arden ☎(0506)21783 ☎(0506)21246 ✿ Fia/Lnc
🛪 *Tullamore Mtr Works* High St ☎(0506)21202 BL

TULLOW Co Carlow 1,945 Map **36** S87
🛪 *Byrne's* ☎(0503)51207 Dat

VIRGINIA Co Cavan Map **35** N68
★★ ⚐ **Park** ☎35 Closed mid Dec–mid Jan 23rm10⇄ 🏠 A7rm 4⇄ 200P ✎ ⚓ B&B(**d**)
🛪 *21.00hrs Ramor Mtrs* ☎69
🛪 *18.30hrs Smith's* Dublin Rd ☎25

WARRENPOINT Co Down 4,278 Map **35** J11
★**Crown** The Square ☎3665 Closed Xmas Day 15rm4⇄ 🏠 100P 𝅘 B&B(**c**)

WATERFORD Co Waterford 33,676 Map **36** S61
★★★**Ardree** ☎(051)3491 tx8684 98⇄ 🏠 500P Lift 𝅘 ✎ B&B(**d**)

★★**Dooley's** ☎(051)3551 26rm4⇄ 🏠 B&B(**c**)
★★**Metropole** ☎(051)74195 21rm2⇄ 🏠 P ○ B&B(**b**)
🛪 *John Kelly* St Catherine St ☎(051)74988 Fia
🛪 *Sheridan Mtr* ☎(051)32891) Frd

WATERVILLE Co Kerry 547 Map **36** V56
★★**Bay View** ☎4 Closed Nov–Etr 29rm6⇄ 🏠 B&B(**b**)(**c**)
★★**Butler Arms** ☎5 Closed 12 Oct–Feb 40rm16⇄ 🏠 P 𝅘 B&B(**b**)(**c**)
🛪 *20.00hrs Concannon's* ☎Waterville10 ✿ BL/Frd/Tri

WESTPORT Co Mayo 3.023 Map **35** L95
★★★**Westport** ☎351 tx6397 49⇄ 🏠 100P 𝅘 B&B(**c**)(**d**)
★★★**Westport Woods** ☎333 tx4757 56⇄ 🏠 120P 𝅘 B&B(**d**)
★★**Clew Bay** ☎173 tx6346 Closed 24–26 Dec 37rm12⇄ 🏠 B&B(**c**)

WEXFORD Co Wexford 13,293 Map **36** T02
★★★★**Talbot** Trinity St ☎(053)22566 tx8658 116rm96⇄ 🏠 60P Lift 𝅘 Pool B&B(**c**)(**d**)
★★★**Ferrycarrig Castle** Ferrycarrig ☎(053)22999 Closed Nov–Mar 40⇄ 🏠 100P Lift B&B(**c**)(**d**)
★★★**White's** ☎(053)22311 100rm60⇄ 🏠 200P Lift 𝅘 B&B(**c**)(**d**)
🛪 *19.00hrs Crescent* Custom House Quay ☎(053)22223 Ren
🛪 *O'Dowd's* The Faythe ☎(053)22998 ✿ Peu/Ren/Sab

WHITEHEAD Co Antrim 2,618 Map **35** J49
★**Royal George** Edward Rd ☎2476 15rm1⇄ 🏠 80P B&B(**b**)
🛪 *18.30hrs Raw Brae S/sta* ☎8532 **R**18.30hrs

WOODENBRIDGE Co Wicklow Map **36** T17
★**Woodenbridge** ☎(0402)5146 Closed Good Fri & Xmas Day 12rm 100P B&B(**b**)

YOUGHAL Co Cork 5,626 Map **36** X17
★★**Hilltop** ☎(024)2577 Closed 16 Dec–14 Mar 50⇄ 🏠 100P 𝅘 ✎ B&B(**c**)(**d**)
★★ ⚐ **Monatrea House & Country Club** ☎(024)4293 tx8403 Closed Nov–mid Mar 15rm7⇄ 🏠 A5 25P ✎ Pool B&B(**b**)(**c**)
🛪 *21.00hrs Sheehan's* ☎(024)2466 ✿

Kinsale, Co. Cork.

ITALY & SAN MARINO

Population 54,683, 136 **Area** 131,000 sq miles **Maps** 28 – 34

How to get there

Although there are several ways of getting to Italy, entry will most probably be by way of France or Switzerland. The major passes, which are closed in winter, are served by road or rail tunnels. The distance to Milan from the Channel ports is approximately 650 – 700 miles, requiring one or two night stops. Rome is 360 miles further south. Car-sleeper services operate during the summer from Boulogne, Brussels or Paris to Milan.

General information

Information in this section is specific to Italy. A wider background is provided in the notes on page 8 with other information which you are advised to read.

AA Port agents

Note Mail sent to these addresses from outside Italy should have the postal code prefixed with the letter I.

16124 Genova (Genoa) Gastaldi & CSpA, Via Cairoli 1, PO Box 1855 ☎283891 (16 lines)
57100 Livorno (Leghorn) Gastaldi & CSpA, Via Grande 164, PO Box 751 ☎(0856)39021/2
98100 Messina (Sicily) Gastaldi & CSpA, 201 Garibaldi Via, ☎(090)55110
80133 Napoli (Naples) Gastaldi & CSpA, Piazza Municipio 81/84 ☎(081) 323001, 324846
90139 Palermo (Sicily) Gastaldi & CSpA, Via Mariano Stabile 2 ☎(091) 589844
96100 Siracusa (Syracuse) (Sicily) Luigi Mazzone & Figli, Via Dei Mille 12 ☎20086

Italy

These are not recommended routes:
the distances are given as a guide only.

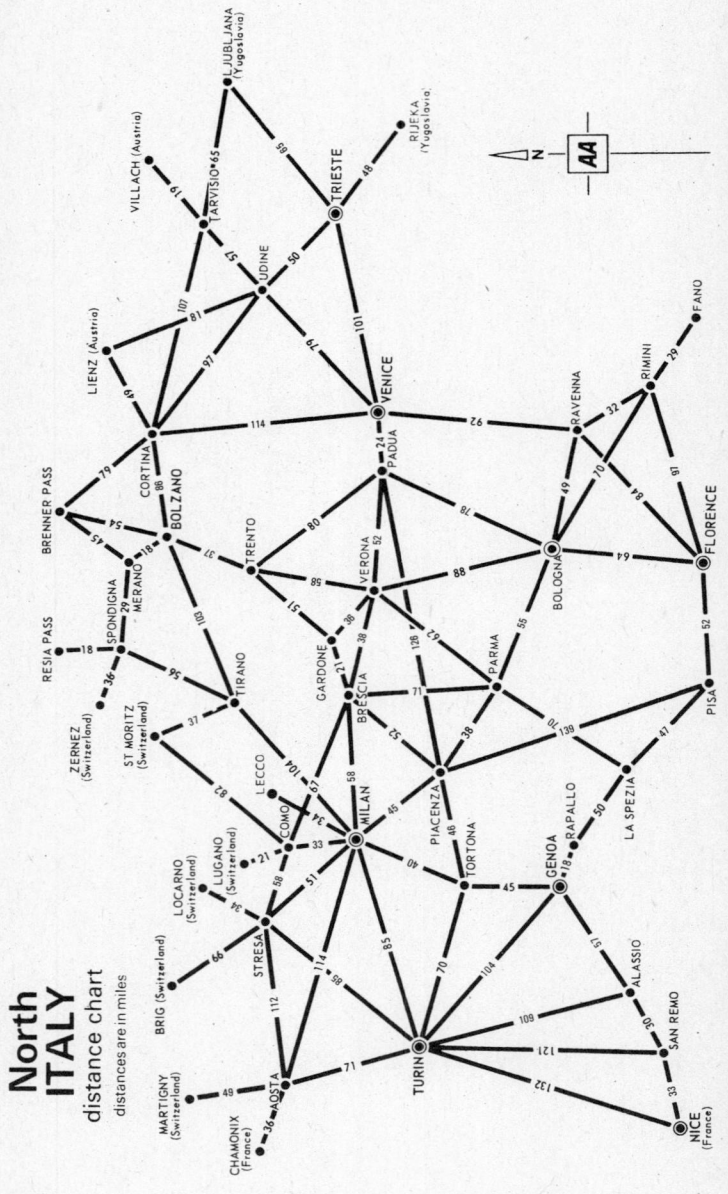

North
ITALY
distance chart
distances are in miles

*These are not recommended routes:
the distances are given as a guide only.*

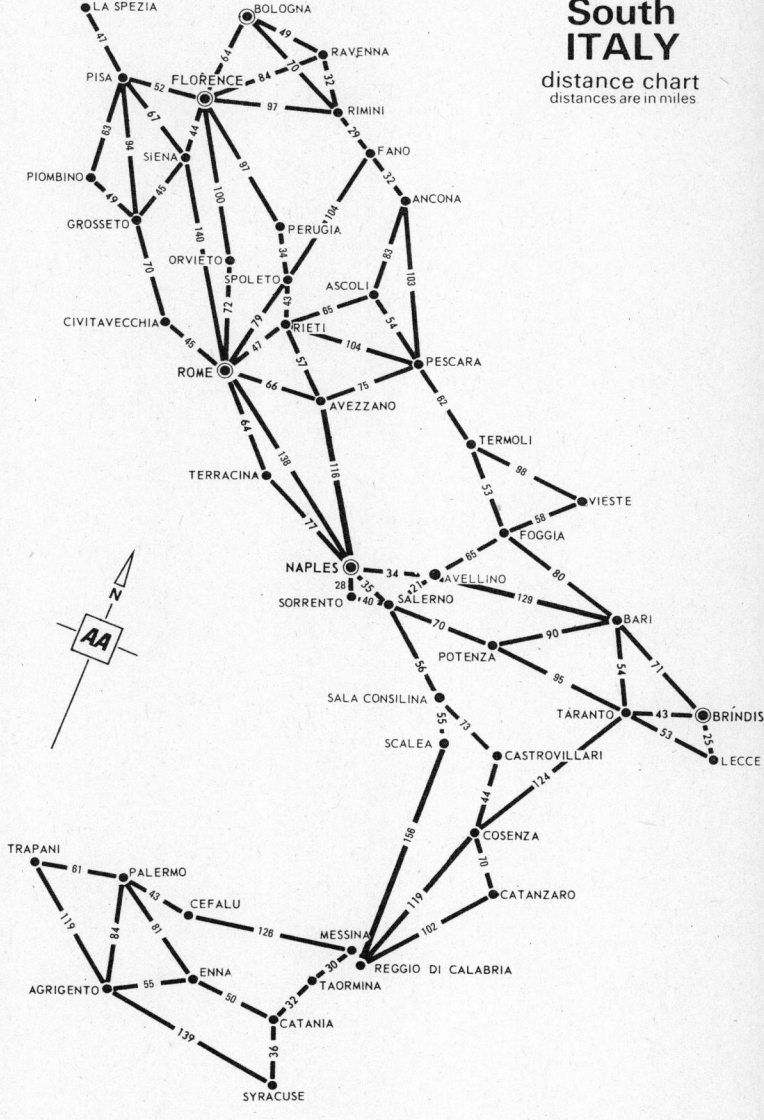

**South
ITALY**
distance chart
distances are in miles

Italy

Accommodation Hotels are classified into categories from *4* to *de luxe,* and there are three categories of pensions. All charges must be agreed by the Provincial Tourist Board *(Ente provinciali per il Turismo).* The Italian State Tourist Office publishes every year an official list of all Italian hotels and pensions *(Annuario Alberghi)* which can be consulted at its London office or major travel agents.

Good accommodation is provided by the Jolly Hotels, of which there are over forty. These are standardised establishments, most of which are included in the gazetteer in the three-star and four-star categories.

Annual events		
	February	**Agrigento** Almond Blossom Festival, folklore gathering
		San Remo Song Festival
	April	**L'Aquila** Good Friday Procession
		Taranto Procession of The Mysteries, strange religious rites
	May	**Cagliari** Feast of Sant' Efisio, celebrated since 1657
		Sassari Costume Cavalcade (Cavalcata Sarda)
	June	**Florence** Football match in 16th-century costume
		Pisa 'Battle of the Bridge' 'fought' in medieval dress
		Brindisi Corpus Christi Festival
	July	**Siena** The Palio Festival, famous for its horse race
		Venice The Feast of the Redeemer, celebrated on the Lagoon
	August	**Venice** Organ concerts in St Mark's Basilica
		Ascoli Piceno Historical pageant and jousting
	September	**Naples** The Piedgrotta Festival, song contests and procession
		Arezzo Joust dating from the 13th century
		Venice Regatta dating from 1300
		Viterbo The procession of the 'Santa Rosa' Tower
	October	**Treviso** Autumn Musical Celebration

A more comprehensive list can be obtained from The Italian State Tourist Office (see page 277).

Breakdowns Try to move the car to the verge of the road, and place a warning triangle on the road at least 50m to the rear of the vehicle to warn following traffic of an obstruction. The Soccorso Stradale Gratuito ACI (Soccorso Autostradale SAS on motorways) is a breakdown service operated by the Automobile Club d'Italia (ACI). This service, which is not available for caravans, can be obtained from public telephones by dialling 116 and from emergency telephones or radio telephones on motorways. In an emergency to call the police, fire or ambulance or to report the theft of a car, dial 123.

To obtain assistance when the breakdown vehicle arrives, you will be asked for your *Carta Carburante* (a fuel and breakdown card obtainable at the frontier or Italian State Tourist offices abroad), which contains two special breakdown coupons.

Although the road service is free, provided a *Carta Carburante* is held, a calling fee will be levied at the following rates:
between 06.00 – 21.00hrs, lire 3,500;
between 21.00 – 06.00hrs, lire 4,500.

Each breakdown coupon entitles you to:
1 Free assistance for up to half an hour (except for calling fee) on the spot from a mechanic, but you must pay for spare parts, petrol and oil.
2 Towage to the nearest ACI workshop. Towage is free up to 40km (24 miles) and a fee of L2,000 is charged for every 10 Kilometres (or part thereof) beyond 40 km. You must pay for the work carried out in repair shops.

Alternatively, requests for assistance on the motorways can be made to the *Servizo Assistenza Vacanze.* This is a service operated by FIAT in conjunction with the ACI and operates during the last two weekends in June and the first two Sundays in September, and daily in July and August. Assistance is free but a call fee, as quoted in the previous paragraph, must be paid. If the repairs take longer than 30mins, the mechanic will call the previous mentioned breakdown service to undertake the repairs.

AA members who have a European *5-Star Service Booklet* may use their Credit Vouchers to settle emergency accounts, in which case the charge would be repayable to the AA by the member on his return home.

British Consulates   00187 Roma, Via XX Settembre 80A, ☎4755441/5 There are also British Consulates in Florence, Milan, Genoa, Turin, Venice, Trieste, Naples, Palermo, Messina, and Cagliari (Sardinia).

Currency and   The unit of currency is the Italian lira. The import of Italian lira bank
Banking   notes is limited to 100,000 – other currency is not restricted. Export of currency is restricted to Italian bank notes up to 100,000 and other currency up to L200,000. To export currency in excess of this amount it must have been declared on form V2 on entry.

Banking hours   Most banks are open from Monday to Friday 08.30 to 13.30hrs.
Shopping hours   Most shops are usually open Monday to Saturday; *food shops* from 08.30 – 13.00hrs and 16.00 – 20.00hrs, closed from 13.00hrs on Mondays; *other shops* from 09.00 – 12.30hrs and 15.30 – 19.30hrs.

Documents
Driving licence   A valid British driving licence, if accompanied by an official Italian translation which can be issued by the AA will be accepted in Italy.

Insurance   Third-party insurance is compulsory for certain boats and engines in Italian waters.

Frontier insurance Short-term third-party insurance can be obtained at the frontier; approximate rates in lire are as follows:

	15 days	*30 days*	*45 days*
cars	14,000	21,000	28,000
motorcycles	7,000	10,500	14,000
trailers	11,200	16,800	22,400
caravans	11,200	16,800	22,400

Frontier insurance for motorboats is carried out by the representatives at each port. Changes are as follows:

	15 days	*30 days*	*45 days*
up to 80hp	3,000	6,000	9,000
80hp to 120hp	5,000	10,000	15,000

These prices should be used only as a guide.

Nationality plates   It is compulsory for foreign registered vehicles to display a distinctive sign at the rear of the vehicle. Failure to comply with this regulation will incur an on-the-spot-fine of 10,000 lire.

Ferries (Internal)   All details are subject to alteration.
Lake Como   **Cadenabbia – Bellagio**
Cadenabbia –Varenna
Bellagio – Varenna
Service frequent daily services between 06.50 – 20.20hrs approx.
Duration 10 minutes Cadenabbia to Bellagio; 30 minutes Cadenabbia to Varenna; 15 minutes Bellagio to Varenna.
Charges

Vehicles	cars	L1,800 – 3,100	*charges include*
		(according to length)	*drivers only*
	motorcycles L1,100 – L1,300		
Passengers		L800 – 1,000	

Lake Maggiore   **Intra-Laveno**
Service   about every 20 mins between 05.40 – 0.30hrs
Duration   20 minutes
Charges

Vehicles	cars	L2,000 – 3,700	*charges include*
		(according to length)	*drivers only*
	motorcycles	L1,300	
Passengers		L600	

Lake Garda   **Torri del Benaco-Marderno**
Service   7 – 11 sailings daily/between 08.40 – 19.50hrs

Duration	30 minutes		
Charges			
Vehicles	cars	L2,400 – 3,000	*charges include*
		(according to length)	*drivers only*
	motorcycles	L1,000	
Passengers		L700	

Medical treatment

Medical benefits in Italy are administered by the National Institute for Sickness Insurance *(Istituto Nazionale per L'Assicurazione Contro le Malattie* known as INAM) which has main offices in each provincial capital, and sub-offices in almost every district. Addresses may be obtained by enquiry at the local post office, town hall or found in the telephone directory.

To obtain medical and dental treatment take form E111 (see page 22) to the INAM office. You will be given a certificate of entitlement and a list of sickness insurance scheme doctors and dentists. Take the certificate to any doctor or dentist on the list and you will be treated free of charge. Without the certificate you will have to pay for treatment and may have difficulty in getting a refund afterwards. If you need prescribed medicines, show the certificate of entitlement to the chemist. Some medicines are free but a small charge is made for others.

If hospital treatment is needed, the doctor will give you a certificate *(proposta di ricovero)* which entitles you to free treatment in certain hospitals. A list of hospitals can be obtained from an INAM office. In an emergency, if you cannot contact the INAM, show form E111 to the hospital authorities and ask them to contact INAM immediately.

Motoring clubs

There are two motoring organisations in Italy. The Touring Club Italiano (TCI) which has its head office at 10 Corso Italia, 20122 Milano, and the Automobile Club d'Italia (ACI) whose head office is at 8 Via marsala, 00185 Rome. Both clubs have branch offices in most leading cities and towns. They will assist motoring tourists on touring matters, road and traffic conditions and AA members should produce their *5-Star Service Booklet* when requesting service. For Breakdown assistance see page 272.

The hours of opening of the TCI are usually between 09.00 and 19.00hrs although some open earlier and close later. A few are closed all day on Mondays or Saturdays. However, all close for three hours for lunch between 12.00 and 16.00hrs.

The ACI offices open between 08.30 and 13.30hrs Monday to Friday. The head office in Rome opens between 08.00 and 14.00hrs Monday to Saturday. A 24-hour information service is in operation although the interpreters are on duty only between 09.00 and 17.00hrs. The Rome telephone number is (06)4212.

Museum card

This card entitles you to visit all the Italian state museums, art galleries, and archaeological sites without payment of the normal entrance fees. A list of establishments is provided with the card. This card can be purchased from any AA service centre.

Petrol

Petrol coupons, which give an appreciable discount on pump prices, are available for tourists. These are obtainable from the AA, the National Tourist Office, and at most major Italian frontiers (with currency other than Lire), but are not sold inside Italy. They are available only on personal application. Each tourist may purchase coupons for up to 400 litres of petrol for a car, 200 litres for a motorcycle of 125cc or more, or 100 litres for a motorcycle under 125cc. Unused coupons are reimbursed by the issuing office.

During the winter, between October and April the opening hours of petrol filling stations are from 07.00 – 12.30hrs and from 15.00 – 19.00hrs. On Sundays and holidays service is further restricted because 75% of filling stations are closed. During the summer, opening hours are longer but many stations will be closed during the lunch time. As a general rule you should keep your tank topped up.

Post and telephone

Rates for mail to the UK are:
Surface mail

Letters	first 20gm	L200
	20 – 50gm	L350
	50 – 100gm	L480
	100 – 250gm	L950
Postcards	up to five words	L120
	fully written	L200
Express surcharge		L400

The *poste restante (Fermo posta)* address in Rome is Posta e Telegrafo, Piazza San Silvestro, 00187 Roma.

Italy

Telephone rates | Telephone communication with the UK is good; the charge is L2,130 for the first three minutes and L710 each further minute. If dialled direct the charge is twelve tokens every minute. There are plenty of public telephones operated by a 50-lire token *(Gettone);* these are available from all tobacco shops, bars and news-stands. Internal trunk calls, although subject to delay, can be dialled direct by using the area code number.

Public holidays

Holidays based on religious festivals are not always fixed on the calender but any current diary will give the actual dates. The Whit holiday should not be confused with the British Spring Holiday.

Fixed holidays

1 January	New Year's Day
19 March	St Joseph's Day
25 April	Liberation Day
1 May	Labour Day
1st Sun in June	Republic Day
15 August	Assumption of the Virgin Mary
1 November	All Saints' Day
1st Sun in November	National Unity Day
8 December	Immaculate Conception
25 December	Christmas Day
26 December	St Stephen's Day

Moveable holidays
Easter Monday
Ascension Day
Feast of St Peter & St Paul (Rome only)

Roads

Motorways reach to most parts of the country. Other main roads are generally good, and there is an exceptional number of bypasses; secondary roads are often poor. Mountain roads are usually well engineered; details of the main passes are given on pages 31–32, 49–55.

Italy's motorways *(autostrada)* were the first in Europe. There are about 3,618 miles of them, and more are under construction. To join a motorway, follow the green signposts; vehicles which cannot exceed 40kph (24mph) and motorcycles under 150cc are prohibited.

Tolls are charged on all motorways except the A3 from Salerno to Reggio, the A19 and A29 in Sicily, the A28 from Portogruaro to Pordenone, and on the Raccordo Autostradale from Ferrara to Porto Garibaldi, Florence to Siena, Val di Chiana to Perugia, Rome to Fiumicino Airport, Rome to Lido di Ostia, Avellino to Salerno, and from Scalo Sicignano (A3) to Potenza.

Motorway telephones | On the *Autostrade* A1 (Milan-Florence-Rome), A8/9 (Milan-the Lakes-Chiasso), A11 (Florence – Pisa N) A3 (Naples – Salerno), A4 (Brescia – Padua), A22 (Bolzano – Verona) and A24 (Rome – L'Aquila) there are radio panels at 1850m (1¼-mile) intervals; each has two buttons, one to call an ambulance and one to call a breakdown vehicle. A light appears on the lower part of the panel when the call is received. If the breakdown occurs between panels, either walk to the nearest panel or wait for a police patrol – you *must not* stop a passing vehicle.

The *Autostrade* A6 (Fossano – Savona) and A10 (Savona – Ventimiglia) have telephone boxes at 2km (1¼-mile) and ½km (⅓-mile) intervals respectively. As soon as the door of the box is opened, you are in contact with the operator who will take action on any message.

On the *Autostrade* A7 (Serravalle – Milan) telephone boxes are also available, but to get help you have to press a button to contact the operator.

Tolls (Pedaggio) | The methods of calculating tolls vary; they are based either on the Italian horsepower, the wheelbase, or the cubic capacity of the vehicle and the distance covered. There is no simple uniform ratio between engine capacity and the Italian rating of horsepower. If there is any doubt the toll booth attendant can be asked to refer to a list, which he should hold, giving the horsepower of all makes of cars. The rates below are given in lire for small (under 10hp Italian), medium – including Minis (10 – 15hp Italian), and large cars (over 15hp Italian).

Toll payment On the majority of the toll motorways a travel ticket is issued on entry, and the toll is paid on leaving the motorway. The travel ticket gives all relevant information about the toll charges, including the toll category of the vehicle. At the exit, the ticket is handed in.

On some motorways – notably A8, A9, A11, A14 (Pescara – Lanciano) and A12 (Rome – Civitavecchia) – the toll is paid at intermediate toll stations for each section of the motorway used.

On a few motorways the destination must be declared and the toll paid on entering the motorway. There is no refund on break of journey.

Italy

		cars small	medium	large	motor-cycles
*A1	Milan – Bologna	2,200	3,500	5,000	1,900
*A1	Milan – Florence (Nord)	3,300	5,100	7,450	2,800
*A1	Milan – Rome	6,100	9,600	14,150	5,200
*A2	Rome – Naples	2,100	3,400	4,900	1,800
A3	Naples – Salerno	350	650	800	300
A4	Turin – Milan	1,000	1,500	2,200	600
A4	Milan – Mestre (Venice)	2,400	3,500	5,100	1,900
A4	Mestre – (Venice) – Trieste	1,000	1,500	2,100	900
A4/5	Milan – Aosta	1,600	2,700	3,500	1,100
A5	Turin – Aosta	1,050	2,050	2,400	900
A6	Turin – Savona	1,350	2,250	3,200	1,050
A7	Milan – Genoa	1,400	2,100	3,150	1,200
A8	Milan – Sesto Calende/Varese	500	900	1,100	400
A8/9	Milan – Como	600	1,100	1,350	500
A10	Genoa – Savona	600	900	1,400	500
A10	Savona – Ventimiglia (Menton)	1,850	2,900	4,000	1,100
A11	Florence – Pisa	900	1,650	1,950	750
A12	Genoa – Livorno	1,800	3,200	4,100	1,550
A12	Rome – Civitavecchia (Nord)	700	1,300	1,400	600
*A13	Bologna – Padua	1,300	2,000	3,000	1,100
*A14	Bologna – Rimini (Sud)	1,200	1,900	2,800	1,100
*A14	Bologna – Pescara	3,800	6,100	8,900	3,200
*A14	Pescara – Bari	3,200	5,100	7,600	2,700
*A14	Bari – Taranto	700	1,100	1,600	600
*A15	Parma – La Spezia	900	1,500	2,200	750
*A16/ 14	Naples – Bari	2,900	4,500	6,600	2,400
A18	Messina – Catana (Nord)	1,150	1,600	1,800	750
A20	Messina – Rocca di C.	1,100	1,750	2,400	950
A20	Cefalu – Buonfornello	250	300	500	200
A21	Turin – Piacenza	1,150	1,700	2,500	1,000
A21	Piacenza – Brescia	500	800	1,150	400
A22	Brenner Pass – Modena	2,800	4,400	6,500	2,400
A23	Palmanova – Udine	150	200	300	150
A24	Rome – L'Aquila	1,000	1,950	2,300	850
A25	Rome – Avezzano	900	1,700	2,000	750
A25	Popoli – Pescara	300	550	650	250
A26	Alessandria – Genoa	1,000	1,500	2,200	800
A26	Alessandria – Santhia	1,200	1,200	1,900	1,000
A27	Mestre (Venice) – Vittorio Veneto	900	1,300	1,700	1,600
*A30	Caserta – Salerno	700	1,000	1,500	500
A31	Vicenza – Piovene Rocchette	350	500	750	300

All prices should be used only as a guide.

*A special tariff reduction has been introduced enabling tourists to pay the lowest tariff *ie* the motorcycle tariff, when travelling on the following motorways: A1 Milan – Rome, A2 Rome – Naples, A13 Bologna – Padua, A14 Bologna – Pescara – Bari – Taranto, A15 Parma – La Spezia, A16/14 Naples – Bari, A30 Caserta – Salerno. To claim the reduced toll tariff make sure you inform the attendant, before he issues a ticket when you enter the motorway, that you are driving a foreign registered vehicle. You will then be issued with a ticket which should be marked with 1 (one) in the box marked classe. You must complete the ticket with your name and surname, the registration number of the vehicle and your signature before arriving at the exit booth to leave the motorway.

Caravans There are varying additional charges, but generally the charge for a caravan is the same as for a medium-to-large-sized car.

Winter conditions   It is possible to approach northern Italy, Milan, and Turin by road or rail tunnels. See Passes and tunnels, pages 31–32, 49–55.

From Switzerland via the Simplon or St Gotthard rail tunnels;
via the Grand St Bernard road tunnel;
via the San Bernardino road tunnel;
also via the Julier and Maloja passes.

From France via the Mont Blanc road tunnel;
via the Fréjus rail tunnel when the Mont Cenis pass is closed.
In favourable weather, via the Lautaret and Montgenèvre passes.
Also via the French Rivera coast, entering at Ventimiglia.

From Austria via the Resia and Brenner passes; wheel chains may be necessary in severe weather.

The Plöcken pass is closed in winter, but the roads entering Italy at Dobbiaco and Travisio are normally free from obstruction.

Roads within the country, apart from those in the Dolomites, are not seriously affected in winter, although during January and February certain highways across the Apennines may be obstructed. Touring in the Dolomites is generally confined to the period from early May to mid October.

Road signs

Signposting is good on most main roads, although signs tend to point across the roads indicated.

Translations of some written signs are given below:

Banchina non transitabile	Shoulder of road not to be driven on
Banchina cedevole	Shoulder of road too soft or sinking under the vehicle wheels
Diveto di accesso	No entry
Entrata	Entrance or turn-in
Crocevia	Cross-roads
Lavori in corso	Road works ahead
Parcheggio	Parking
Passaggio a livello	Level crossing
Rallentare	Reduce speed
Semafori sincronizzati	Synchronised traffic lights (see Traffic lights)
Senso unico	One-way street
Sosta autorizzata/regolamentata	Parking permitted (time in minutes usually indicated)
Sosta vietata	Parking forbidden
Sosta vietata Rimozione Forzata	Parking forbidden. The vehicle will be towed away
Strada dissestata	Ruined or in very bad condition
Svolta	Bend
Uscita	Exit or turn-out
Vietato ingresso veicoli	No entry for vehicles
Vietato transito autocarri	Closed to heavy vehicles
Zona disco	Blue zone

Wheel chains Roads where these are compulsory are marked by a national sign. Chains cannot be hired in Italy, but can be purchased at garages or vehicle accessory shops everywhere. Approximate prices per pair are as follows: iron, L10,000 –20,000; steel/iron, L20,000–30,000. Drivers of vehicles proceeding without wheel chains on roads where they are compulsory are liable to prosecution.

Tourist information offices The Italian State Tourist organisation (ENIT) has an office in London at 201 Regent Street, W1R 8AY ☎01-439 2311. It will be pleased to assist you with any information regarding tourism. In Italy there are three organisations: the *Ente Nazionale Italiano per il Turismo* (ENIT) with offices at frontiers and ports; the *Assessorati Regionali per il Turismo* (ART) and the *Enti Provinciali per il Turismo* (EPT) who will assist tourists through their regional and provincial offices. The *Aziende Autonomedi Cura Soggiorno e Turismo* (AACST) have offices in places of recognised tourist interest and concern themselves exclusively with matters of local interest.

Visitors' registration Police registration is required within three days of entering Italy. If staying at a hotel the management will attend to the formality, but the vistor is responsible for checking that this has been carried out. Your permit of stay will last three months as a tourist. Should you wish to stay for a longer period, an extension must be obtained from the police. In Rome there is a special police information office for assistance to tourists; interpreters can be provided. ☎461950 and 486609.

Motoring regulations

Information in this section is specific to Italy. A wider background is provided in the notes on page 67 with other regulations which you are advised to read.

Accidents **Fire, police, ambulance** (Public emergency service) ☎113.

No particular procedure is required following an accident, excepting that a report must be made to the insurance company within three days.
If the accident involves personal injury it is obligatory that medical assistance is sought for the injured party, and that the incident is reported to the police. On some *autostrade* that are emergency telephone as well as emergency push-button call boxes.

Italy

Compulsory equipment

When vehicles are equipped with snow tyres or chains then amongst other things mud flaps must be fitted behind the rear wheels – this is compulsory for residents and advisable for visitors.

Dimensions restrictions

Private cars and trailers are restricted to the following dimensions and weights:

cars	height	4 metres,
	width	2.5 metres;
caravans	length	6 metres;
	weight	The maximum permitted gross weight is that stated by the manufacturers, or 80% of the gross weight of the towing vehicle – whichever is the lighter.

Drinking and driving

Any driver found to be driving under the influence of alcohol may be sentenced to a term of imprisonment of up to six months and fined from L25,000 to L100,000.

Horn, use of

In built-up area the use of the horn is prohibited except in cases of immediate danger. At night flashing headlights may be used instead of the horn.

Outside built-up areas it is compulsory to use the horn when warning of approach is necessary.

Lights

Full-beam headlights can be used only outside cities and towns. Dipped headlights are compulsory in tunnels and bridges even if they are well lit. Foglights may be used in pairs and in fog or snow when visibility is restricted.

Parking

Parking is forbidden within 5 metres (16½ft) of cross-roads or road intersections, on a main road or one or carrying fast-moving traffic, on or near tram lines, opposite another stationary vehicle, on or within 12 metres (39½ft) of a bus or tram stop. Violators of parking regulations are subject to heavy fines. There is a blue zone (zona disco) in most cities; in such areas parked vehicles must display a disc on the windscreen. Discs are set at the time of parking, and show when parking time expires according to the limit in the area concerned. Disc parking operates 08.00 – 20.00hrs on working days. Discs can be obtained from petrol stations and automobile organisations. There are also green zones *(zona verde)* where parking is absolutely prohibited 08.00 – 09.30hrs and 14.30 – 16.00hrs. Vehicles will be towed away at the owner's expense even if they are not causing an obstruction.

Passengers

No vehicle may carry more passengers than the number for which it was constructed. Passengers must always allow drivers free movement.

Police fines

The police are authorised to impose and collect fines on the spot for violation of traffic regulations. The police must hand over a receipt for the amount of the fine paid. Fines are very heavy for speeding and parking offences.

Priority

Traffic on State highways *(Strade Statali),* which are all numbered and indicated by signs, has right of way, as do public service vehicles and, on postal routes, buses belonging to the service. These bus routes are indicated by a special sign.

If two vehicles are travelling in opposite directions and the driver of each vehicle wants to turn left, they must pass in front of each other (not drive round as in the UK).

Speed

The maximum speed limit in built-up areas, unless otherwise indicated, is 50kph (31 mph). Mopeds are restricted to 40kph (24mph) on all roads unless there is a lower limit. On normal roads limits are 80kph to 110kph; motorways 90kph to 140kph depending on the cc of the vehicle's engine. Limits are signposted. Any infringement of speed regulations can result in punitive fines of up to £400 or imprisonment, and these penalities have been enforced.

Traffic lights

In some places synchronised traffic signals are used; these are preceded by a sign bearing the words *Semefori sincronizzati per velocita . . . . km/ora:* vehicles travelling at the speed shown (. . . . . kph) will not have to stop or slow down at the lights.

Tyres

Snow tyres These may be used on roads where wheel chains are compulsory, provided that they are used on all four wheels.

Spiked or studded tyres Vehicles with spiked tyres may be used provided that:
1 they are used between 15 November and 15 March
2 they do not exceed 120kph (74mph) on motorways, and 90kph (56mph) on other roads.
All signed lower limits must not be exceeded.
3 they must not exceed a total weight of 3,500kg.
4 they are fitted to all wheels, including those of a trailer (if any).
Visitors are also advised to have mud flaps fitted behind the rear wheels.

Warning triangles   These are compulsory for all vehicles except motorcycles. They
must be placed on the road 50 metres (55yd) behind the vehicle (or
a fallen object or load) and must be visible to following traffic from 100 metres (109yd).

Triangles may be hired or purchased at the Italian frontier. A charge of L1,500 is made, for which
a receipt is given. On leaving Italy, the motorist must return the triangle and the receipt in order to
obtain a refund of L1,200.

Cathedral and Leaning Tower of Pisa.

San Marino

Map 30 C2   A small Republic with an area of 23 sq miles and a population of
19,000, situated in the hills of Italy near Rimini. The official
information office in the UK is the Italian State Tourist Office at 201 Regent Street, London W1R
8AY. The chief attraction is the city of San Marino on the slopes of Monte Titano. Its laws,
motoring regulations and emergency telephone numbers are the same as Italy.

Italy/hotels and garages

Prices are in Italian lire

Abbreviations:
c   calle
pza   piazza

ABANO TERME Padova 14,880 (☎049) Map **30** C4
★★★★**Bristol Buja** via Monteortone 2 ☎669390
tx43210 157rm140⇔ 🏥 P Lift sB14100 – 16500
sB⇔15000 – 19000 dB23150 – 26350
dB⇔23000 – 31200 (English breakfast) L10000
D10000 ✆ Pool ♿ ⛰ mountains
   ★★★★**Trieste & Victoria** viale della Terme
☎669101 Closed 6 Nov – 19 Mar 102rm81⇔
P Lift ♪ sB21000 – 23000 sB⇔22000 – 31000
dB38000 – 44000 dB⇔40000 – 54000
L11000 – 15000 D11000 – 15000 ✆ Pool ♿
   ★★★**Milano** viale delle Terme 133 ☎669661 Closed
12 Nov – Mar 98rm47⇔ 🏥 Lift
ACQUAPENDENTE Viterbo 6,000 (☎0763)
Map **31** B3
   ★★**Milano** via Cassia 29 ☎74110 20rm12⇔ 🏥 P
sB6600 – 8500 dB11200 – 13000 dB⇔14200 – 16000
(English breakfast) L8500 – 9500 D10000 – 12000
St%
   ★**Roma** viale del Fiore 13 ☎74016 26rm7⇔4 🏥 P
sB5000 dB8450 dB⇔🏥 11300 (English breakfast)
L5000 D5000 ✆
ÁCQUI TERME Alessandria 22,800 (☎0144)
Map **28** D3
   ★★★**Nuove Terme** pza Italia ☎2106 70rm42⇔7 🏥
Lift
   🛢 **Carrara** (Rogna & Timossi) corso Divisione Acqui 7
☎53735 P VW
AGOGNATE Novara (☎0321) Map **28** D4
   ★★**Meridiana** Autostrada Torino ☎23156 17⇔ 🏥
Lift ✆ Pool
AGRIGENTO See **SICILIA (SICILY)**
ALÁSSIO Savona 14,050 (☎0182) Map **28** D2
   ★★★★**Diana** via Garibaldi 104 ☎42701 tx270655
Closed 21 Oct – 14 Mar 77rm41⇔36 🏥 P Lift ♪
sB⇔🏥16500 – 19500 dB⇔🏥31000 – 43000
(English breakfast) L8500 Pool Beach sea
   ★★★★**Mediterranée** via Roma 63 ☎42564 Closed
Nov – Feb 82rm70⇔ 🏥 P Lift ♪ sB⇔19000 – 23000
dB⇔34000 – 41000 L11000 D11000 St% Beach sea
   ★★★**Curtis-Centrale** corso Europa 32 ☎42437
44rm⇔ 🏥 P ♪ sB⇔6500 – 17500
dB⇔13500 – 19500 L6000 D6000 St% Beach
   ★★★**Flora** Lungomare Cadorna 22 ☎40336 Closed
Nov – Mar 45rm31⇔3 🏥 P Lift ♪ sB12000 – 16000
sB⇔15000 – 18000 dB19000 – 22000
dB⇔🏥22000 – 25000 (English breakfast) L8000
D8000 Beach sea
   ★★**Ideale** corso Dante 45 (DP) ☎40376 Closed 21
Sep – Apr 70rm20⇔ Lift
   ★★★**Majestic** via da-Vinci 300 ☎42721 Closed 16
Oct – 14 Mar 72rm62⇔10 🏥 Lift ♪
sB⇔🏥11000 – 18000 dB⇔🏥16000 – 24000
(English breakfast) L6000 D6000 St% Beach sea
   ★★★**Regina** via Garibaldi 108 ☎40215 Closed
26 Oct – Mar 39rm17⇔20 🏥 Lift Beach sea
   ★★**Alda** via F-Gioia (DP) ☎44085 Closed late Oct
42⇔ A10rm Lift
   ★★**Badano Residence Sur Mer** via Gramsci 30
☎40964 Closed 21 Oct – 14 Jan 18rm3⇔15 🏥 Lift
   ★★**Bellevue** via A-Vespucci 38A ☎42013 Closed
16 Oct – 14 Mar 30rm5⇔12 🏥 A4rm P Lift
sB8500 – 9500 sB⇔🏥10500 – 13500 dB12000 – 13000
dB⇔🏥16000 – 17000 L4500 D4500 Beach sea
   ★★**Londra** via Roma 41 (DP) ☎40380 30⇔ 🏥 Lift
Beach sea
   ★★**Mare** via Boselli 1 ☎40635 47rm6⇔35 🏥 P Lift
sB9500 – 11500 sB⇔🏥12500 – 14500
dB15000 – 18000 dB⇔🏥17000 – 21000
(English breakfast) L6000 D6000 Beach sea
   ★★**Martini** via V-Veneto 31 ☎40436 Closed
26 Oct – Mar 37rm19⇔ Lift
   ★★**Mirafiori** via L-da Vinci 90 ☎40756 30rm10⇔ Lift

   ★★**Toscana** via L-da Vinci ☎40657 70rm40⇔7 🏥
Lift
   ★★**Villa Carlotta** via Adelasia 11 ☎40463 17rm8⇔
🏥 P sB5000 – 6000 dB⇔6000 – 7000
dB9000 – 11000 dB⇔🏥11000 – 13000
(English breakfast) L4500 D5000 Beach sea
   ★**Bel Sit** via Don Boselli 28 ☎40395 Closed
Nov – Mar 48⇔ P Lift sB⇔6500 – 9500 dB⇔18000
L6000 D6000 Beach sea
   ★**Rendez-Vous** via Milano 8 ☎40421 32rm10⇔4 🏥
🏥 Lift Beach sea
ALBA Cuneo 30,450 (☎0173) Map **28** D3
   ★★**Savona** pza Savona ☎2381 110rm60⇔52 🏥 🏥
P Lift ♪ sB8000 – 9600 sB⇔🏥12000 – 13000
dB16000 – 18000 dB⇔🏥21000 – 23000
(English breakfast) L6000 D6000 mountains
ALBISOLA MARINA Savona 6,300 (☎019)
Map **28** D3
   ★★★**Corallo** ☎41784 Closed Nov – 13 Apr
24rm13⇔8 🏥 P sB7500 – 9800
sB⇔🏥9500 – 11500 dB14000 – 17000
dB⇔🏥17500 – 20500 (English breakfast) L7000
D7000 sea
ALLESSÁNDRIA Alessándria 103,000 (☎0131)
Map **28** D3
   ★★**Europa** via Palestro ☎2219 34rm30⇔ 🏥 P Lift ♪
sB11300 – 11500 sB⇔13800 – 14000
dB⇔24600 – 25000 (English breakfast) L7500 – 8500
D7500 – 8500 St%
AMALFI Salerno 6,400 (☎089) Map **33** B3
   ★★★★**Santa Caterina** via Statale ☎871012
62rm59⇔ 🏥 P Lift Pool Beach sea
   ★★★**Aurora** pza Matteotti ☎871209 Closed Nov – 19
Mar 35⇔ 🏥 P Lift sB⇔13500 – 15800
dB⇔21500 – 25500 (English breakfast) L5000 D5000
Beach sea
   ★★★**Luna** Lungomare ☎871002 45⇔ 🏥 Lift Pool
Beach sea
   ★★★**Miramalfi** ☎871247 47rm30⇔17 🏥 🏥 P Lift ♪
sB⇔🏥9900 – 12700 dB⇔🏥19500 – 23000
(English breakfast) L6000 D6000 Beach sea
   ★★**Bellevue** ☎871846 23rm12⇔11 🏥 P ♪
sB⇔🏥10500 – 12500 dB⇔🏥15000 – 17000
(English breakfast) L5000 D5500 Beach sea
   ★★**Marina Riviera** via F-Gioia 22 ☎871104
18rm10⇔ 🏥 P ♪ sB⇔🏥6600 – 9950 sB⇔7450 – 10450
dB12400 – 14400 dB⇔🏥14400 – 16900
(English breakfast) L5000 D5000 Beach sea
At **Lone** (2.5km NE)
   ★★★**Caleidoscopio** ☎871220 Closed 16 Oct – Apr
35rm15⇔8 🏥 P ♪ sB8600 – 10800
sB⇔🏥11500 – 14000 dB15000 – 17200
dB⇔🏥19500 – 24000 (English breakfast) L5000
D5000 Pool Beach sea
At **Minori** (3km E)
   ★★**Caporal** ☎877408 27rm25⇔ A3rm 🏥 P ♪
sB⇔7000 – 7700 dB8400 – 10400
   dB⇔10200 – 11400 (English breakfast) Beach sea
   ★★**Santa Lucia** via Nazionale 44 ☎877142
35rm15⇔20 🏥 P ♪ sB5500 – 6500
sB⇔🏥5800 – 6950 dB⇔🏥9600 – 11100
(English breakfast) L4000 D4000 Beach sea
ANACAPRI See **CAPRI (ISOLA DI)**
ANCONA Ancona 107,150 (☎071) Map **30** D2
   ☆☆**AGIP** SS 16 Adriatica km 293 ☎508241 51 🏥
Lift
   ★★★**Jolly** via XXIX Settembre 14 ☎201171 tx56343
89⇔ P Lift ♪ sB⇔18650 dB⇔28700 L7000 D7000
   ★★★**Passetto** via Thaon di Revel 1 ☎28932
45rm18⇔27 🏥 Lift sea
   🛢**Samet** via de Gasperi 80 ☎31548 M/c Frd
AOSTA Aosta 39,000 (☎0165) Map **28** C4
   ★★★**Ambassador** via Duca degli Abruzzi ☎42230
45rm19⇔26 🏥 🏥
   ☆☆**Motelalp** ☎4000752⇔ P ♪
sB⇔14000 – 16000 dB⇔22000 – 24000
(English breakfast) L6500 – 7000 D6500 – 7000
mountains

★★★ *Valle d'Aosta* corso Ivrea 174 ☎41845 102⇄
🏛 Lift
★★ *Miravalle* Porassan (2km N) (n rest) ☎44310
24rm20⇄ 🏛
★★ *Rayon de Soleil* Strada Gran St-Bernardo (2km
N SS27) ☎2247 Closed Nov – 14 Mar 32⇄ 🏛 P Lift
sB⇄ 8800 – 11800 dB⇄16600 – 20600
(English breakfast) L5500 D5500 mountains
★★ *Turin* via Torino 14 ☎44593 50⇄ 🏛 Lift
★ *Cavallo Bianco* via E-Aubert 15 ☎2214 12rm
§ ♨ *Fabris-Ford* pza Zerbion ☎2619 M/c P Frd
F Gal via Monte Emilius 9 ☎2353 BL/Rov
At **Peroulaz** (13km S)
★★ *Jolie Bergère* ☎4912 42rm4⇄9🏛 🏛

ARABBA Belluno (☎0436) Map **13** A1
★ *Posta* ☎79105 Closed May, Oct & Nov
25rm6⇄4🏛 🏛

ARENZANO Genova 10,500 (☎010) Map **28** D3
★★ *Roma* (n rest) ☎9127314 Closed Oct – mid Apr
45rm8⇄1🏛 P Lift ♪ sB9500 – 11500
dB16400 – 18200 dB⇄🏛 18300 – 21200 St% sea
mountains
★ *Europa* ☎9127384 Closed Oct – 14 Mar 15rm2⇄
🏛 P sB5850 dB9200 dB⇄10700 (English breakfast)
L4000 D4500 sea

AREZZO Arezzo 90,200 (☎0575) Map **30** C2
★★★ *Continentale* pza Guido Monaco 7 ☎20251
80rm45⇄22🏛 Lift ♪ sB6000 – 7000 (room only)
sB⇄🏛 10000 – 11000 (room only)
dB⇄🏛 16000 – 18000 (room only)
♨ *Magi Ezio di Piero & Corrado Magi* Via M-
Perennio 24/1 ☎21264 BL

ARGEGNO Como 800 (☎031) Map **29** A4
★ *Belvedere* ☎821116 Closed 21 Oct – 14 Mar
17rm4⇄7🏛 🏛 P sB8500 – 10500
sB⇄🏛 11500 – 13500 dB15000 – 17000
dB⇄🏛 18000 – 20500 (English breakfast)
L6000 – 6500 D6000 – 6500 lake

ARMA DI TÀGGIA Imperia (☎0184) Map **28** D2
★★★★ *Vittoria Grattacielo* via Lungomare ☎43495
Closed Mar – 14 May & 16 Oct – 19 Dec 77⇄ 🏛 Lift ♪
Pool Beach sea
★★ *Europa* via Stazione 137 ☎43797 30⇄ 🏛

ARONA Novara 16,600 (☎0322) Map **28** D4
At **Fornaci**
★★ *Clipper* via Sempione 18 ☎3364 12rm4⇄ 🏛 lake
ARZACHENA See **SARDEGNA (ISOLA)
(SARDINIA)**

ASCOLI PICENO Ascoli Piceno 56,350 (☎0736)
Map **32** C3
★★★ *Gioli* viale A-de Gaspari ☎4450 38rm8⇄12🏛
🏛

ASSISI Perugia 24,400 (☎075) Map **31** B4
★★★ *Giotto* via Fontebella 41 ☎812209
72rm45⇄14🏛 Lift
★★★ *Subasio* via Frate Elia 2 ☎812206 tx66122
70rm60⇄10🏛 🏛 P Lift ♪ sB10200 sB⇄🏛 14000
dB15750 dB⇄🏛 22250 (English breakfast) L6500
D6500
★★★ *Windsor Savoia* Porta San Francesco (DP)
☎812210 33⇄🏛 🏛 Lift
★★ *Umbra* via degli Archi 2 ☎812240 27rm17⇄ ♪
sB8600 – 9600 sB⇄11800 – 13500 dB13200 – 14700
dB⇄19700 – 21200

ASTI Asti 79,900 (☎0141) Map **28** D3
★★★ *Salera* via del Fortino (DP) ☎211815 54⇄ 🏛
Lift
§ ♨ *G Vignetti* via Ticino 1 ☎55016 M/c P

AVELLINO Avellino 56,800 (☎0825) Map **33** B3
★★★ *Jolly* via Tuoro Capuccini 97A ☎32191
74rm57⇄ P Lift ♪ sB12500 sB⇄19600 dB22000
dB⇄30000 L7500 D7500

BARBARANO See **GARDONE RIVIERA**

BARDOLINO Verona 5,800 (☎045) Map **29** B4
★★★ *Vela d'Or 22* Cisano (DP) ☎623067 tx48444
Closed Oct – Apr 60rm52🏛 A10rm ♨ Pool lake

BARDONÉCCHIA Torino 3,250 (☎0122) Map **28** C3
★★★ *Geneys Splendid* viale Bramafam 41 ☎99001
Closed 21 Apr – Jun & 4 Sep – Nov 60⇄🏛 P Lift ♪
sB⇄🏛 15800 dB⇄🏛 21600 (English breakfast)
L fr6000 D fr6000 mountains

BARI Bari 374,550 (☎080) Map **34** C4
★★★★ *Palace* via Lombardi 13 ☎216551 tx81111
210⇄ 🏛 P Lift ♪ sB⇄35000 – 41000
dB⇄59000 – 68000 (English breakfast)
L10000 – 12000 D10000 – 12000
★★★ *Jolly* via G-Petroni 15 ☎364366 tx81274 164⇄
🏛 Lift ♪ sB⇄23250 dB⇄40300 L8000 D8000
★★★ *Nazioni* Lungomare Nazario Sauro 7 ☎331188
132rm88⇄ Lift sea
★★ *Grand Moderno* via Crisanzio 60 ☎213313
51rm21⇄ Lift ♪ sB7700 – 8500 sB⇄10700 – 13500
dB14900 – 16000 dB⇄18400 – 20500
§ ♨ *L F Tray* 65 Japigia 48 ☎330158 ☎330158 P
Frd (GB)
At **Torre a Mare** (12km)
☆☆☆ *AGIP* ☎300001 95🏛 Lift

BAVENO Novara 4,300 (☎0323) Map **28** D4
★★ *Beau Rivage* via della Vittoria 36 – 38 (DP)
☎24534 Closed Nov – Mar 80rm25⇄ A7rm 🏛 Lift
★★ *Nazionale San Gottardo* via Nazionale 7
☎24529 Closed Nov – Mar 25rm8⇄ Lift lake
★★ *Simplon* ☎24112 tx20217 Closed Nov – Mar
96rm80⇄16🏛 🏛 P Lift sB⇄🏛 16400 – 19800
dB⇄🏛 26800 – 31600 (English breakfast)
L7000 – 8000 D6500 – 9000 ♨ Pool
★★ *Splendid* via Sempione 12 ☎24583 tx20217
Closed Nov ♪ Mar 96rm80⇄16🏛 🏛 P
sB⇄🏛 18500 – 21900 dB⇄🏛 29000 – 34800
(English breakfast) L7500 – 9000 D7500 – 10000 ♨
Pool lake
★ *Ripa* via Sempione ☎24589 Closed Oct – Mar 10rm
🏛 lake
At **Feriolo** (3km NW)
★★ *Carillon* ☎2915 Closed 16 Oct – Mar
20rm2⇄15🏛 🏛

BELGIRATE Novara 550 (☎0322) Map **28** D4
★★★ *Milano* via Sempione 2 ☎7495 tx20490
65rm45⇄ 🏛 P Lift ♪ sB10800 – 14300
sB⇄13800 – 17300 dB18600 – 19600
dB⇄21600 – 26600 (English breakfast) L4800 – 8000
D4800 – 8000 St% Beach sea lake
★★ *Villa Carlotta* (DP) ☎7487 112rm83⇄9🏛 🏛 Lift
Pool lake

BELLÀGIO Como 3,400 (☎031) Map **29** A4
★★★★ *Villa Serbelloni* via Roma 1 ☎950216
tx38330 Closed Nov – Mar 100rm89⇄5🏛 🏛 P Lift ♪
sB23670 – 31650 sB⇄🏛 32790 – 40770
dB34800 – 46200 dB⇄🏛 53040 – 64440 L fr13600
D fr12500 ♨ Pool mountains lake
★★★ *Lac* pza Mazzini ☎950320 Closed Oct – mid Apr
48rm41⇄3🏛 Lift lake
★★ *Belvedere* ☎950410 Closed 11 Oct – Mar
41rm10⇄7🏛 🏛 Lift Pool lake
★★ *Firenze* pza Mazzini ☎950342 Closed Nov – Mar
47rm19⇄ Lift sB10000 – 10500 dB17000 – 18000
dB⇄19000 – 26000 (English breakfast) L5500 D5500
St% mountains lake
★★ *Metropole* pza Mazzini 5 ☎950409 Closed
Nov – Mar 56rm50⇄6🏛 Lift ♪ sB12000 – 14000
sB⇄🏛 16000 – 18000 dB2000 – 22000
dB⇄🏛 22000 – 26000 (English breakfast) L8000
D8000 Pool lake

BELLANO Como 3,700 (☎0341) Map **29** A4
★★ *Meridiana* (DP) ☎821126 29⇄ 🏛 Lift lake

BELLÀRIA IGEA MARINA Forli 11,800 (☎0541)
Map **30** C2
At **Bellaria**
★ *Levante* via C-Colombo 1 ☎44223 Closed
Oct – Apr 32🏛 P Lift sB🏛 9500 – 1200
dB🏛 17000 – 22000 (English breakfast) L5000 – 7000
D5000 – 7000 St% sea
At **Igea Marina**

Italy

★★★**Touring Spiaggia** Lungomare Pinzon 217
(2km S) ☎630419 Closed 11 Sep–May
40rm12⇄28 🕮 P Lift ♪ sB⇄ ▥ 9500–14500
dB⇄ ▥ 13000–19000 (English breakfast)
L5000–7000 D5000–7000 Pool Beach sea
BELLUNO Belluno 36,100 (☎0437) Map **30** C4

🐾B-Moretti via T-Vecellio ☎25789 AR

BÉRGAMO Bérgamo 129,950 (☎035) Map **29** 4A

★★★**Excelsior San Marco** pza Repubblica 6
☎232132 101rm46⇄35 ▥ 🏛 P Lift ♪ sB24000
sB⇄ ▥ 24000 dB⇄ ▥ 38000 (English breakfast)
L9000 D9000
★★★**Grand Moderno** viale P-giovanni XXIII 106
☎233033 96rm27⇄43 ▥ P Lift ♪ sB11500–13500
sB⇄ ▥ 15000–18000 dB20000–22000
dB⇄ ▥ 26000–30000 English breakfast only L8000
D8000
★★**Agnello d'Oro** via Gombito 22 ☎249883
25rm5⇄20 ▥ Lift sB10400 sB⇄ ▥ 10400
dB⇄ ▥ 16800 (English breakfast) L8000 D1000
BIELLA Vercelli 56,000 (☎015) Map **28** D4

★★★**Astoria** viale Roma 9 ☎20545 tx20233
50rm15⇄35 ▥ 🏛 P Lift ♪ sB⇄ ▥ 25000
dB⇄ ▥ 37000 St% mountains
BIVIGLIANO Firenze (☎055) Map **29** B2

★★**Giotto Park** ☎406608 Closed Nov–Feb
38rm5⇄21 ▥ A21rm P ♪ sB10700–11200
sB⇄ ▥ 16300–18300 dB17000–24800
dB⇄ ▥ 20500–27600 (English breakfast) L7000
D7000 🏖
BOLOGNA Bologna 492,725 (☎051) Map **29** B3

★★★★★**Royal Carlton** via Montebello 8 ☎554141
tx51356 254⇄ 🏛 P Lift ♪ sB⇄ ▥ 40500
dB⇄ ▥ 57500 (English breakfast) L12000–18000alc
D12000–18000alc
★★★★**Jolly de la Gare** pza XX Settembre 2
☎264405 tx51076 172⇄ P Lift ♪ sB⇄ ▥ 27850
dB⇄ ▥ 40700 L9500 D9500
★★★★*Milano-Excelsior* via Pietramellara 51
☎239442 tx51213 86rm 🏛 lift
☆☆☆*AGIP* vja M-E-Lepido 203 ☎401131 60 ▥ Lift
☆☆☆**EuroCrest** pza della Constituzione ☎372172
tx51676 164rm 🏛 P Lift ♪ sB⇄ ▥ fr28850
dB⇄ ▥ fr41700 L fr6000 D fr6000 Pool
★★★*Metropolitan* via dell-'Orso 4 ☎272801
40rm30⇄10 ▥ 🏛 Lift
🐾*AMM Sas* (Spett le) via Po 2A ☎492552 M/c
Ren (GB)
Cisa via A-di-Vincenzo 6 ☎370434 BL
C Cesari via della Grada 9 ☎554554 VW (GB)
BOLSENA Viterbo 3,950 (☎0761) Map **31** B3

★★**Columbus** ☎98009 40⇄ 🏛 P ♪ dB⇄ ▥ 20400
(English breakfast) L6000 D6000 lake
★★**Lido Sul Lago** via Cassia ☎98026 12⇄ 🏛 P ♪
sB⇄ ▥ 12000 dB⇄ ▥ 16000 (English breakfast) L6000
D6000 lake
BOLZANO-BOZEN Bolzano 107,100 (☎0471)
Map **12** D1

★★★★**Alpi** via Alto Adige 33–35 ☎25625 tx40156
112rm57⇄37 ▥ 🏛 P Lift ♪ sB16800 sB⇄ ▥ 22800
dB⇄ ▥ 39500 (English breakfast) L6500 D6500
mountains
☆☆☆**AGIP** Ponte Roma ☎33364 18 ▥
★★★**Grifone** pza Walther 7 (DP) ☎27057 tx40081
130rm70⇄20 ▥ Lift Pool
★★★*Laurin* via Laurin 2 ☎47500 tx40081
120rm74⇄ 🏛 Lift Pool
★★★*Cita di Bolzano* pza Walther 21 ☎21240
97rm50⇄ Lift
★★**Figl** pza Grano 9 ☎21412 25rm16⇄4 ▥ Lift ♪
sB8500 dB15000–17000 dB⇄ ▥ 17500–18500
(English breakfast) L5000 D5500
★★*Luna* via Bottai 25 ☎21429 80rm62⇄25 ▥ 🏛
Lift 🏖
★★**Scala** via Brennero 11 ☎41111 70rm25⇄45 ▥ 🏛
P Lift ♪ sB⇄ ▥ 16000 dB⇄ ▥ 29000 L alc D alc Pool
🐾**Bolzano** via Roma 98 ☎36265 BL/Cit (GB)
🔧 🏍*Mich* via Ospedale 2 ☎41119 M/c BL/Rov/Tri

🔧 🏍**1000 Miglia** via Macello 13 ☎26340☎21000
Bed/Opl/Vau
🐾*SAS Motor* via Macello 53 ☎25373 BMW
🐾**E Tasini** via Roma N 61 B ☎916465 Frd
BONASSOLA La Spezia 1,200 (☎0187) Map **29** A2

★★**Lungomare** ☎813632 Closed Oct–Apr
44rm14⇄14 ▥ P sB7500 dB10500 dB⇄ ▥ 12000
(English breakfast) L5000 D5500 St%
BORCA DI CADORE Belluno 750 Map **13** A1
At **Corte di Cadre** (2km E)
★★★*Bolte* ☎82001 Closed Oct–19 Dec & Apr–May
84 ▥ Lift 🏖
BORDIGHERA Imperia 11,900 (☎0184) Map **28** D2

★★★★**Grand del Mare** via Aurelia ☎262201
tx27535 Closed 16 Oct–14 Dec 126rm116⇄10 ▥
A40rm 🏛 P Lift ♪ sB⇄ ▥ 34000–37500
dB⇄ ▥ 63000–70000 (English breakfast) D13500 🏖
Pool Beach sea
★★★★*Jolanda* corso Italia 85 ☎261325 Closed Oct
& Nov 48rm45⇄ P Lift ♪ sB12000–14000
sB⇄ ▥ 16500–18500 dB22000–23000
dB⇄ ▥ 23000–27500 (English breakfast) L fr9000
D fr9000 sea
★★★*Belvedere* via Romana (n rest) 56 ☎261408
Closed 11 Jan–14 Mar & 27 Sep–21 Dec 78rm34⇄
P Lift ♪ sB8800–11800 sB⇄ ▥ 12800–14800
dB16550–21750 dB⇄ ▥ 22550–27750 sea
★★**Excelsior** via Gl-Biamonti 30 ☎261488 Closed
Nov–17 Dec 43rm20⇄10 ▥ 🏛 P Lift ♪
sB7500–10500 sB⇄ ▥ 8500–10500
dB13000–15000 dB⇄ ▥ 19000–21000
(English breakfast) L fr6500 D fr6500 beach sea
★★*Villa Elisa* via Romana 70 ☎261313 Closed
11 Oct–19 Dec 35rm25⇄2 ▥ P Lift ♪ sB8300–9300
sB⇄ ▥ 10300–12800 dB13600–16600
dB⇄ ▥ 18600–21600 (English breakfast) L7500
D7500 sea
🐾*G Renalto* via Ferrara 8 ☎22908 Frd
BÓRMIO Sondrio 4,050 (☎0342) Map **12** D1

★★*Funivia* ☎91341 Closed Oct 41rm19⇄ 🏛 Lift
★★**Posta** via Roma 66 ☎901106 tx35425 Closed 21
Apr–19 Jun & 21 Sep–Nov 55rm33⇄16 ▥ 🏛 Lift ♪
sB⇄ ▥ 10500–12500 dB⇄ ▥ 21000–23000
(English breakfast) L7500 D7500 St% mountains
BRÉSCIA Bréscia 213,130 (☎030) Map **29** B4

☆☆☆*AGIP* viale Bornata 42 ☎361654 42 ▥ Lift
🐾*Astra-Motor* via F-Boario 16 ☎57561 Frd
Brescia Motori via L-Apollonia 17A ☎50051
BL/Rov/Tri
BRESSANONE-BRIXEN Bolzano 16,150 (☎0472)
Map **13** A1

★★★*Elefante* Rio Bianco 4 ☎22288 tx40491 Closed
Nov–Feb 48⇄ A16rm 🏛
★★★**Gasser** via Giardini 19 ☎22105 Closed
23 Oct–Mar 30rm26⇄4 ▥ 🏛 P ♪
sB⇄ ▥ 14000–16500 dB⇄ ▥ 28000–33000
(English breakfast) L6000 D6000 mountains
🔧🏍**F U Lanz** via Stazione 32 ☎22226 ☎22226 🏍 M/c
P Aud/Por/VW (GB)

BREUIL See **CERVÍNIA-BREUIL**

BRINDISI Brindisi 85,100 (☎0831) Map **34** D3

★★★**Internazionale** Lungomare Regina Margherita
☎23475 87rm⇄ ▥ 🏛 P Lift ♪ sB⇄ ▥ 17500
dB⇄ ▥ 27000 (English breakfast) L6500 D6500 sea
★★★**Jolly** corso Umberto 149 ☎22941 tx86078
77rm54⇄ ▥ P Lift ♪ sB13750 sB⇄ ▥ 18700 dB22500
dB⇄ ▥ 29700 L7000 D7000
Giovine Blagio via Cappuccini 70 ☎23037 M/c Opl
🐾*T Marino* via Appia 340 ☎81888 Frd (GB)
BRUNICO-BRUNECK Bolzano 10,800 (☎0474)
Map **13** A1

★★★**Posta** Greben 9 ☎85127 tx40350
64rm34⇄16 ▥ P ♪ sB16000–20000
sB⇄ ▥ 16000–20000 dB26000–27600
dB⇄ ▥ 30000–37000 (English breakfast)
L5000–6000 D5000–6000

CADENÅBBIA Como (☎0344) Map **29** A4
★**Beau-Rivage** via Regina 87 ☎40426 Closed
Nove – Mar 20rm3⇌2 🏠 P sB8400 – 9600
sB⇌ 🏠10300 – 11300 dB15100 – 15900
dB⇌🏠17600 – 19600 (English breakfast) L5500
D6000 ✍ Beach lake

CAGLIARI See **SARDEGNA (SARDINIA)**

CALTAGIRONE See **SICILIA (SICILY)**

CAMAIORE (LIDO DI) Lucca 4,041 (☎0584)
Map **29** B2
★★★**Grand & Riviera** pza Matteotti 64 ☎64571
Closed 11 Oct – 9 May 73rm14⇌32 🏠 🏠 P Lift
♪ sB7000 – 11500 sB⇌🏠 10500 – 18500
dB14000 – 23000 dB⇌🏠18000 – 31000
L10000 – 12000 D10000 – 12000 Beach sea
★★**Pineta Mare** viale C-Colombo 195 ☎64623 33⇌
Lift sea
🏠**L Galletti** via Brancola 2 ☎90024 ☎90024 Jag/Vlo
(GB)

CAMOGLI Genova 7,050 (☎0185) Map **29** A3
★★★★**Cenobio dei Dogi** via Cuneo 34 ☎770041
tx24116 75⇌ 🏠 P Lift ♪ sB⇌22500 – 27500
dB⇌39000 – 49000 L11000 D11000 ✍ Pool Beach
♪ ○ sea
★★**Casmona** via Garibaldi 103 ☎770015 34rm14🏠
A15rm sea

CAMPIONE D'ITALIA See page 380 (Italian enclave
in Switzerland)

CAMPOBASSO Campobasso 44,050 (☎0874)
Map **33** A/B4
P Vitale via XXIV Maggio 95 ☎61069 Aud/MB
Por/VW

CAMPO NELL'ELBA See **ELBA (ISOLA D')**

CANAZEI Trento 1,500 (☎0462) Map **13** A1
★★**Croce Bianca** via Roma 3 ☎61111 tx40012
Closed 27 Dec – 14Apr 30⇌ 🏠 P ♪
sB⇌ 🏠10000 – 14000 dB⇌ 🏠20000 – 24000
(English breakfast) L8000 D8000 mountains

CANDELI See **FIRENZE (FLORENCE)**

CÅNNERO RIVIERA Novara 1,450 (☎0323)
Map **28** D4
★★**Cannero** Lungo Lago ☎78046 Closed Nov –
14 Mar 32rm16⇌16 🏠 🏠 P Lift sB⇌ 🏠 fr8000
dB⇌ 🏠8000 – 10000 Pool ♪ sea lake

CÅORLE Venezia 11,100 (☎0421) Map **30** C4
★★**Excelsior** viale A-Vespucci ☎81515 Closed
Oct – Apr 55rm39⇌16 🏠 P Lift ♪ sB12500 – 14500
sB⇌ 🏠12500 – 14500 dB⇌ 🏠21000 – 23000
(English breakfast) L6000 – 7500 D6000 – 7500
Beach sea
★★**Parigi** ☎81430 Closed Oct – 14 May 56rm45 🏠 P
Lift sB6800 – 9300 dB10600 – 15600
dB⇌12600 – 18600 L5500 D5500 St% Beach sea
♪ 🏠**G Cecotto** via Strada Nuova 64 ☎81315 M/c

CAPO BOI See **VILLASIMIUS** under **SARDEGNA
(SARDINIA)**

CAPRI (ISOLA DI) Napoli 12,350 (☎081) Map **32** D1
★★★★★**Quisisana & Grand** via Carmerelle 2
☎8370788 tx71520 130⇌1 Lift ✍ Pool sea
★★★★**Tiberio Palace** via Croce 13 ☎8370100
Closed Nov – 14 Mar 96rm85⇌11 🏠 Lift ♪
sB⇌ 🏠21300 – 23500 dB⇌ 🏠37900 – 41400
(English breakfast) L8800 D8800 sea
★★**Manfredi Pagano** viale Campi 15 ☎837202
30rm12⇌2 🏠 sea
At **Anacapri**

★★★**San Michele**☎8371427 40rm35⇌ 🏠 P Lift ♪
sB12650 – 13150 sB⇌16650 – 17150
dB23800 – 24300 dB⇌25800 – 26300 L6500 D6500
sea mountains lake

CARBONIN DI DOBBIACO See **CORTINA
D'AMPEZZO**

CARRARA (MARINA DI) Massa Carrara 7,920
(☎0585) Map **29** A2
★★**Mediterraneo** via Genova 2 bis ☎57397
50rm4⇌46 🏠 P Lift ♪ sB7500 – 8500
sB⇌ 🏠11000 – 15500 dB⇌ 🏠18000 – 22000
L6500 – 7000 D6500 – 7000 sea
★★**Paradiso** viale Litoraneo 121 ☎5115 Closed
Oct – 14 May 24rm5⇌ Beach sea

CASERTA Caserta 65,500 (☎0823) Map **33** A3
★★★**Jolly** viale V-Veneto 9 ☎25222 tx71548 92⇌ P
Lift ♪ sB⇌18000 dB⇌29500 L8000 D8000
🏠**Colombo** via Colombo 56 ☎25268 P Cit/Lnc
MB/Ren
♪ 🏠**M Masullo** via Roma 78 – 92 ☎26441
BL/Rov/Tri

CASSINO Frosinone 28,300 (☎0776) Map **32** C2
★★**Florida** pza Diaz 14 ☎22041 30rm10⇌4 🏠 🏠

CASTELLINA IN CHIANTI Siena 2,900 (☎0577)
Map **29** B2
★★**Villa Casalecchi** ☎740240 Closed Nov – 14 Mar
15⇌ P sB⇌13200 (room only) dB⇌21550 (room
only) Pool
At **Ricavo** (4km N)
★★★**Tenuta di Ricavo** (DP & Pn) ☎740221 Closed
Nov – mid Apr 26⇌ P sB⇌25000 – 33000
dB⇌50000 – 66000 ✍ Pool

CASTELVETRANO See **SICILIA (SICILY)**

CASTIGLIENCELLO Livorno 3,3433 (☎0586)
Map **29** B2
★★★**Miramare** via Marconi 8 ☎752435 Closed
Oct – Mar 64rm42⇌18 🏠 A6rm P Lift ♪
sB9500 – 15000 sB⇌ 🏠 15000 – 17500
dB16000 – 20500 dB⇌ 🏠21400 – 27500
L7000 – 9000 D7000 – 9000 sea
★★**Guerrini** via Roma 12 ☎752047 29rm2⇌11 🏠 P
sB7600 – 7800 sB⇌🏠8800 – 9600 dB 13500
dB⇌ 🏠16200 – 17000 L 5500 – 6500 D5500 – 6500

CATANIA See **SICILIA (SICILY)**

CATANZARO Catanzaro 89,700 (☎0961)
Map **34** C2
☆☆☆**AGIP** exit Strada due Mari ☎51791 76 🏠 Lift
♪ 🏠 **Autosabin** via Cassio doro ☎61857 P Frd

CATTÓLICA Forlì 15,850 (☎0541)) Map **30** C2
★★★★**Victoria Palace** via Carducci 24 ☎962921
tx55459 98rm90⇌8 🏠 P Lift ♪ ♪ sB⇌ 🏠12500 – 24000
dB⇌ 🏠22000 – 31000 (English breakfast) L 7500
D7500 Beach sea
★★★**Caravelle** ☎962417 Closed Nov – Mar 45⇌ 🏠
Lift Beach sea
★★★**Diplomat** via del Turismo ☎962975 Closed
16 Sep – 24 May 80⇌ P Lift ♪ sB⇌9000 – 12000
dB⇌16000 – 24000 (English breakfast) L 7000
D7000 sea
★★★**Europa-Monetti** via Curiel 33 (n rest) ☎961159
Closed 16 Sep – 14 May 77rm20⇌50 🏠 🏠 P Lift ♪
sB 11000 – 12500 sB⇌ 🏠12000 – 13500
dB 13000 – 19000 dB⇌ 🏠 15000 – 25000
L 6000 – 7000 D6000 – 7000 Beach
★★★**Gambrinus Mare** viale Oriani ☎961347 Closed
Nov – Apr 42rm33 🏠 P Lift ♪ sB 8000 – 10000
sB⇌🏠9000 – 11000 dB 12000 – 14000

Italy

dB🍴 14000 – 16000 (English breakfast) L6000
D6000 St% Beach sea
★★★**Moderno Majestic** viale d'Annunzio 13 (Pn)
☎961169 Closed 21 Sep – Apr 60 rm53⇄7🍴 A10rm
P Lift ♪ sB10000 – 16000 sB⇄10000 – 16000
dB13000 – 18000 dB⇄🍴13000 – 18000
(English breakfast) L5000 D5000 Beach sea
★★★**Rosa** via Carducci 80 ☎963275 Closed
21 Sep – 19 May 57⇄🍴 🏛 P Lift ♪ sB⇄8000 – 9000
dB15000 – 17000 (English breakfast) L5000 – 6000
D5000 – 6000 Beach sea
★★**Maxim** via Facchini 7 ☎962137 Closed
16 Sep – May 55rm4⇄51🍴 P Lift ♪
sB⇄🍴6900 – 8800 dB⇄🍴13400 – 17000
(English breakfast) L4500 – 5000 D4500 – 5000
★★**Nord-Est** viale Carducci 60 ☎961293 Closed
21 Oct – Apr 72rm16⇄ Lift Beach sea
★★**Senior** viale Del prete (n rest) ☎963443 Closed
Oct – Apr 46rm16⇄46🍴 A10rm P Lift ♪
sB⇄🍴6500 – 8000 dB⇄🍴7500 – 9500
(English breakfast) L4000 – 5000 D4000 – 5000 Pool
★**Bellariva** via Fiume 10 ☎961609 Closed
21 Sep – 4 May 24rm8⇄4🍴 ♪ sB4800 – 6800
sB⇄🍴5300 – 7300 dB9600 – 10600
dB⇄🍴10600 – 11600 (English breakfast)
L3000 – 4000 D4000 – 6000
🛢 ⏚**A Fernando** via del Prete 4 ☎961055 P Aud/VW
(GB)
CAVA DE' TIRENNI Salerno 48,350 (☎089)
Map 33 B3
★★**Victoria** Corso Mazzini 4 ☎841064
42rm10⇄27🍴 🏛 P Lift ♪ sB8300 – 9600
sB⇄🍴10600 – 11600 dB14800 – 16100
dB⇄🍴17600 – 19600 (English breakfast) L5500
D5500 ✒ Beach mountains
CAVAGLIA' Vercelli 3,100 (☎0161) Map 28 D4
★★**Prateria** ☎96115 Closed Dec – Feb 32⇄ 🏛 P
sB⇄10800 dB⇄19600 (English breakfast) Lfr8000
Dfr8000 mountains
CAVI See **LAVAGNA**
CELLE LIGURE Savona 4,800 (☎019) Map 28 D3
★★★**San Michele** Piani ☎990017 Closed Oct – May
57rm50⇄ P Lift ♪ sB15000 – 16500
dB⇄20000 – 24900 L7000 – 9000 D7000 – 9000 Pool
sea
CERIALE Savona 4,210 (☎0182) Map 28 D2
★★**Torelli** Lungomare ☎90040 Closed 15 Oct – Dec
80rm50⇄ P Lift sB⇄8500 – 10500 dB⇄15000
(English breakfast) L4500 D4500 Beach sea
CERNÓBBIO Como 8,250 (☎031) Map 29 A4
★★★★★**Villa d'Este** ☎511471 tx38025 Closed
Nov – Mar 160rm150⇄10🍴 🏛 Lift ✒ Pool 🕯 lake
★★★**Regina Olga** ☎510171 tx38821 67rm50⇄17🍴
🏛 P Lift ♪ sB⇄🍴18200 – 22200
dB⇄🍴30600 – 33850 L7500 D7500 Pool mountains
lake
★**Asnigo** pza San Stefano ☎510062 Closed
Nov – Mar 22rm 10🍴 P sB8800 dB15600 dB🍴19600
(English breakfast) L5500 D5500 lake
CÉRVIA Ravenna 24,150 (☎0544) Map 30 C3
★★**Buenos Aires** Lungomare G-Deledda 130
☎71948 tx55394 Closed Oct – Mar 58rm 🏛 P Lift ♪
sB⇄🍴10500 – 11500 dB⇄🍴17500 – 19000
(English breakfast) L5500 – 7000 D6500 – 7500
Beach sea
★★**K2** viale dei Mille 98 ☎71025 Closed 21 Sep –
19 May 37rm1⇄36🍴 Beach sea
🛢 ⏚**Opel-Cervia** via Oriani 57 ☎991390 🔧 Opl
At **Milano Marittima** (3km N)
★★★★**Aurelia** viale 2 Giugno 18 ☎972082 Closed
Oct – Apr 113⇄🍴 Lift ✒ Pool Beach sea
★★★★**Mare & Pineta** viale Dante ☎992262 Closed
21 Sep – 14 May 197⇄ 🏛 P Lift ♪ sB⇄🍴21000
dB⇄🍴36000 L10000 D10000 ✒ Pool Beach 🌓 sea
🛢 ✒**Europa** viale 2 Giugno 15 ☎92276 P Fia
CERVÍNIA-BREUIL Aosta 2,050 (☎0166)
Map 28 D4
★★★★**Cervinia** ☎94028 Closed May – Nov
78rm74⇄4🍴 🏛 Lift

★★**Valdôtain** Lago Bleu ☎94428 Closed Jun, Oct &
Nov 30⇄🍴 🏛 P Lift sB⇄🍴9500 – 11500
dB⇄🍴17000 – 21000 (English breakfast)
L6000 – 7000 D6000 – 7000 mountains lake
CESENÀTICO Forli 19,500 (☎0547) Map 30 C2
★★★**Britannia** viale Carducci 129 ☎80041 Closed
10 Sep – 25 May 44⇄ 🏛 P Lift ♪
sB⇄🍴11500 – 17500 dB⇄🍴20000 – 29000
(English breakfast) L7000 – 8000 D7000 – 8000
Beach sea
★★★**Grand** pza Costa ☎80012 Closed
16 Sep – May 94rm60⇄ A34rm 🏛 P Lift ♪
sB10000 – 15700 sB⇄12500 – 17700
dB17000 – 27000 dB⇄19000 – 33000
(English breakfast) L9000 – 9500 D9000 – 9500 St%
✒ Beach 🕯
★★★**Internazionale** via Ferrara 7 ☎80231 Closed
Oct – May 50⇄ P Lift ♪ sB⇄9000 – 13500
dB⇄12000 – 17000 (English breakfast) L5000 – 7000
D5000 – 7000 St% ✒ Pool Beach sea
★★★**Torino** viale Carducci 55 ☎80044 Closed
21 Sep – 19 May 48🍴 P Lift ♪ sB🍴6800 – 9200
dB🍴12600 – 15400 (English breakfast) L5000 – 6000
D5000 – 6000 sea
🛢 **Internazionale** viale Carducci 95 ☎81418 Opl
🛢✒**Luciano** via A-Saffi 91 ☎81347 BMW/Lnc/MB
(GB)
CHIÀVARI Genova 31,900 (☎0185) Map 29 A2/3
★★**Mignon** via A-Salietti 7 ☎309420 32rm20⇄ Lift
♪ sB5500 – 6750 sB⇄7000 – 9000
dB⇄11500 – 14600 (English breakfast) L5000 – 6000
D5000 – 6000
★★**Santa Maria** via T-Groppo ☎309621 36rm8⇄ 🏛
Lift sea
★★**Tigullio Rocks** via Aurelia 61 (on SS 1) ☎318193
11rm4⇄4🍴 P sB6600 dB⇄🍴16400 Pool Beach sea
🛢✒**Cantero** corso Dante 90 ☎307018 P (GB)
G-Ughini V Nazario Sauro 13 – 15 ☎308278
☎390549 Aud/MB/VW
CHIAVENNA Sondrio 7,450 (☎0343) Map 12 C1
★★★**Conradi** ☎32300 34rm6⇄6🍴 🏛 Lift
★★**Nazionale** pza Bertacchi 72 ☎32303
17rm1⇄2🍴
CHIÓGGIA Venezia 52,100 (☎041) Map 30 C3
★★**Grande Italia** pza Vigo ☎400515 Closed
7 Nov – 14 Dec 61rm20⇄ Lift sea
🛢✒**Autolagunare** via Orti Est 31 ☎401110 Fia
CHIUSA-KLAUSEN Bolzano 4,050 (☎0472)
Map 13 A1
★**Post Hotel Posta** ☎47514 61rm19⇄6🍴 🏛 P Lift
sB7000 – 8000 sB⇄🍴8500 – 9500 dB13000 – 16000
dB⇄🍴17000 – 19000 (English breakfast)
L5000 – 8000 D5000 – 8000 Pool mountains
CHIVASSO Torino 26,300 (☎011) Map 28 D3
★**Moro** via Roma 17 ☎9102191 39rm7⇄ 🏛
CIRELLA Cosenza 1,207 (☎0985) Map 34 C2
☆**Autostello** ☎86055 82rm12⇄70🍴 A51rm Beach
sea
CITTÀ DELLA PIEVE Perugia 6,500 (☎0578)
Map 31 B3
★★**Barzanti** via Santa Lucia ☎28010 30rm26⇄ P
sB8200 sB⇄9200 dB12400 dB⇄14400
(English breakfast) L5000 D5000 ✒ Pool 🕯
mountains lake
CIVITAVÈCCHIA Roma 46,150 (☎0766) Map 31 B3
SAC Lungomare Garibaldi 42 ☎21830 BL
CLAVIERE Torino 200 (☎0122) Map 28 C3
★★**Bes** ☎8805 Closed 16 Apr – 14 Jun & 16
Sep – Nov 19rm12⇄ 🏛
CÓLICO Como 5,250 (☎0341) Map 29 A4
★★**Isola Bella** via Nazionale 6 ☎940101 44rm22⇄
🏛 P sB7200 sB⇄8200 dB13400 dB⇄14400 St%
mountains lake
★**Gigi** ☎940268 18rm4⇄ 🏛
★**Risi** pza Cavour 1 ☎940123 50⇄ 🏛 P Lift ♪
sB⇄10500 dB⇄19000 (English breakfast) L6000
D6000 lake

COMO Como 98,550 (☎031) Map **29** A4
★★★**Flori** via Per Cernobbio 12 (n rest) ☎557642
49rm41⇌7🗐 P lift ♪ sB12200 sB⇌🗐22500
dB21000 dB⇌🗐34100 (English breakfast) lake
★★**Engadina** viale Rosselli 22 ☎550415
21rm9⇌12🗐 Lift
★★**Firenze** pza Volta 16 ☎272001 (DP) 34rm7⇌4🗐
Lift
★★**Park** viale Rosselli 20 ☎556782 Closed
Dec–Feb 42rm15⇌15🗐 lift
★★**San Gottardo** pza Volta ☎263531 55rm25⇌9🗐
Lift ♪ sB fr9250 sB⇌🗐 fr15000 dB fr15250
dB⇌🗐 fr24000 (English breakfast) L fr7500 D fr7500
mountains lake
★**Tre Re** (DP) ☎265374 33rm13⇌ 🗐
⌷ ⋈ Autorimessa Dante via Dante 59 ☎272545 P
Ren
Grassi & Airoldi via Napoleona 50 ☎266027
BL/Rov/Tri
At **Lipomo** (4km S)
★**MEC** via Provinciale per Lercco (n rest) ☎269227
35rm29⇌ ⋇

CONCA DEI MARINI Salerno 750 (☎089)
Map **33** B3
★★★**Belvedere** ☎871266 Closed Nov–Mar
33rm30⇌3🗐 P lift ♪ sB⇌🗐12000–15000
dB⇌🗐22000–26000 (English breakfast) L7000
D7000 Pool Beach sea mountains

CORTE DI CADORE See **BORCA DI CADORE**

CORTINA D'AMPEZZO Belluno 8,650 (☎0436)
Map **13** A1
★★★★**Corona** corso C-Battisti ☎3251 tx44004
Closed Apr–19 Jun & 11 Sep–19 Dec 56rm40⇌2🗐
A10rm 🗐 Lift
★★★★**Miramonti Majestic** ☎4201 Closed Apr–
9 Jun & 11 Sep–Nov 143rm113⇌30🗐 🗐 Lift ⋇
Pool ⸹
★★★★**Savoia** via Roma 62 ☎3201 tx44004 Closed
Apr–27 Jun & 11 Sep–19 Dec 145⇌ 🗐 lift ⋇ Pool
☆☆☆**AGIP** via Roma 70 ☎839101 28🗐 lift
★★★**Ampezzo** via 29 Maggio 15 ☎4241 Closed 26
Mar–19 May & 26 Sep–9 Dec 80 rm54⇌7🗐 P lift ♪
sB15500–17000 sB⇌🗐21500–24000
dB26000–29000 dB⇌🗐33000–40000
(English breakfast) L7000–9000 D7000–9000
mountains
★★★**Ancora** corso Italia 62 ☎3261 tx44004 Closed
17 Apr–14 Jun & 16 Sep–20 Dec 140rm57⇌7🗐 🗐
P Lift ♪ sB15500–16500 sB⇌🗐20500–23500
dB26000–28000 dB⇌🗐26000–39000
(English breakfast) L7000–10000 D7000–10000
mountains
★★★**Cortina** corso Italia 94 ☎4221 tx44004 Closed
21 Sep–19 Dec & 16 Apr–14 Jun 51⇌ 🗐 P lift ♪
sB18000 sB⇌26000 dB31000 dB⇌42000
(English breakfast) L11000 D11000 mountains
★★★**Cristallo Palace** ☎4281
Closed Apr, May, Oct & Nov 100⇌ 🗐 Lift ⋇ Pool sea
★★★**Europa** corso Italia 207 ☎3221 tx44004 52⇌ P
Lift ♪ sB⇌20000–25800 dB⇌34600–40600
L8000–12000 D8000–12000 mountains
★★★**Parc Concordia** corso Italia 28 ☎4251 tx44004
Closed Apr–24 Jun & 6 Sep–19 Dec 70rm40⇌ 🗐 P
Lift ♪ sB15500–19500 sB⇌20500–29500
dB26000–32000 dB⇌34000–43000
(English breakfast) L8000–11000 D8000–11000
mountains
★★★**Poste** pza Roma 14 ☎4271 tx44044 Closed
21 Oct–19 Dec 82⇌ 🗐 P ♪ sB⇌🗐23000–32600
dB⇌🗐34000–50200 (English breakfast)
L10000–12000 D10000–12000 mountains
★★**Alpes** via la Vera 4 ☎2021 Closed Apr–24Jun &
26 Sep–19 Dec 37rm4 ⇌
★★**Menardi** Majon 114 ☎2400 Closed Apr, May, Oct
& Nov 40rm35⇌ 🗐
★**Tiziano** Campo di Sotto 26 ☎2504 Closed Apr–
14 Jun & 16 Sep–19 Dec 41rm21⇌
⌷ ⋈ Dolomiti corso Italia 182 ☎61077 P Fia/Lnc
(GB)

At **Carbonin di Dobbiaco** (17km NE S51)
★★**Ploner** ☎72240 tx44004 Closed Nov–14 Dec
85rm18⇌10🗐 A21rm 🗐 P sB8500–11500
sB⇌🗐 9500–15150 dB16000–20400
dB⇌🗐18000–26000 L6000 D6500 ⋇ ⌒ mountains

COSENZA Cosenza 102,550 (☎0984) Map **34** C2
★★★**Jolly** Lungo Crati de Seta 2B ☎74481 48⇌ P ♪
sB⇌15750 dB⇌28500 L7000 D7000
At **Rende** (6km NW off S107)
☆☆☆**AGIP** Castiglione Cosentino Scalo ☎839101
65🗐 Lift
⌷ ⋈ AMC Via S Pellico ☎39598 M/c BMW

COSTALUNGA (PASSO DI) Trento Map **13** A1
★★**Passo di Carezza** ☎61023 Closed Oct–14 Jun
43rm10⇌ 🗐
★★**Savoy Tamlon** Carezza Al Lago ☎616824
45rm15⇌15🗐 🗐 P sB10500–12000
sB⇌🗐12500–15000 dB23000–31000
dB⇌🗐30000–34000 (English breakfast)
L6000–7000 D7000–8000 Pool Beach sea
mountains

COURMAYEUR Aosta 2,550 (☎0165) Map **28** C4
★★★★★**Royal** ☎83621 Closed Apr–26 Jun & 11
Sep–21 Dec 80⇌ 🗐 Lift Pool
★★★★**Pavillon** ☎82420 Closed Nov & May 40⇌ 🗐
P Lift ♪ sB⇌21000–26000 dB⇌38000–48000
(English breakfast) L10000–12000 D10000–12000
Pool mountains
★★★**Alpes** ☎89981 Closed 29Sep–5 Dec 56⇌ 🗐
Lift

CREMONA Cremona 82,650 (☎0372) Map **29** A3
★★★**Continental** pza Libertà 27 (DP) ☎430209
51⇌ 🗐 Lift
General Cars via Castelleone 77–79 ☎20343
Bed/Opl/Vau
⌷ ⋈ Cunicar Via Torino ☎66442 BL/Rov/Tri

CÚNEO Cuneo 56,050 (☎0171) Map **28** C/D3
★★★**Augustus Minerva** corso Giolitti 1 ☎65934
67rm47⇌10🗐 Lift
★★**Royal Superga** via Pascal 3 ☎3223 48rm29⇌ 🗐
⌷ ⋈ Cunicar via Torino ☎66442 BL/Rov/Tri

DESENZANO DEL GARDA Brescia 18,750 (☎030)
Map **29** B4
★★★**Mayer & Splendid** pza del Porto ☎9141409
Closed 11 Nov–14 Mar 56rm14⇌28🗐 P Lift
sB6800–7800 sB⇌🗐7800–8800 dB13600–14600
dB⇌🗐14600–15600 (English breakfast) L fr6000
D fr6000 lake
★★★**Ramazzotti** viale dal Molin 78 ☎9141808
tx30395 22rm10⇌ 🗐 P ♪ sB9500 (room only)
sB⇌12000 (room only) dB16000 (room only)
dB⇌19000 (room only)
★★**Barchetta** pza Matteoti 27 ☎9141006 36rm 8⇌
2🗐 lake
★★**Eden** Lungolago Battisti 27 ☎9141416 18rm12⇌
A12rm P sB fr9500 dB fr9500 dB11400–12900
dB⇌15000 L fr6000 D fr6000
★★**Vittorio** Portovecchio 18 ☎9141504 35rm 20⇌
5🗐 lake

DIANO MARINA Imperia 6,950 (☎0183) Map **28** D2
★★★★**Diana Majestic** via degli Oleandri 15 ☎45445
tx28025 Closed 21 Oct–19 Mar 80rm72⇌8🗐 🗐 P
Lift ♪ sB⇌🗐24500–28500 dB⇌🗐33000–39000
(English breakfast) L14000 D14000 Pool Beach sea
★★**Florida** via St-Elmo 21 ☎45226 Closed Oct–14
May 88rm 15⇌73🗐 Lift Beach sea
★★**Riviera** viale Torino 6 ☎45147 Closed 11 Oct–14
Dec 32rm23🗐 P Lift sB8300 dB12000 dB🗐14700
L5000 D6000 sea
★★**Teresa** viale Torino 34 ☎45007 Closed Oct–Apr
138rm52⇌6🗐 Lift Beach sea
⋈ G Ghirardi via Gl-Ardoino 211 ☎45334 M/c P AR
(GB)

ELBA (ISOLA D) Livorno 28,250 (☎0565)
Lacona 140 Map **31** A3
★★★**Capo Sud** ☎964021 Closed Oct–Apr
34rm2⇌32🗐 🗐 P ♪ sB⇌🗐7500–13500

Italy

dB⇄ ⋔ 12500 – 25000 (English breakfast)
L8000 – 9000 D8000 – 9000 ⚓ Beach sea
Marciana-Marina 1,830 Map **31** A3
★★★***Primula*** ☎99010 Closed Nov – Mar
63rm40⇄23 ⋔ ⚓ Beach sea
At **Procchio** (7km SE)
★★★★***Golfo*** ☎907445 tx59690 Closed 16 Oct – 14
May 95rm75⇄20 ⋔ P ♪ sB⇄ ⋔ 16600 – 22200
dB⇄ ⋔ 29200 – 40200 (English breakfast) L11500
D11500 ⚓ Pool Beach sea
At **Spartaia** (5.5km SE)
★★★***Désirée*** ☎907502 tx59220 Closed 16 Oct – 14
Apr 69 ⋔ P ♪ sB⇄ 18300 – 32500 (room only)
dB ⋔ 16800 – 24000 (room only) ⚓ Beach
Marina di Campo 4,308 Map **31** A3
★★★***Iselba*** (DP) ☎97096 Closed 16Oct – 14May
45rm21⇄22 ⋔ Beach Beach sea
Porto Azzurro 2,940 Map **31** A3
★★★**Elba International** ☎968611 tx59669 Closed
Nov – Feb 242⇄ ⋔ ♪ ⚓ Pool Beach ♨
★**Belmare** ☎95012 tx95076 25⇄ P ♪
sB⇄ ⋔ 7700 – 8000 dB⇄ ⋔ 13900 – 15500
(English breakfast) L5000 – 6000 D5000 – 6000 St%
sea
Portoferraio 10,950 Map **31** A3
★★★★***Darsena*** ☎92661 45⇄ Lift sea
★★★**Garden** ☎966043 tx59220 Closed Nov – Mar
60rm20⇄33 ⋔ P ♪ sB12000 – 12500
dB21000 – 22000 ⋔ ⚓ 125000 – 26000
L7000 – 8000 D7000 – 8000 Beach sea
★★★**Hermitage** ☎969932 tx50219 Closed Oct – 9
May 80rm70⇄ P Lift ♪ sB23600 – 29000
dB39200 – 52000 (English breakfast) L11000 – 13000
D11000 – 13000 ⚓ Pool Beach sea
☷ ♨***Bardi Emilio*** viale Elba 157 ☎93583 Frd
ÉMPOLI Firenze 45,500 (☎0571) Map **29** B2
★★**Tazza d'Oro** via del Papa 46 ☎712129 51rm44⇄
⋔ P Lift ♪ sB9200 sB⇄10700 dB13200 dB⇄ 16400
(English breakfast) L fr4800 D fr4800
ERICE See **SICILIA (SICILY)**
FANO Pesaro & Urbino 50,650 (☎0721) Map **30** C2
★★**Astoria** viale Cairoli ☎82474 Closed Oct – Apr
42rm37⇄ P ♪ sB⇄8000 – 8500 dB11000 – 12000
dB⇄12000 – 14000 (English breakfast) L5000 D5000
Beach sea
★★**Excelsior** Lungomare Simonetti 17 ☎82558
Closed 11 Sep – 14 Jun 30rm3⇄27 ⋔ P
sB7800 – 8300 dB12600 – 14600
dB⇄ 15100 – 16600 L8000 D8000 Beach sea
FASANO DEL GARDA See **GARDONE RIVIERA**
FERENTINO Frosinone 16,370 (☎0775) Map **32** C2
★★**Bassetto** via Casilina Sud ☎394931 72⇄ ⋔ Lift
FERIOLE See **BAVENO**
FERRARA Ferrara 155,500 (☎0532) Map **29** B3
★★★**Astra** viale Cavour 55 ☎26234 82rm52⇄ ⋔ P
Lift ♪ sB13530 sB⇄15630 dB22560 dB⇄26960
(English breakfast) L6000 D6000
★★★**Europa** corso Giovecca 49 (n rest) ☎33460
46rm12⇄7 ⋔ ▦ Lift
★★★**San Giorgio** via Garibaldi 93 (n rest) ☎33141
85rm11⇄31 ⋔ ⋒ Lift
☷ ♨***SIRA*** via Bologna 306 ☎93375 M/c Frd
FIÉSOLE Firenze 16,600 (☎055) Map **29** B2
★★★★**Villa San Michele** via Doccia 4 ☎59451
Closed Nov – 14 Mar 30rm30⇄ P ♪ sB⇄54600
dB⇄82800 (English breakfast) L21000 D21000 St%
★★★**Aurora** pza Mino 39 ☎59100 22rm12⇄8 ⋔ P ♪
sB12300 sB⇄ ⋔ 18900 dB22200 dB⇄ ⋔ 34200
English breakfast only L fr8500 D fr8500 mountains
At **San Domenico** (2·5km S)
★★**Bencista** ☎59163 Closed Nov – 20 Mar
35rm9⇄1 ⋔ A1rm ⋒
FINALE LIGURE Savona 14,250 (☎019) Map **28** D2
★★**Moroni** viale delle Palme 20 ☎63333 Closed 11
Oct – 9 May 113rm80⇄33 ⋔ ⋒ Lift Beach sea
★★★**Tritzo** viale Torino 127 ☎63279 Closed 16
Oct – Nov 50rm27⇄4 ⋔ Lift Beach sea
★**Principe** pza Oberdan 8 ☎63330 Closed

16 Oct – 14 Mar 30rm24⇄ Beach sea
At **Varigotti** (6km E)
★★★**Nik-Mehari** via Aurelia 104 ☎698030
A30rm15⇄15 ⋔ ⋒ P Lift ♪ sB⇄ ⋔ 13600 – 15600
dB⇄ ⋔ 17700 – 19700 (English breakfast) L6000
D65000 Beach sea
FIORE (ON LAKE ARVO) See **LORICA**
FIRENZE (FLORENCE) Firenze 464,900 (☎055)
Map **29** B2 **See Plan**
★★★★★**Excelsior Italia** pza Ognissanti 3 (off
Lungarno A-Vespucci) ☎294301 tx57022 Plan **1**
212⇄ ⋒ P Lift ♪ sB⇄44000 – 59000
dB⇄73000 – 83000 (English breakfast) L20000
D20000 St%
★★★★★***Grand*** pza Ognissanti 1 (off Lungarno A-
Vespucci) ☎294401 tx57055 Plan **2** 151 ⇄ ⋒ Lift
★★★★★***Savoy*** pza della Repubblica 7 ☎283313
tx57220 Plan **3** 96⇄ Lift
★★★★**Villa Medici** via il Prato 42 ☎261331
tx57179 Plan **4** 105⇄ ⋒ P Lift ♪ sB⇄39200 – 60900
dB⇄ 64800 – 93300 (English breakfast) L alc D alc
Pool
★★★★**Aerhotel Baglioni** pza Unità Italiana 6
☎218441 tx57225 Plan **5** 194⇄ P Lift ♪ sB⇄36000
dB⇄58000 (English breakfast) L alc D alc
★★★★**Jolly** pza V-Veneto 4 ☎2770 tx57191 Plan **6**
143⇄ P Lift ♪ sB⇄33050 dB⇄59200 L10000
D10000 Pool
★★★★**Londra** via Jacopo da Diacceto 16 – 20
☎262791 tx58152 Plan **7** 105rm100⇄5 ⋔ ⋒ P Lift ♪
sB⇄31500 – 35700 dB⇄ ⋔ 5100 – 57700
(English breakfast) L11000 D11000
★★★★**Minerva** pza Santa M-Novella 16 ☎284555
tx57414 Plan **8** 112rm94⇄18 ⋔ ⋒ P Lift
sB⇄ ⋔ 27900 – 35650 DB⇄ ⋔ 43800 – 57500
(English breakfast) L alc D alc Pool
★★★**Adriatico** vice Maso Finiguerra 9 ☎261781
tx59265 Plan **10** 110rm74⇄36 ⋔ P Lift ♪
sB⇄ ⋔ 19200 dB⇄ ⋔ 32700 (English breakfast)
L7000 D7000
☆☆☆**AGIP** Riccardo Firenze-Marse/Autostrada del
Sole (12km NW) ☎440081 Plan **11** 109 ⋔ Lift
★★★**Berchielli** Lungarno Acciaioli 14 (n rest)
☎211530 Plan **12** 78rm28⇄7 ⋔ Lift ♪
sB10000 – 15250 sB⇄ ⋔ 22650 dB20650 – 28900
dB⇄ ⋔ 31550 – 34800
★★★**Croce di Malta** via della Scala 7 ☎282600
tx57540 Plan **14** 100rm40⇄60 ⋔ Lift ♪
sB⇄ ⋔ 32500 dB⇄ ⋔ 54500 (English breakfast)
L9000 D9000 Pool
★★★***Embassy*** via Nazionale 23 ☎260806 Plan **15**
25rm13⇄4 ⋔ ⋒ Lift
☆☆☆**EuroCrest** viale Europa 205 ☎686841 tx57376
Plan **13** 92⇄ P Lift ♪ sB⇄ ⋔ fr34500 dB⇄ ⋔ fr50000
L fr6000 D fr6000 Pool
★★★***Hermitage*** vicolo Marzio 1 ☎287216 Plan **16**
16rm12⇄
★★★**Kraft** via Solferino 2 ☎284273 Plan **17**
67rm58⇄5 ⋔ Lift ♪ sB23080 sB⇄ ⋔ 30710 dB36350
dB⇄ ⋔ 49430 L9000 D9000 Pool
★★★**Regency** pza d'Azeglio 3 ☎53602 tx58058
Plan **18** 31rm20⇄11 ⋔ ♪ sB⇄ ⋔ 30000
dB⇄ ⋔ 49000 (English breakfast) L9000 – 11500
D9000 – 11500
★★★**Roma** pza Santa M-Novella 8 (n rest) ☎210366
Plan **19** 61rm27⇄5 ⋔ Lift ♪ sB13500 sB⇄ ⋔ 19350
dB24900 dB⇄ ⋔ 33050 (English breakfast)
★★★**Villa Belvedere** via B-Castelli 3 (n rest)
☎222501 Plan **20** Closed Dec – Feb 27rm 25⇄2 ⋔ P
Lift sB⇄ ⋔ 23500 – 25500 dB⇄ ⋔ 39000 – 41000
(English breakfast) ⚓ Pool
★★★**Villa Park San Domenico** via della Piazzola
☎576697 Plan **21** 19⇄ ⋔ Lift
★★***Autostrada*** via L-Giori 23 ☎371925 Plan **22**
45rm30⇄10 ⋔ ⋒ Lift
★★**Basilea** via Guelfa 41 ☎214587 Plan **23**
49rm40⇄ ⋒ P Lift ♪ sB11700 sB⇄14400 dB19000
dB⇄23150 Pool
★★★***David*** viale Michelangelo 1 (n rest) ☎675867
Plan **24** 26rm6⇄5 ⋔

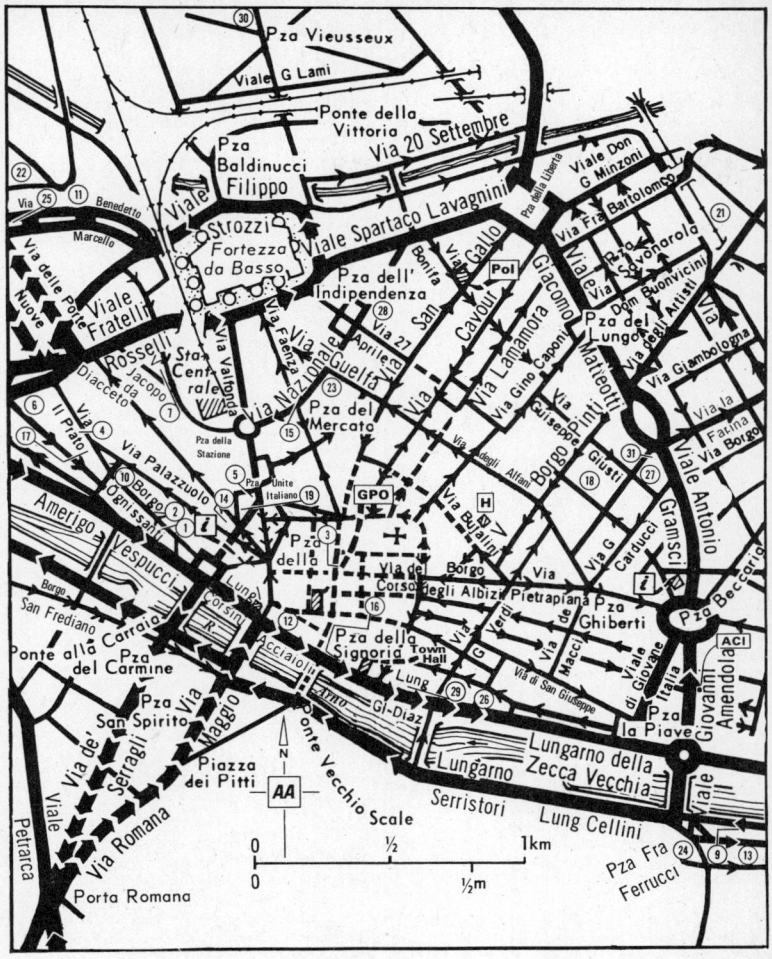

Firenze (Florence)

No.	Hotel	No.	Hotel
1	★★★★★Excelsior Italia	17	★★★Kraft
2	★★★★★Grand	18	★★★Regency
3	★★★★★Savoy	19	★★★Roma
4	★★★★★Villa Medici	20	★★★Villa Belvedere
5	★★★★Aerhotel Baglioni	21	★★★Villa Park San Domenico
6	★★★★Jolly	22	★★Autostrada
7	★★★★Londra	23	★★Basilea
8	★★★★Minerva	24	★★David
9	★★★★Villa Massa (at Candeli 6km SE/ on road to Bagno a Ripoli)	25	★★Franchi
		26	★★Jenning's Riccioli
10	★★★Adriatico	27	★★Liana
11	☆☆☆AGIP	28	★★Rapallo
12	☆☆☆Berchielli	29	★★Rigatti
13	☆☆☆EuroCrest	30	★★Villa Villoresi (at Sesto/ Fiorentino 9km NW)
14	★★★Croce di Malta		
15	★★★Embassy	31	★Losanna
16	★★★Hermitage		

287

Italy

★★**Franchi** via Sgambati 28 ☎372425 Plan **32**
35rm34⇌35 ⋒ 🏠 P Lift sB⇌ ⋒13900 dB⇌ ⋒22100
(English breakfast)
★★*Jenning's Riccioli* Lungarno delle Grazie 2
☎23724 Plan **26** Closed Dec – 14 Mar 65rm60⇌ Lift
★★**Liana** via V-Alfieri 18 ☎587608 Plan **27**
22rm9⇌4 ⋒ 🏠 P Ɔ sB11200 sB⇌ ⋒13900 dB18000
dB⇌ ⋒22150
★★*Rapallo* via Santa Caterind d'Alessandria
☎472412 tx57273 Plan **28** 40rm15⇌10 ⋒ 🏠 Lift
★★*Rigatti* Lungarno Diaz 2 ☎23022 Plan **29** Closed
Dec – 14 Mar 25rm7⇌ Lift
★**Losanna** via V-Alfieri 9 (n rest) ☎587516 Plan **31**
9rm1⇌1 ⋒ 🏠 Lift Ɔ sB7000 dB11500 dB⇌ ⋒14000
(English breakfast) L3500 D3500
Autosalone la Scala Lungarno del Tempio 44
☎677740 P BMW (GB)
🛢 **Europa** Borgognissanti 96 ☎260846 P
Bed/Opl/Vau
🛢 **M Ronchi** via Crimea 8 ☎489855 Frd (GB)
🛢 **Zaniratti** viale Fratelli Rosselli 55 ☎471465
BL/Rov/Tri
At **Candeli** (6km SE on road to **Bagno a Ripoli**)
★★★★ *Villa Massa* ☎630051 Plan **9** 37⇌ A11rm 🏠
Lift Pool lake
At **Sesto Fiorentino** (9km NW)
★★**Villa Villoresi** ☎4489032 Plan **30** 30rm14⇌14 ⋒
P SB14850 sB⇌ ⋒118100 dB24200 dB⇌ ⋒29350
(English breakfast) L fr9100 D fr9100 Pool

FOLIGNO Perugia 51,500 (☎0742) Map **31** B3
★★★**Umbria** via C-Battisti ☎52821 47rm34⇌7 ⋒ 🏠
P Lift Ɔ sB8000 – 8500 sB⇌ ⋒9500 – 13700
dB15500 dB⇌ ⋒ 19000 – 21900 (English breakfast)
L6000 – 6500 D7000 – 75000 mountains

FORIO See **ISCHIA (ISOLA D')**

FERNACI See **ARONA**

FORTE DEI MARMI Lucca 10,400 (☎0584)
Map **29** B2
★★★**Alcione** viale Morin 137 ☎899052 Closed
Oct – May 43rm26⇌6 ⋒ P Lift Ɔ sB 11000 – 12000
sB⇌ ⋒15000 – 17000 dB 17000 – 19000
dB⇌ ⋒20000 – 28000 (English breakfast) L 10000
D10000 Beach sea
★★★**Astoria Garden** via L-da Vinci 10 ☎80754
Closed 16 Sep – 14 May 25rm25⇌ P Ɔ
sB⇌13500 – 16500 dB⇌22000 – 27000
(English breakfast) L 8500 D8500 Beach sea
★★★**Byron** viale Morin 46 ☎80087 Closed Nov – Apr
40rm35⇌ A5rm P Ɔ sB23000 sB⇌ ⋒28000
dB 36000 dB⇌ ⋒41000 (English breakfast) L 10000
D10000 sea mountains
★★★**Raffaelli Park** via Mazzini 37 ☎81494 tx59239
34rm5⇌2 ⋒ A5rm 🏠 P Lift Ɔ sB⇌ ⋒21000 – 31000
dB⇌ ⋒37600 – 50000 (English breakfast) L 10000
D12000 ✈ Pool Beach
★★★**Raffaelli Villa Angela** via G-Mazzini 64
☎80652 tx59239 Closed Nov – Feb 80rm80⇌ A20rm
P Ɔ sB⇌16000 – 24000 dB⇌26000 – 36000
(English breakfast) L 10000 D12000 ✈ Pool Beach
★★**Adams Villa Maria** Lungomare 110 ☎80901
Closed Oct – May 44rm36⇌18 ⋒ A8rm P Lift Ɔ
sB 10000 – 15000 sB⇌ ⋒14000 – 18000
dB 18000 – 26000 dB⇌ ⋒22000 – 30000
(English breakfast) L 3000 – 6000 D3000 – 6000 sea
mountains

FREGENE Roma 1,210 (☎06) Map **31** B2
★★★**Florita** via Castellammare 86 ☎6460435 40⇌ P
Ɔ sB⇌8500 – 12500 dB⇌18000 – 25000 English
breakfast only L 8000 D8000

FROSINONE Frosinone 43,425 (☎0775) Map **32** C2
★★**Palace Hasser** via Brighindi 1 ☎852747 60⇌ ⋒
🏠 P Lift Ɔ sB⇌ ⋒9700 dB⇌ ⋒17900
(English breakfast) L fr4500 Dfr5000 mountains
★**Garibaldi** via Pleblscito 48 (DP) ☎20051 15rm1 ⋒

GABICCE MARE Pesaro & Urbino 5,450 (☎0451)
Map **30** C2
★★**Club de Bona** via Panoramica 33 ☎962622
tx55535 Closed Oct – Apr 50rm10⇌40 ⋒

🏠 P Lift Ɔ sB⇌ ⋒9200 – 11200
dB⇌ ⋒17400 – 20400 (English breakfast) L8000
D8000 Pool Beach sea
★★**Excelsior** via V-Veneto 76 ☎961789 Closed
Oct – Apr 46⇌ 🏠 Lift sea
★★**Valbruna** Redipuglia 1 ☎961843 Closed
Oct – Apr 45rm5⇌5 ⋒ 🏠 Lift Beach sea

GAETA Latina 23,650 (☎0771) Map **32** C2
★★★**Serapo** via Firenze 11, Spiaggia di Serapo
☎460092 103rm87⇌3 ⋒ A31rm 🏠 P Lift Ɔ
sB7400 – 8400 sB⇌ ⋒8900 – 11400
dB12300 – 14800 dB⇌ ⋒15750 – 18300 L5800
D6000 Beach sea

GARDA Verona 3,400 (☎045) Map **29** B4
★★★★**Eurotel** via Gardesann 18 ☎624107 tx48154
150rm120⇌30 ⋒ 🏠 P Lift Ɔ sB⇌ ⋒12000 – 21000
dB⇌ ⋒22500 – 40000 (English breakfast) L85000
D85000 Pool lake
★★★**Regina Adelaide Palace** via 20 Settembre
☎624013 53rm6⇌47 ⋒ P Lift Ɔ sB⇌ ⋒15000
dB⇌ ⋒28000 (English breakfast) L 8000 D8000 lake
★★**Tre Corone** via Lungolago 44 ☎624033 Closed
21 Oct – Feb 25rm6⇌16 ⋒ P Lift Ɔ sB8300
sB⇌ ⋒10100 dB⇌ ⋒178000 (English breakfast)
L 6000 D6000 lake

GARDONE RIVIERA Brescia 2,650 (☎0365)
Map **29** B4
★★★★**Albergo** ☎20261 tx30254 Closed Nov – mid
Apr 200rm143⇌19 ⋒ P Lift Ɔ sB 15500 – 17250
sB⇌ ⋒25500 – 28250 dB27500 – 31500
dB⇌ ⋒40500 – 48500 L 10000 D10000 Pool lake
★★★**Eurotel** via Vittoriale II ☎21161 Closed 16
Sep – 15 Feb 69 rm48⇌21 ⋒ 🏠 Lift ✈ Pool lake
★★★**Lac** corso Repubblica 58 ☎20124 Closed
Nov – Feb 30rm17⇌ Lift lake
★★**Bellevue** via Zanardelli 44 ☎20235
34rm20⇌11 ⋒ 🏠 P sB8100 sB⇌ ⋒9600 dB 14200
dB⇌ ⋒17200 (English breakfast) L 6000 D6000 lake
★**Garda & Suisse** ☎20150 Closed Oct – Mar 19rm 🏠
lake
At **Barbarano** (1km W)
★★★**Astoria** ☎20761 96rm80⇌ 🏠 Lift Pool lake
★★**Barbarano Galeazzi** ☎20256 76rm20⇌
At **Fasano del Gardo** (1.5km NE)
★★*Riccio* ☎21987 27⇌ A7rm Lift

GELA See **SICILIA (SICILY)**

GÊNOVA (GENOA) Génova 807, 150 (☎010)
Map **29** A3
[AA] agents; see page 269
★★★★*Corvetto Plaza* via M-Piaggio II ☎893642
100rm62⇌38 ⋒ 🏠 Lift
★★★★*Savioa Majestic* Stazione Centrale Principe
☎261641 tx27426 120⇌ 🏠 P Lift Ɔ sB⇌33120
dB⇌54240 L 10000 D10000 St%
★*Principessa* via Roccatagliata 4 ☎580909
23rm2⇌ Lift ✈ sea
🚗 *ARA* via Marsilio de Padova 6 ☎317388 Chy/Sim
🚗 *Dllla* viale C & M Rosselli 18r ☎361689 Frd
🚗 *B Koelllker* via S-Piox 79 ☎315306 BL (GB)
🚗 *Oram* via G-Bandi 10 Quarto ☎384653 Jag/Vlo
(GB)
🛢 *XX-Settembre* via D-Fiasella 19 ☎511941 P Cit

GENZANO DI ROMA Roma 16,250(☎06)
Map **31** B2
★★**Villa Robinia** viale Frattelli Rosselli 19
☎9396409 30⇌ P Lift sB⇌7500 dB⇌12800
(English breakfast) L fr4500 Dfr4500 St% Mountains
lake

GHIFFA Novara 2,150 (☎0323) Map **28** D4
★★*Castello di Frino* ☎59181 Closed Oct – Mar
13rm6⇌4 ⋒ A6rm ✈ Pool lake
★★★**Ghiffa** via Belvedere 66 ☎59285 Closed
Oct – Mar 26rm12⇌4 ⋒ P Lift Ɔ sB8500 – 12500
sB⇌ ⋒11250 – 14400 dB1700 – 20000
dB⇌ ⋒19000 – 24700 L 7500 D7500 lake

GIOIA DEL COLLE Bari 27,850 (☎080) Map **34** C3
★★★**Artu** via Circonvallazione Statale 100 ☎830009
23rm10⇌ Lift ✈ Pool

ị ☞ Auto Carrozzeria (F I Capurso) via Santeramo 120 ☎830417 ❀ M/c.P Ren

GIÓIA TÀURO Reggio di Calabria 15,725 (☎0966) Map **34** C1

★★**Park** via Nazionale ☎51159 44rm28⇄5 ⋔ ⋒ P Lift ♪ sB9500 sB⇄⋔16000 dB 16500 dB⇄⋔19900 (English breakfast) L 5500 D5500

GIULIANOVA LIDO Teramo 21,550 (☎085) Map **32** C3

☜**Ubaldo & Forlini** via G-Galilei 180 ☎862771 Bed/Opl/Vau

GOLFO ARANCI See **SARDEGNA (SARDINIA)**

GORÍZIA Gorízia 43,625 (☎0481) Map **30** D4

★★**Transalpina** via Caprin 30 ☎2008 Closed 17 Aug–4 Sep 55⇄ ⋒ Lift

GRADO Gorizia 10,300 (☎0431) Map **30** D4

★★**Hungaria** via Carducci 13 ☎80183 Closed Oct–Apr 47rm4⇄24 ⋔ P sB 7000–8000 sB⇄⋔8500–9000 dB 14000–14500 dB⇄⋔15000–16000 (English breakfast) L 5000 D5000

GRAVEDONA Como 2,850 (☎0344) Map **29** A4

★**Turismo** ☎85227 Closed Dec–Feb 14rm5⇄ ⋒ P sB8000–8500 sB⇄⋔10000–10500 dB13000–13500 dB⇄⋔ 15000–15500 (English breakfast) L5000 D5000 mountains lake

GRAVELLONA TOCE Novara 7,350 (☎0323) Map **28** D4

★**Helios** ☎84096 19rm11⇄ P sB6000–65000 sB⇄7300–7800 dB⇄⋔11950–12950 (English breakfast) L5000 D5000 mountains

GRIGNANO Trieste (☎040) Map **30** D4

★★★★**Adriatico Palace** ☎224241 tx46449 Closed Nov –14 Mar 102rm72⇄30 ⋔ ⋒ P Lift ♪ sB⇄⋔28000–39500 dB⇄⋔31900–41900 (English breakfast) L9500 ☞ Pool Beach sea

GROSSETO Grosseto 66,850 (☎0564) Map **31** A3

☆☆☆**AGIP** exit Roma ☎24100 32 ⋔ ⋒ Lift

★★★**Lorena** via Trieste 3 ☎25501 60⇄ ⋒ P Lift ♪ sB⇄⋔14200–17150 dB⇄⋔23950–29500 (English breakfast) L7000 D7000

ị ☜**O Biagini** via Senese 55 ☎23054 VW (GB)

☜**Morelli** via Privata dei Curiazi 13 ☎23000 BL/Vlo (GB)

GUARDISTALLO Pisa 1,050 (☎0586) Map **29** B2

★★**Villa Elena** ☎655035 20rm3⇄23 ⋔ A10rm ⋒ P sB9500 sB⇄⋔10500 dB16000 dB⇄⋔17000 (English breakfast) L6000 D6000 ☞ Pool sea

IÉSOLO (JESOLO) (LIDO DI) Venezia 21,900 (☎0421) Map **30** C4

★★★★**Las Vegas** via Mascagni 3 (DP) ☎91200 tx41443 Closed Oct–Apr 110⇄ Lift

★★★**Excelsior** via Zara 2 ☎90284 Closed 21 Sep–9 May 80rm30⇄50 ⋔ Lift Beach

★★★**London** via Dalmazia 508 ☎90988 Closed Oct–Apr 84rm76⇄ ⋔ P Lift ♪ sB9500–12000 sB⇄⋔11500–14000 dB16000–20000 dB⇄⋔17000–22000 L4500–6000 D4500–6000 Beach sea

★★★**Oxford** via Zara 25 (DP & Pn) ☎91320 Closed Oct–19 May 60⇄ P Lift ♪ sB⇄15000–18000 dB⇄30000–36000 L5000 D5000 Pool sea

★★★**Ritz** via Zanella 2 ☎90861 Closed Oct–Apr 48 ⋔ Lift Beach sea

★★**Brezza** via Altinate (DP) ☎91932 Closed Oct–19 May 40rm34⇄36 ⋔ ⋒ Lift Pool Beach sea

★★**Palace & Principe** pza Mazzini 38 ☎90341 Closed Oct–27 May 133rm83⇄ Lift

★★**Regina** via Bafile 115 ☎90383 Closed Oct–Apr rm50⇄ ⋔ P Lift ♪ sB⇄⋔ 9500 dB⇄⋔19000 L5000 D5000 Beach sea

★★**Termini** via Altinate ☎90488 tx41433 Closed Oct–Apr 45⇄ P Lift ♪ sB⇄8500–12500 dB⇄13500–21100 (English breakfast) L7000 D7000 St% Pool Beach sea

☜**Brusa** pza Mazzini ☎91344 Frd (GB)

At **Iésolo Pineta** (6kmE)

★★**Danmark** via Oriente 170 ☎961013 tx41433 Closed Oct–Apr 58rm35⇄28 ⋔ P Lift sB⇄⋔11000–12000 dB16000–16400 dB⇄⋔18000–20000 (English breakfast) L5000 D5000 sea

IGEA MARINA See **BELLARIA IGEA MARINA**

IGLESIAS See **SARDEGNA (SARDINIA)**

IMPÉRIA Impéria 41,550 (☎0183) Map **28** D2

☜**Riviera Motori** viale Matteotti 175 ☎20297/20701 BL

ISCHIA (ISOLA D') Napoli 41,350 (☎081) Map **32** C1

Forio 8,230

★**Splendid** (1kmNE) ☎997165 Closed Nov–Mar 40⇄ ☞ Pool sea

Ischia 15,450

★★★★**Grande Albergo delle Terme Jolly** via A-de-Luca ☎991744 tx71268 208⇄ P Lift ♪ sB⇄ 28800 dB⇄51250 L12500 D12500 Pool

★★★**Grand Hotel & Parco Aurora** Lungomare C-Colombo ☎982022 56rm20⇄50 ⋔ A14rm P Lift ♪ sB⇄ ⋔ 14000–16000 dB⇄⋔22000–26000 (English breakfast) L8000 D8000 Pool Beach sea

Lacco Ameno 3,300

★★★★**Reginella** ☎994304 50rm26⇄24 ⋔ ⋒ Lift ☞ Pool

IVREA Torino 29,400 (☎0125) Map **28** D4

★★★**Sirio** via Lago Sirio 47 ☎3646 35rm14⇄21 ⋔ ⋒ Lift lake

★★**Eden** corso Massimo d'Azeglio 67 (n rest) ☎49190 36rm4⇄32 ⋔ ⋒ P Lift ♪ sB⇄⋔9000–9500 dB⇄⋔13000–14000 (English breakfast) mountains

☜**M Peroni** via S-Lorenzo 10 ☎422002 P Aud/VW (GB)

LA Each name preceded by La is listed under the name that follows it.

LACCO AMENO See **ISCHIA (ISOLA D')**

LACONA See **ELBA (ISOLA D')**

LAIGUÉGLIA Savona 2,600 (☎0182) Map **28** D2

★★★**Aquilia** via Asti 1 (DP) ☎49040 Closed 21 Oct–19 Dec 40⇄ ⋒ Lift Beach sea

★★★**Laigueglia** pza Libertà 14 ☎49002 ta Sighel Closed Nov–Mar 55⇄ ⋒ Lift Beach sea

★★★**Royal** via Roma 176 ☎49283 30 ⇄ ⋒ Lift sea

★★**Mariolina** via Concezione 15 ☎49029 22rm18⇄ P sB7800–10800 sB⇄9800–12800 dB13600–15600 dB⇄ 15600–17600 L8000 D8000 Beach sea

★★**San Giorgio** via Dante 190 ☎49166 Closed Oct–Apr 43rm20⇄13 ⋔ Beach sea

★★**Splendid** pza Badaro 4 ☎49325 Closed Nov–Mar 46rm28⇄18 ⋔ Lift ♪ sB⇄⋔18000 dB⇄⋔ 30000 (English breakfast) L10000 D10000 Pool Beach

★★**Villa Ida** via Roma 90 ☎49042 Closed Oct–14 May 40rm16⇄4 ⋔

★★**Windsor** pza 25 Aprile 7 ☎49000 Closed 26 Oct–19 Apr 50rm30⇄20 ⋔ P Lift ♪ sB⇄⋔ 10000–11600 dB16000 dB⇄⋔ 19600 (English breakfast) L4000–5000 D4000–5000 Beach sea

LAINATE Milano 16,460 (☎02) Map **29** A4

☆**Italmotel** via Manzoni 43 ☎9370869 34⇄ P ♪ dB⇄⋔26200 (English breakfast) L7000 D7000 ☞ Pool

LAVAGNA Genova 14,000 (☎0185) Map **29** A2/3

★★**Tigullio** via Matteotti 3 ☎307623 Closed 16 Nov–14 Mar 42rm14⇄6 ⋔ ⋒ Lift sB5700–6500 sB⇄⋔7700–8500 dB11400–12800 dB⇄⋔15400–16800 (English breakfast) L4700–6700 D4700–6700 sea

At **Cavi** (3km SE)

★**Scogliera** (n rest) ☎390072 Closed Oct–24 May 22rm 21 ⋔ P sB7000–9700 sB⋔7000–9700 dB14400–16900 dB⋔ 14400–16900 Beach sea

LECCE Lecce 86,400 (☎0832) Map **34** D3

Italy

★★★**Astor** via 140 Regimento Fanteria 69 ☎26911
66rm46⇄10 🏨 Lift
LEGHORN See **LIVORNO**

LENNO Como 1,600 (☎0344) Map **29** A4
★★**San Giorgio** ☎40415 Closed 16 Oct – Mar
30rm21⇄ 🏨 P Lift 🄳 sB10500⇄17400 dB18000
dB⇄ 26000 (English breakfast) L7500 – 8500
D7500 – 8500 St% ✈ mountains lake
LÉRICI La Spezia 14,500 (☎0187) Map **29** A2
★★★**Doria** via A-Doria (DP) ☎967124
42rm15⇄15 🏨 Lift
★★ **Venere Azzurra** Lungomaree Biaggini 33 (n rest)
☎967210 Closed Nov – Feb 22rm1⇄14 🏨 🏨 sea
LESA Novara 2,550 (☎0322) Map **28** D4
★★**Giardino** ☎7283 40rm15⇄10 🏨 A7rm P Lift 🄳
sB4850 – 6800 sB⇄🏨6650 – 8700 dB10000 – 13200
dB⇄ 🏨 12000 – 16000 (English breakfast)
L3500 – 5500 D3500 – 5500 mountains lake
LÉVANTO La Spezia 6,750 (☎0187) Map **29** A2
★★★**Crystal** via Vallesanta ☎808261 Closed
Oct – Apr 16rm1⇄15 🏨 A9rm 🏨 P Lift 🄳 sB11500⇄15500
dB⇄ 21000 (English breakfast) L8500 D8500 sea
★★**Nazionale** ☎808102 Closed Nov – Mar
23rm6⇄5 🏨 sea
★**Garden** corso Italia 6 ☎808173 Closed Oct – Mar
15rm Lift sB8000 dB13000 (English breakfast) L6000
D6000 sea
LEVICO TERME Trento 5,610 (☎0461) Map **29** B4
★★★**Bellavista** via Emanuele 2 ☎71136 Closed 8
Jan – 14 May & Oct – 24 Dec 78⇄ 🏨 P Lift 🄳
sB⇄🏨9000 – 14000 dB⇄🏨16000 – 24000
(English breakfast) L6000 D7000 Pool lake
LIDO DI CAMAIORE See **CAMAIORE (LIDO DI)**
LIDO DI IESOLO (JESOLO) See **IÉSOLO (LIDO DI)**
LIGNANO SABBIADORO Udine 5,100 (☎0431)
Map **30** C4
At **Lignano Pineta** (5km SW)
★★★**Medusa Splendid** Arco dello Scirocco 13
☎72211 Closed 21 Sep – 14 May 56⇄ P Lift 🄳
sB⇄🏨12000 – 15000 dB⇄🏨18000 – 22000
(English breakfast) L10000 D10000 Pool Beach
At **Lignano Riviera** (7km SW)
★★★**Eurotel** c Mendelssohn 9 ☎729992 Closed 21
Sep – 14 May 59⇄ Lift Pool Beach sea
LIMONE SUL GARDA Brescia 1,000 (☎0365)
Map **29** B4
★★**Azzurro** ☎94000 Closed Nov – Mar 32rm lake
LIPOMO See **COMO**
LIVORNO (LEGHORN) Livorno 177,550 (☎0580)
Map **29** B2
⬜ **AA** agents; see page 269
★★★**Giappone** via Grande 65 (n rest) ☎24751
57rm26⇄14 🏨 P Lift 🄳 sB9500 – 10500
sB⇄🏨12400 – 13600 dB15000 – 17000
dB⇄🏨19200 – 21700
🛢 🅱️ **G Malloggi** via Prov Pisma 631 ☎422230 MB
🛢 **G Scotti** via della Cinta Esterna 36 ☎24007 M/c
At **Stagno** (5km N on SS1)
☆☆☆ **AGIP** ☎93067 49⇄ Lift
LOANO Savona 13,250 (☎019) Map **28** D2
★★★**Garden Lido** Lungomare N-Sauro 9 ☎669666
88rm48⇄40 🏨 🏨 P Lift 🄳 sB⇄🏨17500 – 22000
dB⇄🏨25000 – 34000 (English breakfast)
L10000 – 11000 D10000 – 12000 Pool Beach sea
★★**San Marco** via Private Mazza 9A (n rest)
☎668094 Closed 16 Mar – Apr & 6 Oct – Nov
23rm1⇄4 🏨 Lift sea
★**Aurelia** via Mazza 2 ☎668264 13rm1⇄ Lift sea
LONE See **AMALFI**
MACERATA Macerata 44,250 (☎0733) Map **30** D2
☆☆☆ **AGIP** via Roma ☎31146 51⇄ Lift
MACOMER See **SARDEGNA (SARDINIA)**
MACUGNAGA Novara 800 (☎0324) Map **28** D4
★★**Lagger** Frazione Pecetto ☎65139 21rm17⇄ P
Lift sB6600 – 8000 sB⇄8600 – 10000
dB12600 – 15000 dB⇄🏨14600 – 17000

(English breakfast) L5000 – 6000 D5000 – 6000
mountains
MADERNO Brescia 6,327 (☎0365) Map **29** B4
★★**Milano** Lungolago 12 ☎641223 Closed Oct – mid
Apr 40rm12⇄ lake
MADONNA DE CAMPÍGLIO Trento (☎0465)
Map **29** B4
★★★★**Alpes** ☎41002 Closed Sep – 14 Jul 91⇄ Lift
★★★**Savoia** ☎41004 tx30254 Closed Sep & Aug
57rm47⇄10 🏨 🏨 P Lift 🄳 sB⇄🏨19500 – 26500
dB⇄🏨34000 – 45000 (English breakfast) L10000
D10000 mountains
MAIORI Salerno 6,200 (☎089) Map **33** B3
★★★**San Francesco** via S-Tecla 54 ☎877070
Closed Nov – Feb 44⇄ 🏨 P Lift 🄳 sB⇄8000 – 9000
dB⇄15000 – 17000 (English breakfast) L6000 D6000
Beach sea
MALCÉSINE Verona 3,600 (☎045) Map **29** B4
★★★**Malcesine** pza Pallone 1 ☎600173 Closed
Nov – Mar 43rm17⇄11 🏨 🏨 Lift lake
★★**Bellevue San Lorenzo** Val di Sogno ☎600088
Closed Nov – Mar 25rm7⇄8 🏨 🏨 Lift Pool lake
★★**Vega** ☎600151 Closed Nov – 14 Mar rm20⇄ P
Lift sB⇄13000 – 18000 dB⇄21000 – 28000
(English breakfast) L7500 D7500 mountains lake
MÁNTOVA Mántova 66,600 (☎0376) Map **29** B3
Filippini via Curtatone e Montanara 58 ☎29696
Aud/Por/VW
MARATEA Potenza 4,900 (☎0973) Map **33** B3
★★★★**Santavenere** ☎76160 Closed 11 Oct – mid
Apr 44rm10⇄4 🏨 Beach 🄳 sea
MARCIANA MARINA See **ELBA (ISOLA D')**
MARGHERA See **MESTRE**
MARINA DI CARRARA See **CARRARA (MARINA
DI)**
MARINA DI MASSA See **MASSA (MARINA DI)**
MARINA DI PIETRASANTA See **PIETRASANTA
(MARINA DI)**
MARINA EQUA See **VICO EQUENSE**
MARSALA See **SICILIA (SICILY)**
MASSA (MARINA DI) Massa Carrara 8,820
(☎0585) Map **29** A2
★★★★**Tirreno** via Mazzini 22 ☎20016 Closed
Oct – Apr 45rm33⇄1 🏨 Beach sea
★★★**Marina** viale Magliano 3 ☎20192 Closed
Nov – Apr rm32⇄ P 🄳 sB⇄11500 – 14500
dB⇄17000 – 20000 (English breakfast) L6000 D6000
St% Beach
★**Internazionale** via Siena 1 (Pn) ☎309293 Closed
Oct – 9 May 13rm5⇄ P sB fr12000 Beach 🄳 sea
MATELICA Macerata 8,750 (☎0737) Map **30** C2
☆☆☆ **AGIP** (SS 256 km29) ☎8381 16 🏨
MAZZARÒ See **TAORMINA** under **SICILIA (SICILY)**
MÉINA Novara 2,250 (☎0322) Map **28** D4
★**Bel Sit** via Sempione 86 (DP) ☎6483 12rm3⇄9 🏨
🏨 lake
MENÁGGIO Como 3,350 (☎0344) Map **29** A4
★★★**Bella Vista** via IV Novembre 9 ☎32136 Closed
11 Oct – Mar 39rm26⇄ 🏨 P Lift sB8500 – 10000
sB⇄9500 – 13500 dB13000 – 16000
dB⇄19000 – 22000 (English breakfast) L fr5500
D fr5500 lake
★★★**Victoria** via al Lago 7 ☎32003 Closed
Nov – Mar 98rm58⇄17 🏨 🏨 Lift ✈ Pool lake
★★**Loveno** via N-Sauro 5 ☎32110 Closed Nov – 14
Mar 14rm6⇄3 🏨 A5rm 🏨 P sB6000 – 9500
sB⇄🏨7000 – 10500 dB10000 – 13000
dB⇄14000 – 18000 (English breakfast)
L5000 – 7000 D5000 – 7000 mountains
At **Nobiallo** (1km N)
★★**Miralago** ☎32363 Closed 11 Oct – Mar 28rm25⇄
🏨 P 🄳 sB⇄7800 dB⇄14600 (English breakfast)
L6000 D6000 mountains lake
MENDOLA (PASSO DELLA) Trento e Bolzano
(☎0471) Map **12** D1
★★ **Caldaro** ☎63124 24rm2⇄ 🏨 ✈ Pool

MERANO-MERAN Bolzano 34,600 (☎0473) Map **12** D1
★★★★★**Bristol** via O-Huber 14 ☎23361 tx40662 Closed Nov–Mar 150rm103⇌47⋒ ⌂ P Lift ☽ sB⇌ ⋒19500–32000 dB⇌ ⋒29000–56000 (English breakfast) L fr10500 D fr10500 Pool mountains
★★★**Augusta** via O-Huber 2 ☎30331 tx40632 Closed Nov–Feb 25⇌ ⌂ P Lift ☽ sB⇌17500–20000 dB⇌31000–35000 (English breakfast) L6500 D6500 mountains
☆☆☆***Eurotel*** via Garibaldi 5 ☎24316 tx40471 130rm70⇌60⋒ ⌂ Lift
☆☆☆**Eurotel Astoria** via Winkel 21 (n rest) ☎25442 tx40471 Closed 6 Nov–14 Mar 114rm108⇌6⋒ P Lift ☽ sB⇌ ⋒14000–19000 dB⇌ ⋒24000–31000 Pool mountains
★★★***Mirabella*** via Mirabella 1 ☎26112 Closed Nov–Feb 30rm16⇌14⋒ Lift Pool
★★★**Palace** via Cavour 4 ☎23791 tx40256 102⇌ P Lift ☽ sB⇌ ⋒21500–30000 dB⇌ ⋒39000–54000 (English breakfast) L10500 D10500 St% Pool mountains
★★★**Savoy** via Rezia 1 ☎47600 tx40632 Closed Dec–Feb 54⇌ P Lift ☽ sB⇌17500–23500 dB⇌30000–42000 (English breakfast) L8000 D8000 Pool mountains
★★**Adria** via Gilm 2 ☎26183 Closed Nov–Feb 42rm25⇌20⋒ A9rm P Lift ☽ sB⇌ ⋒11500–14500 dB22000–26000 dB⇌ ⋒24000–27500 L6000 D6500 Pool mountains
★★***Albergo Mendola*** via Winkel 35 ☎22330 Closed Nov–Feb 40rm8⇌26⋒ Lift Pool
★★**Irma** via Belvedere 7 ☎30124 Closed Nov–23 Feb 60rm31⇌31⋒ A2rm ⌂ P Lift ☽ sB8000–11000 sB⇌ ⋒11000–14000 dB12000–14000 dB⇌ ⋒16000–28000 (English breakfast) L5000–6000 D5000–6000 ꝏ Pool mountains
★★**Regina** via Cavour 101 ☎33432 Closed Nov–14 Mar 75rm26⇌43⋒ P Lift ☽ sB11500–13000 dB⇌ ⋒16000–18000 dB22000–27000 dB⇌ ⋒25000–32000 L7500 D7500 Pool mountains
★***Livonia*** Christomannos Strada 31 ☎24126 20rm3⇌12⋒ Pool
★**Westend** (n rest) ☎47654 Closed 11 Nov–14 Mar 22rm4⇌6⋒ P ☽ sB13000–14000 sB⇌ ⋒14500–15500 dB23000–24000 dB⇌ ⋒27000–28000 (English breakfast) L4800 mountains
⚙ **Merano** (O Montolli) via Roma 288 ☎32074 Fia/Frd/Opl/Ren (GB)

MESSINA See **SICILIA (SICILY)**

MESTRE (Venezia) (☎041) Map **30** C4
★★★**Bologna & Stazione** pza Stazione ☎931000 tx41678 131rm23⇌93⋒ P Lift ☽ sB13000–15000 sB⇌ ⋒17000–21000 dB19000–22000 dB⇌ ⋒26000–30000 (English breakfast) L8000 D8000
★★★**Plaza** pza Stazione ☎929388 tx41490 ⌂ P Lift ☽ sB18000 sB⇌ ⋒19000 dB28000 dB⇌ ⋒30000 (English breakfast) L8000 D8000
★★★***Sirio*** via Circonvallazione 109 ☎51728 110rm2⇌78⋒ ⌂ Lift
★★★**Tritone** pza Stazione 16 ☎930955 Closed Dec–Feb 67rm30⇌24⋒ ⌂ P Lift ☽ sB14000 sB⇌ ⋒17000 dB22000 dB⇌ ⋒27000 L7500 D7500
★★**Aurora** pza G-Bruno 15 (n rest) ☎989832 33rm15⇌4⋒ P Lift ☽ sB9700 sB⇌ ⋒12400 dB16500 dB⇌ ⋒20500
★★**Venezia** pza XXVII Ottobre ☎972400 tx41693 100rm50⇌ ⌂ P Lift ☽ sB9700 sB⇌12500 dB16700 dB⇌20700 L4500
Autolambro corso del Popolo 7 ☎986255 M/c P BL/Rov/Tri
Diamani & Giorgio via Torino 40 ☎932844 M/c Frd (GB)
ꝏ***S Lorenzo*** via Giustizia 27 ☎926722 P Bed/Opl/Vau
⚙ ***Roma/Caldera*** via Piave 182 ☎929611 Fia

At **Marghera** (1km S)
★★***Vienna*** via Rizzardi 11 ☎921979 Closed Nov–14 Mar 76rm15⇌15⋒ Lift Pool
⚙ ꝏ***Sartori*** piazzle Autostrada 12 ☎920444

MILANO (MILAN) Milano 1,732,5000 (☎02) Map **29** A4 **See Plan overleaf**
AA agents; see page 269
★★★★★**Duomo** via San Raffaele 1 ☎8833 tx33086 Plan **1** 160⇌ ⌂ P Lift ☽ sB⇌41200 dB⇌56400 (English breakfast) L10000 D10000 St%
★★★★★**Excelsior-Gallia** pza Duca d'Aosta 9 ☎6277 tx32160 Plan **2** 280⇌ ⌂ P Lift ☽ sB⇌33000–43000 dB⇌44000–56000 (English breakfast) L11000 D11000 St%
★★★★★**Palace** pza della Repubblica 20 ☎6336 tx32036 Plan **3** 203rm163⇌29⋒ ⌂ P Lift ☽ sB⇌ ⋒fr58000 dB⇌ ⋒fr77000 St%
★★★★★***Principe & Savoia*** pza della Repubblica 17 ☎6230 tx31052 Plan **4** 358⇌A60rm ⌂ Lift
★★★★**Jolly President** Largo Augusto ☎7746 tx33054 Plan **5** 201⇌ ⌂ Lift ☽ sB⇌45000 dB⇌60000 L10000 D10000
★★★★***Manin*** via Manin 7 ☎667251 tx34385 Plan **6** 106rm100⇌6⋒ Lift
★★★★**Select** via Baracchini 12 (off via A-Albricci) (n rest) ☎8843 tx33256 Plan **7** 140rm70⇌70⋒ P Lift ☽ sB⇌ ⋒31000–41500 dB⇌ ⋒46000–61000
★★★★**Touring** via Torchetti 2 (off via Manin) ☎665653 tx34118 Plan **8** 277rm241⇌36⋒ ⌂ P Lift ☽ sB⇌ ⋒38100 dB⇌ ⋒51250 (English breakfast) L9000 D9000
☆☆☆***AGIP*** Milano Tangenziale Ovest, Assago ☎8465246 Plan **9** 180⋒ Lift
★★★**American** via Finocchiaro Aprile 2 ☎66641 tx33150 Plan **11** 306⋒ ⌂ P Lift ☽ sB ☽19000–21500 dB ⋒30000–34000 (English breakfast) L6500 D6500
★★★**Terminus** viale V-Veneto 32 (n rest) ☎664917 Plan **16** 65rm25⇌4⋒ ⌂ P Lift ☽ sB9000–12000 sB⇌ ⋒13000–16500 dB14000–18000 dB⇌ ⋒19000–27000 (English breakfast) L6000 D6000 St%
★★***Adriatico*** via Conca del Naviglio 20 (n rest) ☎8324141 Plan **14** 105rm7⇌98⋒ ⌂ Lift
☆☆**Dei Fiori** Ingresso Autostrada per Genova (A7) (n rest) ☎8436441 Plan **12** 55rm40⇌13⋒ P Lift ☽ sB⇌ ⋒12400 dB⇌ ⋒18800
☆☆**Eur** Nuouo Strada Vivegawese (n rest) ☎4451951 Not on plan 41rm39⋒ ⌂ P Lift ☽ sB ⋒14500 dB ⋒21500
☆☆**Fini** via del Mare 93 ☎8464041 Plan **13** 78rm24⇌48⋒ ⌂ P Lift ☽ sB fr14000 sB⇌ ⋒fr18000 dB⇌ ⋒fr25400
★★**Gamma** via Valvassor, Peroni (off via Porpora) (n rest) ☎292602 Plan **15** 55⇌ ⌂ P Lift ☽ sB⇌20200 dB⇌29100
ꝏ**Forlanini** via Mecenate 84 ☎5060340 Fia

At **San Donato Milanese** (8km SE on road N9)
☆☆☆***AGIP*** Ingress Autostrada del Sole ☎512941 Plan **10** 275⇌ Lift

MILANO MARTUMA See **CÉRVIA**

MINORI See **AMALFI**

MISURINA Belluno (☎0436) Map **13** A1
★★**Sorapiss** ☎8209 Closed Apr–14 May & Oct–14 Dec 24rm 9⋒ A6rm P sB 7200–9200 dB 12400–14400 dB ⋒15400–17400 (English breakfast) L 6000 D6000 mountains lake

MÓDENA Módena 176,800 (☎059) Map **29** B3
★★★★**Canalgrande** corso Canalgrande 6 ☎217160 tx51480 78rm40⇌38⋒ ⌂ P Lift sB⇌ ⋒28500 dB⇌ ⋒44000 (English breakfast) L 15000 D15000
★★★★**Fini** via E-Est 441 ☎238091 tx51286 100⇌ ⌂ P Lift ☽ sB⇌30000 dB⇌45000 L alc D alc
★★★★***Palace*** via E-Est 65 ☎236091 64rm54⇌ ⌂ Lift
☆☆☆***AGIP*** via E-Est 1014 ☎361249 17⋒
☆☆☆***AGIP*** Raccordo Autostrada Brennero-Modena/Autostrada del Sole (n rest) ☎338221 184⋒ Lift

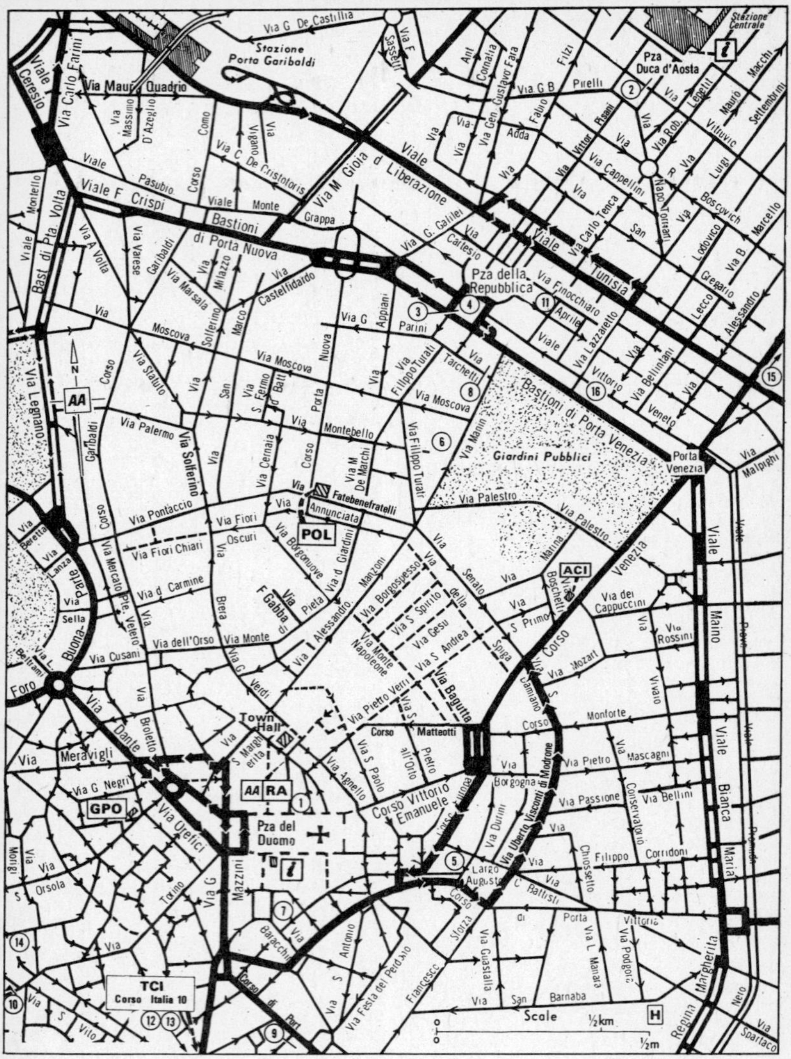

Milan

1	★★★★★Duomo
2	★★★★★Excelsior-Gallia
3	★★★★★Palace
4	★★★★★Principe & Savoia
5	★★★★Jolly President
6	★★★★Manin
7	★★★★Select
8	★★★★Touring
9	☆☆☆AGIP
10	☆☆☆AGIP (at San Donato Milanese/ 8km SE on road No. 9)
11	★★★American
12	☆☆Dei Fiori
13	☆☆Fini
14	★★Adriatico
15	★★Gamma
16	★★★Terminus

★★*Geminiano* ☎231303 23rm11⇌ Lift

î ➻ Barbieri Auto via E-Est 1040 ☎360260 P BL (GB)

&➻**W Bellei** via E-Est 1127 ☎366172 Frd (GB)

MOGLIANO VENETO Treviso 21,650 (☎041) Map **30** C4

★★★★**Villa Condulmer** ☎450001 Closed 11 Jan–Feb 33rm20⇌13 ⋔ P ♪ sB⇌ ⋔19000 dB⇌ ⋔32000–40000 (English breakfast) L10000–12000 D10000–12000 ✎ Pool δ

MOLTRÀSIO Como 2,800 (f031) Map **29** A4

★★**Caramazza** ☎290050 Closed 21 Oct–Mar 20rm 12 ⋔ P Lift sB 9000 sB⋔12000 dB⇌15500 dB ⋔21000 L 6000 D6000 mountains lake

MOLVENO Trento 1,000 (☎0461) Map **29** B4

★★**Miralage** ☎58935 Closed Apr, Oct & Nov 52rm34⇌18 ⋔ P Lift sB⇌ ⋔7000–8800 dB⇌ ⋔11000–15000 (English breakfast) L5000 D5000 Pool lake

★**Cima Tosa** via Scuole 3 ☎586928 Closed 21 Sep–May 32rm8⇌9 ⋔ ⋔ P sB 6200–7500 dB 10400–13000 dB⇌ ⋔12400–15000 (English breakfast) L6000 D6000 mountains lake

MONDOVÌ BREO Cuneo 21,950 (☎0174) Map **28** D3

★★★**Park** via del Vecchio 2 ☎43550 60rm3⇌57 ⋔ P Lift ♪ sB⇌ ⋔12200 dB⇌ ⋔20500 L 4000 D4000

î ➻*Franco Govone* via Piave 6 ☎43111 ☎40355 Cit

MONÉGLIA Genova 2,850 (☎0185) Map **29** A2

★★*Mondial* ☎49339 Closed 16 Oct–14 Mar 36rm4⇌32 ⋔ ⋔ Lift

MONFALCONE Gorizia 30,850 (☎0481) Map **30** D4

★★*Lussino* via Duca d'Aosta 37 ☎72409 23rm3⇌2 ⋔

MONTALTO DI CASTRO Viterbo 6,250 (☎0766) Map **31** B3

☆☆*AGIP* via Aurelia ☎89090 32 ⋔

MONTECATINI TERME Pistoia 21,400 (☎0572) Map **29** B2

★★★★**Croce di Malta** via IV-Novembre 18 ☎79381 Closed Nov–Mar 115 ⇌ A30 rm ⋔ P Lift ♪ sB⇌18000–23000 dB⇌31000–41000 (English breakfast) L12000 D12000 Pool

★★*Lido Palace Risorgimento* via IV Novembre 14 ☎70731 Closed Nov–Mar 56rm44⇌ Lift ♪ sB 8000–10000 sB⇌ ⋔9000–11400 dB 12000–15500 dB⇌ ⋔14000–18000 L 6000 D6000

MONTEGROTTO TERME Padova 8,400 (☎049) Map **30** C4

★★★ **Terme Zurigo** via Neronianal ☎793555 84rm8⇌76 ⋔ Lift Pool

MONTESILVANO MARINA See **PESCARA**

MÙCCIA Maserata 900 (☎0737) Map **32** C4

☆☆*AGIP* Bivio Maddalena (SS 77) ☎43138 38 ⋔

NAPOLI (NAPLES) Napoli 1,224,300 (☎081) Map **32** D2

AA agents, see page 269

★★★★★**Excelsior** via Partenope 48 ☎417111 tx71043 160⇌ ⋔ P Lift ♪ sB⇌44000–49000 dB⇌68000–83000 (English breakfast) L fr18000 Dfr18000 St% sea

★★★★**Vesuvio** via Partenope 45 ☎417044 tx71127 180⇌ ⋔ P Lift ♪ sB⇌23400–36400 dB⇌32800–54800 (English breakfast) L10000 D10000 sea

★★★★*Mediterraneo* Ponte di Tappia 2 ☎312240 221⇌ ⋔ Lift sea

★★★★**Royal** via Partenope 38 ☎400244 tx71167 316rm218⇌98 ⋔ ⋔ P Lift ♪ sB⇌ ⋔32950 dB⇌ ⋔53700 (English breakfast) L 95000 D95000 Pool sea

★★★**Parker's** corso V-Emanuele 135 ☎684866 tx71578 86rm53⇌12 ⋔ ⋔ Lift sea

î *Gallo & Bacialli* Salita Piedignotta 2 ☎660256 P Lnc (GB)

&➻*S Luigi* via Gl-Francesco Pinto 59 ☎514865 Ren

&➻*SVAi* via S-Veniero 17–20 ☎611122 Frd

NERVI Genova 19,147 (☎010) Map **29** A3

★★★*Giardino Rivera* Passeggiata A-Mare ☎378581 35rm22⇌2 ⋔ ⋔ Lift Beach sea

☆☆*Milano* via Somma Donate 39 ☎378292 50rm30⇌4 ⋔ A19rm ⋔ sea

NOBIALLO See **MENÀGGIO**

NOLI Savona 3,100 (☎019) Map **28** D2

★★★**Capo Noli** via Aurelia ☎748945 Closed Oct–14 May 52rm20⇌32 ⋔ Lift sea

★★*Monique* via Colleqio 22 ☎748930 Closed Oct–27 May 32rm4⇌16 ⋔ Lift sea

NOVA LEVANTE-WELSCHNOFEN Bolzano 1,600 (☎0471) Map **13** A1

★★*Posta Cavallino Bianco* Strada Dolomiti ☎61113 Closed 21 Oct–17 Dec 70rm28⇌7 ⋔ ⋔ Lift ✎ Pool

NUMANA Ancona 2,050 (☎071) Map **30** D2

★★**Numana Palace** (Pn) ☎950156 Closed 16 Sep–14 May 110rm3⇌98 ⋔ ⋔ P Lift ♪ dB⇌ ⋔14750–21690 ✎ Pool Beach sea

NUORO See **SARDEGNA (SARDINIA)**

ORA-AUER Bolzano 2,450 (☎0471) Map **13** A1

★★*Elefant* via Nazionale ☎80129 32rm4⇌19 ⋔ Lift sB9200 sB⇌ ⋔10200 dB17400 dB⇌ ⋔18900 (English breakfast) L5500 D5500 mountains

ORBETELLO Grosseto 15,150 (☎0564) Map **31** A3

★★*Nazionale* corso Italia 48 (n rest) ☎867062 33rm10⇌1 ⋔ ⋔

ORISTANO See **SARDEGNA (SARDINIA)**

ORTA SAN GIULIO Novara 1,250 (☎0322) Map **28** D4

★★★**San Rocco** via Gippini 12 ☎90191 41rm36⇌5 ⋔ ⋔ P Lift ♪ (English breakfast) L10000 D10000 lake

ORTISEI-ST ULRICH Bolzano 4,050 (☎0471) Map **13** A1

★★★**Aquila** via Rezia 7 ☎76203 Closed Oct–4 Dec 86rm70⇌1 ⋔ ⋔ P Lift ♪ sB14000–26500 sB⇌ ⋔18000–31500 dB24000–49000 dB⇌ ⋔32000–59000 L6500–8000 D6500–8000 ✎ Pool mountains

★★★**Gardena** ☎76315 50rm46⇌ ⋔ Lift

OSPEDALETTI Imperia 3,300 (☎0184) Map **28** D2

★★★**Floreal** corso Regina-Margherita 83 ☎59638 Closed Oct 26rm12⇌6 ⋔ P Lift sB5500–7500 sB⇌ ⋔6500–8500 dB11000–12000 dB⇌ ⋔12000–15000 L5000 D5000 sea

★★★**Rocce del Capo** Lungomare C-Columbo (n rest) ☎59733 26rm4⇌24 ⋔ ⋔ P Lift ♪ sB14700 sB⇌ ⋔14700 dB⇌ ⋔26900 Pool Beach sea

★★*Petit Royal* via Regina Mergherita 86 ☎59026 Closed Oct–14 Dec 30rm9⇌6 ⋔ Lift sea

PADOVA (PADUA) Pàvova 239,275 (☎049) Map **30** C4

★★★★**Park Villa Altichiero** Strada Altichiero 2 ☎615111 70⇌ Lift Pool

★★★**Biri** pza Stanga (Autostrada Terminal) ☎42442 63rm15⇌48 ⋔ ⋔ P Lift ♪ sB⇌ ⋔12800 (room only) dB⇌ ⋔20100 (room only)

★★★**Europa** Largo Europa 9 ☎661200 57rm24⇌33 ⋔ P Lift ♪ sB⇌ ⋔16500 dB⇌ ⋔28000 (English breakfast) L8000 D8000

★*Maritan* via Gattamelata 8 ☎50118 23rm15⇌11 ⋔ Lift

&➻*C Meneghini* via N-Tommaseo 80 ☎27272 Frd

PAESTUM Salerno 1,457 (☎0828 Map **33** B3

★★**Calypso** Zona Pineta ☎811031 40⇌ ⋔ A10rm ⋔ P ♪ sB⇌ ⋔9500–12000 dB⇌ ⋔13000–18000 (English breakfast) L5000–6000 D5000–6000 Beach sea mountains

★★*Mec* ☎843073 Closed Oct–Mar 40rm16⇌24 ⋔ Lift

PALERMO See **SICILIA (SICILY)**

PALLANZA see **VERBÀNIA**

PARMA Parma 176,650 (☎0521) Map **29** B3

★★**Button** via S-Vitale 7 (n rest) ☎22317 44rm26⇌ ⋔ P Lift ♪ sB9250 sB⇌11750 dB20200

★★*Milano* viale Ponte Botlogo 8 ☎35877 47rm27⇌3 ⋔ ⋔ P Lift ♪ sB fr7350 sB⇌ ⋔fr10950

Italy

dBfr13150 dB⇨ 🍴 fr16800 (English breakfast)
L6000 – 7000 D6000 – 7000
★★*Principe* via E-Est 46 (n rest) ☎40996 43⇨ 🏠 Lift
🅱 🐾*Bottesini* via Golese 30 ☎24219 M/c Hon/Vlo

PEDRACES Bolzano 433 (☎0471) Map **13** A1
★★*Sporthotel Teresa* (1km S) ☎85023 58rm52⇨
🏠 Lift Pool

PEGLI Genova 21,047 (☎010) Map **28** D3
★★★*Mediterraneo* Lungomare 69 (n rest) ☎480185
73⇨ Lift sea

PEROULAZ See **AOSTA**

PERÚGIA Perúgia 134,400 (☎075) Map **31** B4
★★★*Brufani Palace* pza Italia 12 ☎20741
117rm97⇨11 🍴 🏠 Lift
★★★*Rosetta* pza Italia 19 ☎20841 108rm49⇨33 🍴
🏠 P Lift 𝒟 sB10000 sB⇨ 🍴 138000 dB15400
dB⇨ 🍴21900 – 27100 (English breakfast) L7000
D7000
🅱 🐾 *Negri & Ricci* via Romana 35 ☎30676 M/c
BMW

PÉSARO Pésaro Urbine 88,550 (☎0721) Map **30** C2
★★★*Mediterraneo Ricci* Viale Trieste 199 ☎21556
tx56062 58⇨ A15rm P Lift 𝒟 sB⇨8500 – 9500
dB⇨15000 – 17000 (English breakfast) L5000 D5000
Beach
★★*Atlantic* viale Trieste 365 ☎61911 tx56062
Closed Oct – Apr 40rm25⇨ 15 🍴 P Lift 𝒟
sB10000 – 105000 sB⇨ 🍴10000 – 10500
dB⇨ 🍴17000 – 18500 (English breakfast) L7500
D7500 Beach sea
★★*Touring* viale Trieste 203 ☎31093 33⇨ Lift
Beach sea
A *Gabellini* Strada Romagna 119 ☎39124
Aud/Por/VW (GB)
Paole del Monte via Porto Rimini ☎32919 BL (GB)

PESCARA Pescara 131,800 (☎085) Map **32** C/D3
☆☆☆*AGIP* Autostrada Adriatica, Casello Pescara
Nord (DP) ☎968221 85 🍴 Lift
★★★*Carlton* viale Riviera 35 ☎26373
71rm34⇨37 🍴 P Lift 𝒟 sB⇨ 🍴14700 – 16500
dB⇨24900 – 27200 (English breakfast) L6000
D6000 Beach sea
🐾*MADA* via Tiburtina Valeria ☎51342 Frd
At **Montesilvano Marina** (8km NW on S16)
★★★★*Grand Montesilvana* via Riviera 28
☎838330 Closed Oct – May 150⇨ 🏠 Lift Beach sea
★★★*Serena Majestic* ☎835142 tx68279 Closed
Nov – 17 Apr 216rm84⇨128 🍴 🏠 Lift 🐾 Pool Beach

PIACENZA Piacenza 108,800 (☎0523) Map **29** A3
★★★*Croce Bianca* Largo Matteoti 16 ☎21231
85rm30⇨25 🍴
★★*Cappello* via Mentano 8 ☎25721 58rm13⇨9 🍴
🏠 Lift
☆☆*K2* via E-Parmense 133 ☎25381 45rm 35 🍴 🏠 P
Lift 𝒟 sB fr5500 sB 🍴 fr7000 dB fr8500 dB 🍴 fr12500
(English breakfast) L4500 D4500
Agosti & Lunardi via Perletti 5 ☎28920 Jag/Toy
(GB)
Mirani & Toscani via E-Parmense 6 ☎62744 Frd

PIANO DI SORRENTO Napoli 10,050 (☎081)
Map **33** A3
★★★*Nastro Azzurro* (3km S on SS163) ☎8786818
tx73008 Closed 17 Nov – Feb 55rm25⇨28 🍴 🏠 P Lift
𝒟 sB7900 – 8550 sB⇨ 🍴10500 – 11960
dB⇨21600 – 22900 (English breakfast) L fr9500
D fr8500 St% 🐾 Pool mountains

PIAZZA ARMERINA See **SICILLIA (SICILY)**

PIETRA LIGURE Savona 9,525 (☎019) Map **28** D2
★★★★*Royal* via delle Palma 129 ☎647192
105rm85⇨20 🍴 🏠 P Lift 𝒟 sB⇨ 🍴17000
dB⇨ 🍴24000 (English breakfast) L8000 – 8500
D8500 – 10000 Beach sea

PIETRASANTA (MARINA DI) Lucca (☎0584)
Map **29** B2
★★★*Lombardi* Fiumetto ☎20431 Closed Oct – Apr
40rm30⇨3 🍴 Lift 🐾 Pool Beach sea

★★★*Batelli* Motrone ☎20010 Closed Oct – May
42rm38⇨ 🏠 P Lift 𝒟 sB11500 – 14100
sB⇨14500 – 17100 dB17000 – 20200
dB⇨23000 – 26200 (English breakfast) L8000
D8000 – 10000 🐾 Beach sea
★★*Esplanade* Viale Roma 235, Tonfano ☎21151
33⇨ P Lift 𝒟 sB⇨ 🍴9500 – 14500
dB⇨ 🍴20000 – 26360 (English breakfast) D7000
L7000 – 10000 D7000 – 10000 sea
★★*Pinamar* via Catalina 74 ☎20277 Closed Oct – 14
May 20rm16⇨
★★*Venezia* via Firenze 48 (n rest) ☎20731 Closed
Oct – May 34⇨ 🏠 Lift sea

PINETA See **LIGNANO PINETA**

PIOMBINO Livorno 40,500 (☎0565) Map **31** A3
★★*Centrale* pza G-Verdi 2 ☎32581 38rm33⇨ 🏠 Lift
𝒟 sB8500 sB⇨12000 dB⇨21000
(English breakfast) L5500 D5500 St%
E **Blanchetti** pza Constitutione 54 ☎33017 Frd

PISA Pisa 103,400 (☎050) Map **29** B2
★★★*Cavalleri* pza Stazione (n rest) ☎43290
tx59663 102rm58⇨44 🍴 🏠 Lift 𝒟 sB⇨ 🍴29950
dB⇨ 🍴44900 St%
☆☆*California* via Aurelia ☎890726 tx50119 Closed
Nov – Feb 74rm2⇨72 🍴 P 𝒟 sB10500 – 12850
sB⇨ 🍴10500 – 12850 dB⇨ 🍴17500 – 21300
(English breakfast) L6500 D6500 Pool
★★*Kinzica* pza Arcivescovado ☎22300
33rm6⇨14 🍴 𝒟 sB9800 sB⇨ 🍴13000 dB16500
dB⇨ 🍴21000 L5500 D5500
★★*Touring* via G-Puccini 6 (n rest) ☎46374
40rm20⇨ Lift
🐾 *G Finocchi* via Galcesana ☎86147 Aud/VW

PISTICCI Matera 16,850 (☎0835) Map **34** C3
☆☆☆*AGIP* (SS 407 Basentana km 137 & 400)
☎632007 64 🍴 Lift

POLIGNANO A MARE Bari 13,900 (☎080)
Map **34** C4
★*Grotta Polazzese* via Narciso 59 ☎740261
14rm8⇨8 🍴 A2rm 🏠 Lift 𝒟 sB⇨ 🍴12500 – 14500
dB⇨ 🍴23000 – 25000 (English breakfast)
L8000 – 10000 D8000 – 10000 St%

PORDENONE Pordenone 51,025 (☎0434)
Map **30** C4
★★*Moderno* pza XX-Settembre ☎22565
134rm22⇨55 🍴 🏠 Lift
🐾*Automobile* viale Grigoletti ☎32591
BL/Jag/Rov/Tri
🅱 🐾 *Cossetti & Vatta* viale Venezia ☎31474 Ren

PORT'ERCOLE Grosseto (☎0564) Map **31** A/B3
★*Don Pedro* ☎833914 Closed Oct – Feb
44rm16⇨28 🍴 🏠 P Lift 𝒟 sB⇨ 🍴13600 – 17200
dB⇨ 🍴23300 – 28500 (English breakfast)
L7000 – 10000 D7000 – 10000 St% sea

PORTO AZZURRO See **ELBA (ISOLA D')**

PORTO FERRÁIO See **ELBA (ISOLA D')**

PORTOFINO Genova 850 (☎0185) Map **29** A2/3
★★★★*Splendido* ☎69195 tx37057 Closed 11
Jan – 9 Mar 67rm57⇨10 🍴 🏠 P Lift 𝒟
sB⇨ 🍴33500 – 43500 dB⇨ 🍴57000 – 67000
(English breakfast) L16000 D16000 🐾 Pool sea
★★*Piccola* (n rest) ☎69015 Closed Oct – Mar
26rm6⇨16 🍴 P 𝒟 sB⇨ 🍴17000 – 20000
dB24000 – 27000 dB⇨ 🍴31000 – 34000
(English breakfast) sea

PORTO SAN GIÓRGIO Ascoli Piceno 14,900
(☎0734) Map **32** C4
★*Terrazza* via A-Costa ☎4244 36rm2⇨18 🍴 P
Lift 𝒟 sB6800 – 7000 sB⇨ 🍴7800 – 8500
dB12600 – 13500 dB⇨ 🍴13600 – 16000
(English breakfast) L5000 D5000 Beach sea
🐾*Petracci* via Nazionale Adriatica 235 ☎4248

POSITANO Salerno 3,350 (☎089) Map **33** A3
★★★*Montemare* via Positea 58 ☎875010 36⇨ sea
★★★*Savola* via C-Colombo 29 ☎875003 Closed
Oct – Mar 44rm27⇨12 🍴 P Lift 𝒟

sB⇄🏠9500–11000 dB15000–20000
dB⇄🏠19500–25500 (English breakfast)
L6000–8000 D6000–8000 sea
★★Buca di Bacco ☎875004 Closed Nov & Dec
31rm8🏠 Lift sea
★★Maresca ☎875140 Closed 16 Nov–14 Mar
19rm7⇄6🏠 A4rm 🏠 P sB5000–5500
sB⇄🏠5500–6000 dB7800–8500
dB⇄🏠9700–10500 (English breakfast) L3000
D3000 sea
★★Margherita via G-Marconi 31 ☎875188 Closed
Nov–14 Mar 14rm3⇄6🏠 P D sB6000–6800
sB⇄🏠6800–8500 dB12300–14000
dB⇄🏠14500–16000 L5000 D5000 sea mountains
★★Poseidon ☎875014 tx77072 Closed 16
Oct–Mar 54⇄ 🏠 Lift D sB13750–16250
dB25000–28500 L7000 D7000 Pool sea
POTENZA Potenza 60,750 (☎0971) Map **33** B3
🛏 ⋈**L Olita** via del Gallitello ☎26477 ☎24379 🐾 M/c
Bed/Opl/Vau (GB)
POZZUOLI Napoli 60,990 (☎081) Map **32** D1
Pelli via E-Scarfoglio ☎7605322 M/c Bed/Opl/Vau
(GB)
PRAIANO Salerno 1,700 (☎089) Map **33** A/B3
★★Grand Tritone ☎874005 Closed 21 Oct–Mar
77rm40⇄37 🏠 🏠 P Lift D sB⇄🏠10000–15000
dB⇄🏠19000–28000 (English breakfast) L fr8000
D fr7500 Pool Beach sea mountains
★★Tramonto d'Oro ☎874008 35⇄ P Lift D
dB⇄15000–22500 (English breakfast) L fr5500
D fr5500 Pool sea
PROCCHIO See **MARCIANA-MARINA** under **ELBA**
PUGNOCHIUSO See **VIESTE**
RAGUSA See **SICILIA (SICILY)**
RAPALLO Genova 28,600 (☎0185) Map **29** A3
★★★★Savola pza III Novembre 1 ☎50492
63rm37⇄ 🏠 Lift Beach sea
★★★Bel Soggiorno via Gramsci 10 ☎54527
24rm12⇄ Lift
★★★Eurotel via Aurelia Ponente 22 ☎60981
65rm50⇄14🏠 🏠 P Lift sB⇄ 🏠17000–20000
dB⇄🏠26000–30000 (English breakfast) L8000
D8000 Pool sea
★★★Grande Italia Lungomare Castello 1 ☎50492
60rm44⇄10🏠 P Lift D sB10500–11500
sB⇄🏠12500–15000 dB 16000–21000
dB⇄🏠20000–27000 L 7000–7500 D7000–7500
Beach sea
★★★Marsala Lungomare V-Veneto ☎50348
30rm5⇄10🏠 Lift D sB8800 sB⇄🏠11000 dB17000
dB⇄🏠21500 (English breakfast) L6500 D6500 sea
★★★Miramare Lungomare V-Veneto 27 ☎50293
Closed 21 Nov–19 Dec 25rm12⇄ Lift D
sB10400–12100 sB⇄14600–16600
dB18200–21700 dB⇄23200–26000
(English breakfast) D8000 ♂ sea
★★★Moderno & Reale viale Gramsci 6 ☎50601
48rm35⇄5🏠 P Lift D sB12000–14000
sB⇄🏠15000–17000 dB20000–22000
dB⇄🏠26000–28000 (English breakfast) L8000
D7000 St% sea
★★★Riviera via Gramsci 2 ☎50248 26rm25⇄1🏠 P
Lift D sB⇄🏠18700–21700 dB⇄🏠23400–28400
(English breakfast) L8000–9000 D8000–9000 sea
★★Piccoloo via Dante 6-7 ☎54975 Closed Oct–19
Dec 10⇄ Lift sea
★★Bandoni via Marsala 24 ☎50423 18rm5⇄1🏠 Lift
D sB5500–6400 dB11000–12800
dB⇄🏠11500–14500 (English breakfast) L3000
D3000 sea
★Elvezia via Ferraretto 12 (DP) ☎50564 11rm2⇄
sea
🛏 ⋈**E Massa** via G-Mameli 182 ☎50689 BL
RAVELLO Salerno 2,450 (☎089) Map **33** B3
★★★Caruso Belvedere via Toro 52 ☎871527
26rm19⇄1🏠 🏠 sea
★★★Palumbo via Toro 34 ☎857244 47rm30⇄3🏠
A15rm 🏠 P D sB14700–16600

sB⇄🏠17900–21600 dB22500–27800
dB⇄🏠27800–33100 (English breakfast) L8000
D8000 sea
★★Parsifal pza Fontana ☎857144 Closed Nov–Mar
19rm12⇄3🏠 🏠 P sB6700–8700
sB⇄🏠9200–10700 dB10900–12900
dB⇄🏠11400–17400 L7000 D7000 sea
RAVENNA Ravenna 137,050 (☎0544) Map **30** C2
★★★★Jolly Mameli pza Mameli 1 ☎35762 tx55575
75⇄ 🏠 Lift D sB⇄22250 dB⇄36500 L8500 D8500
★★★Bisanzio via Salara 30 ☎27111 40rm27⇄10🏠
P Lift D sB 15500 sB⇄🏠23500 dB28000
dB⇄39000 (English breakfast) St%
★Centrale Byron via IV Novembre 14 (n rest)
☎22225 57rm12⇄42🏠 Lift D sB⇄🏠11500
dB 15000 dB⇄🏠20500 L 4200 D4200
☆Romea via Romea 1 ☎26477 39rm 🏠 P Lift D
sB⇄🏠9750–11250 dB⇄🏠17500–20500
(English breakfast) L 5500 D5500
🛏 ⋈**Ravennate** via M-Perilli 40 ☎39079 ☎28061 P
Fia/Ren (GB)
REGGIO DI CALABRIA Reggio Di Calabria 174,500
(☎0965) Map **34** C1
C Mazzone via San Caterina 12 ☎48600 M/c
Aud/Por/VW
RÉGGIO NELL'EMILIA Réggio Nell'Emilia 129,800
(☎0522) Map **20** B3
★★★★Astoria via Leopoldo Nobili 4 ☎35245 tx5003
100rm60⇄40🏠 🏠 P Lift D sB⇄🏠26200
dB⇄🏠40400 (English breakfast) L8000 D8000
★★★Posta pza C-Battisti 4 (n rest) ☎32944
55rm14⇄24🏠 🏠 P Lift D sB8700–10200
sB⇄🏠13700–16200 dB 17900–19250
dB⇄🏠25400–27400
RENDE See **COSENZA**
RICAVO See **CASTELLINA IN CHINATI**
RICCIONE Forli 30,100 (☎054) Map **30** C2
★★★★Atlantic viale Milano II ☎601155 tx55192
Closed 21 Sep–19 May 65rm35⇄30🏠 🏠 P Lift D
sB⇄🏠20000–34000 dB⇄🏠28000–63000
(English breakfast) L6000–9000 D6000–9000 Pool
Beach sea
★★★Beaurivage viale d'Annunzio 132 ☎41703
Closed 16 Sep–14 May 55rm23⇄32🏠 Lift ♂
★★★Saviole Speaggia viale d'Annunzio 2
☎43252 Closed Oct–9 May 70⇄ Lift Pool Beach sea
★★★Abner's Lungomare Repubblica ☎600601
tx55153 50⇄ P Lift D sB⇄21900–33000
dB⇄32650–46000 (English breakfast)
L6000–12000 D6000–12000 ♂ Beach sea
★★★Arizona via G-d'Annunzio 22 ☎48520 Closed
Oct–Apr 60⇄ P Lift D sB⇄9000–13000
dB⇄10000–15000 (English breakfast)
L8000–10000 D8000–10000 Beach sea
★★★Lungomare viale Milano 7 ☎41601 Closed 19
Sep–24 May 56⇄ P Lift D sB⇄9200–17000
dB⇄144000–24000 (English breakfast)
L7000–8000 D8000–9000 sea
★★★Vienna & Touring viale Gramsci 79 ☎41041 (fr
Oct601700) tx551253 Closed Oct–Apr 🏠 97
rm90⇄7🏠 P Lift D sB⇄🏠17500–23000
dB⇄🏠25000–36000 (English breakfast)
L6000–12000 D6000–12000 ♂ sea
★★Alexandra-Plaza viale Torino 61 ☎615344
tx55153 Closed Oct–Mar 58⇄ P Lift
sB⇄14500–19000 dB⇄23000–28000
(English breakfast) L6000–12000 D6000–12000 ♂
Beach sea
★★Nevada viale Milano 46 ☎601245 Closed 11
Oct–Apr 48⇄🏠 🏠 P Lift D sB⇄🏠11500
dB⇄🏠13000 (English breakfast) L7000 D7000 sea
★★Santo Stefano via Tassoni 5 ☎42391 Closed
Oct–Apr 49rm38⇄4🏠 Lift sea
★Sarti viale Torino 1 ☎42264 tx55192 Closed
Oct–Apr 54⇄ sea
🛏 ⋈**Morelli & Muccioli** via R-Molari 26 ☎41436 P
Aud/VW (GB)

Italy

RIMINI Forli 123,3000 (☎0541) Map **30** C2
★★★**Ambasciatori** viale Vespucci 22 ☎27642
tx55132 70rm50⇌20 ⋒ ⋒ P Lift ♪
sB⇌ ⋒18000 – 23000 dB⇌ ⋒34000 – 51000
(English breakfast) L12000 D12000 ⚓ Pool Beach
sea
★★★**Fantasy** viale Regina Elena 93 ☎24922 Closed
Oct – Apr 65 ⋒ Lift Beach sea
★★★**France** viale Regina Margherita 48 ☎32237
Closed Oct – 19 May 65⇌ P Lift ♪
sB⇌10000 – 14000 dB⇌ ⋒18000 – 24000
(English breakfast) L5500 D5500 Pool Beach ♂ sea
★★★**President** via Tripoli 270 ☎25741 Closed
Oct – Apr 50rm15⇌35 ⋒ ⋒ Lift ♪ sB8000 – 11000
sB⇌ ⋒9000 – 12000 dB⇌ ⋒16500 – 19500
(English breakfast) L fr6000 Dfr6000
★★**Alpen** viale Regina Elena 203 ☎80662 Closed
Oct – Apr 60rm4⇌40 ⋒ P Lift ♪ sB6200 – 9300
sB⇌ ⋒6700 – 10100 dB10400 – 13000
dB⇌ ⋒11400 – 15000 (English breakfast) L4000
D4000 sea
★★**Constellation** viale Regina Elena 73 ☎55071
Closed Oct – Apr 35⇌ ⋒ Lift sea
★★**Gran Bretagna** viale Carducci 2 ☎22613 Closed
21 Sep – 24 May 29rm12 ⋒
∫⚓**Grattacielo** viale P-Amedeo 11 ☎24610 P Opl
∬ ∫⚓**E Sartini** viale le P-Amedeo 13 ☎27548 P Fia
(GB)
∫⚓**F Sartini** Nuova Circonvallazione N 22 ☎770311
M/c Fia (GB)
At **Rivazzura** (4km SE)
★★★**Grand Meeting** viale Regina Margherita 46
☎32123 Closed Oct – Apr 50⇌ ⋒ P Lift ♪
sB⇌8000 – 12000 (room only) dB⇌12000 – 18000
(room only) Beach sea
★★★**Little** via Gubbio 16 ☎33258 Closed Oct – 19
May 45 ⋒ P Lift ♪ sB ⋒9000 – 13500
dB ⋒16000 – 23000 (English breakfast) L 3000 – 6000
D3000 – 6000 mountains

RIVA DEL GARDA Trento 12,7000 (☎0464)
Map **29** B4
★★★**Grand Riva** pza Garibaldi 10 ☎52340 tx40278
Closed 11 Oct – 9 Apr 140rm80⇌ ⋒ Lift lake
★★★**Lac & Parc** viale Rovereto 38 ☎52122 tx40258
Closed Nov – 14 Mar 170rm140⇌30 ⋒ P Lift ♪
sB⇌ ⋒18000 – 22000 dB⇌ ⋒32000 – 39000
(English breakfast) L8000 – 9000 D8000 – 9000 ⚓
Pool mountains lake
★★★**Marina** ☎52736 Closed Oct – Mar
30rm3⇌15 ⋒ Lift Pool lake lake
★★**Bellavista** ☎52334 Closed 16 Oct – Apr 28rm6⇌
⋒ Lift lake
★★**Centrale** pza III Novembre 27 ☎52344 Closed 6
Oct – mid Apr 70rm 12⇌ Lift

ROCCARASO L'Aquila 1,600 (☎0864) Map **32** C2
☆☆ **AGIP** SS17 dell'Appennino l'Abruzzese
☎62443 ⋒ Lift

ROLLE (PASSO DI) Trento (☎0439) Map **13** A1
★**Passo Rolle** ☎68216 22rm3⇌ P sB4200 – 4700
dB8400 – 10400 dB⇌10400 – 14400
(English breakfast) L7000 D7000 mountains

ROMA (ROME) Roma 2,856,350 (☎06) Map **31** B2
See Plan
★★★★★**Bernini-Bristol** pza Barberini 23 ☎463051
tx61554 Plan **1** 125⇌ ⋒ P Lift ♪ sB⇌34850 – 51150
dB⇌57100 – 78250 (English breakfast) L10000
D10000
★★★★★**Grand Flora** via V-Veneto 191 ☎462151
Plan **2** 177rm151⇌26 ⋒ ⋒ Lift
★★★★**Hassler-Villa Medici** pza Trinita dei Monti 6
☎6792651 tx61208 Plan **3** 100⇌ ⋒ Lift
★★★★**Boston** via Lombardia 47 ☎4751592 tx63295
Plan **4** 120⇌ ⋒ P Lift ♪ sB⇌33000 dB⇌45000
(English breakfast) L fr8000 D fr8000
★★★★**Commodore** via Torino 1 (n rest) ☎4751515
tx63170 Plan **5** 65rm40⇌25 ⋒ ⋒ Lift
★★★★**Eliseo** via di Porta Pinciana 30 (DP) ☎460556
tx61693 Plan **6** 60⇌ Lift

★★★★**Jolly** corso d'Italia 1 ☎8495 tx63293 Plan **7**
200⇌ ⋒ Lift ♪ sB⇌40000 dB⇌60000 L10000
D10000
★★★★**Quirinale** via Nazionale 7 ☎489101 tx61332
Plan **8** 200rm180⇌15 ⋒ ⋒ Lift ♪
sB⇌29000 – 40000 dB⇌ ⋒47000 – 65000 English
breakfast only L fr9500 D fr9500
★★★★**Ville** via Sistina 69 (DP) ☎688941 Plan **9** ⋒
Lift
☆☆**AGIP** via Aurelia (8km W road No 1) ☎626843
Plan **10** 222⇌ Lift
★★★**Britannia** via Napoli 64 (n rest) ☎463153
tx62292 Plan **11** 32⇌ P Lift ♪ sB⇌21000
dB⇌32000 (English breakfast)
★★★**Columbus** via delle Conciliazione 33
☎6564874 tx64010 Plan **12** 110⇌80 ⋒ Lift
★★★**Continental** via Cavour 5 (n rest) ☎462141
tx61421 Plan **13** 260rm132⇌105 ⋒ ⋒ Lift
★★★**Dinesen** via de Porta Pinciana 18 (n rest)
☎471410 Plan **14** 50rm25⇌ Lift
★★★**Lord Byron** via de Notaris 5 ☎3609541
tx62217 Plan **15** 50rm30⇌20 ⋒ ⋒ P Lift ♪
sB⇌32000 – 43000 dB⇌ ⋒52000 – 75000
(English breakfast) L fr1000 D fr1000 St%
★★★**Nord-Nuova** via G-Amendola 3 ☎465441
tx61550 Plan **16** 160rm128⇌10 ⋒ P Lift ♪
sB⇌18700 dB⇌ ⋒30900 L6800 D6800
★★★**Park** via A-Morelli 5 (n rest) ☎870184 Plan **18**
28rm25⇌8 ⋒ P Lift ♪ sB⇌ ⋒14800 – 16350
dB⇌ ⋒18800 – 22700 (English breakfast) St%
★★★**Regina-Carlton** via V-Veneto 72 ☎4758841
tx59142 Plan **19** 134rm123⇌11 ⋒ ⋒ P Lift ♪
sB⇌38200 – 42100 dB⇌ ⋒54000 – 63300
(English breakfast) L fr11000 D fr11000
★★★**Rivoli** via Taramelli 7 (off viale B-Buozzi)
(n rest) ☎878140 Plan **20** 50rm46⇌ Lift
★★**Alba** via Leonina 12 (n rest) ☎484471 Plan **22**
30⇌ ⋒ P Lift ♪ sB⇌11700 dB⇌16600 – 17500
★★**Ariston** via Turati 16 (n rest) ☎7310341 Plan **23**
110rm75⇌ Lift ♪ sB10500 sB⇌14000 dB19000
dB⇌24000
★★**Astrid** Largo A-Sarti 4 (n rest) ☎3610048 Plan **24**
Closed Nov 20rm Lift sB fr10000 dB fr16700
★**Margutta** via Laurina 34 (n rest) ☎6798440
Plan **28** 25rm4⇌18 ⋒ P Lift ♪ sB10700
sB⇌ ⋒12000 dB14900 dB⇌ ⋒17500
(English breakfast)
★**Scalinata di Spagna** pza Trinita dei Monti 17
(n rest) ☎6793006 Plan **29** 14rm7⇌7 ⋒ ♪
sB⇌ ⋒15000 – 16000 dB⇌ ⋒24500 – 26000
∫⚓**Bellancauto** pza Villa Carpegna 52 ☎6223359
Chy/Sim
∫⚓**Marchi Orlando** Circonvallazione Trionfale 133
☎3599893 M/c Jag/Ska/Toy
At **Storta (La)** (16km NW road No. 2)
☆**Bela** via Cassia 1801 ☎6990232 Plan **25**
44rm18⇌25 ⋒ ♪ sB⇌ ⋒14500 – 1500
dB⇌ ⋒19300 – 20200 (English breakfast) L4900
D4900 ⚓ Pool

ROVIGO Rovigo 51,250 (☎0425) Map **30** C3
★★**Bologna** viale Regina-Margherita 6 ☎22406
14rm4⇌2 ⋒ sB7300 dB12800 dB⇌ ⋒15000
(English breakfast) L4500 – 5000 D4500 – 5000

ST VINCENT Aosta 4,750 (☎0166) Map **28** D4
★★★**Billia** viale Piemonte ☎3446 134⇌ ⋒ Lift ⚓
Pool
∫⚓**Fabris-Ford** pza Zerbion ☎2619 P Frd (GB)

SALERNO Salerno 159,300 (☎089) Map **33** B3
★★★★**Jolly delle Palme** Lungomare Trieste 1
☎225222 tx77050 106 ⇌ P Lift ♪ sB⇌20250
dB⇌33500 L8500 D8500
∬ **G Jannone** via Picenza 12 ☎351229 BL/Jag
Rov/Tri
At **Vietri Sul Mare** (3km W)
★★★★**Lloyd's Bala** via dei Marinis ☎210145
tx77043 120rm110⇌10 ⋒ A10rm ⋒ P Lift ♪
sB⇌ ⋒27200 – 32400 dB⇌ ⋒44000 – 52800
(English breakfast) L10900 D10900 Pool Beach sea

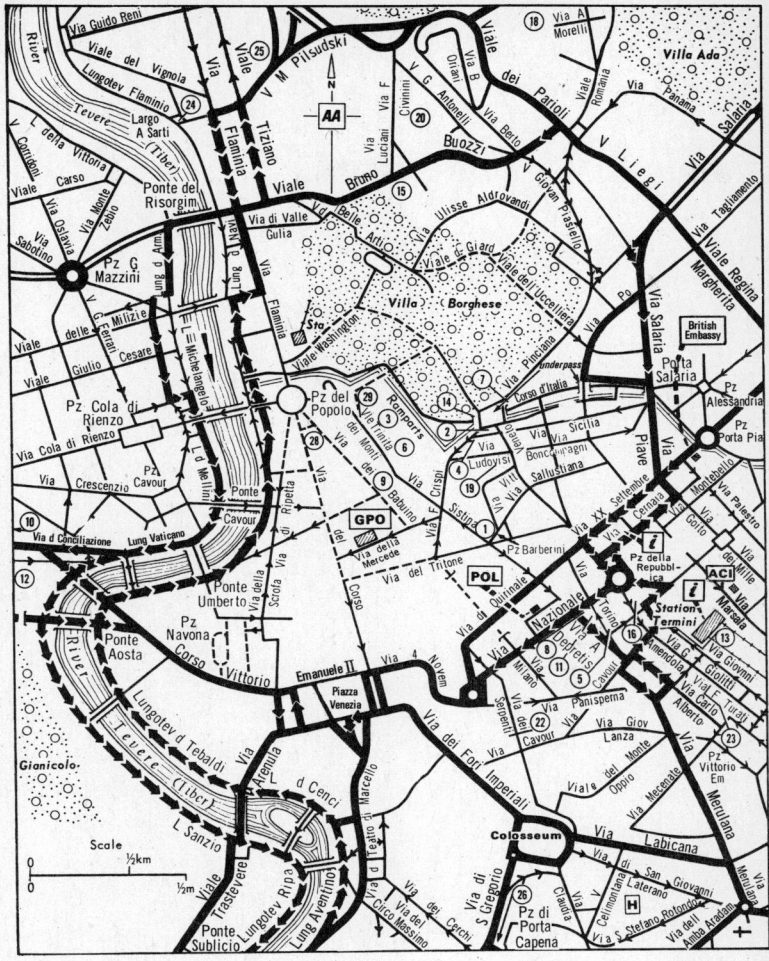

Roma (Rome)

1	★★★★★Bernini-Bristol		15	★★★Lord Byron
2	★★★★★Grand Flora		16	★★★Nord-Nuova
3	★★★★★Hassler Villa Medici		18	★★★Park
4	★★★★Boston		19	★★★Regina Carlton
5	★★★★Commodore		20	★★★Rivoli
6	★★★★Eliseo		22	★★Alba
7	★★★★Jolly		23	★★Ariston
8	★★★★Quirinale		24	★★Astrid
9	★★★★Ville		25	☆Bela (at La Storta 16km NW
10	☆☆☆AGIP			on road No. 2)
11	★★★Britannia		28	★Margutta
12	★★★Columbus		29	★Scalinata di Spagna
13	★★★Continental			
14	★★★Dinesen			

Italy

SALÒ Brescia 10,650 (☎0365) Map **29** B4
★★★**Duomo** via Duomo 18 ☎21026 28⇄ P Lift
sB⇄🍽12200 dB⇄🍽20200 (English breakfast)
L6000 D6000 mountains lake
★**Ideal** via Pietro de Salò 11 (DP) ☎20873 Closed
Nov – Mar 28rm18⇄4🍽 A8rm 🏠 lake
SALSOMAGGIORE TERME Parma 17,900
(☎0524) Map **29** A3
★★★★**Porro** viale Porro 10 ☎78221 tx53639
85rm38⇄40🍽 P Lift ♪ sB⇄🍽19500 – 21500
dB⇄🍽36000 – 38500 (English breakfast) L10000
D10000 Pool
SAN BARTOLOMEO AL MARE Imperia 2,500
(☎0183) Map **28** D2
★**Mayola** 400739 Closed 11 Oct – Apr 80rm60🍽 🏠 P
Lift ♪ sB7800 – 8800 dB11100 – 13100
dB🍽12100 – 14100 (English breakfast) L5000 D5000
Beach sea
SAN BENEDETTO DEL TRONTO Ascoli Piceno
44,600 (☎0735) Map **32** C3
★★**Pierrot** Lungomare Rinascimento 15 ☎65386
Closed Oct – Apr 45🍽 Pool Beach sea
★**Arlecchino** viale Trieste 24 ☎2959 24⇄ 🏠 Pool
Beach ○ sea
🏠 🕭**G E Tommassini** corso Mazzini 249 ☎5608
Aud/VW
SAN CANDIDO INNICHEN Bolzana 3,000 (☎0474)
Map **13** A1
★★**Park Sole Paradiso** ☎73120 Closed Oct Nov & 5
Apr – May 50⇄ 🏠
SAN DOMENICO See **FIESOLE**
SAN DONATO MILANESE See **MILANO**
SAN GIMIGUANO Siena 7,600 (☎0577) Map **29** B2
★★**Cisterna** pza della Cisterna 23 ☎940328 42rm
Lift sB 10250 sB⇄🍽11500 dB 17400 dB⇄🍽21000
L6500 D6500 mountains
SAN MAMETE See **VALSOLDA**
SAN MARTINO DI CASTROZZA Trento 328
(☎0439) Map **31** A1
★★★**San Martino** ☎68011 Closed 10 Sep – 11 Dec
& 5 Apr – 19 Jun 46rm42⇄ 🏠
★★**Savole** ☎68094 Closed 11 Apr – Jun & 11
Sep – 19 Dec 73⇄ 🏠 P Lift ♪ sB⇄14000 – 19000
dB⇄27000 – 31000 (English breakfast)
L9000 – 12000 D9000 – 12000 mountains
★**Belvedere** ☎68000 tx44043 Closed 11 Apr – 24
Jun & 4 Sep – 19 Dec 30rm26⇄ P Lift ♪
sB⇄9800 – 16800 dB 17600 – 27600 Lfr5500
Dfr5500 mountains
SAN REMO Imperia 64,800 (☎0184) Map **28** D2
★★★★**Royal** corso Imperatrice ☎84321 tx27511
Closed Oct – 15 Dec 141rm132⇄9🍽 🏠 P Lift ♪
sB⇄🍽25500 – 38500 dB⇄🍽43000 – 73000
(English breakfast) L fr13000 Dfr13000 🏊 Pool sea
★★★★**Miramare** corso Matuzia 9 ☎882381
79rm70⇄ P Lift ♪ sB11000 – 15000
sB⇄15000 – 22000 dB 20000 – 28000
dB⇄26000 – 38000 L10000 D10000 St% Pool sea
★★★★**Savoy** via Nuvoloni 40 ☎84921 Closed
Oct – 19 Dec 160rm140⇄ 🏠 Lift Pool sea
★★★**Astoria West End** corso Matuzia 8 ☎70791
94rm77⇄ P Lift ♪ sB⇄22800 – 27800
dB⇄38600 – 45600 (English breakfast) L9800
D9800 sea
★★★**Europa & Pace** corso Imperatrice 27 ☎70605
80rm40⇄🍽 🏠 P Lift ♪ sB 10000 – 14000
sB⇄14000 – 20000 dB 18000 – 25600
dB⇄🍽26000 – 34000 (English breakfast) L9000
D9000 sea
★★★**Grand Londra** corso Matuzia 2 ☎79961
tx28420 Closed 3 Oct – 21 Dec 200rm192⇄ 🏠 P Lift
♪ sB 28750 dB⇄38600 L9500 D9500 Pool sea
★★★**Parco** corso Mazzini 199 ☎85305 Closed 21
Oct – 19 Dec 30rm15⇄15🍽 🏠 P Lift ♪
sB⇄🍽11500 – 13750 dB⇄🍽21000 – 24700
(English breakfast) L7500 D7500 St% sea
★★★**Residence Principe** via Asquasciati 48
☎83565 58rm48⇄10🍽 🏠 P Lift ♪

sB⇄🍽14000 – 17000 dB⇄🍽24000 – 31000
(English breakfast) L8000 D8000 sea
★★**Beau Rivage** corso Trieste 49 ☎85146 30🍽 P
Lift ♪ sB⇄🍽10000 dB⇄🍽18600 (English breakfast)
L5500 D5500 sea
☆**Bobby** via Marconi 146 ☎60256 74rm20⇄54🍽
🏠 P Lift ♪ sB⇄🍽17000 dB⇄🍽32500
(English breakfast) L8000 D8000 Pool sea
★★**King** corso Cavallotti 92 ☎86054 26rm10⇄16🍽
P ♪ sB⇄🍽11000 – 13000 dB⇄🍽22000 – 24000
(English breakfast) L6000 D6000 sea
★★**Morandl** corso Matuzia 25 ☎85275
32rm22⇄5🍽 🏠 P Lift ♪ sB9800 – 10800
sB⇄🍽12300 – 13800 dB17000 – 20400
dB⇄🍽21600 – 24600 (English breakfast) L7000
D7000 Beach sea
★★**Paradiso** corso Imperatrice ☎85112 tx27620
41rm22⇄17🍽 🏠 P Lift ♪ sB⇄🍽13800 dB20600
dB⇄🍽24900 (English breakfast) L7500 D7500 sea
🏠 **Toselli** corso Matuzia 51 ☎85572 P
Bed/MB/Opl/Vau
SANTA CATERINA VALFURVA Sondrio (☎0342)
Map **12** D1
★★**Sobretta** (DP) ☎935505 Closed May – 27 Jun &
21 Sep – Nov 27rm12⇄8🍽 🏠
SANTA CRISTINA VAL GARDENA Bolzano 1,600
(☎0471) Map **13** A1
★★**Posta** ☎76678 Closed Nov 60rm30⇄ 🏠 Lift 🍴
Pool
SANTA MERGHERITA LIGURE Genova 12,9000
(☎0185) Map **29** A3
★★★★★**Imperial-Palace** via Pagana 19 ☎88991
tx28398 Closed Nov – 19 Dec 105 P Lift ♪
sB⇄31600 – 48600 dB⇄53200 – 79200
(English breakfast) L 12000 – 15000 D12000 – 15000
Pool Beach sea
★★★★**Miramare** via Milite Ignoto 30 ☎87014 73⇄
🏠 Lift Pool Beach sea
★★★**Continentale** via Pagana 8 (DP) ☎86512 61⇄
🍴 Pool ♪ ○
★★★**Laurin** corso Marconi 3 ☎89971 Closed 21
Nov – 20 Dec 41⇄ Lift sea Beach
★★★**Mediterraneo** via Vittoria 18 A ☎86881
25rm13⇄ Lift
★★★**Metropole** via Pagana 2 ☎86134 Closed 7
Nov – 19 Dec 50rm44⇄ A12rm 🏠 P Lift ♪
sB⇄19000 – 22300 dB⇄32500 – 38000
(English breakfast) L9000 D10000 Beach sea
★★★**Park Suisse** via Favale 31 ☎89571 tx28549
70rm54⇄16🍽 🏠 P Lift ♪ sB⇄🍽23000 – 27000
dB⇄🍽41000 – 48000 (English breakfast) L 11000
D11000 🍴 Pool ♪ ○ sea
★★★**Regina Elena** Lungomare Milite Ignoto 44
☎87004 tx28563 64rm56⇄8🍽 🏠 P Lift ♪
sB⇄19600 – 27600 dB⇄🍽34200 – 48200 L 12000
D12000 Beach sea
★★★**Tigullio** corso E-Rainusso 3 (n rest) ☎87455
40⇄ Lift 🍴 Pool 🍴
★★**Villa Anita** viale Minerva ☎86543 20rm3⇄7🍽
A5rm 🏠 P sB 10500 sB⇄🍽12500 dB 17000
dB⇄🍽19000 (English breakfast) L fr6500 Dfr6500
sea
★**Europa** via Trento 5 ☎87187 16rm2⇄ 🏠 P
dB 1400 – 14100 dB⇄15400 L fr6000 Dfr6000
SAPRI Saterno 7,580 (☎0973) Map **33** B3
★★**Tirreno** corso Italia ☎31157 56rm7⇄19🍽 🏠 P
Lift ♪ sB5500 – 7000 sB⇄🍽6500 – 8200
dB 10000 – 11800 dB⇄🍽11000 – 13600
(English breakfast) L5000 D5000 sea
🏠 🕭**Comisso** via Pisacane 22 ☎31370 ☎31356
M/c P Frd
SARDAGNA See **TRENTO**
SARDEGNA (ISOLA) (SARDINIA) 135,750
Map **31** Inset
Arzachena Sassari 6,340 (☎789) Map **31** A2
★★★★**Romazzino** costa Smeralda ☎96020
tx79059 Closed Nov – Apr 85⇄ P Lift ♪
sB⇄41500 – 63000 dB⇄57000 – 84000

(English breakfast) L 16000 D16000 ⚓ Pool Beach sea

Cagliari Cagliari 225,900 (☎070) Map **31** A1
★★★★**Jolly Regina Margherita** viale Regina Margherita 44 ☎651971 tx79050 126 rm104⇌ P Lift ♪ sB14050 sB⇌21250 dB24100 dB⇌36500 L8000 D8000
☆☆☆**AGIP** Circonvallazione Nuova ☎494003 57 🍴 Lift

Golfo Aranci Sassari (☎0789) Map **31** A2
★★**Margherita** ☎46906 25rm4⇌7 🍴 Beach sea

Iglesias Cagliari 29,000 (☎0781) Map **31** A1
★★★**Artu** pza Quintino Sella 12 ☎2492 22rm4⇌5 🍴 🏛

Macomer Nuoro 10,350 (☎0785) Map **31** A2
☆☆**AGIP** (SS 131 di Carlo Felice 145km) 30 🍴
Nuoro Nuoro 33,850 (☎0784) Map **31** A2
☆☆☆**AGIP** via Trieste ☎34071 57 🍴 Lift

Sassari Sassari 112,800 (☎079) Map **31** A2
★★★★**Jolly Grazia Deledda** viale Dante 47 ☎271235 tx79056 140⇌ P Lift ♪ sB⇌25500 dB⇌44000 L8000 D8000 Pool
☆☆☆**AGIP** Loc Serra Secca ☎271440 57 🍴 Lift
★★**Jolly** via Mancini 2 (n rest) ☎273101 59⇌ 🏛 P ♪ sB11600 sB⇌16650 dB20500 dB⇌28550

Villasimius Cagliari 2,150 (☎070) Map **31** A1
★★★**Timi-Ama** ☎79228 Closed Oct – 14 May 64⇌ P ♪ sB⇌11000 – 16000 dB⇌19000 – 26500 (English breakfast) L9500 D9500 ⚓ Beach sea
At **Cupo Bol** (6km W)
★★★**Grand Copo Bol** (DP & Pn) ☎79225 tx79266 Closed 21 Oct – Apr 103rm67⇌34 🍴 Lift ⚓ Pool Beach sea

SARZANA La Spezia 19,200 (☎0187) Map **29** A2
☆☆**AGIP** Nuova Circonvallazione ☎61491 51 🍴 Lift

SASSARI See **SARDEGNA (SARDINIA)**

SAVONA Savona 80,380 (☎019) Map **28** D3
☆☆☆**AGIP** via Nizza-Loc Zinola ☎801961 60 🍴 Lift
★★★**Miramare** via Giordano 5 ☎803333 22⇌ 🏛 P Lift ♪ sB⇌17000 – 19000 dB⇌32000 (English breakfast) L7000 D7000 St% Beach sea
★★**Riviera-Suisse** via Paleocapa ☎20683 54rm36 🍴 🏛 Lift
C M Spirito corso Viglienzoni 8F ☎806860 Chy/Sim

SCIACCA See **SICILIA (SICILY)**

SELVA DI VAL GARDENA Bolzano 2,250 (☎0471) Map **13** A1
★★**Solaia** ☎75104 Closed 21 Oct – Nov & 21 Apr – 19 Jun 30 ⇌ 🏛 P sB⇌20000 – 265000 dB⇌40000 – 53000 English breakfast only L12000 – 15000 D12000 – 15000

SENIGÀLLIA Ancona 39,650 (☎071) Map **30** D2
★★★**Ritz** Lungomare Dante Alighieri 142 ☎63563 tx56044 Closed 16 Oct – Apr 150rm60⇌90 🍴 P Lift ♪ sB⇌14600 – 17200 dB⇌22000 – 28600 (English breakfast) L8000 D8000 St% Pool Beach sea
★★**Grand Excelsior** Lungomare Dante Alighieri 148 ☎61491 Closed Oct – Apr 94rm90 🍴 Lift sea
🅱 ➡ **G E Luzi & Figli** via Podesti 156 ☎62035 ☎64806 P Aud/Por/VW

SESTO CALENDE Varese 10,550 (☎0331) Map **28** D4
★★**Tre Re** pza Garibaldi 25 ☎924229 Closed Dec – Feb 36rm32⇌4 🍴 P Lift ♪ sB⇌14000 – 14500 dB⇌ 🍴22000 – 23500 (English breakfast) L12000 D9000 St% lake

SESTO FIORENTINO See **FIRENZE**

SESTRIERE Torino 700 (☎0122) Map **28** C3
★★★**Duchi d'Aosta** colle del Sestriere ☎7123 Closed 16 Apr – 4 Dec 173rm99⇌ Lift
★**Torre** colle del Sestriere ☎7041 Closed 10 Apr – 2 Dec 150rm Lift

SESTRI LEVANTE Genova 21,650 (☎0185) Map **29** A2

★★★**Villa Balbi** viale Rimembranze 1 ☎42941 Closed Oct – Apr 105rm80⇌25 🍴 P Lift ♪ sB⇌ 🍴16000 – 20000 dB⇌ 🍴26000 – 32000 (English breakfast) L10000 – 12000 D10000 – 12000 Pool Beach sea
★★★**Miramare & Europa** via Cappellini 3 ☎41055 Closed Nov – Mar 37rm23⇌10 🍴 Lift Beach sea
★★★**Vis a Vis** via della Chiusa 28 ☎42661 50⇌ P Lift ♪ sB⇌11600 – 13600 dB⇌21200 – 23200 L fr7000 D fr7000 sea
★★**Eden** viale delle Palme ☎41792 Closed 11 Oct – Feb 25rm20⇌15 🍴
★★**Helvetia** via Cappuccini 17 ☎41175 Closed 16 Oct – 14 Mar 28⇌ P Lift ♪ sB⇌16500 dB⇌20500 (English breakfast) L7000 D7000 Beach sea
★★**Mimosa** via Antica Romans Occidentale ☎41449 25rm22⇌ Pool
★**Darla** via Rimenbranze 46 ☎41139 23rm5⇌14 🍴 🏛 Lift ♪ sB8700 sB⇌ 🍴11100 dB14400 dB⇌ 🍴17400 (English breakfast) L5500 D5500 sea

SETTIMO See **TORINO**

SICILIA (SICILY) 4,819,000 Map **33** Inset
AA agents; see page 269

Agrigento Agrigento 49,150 (☎0922) Map **33** A1
★★★**Jolly dei Templi** Contrada Angeli (SS 115) ☎76144 tx91086 146⇌ P Lift ♪ sB⇌ 🍴192500 dB⇌29500 L8000 D8000 Pool
P Capizzi viale della Vittoria 115 ☎26854 M/c BL

Caltagirone Catania 38,780 (☎0933) Map **33** B1
★★★**Artu** pza San Luigi ☎22360 23rm4⇌5 🍴 🏛

Castel Vetrano Trapani 30,650 (☎0924) Map **33** A1
★★★**Zeus** via le V-Veneto ☎41389 50rm31⇌5 🍴 🏛 P Lift ♪ sB7500 – 8950 sB⇌ 🍴10400 – 12250 dB12000 – 14800 dB⇌ 🍴18500 – 21750 (English breakfast) L5500 – 6000 D5500 – 6000

Catánia Catania 399,650 (☎095) Map **33** B1
☆☆☆**AGIP** Ognina (SS 114) ☎424003 45 🍴 Lift
★★★**Jolly Trinacria** pza Trento 13 ☎316933 tx97080 159⇌ P Lift ♪ sB⇌25250 dB⇌38500 L8500 D8500

Erice Trapani 28,350 (☎0923) Map **33** A1
★★★**Ermione** ☎29400 45rm5⇌40 🍴 P Lift ♪ sB⇌ 🍴13700 – 14400 dB⇌ 🍴24250 – 25000 L7000 D7000 sea mountains

Gela Caltanissetta 71,725 (☎0933) Map **33** B1
☆☆☆**AGIP** Giardinelli (SS 117 bis) ☎933032 91 🍴 Lift
☆**Motel delle Mimose** via Indipendeza 11 ☎30232 7 🍴 🏛

Marsala Trapani 81,750 (☎0923) Map **33** A1
☆☆**AGIP** exit Mazara del Vallo (SS 115) ☎951611 32 🍴

Messina Messina 259,900 (☎090) Map **33** B2
★★★★**Jolly dello Stretto** via Garibaldi 126 ☎43401 tx98074 99⇌ P Lift ♪ sB⇌18250 dB⇌32500 L8500 D8500

Palermo Palermo 661,250 (☎091) Map **33** A1
★★★★**Jolly del Foro Italico** ☎235842 tx91076 290⇌ 🏛 P Lift ♪ sB⇌22750 sB⇌34000 L8000 D8000 Pool
★★★**Palme** via Roma 398 ☎215570 180⇌ 🏛 Lift
☆☆☆**AGIP** via della Regione Sicilinna 2620 ☎403102 100 🍴 Lift
RAF viale Michelangelo 2040 ☎400900 Frd

Piazza Armerina Ellna 22,200 (☎0935) Map **33** B1
★★★**Jolly** via C-Altacura ☎81446 58rm53⇌ P Lift ♪ sB12250 sB⇌16250 dB20500 dB⇌28500 L700 D700

Ragusa Ragusa 63,550 (☎0932) Map **33** B1
★★★**Jonio** Strada Nazionale 115 ☎24322 49hm10⇌6 🍴 🏛 P ♪ sB7700 sB⇌ 🍴11000 dB14000 dB⇌ 🍴19500 (English breakfast) L4500 D4500
🅱 ➡ **C.A.I.** via R-Morandi 1-15 ☎24047 Cit (GB)

Italy

Sciacca Agrigento 33,600 (☎0925) Map **33** A1
☆☆☆*AGIP* Via Figuli (SS115) ☎21978 38 🏠

Siracusa (Syracuse) Siracusa 116,750 (☎0931)
Map **33** B1
★★★★*Grand Villa Politi* via M-Politi Laudien 3
☎32100 93⇌ Lift ✒ Pool sea
☆☆☆*AGIP* viale Teracati 30–32 ☎66944 76 🏠 Lift
★★*Jolly* corso Gelone 43 ☎64744 tx98108 102⇌
P Lift ♪ sB⇌23150 dB⇌35500 L8500 D8500

Taormina Messina 9,950 (☎0942) Map **33** B1
★★★★★*San Domenico Palace* pza San Domenico
5 ☎23701 tx98013 101⇌ 🏠 Lift ✒ Pool Beach sea
★★★*Jolly Diodoro* via Bagnoli Croce 75 ☎23312
tx98028 103⇌ P Lift ♪ sB⇌24250 dB⇌45500
L11500 D11500 Pool sea
★★★*San Pancrazio* via L-Pirandello 22 (n rest)
☎23252 tx98062
Closed 8 Jan – 9 Mar 18rm12⇌3 🏠 P ♪ sB6600
sB⇌8450 dB11500 dB⇌ 🏠 15600
(English breakfast) sea
★★*Villa Paradiso* via Roma 6 ☎23922 tx98062
Closed 7 Nov – 19 Dec 33rm28⇌5 🏠 Lift ♪
sB⇌ 🏠 13400 – 16600 dB⇌ 🏠 26800 – 31200
(English breakfast) L10000 – 11000 D10000 – 11000
sea mountains
At **Mezzarò** (5.5km E)
★★★★*Mazzarò Sea Palace* (N16) ☎24004 tx98041
Closed 16 Nov – Feb 78rm55⇌28 🏠 Lift ♪
sB⇌ 🏠 21920 – 38370 dB⇌ 🏠 40890 – 66840
(English breakfast) L16500 D16500 St% Pool Beach
sea
★★★★*Villa Sant' Andrea* via Nazionale 137
(DP&Pn) ☎23125 tx98077 Closed Nov – 14 Mar
40rm36⇌4 🏠 P ♪ sB⇌ 🏠 25500 – 42000
dB⇌ 🏠 51000 – 84000 L12000 D12000 Beach sea

SIENA Siena 65,500 (☎0577) Map **29** B2
★★★★*Park* via Marciano 16 ☎44803 52⇌ 🏠 Lift
★★★*Moderno* via Baldassare Peruzzi 19 ☎288453
68rm10⇌40 🏠 P Lift ♪ sB11260 sB⇌ 🏠 14260
dB19420 dB⇌ 🏠 23620 (English breakfast) L5500
D5500
★★★*Palazzo Ravizza* Pian dei Mantellini 34
☎280462 27rm14⇌1 🏠 P Lift ♪ sB11100
sB⇌ 🏠 14100 dB19500 dB⇌ 🏠 23900 L6000
★★*Albergo Senese* via Camollia 86 ☎48324
30rm3⇌ Lift ♪ sB9000 sB⇌14000 dB15500
dB⇌20000

SIRACUSA (SYRACUSE) See **SICILLIA (SICILY)**

SIRMIONE Brescia 3,550 (☎030) Map **29** B4
★★★*Cortine Palace* via Grotte 12 ☎916021
tx30395 Closed 21 Oct – 5 Apr 54rm40⇌14 🏠 Lift
Pool lake
★★★*Florida* via Colombare ☎919018 Closed
Nov – Feb 28rm22⇌ P ♪ sB11000 sB⇌19000
(English breakfast) L8500 D8500 Pool lake
★★★*Sirmione* pza Castello ☎916331 Closed 7
Nov – Mar 82rm70⇌ Lift Pool lake
★★★*Terme* viale Marconi (Pn) ☎916261 Closed
Nov – 6 Apr 68rm49⇌4 🏠 Lift Pool lake
★★*Lac* via Colombare 54 ☎916026 Closed
Nov – Feb 28rm20⇌8 🏠 A7rm P sB8350 sB⇌ 🏠 9850
dB15100 dB18450 (English breakfast) L7000 D7000
lake

SOLDA-SULDEN Bolzano (☎0473) Map **12** D1
★★*Grand* ☎75422 Closed Oct, Nov, & May
110rm23⇌ 🏠 ✒
★*Posta Ortler* ☎75424 Closed 21 Sep – 19 Dec & 21
Apr – 19 Jun 42rm4⇌5 🏠 A22rm 🏠

SÓNDRIO Sóndrio 23,450 (☎0342) Map **29** A4
★★★*Posta* pza Garibaldi 19 ☎22734 37rm12⇌3 🏠
🏠 Lift

SORI Genova 4,813 (☎0185) Map **29** A3
★★*Rondini* via Crispi 33 ☎78944 Closed 16
Oct – mid Apr 15rm7⇌1 🏠 Beach sea

SORRENTO Napoli 16,150 (☎081) Map **33** A3
★★★★*Europa Palace* via Correale 34 ☎8781501
72rm57⇌10 🏠 A10rm P Lift ♪ sB⇌ 🏠 11500

dB14400 dB⇌ 🏠 20100 (English breakfast) L6000
D6000
★★★★*Excelsior Vittoria* pza Tasso 34 ☎8781900
tx73368 🏠 P Lift ♪ sB⇌20500 – 26900
dB⇌31400 – 53000 (English breakfast) L13000
D13000 Pool Beach sea
★★★★*Imperial Tramontano* via V-Veneto
☎8781940 tx71345 104rm75⇌29 🏠 Lift Pool Beach
sea
★★★*Aminta Grand* via Nastro Verde 7 ☎8781821
Closed Nov – Mar 73rm62⇌11 🏠 🏠 P Lift ♪
sB⇌ 🏠 17000 – 19000 dB⇌ 🏠 26000 – 29500 (English
breakfast) L7500 D8600 Pool sea
★★★*Bellevue Syrene* pza della Vittoria 5
☎8781024 51rm27⇌15 🏠 Lift Beach sea
★★★*Cocumella* via Cocumella 7 ☎8781660 Closed
Nov – Feb 60rm35⇌14 🏠 Lift ✒ Pool Beach sea
★★★*Eden* via Correale 25 ☎8781909 Closed
Nov – Mar 58rm36⇌22 🏠 A16rm 🏠 sB fr9250
sB⇌ 🏠 fr12400 dB⇌ 🏠 fr20200 (English breakfast)
L6500 D6500 ♪ ∩ sea mountains
★★★*Vesuvio* corso Italia 248 ☎8781804
37rm10⇌12 🏠 P Lift ♪ sB7600 – 10800
sB⇌ 🏠 10800 – 12800 dB14000 – 18350
dB⇌ 🏠 15000 – 22200 (English breakfast) L6500
D5000 – 6500 Beach
🍴 ✒*Porto* via L-de-Maio ☎8781036

SPARTAIA See **MARCIANA-MARINA** under **ELBA**

SPÉZIA (LA) La Spézia 122,800 (☎0187) Map **29** A2
★★★★*Jolly del Golfo* via XX Settembre 2 ☎27200
tx37047 110⇌ P Lift ♪ sB⇌24300 dB⇌40500
L8000 D8000
🍴*Cozzani & Rossi* pza Caduti per la Libertà 6
☎25386 BL (GB)
🚗 🍴*Auto Per Tutti* via Manzoni 31 ☎501324 Frd

SPOLETO Perugia 37,000 (☎0743) Map **31** B3
☆☆*AGIP* via Flamina (SS3) ☎49368 57 🏠 Lift

SPOTORNO Savona 4,460 (☎019) Map **28** D2
★★★*Royal* Lungomare Kennedy ☎745074 tx27179
Closed 5 – 10 Oct & 15 – 20 Apr 100rm85⇌10 🏠 P Lift
♪ sB⇌ 🏠 18500 – 24000 dB⇌ 🏠 27000 – 44000
(English breakfast) L11000 – 12000 D11000 – 12000
Beach sea
★*Villa Teresina* via Imperia ☎74560 Closed
Oct – Mar 26rm A4rm P sB6000 – 7000
dB6500 – 12000 (English breakfast) L4000 D4500

STAGNO See **LIVORNO**

STORTA (LA) See **ROMA (ROME)**

STRESA Novara 5,100 (☎0323) Map **28** D4
★★★★★*Grand Hotel et des Iles Borromees*
Lungolago 1 ☎30431 tx20377 145rm116⇌7 🏠 P Lift
♪ sB⇌ 🏠 21500 – 37500 dB⇌ 🏠 37000 – 62000 L alc
D alc St% ✒ Pool lake
★★★★*Bristol* via Nazionale del Sempione 73
☎31185 tx20217 Closed Nov – 19 Mar
210rm190⇌20 🏠 P Lift sB⇌ 🏠 19600 – 23000
dB⇌ 🏠 30200 – 36000 (English breakfast)
L7500 – 10500 D8000 – 12000 ✒ Pool lake
★★★★*Regina Palazzo* Lungolago 27 ☎30171
tx20381 Closed Nov – Mar 130rm118⇌12 🏠 🏠 P Lift
♪ sB⇌ 🏠 27000 – 29000 dB⇌ 🏠 44000 – 47000
(English breakfast) L11000 D11000 ✒ Pool
mountains lake
★★★*Astoria* Lungolago ☎30259 tx20381 Closed 16
Oct – 9 Apr 98rm59⇌39 🏠 🏠 P Lift ♪
sB14000 – 16000 sB⇌ 🏠 19000 – 21000
dB⇌ 🏠 29000 – 33000 (English breakfast) L10000
D10000 ✒ Pool mountains lake
★★★*Palma* Lungalago ☎30266 tx20381 Closed
Oct – Feb 125rm115⇌10 🏠 🏠 P Lift ♪
sB⇌ 🏠 14500 – 20000 dB⇌ 🏠 22000 – 33500
(English breakfast) L9000 D9000 Pool lake
★*Italia & Svizzera* Lungolago ☎30540 34rm14⇌ P
Lift ♪ sB8000 – 9000 sB⇌10000 – 12500
dB14000 – 16000 dB⇌16000 – 19000
(English breakfast) L5000 D5000 St% lake

★★**Lido la Perle Nera** pza Stazione Funivia ☏30384
Closed 16 Oct – 14 Mar 27rm20⇆1 🛆 P
sB8000 – 95000 sB⇆ 🛆 10200 – 12800
dB16000 – 18000 dB⇆ 🛆 19300 – 24000
(English breakfast) L7000 D7000 lake
★★*Milano & Speranza au Lac* pza Imbarcadero
☏31190 Closed Nov – Feb 171rm103⇆54 🛆 A87rm
🛆 Lift ➘ lake
★★*Parco* via Gignous 1 (DP) ☏30335 Closed
Oct – Mar 41⇆ A18rm 🛆 Lift lake
★★**Royal** via Nazionale del Sempione ☏30471
tx20396 Closed Oct – mid Apr 43rm32⇆8 🛆 P
sB8500 – 10000 sB⇆ 🛆 1000 – 13000
dB15000 – 18000 dB⇆ 🛆 18000 – 22000 L7000
D7000 mountains lake
★*Elena* pza L-Cadorna 16 (n rest) ☏31043 14rm3⇆
🛆 Lift
★**Flora** via Nazionale del Sempione 30 ☏30524
Closed Oct – Mar 21rm7⇆9 🛆 sB7300 – 9300
sB⇆ 🛆 8300 – 10300 dB13600 – 17600
dB⇆ 🛆 15600 – 19600 (English breakfast) L6000
D6000 mountains lake

SUNA See **VERBÀNIA**

SUSA Torino 7,356 (☏0122) Map **28** C3
★★**Napoleon** ☏2704 45rm41⇆4 🛆 🛆 P Lift
sB⇆ 🛆 11000 dB⇆ 🛆 19000 (English breakfast)
L6500 D6500 mountains

SYRACUSE See **SIRACUSA** under **SICILIA**
(SICILY)

TAORMINA See **SICILIA (SICILY)**

TÀRANTO Tàranto 238,750 (☏099) Map **34** C3
★★★★**Jolly Mar Grande** viale Virgilio 90 ☏330861
tx860979 89rm82⇆ P Lift ➘ sB⇆ 🛆 19500
dB23950 dB⇆ 🛆 33100 L7500 D7500 Pool

TERRACINA Latina 35,350 (☏0733) Map **32** C2
★★**Palace** Lungomare Matteotti ☏727285
78rm18⇆60 🛆 🛆 P Lift ➘ 🛆 7400 – 8900
dB⇆ 🛆 132000 – 15800 (English breakfast) L5000
D5000 ➘ Beach sea

TIRANO Sondrio 8,750 (☏0342) Map **29** A4
★**Posta & Stelvio** via Lungo Adda 4 Novembre 1
(n rest) ☏702555 Closed Oct – Dec 36rm3⇆9 🛆 🛆 P
Lift ➘ sB8800 sB⇆ 🛆 10800 dB15600 dB⇆ 🛆 19100
(English breakfast) mountains

TOLMEZZO Udine 10,340 (☏0433) Map **13** B1
🛄C *Automezzi Tolmezzo* via Paluzza 7 ☏2151 M/c
Fia

TONALE (PASSO DEL) Brescia (☏0364)
Map **12** D1
★★**Redivalle** ☏91349 Closed Oct – Nov & May – Jun
56rm50⇆ 🛆 P ➘ sB⇆ 🛆 13000 – 15500
dB18000 – 24000 dB⇆ 🛆 22000 – 27000
(English breakfast) L5000 – 6000 D5000 – 6000
mountains

TORBOLE Trento 802 (☏0464) Map **29** B4
★★**Ifigenia** via Lungolago Verona 39 ☏55134
Closed 11 Oct – Mar 44rm32⇆ 🛆 Lift sB6500 – 9500
sB⇆ 🛆 8500 – 11500 dB11000 – 17000
dB⇆ 🛆 15000 – 21000 (English breakfast) L6000 D6000
lake
★★*Lago di Garda* via Lungolago Verona ☏55135
taGianflippi Closed Nov – mid Apr 38rm10⇆ Lift lake

TORINO (TURIN) Torino 1,202,850 (☏011)
Map **28** D3
★★★★★**Jolly Principi di Piemonte** via P-Gobetti 15
(off via Roma) ☏519693 tx23120 103⇆ P Lift ➘
sB⇆ 45850 dB⇆ 65200 L11500 D11500
★★★★**Jolly Ambasciatori** corso V-Emanuele 104
☏5752 tx23296 197⇆ 🛆 P Lift ➘ sB⇆ 36900
dB⇆ 54450 L10000 D10000
★★★★**Turin Palace** via Sacchi 8 ☏548585 tx23411
125⇆ 🛆 P Lift ➘ sB⇆ 36250 dB⇆ 51500
(English breakfast) L alc D alc
★★★**Patria** via Cernaia 42 (n rest) ☏519903
108rm75⇆10 🛆 🛆 P Lift ➘ sB12500 sB⇆ 🛆 18500
dB21000 dB⇆ 🛆 29000 (English breakfast)
🛄 *B Koelliker* via Barletta 133 – 135 ☏353632
BL/Jag Rov/Tri
At **Settimo** (8km NE on Autostrade to Ivrea)

☆☆☆*AGIP* ☏8001855 100 🛆 Lift

TORRE A MARE See **BARI**

TORRI DEL BENACO Verona 2,500 (☏045)
Map **29** B4
★★**Continental** ☏626195 Closed Oct – Mar
30rm4⇆26 🛆 🛆 P ➘ sB⇆ 🛆 9500 dB⇆ 🛆 19000
L6000 D6000 Beach sea

TREMEZZO Como 1,400 (☏0344) Map **29** A4
★★★**Grand Tremezzo** Grande Parco ☏40446
tx38128 Closed 11 Oct – Mar 100rm90⇆10 🛆 🛆 P
Lift ➘ sB⇆ 🛆 18500 – 20500 dB⇆ 🛆 28000 – 31000
(English breakfast) L8000 D8000 ➘ Pool 🛆 lake
★★**Bazzoni** via Regina ☏40403 150rm75⇆15 🛆 Lift
lake

TRENTO Trento 95,850 (☏0461) Map **29** B4
★★★**Grand Trento** via Alfieri 21 ☏26297
95rm15⇆73 🛆 Lift
★★**Venezia** pza Duomo 45 ☏26335 50rm25⇆ P Lift
➘ sB7000 – 7500 sB⇆ 🛆 10500 – 11500
dB14000 – 15000 dB⇆ 🛆 16000 – 17000
(English breakfast) L6000 D6000
E Franceschi via Brennero 264 ☏80110
Bed/Opl/Vau (GB)
Mille Miglia via Muredei 8 ☏21986 Frd
At **Sardagna** (4km W)
☆☆☆*AGIP* via Brennero 168 (SS 12) ☏81117 45 🛆
Lift

TREVISO Treviso 91,450 (☏0422) Map **30** C4
★★★**Continental** via Roma 16 ☏57216
87rm30⇆57 🛆 🛆 P Lift ➘ sB⇆ 🛆 17500 – 18500
dB⇆ 🛆 29000 – 32000 (English breakfast)
🛄*Bobbo* via della Repubblica 270 ☏62396 Peu/Vlo
(GB)
🛄 🛄*Sile motori* viale della Repubblica 278 ☏62743
BL/Rov/Tri
🛄 🛄*Socaart* viale della Repubblica 19 ☏63725 M/c
Frd (GB)
🛄 🛄*Trevisaute* viale Felissent 58 ☏63265
Bed/Opl/Vau

TRICESIMO Udine 6,450 (☏0432) Map **30** C4
★★**Boschetti** pza Mazzini 9 ☏851230 32⇆ P Lift ➘
sB⇆ 13500 dB⇆ 23000 (English breakfast) L 12000
D12000

TRIESTE Trieste 271,550 (☏040) Map **30** D4
★★★★**Jolly Cavour** corso Cavour 7 ☏7694 tx46139
179rm165⇆ 🛆 Lift ➘ sB 132200 sB⇆ 🛆 27200
dB 25400 dB⇆ 🛆 40400 L8500 D8500
☆☆☆*AGIP* Duino Service Area (On Autostrada A4
24km NW via SS14) ☏208273 80 🛆 Lift
☆☆☆*Valrosandra* ☏226221 76⇆ 🛆 Pool
★★**Colomba** via Geppa 18 (n rest) ☏69434 40⇆ P
Lift ➘ sB⇆ 🛆 16100 – 17100 dB⇆ 🛆 27200 – 28200
★**Citta di Parenzo** via degli Artisti 8 (n rest) ☏30119
43rm4⇆4 🛆 Lift ➘ sB8000 – 10300 sB⇆ 🛆 13000
dB15000⇆18000 dB⇆ 🛆 22000
F Antonucci via Villan de Bacchino 2 ☏414396 Fia
Filotecnica Giuliana via F-Severo 42 – 48 ☏569121
BL/Vlo (GB)
A Grandi via Flavia 120 ☏817201 Fia (GB)
🛄*Regina* (G Cibin) via Raffineria 6 ☏725345 M/c P
Bed/BMW Opl/Vau (GB)

TURIN see **TORINO**

ÙDINE Udine 103,500 (☏0432) Map **30** C4
☆☆☆*AGIP* viale Ledra 24 (SS 13) ☏63841 105 🛆 Lift
★★★**Astoria** pza XX-Settembrè 10 ☏207091
tx45120 80⇆ 🛆 Lift
★★★**Cristallo** pza d'Annunzio ☏205951
81rm36⇆45 🛆 🛆 Lift
🛄*Autofriulana* viale Europa Unita 33 ☏56330 P
BL/Rov/Tri
Edera via della Cisterna 18 ☏205358 Chy/Sim
🛄*Furgiuele & Baldelli* viale Venezia 383 ☏32169 P
Frd (GB)
🛄*Nord* viale L-da-Vinci ☏55669 Ren

VALSOLDA Como 2,500 (☏0344) Map **29** A4

Italy

At **San Mamete**
★★**Stella d'Italia** ☎68139 Closed 11 Oct – 9 Apr
38rm24⇌ 🏠 P Lift sB9300 – 11000 dB 16600 – 20200
dB⇌20200 – 25000 L fr8000 Dfr8000 mountains lake

VALTOURNANCHE Aosta 2,025 (☎0166)
Map **28** D4
★★**Tourist** (Pn) ☎92070 Closed May – 14 Jun & 16
Sep – Nov

VARALLO Vercelli 7,950 (☎0163) Map **28** D4
☆☆☆**AGIP** d'Alagna (SS 299) ☎52447 38 🗇 Lift

VARAZZE Savona 15,200 (☎019) Map **28** D3
★★**Delfino** via Colombo 48 ☎97073 25rm11⇌3 🗇
A14rm 🏠 P Lift ♪ sB7500 – 10000 dB 17000
dB⇌19000 (English breakfast) L 7000 D7000
Beach sea
★★**Europa** via Garibaldi 10 ☎96683 36rm19⇌ P
sB 9500 sB⇌ 🗇 11500 dB 17000 dB⇌ 🗇 18000
(English breakfast) L 6500 D6500 St%

VERENNA Como 800 (☎0341) Map **29** A4
★★**Olivedo** ☎830115 Closed 6 Nov – 14 Dec
25rm6⇌ A4rm P sB 6500 – 9500 sB⇌ 🗇 9500 – 11500
dB 13000 – 15000 dB⇌ 🗇 17000 – 20000 L fr5500
Dfr5500 St% lake
★★**Royal Victoria** pza San Giorgio 5 ☎83102
Closed 11 Oct – Apr 65rm12⇌ 🏠 lake

VARESE Varese 87,950 (☎0332) Map **28** D4
★★★**Palace** via L-Manara 11 ☎230120 tx38163
Closed Dec – Feb 100rm60⇌30 🗇 Lift ⚓ lake

VARIGOTTI See **FINALE LIGURE**

VASTO Chieti 26,490 (☎0873) Map **33** A/B4
★★★**Panoramic** via G-Smargiassi ☎2152
47rm19⇌28 🗇 🏠 Lift sea

VENÉZIA (VENICE) Venézia 365,450 (☎041)
Map **30** C4
See also **Mestre** and **Marghera**
No road communications in city. Vehicles may be left
in garages in piazzale Roma at end of causeway from
mainland or at open parking places on the mainland
approaches. Garages will not accept advance
bookings. Transport to hotels by waterbus, etc, for
which there are fixed charges for fares and
porterage. Hotel rooms overlooking the Grand Canal
normally have a surcharge.
★★★★★**Europa & Britannia** Canal Grande-San
Marco 2159 ☎700477 tx41123 140rm130⇌10 🗇 Lift
⚓ Pool Beach ♭ sea
★★★★★**Gritti Palace** Campo Santa Maria del Giglio
☎26044 tx41125 101⇌ Lift ♪ sB⇌62000 – 74000
dB⇌86000 – 98000 (English breakfast) L alc Dalc
St% Pool ♭ ∩
★★★★★**Royal Danieli** Riva degli Schiavoni ☎26480
tx41077 250⇌ Lift ♪ sB⇌65000 – 69000
dB⇌90000 – 102000 (English breakfast) L 16000
D16000 St% sea
★★★★**Europa & Regina** Canal Grande-San Marco
2205 ☎700477 tx41123 200rm188⇌12 🗇 Lift ♪
sB⇌38500 – 45500dB⇌ 🗇 62000 – 75000
(English breakfast) L alc Dalc St%
★★★★**Gabrielli-Sandwirth** Riva degli Schiavoni
☎31580 tx41228 Closed Nov – 15 Mar 123rm96⇌
Lift
★★★★**Luna** pza San Marco ☎89040 tx41236
122rm111⇌ Lift
★★★★**Monaco & Gran Canale** Canal Grande-San
Marco 1325 ☎700211 82rm66⇌9 🗇 Lift
★★★**Cavalletto** San Marco 1107 ☎700955 tx41684
81rm54⇌27 🗇 Lift ♪ sB⇌ 🗇 17500 – 21000
dB⇌ 🗇 30500 – 35500 L 8100 D8100 St%
★★★**Concordia** c Larga San Marco 367 ☎706866
tx42069 60rm55⇌5 🗇 Lift ♪ sB⇌ 🗇 23800 – 32400
dB⇌ 🗇 31700 – 44800 (English breakfast) L 10000
D10000
★★★**Saturnia & International** via XXIII Marzo 2399
☎708377 tx41355 96rm56⇌40 🗇 Lift ♪
★★★**Savoia & Jolanda** Riva degli Schiavoni 4187
☎24130 91rm52⇌ Lift
★★**Antico Panada** c Larga San Marco 656 ☎709088
tx42069 47rm12⇌18 🗇 ♪ sB 11400 – 14300
sB⇌ 🗇 13900 – 17600

dB21200 – 26500 dB⇌ 🗇 24900 – 31400 L 7000
D7000
★★**Calcina** Zatters 780 ☎27045 30rm15⇌5 🗇
A10rm ♪ sB fr10300 sB⇌ 🗇 fr13300 dB fr18600
dB⇌ 🗇 fr23000 (English breakfast) L fr6000 dFr6000
sea
★★**Flora** via XXII Marzo 2238A ☎25324 Closed 16
Nov – Feb 47rm45⇌ Lift ♪ sB⇌19000 – 22000
dB 24000 – 28000 dB⇌ 🗇 30000 – 35000
★★**Giorgione** Santi Apostoli 4587 ☎25810
57rm50⇌7 🗇 Lift ♪ sB⇌ 🗇 26500 – 28500
dB⇌ 🗇 38000 – 42000 (English) L 9000 D9000
★★**Metropole** Riva degli Schiavoni 4149 ☎705044
tx41340 64⇌ 🗇 Lift ♪ sB⇌ 🗇 23000 – 42000
dB⇌ 🗇 35000 – 63000 (English breakfast) L 14000
D14000
★★**San Marco** pza San Marco 877 ☎22447
60rm6⇌39 🗇 Lift ♪ sB12400 – 16200
sB⇌ 🗇 15400 – 18300 dB23800 – 28500
dB⇌ 🗇 27800 – 35400 (English breakfast) L7600
D7600

VENÉZIA LIDO Venézia 13,296 (☎041) Map **30** C4
There is a car ferry service from Venice (piazzala
Roma).
★★★★★**Excelsior Palace** Lungomare Marconi
☎60201 tx41023 272⇌ 🏠 Lift
★★★★**Bains** Lungomare Marsconi 17 (DP) ☎65921
tx41142 Closed Oct – Apr 293rm233⇌60 🗇 Lift ⚓
Pool Beach sea
★★★**Adria Urania & Villa Nora** viale Dandolo 29
☎760120 tx41666 Closed Nov – mid Apr 73rm62⇌ P
Lift ♪ sB20000 sB⇌ 🗇 27000 dB38000
dB⇌ 🗇 48000 (English breakfast) L8000 – 10000
D8000 – 10000 Beach
★★**Buon Pesce** Riviera San Nicolo 50 (n rest)
☎760533 Closed 16 Oct – Mar 28rm15⇌2 🗇 A5rm 🏠
P sB12800 sB⇌ 🗇 16000 dB23400 dB⇌ 🗇 27800
(English breakfast)
★★**Centrale** via M-Bragadin 30 (DP) ☎760052
Closed Oct – Mar 38rm24⇌ Lift
★**Villa Pannonia** via Doge Michiel 48 ☎760162
Closed Nov – Mar 31rm13 🗇 ♪ sB13000 (room
only) dB24000 (room only) dB 🗇 28000 (room only)
L5000 D5000

VENTIMÍGLIA Imperia 26,950 (☎0184) Map **28** D2
★★**Posta** via Cavour 56 ☎351218 Closed
11 Nov – 19 Dec 21rm3⇌15 🗇 ♪ sB6500 dB11500
dB⇌ 🗇 12500 (English breakfast) L6000 D6000
★★**Terminus Svizzero** pza C-Battisti 34 ☎31138
28rm5⇌6 🗇 🏠
♭ ∿**G. Revelli** via Nervia 2 ☎32459 M/c BMW/Sim
(GB)

VERBANIA Novara 34,700 (☎9323) Map **28** D4
At **Pallanza** (2km W)
★★★**Majestic** via V-Veneto 32 ☎42453 tx20393
Closed Nov – Mar 100rm95⇌ 🏠 P Lift ♪
sB⇌18500 – 22500 dB21000 – 25000
dB⇌ 🗇 30000 – 35000 (English breakfast) L8500 D8500
⚓ Pool lake
★★**Albergo San Gottardo** viale delle Magnolie
☎42119 Closed Oct – 14 Mar 40rm3⇌23 🗇 🏠 P Lift
♪ sB7000 – 7500 sB⇌ 🗇 8500 – 9500
dB13000 – 14000 dB⇌ 🗇 16500 – 18000 L6500
D6500 lake
★★**Belvedere** pza IV-Novembre 10 ☎503202
Closed Nov – mid Apr 58rm40⇌10 🗇 A35rm P Lift ♪
sB10000 – 11800 sB⇌ 🗇 12000 – 14000
dB17000 – 20000 dB⇌ 🗇 20000 – 24000 L6500
D6500 lake

At **Suna** (1.5km NW)
★★**Pesce d'Oro** ☎502330 Closed Oct – Apr
24rm6⇌2 🗇 P sB6950 dB10250 dB⇌ 🗇 13400
(English breakfast) L5500 D5500 lake

VERCELLI Vercelli 56,500 (☎0161) Map **28** D3
★★★**Viotti** via Marsala 7 ☎61602 56rm22⇌34 🗇 Lift
★**Savoia** viale Garibaldi 14 ☎65047 tx8500
38rm3⇌1 🗇

302

VERONA Verona 270,850 (☎045) Map **29** B4
★★★★**Colomba d'Oro** via C-Cattnneo 10 ☎21510
58rm58⇌12🍽 🏠 P ♪ sB⇌🍽23600–27100
dB⇌🍽41200–46200 (English breakfast)
★★★★**Due Torri** pza Sant' Anastasia 4 ☎34130
tx48524 100rm68⇌32🍽 🏠 P Lift ♪ sB⇌🍽35200
dB⇌🍽55600 (English breakfast) L12000 D12000
St%
★★★**Accademia** via Scala 12 ☎21643
90rm50⇌40🍽 🏠 P Lift ♪ sB⇌🍽fr21500
dB⇌🍽fr35000 (English breakfast)
☆☆★**AGIP** via Unita d'Italia 346 ☎521271 68⇌ Lift
★★★**Nuovo Hotel San Pietro** via Santa Teresa 1
☎582600 tx48523 58⇌🍽 🏠 P Lift ♪ sB⇌🍽18450
dB⇌🍽30100 (English breakfast)
★★**Capuleti** via del Pontiere 26 ☎32970 36rm18⇌
Lift ♪ sB9500 dB16000 dB⇌🍽20000
(English breakfast) L6000 D6000
★★**Italia** via G-Maneli 54 ☎48028 Closed 26 Dec–9
Jan 50rm3⇌35🍽 🏠 P Lift ♪ sB95000 sB⇌🍽11500
dB16000 dB⇌🍽20000 (English breakfast) L6000
D6000
🛢 🏍**Auto-Motor** Stradone Santa Lucia 21 ☎500344
Aud/Por/VW (GB)
🏍**SVAE** via Torricelli 3 Z.A.I, ☎508088 Frd (GB)
VIARÉGGIO Lucca 57,800 (☎0584) Map **29** B2
★★★★**Palace** via F-Gioio 2 ☎46134 78rm60⇌18⇌
P Lift ♪ sB⇌🍽17500–22500 dB⇌🍽35000–45000
L85000 D85000 sea
★★**Excelsior** viale Carducci 88 (DP) ☎50726
Closed Oct–Apr 106rm63⇌ Lift Beach sea
★★**Garden** ☎44025 43rm20⇌20🍽 Lift
🏍**Autosalone Lupori** via Galvani 9 ☎42266
☎42266 🕏 P Cit (GB)
🛢 🏍**F Fazioili & Figlio** via M-Buonarroti 67 ☎42580
P Bed/Opl/Vau (GB)

🛢 🏍**Pecchia** viale del Tigli 8 ☎443312 ☎43312 🕏
Cit
VICENZA Vicenza 119,650 (☎0444) Map **29** B4
☆☆★**AGIP** via degli Scoligeri ☎45155 66🍽 Lift
★★★**Jolly Campo Marzio** viale Roma 21 ☎24560
35⇌ P Lift ♪ sB⇌20250 dB⇌30500 L7000 D7000
★★**Jolly Stazione** viale Milano 92 ☎22209
74rm38⇌ P Lift ♪ sB10650 sB⇌16150 dB20300
dB⇌24300
V Americana viale San Lazzaro 15 ☎563101 M/c
Bed/Dat/Opl Vau (GB)
Sabema viale della Pace 50 ☎500348 M/c P BMW
VICO EQUENSE Napoli 15,190 (☎081) Map **33** A3
★★**Oriente** ☎8798143 53rm49⇌ 🏠 P ♪
sB4000–4500 dB⇌10000–12000 L fr3000 D fr3000
sea
At **Marina Equa** (2.5km SW)
★★★★**Axidie** ☎8798181 Closed Nov–Mar
30rm15⇌15🍽 🏊 Pool Beach sea
VIESTE Foggia 12,044 (☎0884) Map **34** C4
★★★**Ulivi** ☎79061 202🍽 Lift
At **Pughochiuso** (12km S)
★★★**Faro** ☎79011 191⇌ Lift
VIETRI SUL MARE See **SALERNO**
VILLASIMIUS See **SARDEGNA (SARDINIA)**
VIPITENO-STERZING Bolzano 4,900 (☎0472)
Map **12** D1
★★**Aquila Nera** pza Città 1 ☎65120 35rm3⇌6🍽 🏠
Pool
★★**Corona-Krone** Città Vecchia 139 ☎65210
43rm19⇌ 🏠
VITERBO Viterbo 56,600 (☎0761) Map **31** B3
★★**Leon d'Oro** via della Cava 36 ☎31012 48rm30⇌
🏠 Lift ♪ sB6000 sB⇌🍽8350 dB10500
dB⇌🍽13500 L5500 D5500
🛢 🏍**Tedeschi** via I-Garbini 84 ☎32109 M/c Frd

Isola D'Elba (Livorno)

San Marino

Prices are in Italian lire
★★★**Grand** via Lungomente 28 Luglio ☎992400
Closed 11 Nov–19 Mar 54rm39⇌15🍽 🏠 P Lift ♪
sB⇌🍽16000 dB⇌🍽24000 (English breakfast)
L7000–12000 D5500–9000 mountains
★★★**Titano** via Marzo 25 ☎991007 66rm24⇌20🍽
🏠 Lift

★★**Excelsior** via J-Istriani ☎991163 25rm3⇌15🍽
🏠
★**Tre Penne** via G-di Simone delle Penne ☎992437
Closed Dec–Feb 12rm4⇌5🍽 🏠 P sB75000–8000
sB⇌🍽8500–10000 dB12000–13500
dB⇌🍽16500–17500 (English breakfast)
L4500–6000 D4500–6000

LUXEMBOURG

Population 357,300 **Area** 1,000 sq miles **Map** 10 D4, 11 A4

How to get there

Luxembourg is easily approached through either Belgium or France. Luxembourg City is just over 200 miles from Ostende, about 260 miles from Boulogne or Calais, and is therefore within a day's drive of the Channel coast.

General information

Information in this section is specific to Luxembourg. A wider background is provided in the notes on page 8 with other information which you are advised to read.

Accommodation A national guide to hotels, inns, restaurants, and boarding houses in the Grand Duchy can be obtained free of charge from the National Tourist Office.

Details of holiday flats and chalets are also available from this source.

Luxembourg

Annual events	March	**Luxembourg** 'Europleinair' Camping Fair
	April	**Grevenmacher** Easter Exhibition **Luxembourg** 'Emaischen' traditional festival **Grevenmacher** Wine Fair
	May	**Luxembourg and Diekirch** Procession of the Octave of Our Lady of Luxembourg **Luxembourg** International Fair **Wiltz** Broom Festival with folklore procession **Echternach** Dancing procession **Wormeldange** Wine Fair
	June	**Luxembourg** National Day (23 June) **Luxembourg** 'Tour de Luxembourg' International Cycle Race
	July	**Nationwide** concerts, folklore events, gymnastic shows and exhibitions (July – August) **Wiltz** Open Theatre Festival **Nospelt** 'Fortnight of Pottery and Ceramics' (July – August)
	August	**Rosport** Procession of the Holy Virgin **Luxembourg** The 'Schobermesse' Fair and Market (August/September)
	September	**Schwebsingen** Wine Festival **Grevenmacher** Wine and Grape Festival with folklore procession

A more comprehensive list can be obtained from the Luxembourg National Tourist Office (see page 306).

Breakdowns

Try to move the vehicle to the verge of the road and place a warning triangle to warn following traffic. The Automobile Club du Grand-Duché de Luxembourg (ACL) operates a 24-hour road assistance service which can be utilised by AA members: ☎311031 at any time. This service operates throughout the whole country. The service permits up to half-an-hour's on-the-spot breakdown assistance free to AA members upon production of the *European 5-Star Service Booklet*.

The vehicles of the ACL are yellow in colour and bear a black inscription *'Automobile Club, Service Routier'*. This service should not be confused with the *Secours Automobile Luxembourg* which is a commercial enterprise whose representatives will charge for all services rendered and will not accept Credit Vouchers. This enterprise is not connected with the AA or any other motoring organisation.

British Consulate

Luxembourg, 28 Boulevard Royal ☎29864/5/6

Currency and banking

The unit of currency is the Luxembourg franc, divided into 100 centimes. There are no restrictions on the amount of foreign or local currency which can be taken into or out of the country, but because of the limited market for Luxembourg notes in other countries, it is advisable to change them before leaving. Belgian currency is also used in Luxembourg.

Banking hours

From Monday to Friday 09.00 – 12.00hrs and 13.30 – 13.30hrs. Banks are usually closed on Saturdays.

Shopping hours

While some shops are closed Monday mornings, the usual hours of opening are: from Monday to Saturday 08.30 – 12.00hrs, 14.00 – 18.30hrs.

Documents

Yachts and other pleasure craft must be imported under cover of a Carnet except pleasure craft with or without motor, of any length, which enter and must leave by water.

Medical treatment

Medical benefits in Luxembourg are administered by the National Sickness Insurance Office, 10 rue de Strasbourg, Luxembourg, which has agencies throughout the Grand Duchy. To obtain medical treatment form E111 should be presented to the local Sickness Insurance Office, which will provide the necessary document to be taken to any doctor or dentist. The medical practitioner will charge a fee (a receipt should be obtained) which is generally refunded by the local Sickness Insurance Office. Similarly you will have to pay initially for any medicines that are prescribed; a proportion of the cost may be refunded. Hospital treatment normally will be free after a certificate provided by the

Luxembourg

doctor is presented with form E111 to the local Sickness Insurance Office. In emergencies admission to hospital can be made without prior authorisation.

Motoring club

The **Automobile Club du Grand-Duché de Luxembourg** (ACL) has its head office at 13 Route de Longwy, Helfenterbruck/Bertrange, Luxembourg ☎311031. AA members should produce their *5-Star Service Booklet* when seeking assistance.

ACL office hours are 08.30–12.00hrs and 13.30–18.00hrs from Monday to Friday; closed Saturday and Sunday.

Post and telephone

Rates for post to the United Kingdom are:

Airmail and surface mail		Fr
Postcards		5
Letters	up to 20gm	8
	20–50gm	14
	50–100gm	18
	100–250gm	40

Telephone rates

The charge for a 3-minute telephone call to the UK is Fr56.25; for each additional minute Fr18.75. A local call costs Fr3.

Public holidays

Holidays based on religious festivals are not always fixed on the calendar but any current diary will give actual dates. The Whit period (a religious holiday) should not be confused with the British Spring Holiday.

Fixed holidays

1 January	New Year's Day
1 May	May Day
23 June	National Day
15 August	Assumption
1 November	All Saints' Day
25 December	Christmas Day
26 December	St Stephen's Day

In addition, banks, shops, and public administration close on certain other days which are not public holidays.

25 February	Carnival Monday
2 November	All Souls' Day

Moveable holidays

Easter Monday
Ascension Day
Whit Monday
Shrove Monday
Local Luxembourg City Holiday

Roads

There is a comprehensive system of good main and secondary roads.

Motorways

Only short sections, totalling 44.4km (28 miles), are at present open, 7km between Luxembourg and the airport, 15km between Luxembourg and Esch-sur-Alzette, 15km between Luxembourg and Dudelange, and 4km of the Luxembourg by-pass, but a future network of 160km is planned.

Tourist information offices

Office National du Tourisme (National Tourist Office), local authorities, and tourist information societies *(Syndicats d'Iniatives)* organise information offices at the following addresses:

	Telephone
Luxembourg Air Terminal, place de la Gare	481199
Luxembourg, place d'Armes (Cercle)	22809
Echternach, Porte St Willibrod	72230
Diekirch, place Guillaume	83023
Ettelbruck, Town Hall	82068
Clervaux, 93 Grand rue	92072
Larochette	87676
Viaden, Victor Hugo House	84257
Wiltz, Castle	96199
Mondort-les-Bains, Casino	67018 or 67575
Grevenmacher, Town Hall	75311
Esch-sur-Alzette, Town Hall	52101
Beaufort	86081

Visitors' regulations

Visitors staying up to three months are required to enter their names in the hotel or camp site register. Visitors staying with private persons are required to notify the Administration Communale within 48 hours of their arrival.

Motoring regulations

Information in this section is specific to Luxembourg. A wider background is provided in the notes on page 67 with other regulations which you are advised to read.

Accidents **Fire, police, ambuiance** ☎012 – Civil Defence emergency service *(Secours d'urgence)*.

There are no firm rules to adopt following an accident. However, in most cases the recommendations on page 67 are advisable.

Dimensions Private cars and trailers are restricted to the following dimensions:

cars Height 4 metres;
    width 2.50 metres;

car and trailer overall length 18 metres;

caravan weight 75% of towing vehicle.

Drinking and driving A person suspected of driving while under the influence of alcohol may have to undergo a breath test. A driver, if convicted, faces severe penalties including heavy fines and/or imprisonment.

Horn, use of *In built-up areas* it is prohibited to use the horn except to avoid an accident.

Outside built-up areas use the horn instead of the lights, during the day, to warn of approach.

Lights It is prohibited to drive on sidelights only. At night and also during the day when necessary, vehicles parked on a public road must have their sidelights on if the public lighting does not enable them to be seen from a sufficient distance. Vehicles equipped with a side parking light may use this instead of sidelights. Should fog or snow reduce visibility to less than 100 metres, vehicles stopped or parked outside a built-up area must be illuminated by dipped headlights or foglights. Two foglights may be used at the same time as sidelights but headlights together with fog or spot lights may not be used at the same time. Outside built-up areas at night it is compulsory to flash one's headlights before overtaking another vehicle, at places where visibility is restricted, and whenever road safety requires it.

Overtaking Outside built-up areas at night it is compulsory to flash one's headlights before overtaking another vehicle. During the day use the horn instead of lights.

Parking Spending the night in a vehicle or trailer on the roadside is prohibited. Parking is forbidden on or near tramlines, opposite another stationary vehicle, and within 12 metres (39½ft) of a bus or tram stop. In the city of Luxembourg (in the centre and the railway station area), Esch-sur-Alzette, Dudelange, and Wiltz, there are short-term parking areas known as blue zones. In these areas parked vehicles must display a disc on the windscreen; discs are set at the time of parking and show when parking time expires according to the limit in the area concerned. Discs are available free of charge from the ACL, the Luxembourg Communal Administration, principal banks, petrol companies, and other firms. Discs of other countries may be used if they conform; Parisian ones do, those used in the United Kingdom do not. In special parking zones a vehicle must be moved at least 150 metres before re-parking. Park on the right-hand side of the road in the direction of the traffic flow unless parking is prohibited on this side.

A disabled driver may obtain special concessions for parking if he applies to the Administration Communale or police station.

Police fines The police are authorised to impose and collect on-the-spot fines from any motorist infringing traffic regulations. The officer collecting the fine should issue an official receipt. Refusal to pay results in court proceedings and non-residents may be arrested or detained.

Speed The placename indicates the beginning and end of a built-up area. The following speed limits for cars are in force if there are no special signs:

built-up areas 60kph (37mph)
main roads without any signs 90kph (56mph)
main roads indicated by signs 120kph (74mph)
motorways 120kph (74mph)
All lower signposted speed limits must be adhered to.

Tyres **Spiked tyres** The use of spiked tyres is prohibited.

Warning triangles These are compulsory for all vehicles (except motorcycles). They must be placed about 30 metres (33yd) behind the vehicle, fallen object or load on the road.

Luxembourg/hotels and garages

Prices are in Belgian francs
See French section for abbreviations

BEAUFORT 900 Map **11** A4
★★**Meyer** ☎86262 tx1524 Closed 16 Jan–14 Mar
44rm29⇆15🛏 🅿 Lift sB800–850 sB⇆🛏800–850
dB⇆🛏1450–1500 L500–600 D500–600

BERDORF 950 Map **11** A4
★★**Ermitage** ☎79184 Closed Oct–mid Apr 16rm8⇆
A9rm 🅿

CLERVAUX 1,550 Map **11** A4
★★**Abbaye** r Principale ☎91049 Closed 9 Nov–19
Dec & Jan–7 Apr 50rm12⇆8🛏 A5rm 🅿 Lift
sB480–590 sB⇆🛏630–790 dB620–980
dB⇆🛏930–1380 (English breakfast) L200–500
D200–550
★★**Claravallis** av de la Gare 33 ☎91034
21rm7⇆2🛏 🅿
★★**Grand Central** pl du Château ☎91105 Closed
Dec–14 Feb 32rm15⇆5🛏 🅿 Lift sB645–845
sB⇆🛏795–845 dB840–990 dB⇆🛏1090–1190
L350–600 D350–600
★★**Koener** Grand r 14 ☎91002 Closed Nov–Mar
24rm10⇆🅿 P sB500–750 sB⇆🛏1000 dB780–900
dB⇆🛏1000–1200 L400–800 D400–800
★★**Parc** ☎91068 12rm3⇆2🛏 🅿

DIEKIRCH 5,600 Map **11** A4
★**Beau-Sèjour** espl 12 ☎83403 Closed 16 Oct–14
Nov 38rm4⇆4🛏
★**Hiertz** r Clairefontaine 1 ☎83562 7rm4⇆

DOMMELDANGE Map **11** A4
☆☆☆**Novotel-Luxembourg** rte d'Echternach (E42)
☎435643 tx1418 121⇆ P Lift sB⇆fr131 dB⇆fr131
🖈 Pool

ECHTERNACH 4,200 Map **11** A4
★★★**Bel-Air** r de Berdorf ☎729383 tx2640 Closed
15 Nov–11 Dec 42⇆ 🅿 P Lift sB⇆1000–1600
dB⇆1600–2300 (English breakfast) L600–1500
D600–1500 🖈
★★**Commerce** pl du Marché 16 ☎72301
50rm8⇆1🛏 A10rm 🅿 Lift
★★**Parc** r Hôpital 9 ☎729481 Closed 16 Nov–
14 Feb 35rm25⇆4🛏 🅿 P sB600–700
sB⇆🛏850–1100 dB900–1050 dB⇆🛏1250–1350
D350–400 Pool
★**Marmann** r de Luxembourg 7 ☎72188 25rm2⇆ 🅿
★**Universal et Cheval Blanc** ☎72142 Closed
Nov–Mar 33rm20⇆ P sB500–600 sB⇆600 dB800
dB⇆960 L250–500 D250–500

EHNEN 410 Map **11** A4
★★**Simmer** ☎76030 Closed 16 Jan–Feb
23rm18⇆2🛏 🅿 P sB700 sB⇆🛏900 dB900
dB⇆🛏1300 river
★**Moselle** r du Vin 131 ☎76022 Closed Dec–16 Jan
22rm6⇆7🛏 🅿 Lift

ESCH-SUR-ALZETTE 27,800 Map **11** A4
🖘**Grand du Centre** r de la Libération 42 ☎53937 P
Opl

ESCH-SUR-SÛRE 300 Map **10** D4
★**Moulin** ☎89107 Closed Jan & Feb 33rm31🛏

ETTELBRUCK 6,050 Map **11** A4
★★**Central** r de Bastogne 25 ☎819351 Closed 16
Dec–14 Jan 28rm3⇆9🛏 A6rm 🅿 Lift ♪ sB530–830
sB⇆🛏780–830 dB860–1010 dB⇆🛏960–1060
L190–660 D300–660
🖪 🖘P **Wengler** av des Alliés 36 ☎82157 P Frd (GB)

FINDEL AIRPORT See **LUXEMBOURG**

GREVENMACHER 3,050 Map **11** A4
★**Poste** r de Trèves 28 (n rest) ☎75136 11rm1⇆🛏
sB410–445 dB555–640 dB⇆🛏890–900
(English breakfast)

GRUNDHOF Map **11** A4
★★**Brimer** ☎86251 tx1308 Closed 6 Nov–14 Feb
23rm18⇆5🛏 🅿 P sB⇆🛏1000 dB⇆🛏1250 L375
D375 river
★**Ferring** rte Mullertal 33 ☎86015 25rm16🛏 🅿 P Lift
sB600–700 sB⇆700 dB800–900 dB1000
(English breakfast) L450–700 D450–700

HALLER 170 Map **11** A4
★★**Hallerbach** ☎86151 25rm14⇆1🛏 🅿

HEINERSCHEID 1,000 Map **11** A4
★**Wegener** ☎98503 14rm 🅿

HESPÉRANGE See **LUXEMBOURG**

KAUTENBACH 250 Map **11** A4
★**Hatz** ☎96561 Closed 15 Nov–15 Dec 11rm6🛏 P
sB430 dB660 dB🛏760 L150–450 D150–450

KIRCHBERG See **LUXEMBOURG**

LAROCHETTE 1,450 Map **11** A4
★★**Château** r Medernach 1 ☎87009 Closed 10–31
Jan 45rm14⇆3🛏 A14rm 🅿 Lift sB480–500
sB⇆🛏930 dB790–830 dB⇆🛏1120–1350
L260–500 D350–600
★★**Poste** ☎87006 Closed Jan 40rm16⇆2🛏 sB580
sB⇆🛏995 dB880–950 dB⇆🛏1300–1380
L450–950 D450–950

LUXEMBOURG 78,825 Map **11** A4
★★★**Kons** pl de la Gare ☎486021 tx2306
141rm67⇆39🛏 Lift sB750–800
sB⇆🛏950–1100 dB1210 dB⇆🛏1650 L350 D350
★★★**Central Molitor** av de la Liberté 28 ☎489911
tx2613 36⇆ Lift ♪ sB⇆970–1080 dB⇆1300–1480
(English breakfast) L320–440 D320–440
★★★**Dauphin** av de la Gare 42 ☎488282
37rm20⇆17🛏 Lift
★★★**Rix** bd Royal 20 ☎27545 20rm9⇆6🛏 Lift
★★**Continental** Grande r 86 ☎23616 43rm14⇆4🛏
A37rm 🅿 Lift
★★**Empire** pl de la Gare 34 ☎485252 42rm5⇆15🛏
Lift sB600 sB⇆🛏700 dB800 dB⇆🛏900 L450–600
D450–600
★★**Graas** av de la Liberté 78 ☎484445 (n rest)
32rm2⇆ Lift sB350–500 dB600–780 dB⇆🛏850–900

Kautenbach in the Ardennes

★**Français** pl d'Armes 14 ☎23009 23rm 19🛊 🌙
sB800 – 920 sB🛊800 – 920 dB900 – 1090
dB🛊980 – 1090

★*Wellington* r M-Rodange 1 (n rest) ☎488235 16rm
➤➤**Grand Garage de la Pétrusse** r des Jardiniers
13 – 15 ☎22664 ☎22664 BL (GB)

🛢 **H Frères** rte d'Esch 106 ☎24998 Lnc (GB)

🛢 ⚡**P Lentz** rte d'Arlon 257 ☎20925 Vau (GB)

At Findel Airport (6km E on N2 & E42)

★*Airfield* rte Trèves 6 ☎431934 7🛁 🏛

At Hespérange (5km SE)

🛢 ⚡**J P Engel** rte de Thionville 326 ☎36179 P
Chy/Sim/Vlo (GB)

At Kirchberg

☆☆☆☆**Holiday Inn** ☎435051 ta Holinnlu tx2751
260🛁🛊 P Lift 🌙 sB🛁🛊1400 dB🛁🛊1800
(English breakfast) Pool

At Strassen (2km W on N9)

★★**Dany** rte d'Arlon 72 ☎318062 17rm6🛁17🛊 🏛 P
sB🛁🛊695 – 1485 dB🛁🛊 🛊fr1420 (English breakfast)
L300 D450 Pool ○

MARTELANGE 135 Map **10** D4

★**Maison Rouge** rte d'Arlon ☎64006 Closed Oct
12rm 🏛 P sB 475 dB800 – 900 L 400 – 800 D400 – 800

MERSCH 4,400 Map **11** A4

★*7 Châteaux* r d'Arlon 3 ☎32093 16rm 🏛

★**Marisca** pl Étoile 1 ☎328456 Closed Oct
19rm2🛁6🛊 🏛 P sB 450 sB🛁 🛊550 dB 750
dB🛁🛊1000 L250 – 500 D250 – 500

MONDORF-LES-BAINS 2,450 Map **11** A4

★★★*Grand Chef* av des Bains 36 ☎68012 Closed
16 Oct – mid Apr 46rm27🛁9🛊 🏛 Lift

STRASSEN See **LUXEMBOURG**

VIANDEN 1,500 Map **11** A4

★★**Colette** Grand r 68 – 70 ☎84004 Closed
Nov – mid Apr except Xmas 17rm6🛁6🛊 🏛 sB 700
sB🛁🛊900 dB900 – 1100 dB🛁🛊1100 – 1350
(English breakfast) L alc Dalc

★★*Heintz* Grande r 55 ☎84155 Closed 6 Nov – Feb
30rm25🛁 🏛 Lift Pool

★**Oranienburg** Grande r 126 ☎84153 Closed Jan
55rm20🛁4🛊 A8rm 🏛 P Lift sB390 – 440
sB🛁🛊490 – 540 dB680 – 780 dB🛁🛊830 – 930
L350 – 800 D350 – 800

WILTZ 4,050 Map **10** D4

★★**Vieux Château** Grande r 1 ☎96018 13rm2🛁4🛊
P sB745 – 820 sB🛁🛊820 dB 1075 – 1180
dB🛁🛊1180 (English breakfast) L350 – 900
D350 – 900

The Castle at Wiltz

NETHERLANDS

Population *13,077,000* **Area** *14,400 sq miles* **Maps** *3 & 4*

How to get there

There are direct ferry services to the Netherlands. Services operate from Harwich to the Hook of Holland, Hull to Rotterdam (Europoort), Felixstowe to Rotterdam (Europoort), Great Yarmouth to Scheveningen (The Hague) and Sheerness to Flushing (Vlissingen); the sea journey can take between 7 and 14hrs depending upon the port of departure. Alternatively one of the short Channel crossings can be used, and the the Netherlands can be easily reached by driving through France and Belgium. The distance from Calais to The Hague is just under 220 miles and is within a day's drive.

General information

Information in this section is specific to the Netherlands. A wider background is provided in the notes on page 8 with other information which you are advised to read.

AA agents   All representatives are under appointment by Koninklijke Nederlandsche Toeristenbond, ANWB.

Hague (The) ANWB, Wassenaarseweg 220 ☎ (070) 264426.

*These are not recommended routes:
the distances are given as a guide only.*

NETHERLANDS

distance chart
distances are in miles

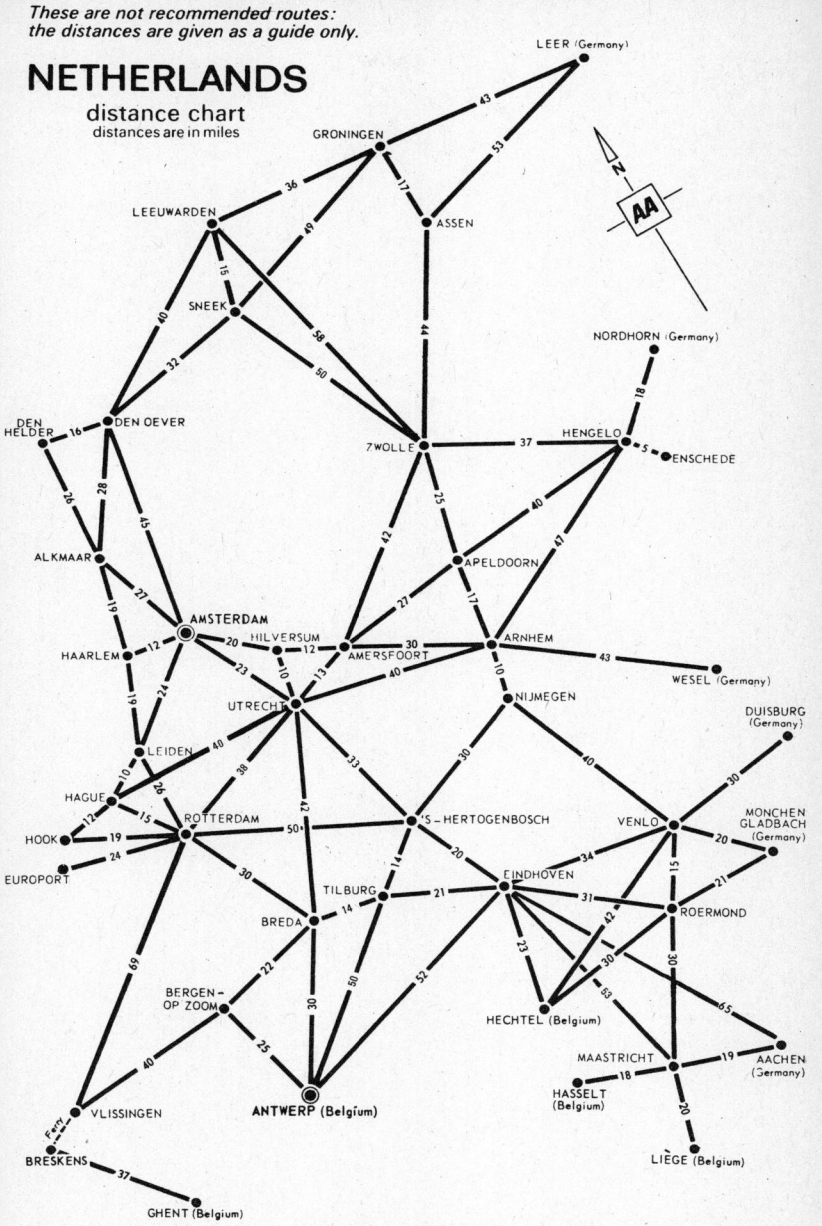

Netherlands

Accommodation   The official hotel guide includes details of the most important hotels in the Netherlands. Information on other types of accommodation such as guesthouses, furnished rooms, and bungalows can be obtained from tourist information offices (VW).

Hotels are officially classified and the category is exhibited outside each. Room prices must by law be indicated in hotel reception and in each bedroom but they are not subject to official control. The service charge amounts to 15%, and it is usual for this to be included in the charges as well as the value added tax.

The National Reservation Centre will secure accommodation free of charge. Application may be made direct, by post, telephone or telex to NCR Amsterdam, PO Box 3387, Hoofdpostkantor, NZ Voorburgwal 182, Amsterdam 1001 ☎ 020 211 211, tx 15754. Applications for reservations may also be made to one of the VVV offices, which will book a room for a small charge.

Annual events

May	**Scheveningen** Opening of the Herring Season	
	Alkmaar Cheese Market, Fridays (May/Sep)	
	Gouda Cheese Market, Thursdays (May/Sep)	
June	**Amsterdam, The Hague, Rotterdam** Holland Festival	
	Assen International TT Motorcycle Races	
July	**Kinderdijk** Windmill Open Days (July/Aug)	
August	**Laren** International Jazz Festival	
	Zandvoort Dutch Grand Prix (Formula 1)	

A comprehensive list can be obtained from the National Tourist Office (see page 314)

Breakdowns   If your car breaks down, try to move it to the verge of the road so that it obstructs the traffic flow as little as possible, and place a warning triangle behind the vehicle to warn following traffic of the obstruction (see page 315)

Patrol services   The Royal Dutch Touring Club ANWB, maintains a nationwide road patrol service called *Wegeneacht* (the watch on the road), similar to AA Road Patrol Service. The service operates on main roads between 07.00 and 23.00hrs, and on less important roads if circumstances permit.

For instance, stop a passing car during the above hours, or use a yellow telephone to telephone the ANWB Head Office which has an Emergency Centre ☎ (070) 264426 operating a 24-hour service.

AA members should produce their *5-Star Service Booklet* if they call upon this service.

British Consulates   Amsterdam OZ, Johannes Vermeerstraat 7 ☎ 736128. There is also a British Consulate in Rotterdam.

Currency and banking   The unit of currency is the guilden (Fl), which is also known as the guilder and is divided into 100 cents. There are no restrictions limiting the import of currency. All imported currency may be freely exported, as well as any currency exchanged in, or drawn on an account established in, the Netherlands.

Banking hours   In all cities and towns, banks are open from Monday to Friday 09.00–15.00hrs on Saturday. At all ANWB offices, money can be exchanged from Monday to Friday 08.45–16.45hrs, and on Saturdays 08.45–12.00hrs; there are also exchange offices at the principal railway stations (eg Amsterdam, Arnhem, Eindhoven, The Hague, Hook of Holland, Maastricht, Rosendaal, Rotterdam, Utrecht, and Venlo).

Shopping hours   *Stores* Monday 13.00–17.30hrs, Tuesday–Saturday 09.00–17.30hrs; *Food shops* 08.00–18.00hrs.

Most *food shops* close for one half day per week. This varies according to location.

Ferries (internal)   All particulars are subject to alterations. In many cases sailings are augmented to meet traffic demands.

Vlissingen (Flushing)–Breskens *Map 3 B2*
There is a frequent daily service. Last sailings:
From Vlissingen – 23.10hrs *Duration* 20 minutes
From Breskens – 23.35hrs

Charges (single journey)	15 May–15 Sep	16 Sep–14 May
Vehicles	Fl	Fl
Car (including driver)	5.75	4.00
Passengers	1.00	1.00
Children (4–10 years)	0.50	0.50
Children (under 4)	free	free

Kruiningen-Perkpolder *Map 3 B2*
There is a frequent daily service. Last sailings:
Duration 15-20 minutes

From Kruiningen–	23.05hrs Monday–Friday
	22.25hrs Saturday–Sunday
From Perkpolder–	23.25hrs Monday–Friday
	22.45hrs Saturdays–Sunday

Charges as for Vissingen (Flushing)–Breskens above

Den Holder-Texel *Map 4 C3*
There is a regular service in both directions until 21.05hrs.
Duration 15 minutes

Charges (return journey)

Vehicles	Fl
Car	17.25
Motorcycles	2.50
Passengers	3.75
Children (4–9 years)	1.75
Children (under 4)	free

Further internal services operate as follows:

Zijpe-Anna Jacoba *Map 3 B2*
Frequent sailings in each direction until 23.00hrs
Duration 7 minutes

Maassluis-Rozenburg *Map 4 C2*
Regular service until 00.30hrs
Duration 5 minutes

Medical treatment   As a member of the EEC, the Netherlands provides medical benefits to persons of affiliated countries. Most doctors and dentists are affiliated to the Sickness Fund (ANOZ) and will provide free treatment on production of form E111 (see page 22). Drugs are also free if they are supplied by a doctor or by an approved chemist to which you have taken the doctor's prescription. Urgent hospital treatment is usually provided free on production of E111; ask the authorities to obtain the necessary authority from the ANOZ in Utrecht within two days. The medical benefits are administered by the Netherlands General Sickness Insurance Fund, *Algemeen Nederlands Onderling Ziekenhuis* (ANOZ), Kaap Hoorndreef 24–28, Utrecht ☎ 030–317541.

Motoring club

The **Koninklijke Nederlandsche Toeristenbond (ANWB)** has its headquarters at Wassenaarseweg 220, The Hague, and offices in numerous provincial towns. They will assist motoring tourists generally and supply road and touring information. AA members should produce their *5-Star Service Booklet* when requesting service. Offices are usually open between 08.45 and 16.45hrs Monday to Friday, and 08.45 and 12.00hrs on Saturdays. Traffic information may be obtained by telephoning (070) 264455 and the ANWB Emergency Centre in Amsterdam is open 24hrs a day, seven days a week ☎ (070) 264426.

Post and telephone   **Air mail rates** to the UK are:

Postcards	Fl 0.45
Letters up to 20gm	Fl 0.75
20 to 50gm	Fl 1.30
50 to 100gm	Fl 2.75

The address of the *poste restante office* in Amsterdam is Hoofdpostkantoor, NZ Voorburgwal.

Telephone rates   STD calls can be made to all the major cities in the UK; the cost is Fl0.85 for each minute. Calls can be made from all main post offices. There is an English-speaking instruction service available by dialling 008. All internal calls can be made automatically, and many calls to Belgium, Luxembourg, and West Germany can be made automatically from most parts of the country. Local calls cost 25 cents.

Public holidays   Holidays based on religious festivals are not always fixed on the calender but any current diary will give actual dates. The Whit period (a religious holiday) should not be confused with the British Spring Holiday.

Fixed holidays

1 January	New Year's Day
25, 26 December	Christmas

Netherlands

Moveable holidays	Good Friday
	Easter Monday
	Ascension Day
	Whit Monday

Roads   There is a network of motorways carrying most inter-city and long-distance traffic. Other main roads usually only have two lanes but are well surfaced. Signposting is good; in some places there are special by-way tours signposted by the ANWB. The best way to see the countryside is to tour along minor roads, often alongside canals, with the aid of large-scale maps.

Motorways   There are about 1,023 miles of motorway open and more are being built, a very comprehensive network of 1,864 miles is planned. No tolls are charged (but see Toll bridges and tunnels). Nearly all the motorways are part of the European international network.

Toll bridges

	car	Car/caravan
Zeeland (Oosterschelde) bridge	Fl 3.50	Fl 5.00
Waalbrug (near Tel)	Fl 1.75	Fl 4.50

Toll tunnels   **Benelux Tunnel** (Vlaardingen near Rotterdam) car Fl 1.00 car/caravan Fl 2.50

Kiltunnel ('s-Gravendeel-Dordrecht) car Fl 3.50 car/caravan Fl6.00

All toll charges should be used only as a guide.

Road signs   Translations of some written signs to be seen on the road are given below:

Bushalte	Bus stop
Doorgaand rijverkeer gestremd	No through way
Doorgaand verkeer	Through traffic
Een file	Single lane
Fietspad	Cycle path – motor vehicles prohibited
Langzaam rijden	Slow down
Opspattend grind	Loose grit
Pas op; filevorming	Attention; single-lane traffic ahead
Rijwiepad	Cycle path – motor vehicles prohibited
Tegenliggers	Two-way traffic
Voetpad	Footpath – vehicles prohibited
Wegomlegging	Detour
Werk in uitovering	Roadworks

Tourist information offices   The Netherlands National Tourist Office (NBT), Savory & Moore House, 143 New Bond Street, London W1Y 0QS ☎ 01-499 9367 will be pleased to assist you with any information regarding tourism and has branch offices (VVV) in all towns and large villages in the Netherlands. They can be recognised by the sign illustrated on the left (blue with white lettering).

There are three types of these branch offices: Travel Offices giving detailed information about the whole of the Netherlands; Information Offices giving general information about the Netherlands and detailed information about their own region, and Local Information Offices giving detailed information about that locality.

Visitor's registration   Unless a visitor is staying in Netherlands for more than eight days there is no need to register.

Motoring regulations

Information in this section is specific to the Netherlands. A wider background is provided in the notes on page 67 with other regulations which you are advised to read.

Accidents   **Fire, police, ambulance** Amsterdam and The Hague ☎ 222222, Rotterdam ☎ 94. Numbers for other towns are in the front of the local telephone directories. If necessary, contact the State Police Emergency Centre ☎ (03438) 4321.

In the event of a serious or complicated accident, especially when personal injury has been sustained, the police should be called before the vehicles are removed.

Crash helmets   It is obligatory for drivers and passengers of motorcycles to wear crash helmets.

Dimensions　　　　Private cars are restricted to the following dimensions:
Cars　　　　　　　　　　height including load 4 metres
　　　　　　　　　　　　　width 2.20 metres on 'B' roads,
　　　　　　　　　　　　　2.50 metres on 'A' roads;
cars and trailers　　　　overall length 18 metres.

Drinking and driving　　Drivers suspected of having consumed alcohol may be required to
undergo a blood test. Penalties for persons found guilty of driving
under the influence of alcohol include a term of imprisonment and a driving ban of up to five
years.

Firearms　　　　The Dutch laws concerning the possession of firearms are the most
stringent in Europe. Any person crossing the frontier with any type of
firearm will be arrested. The law applies also to any object which, on superficial inspection,
shows any resemblance to real firearms (eg plastic imitations, etc). If you wish to carry firearms,
real or imitation, of any description into the Netherlands, seek the advice of the Netherlands
Consulate.

Lights　　　　Dipped headlights must be used at all times in built-up areas and
outside built-up areas when meeting oncoming traffic. In fog or
falling snow, foglights may be used in pairs in conjunction with sidelights only. Headlights should
be flashed as a warning of approach at night provided that they do not inconvenience other
traffic. All vehicles parked on a public road must have their side lights on if not within 30 metres
(33 yards) of a street lamp.

Parking　　　　Vehicles must not stop where there are signs reading *Stopverbod*
(no waiting). You can stop elsewhere provided that you keep to the
extreme right of the road and do not interfere with other traffic. You are allowed to stop to let
passengers in and out at bus stops. Parking meters and/or parking discs are used in many
towns. Discs can be obtained from police stations and must be displayed on the windscreen.

They must be set at the time of parking and show when parking time lapses according to the limit
in the area concerned. Failure to observe zonal regulations could result in a fine or the vehicle
being towed away.

Spending the night in a vehicle or trailer on the roadside is not permitted.

Passengers　　　　Children under six years must not be carried on the front seats.
Children 6–12 years may occupy the front seat provided they wear a
safety belt.

Police fines　　　　In some districts the police are empowered to impose and collect
on-the-spot fines from motorists infringing local traffic regulations.

Priority　　　　Regulations in the Netherlands take account of the very large
number of cyclists for whom special tracks are provided on a
number of roads. Motor vehicles generally have priority over this slower moving traffic except
when controlled by the appropriate road signs. However, cyclists proceeding straight ahead at
intersections have priority over all turning traffic. Visitors should be particularly alert.

Speed　　　　The placename indicates the beginning and end of a built-up area.
The following speed limits for cars are in force if there are no special
signs. Built-up areas 50kph (31mph). Outside built-up areas it is 100kph (62mph) on motorways
and 80kph (49mph) on other roads. Car/trailer combinations are limited to 80kph (49mph).

Tyres　　　　Although residents are not permitted to use spiked tyres, visitors
may do so provided that they do not exceed 80kph (49mph), and if
spikes are allowed in their home country.

Warning triangles　　These are compulsory for all vehicles except motorcycles; they
must be used at night if a stopped vehicle's lighting system fails, and
by day if a vehicle is not readily visible.

Netherlands/hotels and garages

Prices are in florins (guilden)
Abbreviations:
bd   boulevard
pl   plein
str   straat

AALSMEER Noord-Holland 20,800 (☎02977)
Map **4** C3
🛏 🕭**Boom** 220 Oosteinderweg ☎25667 BL (GB)

ALKMAAR Noord-Holland 65,200 (☎072) Map **4** C3
☆☆☆**Alkmaar** 2 Arcadialaan ☎120744 92rm5⇌ P 🌙
sBfr48 dB⇌86–124
🛏 🕭**Klaver** 29–30 Heldersweg ☎127033 P BL
(GB)
🛏 🕭**W Schmidt** 1 Nassaupl ☎113545 Frd (GB)

ALMELO Overijssel 62,650 (☎05490) Map **4** D3
☆☆☆**Postiljon** 1 Aalderinkssingel ☎15261 tx44417
50rm4⇌46🍴 P 🌙 sB⇌🍴fr56 dB⇌88 L fr7 Dfr13
🛏 🕭**Almelo** 107 Wierdensestr ☎12472 Frd (GB)
🛏 **Konink** 1 H-R-Holst Laan ☎11064 ☎61890
Aud/Por/VW (GB)

AMERSFOORT Utrecht 87,800 (☎033) Map **4** C3
★★★**Witte** 2 Utrechtseweg ☎14142 17rm10⇌5🍴 P
🌙 sBfr60 sB⇌🍴70–90 dB⇌🍴110–120 L fr13
Dfr40
★★**Berg** 225 Utrechtseweg ☎16110 22rm13🍴 🏛 🏊
🛏 🕭**Lips** 12 Kapelweg ☎14841 Ren
🛏 🕭**J J Molenaar's** 2 Barchman Wuytierslaan
☎30304 BL/Jag/Rov/Tri/(GB)

AMSTERDAM Noord-Holland 751,200 (☎020)
Map **4** C3 **See Plan**
★★★★★**Amstel** 1 Prof-Tulppl ☎226060 tx12545
Plan **1** 118⇌ 🏛 Lift
★★★★★**Amsterdam Hilton** 138 Apollolaan
☎780760 tx11025 Plan **2** P Lift 🌙 sB⇌136–179
dB⇌177–223 L fr28 Dfr28
★★★★**Apollo** 2 Apollolaan ☎735922 tx14084
Plan **3** 220⇌ P Lift sB⇌131–165dB⇌177–220
(English breakfast) Lalc Dalc
★★★★**Adda Park** 25 Stadhouderskade ☎717474
tx11412 Plan **4** P Lift 🌙 sB⇌85–110
dB⇌🍴135–165 (English breakfast) L20–25
D20–25
★★★★**American** 97 Leidsekade ☎245322 tx11379
Plan **5** Lift
★★★★**Caransa** 19 Rembrandtspl ☎229455 tx13342
Plan **6** 66⇌ Lift 🌙 sB⇌🍴85–125
dB⇌🍴116–165 L27–28 D27–28
★★★★**Carlton** 2 Vijzelstr (n rest) ☎222266 tx11670
Plan **7** 144⇌ 🏛 Lift
★★★★**Doelen** 24 Nieuwe Doelenstr ☎220722
tx14399 Plan **8** 86⇌ Lift 🌙 sB⇌🍴85–125
dB⇌🍴116–165 L27–28 D27–28
☆☆☆**EuroCrest** 2 De Boelelaan ☎429855 tx13647
Plan **9** 260⇌ Lift
★★★★**Krasnapolsky** 9 Dam ☎263163 tx12262
Plan **10** 300rm270⇌ 🏛 P Lift 🌙 sBfr70
sB⇌🍴100–121 dBfr90 dB⇌156–177 L17 D22
★★★★**Port Van Cleve** 178–180 Nieuw Zyds
Voorburgwai ☎244860 tx13129 Plan **11** 110⇌ Lift 🌙
sB⇌90–100 dB⇌115–165 (English breakfast)
L fr23 Dfr25
★★★★**Pulitzer** 315–331 Prinsengracht ☎228333
tx16508 Plan **12** 176⇌ P Lift 🌙 sB⇌🍴126–141
dB⇌🍴172–187 L20 D28
★★★**Amster Centre** 255 Herengracht ☎221727
tx15424 Plan **13** 110⇌ Lift 🌙 sB⇌🍴75–95
dB⇌🍴107–140 L20 D20
★★★**Centraal** 7 Stadhouderskade ☎185765
tx12601 Plan **14** 119rm104⇌ Lift
★★★**Delphi** 101–105 Apollolaan ☎795152 tx16659
Plan **15** 51rm43⇌ P Lift 🌙 sB55 sB⇌83–88 dB88
dB⇌110–125
☆☆☆**Euromotel Amsterdam** 20 Oude Haagseweg
☎179005 tx15524 Plan **16** 157⇌🍴 P Lift 🌙
sB⇌🍴65–72 dB⇌🍴95–104 L Fr15 D Fr17
★★★**Euromotel E.9.** 10 J-Muyskensweg ☎658181
tx13382 Plan **17** 140rm128🍴 P 🌙 sB⇌🍴57 dB64
dB🍴90

★★★**Schiller** 26–36 Rembrandtspl ☎231660
tx14058 Plan **19** 89rm80⇌ Lift 🌙 sB⇌75–95
dB⇌107–140 L20 D20
★★**Ams Hotel Terdam** 23 Tesselschadestr
☎126876 Plan **19** 60rm35⇌5🍴 A40rm Lift
★**Piet Hein** 53 Vossiusstr (n rest) ☎727205
Plan **20** Closed 16 Dec–14 Mar 21rm16🍴 P 🌙 sB58
sB🍴75 dB102 dB🍴123
★★**Roode Leeuw** 93–94 Damrak ☎240396 Plan **21**
80rm48⇌3🍴 Lift 🌙 sB52 sB⇌🍴63 dB78
dB⇌🍴105 L15 D18
★**De Amstel** 28 Weesperzijde (n rest) ☎946407
Plan **22** 22rm 12🍴
★**Gerstekorrel** 22 Damstr ☎241367 Plan **23** Closed
24 Dec–1 Jan 25rm8🍴 A6rm 🌙 sB38–45 sB🍴45
dB70 dB🍴90 L18–22 D18–22
★**Leijdsche Hof** 14 Leidsegracht (n rest) ☎232148
Plan **24** 12rm4🍴 A🚭 sB30–50 dB55 dB🍴60–65
🕭**AEM** 399 Overtoom ☎181234 P Vau
🛏 🕭**Asmoco** 39 Iste Ringdijkstr ☎101949
BMW/(GB)
🛏 🕭**J C Doorn** 93 Vuurwerkweg ☎273030 Chy/Sim
🛏 🕭**Sieberg** 93 Stadhouderskade ☎717944

APELDOORN Gelderland 134,100 (☎055)
Map **4** C3
★★★**Keizerskroon** 7 Koningstr ☎217744 60rm48⇌
P Lift 🌙 sB57 sB⇌81–87 dB102 dB⇌120–143 L13
D31
★★**Bloemink** 56 Loolaan ☎214141 tx49253
33rm11⇌15🍴
★**Suisse** 15 Stationspl ☎212040 12rm
🛏 🕭**Nefkens** 41 Deventerstr/Edisonlaan 270
☎219564☎219564 Peu (GB)
🛏 🕭**Bakker** 21 Gazellestr ☎214208 P Ren

ARCEN EN VELDEN Limburg 7,650 (☎04703)
Map **4** D2
★**Maas** 18 Schansstr ☎1556 24rm2⇌7🍴 🏛

ARNHEM Gelderland 126,100 (☎085) Map **4** C2
★★★**Groot Warnsborn** 277 Bakensbergseweg
☎455751 tx45596 29rm14⇌15🍴 A14rm 🏛
★★★**Haarhuis** 1 Stationspl ☎427441 tx45357
98rm45⇌53🍴 🏛 P Lift 🌙 sB⇌🍴45–60
dB⇌🍴80–95 L13–18 D15–25
☆☆☆**Postiljon** 20 Europaweg ☎453741 tx45028
30rm28🍴 P 🌙 sB🍴56–68 dB🍴88 L alc D alc
★★★**Rijn** 10 Onderlangs ☎434642 tx45982 28⇌ 🏛
P 🌙 sB⇌75–100 dB⇌120–140 L20 D25 lake
★★**Leeren Doedel** 467 Amsterdamseweg, La rte
d'Ede ☎332344 10rm3⇌ P sB38 sB⇌46 dB75
dB⇌85 L13 D20 ♨
★**Rijnzicht** 123 Utrechtseweg (n rest) ☎420865
Closed Nov–Feb 12rm3🍴
🛏 🕭**J Reymes** 5A Amsterdamseweg ☎450247 (GB)
🛏 **Rosier & Meijer** 10 Velperweg ☎629033 Frd (GB)

ASSEN Drenthe 43,800 (☎05920) Map **4** D3
🚗 🚐**AZA** 17–19 Beilerstr ☎15249 M/c P MB

BAARN Utrecht 25,050 (☎02154) Map **4** C3
★**Promenade** 1 Amalialaan ☎2913 17rm2⇌
🛏 **M Koog** 57A Eemnsser ☎12619 P Chy/Sim

BEEK Limburg 12,650 (☎04402) Map **4** C2
☆☆☆**Euromotel Limburg** Beek-Maastricht (E9)
☎2462 tx56059 62rm20⇌42🍴 P 🌙 sB⇌🍴54–60
dB🍴78–90 L14 D17

BERGEN AAN ZEE Noord-Holland 350 (☎02208)
Map **4** C3
★★★**Nassau-Bergen** 4 Van de Wijckpl ☎2345
32rm8⇌10🍴 P sB63–68 sB⇌🍴73 dB113–117
dB⇌🍴130–144 (English breakfast) L18 D30–35
Pool sea
★**Prins Maurits** 7 Van Hasseltstr ☎2364 Closed 16
Oct–14 Mar 24rm12⇌3🍴 🏛 P dB50–70
dB⇌🍴75–85 D15

BERG-EN-DAL Gelderland 2,000 (☎08895)
Map **4** C/D2
★★★**Park 'Val Monté** 5 Oude Holleweg ☎1704
tx48428 92rm53⇌37🍴 P 🌙 sB44 sB⇌🍴54–94
dB⇌108–118 L19 D24

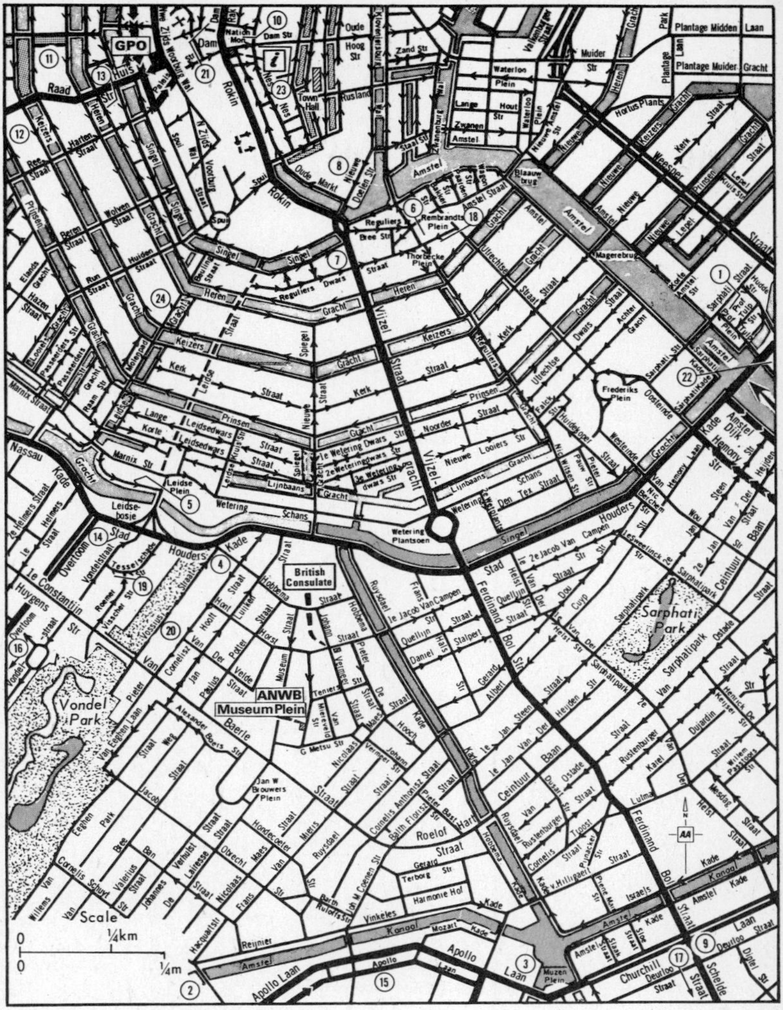

Netherlands

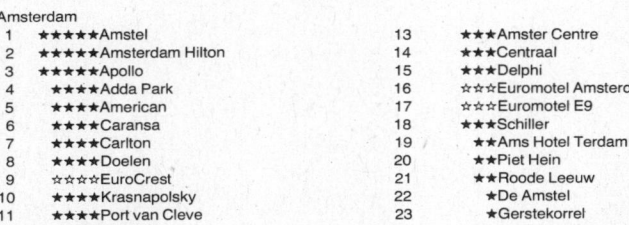

Amsterdam

No.	Hotel	No.	Hotel
1	★★★★★Amstel	13	★★★Amster Centre
2	★★★★★Amsterdam Hilton	14	★★★Centraal
3	★★★★★Apollo	15	★★★Delphi
4	★★★★Adda Park	16	☆☆Euromotel Amsterdam
5	★★★★American	17	☆☆☆Euromotel E9
6	★★★★Caransa	18	★★★Schiller
7	★★★★Carlton	19	★★Ams Hotel Terdam
8	★★★★Doelen	20	★Piet Hein
9	☆☆☆EuroCrest	21	★★Roode Leeuw
10	★★★★Krasnapolsky	22	★De Amstel
11	★★★★Port van Cleve	23	★Gerstekorrel
12	★★★★Pulitzer	24	★Leijdsche Hof

317

BERGEN-OP ZOOM Noord-Brabant 40,800 (☎01640) Map **4** C2
★★★**Gouden-Leeuw** 14 Fortuinstr ☎35000 tx54765 22rm5⇌17 🏠 🎱 P ♪ sB⇌ 🍴50–60 dB⇌ 🍴96–116 (English breakfast)
★**Draak** 37 Grote Markt ☎33661 27rm4⇌
★**Schelde** 56 Antwerpsestr ☎33390 18⇌3 🍴
🛢 🅟**Difoga** 25 Bredasestr ☎35910 Frd
🛢 🅟**Swagemakens** 50 Moerstraatsebaan ☎36285 AR (GB)
🛢 🅟**Vos** 10–12 Ravelstr ☎42050 ☎42050 Cit (GB)
BEVERWIJK Noord-Holland 37,551 (☎02510) Map **4** C3
🛢 🅟**Admiraal & Zn** 1 Laan der Nederlanden ☎36050 P Cit (GB)
🛢 🅟**Wijkeroog** 6 Bullerlaan ☎41664 P BL (GB)
BILTHOVEN Utrecht 16,050 (☎030) Map **4** C3
★★**Heidepark** 22–24 J-Steelaan ☎782477 18rm8⇌7 🍴 P ♪ sB45–60 sB⇌ 🍴60 dB80–90 dB⇌ 🍴80–90
BLOEMENDAAL Noord-Holland 17,950 (☎023) Map **4** C3
★★**Iepenhove** 4 Hartenlustlaan ☎258301 48rm4⇌20 🍴 P Lift sB34–45 sB⇌ 🍴40–51 dB62–78 dB⇌ 🍴68–96 L20 D35
🛢 🅟**Van Loon's** 30–44 Korte Kleverlaan ☎259311 ☎259311 P Lnc/Ren/Sab (GB)
BORN Limburg 7,350 (☎04498) Map **4** C1
☆☆☆**Eurocrest** 6 Julianaweg ☎1666 tx56248 49rm17⇌32 🍴
BOSKOOP Zuid-Holland 13,000 (☎01727) Map **4** C2
★★**Florida** 1 A-P Van Neslaan ☎2282 9rm7⇌ 🎱
🛢 🅟**Eerste Boskoops** 2-6 Plankier ☎2110 P MB/Opl (GB)
BREDA Noord-Brabant 118,100 (☎01600) Map **4** C2
☆☆☆**Euromotel Brabant** 4–6 Heerbaan ☎149754 tx54263 82rm22⇌60 🍴 P Lift ♪ sB⇌ 🍴74–79 dB⇌ 🍴97 L13 D18 Pool
☆**Euromotel** 20 Roskam (4km S) ☎222177 tx54126 80rm20⇌60 🍴 P ♪ sB⇌ 🍴63–78 dB⇌ 🍴81–96 L5–10 D18–25
🛢 🅟**Nefkens Breda** 20 Loevesteinstr ☎659211 Peu (GB)
🛢 🅟**Van Nunen** 442–444 Haagweg ☎134223 BL (GB)
🛢 🅟**Valkenberg** 8–12 Valkenstr ☎222371 Cit (GB)
At **Ginneken** (2km S)
★★★**Mastbosch** 20 Burgemeester Kerstenslaan ☎650050 tx54406 47rm43⇌4 🍴 Lift
BRESKENS Zeeland 4,200 (☎01172) Map **3** B2
★★**Wapen van Breskens** 33 Grote Kade ☎1401 18rm6 🍴 A3rm 🎱 P sB25 sB 🍴45 dB50 dB 🍴90 L Fr5 D Fr15 sea
🛢 🅟**Vroon's** 11 Mercuriusstr ☎1729 P Frd
BUNNIK See **UTRECHT**
BUSSUM Noord-Holland 37,850 (☎02159) Map **4** C3
★**Gooiland** 16–18 Stationsweg ☎43724 14rm2⇌3 🍴 P ♪ sB34–43 sB⇌ 🍴38–43 dB75–85 dB⇌ 🍴75–85 (English breakfast) L13 D23
🛢 🅟**Van Meurs** 84–86 Huizerweg ☎34047 Ren (GB)
DELDEN Overijssel 6,350 (☎05407) Map **4** D3
★★**Zwaan** 2 Langestr ☎1206 19rm2⇌7 🍴 A6rm 🎱 P sB30–40 sB⇌ 🍴45–65 dB60–70 dB⇌ 🍴87–95 L12–20 D20–25 Pool ♡
DELFT Zuid-Holland 86,150 (☎015) Map **4** C2
★**Central** 6 Wijnhaven ☎123442 15rm10 🍴
🛢 🅟**P H Blansjaar** 51 H-de Grootstr ☎120751 P Aud/Chy/Vau
🛢 🅟**Kinesis** 281 Vulcanusweg ☎569202 Frd (GB)
DEN HAAG See **HAAG (DEN) (HAGUE, THE)**
DEN HELDER Noord-Holland 60,421 (☎02230) Map **4** C3
🛢 🅟**Ceres** 139 Baljuwstr ☎30000 Peu (GB)

DEVENTER Overijssel 65,600 (☎05700) Map **4** D3
★★★**Postiljon** 121 Deventerweg ☎24022 48⇌ 🍴 P Lift ♪ sB⇌ 🍴55–63 dB⇌ 🍴80 L13 D20 lake
🛢 🅟**Hardonk's** 6 Gl-Gibsonstr ☎13945 Bed/MB/Vau
DOETINCHEM Gelderland 34,950 (☎08340) Map **4** D2
🛢 🅟**Gelderse-Auto** 10 Keppelseweg ☎33250 P Frd
DOMBURG Zeeland 3,900 (☎01188) Map **3** B2
★★★**Bad** 3 Domburgseweg (Pn) ☎1241 Closed 6 Sep–9 May 65rm25⇌2 🍴 A20rm
DORDRECHT Zuid-Holland 101,850 (☎078) Map **4** C2
★★★**Bellevue-Groothoofdspoort** 37 Boomstr ☎37900 20rm10⇌10 🍴 P ♪ sB⇌ 🍴53–73 dB⇌ 🍴110 L18 D18 river
🛢 🅟**AVD Ban** 51 Dubbelsteynlaan ☎61600 P BL/BMW
🛢 🅟**H W Van Gorp & Zonnen** 296 A-Cuypsingel ☎42044 Bed/Peu
🛢 🅟**Kern's** 1 Copernicusweg ☎71633 Ren
DRACHTEN Friesland 33,950 (☎05120) Map **4** C/D2
🛢 🅟**Siton** 25 de Knobben ☎14455 Opl
DRONTEN Gelderland 16,550 (☎03210) Map **4** C3
🛢 🅟**Visser** 1 de Ketting ☎3114 Bed/Opl/Vau
EDAM Noord-Holland 21,550 (☎02993) Map **4** C3
★**Dam** 1 Keizersgracht ☎71766 10rm1 🍴 P sB30–43 sB 🍴45 dB60–75 dB 🍴75 L1 D13
🛢 🅟**Griep & Frikkee** 4–6 Schepenmakersdijk ☎1602 ☎1772 Ren
EDE Gelderland 79,900 (☎08380) Map **4** C2
🛢 🅟**Van der Volk** 30 Klaphekweg ☎30201 ☎30201 P Frd (GB)
🛢 🅟**G Van Silfthout** 1 Proosdijweg ☎14041 P Ren
At **Veerendaal** (8 km W)
🛢 🅟**Lagendijk** 81 Buurtlaan Oost ☎10546 ☎14397 M/c P Bed/Vau (GB)
EEMNES See **LAREN**
EERNEWOUDE Friesland 300 (☎05117) Map **4** C/D3
★★★**Princenhof** 15 Piet Miedemaweg ☎9206 Closed 11 Oct–Mar 47rm23⇌16 🍴 A3rm lake
EGMOND AAN ZEE Noord-Holland 5,750 (☎02206) Map **4** C3
★★★**Bellevue** Strandboulevard (A7) ☎1387 36rm30⇌2 🍴 A6rm Lift ♪ sB44–63 sB⇌ 🍴44–63 dB87–102 dB⇌ 🍴96–125 L Fr10 D Fr23 sea
🛢 🅟**J A Karels** 17 Trompstr ☎1250 ⚙ BL (GB)
EINDHOVEN Noord-Brabant 192,600 (☎040) Map **4** C2
★★★★**Cocagne** 47 Vestijk ☎444755 tx51245 205⇌ 🎱 P Lift ♪ sB⇌ 🍴100–108 dB⇌ 🍴154–189 L Fr20 D Fr30
☆☆☆☆**Holiday Inn** 1 Veldmarschalk Montgomerylaan ☎433222 tx51775 200rm P Lift sB95 dB135 L8–25 D15–35 Pool
🛢 **Van Laarhoveb's Auto** 10 Bruggelaan ☎413615 BL (GB)
🛢 🅟**L Lang** 57 Keizer Karel V Singel ☎518402 Fia/Lnc (GB)
🛢 🅟**Van der Meulen-Ansems** 27 Vestdijk ☎444550 Frd
🛢 🅟**T Vlemmings** 23 Stratumsedijk ☎116336 Bed Sab/Vau
EMMELOORD Overijssel 13,550 (☎05270) Map **4** C3
🛢 🅟**Gorter** 50 Kampwal ☎3541 P Bed/BL/Opl/Vau (GB)
EMMEN Drenthe 86,725 (☎05910) Map **4** D3
🛢 🅟**Jong** 5–7 Statenweg ☎22330 ☎22330 Cit (GB)
🛢 🅟**Misker** 4 Odoornerweg ☎18288 BL (GB)
ENKHUIZEN Noord-Holland 13,450 (☎02280) Map **4** C3
★**Port van Cleve** 74 Dijk ☎2510 15rm7⇌6 🍴 P sB Fr35 (room only) sB⇌ 🍴40–60 (room only) dB Fr50 (room only) dB⇌ 🍴55–75 (room only) L Fr8 D Fr15

Netherlands

🍴 ⬧❉**Watses** 273–275 Westerstr ☎2708 Frd (GB)

ENSCHEDE Overijssel 141,600 (☎053) Map **4** D3

★★★**Memphis** 55 Tromplaan ☎318244
37rm26⇔9🛏 P Lift 🍴 sB38–73 sB⇔🛏73–83
dB Fr75 dB⇔🛏110–140 L Fr20 D Fr20

★★**Park** 200 Hengelosestr ☎353855 17rm5🛏 P 🍴
sB Fr43 sB🛏53 dB Fr85 dB🛏105 D20

🍴 ⬧❉**Auto-Fischer** 137 Oldenzaalsestr☎354555
☎354555 Frd (GB)

🍴 ⬧❉**C Jassles** 74 Hengelostr ☎327025 P
BL/Jag/Rov/Tri

Krupers 51–53 Hoogstr ☎315434 M/c only
BMW/Hon (GB)

FLUSHING See **VLISSINGEN**

GINNEKEN See **BREDA**

GOES Zeeland 28,550 (☎01100) Map **3** B2

★★**Korenbeurs** 17 Grote Markt ☎27110
30rm6⇔7🛏 sB32 (room only) sB⇔🛏35–40 (room
only) dB Fr64 dB⇔🛏68–90 L5–20 D15–25

★**Ockenburgh** 104 Van de Spiegelstr ☎16303
12rm1🛏 🏛

🍴 ⬧❉**Adria** 1 Marconistr ☎20440 Frd (GB)

⬧❉**Van Fraassen** 79 Voorstad ☎27353 Cit

⬧❉**B V Oeveren** 51 Couwerverstr ☎16100
BL/MB/Rov/Tri

🍴 ⬧❉**Van Strien** 92 Van de Spiegelstr ☎14840 M/c P
Aud/VW (GB)

GORINCHEM Zuid-Holland 28,350 (☎01830)
Map **4** C2

☆☆**Gorinchem** 10 Van Hogendorpweg ☎22400
15rm⇔🛏 P 🍴 sB⇔🛏63 dB⇔🛏96

🍴 ⬧❉**Romeyn & Van Zanten** 33 Concordiaweg
☎24455 ☎24455 P Frd (GB)

🍴 ⬧❉**Noordegraaf's** 184 Raam ☎17795 Cit

GROESBEEK Gelderland 18,100 (☎08891)
Map **4** C2

★★**Wolfsberg** 12 Mooksebaan ☎1327
19rm1⇔12🛏 🏛 P sB37 sB⇔🛏41 dB70–74
dB⇔🛏82–86 L10–30 D18–30

GRONINGEN Groningen 163,400 (☎050) Map **4** D4

☆☆**Euromotel Groningen** 7 Expositielaan
☎258400 tx53795 109rm⇔🛏 P Lift 🍴 sB⇔🛏65
(room only) dB⇔🛏90 (room only) L18–20 D25–35

☆☆**Clingendael** 156 Donderslaan ☎252040
tx53394 59rm10⇔49🛏 P 🍴 sB⇔🛏55–70
dB⇔🛏80–100

★★**Grande Frigge** 72 Heerstr ☎136342
86rm20⇔40🛏 Lift

🍴 ⬧❉**'A-Z'** 22 Friesestraatweg ☎120012 P Hon

🍴 ⬧❉**Geba** 1 Flemingstr ☎250015 BL (GB)

🍴 ⬧❉**Gronam** 130 Rijksweg, Oosterhoogebrug
☎411552 ☎344996 Frd (GB)

🍴 ⬧❉**J K Oosterhuis** 11–12 Westerkade ☎120246
Toy

GULPEN Limburg 4,450 (☎04450) Map **4** C1

At **Wittem** (1.5 km E)

★★**Kasteel Wittem** 3 Wittemerallee ☎1208 8⇔

HAAG (DEN) (HAGUE, THE) Zuid-Holland 479,400
(☎070) Map **4** C2

☐AA☐ agents; see page 310

★★★★★**Promenade** 1 Van Stolkweg ☎574121
tx31162 100⇔ 🏛 P Lift 🍴 sB⇔135 dB⇔170 L alc D
alc

★★★★**Bel Air** 30 J-de Wittlaan ☎572011 tx31444
350⇔ P Lift 🍴 sB⇔96 dB⇔136 (English breakfast)
L Fr25 D Fr25 Pool

★★★★**Grand Central** 6 Lange Poten ☎469414
tx32000 137rm123⇔14🛏 Lift 🍴 sB⇔🛏80–85
dB⇔🛏115–133 L Fr16 d Fr18

★★★★**Indes** 54/56 Lange Voorhout ☎469553
tx31196 77rm P Lift 🍴 sB⇔🛏110–145

dB⇔🛏165–195 L & alc D & alc

★★★**Parkhotel de Zalm** 53 Molenstr (Off
Noordeinde) (n rest) ☎624371 tx33005
132rm88⇔21🛏 P Lift 🍴 sB40–50 sB⇔🛏68–73
dB⇔🛏120–130

★**Esquire** 59–61 V-Aerssenstr ☎503840 10rm4🛏 P
🍴 sB35 dB60 dB🛏80

🍴 ⬧❉**Auto-Haag** 2 Calandpl ☎889255 Ren (GB)

🍴 ⬧❉**Case** 6 Pletterijstr ☎858780 Chy (GB)

🍴 ⬧❉**Centraal** 10 Prinses Margrietplantsoen
☎814131 Frd (GB)

🍴 ⬧❉**Gemex** 49–51 Reinkenstr ☎603588 P BL (GB)

🍴 ⬧❉**Internationale** 15 Scheldestr ☎850300
Hon/Sab/Vlo (GB)

🍴 ⬧❉**Zoet** 1B Koninginnegracht ☎185165 Chy

At **Rijswijk** (3 km SE)

☆☆☆**Hoornwijck** 2 J-Thijssenweg ☎903130
tx32358 74rm30⇔44🛏 🏛

At **Scheveningen**

★★★★**Europa** 2 Zwolsestr ☎512651 tx33138 🏛 Lift
⌒ sea

★★★**Badhotel** 15 Gevers Deijnootweg ☎512221
96rm76⇔20🛏 P Lift 🍴 sB⇔🛏43–66 dB⇔🛏86–96
L Fr15 d Fr20

★★**Eurotel** 63 Gevers Deijnootweg ☎512821
tx32799 83rm59⇔24🛏 P Lift 🍴 sB⇔🛏70–93
dB⇔🛏125 L18 D20 St% sea

★★**Bali** 1 Badhuisweg ☎514371 34rm8⇔2🛏 A12rm

HAARLEM Noord-Holland 164,700 (☎023)
Map **4** C3

★★★**Lion d'Or** 34–36 Kruisweg ☎321750
35rm9⇔13🛏 P Lift 🍴 sB57–58 sB⇔🛏82–93
dB83–85 dB⇔🛏108–120 L Fr20 D Fr20

🍴 ⬧❉**E Kimman** 2 ☎339069 BL (GB)

HARDET Gelderland (☎05255) Map **4** C3

★★**Val Ouwe** 94 Eperweg ☎1341 11rm3⇔4🛏 🏛 P
sB Fr38 sB⇔🛏 fr45 dB fr75 dB⇔🛏 Fr90

HAGUE (THE) See **HAAG (DEN)**

HARDERWIJK Gelderland 28,550 (☎03410)
Map **4** C3

★★**Baars** 52 Smeepoortstr ☎12007 18rm8⇔10🛏 🏛
P 🍴 sB⇔🛏 fr48 sB⇔🛏 fr85 L18 D23

HAREN Groningen 18,700 (☎050) Map **4** D4

☆☆**Postiljon** 33 Emmalaan ☎347041 tx53688
57rm24⇔33🛏

HARLINGEN Friesland 14,500 (☎05178)
Map **4** C3/4

★**Zeezicht** 1 Zuiderhaven ☎2536 10rm sea

🍴 ⬧❉**W Molenaar** 54 Heiligeweg ☎2925 P Frd

HEELSUM Gelderland (☎08373) Map **4** C2

★★★**Klein Zwitserland** 5 Klein Zwitserlandlaan
☎9104 tx45627 62rm32⇔29🛏 🏛 P Lift 🍴
sB⇔🛏63–88 dB⇔🛏125–220 L20–45 D45–85 🏊
Pool

HEEMSTEDE Noord-Holland 27,400 (☎023)
Map **4** C3

🍴 ⬧❉**Barnhoorn** 21 Roemer Visscherpl ☎242250
Toy

HEERENVEEN Friesland 34,950 (☎05130)
Map **4** C3

☆☆☆**Postiljon** 65 Schans ☎24041 44rm4⇔40🛏 🏛

🍴 ⬧❉**Vriesema** 1 Schans ☎32333 M/c BL/Rov/Tri
(GB)

HEERLEN Limburg 71,500 (☎045) Map **4** C/D1

★★★**Grand** 17 Wilhelminapl ☎713846
67rm15⇔17🛏 P Lift 🍴 sB38–55 sB⇔🛏60–85
dB75 dB⇔🛏105–140 L9–20 D22–65

🍴 ⬧❉**Canton-Reiss** 34 Valkenburgerweg ☎718040
Bed/Opl/Vau

🍴 ⬧❉**Sondagh** 19–21 Looierstr ☎711399 P Cit (GB)

🍴 ⬧❉**Van Haaren** 25 Schandelerboord ☎711152 Frd

🍴 ⬧❉**Heynen** 1 Frankenlaan ☎713600 Ren (GB)

🍴 ⬧❉**Vencken** 60–64 Heesbergstr/Kruisstr 13
☎412641 Aud/VW (GB)

HELMOND Noord-Brabant 59,250 (☎04920)
Map **4** C2

Netherlands

★★★ **West-Ende** 1 Steenweg ☎24151 Closed 25 Dec – 1 Jan 36rm12⇄12🅿 Lift
🛏 ᐳᐸ**Alards** 31 Gerwenseweg ☎22608 P BL/Rov
🛏 ᐳᐸ**J Gorp** 220 Engelseweg ☎39670 Cit

HENGELO Overijssel 72,300 (☎05400) Map **4** D3
★★★ **Lansink't** 18 Storkstr ☎10066 Closed 25 Dec – 1 Jan 22rm8⇄14 🅿 🏛
★**Kroon** 62 Deldenerstr ☎12872 32rm13 🅿 P sB33 sB🖪38 dB65 dB🖪75 L alc D13
🛏 ᐳᐸ**G Ter Haar** 140 – 142 Breemarsweg ☎13901 BL
🛏 ᐳᐸ**W Noordegraaf** 19 – 23 Oldenzaalsestr ☎14444 M/c Frd (GB)

'S-HERTOGENBOSCH Noord-Brabant 86,200 (☎073) Map **4** C2
★★★ **Eurotel** 63 Hinthamerstr ☎137777 42⇄ 🏛 P Lift ᐳ sB⇄55 – 60 dB⇄80 – 85 Lfr15
🛏 ᐳᐸ**Lautenslager Auto** 7 Havenstr ☎130636 Fia/Ska (GB)

HILVERSUM Noord-Holland 94,050 (☎02150) Map **4** C3
★★**Hof Van Holland** 1 Kekbrink ☎46141 tx43399 30rm16⇄14🖪 P Lift ᐳ sB⇄ 🖪75 dB⇄ 🖪100 – 110 D25
🛏 ᐳᐸ**H Donkelaar** 26A-E Vaartweg ☎48917 M/c only P BMW (GB)
🛏 ᐳᐸ**H Koster** 42 Langestr ☎71156 BMW (GB)
🛏 ᐳᐸ**J K Poll** 2 Zeverijnstr ☎47841 Frd

HOLTEN Overijssel 8,850 (☎05483) Map **4** D3
★★**Hoog Holten** 25 Holterberg ☎1306 27rm8🖪 ᐟᐠ
★★**Lösse Hoes** 46 Holterberg ☎1353 18rm17⇄17🖪 A16rm P sB46 – 49 sB⇄ 🖪49 – 55 dB92 – 115 dB⇄ 🖪99 – 115 (English breakfast) Lfr10 Dfr35 ᐟᐠ Pool 🛇 ∩

HOOGERHEIDE Noord-Brabant 6,300 (☎01646) Map **4** C2
★★**Pannenhuis** 100 Antwerpsestraatweg ☎2540 Closed 25 Dec – 1 Jan 28rm13🖪 A4rm 🏛 P sB25 – 30 sB🖪30 – 35 dB50 – 65 dB🖪55 – 70 L fr8 D fr15
🛏 ᐳᐸ**P J Wils** 88 Raadhuisstr ☎2530 BL/Tri

HOORN Noord-Holland 24,650 (☎02290) Map **4** C3
★**Keizerskoon** 31 Breed ☎14401 26rm 🏛
🛏 ᐳᐸ**Koopmans** 5 Dampten ☎16912 ☎17393 M/c Hon/Ska
🛏 ᐳᐸ**Van der Linden & Van Sprankhuizen** 11 Berkhouterweg ☎12910 P Opl/Vau (GB)

KAMPEN Overijssel 29,500 (☎05202) Map **4** C3
★★★**Stadsherberg** 48 Ijsselkade ☎12645 tx42110 16rm7⇄9🖪 P Lift sB⇄ 🖪53 – 65 dB⇄ 🖪90 – 100 L10 – 18 D18 – 45
★★ **Van Dijk** 30 Ijsselkade (n rest) ☎14925 28rm8⇄1🖪 A6rm
🛏 ᐳᐸ**J H R Van Noort** 33 – 37 Oudestr ☎12241 Frd (GB)
🛏 ᐳᐸ**Westerhof** 2 Ysseldijk ☎13386Chy/Sim (GB)

KOOG (DE) Texel (☎02228) Map **4** C3
★★★**Opduin** 22 Minister Ruyslaan ☎445 tx57555 46rm32🖪 A8rm 🏛 P Lift sBfr44 sB🖪fr60 ᐟᐠ Pool

LAREN Noord-Holland 13,650 (☎02153) Map **4** C3
At Eemnes (2km E)
☆☆**Witte Bergen** 2 Rijksweg ☎86754 tx73041 61rm42⇄19🖪 🏛 P sB⇄ 🖪47 – 57 dB⇄ 🖪58 – 68 L alc D alc

LEEUWARDEN Friesland 85,100 (☎05100) Map **4** C4
★★★**Oranje** 4 Stationsweg ☎26241 54rm7⇄27🖪 P Lift ᐳ sB52 – 69 sB⇄ 🖪62 – 82 dBFr101 dB⇄ 🖪117 – 133 Lfr14 Dfr19
★★**Euro** 19 Europapl ☎31113 61rm13⇄31🖪 A3rm P Lift ᐳ sB39 – 52 sB⇄ 🖪47 – 52 dB93 – 103 dB⇄ 🖪93 – 103 (English breakfast) Lfr8 D fr15
🛏 ᐳᐸ**Molenaar** 2 Keidam ☎61115 ☎81441 BL/Jag/Rov/Tri
🛏 ᐳᐸ**Nagelhout** 2 Brandemeer ☎63633 Toy (GB)
🛏 ᐳᐸ**Rosier's** 162 Spanjaardslaan ☎20043 Ren
🛏 ᐳᐸ**Zeeuw** 2-II Valeriusstr ☎31444 Frd (GB)

LEIDEN Zuid-Holland 99,900 (☎071) Map **4** C3
☆☆☆**Holiday Inn** 10 Haagse Schouwweg ☎769310 tx32541 190⇄ 🏛 P Lift sB⇄ 🖪90 – 95

dB⇄ 🖪130 – 140 (English breakfast) L8 D15 ᐟᐠ Pool
★**Karrewiel't** 55 Steenstr ☎122509 11rm3🖪
🛏 ᐳᐸ**Leidse Autoboxen** (LAG) 37 Van Oldenbarneveldtstr ☎151683 P BL (GB)
🛏 ᐳᐸ**Poot** 132 Lammenschansweg ☎764800 BL (GB)

LEUSDEN Utrecht (☎033) Map **4** C2/3
★★ **Treek** 23 Trekerweg ☎1425 16rm2⇄7🖪 🏛 Lift

LEUVENUM Gelderland 150 (☎05770) Map **4** C3
★★**Roode Koper** 82 Van Sandbergweg ☎7393 26rm7⇄9🖪

LOCHEM Gelderland 17,300 (☎05730) Map **4** D3
★★★**Adbo** 3 Paaschberg ☎4051 Closed 4 Jan – Mar 35rm1⇄34🖪 P Lift sB⇄ 🖪48 – 58 dB⇄ 🖪55 – 75 (English breakfast) D10 – 20 D15 – 30
🛏 ᐳᐸ**Van de Straat** 36 Tramstr ☎1652 M/c P BL (GB)

MAARSBERGEN Utrecht 1,525 (☎03433) Map **4** C2
☆☆**Maarsbergen** 44 Woudenbergseweg ☎341 tx47986 15🖪 P ᐳ dB⇄ 🖪47 – 50 dB🖪64 L8 D14

MAASTRICHT Limburg 111,050 (☎043) Map **4** C1
★★★**Casque** 52 Vrijthof ☎14343 tx56657 40rm20⇄15🖪 🏛 P Lift ᐳ sBfr46 sB⇄ 🖪fr72 dB⇄ 🖪92 – 100 (English breakfast) L19 – 49 D19 – 49
★★★**Derlon** 6 0 L-Vrouwespl ☎12542 tx56256 30rm16⇄4🖪70 – 78 dB73 – 78 dB⇄ 🖪90 – 113 D25
★★**Dominicain** 16 Helmstr (n rest) ☎14656 16rm7⇄2🖪 Lift sB30 – 40 (room only) sB⇄ 🖪35 – 45 (room only) dB60 – 80 (room only) dB⇄ 🖪70 – 80 (room only)
🛏 ᐳᐸ**Straten** 170 Via Regia ☎32500 Aud/Vw (GB)

MIDDELBURG Zeeland 36,400 (☎01180) Map **3** B2
★★★**Commerce** 1 Loskade (n rest) ☎36051 31rm9⇄14🖪 A4rm P Lift sBfr75 (room only) sB⇄ 🖪fr47 (room only) dB70 (room only) dB⇄ 🖪85 (room only)
★★**Nieuwe Doelen** 3 – 7 Loskade ☎12121 30rm12🖪 Lift sBfr43 (room only) sB🖪45 – 50 (room only) dBfr85 (room only) dB🖪90 – 100 (room only) L fr20 D fr25
★**Huifkar** 19 Markt ☎12998 8rm4🖪 P sB35 – 45 sB⇄ 🖪55 – 75 dB65 – 85 dB⇄ 🖪85 – 95 L7 – 45 D13 – 65
🛏 ᐳᐸ**Louisse** 1 Kalverstr ☎25851 Opl (GB)

MIDDELHARNIS Zuid-Holland 14,250 (☎01870) Map **3** B2
🛏 ᐳᐸ**Auto Service** 41 – 43 Kastanjelaan ☎3094 Chy/Sim
🛏 ᐳᐸ**Knöps** 113 Langeweg ☎2043 Bed/Opl/Vau (GB)

MOOK-EN-MIDDELAAR Limburg 5,800 (☎08896) Map **4** C2
★★★**Plasmolen** 170 Rijksweg ☎1444 30rm21⇄6🖪 🏛 P ᐳ sB28 – 40 sB⇄ 🖪48 – 65 dB40 – 50 dB⇄ 🖪79 – 92 L15 – 45 D20 – 50 ᐟᐠ lake
★★**Schans** 95 Rijksweg ☎1209 12rm1⇄5🖪 🏛

NAARDEN Noord-Holland 17,350 (☎02159) Map **4** C3
☆☆☆**Euro** 92 Amersfoortsestraatweg ☎44641 tx43465 50rm49🖪 A12rm P ᐳ sBfr55 sB🖪fr55 dB🖪fr80

NIJMEGEN Gelderland 148,500 (☎080) Map **4** C2
🛏 ᐳᐸ**Jansen & Erdeveen** ☎224800 Ren (GB)
🛏 ᐳᐸ**Vossen** 119 – 123 Molenweg ☎770144 BL/Rov/Tri
🛏 ᐳᐸ**T Wolf's** 8 Waalkade ☎225111 Frd (GB)

NIJVERDAL Overijssel 18,925 (☎05486) Map **4** D3
🛏 ᐳᐸ**Blokken** 27 Bergleidingweg ☎12959 BL/Tri
🛏 ᐳᐸ**H Valk** 19 – 21 Boomcateweg ☎12487 Bed/Vau (GB)

NOORDGOUWE Zeeland (☎01112) Map **3** B2
🛏 ᐳᐸ**Akkerdaas** 2 Kloosterweg Bed/Opl/Vau (GB)

NOORDWIJK AAN ZEE Zuid-Holland 22,400 (☎01719) Map **4** C3
★★★**Palace** 3 Koningin-Wilhelmina bd ☎19231 tx32010 91rm29⇄75🖪 A36rm Lift ᐳ sB38 – 43 sB⇄ 🖪43 – 68 dB75 – 85 dB⇄ 🖪115 – 125 (English breakfast) L20 D30 sea

★★**Clarenwijck** 46 Koningen-Astrid bd ☎12727
25rm15⇄3 🈸 P ⅅ sB30−35 sB⇄🈸40−45 dB60−70
dB⇄🈸80−90 D23 sea
★★**Huis ter Duin** 5 Koningin-Astrid bd (DP) ☎19220
tx31713 Closed 12 Sep−30 Dec 89⇄ 🏛 Lift ➳ Beach
♨ sea
★★**Noordzee** 8 Koningin-Wilhelmina bd ☎19205
tx32504 90rm14⇄67 🈸 P Lift ⅅ sB58−68
sB⇄🈸68−88 dB100−125 dB⇄🈸125−175 L6−30
D fr14 Pool Beach sea
★★**Zinger** 1 bd Zeereep ☎19330 46rm13⇄27 🈸 P
ⅅ sB fr38 sB⇄🈸63−95 dB fr75 dB⇄🈸107−140
(English breakfast) L15−23 D25−50 sea
★**Duinlust** 1 Koepelweg ☎12916 Closed Oct−Mar
25rm P sB30−45 dB60−95 L15 D20
🛏 ⅋ο**Beuk** 19 Golfweg ☎19213 Fia/Lnc (GB)
OISTERWIJK Noord-Brabant 16,300 (☎04242)
Map 4 C2
🛏 ⅋ο**Spoormakers** 80 Kerkstr ☎4683 P Fia (GB)
OLDENZAAL Overijssel 26,650 (☎05410) Map 4 D3
🛏 ⅋ο**Olde Monnikhof** 20 Vos de Waelstr ☎14461
Opl (GB)
🛏 ⅋ο**Munsterhuis** 4 Ollemolenstr ☎15661 P Ren
(GB)
OMMEN Overijssel 16,150 (☎05291) Map 4 D3
★★**Zon an de Vecht** 1 Voorbrug ☎1141
20rm2⇄5 🈸 🏛 ◯
🛏 ⅋ο**Leerentveld** 1 Hammerweg ☎2500 ☎1475
Chy/Sim (GB)
OOSTBURG Zeeland 18,500 (☎01170) Map 3 B2
★**Commerce** 20 Burchstr ☎2912 22rm 🏛
OOSTERBEEK Gelderland 13,800 (☎085)
Map 4 C2
★★★**Bilderberg** 261 Utrechtseweg ☎333060
55rm40⇄ 🏛 Lift
★★**Strijland** 6 Stationsweg ☎332136 Closed mid
Dec−Jan 30rm6⇄14 🈸 P sB⇄🈸58 dB⇄🈸84−93
L11 D19
★**Dreyeroord** 12 Graaf Van Rechterenweg
☎333169 28rm4⇄14 🈸 A8rm P Lift sB38−48
sB⇄🈸48−55 dB70−96 dB⇄🈸88−110
(English breakfast) L10 D15
🛏 ⅋ο**Hoog en Laag** 84 Utrechtseweg ☎334751 Toy
OSS Noord-Brabant 45,650 (☎04120) Map 4 C2
★**Alem** 81 Molenstr ☎22114 18rm P sB25 dB45
(English breakfast) L13 D19
🛏 ⅋ο**J Putters** 38 Hertogensingel ☎23600 P AR/MB
(GB)
🛏 ⅋ο**Uyting & Smits** 27 Oude Molenstr ☎26925 P
Bed/Opl/Vau
OVERVEEN Noord-Holland (☎023) Map 4 C3
★★**Roozendaal** 260 Bloemendaalseweg ☎324517
13rm2⇄11 🈸
PAPENDRECHT Zuid-Holland 24,200 (☎078)
Map 4 C2
☆☆☆**Staatse Schans** 2 Lange Tiendweg ☎52099
tx23631 33rm26⇄7 🈸 A26rm P Lift ⅅ
sB⇄🈸75−100 dB⇄🈸100−155 L10−35 D18−45
POELDIJK Zuid-Holland 4,150 (☎01749) Map 4 C2
★★**Verburgh** 2 Julianstr (DP & Pn) ☎45209
16rm10 🈸 A10rm P sB55−75 dB110−150 L15 D fr20
RENKUM Gelderland 34,550 (☎08373) Map 4 C2
★★**Nol in't Bosch** 60 Hartenseweg ☎9101
30rm8⇄14 🈸
RIJSWIJK See HAAG (DEN) (HAGUE, THE)
ROERMOND Limburg 36,700 (☎04750) Map 4 D2
🛏 ⅋ο**Nedam** 802 Oranjelaan ☎23351 P Opl/Vau
(GB)
🛏 ⅋ο**Opheij** 29−31 W-II-Singel ☎12125 BL/Hon
(GB)
ROOSENDAAL Noord-Brabant 51,700 (☎01650)
Map 4 C2
★★**Central** 9 Stationspl ☎35650 19rm11⇄4 🈸 🏛
🛏 ⅋ο**Van Poppel** 9 Van Beethovenlaan ☎45350 P BL
(GB)
ROTTERDAM Zuid-Holland 614,800 (☎010)
Map 4 C2

★★★★**Atlanta** 4 Aert Van Messtr ☎110420 tx21595
185rm158⇄27 🈸 P Lift ⅅ sB⇄🈸88−97
dB⇄🈸101−133 (English breakfast) L fr33alc
D fr33alc
★★★★**Central** 12 Kruiskade ☎140744 tx24040
75rm35⇄40 🈸 Lift
★★★★**Park** 70 Westersingel ☎363611 tx22020 96⇄
P Lift ⅅ sB⇄90−115 dB⇄160−190
(English breakfast) L23 D25
★★★★**Rijn** 1 Schouwburgpl ☎333800 tx21640
140rm20⇄120 🈸 P Lift ⅅ sB⇄🈸75−135
dB⇄🈸145−160
☆☆☆**Euromotel Rotterdam** 61 Vliegveldweg
☎158000 tx22064 100rm60⇄40 🈸 P Lift ⅅ
sB⇄🈸61 dB⇄🈸88 (English breakfast) L14 D16 lake
★★★**Savoy** 81 Hoogstr ☎1392800 tx21525 100⇄ P
Lift ⅅ sB⇄77−88 dB⇄101−106 (English breakfast)
L fr33 D fr33
★★**Baan** 345 Rochussenstr (n rest) ☎770555
14rm7 🈸 P sB32−35 sB⇄🈸40−45 dB45−50
dB⇄🈸60−75 lake
★**Pax** 110 Schiekade (n rest) ☎653107 35rm16 🈸
A12rm 🈸 P Lift sB38 dB63 dB⇄🈸80
★★**Witte Paard** 245 Groenezoom ☎192020
9rm2⇄1 🈸 P ⅅ sB52−56 sB⇄🈸69−83 dB fr76
dB⇄🈸fr107 L alc D alc
★★**Holland** 7 Provenierssingel (n rest) ☎653100
24rm2⇄2 🈸 A4rm ⅅ sB43 dB73 dB⇄🈸100
🛏 ⅋ο**Dunant** 22−40 Dunantstr ☎766166 Toy (GB)
🛏 ⅋ο**Excelsior** 12 Boezemsingel ☎144644 BL (GB)
🛏 ⅋ο**Gam Rotterdam** 21−23 Smirnoffweg ☎298211
☎298211 P MB/VW (GB)
🛏 ⅋ο**Hoogenboom** 5 Geijssendorffferweg ☎298844
Aud/VW

ROZENDAAL Gelderland (☎08302) Map 4 C/D2
★★★**Roosendael** 1 Beekhuizenseweg ☎629123
Closed 17 Jul−7 Aug 16⇄ 🈸 P sB⇄🈸52−72
dB⇄88−168 (English breakfast) L30 D40
SASSENHEIM Zuid-Holland 12,734 (☎02522)
Map 4 C3
★**Bruine Paard** 241 Hoofdstr ☎11151 10rm P
sB25−30 dB50−55 L fr6 D fr15
SCHERPENZEEL Gelderland 7,750 (☎03497)
Map 4 C2
★★**Witte Holevoet** 282 Holevoetpl ☎1336 Closed
1−15 Jul 9rm4⇄2 🈸 P sB40−50 sB⇄🈸50 dB60
dB⇄🈸75 (English breakfast) L fr30 D fr50
SCHEVENIGEN See HAAG (DEN) (HAGUE, THE)
SITTARD Limburg 34,300 (☎04490) Map 4 C1
🛏 ⅋ο**Cartigny** 208−210 Rijksweg Zuid ☎5900 Sim
SLUIS Zeeland 3,150 (☎01178) Map 3 B2
★**Korensbeurs** 1 Kade ☎1402 16rm5⇄5 🈸
sB45−55 sB⇄🈸fr55 dB fr110 dB⇄🈸fr110
(English breakfast) L10 D fr28
★**Sanders de Paauw** 42 Kade ☎1224 10rm5⇄5 🈸
🏛 P sB28−30 sB⇄🈸60−70 dB55−60
dB⇄🈸70−80 English breakfast only L13−25
D25−60
SNEEK Friesland 28,150 (☎05150) Map 4 C3
★★**Wijnberg** 23 Markstr ☎12421 Closed Jul & Aug
36rm5⇄31 🈸 A13rm 🏛 P sB fr28 sB⇄🈸fr33 dB fr55
dB⇄🈸65−95 L fr8 D fr20
🛏 ⅋ο**Bonnema** 64 Stationstr ☎13175 24rm4⇄4 🈸 P
sB38−43 sB⇄🈸43 dB75−85 dB⇄🈸85−95 L8
D14−25
🛏 ⅋ο**Fritsmas** 16B Oude Koemarkt ☎12030 M/c P
Opl
🛏 ⅋ο**F Ozinga's** 16 Parkstr ☎13344 Frd (GB)
🛏 ⅋ο**H de Vries** 26 Oosterkade ☎13291 ☎13092
Ren (GB)
TEGELEN Limburg 18,400 (☎077) Map 4 D2
🛏 ⅋ο**Linssen** 139 Roermondseweg ☎31427
☎31421 ⅌ P Chy/Peu
TERNEUZEN Zeeland 33,750 (☎01150) Map 3 B2
ℹ ⅋ο**R R Visser** Parkeerterrein ☎7900 Bed/Vau
TILBURG Noord-Brabant 151,550 (☎013) Map 4 C2

Netherlands

★★Postelse Hoeve 10 Dr-Deelenlaan ☎671977
19rm7 🚿 P ⅅ sB43–48 sB⇌🚿48 dB75 dB⇌🚿80
L fr10 D fr18

🛏 🕭O **H J Groot Eerste** 78 Lage Witsiebaan ☎681916
Bed/Chy/Vau (GB)

🛏 🕪 **W A Holland** 100 Hart van Brabantlaan
☎422600 P BL/Jag/Rov/Tri

UTRECHT Utrecht 250,900 (☎030) Map **4** C2
☆☆☆☆**Holiday Inn** 24 Jaarbeurspl ☎910555
tx47745 235⇌ P Lift ⅅ sB⇌🚿120 dB⇌🚿165 English
breakfast only L10–25 D25 Pool

★★★Pays Bas 10 Janskerkhof ☎333321 tx47485
46rm12⇌9🚿 Lift

★★Hes 2 Maliestr ☎316424 tx47485 20rm9⇌10🚿 P
Lift ⅅ sB48 sB⇌🚿 🚿73–83 dB⇌🚿 95–115 L15 D25

🛏 🕭O **Arijjansen Kanaleneiland** 71 M-Pololaan
☎883520 BL/MB/Sab (GB)

🛏 🕭O **Van Meeuwen's** 42–44 Weerdsingel OZ
☎719111 Bed/Vau (GB)

🛏 🕪 **Renault** 71–73 Maliebaan ☎333435 ☎333435
Ren (GB)

🛏 🕭O **Stichtse** 128 Leidseweg ☎931744 Frd
At **Bunnik** (8km SE)
☆☆☆**Postiljon Utrecht** 8 Motorestoweg ☎(03405)
2744 tx70298 A19rm4⇌15🚿 P ⅅ sB🚿57 dB fr79
dB⇌🚿84–89 🚿

VALKENBURG Limburg 12,800 (☎04406)
Map **4** C1

★★★★Prinses Juliana 11 Broekhem ☎12244
Closed Jan 44rm14⇌20🚿 A14rm 🏛 P Lift ⅅ
sB30–48 sB⇌🚿65–70 dB60–75 dB⇌🚿85–170
L alc D alc

★★★ Grand Voncken 1 Walrampl ☎12841
54rm35⇌3🚿 Lift

★★ Bouwes Vossen 7 Nieuweweg ☎15341 Closed
Oct–Apr 28rm5🚿

🛏 **Auto-Caubo** 25–33 Oud-Valkenburgerweg
☎15041 P

🛏 🕭O **Nerum** 25 Neerhem ☎15041 P Aud/VW (GB)

🛏 **Poot** 104–106 Hoofdstr ☎16947 P BL/Rov/Tri

VEENDAM Groningen 26,200 (☎05987) Map **4** D3

🛏 🕭O **Bakker** 55B Kerkstr ☎2288 P Bed/Vau

VEENENDAAL See EDE

VEERE Zeeland 4,300 (☎01181) Map **3** B2

★Campveerse Toren 2 Kade ☎291 6rm4⇌ A10rm
P sB30–50 dB45–75 dB⇌🚿75 L30–50 D30–50 sea

VELP Gelderland 21,280 (☎08302) Map **4** D2
☆☆☆ **EuroCrest** 70 Prés-Kennedylaan ☎62910
tx45527 74rm38⇌36🚿 Lift

★★Beekhuizen 70 Beekhuizenseweg ☎619591
24rm P Lift sB40–50 (room only) dB40–50 (room
only) L fr18 D fr28

VENLO Limburg 61,700 (☎077) Map **4** D2

★★★★Bovenste Molen 12 Bovenste Molenweg
☎41045 tx58393 65⇌ P Lift ⅅ sB⇌🚿88 dB⇌🚿130 L25
D33 Pool

★★Wilhelmina 1 Kaldenkerkerweg ☎16251
tx58710 41rm25⇌7🚿 P Lift ⅅ sB40 sB⇌🚿45–50
dB⇌🚿85–114 L alc D alc

★ Deckers 44 Mgr-Nolenspl ☎16858 10rm

🛏 🕪 **AML** 53E Wezelseweg ☎96666 ☎96666 P MB
(GB)

🛏 🕭O **J Van Gorp** 10 F-Bolstr ☎16752 Cit (GB)

🛏 🕭O **L Van den Hombergh** 18 Straelseweg ☎11441
P Frd

🛏 🕭O **Nefkens & Zonen** 52 Straelseweg ☎12474 Peu

🛏 🕭O **K Peters** 30 Burg Bloemartstr ☎10455 Vlo (GB)

VENRAY Limburg 31,550 (☎04780) Map **4** C2

🛏 🕭O **Van Haren** 24 Maaheeseweg ☎5300 P Frd (GB)

VIERHOUTEN Gelderland 900 (☎05771) Map **4** C3

★★★Mallejan 70 Nunspeterweg ☎241 46rm42⇌ 🏛
P Lift ⅅ sB68 aB⇌🚿68 dB⇌🚿125–135 L fr20 D30–35
🛎 ⌂

VLAARDINGEN Zuid-Holland 78,350 (☎010)
Map **4** C2

★★★Delta 15 Maasbd ☎345477 tx23154 78⇌ P Lift
ⅅ sB⇌🚿93–113 dB⇌🚿135–155 L alc D alc Pool

VLISSINGEN (FLUSHING) Zeeland 43,850
(☎01184) Map **3** B2

★★★Britannia 44 bd Evertsen ☎13255 35⇌ P Lift
ⅅ sB⇌🚿75–95 dB⇌🚿95–115 L18 D28 sea

★★★Strand 4 bd Evertsen ☎12297 40rm10⇌30🚿
P Lift ⅅ sB33–39 sB⇌🚿53–60 sB⇌🚿99–114 D29
sea

🛏 🕭O **P Kruger** 754 Prés-Rooseveltlaan ☎12008
Chy/Sim (GB)

🛏 🕭O **Muynck's** 237 P-Krugerstr ☎19010

VOLENDAM Noord-Holland 13,950 (☎02993)
Map **4** C3

★★ Van Diepen 35 Haven ☎3705 18rm10🚿 🏛 sea

WAGENINGEN Gelderland 26,466 (☎08370)
Map **4** C2

🛈 🕪 **Van der Kolk** 21 Stationstr ☎19055 ☎19055 ⊜
P Frd (GB)

WARNSVELD Gelderland 7,100 (☎05750)
Map **4** D3

★★★Kap 166 Rijiksstraatweg ☎22873 21rm5⇌7🚿
🏛 P sB26–28 dB52–56 dB⇌🚿63–69 L1 ⌊–23
D18–35 ⌂

WASSENAAR Zuid-Holland 28,250 (☎01751)
Map **4** C3

★★Bianca 1 Gravestr ☎19206 14rm10🚿 A5rm P
sB35–55 sB🚿55 dB60 dB🚿75 D fr20

★★Duinoord 26 Wassenaarse Slag ☎12961
20rm5⇌4🚿 P sB29–31 (room only) sB⇌🚿39–44
(room only) dB52–60 (room only) dB⇌🚿65–99
(room only)

🛏 🕭O **Blankespoor** 29–31 Oostdorperweg ☎12405
BL (GB)

🛏 🕭O **Jansen** 773 Rijksstraatweg ☎79940 Aud/VW

WITTEM See GULPEN

ZAANDAM Noord-Holland 69,300 (☎075) Map **4** C3
🕪 **Hoogwout** 16 Hobbemastr ☎162337 ☎162337 P
(GB)

🛏 🕪 **Verenigde** ☎172751 ☎172751 Frd (GB)

ZANDVOORT Noord-Holland 16,300 (☎02507)
Map **4** C3

★★★★Bouwes 7 Badhuispl (DP) ☎5041 tx41096
59🚿 Lift sea

★★★Bouwes Palace 2 Burg van Fenemapl ☎5041
tx41096 85🚿 🏛 P Lift ⅅ sB🚿 fr58 dB🚿 fr115 L13
D20 Pool sea

★★Bernsen 70 Hogeweg (n rest) ☎2202 Closed 11
Sep–Mar 13rm6🚿 sB23–24 dB47–50
dB⇌🚿52–54

★Hoogland 5 Westerpaskstr ☎5541 Closed
Dec–Jan 26rm1⇌24🚿 P ⅅ sB35–45 sB⇌🚿45
dB70 dB⇌🚿85–95

ZEIST Utrecht 58,650 (☎03404) Map **4** C2

★★★Kerckebosch't 31 Arnhemse Bovenweg
☎14772 tx40827 31rm13⇌13🚿

🛏 🕭O **J J Molenaar's** 109 2E Hogweg ☎18041 P
BL/Jag Rov/Tri

🛏 **Philippo** 21–23 Laa van Cattenbroeck ☎14529
Toy (GB)

ZUTPHEN Gelderland 28,200 (☎05750) Map **4** D3

★★'s-Gravenhof Kuiperstr 11 ☎131913 Closed Sun
16rm3⇌3🚿 P sB fr35 sB⇌🚿 fr40 dB fr80
dB⇌🚿 fr100 L15 D23

🛏 🕭O **H Nijendijk** 32–34 Spittaalstr ☎15257 BL/Tri
(GB)

🛏 🕭O **Welmers** 2 H-Dunantweg ☎12537 P Fia (GB)

ZWOLLE Overijssel 77,850 (☎05200) Map **4** D3
☆☆☆**Postiljon** 1 Hertsenbergweg ☎16031 tx42180
72rm8⇌64🚿 P Lift ⅅ sB⇌🚿63–73 dB⇌🚿70–111
L10–30 D15–50

★★★Wientjes 7 Stationsweg (n rest Sun) ☎11200
tx42640 53⇌ P Lift ⅅ sB⇌🚿9 ⌊–108 dB⇌🚿135–175
L fr15 D fr25

🛏 🕪 **All Round** 7–9 Ceintuurbaan ☎42300 ☎42300
Lnc/Maz (GB)

🛏 🕭O **Autobedrijf Smit** 3 Ceintuurbaan ☎32555 Opl

🛏 🕭O **Spaay** 44 Assendorpdijk ☎13183 BL/Jag
Rov/Tri

🛏 🕭O **Vapro** Katwolderweg 28 ☎14909 Bed/Dat/Vau
(GB)

PORTUGAL

Population 8,545,120 **Area** 34,500 sq miles **Maps** 17, 18, 23 & 24

How to get there

The usual approach to Portugal is via France and Spain, entering Spain on the Biarritz to San Sebastián road at the western end of the Pyrenees. The distance from the Channel ports to Lisbon, the capital, is nearly 1,300 miles, a distance which will require three or four night stops. The driving distance can be shortened by using one of the car/sleeper services from Boulogne or Paris to Biarritz. Alternatively you can ship your vehicle to Spain by the Plymouth to Santander car ferry, then travel onwards by road. Santander to Lisbon is about 550 miles and this will require one or two night stops.

General information

Information in this section is specific to Portugal. A wider background is provided in the notes on page 8 with other information which you are advised to read.

AA Port agents   **Lisbon 2** Sociedade Comercial Garland, Laidley SARL, Travessa do Corpo Santo, 10–20, PO Box 2127 ☎363191/5.
Oporto Sociedade Comercial Garland, Laidley SARL, 131 rua Infante D Henrique, ☎27091/27095

Stay at
a pousada.
The historic inns of Portugal.

There are twenty two pousadas in Portugal. Many are ancient castles, convents and abbeys – and set in some of Portugal's most spectacular countryside.

For more information on pousada holidays, please write to the Portuguese National Tourist Office, New Bond Street House, 1, New Bond Street, London W.1. Or telephone 01-493 3873.

Portugal

These are not recommended routes:
the distances are given as a guide only.

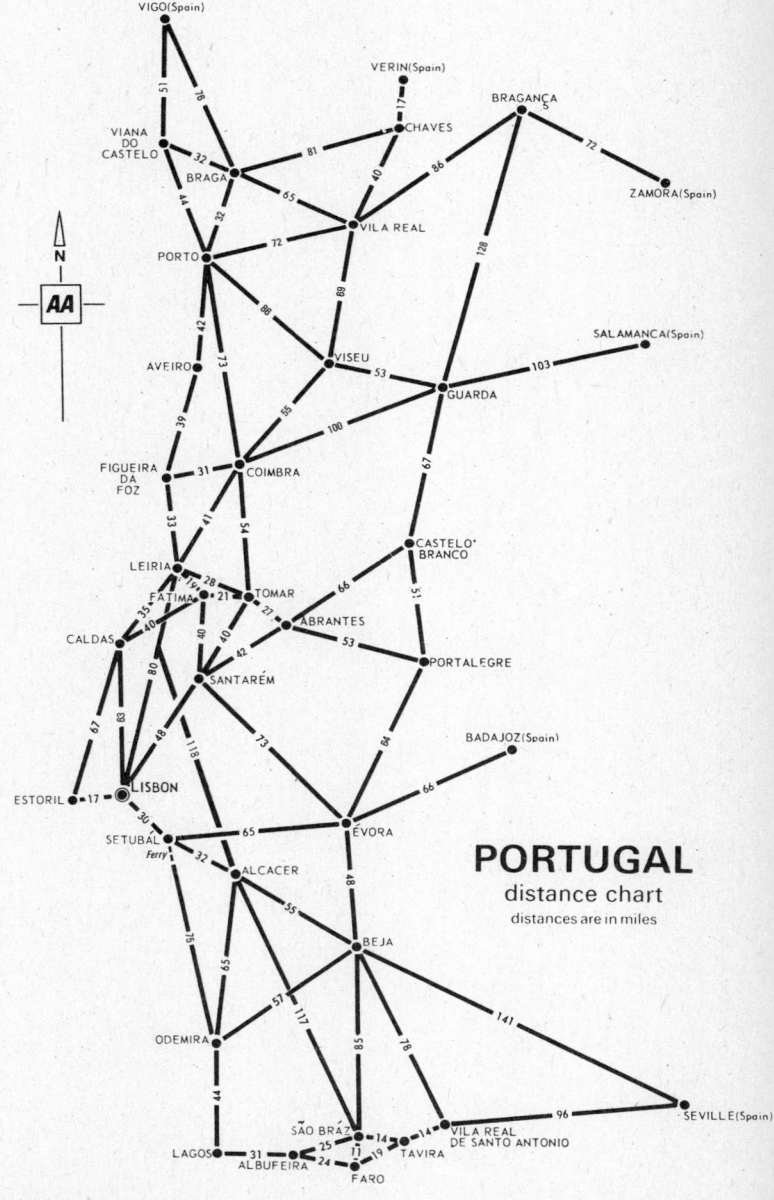

PORTUGAL
distance chart
distances are in miles

Portugal

Accommodation   A list of hotels is available from the Tourist Office in London. Hotels are officially approved and classified by the office of the Secretary of State for Information and Tourism. Details of officially authorised charges must be exhibited in the reception area, and in every bedroom. The cost of meals served in bedrooms, other than breakfast, is subject to an increase of 10%. Children under eight years of age are granted a discount of 50% on prices of meals.

While commendations and complaints about hotels are an important source of information to us, members may also like to know that an official complaints book, which must be kept in all establishments, enables guests to record their comments.

Complaints may also be made to local Tourism Delegations and Boards or to the State Tourism Department, Palácio Foz, Praça dos Restauradores, Lisbon. The Government has encouraged the building of well-equipped hotels, particularly in the Algarve region. Tourist inns known as *pousadas* and *estalagens* are controlled by the *Direcção General de Turismo*, the official Portuguese tourist organisation; details of most of these are included in the gazetteer.

Pousadas are Government-owned but privately run. They have been specially built or converted, and are often located in the more remote touring areas where there is a lack of other hotels. Visitors may not usually stay more than five nights.

Estalagens are small, well-equipped wayside inns (although there are some in towns), privately-owned and run, and normally in the one-or two-star category.

Annual events

March	**Braga** Grand religious ceremonies and processions for Holy Week
April	**Loule** Fair of Our Lady of Piety
May	**Sesimbra** Procession of Our Lord Jesus of the Wounds
June	**Santarém** Great Annual Fair at Ribatejo
	Evora Annual Fair of St John
	Lisbon Festival of Popular Saints
	Sintra Fair of St Peter and San Pedro de Penaferrim
July	**Vila Franca de Xira** Great Festival of Red Waistcoat
	Faro Fair of Our Lady of Carmo
	Covilhã Fair and Festival of St James
August	**Guimarães** Great Festival and Fair of St Walter
	Rio Caldo (Terras do Bouro) Pilgrimage of St Benedict of the Open Door
September	**Lamego** Pilgrimage of Our Lady of the Needy (Sra dos Remedios)
	Nazare Great Annual Festival of Our Lady of Nazaré
November	**Golegã** St Martin's Annual Fair (horse show)

A more comprehensive list of events can be obtained from the National Tourist Office (see page 328).

Breakdowns   If your car breaks down, try to move it to the verge of the road so that it obstructs the traffic flow as little as possible and place a warning triangle. Should you break down or need assistance on the Lisbon Tagus Bridge (on the southern approach to Lisbon), keep the vehicle as near to the right-hand side of the bridge as possible, remain in the vehicle and hang a white handkerchief out of the window. You must wait inside the vehicle until the road patrol arrives. Vehicles must not be towed, except by purpose-built vehicles, or pushed by hand on the bridge. If you run out of petrol you can buy 10 litres (2gal 1½pt) at a cost of Esc 400 from the bridge authorities.

If you require roadside assistance you should telephone the nearest breakdown centre operated by the *Automovel Club de Portugal* (ACP) who will help you but will charge for their services. AA members should produce their *5-Star Service Booklet*. The ACP operates a 24-hour breakdown service in the following locations: Lisbon ☎777354 & 775475, Coimbra ☎(0039) 26813 and Oporto ☎(02) 29271/2.

British Consulates   **Lisbon** rua São Domingos à Lapa 35/39 ☎661191, 661122, 661147. There are also British Consulates in Figuera da Foz, Oporto, Portimão, and Vila Real de S. Antonio.

Currency and banking   The unit of currency is the escudo, which is divided into 100 centavos; 1,000 escudos are known as 1 conto; one escudo is written 1$00 (with the dollar sign). One escudo fifty centavos is written 1$50.

It is prohibited to import or export more than Esc 1,000 in Portuguese currency. There is no restriction on the importation of foreign currencies or travellers' cheques, which must be declared at the Customs on entry if it exceeds Esc20,000. Amounts in excess of this figure may only be exported if they tally with the amount declared on entry.

Portugal

Banking hours	Banks are usually open from Monday to Friday 09.00–12.00hrs and 14.00–15.30hrs.

Shopping hours Shops are usually open Monday to Friday 09.00–13.00hrs and 15.00–19.00hrs and Saturday 09.00–13.00hrs. Markets are open Monday to Saturday 07.00–13.00hrs.

Documents

Insurance — It is expected that third party insurance will become compulsory during 1979. Meanwhile a Green Card is recognised and should be carried.

Nationality plate — The penalty for failure to display a nationality plate, or for displaying one of the wrong size or type, is a fine of Esc200.

Ferries All details are subject ot alteration.
Vila Real de Santo Antonio–Ayamonte (Spain)
Map 23 B2 **(Across River Guadiana)**
Service There is an hourly service from 09.00 to 20.00hrs, or when at least two cars have cleared Customs.
Additional services are available on request (double fare payable).
Duration 15 minutes
Charges

Vehicles	cars	Esc80–230	or the equivalent
Passengers		Esc9	in Spanish currency

Small river boats are used, and the loading of caravans may be difficult and complicated. Only small numbers of vehicles can be carried on each service.

Medical treatment There is no free medical treatment for visitors.

Motoring club **The Autómovel Club de Portugal** (ACP) which has its headquarters at rua Rosa Araújo 24–26, Lisbon has offices in a number of provincial towns. They will assist motoring tourists generally and supply information on touring and other matters. Some of their more specialised services may have to be paid for but if you are an AA member you should produce your *5-Star Service Booklet*.
ACP offices are normally open 09.30–12.45 and 14.30–17.00hrs Monday to Friday; English and French are spoken. Offices are closed on Saturday and Sunday but the ACP operates a 24-hour breakdown service in and around Lisbon, Coimbra and Oporto (see Breakdowns).

Post/telephone Rates for mail to the United Kingdom are:

Airmail and surface mail	Esc
Postcards	9.00
Letters 5–20gm	12.50
20–50gm	23.00
50–100gm	30.00

Post offices are open 24 hours in Lisbon at Praça dos Restaudores and at the airport, and Oporto at the Município.
The address of the *poste restante* office in Lisbon is Praça do Comércio.

Telephone rates — The cost of a 3-minute call to the UK is Esc90. A local call costs Esc1.50. Trunk services are available and there are English-speaking operators for international calls. In Lisbon and Oporto there is an automatic dialling system in use. Public call boxes are red.

Public holidays Holidays based on religious festivals are not always fixed on the calendar but any current diary will give actual dates. The Whit period (a religious holiday) should not be confused with the British Spring Holiday.

Fixed holidays		
	1 January	New Year's Day
	25 April	Day of Freedom
	1 May	Labour Day
	10 June	National Day
	13 June	St Athony's Day (Lisbon only)
	24 June	St John's Day (Oporto only)
	15 August	Assumption
	5 October	Republic Day
	1 November	All Saints' Day
	1 December	Independence Day
	8 December	Immaculate Conception
	24, 25 December	Christmas
Moveable holidays	Shrove Tuesday	
	Good Friday	
	Corpus Christi	

Portugal

Roads
Main roads and most of the important secondary roads are good, as are the mountain roads of the north-east.

Motorways
There are about 63 miles of motorway *(auto estrada)* open; more sections are under construction and 200 miles of toll motorways are planned. Most of the motorways are part of the European international network. The main stretches open to traffic are:

E3	Lisbon – Vila Franca de Xira – Carregado (toll: Esc12.50 – 17.50)	
E4	Lisbon (Tagus Bridge) – Fogueteiro – Palmela (for Setúbal) toll: Esc30 for cars; plus bridge tolls; (see below)	
E50	Porto (Oporto) bypass	

Lisbon Tagus Bridge Pedestrians, bicycles, and bicycles with auxiliary motors of less than 50cc, are prohibited. Drivers must maintain a speed of 30 – 60kph (18 – 37mph) on the bridge. Speed is checked by radar. Heavy vehicles must keep at least 20 metres (66ft) behind the preceding vehicle.

Toll bridges
River Tagus bridges *Map 23 A4*

Lisbon Tagus Bridge

	Esc
Cars	
up to 3.30 metres	10
3.30 – 4.70 metres	20
over 4.70 metres	25
Caravans/trailers	*plus* 15
Motorcycles – over 50cc	10
under 50cc not permitted	

Ponte De Vila Franca

	Cars
	7.50 Single
	12.50 Return

Winter conditions
The winter months in the northern provinces are usually rainy, but snow is rare except in the Estrela mountains.

Tourist information centres
The Portuguese National Tourist Office, 1/5 New Bond Street, London W1Y 9PE ☎01-493 3873, will be pleased to assist you with information regarding tourism. Within Portugal an office of the Dirrecção General de Turismo is in Lisbon at Palacio Foz, Praça dos Restauradores ☎363314 and local information offices will be found in most provincial towns under this name or one of the following: Comissão Municipal de Tourismo, Junta de Turismo or Câmara Municipal.

Visitors' registration
A visitor staying overnight should report to the police, but this is often done by the hotel or camp site management who complete the registration form. If you are staying with friends the host should notify the authorities.

Motoring regulations

Information in this section is specific to Portugal. A wide background is provided in the notes on page 67 with other regulations which you are advised to read.

Accidents
Fire, police and **ambulance** Public emergency service ☎115.
There are no firm rules of procedure after an accident, however, the recommendations on page 67 are advised.

Crash helmets
It is compulsory for all riders of motorcycles to wear crash helmets.

Dimensions
Private cars and trailers are restricted to the following dimensions and weights:

Cars   height 4 metres;
width 2.5 metres;

Trailers   length 12 metres; weights (unladen) 750kg (14cwt 85lb)

if the towing vehicle's engine is 2,500cc or less; 1,500kg (1ton 9cwt 59lb) for vehicles with an engine capacity in excess of 2,500cc but under 3,500cc.
Vehicle/trailer combination length 18 metres.

Drinking and driving
Although Portugal has no regulations on driving after drinking, visitors should apply the safe rule – 'If you drink – don't drive'.

Lights
Parking lights must be used in badly-lit areas and when visibility is poor. The use of headlights is prohibited in built-up areas.

Overtaking   Vehicles more than 2 metres wide must stop, if need be, to facilitate passing.

Parking   Parking is forbidden in the following places: within 20 metres (66ft) of a junction, bend, or rise with limited visibility, on a main road outside a built-up area, and within 5 metres (16½ft) of any other cross-roads or road intersection; on a main road or one carrying fast-moving traffic; on or near tram lines; opposite another stationary vehicle; within 15 metres (48½ft) of a bus stop and 3 metres (10ft) off a tram stop. At night parking is prohibited on all roads outside built-up areas.

Vehicles parked on the side of the road must be left facing in the direction of the traffic flow, except where regulations decree otherwise or where parking is allowed on only one side of the road.

Spending the night in a vehicle by the roadside is prohibited.

There are short-term parking areas known as blue zones in some towns; in these areas, parked cars must display a disc on the windscreen. Discs are set at the time of parking, and show when parking time expires according to the limit in the area concerned. They are obtainable free of charge from the local police or the motoring club. Failure to observe zonal regulations could result in a fine or the vehicle being towed away There are a few parking meters in Oporto.

Police fines   Police are empowered to impose on-the-spot fines of up to Esc1,000. The officer collecting the fine should issue an official receipt.

Speed   The beginning of a built-up area is marked by a sign bearing the placename; there are no signs showing the end – the only indication is the sign for the beginning of the area (on the other side of the road) for motorists coming from the other direction. In built-up areas the limit is 60kph (37mph), or 50kph (31mph) for vehicles towing trailers. Outside built-up areas private vehicles must not exceed 120kph (74mph) on motorways and 90kph (56mph) on other roads. Vehicles towing trailers must not exceed 70kph (43mph) outside built-up areas. There is a minimum speed limit of 40kph (24mph) on motorways, except where otherwise signposted.

Leaflets giving details in English are handed to visitors at entry points. Also see Motorways, opposite.

Warning triangles   Triangles are compulsory for all vehicles except motorcycles, mopeds, and scooters. They must be placed 30 metres (33yd) behind the obstacle and must be visible to following traffic from 100 metres (109yd).

Sines, near Lisbon.

Prices are in escudos
Abbreviations:
av   avenida
Capt   Capitão
Cdt   Comandante
esp   esplanade
r   rua

ABRANTES Santarém 9,050 Map **23** B4
★★★ *Turismo* Largo de Santo António ☎256 24⇄ 🏛
⏍ Pool lake
🏚 *J Dos Santos Bioucas* Estrada Nacional 2
☎160 P Aud/BL/MB
ALBERGARIA A VELHA Aveiro 3,620 (☎0034)
Map **17** A2
☆ *Alameda* Estrada Nacional (n rest) ☎52409 18⇄
🏛
ALBUFEIRA Faro 7,480 Map **23** A2
★★★★ *Balaia* Praia M-Luisa ☎52681 tx18298 186⇄
P Lift sB⇄1250 dB⇄1650 (English breakfast) L450
D450 ⏍ Pool Beach sea
★★★ *Sole e Mar* ☎52121 tx8217 74⇄ Lift
★★ *Estalagem do Cerro* ☎52191 50rm50⇄11 🏚 Lift
🌙 sea
★★ *Estalagem Mar à Vista* Cerro de Piedade
☎52154 42rm32⇄6🏚 Lift
ALCÁCER DO SAL Setúbal 13,190 Map **23** A3
★★ *Estalagem da Barrosinha* Estrada Nacional 5
☎62363 15rm12⇄
ALCOBAÇA Leiria 4,800 (☎0044) Map **23** A4
🏚 *Assessor* Quinta da Roda ☎42302 Aud/BL/Sab
ALIJÓ Vila Real 2,200 (☎0099) Map **17** B2
★ *Pousada Barão de Forrester* ☎62215
12rm3⇄3🏚 🏛
ALJUBARROTA Leiria 5,795 Map **17** A1
★ *Estalagem do Cruzeiro* ☎42112 13rm6⇄2🏚
A4rm 🏛
ALPEDRINHA Castelo Branco 1,410 Map **17** B1
★*Estalagem São Jorge* ☎57154 Closed Oct
11rm9⇄4🏚 sB335–450 sB⇄🏚385–500
dB470–600 dB⇄🏚520–650 (English breakfast)
L180–220 D180–220 St% mountains
AMARANTE Porto 4,000 (☎0025) Map **17** B2
At **Serro do Marão** (25km E on N15 to Vila Real)
★★ *Pousada de São Gonçalo* ☎46113 18rm14⇄ 🏛
ARMAÇÃO DE PÊRA Faro 1,790 (☎0082)
Map **23** A2
★★★ *Estalagem Algar* av Beira-Mar ☎55353
Closed Nov–Feb 18⇄
★★★ *Garbe* ☎55187 tx18285 104rm85⇄ Lift Pool
AVEIRO Aveiro 19,460 (☎0034) Map **17** A2
★★ *Arcada* r Viana do Castelo 4 ☎23001 55rm41⇄
Lift 🌙 sB fr270 sB⇄fr360 dB fr390 DB⇄fr690
🏚 🏚 *Stand Justino* Largo L-de Camões 2 ☎23593
Bed/Opl/Vau (GB)
AZEITÃO Setúbal Map **23** A3
★ *Estalagem Quintas des Torres* ☎2080001
12rm10⇄ A2rm
BARCELOS Braga 4,150 (☎0023) Map **17** A2
🏚 *Avenida* (C E Barbosa) ☎82019 P Cit/Ren
🏚 *E T Machado & Filhos* Campo 5 de Outubre 44
☎82166
BEJA Beja 19,190 (☎0079) Map **23** B3
🏚 🏚 *Stand Castilho* r G-Palma 21 ☎22591 P BL
BRAGA Braga 37,630 (☎0023) Map **17** A2
🏚 *Ranhada & Teixeira* Largo 1 de Dezembro 20,
Apartado 19 ☎22912 P Frd (GB)
BRAGANÇA Bragança 10,970 Map **18** C2
★★ *Pousada de São Bartolomeu* Estrada de
Turismo ☎22493 15rm10⇄2🏚 A5rm 🏛
BUÇACO Aveiro 3,696 (☎0031) Map **17** A1
★★★★ *Palace* ☎93101 93⇄ 🏛 Lift
CALDAS DA RAINHA Leiria 15,010 (☎0012)
Map **23** A4
★*Central* Largo do Dr-J- Barbosa 22 ☎22078
40rm7⇄7🏚 🌙 sB260 sB⇄🏚430 dB425 dB⇄🏚645
(English breakfast)

🏚 🏚 *Auto Mecanica* r Tenente Cl-Santos Costa 22
☎22947 BL/Cit/ MB
🚙 🏚 *A Flores* r Heróis da Grande Guerra 104
☎23011 P AR/Hon/Peu/Ren
🏚 *Leira* r Capt F-de-Sousa ☎22561 Frd
CANAS DE SENHORIM Viseu 2,075 (☎0032)
Map **17** B1
At **Urgeiriça** (1km NE on N234)
★★★ *Urgeiriça* ☎67267 76rm54⇄5🏚 A17rm P 🌙
sB290–300 SB⇄🏚450–600 dB450
dB⇄🏚600–750 L200 D200 ⏍ Pool 🕉 mountains
CARAMULO Viseu (☎0032) Map **17** A1
★ *Estalagem de São Jerónimo* ☎86291 6⇄ 🏛
CARCAVELOS Lisboa 7,300 Map **23** A4
★★ *Estalagem Rota do Sol* r Jorge-V ☎2470152
15rm6⇄6🏚
CASCAIS Lisboa 20,540 Map **23** A4
★★★★ *Estoril Sol* Estrada Marginal ☎282831
tx12624 404⇄ 🏛 P Lift 🌙 sB⇄900–1100
dB⇄🏚1600–2100 (English breakfast) L320 D320 Pool
🕉 sea
★★★ *Baia* Estrada Marginal ☎281033 59⇄ 🏛 Lift
sea
★★★ *Estalagem Albatroz* r F-Aronca 100–102
☎282821 16rm15⇄1🏚 A5rm P Lift 🌙
sB⇄🏚570–630 dB⇄🏚810–900
(English breakfast) L alc D alc sea
★★★ *Nau* r Dr-I-Doyle Lote 14 ☎282861 60⇄ Lift 🌙
sB⇄260–645 dB⇄420–700 (English breakfast) sea
★★ *Estalagem Solar do Carlos* r Latino Coelho 8
☎280961 9rm6⇄
🚙 🏚 *Auto Rali* av J-F-Ulrich ☎2868431 Frd (GB)
🏚 *Reparadora de Cascais* r das Amendoeiras-Torre
☎289045 BL (GB)
At **Praia do Guincho** (4km W)
★★★★ *Guincho* ☎2850491 36⇄ 🏛 Lift ⏍ Beach
sea
★★ *Estalagem Muchaxo* ☎2850221 24⇄ Pool
Beach sea
★★ *Estalagem Mar do Guincho* ☎2850251 13⇄ P
dB⇄580–710 (English breakfast) L180 D180 sea
CASTELO BRANCO Castelo Branco 21,730
Map **17** B1
🚙 *Mocambicana* Estrada da Cruz de Montalvão
☎1310 P Chy/Sim
🏚 🏚 *S Cristóvão* av Ml-Carmona 74–80 ☎283 P
Fia/MB (GB)
CASTELO DO BODE See **TOMAR**
CASTELO DE VIDE Portalegre 3,420 (☎0045)
Map **23** B4
★★ *Estalagem de São Paulo* ☎111 43⇄ 🏛
CHAVES Vila Real 11,470 (☎0091) Map **17** B2
★★ *Estalagem Santiago* r do Olival (n rest) ☎22545
31⇄
🏚 *Auto Mecânica de Chaves* r do Sabueeiro
☎22485 P BL
COIMBRA Coimbra 24,350 (☎0039) Map **17** A1
★★★ *Bragança* Largo das Ameias 10 ☎22171
taBrazanzotel 83rm57⇄26🏚 Lift
🏚 *Auto Garagem de Coimbra* Largo das Ameias 11
☎22038 P Frd
🏚 *Carvalho & Sobrinho* r M-Almeida e Sousa
☎27071 Ren
🚙 *S José* av F-de Magalhaes 216 ☎25578 P
BL/Tri
COLARES Sintra 5,500 Map **23** A4
★ *Estalagem do Conde* Quinta do Conde ☎2991652
11⇄🏚 P sB⇄🏚400–550 dB⇄🏚600–700
(English breakfast) L fr220 D fr220 sea mountains
At **Praia das Maçãs** (4km NW by N375)
★★★ *Miramonte* ☎2991230 taClaygate 90⇄ P 🌙
sB⇄620 dB⇄720 (English breakfast) L200 D200
Pool mountains
COSTA DA CAPARICA Setúbal 2,660 Map **23** A4
★★ *Estalagem Colobri* ☎3200776 25⇄🏚 Lift
★★ *Estalagem Rosa dos Ventos* r Dr-C-Freire
☎2400303 taRosaventes Closed Nov–Apr
27rm20⇄7🏚

COVILHĂ Castelo Branco 25,280 (☎0059)
Map **17** B1
&🅓**J Valente & Imãos** r Rui Faleira 37–39 ☎22746 P
Frd (GB)

CURIA Aveiro 2,810 (☎0031) Map **17** A1
★★★**Palace** ☎52131 Closed 16 Oct–Apr
225rm90⇌ 🏛 Lift 🛥 Pool

ELVAS Portalegre 14,550 Map **23** B3
★★**Estalagem D Sancho II** Praça da República 20
☎22686 24rm Lift
★**Pousade de Santa Luzia** (outside the walls of
Elvas on the main road from Borba to Badajaz).
☎22194 11rm P ♪ sB440 dB500 L270 D270
🛈 &🅓**Autunes & Guerra** av Badajoz ☎22341 M/c P
Bed/Opl/Vau

ERICEIRA Lisboa 2,570 Map **23** A4
★★**Estalagem Morais** r M-Bombarda 3 ☎54611
40rm21⇌19🕮 Lift Pool sea

ESPINHO Aveiro 11,640 (☎02) Map **17** A2
★★★**Praia Golfe** ☎920630 119⇌ 🏛 Lift Pool 🕈 sea

ESPOSENDE Braga 1,530 (☎0023) Map **17** A2
★★**Suave Mar** av E-Duarte Pacheco ☎89445
46rm33⇌13🕮 P ♪ sB310–450 sB⇌🕮400–500
dB440–510 dB⇌🕮500–770 L200 D200 🛥 Pool sea

ESTORIL Lisboa 15,740 Map **23** A4
★★★★★**Palacio** ☎260400 tx12757 170⇌ Lift Pool
🕈 sea
★★★★**Cibra** Estrada Marginal ☎2681811 89rm89⇌
A11rm P lift ♪ sB⇌680–705 dB⇌1000–1050
(English breakfast) L250 D250 sea
★★★**Estalagem Claridade** r Mouzinho de
Albuquerque 14 ☎2683434 10rm10⇌1🕮
dB⇌🕮780 (English breakfast) L180 D180
★★★**Estalagem Lennox Country Club** r Infante de
Sagres 5 (DP & Pn) ☎2680424 tx16470 17⇌ P Lift
sB⇌765–1350 dB⇌1530–2700 (English breakfast)
L275–300 d300–350 Pool sea
★★**Founder's Inn** (Albergaria do Fundador)
r D A-Henriques 11 ☎2682221 12⇌🕮 sB⇌🕮550
dB⇌🕮800 L80 D100 sea
At **Monte-Estoril**
★★★**Atlântico** Estrada Marginal ☎2680270 101⇌
🏛 Lift Pool sea
★★★**Grande** av Sabória ☎2684609 73rm67⇌6🕮
Lift 🛥 Pool sea
★★★**Miramar** r da Pinheiro 1 ☎2684050
49rm45⇌4🕮 P Lift ♪ sB⇌🕮330–380
dB⇌🕮450–570 (English breakfast) L200 D200 Pool
sea mountains
🅓 **Gomes** Largo de Ostende 4 ☎2680021 BL

ESTREMOZ Évora 9,570 Map **23** B3
★★★**Pousada da Rainha Santa Isabel** Castelo de
Estremoz ☎22618 23⇌ Lift

ÉVORA Évora 35,410 (☎0069) Map **23** B3
★★★★**Pousada Dos Lóios** ☎24051 29rm28⇌
★★★**Planicie** r M-Bombarda 40 ☎24026 33⇌ Lift
sea
🅓 &🅓**Lagril** r Dr-A-José de Almeida 5 ☎22083
Chy/Sim

FARO Faro 21,580 (☎0089) Map **23** A/B2
★★★★**Eva** av da República ☎24054 tx18224
150rm150⇌26🕮 P Lift ♪ sB⇌🕮540–1190
dB⇌🕮870–1270 (English breakfast) L fr300 D fr300
Pool sea
★★★**Faro** Praça D-F-Gomes 2 ☎22076
52rm36⇌16🕮 P Lift ♪ sB365–690 sB⇌🕮405–755
dB515–785 dB⇌🕮555–925 (English breakfast)
L200–300 D200–300 sea
★★**Albacor** r Brites de Almeida 25 ☎22093
38rm38⇌2🕮 Lift ♪ sB⇌🕮420–550
dB⇌🕮560–720
🅓 &🅓**Auto-Gharb** r do Alportel 121A ☎23071 Cit (GB)
🅓 &🅓**Farauto** Largo do Mercado 51 ☎23032 M/c
Bed/Opl/Vau (GB)
🅓 &🅓**Monumental** r D-João de Castro 4–6 ☎26406 P
Chy/Sim

🅓 &🅓**H D Santos** r dos Bombeiros Portugueses 13
☎24330 BL/Tri
🅓 &🅓**UTIC** r Dr-Francisco de Sousa Vaz ☎24936 Ren
At **Praia de Faro** (8km SW)
★★**Estalagem Aeromar** ☎23542 Closed Dec & Jan
20⇌

FÁTIMA Santarém 6,430 (☎0049) Map **17** A1
★★★**Fátima** ☎97751 76⇌ P Lift ♪ sB⇌555
dB⇌860 L200 D200
★★**Estalagem Os Três Pastorinhas** Cova da Iria
☎97629 92⇌ 🏛 P Lift ♪ sB⇌395–460
dB⇌670–740 L fr180 D fr180

FIGUEIRA DA FOZ Coimbra 14,560 (☎0033)
Map **17** A1
★★★★**Figueira** av Dr-O-Salazar ☎22146
110rm54⇌56🕮 Lift sea
★★**Portugal** r da Liberdade 41 (n rest) ☎22176
Closed Oct–Jun 50rm15⇌15🕮 🏛

FOZ DO ARELHO Leiria 650 (☎0012) Map **23** A4
★★**Facho** ☎97110 45rm25⇌ 🏛 lake

FUNDÃO Castelo Branco 5,080 (☎0059) Map **17** B1
★★**Estalagem da Neve** r de São Sebastião ☎52215
12rm9⇌
🅓 &🅓**Maful** r A-Pinto ☎52372 P BL/Toy

GUARDA Guarda 14,590 Map **17** B1
★★★**Turismo** Largo de São Francisco ☎22206
110⇌ 🏛 P Lift ♪ sB⇌435–525 dB⇌700–810 L alc
D alc Pool mountains
★★**Aliança** r V-da-Gama ☎22135 6rm16⇌ A10rm
★★**Filipe** r V-da-Gama 9 ☎22659 32rm8⇌4🕮 Lift ♪
sB250–285 sB⇌🕮300–500 dB380–440
dB⇌🕮550–790 L fr165 D fr165 mountains
🅓 &🅓**Auto Neofar** r D-Luis I 20–22 ☎22957 M/c P
Frd (GB)
🅓 &🅓**J Carvalho dos Santos** Largo Serpa Pinto 13
☎21121 M/c P BMW/VW (GB)
&🅓**Graca Morais** r Vasco da Gama ☎22259 P
Chy/Hon/Maz Ren/Sim

LAGOS Faro 10,360 (☎0082) Map **23** A2
★★★**Meja Prajor** (DP) ☎62001 tx18289 65⇌ Lift 🛥
Pool Beach ◯ sea
★★★**São Cristóvão** Praço D-João II ☎63051 80⇌
Lift lake
★★**Residential Mar Azul** (n rest) ☎62181 17rm14⇌
♪ sB fr220 sB⇌fr390 dB fr340 dB⇌fr450 sea
★★**Pensão Dona Ana** Praia de Dona Ana ☎62322
Closed Nov–Mar 11rm5⇌

LAMEGO Viseu 10,350 (☎0032) Map **17** B2
🅓 &🅓**Calauto** r D-João da Silva Campos Neves
☎62445 P BL (GB)

LECA DO BALIO Porto Map **17** A2
★★★**Estalagem Via Norte** Estrada via Norte
☎9480294 12⇌ 🏛 P ♪ sB⇌🕮775 dB⇌🕮1250
L225 D225 Pool

LEIRIA Leiria 10,290 (☎0044) Map **17** A1
★★★**Euro-Sol** r Dr-J-Alves da Silva ☎24101 54⇌ 🏛
P Lift ♪ 🕮fr560 dB⇌🕮870 (English breakfast)
L fr225 D fr225 Pool mountains
★★**Estalagem Claras** av Heróis de Angola ☎22373
11⇌
★**Central** r V-da-Gama 5 ☎22442 41⇌
🅓 &🅓**Auto Industrial** r Capt-Mouzinho de
Albuquerque ☎24061 Bed/Opl/Vau (GB)
🅓 &🅓**Auto-Leiria** av dos Combatentes ☎24191 Frd

LISBOA (LISBON) Lisboa 782,270 Map **23** A4 **See
Plan overleaf**
[AA] agents; see page 323
★★★★★**Ritz** r R-da Fonseca ☎684131 tx12589
Plan **1** 306⇌ 🏛 P Lift ♪ sB⇌1662–2438
dB⇌2172–2930 (English breakfast) L alc D alc
★★★★**Avenida Palace** r de Dezembro 123 ☎30154
tx1815 Plan **2** 95⇌ Lift
★★★★**Eduardo VII** av Fontes Pereira de Mello 5
☎530141 taEduardotel Plan **3** 100⇌ Lift

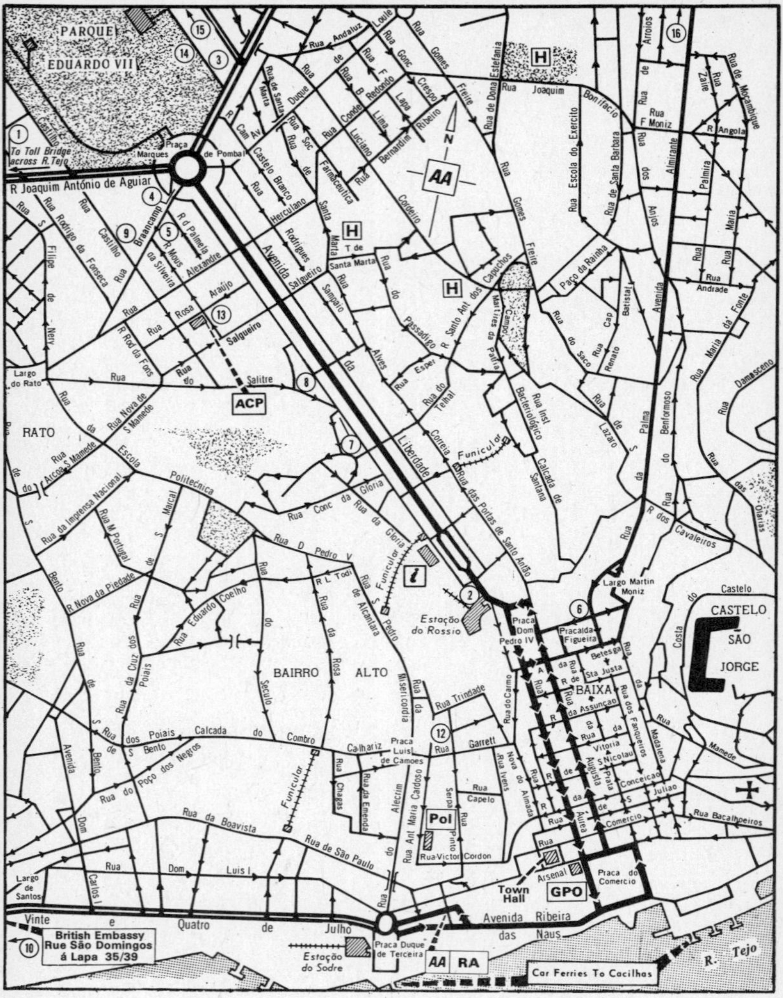

Portugal

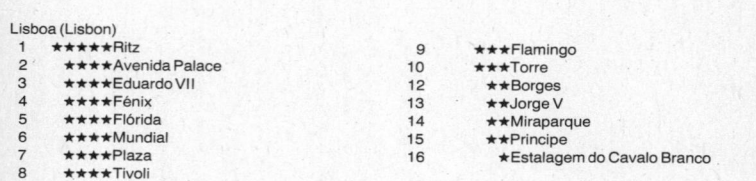

Lisboa (Lisbon)

1	★★★★★Ritz		9	★★★Flamingo
2	★★★★Avenida Palace		10	★★★Torre
3	★★★★Eduardo VII		12	★★Borges
4	★★★★Fénix		13	★★Jorge V
5	★★★★Flórida		14	★★Miraparque
6	★★★★Mundial		15	★★Principe
7	★★★★Plaza		16	★Estalagem do Cavalo Branco
8	★★★★Tivoli			

★★★★*Fénix* Praça Marquês de Pombal 8 ☎535121
ta Hausa tx1170 Plan **4** 125 Lift
★★★★*Flórida* r Duque de Palmela 32 ☎576145
tx12256 Plan **5** 108 P Lift ♪ sB 864 – 1042
dB 1197 – 1463 (English breakfast) L332 D332
★★★★*Mundial* r D-Duarte 4 ☎863101 tx12308
Plan **6** 146 P Lift ♪ dB 665 – 931
(English breakfast) L266 D266
★★★★*Plaza* Travessa do Salitre 7 (off av da
Liberdade) ☎33922 taCondotel tx16402 Plan **7**
100 P Lift ♪ sB 1330 dB 1552
(English breakfast) L332 D332

★★★★**Tivoli** av da Liberdade 185 ☎530181 tx12588 Plan 8 344⇄🍴 🎱 P Lift 🌙 sB⇄🛏1055 dB⇄🛏1375 (English breakfast) L240 D240

★★★**Flamingo** r Castilho 41 ☎53291 Plan 9 35⇄🍴 P Lift 🌙 sB⇄🛏525–700 dB⇄🛏810–1010 (English breakfast) L240 D240

★★★**Torre** r dos Jeronimos 8 ☎636262 Plan 10 52⇄ Lift

★★**Borges** r Garrett 108 ☎361951 Plan 12 105rm55⇄50 🛏 P Lift 🌙 sB⇄🛏475–635 dB⇄🛏570–870 (English breakfast) L fr200 D fr200

★★**Jorge V** r Mouzinho da Silveira 3 (n rest) ☎562525 taAvrotel Plan 13 49⇄🍴 P Lift 🌙 sB⇄515 dB⇄780

★★**Miraparque** av Sidónio Pais 12 ☎578070 tx16745 Plan 14 100⇄ Lift 🌙 sB⇄360–560 dB⇄670–820 (English breakfast) L fr200 D fr200

★★**Principe** av Duque d'Ávila 199 ☎536151 Plan 15 54⇄ Lift

★**Estalagem do Cavalo Branco** av A-Gago Continho 146 ☎726121 Plan 16 24⇄

🛅 🕭**A M Almeida Comercio Industria** r A-da Silva, Portela da Ajuda ☎681738 BL (GB)

🛅 🕭**Angolana** r Visconde Seabria 10A ☎770425 M/c P

🚲 🕭**Conde Barão** av 24-Julho 62, Arpartado 2734 ☎671011 M/c P (Lucas Apont) (GB)

🕭**J J Goncalves** r A-Patricio 11E ☎767095 BL/Jag/ ˙ri

🛅 🕭**J J Conçalves** r das Laranjeiras 12 ☎782071 BL

🕭**Martins e Almeida** av Visconte Valmor 70A ☎773871 Jag

🛅 🕭**J Mendes Coelho** r G-Freire 5A–F ☎539801 Frd (GB)

🛅 🕭**Sovendo** r Cova da Mourva 2 ☎607116 Cit (GB)

LUSO Aveiro 2,480 (☎0031) Map **17** A1

★★★★**Termas** ☎93450 taBanhos Closed 16 Oct–Apr 157rm81⇄76🛏 Lift 🌙 sB⇄🛏345–525 dB⇄🛏505–810 L240 D240 🏊 Pool mountains

★★**Estalagem do Luso** r Dr-L-Pais Almoches ☎93114 8⇄ 🏊

MACEDO DE CAVALEIROS Bragança 3,240 Map **17** B2

★**Estalagem Caçador** Largo Pinto de Azevedo ☎56 21rm6⇄ sB355 sB⇄500 dB570 dB⇄880 L185 D185

MANGUALDE Viseu 4,840 (☎0032) Map **17** B1

★★**Estalagem Cruz de Mata** Estrada Nacìonal ☎62556 12⇄

MONTE ESTORIL See **ESTORIL**

MONTE GORDO Faro Map **23** B2

★★★**Das Caravelas** r ☎460 tx18220 87⇄ P Lift 🌙 sB⇄450–650 dB⇄750–900 (English breakfast) L240–300 D240–300 🏊 Pool Beach sea

★★★**Dos Navegadores** r Goncalso Velho ☎2490 tx18254 104⇄ Lift 🏊 Pool

★★★**Vasco da Gama** r ☎321 tx18220 200⇄ P Lift 🌙 sB⇄🛏460–830 dB⇄🛏620–1160 (English breakfast) L285–350 D285–350 🏊 Pool Beach sea mountains

MONTES DE ALVOR See **PORTIMÃO**

NAZARÉ Leiria 8,550 Map **17** A1

★★★**Dom Fuas** Estrada da Foz ☎46396 40⇄ Lift 🌙 dB⇄🛏740–900 (English breakfast) L fr200 D fr200 sea

★★★**Nazaré** Largo A-Zuquete ☎46311 tx16116 50rm P Lift 🌙 sB525 dB810 (English breakfast) L fr240 D fr240 sea

★★★**Praia** av V-Guimarães 39 ☎46423 40⇄ Lift sea

ÓBIDOS Leiria 4,720 (☎0012) Map **23** A4

★★**Estalagem do Convento** r Dr-j-de-Ornelas ☎95217 13⇄

★**Pousada do Castelo** (on the Caldas da Rainha-Torres Vedras–Lisbon Road) ☎95105 6rm3⇄

OEIRAS Lisboa 14,880 Map **23** A4

☆☆**Continental** Estrada Marginal ☎2431186 tx12669 140⇄ 🎱 Pool Beach sea

OFIR Braga (☎0023) Map **17** A2

★★★**Estalagem do Parque do Rio** ☎89521 Closed Nov–Mar 36rm30⇄6🛏 Lift 🏊 Pool

★★★**Pinhal** Estrado do Mar ☎89473 100⇄ Lift 🏊 Pool lake

OLHÃO Faro 10,830 (☎0089) Map **23** B2

★**Caique** r Dr-O-Salazar 37 ☎72167 40⇄🎱

OLIVEIRA DO HOSPITAL Coimbra 2,260 Map **17** B1

★★**Pousada Santa Barbara** ☎52252 18rm16⇄2🛏 P 🌙 sB⇄🛏550–600 dB⇄🛏700–750 (English breakfast) L220–275 D220–275 mountains

OPORTO See **PORTO**

PAREDES Porto Map **17** A2

🕭**Ruzo Estacão de Servicio e Sorcar** ☎22164 P BL/Fia/Sim

PENAFIEL Porto Map **17** B2

🛅 🕭**Central de Penafiel** av de J-Júlio 213 ☎22071 P VW

🕭**Sameiro** r da Vista Alegre ☎22241 P BL

PENICHE Leiria 12,500 Map **23** A4

🛅 🕭**Patricio** av DR-A-O-Salazar 14 ☎99233 P BL (GB)

PORTALEGRE Portalegre 13,140 Map **23** B4

★**Alto Alentejo** r 19 de Junho 59 ☎330 23rm4⇄4🛏 A8rm

🚲 🕭**Auto Portalegre** r 1 de Maio 94 ☎167 M/c P Frd (GB)

🛅 🕭**Rodrigues & Figueira** av Frei Amador Arrais Lote 2 ☎1072 AR/Bed/Hon Opl/Peu/Vau (GB)

PORTIMÃO Faro 18,210 (☎0082) Map **23** A2

★★★★**Alvor Praia** Praia dos Três Irmãos (5km SW) ☎24020 tx18299 241⇄🛏 🎱 P Lift 🌙 sB⇄🛏978–1190 dB⇄🛏1488–1828 (English breakfast) L595 D595 🏊 Pool sea

★★**Estalagem Miradeiro** r Machado Santos ☎23011 30⇄

★**Estalagem Mira-Fola** r V-Vaz das Vacas 33 ☎22011 25rm13⇄ Lift

🛅 🕭**Anibal as Gloria** Avenida 3 ☎22337 P Ren (GB)

🛅 🕭**Farauto** r D-Carlos 1 ☎23083 Bed/Opl/Vau (GB)

🛅 🕭**Pardal e Antónia** r D-Carlos 1 ☎23227 P Chy/Sim

🕭**Porti Pepar Automoveis Portimao** av D-Alfonso Henriques ☎22228 P Cit/VW (GB)

At **Montes de Alvor** (5km W on N 125)

★★★★**Penina Golf** ☎22051 tx18207 214⇄ 🎱 P Lift 🌙 sB⇄🛏1100–1828 dB⇄🛏1360–2720 (English breakfast) L468 D468 🏊 Pool lake

PORTO (OPORTO) Porto 310,440 (☎02) Map **17** A2

★★★★**Infante de Sagres** Praça Filipa de Lencustre 62 (off av dos Aliados) ☎28101 tx22378 🎱 Lift 🌙 sB⇄fr 1255 dB⇄fr 1700 (English breakfast) L fr300 D fr300

★★★**Grande da Batalha** Praça de Batalha 116 ☎20571 tx25131 147rm70⇄72🛏 Lift

★★★**Grand do Porto** r da Santa Catarina 197 ☎28176 tx22553 100rm95⇄5🛏 P Lift 🌙 sB⇄🛏475–550 dB⇄🛏600–650 L200–240 D200–240

★★★★**Império** Praça da Batalha 130 (Off R São Ildefoso) ☎26861 100⇄ 🎱 P Lift 🌙

🛅 🕭**A M Almeida** r Costa Cabral 954 ☎495045 BL/Rov

🕭**Filinto Mota** r do Godim 777 ☎562202 Cit

🛅 🕭**M A de Freitas** r de Heróismo 291 ☎54155 P Frd (GB)

🛅 🕭**J J Gonçalves** r do Heróismo 333 ☎53179 BL (GB)

🛅 🕭**Moto Meca** r M-Pinto de Azevedo 574 ☎63066 Bed/Opl/Vau (GB)

🚲 🕭**Palhinhas** Camp Lindo 328 ☎485185 P Cit

🛅 🕭**Stock** r de Sta Catarina 1891–1899 ☎488785 Maz

PRAIA DA ROCHA Faro 2,085 (☎0082) Map **23** A2

★★★★**Algarve** ☎24001 tx18247 163⇄ P Lift 🌙

Portugal

sB⇄ ⏹fr931 dB⇄ ⏹fr1286 L465 D465 ✎ Pool sea
★★★*Estalagem Mira Sol* ☎24046 38⇄
★★*Bela Vista* ☎24055 27⇄ Lift
★★*Estalagem Alcala* ☎24062 20⇄ sea
★★★*Estalagem São José* ☎24037 25rm25⇄ A14rm
P ♪ sB⇄275–560 dB⇄740–870 L160–200
D160–200 sea mountains
PRAIA DA SALEMA Faro (☎0082) Map **23** A2
★★*Estalagem Infante do Mar* ☎65137 30⇄ Pool
PRAIA DAS MAÇÃS See **COLARES**
PRAIA DE FARO See **FARO**
PRAIA DE SANTA CRUZ Lisboa (☎0011)
Map **23** A4
★★*Estalagem de Santa Cruz* r J-P-Lopes ☎8 32⇄
Lift sea
PRAIA DO GUINCHO See **CASCAIS**
RIBA DE AVE Braga 2,800 Map **17** A2
★*Estalagem de São Pedro* av da Fábrica ☎38
9rm1⇄
RIO DE MOURO Lisboa 10,410 Map **23** A4
★★*Estalagem Gruta do Rio* av Gago Coutinho 1–3
☎2960535 6rm3⇄3 ⏹ 🏠 lake
SAGRES Faro 1,200 (☎0082) Map **23** A2
★★*Estalagem Descobertas* Estrada Marginal
☎64251 17⇄
★★*Baleeira* ☎64212 tx18267 114⇄ ⏹ P ♪
sB⇄ ⏹275–545 dB⇄ ⏹420–840
(English breakfast) L240 D240 Pool sea
★★*Pousada do Infante* Ponta da Atalaia ☎64222
15⇄ P ♪ sB⇄550–650 dB⇄700–1100
L210–275 D210–275 Beach sea
SANTA CLARA-A-VELHA Beja 2,570 Map **23** A2
★★*Pousada de Santa Clara* Barragem Marcella
Caetrano ☎52250 6⇄ lake
SANTA LUZIA See **VIANNA DO CASTELO**
SANTARÉM Santarém 20,030 (☎0043) Map **23** A4
★★*Abidis* r Guilherme de Azevedo 4 ☎22017
28rm6⇄
SANTIAGO DO CACÉM Setúbal 5,890 (☎0017)
Map **23** A3
★*Pousada de São Tiago* estrada National (on main
rd on descent into town) ☎22459 4rm4⇄ A3rm P ♪
sB490–540 sB⇄540–590 dB730 dB⇄730
(English breakfast) L275 D275 Pool
SÃO BRAS DE ALPORTEL Faro 7,600 Map **23** B2
★*Pousada de São Bras* (in Serra da Caldeirão, on
main rd 5km N) ☎42305 16⇄ ⏹ P sB⇄ ⏹500–700
dB⇄ ⏹620–820 (English breakfast) L200–270
D200–270 mountains
SERÉM Aveiro 1,108 Map **17** A2
★★*Pousada de Santo Antonio* Mourisca do Vouga
☎52230 12⇄ ⏹ Pool
SERPA Beja 7,990 (☎0079) Map **23** B3
★★*Pousada de Sao Gens* ☎52327 18rm12⇄18 ⏹
P sB⇄490–655 sB⇄ ⏹490–655 dB⇄ ⏹560–740
L185–250 D185–250
SERRA DO MARÃO See **AMARANTE**
SESIMBRA Setúbal 16,610 Map **23** A3
★★★★*Do Mar* ☎2233326 tx13883 119⇄ P Lift ♪
(English breakfast) Pool sea
★★★★*Espadarte* Esplanada do Atlantico
☎2233189 80⇄ Lift ♪ dB⇄ ⏹505–565
dB⇄ ⏹810–910 L240 D240 sea
★★*Náutico* r Biarro Infante D-Henrique (n rest)
☎2233233 15⇄ A3rm sea
SETÚBAL Setúbal 58,580 (☎04) Map **23** A3
★★★★*Esperancea* av L-Todi 220 ☎25151
76rm54⇄23 ⏹ Lift sea
★★*Pousada de São Filipe* ☎23844 15⇄ sea
ⓘ 🛇*Bocage* av Portela 43 ☎23169 BL (GB)
🛇*Gemoraute* Estrada da Graca 222 ☎29012 M/c P
Bed/Opl/Vau (GB)
🛢 *A Marquês dos Santos* av Combatentes da
Grande Guerra 81 ☎23131 M/c Frd (GB)
SINES Setúbal 7,000 (☎0017) Map **23** A3
★★★*Malhada* r do Farol ☎62105 37⇄

SINTRA Lisboa 15,990 Map **23** A4
★★★★*Palácio de Seteais* r B do Bocage 8
☎2933220 18rm⇄ ⏹ P Lift ♪ sB⇄ ⏹1275–1400
dB⇄ ⏹1725–1900 (English breakfast) L350 D350
★★*Estalagem da Raposa* r Dr-Alfredo Costa 3
☎2930465 8rm6⇄
TAVIRA Faro 10,260 (☎0081) Map **23** B2
★★★*Eurotel– Tavira* Quinta das Oliveiras ☎22041
tx12546 80⇄ Lift ✎ Pool ◯ sea
TOMAR Santarém 16,470 (☎0049) Map **23** B4
★★*Estalagem de Santa Iria* Parque do Mouchão
☎32427 10rm7⇄
At **Castelo do Bode**
★*Pousada São Pedro* ☎38159 17⇄ Pool ◯ lake
TORRES VEDRAS Lisboa 14,830 (☎0011)
Map **23** A4
🛢 🛇*Atlântica* r Santos Bernardes 21 ☎22155 P
Aud/BL/MB/VW
ⓘ 🛇*Foroeste* Parque do Choupal ☎23115 Frd (GB)
ⓘ 🛇*Torreense* Praça do Imperio ☎22021 M/c P
Chy/VW
UGEIRIÇA See **CANAS DE SENHORIM**

VALE DO LOBO Faro (☎0089) Map **23** A2
★★★★*Dona Filipa* ☎94141 tx18248 129⇄ P Lift ♪
Pool Beach 🔥 ◯
VALENÇA Viano do Castelo 1,810 (☎0021)
Map **17** A3
★★*Pousada de São Teotónio* ☎22252 16⇄ ⏹
A4rm 🏠 P sB⇄ ⏹550–600 dB⇄ ⏹700–750
L210–275 D210–275 mountains
VIANA DO CASTELO Viano do Castelo 13,780
(☎0028) Map **17** A3
★★★★*Parque* Azenhas do D-Prior ☎24151 120⇄ P
Lift ♪ dB⇄ ⏹690–1090 L fr250 D fr250 ✎ Pool sea
mountains
★★*Aliança* ☎23002 40rm15⇄ sea
★★*Rali* av Alfonso III ☎22176 39⇄ Lift ✎ Pool ◯
🛢 🛇*Auto-Vianense* av Camões 25–27 ☎22092
Chy/VW (GB)
🛢 🛇*S.A.* r de Aveiro 156 ☎22749 P BL/Tri
At **Santa Luzia** (2km NW; also funicular connection)
★★★*Santa Luzia* ☎22192 48⇄ 🏠 Lift ✎ Pool sea
VILA DE FEIRA Aveiro 5,220 (☎0026) Map **17** A2
★★*Estalagem de Santa Maria* r dos Condes de
Feijo ☎96130 18rm8⇄ lake
VILA DO CONDE Porto 15,870 (☎0022) Map **17** A2
★★*Estalagem do Brasão* r J-M de Melo ☎64016
24⇄ P ♪ sB⇄290–400 dB⇄460–650 (English
breakfast) L120–160 D120–160 ✎ ◯
ⓘ 🛇*J Félix & Filhos* r 5 de Outubro ☎63328 P
AR/BL/Hon/Opl (GB)
VILA FRANCA DE XIRA Lisboa 16,280 (☎0013)
Map **23** A4
★*Estalagem do Gado Bravo* Estrada do Cabo
☎324 8rm5⇄
★*Estalagem Leziria* r Palha Blanco ☎129 20rm6⇄
lake
🛢 🛇*G Cunha* Praceta da Justica 19–20 ☎22529 BL
VILA REAL Vila Real 13,250 (⇄0099) Map **17** B2
★★*Tocaio* av Carvalho Araujo 45 ☎23106 52⇄ 🏠
Lift
🛢 *Correira, Silva & Pureza* Timpeira ☎23108
Chy/Sim
🛢 🛇*C Sousa & Camilo* Praço Diago Cão ☎23035
Cit (GB)
VISEU Viseu 19,530 (☎0032) Map **17** B2
★★★*Grão Vasco* ☎23511 90⇄ ⏹ P Lift ♪
sB⇄ ⏹530–650 dB⇄ ⏹840–1030 L alc D alc Pool
🛢 🛇*Gavis* av Emidio Navarro ☎23725 P
BMW/Maz/VW
Guedes & Filhos r 5 de Outubro 79 ☎23905 M/c P
Chy/Sim
ⓘ 🛇*Lopes* r da Paz 21 ☎23561 P Frd (GB)
ⓘ 🛇*Lopes & Figueiredo* av da Belgica ☎25151 M/c
P BL/Fia/Tri

SPAIN & ANDORRA

Population 34,032,801 **Area** 196,700 sq miles **Maps** 17–26

How to get there

From the Channel ports, Spain is approached via France. The two main routes are at either end of the Pyrenees Mountains, the Biarritz to San Sebastián road, or motorway at the western end for central and southern Spain or the Perpignan to Barcelona road, or motorway at the eastern end for the Costa Brava. The distance from Calais to Madrid is over 970 miles and usually requires two or three night stops. It is possible to shorten the road journey by using the car sleeper services between Boulogne or Paris and Biarritz or Narbonne. There is also a direct ferry service from Plymouth to Santander.

General·information

Information in this section is specific to Spain. A wider background is provided in the notes on page 8 with other information which you are advised to read.

Port agent   Santander 21 Viajes Ecuador SA, Calle Lealtad ☎215708;
Town Office – Santander 17, Calle J Monasterio ☎225965.

Spain

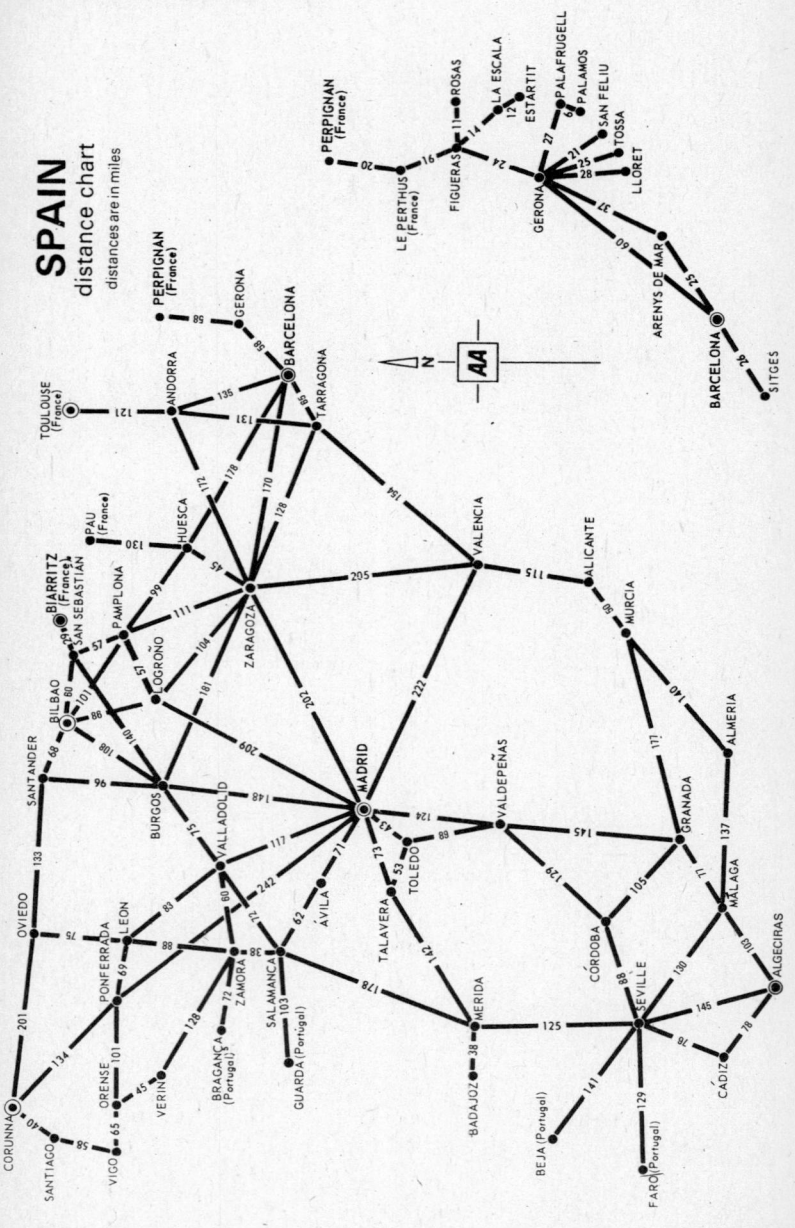

SPAIN
distance chart
distances are in miles

These are not recommended routes:
the distances are given as a guide only.

Accommodation   Spain has some of the most attractively furnished hotels in Europe – especially luxury hotels converted from former monasteries or palaces. Provincial hotels are pleasantly old-fashioned; usually the plumbing and lavatories are just about adequate, and do not compare with those in modern hotels in coastal resorts. Hotels are officially classified, and the category exhibited outside each. Charges must be approved by the State Tourism Department (*Administrácion Turística Española*). Establishments are now permitted to charge for breakfast whether taken or not. While commendations or complaints about hotels are an important source of information to us. AA members may also like to know that Spanish hotels must keep an official complaints book. During the past ten years, the government has undertaken the building of state hotels, including *albergues* and *paradores*, details of which are given in the gazetteer.

Albergues are modern wayside inns catering for the passing motorist, and are classified as motels. Accommodation is limited, and you cannot usually stay for more than 48 hours. There are facilities for garaging, minor repairs, and refuelling.

Paradores are fully-appointed tourist hotels, usually on the outskirts of towns or in the country. Some are newly built, but others are converted country houses, palaces, or Moorish castles. They offer very good value for money. A stay must normally be limited to ten days. Bookings should be made by contacting the manager of the individual establishments. When closed they should be addressed to *Administrácion Turística Española, DGEAT, Secretaria de Estado de Turismo, Av Generalisimo 31, Madrid 16*.

Annual events

February	**Bocairente (Valencia)** Moors and Christians festivals
March	**Valencia** San José Fallas
April	**Vich (Barcelona)** Mercat del Ram
May	**Jerez de la Frontera (Cádiz)** Horse Fair
June	**Calella (Barcelona)** Aplec de la Sardana Festival
July	**Pamplona (Navarra)** San Fermin Festival (including running bulls)
	Anguiano (Logroño) Dance of the Stilts
August	**Elche (Alicante)** Mystery of Elche
	Betanzos (La Coruña) San Roque Festivals
September	**Logroño** Riojana Wine Harvest Festival
	Barcelona Festival of Our Lady of Mercy

Breakdowns   If your car breaks down, try to move it to the verge of the road so that it obstructs the traffic flow as little as possible and place a warning triangle 30 metres behind the vehicle to warn following traffic. A 24-hour breakdown service is run by the Spanish Motoring Club (RACE) in collaboration with a private firm (ADA) in the Madrid area only. This service is available to touring motorists and AA members should produce their *5-Star Service Booklet* when seeking assistance. To obtain assistance telephone 4554646, 4554787, 2340300 or 2534353.

Elsewhere in Spain there is no road patrol service and if you need help you must make your own arrangements with a garage. If you wish to use *5-Star Service* credit vouchers ensure that the garage will accept them in payment before allowing any work to be undertaken.

British   Madrid 4, Calle de Fernando el Santo 16 ☎ 4190200 (12 lines).
Consulates   There are also British Consulates in Barcelona, Palma (Majorca), Tarragona, Ibiza, Bilbao, Las Palmas (Canaries), Santa Cruz (Tenerife), Seville, Algeciras, Cadiz, Jerez de La Frontera, Malaga, Alicante and Vigo.

Currency and   The unit of currency is the peseta, which is divided into 100
banking   centimos.
    There are no restrictions on importing or exporting foreign currencies, travellers' cheques, etc, if a declaration is made to the Customs on entry. Travellers' cheques, etc, may be changed only at banks, authorised travel agencies, or hotels. Spanish bank notes to a maximum value of 50,000 pesetas may be imported, but not more than 3,000 pesetas in bank notes may be exported.

Banking hours   Banks are usually open 09.00–14.00hrs Monday to Saturday. There are exchange offices at travel agents which are open 09.00–13.00hrs and 16.00–19.00hrs from Monday to Friday, and 09.00–13.00hrs on Saturday.

Shopping hours   Shops are open Monday to Saturday: *foodshops* 09.00–13.30 and 16.30–20.00hrs; *stores* 09.30–13.30hrs and 16.30–20.00hrs (17.00–20.30hrs from June to September).

Spain

Customs Tourists should be warned that it is likely that the Spanish Customs authorities will demand a heavy deposit against duty and taxes on portable articles of high value such as musical instruments, portable radios and television sets, cassette recorders etc. Such an outlay may not be budgeted for and may cause inconvenience particularly since any deposit placed may not be readily available for refund when leaving the country.

Documents

Driving licence A British driving licence is acceptable in Spain but only if accompanied by an official translation stamped by a Spanish Consulate. It is recommended that you carry an International Driving Permit which costs less than the official stamping and translation.

Insurance **Frontier insurance** If you do not hold insurance cover, you must take out a short-term insurance policy which is issued by offices of the Guarantee Syndicate for Special Automobile Risks, by tourist offices, and by Customs offices.

Bail bond An accident in Spain can have very serious consequences, including the impounding of the car, and property, and the detention of the driver pending trial. A bail bond can often facilitate release of person and property, and you are advised to obtain one of these from your insurer, for a nominal premium, together with your Green Card. A bail bond is a written guarantee that a cash deposit of usually up to £1,000 will be paid to the Spanish Court as surety for bail, and as security for any fine which may be imposed, although in such an event you will have to reimburse any amount paid by your insurers. In very serious cases the Court will not allow bail and it has been known for a minor Spanish court to refuse to accept bail bonds, and to insist on cash being paid by the driver. Nevertheless, motorists are strongly advised to obtain a bail bond and to ensure that documentary evidence of this (in Spanish) is attached to the Green Card.

Nationality plate The penalty for failure to display a nationality plate, or for displaying one of the wrong size or type, is a fine of approx Pta500.

Ferries **Ayamonte–Vila Real de Santo António** (Portugal) across the River Guadiana. See Portugal page 327.

Medical treatment There is no free medical treatment for visitors.

Motoring club The **Real Autómovil Club de España** (RACE) which has its headquarters at General Sanjurjo 10, Madrid 3 ☎4473200 is associated with local clubs in a number of provincial towns. These clubs will assist motoring tourists generally and supply road and touring information. AA members should produce their *5-Star Service Booklet* when requesting service. Motoring club offices are normally open from 09.00–13.00hrs only and are closed on Sundays and public holidays.
For RACE road assistance, see Breakdowns.

Post/telephone

Rates to the UK are:	Pta
Postcards	9.00
Letters up to 20gm	12.00

The address of the *poste restante* office in Madrid is Edificio de Correos y Telegrafos, Lista de Correos, Plaza de Cibeles, Madrid 14.

Telephone rates An automatic call to the UK, or one through the operator, costs approximately Pta243 for the first three minutes and Pta78 for each additional minute. The internal telephone system connects all principal towns, but long delays on trunk calls are not unusual. Local calls are covered by a flat rate of Pta5; hotels, restaurants, etc, usually make an additional charge.

Public holidays Holidays based on religious festivals are not always fixed on the calendar but any current diary will give actual dates. The Whit period (a religious holiday) should not be confused with the British Spring Holiday.

Fixed holidays		
	1 January	New Year's Day
	6 January	Epiphany
	19 March	St Joseph's Day
	1 May	St Joseph the Worker
	15 May	Madrid only
	25 July	St James of Spain

	15 August	Feast of the Assumption
	12 October	Our Lady of El Pilar
	1 November	All Saints' Day
	9 November	Madrid only
	8 December	Immaculate Conception
	25 December	Christmas Day
Moveable holidays	Maundy Thursday	
	Good Friday	
	Corpus Christi	

Roads

The surfaces of the main roads vary, but on the whole are good; traffic is light. The roads are winding in many places and at times it is not advisable to exceed 30–35mph. Secondary roads are often rough, winding, and encumbered by slow, horse-drawn traffic. All main roads are prefixed N; six of those radiating from Madrid are numbered in roman numerals. Secondary roads are prefixed C.

Holiday traffic   Holiday traffic, particularly on the coast road to Barcelona and Tarragona and in the San Sebastián area, causes congestion which may be severe at weekends.

Motorways   There are approximately 1,228 miles of motorway (*autopista*) open, and more are under construction; a network of about 1,800 miles of toll *autopista* is planned. Apart from a few stretches of toll-free motorways in the Madrid and Barcelona areas, tolls are charged on most of the other sections. The main toll motorways are as follows:

A1	**Irún–San Sebastián**	toll: cars Pta40, car and caravan Pta100
A1/A8	**San Sebastián–Bilbao**	toll: cars Pta280, car and caravan Pta565
A1	***Burgos–Miranda de Ebro**	
A2	**Barcelona–Lérida**	toll: cars Pta265, car and caravan Pta325
A2	**Lérida–Zaragoza**	toll: cars Pta225, car and caravan Pta225
A2/A7	**Barcelona–Tarragona**	toll: payable in three stages cars Pta150, car and caravan Pta275
A4	**Cádiz–Seville**	toll: payable in three stages, and includes Puente Carranza, cars Pta235, car and caravan Pta460
A6	**Villalba–Guadarrama** Tunnel–Adanero	toll: cars Pta275, car and caravan Pta440
A7	**Tarragona–Valencia**	toll: cars Pta540, car and caravan Pta1040
A7	**Silla–Gandia**	toll: cars Pta140, car and caravan Pta240
A7	***Gandia–Altea**	
A7	**Altea–Alicante**	toll: cars Pta125, car and caravan Pta220
A15	**Pamplona–Castejoṅ**	toll: cars Pta155, car and caravan Pta240
A17	**Barcelona–La Junquera (Frontier)** toll: payable in two stages, cars Pta235, car and caravan Pta380	
A19	**Barcelona–Mongat–Mataró**	toll: cars Pta45, car and caravan Pta70
A68	***Bilbao–Zaragoza**	

* **Note** The toll charges for these sections are not available at the time of going to press.

Spain

Winter conditions   Most roads across the Pyrenees are either closed or affected by winter weather, but the roads or motorways to Biarritz and Perpignan in France avoid the mountains. The main routes into Portugal are unaffected.

Within the country, motoring is not severely restricted although certain roads may be temporarily blocked, particularly in January and February. The most important roads likely to be affected are San Sebastián–Burgos–Madrid and Granada–Murcia, but these are swept immediately there is a snowfall. On the Villacastin–Madrid road there is a tunnel under the Guadarrama Pass. Roads likely to be affected by heavy snowfall are:

Pass	Road
Pajares	León–Gijon
Reinosa	Santander–Palencia
Escudo	Santander–Burgos
Somosierra	Burgos–Madrid
Orduña	Bilbao–Burgos
Barazar	Bilbao–Vitoria
Piqueras	Logroño–Madrid
Navacerrada	Madrid–La Granja

The Real Automóvil Club de España will give you up-to-date information about road conditions. See also Passes and tunnels, page 31.

Road signs   Translations of some written signs to be seen on the road are given below:

Aduana	Customs
Al paso	Drive slowly
Atencion a la Senalizacion	Watch out for road signs
Camineros	Roadman's hut
Cañada	Beware of cattle
Cedo el paso	Give way
Cuidado (or, Precaución)	Caution
Despacio	Slow
Desvio	Diversion
Direccion unica	One-way street
Estacionamiento de automoviles	Car park
Estacionamiento prohibido	Parking prohibited
Llevar la derecha (la izquierda)	Drive on the right (the left)
Obras	Workmen
Paso prohibido	No thoroughfare
Peligro	Danger
Curva peligroso	Dangerous bend
Vuelta permitida	Turning permitted

Tourist information offices   The Spanish National Tourist Office, Metro House, St James's Street, London SW1 ☎01–499 0901, will be pleased to assist you with information regarding tourism and there are branch offices in most of the leading Spanish cities, towns and resorts. Local offices are normally closed at lunchtime.

Visitors' registration   There are no police formalities for a stay of less than three months.

Motoring regulations

Information in this section is specific to Spain. A wider background is provided in the notes on page 67 with other regulations which you are advised to read.

Accidents　　**Fire, police, ambulance**. In Madrid and Barcelona dial 091 for **police**, and 2323232 for **fire** service; in other towns call the operator.

Ambulance　　There is an assistance service for the victims of traffic accidents which is run by the Central Traffic Department. At the moment the service operates day and night on the N1 Madrid–Irún road, on the N11 road in the province of Lerida, on some roads in the provinces of Valencia (N111, N340, N332, and N430) and Vizcaya (N625, N634, N240, C639, C6211, C6315, C6318, and C6322).
There is an SOS telephone network on these roads; motorists in need of help should ask for *auxilio en carretera* (road assistance). The special ambulances used are in radio contact with the hospitals participating in the scheme.
There are no firm rules of procedure after an accident; however, in most cases, the recommendations on page 67 are advisable.

Dimensions　　Private cars and trailers are restricted to the following dimensions:
cars　　height 4 metres;
width 2.5 metres;
vehicle/trailer combinations　　length 18 metres.

Drinking and driving　　A driver suspected of driving while under the influence of alcohol may be required to undergo a breath test. If the test indicates a level in excess of 0.8% the driver will be considered to be under the influence of alcohol. A heavy fine, together with the withdrawal of the driving licence, will be imposed on a person found guilty.

Lights　　Passing lights (dipped headlights) are compulsory on motorways and fast dual carriageways even if they are well lit. The use of full headlights in built-up areas is prohibited but it is also an offence to travel with faulty sidelights. You are advised to carry an adequate supply of spare bulbs.

Overtaking　　Both at night and during the day, drivers who are about to be overtaken must operate their right-hand indicator light to show the driver following that his intention to overtake has been understood. Outside built-up areas drivers about to overtake must sound their horn during the day and flash their lights at night. Stationary trams must not be overtaken while passengers are boarding or alighting.

Parking　　Parking is forbidden in the following places: within 5 metres (16½ft) of cross-roads or an intersection; near a level crossing; on or near a pedestrian crossing; within 5 metres of the entrance to a public building; on a main road or one carrying fast-moving traffic; on or near tram lines; within 7 metres (23ft) of a tram or bus stop. You must not park on a two-way road if it is not wide enough for three vehicles. In one-way streets, vehicles are parked alongside buildings with even numbers on even dates and on the opposite side on odd dates; any alteration to this system is announced by signs or notices in the press.
Drivers may stop their vehicles alongside another parked vehicle if there is no space free nearby and the flow of traffic is not obstructed, but only long enough to let passengers in or out or to load or unload goods.
In some cities, there are short-term parking areas known as blue zones indicated by signs. In these areas parked cars must display a disc on the windscreen; discs are set at the time of parking, and show when parking time expires according to the limit in the area concerned. The maximum parking period is 1½hrs during the day; there is no parking limit 21.00–08.00hrs. Parking discs are available from town halls and some hotels, travel agencies, etc. Foreign parking discs are recognised if they carry the same indications as Spanish discs.
It is forbidden to park facing oncoming traffic. Vehicles wrongly parked may be towed away.

Madrid　　You may not park for more than 90 mins in central Madrid, except after 21.00hrs. The police supply parking discs for use in the Madrid blue zone; discs must be displayed on the inside of the windscreen on the side nearest the pavement. Except on Sundays and bank holidays (when shops are closed) there is a limited parking period, as shown on the disc, from 08.00hrs to 21.00hrs. After 21.00hrs parking is allowed until 10.00hrs next day; the disc must still be displayed, and must show the exact time of arrival unless the vehicle is to be collected before 08.00hrs.
If the authorised period is exceeded, the police can tow the vehicle away. A driver whose vehicle has been towed away should contact the Municipal Office, Avenida de Valladolid 6 ☎2472635. Failure to comply with the regulations can result in a fine of up to 500 pesetas, which includes towing costs.

Spain

Motorcycles, scooters, and mopeds need not use discs if they are parked in special parking places. Vehicles weighing more than 2,000kg (1 ton 19cwt 41lb) are not allowed in the zone between 09.00 and 14.00hrs, and 16.00 and 22.00hrs.

Passengers   It is recommended that children under the age of fourteen travel in the rear seat of a vehicle.

Police fines   The police are authorised to impose on-the-spot fines on any motorist infringing the local traffic regulations. They are very active in this respect and are not very sympathetic even with visiting tourists. The officer collecting the fine should issue an official receipt. Visiting motorists must pay their fines immediately (which gives a reduction of 20% in most cases), unless they give the name of a person or corporation in Spain which will guarantee payment of the fine. If not, the vehicle will be held until the fine is paid. A fine may be levied on a motorist who does not carry his driving licence or IDP.

Speed   In built-up areas vehicles are limited to 60kph (37mph) except where signs indicate a lower limit. Outside built-up areas cars are limited to 100kph (62mph) on motorways, roads with two or more lanes in each direction or roads with an additional lane for slow vehicles and 90kph (56mph) on other roads. Vehicles towing a caravan or trailer are limited to 50kph (31mph) inside built-up areas and 80kph (49mph) outside built-up areas if the weight of the caravan exceeds half the unladen weight of the towing vehicle.

Traffic lights   In some cases the green light remains on with the amber light when changing from green to red. Two red lights, one above the other, mean 'no entry'. Usually, lights on each side of cross-roads operate independently and must be obeyed independently.

A policeman with a whistle may over-ride the traffic lights, and he must be obeyed.

Turning   Unless there is a 'turning permitted' sign, three-point turns and reversing into side streets are prohibited in towns.

Tyres   **Spiked tyres** Spikes on tyres must be 10mm in diameter and not more than 2mm in length.

Warning triangles   Vehicles weighing more than 3,500kg (3tons 8cwt 100lb) and passenger vehicles with more than nine seats (including the driver's) must be equipped with two warning triangles. A triangle must be placed 30 metres (33yds) in front of and behind the obstacle. Both must be visible from a distance of at least 100 metres (109yds).

Andorra

Maps 20 & 22   Andorra is an independent Republic covering 180 sq miles with a population of 25,000. It is situated high in the Pyrenees between France and Spain and jointly administered by these two countries. French and Spanish are both spoken and the currency of either country is accepted. General regulations for France and Spain apply to Andorra with the following exceptions:

Accidents   **Fire** and **ambulance** ☎18 **police** ☎21222

Breakdowns   The Automobile Club d'Andorra ☎20890 will offer advice and assistance in the event of a breakdown. However, owing to many unnecessary journeys made in the past, the motorist is now asked to go to the garage and personally accompany the mechanic or breakdown vehicle to his car.

British Consulate   Andorra comes within the Consular District of the British Consul-General at Barcelona.

Medical treatment   There is no free medical treatment for visitors.

Prices are in pesetas
Abbreviations:

av	avenida
c	calle
Cdt	Commandant
ctra	carretera
Gl	Generalísimo
pl	plaza
ps	paseo

AIGUA-BLAVA See **BAGUR**

ALARCÓN Cuenca 400 Map **25** B4

★★ *Parador Marqués de Villena* av Amigo Castillo
☎331350 11⇆ ☖ Lift

ALBACETE Albacete 93,230 (☎967) Map **25** B3

★★★ *Llanos* av Rodrígues Acosta 9 ☎223750
99rm94⇆5 ⋔ ☖ P Lift ♪ sB⇆ ⋔1110–1350
dB⇆ ⋔1788–2150 D fr700

★★★ *Parador Nacional de la Mancha* (ctra National
301km 260) ☎229450 70⇆ P ♪ sB⇆ ⋔1300–1565
dB⇆ ⋔1870–2215 D500 ✒ Pool

ALBUFERETA (LA) See **ALICANTE**

ALCANAR Tarragona 7,070 Map **21** B2

★★ *Biarritz* (n rest) ☎737025 Closed Oct–May 24⇆
P sB⇆ ⋔407–492 dB⇆ ⋔769–929 ✒ Pool Beach
sea

ALCAÑIZ Teruel 10,820 (☎974) Map **21** B2

★★★ *Parador Nacional de la Concordia* ☎130400
12⇆ P Lift ♪ sB⇆ ⋔1249–1529 dB⇆ ⋔1655–2005
L500 D500 mountains

🅱 &⊃ *Agulló* av B-Esteban 28 ☎130825 BL/MB (GB)

ALGECIRAS Cádiz 81,660 (☎956) Map **24** C1

★★★★ *Reina Cristina* ps de las Conferencias
☎671390 tx78057 114⇆ ☖ Lift ✒ Pool sea

☆ *Alarde* Alfonso XI-4 (n rest) ☎660408 68⇆ P Lift
♪ sB⇆812 dB⇆1603

☆ *Sollmar* Málaga road (3km N on N340) ☎660650
Closed Nov–Feb) 14⇆ sea

🅱 &⊃ *M G Gaggero* c Zorrilla 34 ☎673769 M/c

🅱 &⊃ *Mecanicos* ctra Cádiz-Málaga 21 ☎660950
BL/Rov

ALHAMA DE ARAGÓN Zaragoza 1,590
Map **19** B1/2

★★★ *Termas & Parque* GL-Franco 20 ☎1 Closed 16
Oct–8 Apr 149rm ☖ Lift Pool

ALICANTE Alicante 184,720 (☎965) Map **26** C2

★★★★ *Meliá Alicante* Playa de El Postiguet
☎205000 tx66131 580⇆ ☖ Lift Pool sea

★★★ *Gran* Navas 41 ☎214401 72⇆ ☖ Lift

★★★ *Palas* c de Cervantes 5 ☎209309 60rm120⇆
A60rm ☖ P Lift ♪ sB⇆750 dB⇆1310 L475 D475 sea

★★ *Benacantil* San Telmo 7 (n rest) ☎207423
47rm12⇆35 ⋔ Lift sea

★★ *Cabo* Playa de San Juan ☎650100 Closed 16
Sep–14 Jun 35⇆ Lift

★★ *Gran Sol* rambla Méndez Núñez 3 (n rest)
☎203000 150⇆ Lift ♪ sB⇆1410 dB⇆2270 sea

🅱 &⊃ *V M Llavador* c Reyes Católicos 41 ☎221109
BL

🅱 &⊃ *Nuevo* T-Aznar Domenech 7 ☎283932
☎283932 Chy

At **Albuferata (La)** (3km N)

★★★ *Villa Linda* (DP) ☎262208 34rm29⇆5 ⋔ ☖
Pool

ALMERÍA Almería 114,510 (☎951) Map **25** B1

★★★ *Costacabana* (4km E near airport) ☎222063
102⇆ Lift ✒ Pool Beach sea

★★★ *Costasol* ps del Gl-Franco 58 (n rest) ☎234011
55⇆ Lift

★★★ *Perla* pl del Carmen 7 ☎238877 44⇆ ♪
sB⇆ ⋔487–590 dB⇆ ⋔830–1000

🅱 &⊃ *Automecanica Almeriense* Paraje Los
Callejones ☎237033 P

ALMUÑÉCAR Granada 13,250 (☎958) Map **25** A1

★★★ *Portamar* Playa Puerto del Mar ☎630210 72⇆
☖ Lift Beach sea

ALMUNIA DE DOÑA GODINA (LA) Zaragoza 4,910
(☎976) Map **19** B2

★ *Patio* av del Generalísimo 6 ☎600608 11rm5⇆ ☖
P Lift ♪ sB265–300 dB490 dB⇆605 (English
breakfast) L250 D225

ALMURADIEL Cuidad Real Map **25** A3

★★★ *Podencos* (ctra NIV-km 232) ☎363738
80rm68⇆3 ⋔ ☖

ALQUERÍA DEL NIÑO PERDIDO See
VILLARREAL DE LOS INFANTES

ALSASUA Navarra 7,050 (☎948) Map **19** B3

★★ *Alaska* Ctr Madrid-Irún (7km) 402 ☎560100
Closed Jan–Feb 30⇆ ☖ P ♪ sB⇆ ⋔823–923
dB⇆ ⋔1346–1496 (English breakfast) L476 D476
Pool mountains

🅱 &⊃P Celaya Urrestarazu ctra Gl-Irún-Madrid
☎560233 ⊛ M/c P Cit/Peu (GB)

At **Ciordia** (6.4km SW on NI)

★★ *Alzania* ☎560550 36⇆ ☖ Lift

ANDRAITX See **MALLORCA** under **BALEARES
(ISLAS DE)**

ANTEQUERA Málapa 40,910 (☎952) Map **24** D1

☆☆ *Albergue Nacional* Parque M-Cristina ☎841740
17rm14⇆

ARANDA DE DUERO Burgos 18,370 (☎947)
Map **19** A2

☆☆☆ *Bronces* ctra Madrid-Irún ☎500850
30rm27⇆3 ⋔ ☖

Electro-Sanz ctra Madrid-Irún km 160, av C-Miralles
61 ☎501134 BL

ARANJUEZ Madrid 29,550 (☎91) Map **25** A4

L Checa ctra Andaluza 26 ☎8910207 Chy

ARCANTE See **VITORIA**

ARCOS DE LA FRONTERA Cádiz 25,970
Map **24** C1

★★★ *Parador Nacional Casa de Corregidor* pl
d'España ☎362 21⇆

ARENAS DE CABRALES Oviedo Map **18** D4

★ *Naranjo de Bulnes* ☎845024 Closed Oct–Mar
20rm8⇆1 ⋔ sB245–290 sB⇆ ⋔325–390
dB400–485 dB⇆ ⋔550–670 L fr262 D fr262
mountains

ARENYS DE MAR Barcelona 8,330 (☎93)
Map **22** D3

★★ *Floris* playa Cassá 80–82 ☎7920384
32rm22⇆10 ⋔ Lift ♪ sB⇆D416–506
dB⇆ ⋔712–857 L298 D298 sea

★ *Impala* Apartado 20 (n rest) ☎7921504 Closed
Oct–May 52rm14⇆38 ⋔ P ♪ sB⇆ ⋔501–606
dB⇆ ⋔897–1162 Pool sea mountains

ASTORGA León 11,790 (☎987) Map **18** C3

★★ *Cantábrico* pl de la Aduana 1 (n rest) ☎615250
30rm6⇆6 ⋔ ☖

🅱 &⊃ *M Alonso* ctra Madrid-Coruña 60 ☎615259
☎616056 M/c P BL

ÁVILA Ávila 1,131 (☎918) Map **18** D1

★★★★ *Palacio Valderrábanos* pl Catedral 6
☎211025 73⇆ P Lift ♪ sB⇆ ⋔1070–1300
dB⇆ ⋔1900–2300 L600 D600

★★★ *Parador Nacional de Gredos* ☎340048 72⇆
☖ P Lift ♪ sB⇆1075–1165 dB⇆ ⋔1810–2200 L500
D500

★★★ *Parador Nacional Raimundo de Borgoña*
☎211340 taParal 27⇆ P Lift sB⇆770–935
dB⇆1445–1750 L475 D475

★★ *Cuatro Postes* ☎212944 36rm35⇆ P Lift ♪
sB453–543 sB⇆453–543 dB⇆798–951 L369
D369

★★ *Reina Isabel* av J-Antonio 17 ☎220200
44rm13⇆ ♪ sB489 sB⇆fr633 dB⇆fr769 dB⇆fr1058
(English breakfast) L fr369 D fr369

AYAMONTE Huelva 13,100 (Pr 955) Map **23** B2

★★★ *Parador Nacional Costa de la Luz* ☎320700
taParal 20⇆ Pool sea

BADAJOZ Badajoz 101,710 (☎924) Map **23** B3

★★★ *Gran Zurbaran* ps Castelar ☎223741 215⇆ ☖
P Lift ♪ sB⇆ ⋔1300–1550 dB⇆ ⋔2040–2400
L fr550 D fr550 ✒ Pool

🅱 &⊃ *Inbasa* ctra Sevilla ☎224547 P MB

Spain

BAGUR Gerona 2,230 (☎972) Map **22** D3
★★**Sa Riera** Playa de Sa Riera ☎623000
44rm20⇌24🛏 ♪ sB⇌🍴424–489 dB⇌🍴698–888
L357 D357 sea
At **Aigua-Blava** (2km SE)
★★★**Aigua-Blava** Playa de Fornells ☎622058
Closed 18 Oct–17 Mar 85rm78⇌7🍴 P ♪
sB⇌🍴1170–1290 dB⇌🍴1690–2400 L650 D650
🏊 Pool sea
★★★**Parador Nacional de la Costa Brava**
☎312162 ta Paral 40⇌ Lift
At **Playa d'Alguafreda** (5km NE)
★★★★★**Cap sa Sal** ☎312100 Closed Oct–May
230⇌ Lift Pool sea

BAILÉN Jaén 13,230 Map **25** A2
☆☆☆**Albergue Nacional** (1km S on NI) ☎372 40⇌

BALAGUER Lérida 11,680 (☎973) Map **22** C3
★★★**Conde Jaime de Urgel** c Urgel 2 ☎445604
60rm57⇌3🍴 🏡 P Lift ♪ sB⇌🍴1020–1240
dB⇌🍴1720–2080 L fr600 D fr600 Pool mountains
lake

BALEARES (ISLES DE)

IBIZA Map **22** Inset

SAN ANTONIO
★★★**Tanit** Cala Gracio ☎341300 386⇌ 🏊 Pool
Beach ∩ sea

SANTA EULALIA DEL RÍO 9,300 (☎971)
★★★**S'Armagassa** ☎330051 Closed Oct–Apr
217⇌ 🏡 Lift 🏊 Beach sea

MALLORCA (MAJORCA)
Andraitx 3,800 Map **22** C1
At **Camp de Mar** (5km S)
★★★**Camp de Mar** ☎671000 Closed Dec–Mar 75⇌
🏡 P Lift sB⇌🍴740–1040 dB⇌🍴1380–1780
(English breakfast) L550 D550 🏊 Pool sea
Cala Ratjada (☎971) Map **22** D1

★★★**Son Moll** Playa Son Moll ☎563100 Closed
Nov–Mar 118⇌ Lift ♪ sB⇌655 dB⇌1120 (English
breakfast) L357 D357 Pool sea
Formentor (☎971) Map **22** D2
★★★★★**Formentor** ☎531300 tx68523 132⇌ P ♪
sB⇌1410 dB⇌2320 L1000 D1000 🏊 Pool Beach ∩
sea mountains
Magaluf (☎971) Map **22** C1
★★★★**Meliá** ☎681050 Closed Nov–Mar 271⇌ Lift
🏊 sea
Paguera 90 (☎971) Map **22** C1
★★★**Villamil** ☎686050 tx68841 103⇌ P Lift ♪
sB⇌2020 dB⇌fr3440 L fr550 D fr550 🏊 Pool sea
★★★**Bahía** av de Paguera 3A ☎686100 54⇌ 🏊
Pool sea
Palma de Mallorca 234,100 (☎971) Map **22** C1
★★★★★**Meliá Mallorca** c Monseñor Palmer
☎233740 tx68538 240⇌ Lift Pool
★★★★★**Son Vida** (6km NW) ☎232340 tx68651
169⇌ Lift 🏊 Pool ♨ ∩ sea
★★★★**Victoria** av Calvo Sotelo 21 ☎232542
tx68558 172⇌ Lift Pool sea
★★★**Alcina** ps Marítimo ☎231140 91⇌ Lift ♪
sB⇌596–826 dB⇌876–1236 L fr440 D fr440 sea
★★★**Maricel** C'as Catalá Beach ☎402712
55rm55⇌3🍴 A8rm 🏡 P Lift ♪ sB1100–1600
sB⇌🍴1100–1600 dB⇌🍴2400–3200 L650 D650
🏊 Pool Beach sea
★★★**Paso** Son Armadems 93 ☎237602 tx68652
254⇌ P Lift sB⇌🍴680 dB⇌🍴1060 L fr350 D fr350
Pool mountains
🚗**Oliver** c G-Llabres 12 ☎273581 Bed/Opl/Vau
🚗🚗**Minaco** Aragón 27 ☎463540 Peu/Rov (GB)
At **Playa de Palma** (Ca'n Pastilla)
★★★**Acapulco** ☎261800 100rm93⇌7🍴 Lift Pool
sea
★★**Oasis** ☎260150 110⇌ 🏡 P Lift ♪ sB⇌670–790
dB⇌1030–1244 (English breakfast) L270 D270 Pool
Beach sea

Barcelona

1 ★★★★★	Avenida Palace	
2 ★★★★★	Ritz	
3 ★★★★★	Rotonda	
4 ★★★★	Condado	
5 ★★★★	Christina	
6 ★★★★	Diplomatic	
7 ★★★★	Majestic	
8 ★★★★	Manila	
9 ★★★★	Presidente	
10 ★★★★	Regente	
11 ★★★	Astoria
12 ★★★	Dante
13 ★★★	Derby
14 ★★★	Florida (at Mont-Tibidabo 12km NW)
15 ★★★	Meśon Castilla
16 ★★★	Regina

Spain

At **Playa de Palma Nova** (16km SW)
★★★ **Hawaii** ☎681150 204⇄ Lift Pool Beach sea
Pollensa 9,960 (Pr 971) Map **22** D1/2
At **Cala San Vicente**
★★★★ **Molins** ☎530200 Closed 6 Jan – 4 Feb
100rm97⇄3 🏛 P Lift ♪ sB⇄🍴1030 dB⇄🍴1575
L575 D575 🍴 Pool sea
At **Puerto de Pollensa** (6km NE)
★★★ **Capri** ps Anglada Camarasa ☎531600 Closed
Nov – Mar 33rm28⇄5 🍴 🏛 P Lift ♪ sB⇄🍴485 – 620
dB⇄🍴795 – 1035 L405 D405
★★★ **Miramar** ps de Anglada Camarasa ☎531400
Closed Nov – Mar 70⇄ 🏛 P Lift ♪ sB⇄495 – 595
dB⇄830 – 1010 L fr440 🍴 Beach sea
★★★ **Uyal** ps de Londres ☎531500 Closed Nov – Mar
83⇄ Lift Beach sea
MENORCA (MINORCA) Map **22** Inset
Mahón 19,280 (☎971)
At **Villacarlos** (3km W)
★★★★ **Agamenon** Fontanillas ☎362150 Closed
Nov – Feb 75⇄ P Lift ♪ sB⇄620 – 795
dB⇄1000 – 1270 (English breakfast) L460 D460 Pool
sea
★★★ **Rey Carlos III** Miranda de Cala Corp ☎363100
Closed Nov – Mar 87⇄ 🏛 Lift Pool sea
BAÑEZA (LA) León 8,840 Map **18** C3
☆ **Albergue Nacional** (1km NW) ☎641850 12rm4⇄
🏛
BAÑOLAS Gerona 10,020 (☎972) Map **22** D3
★★ **Lago** 19⇄ 🏛 lake
★★ **Mundial** pl España 23 (n rest) ☎570078 38rm8⇄
🏛
BAÑOS DE MONTEMAYOR Caceres 1,020
Map **18** C1
★★ **Balneario** Calvo Sotelo 24 ☎579 Closed
Oct – May 100rm40⇄ 🏛 Lift
BARAJAS See **MADRID**
BARCELONA Barcelona 1,745,140 (☎93)
Map **22** C3 **See Plan**
    AA agents; see page 335
★★★★ **Avenida Palace** av J-Antonio 605
☎3019600 tx54734 Plan **1** 225⇄ Lift
★★★★ **Ritz** av J-Antonio 668 ☎3185200 tx52739
Plan **2** 200rm192⇄10🍴 P Lift ♪ sB⇄ fr2400
dB⇄ 4050 (English breakfast) L1000 D1000
★★★★ **Rotonda** ps de San Gervasio 53 ☎2470400
Plan **3** 100⇄ 🏛 Lift
★★★★ **Condado** Aribau 201 ☎2172500 Plan **4** 90⇄
Lift
★★★★ **Christina** av Gl-Franco 458 ☎2176800
Plan **5** 125⇄ 🏛 Lift
★★★★ **Diplomatic** vía Layetana 122 ☎3173100
tx54701 Plan **6** 225⇄ 🏛 P Lift ♪ sB⇄2725
dB⇄4850 L1000 D1000 Pool
★★★★ **Majestic** ps de Gracia 70 ☎2154512 tx52211
Plan **7** 350⇄ 🏛 Lift Pool
★★★★ **Manila** Rambla de los Estudios 111
☎3186200 tx54634 Plan **8** 250⇄ 🏛 Lift
★★★★ **Presidente** av del Generalisimo 570
☎2273141 tx52180 Plan **9** 161⇄ 🏛 Lift Pool
★★★★ **Princesa Sofia** pl Pío XII ☎2591700 tx51032
Not on plan 511⇄ 🏛 Lift
★★★★ **Regente** Rambla de Cataluña 76 ☎2152570
Plan **10** 66⇄ Lift Pool
★★★ **Astoria** c Paris 203 (off c de Urgel) (n rest)
☎2185600 Plan **11** 108⇄ 🏛 Lift
★★★ **Dante** c Mallorca 181 (n rest) ☎3232254
tx52588 Plan **12** 81⇄ 🏛 P Lift sB⇄1200 – 1400
dB⇄2300 – 2700 🍴 Pool Beach ∫ ◯
★★★ **Derby** Loreto 21 ☎2393007 Plan **13** 116⇄ 🏛
Lift
★★★ **Mesón Castilla** Valdoncella 5 (n rest)
☎3182182 Plan **15** 55⇄ 🏛 Lift
★★★ **Regina** c Vergara 4 (off pl de Cataluña) (n rest)
☎3013232 tx51939 Plan **16** 102⇄ Lift ♪ sB⇄951
dB⇄1769
🛏 **M Aguilar** c Mallorca 27 – 31 ☎2397275
Bed/Opl/Vau (GB)
🛵 **Benedito** Córcega 418 ☎2587405 P BL
🛏 🛵 **California** c Mallorca 419 ☎2363545 M/c P

🛏 🛵 **Layetana** Travesera de Gracia 17 – 29
☎3212327 Frd
🛵 **F Roca** Diputación 43 ☎3251550 M/c
Chy/Jag/Rov/RR/Sim
🛵 **Romagosa** c Bolivia 243 – 245 ☎3071957 (Closed
Fri & wknds) Peu/Rov
🛏 🛵 **Ryvesa** Aragón 179 ☎2531600 BL (GB)
🛏 🛵 **G Salamanca** c Laforja 75 ☎2284496 M/c P
Hon
At **Mont-Tibidabo** (12km NW)
★★★ **Florida** (n rest) ☎2475000 Plan **14** Closed
Sep – May 52⇄ Lift
BAYONA Pontevedra 7,890 Map **17** A3
★★ **Parador Nacional del Conde de Gondomer** ría
de Vigo ☎142 ta Paral 66⇄ 🏛 🍴 Pool Beach sea
BENAJARAFE See **TORRE DEL MAR**
BENALMADENA Málaga (☎952) Map **24** D1
★★★ **Siroco** ☎443040 tx77135 252⇄ P Lift ♪
sB⇄🍴735 – 1105 dB⇄🍴1350 – 1700 (English
breakfast) L530 D530 🍴 Pool sea mountains
★★ **Delfin** ctra de Cádiz ☎441640 78⇄ Lift Pool sea
BENAVENTE Zamora 11,780 (☎988) Map **18** C2
★★★ **Martín** ctra Madrid (2km SE) ☎631850
30rm8⇄8 🍴 🏛
BENICARLÓ Castellón 12,830 (☎964) Map **21** B2
☆☆☆ **Albergue Nacional** ctra de Peñiscola
☎470100 ta Paral 108⇄9 🏛 🍴 Pool sea
★★ **Sol** av Magallanes 90 ☎471349 Closed
Oct – May 16⇄ A8rm 🏛 sea
BENICASIM Castellón 2,920 (☎964) Map **21** B1
★★★★ **Azor** ps Marítimo ☎300350 tx65503 Closed
Nov – Feb 88⇄ P Lift ♪ sB⇄🍴950 – 1450
sB⇄🍴1600 – 2000 L625 D625 🍴 Pool ◯ sea
★★★ **Voramar** ☎300150 Closed 11 Oct – mid Apr
55⇄ 🏛 Lift Beach sea
BENIDORM Alicante 12,120 (☎965) Map **26** D2
★★★★ **Gran Delfin** Playa de Poniente ☎853400
Closed Oct – Mar 99⇄ 🏛 Lift 🍴 Pool sea
★★★ **Europa** Rincón de Loix ☎360800 Closed
Dec – 14 Mar 48rm43⇄5🍴 Lift Pool sea
★★★ **Planesia** pl de San Jaime 2 ☎360303 Closed
Nov – Mar 36⇄ Lift sea
☆ **Marola** La Cala ☎360932 Closed Nov – Mar 20⇄
🏛 sea
★★ **Presidente** av Filipinas ☎853950 228⇄ Lift Pool
sea
🛵 **Autonautica** ctra Alicante-Valencia, km 116,700
☎853562 ☎853566 Frd (GB)
BIELSA Huesca 620 Map **21** B4
★★ **Parador Monte Perdido** Valle de Pineta (14km
NE) ☎23 16⇄ 🏛 Lift
BILBAO Vizcaya 410,490 (☎944) Map **19** B3 **See
Plan**
★★★★ **Aranzazu** R-Arias 66 ☎4413100 tx32164
Plan **1** 🏛 P Lift ♪ sB⇄2190 dB⇄3000 (English
breakfast) L700 D700
★★★★ **Avenida** av H-de Saracho 2 ☎4334000
tx31040 Plan **2** 116⇄ P Lift ♪ sB⇄1150 – 1400
dB⇄1900 – 2300 L360 D360
★★ ★★ **Carlton** pza F-Moyúa 2 (n rest) ☎4162200
tx32233 Plan **3** 146⇄ Lift
★★★★ **Ercilla** Ercilla 37 ☎4438800 tx32449 Plan **4**
350⇄ 🏛 P Lift ♪ sB⇄2050 dB⇄3075 L700 D700
🛵 **Rotarduy** Alameda de Urquijo 85 ☎419900 Peu
BLANES Gerona 16,020 (☎972) Map **22** D3
★★★★ **Park Hotel Blanes** ☎330250 Closed 11
Oct – Apr 131rm126⇄5🍴 🏛 Lift 🍴 Pool Beach ◯
sea
★★★ **Pop Coronat** ps de la Maestranza 97 ☎330050
34rm22⇄12🍴 Lift sea
★★ **Horitzo** ps Marítimo 11 ☎330400
122rm95⇄27🍴 🏛 Lift sea
★★ **San Francisco** ☎330477 (Pn) Closed Nov – May
32⇄ Lift ♪ sB⇄ Pool 750 – 810 dB⇄🍴1500 – 1620 sea
BURGOS Burgos 119,920 (☎947) Map **19** A3
★★★★ **Almirante Bonifaz** Vitoria 22 – 24 ☎206943
tx39430 76⇄ Lift ♪ sB⇄🍴1120 – 1630
dB⇄1540 – 2880 L650 D650

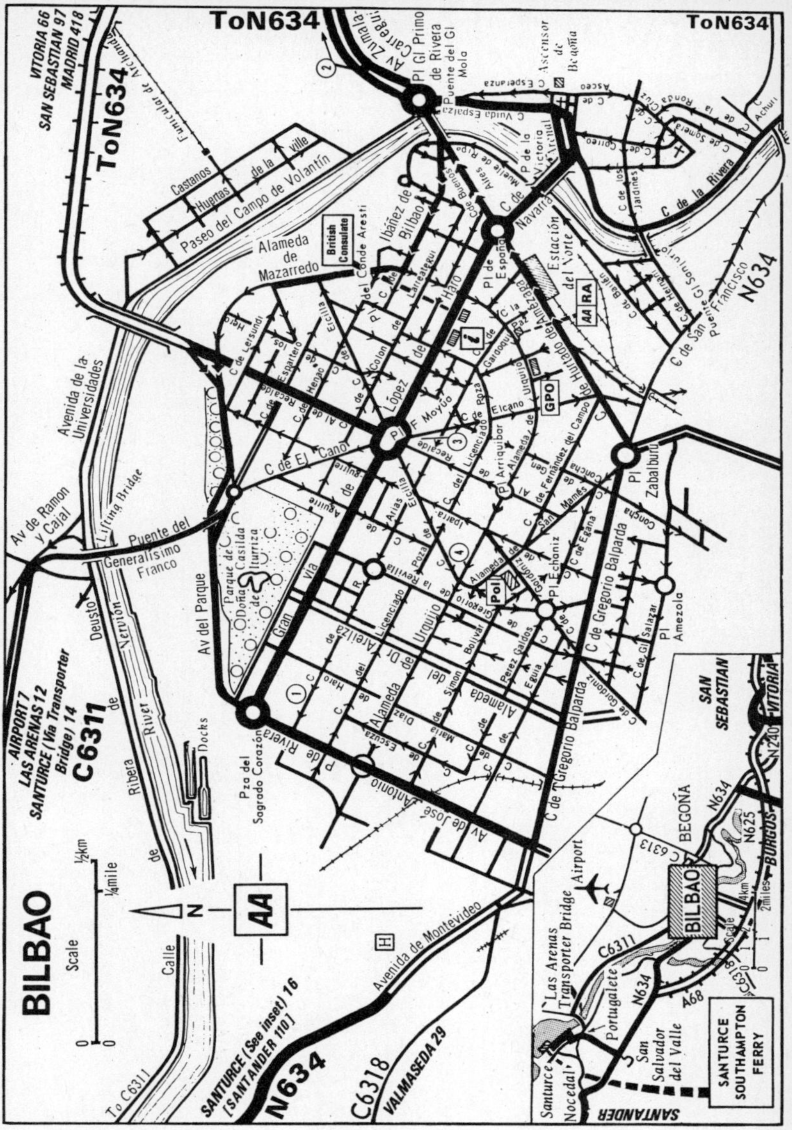

Bilbao
1 ★★★★ Aranzazu
2 ★★★★ Avenida
3 ★★★★ Carlton
4 ★★★★ Ecrilla

★★★★**Landa Palace** (2km S on NI) ☎206343 39🏠
🏠 P Lift ⟂ sB⇄🏠2280 dB🏠3660 (English breakfast)
L fr850 D fr850
★★★★**Condestable** Vitoria 8 ☎200644 77⇄ 🏠 Lift
🛏 🚗**J Barrios** c de Vitoria 113 ☎224900 Fia/Lnc/Vlo
(GB)
🛏 🚗**Mecanico 'Suizo'** San Agustin 5 ☎202364 P
Aud/VW (GB)
🛏 🚗**Pedro** av Vitoria 105 ☎224528 P Chy
BURRIANA Castellón 22,650 (☎964) Map **26** D4
★★★**Aloha** (Playa 2.5km W) ☎510104 Closed
Oct – 14 Mar 30⇄ Lift Pool sea
CABRERA (LA) Madrid 701 (☎91) Map **19** A1
★★**Mavi** ctra de Madrid-Irún 58 ☎8688000
43rm12⇄31🏠 P ⟂ sB365 – 440 sB⇄395 – 475
dB⇄🏠640 – 825 L357 D357 mountains
CÁCERES Cáceres 55,060 (☎927) Map **24** C4
★★★**Alcántara** av Virgen de Guadalupe 14
☎221700 67⇄ Lift ⟂ sB⇄694 – 839
dB⇄1238 – 1588 L fr410 D fr410
CADAQUES Gerona 1,270 (☎972) Map **22** D3
★★★**Llané Petit** Dr-Bartomens 36 ☎258050 Closed
Oct – Mar 35⇄ 🏠 Lift
★★★**Playa-Sol** ☎258100 50⇄ 🏠 P Lift ⟂
sB⇄🏠1025 – 1170 dB⇄🏠1950 – 2240 Pool sea
CÁDIZ Cádiz 135,740 (☎956) Map **24** C1
★★★**Atlantico** Parque Genovés (n rest) ☎212301
ta Paral A48⇄ P Lift ⟂ dB⇄🏠1905 – 2255 sea
🛏 🚗**SAINA** av del Puente ☎231604 Ren
CALAFELL Tarragona 3,360 (☎977) Map **22** C2
★★★**Miramar** av San Juan de Dios 107 ☎662304
Closed Nov – Mar 212rm200⇄ P Lift ⟂ sB481 – 576
sB⇄🏠541 – 651 dB852 – 1012 dB⇄🏠972 – 1162
(English breakfast) L416 D416 Pool sea
CALA RATJADA See **MALLORCA** under
BALEARES (ISLAS DE)
CALA SAN VICENTE See **POLLENSA** under
MALLORCA under **BALEARES (ISLAS DE)**
CALATAYUD Zaragoza 17,220 (☎976)
Map **19** B1/2
🛏 🚗**Vicor** A-Simón 3 ☎881863 🚗 (GB)
CALDETAS Barcelona 1,050 (☎93) Map **22** D3
★★★★**Colón** ps 16 ☎7910351 82⇄ P Lift ⟂
sB⇄1110 sB⇄1920 L500 D500 Pool Beach sea
mountains
CALELLA Barcelona 9,700 (☎93) Map **22** D3
★★★**Las Vegas** ctra de Francia ☎7690850 Closed
16 Oct – 14 May 110rm65⇄45🏠 P Lift ⟂
sB⇄440 – 535 dB⇄785 – 1050 L325 D325 Pool sea
★★★★**Mont-Rosa** ps de las Rocas ☎7690508
Closed Nov – Apr 120rm96⇄24🏠 P Lift ⟂
sB⇄🏠543 – 655 dB⇄🏠910 – 1090 (English
breakfast) L fr369 D fr369 Pool sea
★★★**Velamar** Bruguera 49 ☎7690509 Closed
Oct – May 74rm24⇄50🏠 A39rm 🏠 ⟂ D
sB⇄🏠325 – 375 dB⇄🏠625 – 665 L250 D250 Pool
CALELLA DE PALAFRUGELL See
PALAFRUGELL
CALPE Alicante 3,400 (☎965) Map **26** D3
★★★**Venta la Chata** (4km N) ☎830308 17⇄ 🏠 ⟂ sea
CAMBADOS Pontevedra 10,640 Map **17** A3
★**Parador Nacional del Albariño** ps de Cervantes
☎171 ta Paral 8⇄
CAMP DE MAR See **ANDRAITX** under **MALLORCA**
under **BALEARES (ISLAS DE)**
CARDONA Barcelona 7,000 (☎ 93) Map **22** C3
★★★**Parador National Duques de Cardona**
☎8691275 ta Paral 65⇄ P Lift ⟂ sB⇄🏠1175 – 1440
dB⇄🏠1655 – 2005 L500 D500
CAROLINA (LA) Jaén 15,770 (☎953) Map **25** A2/3
★★★**Perdiz** (ctra N IV) ☎660300 tx27578 89⇄ 🏠 P
sB⇄1500 – 1800 dB⇄2000 – 2325 L600 D600 Pool
mountains
CASTELLDEFELS Barcelona 13,220 (☎93)
Map **22** C3

★★★**Catite** ps Garbi 134 ☎6651700 Closed
Oct – Apr 31rm25⇄16🏠 Pool sea
★★★**Neptuno** ☎6651400 42rm25⇄17🏠 A3rm Lift
⟂ Pool sea
★★★**Rancho** ps de la Marina 212 ☎6651900 60⇄
Lift ⟂ Pool sea
CASTELLÓN DE LA PLANA Castellón 93,970
(☎964) Map **21** B1
★★★**Mindoro** Moyano 4 ☎222300 114⇄ 🏠 P Lift ⟂
sB⇄1390 dB⇄2200
🛏 🚗**Tagerbaf** Hños Vilafaña 13 ☎216653 ☎216653
🚗 P Cit/MB/Ren/Sim (GB)
At **Grao de Castellón** (5km E)
★★★★**Golf** Playa del Pinar ☎221950 65⇄ 🏠 Lift ⟂
Pool Beach 🛏 sea
★★★**Turcosa** av Buenavista ☎222150 70⇄ Lift sea
CASTRO URDIALES Santander 12,400 (☎944)
Map **19** A3
★★**Rocas** av de la Playa ☎860400 61 ⇄ 🏠 Lift sea
CAZORLA Jaén 9,370 Map **25** A2
★**Parador Nacional el Adelantado** (25km SE)
☎295 ta Paral 30rm16⇄ A8rm 🏠 ○
CERVERA DE PISUERGA Palencia 2,000 (Pr 988)
Map **18** D3
★★★**Parador Nacional de Fuentes Carrionas**
☎870075 ta Paral 80⇄ 🏠 P Lift ⟂
sB⇄🏠1175 – 1440 dB⇄🏠1655 – 2005 L fr500
D fr500 lake
CESTONA Guipúzcoa 4,380 (☎943) Map **19** B3
★★★★**Arocena** ☎867040 Closed 11 Oct – 9 Jul
109rm82⇄27🏠 🏠 P Lift ⟂ sB⇄🏠806 -856
dB⇄🏠1237 – 1402 L550 D550 ⟂ Pool mountains
lake
CIORDIA See **ALSASUA**
CIUDAD REAL 42,000 (☎926) Map **25** A3
🛏 🚗**Calatrave** ctra Carrion km 242 ☎220315 MB
CIUDAD RODRIGO Salamanca 13,320 (☎923)
Map **18** C3
★★★**Parador Nacional Enrique II** pl del Castillo 1
☎460150 ta Paral 34rm24⇄
🛏 🚗**F M Rubio** av España 20 & ctra Salamanca
☎460943
COMARRUGA Tarragona (☎977) Map **22** C2
★★★**Europa** ☎661850 Closed Nov – 14 Apr 162⇄ P
Lift ⟂ sB⇄1015 – 1225 dB⇄1710 – 2050 L650 D650
⟂ Pool sea
COMILLAS Santander 2,410 Map **19** A4
★★★**Casal del Castro** San Jeronimo ☎89 Closed
Oct – May 45⇄ Lift ⟂
CONDADO DE SAN JORGE See **PLAYA DE ARO**
CONTRERAS Cuenca Map **26** C3
★★**Venta de Contreras** ☎Villagordo del Cabriel 10
Closed Dec – Feb 9rm3⇄4🏠 A3rm 🏠 Pool lake
CÓRDOBA Córdoba 235,630 (☎957) Map **24** D2
★★★★★**Meliá Córdoba** Jardines de la Victoria
☎226380 106⇄ 🏠 Lift Pool
★★★★**Gran Capitán** av América 3 – 5 ☎221955
99⇄ 🏠 Lift
★★★★**Parador Nacional de la Arruzafa** av de la
Arruzafa ☎226240 ta Paral 56⇄ Lift ⟂ Pool
★★★**Cordobés** Medina Azahara 7 ☎235500 103⇄
Lift
★★**Marisa** Cardenal Herrero 10 (n rest) ☎226317
16rm4⇄12🏠 ⟂ sB⇄🏠455 – 545 dB⇄🏠830 – 1040
★★**Zahira** Conde del Robledo 1 (off av del Gran
Capitan) (n rest) ☎226260 100⇄ Lift
★**Brillante** ctra el Brillante 91 (DP) ☎275800
32rm9⇄12🏠 Lift
CORUÑA (LA) (CORUNNA) La Coruña 189,650
(☎981) Map **17** B4
★★★★**Finisterre** ps del Parrote ☎223075 Closed
Oct – Jun 135⇄ Lift ⟂ Pool sea
🛏 🚗**L R Amada** Gl-Sanjurjo 117 – 119 ☎283400
Cit/Rov
At **Santa Cruz** (7.5km SE)

★★★ *Porto Cobo* Playa de Santa Cruz ☎614100
58⇌ Lift Pool Beach sea
COVARRUBIAS Burgos 980 Map **19** A2
★★★ *Arlanza* pl de Doña-Urraca ☎28 31rm29⇌2🕅
Lift
CUENCA Cuenca 34,490 (☎966) Map **25** B4
★★★ *Torremangana* San Ignacio de Loyola 9
☎223351 112⇌ 🏛 Lift
CULLERA Valencia 15,740 (☎963) Map **26** D3
★★★ *Sicania* ctra El Faro, Playa del Raco ☎1520143
Closed Nov 117⇌ 🏛 P Lift ♪ sB⇌🕅1140 – 1440
dB⇌ 2080 – 2580 L fr600 d fr600 Beach sea
DALIAS Almería Not on atlas
★★★★ *Golf Almerimar* ☎480950 38⇌ 🛥 Pool ♭ ♫
sea
DAROCA Zaragoza 2,900 Map **19** B1
★★ *Daroca* Mayor 34 ☎253 20⇌ Lift
DENIA Alicante 16,500 (☎965) Map **26** D3
At **Playa de las Marinas** (1km N)
★★ *Angeles* ☎780458 Closed Oct – 29 May 59⇌ 🛥
Beach sea
DEVA Guipúzcoa 4,490 (☎943) Map **19** B3
★★ *Miramar* J-J-Aztiria 36 ☎601144 60⇌ 🏛 P Lift ♪
sB⇌🕅830 – 990 dB⇌🕅1520 – 1730 (English
breakfast) L610 D610 🛥 Pool Beach ♭ ♫ sea
EL Each name preceded by El is listed under the
name that follows it.
ESCALA (LA) Gerona 3,120 (☎972) Map **22** D3
★★★ *Barca* E-Serra 25 ☎770162 Closed 16
Sep – May 26⇌ ♪ sB⇌🕅332 – 442 dB⇌🕅559 – 739
(English breakfast) L260 D260
★★★ *Bonaire Juvines* ps L-Albert 4 ☎770068
Closed Nov – Feb 32⇌ A12rm Lift ♪
dB⇌🕅1033 – 1203 L375 – 387 D375 – 385 Pool Beach
sea mountains
★★★ *Nieves Mar* ps Marítimo ☎070300 Closed 16
Nov – 14 Jan 80⇌ Lift 🛥 Pool sea
★★★ *Voramar* ps L-Albert 2 ☎770108 Closed 3
Oct – 24 Mar 42rm40⇌ Lift Pool Beach sea
★★ *Marquesado* ps L-Albert 2 (n rest) ☎770150
Closed Oct – May 32⇌ 🏛 Pool sea
ESCORIAL (EL) See **SAN LORENZO DE EL
ESCORIAL**
ESTARTIT Gerona (☎972) Map **22** D3
★ *Vila* Santa Ana 34 ☎758113 Closed Oct – Apr
58rm6⇌28🕅 A20rm
ESTELLA Navarra 10,370 (☎948) Map **19** B3
★★ *Tatan* ps de las Llanos (n rest) ☎550025
19rm8⇌8🕅
ESTEPONA Málaga 21,160 (☎952) Map **24** C1
★★★★ *Atalaya Park* (DP & Pn) ☎811644 tx77210
446⇌ P Lift ♪ dB⇌🕅2028 – 2725 🛥 Pool Beach
♭ ♫ sea
★★★ *Santa Marta* Apartado 2 ☎811340 Closed
Oct – Apr 40rm37⇌1🕅 P ♪ sB990

sB⇌🕅990 dB1320 dB⇌🕅1320 (English breakfast)
L500 D500 🛥 Pool Beach sea
★ *Buenavista* Gl-France 119 ☎800137
37rm20⇌2🕅 🏛 Lift ♪ sB285 – 330 dB455 – 515
dB⇌🕅625 – 665 L fr265 D fr265 sea
FERROL DEL CAUDILLO (EL) La Coruña 87,740
(☎981) Map **17** B4
★★★ *Nacional Parador San Francisco* Almirante
Vierna 1 ☎353400 27rm23⇌4🕅 🏛
Castelos av Generalísimo 336 ☎312417 Frd (GB)
FIGUERAS Gerona 22,090 (☎972) Map **22** D3
★★★★ *President* ctra Nacional II de Madrid a Francia
☎501700 75rm56⇌19🕅 🏛 P Lift sB⇌🕅770 – 850
dB⇌🕅1325 – 1390 L425 D425
☆☆☆ *Ampurdán* ctra Madrid-Francia (1.5km N on
NII) ☎500592 48⇌ 🏛 Lift
★★★ *Duran* c Lasuaca 5 ☎501250 67rm57⇌1🕅 🏛
Lift ♪ sB607 sB⇌🕅859 dB951 dB⇌🕅1416 L415
D415
★★★ *Rallye* Cruce ctra Francia ☎501300 20rm16⇌
🏛 P Lift ♪ sB490 sB⇌610 – 740 dB⇌1020 – 1220
L415 D415 mountains
★★ *Trave* ctra de Olot (DP) ☎500591 59rm38⇌21🕅
A25rm 🏛
H J Bordas pl Alcázar 6
🛢 ⊗ *Central* av J-Antonio 1 ☎500667 BL/Frd
🛢 *Victoria* pl de la Victoria 12 ☎500293 Rov (GB)
FORMENTOR See **MALLORCA** under **BALEARES
(ISLAS DE)**
FORNELLS DE LA SELVA See **GERONA**
FUENGIROLA Málaga 20,600 (☎952) Map **24** D1
★★★★ *Mare Nostrum* ctra de Cádiz ☎462140
Closed Nov – Apr 246⇌ 🏛 Lift 🛥 Pool Beach sea
★★★ *Florida* Playa Florida ☎461847
116rm108⇌8🕅 🏛 P Lift ♪ sB⇌🕅622 dB⇌🕅1049
(English breakfast) L400 D400 Pool Beach sea
mountains
🛢 ⊗ *Pauli* ☎462058 P Aud/MB/Opl/VW
FUENTE DÉ Santander Map **18** D3
★★ *Parador Nacional del Río Deva* ☎Camaleño 7
10⇌
FUENTERRABÍA Guipúzcoa 10,470 (☎943)
Map **19** B3
★★ *Guadalupe* Ciudad de Peñíscola (n rest)
☎641650 Closed Oct – 14 May 35rm22⇌13🕅 P ♪
sB⇌🕅650 dB⇌🕅1225 – 1565 Pool
★★ *Parador Nacional el Emperador* pl de Armas del
Castillo ☎641873 16⇌
At **Jaizkibel** (8km SW)
★★★ *Jaizkibel* Monte Jaizkibel ☎641100 13rm6⇌
🏛 sea
GANDÍA Valencia 36,340 (☎963) Map **26** D3
At **Playa de Gandía** (4km E)
★★★★ *Bayren* ps de Neptuno (DP) ☎2840300
164⇌ 🏛 Lift 🛥 Pool Beach sea
GELIDA Barcelona 2,680 Map **22** C3
★ *San Jorge* Cuartel Oeste ☎7790031 16rm 🏛 P ♪
Pool mountains

Spain

GERONA Gerona 50,340 (☎972) Map **22** D3
★★*Ultonia* av Jaime 22 (n rest) ☎203850
45rm43⇄2♿ Lift
★★*Europa* Julio Gattera 23 (n rest) ☎202750
26rm12⇄14♿ Lift
★★*Peninsular* Gl-Primo de Rivera 1 (n rest)
☎203800 68rm22⇄ Lift
🛢 🏪*Blanch* Ronda San António Maria Claret 10
☎204381 ☎202824 BL
At **Fornells de la Selva** (5km S off NII)
★★★*Fornells Park* ☎209925 52⇄ P Lift 🌙
sB⇄662–765 dB⇄1139–1319 L467 Pool
mountains

GETAFE See **MADRID**

GIJÓN Oviedo 187,610 (☎985) Map **18** D4
★★★★*Hernan Cortés* F-Vallin 5 ☎346000
109rm92⇄17♿ Lift sea
★★*Parador Molino Viejo* Parque de
Isabel la Católica 19 ☎354945 6⇄

GRANADA Granada 190,430 (☎958) Map **25** A1
★★★★★*Meliá Granada* Ganivet 5 ☎227400
tx78429 221⇄
★★★★*Alhambra* Penapartida 2 ☎221468 tx78400
133rm117⇄16♿ P Lift 🌙 sB930–1130
sB⇄1480–1850 dB1980–2410
dB⇄1420–1710 (English breakfast) L660 D660
mountains
★★★*Brasilia* Recogidas 7 ☎227448 60⇄ Lift
★★★*Guadalupe* de los Alijares ☎223423
86rm82⇄4♿ A43rm P Lift 🌙 sB⇄830–1010
dB⇄1350–1685 (English breakfast) L450 D450
mountains
★★★*Kenia* Molinos 65 ☎227507 19⇄ P 🌙
sB⇄543–678 dB⇄1046–1286 L fr450 D fr450
mountains
★★★*Parador Nacional de San Francisco* (In the
Alhambra) ☎221493 taParal 26⇄ P 🌙 sB⇄1615
dB⇄1280 L500 D500 mountains
★★*Inglaterra* Cetti Merien 4 (off Gran vía de Colón)
(n rest) ☎221558 50rm45⇄5♿ Lift 🌙 sB⇄565
dB⇄845 (English breakfast)
★*America* Real Alhambra 53 ☎221717 Closed 11
Nov–Mar 13rm5⇄3♿ P 🌙 sB335–400
sB⇄415–495 dB645–765 dB⇄720–866 L365
D365 mountains
🛢 🏪*Autiberia* ps de Ronda 103 ☎235448 BL/Rov
🛢 🏪*Auto-Dibesa* Calvo Sotelo 37 ☎276750 P Cit
(GB)
🛢 🏪*Servicio Union* c Cisne 5 ☎233100 M/c Peu
(GB)
At **Siema Nevada** (40km SE)
★★★*Sol & Nieve* ☎480300 70rm 3⇄37♿ 🏛 Lift 🏊
Pool

GRAO DE CASTELLÓN See **CASTELLÓN DE LA
PLANA**

GREDOS Avila Map **18** C/D1
★★*Parador Nacional* ☎El Barco de Ávila 550 68⇄
Lift

GUADALAJARA Guadalajara 31,920 (☎911)
Map **19** A1
★★★*Pax* ctra Madrid-Barcelona ☎221800 61⇄ 🏛
Lift 🏊 Pool
★*Reloj* Dr-Mayoral 11 (n rest) ☎211525 20rm8⇄ P
🌙 sB204–244 sB⇄252–304 dB356–424
dB⇄468–563 L261 D261
Taberné ingeniere Mariñvo 27 ☎211038 M/c (GB)
🛢 *Taberné* ctra Nacional Madrid-Barcelona
km51400 ☎213066 (GB)

GUADALUPE Cáceres 3,070 Map **24** D4
Hospederia del Monasterio (Monastery where
accommodation is provided by the monks) ☎36700
38rm19⇄13♿
★★*Parador Nacional de Zurbaran* Marqués de la
Romana 10 ☎367075 20⇄ 🏛 P Lift 🌙 sB⇄750–910
dB1120–1345 L475 D475 Pool

HUELVA Huelva 96,690 (☎955) Map **23** B2
★★★*Tartessos* Gran Vía 13 (n rest) ☎216700 82⇄
Lift 🌙 sB⇄980 dB⇄1730

HUESCA Huesca 33,190 (☎974) Map **20** C2
★★★*Pedro I de Aragón* ps de Gl-Franco 34
☎220300 52⇄ Lift
🛢 *Autoloto* Alcampel ☎211113 BL
🛢 🏪*Commercial Niagara* (AC Loriente)
Ramón y Cajal 73 ☎222414 ☎223861 P

IGUALADA Barcelona 27,940 (☎93) Map **22** C3
★★★*America* (ctra NII) ☎8031000 52rm38⇄14♿ P
Lift 🌙 sB⇄742–962 dB⇄1399–1699 L500
D500 Pool mountains

IRÚN Guipúzcoa (☎943) Map **19** B3
★★*Lizaso* Márires de Guadalupe 5 (n rest) ☎611600
20rm4⇄4♿ P 🌙 sB350–420 dB605–715
dB⇄735–880
★*Paris* (n rest) ☎616545 Closed 11 Nov–Mar
22rm1⇄6♿

JACA Huesca 11,130 (☎974) Map **20** C3
★★★*Gran* ps Generalísimo-1 ☎360900
80rm35⇄45♿ 🏛 P Lift 🌙 sB⇄650–790
dB⇄1160–1595 L550 D550 🏊 Pool mountains

JAÉN Jaén 78,160 (☎953) Map **25** A2
★★*Nervión* Madre Soledad Torres Acosta 3 (n rest)
☎234688 42rm24⇄18♿ Lift
★★*Rey Fernando* pl Coca de la Piñera 7 ☎211840
36rm28⇄8♿ 🏛 P Lift 🌙 sB495–600
sB⇄555–670 dB890–1075 dB⇄985–1180
L385 D385
🏪*Lopez* av de Madrid 15 ☎220132 Ska
🛢 🏪*San Cristóbal y Ada* av Gl-Franco 14 ☎223635
☎223635 (GB)

JAIZKIBEL See **FUENTERRABÍA**

JARANDILLA DE LA VERA Cáceres 3,040
Map **18** C1
★★★★*Parador Nacional de Carlos V* ☎560117
taParal 16⇄ P 🌙 sB⇄640–880 dB⇄900–1125
(English breakfast) L475 D475 Pool mountains

JÁVEA Alicante 7,130 Map **26** D3
★★★★*Parador Nacional Costa Blanca* ☎790200
taParal 60⇄ 🏛 P Lift 🌙 sB⇄1175–1340
dB⇄1655–2005 L500 Pool sea
🛢 🏪*Jávea* av de Ondara 11 ☎790178 BL/Chy (GB)

JEREZ DE LA FRONTERA Cádiz 149,870 (☎956)
Map **24** C1
★★★★*Cisnes* J-António Primo de Rivera 25 (n rest)
☎343541 63rm52⇄8♿ Lift
★★*Aloha* ☎332500 30⇄ Pool

JUNQUERA (LA) Gerona 1,960 (☎972) Map **22** D4
★★★*Puerta de España* ctra Nacional II ☎540120
26⇄ P 🌙 sB⇄587–677 L355 D355 mountains
★★*Mercé Park* ctra Nacional II (4km S) ☎502704
48rm42⇄6♿ P Lift 🌙 sB⇄653 dB⇄1208 L400
D400 mountains lake

LA Each name preceded by La is listed under the
name that follows it.

LAREDO Santander 10,260 (☎942) Map **19** A4
★*Romona* av J-António 4 ☎605336 Closed Nov
28rm220⇄ A15rm 🌙 sB420–450 sB⇄495–615
dB690–725 dB⇄890–950 (English breakfast)
L395 D395

LECUMBERRI Navarra 650 (☎948) Map **19** B3
★★*Ayestaran* ctra 64 ☎504127 120rm50⇄15♿
A94rm 🏛 P Lift sB288 sB⇄318 dB461 dB⇄621
(English breakfast) L243 D243 🏊 Pool mountains
lake

LEÓN León 105,240 (☎987) Map **18** D3
★★★★*Conde Luna* Independencia ☎216700 150⇄
🏛 Lift Pool
★★★★*San Marcos* pl San Marcos ☎237300
tx89809 258⇄ P Lift 🌙 sB⇄2060 dB⇄3420
(English breakfast) L900 D900 🏊 Pool Beach 🎣 ♁
★★★*Oliden* Playa de Santo Domingo 4 (n rest)
☎227500 50rm45⇄5♿ Lift
★★*Ríosol* av de Palencia 3 ☎223650 141⇄ Lift 🌙
sB⇄639 dB⇄1107 L431 D431 mountains

LÉRIDA Lérida 90,880 (☎973) Map **21** B3
★★★*Condes de Urgel* av de Barcelona 2 ☎202300
105⇄ Lift

350

★★*Principal* pl Paheria 8 (n rest) ☎240900
45rm12⇌33 ⋒ Lift
🅿 ᴓMoncasI av de las Garrigas 38 ☎201650 P
LLAFRANCH See **PALAFRUGELL**
LLANES Oviedo 15,510 Map **18** D4
★★*Penablanca* Pidal 1 (n rest) ☎400166 Closed 16
Sep – 14 Jun 30rm 10⇌20 ⋒ ⅅ sB721 – 749
sB⇌⋒477 – 822 dB1007 – 1214 dB⇌⋒1094 – 1220
sea mountains
LLANSÁ Gerona 2,680 (☎972) Map **22** D3
At **Peurto de Llansá** (2km NE)
★★★*Mendisol* Playa de Grifeu ☎380100 Closed
Oct – Feb 35⇌ ⋒ P ⅅ sB⇌558 – 718 dB⇌876 – 1196
(English breakfast) L393 D393 sea mountains
★★*Berna* ☎380150 Closed 16 Sep – 14 May
45rm35⇌10 ⋒ ⅅ sB⇌⋒603 dB⇌⋒1009 L fr339
D fr339 sea
★*Miramar* ps Marítimo 2 ☎380132 Closed Oct – Mar
31rm
LLORET DE MAR Gerona 7,060 (☎972) Map **22** D3
★★★★*Monterrey* ctra de Tossa ☎364050 Closed
mid Oct – Mar 228⇌ P Lift ⅅ sB⇌⋒1480 – 1830
dB⇌⋒2960 – 3360 (English breakfast) L800 D800 ⚊
Pool sea
★★★★*Rigat Park* Playa de Fanals ☎365200
tx51801 Closed Oct – mid Apr 100⇌ P Lift ⅅ
sB⇌⋒1675 – 2175 dB⇌⋒2850 – 3350 ⚊ Pool
Beach sea
★★★★*Santa Marta* Playa de Santa Cristina
☎364904 Closed Nov – Feb 78rm74⇌4 ⋒ A18rm ⋒
Lift ⚊ Pool Beach sea
★★★*Anabel* Carmen 35 ☎334108 230⇌ P ⚊ Pool
★★★*Solterra Playa* pl de España ☎364462
53rm52⇌1 ⋒ Lift
★★*Excelsior* ps M-J-Verdaguer 16 ☎364137
Closed Nov – Mar 45⇌ P Lift ⅅ sB⇌⋒625 – 700
dB⇌⋒1250 – 1400 L400 – 425 D400 – 425 sea
★★*Fanals* ctra de Barcelona ☎364112 Closed
Oct – mid Apr 84rm50⇌34 ⋒ ⋒ P Lift ⅅ
sB⇌⋒445 – 940 dB⇌⋒860 – 1260
(English breakfast) L430 D430 ⚊ Pool
★★*Mariana* ctra Tossa ☎364180 Closed Oct – May
14rm9⇌
★★*Santa Rosa* Seria del Barral ☎364362 Closed
Dec – Mar 132⇌ ⋒ P Lift ⅅ sB⇌⋒470 – 595

dB⇌ ⋒905 – 1055 (English breakfast) L285 D285
Pool sea mountains
🅿 **Celler** San Pedro 102 ☎365397 BL
LOGROÑO Logroño 84,460 (☎941) Map **19** B3
★★★★*Carlton Rioja* av Rey J-Carlos 15 ☎222600
120⇌ Lift
★★*Gran* Gl-Vara de Rey 5 (n rest) ☎212100 83⇌ ⋒
P Lift ⅅ sB⇌⋒536 – 648 dB⇌⋒1081 – 1307
LOS Each name prededed by Los is listed under the
name that follows it.
LUARCA Oviedo 19,600 (☎985) Map **18** C4
★*Gayoso Tres Estrellas* Parque ☎640050 27⇌ Lift
MADRID Madrid 3,146,070 (☎91) Map **19** A1 **See
Plan overleaf**
🄰🄰 agents; see page 335
★★★★★*Meliá Castilla* Capitan Haya 37 ☎2708000
tx23142 Plan **1** 1000⇌ ⋒ Lift Pool
★★★★★*Meliá* Princesa 27 ☎2418200 tx22537
Plan **2** 250⇌ ⋒ Lift
★★★★★*Palace* pl de las Cortés 7 ☎2326300
tx27704 Plan **3** 500⇌ ⋒ P Lift ⅅ
sB⇌⋒3005 – 3645 dB⇌⋒3930 – 5450
(English breakfast) L1000 D1000
★★★★★*Plaza* pza de España 8 (n rest) ☎2471200
tx27383 Plan **4** 420⇌ Lift Pool
★★★★★*Ritz* pl de la Lealtad 5 ☎2212857 tx43986
Plan **5** 175⇌ ⋒ Lift ⅅ sB⇌4000 – 4375
dB⇌5200 – 6200 (English breakfast) L alc D alc
★★★★★*Wellington* Veláquez 8 ☎2754400 tx22700
Plan **7** 325⇌ ⋒ Lift Pool
★★★★*Castellana* ps Castellana 57 (n rest)
☎4100200 taGrandmet tx27686 Plan **8** 278⇌ ⋒ P
Lift sB⇌2035 – 2135 dB⇌2770 (English breakfast)
★★★★*Emperador* av J-António 53 (n rest)
☎2472800 Plan **9** 240⇌ Lift ⅅ sB⇌2300 sB⇌3075
(English breakfast) Pool
★★★★*Emperatriz* López de Hoyos 4 ☎2761910
tx43640 Plan **10** 170⇌ P Lift ⅅ sB⇌1770 dB⇌2725
(English breakfast) L700 D700
★★★★*Gran Vía* av J-António 25 ☎2221121 Plan **11**
162⇌ Lift
★★★★*Sanvy* c Goya 3 ☎2760800 Plan **12** 109⇌ ⋒
Lift Pool
★★★★*Villa Magna* Paseo de la Castellana 22
☎2614900 tx22914 200rm 350P

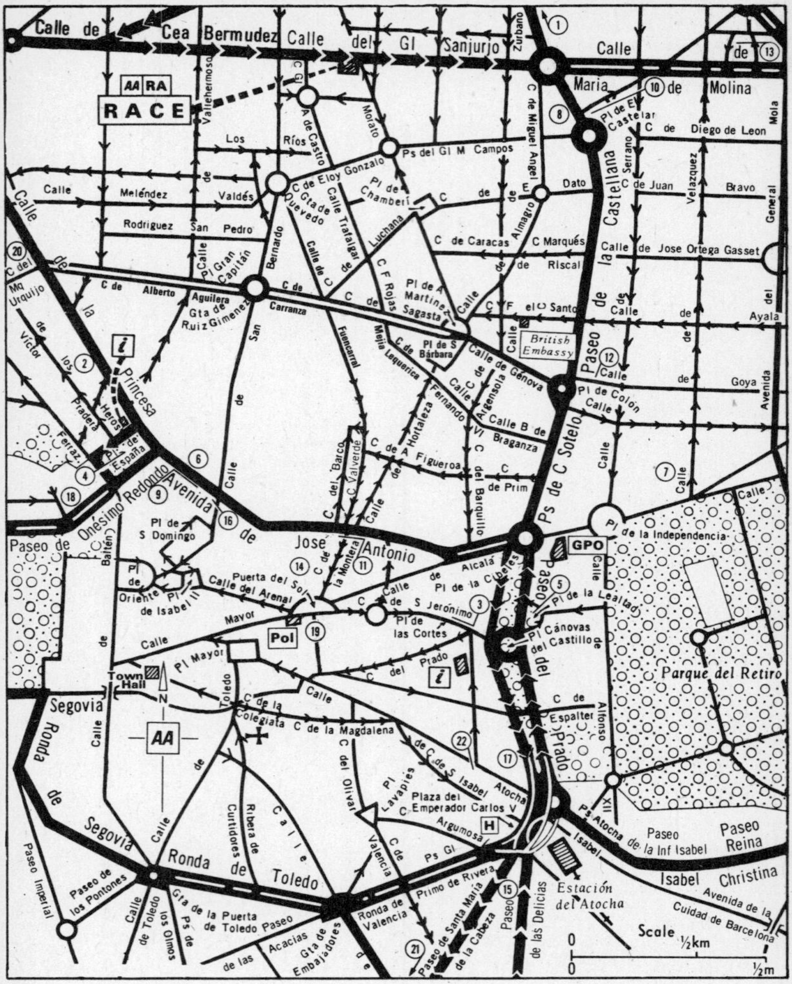

Spain

Madrid

1	★★★★★	Meliá Castilla
2	★★★★★	Meliá
3	★★★★★	Palace
4	★★★★★	Plaza
5	★★★★★	Ritz
6	★★★★★	Washington
7	★★★★★	Wellington
8	★★★★	Castellana
9	★★★★	Emperador
10	★★★★	Emperatriz
11	★★★★	Gran Vía
12	★★★★	Sanvy
13	★★★	Balboa
14	★★★	Carlos-V
15	★★★	Carlton
16	★★★	Lope de Vega
17	★★★	Nacional
18	★★★	Principe Pío
19	★★★	Residencia Madrid
20	★★★	Tirol
21	☆☆☆	Olivos (at Getafe 12.5km S)
22	★★	Mercator

Spain

★★★*Balboa* Núnez de Balboa 112 ☎2625440
Plan **13** 110⊷ 🏛 Lift
★★★*Carlos-V* c Maestro Victoria 5 (off c de la Arenal)
(n rest) ☎2314100 Plan **14** 67⊷ Lift
★★★*Carlton* ps de la Delicias 28 ☎2397100 Plan **15**
150⊷ P Lift ♪ sB⊷1300 dB⊷2250
(English breakfast) L725 D725
★★★*Centro Norte* Mauricio Ravel 10 ☎7333450
tx42598 Not on plan 179rm P Pool
★★★*Lope de Vega* av J-Antónlo 59 (n rest)
☎2477000 Plan **16** 50⊷ Lift
★★★*Nacional* ps del Prado 48 ☎2273010 Plan **17**
189rm146⊷43 🏛 Lift
★★★*Principe Pío* ps de Onésimo Redondo 16
☎2470800 Plan **18** 200rm190⊷10 🏛 Lift
★★★*Residencia Madrid* Carretas 10 (off Puerto de
Sol) (n rest) ☎2216520 Plan **19** 71⊷ Lift ♪ sB⊷889
dB⊷1518
★★★*Tirol* Marqués de Urquljo 4 (n rest) ☎2481900
Plan **20** 92rm84⊷ 🏛 Lift
★★*Mercator* Atocha 123 (n rest) ☎2392600 Plan **22**
90⊷ 🏛 Lift
🏍*Pardal* F-de-la Hoz 50 ☎4198201 Chy/Rov
🛢 🏍*Standard* A-López 88 ☎2698806 P BL/Tri
At **Barajas** (15km N on NI)
★★★★*Barajas* ☎2054840 tx22255 Not on plan
230⊷ P Lift ♪ sB⊷2725 – 3425 dB⊷fr4550
(English breakfast) L1050 D1050 Pool
At **Getafe** (12.5km S off NIV)
☆☆☆*Olivos* ☎6956700 Plan **21** 100⊷ 🏛 Pool
MAGALUF See **MALLORCA** under **BALEARES
(ISLAS DE)**
MAHON See **MENORCA** under **BALEARES (ISLAS
DE)**
MÁLAGA Málaga 374,450 (☎952) Map **24** D1
★★★★*Málaga Palacio* av Cortina del Muelle
☎211571 tx77021 235⊷ Lift Pool sea
★★★★*Gaviota* ps de Salvador Rueda ☎250150
25⊷ 🏛 Lift Pool sea
★★★*Naranjos* ps Sancha 29 (n rest) ☎224316
tx77061 38rm35⊷3 🏛 Lift sea
★★*Parador Nacional de Gibralfaro* ☎221902 12⊷
★★*Niza* Marqués de Larios 2 ☎217761 53rm30⊷
Lift
★★*Penón* Marqués de Larios 4 ☎213602
29rm10⊷12 🏠 Lift
🛢 🏍*Talllefer* ctra la Union ☎222940
MALLORCA See **BALEARES (ISLAS DE)**
MANZANARES Ciudad Real 15,690 (☎926)
Map **25** A3
☆*Albergue Nacional* (2km S) ☎610400 taParal
42⊷ P sB⊷630 – 760 dB⊷1060 – 1270 L 475 D475
★*Cruce* ctra Madrid-Cádiz km 173 (DP) ☎611900
40rm36⊷4 🏠 Pool
🛢 🏍*J Serrano Calvlllo* ctra Madrid-Cádiz km 171
☎611192 P BL
MAQUEDA Toledo 510 Map **25** A4
★★★*Cazador* ctra Madrid-Badajoz ☎20
30⊷ A15rm 🏛 Pool
MARBELLA Málaga 33,200 (☎952) Map **24** D1
★★★★★*Mellá Don Pepe* ctra de Cádiz ☎770300
tx77055 226⊷ 🏛 Lift ✈ Pool ᘒ sea

★★★★★*Monteros* (DP) ☎771700 tx77059 168⊷
Lift ✈ Pool Beach ᘒ ∩ sea
★★★★*Chapas* rte de Málaga km198 ☎831375
taLuzhotel tx77057 Closed Nov – Feb 117⊷ P Lift ♪
sB⊷1250 – 1360 dB⊷2050 – 2220
(English breakfast) L 650 D650 mountains
★★★★*Golf Guadalmina* ☎811744 tx77058 80⊷ P
♪ dB⊷3100 (English breakfast) L 900 D900 ✈ Pool
Beach ᘒ ∩ sea
★★★★*Guadalpin* ctra Cádiz – Málaga ☎771100
103⊷ pool
★★★*Artola* ctra de Cádiz ☎831390 Closed
Dec – Feb 50rm50⊷2 🏠 ᘒ P Lift ♪ sB⊷ 🏠1045
dB⊷ 🏠1790 (English breakfast) L390 D390 ✈ Pool
Beach ᘒ sea
★★★*Fuerte* Castillo de San Luis ☎771500 taForotel
110⊷ P Lift sB⊷985 – 1235 dB⊷1770 – 1870
(English breakfast) L 625 D625 ✈ Pool Beach sea
★★★*San Cristóbal* Ramón y Cajal 16 ☎771250
109⊷ Lift sea
🛢 🏍*Auto Servicios Andaluces* ctra de Cádiz-
Málaga km188.8 ☎771896 BL (GB)
MATARÓ Barcelona 73,130 (☎93) Map **22** D3
★★★*Castell de Mato* (N II) ☎7901681 52⊷ Lift
MAZAGÓN Huelva Map **23** B2
★★★*Parador Nacional Cristóbal Colón* ☎303
20⊷ A10rm Pool sea
MEDINACELI Soria 1,440 Map **19** B1
★★*Duque de Medinaceli* (N II) (DP) ☎326111
13rm2⊷3 🏠 🏛 Pool
🏍*Vincento Martinez Medina* ctra Madrid-Zaragoza
km 150 ☎326029 ☎326029 M/c P
MENORCA See **BALEARES (ISLAS DE)**
MÉRIDA Badajoz 40,060 (☎924) Map **24** C3
★★★*Emperatriz* pl España 19 ☎302640 43⊷
★★★*Parador Nacional Vía de la Plata* pl de Queipo
de Llano 3 ☎301540 taParal 95⊷ 🏠 🏛 P
sB⊷ 🏠1650 dB⊷ 🏠2250 D600
MIERES Oviedo Map **18** C/D4
🛢 🏍*Tunon* Peligene Industrial ☎472144 Chy/Rov
MIJAS Málaga 9,320 Map **24** D1
★★★*Mijas* Urbanización Tamisa ☎463940 106⊷
A15rm ✈ Pool sea
MINGLANILLA Cuenca 2,950 Map **26** C3
🛢 🏍*Marco* ctra Madrid-Valencia ☎36 ⊷80 P Chy
MOJÁCAR Almería 1,812 Map **25** B1
★★★*Moresco* ☎478025 closed Nov – Mar 147⊷ Lift
Pool sea
★★★*Parador Nacional Reyes Católicas* ☎478250
taParal 99⊷ P ♪ sB⊷1495 dB⊷1965 L500 D500
MOLAR (EL) Madrid 1,900 (☎91) Map **19** A1
🛢 🏍*M Sato* ctra de Francia km 42 ☎6210081 M/c P
Ren
MONACHIL Granada Map **25** A1
★★★*Parador Nacional Sierra Nevada* ☎480200
taParal 32rm10⊷22 🏠 🏛 P ♪ sB⊷ 🏠1270 – 1560
dB⊷ 🏠1580 – 2110 L 475 D475 mountains
MONTBLANCH Tarragona 5,020 (☎977)
Map **22** C3
★★*Ducal* av Gl-Mola ☎860025 40rm20⊷20 🏠 🏛
🛢 🏍*Vidal* Arrabal de Santa Ana 26 ☎860021 P BL

HOTEL CENTRO NORTE

Telegramadr. CENTROTEL — Telex 42 598 CNOR-E
Phone 91/733 3450 733 2300 Calle (street) Mauricio Revel, 10 MADRID-16

500m from motorway M-30, 5km to the airport. 179 rooms air-conditioned, with background music and telephone. Parking. 6,000m garden. Swimming-pool for adults and children. Lounges — conference and banquet-hall — English bar — cafeteria — self-service. Large shopping-centre with restaurant, discotheque, pub, hairdresser, sauna, etc.

nt

Spain

MONSTENY Barcelona 310 Map **22** D3
★★★*San Bernat* ☎8670651 18⇌ 🏠 ○
MONTSERRAT Barcelona 730 (☎93) Map **22** C3
★★★*Abat Cisneros* pl del Monasterio 10 ☎8350201
41rm31⇌10🝙 P Lift 𝄐 sB⇌🝙939 dB 1478
dB⇌🝙1578 L 606 D606
MONT-TIBIDABO See **BARCELONA**
MOTILLA DEL PALANCAR Cuenca 4,270
Map **25** B4
★★★*Sol* ctra Madrid-Valencia 11 ☎331025
37rm19⇌18🝙 🝙
MOTRIL Graada 31,720 (☎958) Map **25** A1
★★★*Costa Nevada* ctra de Granada ☎600500 65⇌
⤳ Pool
🛢 ⅍*Litoral* R-Acosta 11 ☎601296 BL/Chy/Rov
MURCIA Murcia 243,760 (☎968) Map **26** C2
★★★*7 Coronas Meliá* Ronda de Garay 3 ☎217771
124⇌ 🏠 Lift
🛢 ⅍*T Guillen Guillen* ctra de Alicante 119 ☎241212
P Peu
NAVALMORAL DE LA MATA Cáceres 9,710
(☎927) Map **24** D4
★*Moya* Apartado 110 ☎530500 40rm16⇌5🝙 🏠 P
𝄐 sB303–363 sB⇌🝙398–478 dB536–631
dB⇌🝙646–771 L 295 D295 mountains
🛢 ⅍*Moya* ctra Madrid-Lisbon km180 ☎531462 P
Ren
NERJA Málaga 8,570 (☎952) Map **25** A1
★★★★*Parador Nacional* ☎520050 taParal 40⇌ P
Lift 𝄐 Pool sea mountains
★★★*Portofino* Puerta de Mar 2 ☎520150 Closed
Nov–19 Mar 12⇌
NUEVALOS Zaragoza Map **19** B1
★★★*Monasterio de Piedra* (3km S) ☎2
taPor Ateca Closed Nov–Mar 61⇌ P 𝄐 sB⇌680
dB⇌1085 L 425 D425 ⤳ Pool mountains
OJÉN Málaga Map **24** D1
★*Refugio Nacional de Cazadores de Juana*
☎826140 9⇌ 🏠
OLITE Navarra 2,900 (☎948) Map **22** D3
★★★*Parador Principe de Viana* ☎740000
34rm10⇌
OLOT Gerona 21,225 (☎972) Map **22** D3
★★★*Montsacopa* c Mulleras ☎260762
72rm34⇌1🝙 🏠 Lift
🛢 🛲*Maso* av Gerona 7 ☎261575 P Aud/Rov/VW
🛢 🛲*Ferran* Jose Ayats 9 ☎261546
ORENSE Orense 7,3350 (☎988) Map **17** B3
★★*Barcelona* av Pontevedra 13 (DP) ☎220800
47rm⇌10🝙 Lift
★★*Parque* Parque de San Lázaro 24 (n rest)
☎213200 50rm14⇌22🝙 Lift
OROPESA Toledo 3,580 Map **24** D4
★★★*Parador Nacional de Virrey Toledo* pl del
Palacio 1 ☎21 taParaloro 44⇌ P Lift 𝄐
sB⇌1175–1440 dB⇌1655–2005 L 500 D500
mountains
OVIEDO Oviedo 154,120 (☎985) Map **18** C4
★★*España* Jovellanos 2 (n rest) ☎222345 100⇌ 🏠
Lift
★★*Principado* San Francisco 8 ☎217792
100rm83⇌17🝙 Lift 𝄐 sB⇌🝙845–1030
dB⇌🝙1420–1720 L fr525 Dfr525
★*Pasaje* Palacio Valdés 1 ☎214580 36rm6⇌1🝙 Lift
PAGUERA see **MALLORCA** under **BALEARES**
(ISLAS DE)
PALAFRUGELL Gerona 12,260 (☎972) Map **22** D3
★★★*Cavallers* c Callavers 1 ☎300362 Closed
Oct–May 17rm15⇌2🝙
⅍*J M Suquet* Bagur 19 ☎300248 P Cit
At **Calella de Palafrugell** (5km SE)
★★★★*Alga* ☎300058 54⇌ Lift ⤳ Pool sea
★★★*Garbi* Mirto ☎300100 Closed Oct–Mar
36rm36⇌ A6rm P Lift 𝄐 sB⇌680–870
dB⇌🝙1136–1360 Pool sea
★★★*Mestral* ☎300258 Closed Oct–Apr 59⇌ Lift ⤳
Pool sea

★★*Mediterraneo* Playa Baños ☎300150 Closed
Oct–Apr 38rm20⇌18🝙 P 𝄐 sB⇌🝙398–453
dB⇌🝙741–916 L 387 Beach sea
★★*Torre* Canadell ☎300300 Closed 16 Oct–Apr
58rm38⇌ sea
At **Llafranch** (6km E)
★★★*Paraiso* (DP) ☎300450 Closed 21 Sep–19
May 55⇌ 🏠 Lift ⤳ Pool
★★★*Terramar* ☎300200 Closed Nov–mid Apr
56rm53⇌🝙3🝙 🏠 P Lift 𝄐 sB 1025–1250
sB⇌🝙1225–1550 dB⇌🝙2050–2400 L 400–500
D400–500 sea
★★*Llafranch* ps Cypsele 35 ☎300208 28rm24⇌
sea
★*Levante* San Francisco de Blanes (DP) ☎300366
Closed 2 Nov–2Dec 20rm8⇌12🝙 sea
At **Tamariu** (4km SE)
★★★*Hostalillo* Bellavista 11 (DP) ☎300158 Closed
21 Sep–19 May 72⇌ 🏠 Lift sea
★★*Tamariu* ps del Mar 3 ☎300108 Closed
Oct–Mar 48rm40⇌8🝙 A23rm 🏠 P 𝄐
sB⇌🝙405–500 dB⇌🝙810–1000
(English breakfast) L 375–450 D350–425
PALAMÓS Gerona 10,090 (☎972) Map **22** D3
★★★*Trias* ps del Mar 16 ☎314100 Closed Nov–Feb
77rm67⇌10🝙 🏠 Lift Pool sea
★★*Marina* av de Generalísimo 48 ☎314250
62rm34⇌28🝙 𝄐 sB⇌🝙520–675
dB⇌🝙855–1090 L 400 D400
★★*San Juan* c Mayor de San Juan 30 ☎314208
Closed Oct–Mar 31rm23⇌8🝙 sB⇌🝙750–990
dB⇌🝙1320–1510 (English breakfast) L 400 D400
Pool sea
★★*Vostra Llar* av J-António 16 ☎314262 Closed
Oct–May 30
⅍*Central* ctra a San Felíu 6 ☎314466 Fia
At **San Antonio de Calonge** (2.5km S)
★★★*Lys* ctra de San Felíu (DP) ☎314150 Closed 26
Sep–19 May 204rm16⇌11🝙 A5rm
★★★*Rosa dels Vents* ps del Mar ☎314216 closed
16 Oct–19 May 70⇌ 🏠 P Lift 𝄐 sB⇌629–952
dB⇌1433–1781 (English breakfast) L 476 D476 ○
sea
★★★*Rosamar* ps del Mar 33 ☎314165 Closed 11
Oct–Apr 74⇌ 🏠 P Lift 𝄐 sB⇌450–900
dB⇌1200–1600 (English breakfast) L 350 D350
Beach sea
★★*Petit* c Progreso 10 ☎314062 Closed Oct–Apr
25⇌
PALMA DE MALLORCA See **MALLORCA** under
BALEARES (ISLAS DE)
PAMPLONA Navarra 147,170 (☎948) Map **19** B3
★★★★*Tres Reyes* Jardines de la Taconera
☎226600 tx36720 180⇌ 🏠 Lift 𝄐 sB⇌2280–2800
dB⇌3200–3900 L fr860 Dfr860 Pool mountains
★★*Yoldi* av San Ignacio 11 ☎224800 26rm24🝙 Lift
sB492–572 sB⇌🝙552–642 dB849–1024
dB🝙959–1139 (English breakfast) L 428
★*Hostal Valerio* av de Zaragoza 5 ☎245466
16rm1⇌ Lift 𝄐 sB329–384 dB563–653
dB⇌688–793 L 345 D345
🛲*Redin* Arrieta 9 ☎246848 ☎245122 (GB)
PANCORBO Burgos 750 (☎947) Map **13** A3
★★★*El Molino* ctra G-Madrid-Irún km305 ☎320266
48⇌ Pool
PEÑISCOLA Castellón 2,720 Map **21** B2
★★★*Hosteria del Mar* ctra Benicarló ☎480600
tx64550 85⇌ P Lift 𝄐 sB⇌1122–1375
dB⇌1774–2150 L 500 D500 ⤳ Pool Beach sea
PINEDA DE MAR Barcelona 7,780 (☎93) Map **22** D3
★★*Mont Palau* ps Marítimo ☎7623387 Closed
Dec–Feb 99rm80⇌10🝙 A17rm Lift
★★*Taurus Park* ps Marítimo ☎7623350 Closed
Nov–Apr 417⇌ Lift sB⇌857 dB⇌1654 L244 D244
⤳ Pool Beach ○ sea
PLASENCIA Cáceres 27,170 (☎927) Map **18** C1
★★★*Alfonso VIII* c Alfonso VIII 32 ☎410250 56⇌
Lift 𝄐 sB⇌🝙762–926 dB⇌2116–1830 L435
D435

PLAYA D'AIGUAFREDA See **BAGUR**

PLAYA DE ARO Gerona 493 (☎972) Map **22** D3
★★★*Cliper* ☎817000 Closed 16 Oct – Apr 40⇄ ☽
sB⇄405 – 520 dB⇄810 – 1040 L350 – 400
D350 – 400 sea mountains
★★★*Cosmopolita* ps del Mar ☎817350 Closed
Dec – mid Apr 91⇄7🛏 Lift Beach sea
★★★*Miramar* ☎817150 Closed Nov – Apr 45⇄ 🏠 P
Lift ☽ sB⇄505 – 556 dB⇄876 – 1004
(English breakfast) L235 D235 sea
★★★*Rosamar* pl del Los Martires (DP) ☎817304
Closed Oct – 14 May 61rm54⇄7🛏 Lift
★★★*Xaloc* ☎817300 Closed Nov – Apr 45⇄ 🛏 P ☽
sB⇄🛏392 dB⇄🛏754 (English breakfast) L298
D298 Beach sea
★★*Bell Repos* Virgen del Carmen ☎81700 Closed
21 Oct – 19 May 40rm27⇄2🛏 🏠 sea
★★*Pins* ☎817219 60⇄ Lift
★★*Residencia Japet* ctra de Palamós ☎817366
48rm26⇄22🛏 P ☽ sB⇄🛏484 – 534
dB⇄🛏813 – 888 L369 D369
At **Condado de San Jorge** (2km NE)
★★★*Cap Roig* ☎315351 tx57204 Closed 21
Nov – Feb 160⇄ 🏠 Lift 🏊 Pool sea
★★★*Park Hotel San Jorge* ☎327316 Closed 21
Oct – 26 May 85rm80⇄5🛏 Lift 🏊 Beach sea

PLAYA DE GANDÍA See **GANDÍA**

PLAYA DE LAS MARINAS See **DENIA**

PLAYA DE PALMA (CA'N PASTILLA) See **PALMA
DE MALLORCA** under **MALLORCA** under
BALEARES (ISLAS DE)

PLAYA DE PALMA NOVA See **PALMA DE
MALLORCA** under **MALLORCA** under **BALEARES
(ISLAS DE)**

POBLA-DE-SEGUR Lérida 500 Map **22** C3
🛏 🍴*San Cristóbal* av Estación 2 ☎680524
☎680360 P

POLLENSA See **MALLORCA** under **BALEARES
(ISLAS DE)**

PONFERRADA León 45,260 (☎987) Map **18** C3
★★*Madrid* J-Antonio 50 ☎411550 54rm41 ⇄13🛏 P
Lift sB⇄🛏635 – 691 dB⇄🛏1149 L381 D381
★*Maran* A-Lopez Pelaez 29 (n rest) ☎411800
24rm2⇄15🛏

PONTEVEDRA Pontevedra 52,450 (☎986)
Map **17** A3
★★★*Parador Nacional Casa del Baron* Maceda 21
☎852195 27⇄
🛏 *S Varela Pasarin* C Benito Corbal 36 ☎850735
PORT-BOU Gerona 2,360 (☎972) Map **22** D4
★*Costa Brava* J-Antonio 26 ☎390003 Closed
Oct – May 34rm P sB289 – 350 dB528 – 645
L315 – 380 D315 – 380

POTES Santander 1,210 Map **18** D3
★★*Parador Nacional* ☎730001 taParal 78⇄ P ☽
sB⇄1175 – 1440 dB⇄1620 – 1965 L500 D500
mountains

PREMIÁ DE MAR Barcelona 11,280 (☎93)
Map **22** D3
★★*Premiá* c San Miguel 46 (n rest) ☎7510997 23⇄
PUEBLA DE SANABRIA Zamora 1,590 (☎988)
Map **18** C3
☆☆*Albergue Nacional* ☎620001 24rm18⇄ 🏠
PUERTO DE LLANSÁ See **LLANSA**
PUERTO DE PAJARES Oviedo (☎985)
Map **18** C/D3
★★*Parador Nacional de Pajares* ☎490100
29rm7⇄3🛏 🏠
PUERTO DE POLLENSA See **POLLENSA** under
MALLORCA under **BALEARES (ISLAS DE)**
PUERTO DE SANTA MARÍA (EL) Cadiz 42,150
(☎956) Map **24** C1
☆☆☆*Meliá el Caballo Blanco* (2.5km S on ctra de
Cádiz) ☎863745 89⇄ Lift 🏊 sea
★★★*Fuentebravia* ctra de Rota ☎851717 taParador
90⇄7 Lift ☽ sB⇄1660 – 1900 dB⇄2510
(English breakfast) L fr840 D fr840 Pool Beach sea
🚗*Auto Guadalete* c F-Zamacola 5 ☎864692 P
BL/Chy (GB)
PUERTO LAPICE Ciudad Real 1,300 Map **25** A3
★★*Puerto* ctra Madrid-Cádiz ☎576000 37rm 🏠 P
sB387 – 466 dB690 – 827 L357 D357 mountains
PUERTO LUMBRERAS Murcia 7,990 (☎968)
Map **25** B2
☆☆*Albergue Nacional* (On N340) ☎402025
19rm11⇄ 🏠
PUERTOMARIN Lugo 2,960 Map **17** B3
★★★*Parador Nacional*
PUIGCERDA Gerona 5,530 (☎972) Map **22** C4
★★*Maria Victoria* Florenza 9 ☎880300 ta Marvic
50rm34⇄16🛏 P Lift sB⇄🛏563 – 817
dB⇄🛏807 – 1093 (English breakfast) L392 – 500
D392 mountains
★★*Martinez* ctra de Llivia ☎880250 15⇄ P ☽
sB⇄530 – 602 dB⇄975 – 1119 (English breakfast)
mountains
REINOSA Santander 10,900 Map **19** A3
🍴*Hermanos Hidalgo* Pozo Pozmieo ☎751883
☎751822 🍴 M/c P
REUS Tarragona 59,100 (☎977) Map **22** C2
🛏 🍴*Rull* av 15 de Enero25 ☎302269 (GB)
RIBADEO Lugo 8,970 (☎982) Map **18** C4
☆☆*Albergue Nacional* ☎110825 49⇄ 🏠 Lift sea
★*Eo* av de Asturias 5 (N rest) ☎110750 Closed
Oct – Mar 24⇄ P ☽ sB⇄714 dB⇄1008 Pool sea
RIBADESELLA Oviedo 7,110 Map **18** D4
★★★*Gran de Sella* La Plage (DP) ☎860150 Closed
Nov – Feb 73⇄ Lift 🏊 Pool sea
RIBAS DE FRESER Gerona 3,130 (☎972)
Map **22** C/D3
★★*Cataluña* San Quintin 37 ☎727017 26rm4⇄12🛏
🏠 Pool

Spain

★★*Montagut* Aguas de Ribas ☎727021 Closed 16 Sep – Jun 100rm32⇄16🍴 🏛 ✶ Pool
★★*Prats* San Quintin 20 (DP) ☎727001 25rm20⇄3🍴

RINCÓN DE LA VICTORIA Málaga 6,061 Map **24** D1
★★★*Elimar 2* Quiepo de Llano 84 ☎401200 80⇄ 🏛 Lift

RONDA Málaga 30,080 (☎952) Map **24** C1
★★★*Reina Victoria* c Jerez 39 ☎871240 89rm78⇄11🍴 P Lift 🌙 sB⇄🍴695 – 835 dB⇄🍴1330 – 1605 L505 D595 Pool mountains
ROSAS Gerona 6,190 (☎972) Map **22** D3
★★★*Coral Playa* ctra Playa ☎256250 Closed 11 Oct – Mar 125rm110⇄15🍴 Lift
★★★*Vistabella* Playa de Cañyellos Petites ☎256200 Closed Oct – mid Apr 43⇄ P 🌙 sB⇄🍴965 dB⇄1625 L580 D580 Pool Beach sea
★★*Terraza* Playa ☎256154 Closed Nov – 14 Mar 85rm62⇄13🍴 🏛 Lift ✶ Pool Beach sea
⋆*Goya* Riera Ginjolers (DP) ☎256123 Closed Oct – 14 May 68rm38⇄30🍴 ✶ Pool
RUBENA Burgos 190 Map **19** A3
★★*Fuente de Ray* ctra Madrid-Francia ☎1 11rm2⇄
SABIÑÁNIGO Huesca 8,610 (☎974) Map **21** B4
★★*Pardina* ☎480975 64rm51⇄ P Lift 🌙 sB600 – 730 dB1060 – 1280 L460 D460 Pool mountains lake
🛈 ✷*Arranz* Zaragoza 9 ☎480043 BL

S'AGARO Gerona 160 (☎972) Map **22** D3
★★★★★*Gavina* ☎321100 tx57132 74⇄ Lift ✶ Pool Beach sea
★★★*Caleta Park* playa de St-Pol (Pn Jul & Aug) ☎320012 Closed Nov – mid Apr 105rm95⇄10🍴 P Lift 🌙 sB⇄🍴800 – 1200 1800 – 2500 Jul & Aug dB⇄🍴1700 – 2700 (3600 – 5000 Jul & Aug) (English breakfast) L680 – 780 D680 – 780 Pool sea
SALAMANCA Salamanca 125,220 (☎923) Map **18** C2
★★★*Gran* pl Poeta Iglesias 3 ☎213500 94⇄ 🏛 Lift
★★★*Monterrey* J-Antonio 73 ☎214400 98rm84⇄ 🏛 Lift Pool
★★*Clavero* Consuelo 15 ☎218108 39rm19⇄6🍴
🛈 ✷*M N Bermejo* av Italia 11 – 13 ☎223539 M/c P BL/Chy
Paz av Pérez Almeida 69 ☎220546 ☎227852 P
🛈 ✷*Vicente Sanchez Marcos* av Mirat 15 ☎222450 Cit/Peu
At **Santa Maria de Tormes** (4km E)
★★★*Jardín Regio* ☎6 108⇄ 🏛 Lift ✶ Pool
SALER (EL) See **VALENCIA**
SALOU Tarragona 4,700 (☎977) Map **22** C2
★★★*Picnic* ctra Salou-Reus ☎380158 54rm 46⇄ A10rm P 🌙 sB485 – 555 sB⇄585 – 655 dB822 – 900 dB⇄🍴952 – 1060 (English breakfast) L350 D350 Pool
★★★*Salou Park* Busellas 35, cala Capellans ☎380208 Closed Oct – Apr 102⇄ P Lift 🌙 sB⇄1010 – 1360 dB⇄1520⇄2320 L700 D700 Pool sea
★★*Gaviotas* pl de España (DP) ☎380362 Closed 21 Dec – Jan 18⇄ 🏛 sea
★★*Planas* pl Bonet 2 ☎380108 Closed Oct – Mar 100rm98⇄2🍴 Lift 🌙 sB●⇄592 – 653 dB⇄🍴1039 – 1144 (English breakfast) L369 D369 sea
🛈 ✷*International* C P-Martell ☎380614 M/c P
SAN ANTONIO DE CALONGE See **PALAMÓS**
SAN FELIÚ DE GUIXOLS Gerona 12,510 (☎972) Map **22** D3
★★★★*Murla Park* ps Generalísimo 21 – 23 ☎320450 91rm80⇄11🍴 P Lift sB⇄🍴930 – 1230 dB⇄🍴1960 – 2360 (English breakfast) L650 D650 Pool sea
★★★★*Reina Elisenda* ps Generalísimo 6 ☎320700 Closed Oct – Apr 70⇄ Lift ✶ Pool
★★★*Montecarlo* Montaña de San Elmo ☎320000 Closed Oct – May 60⇄ Lift sea

★★★*Montjoi* San Elmo (DP) ☎320300 tx57139 Closed Oct – Mar 64⇄ 🏛 Lift Pool sea
★★★*Murla* Gl-Mola 48 ☎320450 92rm81⇄11🍴 Lift Pool sea
★★★*Rex* Rambla J-Antónió 18 ☎320312 Closed 21 Sep – May 25rm23⇄2🍴 Lift 🌙 sB⇄🍴500 – 720 dB⇄🍴1120 – 1325 sea mountains
★★*Ideal* c Especieros 6 ☎320612 closed Nov – Apr 24⇄
★★*Jecsalis* ctra Gerona 9 ☎320258 Closed Oct – May 63rm20⇄43🍴 🏛 Lift
★★*Nautilus* pl San Pedro 5 ☎320516 Closed Nov – Apr 22rm19⇄3🍴 Lift 🌙 sB⇄1062 – 1197 dB⇄🍴1059 – 1192 L339 D339 Beach sea
★★*Noies* Rambla J-Antónió 10 ☎320400 Closed Oct – Apr 50rm50⇄ A10rm Lift 🌙 sB⇄600 – 900 dB⇄1000 – 1400 L400 D400 ✶ sea
★★*Turist* San Ramón 39 ☎320841 Closed Nov – Mar 23rm10⇄ A9rm 🏛 P sB371 dB682 dB⇄808 L310 D310 sea mountains
🛈*Metropol* ctra Gerona 7 ☎320982 Ren
SAN LORENZO DE EL ESCORIAL Madrid 7,450 (☎91) Map **18** D1
★★★★*Victoria Palace* Juan de Toledo 4 ☎2961200 90⇄ 🏛 Lift Pool
★★★*Miranda & Suizo* Floridablanca 20 ☎2960000 50⇄ Lift
SAN PEDRO DE ALCÁNTARA Málaga (☎952) Map **24** D1
★★★*Cortijo Blanco* ☎811440 Closed Nov – Mar 119rm86⇄33🍴 ✶ Pool
SAN POL DE MAR Barcelona 2,040 (☎93) Map **23** D3
★★★*Gran Sol* ctra de Francia (DP) ☎7600051 41⇄ Lift ✶ Pool Beach sea
★★★*Torre Martina* ctra Madrid-Francia km670 ☎8905125 Closed 11 Oct – Apr 35⇄ sea
SAN ROQUE Cádiz 17,730 (☎956) Map **24** C1
★★★*Rio Grande* ctra Cádiz-Málaga ☎780100 22⇄
SAN SEBASTIÁN Guipúzcoa 165,830 (☎943) Map **19** B3
★★★★*Londres & Inglaterra* Zubieta 2 ☎444133 153⇄ Lift sea
★★★*Gudamendi* (4km W) ☎214000 taArtaze tx36121 20⇄ P 🌙 sB⇄1300 – 1592 dB⇄1820 – 2210 L625 D625 sea mountains
★★★*Monte Igueldo* Monte Igueldo ☎210211 121⇄ 🏛 Lift Pool sea
★*Juaristi Residencia* Sanchez Toca 1 ☎467533 Closed 16 Oct – 14 Apr 20rm10🍴 🌙 sB411 dB fr594 dB🍴707
🛈 *Amara* C Amara 24 ☎464737 Frd/Vlo (GB)
🛈 ✷*Gruas Espana* av Isabel 11 – 15 ☎458352 ☎458352 M/c P (GB)
SANTA CRISTINA DE ARO Gerona 980 Map **22** D3
★★★★*Costa Brava Golf* ☎837052 tx57252 Closed Oct 91rm84⇄7🍴 P Lift 🌙 sB⇄🍴1375 – 2000 dB⇄🍴2550 – 3000 L fr600 D fr600 ✶ Pool ◯
★★*Riu d'Or* Taulera 2 Closed Oct – May 16⇄ 🏛 ✶ Pool
SANTA CRUZ See **CORUÑA (LA)**
SANTA CRUZ DE MUDELA Ciudad Real Map **25** A3
🛈 ✷*Izquierdo* ctra Madrid-Cádiz km217 ☎342022 P Cit
SANTA EULALIA DEL RÍO See **IBIZA** under **BALEARES (ISLAS DE)**
SANTA MARÍA DE HUERTA Soria 1,010 Map **19** B1
★★★*Albergue Nacional* ☎2520 40⇄ 🏛
SANTA MARTA DE TORMES See **SALAMANCA**
SANTANDER Santander 149,700 (☎942) Map **19** A4
★★★★*Bahia* av Alfonso XIII 5 ☎221700 tx35859 181rm162⇄19🍴 Lift 🌙 sB⇄🍴1580 – 1975 dB⇄🍴2280 – 2850 (English breakfast) L720 – 900 D720 – 900 sea
★★*Colón* pl de las Brisas ☎272300 Closed 10 Sep – 19 Jun 43rm6⇄ 🍴 sea

🛏 **Gallo** Magallanes 19–23 ☎232237 P Vlo (GB)

🛏 🍴 **Sancho** c Castilla 62 ☎370017 M/c Frd/MB

🍴 🅿 **Vidal de la Pena** ps de Pereda ☎212150
Ren/Rov (GB)

SANTIAGO DE COMPOSTELA La Coruña 70,890
(☎981) Map **17** B4

★★★★★ **Los Reyes Católicos** pl de España 1
☎582200 tx86004 157rm105➪52🍴🏨 P Lift ♪
sB➪🍴1840–2800 dB➪🍴2540–3740
(English breakfast) L900 D900

★★★ **Peregrino** av R-de Castro ☎591850 148➪ Lift
Pool

SANTILLANA DEL MAR Santander 3,920
Map **19** A4

★★★ **Parador de Gil Blas** ☎818000 tzParal
24rm24➪ A21rm 🏨 P ♪ sB455–540 sB➪770–935
dB800–945 dB➪1325–1600 L475 D475

★★ **Altamira** Canton 1 ☎818025 Closed Nov–Mar
27rm16➪ P ♪ sB345–410 dB560–660
dB➪720–865 L335 D335

SANTO DOMINGO DE LA CALZADA Logroño
5,640 (☎941) Map **19** A3

★★ **Parador Nacional** ☎340300 27➪

SEGOVIA Segovia 41,880 (☎911) Map **18** D1

★★★ **Parador National de Segovia** ☎415090 ta
Paral 80➪ 🏨 P Lift ♪ sB➪1175–1440
dB➪1655–2005 L500 D500 Pool

★★★ **Sirenas** J-Bravo 30 ☎411897 52rm48➪4🍴 🏨
Lift ✈ Pool

SEO DE URGEL Lérida 8,010 (☎973) Map **22** C4

★ **Andria** av J-António 1 ☎350300 25rm12➪1🍴 🏨

★ **Avenida** av Gl-Franco 18 ☎350104 39rm7➪12🍴
P Lift sB289–329 dB493–558 dB➪🍴598–718 L291
D291 mountains

🛏 🅿 **Carrillo** av Guillermo 5 ☎350570 BL

SEVILLA (SEVILLE) Sevilla 548,070 (☎954)
Map **24** C2

★★★★★ **Luz Sevilla** Martín Villa 2 ☎222991 tx72112
150➪ 🏨 Lift sB➪2275 dB➪3650 L800 D800

★★★★ **Alfonso XIII** San Fernando 2 ☎222850
tx72191 300➪ 🏨 Lift Pool

★★★★ **Colón** J-Canalejas 1 ☎222900 tx72726
262➪🍴 Lift ♪ sB➪🍴1630–2000
dB➪🍴2700–3300 (English breakfast) L800 D800

★★★★ **Inglaterra** pl Nueva 7 ☎224970 tx72244 🏨
Lift ♪ sB➪2150 dB➪3600 (English breakfast) L800
D800

★★★ **Acuarium** Urbanización Santa Isabel
☎258207 44➪ Lift

★★★ **Fleming** Sierra Nevada 3 ☎361900 90➪ A6rm
Lift

★★ **Doña María** don Remondo 19 (n rest) ☎224990
taMaryhotel 61➪ Lift ♪ sB➪1325–1625
dB➪2050–2500 Pool

★ **Simon** Garcia de Vineusa 19 (off av Quiepo de
Llano) ☎226660 48rm20➪

🛏 🅿 **R Falcon** Almaden de la Plata 19 ☎352284 P
Bed/Opl/Vau (GB)

SIERRA NEVADA See **GRANADA**

SIGÜENZA Guadalajara 6,000 (☎911) Map **19** B1

★★★ **Parador Nacional Castillo de Sigüenza**
☎390100 ta Paral 82➪ P Lift ♪ sB➪1175–1440
dB➪1655–2005 L500 D500

SITGES Barcelona 11,450 (☎93) Map **22** C2/3

★★★ **Antemare** Tercio Nuestra Señora de
Montserrat ☎8940600 72➪ Lift Pool sea

★★★ **Platjador** ps Ribera 35 ☎8940312 Closed
Dec–Feb 44➪ Lift ♪ sB➪523–671 dB➪916–1101
(English breakfast) L340 D340 sea

★★★ **Terramar** ps Calvo Sotelo ☎8940050 Closed
Oct–Apr 209➪ P Lift ♪ sB➪1650–1800
dB➪3300–3600 (English breakfast) L alc D alc ✈
Pool Beach 🏖 sea

★★ **Arcadia** c Socias ☎8940900 Closed Oct–May
38➪ 🏨 Lift sea

★★ **Luna Playa** Puerto Alegre 51 ☎8940430 12➪ P
Lift ♪ sB➪🍴723 dB➪🍴1435 sea

★★ **Sitges** San Gaudencio 5 (n rest) ☎8940072
Closed Nov–Apr 52rm11➪17🍴 P Lift ♪ sB306–362
dB520–609 dB➪🍴620–734 (English breakfast)

★ **Romantic** San Isidro 23 ☎8940643 Closed
Nov–Apr 55rm40➪ ♪ sB457–507 sB➪482–532
dB489–539 dB➪514–564 (English breakfast) L250
D250

SOMOSIERRA Madrid 150 Map **19** A1

★★ **Mora** ☎619➪ 🏨

SORIA Soria 25,030 (☎975) Map **19** B2

★★★ **Mesón Leonor** ps del Mirón ☎220250 60➪
A19rm 🏨

★★ **Parador Nacional Antonio Machado** parque del
Castillo ☎213540 14➪ 🏨

🛏 **G Ruiz Pedroviejo** C Sorovega 8 ☎213243

SUANCES-PLAYA Santander 5,050 Map **19** A4

★ **Lumar** ctra de Tagle ☎214 Closed 16 Sep–14 Jun
31rm3➪23🍴 sea

TALAVERA DE LA REINA Toledo 45,330 (☎925)
Map **24** D4

★★ **Auto-Estación** av Toledo 1 ☎800300
40rm31➪9🍴 🏨 ♪ sB➪🍴351–406
dB➪🍴562–662 (English breakfast) L250 D250

★★ **Talavera** av G-Ruiz 1 ☎800200 80rm80➪20🍴
Lift ♪ sB➪🍴455–470 dB➪🍴fr800 Lfr262 Dfr262

TAMARIU See **PALAFRUGELL**

TARIFA Cádiz 15,830 (☎956) Map **24** C1

★★★ **Mesón de Sancho** Apartado 25, ctra Cádiz-
Málaga (11km NE) ☎684900 36rm36➪ A20rm P ♪
sB➪831 dB➪1101 (English breakfast) L417 D417 ✈
Pool mountains

☆☆ **Balcón de España** ctra de Cádiz (8km N) (n rest)
☎684326 Closed Nov–Mar 38➪ P ♪ sB➪785
dB➪1267 (English breakfast) L535 D535 ✈ Pool

★★ **Dos Mares** ctra Cádiz-Málaga km 78 ☎684117
Closed Nov–Mar 19➪ P ♪ sB➪587–747
dB➪874–999 L387 D387 ✈ Beach ◯ sea

TARRAGONA Tarragona 78,240 (☎977) Map **22** C2

★★★★ **Imperial Terraca** Rambla de San Carlos
☎203040 tx56441 170➪ 🏨 P Lift ♪ sB➪🍴1415
dB➪🍴2380 L675 D675 ✈ Pool sea

★★★ **Lauria** Rambla Generalísimo 20 ☎203740
ta Reslau 72➪ P Lift ♪ dB➪1590 Pool sea

★★★ **Astari** via Augusta 97 ☎203840 Closed Nov–Apr
83rm59➪24🍴 🏨 P Lift ♪ sB➪🍴735–785
dB➪🍴1170–1370 (English breakfast) L375 D375
Pool sea

★ **Nuria** via Augusta 217 (DP) ☎202840 Closed
Nov–14 Mar 61rm51➪ 🏨 Lift sea

🛏 🅿 **Minicar** Cdt Rivadulla 40 ☎211865 P

🛏 🅿 **Tarrauto** Ramen y Cajal 40 ☎211315 P Chy

TERUEL Teruel 21,600 (☎974) Map **26** C4

★★★ **Parador Nacional** ctra de Zaragoza ☎602553
41rm40➪ A11rm 🏨 Lift

★★★ **Civera** av de Sagunto 23 ☎602300 73➪ P Lift ♪
sB➪525–635 dB➪940–1135 mountains

🛏 **B-Z-Coll** Ronda 18 de Julio 5 ☎601235

🅿 **J Z Coll** (ctra N234 km 123) ☎601061 BL/Frd
(GB)

TOJA (ISLA DE LA) Pontevedra 8,100 (☎986)
Map **17** A3

★★★★ **Gran** ☎730025 Closed Sep–Jun
214rm204➪10🍴 🏨 Lift ✈ Pool Beach 🏖 sea

TOLEDO Toledo 44,380 (☎925) Map **25** A4

★★★ **Parador Conde de Orgaz** ☎221850 20➪

TORDESILLAS Valladolid 6,600 Map **18** D2

★★★ **Montico** (5km E on N122) ☎770551 34➪ 🏨 P
sB➪1310 dB➪2070 L780 D780 ✈ Pool

TORRE DEL MAR Málaga (☎952) Map **24** D1
At **Benajarafe** (9km W)

★★ **España** ctra Málaga-Almería km267 ☎513000
20➪ 🏨

TORREDEMBARRA Tarragona 3,750 (☎977)
Map **22** C2

★★★ **Costa Fina** av Virgen de Montserrat ☎640075

Spain

Closed Jan–May 48⇄ 🏠 P Lift ♪ sB⇄577–696
dB⇄904–1079 L392 D392 🏊 sea

TORREMOLINOS Málaga 5,000 (☎952) Map **24** D1
★★★★ *Carihuela Palace* av de Montemar ☎380200
tx77124 107⇄ Lift 🏊 Pool Beach sea
★★★★ *Meliá Torremolinos* av de Montemar
☎380500 tx77060 284⇄ 🏠 Lift 🏊 Pool sea
★★★★ *Pez Espada* av de Montemar ☎380300
tx77047 149⇄ P Lift ♪ sB⇄1240–2580
dB⇄2280–3760 (English breakfast) L700–900
D700–900 🏊 Pool Beach ♪ sea
★★★ *Edén* Las Mercedes ☎384600 100⇄ Lift Pool
Beach sea
★★★ *Isabel* ps Marítimo 97, Playa del Lido (n rest)
☎381744 40⇄ P Lift ♪ sB⇄ 🏠787–957
dB⇄ 🏠1174–1410 (English breakfast) Pool Beach
sea
★★★ *Mercedes* Los Tajos ☎380100 tx77004 95⇄
Lift Pool sea
★★★ *Nidos* c los Nidos ☎384633 tx77151 198⇄ P
Lift ♪ sB⇄ 🏠539–659 dB⇄ 🏠903–1098
(English breakfast) L333 D333 Pool Beach sea
★★★ *Parador Nacional del Golf* ☎381255 40⇄
Pool Beach ♪ sea
★★★ *Pinar* ctra de Cádiz 134 ☎382644 73⇄ 🏊 Pool
★★★ *Tropicana* Trópico 2 ☎386600 tx77107 Closed
Nov–Feb 86⇄ Lift Pool Beach sea
★★ *Panorama* c Mercedes 14 ☎386277
53rm52⇄1 🏠 🏠 P Lift ♪ sB645–645 dB⇄865–990
(English breakfast) L fr350 D fr350 Pool sea
🍴 ✆ *Salamanca* av C-Alessandri 27 ☎381151 M/c
Opl/RR
🍴 ✆ *Unidos* c Borbollon ☎382875 M/c

TORREVIEJA Alicante 9,750 (☎965) Map **26** C2
★★ *Berlin* 41 Torre del Moro ☎711537 32⇄ Pool

TORTOSA Tarragona 46,380 (☎977) Map **21** B2
🍴 *Moderno* Ronda Docks22, Cuatro Caminos
☎441138 ☎441081 (GB)

TOSSA DE MAR Gerona 2,520 (☎972) Map **22** D3
★★★ *Alexandra* av de la Palma ☎340150 Closed 16
Oct–Mar 76rm72⇄4 🏠 Lift Pool sea
★★★ *Ancora* av de la Palma ☎340299 Closed
Oct–May 60rm30⇄30 🏠 P ♪ sB⇄ 🏠395–545
dB⇄ 🏠790–1180 (English breakfast) L375 D375 🏊
○ sea
★★★ *Florida* av de la Palma 21 ☎340308 Closed 11
Oct–Apr 45⇄ P Lift ♪ sB⇄500–750
dB⇄850–1300 (English breakfast) L400–450
D400–450 🏊
★★★ *Mar Menuda* Playa de Mer Menuda ☎341000
talmmsa Closed Oct–11 May 40⇄ P Lift ♪
sB⇄669–809 dB⇄1298–1558 (English breakfast)
L470 D470 🏊 Pool sea mountains
★★★ *Terranova* c Givarola (n rest) ☎340289 Closed
6 Sep–14 Jun 113rm86⇄ ♪ sB⇄ 🏠425–490
dB⇄ 🏠680–780 Pool sea mountains
★★★ *Voramar* av de la Palma (n rest) ☎340354
Closed 16 Sep–14 May 63rm57⇄6 🏠 ♪
sB⇄ 🏠700–885 dB⇄ 🏠750–900 mountains
★★ *Corisco* J-António 8 (n rest) ☎340174 Closed
Nov–Feb 28rm19⇄9 🏠 Lift ♪ sB454–569
dB693–883 dB⇄ 🏠788–1073 L387 D387 sea
★★ *Hacienda* (DP) ☎340216 Closed Oct–Apr 16⇄
★★ *Sulzo* c Llagostera (n rest) ☎340258 Closed Oct–Apr
★★ *Villa Romana* (n rest) ☎340258 Closed Oct–Apr
38rm17⇄21 🏠 A10rm 🏠 P Lift ♪ sB⇄ 🏠430–545
dB⇄ 🏠695–880 sea
★ *Cap d'Or* ps del Mar ☎340081 Closed Nov–Mar
12rm8⇄4 🏠 sea
★ *San Francisco* (DP) ☎340149 Closed 21 Oct–14
May 22rm6⇄16 🏠

⌂ ⇝ *Nautica* ctra San Feliá ☎340377 Fia

TRUJILLO Cáceres 10,950 (☎927) Map **24** C4

★*Madrid-Lisboa* ctra Madrid-Portugal ☎48258
23rm5⇌11 ⋔ 🏛

TUDELA Navarra 20,940 (☎948) Map **19** B2

★★*Morase* ☎821700 26rm23⇌3 ⋔ P 🍴
sB⇌ ⋔472–577 dB⇌ ⋔749–954 L386 D386 St%

★*Tudela* ctra de Zaragoza ☎820558 16rm12⇌4 ⋔
🏛 P 🍴 sB450 sB⇌ ⋔470–550 dB635–735
dB⇌ ⋔800–925 (English breakfast) L fr385 D fr385

Auto Diesel Navascues av del Instituto ☎820209
Fre (GB)

ÚBEDA Jaén 30,190 (☎953) Map **25** A2

★★★*Parador Nacional Condestable Dávalos* pl
Váquez de Molina 1 ☎750345 25⇌ 🏛

VALDEPEÑAS Ciudad Real 24,400 (☎926)
Map **25** A3

✩✩✩*Meliá El Hildago* ctra Andalusia (7km N)
☎311640 54⇌ 🏛 Lift Pool

★*Vista Alegre* ctra Madrid-Cádiz ☎312040 17⇌

VALENCIA Valencia 653,690 (☎96) Map **26** C/D3

★★★★*Reina Victoria* c de las Barcas 4 ☎3211360
100⇌ P Lift 🍴 sB⇌ fr1610 dB⇌ fr2770
(English breakfast) L fr635 D fr635

★★★*Alhambra* c del Convento de San Francisco 2
(nr pl de Caudillo) ☎3212040 65⇌ Lift

★★★*Excelsior* Hermanas Chabás 5 (off pl de
Caudillo) ☎3213040 65⇌ Lift

★★*Bristol* Abadia de San Martín 3 (off c San
Vicente) (n rest) ☎3224895 Closed 11 Dec–14 Jan
40rm20⇌20 ⋔ Lift 🍴 sB⇌ ⋔677–762
dB⇌ ⋔1114–1224

⌂ &o **Auto Montalt** c San Vicente 118 ☎3268100 M/c
Frd (GB)

⌂ &o **Basset** c S-Vicente 79–81 ☎3214581 Fia/Lnc

At **Saler (El)** (12km S)

★★★*Parador Nacional Luis Vives* ☎3236850 40⇌
Pool Beach 🏖 sea

VALLADOLID Valladolid 236,340 (☎983)
Map **18** D2

★★★★*Olid Meliá* pl San Miguel 10 ☎254204
tx26312 237⇌ 🏛 Lift

★★★*Conde Ansurez* María de Molina 9 (n rest)
☎222278 76⇌ Lift 🍴 sB⇌ ⋔1195–1455
dB⇌ ⋔1960–2370

⌂ &o *Willi* av Gijon ☎271875 Peu/Vlo

VERÍN Orense 8,870 (☎988) Map **17** B3

★★★*Parador Nacional de Monterrey* ☎410075
23⇌ Pool

VICH Barcelona 25,910 (☎93) Map **22** D3

★★★*Parador Nacional* (15km NE) ☎309 31⇌ Lift
lake

★★*Colón* ps J-Antonio 1 ☎8891917 38rm30⇌4 ⋔
🏛 P 🍴 sB270–330 sB⇌ ⋔370–420
dB⇌ ⋔690–760 (English breakfast) L270 D270

VIELLA Lerida 2,140 (☎973) Map **22** C4

★★★*Parador Nacional de Aran* ☎640100 135⇌ 🏛
Lift Pool

VIGO Pontevedra 197,140 (☎986) Map **17** A3

★★★★*Bahia d Vigo* av Cánovas del Castillo 5
☎226700 tx83014 107⇌ 🏛 Lift sea

VILAFRANCA DEL PENEDÉS Barcelona 17,700
(☎93) Map **22** C3

⌂ ⇝ *S Romeu* av Barcelona 2 ☎8920910 P

VILLACARLOS See **MENORCA** under **BALEARES
(ISLAS DE)**

VILLACASTÍN Segovia 1,730 (☎911) Map **18** D1

✩✩✩*Albergue Nacional* ☎107000 13⇌ P 🍴
sB⇌770–935 dB⇌1120–1345 L475 D475

Church of San Lorenzo, Cordoba

Spain and Andorra

VILLAFRANCA DEL BIERZO León 6,120 (☎987)
Map **18** C3
★★★*Parador Nacional Villafranca del Bierao* (DP)
☎540175 40⇄ A12rm 🏠
VILLAJOYOSA Alicante 16,260 (☎965)
Map **26** C/D2
★★★★*Montiboli* ☎890250 49⇄ 🏠 P Lift ♪
sB⇄1795–2605 L1147 D1147 ✔ Pool
VILLALBA Lugo 17,300 Map **17** B4
★★*Parador Nacional Condes* ☎510011 6⇄ P Lift
– dB⇄1120–1345 L475 D475
VILLANUEVA Y GELTRÚ Barcelona 35,710 (☎93)
Map **22** C2
★*Solvi 70* ps Ferrer pl 1 ☎8933243 29rm23⇄ 🏠
sB⇄407 dB⇄704 L300 D300 sea
🍴 ✔*Nautilsport* Gas 11-15 ☎8931516 P
VILLARREAL DE LOS INFANTES Castellón 33,220
(☎964) Map **26** D4
At **Alqueria de Niño Perdido** (4km S on N340)
☆☆☆*Ticasa* ☎510200 26⇄ ✔ Pool
VINAROZ Castellón 13,730 (☎964) Map **21** B2
★★*Duc de Vendome* (1.5km on N340) ☎450944
12⇄ 🏠 sea
★★*Roca* ctra Valencia Barcelona ☎450350 36⇄ 🏠
P ♪ sB⇄640 dB⇄960 (English breakfast) L345
D345
🍴 ✔*Aragón* San Agustin 11 ☎450893 P Cit
VITORIA Alava 136,870 (☎973) Map **19** B3
★★★★*Canciller Ayala* Ramón y Cajal 6 ☎220800
tx32471 185rm161⇄24 🏠 Lift
★★*Fronton* San Prudencio 7 ☎211400
36rm8⇄28 🏠 Lift
At **Arcaute** (4km)
★*Iradier* (NI) ☎217100 Closed Nov–Jan
27rm20⇄7 🏠 🏠

ZAFRA Badajoz 11,980 (☎924) Map **24** C3
★★★*Parador Nacional Hernan Cortés* pl de M-
Cristina ☎550200 26rm21⇄5 🏠
On N432 Badajoz road (16km NW)
🍴 ✔F Alvarez Ruiz Pasaje de Feria ☎551160
☎550811 P Cit/Peu
ZAHARA DE LOS ATUNES Cadiz Map **24** C1
★★★*Residencia Cortijo de la Plata* ☎430150
Closed 16 Oct–14 Apr 14rm10⇄4 🏠 P sB575–655
sB⇄🏠700–800 dB792–950 dB⇄🏠1070–1300
sea
ZAMORA Zamora 49,030 (☎988) Map **18** C2
★★*Cuatro Naciones* av J-Antónío 7 ☎512275
40rm30⇄10 🏠 Lift
★★*Parador Nacional Condes de Alba & Alíste* pl
de Cánovas ☎514497 19⇄ 🏠 P ♪ sB⇄1300–1565
dB⇄1980–2350 L500 D500 mountains
ZARAGOZA Zaragoza 479,850 (☎976) Map **20** C2
★★★★*Corana de Aragón* vía Imperial ☎224945
tx58067 237⇄ 🏠 Lift Pool
★★★★*Gran* c Costa 5 ☎221901 tx58010 169⇄ Lift
★★★*Goya* Requeté Aragónés 6 (off ps de la
Independencia) ☎229331 150⇄ 🏠 Lift
★*Conde Blanco* Predicadores 84 ☎238600 84⇄ 🏠
P Lift sB⇄481–551 dB⇄807–982
On NII Madrid road (8km SW)
★★*Cisne* 61rm47⇄4 🏠 P ♪ sB 🏠720–895
dB⇄1340–1695 L alc D alc Pool mountains
ZARAUZ Guipúzcoa 11,640 (☎943) Map **19** B3
★★★*Nautico-Playa* Vizconde Zolina 11 ☎841303
Closed Oct–Apr 74⇄ Lift sea
★★★*Zarauz* av de Navarra 4 ☎830200 Closed 16
Sep–14 Jun 82⇄ P Lift ♪ sb⇄990–1335
dB⇄1725–2090 L575 D575 sea mountains
★★*Alameda* Travesia Alameda (DP) ☎830143
Closed 4 Sep–3 May 26rm4 🏠

Andorra

Prices are in Spanish pesetas.
(☎ from France 078 ☎ from Spain 9738)
ANDORRA LA VELLA 2,463 Map **22** C4
★★★*Andorra Palace* Prat de la Creu ☎21072 140⇄
Lift ✔ Pool
★★★*Park* ☎20979 bx203 80rm48⇄32 🏠 A40rm ⇄ P
♪ sB1255–1450 sB⇄🏠1895–2325 dB1585–1825
dB⇄🏠2450–2930 (English breakfast) L710 D710
St% ✔ Pool mountains
★★★*Internacional* Mossen Tremosa 2 ☎21422
50rm30⇄20 🏠 Lift
★★*Mirador* c de la Vall ☎20920 30rm ♪
sB⇄🏠725⇄825 dB⇄🏠1180–1300 Lfr575 D fr500
mountains
★★*Pyrénées* av Princep Benllock 20 ☎20508 tx209
81rm53⇄ P Lift sB800 sB⇄1000 dB1000 dB⇄1400
(English breakfast) L500 D500 mountains
★★*Riberpuig 'la Truita'* ☎20773 120rm60⇄ Lift
Pool
🍴 ✔*CIMEX* av de Mitnavilaa 3–9 ☎20471 M/c P Fia
(GB)
✔*Sud-América* av Merixtell 94 ☎20626 P AR/Por
(GB)

ENCAMP 806 Map **22** C4
★★★*Oros* pl de Encamp ☎31222 54rm14⇄40 🏠 🏠
Lift

ESCALDES (LES) 2,300 Map **22** C4
★★★*Catalunya* ☎21315 tx203 35rm20⇄10 🏠 P ♪
sB375–500 sB⇄🏠600–725 dB750–1000
dB⇄🏠1050–1250 (English breakfast)

L320–350 D320–350 mountains
★★★*Roc Blanc* pl dels Co-Princeps 5 ☎21486 tx224
100rm85⇄ P Lift ♪ sB885 sB⇄1685 dB⇄2470
(English breakfast) L700 D700 ✔ Pool mountains
★★★*Tudel* pl dels Co-Princeps ☎20563
60rm12⇄40 🏠 Lift
★★*Lina Pla Pujol* ☎20934 15rm6 🏠
★★*Pla* ☎21432 Closed Sep–9 Jun 32rm17⇄ Lift
sB430–530 sB⇄580 dB660–760 dB⇄960
(English breakfast) L260–400 D260–400 mountains
★★*Refugi* av Carlemany 36 ☎21435 54rm10⇄ 🏠
Lift
★★*Valira* ☎20565 50rm45⇄3 🏠 Lift
🍴 ✔*Central* av Carlemany 34 bis ☎20501 P BL/Cit
🍴 ✔*Internaciónal* av Carlemany 65 ☎21492 Peu
PAS DE LA CASA Map **22** C4
★*Vendaval* ☎51142 16rm1⇄6 🏠

SANTA COLOMA (3.5KM SW of **Andorra la Vella**)
Map **22** C4
★★★*Roureda* av d'Enclar 18 ☎20681 Closed
Oct–Apr 36⇄ P sB⇄825 dB⇄1500 L525 D525 Pool
mountains
SANT JULIÀ DE LÒRIA 1,392 Map **22** C4
★★★*Co-Princeps* ☎41002 Closed 16 Oct–14 Mar
75⇄ P Lift ♪ sB⇄650–970 dB⇄1200–1540
(English breakfast) L400–550 D400–550 mountains
★★*Sardane* pl Major 2 ☎41018 Closed Oct–14 Mar
25rm23⇄2 🏠 A4rm P sB704 sB⇄🏠822 dB1492
dB⇄🏠1492 (English breakfast) L638 D638
mountains

SWITZERLAND & LIECHTENSTEIN

Population 6,385,000 **Area** 15,950 sq miles **Maps** 11, 12, 27, 28, 29.

How to get there

From Great Britain, Switzerland is usually approached via France. The distance from the Channel ports to Bern, the capital is approximately 470 miles, a distance which will normally require only one night stop.

General information

Information in this section is specific to Switzerland. A wider background is provided in the notes on page 8 with other information which you are advised to read.

AA agents
The AA has no agent in Switzerland but is allied to the Touring Club Suisse whose head office is at 9 rue Pierre Fatio, Geneva 3 ☎357611.

Accommodation
Hotels are now officially classified and the Guide to Swiss Hotels, published annually by the Swiss Hotel Association, groups hotels according to prices. The guide, which also contains details of spas and facilities for sports, is available from the Swiss National Tourist Office in London and local tourist offices which issue hotel guides on a regional basis.

Prices generally include service and taxes provided that children do not occupy separate rooms, reductions of up to 50% are granted for children up to six years of age, and up to 30% for those over six and up to twelve years. The electronic hotel-reservations panels at the Tourist Office, Zürich, Kloten Airport, open daily from 06.30 to 23.30hrs, and at Zürich's main railway station, enable passengers to see at a glance which hotels have rooms available and to make immediate contact with the hotel selected in order to make a reservation.

*These are not recommended routes:
the distances are given as a guide only.*

SWITZERLAND
distance chart
distances are in miles

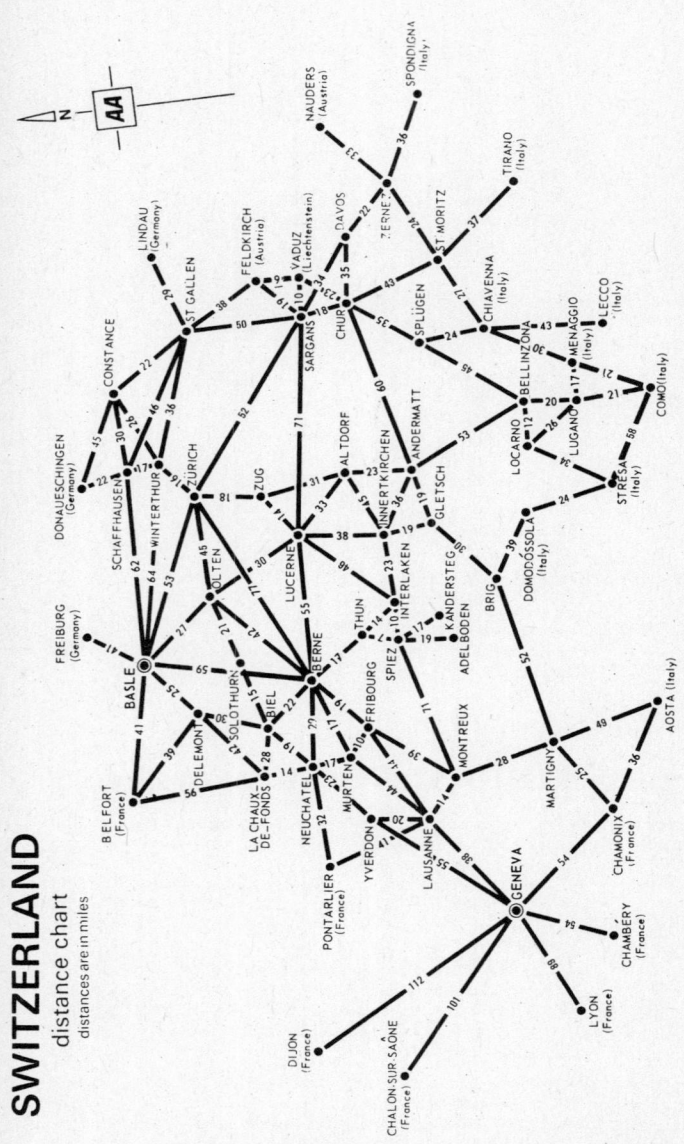

Annual events	February	**Basel** Carnival
	March	**Geneva** International Motor Show
	April	**Basel** Swiss Industries Fair
		Montreux 'Golden Rose of Montreux' International TV Festival
	June	**Berne** Arts Week
		Geneva Rose weeks
		Zürich June festival weeks (opera, plays, concerts, exhibitions, etc)
		Mürren International High Alpine Ballooning weeks
	July	**Locarno** International Film Festival
		Interlaken William Tell Festival, plays (July/August)
	August/ September	**Lucerne** International Festival of Music
	August	**Geneva** Geneva festival
		Gstaad Yehudi Menuhin Festival
	September	**Lausanne** National Autumn Trade Fair
		Montreux-Vevey International Music Festival
	October	**Geneva** Exhibition of Watches and Jewellery
	November	**Lausanne** West Swiss Antiques Fair
	December	**Arth, Küssnacht a R** Festival of St Nicholas processions

A comprehensive list of annual events can be obtained from the Swiss National Tourist Office (see page 366).

Breakdowns

The major motoring club, the Touring Club Suisse, operates a patrol service and a day and night breakdown service but it is likely that you will be charged for any service. The service *(Touring Secours)* operates from several centres throughout the country and can be summoned by telephone. The number is being standardised to 140 and it is as well to try this number first, but if the call is not successful proceed as follows:

note the first three figures (two in the Zürich zone) on the instrument from which you are making your call. Find the corresponding number in the places on the map below and ring the centre indicated by the arrow.

When calling, give the operator the password *Touring Secours, Touring Club Suisse*, and state your location and if possible the nature of the trouble. The operator will state within a short time whether it will be a black and yellow patrol car or garage assistance, and how soon help can be expected.

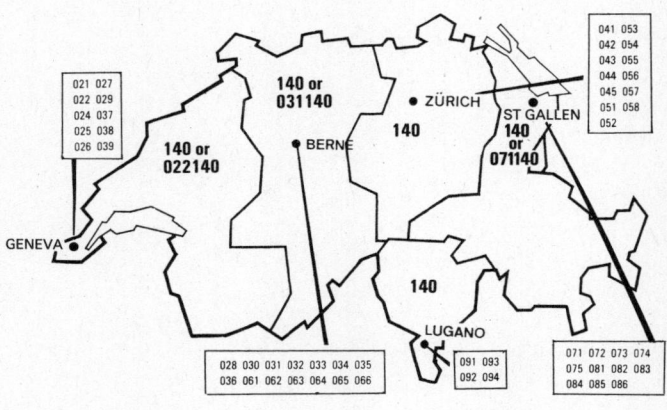

British Consulates

3005 Berne, Thunstrasse 50 ☎(031) 445021/8. There are also British Consulates in Basel, Geneva, Montreux, Zürich and Lugano.

Switzerland

Currency and banking	
Currency and banking Banking hours	The unit of currency is the Swiss franc, divided into 100 centimes or rappen. There are no restrictions on the import or export of currency. Basel 08.15–16.30hrs (Wednesday 18.30) Berne 08.00–16.30hrs (Thursday 18.00) Geneva 08.30–16.30hrs (Wednesday 17.30) Lausanne 08.30–12.30, 13.30–16.30hrs (Friday 17.30) Lugano 08.30–12.30, 13.30–16.00hrs Zürich 08.30–16.30hrs (Monday 18.00)

There are exchange offices in nearly all TCS offices open during office hours. At railway stations in large towns, and at airports, exchange offices are open 08.00–20.00hrs (these hours may vary from place to place). Banks are closed on Saturdays and Sundays.

Shopping hours   Shops are open in general 08.30–18.30hrs from Monday to Friday, and 08.30–16.00hrs on Saturdays with the exception of *food stores* which close at 17.30hrs.

Documents

Insurance   **Frontier insurance** If you do not hold insurance cover, frontier insurance (blue certificate) should be effected at the Customs border house.

Nationality plate (distinguishing sign)   If no plate or sticker is displayed on a foreign, temporarily imported vehicle the police will impose an on-the-spot fine of up to Fr100. British visitors should display the standard GB sign.

Ferries (internal)   *All particulars are subject to alteration*
Sailings are often augmented to meet traffic demands.

Bodensee
(Lake Constance)   See Germany, page 230.

Lake Lucerne   **Beckenried–Gersau** *Map 11 B1*
(Available from 15 March to 9 November only)
Service about 12 sailings 07.00–19.00hrs.
Duration 15 minutes
Maximum weight 10 tons

Charges		*Single*	*Return*
Cars not over	600kg	Fr8	Fr14
	1,000kg	9	16
	1,300kg	10	17
	1,500kg	11	19
	2,000kg	12	21
Motorcycles –	solo	6	10
	with sidecars	8	14
Passengers		2	3
Children		1	2

Charges include drivers' fares.

Lake Zürich   **Horgen–Meilen** *Map 11 B2/12 C2*
Service sailings every half hour 06.15–19.45hrs.
Duration 10 minutes
Charges *Vehicles* – cars (including drivers) Fr5 single motorcycles (not including drivers) Fr2;
Passengers – Fr1.00 single.

Medical treatment   There is no free medical treatment for visitors.

Motoring club    The **Touring Club Suisse** has branch offices in all important towns and has its head office in 1211 Geneva 3, at 9 rue Pierre-Fatio. The telephone number is (022) 357611. The TCS will extend a courtesy service to all motorists but their major services will have to be paid for. The club is affiliated with the AA whose members should produce their *5-Star Service Booklet* when requesting service.

TCS offices are usually open from 08.30 to 12.00hrs and 13.30 to 17.00hrs, during the week and between 08.00 and 11.30hrs on Saturday mornings (summer only). They are not open on Sunday. The club maintains a 24-hour, seven-day a week emergency centre at their head office which can be contacted by telephone (022) 358000.

Post and telephone			Fr
Post and telephone	The rates for mail to the UK are:		Fr
	Surface mail	Postcards	0.70
		Letters 5–20gm	0.80
		20–50gm	1.60
	Air mail	Enquire at local post offices.	
		The address of the *poste restante* in Bern is Postlagernd, Schanzenpost, Bern 1.	

Switzerland

Hours of opening Post offices in towns are open from Monday to Friday 07.30–12.00hrs and 13.45–18.30hrs. On Saturdays they generally close at 11.00hrs.

Telephone rates The telephone service is an extremely good one with subscriber dialling available throughout the country and for calls to many foreign countries. A 3-minute call to Britain costs Fr6.00 and Fr2.00 for each additional minute. A local call costs 40cts and there are reductions at certain hours during the day and at weekends.

Public holidays Public holidays based on religious festivals are not always fixed on the calendar but any current diary will give actual dates. The Whit period (a religious holiday) should not be confused with the British Spring Holiday.

Switzerland has a long list of public holidays varying from canton to canton, even from town to town, depending upon the predominant religious aspects of the area, only three, Christmas Day, New Year's Day and Ascension Day, are recognised throughout the country. The following list is therefore not complete but it is representative and qualified generally.

Fixed holidays		
	1 January	New Year's Day
	2 January	Bank Holiday
	1 May	Labour Day (not all cantons)
	1 August	National Day (not a full day in all cantons)
	1 November	All Saints' Day (Roman Catholic areas)
	25 December	Christmas
	26 December	Boxing Day (not in all cantons)

Moveable holidays		
	Good Friday	(except Tessin)
	Easter Monday	(except Obwald)
	Ascension Day	
	Whit Monday	
	Corpus Christi	(Roman Catholic areas)

Roads The road surfaces are generally good, but many main roads are narrow. A network of motorways is being built (see below). There is ample scope for touring and it is quite easy to negotiate the popular passes in summer; of these the St Gotthard, Simplon, and Susten, which provide good routes to the south, are outstanding. See pages 31–55 for details of mountain passes and pages 55–58 for road and rail tunnels; note also Priority, page 367.

Signposting is excellent and warnings of any obstructed roads are prominently displayed. Main roads are numbered. Near towns and on some mountain circuits, traffic congestion may be severe at weekends. At the beginning and end of the German school holidays (see page 226) traffic increases considerably.

Alpine postal roads On any stretch of mountain road, the driver of a private car may be asked by the driver of a postal bus, which is painted yellow, to reverse, or otherwise manoeuvre to allow the postal bus to pass.

If postal buses run in convoys, then each one except the last carries a red circular sign with a white diagonal bar. These vehicles are often driven at high speed, although by very experienced drivers, and other road users must take great care. Postal bus drivers often sound a distinctive three-note horn and no other vehicles may use this type of horn in Switzerland.

Motorways There are approximately 582 miles of toll-free motorway (Autobahn or autoroute) and more are under construction; a network of 1,143 miles is planned.

Motorways are numbered N (national road) and are divided into classes 1, 2 and 3; they vary from the usual two-lane dual carriageway to 25ft-wide two-lane roads with limited access points. To join a motorway, follow the green and white signposts, or signposts with the motorway symbol. Vehicles unable to exceed 60kph (37mph) and motorcycles under 50cc are forbidden. The only speed restrictions are for vehicles towing trailers (see Speed page 368) but, as an experiment, certain sections have a recommended maximum limit.

Motorway telephones These are placed 2km (1¼ miles) apart along all motorways, and give an automatic connection with the motorway control police. Ask for TCS patrol assistance. A patrol will normally be sent, but if one is not available, help will be sent from a TCS affiliated office.

Weather services The Touring Club Suisse operates a weather service to give up-to-the-minute conditions of mountain passes. The information appears on notices placed at strategic points along the roads leading up to the passes. When the weather is exceptional, special bulletins are issued by the TCS through the press and broadcasting services. By dialling 163 on the national telephone system, you can also get road/weather reports in French, German, or Italian, according to the canton from which the call is made.

Switzerland

Winter conditions   *Entry from France and Germany:* the main entries are seldom affected, although the Faucille pass on the Dijon–Geneva road, and also minor routes through the Jura, Vosges, and Black Forest may be obstructed.

To Italy: from western Switzerland – during the winter months this is via the Grand St Bernard road tunnel or the Simplon or St Gotthard rail tunnels (see pages 55, 56); wheel chains are sometimes necessary on the approach to the Grand St Bernard road tunnel. From eastern Switzerland, the San Bernardino road tunnel (see page 55) or the Julier or Maloja passes can be used.

To Austria: the route across northern Switzerland via Liechtenstein is open all the year.

Within the country: the main highways linking Basel, Zürich, Lucerne, Berne, Lausanne, and Geneva are unaffected. The high passes are usually closed in the winter months but it is generally possible to drive within reasonable distance of all winter sports resorts. According to weather conditions, wheel chains or snow tyres may be necessary.

Wheel chains   These are generally necessary on journeys to places at high altitudes. Roads with a sign 'chains compulsory' (a tyre with chains on it drawn on a white board which also includes the name of the road) are closed to cars without wheel chains. It is a punishable offence to drive without this equipment. On other roads (indicated by a rectangular sign with the words *Chains a neige ou pneus a neige* – Wheel chains or snow tyres) drivers of cars not fitted with them may be accused of breaking the law if they hold up traffic.

Tourist information offices   The Swiss government maintains an excellent information service in London at the Swiss National Tourist Office, Swiss Centre, 1 New Coventry Street, W1V 3H6, ☎01–734 1921. In all provincial towns and resorts throughout the country there are tourist information offices who are pleased to help tourists with local information and advice.

Visitors' registration   A visitor staying overnight should report to the police, but this is often done by the hotel or camp site management who complete the registration form. If staying with a friend or relative at a private address, the host should notify the authorities.

Motoring regulations

Information in this section is specific to Switzerland. A wider background is provided in the notes on page 67 with other regulations which you are advised to read.

Accidents   **Fire** ☎118 **Police, ambulance** ☎117 except in the following departments – Rapperswil (055) and Sargans (085) – where the number is 17 or 18. The three-digit number system is being extended to all areas of the country. In provincial areas ☎111 (11); this connects you with the postal services, who will then connect you with the police giving you precedence over other callers. If you have no change to put in a telephone slot, ☎112 (12) to call the post office line-fault department, who will immediately inform the police.

The most important principle is that all persons involved in an accident should ensure, as far as is possible, that the traffic flow is maintained. Should the accident have caused bodily injuries, the police must be called immediately. Those injured should be assisted by the persons at the scene of the accident until the arrival of medical help. It is not necessary to call the police if the accident has only caused material damage, although the party at fault should immediately report the damage and exchange particulars. If this is not possible, he must advise the police.

Dimensions   Private cars and trailers are restricted to the following dimensions:

cars	height	4 metres;
	width	2.30 metres;
caravans	length	6 metres including tow bar;
	width	2.10 metres.

Luggage trailers may not be wider than the towing vehicle. Special regulations apply to four-wheel-drive vehicles towing trailers.

The Swiss Customs Officials can authorise slightly larger limits for foreign caravans for direct journeys to their destination and back, eg:

width	maximum 2.20 metres (7ft 2in);
length	maximum 6.50 metres (21ft 4in) if Alpine passes are used;
	maximum 7.00 metres (23ft) if no Alpine passes are used.

A charge of Fr5 is made for these special permits.

It is dangerous to use a vehicle towing a trailer on some mountain roads; motorists should ensure that roads on which they are about to travel are suitable for the conveyance of car/trailer combinations.

Drinking and driving   A blood test may be required if there is definite suspicion that the driver is under the influence of alcohol. A driver is considered to be intoxicated if the amount of alcohol in his blood exceeds 0.8%. The penalty is either a fine or a prison sentence, and the withdrawal of the offender's driving licence for a period of at least two months.

Hazard warning lights   The use of hazard warning lights is permissible but they should supplement, and not take the place of, a warning triangle which must always be used to give advance warning of an obstruction.

Lights   Driving on sidelights only is prohibited. Spotlights are forbidden. Foglights can be used only in pairs of identical shape, brilliance, and colour, dipped headlights must be used in cities, and towns. Dipped headlights must be used at all times in tunnels, whether they are lit or not, and failure to observe this regulation can lead to a fine. Switzerland has a 'tunnel' road sign (a red triangle showing a tunnel entrance in the centre) which serves to remind drivers to turn on their dipped headlights. In open country, headlights must be dipped at least 200 metres (220yd) in front of any pedestrian or oncoming vehicle (including trains parallel to the road), when requested to do so by the driver of an oncoming vehicle flashing his lights, or when reversing, travelling in lines of traffic or stopping. Dipped headlights must be used when waiting at level crossings, traffic signals, or near roadworks. Dipped headlights must be used in badly-lit areas when visibility is poor.

Drivers of motorcycles and mopeds must use dipped headlights even during good daylight.

Parking   Parking restrictions are indicated by international signs or by broken yellow lines or crosses at the side of the road, or yellow markings on pavements or poles. Parking is forbidden where it would obstruct traffic or view on a main road or one carrying fast-moving traffic, and on or within 1.5 metres (5ft) of tram lines. Stopping is forbidden, even for passengers to get in or out of a vehicle or for unloading goods, in places marked by a continuous yellow line at the side of the road or red markings on pavements or poles. When parked on a slope or incline, use the handbrake and place chocks or wedges under the wheels. If you have to stop in a tunnel you must immediately switch off your engine. You cannot spend the night in a vehicle or trailer on the roadside in the canton of Tessin.

Blue zones   In some large towns, there are short-term parking areas known as blue zones. In these areas parked vehicles must display a disc on the windscreens; discs are set at the time of parking, and show when parking time expires. restrictions apply 08.00–19.00hrs on weekdays throughout the year. Discs can be obtained free of charge from the TCS, the police, some large shops, or tobacconists' shops. Failure to observe zonal regulations could result in a fine or the vehicle being towed away.

Red zone   In Lausanne, a red zone system is in operation; for this, adjustable discs entitling up to 15 hours' parking are available free from the local TCS office, the tourist information office, or the parking attendant. These discs may be used for either red or blue zones, one side of the disc to be used for the blue zone and the other for the red zone. Failure to observe zonal regulations could result in a fine or in the vehicle being towed away.

Passengers   Children under twelve years of age are not allowed to travel in the front seats of a vehicle.

Police fines   The police are empowered to impose on-the-spot fines on any motorists contravening the local traffic regulations; for more serious infringements, the case would be taken to court. The officer collecting the fine should issue an official receipt. Fines are extended to include other regulations; eg displaying an L sign when the learner driver is not at the wheel; having an illegible number plate; not carrying a driving licence.

Priority   When the road is too narrow for two vehicles to pass, vehicles towing trailers have priority over other vehicles; heavy vehicles over light vehicles. If two vehicles of the same category cannot pass, the vehicle nearest to the most convenient stopping point or lay-by must reverse. On mountain roads if there is no room to pass, the descending vehicle must manoeuvre to give way to the ascending vehicle – unless the ascending vehicle is obviously nearer a lay-by. If two vehicles are travelling in opposite directions and the driver of each vehicle wants to turn left, they must pass in front of each other (not drive round). Drivers turning left may pass in front of traffic islands in the centre of an intersection. Lanes reserved for buses have been introduced; these are marked with either a continuous or broken yellow line and the word 'bus'. Bus lanes may be supplemented with the sign 'Bus lane only – *Voie reservee aux bus*' (a circular blue sign with the white silhouette of a bus superimposed on it). Only the broken yellow line may be crossed, either at a junction when turning or to enter the premises of a company.

Speed Because the country is mountainous with many narrow and twisting roads, it is not safe to maintain a high speed. Built-up areas are indicated by signs bearing the placename: in these areas the limit is 60kph (37mph) for all vehicles.

Outside built-up areas the limit is 100kph (62mph) except on motorways where vehicles are subject to a limit of 130kph (80mph). Car/caravan or luggage trailer combinations are restricted to 80kph (49mph) on all roads outside built-up areas. These limits do not apply if another limit is indicated by signs or if the vehicle is subject to a lower general speed limit.

Tyres Spiked or studded tyres. These may be used on light motor vehicles and on trailers drawn by such vehicles from 1 November to 31 March provided they are fitted to all four wheels and a speed of 80kph (49mph) is not exceeded. They are prohibited on motorways and fast motor roads. Spiked or studded tyres may not be substituted for wheel chains when these are compulsory. On-the-spot fines of Fr30 are imposed for the use of spiked or studded tyres after 31 March.

Warning triangles It is compulsory to use a warning triangle to give advance warning of an obstruction and one should be used if a vehicle is stopped on the road for any reason. It should be placed on the roadside at least 50 metres (55yd) behind the stopped vehicle or obstruction but on motorways the distance should be increased to 150 metres (164yd).

If vehicles are fitted with hazard warning lights these may also be used in conjunction with a triangle but their use in no way effects the obligation to place a triangle in position.

The Limmatquai, a favourite meeting place in Zurich.

Liechtenstein

Map 12 D1/2 The principality of Liechtenstein has a population of 23,000 and an area of 65 sq miles. Although it is an independent state it is represented in diplomatic and other matters by Switzerland. Vaduz is the capital.

Traffic regulations, insurance laws, and the monetary unit are the same as for Switzerland and prices are adjusted to match those in the major country.

Prices are in Swiss francs
Abbreviations:

pl	place, Platz
pza	piazza
r	rue
rte	route
Str	Strasse

AARAU Aargau 17,045 (☎064) Map **11** B2
★***Goldenen Löwen*** Rathauspl ☎221531 10rm
8 ⚐ ***F Brack*** Buchserstr 19 ☎221851 P Frd
8 ⚐ **Hohglas** (F Glaus) Entfelderstr 8 ☎221332 Bed/Dat/Opl/Vau (GB)
ADELBODEN Bern 2,900 (☎033) Map **11** B1
★★★★**Nevada Palace** ☎732131 tx32384 Closed Oct–14 Dec & 16 Apr–16 Jun 76rm33⇌11 ⋒ ⌂ P Lift ☽ sB46–66 sB⇌ ⋒66–136 dB92–132 dB⇌ ⋒132–272 (English breakfast) L30–35 Dfr35 ⚘ Pool mountains
★★**Park Bellevue** ☎731621 Closed 21 Oct–19 Dec & 21 Apr–May 44rm21⇌4 ⋒ P Lift sB41–66 sB⇌ ⋒61–81 dB82–132 dB⇌ ⋒102–152 (English breakfast) Lfr16 Dfr22 ⚘ Pool mountains
★**Alpenrose** ☎731161 Closed Oct–Nov & May 35rm8⇌3 ⋒ A4rm ⌂ P sB28–36 sB⇌ ⋒39–52 dB56–72 dB⇌ ⋒78–104 (English breakfast) L14–16 D17–24 mountains
★***Bären*** ☎732151 12rm
★***Edelweiss*** ☎732241 Closed 16 Apr–14 Jun & Oct–19 Dec 32rm Lift
ADLISWIL See **ZÜRICH**
AIGLE Vaud 4,300 (☎025) Map **11** A1
★★**Nord** pl du Centre ☎261055 18rm4⇌4 ⋒ P Lift sB25–30 sB⇌ ⋒35–45 dB45–50 dB⇌ ⋒60–80 (English breakfast) L16–30 D16–30 mountains
AIROLO Ticino 1,880 (☎094) Map **11** B1
★★★***Alpes*** ☎881722 25rm7⇌3 ⋒ Lift
★★***Motta & Poste*** ☎881917 24rm3⇌8 ⋒ Lift
8 ⚐ **Airolo** (A Piccinonno) ☎881765 P AR/Cit (GB)
8 ⚐ **Gottardo** (E Brasi) ☎881177 P Toy (GB)
8 ⚑ **Wolfisberg** via San Gottardo ☎881195 ☎881195 ⚙ M/c P BL/Vlo
ALTDORF Uri 6,600 (☎044) Map **11** B1
★**Schwarzer Löwen** Gotthardstr ☎21007 19rm5⇌ ⌂ Lift sB30–40 sB⇌40 dB60–80 dB⇌80 (English breakfast) L8–22 D8–22 mountains
★***Wilhelm Tell*** Gemeindehauspl ☎21020 20rm1 ⋒
8 ⚐ ***Central*** (B Musch) Gotthardstr 54 ☎22355 Cit/Dat/Vlo
ALTERSWIL Fribourg Map **11** B1
8 ⚑ ***A Piller*** Hofmatt ☎441237 BL
AMBRI-PIOTTA Ticino 400 (☎094) Map **12** C1
★★***Poste*** rte Internatinale du St-Gotthard ☎891221 Closed Nov–Mar 45rm3⇌3 ⋒ ⌂ Lift
AMSTEG Uri 600 (☎044) Map **11** B1
★★★***Stern & Post*** Gotthardstr ☎64190 tx78445 40rm20⇌ ⌂ Lift
ANDERMATT Uri 1,300 (☎044) Map **11** B1
★★★**Badus** ☎67286 23rm11⇌9 ⋒ ⌂ P Lift sB29–35 sB⇌ ⋒32–40 dB58–70 dB⇌ ⋒64–80 L6–18 D6–18 ∩ mountains
★★★***Schweizerhof*** ☎67189 28rm15⇌ ⌂
★★**Alpenhof** Gotthardstr ☎67239 Closed Nov & May 25rm2⇌2 ⋒ ⌂ P sB24–31 sB⇌ ⋒30–34 dB46–50 dB⇌ ⋒60–68 (English breakfast) L16 D20 ⚘ mountains
★★**Helvetia** ☎67515 30rm18⇌12 ⋒ P Lift sB⇌ ⋒38 dB64 dB⇌ ⋒72–76 (English breakfast) L9–18 D9–18
★★**Krone** ☎67206 tx78446 52rm11⇌15 ⋒ P Lift sB32–40 sB⇌ ⋒42–50 dB64–80 dB⇌ ⋒84–100 (English breakfast) Lfr9 Dfr17 mountains
★★**Monopol Metropol** ☎67575 tx78443 Closed 16 Oct–Nov 31rm20⇌2 ⋒ ⌂ P Lift sB30–38 sB⇌ ⋒36–54 dB60–76 dB⇌ ⋒72–108 L12–18 D16–24 Pool mountains
★★***St Gotthard*** ☎67204 Closed Nov 27rm9⇌ ⌂
★***Löwen*** ☎67223 Closed 16 Oct–14 May 21rm
★***Schlüssel*** Gotthardstr ☎67198 25rm ⌂
8 ⚑ **L Loretz** ☎67243 ☎67243 P Ren (GB)
At **Hospental** (2km SW)
★★**Meyerhof** ☎67207 Closed Nov & May 33rm2⇌ ⌂ P sB26–30 dB50–60 dB⇌70–80 L15–20 D15–20 mountains
APPENZELL Appenzell 5,000 (☎071) Map **12** C2
★★***Hecht*** ☎871025 35rm10⇌ Lift
★★**Santis** ☎872644 32rm15⇌15 ⋒ A20rm ⌂ P Lift sB42–52 sB⇌ ⋒52–62 dB⇌ ⋒99–109 Lfr18 Dfr20 mountains
8 ⚑ **W Baumann** Weissbadstr ☎871466 ☎871466 Dat/Peu (GB)
ARBON Thurgau (☎071) Map **12** C2
★★★**Metropole** Bahnhofstr 49 ☎463535 tx77247 Closed 19 Dec–7 Jan 70rm18⇌21 ⋒ P Lift ☽ sB⇌ ⋒52–70 dB⇌ ⋒86–114 (English breakfast) L alc D alc Pool lake
★**Frohsinn** ☎461046 Closed 10 Sep–10 Oct 7rm P sB20–22 dB40–42 L12–15 D12–15 lake
★**Rotes Kreuz** ☎461914 24rm2⇌7 ⋒ P sB29–37 sB⇌ ⋒fr35 dBfr58 dB⇌ ⋒70–74 Lfr11 mountains lake
ARLESHEIM Basel (☎061) Map **11** B2
★**Ochsen** ☎725225 27rm3⇌10 ⋒ A1rm ⌂ P sB27–30 sB⇌ ⋒40–45 dB54–60 dB⇌ ⋒75–83 mountains
AROLLA Valais (☎027) Map **28** C4
★★***Grand & Kurhaus*** ☎831161 Closed mid Apr–Jun & Sep–Xmas 70rm29⇌ Lift
AROSA Graubünden 2,600 (☎081) Map **12** C1
★★★★***Kulm*** ☎310131 tx74279 Closed 18 Sep–24 June & 16 Oct–25 Nov 150rm120⇌30 ⋒ Lift ⚘ Pool
★★★**Alexandria-Palace** (DP & Pn) ☎310111 tx74261 Closed Nov & May 159⇌ ⌂ P Lift ☽ sB⇌50–163 dB⇌100–326 L22 D28 Pool mountains
★★★***Cristallo*** ☎312261 tx74270 Closed May & Oct–Nov 40rm28⇌8 ⋒ Lift
★★★***Post & Sport*** ☎311361 75rm45⇌ lake
★★★***Seehof*** (DP) ☎311541 tx74277 Closed 18 Dec–mid Apr 78rm40⇌ Lift lake
★★★**Sporthotel Valsana** (Pn) ☎310275 tx96rm52⇌9 ⋒ P Lift ☽ sB75–80 sB⇌ ⋒115–145 dB65–95 dB⇌ ⋒105–135 mountains lake
8 ⚑ ***Grand Dosch*** ☎312222 P AR/MB/Opl
ARTH-AM-SEE Schwyz 6,300 (☎041) Map **11** B1
8 ⚐ **Rigi** (O Kenel) Zugerstr ☎821223 Chy/Sim (GB)
ASCONA Ticino 3,000 (☎093) Map **28** D4
★★★★**Acapulco au Lac** Lago Maggiore ☎354521 tx79399 Closed Nov–Feb 44rm36⇌4 ⋒ P Lift sB⇌ ⋒66–103 dB⇌ ⋒97–183 (English breakfast) L alc D alc Pool lake
★★★**Ascona** ☎351135 tx73577 Closed 7 Jan–9 Mar 55rm27⇌23 ⋒ P Lift sB⇌ ⋒50–85 dB⇌ ⋒60–200 L alc D alc Pool mountains lake
★★★***Schweizerhof*** via Locarno ☎351214 Closed Nov–Feb 70rm11⇌4 ⋒ ⌂ Lift Pool
★★★**Tamaro au Lac** ☎353939 tx79379 Closed Dec–Jan 47rm19⇌9 ⋒ A13rm ⌂ Lift sB25–40 sB⇌ ⋒35–60 dB50–80 dB⇌ ⋒70–120 (English breakfast) L10–20 D10–20 lake
★**Piazza au Lac** ☎351181 Closed Dec–Feb 22rm7⇌ A5rm sB28–35 dB56–70 dB⇌64–90 lake
8 ⚐ **C Buzzini** via Cantonale 124 ☎352414 Aud/VW
8 ⚐ **Cristallina** (F Bianda) via Circonvallazione ☎351320 M/c P BL/Jag/Rov (GB)
8 ⚐ **Storelli** via Cantonale ☎352196 Toy
AVENCHES Vaud (☎037) Map **11** A1
8 ⚐ ***J P Divorne*** rte de Berne 6 ☎751263 P Opl
BAAR Zug 7,000 (☎042) Map **11** B2
★★***Lindenhof*** Dorfstr ☎311220 8rm3⇌2 ⋒ Lift
BADEN Aargau 14,000 (☎056) Map **11** B2
★★**Verenahof** Kurpl ☎225251 106rm39⇌10 ⋒ A24rm ⌂ P Lift ☽ sB46–66 sB⇌ ⋒66–106 dB82–112 dB⇌ ⋒122–192 (English breakfast) L24–35 D20–28 Pool river
★**Bären** Bäderstr 36 ☎225178 60rm30⇌ ⌂ P Lift ☽ sB32–48 sB⇌50–75 dB64–96 dB⇌90–150

(English breakfast) L18–28 D18–28 Pool mountains
★**Park** Haselstr 9 ☎225353 14rm2⇄8 🛏 Lift sB fr35
sB⇄🛏47–50 dB fr64 dB⇄🛏70–85
(GB)
🛢 &🖎**Kappelerhof** (J Miller) ☎227326 P Aud/VW

BAD-RAGAZ-PFAFERS See **RAGAZ-PFAFERS (BAD)**

BÂLE See **BASEL**

BALSTHAL Solothurn 5,200 (☎062) Map **11** B2
★*Kreuz* Hauptstr ☎713412 18rm3⇄7🛏 🏠 lift
★*Rössli* ☎715858 9rm

BASEL (BÂLE) Basel 238,500 (☎065) Map **11** B2
See Plan
★★★★★**Drei Könige** Blumenrain 8 ☎255252
tx62937 Plan **1** 80rm78⇄ 🛏 Lift P 🌙 sB⇄90–125
dB⇄155–220 (English breakfast) L alc D alc
★★★★★**Euler** Centralbahnpl 14 ☎234500 tx62215
Plan **2** 70rm67⇄3🛏 🏠 Lift 🌙 sB⇄99–134
dB⇄🛏172–237 (English breakfast) L35–65
D35–65
★★★★**International** Steinentorstr 25 ☎221870
tx62370 Plan **3** 160rm148⇄12🛏 🏠 P Lift 🌙
sB⇄🛏70–130 dB⇄🛏110–180 L15–20 D20–30
Pool
★★★★**Schweizerhof** Centralbahnpl 1 ☎222833
tx62373 Plan **4** 75rm70⇄ P Lift 🌙 sB⇄80–110
dB⇄120–160 L alc D alc
★★★**Bernina** Innere Margarethenstr 14 (n rest)
☎237300 tx63813 Plan **5** 35rm20⇄15🛏 🏠 Lift 🌙
sB35–50 sB⇄🛏50–80 dB55–80 dB⇄🛏80–140
L10–20 D10–20
★★★**Cavalier** Reiterstr 1 ☎392262 Plan **6**
27rm18⇄9🛏 Lift sB38–53 sB⇄🛏38–53
dB⇄🛏65–91
★★★**Drachen** Aeschenvorstadt 24☎239090
tx62346 Plan **7** 43rm17⇄19🛏 🏠 Lift
★★★**Europe** Clarastr 35–43 ☎268080 tx64103
Plan **8** 173rm44⇄129🛏 P Lift sB40–50
sB⇄🛏75–90 dB⇄🛏120–140
★★★**Excelsior** Aeschengraben 13 ☎225300 Plan **9**
50⇄ P Lift 🌙 sB⇄54–65 dB⇄92–110
(English breakfast) L7–14
★★★**Touring & Red Ox** Ochsengasse 2 ☎329393
tx62480 Plan **10** 104rm40⇄20🛏 🏠 Lift
★★**Greub** Centralbahnstr 11 (n rest) ☎231840
Plan **11** 50rm7⇄1🛏 🌙 sB25–38 sB⇄🛏40–60
dB50–68 dB⇄🛏70–100 (English breakfast)
★★**Jura** Centralbahnpl 11 ☎231800 Plan **12**
65rm7⇄27🛏 P Lift 🌙 sB28–38 sB⇄🛏54–60
dB50–68 dB⇄🛏90–100 L11–20 D11–20
★★**Krafft** Obere Rheingasse 12 ☎268877 tx64360
Plan **13** 56rm16⇄11🛏 🏠 Lift 🌙 sB31–38
sB🛏46–51 dB52–68 dB⇄🛏82–100
(English breakfast) L alc D alc river
★★*Merkur* Theaterstr 24 ☎233740 Plan **14**
25rm4⇄3🛏
★★**St-Gotthard-Terminus** Centralbahnstr 13
☎225250 Plan **15** 40rm9⇄4🛏 Lift 🌙 sB35–40
sB⇄🛏45–53 dB60–75 dB⇄🛏85–88
(English breakfast) L7–22 D12–24
★★**Victoria am Bahnhof** Centralbahnpl 3–4
☎225566 tx63362 Plan **16** 110rm18⇄44🛏 P Lift 🌙
sB30–40 sB⇄🛏55–75 dB60–70 dB⇄🛏90–126
★**Bristol** Centralbahnstr 15 ☎223822 Plan **17**
30rm4⇄2🛏 🏠 P Lift 🌙 sB28–34 sB⇄🛏40–45
dB48–56 dB⇄🛏60–70 L7–28 D7–28
★*Helvetia* Küchengasse 13 ☎230688 Plan **18**
25rm5🛏
★**Hospiz Engelhof** Nadelberg/Stiftsgasse 1 (n rest)
☎252244 Plan **19** 48rm2⇄ P Lift sB26–36
sB⇄🛏38–46 dB56–64 dB⇄74–76
(English breakfast)
★**Rochat** Petersgraben 23 ☎258140 Plan **20**
40rm6⇄10🛏 P lift 🌙 sB25–30 sB⇄🛏34–42 dB48
dB⇄🛏52–66
★**Steinbock** Centralbahnstr 19 ☎225844 Plan **22**
26rm4🛏 Lift sB28–35 dB50–60 dB🛏64–70
🛢 🖎*Americaine Autos* (AAA) Brüglingerstr 2
☎342233 Bed/Dat/Vau

🛢 &🖎*Autavia* Hardstr 14 ☎427878 Frd
🛢 &🖎**Delta** St-Johanns Ring 30 ☎449910 Hon/Sab
(GB)
🛢 *Dreispitz* (G Kenk) Reinacherstr 28 ☎345555 BL
🛢 *Dufour* Dufourstr 36 ☎231214 (GB)
🛢 *Grospeter* Grospeterstr 12 ☎356070 Opl (GB)
🛢 &🖎*St-Johann* Ryffstr 16 ☎438450 BL/Fia
🛢 *C Scholotterbeck* Viaduktstr 40 ☎220050
Cit/Jag/RR
🛢 &🖎**Settelen** Türkheimerstr 17 ☎383800 ☎222220
Vlo/Toy/Tri (GB)
🛢 *G Uecker* Näfelserstr 19 ☎385076 Chy/Sim

BEATENBERG Bern 1,323 (☎036) Map **11** B1
★*Beauregard* ☎411341 Closed 26 Apr–14 May &
Nov–19 Dec 22rm6🛏 lake
★*Jungfraublick* ☎411581 taZähler 20rm lake

BECKENRIED Nidwalden 2,000 (☎041) Map **11** B1
★★**Edelweiss** ☎641252 30rm4⇄4🛏 P sB30–33
sB⇄🛏40–45 dB56–62 dB⇄🛏70–76
(English breakfast) L14–18 D14–18 sea mountains
lake
★*Mond* ☎641204 35rm20⇄ P Lift L fr11 Dfr12
(English breakfast) sea mountains lake
★*Nidwaldnerhof* ☎641484 Closed Oct–Apr 56rm P
sB24–38 dB40–70 (English breakfast) L15 D15
Pool mountains lake
★*Sonne* ☎641205 25rm 🏠 P sB20–25 dB40–50
L12–14 D12–14 mountains lake

BELLINZONA Ticino 13,400 (☎092) Map **29** A4
★★★*Unione* Via Gl-Guisan ☎255577 tx73474
35rm21⇄9🛏 P Lift sB30–37 sB⇄🛏50–57
dB64–74 dB⇄🛏83–94 L18–24 D18–24
🛢 &🖎*Ferrari* via Lugano 31 ☎251668 P Toy (GB)
🛢 *Gottardo* viale Portone 6 ☎252818 BL/Tri

BELVÉDÈRE See **FURKA PASS**

BERGUN Graubünden 608 (☎081) Map **12** C1
★*Weisses Kreuz* Bern 1,323 ☎731161 Closed 16 Apr–May &
Nov–14 Dec 34rm8⇄20🛏 🏠 P sB⇄🛏44–67
dB63–88 dB⇄🛏81–126 L16–22 D16–22
mountains

BERLINGEN Thurgau (☎054) Map **12** C2
★*Seestern* ☎82404 Closed 26 Dec–Jan 9rm 1🛏
lake

BERN (BERNE) Bern 164,800 (☎031) Map **11** B1
★★★★★**Bellevue Palace** Kochergasse 3-5
☎224581 tx 32124 115⇄ 🏠 P Lift 🌙 sB⇄65–95
dB⇄140–200 (English breakfast) L24–32 D24–32
mountains
★★★★★**Schweizerhof** Bahnhofpl 11 (Nr Station)
☎224501 tx32188 120rm110⇄ P Lift 🌙 sB⇄50–65
sB⇄85–125 dB100–120 dB⇄140–230
(English breakfast) L25–30 D25–30alc
★★★★**Savoy** Neuengasse 26 ☎224405 tx32445
77rm25⇄18🛏 Lift
★★★**Bären** Schauplatzgasse 4 ☎223367 tx33199
57rm23⇄34🛏 P Lift 🌙 sB⇄🛏60–70
dB⇄🛏86–108 L18–25 D18–25
★★★**Bristol** Schauplatzgasse 10 (Off Bärenpl)
☎220101 tx33199 87rm19⇄36🛏 Lift 🌙 sB35–41
sB⇄🛏57–62 dB62–68 dB⇄🛏86–98
(English breakfast) L alc D alc
★★★**Touring** Eigerpl ☎458666 tx33356
56rm16⇄31🛏 Lift
★★**Continental** Zeughausgasse 27 (off
Weisenhauspl) (n rest) ☎222626 tx33055
38rm5⇄9🛏 Lift 🌙 sB32 sB⇄🛏52 dB56 dB⇄🛏90
(English breakfast)
★**Goldener Schlüssel** Rathausgasse 72 ☎220216
A30rm P 🛏 sB31–33 dB58–60 L8–16 D9–20
★**Stamm** Bernastr 6 ☎430684 13rm sB24–26
dB46–50
★**Volkshaus** Zeughausgasse 9 ☎222976 tx33055
70rm2⇄1🛏 P Lift 🌙 sB26–31 sB⇄🛏45 dB50–58
dB⇄🛏80–84 (English breakfast) L13–15 D13–15
🛢 &🖎*Auto Marti* Eigerpl 2 ☎451515 BMW (GB)
🛢 &🖎*Citroen (Suisse)* Freiburgstr 447 ☎553311
☎552511 Cit (GB)
🛢 &🖎*Egghölzli* Egghölzlstr 1 ☎446366 P
Bed/Hon/Peu/Vau

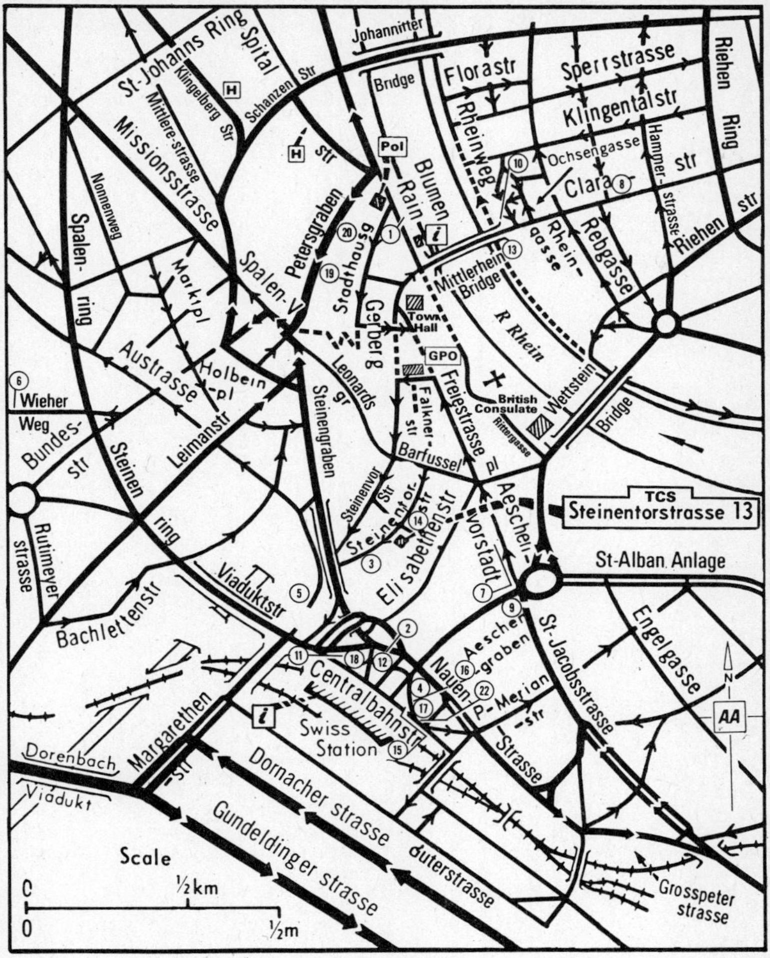

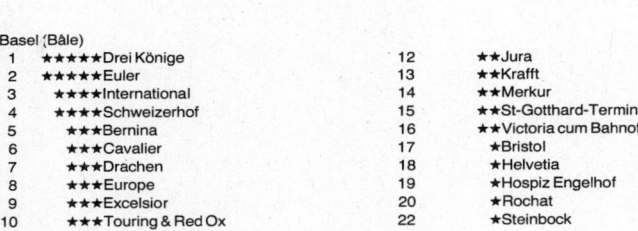

Basel (Bâle)

1	★★★★★Drei Könige		12	★★Jura
2	★★★★★Euler		13	★★Krafft
3	★★★★International		14	★★Merkur
4	★★★★Schweizerhof		15	★★St-Gotthard-Terminus
5	★★★Bernina		16	★★Victoria cum Bahnof
6	★★★Cavalier		17	★Bristol
7	★★★Drachen		18	★Helvetia
8	★★★Europe		19	★Hospiz Engelhof
9	★★★Excelsior		20	★Rochat
10	★★★Touring & Red Ox		22	★Steinbock
11	★★Greub			

Switzerland

🕶 **Rodtmatt** Rodtmattstr 103 ☎423330 BL Maz/Sab (GB)

🕶 ⛴**Willy** Freiburgerstr 443 ☎552511 ☎552511 P Frd (GB)

At **Gümligen** (6km E)

🕶 😐**Schwarz** ☎523636 P Vlo

At **Muri** (3km SE on N6)

☆☆**Krone** ☎521666 12rm4⇋8∣ 🏨 P sB⇋ 55−75 dB⇋ 75−95 L 12−25 D12−25

🕶 😐**F & H Schwarz** Thunstr 25 ☎521600 P BL

At **Wabern** (2km S)

🕶 😐**Wabern** Seftigenstr 198 ☎542622 P BL (GB)

BEVAIX Neuchâtel (☎038) Map **11** A1

☆**Bevaix** ☎461464 22⇋ 🏨 P Lift sB∣27 dB∣50 mountains lake

BEX-LES-BAINS Vaud 4,800 (☎025) Map **28** C4

★★**Salines** ☎52453 Closed 16 Oct−Apr 100rm12⇋ 🏨 Lift ⛴ Pool

☆**St-Christophe** ☎36777 15rm10∣

😐**Rallye** (W Dreier) r Servannaz ☎51225 P Sab/Toy

BIASCA Ticino (☎092) Map **12** C1

★★**Poste** via Stazione ☎722121 10rm 🏨 P sB22−27 dB44−54 (English breakfast) L17−22 D17−22 mountains

🕶 😐**Maggetti** via San Gottardo ☎721266 Chy Sim

BIEL (BIENNE) Bern 59,200 (☎032) Map **11** B1/2

★★★★**Elite** pl Gl-Guisan ☎225441 tx34101 60rm40⇋20∣ P Lift sB⇋∣61−80 dB⇋∣95−120 (English breakfast) L fr20 Dfr20

★★★**Continental** r d'Aarberg 29 ☎223255 tx34440 70rm40⇋30∣ P Lift ♫ sB⇋∣ 55−65 dB⇋∣ 86−96 (English breakfast) L 10−26 D 10−26 mountains lake

★**Bären** Nidaugasse 22 ☎224573 20rm8⇋ 🏨 Lift sB29 sB⇋37 dB48 dB⇋56

🕶 😐**City** (Bienne H S Dubach) Oberer quai 32 ☎236388 BL/Chy/Sim (GB)

🕶 😐**Giro** Solothurnstr 126 ☎421542 BL/Maz

🕶 😐**Mühle** Heilmannstr 16 ☎222201 P BL/Ren/Tri

🕶 😐**Progress** Portstr 32 ☎259666 AR/Bed/Vau (GB)

At **Bözingen** (3km)

🕶 😐**Grand Garage du Jura** Goufistr 18 & Renferstr 1 ☎419333 P Frd (GB)

BISSONE Ticino (☎091) Map **29** A4

★★★**Lago di Lugano** ☎688591 tx79378 90⇋ P Lift ♫ sB⇋57−102 dB⇋89−134 (English breakfast) L18−22 D18−22 Pool lake

BIVIO Graubünden 190 (☎081) Map **12** C1

★★★**Post** ☎751275 Closed Nov 41rm11⇋2∣ A15rm 🏨 P sB31−41 dB⇋∣41−54 dB61−77 dB⇋∣81−107 L15−23 D15−23 mountains

BLONAY-SUR-VEVEY Vaud (8km N of Montreux) 1,360 (☎021) Map **11** A1

★★**Bahyse** ☎531322 20rm2⇋ 🏨

★**Beaumont** ☎531244 Closed 16 Oct−19 Dec 38rm 🏨 lake

BOLLINGEN St-Gallen (☎055) Map **12** C2

☆☆**Schiff** am oberen Zürichsee ☎271813 18∣ 🏨 P ♫ sB∣33 dB∣60 (English breakfast) D7−24 St% mountains lake

BÖNIGEN Bern 1,750 (☎036) Map **11** B1

★★**Seiler au Lac** ☎223022 tx32364 Closed 16 Oct−19 Dec 50rm15⇋12∣ 🏨 P Lift sB33−51 sB⇋∣46−61 dB⇋∣89−119 (English breakfast) L15−20 D20−25 mountains lake

BÖZINGEN See **BIEL (BIENNE)**

BRÈ See **LUGANO**

BRESTENBERG Aargau 1,450 (☎064) Map **11** B2

★★**Shloss** ☎541131 23rm5⇋5∣ Lift ⛴ lake

BRIENZ Bern 2,900 (☎036) Map **11** B1

★★**Bären** ☎512412 33rm4⇋6∣ 🏨 Lift Pool

★★**Gare** ☎512712 12rm3⇋ lake

★★**Schönegg** ☎511113 15rm6⇋2∣ P sB27−30 sB⇋∣37−46 dB54−60 dB⇋∣74−88 ⛴ Pool mountains lake

★**Weisses Kreuz** Tachstr ☎511781 55rm lake

BRIG (BRIGUE) Valais 3,900 (☎028) Map **11** B1

★★★**Europe** (n rest) ☎31323 25rm5⇋4∣ Lift

★★★**Sporting** (n rest) ☎32363 33rm6⇋15∣ 🏨 Lift

★★**Brigerhof** Rhônesandstr 18 ☎31607 Closed Dec−Mar 29rm5⇋24∣ 🏨 Lift

★★**Müller** Kantonstr ☎32295 Closed Nov−Mar 60rm12⇋5∣ 🏨 Lift

★★**Victoria-Terminus** ☎231503 Closed Nov 40rm19⇋15∣ 🏨 P Lift ♫ sB36−40 sB⇋∣40−54 dB75−85 dB⇋∣85−100 (English breakfast) L16−19 D18−25 mountains

At **Glis** (2km E)

⛴**Saltina** (H Schwery) ☎232562 ☎232562 M/c P BL/Toy (GB)

BRISSAGO Ticino 1,940 (☎093) Map **28** D4

★★**Mirto & Belvédère au Lac** ☎651328 Closed Nov−Feb 30rm9⇋21∣ 🏨 P Lift ♫ sB⇋∣28−46 dB⇋∣56−92 lake

BRUGG Aargau 5,508 (☎056) Map **11** B2

★★★**Rotes Haus** Hauptstr 7 ☎411479 tx53084 26rm16⇋7∣ P Lift sB20−22 sB⇋25−27 dB40−44 dB⇋50−54 L5−20alc D5−20alc

BRUNNEN Schwyz 1,850 (☎043) Map **11** B1

★★**Bellevue** ☎311318 Closed Nov−Feb 50rm14⇋9∣ 🏨 Lift lake

★★**Elite** ☎311024 Closed Nov−Mar 75rm50⇋15∣ 🏨 P Lift sB31−36 sB⇋∣46−51 dB62−72 dB⇋∣92−102 (English breakfast) L17−24 D16−22 lake

★★**Metropole** ☎311039 Closed Dec−Feb 12rm1⇋8∣ 🏨 Lift lake

★★**Schmid** ☎311882 Closed Nov−Mar 24rm8⇋ Lift

★★**Waldstätterhof** ☎331133 tx78378 101⇋ 🏨 P Lift ♫ sB⇋∣61−81 dB⇋∣121−171 (English breakfast) L20 D24 ⛴ mountains lake

★★**Weisses Kreuz** ☎311736 30rm3∣ lake

★★**Weisses-Rössli** ☎311022 30rm4⇋ 🏨

★**Alpina** ☎311813 23rm7⇋ 🏨 P sB27−35 dB54−70 dB⇋38−52 L12−16 D12−16 mountains

★**Wolfsprung** ☎311173 Closed Nov−mid Apr 10rm3⇋ lake

🕶 **Inderbitzin** Gersauerstr 17 ☎311313 P MB

🕶 **J Strüby** Schwyzerstr 11, Ingenbohl ☎311304 Frd (GB)

BUCHS St-Gallen 5,300 (☎085) Map **12** C2

★★**Chez Fritz Bahnhof** ☎61377 15rm1⇋ 🏨 sB fr30 sB⇋fr41 dB fr60 dB⇋fr80 (English breakfast) L15−20 D15−20

😐**Sulser** St-Gallerstr 19 ☎61414 Opl

BULLE Fribourg 5,300 (☎029) Map **11** A1

★★★**Alpes** ☎29292 30rm5⇋25⇋ Lift

★★**Rallye** rte de Riaz 8 ☎28498 19rm15∣ A4rm 🏨 P Lift sB∣30 dB∣55 L9−24 D9−24 mountains

BURGDORF Bern (☎034) Map **11** B1

🕶 **Central** ☎223406 P Cit/Vau

BÜRGENSTOCK Nidwalden (☎041) Map **11** B1

★**Waldheim** ☎641306 54rm6⇋5∣ 🏨 Lift Pool

BUSSIGNY See **LAUSANNE**

CAMPIONE D'ITALIA See **LUGANO**

CAROUGE See **GENÈVE (GENEVA)**

CASSARATE See **LUGANO**

CASTAGNOLA See **LUGANO**

CELERINA Graubünden 713 (☎082) Map **12** C1

★★★**Cresta Palace** ☎33564 tx74461 Closed Oct & May 98rm52⇋20∣ 🏨 P Lift ♫ sB43−83 sB⇋∣53−123 dB76−156 dB⇋∣116−236 (English breakfast) L 22−32 D26−38 ⛴ Pool mountains

★★★**Cresta Kulm** ☎33373 Closed 16 Sep−19 Nov & 16 Apr−14 Jun 50rm27⇋6∣ A5rm 🏨 P Lift ♫ sB35−47 sB⇋∣45−57 dB70−104 dB⇋∣110−134 L 19−20 D19−20 mountains

CHAM Zug (☎042) Map **11** B2

😐**Ettmüller** Steinhauserstr ☎365370 Cit (GB)

CHAMPÉRY Valais 861 (☎025) Map **28** C4

★★★**Champéry** ☎84245 tx25980 Closed Apr−14 Jun & 16 Sep−14 Dec 55rm30⇋5∣ 🏨 P sB44−64

sB⇌ ⌂ 59 – 72 dB 76 – 110 dB⇌ ⌂ 102 – 140
(English breakfast) L 21alc D21alc mountains
★★**Alpes** ☎84222 Closed May & Oct – 14 Dec
24rm20⇌10 ⌂
★★**Beau-Séjour** ☎84343 (fr Mar '79 791701) Closed
7 Sep – 11 Apr 25rm6⇌ ⌂ P sB31 – 41 sB⇌44 – 62
dB 62 – 82 dB⇌ 77 – 123 (English breakfast) L 14 – 18
D14 – 18 mountains
★★**Parc** ☎84235 (fr Mar'79 791313) tx25980
16 Sep – 14 Dec & 16 Apr – 14 Jun 40rm5⇌20 ⌂
A5rm sB36 – 61 sB⇌ ⌂36 – 61 dB 63 – 102
dB⇌ ⌂ 63 – 102 mountains
CHAMPEX Valais 73 (☎026) Map **28** C4
★★★**Alpes & Lac** ☎41151 Closed Oct – May
65rm45⇌2 ⌂ ⌂ P Lift sB 30 – 40 sB⇌ ⌂40 – 75
dB60 – 80 dB⇌ ⌂ 80 – 120 (English breakfast)
L20 – 25 D20 – 25 ⚓ mountains lake
CHÂTEAU-D'OEX Vaud (☎029) Map **11** B1
★★★**Beau-Séjour** ☎47423 Closed Nov
48rm20⇌4 ⌂ ⌂ Lift
★★★**Chalet du Bon Accueil** ☎46320 tx46318
Closed 10 Oct – 5 Dec 17rm12⇌ P D sB36 – 51
sB⇌46 – 61 dB61 – 101 dB⇌81 – 121
(English breakfast) L 12 – 25 D20 – 30 mountains lake
★★★**Victoria** (n rest) ☎46434 tx36418 Closed mid
Apr – May & Nov – Xmas 18⇌ ⌂ ⌂ P Lift D
sB⇌37 – 59 dB⇌137 – 160 (English breakfast) L 20
D20 Pool mountains
★★**Ermitage** ☎46003 Closed Nov 27rm8⇌
🗋 **Burnand** ☎47539 P BL/Cit Vlo
🗎 **Pont** Petit Pré ☎46173 ☎46173 M/c P
Bed/Opl/Vau (GB)
CHAUMONT See **NEUCHÂTEL**
CHAUX-DE-FONDS (LA) Neuchâtel 38,900 (☎039)
Map **11** A1
★★★**Club** r du Parc 71 ☎235300 tx35548 40⇌ Lift
🗎 **Étoile** r F-Courvoisier 28 ☎231362 Chy Sim
(GB)
🗋 **Metropole** r du Locle 64 ☎269595 ☎268181
AR/BL/Jag

🗎 **Trois Rois** bd des Eplatures 8 ☎268181
☎268181 Frd/Lnc (GB)
CHERNEX See **MONTREUX**
CHEXBRES Vaud 1,343 (☎021) Map **11** A1
★★★**Bellevue** ☎561481 27rm14⇌P Lift sB32 – 36
sB⇌38 – 42 dB64 – 72 dB⇌76 – 82 L 20 – 25 D20 – 25
mountains lake
★★★**Signal** ☎562525 Closed Dec – Feb
82rm64⇌18 ⌂ ⌂ P Lift D sB⇌ ⌂38 – 75
dB⇌ ⌂72 – 150 (English breakfast) L 17 – 26 D18 – 25
⚓ Pool mountains ◯ lake
★★**Cécil** ☎561292 25rm10⇌2 ⌂ P Lift sB 30 – 32
sB⇌ ⌂35 – 42 dB60 – 64 dB⇌70 – 84 Pool
mountains lake
CHUR (COIRE) Graubünden 24,800 (☎081)
Map **12** C1
★★★**City** Martinspl 4 ☎225444 tx74583
75rm25⇌25 ⌂ Lift
★★★**Duc de Rohan** Masanserstr 44 ☎221022
tx74161 35rm32⇌1 ⌂ ⌂ Lift D sB39 – 43
sB⇌ ⌂56 – 61 dB69 – 75 dB⇌ ⌂96 – 104 Pool
mountains
★★**ABC** Bahnhofpl (n rest) ☎226033 tx74580
38rm8⇌20 ⌂ ⌂ P Lift D sB32 – 34 sB⇌ ⌂40 – 50
dB60 – 64 dB⇌ ⌂78 – 96 mountains
★★**Drei Könige** Reichsgasse 18 ☎221725
60rm10⇌5 ⌂ ⌂ P Lift sB31 – 34 sB⇌ ⌂40 – 44
dB60 – 66 dB⇌ ⌂80 – 82 L 15 – 18 D15 – 18
mountains
★☆**Sommerau** Emerstr ☎225545 tx74172
45rm21⇌24 ⌂
★★**Stern** Reichsgasse 11 ☎223555 tx74198
51rm13⇌33 ⌂ ⌂ P D sB34 sB⇌ ⌂42 – 45 dB60
dB⇌ ⌂76 – 84
★★**Weisses Kreuz** Vazerolgasse 19 ☎223112
22rm4⇌
🗋 **Autocenter Tribolet** Rossbodenstr 14
🗋 **Calanda** Kasernenstr 30 ☎221414 Fia/Lnc
(GB)

🛢 &⃝*Comminot* Rossbodenstr 24 ☎223737 P Peu
Rov
🛢 &⃝*Grand Garage Dosch* Kasernenstr ☎215171
Bed/Opl/Vau (GB)
🛢 ⋈*Lidoc* St-Margrethenstr 9 ☎221313 ☎221313 P
AR/Bed/MB/Opl/Vau (GB)
CLARO Ticino (☎092) Map **29** A4
☆*San Gottardo* ☎63566 35rm28 🏚
COLLONGE-BELLERIVE Genève Map **28** C4
★★*Bellerive* ☎521282 Closed 21 Dec–Jan 7rm6⇄
lake
COPPET Vaud (☎022) Map **11** A1
🛢 &⃝*Port* (P Keller) rte de Suisse ☎761212 P
BL/Maz (GB)
CORNAREDO See **LUGANO**
COUVET Neuchâtel 2,897 (☎038) Map **11** A1
★*Aigle* Grande r 27 ☎632644 11rm P sB25 dB 40
(English breakfast) L 10 D10 mountains
CRANS-SUR-SIERRE Valais 1,750 (☎027)
Map **28** C4
★★★★*Alpina & Savoy* ☎412142 tx34138
16 Sep–14 Dec & 16 Apr–14 Jun 61rm60⇄1 🏚 P
Lift sB⇄🏚35–80 dB⇄🏚70–160 (English breakfast)
L 25–32 D25–32 Pool ♨ mountains lake
★★★*Elite* ☎414301 Closed mid Apr–May &
Oct–Nov 30⇄ P Lift sB⇄🏚41–51 dB⇄🏚82–92
(English breakfast) L 15–20 D15–20 Pool mountains
lake
★★★*Robinson* ☎411353 16rm12⇄4🏚 P Lift
sB⇄🏚41–61 dB⇄🏚72–112 (English breakfast)
L 18 D20 mountains
★★★*Royal* ☎413931 tx38227 Closed 16 Apr–
9 May & 11 Sep–9 Dec Lift
★★★*Splendide* ☎412056 Closed May & Nov
32rm28⇄2🏚 🏚 Lift
CULLY See **LAUSANNE**
DÄRLIGEN Bern 361 (☎036) Map **11** B1
★*Strandbad* ☎227544 40rm2⇄6🏚 lake
DAVOS Graubünden 7,378 (☎083) Map **12** C1
At **Dorf**
★★★*Meierhof* Promenade (DP) ☎61285 tx74363
44rm19⇄ 🏚 Lift
At **Laret** (8km NE)
★*Tischiery's Im Landhaus* (DP) ☎52121 Closed 16
Apr–9 Jun & 16 Oct–Nov 30rm6⇄ 6🏚 🏚 P
sB30–60 sB⇄🏚40–60 dB60–120 dB⇄🏚fr70
(English breakfast) mountains
At **Platz**
★★★*Morosani Post* Promenade 42 ☎21161
tx74350 Closed 26 Oct–25 Nov & 19 Apr–17 May
90rm60⇄ 🏚 P Lift 🌙 sB40–81 sB⇄58–126
dB80–162 dB⇄100–252 (English breakfast) L18
D25 Pool mountains
★★★*Schweizerhof* Promenade ☎21151 tx74324
Closed 23 Apr–25 May & Oct–Nov 105rm90⇄ 🏚 P
Lift 🌙 sB35–47 sB⇄55–65 dB70–84
dB⇄100–130 (English breakfast) L18 D22 Pool
mountains
★*Belmont* Tanzbühlstr 2 (n rest) ☎35032 Closed
Oct–Nov & May–Jun 25rm P sB30–40 dB58–78
mountains
DÉLÉMONT Bern 7,500 (☎066) Map **11** B2
★*Bonne Auberge* Grande r 32 ☎221758 Closed Jan
& Feb 9rm2⇄4🏚 🏚
★*Central* Grande r 10 ☎223363 Closed 26 Dec–
14 Jan 10rm7🏚 Lift sB25 sB🏚25 dB50 dB🏚50 L13
D13
🛢 ⋈*Gare* (Willemin) rte de Moutier 65 ☎222461
☎222461 Ren (GB)
🛢 ⋈*Mercay* r de la Maltière 20 ☎221745 BMW/Fia
🛢 &⃝*Stand* (Hulmann) r du Stand ☎222424
☎222424 P Aud/Lnc/MB VW (GB)
DÜRRENAST See **THUN (THOUNE)**
EBIKON See **LUZERN (LUCERNE)**
EBLIGEN Bern (☎036) Map **11** B1
★*Hirschen* ☎511551 Closed Nov–Mar 14rm3⇄5🏚
P sB32–41 sB⇄🏚37–46 dB56–70 L14–15
D14–15 mountains lake
ECHALLENS Vaud (☎021) Map **11** A1

At **Villars-le-Terroir**
☆☆*Beauregard* ☎811917 20⇄ 🏚
ECLEPENS Vaud (☎021) Map **11** A1
★*Auberge Communale* ☎877193 6rm1⇄4🏚 🏚 P
sB23–30 sB⇄🏚23–30 dB45–55 dB⇄🏚45–55
(English breakfast) L12–18 D10–16
EGERKINGEN Solothurn (☎062) Map **11** B2
☆☆*AGIP* (Autobahn Crossroads N1/N2) ☎612121
tx68644 80rm40⇄30🏚 🏚
🛢 ⋈*Reinhart* ☎611250 ☎611250 Frd/Toy (GB)
EINIGEN Bern (☎033) Map **11** B1
☆*Hirschen* ☎543272 23rm20 🏚 🏚 lake
EINSIEDELN Schwyz (☎055) Map **12** C1
★★*Drei Könige* ☎532441 52rm14⇄37🏚 🏚 Lift
EMMENBRÜCKE See **LUZERN (LUCERNE)**
ENGELBERG Obwalden 2,600 (☎041) Map **11** B1
★★★*Bellevue* ☎941213 tx78555 Closed Nov
90rm45⇄ 🏚 Lift ♨
★★*Hess* ☎941366 tx72347 Closed 31 Oct–17 Dec
48rm23⇄13🏚 P Lift 🌙 sB41–47 sB⇄🏚51–72
dB72–84 dB⇄🏚92–134 (English breakfast)
L15–17 D15–17 mountains
★*Engelberg* Dorfstr 14 ☎941168 30rm6⇄8🏚
ENTLEBUCH Luzern (☎041) Map **11** B1
★★*Drei Könige* ☎721227 13rm3⇄1🏚 🏚
ESTAVAYER-LE-LAC Fribourg (☎037) Map **11** A1
★*Lac* ☎631343 Closed Jan 18rm6⇄2🏚 Pool lake
ETOY-BUCHILLON Vaud (☎021) Map **11** A1
☆☆*Péchers* rte du Lac Genève-Lausanne ☎763277
Closed Jan 14rm2⇄12🏚 🏚 Pool lake
EVOLÈNE Valais 1,300 (☎027) Map **28** C4
★★*Hermitage* ☎831232 Closed Jan–May &
17 Sep–24 Dec 22rm12⇄ 🏚
★*Dent-Blanche* ☎831105 Closed 16 Apr–May &
Oct–19 Dec 🏚
★*Eden* ☎831112 Closed Nov 18rm 🏚
★*Evolène* ☎831202 45rm15⇄3🏚 P 🌙 sB23–32
sB⇄🏚29–42 dB46–64 dB⇄🏚58–84
(English breakfast) L13–18 D13–18 ♨ Pool
mountains
FAIDO Ticino 1,200 (☎094) Map **12** C1
★★*Faido* ☎381555 17rm2⇄ 🏚 Lift
★★*Milan* ☎381307 Closed Nov–Mar 41rm21⇄ 🏚 P
Lift sB31 sB⇄🏚38 dB52 dB⇄🏚66 L17–20 D17–20
mountains
FAULENSEE Bern 262 (☎033) Map **11** B1
★★*Bellerive* ☎543774 Closed Mar & Nov
27rm11⇄6🏚 🏚 Pool lake
☆☆*Faulensee* ☎542888 Closed Nov–Feb
18rm2⇄14🏚 P sB26–28 sB⇄🏚30–37 dB52–56
dB⇄🏚60–74 ♨ mountains lake
☆*Sternen* ☎541306 Closed Nov 16rm1⇄5🏚 P
sB32–37 sB⇄🏚41–46 dB37–40 dB⇄🏚45–48
L8–28 D8–28 mountains lake
FIESCH Valais 520 (☎028) Map **11** B1
★*Glacier & Poste* ☎81102 40rm6⇄ 🏚 Lift
FILZBACH Glarus 393 (☎058) (2km W of
Obstalden) Map **12** C1
★*Rössli* Kerenzerbergstr ☎321818 15rm
★*Seeblick* ☎321455 10rm P sB23–25 dB45–50
mountains lake
FLEURIER Neuchâtel 3,413 (☎038) Map **11** A1
★*Commerce* ☎611733 26rm 🏚 Lift
🛢 &⃝*L Duthé* r de Temple 34 ☎611637 P
Aud/Ren/VW
🛢 &⃝*C Hotz* r de l'Industrie 19 ☎612922 P
BMW/Chy/Cit
FLIMS-WALDHAUS Graubünden (☎081)
Map **12** C1
★★★★*Park Waldhaus* ☎391181 tx74125 Closed
Nov & May 200rm180⇄ 🏚 P Lift 🌙 sB87–107
sB⇄102–182 dB174–214 dB⇄204–364 L fr32
Dfr35 ♨ Pool mountains lake
★★★*Schloss* ☎391245 Closed May & Oct–Nov
40rm14⇄10🏚 A18rm 🏚 Lift
★★★*Segnes* ☎391281 tx74125 Closed 16 Oct–
14 Dec & 16 Apr–19 May 70rm40⇄10🏚 P 🌙
sB33–47 sB⇄🏚41–61 dB66–86 dB⇄🏚82–114

(English breakfast) L 13 – 23 D13 – 23 ☙ Pool
★★**Alpes** Hauptstr ☎390101 tx74565 90 ⇌ 🏛 P Lift
♪ sB ⇌ 50 – 80 dB ⇌ 80 – 120 L 8 – 20 D8 – 20 Pool
★★**National** ☎391224 Closed mid Apr – 26 May &
mid Oct – mid Dec 24rm6 ⇌ 6 🏛 P Lift sB 29 – 39
sB ⇌ 🏛 35 – 50 dB50 – 76 dB ⇌ 🏛 66 – 100
(English breakfast) L 15 – 22 D15 – 22
FLÜELA-PASS Graubünden (☎083) Map **12 C1**
☆*Flüela-Hospiz* ☎36864 Closed Nov – Apr 10rm
lake
FLÜELEN Uri 1,700 (☎044) Map **11 B1**
★★*Hirschen* Axenstr (DP) ☎21201 30rm 🏛 lake
★*Weisses Kreuz* ☎21717 Closed Dec – Mar
34rm1 ⇌ 6 🏛 🏛 P sB22 ⇌ 28 – 36 dB36 – 48
dB ⇌ 🏛 52 – 60 (English breakfast) L 6 – 18 alc
D6 – 18alc lake
🅗 ✺*Signist* ☎21260 P Fia/Ren
FOUNEX Vaud (☎022) Map **11 A1**
☆☆**Founex** ☎762535 tx23623 108rm44 ⇌ 64 🏛 P Lift
sB ⇌ 47 – 75 dB ⇌ 63 – 80 (English breakfast) L alc
Dalc Pool mountains lake
FRAUENFELD Thurgau 14,700 (☎054) Map **12 C2**
🅗 ✺*Lüthi* Zürcherstr 332 ☎76221 BL/Chy/Dat/Sim
(GB)
FRIBOURG Fribourg 29,000 (☎037) Map **11 B1**
🅗 ✺*Central* r de l'Industrie 7 ☎223505 Frd
🅗 *Gendre* rte de Villars 105 ☎240331 ☎240331
Aud/Por/VW
🅗 ✺*Piller* r Guillimann 24 – 26 ☎223092 Cit/Lnc
FRICK Aargau (☎064) Map **11 B2**
★*Engel* ☎611314 15rm8 🏛 P sB22 sB ⇌ 25 dB 44
dB 🏛 50 L alc D alc
FRUTIGEN Bern 5,700 (☎033) Map **11 B1**
★*Simplon* ☎711041 35rm1 ⇌
🅗 ✺ *Bahnhof* ☎711414 P Aud/Frd/VW
🅗 ✺*Widi* (O Stucki) ☎711053 ☎711053 ☒ P Opl
(GB)
FÜRIGEN Nidwalden (☎041) (5km N of **Stans**)
Map **11** B1
★★*Fürigen & Bellevue* ☎611254 96rm80 ⇌ 🏛 Lift
☙ lake
FURKA PASS Uri (☎044) Map **11 B1**
★*Furkablick* ☎67297 Closed Nov – May 20rm 🏛
sB30 – 32 dB 60 – 62 (English breakfast) L alc Dalc
mountains
At **Belvédère**
★★*Seiler's Belvédère* ☎82530 Closed 26 Sep –
14 Jan 40rm10 ⇌
GANDRIA See **LUGANO**
GENÈVE (GENEVA) 170,000 (☎022) Map **28 C4**
See Plan overleaf
AA agents; see page 361
★★★★★**Bergues** quai-des-Bergues 33 ☎315050
tx23383 Plan **1** 130rm119 ⇌ 11 🏛 P Lift ♪
sB ⇌ 🏛 100 – 140 dB ⇌ 🏛 150 – 230
(English breakfast) L 35 D40 lake
★★★★★*Président* quai Wilson 47 ☎311000
tx22780 Plan **2** 270 ⇌ 🏛 P Lift ♪ sB ⇌ 180 – 237
dB ⇌ 249 (English breakfast) L 52 & alc D52 & alc
mountains lake
★★★★★**Rhône** quai Turrettini 3 ☎319831 tx22213
Plan **3** 350rm320 ⇌ 30 🏛 🏛 P Lift ♪ sB ⇌ 🏛 95 – 130
dB ⇌ 🏛 170 – 200 (English breakfast) L fr37 Dfr37 lake
★★★★★**Richemond** Jardin Brunswick ☎311400
tx22598 Plan **4** 150rm120 ⇌ 30 🏛 P Lift ♪
sB ⇌ 🏛 126 – 145 dB ⇌ 🏛 216 – 257
(English breakfast) L 35 D35 St% mountains lake
★★★★*Beau Rivage* quai-du-Mont-Blanc 13
☎310221 tx23362 Plan **5** ⇌ 🏛 P Lift ♪ sB ⇌ 110 – 145
dB ⇌ 180 – 250 (English breakfast) L fr35&alc
Dfr35&alc mountains lake
★★★★*Paix* quai-du-Mont-Blanc 11 ☎326150
tx22552 Plan **6** 109rm83 ⇌ 26 🏛 Lift lake
★★★*Ambassador* quai des Bergues 21 ☎317200
tx23231 Plan **7** 92rm ⇌ 🏛 🏛 Lift lake
★★★*Angleterre* quai-du-Mont-Blanc 17 ☎328180
tx22668 Plan **8** 64 ⇌ 🏛 P Lift ♪ sB ⇌ 🏛 90 – 145
dB ⇌ 🏛 135 – 210 (English breakfast) L fr25 Dfr25
mountains lake

★★★**Berne** r de Berne 26 ☎316000 tx22764 Plan **9**
80 ⇌ Lift ♪ sB ⇌ 🏛 60 – 75 dB ⇌ 🏛 80 – 110
(English breakfast) L fr18 Dfr18
★★★*Century* av de Frontenex 24 (n rest) ☎368095
tx23223 Plan **10** 140rm105 ⇌ 15 🏛 Lift
★★★*Cornavin* bd J-Fazy 33 (n rest) ☎322100
tx22853 Plan **11** 125rm50 ⇌ 65 🏛 P Lift ♪
sB ⇌ 🏛 68 – 95 dB ⇌ 🏛 95 – 125
★★★*Eden* r de Lausanne 135 ☎326540 tx23962
Plan **12** 54rm27 ⇌ 27 🏛 🏛 P Lift ♪ sB ⇌ 🏛 60 – 70
dB ⇌ 🏛 80 – 90 (English breakfast) L 18 D18 lake
★★★*Grand-Pré* r du Grand-Pré 35 (n rest) ☎339150
tx23284 Plan **13** 100rm50 ⇌ 50 🏛 🏛 Lift
★★★*Lutetia* r de Carouge 12 ☎204222 tx28845
Plan **14** 42 ⇌ Lift
★★★*Méditerranée* r de Lausanne 14 ☎316250
tx23630 Plan **15** 167rm161 ⇌ 6 🏛 P Lift ♪
sB ⇌ 🏛 80 – 100 dB ⇌ 🏛 130 – 150 (English breakfast)
L 16 – 40 D16 – 40
★★★*Résidence* rte de Florissant 11 ☎461833
tx28526 Plan **16** 122rm110 ⇌ P Lift ♪ sB44 – 54
sB ⇌ 🏛 57 – 80 dB80 – 90 dB ⇌ 🏛 100 – 140
(English breakfast) L alc Dalc ☙
★★*Ariana* r J R-Chouet 7 (n rest) ☎339950
51rm17 ⇌ 37 🏛 P Lift sB39 sB ⇌ 🏛 49 – 55 dB51
dB ⇌ 🏛 69 – 85
★★*Epoque* r Voltaire 10 ☎452550 tx22940 Plan **18**
54rm18 ⇌ 36 🏛 🏛 Lift
★★*Montbrillant* r Montbrillant 2 ☎337784 Plan **19**
34rm6 ⇌ 6 🏛 P Lift sB30 – 33 sB ⇌ 🏛 49 dB 50
dB ⇌ 🏛 58 – 90
★★*Parc* av Krieg 42 ☎479041 Plan **20**
63rm24 ⇌ 21 🏛 🏛 Lift Pool
★★*Touring-Balance* pl Longemalle 13 ☎287122
tx27634 Plan **21** 58rm27 ⇌ 13 🏛 Lift ♪ sB40 – 45
sB ⇌ 🏛 60 – 70 dB 60 – 70 dB ⇌ 🏛 80 – 100
(English breakfast) L 20 D18 lake
★*Adris* r Gevray 6 – 8 (n rest) ☎315225 Plan **22**
22rm7 ⇌ Lift ♪ sB30 sB ⇌ 50 dB60 dB ⇌ 80
🅗 ✺*Acacias Motors* r Boissonnas 11 ☎433600 Chy
(GB)
🅗 ✺*Athénée* rte de Meyrin 122, Cointrin ☎960044
BMW/RR/Sab (GB)
🅗 ✺*Autobritt* r Ancien Port 4 ☎320010 BL (GB)
🅗 ✺*Autos-Import* r Viguet 1, Acacias ☎425804 P
BMW (GB)
🅗 *Bouchet* (C Roqivue) rte de Meyrin 54 – 56,
Cointrin ☎968900 BL (GB)
🅗 ✺*E Frey* rte des Acacias 23 ☎21010 ☎21010
BL/MB/Toy (GB)
✺*Metropole* rte du Pont-Butin, Petit-Lancy
☎921322 Frd (GB)
🅗 ✎ *Nouveau* r Pré Jérome 21 – 23 ☎202111 M/c
BMW (GB)
Tranches (Blanc & Paiche) bd des Tranchées 50
☎468911 Maz (GB)
At **Carouge** (2km S)
🅗 ✺*Claparede Val d'Arve* rte de Veyrier 90
☎429950 ☎431710 P BL/Fia/Jag
At **Mies** (10km N on No 1)
☆*Buna* ☎551535 Not on plan 6 🏛 P sB 🏛 41 dB 🏛 56
L fr9 D fr9 Pool mountains
At **Vésenaz** (6km NE on No 37)
★*Tourelle* rte d'Hermance 26 ☎521628 Not on plan
24rm10 ⇌ 8 🏛 P sB30 – 35 sB ⇌ 🏛 45 – 60 dB45 – 50
dB ⇌ 🏛 60 – 90 mountains lake
GENÈVE AIRPORT (7km N)
At **Fernay Voltaire** (in France, 4km from airport)
☆☆☆**Novotel Genève Aéroport** rte le Meyrin
☎(023) 408523 from Switzerland (50) 408523 from
France tx385046 79 ⇌ P Lift sB ⇌ fr134 dB ⇌ fr154
(French francs) English breakfast only ☙ Pool
GERSAU Schwyz 1,890 (☎041) Map **11 B1**
★★*Beau-Rivage* ☎841223 Closed Nov – Feb
34rm4 ⇌ 20 🏛 P Lift sB20 – 30 (room only)
sB ⇌ 🏛 30 – 45 (room only) dB40 – 60 (room only)
dB ⇌ 🏛 60 – 90 (room only) lake
★★*Bellevue* (n rest) ☎841120 23rm5 ⇌ P sB30 – 35
dB56 – 70 dB ⇌ 70 – 86 Pool lake

Switzerland

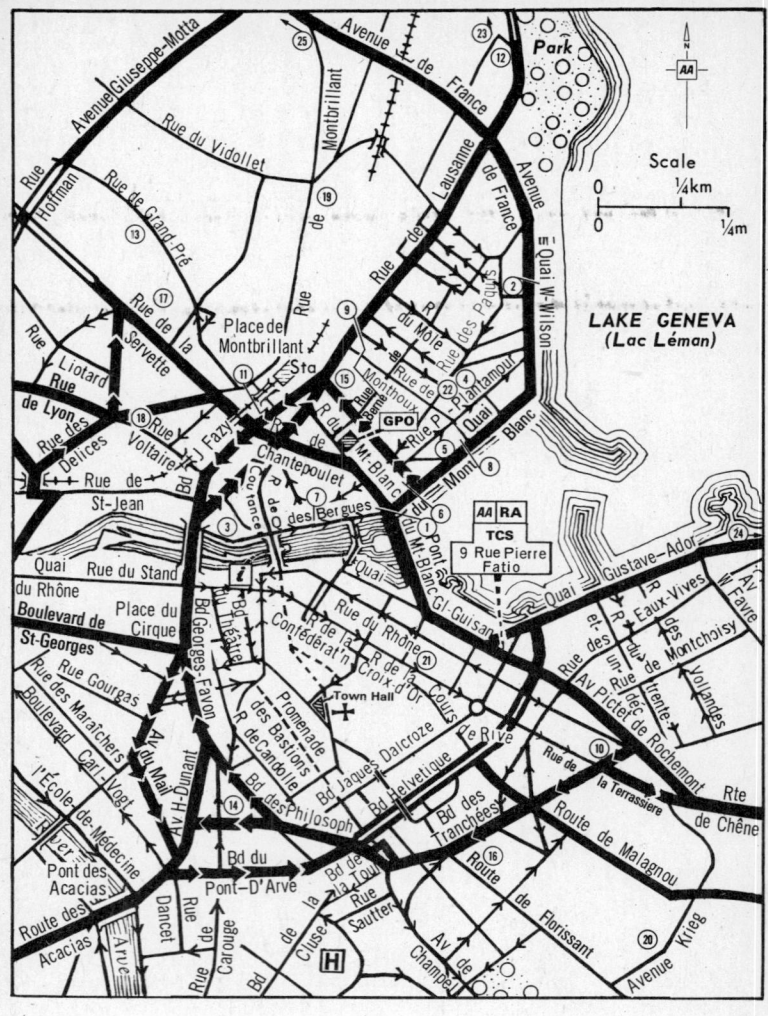

Genève (Geneva)

1	★★★★★Bergues	14	★★★Lutetia
2	★★★★★Président	15	★★★Méditerranée
3	★★★★★Rhône	16	★★★Résidence
4	★★★★★Richemond	17	★★Ariana
5	★★★Beau Rivage	18	★★Epoque
6	★★★Paix	19	★★Montbrillant
7	★★★Ambassador	20	★★Parc
8	★★★Angleterre	21	★★Touring-Balance
9	★★★Berne	22	★Adris
10	★★★Century	23	☆Motel de la Buna (at Mies 10km N on No 1)
11	★★★Cornavin	24	★Tourelle (at Vésenaz 6km NE on No 37)
12	★★★Eden	25	☆☆☆Novotel Genèva Aeróport
13	★★★Grand-Pré		

★★*Müller* am Vierwaldstättersee ☎841212 tx78641 Closed Nov–Mar 75rm30⇌ 🏡 Lift ✒ Lake

★*Seehof du Lac* ☎841245 Closed Oct–Mar 24rm

GIESSBACH Bern (☎036) Map **11** B1

★★*Park* ☎511515 Closed Oct–14 May 80rm 🏡 Lift ✒ Pool lake

GISWIL Obwalden 2,700 (☎041) Map **11** B1

★*Krone* Brünigstr ☎681151 97rm16⇌24🏔 🏡

GLARUS Glarus 5,800 (☎058) Map **12** C1

★★*Glarnerhof* Bahnhofstr 2 ☎614106 32rm16⇌ 🏡 Lift

Central Landsgemeindepl ☎611834 P Opl/Rov (GB)

GLATTBRUGG See **ZÜRICH AIRPORT**

GLETSCH Valais (☎028) Map **11** B1

★★*Glacier du Rhône* ☎731515 Closed Oct–14 Jun 110rm15⇌ 🏡25rm 🏡

GLION See **MONTREUX**

GLIS See **BRIG (BRIGUE)**

GOLDSWIL Bern 610 (☎036) (2km E of **Interlaken**) Map **11** B1

★*Park* ☎222942 56rm4⇌ A7rm 🏡 P sB23–27 dB45–49 dB⇌🏔59–67 L9–12 D9–12

🛢 ✒*Burgseeli* Haupstr ☎221043 Toy/Vau

GÖSCHENEN Uri (☎044) Map **11** B1

★*St Gotthard* ☎65263 25rm2⇌2🏔 🏡 P sB23–24 sB⇌🏔25–26 dB45–47 dB⇌🏔50–52 L7–25 D7–25

GRÄCHEN Valais (☎028) Map **28** D4

★★*Beausite* ☎562656 Closed Nov 42rm6⇌3🏔 🏡 Lift Pool

★*Grächerhof & Schönegg* ☎40172 35rm

GREPPEN Luzern 349 (☎041) Map **11** B1

★*St-Wendelin* ☎811016 Closed Dec–Feb 14rm 🏡 P sB24–26 dB48–52 L13–24 D13–24

GRINDELWALD Bern 3,100 (☎036) Map **11** B1

★★★★*Regina* ☎531515 tx32663 Closed 16 Oct–14 Dec 100rm80⇌20🏔 🏡 Lift ✒ Pool lake

★★★*Belvédère* ☎531818 tx32217 Closed Oct–May 65rm40⇌6🏔 P Lift sB50–65 sB⇌🏔65–80 dB100–120 dB⇌🏔130–150 L22–26 Pool

★★★*Parkhotel Schönegg* ☎531853 tx33645 Closed Nov 70rm45⇌5🏔 A6rm 🏡 P Lift ♪ sB43–68 sB⇌🏔63–83 dB86–136 dB⇌🏔112–166 (English breakfast) L20–28 D20–28 Pool

★★★*Schweizerhof* ☎532202 tx32217 Closed 21 Apr–24 May & Oct–19 Dec 45rm39⇌3🏔 🏡 P Lift sB54–64 sB⇌🏔64–79 dB⇌🏔117–147 L18–24 D18–24 mountains

★★★*Sunstar* ☎545417 tx32530 Closed 10 Apr–May & 16 Oct–16 Dec 168rm143⇌25🏔 A33rm 🏡 Lift ✒ Pool

★★*Derby* ☎545461 tx32897 Closed last 2 wks Nov 78rm34⇌27🏔 A32rm 🏡 Lift ✒

☆☆*Grindelwald* ☎532131 tx3818 Closed Nov 18⇌ 🏡

★★*Hirschen* ☎532777 30rm15⇌5🏔 🏡 P Lift sB31–41 sB⇌🏔36–56 dB62–82 dB⇌🏔72–112 L12–18 D12–18

★*Alpenblick* ☎531105 16rm 🏡

🛢 ✒*Rothenegg* Rothenegg ☎531507 ☎531507 Aud/Rov/VW (GB)

GROSSHÖCHSTETTEN Bern 1,700 (☎031) Map **11** B1

★*Löwen* Dorfstr ☎910210 4rm 🏡 P sB fr27 dB fr50 (English breakfast) L fr12 D fr12

GRUYÈRES Fribourg (☎029) Map **11** A1

★★*Gruyerotel* ☎61933 35⇌ 🏡 P Lift sB⇌🏔38–53 dB⇌🏔70–95 L alc D alc mountains

★★*Hostellerie St-Georges* ☎62246 Closed Nov–Feb 14rm

GSTAAD Bern 1,700 (☎030) Map **11** B1

★★★*Bellevue* ☎43264 tx33632 Closed May & Nov 55rm47⇌8🏔 🏡 P Lift ♪ sB⇌🏔50–120 dB⇌🏔100–240 (English breakfast) L20 D20 ✒ Pool

★★*National-Rialto* Hauptstr ☎43474 30rm13⇌6🏔 🏡 P Lift ♪ sB30–40 sB⇌🏔40–65 dB60–80 dB⇌🏔80–130 (English breakfast) L fr30 Dfr30

★★*Olden* ☎43444 16rm14⇌2🏔 A4rm 🏡 P sB32–56 sB⇌🏔41–86 dB64–112 dB⇌🏔82–172 (English breakfast) L16–28 D16–28

★*Rössli* ☎43412 Closed May 27rm10⇌4🏔 A4rm 🏡 P sB26–50 sB⇌🏔35–60 dB52–100 dB⇌🏔70–120 L16–24 D16–24

GSTEIG (LE CHÂTELET) Bern 740 (☎030) Map **11** B1

★*Viktoria* ☎51034 12rm4⇌4🏔 🏡 P ♪ sB30–36 sB⇌🏔33–40 dB62–76 dB⇌🏔64–80 (English breakfast) L12–20 D12–20

GSTEIN-GABI Valais (☎028) Map **28** D4

★★*Weissmies* Simplonstr ☎291116 20rm2⇌ A2rm 🏡 P sB25–30 sB⇌🏔30–33 dB54–56 dB⇌🏔64–68 L9–13 D9–13

GÜMLIGEN See **BERN**

GUNTEN Bern 323 (☎033) Map **11** B1

★★*Hirschen am See* ☎512244 Closed Oct–Apr 68rm40⇌28🏔 🏡 P Lift sB⇌🏔65–72 dB⇌🏔123–143 (English breakfast) L18–25 D18–25 lake

★★*Lac* ☎511421 Closed Oct–14May 62rm12⇌6🏔 🏡 Lift lake

★*Bellevue* ☎511121 Closed 16 Nov–Feb 30rm3 ⇌ 🏡 P sB20–30 dB40–55 dB⇌🏔70–90 L14–17 D14–17 lake

GURTNELLEN Uri (☎044) Map **11** B1

★*Gotthard* ☎65110 14rm1⇌2🏔 🏡 P sB26–31 sB⇌🏔31–36 dB51–57 dB⇌🏔61–72 (English breakfast) L10–16 D10–16

GUTTANNEN Bern 557 (☎036) Map **11** B1

★*Bären* ☎731261 24rm 🏡 P sB18–20 dB35–40 L10–16 D10–16

GWATT Bern (☎033) Map **11** B1

★*Lamm* ☎362233 16rm

HANDEGG Bern (☎036) Map **11** B1

★*Handeck* ☎731131 Closed Nov–Apr 44rm9⇌4🏔 A22rm 🏡

HEIDEN Appenzell 3,100 (☎071) Map **12** C2

★★★*Heiden* Dorfpl (DP Pn) ☎911115 60rm12⇌30🏔 🏡 Lift Pool lake

★★*Krone* ☎911127 tx71101 Closed Nov–Feb 35rm16⇌6🏔 🏡 Pool lake

HERGISWIL Nidwalden 2,900 (☎041) Map **11** B1

★★★*Pilatus* ☎951555 74rm26⇌14🏔 P Lift sB27–45 sB⇌🏔35–60 dB54–90 dB⇌🏔70–110 (English breakfast) L17–20 D17–20 Pool lake

★★*Belvédère* ☎951185 tx78444 Closed Nov–Mar 59rm10⇌8🏔 P Lift Pool lake

★★*Friedheim* Kantonstr ☎951282 35rm3⇌ 🏡 Lift Pool lake

HERTENSTEIN Luzern 38 (☎041) (2km W of **Weggis**) Map **11** B1

★★★*Hertenstein* ☎931444 tx72284 Closed Nov–Mar 70rm57⇌ 🏡 P Lift ♪ sB fr37 sB⇌🏔fr50 dB fr33 dB⇌🏔fr46 Pool lake

HILTERFINGEN Bern 2,500 (☎033) Map **11** B1

★*Schönbühl* ☎432143 Closed Nov–Mar 22rm4🏔 sB27–33 sB🏔35–41 dB54–66 dB🏔70–77 L8–20 D8–20 lake

HORW Luzern 4,700 (☎041) Map **11** B1

★★*Waldhaus* ☎421154 29rm6⇌2🏔 🏡 Pool ○ lake

HOSPENTAL See **ANDERMATT**

HÜNIBACH See **THUN**

ILANZ Graubünden 1,590 (☎086) Map **12** C1

★*Casutt* ☎21131 14rm5🏔 P sB27–30 sB⇌🏔31–38 dB54–60 dB⇌🏔64–76 L9–15 D9–15

🛢 ✒*Spescha* ☎21424 P Cit/Frd (GB)

IMMENSEE AM ZUGERSEE Schwyz 1,380 (☎041) Map **11** B1

Switzerland

★★**Rigi-Royal** ☎811161 80rm24⇌12🛏 A12rm 🏦 P
♪ sB29−33 sB⇌🛏37−43 (English breakfast) L12.
D12 Pool lake

INNERTKIRCHEN Bern 1,194 (☎036) Map **11** B1
★**Hof & Post** ☎711951 25rm 🏦

INTERLAKEN Bern 4,368 (☎036) Map **11** B1
★★★★**Beau-Rivage** Höheweg 211 ☎224621
tx32827 Closed Nov−Mar 113rm87⇌ A3rm 🏦 P Lift
♪ sB42−89 sB⇌🛏80−120 dB40−85 dB⇌🛏76−115
(English breakfast) L20−29 D20−29 Pool lake
★★★★**Victoria-Jungfrau** Höheweg 41 ☎212171
tx32602 Closed Apr & Nov−mid Dec 220⇌ 🏦 P Lift
♪ sB⇌fr95 dB⇌fr170 ♪ Pool
★★★**Bellevue Garden** Marktgasse 59 ☎224431
tx32102 Closed Oct−Apr 60rm30⇌ P Lift sB33−47
sB⇌🛏45−63 dB60−90 dB⇌🛏74−120 L20−22
D20−22
★★★**Bernerhof** Bahnhofstr 16 ☎223131 tx32338
36rm12⇌24🛏 🏦 P Lift ♪ sB⇌🛏59−75
dB⇌🛏88−120 (English breakfast) L16−18 D16−18
Pool
★★★**Carlton** Höheweg 92 ☎223821 tx33655 Closed
Oct−14 Apr 50rm30⇌3🛏 🏦 P Lift ♪ sB34−46
sB⇌🛏43−58 dB61−91 dB⇌🛏76−115
(English breakfast) L15−21 D15−21
★★★**Eurotel** Rugenparkstr 13 (n rest) ☎226233
tx32257 Closed 22 Oct−17 Dec 40rm21⇌11🛏 P Lift
sB35−46 sB⇌🛏46−58 dB50−72 dB⇌🛏72−96
★★★**Goldey** Goldey 85 Anterseen (n rest) ☎224445
Closed 16 Oct−Apr 39rm18⇌21🛏 P Lift
sB⇌🛏43−63 dB⇌🛏74−126 (English breakfast)
D22−28
★★★**Jura** Bahnhofpl 45 ☎228812 80rm14⇌Lift
★★★**Krebs** Bahnhofstr 4 ☎227161 Closed 11
Oct−27 Apr 55rm40⇌6🛏 🏦 P Lift ♪ sB33−45
sB⇌🛏50−60 dB65−85 dB⇌🛏90−110 L19−25
D19−25
★★★**Lac** Höheweg 225 ☎222922 tx33773
46rm31⇌3🛏 🏦 Lift
★★★**Royal St-Georges** Höheweg 139 ☎227575
tx33975 Closed Nov−Mar 125rm66⇌35🛏 🏦 P Lift
♪ sB28−47 sB⇌🛏43−63 dB56−94
dB⇌🛏76−126 (English breakfast) Lfr16 Dfr20
★★**Beau Site** Seestr 16 ☎228181 tx33977
55rm24⇌ 🏦 P Lift ♪sB27−40 sB⇌🛏52−65 dB50−80
dB⇌🛏80−104 (English breakfast) L6−20 D6−20
★★**Belvédère** Höheweg 95 ☎223221 tx33699
Closed 16 Oct−14 Apr 50rm25⇌6🛏 🏦 P Lift ♪
sB33−47 sB⇌🛏43−63 dB56−94 dB⇌🛏76−126
(English breakfast) L18−22 D18−22
★★**Interlaken** Höheweg 74 ☎222012 Closed
Oct−Apr 75rm12⇌ 🏦 Lift
☆★**Marti** Brünigstr ☎222602 Closed mid Oct−mid
Apr 25rm 21 🛏 A4rm P ♪ sB27−44 sB🛏41−54
dB50−60 dB🛏70−81 (English breakfast) L5−16
D5−16 lake
★★**National** Jungfraustr 46 ☎223621 tx33987
Closed 16 Oct−Apr 46rm27⇌8🛏 P Lift ♪ sB54−69
sB⇌🛏54−69 dB98−128 dB⇌🛏98−128 L19−22
D19−22
★★**Nord** Höheweg 70 ☎222631 tx33001
68rm21⇌8🛏 🏦 P Lift ♪ sB28−40 sB⇌🛏37−52
dB46−80 dB⇌🛏63−104 (English breakfast)
L15−20 D15−20 mountains
★★**Oberland** Postgasse 1 ☎229431 tx32828
68rm6⇌10🛏 P Lift ♪ sB33−46 sB⇌🛏41−58
dB65−91 dB⇌🛏81−115 (English breakfast) Lfr15
Dfr15
★★**Splendid** Höheweg 33 ☎227612 40rm7⇌1🛏 Lift
★★**Strand Hotel Neuhaus** Seestr 121 ☎228282
tx33996 Closed 16 Oct−Mar 52rm6⇌35🛏 P ♪
sB28−40 sB⇌🛏37−52 dB46−78 dB⇌🛏64−104
Lfr12 Dfr12 ⏚ lake
★★**Weisses Kreuz** Höheweg 2 ☎225951
73rm25⇌9🛏 Lift
★**Anker** Marktgasse 57 ☎221672 18rm sB25−30
dB30−35 (English breakfast) L8 D8
★**Harder-Minerva** Harderstr 15 ☎222361
25rm2⇌10🛏 P sB25−35 sB⇌🛏34−47 dB40−70

dB⇌🛏57−94 (English breakfast) L7−22 D7−22
mountains
★**Merkur** Bahnhofpl 35 ☎226655 tx32953
36rm16⇌20🛏 P Lift ♪ sB⇌🛏37−52
dB⇌🛏63−104 (English breakfast) L14−18 D14−18
🛢 🆘**Bohren & Urfer** Rugenparkstr 34 ☎223231 P
Cit/Fia (GB)
🛢 🆘**Harder** Harderstr 25 ☎223651 ☎223651
(222333 Sun) MB/Vau (GB)
🛢 🆘**National** Centralstr 34 ☎222143 P Chy/Sim/Tri
🛢 🆘 **Touring** Seestr 109 ☎221515 ☎222333
Toy/Vlo
🛢 🆘**Waldegg** (Oertel-Balmer) Waldeggstr 34A
☎221939 ☎221939 P BL (GB)

KANDERSTEG Bern 913 (☎033) Map **11** B1
★★★★**Royal Bellevue** ☎751212 tx32332 Closed
16 Apr−14 May & Nov−14 Dec 35⇌ 🏦 P Lift ♪
sB⇌🛏70−100 dB⇌🛏140−260 (English breakfast)
L9−45 D9−45 ⏚ Pool ◯
★★★**Park Gemmi** ☎751117 tx32771 Closed May &
Nov 40rm15⇌ 🏦 P Lift sB25−35 sB⇌🛏45−55
dB50−70 dB⇌🛏90−110 (English breakfast) L15−25
D15−25 Pool
★★★**Schweizerhof** ☎751241 Closed Apr−16 Dec
53rm14⇌ 🏦 P Lift sB30−35 sB⇌35−40 dB60−70
dB⇌🛏70−80 L15−18 D15−18 ⏚
★★**Adler** ☎751121 Closed 21 Oct−13 Dec
20rm10⇌4🛏 sB38−42 sB⇌🛏46−51 dB42−46
dB⇌🛏50−55 (English breakfast) L5−26 D5−26
★★**Alpenrose** ☎751170 Closed Oct−14 Dec
28rm5⇌5🛏 A15rm P sB34−36 dB65−67
dB⇌🛏77−81 Lfr15 Dfr15 mountains
★★**Bernerhof** Hauptstr 2 ☎751142 Closed 16 Apr−14
May & Nov−14 Dec 45rm10⇌8🛏 🏦 Lift
★**Doldenhorn** ☎751251 30rm3⇌5🛏 A7rm 🏦 P
sB28−33 sB⇌🛏34−42 dB50−60 dB⇌🛏62−78
(English breakfast) L12−16 D12−16

KERZERS Fribourg (☎031) Map **11** B1
★**Löwen** ☎955117 15rm2⇌2🛏 P sB22−25
sB⇌🛏27−31 dB42−50 dB⇌🛏52−58 L7−12
D10−16 Pool mountains

KLOSTERS Graubünden 3,000 (☎083) Map **12** C1
★★★★**Grand Vereina** ☎41161 tx74359 Closed 21
Mar−19 Jun & 6 Sep−17 Dec 105rm80⇌3🛏 🏦 P Lift
♪ sB45−80 sB⇌🛏60−130 dB90−160
dB⇌🛏120−260 (English breakfast) L20−28
D20−28 D20−28 ⏚ Pool mountains
★★★**Alpina** ☎41233 30rm12⇌ 🏦 Lift
★★★**Silvretta** ☎41353 tx74336 Closed 16 Apr−
9 Dec 120 rm90⇌6🛏 Lift
★**Sport-Hof** ☎41460 Closed May 14rm4⇌3🛏 🏦 P
sB25−40 sB⇌🛏35−50 dB50−80 dB⇌🛏70−100
mountains

KRATTIGEN BEI SPIEZ Bern (☎033) Map **11** B1
★★**Bellevue-Bären** ☎543929 35rm3⇌12🛏 A8rm
🏦 P Lift sB27−39 sB⇌🛏38−49 dB54−77
dB⇌🛏76−97 L7−25 D7−25 lake
★**Seeblick** (n rest) ☎542969 20rm P sB26 dB49
lake

KREUZLINGEN Thurgau 12,600 (☎072) Map **12** C2
🛢 🆘**Amag** Hauptstr 99 ☎722424 M/c Aud/VW (GB)

KRIENS See **LUZERN (LUCERNE)**

KÜSNACHT See **ZÜRICH**

KUSSNACHT AM RIGI Schwyz 5,700 (☎041)
Map **11** B1
★★**Hirschen** (n rest) ☎811027 40rm30⇌10🛏 🏦 P
Lift sB fr30 sB⇌🛏40−46 dB54−62 dB⇌🛏70−82
(English breakfast) L15−20 D15−20
☆**Picnic** ☎811555 Closed 16 Dec−Feb 12rm2⇌1🛏
🏦 lake
★**Tell's Hohle Gasse** ☎811429 30rm2⇌ 🏦
🆘**Aebi** Hürtelstr ☎811050 M/c Aud/RR/VW
La Each place preceded by La is listed under the
name that follows it.
LACHEN Schwyz 3,458 (☎055) Map **12** C2
★★**Bären** ☎631602 16rm4⇌1🛏 🏦 P Lift sB28−30
sB⇌🛏34−36 dB56−60 dB⇌🛏72−76
(English breakfast) L10−19 D10−19

LANGENBRUCK Basel (☎062) Map **11** B2
★**Bären** ☎601414 20rm12⇌ A11rm 🏠 P sB fr25
sB⇌40 – 51 dB45 – 52 dB⇌70 – 92 L7 – 30 D7 – 30

LARET See **DAVOS**

LAUSANNE Vaud (☎021) Map **11** A1

At **Bussigny**
☆☆☆**Novotel Lausanne Ouest** r des Condemines
☎892871 tx25752 100⇌ P Lift sB⇌fr69 dB⇌fr104
English breakfast only Pool

At **Cully** (8.5km SE)
☆☆**Intereurop** ☎992091 tx25973 Closed Nov – Feb
61rm60⇌ P Lift ♪ sB⇌40 – 45 dB⇌70 – 80 L 8 D8
mountains lake

At **Ouchy**
★★★★★**Beau-Rivage** chemin-de-Beau-Rivage
☎263831 tx24341 220⇌ 🏠 P Lift ♪ sB⇌75 – 150
dB⇌ 🍴110 – 200 (English breakfast) D30 ✎ Pool
mountains lake
★★★★**Palace** Grand Chêne 7 – 9 ☎203711
tx24171 200⇌ 🏠 P Lift ♪ sB⇌70 – 140
dB⇌100 – 200 (English breakfast) Lfr32 Dfr38
mountains lake
★★★★**Continental** pl de la Gare 2 ☎201551
tx24500 120⇌ P Lift ♪ sB⇌59 – 80 dB⇌99 – 140
(English breakfast) L alc D alc mountains lake
★★★★**Royal Savoy** av d'Ouchy 40 ☎264201
tx24640 120rm108⇌10 🍴 🏠 Lift Pool ○ lake
★★★**Alpha-Palmiers** ☎23031 tx24999
131rm112⇌19 🍴 P Lift ♪ sB38 – 43 sB⇌ 🍴64 – 69
dB65 – 75 dB⇌ 🍴99 – 109 (English breakfast) Lfr15
D fr15 lake
★★★**Carlton** av de Cour 4 ☎263235 tx24800
53rm43⇌10 🍴 P Lift ♪ sB⇌ 🍴60 – 75
dB⇌ 🍴85 – 120 (English breakfast) L28 D30
mountains lake
★★★**City** r Caroline 5 (n rest) ☎202141 tx24400
65rm17⇌4 🍴 Lift ♪ sB32 – 37 sB⇌ 🍴54 – 59
dB56 – 66 dB⇌ 🍴82 – 92 mountains lake
★★★**Jan** av de Beaulieu 8 ☎361161 tx24485
60rm34⇌9 🍴 🏠 P Lift ♪ sB35 – 45 sB⇌ 🍴55 – 65
dB55 – 70 dB⇌ 🍴85 – 95 L10 – 18 D16 – 18
★★★**Mirabeau** av de la Gare 31 ☎206231 tx25030
72rm38⇌ P Lift ♪ sB fr40 sB⇌70 dB fr70 dB⇌100
(English breakfast) Lfr15 Dfr15 ○ mountains lake
★★★**Paix** av B-Constant 5 ☎207171 tx24080
130rm100⇌ 🏠 Lift
☆☆**Parking** av du Rond Point 9 ☎271211 tx25300
100⇌ 🏠 P Lift ♪ sB38 – 43 sB⇌64 – 69 dB65 – 75
dB⇌99 – 109 (English breakfast) Lfr15 D fr15
mountains lake
★★★**Terminus** av de la Gare 52 ☎204501 tx24454
80rm50⇌30 🍴 🏠 Lift
★★★**Victoria** av de la Gare 46 (n rest) ☎205771
tx25030 65rm45⇌5 🍴 🏠 P Lift ♪ sB40 – 45
sB⇌ 🍴70 – 85 dB60 – 75 dB⇌ 🍴90 – 120
(English breakfast) L15 D15 mountains lake
★**Angleterre** pl du Port 9 ☎264145 Closed Jan
36rm13⇌6 🍴 P ♪ sB32 – 35 sB⇌ 🍴55 – 65 dB48 – 55
dB⇌ 🍴65 – 95 (English breakfast) L15 D15
mountains lake
★**France** r de Mauborget 1 (n rest) ☎233131 50rm P
Lift ♪ sB30 – 35 dB50 – 55
🛢 🔧**Autonor Garage de Bellevaux** rte A-Fauquez
91 ☎373960 P BL (GB)
🔧**City-Carrosserie** (E Frey) rte de Genève 60
☎242600 ☎203071 BL/BMW (GB)
🛢 🔧**Edelweiss** av de Morges 139 ☎253131 P
Bed/Opl
🛢 🔧**Gare** (E Frey) ☎203761 ☎203071 P BL/BMW
(GB)
🛢 🔧**L Jan** Petit-Rocher 6 ☎361161 P BL/Chy/Tri
(GB)
🔧**Occidental** av de Morges 7 ☎258225
🔧**Tivoli** av Tivoli 3 ☎203071 ☎203071
BL/BMW/Jag Tri (GB)

At **Pully**
★★★**Montillier** av de Lavaux 35 ☎287585 53rm21⇌
Lift lake

At **Renens**
🛢 🔧**Étoile** rte de Cossonay 101 ☎349691 P
Fia/Lnc/MB (GB)

At **St-Sulpice**
☆**Pierrettes** ☎254215 21 🍴 P sB⇌ 🍴40 – 51
dB⇌ 🍴58 – 76 (English breakfast) L alc D alc
mountains lake

LAUTERBRUNNEN Bern 2,880 (☎036) Map **11** B1
★★**Jungfrau** ☎553434 tx33615 26rm12⇌ A6rm 🏠
P sB34 – 44 sB⇌40 – 52 dB66 – 92 dB⇌77 – 102
(English breakfast) Lfr14 Dfr14 Pool mountains
★★**Silberhorn** ☎551471 28rm19⇌ P sB25 – 40
sB⇌35 – 45 dB50 – 78 dB⇌65 – 90 L10 – 25 D10 – 25
★★**Staubbach** ☎551381 tx33755 34rm19⇌ 🏠 P Lift
sB30 – 40 sB⇌40 – 55 dB60 – 80 dB⇌80 – 100
(English breakfast) L17 – 30 D17 – 30
★**Oberland** ☎551241 tx33985 31rm8⇌2 🍴 A5rm
sB31 – 41 sB⇌38 – 48 dB55 – 75 dB⇌67 – 99
L10 – 20 D10 – 20 mountains
★**Trümmelbach** (n rest) ☎553232 Closed Oct – Apr
10rm2⇌ 🏠
Le Each name preceded by Le is listed under the
name that follows it.

LEISSIGEN Bern (☎036) Map **11** B1
★**Kreuz** ☎471231 30rm10⇌20 🍴 P Lift
sB⇌ 🍴40 – 45 dB⇌ 🍴64 – 70 lake

LENK Bern 1,871 (☎030) Map **11** B1
★★★**Park Bellevue** ☎31761 Closed Apr & Oct –
19 Dec 78rm29⇌2 🍴 🏠 Lift Pool
★★★**Wildstrubel** ☎31506 tx33225 Closed Apr – 26
May & Oct – 15 Dec P Lift sB41 – 56 sB⇌ 🍴46 – 76
dB82 – 112 dB⇌ 🍴92 – 152 L18 – 30 D18 – 30

LENZERHEIDE Graubünden 183 (☎081)
Map **12** C1
★★★**Park** ☎341525 Closed May, Oct & Nov
36rm17⇌6 🍴 P Lift sB25 – 40 dB50 – 80
dB⇌ 🍴65 – 100 (English breakfast) L13 – 22 D13 – 22
Pool
★★★**Post** ☎341160 56rm30⇌ A44rm P sB30 – 40
sB⇌35 – 50 dB34 – 44 dB⇌39 – 44
(English breakfast) L14 – 18 D14 – 18 ✎ Pool ♨
mountains

At **Valbella**
★★**Waldhaus** ☎341109 45rm ⇌4 🍴 lake

LEYSIN Vaud (☎025) Map **11** A1
★**Mont Riant** ☎62235 Closed May, Oct & Nov
19rm2⇌8 🍴 P Lift sB26 – 43 sB⇌ 🍴37 – 53 dB48 – 78
dB⇌ 🍴70 – 98 (English breakfast) L14 – 22 D14 – 22
mountains

LIESTAL Basel 10,300 (☎061) Map **11** B2
★★★**Engel** Kasernenstr 10 ☎912511 tx62086
36rm12⇌15 🍴 A12rm 🏠
★**Bahnhof** Bahnhofpl 14 ☎910072 15rm 🏠
★**Radackerhof** Rheinstr 93 ☎943222 32rm 8 🍴
A14rm P sB31 – 35 sB🍴35 – 40 dB58 – 69
dB 🍴69 – 79 (English breakfast) Lfr6 Dfr6
🛢 🔧**Peter** Gasstr 11 ☎919140 ☎919140 Frd
🛢 🔧**Rheingarage Buser** Rheinstr 95 ☎945025 P
Vlo (GB)

LOCARNO Ticino 10,200 (☎093) Map **28** D4
★★★★★**Palma au Lac** Lungolago Motta ☎336771
tx79322 140rm80⇌14 🍴 🏠 P Lift ♪ sB35 – 55
sB⇌ 🍴60 – 115 dB60 – 90 dB⇌ 🍴100 – 200
(English breakfast) L30 D30 ✎ Pool mountains lake
★★★★**Reber au Lac** via Verbano (off via San
Gottardo) ☎336723 tx79024 93rm55⇌8 🍴 🏠 Lift ♪
Pool lake
★★★**Lac** pza Grande ☎312921 tx73098
33rm16⇌17 🍴 P Lift ♪ sB⇌ 🍴41 – 56
dB⇌ 🍴91 – 116 mountains lake
★★★**Park** via Gottardo ☎334554 tx79773 Closed
Nov – Feb 85rm49⇌3 🍴 🏠 P Lift ♪ sB42 – 62
sB⇌ 🍴62 – 92 dB83 – 123 dB⇌ 🍴123 – 183

(English breakfast) L31–34 D28–31 Pool mountains lake

★★★**Quisisana** via del Sole 17 ☎336141 73rm37⇄8🅿 P Lift sB36–56 sB⇄🍴46–81 dB72–107 dB⇄🍴87–157 (English breakfast) L23–32 D23–32 Pool lake

★★**Belvédère** via al Sasso ☎311154 Closed Nov–14 Mar 50rm15⇄ P Lift sB32–43 sB⇄40–55 dB64–86 dB⇄80–120 (English breakfast) L fr20 D fr20 mountains lake

★★**Montaldi** pza Stazione ☎336633 65rm22⇄ A15rm Lift

🗋 🕭**Léomotor** via Ciseri 19 ☎314880 Cit/Fia/Lnc (GB)

🗋 🕭**5 Vie** pza 5 Vie ☎311616 Cit

At Muralto (1km W)

🗋 🕭**Starnini** via Sempione 11 ☎333355 P BL/Chy/Rov/Sim/Tri/ (GB)

LOCLE (LE) Neuchâtel (☎039) Map **11** A1

🗋 **Trois Rois** r de France 51 ☎312431 ☎268181 Lnc

LUCERNE See **LUZERN**

LUGANO Ticino 21,000 (☎091) Map **29** A4

★★★★**Arizona** via Massagno 20 ☎229343 tx79087 53rm47⇄ P Lift ♪ sB36–46 sB⇄56–76 dB82–102 dB⇄102–132 (English breakfast) L18–22 Dfr18 Pool mountains lake

★★★★**Excelsior** Riva V-Vela ☎228661 tx79151 81rm65⇄16🍴 P Lift ♪ sB⇄🍴70–92 dB⇄🍴100–140 (English breakfast) L25 D25 mountains lake

★★★★**Splendide-Royal** Riva A-Caccia 7 ☎542001 tx73032 73rm66⇄ A10rm 🏛 Lift Pool

★★★**Bellevue au Lac** Riva A-Caccia 10 ☎543333 tx79440 Closed Dec–Feb 70rm57⇄13🍴 🏛 P Lift ♪ sB⇄🍴63–70 dB⇄🍴116–130 (English breakfast) L20–30 D14–20 Pool lake

★★★**Gotthard Terminus** via Cl-Maraini 1 ☎227777 tx73761 60rm20⇄20🍴 🏛 P Lift ♪ sB34–46 sB⇄🍴46–61 dB62–88 dB⇄🍴92–122 (English breakfast) L fr18 Dfr16 mountains lake

★★★**International** via Nassa 68 ☎227541 tx64017 Closed Nov–Feb 80rm55⇄2🍴 🏛 P Lift ♪ sB32–39 sB⇄🍴50–62 dB50–72 dB⇄🍴76–124 (English breakfast) L17–18 D17–18 mountains lake

★★**Continental Beauregard** Basilea 28–30 ☎561112 tx79222 Closed Nov–Feb 75rm50⇄ A25rm P Lift ♪ sB34–44 sB⇄44–64 dB58–83 dB⇄88–118 (English breakfast) L fr14 Dfr15 mountains lake

★★**Everest** via Ginevra 7 (n rest) ☎229555 45rm12⇄12🍴 🏛 P Lift ♪ sB35–38 sB⇄🍴55–65 dB65–75 dB⇄🍴95–120 (English breakfast)

★★**Walter** pza R-Rezzonico 7 ☎227425 40rm21⇄10🍴 Lift ♪ sB36 sB⇄🍴46 dB65 dB⇄🍴82 L15–18 D15–18 mountains lake

🗋 🕭**Cencini** via Ceresio 2 ☎512826 P BMW Jag (GB)

🗋 🕭**Centro Mercedes** via Cantonale 24 ☎220732 MB (GB)

🗋 🕭**N Crescionini** via Franscini 8 ☎28343 Opl

🗋 🕭**Stazione** (R Morganti) via San Gottardo 13 ☎228251 P Bed/Vau (GB)

At Brè (5km E)

★**Brè** (n rest) ☎514761 Closed Dec–Feb 20rm5⇄ 🏛

At Campione d'Italia (10km S) (Italian enclave; prices in Swiss francs)

★★★**Grand** ☎687031 45rm17⇄28🍴 🏛 Lift lake

At Cassarate

★★★★**Castagnola au Lac** ☎512213 76rm57⇄ 🏛 P Lift ♪ sB45–60 sB⇄65–90 dB90–110 dB⇄130–180 (English breakfast) L23–26 D23–26 ⚓ Pool lake

★**Atlantic** via Concordia 12 (n rest) ☎512921 25rm4⇄4 Lift

🗋 🕭**M Vismara** via Concordia 2 ☎512614 Frd (GB)

At Castagnola (2km E)

★★★**Belmonte** ☎514033 tx79517 Closed Nov–Feb 40rm15⇄15🍴 🏛 P Lift ♪ sB35–55 sB⇄🍴55–70 dB60–90 dB⇄🍴90–140 L20–25 D20–25 Pool mountains lake

★★**Carlton** ☎513812 tx64003 Closed 26 Oct–19 Mar 60rm15⇄35🍴 🏛 P Lift sB32–42 sB⇄🍴40–54 dB60–80 dB⇄🍴76–104 (English breakfast) L16–22 D16–22 Pool lake

★★**Helvetia** (n rest) ☎514121 Closed Dec–Feb 37rm4⇄ 🏛 Lift lake

At Cornaredo

🗋 🕭**R Camenisch** Pista del Ghiaccio ☎519725 BL/Maz/Tri (GB)

At Gandria (5km E)

★**Moosmann** ☎517261 Closed Nov–19 Mar 30rm17⇄ lake

At Maroggia-Melano (10km S)

☆**Lido** ☎687971 28⇄ P sB⇄🍴43–48 dB⇄🍴85–95 L fr16 Dfr16 Pool

At Melide (6km S)

★★**Riviera** ☎687912 21⇄ Lift Pool lake

At Paradiso

★★★★**Admiral** via Geretta 15 ☎542324 tx73177 92rm81⇄11🍴 🏛 Lift Pool

★★★★**Eden** Riva Paradiso 7 ☎542612 tx79156 75⇄ 🏛 Lift Pool

★★★**Beau Rivage** ☎542912 Closed 16 Oct–Mar 92rm67⇄10🍴 P Lift ♪ sB41–51 sB⇄🍴56–66 dB72–92 dB⇄🍴102–122 L15–25 D14–20 Pool lake

★★★**Conca d'Oro** Riva Paradiso ☎543131 Closed Nov–Feb 35rm18⇄ P Lift sB35–43 sB⇄45–55 dB69–79 dB⇄91–99 L20 D18 mountains lake

★★★**Flamingo** viale Funicolare San Salvatore ☎541321 Closed Dec–Feb 20rm12⇄ Lift

★★★**Lac Seehof** ☎541921 tx79555 Closed Nov–Mar 54rm30⇄24🍴 P Lift ♪ sB⇄🍴63–78 dB⇄🍴105–151 (English breakfast) L21–28 D21–28 Pool lake

★★★**Meister** viale Funicolare 11 (DP) ☎541412 tx79365 Closed Nov–Mar 82rm51⇄ 🏛 Lift Pool lake

★★★**Paix** via Cattori 18 ☎542331 Closed Nov–mid Apr 87rm48⇄25🍴 Lift Pool lake

★★**Primerose** Riva Paradiso 6 ☎542841 Closed Dec–Feb 27rm14⇄ A3rm P Lift ♪ sB32–36 sB⇄36–42 dB63–71 dB⇄71–83 (English breakfast) L16–18 D16–18 mountains lake

★★**Victoria** ☎542031 Closed 21 Oct–mid Apr 35rm6⇄ Lift lake

🗋 🕭**Mazzuchelli-Auto** Riva Paradiso 26 ☎543412 Lnc/RR (GB)

At Vezia (3km NW)

☆**Vezia** ☎563631 Closed Jan 75rm 25🍴 🏛 P sB fr24 sB 🍴fr38 dB fr34 dB 🍴fr68 (English breakfast) L alc Dalc Pool

LUNGERN AM SEE Obwalden (☎041) Map **11** B1

★**Rössli** ☎691171 17rm P sB22–27 dB40–50 dB⇄45–55 (English breakfast) L10–12 D10–12 lake

LUZERN (LUCERNE) Luzern 67,500 (☎041) Map **11** B1 **See Plan**

★★★★★**Carlton-Tivoli** Haldenstr 57 ☎232333 tx72456 Plan **1** Closed Nov–Mar 100⇄ 🏛 P Lift ♪ sB⇄65–97 dB⇄116–180 (English breakfast) L12 D22–25 ⚓ Pool lake

★★★★★**Grand National** Maldenstr 4 ☎243322 tx78130 Plan **2** Closed May 80⇄ 🏛 P Lift ♪ sB⇄100–130 dB⇄175–230 L fr35 Dfr35 Pool lake

★★★★★**Palace** Haldenstr 10 ☎221901 tx78155 Plan **3** 175⇄ 🏛 P Lift ♪ sB60–120 dB⇄106–230 (English breakfast) L fr26 Dfr36 lake

★★★★★**Schweizerhof** Schweizerhof quai 3 ☎225801 tx78277 Plan **4** 180rm125⇄ P Lift ♪ sB49–64 sB⇄🍴79–110 dB82–110 dB⇄🍴126–200 L fr32 Dfr32 lake

★★★★**Astoria** Pilatusstr 29 ☎235323 tx78220 Plan **5** 100rm65⇄35🍴 P Lift ♪ sB⇄🍴43–65 dB⇄🍴90–130 (English breakfast) L18 D18

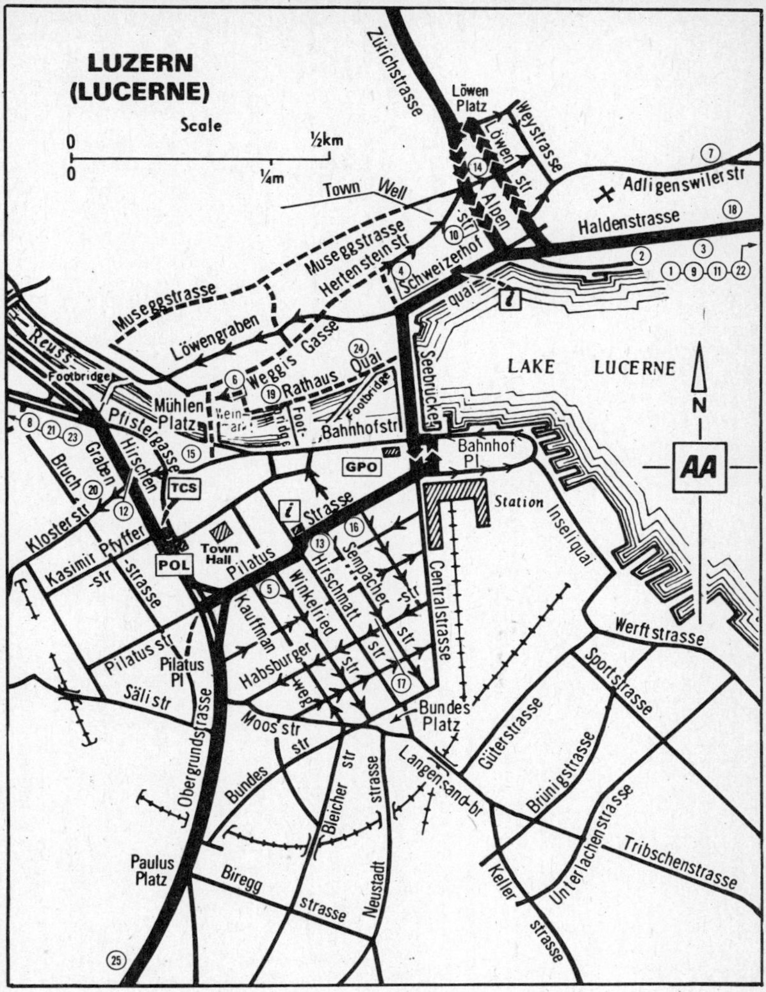

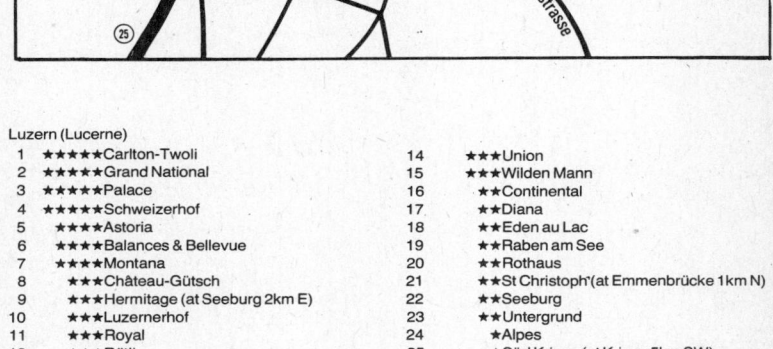

LUZERN
(LUCERNE)

Scale

0   ½km

0   ¼m

Town Well

Luzern (Lucerne)

1	★★★★★	Carlton-Twoli
2	★★★★★	Grand National
3	★★★★★	Palace
4	★★★★★	Schweizerhof
5	★★★★	Astoria
6	★★★★	Balances & Bellevue
7	★★★★	Montana
8	★★★★	Château-Gütsch
9	★★★	Hermitage (at Seeburg 2km E)
10	★★★	Luzernerhof
11	★★★	Royal
12	★★★	Rütli
13	★★★	Schillen
14	★★★	Union
15	★★★	Wilden Mann
16	★★	Continental
17	★★	Diana
18	★★	Eden au Lac
19	★★	Raben am See
20	★★	Rothaus
21	★★	St Christoph'(at Emmenbrücke 1km N)
22	★★	Seeburg
23	★★	Untergrund
24	★	Alpes
25	☆	Süd Kriens (at Kriens 5km SW)

★★★★**Balances & Bellevue** Weinmarkt 7 ☎231833
tx78183 Plan **6** Closed Nov – 14 Apr 80⇌ P Lift ♪
sB⇌70 – 86 dB⇌90 – 160 (English breakfast) L alc
D alc lake

★★★★**Montana** Adligenswilerstr 22 ☎225791
tx78591 Plan **7** Closed Nov – Mar 70⇌ ⋔ P Lift ♪
sB⇌65 – 80 dB⇌120 – 150 (English breakfast)
L22 – 25 D22 – 25 lake

★★★ *Château Gütsch* Kanonenstr ☎233883
tx78233 Plan **8** 40rm37⇌ Lift Pool lake

★★★**Luzernerhof** Alpenstr 3 ☎224444 Plan **10**
85rm45⇌26 ⋔ Lift

★★★*Royal* Rigistr 22 ☎231233 Plan **11** Closed
Nov – Mar 56rm37⇌ Lift lake

★★★**Rütli** Hirschengraben 38 ☎224162 Plan **12**
71rm31⇌35 ⋔ Lift ♪ sB36 – 46 sB⇌⋔43 – 53
dB70 – 92 dB⇌⋔80 – 102 (English breakfast)
L15 – 20 D15 – 20

★★★*Schiller* Sempacherstr 4 ☎224821 tx78621
Plan **13** 80rm26⇌26 ⋔ ⋔ Lift

★★★**Union** Löwenstr 16 ☎220212 tx78163 Plan **14**
120rm80⇌ A40rm P Lift – sB36 – 50 sB⇌52 – 72
dB61 – 89 dB⇌93 – 139 (English breakfast) L fr8
D fr18 lake

★★★*Wilden Mann* Bahnhofstr 30 ☎231666 tx78233
Plan **15** 55rm40⇌3 ⋔ Lift lake

★★**Continental** Morgenstr 4 ☎237566 tx78553
Plan **16** 73rm9⇌34 ⋔ P Lift ♪ sB33 – 42
sB⇌⋔40 – 54 dB59 – 71 dB⇌⋔68 – 96
(English breakfast) L13 D13

★★**Diana** Sempacherstr 16 ☎232623 Plan **17**
Closed Nov – Mar 40rm5⇌35 ⋔ ⋔ P Lift ♪
sB⇌⋔47 – 59 dB⇌⋔90 – 104 L15 D15 lake

★★**Eden au Lac** Holdenstr 47 ☎220806 tx78160
Plan **18** Closed Nov – Mar 39rm21⇌ ⋔ P Lift
sB35 – 47 sB⇌45 – 57 dB59 – 83 dB⇌79 – 103 L16
D16 lake

★★**Raben am See** Kornmarkt 5 ☎220734 Plan **19**
37rm12⇌3 P Lift ♪ sB25 – 35 sB⇌⋔33 – 42
dB49 – 63 dB⇌⋔65 – 73 L7 – 21 D7 – 21

★★**Rothaus** Klosterstr 4 ☎235015 Plan **20** 50⇌ P
Lift ♪ sB⇌27 – 43 dB⇌48 – 80 L12 – 19 D12 – 19

★★**Seeburg** ☎311922 tx78270 Plan **22** 120rm90⇌
⋔ P Lift ♪ sB42 – 47 sB⇌⋔55 – 72 dB74 – 82
dB⇌⋔100 – 130 (English breakfast) L19 – 22
D23 – 26 mountains lake

★★*Untergrund* Baselstr 57 (n rest) ☎224751
Plan **23** 80rm50⇌1 ⋔ Lift

★*Alpes* Rathausquai 5 ☎225825 Plan **24** 30 ⋔ Lift
sB⇌⋔35 – 52 dB⋔70 – 94 L10 – 20 D10 – 20 mountains
lake

🅿 **City-Parking** Zürichstr 35 ☎365151 P (GB)

🅿 ⋙*Epper Luzern* Horwerstr 81 ☎411122
Jag/Peu/Rov (GB)

🅿 ⋙**Koch Panorama Luzern** Löwenstr 18 ☎226666
M/c Chy/Sim (GB)

🅿 ⋙*Letzi* Hirschengraben 48 ☎238022 P Opl

ℹ ⋙**Macchi** Maihofstr 61 ☎363344 BL/Maz/Rov
Sab/Tri (GB)

🅿 **Ottiger** Spitalstr 8 ☎365555 Fia/MB (GB)

🅿 **Schwerzmann** Kauffmannweg 24 &
Habsburgerstr 29 ☎228181 BL/Jab/Rov Tri (GB)

At **Ebikon** (4.5km NE)

🅿 ⋙*Zai* Luzernerstr 57 ☎367500 Dat/MB

At **Emmenbrücke** (1km N)

★★**St-Christoph** ☎531308 Plan **21** 14rm2⇌1 ⋔ P
sB24 – 30 dB44 – 54 dB⇌⋔56 – 68 L fr12 D fr12

★★**Emmenbaum** Gerliswilstr 8 ☎552960 Not on plan
Closed Jan 9rm P sB25 – 30 dB50 – 60
(English breakfast) L8 – 16 D6 – 20

★**Landhaus** ☎531737 Not on plan 30rm4⇌ ⋔ P
sB30 – 34 sB⇌34 – 44 dB48 – 55 dB⇌58 – 76 L16 – 24
D16 – 24 mountains

At **Kriens** (5km SW)

☆*Süd Kriens* Autobahn Luzern-Süd ☎413546
Plan **25** Closed Dec 38 ⋔ ⋔

At **Seeburg** (2km E)

★★★**Hermitage** Seeburgstr 72 ☎313737 Plan**9**
35rm21⇌ A24rm ⋔ P Lift ♪ mountains lake

LYSS Bern (☎032) Map **11** B1

🅿 ⋙*Aebi* Bernstr 38 – 40 ☎844994 ☎841172 M/c P
Cit

MALOJA Graubünden 100 (☎082) Map **12** C1

★★**Maloja-Kulm** ☎43105 Closed 21 Oct – 9 Dec
30rm8⇌6 ⋔ P Lift sB37 – 42 sB⇌⋔49 – 54
dB72 – 75 dB⇌⋔98 – 103 (English breakfast)
L12 – 25 D12 – 28 ○ mountains

★*Sporthotel Maloja* ☎43126 Closed Nov
18rm4⇌3 ⋔ P sB30 – 35 dB⇌⋔86 – 100
(English breakfast) L14 – 18 D14 – 18 mountains

MARLY See FRIBOURG

MAROGGIA-MELANO See LUGANO

MARTIGNY Valais 7,000 (☎026) Map **28** C4

★★★★**Rhône** av du Grand St-Bernard ☎21717
tx38341 41rm13⇌28 ⋔ ⋔ P Lift sB⇌⋔35 – 50 (room
only) dB⇌⋔60 – 80 (room only) mountains

★★★*Centrale* ☎21184 tx38341 30rm21⇌
⋔ P Lift sB26 – 30 sB⇌38 – 45 dB40 – 45 dB⇌65 – 70
L14 – 22 D16 – 24 mountains

★★★*Forclaz* av du Léman 15 ☎22701 Closed
Nov – Apr 36rm22⋔ ⋔ Lift

★★★*Poste* ☎21444 32rm22⇌7 ⋔ ⋔ Lift

★★*Kluser* ☎22641 38rm15⇌

★★*St-Bernard* ☎22612 35rm7⇌1 ⋔ ⋔

★*Suisse* av de la Gare ☎21572 30rm10 ⋔ ⋔ Lift

☆*Sports* ☎22078 21 ⋔ ⋔

🅿 ⋙**Mont-Blanc** (Boisset & Moulin) av du Grand
St-Bernard ☎21181 P Ren (GB)

MEGGEN Luzern 2,200 (☎041) Map **11** B1

★★**Balm** ☎371135 Closed 16 Dec – 14 Jan 20rm5⇌
P sB25 – 27 (room only) dB50 – 55 (room only)
dB⇌70 – 75 (room only) L5 – 25alc D5 – 25alc
mountains lake

★*Splendid* ☎372625 Closed Dec – Feb 22rm4⇌
Pool lake

MEIRINGEN Bern 3,700 (☎036) Map **11** B1

★★**Löwen** ☎711407 20rm3⇌10 ⋔ P sB25 – 28
dB50 – 56 dB⇌⋔56 – 70 L15 – 20 D15 – 20 mountains

★*Baer* Hauptstr ☎712112 33rm

★*Post* Hauptstr ☎711221 27rm

★*Weisses Kreuz* ☎711216 32rm

ℹ ⋙*E Boss* ☎711631 ☎711631 P Frd/MB (GB)

MELIDE See LUGANO

MERLIGEN Bern 454 (☎033) Map **11** B1

★★★★**Beatus** ☎512121 tx32447 Closed Dec – Mar
78rm53⇌25 ⋔ ⋔ P Lift ♪ sB⇌⋔80 – 128
dB⇌⋔136 – 236 (English breakfast) L26 – 30
D26 – 30 ○ Pool mountains lake

☆*Mon Abri* ☎511399 38 ⋔ A10rm lake

🅿 K Wittwer Thunersee ☎512222 Cit/Jag/Sab (GB)

METTENDORF Thurgau (☎054) Map **12** C2

ℹ ⋙W Debrunner Hauptstr 90 ☎99119 ☎99696 P
Bed/Opl/Toy Vau (GB)

MEYRIEZ See MURTEN

MIES See GENÈVE

MINÚSIO Ticino (☎093) Map **28** D4

★★★★**Esplanade** via delle Vigne ☎332121 tx79470
⋔ P Lift ♪ sB42 – 62 sB⇌⋔57 – 97 dB73 – 123
dB⇌⋔103 – 193 (English breakfast) L fr30 D fr30
Pool mountains lake

★★*Remorino* (n rest) ☎331033 Closed Nov – Feb
25rm15⇌10 ⋔ P Lift sB⇌⋔35 – 60 dB⇌⋔70 – 120
(English breakfast) ○ lake

★*Navegna-au-Lac* via la Riva (DP) ☎332222
18rm16⇌1 ⋔ A4rm ⋔ lake

🅿 ⋙*Rivapiana* via R-Simen 56 ☎334056 M/c BMW
(GB)

MONTANA-VERMALA Valais 1,750 (☎027)
Map **28** C4

★★★**Mirabeau** ☎413912 tx38365 Closed May & Oct
& Nov 52rm34⇌10 ⋔ ⋔ P Lift ♪ sB25 – 30
sB⇌⋔40 – 60 dB50 – 60 dB⇌⋔80 – 100
(English breakfast) L22 – 24 D25 mountains

★★★*St-Georges* ☎412414 Closed May & Nov
52rm29⇌8 ⋔ ⋔ Lift

★★**Bellavista** ☎414133 15⇌ Lift dB⇌70 – 80 (room
only) mountains

★★**Eldorado** ☎411333 Closed Oct–14 Dec
35rm30⇌1 🏠 P Lift sB28–34 sB⇌ 🍴38–54
dB55–69 dB⇌ 🍴75–107 (English breakfast)
L21–26 D19–24 🍴 Pool mountains
★★*Lac* ☎413414 Closed May & Nov 35rm1⇌ 🏠
lake
📻 ⚭*Lac* ☎411818 ☎411818 P AR/Ren
MONTREUX Vaud 12,300 (☎021) Map **11** A1
★★★★★**Eurotel** ☎622951 tx24666
150rm110⇌40 🍴 Lift ♪ sB⇌ 🍴68–73
dB⇌ 🍴126–176 (English breakfast) L24–29
D24–29 Pool Mountains lake
★★★★*Excelsior* r Bon Port 21 ☎613305 tx24720
85rm75⇌11 🍴 🏠 Lift Pool lake
★★★★*Palace* av des Alpes ☎613231 tx24235
210rm145⇌ 🏠 🍴 Pool
★★★*Bonivard* r Bonivard 1 ☎613358 76rm40⇌ 🏠
lake
★★★*Eden* r du Théâtre 11 ☎612601 tx25200 105⇌
🏠 P Lift ♪ sB⇌67–117 dB⇌114–194
(English breakfast) L27 D28–33 Pool mountains lake
★★★*Golf* r Bon Port 35 ☎614133 60rm 🏠 P Lift ♪
sB⇌45–74 dB⇌82–128 (English breakfast)
L18–25 D18–25 mountains lake
★★★*Lorius* Grande r 89–91 ☎613404 65rm15⇌
Lift 🍴 Pool lake
★★★**National** chemin du National 2 ☎622511
tx24650 70rm38⇌9 🍴 P Lift ♪ sB51–86
sB⇌ 🍴61–106 dB92–152 dB⇌ 🍴102–182 L20–30
D24–30 Pool mountains lake
★★★*Suisse & Majestic* av des Alpes 43 ☎612331
tx24674 155rm125⇌ Lift lake
★★**Bon Accueil** Grande r 80 ☎620551 tx25250
39rm24⇌15 🍴 P Lift ♪ sB⇌ 🍴56–66
dB⇌ 🍴100–120 L7–12 D7–12 mountains lake
★★**Europe** av des Alpes ☎614622 Closed Dec–Feb
103rm80⇌ 🏠 P Lift ♪ sB36–51 sB⇌46–76
dB62–92 dB⇌87–132 L15–20 D15–20 mountains
lake
★★**Palmiers** r Stravinsky 2 ☎612242 tx25292
Closed Nov–Feb 32rm8⇌5 🍴 Lift sB30–40
SB⇌ 🍴40–50 dB50–70 dB⇌ 🍴70–90
(English breakfast) L12–15 D15–18 mountains lake
★★*Parc & Lac* Grande r 38 ☎623738 Closed
Nov–Feb 65rm24⇌4 🍴 Lift lake
★★**Terminus** r de la Gare 22 ☎612563 tx24691
58rm21⇌ P Lift sB30–40 sB⇌40–50 dB50–60
dB⇌70–80 L alc D alc mountains lake
📻 ⚭**Central** Grande r 106 ☎612246 Opl/Vau (GB)
⚭**G Dubuis** rte des Colondalles 18 ☎616395 Vlo
📻 ⚭*L Mettraux* av du Théâtre 7 ☎613463
Frd/Jag/Rov
At **Chernex** (2km NE)
★*Iris* ☎624252 23rm4⇌4 🍴 🏠 lake
At **Glion** (3km E)
★★★*Victoria* (Pn) ☎625121 66rm31⇌10 🍴 🏠 Lift
Pool lake
At **Rennaz** (12km S)
☆*Rennaz-Montreux* ☎601541 20 🍴
At **Villeneuve** (4km S)
★*Byron* ☎601061 44rm18⇌7 🍴 P Lift sB35–55
sB⇌45–75 dB60–90 dB⇌85–130
(English breakfast) L fr26 D fr26 mountains lake
MORCOTE Ticino 600 (☎091) Map **28** D4
★*Rivabella* ☎691314 Closed Nov–Mar 11rm4⇌1 🍴
🏠 lake
MORGES Vaud 6,500 (☎021) Map **11** A1
★★**Lac** St-Jean ☎716371 tx25265 Closed 21
Dec–Jan tx25265 Closed 21 Dec–Jan 27rm18⇌7 🍴
P Lift sB fr32 sB⇌ 🍴58–75 dB⇌ 🍴76–136 L fr34
D fr34 mountains lake
MORGINS Valais (☎025) Map **28** C4
★*Beau-Site* ☎83138 15rm
MORSCHACH Schwyz 600 (☎043) Map **11** B1
★*Fronalp* (DP) ☎311122 75rm 🏠
MÜNCHENBUCHSEE Bern (☎031) Map **11** B1
☆**Bern-Biel** ☎860199 27⇌ 🍴 🏠 P sB⇌ 🍴31–34
dB⇌ 🍴51–57 mountains lake

MÜNSINGEN Bern (☎031) Map **11** B1
☆**Münsingen** (n rest) ☎920422 33⇌ P sB⇌37–45
dB⇌60–70 mountains
MÜNSTER Valais (☎028) Map **11** B1
📻 ⚭*Grimsel* ☎82350 M/c P Cit/Frd
MURALTO See **LOCARNO**
MURI See **BERN**
MÜRREN Bern 318 (☎036) Map **11** B1
No road connection: take funicular from
Lauterbrunnen or **Stechelberg**
★★★*Eiger* ☎551331 tx32966 Closed 23 Apr–8 Jun
& 19 Aug–Nov 50rm25⇌ Lift sB41–63 sB⇌51–86
dB72–116 dB⇌92–182 (English breakfast) L fr15
D fr20 Pool mountains
MÜRTEN (MORAT) Fribourg 2,800 (☎37)
Map **11** A/B1
★★*Bâteau* ☎712644 Closed Nov–Feb 15rm3⇌
lake
★★**Weisses Kreuz** Rathausgasse ☎712641 Closed
Jan 30rm8⇌ Lift
At **Meyriez** (1km S)
★★★★*Vieux Manoir au Lac* ☎711283 tx36442
Closed Dec & Jan 23rm15⇌2 🍴 🏠 P Lift ♪ sB43–58
sB⇌ 🍴63–78 dB76–106 dB⇌ 🍴106–166
(English breakfast) L36–56 D36–56 lake
MUSTAIR Graubünden 800 (☎082) Map **12** D1
★★*Münsterhof* ☎85541 19rm1⇌1 🍴 P sB27–30
dB⇌ 🍴59–69 L9–18 mountains
NÄFELS Glarus (☎058) Map **12** C1
★★**Schwert** ☎341722 10rm6⇌2 🍴 🏠 P Lift sB36
sB⇌ 🍴41 dB72 dB⇌ 🍴77 (English breakfast) L19
D24 🍴 Pool
📻 ⚭**J Felber** Hauptstr ☎341031 Frd (GB)
NEUCHÂTEL Neuchâtel 33,500 (☎038) Map **11** A1
★★★**Beau Lac** quai L-Robert 2 ☎258822 tx35122
52rm18⇌23 🍴 P Lift ♪ sB fr34 sB⇌ 🍴60–68
dB fr58 dB⇌ 🍴88–114 (English breakfast) L12–29
D12–23 mountains lake
★★★**Touring** ☎255501 50rm32⇌6 🍴 P Lift ♪
sB33–41 sB⇌ 🍴35–51 dB57–64 dB⇌ 🍴65–97
L fr8 D fr8alc lake
★★*Central* Treille 9 ☎241313 31rm15⇌16 🍴 Lift
lake
★★*City* pl Piaget 12 ☎255412 35rm3⇌ Lift
📻 ⚭*Cote* (R Waser) r de Neuchâtel 15 ☎317573
BL/Rov/Tri (GB)
📻 ⚭*M Faccinetti* av Portes-Rouges 1 ☎242133
(Closed wknds) Bed/Fia
📻 ⚭*Trois Rois* P A-Mazel 11 ☎258301 ☎258301
Frd/Lnc (GB)
At **Chaumont**
★★*Chaumont & Golf* ☎334141 Closed Nov–19 Mar
32rm9⇌ Lift
NEUHAUSEN AM RHEINFALL Schaffhausen
10,300 (☎053) Map **11** B2
★★★*Bellevue* ☎22121 27rm20⇌ 🏠 P Lift sB39–45
sB⇌55–65 dB6–81 dB⇌83–113 L15–25 D15–25
river
NEUVEVILLE (LA) Bern 2,800 (☎038) Map **23** A1
★*Fauçon* Grande r ☎513125 10rm1⇌ A5rm 🏠 P
sB28–31 L8–25 D8–25 🍴 Pool
☆*Neuveville* ☎512060 21rm18⇌ 🍴 P sB27–31
sB 🍴33–39 dB44–48 dB 🍴54–58 L6–12 D6–12
mountains lake
NIEDERURNEN Glarus 3,000 (☎058) Map **12** C1
★*Mineralbad* Badstr ☎211703 7rm 🏠
NYON Vaud 6,100 (☎022) Map **11** A1
★★★*Beau-Rivage* r de Rive 49 ☎613232 tx27439
Closed Jan 46rm23⇌6 🍴 🏠 Lift lake
★★★*Clos de Sadex* rte de Lausanne 21 ☎612831
18rm14⇌ A5rm sB42–46 sB⇌65–110 dB76–82
dB⇌106–150 (English breakfast) L25–45 D25–45
lake
★★★*Nyon* r de Rive 15 ☎611931 tx23591 Closed
Nov 22rm5⇌7 🍴 P Lift sB28–35 sB⇌ 🍴39–60
dB50–65 dB⇌ 🍴60–95 mountains lake

Switzerland

Ⓢℒ**L Jaques** rte de Lausanne ☎612902 Aud/VW (GB)

Ⓢ **Quai** (R Dubler) quai des Alpes ☎614133 Chy/Lnc/Sim

OBERHOFEN Bern 1,500 (☎033) Map **11** B1
★★★*Moy* Staatstr ☎431514 Closed Oct – 14 May 60rm11⇌12🏠 🏛 P Lift sB28 – 40 sB⇌🏠42 – 50 dB56 – 74 dB⇌🏠74 – 98 L18 – 30 D18 – 30 Pool mountains lake
★★*Montana* ☎431661 Closed 11 Oct – Mar 30rm2⇌ 🏛 Lift
★*Kreuz* Hauptstr ☎431448 30rm4⇌4🏠 P Lift sB29 – 35 dB54 – 69 dB⇌🏠70 – 81 (English breakfast) L12 – 18 D12 – 18 ⤴ Pool mountains lake
★*Landte* ☎431553 Closed Dec – Jan 20rm2⇌5🏠 lake

OERLIKON See **ZÜRICH**

OLTEN (see also **EGERKINGEN**) Solothurn 20,000 (☎062) Map **11** B2
★★★*Schweizerhof* Bahnhofquai 18 ☎214571 tx68313 45rm13⇌4🏠 🏛 Lift
Ⓢℒ**City** (F Widmer) Baslerstr 90 ☎212333 AR/BL (GB)
🛈ℒ*Moser* Baslerstr 47 ☎214280 Chy/Sim At **Starrkirch** (2km)
Ⓢℒ**Elite** (Pilloud) Aarauerstr 235 ☎221212 Frd

OUCHY See **LAUSANNE**

PARADISO See **LUGANO**

PARPAN Graubünden 89 (☎081) Map **12** C1
★*Alpina* Hauptstr ☎351184 Closed 21 Apr – May & Nov – 14 Dec 45rm16⇌ 🏛 P Lift 𝄐 sB29 – 38 sB⇌43 – 50 dB58 – 76 dB⇌86 – 100 (English breakfast) L17 – 22 D17 – 22 mountains

PAYERNE Vaud (☎037) Map **11** A1
Ⓢℒ**Promenade** (A Ischi) pl du Gl-Guisan 2 ☎612505 Frd (GB)

PERLY Genève Map **28** C4
Ⓢ **Touring** (L Castrucci) rte St-Julien 266 ☎712540

PFÄFFIKON Schwyz 1,900 (☎055) Map **12** C2
★*Höfe* 7rm4🏠
★*Sternen* ☎481291 26rm1⇌ A9rm 🏛 P sB23 – 35 sB⇌30 dB46 – 48 L9 – 18 D7 – 18

POMPAPLES Vaud (☎021) Map **11** A1
★*Milieu du Monde* ☎877205 8rm

PONTE TRESA Ticino 473.(☎091) Map **28** D4
★★★*Zita* ☎711825 33rm23⇌ A4rm 🏛 P Lift sB32 – 36 sB⇌36 – 42 dB64 – 72 dB⇌72 – 84 (English breakfast) L12 – 18 D12 – 18 Pool ⤴ ᵟ lake
☆*Ponte Tresa* ☎96544 29rm11🏠 Pool lake

PONTRESINA Graubünden 774 (☎082) Map **12** C1
★★★*Kronenhof-Bellavista* ☎66333 tx74488 Closed 16 Apr – 14 Jun & 16 Sep – 14 Dec 150rm74⇌ 🏛 Lift ⤴ Pool
★★★*Müller* (DP) ☎66341 Closed Oct – Dec 51rm20⇌10🏠 A11rm 🏛 Lift
★★★*Schweizerhof* Berninastr (n rest) ☎66412 tx74442 Closed 8 Apr – 2 Jun & 16 Oct – 1 Dec 85rm44⇌20🏠 🏛 P Lift 𝄐 sB41 – 74 sB⇌🏠56 – 89 dB72 – 108 dB⇌🏠102 – 158 (English breakfast) L10 – 25 D15 – 35 mountains
★★*Steinbock* (DP) ☎66371 26rm4⇌1🏠 🏛 ⤴

PORRENTRUY Bern 6,500 (☎066) Map **11** A2
★★*Cheval-Blanc* r Traversière 15 ☎661141 32rm7⇌3🏠 Lift
Ⓢℒ*Gare* r Cuenin 21 ☎661408 ⛽ P Ren
Ⓢ↩*Ponts* Sur les Ponts 15 ☎661206 P Bed/Opl/Vau
Ⓢℒ*St Germain* (L Vallet) r du Jura 5 ☎661913 ☎665448 M/c P Frd

PORTO-RONCO Ticino (☎093) Map **28** D4
★*Eden* (n rest) ☎355142 Closed Nov – Feb 14rm2⇌ P sB22 – 26 (room only) dB40 – 52 (room only) dB⇌78 (room only) mountains lake

POSCHIAVO Graubünden 4,304 (☎082) Map **12** C1
At **Prese (Le)** (4.5km S)

★★★*Prese* ☎50333 Closed Nov – Apr 30rm24⇌1🏠 P Lift sB33 – 53 sB⇌🏠43 – 63 dB43 – 63 dB⇌🏠58 – 78 L22 – 27 D21 – 27 ⤴ Pool mountains lake

PULLY See **LAUSANNE**

RAGAZ-PFÄFERS (BAD) St-Gallen 2,600 (☎085) Map **12** C1
★★★★*Quellenhof* ☎90111 tx74197 Closed Nov – Mar 135rm80⇌21🏠 🏛 Lift ⤴ Pool ᵟ
☆☆*Touring Mot* ☎92355 62rm6⇌ ⤴ Pool
★*Park* ☎92244 Closed Nov – Mar 65rm2🏠 A20rm 🏛 P 𝄐 sB30 – 40 sB🏠39 – 45 dB60 – 76 dB🏠74 – 88 (English breakfast) L14 – 22 D14 – 22 mountains

RARON Valais (☎028) Map **11** B1
☆*Simplonblick* ☎441274 tx38661 19⇌ sB⇌19 – 21 (room only) dB⇌32 – 36 (room only) Pool mountains

REIDEN Luzern (☎062) Map **11** B2
★★★*Sonne* ☎812121 32rm15⇌10🏠 🏛 Lift

RENENS See **LAUSANNE**

RENNEZ See **MONTREUX**

RHEINFELDEN Aargau 4,600 (☎061) Map **11** B2
★★*Schwanen* Kaiserstr 8 ☎875344 Closed 16 Nov – Feb 70rm25⇌ 🏛 Lift
★*Ochsen* ☎875101 Closed Dec – Feb 30rm3🏠 🏛
★*Storchen* Marktgasse 61 ☎875322 30rm12🏠 Lift
Ⓢℒ*Grell* Kaiserstr 30 ☎875051 P Frd

RINGGENBERG Bern 1,800 (☎036) (4km NE of Interlaken) Map **11** B1
★★*Alpina* 222031 19rm10⇌ sB24 – 33 dB48 – 66 dB🏠62 – 72 (English breakfast) L fr6 Dfr14 mountains lake

ROLLE Vaud (☎021) Map **11** A1
★★*Tête Noire* ☎752251 20rm15⇌ lake

ROMANSHORN Thurgau 6,650 (☎071) Map **12** C2
★★*Bodan* ☎631502 60🏠 lake

RORSCHACH St-Gallen 12,800 (☎071) Map **12** C2
★★★*Anker* Hauptstr 71 ☎414243 tx77454 35rm10⇌14🏠 🏛 Lift lake
Ⓢ↩*Central* ☎412222 ☎412312 P Aud VW

SAANENMOSER PASS Bern 200 (☎030) Map **11** B1
★★★*Golf & Sport* ☎43222 Closed May, Oct& Nov 52rm17⇌6🏠 🏛 P Lift 𝄐 sB37 – 45 sB⇌🏠47 – 73 dB74 – 85 dB⇌🏠94 – 139 (English breakfast) L23 – 26 D25 – 30 ⤴ mountains

SAAS-FEE Valais 600 (☎028) Map **28** D4
★★*Beau-Site* ☎48102 tx38284 Closed 21 Apr – 14 Jun & 21 Sep – 14 Dec 80rm15⇌ lake
★★*Bergfreude* (DP) ☎48137 25rm5⇌8🏠

SACHSELN AM SARNERSEE Obwalden 2,500 (☎041) (3km S of **Sarnen**) Map **11** B1
☆☆☆*Kreuz* ☎661466 71rm19⇌26🏠 🏛 Lift

ST-BLAISE Neuchâtel 1,900 (☎038) Map **11** A1
★*Cheval-Blanc* Grande r 18 ☎333007 12rm4⇌8🏠 🏛

ST-GALLEN St-Gallen 76,300 (☎071) Map **12** C2
★★★★*Walhalla* Poststr 27 ☎222922 tx77160 57⇌🏠 Lift
★★★*Hecht* am Bohl 1 ☎226502 tx77173 58rm17⇌15🏠 Lift
★★★*Im Portner* Bankgasse 12 ☎229744 18rm12⇌6🏠 Lift
Ⓢℒ*Capitol* Rorschacherstr 239 ☎242218 BL/Tri
Ⓢ↩*City* Lerchenfeld ☎291131 ⛽ P Aud/Por/VW (GB)
Ⓢ H *Erb* Fürstenlandstr 149 ☎273333 Bed/Sim/Vau (GB)
Ⓢℒ*Lutz* Fürstenlandstr 25 ☎282121 Chy/Cit/Dat
Ⓢℒ*Lutz* Vadianstr 57 ☎232382 Chy/Cit/Dat

ST-GOTTHARD PASS Ticino (☎094) Map **11** B1
★*Monte Prosa* ☎881235 tx78446 Closed 21 Oct – 14 May 22rm 🏛 lake

ST IMIER Bern (☎039) Map **11** A1
★*Sport Mont Soleil* ☎412555 A24rm P 𝄐 sB23 – 28 dB46 – 51 ⤴ ○ mountains

ST-LUC Valais 240 (☎027) Map **28** D4
★★**Bella-Tola** ☎651444 Closed Oct – May
42rm13⇌8🛁 🏥 P Lift sB30 – 33 sB⇌🛁35 – 45
dB60 – 65 dB⇌🛁70 – 85 (English breakfast) L19 – 22
D19 – 22 mountains
★★**Cervin** ☎651393 Closed 7 Sep – 11 Apr
66rm12⇌ 🍸

ST-MAURICE Valais 2,700 (☎025) Map **28** C4
★**Alpes** ☎36223 8rm P sB20 – 25 dB24 – 30 L10 – 15
D10 – 15 mountains
✦**Ecu du Valais** ☎36386 25rm10⇌

ST-MORITZ Graubünden 2,600 (☎082) Map **12** C1
★★★★★**Crystal** ☎21165 tx74449 Closed Nov 110⇌
Lift Pool
★★★★**Kulm** ☎21151 tx74472 Closed 11 Apr – 24
Jun & 11 Sep – 24 Nov 215⇌ 🏥 P Lift 🌙 sB⇌80 – 200
dB⇌130 – 350 (English breakfast) 🏊 Pool mountains
lake
★★★★**Carlton** ☎21141 tx74454 Closed May – Oct
120⇌ 🏥 P Lift 🌙 sB⇌90 – 170 (room only) L35 – 42
D35 – 42 🏊 Pool mountains lake
★★★★**Suvretta-House** ☎21121 tx74491 Closed 26
Mar – 23 Jun & 18 Sep – Nov 230rm214⇌ 🏥 P Lift 🌙
🏊 Pool mountains lake
★★★**Bellevue** ☎22161 tx74448 42rm10⇌30🛁 🏥 P
Lift 🌙 sB35 – 48 sB⇌🛁45 – 75 dB⇌🛁80 – 140
(English breakfast) L10 – 30 D10 – 30 ♉ mountains
lake
★★★**Belvédère** ☎33905 tx74435 (n rest Jun – Sep)
Closed May, Oct & Nov 75rm55⇌15🛁 P Lift 🌙
sB46 – 61 sB⇌🛁56 – 91 dB91 – 121 dB⇌🛁111 – 181
(English breakfast) Dalc 🏊 Pool mountains lake
★★★**Calonder** (n rest) ☎33651 tx74435 Closed
16 Apr – Jun & 16 Sep – Nov Lift 54rm25⇌ 🍸
★★★**Casper Badrutt** ☎34012 Closed mid Apr – Jun
& Sep – 4 Dec 63rm30⇌ 🏥 Lift lake
★★★**Neues Post** ☎22121 tx74430 85rm44⇌13🛁 P
Lift 🌙 sB40 – 50 sB⇌🛁50 – 95 dB70 – 100
dB⇌🛁90 – 190 (English breakfast) L fr16 D fr19
mountains lake
★★**Bären** Hauptstr ☎33656 90rm50⇌ 🏥 Lift Pool
★★**Margna** Bahnhofstr ☎22141 tx74402 Closed 13
Apr – 5 Sep 71rm27⇌15🛁 🏥 Lift lake
🍴**M Conrad** ☎33788 P BL/Fia/Lnc
🅱 🚗**Grand Dosch** ☎81200 P AR/MB/Opl

At **St-Moritz-Bad** (1km S)
★**National** (DP) ☎33274 Closed May – 14 Jun &
Oct – Nov 30🛁 Lift lake

At **St-Moritz-Champfér** (3km SW)
★★★★**Eurotel** ☎21175 tx74458 Closed 25 Apr – 10
Jun & 26 Sep – 28 Oct 150rm112⇌26🛁 🏥 Lift 🏊
Pool
★★**Chesa Guardalej** ☎34781 Closed May
36rm33⇌3🛁 Lift lake

ST-SULPICE See **LAUSANNE**

STE-CROIX Vaud (☎024) Map **11** A1
★**Jura** r du Jura ☎612145 12rm3⇌ 🏥 P sB27 – 31
sB⇌29 – 33 dB54 – 62 dB⇌58 – 66
(English breakfast) L12 – 22 D16 – 22 ♉ mountains

SAMEDAN Graubünden 1,700 (☎082) Map **12** C1
★★★**Bernina** Hauptstr ☎65421 tx74486 Closed Nov
& May 80rm60⇌ 🏥 P Lift 🌙 sB38 – 48 sB⇌52 – 78
dB71 – 91 dB⇌101 – 151 (English breakfast) L18 – 21
D22 – 26 🏊 ♉ ♉ mountains
🅱 🚗**Gebruder Pfister** ☎65666 P Chy/Frd/Sim/Vlo
(GB)
🅱 🚗**Palü** Hauptstr ☎65331 P BL/Jag/MB/Toy/Tri

SANTA MARIA Graubünden 400 (☎082) Map **12** D1
★**Schweizerhof** Hauptstr ☎85124 Closed Nov – Apr
32rm10⇌10🛁 🏥 P Lift sB34 – 43 sB⇌🛁38 – 48
dB67 – 84 dB⇌🛁75 – 95 L6 – 18 D6 – 18 mountains

SARGANS St-Gallen 2,100 (☎085) Map **12** C1
★★**Post** ☎21214 15rm3⇌7🛁 🏥 P sB20 sB⇌🛁23
dB39 dB⇌🛁46 – 50 L8 – 19 D8 – 19 mountains

SARNEN Obwalden (☎041) Map **11** B1
At **Wilen**

★★**Wilerbad am Sarnersee** ☎661292 87rm20⇌8🛁
🏥 Lift Pool

SCHAFFHAUSEN Schaffhausen 31,000 (☎053)
Map **11** B2
★★**Bahnhof** Bahnhofstr 46 ☎54001 44rm38⇌6🛁
Lift 🌙 sB⇌🛁40 – 50 dB⇌🛁70 – 90 L12 – 20 D12 – 20
★★**Kronenhof** Kirchofpl 7 (off Vordergasse)
☎56631 30rm8⇌18🛁 Lift
★★**Park-Villa** Parkstr 18 ☎52737 30rm18⇌ A5rm 🏥
P sB32 – 38 sB⇌45 – 55 dB50 – 62 dB⇌70 – 100
(English breakfast) L14 – 18 D14 – 18 🏊 river
★**Kreuz** Mühlenstr 88 ☎51982 17rm3⇌1🛁
🅱 🚗**Auto-Ernst** Schweizersbildstr 61 ☎33322 P
BMW/Frd (GB)

SCHOENRIED Bern (☎030) (4km NE of **Saanen**)
Map **11** B1
★★★**Ermitage & Golf** ☎42727 Closed Nov & May
35rm20⇌10🛁 🏥 sB30 – 47 sB⇌🛁40 – 57 dB60 – 90
dB⇌🛁80 – 110 (English breakfast) L6 – 25 D6 – 25 🏊
Pool mountains

SCHWANDEN Glarus (☎058) Map **12** C1
★**Adler** ☎811171 Closed 29 Dec – 14 Jan 11rm1⇌

SEEBURG See **LUZERN (LUCERNE)**

SERVION Vaud (☎021) Map **11** A1
☆☆**Fleurs** ☎932054 32rm14🛁 P sB30 – 35 sB🛁35
dB45 – 50 dB🛁50 – 55 (English breakfast) L fr8 D fr8
mountains

SIERRE (SIDERS) Valais 7,200 (☎027) Map **28** C4
★★**Arnold** rte du Simplon ☎551721 32rm3⇌6🛁 🏥
Lift
★★**Atlantic** ☎552535 37rm25⇌12🛁 Lift Pool
★**Victoria** rte de Sion 5 ☎551007 16rm2⇌2🛁 P
sB23 – 32 sB⇌🛁33 – 42 dB49 – 62 dB⇌🛁61 – 77
(English breakfast) L13 – 20 D13 – 20 mountains
🅱 🍴**International** (J Trivério) av M-Hubert 20
☎551436 ☎555544 P Chy/Sim (GB)
🅱 🍴**Rawyl** rte du Simplon ☎550308 P Frd

SIGRISWIL Bern 3,920 (☎033) (3km NE of **Gunten**)
Map **11** B1
★**Adler** ☎512424 29rm11⇌10🛁 🏥 P Lift 🌙
sB30 – 34 sB⇌🛁41 – 46 dB59 – 65 dB⇌🛁79 – 89
(English breakfast) L14 – 18 D15 – 18 🏊 ♉ mountains
lake

SIHLBRUGG Zürich (☎01) Map **11** B2
☆☆**Sihlbrugg** (n rest) ☎7299600 18rm8⇌10🛁 🏥 P
🌙 sB⇌🛁30 – 34 dB⇌🛁49 – 55 (English breakfast)

SILS-MARIA Graubünden 118 (☎082) Map **12** C1
★★★★**Waldhaus** ☎45331 tx74444 Closed 26
Apr – May & 21 Oct – 14 Dec 150rm90⇌14🛁 🏥 P Lift
🌙 sB40 – 77 sB⇌🛁70 – 117 dB70 – 134
dB⇌🛁94 – 224 (English breakfast) L25 – 40 D30 – 40
🏊 Pool mountains lake
★★**Maria** Hauptstr ☎45317 40rm11⇌2🛁 🏥

At **Sils-Baseglia**
★★★**Margna** ☎45306 tx74496 Closed May & Nov
73rm53⇌7🛁 P Lift 🌙 sB46 – 76 sB⇌🛁61 – 101
dB⇌🛁122 – 202 L22 – 28 D25 – 32 🏊 mountains lake
★**Privata** ☎45247 Closed 16 Apr – May & 21 Oct – 19
Dec 20rm
★**Seraina** ☎45292 40rm10⇌2🛁

SILVAPLANA Graubünden 333 (☎082) Map **12** C1
★★**Sonne** ☎48152 57rm26⇌11🛁 Lift lake
★**Corvatsch** ☎48162 Closed May 16rm P sB36 – 41
dB72 – 82 L10 – 18 D10 – 18 mountains lake

SIMPLON-DORF Valais (☎028) Map **28** D4
★**Poste** ☎291121 30rm A15rm 🏥 P 🌙 sB18 – 21
sB⇌🛁22 – 25 dB38 – 42 dB⇌🛁42 – 44 mountains

SIMPLON-KULM Valais (☎028) Map **28** D4
★★**Bellevue** ☎291331 Closed 16 Oct – Feb
45rm3⇌3🛁 🏥 P Lift 🌙 sB25 – 36 sB⇌🛁35 – 46
dB50 – 72 dB⇌🛁70 – 92 (English breakfast) L12 – 20
D18 – 30 mountains

SION (SITTEN) Valais 16,000 (☎027) Map **28** C4
★★★**Rhône** r du Scex 10 ☎228291 tx38104 44⇌ 🏥
P Lift 🌙 sB⇌🛁36 – 42 dB⇌🛁63 – 78 mountains

★★**Continental** rte de Lausanne 116 ☎224641 24rm2⇌22⋒ P ☽ sB⇌⋒33–37 dB⇌⋒63–67 (English breakfast) L alc D alc mountains

★★**Touring** av de la Gare ☎231551 27rm13⇌14⋒ ⌂ P Lift sB31–46 sB⇌⋒36–46 dB62 dB⇌⋒62–90 L15–20 D15–25

⛽ ∞**Aviation** rte Cantonale-Corbassières ☎223924 Maz/Vlo (GB)

⛽ ∞***Hediger*** Batassé ☎220131 Chy/Sim

⛽ ∞**Kaspar** r du Tunnel 22 ☎221271 ☎221271 AR/Frd

⛽ ∞**Nord** av Ritz 35 ☎223413 ☎223413 Ren

⛽ ∞**Tourbillon** (Couturier) av de Tourbillon 23 ☎222077 Peu (GB)

SISIKON Uri (☎044) (7km S of **Brunnen**) Map **11** B1

★★★***Tellsplatte*** ☎21612 Closed Nov–Mar 40rm8⇌30⋒ ⌂ Lift lake

SOLOTHURN (SOLEURE) Solothurn 18,400 (☎065) Map **11** B2

★★★***Krone*** Hauptgasse 64 ☎24438 35rm16⇌ ⌂

⛽ **Howald Otto** Engistr 13 ☎223718 AR/Jag/Ren (GB)

⛽ ∞**Autogarage** (Stauffer) Steingrubenstr 19 ☎226333 BMW/Fia

SPIEZ Bern 6,600 (☎033) Map **11** B1

★★★**Eden** Seestr ☎541154 Closed Nov–Feb 57rm40⇌ A4rm ⌂ P Lift ☽ sB36–53 sB⇌43–63 dB66–96 dB⇌76–126 L18–24 D20–26 ⛳ Pool mountains lake

★★**Alpes** Seestr 38 ☎543354 43rm12⇌12⋒ A4rm ⌂ P Lift sB33–42 sB⇌⋒38–53 dB61–83 dB⇌⋒75–107 L18 D18 ⛳ Pool mountains lake

★★**Erica** (n rest) ☎541735 Closed Oct–Mar 26rm4⇌ P ☽ sB24–38 sB⇌33–48 dB46–72 dB⇌60–88 mountains lake

★★**Terminus** Bahnhofpl ☎543121 64rm28⇌10⋒ P Lift sB27–37 sB⇌⋒32–47 dB50–72 dB⇌⋒64–92 L10–20 D10–20 mountains lake

★***Krone*** Seestr 28 ☎544131 14rm ⌂ lake

STANS Nidwalden 4,000 (☎041) Map **11** B1

★★***Stanserhof*** Stansstaderstr 20 ☎614122 23rm10⇌1⋒ Lift

STANSSTAD Nidwalden 1,400 (☎041) (11km S of **Luzern**) Map **11** B1

★★★**Freienhof** ☎613531 50rm35⇌35⋒ ⌂ P Lift sB26–38 sB⇌⋒32–48 dB52–76 dB⇌⋒64–96 (English breakfast) L15–25 D15–25 ⛳ mountains lake

★★**Schützen** Stanserstr 23 ☎611355 tx72333 50rm25⇌3⋒ ⌂ P Lift sB38–42 sB⇌⋒54–66 dB72–84 dB⇌⋒97–122 (English breakfast) L10–30 D20–40 ⛳ Pool ♁ ∩ mountains

★★***Winkelried*** ☎612622 46rm15⇌20⋒ Lift lake

STARRKIRCH See **OLTEN**

STECKBORN Thurgau (☎054)) Map **12** C2

⛽ ⋙***Bürgi's Erben*** Bahnhofstr ☎82251 P BL/Dat/Sab

SURSEE Luzern 4,300 (☎045) Map **11** B2

★★***Hirschen*** Oberstadt 10 ☎211048 13rm2⇌4⋒ ⌂ Lift

★***Bellevue*** Mariazell ☎211844 16rm1⋒ Pool lake

★***Brauerei*** ☎211083 9rm

⛽ ∞**Central** (L Muller) Luzernstr 18 ☎211144 Frd (GB)

TAFERS Fribourg (☎037) Map **11** B1

⛽ ⋙***Touring*** (O Schweingruber) ☎441750 M/c Opl

TARASP-VULPERA See **VULPERA (TARASP)**

TEGNA Ticino (☎093) Map **28** D4

☆☆**Betulla** (n rest) ☎811851 11rm6⇌5⋒ P sB35–38 sB⇌⋒45–50 dB45–55 dB⇌⋒70–78 Pool ∩ mountains

TEUFEN Appenzell 4,400 (☎071) (6km S of **St-Gallen**) Map **12** C2

★***Linde*** ☎331419 14rm ⌂

★***Ochsen*** ☎332188 14rm

THALWIL Zürich 11,500 (☎01) Map **11** B2

★★**Thalwilerhof** Bahnhofstr 16 ☎7200603 26rm3⇌4⋒ ⌂ P Lift sB28–30 sB⇌⋒35–40 dB46–50 dB⇌⋒65–80 L8–20 D8–20 mountains lake

THIELLE Neuchâtel (☎038) Map **11** A1

☆☆☆**Novotel Neuchâtel Est** rte de Berne ☎335757 tx35402 60⇌ P Lift sB⇌fr47 dB⇌dr72 Pool

THUN (THOUNE) Bern 29,100 (☎033) Map **11** B1

★★★★**Elite** Bernstr 1–3 ☎232823 tx32281 39rm14⇌25⋒ ⌂ P Lift ☽ sB⇌⋒34–47 dB⇌⋒64–90 (English breakfast) L7–25 D7–25 ⛳ Pool mountains

★★★**Beau-Rivage** ☎222236 Closed Dec–Mar 30rm18⇌ ⌂ P Lift sB35–47 sB⇌⋒41–62 dB63–88 dB⇌⋒73–113 (English breakfast) L20 D20 Pool mountains lake

★★★***Falken*** Bälliz 46 Closed 23 Dec–24 Jan 30rm8⇌12⋒ Lift

★★★***Freienhof*** Freienhofgasse 3 (DP) ☎224672 65rm32⇌32⋒ ⌂ Lift

★★**Bellevue** Hofstettenstr 25 ☎225301 Closed Oct–Apr 45rm8⇌ P Lift sB30–48 sB⇌35–58 dB60–86 dB⇌70–106 (English breakfast) L13–15 D18–20 Pool mountains lake

★**Metzgern** Rathauspl ☎222141 8rm sB28 dB56 L7–20 D7–20

∞**City** (G Wenger) Kyburgstr ☎229577 Cit/Lnc/Maz (GB)

⛽ ⋙**Moser** Gwattstr 24 ☎341515 Aud/Chy/MB Por/VW/Vlo (GB)

⛽ ∞**Touring** Schlossmattstr 10 ☎224455 MB/Toy (GB)

At **Dürrenast** (2km S)

★★★***Holiday*** Gwattstr 1 ☎365757 55rm6⇌49⋒ Lift lake

At **Hünibach** (1km SE)

⛽ ∞**K Schick** Staatsstr 134 ☎225833 BMW/Ren (GB)

THUSIS Graubünden 1,600 (☎081) Map **12** C1

★★***Post & Viamala*** ☎811412 31rm8⇌3⋒ ⌂

⛽ **Viamala** Hauptstr ☎811822 M/c P Frd/Opl (GB)

TIEFENCASTEL Graubünden 327 (☎081) Map **12** C1

★★**Posthotel Julier** Julierstr ☎711415 50rm30⇌ ⌂ P Lift sB23–28 sB⇌30–38 dB45–50 dB⇌55–70 (English breakfast) L fr14 D fr14 mountains

★**Albula** ☎711121 23rm6⇌10⋒ P sB25–27 sB⇌⋒28–30 dB40–42 dB⇌⋒52 (English breakfast) L12–18 D12–18 mountains

TRAVERS Neuchâtel 1,653 (☎038) Map **11** A1

★**Cret** ☎631178 Closed Feb 6rm sB23 dB46 L10–25 D10–25

TSCHIERTSCHEN Graubünden 174 (☎081) Map **12** C1

★***Bruesch*** ☎321130 Closed May–14 Jun & Oct–14 Dec 25rm

UNTERWASSER St-Gallen 670 (☎074) Map **12** C2

★★★**Sternen** ☎52424 65rm25⇌ ⌂ P Lift ☽ sB25–36 sB⇌45–52 dB50–72 dB⇌90–104 (English breakfast) L12–28 D15–28 ⛳ Pool mountains

VALBELLA See **LENZERHEIDE**

VALLORBE Vaud 3,900 (☎021) Map **11** A1

★***France*** ☎831022 16rm

☆**Jurats** ☎831991 16⋒ P sB⋒31–37 dB⋒56 mountains

⛽ ∞**Moderne** r de la Poste 41 ☎831156 P Aud/VW

VERBIER Valais (☎026) Map **12** C4

★★★***Grand Combin*** ☎71515 Closed 7 Sep–11 Apr 35rm25⇌5⋒ Lift

⛽ ⋙**Verbier** (A Stuckelberger) ☎76666 ☎76666 M/c P (GB)

VERNAYAZ Valais (☎026) Map **28** C4

★**Victoria** ☎81416 12rm ⌂ P sB19–21 dB39–42 L4–12 D4–12 mountains

VERRIERES (LES) Neuchâtel 1,200 (☎038) Map **11** A1

★**Gare** pl de la Gare ☎661633 6rm4⇌ ⌂ P

sB16–25 sB⇌25 dB50 dB⇌50 (English breakfast)
L10–15 D10–15 mountains
VERSOIX Genève (☎022) Map **28** C4
★*Pavillon* rte de Lausanne 66 ☎551032 17rm A4rm
lake
VESENAZ See **GENÈVE**
VEVEY Vaud 16,300 (☎021) Map **11** A1
★★★★*Trois Couronnes* r d'Italie 49 ☎513005
tx25270 90⇌ P Lift ♪ sB⇌60–110 dB⇌100–200
(English breakfast) L40 D40 mountains lake
★★★*Comte* av des Alpes ☎541441 tx25245
41rm22⇌4🍴 Lift sB41–56 sB⇌🍴61–66 dB42–57
dB⇌🍴62–67 L25 D35 mountains lake
★★★*Lac* r d'Italie ☎511041 tx25577 58rm46⇌ 🏠
P Lift ♪ sB25–50 sB⇌55–85 dB50–80
dB⇌80–160 L25–35 D25–35 ℘ Pool ⅃ ∩
mountains lake
★*Famille* ☎513931 tx26475 61rm37🍴 🏠 P Lift
sB30–34 sB🍴34–44 dB32–40 dB🍴36–50
(English breakfast) L9–12 D8–10 mountains
VEZIA See **LUGANO**
VILLARS-LE-TERROIR See **ECHALLENS**
VILLARS-SUR-OLLON Vaud (☎025) Map **28** C4
★★*Montesano et Régina* ☎32551 tx24727 Closed
May; Oct & Nov 85rm24⇌4🍴 Lift
VILLENEUVE See **MONTREUX**
VILLMERGEN Schwyz (☎057) Map **11** B2
🛢 *R Huber* Hauptstr ☎61379 ☎68857 P
Aud/MB/Rov
VIRA-GAMBAROGNO Ticino (☎093) (13.5km SE of
Locarno) Map **29** A4
☆☆☆*Bellavista* ☎611116 62rm16⇌46🍴 Lift Pool
lake
VIRA-MEZZOVICO Ticino (☎091) Map **29** A4
☆*Mezzovico* ☎98364 89rm24⇌18🍴 Pool
VISP Valais 2,300 (☎028) Map **28** D4
★★★*Touring* pl de la Gare (n rest) ☎62626
55rm16⇌11🍴 🏠 Lift
🛢 🎤*Moderne* ☎464333 ☎464333 P Fia/MB (GB)
🛢 ⚡*Touring* Kantonstr ☎462562 P Aud/Por/VW
(GB)
VITZNAU Luzern 1,000 (☎041) Map **11** B1
★★★★*Park* ☎831322 tx78340 Closed Nov–Mar
90rm70⇌ 🏠 Lift ℘ Pool ⅃ lake
★★★*Vitznauerhof* ☎831315 tx72241 Closed
Nov–Mar 61rm45⇌ P Lift ♪ sB41–54 sB⇌51–71
dB82–108 dB⇌102–142 (English breakfast) L20
D23 ℘ mountains lake
★★*Terrasse Terminus* ☎831033 Closed Nov–mid
Apr 30rm16⇌ P Lift sB38–40 sB🍴46–48 dB68–72
dB🍴84–88 (English breakfast) L15–22 D alc
mountains lake
VULPERA (TARASP) Graubünden 300 (☎084)
Map **12** C1
↙ ★★*Schweizerhof* (Pn) ☎91331 tx74427 Closed
May, Oct & Nov 80rm50⇌ 🏠 Lift ℘ Pool ⅃ lake
★★★*Waldhaus* (Pn) ☎91101 tx74427 Closed
Nov–Apr 120rm90⇌ 🏠 Lift ℘ Pool ⅃ lake
WABERN See **BERN**
WÄDENSWIL Zürich 11,700 (☎01) Map **11** B2
★★★*Lac* ☎7800031 23rm5⇌9🍴 Lift lake
★*Engel* Engelstr 2 ☎7800011 12rm 🏠 P sB31 dB55
L9–10 D10–15 mountains lake
🛢 ⚡*Zentrum* (B & C Weber) Seestr 114 ☎7808080
BL/BMW/Opl Toy (GB)
WASSEN Uri 900 (☎044) Map **11** B1
★★*Krone* Gotthardstr ☎65334 Closed Nov–Feb
15rm2⇌4🍴 🏠 P ♪ sB31–41 dB35–70
dB⇌🍴41–50 (English breakfast) L10–22 D10–22
mountains
★★*Post* (n rest) ☎65231 Closed Nov–Mar 25rm2⇌
★*Alpes* ☎65233 14rm5⇌1🍴 🏠 P sB31–36
sB⇌🍴36–41 dB52–62 dB⇌🍴67–72
(English breakfast) L5–25 D5–25 mountains
🎤*K Calcagni* ☎65663 ☎65663 ☸ P BMW/Frd/MB

WATTWIL St-Gallen 6,400 (☎074) Map **12** C2
✦*Toggenburg* Dorfpl 2 ☎71242 10rm
WEGGIS Luzern 2,300 (☎041) Map **11** B1
★★★*Albana* ☎932141 tx78637 70rm60⇌ 🏠 P Lift
sB35–45 sB⇌🍴50–65 dB60–80 dB⇌🍴80–120
(English breakfast) L18 D23 ℘ lake
★★★*Beau Rivage* Gotthardstr ☎931422 tx72525
Closed Nov–Feb 42rm24⇌16🍴 🏠 P Lift
sB⇌🍴45–65 (room only) dB⇌🍴90–130
(room only) Pool
★★★*Park* ☎931313 Closed Nov–Mar 66rm42⇌ 🏠
P Lift ♪ sB30–45 sB⇌45–65 dN56–86 dB80–120
(English breakfast) L18–25 D18–25 ℘ mountains
lake
★★★*Waldstätten* ☎931341 tx72428 41⇌ Lift lake
★★*Bühlegg* ☎932123 Closed Nov–Apr 20rm10⇌ P
Lift sB32–39 sB⇌🍴36–50 dB62–72 dB⇌🍴fr72
L fr18 D fr20
★★*Central am See* ☎931317 Closed Dec & Jan
50rm 🏠 P Lift sB32–47 sB⇌🍴40–61 dB63–91
dB⇌🍴79–111 L15–22 D15–22 Pool mountains
lake
★★*Post Terminus* ☎931251 Closed Oct–Apr
84rm4⇌ Lift lake
★*Rigi* Seestr ☎932151 Closed Nov–Apr
45rm2⇌6🍴 A30rm P sB30–41 sB⇌🍴37–48
dB56–76 dB⇌🍴70–90 L14–20 D14–20 mountains
lake
★*Felsberg* ☎931136 Closed Oct–Apr 20rm9🍴 lake
★*Frohburg* ☎931022 Closed Dec–Feb 20rm17⇌ P
sB28–45 sB⇌🍴40–65 dB56–90 dB⇌🍴80–130
English breakfast only D15–19 mountains lake
★*National* Seestr ☎931225 tx78395 Closed
Nov–Feb 37rm31⇌4🍴 🏠 P Lift sB34–47
sB⇌🍴42–61 dB63–87 dB⇌🍴79–115
(English breakfast) L14–22 D14–22 ℘ Pool ⅃
mountains lake
★*Rössli* Seestr ☎931106 tx78395 Closed Nov–14
Mar 40rm15⇌ 🏠 P Lift sB29–39 sB⇌🍴35–45
dB54–77 dB⇌🍴69–89 (English breakfast) L fr10
D fr12 mountains lake
★*Seehotel du Lac* ☎931151 Closed Nov–Mar
32rm25⇌1🍴 P Lift sB345–44 sB⇌🍴40–58
dB68–88 dB⇌🍴80–116 L12–18 D12–18
mountains lake
WENGEN Bern 1,230 (☎036) Map **11** B1
No road connection; take train from **Lauterbrunnen**
★★★*Palace National* ☎552612 tx32702 Closed mid
Apr–19 Jun & 11 Sep–17 Dec Lift ℘
★★★*Waldrand* ☎552855 tx32340 Closed 16
Apr–24 May & 26 Sep–14 Dec 50rm40⇌3🍴 Lift ♪
sB42–72 sB⇌🍴52–82 dB84–144 dB⇌🍴104–164
(English breakfast) L fr18 D fr20 mountains
WENGERNALP Bern (☎036) Map **11** B1
No road connection; take train from **Lauterbrunnen**
★*Jungfrau* ☎551622 Closed May–Oct 25rm16⇌
WIL St-Gallen 11,000 (☎073) Map **12** C2
★★★*Derby Bahnhof* Bahnhof pl 1 ☎222626
tx77252 28rm13⇌4🍴 lake
🛢 🎤*Bahnhof* Untere Bahnhofstr 9 ☎221112
BL/Ren/Tri
WILDERSWIL Bern 1,700 (☎036) (2km S of
Interlaken) Map **11** B1
★★*Bären* ☎223521 Closed Nov 60rm6⇌2🍴 A39rm
🏠 lift lake
☆☆*Luna* ☎228414 16rm8⇌8🍴
★*Alpenrose* ☎221024 Closed Nov–Mar
40rm5⇌6🍴 A8rm
★*Viktoria* ☎221670 14rm P sB19–21 dB36–40
(English breakfast) L fr8 D fr12 mountains
WILDHAUS St-Gallen 1,200 (☎074) Map **12** C2
★★*Acker Montana* ☎52221 tx71208 Closed Nov
110rm58⇌52🍴 🏠 P Lift ♪ sB⇌🍴51–81
dB⇌🍴92–152 (English breakfast) L17 D27 ℘ Pool
mountains
★★*Hirschen* ☎52252 90rm30⇌45🍴 A25rm P Lift
sB31–106 sB⇌🍴48–106 dB51–142
dB⇌🍴81–142 (English breakfast) L8–30 D8–30 ℘
Pool mountains

Switzerland

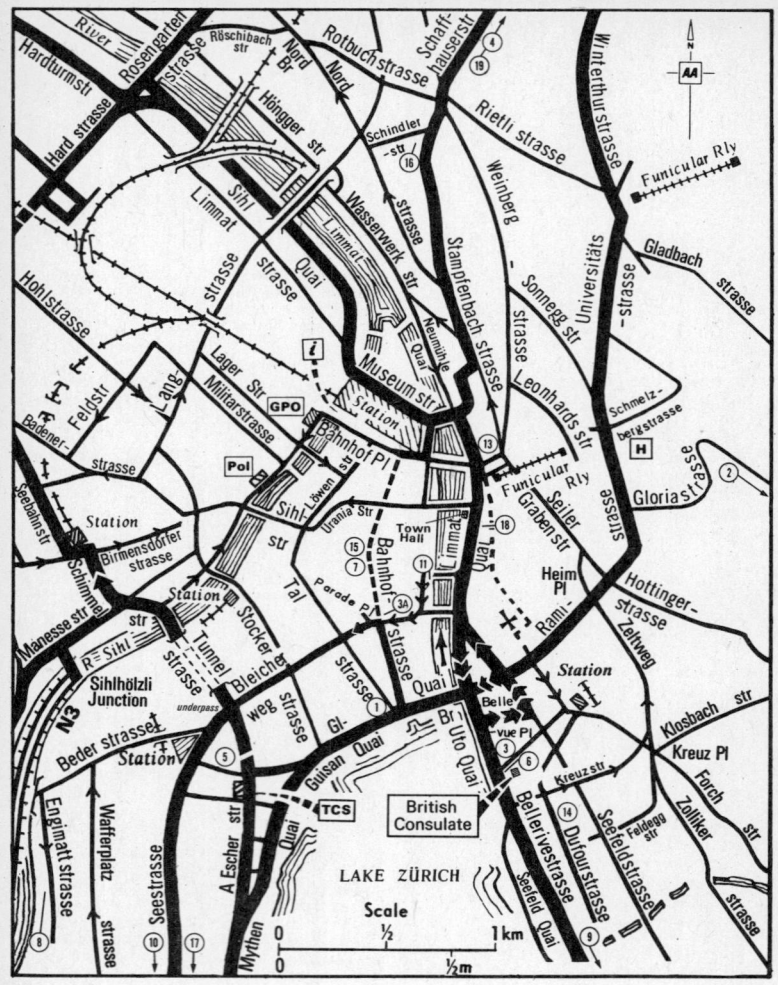

Zurich

1	★★★★★Baur au Lac	10	★★★★Park
2	★★★★★Dolder	11	★★★★Zum Storchen
3	★★★★★Eden au Lac	13	★★★Central
3A	★★★★★Savoy Bauren Ville	14	★★★Excelsior
4	★★★★Airport (at Glattbrugg 8km NE on N4)	15	★★★Glockenhof
5	★★★★Ascot	16	★★Burma
6	★★★★Bellerive au Lac	17	★★Jolie Ville Motor Inn (at Adilswil 4km SE on
7	★★★★Carlton Elite	18	★★Krone
8	★★★★Engematthof	19	★★Sternen Oerlikon (at Oerlikon 4km N)
9	★★★★Ermitage au Lac (at Küsnacht 12km S on N17)		

WILEN See **SARNEN**

WINTERTHUR Zürich 80,400 (☎052) Map **12** C2

★★★★**Garten** Stadthausstr 4 ☎232231 tx75201
55⇆ 🏚 P Lift ♪ sB⇆60−65 dB⇆95−107

★★★**Krone** Marktgasse 49 (n rest) ☎232521
38rm17⇆15🏚 🏚 P Lift sB39−57 sB⇆🏚50−57
dB72−88 dB⇆🏚78−88 (English breakfast) L 10−25
D10−25

🗋 ⏄**Eulach** Technikumstr 67 ☎222333 Bed/Opl

🗋 ⏄**Riedbach** Frauenfeldstr 9 ☎272222 P
BL/BMW/Ren

🗋 ⏄**A Siegenthaler** Frauenfeiderst 44 ☎272900
Chy/Sim

YVERDON Vaud 16,400 (☎024) Map **11** A1

★★**Prairie** av des Bains 9 ☎211919 35rm14⇆8🏚 P
Lift sB44−46 sB⇆🏚51−56 dB79−83 dB⇆🏚89−96
(English breakfast) L 18−27 D18−27 ⏅

🗎 ⏄**Belair** av des Sports 13 ☎213381 Frd

🛏 *&Remparts* Champs Lovat 1 ☎213535 Peu/Vau

ZERMATT Valais 1,400 (☎028) Map **28** D4

No road connection; take train from **Täsch** or **Visp**

★★★★**Mont Cervin** ☎661121 tx38329 Closed 22 Apr–Jun & 25 Sep–Nov 135rm93⇌19⋔ A23rm Lift ♪ sB58–78 sB⇌⋔70–115 dB110–150 dB⇌⋔140–230 (English breakfast) L28 D34 Pool mountains

★★★**Beau-Site** ☎671271 tx38361 Closed May, Oct & Nov 67⇌ 🏠 Lift sB⇌45–100 dB⇌80–170 (English breakfast) L10–18 D12–20 ✍ Pool mountains

★★★**National Bellevue** (Pn) ☎77161 Closed Oct–Nov 93rm56⇌14⋔ Lift ✍

★★★**Schweizerhof** (Pn) ☎77521 tx38201 Closed May & Nov 48rm38⇌ Lift ✍

★★★**Zermatterhof** ☎661101 tx38275 Closed Nov 95rm69⇌9⋔ Lift ♪ sB55–100 dB⇌⋔70–125 dB110–150 dB⇌⋔130–250 (English breakfast) Lfr15 Dfr34 ✍ Pool mountains

★★**Dom** ☎671371 47rm34⇌4⋔ Lift sB24–46 sB⇌⋔32–56 dB48–91 dB⇌⋔64–111 (English breakfast) L12–15 D15–19 mountains

ZERNEZ Graubünden 740 (☎082) Map **12** C1

★★ *C* *Baer & Post* Curtinstr (DP) ☎81141 Closed Nov 19rm5⇌14⋔ A12rm 🏠 Pool

ZUG Zug 19,800 (☎042) Map **11** B2

★★★**City Ochsen** Kolinpl ☎213232 35rm31⇌3⋔ P Lift sB⇌55–68 dB⇌⋔88–110 L19 D19 Pool

★**Guggithal** Zugerbergstr 212821 tx65134 33rm23⇌9⋔ 🏠 P Lift sB⇌⋔50–65 dB⇌⋔75–105 mountains lake

★*Rössli* Vorstadtstr 8 ☎210394 Closed 20 Dec–15 Jan 18rm10⇌ Lift lake

🛏 *&Kaiser* Baarerstr 50 ☎212424 BL/MB/Tri

🛏 *&C Keiser* Grabenstr 18 ☎211818 P Ren

🛏 *Spatz* Chamerstr 75 ☎212818 ☎212851 P Fia/Maz

ZUOZ Graubünden 780 (☎082) Map **12** C1

★★★*Engiadina* Hauptstr ☎71355 40rm12⇌3⋔ 🏠 Lift

ZÜRICH Zürich 440,200 (☎01) Map **11** B2 **See Plan**

★★★★★**Baur au Lac** Talstr 1 ☎211650 tx53567 Plan **1** 170⇌ 🏠 P Lift ♪ sB⇌⋔100–140 dB⇌⋔190–240 (English breakfast) L38 D40 mountains lake

★★★★★**Dolder** Kurhausstr 65 ☎326231 tx53449 Plan **2** 194⇌ A64rm 🏠 P Lift ♪ sB⇌100–140 dB⇌⋔160–240 (English breakfast) L38 D40 ✍ Pool 𝄢 mountains lake

★★★★★**Eden au Lac** Utoquai 45 ☎479404 tx52440 Plan **3** 50rm41⇌9⋔ P Lift ♪ sB⇌⋔100–125 dB⇌⋔160–200 (English breakfast) L alc D alc mountains lake

★★★★★**Savoy Baur en Ville** Poststr 12 ☎2115360 taSavoy tx812845 Plan **3A** 114⇌ P Lift ♪ sB⇌100–140 dB⇌175–240

★★★★**Ascot** Lavaterstr 15 ☎2011800 tx52783 Plan **5** 60⇌ P Lift ♪ sB⇌90–100 dB⇌130–170 (English breakfast) L alc D alc

★★★★*Bellerive au Lac* Utoquai 47 ☎327010 tx53272 Plan **6** 60rm42⇌8⋔ P Lift ♪ sB⇌⋔85–95 dB⇌⋔130–155 (English breakfast) L28 D28 mountains lake

★★★★*Carlton Elite* Bahnhofstr 41 ☎2116560 tx52781 Plan **7** 72⇌ Lift

★★★*Engematthof* Engimattstr 14 ☎2012504 tx56327 Plan **8** 79rm31⇌48⋔ 🏠 P Lift ♪ sB⇌⋔61–81 dB⇌⋔102–122 L17–25 D17–25 ✍

★★★★*Park* Kappelistr 41 ☎2016565 tx56909 Plan **10** 56rm35⇌18⋔ Lift lake

★★★★**Zum Storchen** Weinpl 2 ☎2115510 tx813354 Plan **11** 77rm54⇌23⋔ Lift ♪ sB⇌⋔95–135 dB⇌⋔160–230 (English breakfast) L alc D alc

★★★*Central* Centralpl ☎326820 tx54909 Plan **13** 64rm40⇌18⋔ Lift

★★★*Excelsior* Dufourstr 24 (n rest) ☎342500 tx59295 Plan **14** 40rm21⇌13⋔ Lift

★★★*Glockenhof* Sihlstr 31 ☎2115650 tx52466 Plan **15** 104rm92⇌12⋔ Lift

★★*Burma* Schindlerstr 26 ☎261008 Plan **16** 23rm3⇌ P Lift sB34–38 dB56–60 dB⇌73–78 L7–12

★★**Krone** Limmatquai 88 ☎324222 Plan **18** 25rm2⇌ Lift sB35–38 dB65–69 dB⇌75–85

&Canonica Albisriederstr 401 ☎549824 P BL (GB)

🛏 *&E Frey* Badenerstr 600 ☎545700 P BL/Jag/Rov/Tri

🛏 *&J H Keller* Vulkanstr 120 ☎642410 Hon

🛏 *&Riesbach* Dufourstr 182 ☎552211 ☎322503 P Frd (GB)

🛏 *&Witikon* Witikonerstr 311 ☎539733 BMW (GB)

At **Adliswil** (4km SE on N4)

★★*Jolie Ville Motor Inn* ☎7108585 tx52507 Plan **17** 70rm35⇌35⋔ A35rm

At **Küsnacht** (12km S on N17)

★★★★*Ermitage au Lac* Seestr 80 ☎9105222 Plan **9** Closed 16 Dec–14 Feb 25⇌ Lift Pool lake

At **Oerlikon** (4km N)

★★**Sternen Oerlikon** Schaffhauserstr 335 ☎467777 tx56999 Plan **19** 52rm15⇌22⋔ 🏠 Lift ♪ sB41 sB⇌⋔55 dB70 dB⇌⋔90 (English breakfast) L12–25 D12–25

ZÜRICH AIRPORT

At **Glattbrugg** (8km NE on N4)

★★★★**Airport** Oberhauserstr 30 ☎8104444 tx52387 Plan **4** 47rm27⇌20⋔ 🏠 P Lift sB⇌⋔70–75 dB⇌⋔110 Pool

🛏 *&Barbieri* Glatthofstr 3 ☎8106601 BL/Rov/Tri (GB)

ZWEISIMMEN Bern 1,500 (☎300) Map **11** B1

★★*Bristol* Bahnhofstr ☎21208 32rm1⇌ 🏠

★★*Krone* Lenkstr ☎22626 40rm30⇌6⋔ 🏠 Lift

☆*Sport* Saanenstr ☎21431 20⇌

Liechtenstein

Prices are in Swiss francs.

BENDERN (☎075) Map **12** C2

🛏 *&Auto Center* Landstr 755 ☎32070 P Maz

SCHAAN 2,300 (☎075) Map **12** C2

★★*Linde* Lindenpl ☎21704 23rm4⇌7⋔ P SB23–25 sB⇌⋔29–35 dB42–46 dB⇌⋔54–68 L8–18 D8–18 mountains

🛏 *Fanal* (A Netzer) Feldkircherstr 52 ☎24604 Chy/Sim (GB)

TRIESENBERG 1,400 (☎075) (5km SE of **Vaduz**) Map **12** C1/2

★*Masescha* ☎22337 Closed Nov–Jan 7rm 🏠 P sB25 dB50 L10 D10–20 mountains

VADUZ 3,000 (☎075) Map **12** C1/2

☆☆*Motel Triesen* ☎22666 32rm6⇌26⋔ 🏠 P sB30–45 sB⇌⋔35–45 dB50–58 dB⇌⋔55–68 (English breakfast) L12–22 D12–22 mountains

★★*Real* ☎22222 tx77809 10rm6⇌4⋔ P Lift ♪ sB⇌⋔60 dB⇌⋔80–120 L alc D alc

★★*Sonnenhof* Marestr ☎21192 tx77781 Closed 16 Jan–14 Feb 🏠 P Lift ♪ sB⇌75–100 dB⇌120–180 ✍ Pool mountains

★*Engel* ☎21057 19rm9⇌6⋔ P Lift sB38–50 sB⇌⋔43–50 dB60–73 dB⇌⋔63–73 (English breakfast) L20 D20 mountains

★*Löwen* Herrengasse ☎21408 11rm1⇌ P ♪ sB28–34 sB⇌⋔46 dB60–64 dB⇌82 (English breakfast) L9–24 D9–24 mountains

🛏 *&Muhlehol 3* Hauptstr 584 ☎21668 P AR/Ren

White star establishments

White stars denote motels, motor hotels and some purpose-built hotels.

AUSTRIA

✩✩	Wallersee	Eugendorf
✩✩	Gallina	Frastanz
✩✩	ATS	Leibnitz
✩✩✩	EuroCrest	Linz an der Donau
✩✩✩	Euromotel Mondsee	Mondsee
✩	Salzburger	Salzburg

BELGIUM

✩✩✩	EuroCrest	Antwerpen
✩✩✩	Eurotel Antwerpen	Antwerpen
✩✩✩	Novotel Antwerpen	Antwerpen
✩✩✩✩	Sofitel	Antwerpen (at Aartselaar)
✩✩	Beveren	Beveran-Wass
✩✩	Dennenhof	Brasschaat-Polygoon
✩✩✩✩	Sofitel	Bruxelles Airport (at Diegem)
✩✩✩	Novotel Bruxelles Airport	Bruxelles Airport (at Diegem)
✩✩	Casteau EuroCrest	Casteau
✩✩✩✩	Holiday Inn	Gent (Gand)
✩✩✩✩	Ramada Inn	Liège (Luik)
✩✩	Euromotel	Liège (Luik) (at Herstal)
✩✩✩✩	Sofitel	Wepion

FRANCE

✩✩	Ibis Cap d'Agde	Agde (at Cap d'Agde)
✩✩✩	Novotel Beaumanoir	Aix-en-Provence
✩✩✩	Novotel Sud	Aix-en-Provence
✩✩	Relais du Soleil	Aix-en-Provence (at Celony)
✩✩✩	Novotel Amiens Est	Amiens (at Boves)
✩✩✩	Novotel Angoulême Nord	Angoulême (at Champniers)
✩✩	PM 16	Angoulême (at Champniers)
✩✩✩	Mercure	Annecy
✩✩	Côte d'Azur	Antibes
✩✩	Mercator	Antibes
✩✩✩	Cantarelles	Arles
✩✩✩	Grill	Arras (at Fresnes-les-Montauban)
✩✩✩	Novotel	Aulnay-sous-Bois
✩✩✩✩	Holiday Inn	Avignon
✩✩✩	Novotel Avignon-Sud	Avignon
✩✩✩✩	Sofitel	Avignon (at Avignon Nord Autoroute Junc; (A7)
✩✩	PLM	Beaune
✩✩	Samotel	Beaune
✩✩✩	Mercure	Beauvais
✩✩	Motel 7	Bedarrides
✩✩✩	Mercure	Belfort (at Danjoutin)
✩✩✩	Novotel Dunkerque	Bergues
✩✩✩	Novotel	Besançon
✩✩✩	Mercure	Besançon (at Château Farine)
✩✩	Toit de Chaume	Bessines-sur-Gartempe
✩✩✩	Novotel Bordeaux-le-Lac	Bordeaux
✩✩✩	Sofitel	Bordeaux
✩✩	Ibis	Bordeaux
✩✩✩	Bordeaux EuroCrest	Bordeaux (at Gradignan)
✩✩✩	Novotel Bordeaux Aéroport	Bordeaux (at Merignac)
✩✩	Ibis Boulogne	Boulogne-sur-Mer
✩✩✩	Novotel	Brest
✩✩✩	Ibis Brest	Brest (at Plougastel-Daoulas)
✩✩✩	Novotel	Caen
✩✩	Ibis Caen	Caen (at Herouville St Clair)
✩✩	Horizon	Cagnes-sur-Mer (at Cros-de-Cagnes)
✩✩	Mediterranée	Cagnes-sur-Mer (Villeneuve-Loubet)
✩✩	Croque Sel	Carcassonne
✩✩✩	Mercure	Chalon-sur-Saône
✩✩	Ibis Chambéry	Chambéry (at Chamnord)
✩✩✩	Mercure	Charleville-Mézièrs (at Villers-Semeuse)
✩✩✩	Novotel	Chartres
✩	Girafe	Château-Thierry
✩✩	Ibis Châtellerault	Châtellerault
✩✩✩	Novotel Colmar	Colmar
✩✩	Stella di Mare	Ajaccio Corse (Corsica)
✩✩✩	Novotel Montchannin-Creusot-Montceau	Creusot (Le) (at Monchanin)
	Relais St-Europe	Crouzille (La) (at Nantiat)
✩✩	Ibis Dieppe	Dieppe
✩✩✩	Novotel Dijon-Sud	Dijon (at Marsanny)
✩✩✩	Novotel Paris-Evry	Evry
✩✩✩	Novotel Fontainbleu Ury	Fontainbleu (at Ury)
✩	Escale	Frayssinet
✩✩✩	Novotel Grenoble-Voreppe	Grenoble (at Voreppe)
✩✩✩	Novotel Henin-Douai	Henin Beaumont (at Noyelles-Godault)
✩✩	Delta	Houches (Les)

White star establishments

Stars	Establishment	Location
☆☆☆	Motellerie	Lille (at Englos)
☆☆☆	Novotel Lille-Lomme	Lille (at Englos
☆☆☆☆	Holiday Inn	Lille (at Marcq en Baroeul)
☆☆☆	Novotel Lille Aéroport	Lyon (at Bron)
☆☆☆☆	Holiday Inn	Lyon (at Dardilly)
☆☆☆	International	Lyon (at Dardilly)
☆☆☆	Novotel Lyon Nord	Lyon (at Dardilly)
☆☆☆	Novotel Mâcon Nord	Mâcon
☆☆☆	Sofitel	Mâcon (at St-Albain)
☆☆☆	Vielle Ferme	Mâcon (at Sancé-lès-Mâcon)
☆	Esterel	Mandelieu
☆☆☆	Novotel Marseille Est	Marseille (at Penne-St Menet (La))
☆☆☆	Novotel Marseille Aéroport	Marseille Airport (at Vitrolles)
☆☆	Ibis Melun	Melun
☆☆☆	Novotel	Metz (at Hauconcourt)
☆☆	Bois Fleuri	Mont-de-Marson
☆☆	Euromotel	Montélimar
☆☆	Ibis	Montpellier
☆☆	Euromotel	Montpellier (at Perols)
☆☆	K	Mont-St-Michel (Le)
☆☆	Ibis	Moutiers
☆☆☆	Mercure	Mulhouse (at Sausheim)
☆☆☆	Novotel	Mulhouse (at Sausheim)
☆☆☆	Novotel Nancy-Sud	Nancy (at Houdemont)
☆☆☆	Mercure Nancy Ouest	Nancy (at Laxou)
☆☆☆	Novotel Nancy Ouest	Nancy (at Laxou)
☆☆☆	Sofitel	Nancy (at Laxou)
☆☆☆	Mercure	Nantes (at Carquefou)
☆☆☆	Novotel Nantes Carquefou	Nantes (at Carquefou)
☆☆☆	Novotel Narbonne Sud	Narbonne
☆☆☆	Euromotel	Nemours
☆☆	Relais St-Eutrope	Nepoulas par Campreignac
☆☆	Européen	Neuf-Brisach (at Volgelgrun)
☆☆☆	Massenet	Nice
☆☆☆	Novotel Nice Cap 3000	Nice (at St-Laurent de Var)
☆☆☆	Novotel Nîmes Ouest	Nîmes
☆☆	Marguerittes	Nîmes (at Marguerittes)
☆☆☆	Ile de Lumière	Cotinière (La) Oléron (Ile d')
☆☆☆	Novotel Oléron S-Trojan	St-Trojan-les-Bains (Ile d' Oléron)
☆☆☆	Euromotel Orange	Orange
☆☆☆	Novotel Paris-Orgeval	Orgeval
☆☆	Ibis	Orléans (at Saran)
☆☆☆	Novotel Orléans Sud	Orléans (at Source (La))
☆☆☆	Mercure	Orsay (at Courtabeuf)
☆☆☆	Novotel Massy-Palaisseau	Palaisseau
☆☆☆	Novotel Paris Bagnolet	Paris (at Bagnolet)
☆☆	Ibis	Paris (at Bagnolet)
☆☆☆	Novotel Créteil-le-Lac	Paris (at Créteil)
☆☆	Ibis Paris Porte d'Orleans	Paris (at Montrouge)
☆☆☆	Novotel Paris Nord Aéroport	Paris Airports Le Bourget Airport
☆☆☆☆	Sofitel	Paris Airports Charles-de-Gaulle Airport (at Roissy)
☆☆☆	Novotel Pau Lescar	Pau (at Lescar)
☆☆	Ibis	Périgueux
☆☆☆☆	Sofitel	Péronne (at Asseveillers)
☆☆☆	Novotel Perpignan	Perpignan (at Rivesaltes)
☆☆☆	Relais Poitiers	Poitiers (at Chasseneuil)
☆	Portes du Midi	Pont-de-l'Isère
☆☆☆	Novotel	Pontoise (at Cergy)
☆	Bruyères	Rabot (Le)
☆☆☆	Mercure Reims Est	Reims
☆☆☆	Novotel	Reims (at Tinquex)
☆☆☆	Novotel Rennes Alma	Rennes
☆	Château	Rocamadour
☆☆☆	Novotel Rouen Sud	Rouen (at St Etienne du Rouvray)
☆☆☆	Novotel	Saclay
☆☆☆	Novotel St Avold	St Avold
☆☆☆	Novotel St Étienne Airport	St Etienne Airport
☆☆☆	Basques	St Jean de Luz
☆☆☆	Novotel Val-Thorens	St Martin de Belleville
☆☆	Royal Bon Repos	Ste-Maxime-sur-Mer
☆☆	Ibis	Sallanches
☆☆☆	Sofitel	Salon-de-Provence (at Lancon de Provence)
☆☆☆	Euromotel Perpignan Rousillon	Salses
☆☆☆	PLM Pont de l'Europe	Strasbourg
☆☆	Ibis Strasbourg	Strasbourg
☆☆☆	Mercure Strasbourg Sud	Strasbourg (at Ilkirch)
☆☆☆	Novotel Strasbourg Sud	Strasbourg (at Ilkirch)
☆☆☆	Mercure St-Witz	Survilliers
☆☆☆	Novotel Paris Survillers	Survilliers
☆☆	Ibis	Toulouse
☆☆☆	Novotel Toulouse Purpan	Toulouse Airport
☆☆☆	Novotel Neville en Ferrain	Tourcoing
☆☆	Ibis	Tourcoing
☆☆☆	Novotel Troyes Aéroport	Troyes Airport (at Barberey)
☆☆	Ibis	Valence-d'Agen
☆☆☆	Novotel Valence Sud	Valence sur Rhône

White star establishments

☆☆☆	Motellerie	Valenciennes
☆☆☆	Novotel Valenciennes-Ouest	Valenciennes
☆☆	Km 500	Vienne (at Chonas l'Amballon)
☆☆	Ibis Villefranche-sur-Saône	Villefranche-sur-Saône

GERMANY

☆	Motel Nadermann	Ahhorn
☆☆	Rasthaus Pfefferhohe	Alsfeld
☆☆☆☆	Holiday Inn-Turmhotel	Augsburg
☆☆☆	Bonn	Bonn (at Röttgen)
☆☆	Ebertor	Boppard
☆☆☆	EuroCrest	Bremen
☆	Atlas	Bremen (at Brinkum)
☆☆	Annenriede	Delmonhorst
☆☆☆	EuroCrest	Frankfurt am Main
☆	An der Lahn	Giessen
☆☆☆	EuroCrest	Hamburg
☆	Hamburg	Hamburg
☆☆☆	EuroCrest	Hannover
☆☆☆	Park Kronsberg	Hannover
☆☆	Treffpunkt	Hannover
☆☆☆☆	Holiday Inn	Hannover Airport
☆☆☆	EuroCrest	Heidelberg
☆☆☆	Center Kirchheim	Kirchheim
☆☆☆	EuroCrest	Köln (Cologne) (at Köln Lindenthal)
☆	Waldklause	Lübeck (at Ratekau)
☆	Weber	Mannheim (at Sandhofen)
☆☆☆☆	Holiday Inn	Mönchengladbach
☆☆	Heiligenroth	Montabaur
☆☆☆	Euro	Müllheim
☆☆☆	EuroCrest	München (Munich)
☆☆☆	Novotel Düsseldorf-Neuss	Neuss (at Neuss-Erfttal)
☆☆☆	EuroCrest	Nürnberg (Nuremberg)
☆☆☆	EuroCrest	Ratingen
☆☆☆	Novotel	Saarbrücken
☆☆☆	Stuttgart EuroCrest	Sindelfingen
☆	Rauchfang	Titisee
☆	Stadt Tübingen	Tubingen
☆☆☆☆	Holiday Inn	Walldorf
☆	Wiedenbrück	Wiedenbrück
☆	Ferien	Zwischenahn (Bad)

ITALY

☆☆☆	AGIP	Ancona
☆☆☆	Motelalp	Aosta
☆☆☆	AGIP	Bari (at Torre a Mare)
☆☆☆	AGIP	Bologna
☆☆☆	EuroCrest	Bologna
☆☆☆	AGIP	Bolzano-Bozen
☆☆☆	AGIP	Brescia
☆☆☆	AGIP	Catanzaro
☆	Autostello	Cirella
☆☆☆	AGIP	Cosenza (at Rende)
☆☆☆	AGIP	Firenze (Florence)
☆☆☆	EuroCrest	Firenze (Florence)
☆☆☆	AGIP	Grosseto
☆	Italmotel	Lainate
☆☆☆	AGIP	Livorno (Leghorn) (at Stagno)
☆☆☆	AGIP	Macerata
☆☆☆	AGIP	Matelica
☆☆☆	Eurotel	Merano-Meran
☆☆☆	Eurotel Astoria	Merano-Meran
☆☆☆	AGIP	Milano (Milan)
☆☆	Dei Fiori	Milano (Milan)
☆☆	Eur	Milano (Milan)
☆☆	Fini	Milano (Milan)
☆☆☆	AGIP	Milano (Milan) (at San Donato Milanese)
☆☆☆	AGIP	Modena
☆☆☆	AGIP	Modena
☆☆☆	AGIP	Montalto di Castro
☆☆	Milano	Nervi
☆☆☆	AGIP	Pescara
☆☆	K2	Piacenza
☆☆	California	Pisa
☆☆☆	AGIP	Pisticci
☆	Romea	Ravenna
☆☆☆	AGIP	Roccaraso
☆☆☆	AGIP	Roma (Rome)
☆	Bela	Roma (Rome) (at Storta La)
☆☆	Bobby	San Remo
☆☆☆	AGIP	Cagliari Sardegna (Isola) (Sardinia)
☆☆☆	AGIP	Macomer Sardegna (Isola) (Sardinia)
☆☆☆	AGIP	Nuoro Sardegna (Isola) (Sardinia)
☆☆☆	AGIP	Sassari Sardegna (Isola) (Sardinia)
☆☆☆	AGIP	Sarzana
☆☆☆	AGIP	Savona
☆☆☆	AGIP	Catania Sicilia (Sicily)
☆☆☆	AGIP	Gela Sicilia (Sicily)
☆	Motel delle Mimose	Gela Sicilia (Sicily)
☆☆☆	AGIP	Marsala Sicilia (Sicily)
☆☆☆	AGIP	Palermo Sicilia (Sicily)
☆☆☆	AGIP	Sciacca Sicilia (Sicily)
☆☆☆	AGIP	Siracusa (Syracuse) Sicilia (Sicily)
☆☆☆	AGIP	Spoleto
☆☆☆	AGIP	Torino (Turin) (at Settimo)
☆☆☆	AGIP	Trento (at Sardegna)
☆☆☆	AGIP	Trieste
☆☆☆	Valrosandra	Trieste
☆☆☆	AGIP	Udine
☆☆☆	AGIP	Varallo
☆☆☆	AGIP	Verona
☆☆☆	AGIP	Vicenza

LUXEMBOURG

☆☆☆	Novotel Luxembourg	Dommeldange
☆☆☆☆	Holiday Inn	Luxembourg (at Kirchberg)

White star establishments

NETHERLANDS

✫✫✫	Alkmaar	Alkmaar
✫✫✫	Postiljon	Almelo
✫✫✫✫	EuroCrest	Amsterdam
✫✫✫	Euromotel Amsterdam	Amsterdam
✫✫✫	Euromotel E9	Amsterdam
✫✫✫	Postiljon	Arnhem
✫✫✫	Euromotel Limberg	Beek
✫✫✫	EuroCrest	Born
✫✫✫	Euromotel Brabant	Breda
✫	Euromotel Breda	Breda
✫✫✫✫	Holiday Inn	Eindhoven
✫✫✫	Gorinchem	Gorinchem
✫✫✫	Euromotel	Groningen
✫✫	Clingendael	Groningen
✫✫✫	Hoornwijck	Haag (Den) (Hague, The) (at Rijswijk)
✫✫✫	Postiljon	Haren
✫✫✫	Postiljon	Heerenveen
✫✫✫	Witte Bergen	Laren (at Eemnes)
✫✫✫✫	Holiday Inn	Leiden
✫✫	Maarsbergen	Maarsbergen
✫✫✫	Euro	Naarden
✫✫✫	Staatse Schans	Papendrecht
✫✫✫	Euromotel Rotterdam	Rotterdam
✫✫✫✫	Holiday Inn	Utrecht
✫✫✫	Postiljon	Utrecht (at Bunnik)
✫✫✫	EuroCrest	Velp
✫✫✫	Postiljon	Zwolle

PORTUGAL

✫	Alameda	Albergaria a Velha
✫✫	Motel Continental	Oeiras

SPAIN

✫	Solimar	Algeciras
✫✫	Albergue Nacional	Antequera
✫✫✫	Bronces	Aranda de Duero
✫✫✫	Albergue Nacional	Bailén
✫	Albergue Nacional	Bañeza (La)
✫✫✫	Albergue Nacional	Benicarló
✫✫	Marola	Benidorm
✫✫✫	Ampurdan	Figueras
✫✫✫	Olivos	Madrid (at Getafe)
✫✫	Albergue Nacional	Manzanares
✫✫	Albergue Nacional	Puebla de Sanabria
✫✫✫✫	Meliá el Caballo Blanco	Puerto de Santa María (El)
✫✫	Albergue Nacional	Puerto Lumbreras
✫✫	Albergue Nacional	Ribadeo
✫✫	Balcón de España	Tarifa
✫✫✫	Motel Meliá El Hidalgo	Valdepeñas
✫✫✫	Albergue Nacional	Villacastin
✫✫✫	Parador Nacional Villafranca del Bierzo	Villafranca del Bierzo
✫✫✫	Ticasa	Villarreal de Los Infantes (at Alqueria del Niño Perdido)

SWITZERLAND

✫✫	Krone	Bern (Berne) (at Muri)
✫	Bevaix	Bevaix
✫	St-Christophe	Bex-les-Bains
✫✫	Schiff	Bollingen
✫✫	Sommerau	Chur (Coire)
✫	San Gottardo	Claro
✫✫	Beauregard	Echallens (at Villars-le-Terrair)
✫✫	AGIP	Egerkingen
✫	Hirschen	Einigen
✫✫	Péchers	Etoy-Buchillon
✫✫	Motel Faulensee	Faulensee
✫✫	Founex	Founex
✫	Motel de la Buna	Genève (Geneva) (at Mies)
✫✫✫	Novotel Genève Aéroport	Genève Airport (at Fernay Voltaire, in France)
✫✫	Grindelwald	Grindelwald
✫✫	Marti	Interlaken
✫	Picnic	Kussnacht am Rigi
✫✫✫	Novotel Lausanne Ouest	Lausanne (at Bussigny)
✫✫	Intereurop	Lausanne (at Cully)
✫✫✫	Parking	Lausanne (at Ouchy)
✫	Pierrettes	Lausanne (at St-Sulpice)
✫✫	Lido	Lugano (at Maroggia-Melano)
✫	Vezia	Lugano (at Vezia)
✫	Süd Kriens	Luzern (Lucerne) (at Kriens)
✫	Sports	Martigny
✫	Mon Abri	Merligen
✫	Rennaz-Montreux	Montreux (at Rennaz)
✫✫	Bern-Biel	Münchenbuchsee
✫	Münsingen	Münsingen
✫	Neuveville	Neuveville (La)
✫	Ponte Tresa	Ponte Tresa
✫✫	Touring Mot	Ragaz-Pfäfers (Bad)
✫	Simplonblick	Raron
✫✫✫	Kreuz	Sachseln am Sarnersee
✫✫	Fleurs	Servion
✫✫	Sihlbrugg	Sihlbrugg
✫✫	Betulla	Tegna
✫✫✫	Novotel Neuchâtel Est	Thielle
✫	Jurats	Vallorbe
✫✫✫	Bellavista	Vira-Gambarogno
✫	Mezzovico	Vira-Mezzovico
✫✫	Luna	Wilderswil
✫	Sport	Zweisimmen

LIECHTENSTEIN

✫✫✫	Triesen	Vaduz

Accommodation report (confidential)

to The Automobile Association,
Hotel & Information Services, Fanum House, Basingstoke,
Hants RG21 2EA.

town, country, hotel

your star rating   location   date of stay

food   rooms

service   sanitary arrangements   value for money

general remarks

town, country, hotel

your star rating   location   date of stay

food   rooms

service   sanitary arrangements   value for money

general remarks

town, country, hotel

your star rating   location   date of stay

food   rooms

service   sanitary arrangements   value for money

general remarks

name (block letters)

address (block letters)

| membership no. | for office use only |
| | acknowledged   recorded |

Garage report (confidential)

to   The Automobile Association,
Hotel & Information Services, Fanum House, Basingstoke,
Hants RG21 2EA.

town, country, garage

address

telephone no.

agents for   were AIT vouchers   recommended
                                    used for payment

remarks

town, country, garage

address

telephone no.

agents for   were AIT vouchers   recommended
                                    used for payment

remarks

town, country, garage

telephone no.

agents for   were AIT vouchers   recommended
                                    used for payment

remarks

name (block letters)

address (block letters)

membership no.

| for office use only | |
| acknowledged | recorded |

Road report

to   The Automobile Association,
Overseas Routes,
Fanum House, Basingstoke,
Hants RG21 2EA.

section of road

from   to

passing through   road no.

names shown on signposts

remarks: *ie* surface, width, estimated gradient, description of landscape

section of road

from   to

passing through   road no.

names shown on signposts

remarks: *ie* surface, width, estimated gradient, description of landscape

vehicle used   date of journey

name (block letters)

address (block letters)

membership no.	for office use only acknowledged	recorded

Application for route planning services

The publications available are described on pages 30–31. A suggested route can be marked on the Country and European Route Planning maps. If this is required, please complete section 6 overleaf. Please state also if your vehicle is other than a private car.
When you have completed the application form please send with your remittance, which should be by crossed cheque or postal order to:
The Automobile Association, Fanum House, Basingstoke, Hants RG21 2EA.

Please complete in BLOCK CAPITALS

Mr/Mrs/Miss   Initials   Surname

Address to which route maps should be sent:

County/Postcode

Date of application	Telephone numbers: Home Business
Membership number	European port of landing

1 **European Throughroute Maps** – each map extends as far north as Copenhagen and eastwards as far as Berlin, Prague, Budapest, Bucharest, Athens and Istanbul. Specially suitable for journeys using main routes from the ports listed. Routes from other ports can be marked on the Country or European Route planning maps. Please complete Section 6 overleaf.

Please tick box(es) of map(s) required.	Sale price per map	Total price of maps
Boulogne Calais Cherbourg Dieppe Le Havre Ostende/ Zeebrugge	45p each	£ p
2 **European Route Planning Map** – cover same area as the Throughroute maps described above.	45p each	

continued overleaf

	Please tick box(es) of map(s) required.	Sale price per map	Total price of maps	
			£	p

3 Country Maps

Map 1 France

Map 2 Spain & Portugal

Map 3 Belgium, Netherlands, Luxembourg & Germany

Map 4 Switzerland, Austria & Italy
5, 6, 7 (not available in 1979)

Area Route Planning Maps

Map 8 Southern Scandinavia

Map 9 Northern Scandinavia

45p each

4 Town Plans

Books of plans of the larger towns and cities

Book 1 France

Book 2 Spain & Portugal

Book 3 Belgium, Netherlands, Luxembourg & Germany

Book 4 Switzerland, Austria & Italy

45p each

5 Route Books
A new series of itinerary books with route descriptions

Book 1 France

Book 2 Spain & Portugal

Book 3 Belgium, Netherlands, Luxembourg & Germany

Book 4 Switzerland, Austria & Italy

£1.35 each

Total remittance enclosed	£	p

6 If you require us to suggest a route and indicate it on the map(s), please list the placenames (in BLOCK CAPITALS) in the order in which they will be visited. If you require route information for countries other than those listed above, please give details here.

Please tick (✓) this box if a caravan is being towed

Date of departure

For office use only:
A/C No. 7710/672

Index

Pollution Reports are constantly appearing in newspapers concerning the pollution of sea waters at European coastal resorts — particularly on the shores of the Mediterranean. In some areas the position is so bad as to constitute a severe health hazard. If a popular resort has a pollution problem it will obviously do little to publicize the fact, but you may see small signs on the beach forbidding bathing. If you see any of the following signs you should keep out of the sea — and in any case you should take great care:—

In French, *Défense de se baigner* or *Il est défendu de se baigner;* in Italian, *Vietato bagnarsi* or *È vietato bagnarsi;* and in Spanish *Prohibido bañarse* or *Se prohibe bañarse* all mean 'No bathing' or 'bathing prohibited'.